THE CAMBRIDGE HISTORY OF

WESTERN MUSIC THEORY

The Cambridge History of Western Music Theory is the first comprehensive history of Western music theory to be published in the English language. A collaborative project by leading music theorists and historians, the volume traces the rich panorama of music-theoretical thought from the Ancient Greeks to the present day. Recognizing the variety and complexity of music theory as an historical subject, the volume has been organized within a flexible framework. Some chapters are defined chronologically within a restricted historical domain whilst others are defined conceptually and span longer historical periods. Together the thirty-one chapters present a synthetic overview of the fascinating and complex subject that is historical music theory. Richly enhanced with illustrations, graphics, examples and cross-citations as well as being thoroughly indexed and supplemented by comprehensive bibliographies of the most important primary and secondary literature, this book will be an invaluable resource for students and scholars alike.

THOMAS CHRISTENSEN is Professor of Music and the Humanities at the University of Chicago. He is the author of *Rameau and Musical Thought in the Enlightenment* (Cambridge University Press, 1993). Elected in 1999 as president of the Society for Music Theory, Professor Christensen has also held appointments at the University of Iowa and the University of Pennsylvania.

THE CAMBRIDGE HISTORY OF

MUSIC

The Cambridge History of Music comprises a new group of reference works concerned with significant strands of musical scholarship. The individual volumes are self-contained and include histories of music examined by century as well as the history of opera, music theory and American music. Each volume is written by a team of experts under a specialist editor and represents the latest musicological research.

Published titles

The Cambridge History of American Music
Edited by David Nicholls

The Cambridge History of Nineteenth-Century Music
Edited by Jim Samson

The Cambridge History of Western Music Theory
Edited by Thomas Christensen

THE CAMBRIDGE HISTORY OF WESTERN MUSIC THEORY

*

EDITED BY
THOMAS CHRISTENSEN

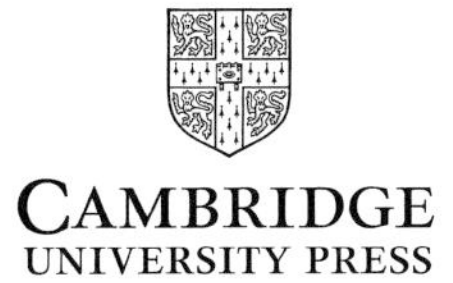

PUBLISHED BY THE PRESS SYNDICATE OF THE UNIVERSITY OF CAMBRIDGE
The Pitt Building, Trumpington Street, Cambridge, United Kingdom

CAMBRIDGE UNIVERSITY PRESS
The Edinburgh Building, Cambridge CB2 2RU, UK
40 West 20th Street, New York, NY 10011-4211, USA
477 Williamstown Road, Port Melbourne, VIC 3207, Australia
Ruiz de Alarcón 13, 28014 Madrid, Spain
Dock House, The Waterfront, Cape Town 8001, South Africa

http://www.cambridge.org

First published 2002
Reprinted 2004

Printed in the United Kingdom at the University Press, Cambridge

Typeface Renard Beta 9/12.5 pt *System* QuarkXPress™ [SE]

A catalogue record for this book is available from the British Library

Library of Congress Cataloguing in Publication data

The Cambridge history of Western music theory / edited by Thomas Christensen.
p. cm. – (The Cambridge history of music)
Includes bibliographical references and index.
ISBN 0 521 62371 5 (hardback)
1. Music theory – History. I. Christensen, Thomas Street. II. Series.
ML3800.C165 2001
781′.09–dc21 00-050366

ISBN 0 521 62371 5 hardback

Contents

Plates

Figures

Contributors

GREGORY BARNETT is Assistant Professor of musicology at the University of Iowa, having received his Ph.D. from Princeton University in 1999. He is currently completing a book on Italian instrumental music of the late seventeenth century for the University of California Press. Recent articles include "Modal Theory, Church Keys, and the Sonata at the End of the Seventeenth Century" (1998) and "The Violoncello da Spalla: Shouldering the Cello in the Baroque Era" (1998).

IAN BENT is Anne Parsons Bender Professor of Music at Columbia University. He is general editor of the series Cambridge Studies in Music Theory and Analysis, and senior editor for *The New Grove Dictionary of Music and Musicians*, 2nd edition (2001); author of the books *Analysis* (1987) and *Music Analysis in the Nineteenth Century*, 2 vols. (1994); and editor of the volumes *Source Materials and the Interpretation of Music* (1981) and *Music Theory in the Age of Romanticism* (1996).

ANNA MARIA BUSSE BERGER is Professor of Music at the University of California, Davis. She has published extensively on aspects of historical music notation, theory, and memory, including her book *Mensuration and Proportion Signs: Origins and Evolution* (1993). Her article "The Myth of *diminutio per tertiam partem*" (*Journal of Musicology* 1990) won the Alfred Einstein Award of the American Musicological Society in 1991.

DAVID W. BERNSTEIN is Professor of Music at Mills College. His research interests have ranged from Arnold Schoenberg's tonal theories and the history of music theory to the thought of John Cage and issues of the avant-garde. Along with Christopher Hatch, he has edited a book of essays exploring interrelationships between theory, analysis, and the history of ideas, entitled *Music Theory and the Exploration of the Past* (1993).

LESLIE DAVID BLASIUS is Assistant Professor of Music Theory at the University of Wisconsin-Madison. He received his Ph.D. from Princeton University, and is the author of two books, *Schenker's Argument and the Claims of Music Theory* (1996) and *The Music Theory of Godfrey Winham* (1997).

CALVIN M. BOWER, Professor and Fellow in the Medieval Institute of the University of Notre Dame, has read and studied medieval theory for over forty years. His annotated translation of Boethius's *De institutione musica* serves as a foundational work in the history of music theory, and the *Glossa maior in institutionem musicam*, which he edited with Michael Bernhard, documents the reception of ancient theory in the Middle Ages.

SCOTT BURNHAM is Professor of Music and Chair of the Music Department at Princeton University. He has published on a range of topics concerning the criticism and analysis of tonal music, including the book *Beethoven Hero* (1995), a study of the values and reception of Beethoven's heroic style. He is also the translator of A. B. Marx, *Musical Form in the Age of Beethoven* (1997) and co-editor of *Beethoven and His World* (2000).

DAVID BUTLER is Professor at, and Associate Director of, The School of Music at The Ohio State University. He has published extensively on music cognition and perceptual theories of Western tonality, including the book *Musician's Guide to Perception and Cognition* (1992).

WILLIAM E. CAPLIN is Associate Professor of Music at McGill University, Montreal. His research interests include the history of harmonic and rhythmic theories in the modern era and theories of musical form. His book *Classical Form: A Theory of Formal Functions for the Instrumental Music of Haydn, Mozart, and Beethoven* (1998) won the 1999 Wallace Berry Award from the Society for Music Theory.

THOMAS CHRISTENSEN is Professor of Music and the Humanities at the University of Chicago and Chair of the Music Department. He has published widely on topics of early-modern historical music theory and aesthetics, including *Rameau and Musical Thought in the French Enlightenment* (1993; winner of the Wallace Berry Award from the Society for Music Theory, 1994) and *Aesthetics and the Art of Musical Composition in the German Enlightenment* (1995, in collaboration with Nancy Baker). Elected president of the Society for Music Theory in 1999, he has also held appointments at the University of Iowa and the University of Pennsylvania.

ALBERT COHEN is William H. Bonsall Professor of Music Emeritus at Stanford University, having previously held appointments at the University of Michigan and the State University of New York at Buffalo. He earned the BS degree in Violin from the Juilliard School of Music, and the Ph.D. in Musicology from New York University. His major research specialities are the history of music theory and French Baroque music, in which he has published extensively. His most recent publication is an edition of the "Ballet Royal de Flore" (1669), appearing in vol. 1 (2001) of the new *Œuvres complètes* of J.-B. Lully, being issued by Olms Verlag.

DAVID E. COHEN is Assistant Professor of Music at Harvard University, having previously taught at Tufts University. A Ph.D. graduate from Brandeis University (1994), his research focuses upon medieval music theory, as well as topics of eighteenth-century music theory.

NICHOLAS COOK is Research Professor of Music at the University of Southampton; he has also taught in Hong Kong and Sydney. His publications cover a wide range of musical topics from analysis and aesthetics to psychology and pop music. Among his most recent books are *Analysing Musical Multimedia* (1998) and *Music: A Very Short Introduction* (1998). He is Editor of *Journal of the Royal Musical Association.*

JOHN COVACH is Associate Professor of Music at the University of North Carolina at Chapel Hill. A graduate of the University of Michigan (1993), his research has concerned aspects of early twentieth-century musical thought, as well as issues of theory and analysis related to popular music.

WILLIAM DRABKIN is Reader in Music at the University of Southampton. His writings include a handbook on Beethoven's *Missa solemnis* (1991), an introduction to Schenkerian analysis in Italian (1995), and a study of Haydn's early quartets (2000). In 2001 he was awarded a British Academy grant for research on the application of Schenkerian theory to string quartets.

JONATHAN DUNSBY is Professor of Music at the University of Reading, having previously held appointments at King's College London and the University of Southern California. His books include *Schoenberg Pierrot Lunaire* (1992), *Performing Music: Shared Concerns* (1995), and *Music Analysis in Theory and Practice*, co-authored with Arnold Whittall (1987). He was Founding Editor (1982–86) of the journal *Music Analysis.*

SARAH FULLER is Professor of Music at the State University of New York at Stony Brook. Her research has focused on medieval and Renaissance music theory, analysis of early music, and relations betweeen music theory and musical repertory, especially with regard to early polyphony and the music of Guillaume de Machaut. Recent articles have appeared in *Early Music History*, *Journal of Music Theory*, *Journal of the American Musicological Society*, and *The Musical Quarterly.*

ROBERT GJERDINGEN teaches in the School of Music at Northwestern University. He has published in the area of music cognition, including *A Classic Turn of Phrase: Music and the Psychology of Convention* (1988), and is currently Editor of the journal *Music Perception.* He was trained at the University of Pennsylvania under Leonard B. Meyer, Eugene Narmour, and Eugene K. Wolf.

BURDETTE GREEN is Associate Professor of Music at the Ohio State University. He specializes in the history of theory and aesthetics and is a founding member of the Society for Music Theory.

PENELOPE GOUK is a Wellcome Researcher in the History of Medicine at the University of Manchester. She has published extensively on early modern intellectual and material culture, and is currently working on music and healing and the use of musical models in medical and scientific thought. Her most recent publications include *Music, Science and Natural Magic in Seventeenth-Century England* (1999) and an edited volume on "Musical Healing in Cultural Contexts" (2000).

JAN HERLINGER is the Derryl and Helen Haymon Professor of Music at Louisiana State University. He has published critical editions and translations of treatises by Marchetto of Padua and Prosdocimo de' Beldomandi, as well as numerous articles on topics concerning medieval music theory and its transmission. His interests also include twentieth-century music and aesthetics.

BRIAN HYER is Associate Professor of Music at the University of Wisconsin-Madison. He has published widely on the anthropology of music theory from the eighteenth through the twentieth century.

CRISTLE COLLINS JUDD is Associate Professor of Music Theory at the University of Pennsylvania. She has published extensively on the motets of Josquin des Prez, analysis of early music, and history of music theory, including an edited volume, *Tonal Structures in Early Music* (1998), and her book *Reading Renaissance Music Theory: Hearing with the Eyes* (2000). Her current projects include a study of music and dialogue in the Renaissance and an exploration of nineteenth-century translations of theory treatises into English.

HENRY KLUMPENHOUWER is Associate Professor of Music at the University of Alberta. He has published on atonal theory, Neo-Riemannian theory, and on Marxist approaches to cultural critique.

JOEL LESTER, Dean of Mannes College of Music and Professor Emeritus of The City College and Graduate School of the City University of New York, is a violinist and scholar whose books on the history of theory include *From Modes to Keys: German Theory, 1592–1802* (1986) and *Compositional Theory in the 18th Century* (1992; winner of the Wallace Berry Award from the Society for Music Theory, 1993). His most recent book is *Bach's Works for Solo Violin: Style, Structure, Performance* (1999; winner of the ASCAP-Deems Taylor Award, 2000).

JUSTIN LONDON is Associate Professor of Music at Carleton College in Northfield, Minnesota. He has published various articles and reviews on rhythm and meter, music perception and cognition, and musical aesthetics, including the entry "Rhythm" in *The New Grove Dictionary of Music and Musicians*, 2nd edition (2001).

THOMAS J. MATHIESEN, Professor of Music History at Indiana University, is director of the *Thesaurus Musicarum Latinarum* and general editor of *Greek and Latin Music Theory*. He is the author of several books and numerous articles on ancient Greek and medieval music and music theory. His most recent book, *Apollo's Lyre: Greek Music and Music Theory in Antiquity and the Middle Ages* (1999), was honored by both the Society of Music Theory (Wallace Berry Award, 2000) and the American Musicological Society (Otto Kinkeldey Award, 2000).

PATRICK MCCRELESS is Professor of Music Theory at Yale University. He has also taught at the Eastman School of Music of the University of Rochester, and at the

University of Texas at Austin. He has published a book, *Wagner's Siegfried: Its Drama, Its History, and Its Music*, as well as articles on such topics as chromaticism in nineteenth-century music, literary-critical approaches to music analysis, and the music of Shostakovich.

CATHERINE NOLAN is Associate Professor of Music Theory at the University of Western Ontario, where she was appointed in 1990 after receiving her Ph.D. from Yale University. Her research interests center on mathematical models in music theory and on the late music of Anton Webern.

RUDOLF RASCH is Associate Professor of Musicology at the University of Utrecht. He has published widely concerning the musical history of the Netherlands (especially during the seventeenth and nineteenth centuries) and the history and theory of tuning and temperament systems. He is presently preparing a general book about the musical history of the Dutch Republic, as well as an edition of the musical correspondence of Constantijn Huygens.

LEE ROTHFARB is department chair and Associate Professor of Music Theory at the University of California, Santa Barbara. Previous appointments include Harvard University, Tulane University, and the University of Michigan. His publications include essays on Ernst Kurth and August Halm, and two books, *Ernst Kurth as Theorist and Analyst* (1988; winner of the Outstanding Publication Award of the Society for Music Theory) and *Ernst Kurth: Selected Writings* (1991).

PETER SCHUBERT is Associate Professor in the Faculty of Music at McGill University in Montreal. He has published widely on questions of Renaissance music theory and is active as a choir conductor. His textbook *Modal Counterpoint, Renaissance Style* was published in 1999.

ROBERT W. WASON is Professor of Music Theory and Affiliate Faculty in Jazz Studies and Contemporary Media at the Eastman School of Music, University of Rochester. He is the author of *Viennese Harmonic Theory from Albrechtsberger to Schenker and Schoenberg* (1985), and a number of articles concerning the history of music theory and twentieth-century musical topics.

Acknowledgments

It is my pleasant duty to acknowledge here the help I have received from many colleagues in the long, arduous process of organizing and editing this history. First, I must thank Professor Ian Bent of Columbia University who originally conceived of this project, and invited me to assume editorial control. Ian has offered unceasing encouragement and advice through all stages of its conception. The *Cambridge History of Western Music Theory* is in many respects the fruition of his vision. Second, I must thank Penny Souster of Cambridge University Press. Without her energy, enthusiasm, and determination, this project could not have proceeded as efficiently as it has. I am profoundly in debt to her unfailing support and friendship.

In the course of conceiving the scope and organization of this history, I have had helpful discussions with so many colleagues that it is impossible to thank them all individually here. Virtually every contributor in these pages has to one degree or another helped me in the shaping of the project by offering their wisdom and knowledge, helping me resolve numerous conceptual problems of natures both *theorica* and *practica*. But I must single out for their advice at particularly seminal moments in the early stages of this volume, Harry Powers, Jonathan Dunsby, David Cohen, and the late Claude V. Palisca. I must also collectively give thanks to my authors for their patience in putting up with my repeated bibliographic queries, suggestions for revisions, scholarly kibitzing, and other editorial meddling with their texts.

With deepest gratitude I am pleased to acknowledge here the critical support I received from the University of Iowa where I was awarded a faculty scholarship in 1996 allowing me course release over the following two years to work on this project. The Director of the School of Music, David Nelson, was especially generous in providing both financial as well as moral support. I am equally indebted to the Dean of Arts and Humanities at the University of Chicago, Philip Gossett, and his successor, Janel Mueller, who both continued this support when I was privileged to move to that institution in the spring of 1999. Last, I must thank several of my graduate assistants at the University of Chicago who were indispensable in the final stages of production. Robert Cook set most of the graphics with uncanny skill and precision, while Peter Martens and Yonatan Malin took on the momentous task of editing all the bibliographies as well as aiding me in compiling the index.

Thomas Christensen

Abbreviations

Journals

Acta *Acta Musicologica*, International Musicological Socety, Basel, Bärenreiter et al., 1928–

JAMS *Journal of the American Musicological Society*, University of Chicago Press, et al., 1948–

JM *Journal of Musicology*, Greenfield, OH, and St. Joseph, MI, Music Science Press, 1982–

JMT *Journal of Music Theory*, New Haven, Yale University Press, 1957–

MA *Music Analysis*, Oxford, B. Blackwell, 1982–

MP *Music Perception*, Berkeley, University of California Press, 1983–

MTS *Music Theory Spectrum* (The Journal of the Society for Music Theory), University of California Press, 1979–

Reference works

AfMw *Archiv für Musikwissenschaft*, Bückeburg, Fürstliches Institut für Musikwissenschaftliche Forschung, 1918–27; Trossingen, Hohner-Stiftung, 1952–61; Wiesbaden, F. Steiner, 1962–

CSM *Corpus Scriptorum de Musica*, Rome, American Institute of Musicology, 1950–

CS *Scriptorum de musica medii aevi novam seriem a Gerbertina alteram collegit nuncque*, ed. E. de Coussemaker, 4 vols., Paris, A. Durand, 1864–76; facs. Hildesheim, G. Olms, 1963

GMt *Geschichte der Musiktheorie*, 10 of 15 vols. to date, ed. F. Zaminer, Staatliches Institut für Musikforschung Preussischer Kulturbesitz Berlin, Darmstadt, Wissenschaftliche Buchgessellschaft, 1984–

vol. I *Ideen zu einer Geschichte der Musiktheorie: Einleitung in das Gesamtwerk* (1985)

vol. II *Vom Mythos zur Fachdiszipline. Antike und Byzanz* (forthcoming)

vol. III *Rezeption des antiken Fachs im Mittelalter* (1990)

vol. IV *Die Lehre vom einstimmigen liturgischen Gesang* (2000)

vol. V *Die mittelalterliche Lehre von der Mehrstimmigkeit* (1984)

vol. VI *Hören, Messen, und Rechnen in der früheren Neuzeit* (1987)
vol. VII *Italienische Musiktheorie im 16. und 17. Jahrhundert: Antikrezeption und Satzlehre* (1989)
vol. VIII *Deutsche Musiktheorie des 15. bis 17. Jahrhunderts*, Part I (forthcoming) Part II *Von Calvisius bis Mattheson* (1994)
vol. IX *Entstehung nationaler Traditionen: Frankreich–England* (1986)
vol. X *Die Musiktheorie im 18. und 19. Jahrhundert*, Part I *Grundzüge einer Systematik* (1984)
vol. XI *Die Musiktheorie im 18. und 19. Jahrhundert*, Part II *Deutschland* (1989)
vol. XII *Die Musiktheorie im 18. and 19. Jahrhundert* Part III (forthcoming)
vol. XIII *Von der musikalischen Akustik zur Tonpsychologie* (forthcoming)
vol. XIV/XV *Musiktheorie im 20. Jahrhundert* (forthcoming)

GS *Scriptores ecclesiastici de musica sacra potissimum*, 3 vols., ed. M. Gerbert, St. Blasien, 1784; facs. Hildesheim, G. Olms, 1963

HmT *Handwörterbuch der musicalischen Terminologie*, ed. H. H. Eggebrecht, Stuttgart, F. Steiner, 1973–

MANC *Music Analysis in the Nineteenth Century*, 2 vols., ed. I. Bent (vol. I: *Fugue, Form and Style*, vol. II: *Hermeneutic Approaches*), Cambridge University Press, 1994

MGG *Die Musik in Geschichte und Gegenwart; allgemeine Enzyklopädie der Musik*, ed. F. Blume, 17 vols., Kassel, Bärenreiter, 1949–86

MGG2 *Die Musik in Geschichte und Gegenwart: allgemeine Enzyklopädie der Musik*, 2nd edn., ed. L. Finscher, 21 vols., Kassel, Bärenreiter; Stuttgart, Metzler, 1994–

MSD *Musicological Studies and Documents*, ed. A. Carapetyan, American Institute of Musicology, Neuhausen-Stuttgart, Hänssler, 1957–

NG *The New Grove Dictionary of Music and Musicians*, ed. S. Sadie, 20 vols., London, Macmillan; Washington, D.C., Grove's Dictionaries of Music, 1980

NG2 *The New Grove Dictionary of Music and Musicians*, 2nd edn., ed. S. Sadie, 29 vols., London, Macmillan, 2001

SR *Source Readings in Music History*, ed. Oliver Strunk; rev. edn., ed. Leo Treitler, New York, Norton, 1998

Introduction

THOMAS CHRISTENSEN

Music theory, Carl Dahlhaus has warned us, is a subject that notoriously resists its own history. How, he challenges us, is it possible to write any meaningful history of a discipline whose subject matter has shifted so dramatically over time?[1] Topics of musical pedagogy that we today take for granted as integral to music theory were not always so considered – rules for writing counterpoint or realizing a figured bass, for instance. Conversely, many of the traditional components that made up the quadrivial science of *musica theorica* are now considered peripheral subjects lying precariously close to occult and esoteric thought, or more benignly, perhaps, as part of some mathematical or acoustical subdiscipline. Nor are these contrasting allegiances mutually exclusive at any given historical period. Widely diverging conceptions of music theory can often be found jostling with one another in the same historical culture, within the *oeuvre* of the same writer, and occasionally even in the same publication.

As a pointed illustration of this diversity, we might consider three texts stemming from the same decade of the early seventeenth century: Thomas Campion's *A New Way of Making Fowre Parts in Counter-point by a Most Familiar, and Infallible Rule* (London, c. 1618), René Descartes's *Musicae Compendium* (c. 1618; printed Utrecht, 1650), and Robert Fludd's *Utriusque Cosmi, maioris scilicet et minoris metaphysica* (Oppenheim, 1617–21). Each of these works has been classified as "music theoretical" (although ironically, none of them actually employs the title "music theory").[2] Yet it is certainly not the case that all three works represent similar kinds of theory. Campion's modest treatise is an eminently practical guide for the novice composer looking for a quick and "easie" means of harmonizing a given bass line using a number of simple rules of thumb. Descartes's treatise, even shorter than Campion's, is on the contrary quite learned. The *Compendium* is a classic text of musical "canonics" – the science of plotting and measuring musical intervals on the monochord. Unlike Campion's text, it has no practical function except perhaps as a test case of the young philosopher's nascent deductivist method of geometrical reasoning. Finally, Fludd's mammoth treatise of Rosicrucian lore and gnostic learning is an unapologetic paean to the harmonic cosmos

1 Dahlhaus, "Was heisst 'Geschichte der Musiktheorie'?," p. 28.

2 As trivial evidence, we may note that all three authors and these works are listed and discussed in the recent dictionary of historical music theory: Damschroder and Williams, *Music Theory from Zarlino to Schenker*.

of Plato's *Timaeus*. Given the profoundly different contents and intended readership of each of these works, we may well ask ourselves how they could be unified within a single disciplinary paradigm we call "music theory." What conceptual boundary can we circumscribe that would help us define and delimit the contents of historical music theory?

Such questions are by no means without consequence with regard to the present volume. For the ambitious – and perhaps presumptuous – attempt to present the history of Western music theory within a single, synoptic volume of essays promises that there is indeed a relatively unified discipline we can call music theory that is both intellectually coherent and conceptually stable. Does such a discipline actually exist? Is "music theory" ultimately an intelligible and meaningful historical subject?

I

It might be helpful as a first step to begin with some Greek etymology. In pre-Socratic usage, *theoria* (θεωρία) is a visual term. It entails the action of seeing or observing. A *theoros* (θεωρός) is a spectator at a theater or games. A *theoros* could also be a witness in a legal dispute or a delegate or ambassador conveying information that he attests to have witnessed.[3] (Although the two terms are etymologically unrelated, a number of Greek writers also noted the striking similarity of the word to *theos* – a god and divine observer, the seer who sees all.)

It was Plato who first called the philosopher a special kind of *theoros*. In the *Republic*, Glaucon points out to Socrates the parallels between the observer at a theater and the philosopher, whom Socrates had just defined as possessing a restless curiosity and "taste for every sort of knowledge."[4] Like the theater audience, the philosopher too is an observer, curious about – but detached from – the events of which he is a spectator. Socrates agrees that the parallel is certainly striking, but he ultimately considers it deficient. For the real goal of the philosopher is different from that of the theatergoer. His wish is not to be entertained or to have his senses ravished; rather, it is to gain *episteme*–the knowledge of the true and good. "And this is the distinction I draw between the sight-loving, art-loving practical class and those of whom I am speaking, and who are alone worthy of the name of philosopher."

In characteristic dialectical fashion, Aristotle contrasted the kind of *episteme* gained by *theoria* with the practical knowledge (πρακτική) gained through *ergon* (ἔργον). This was to be a fateful pairing, for henceforth, theory and practice would be dialectically juxtaposed as if joined at the hip. In Aristotle's conceptual schema, the end of *praktike* is change in some object, whereas the end of *theoria* is knowledge of the object itself.[5]

3 Lobkowicz, *Theory and Practice: History of a Concept from Aristotle to Marx*, p. 15.

4 Plato, *Republic*, 5.18–20 (4736–4776) (Jowett trans.).

5 Aristotle, *Metaphysics*, ii. i. 5–7.

This is not to say that it was impossible to combine the two; on the contrary, Aristotle considered *theoria* not so much opposed to *praktike* as a higher form of *praktike*, while *praktike* was conversely a kind of applied theory.[6] Still, there is a fundamental epistemological distinction drawn between the two as principles of action. To recast these categories in related Aristotelian terminology, we could say that *theoria* is the discipline of final causes (that why a thing is made) and *praktike* that of formal causes (that into which a thing is made).[7]

It is helpful to understand these original meanings of *theoria*. For in its most fundamental sense, music theory is a science of final causes. Strictly speaking, music theory is not concerned with "formal" or "efficient" causes (how a piece of music is composed or performed). Instead, theory is to concern itself with basic ontological questions: what is the essential nature of music? What are the fundamental principles that govern its appearances? (Aristotle would have spoken of music's "forms.") The great medieval transmitter of ancient Greek thought Anicius Manlius Severinus Boethius (c. 480–523/26) famously divided this kind of musico-logy (literally, the "knowledge of music") into three parts: *musica mundana*, *musica humana*, and *musica instrumentalis*. All these kinds of "music" were united by "harmonia," the proper concordance of magnitudes and multitudes. *Musica mundana* concerned the macrocosmic harmony of the universe – the motion of the planets and the rhythms of the four seasons; *musica humana* concerned the microcosmic harmony of the body and soul – the disposition of the four humors and temperaments; and *musica instrumentalis* concerned the sounding harmony of "songs" made by singers and instrumentalists. For Boethius, a faithful student of Platonic thought, it was number and proportion that were the "final" cause governing each of these three kinds of harmony. The true philosopher of *ars musica*, the true musical *theoros*, was the one who understood this numerical basis of harmony beyond the shadows of its profane resonance in *musica instrumentalis*. And the discipline within which one studied the proportions underlying music in all its macrocosmic and microcosmic manifestations – and hence music theory in its most fundamental and authentic sense – was termed by ancient writers as "harmonics."

It is worth noting that no early writers actually used the double cognate "music theorist" to designate a student of harmonics. In a locution drawn from Plato, but extended by generations of medieval exegetes, Boethius simply called one who aspired to the true knowledge of music a "musician" (*musicus*, from the Greek *mousikos*). In one of the most widely repeated aphorisms from the Middle Ages, Guido of Arezzo could contrast a "musicus" who understood the philosophical nature of music with the ignorant singer ("cantor") who could only sound the notes: "Musicorum et cantorum

6 Ball, "On the Unity and Autonomy of Theory and Practice," p. 65.

7 A third form of activity discussed by Aristotle that is also related to music was *poiesis*, whose end is the object made, and hence a discipline of "efficient" causes – that by which a thing is made. But it would not be until the sixteenth century that *musica poetica* began to be taught as a distinct compositional discipline on a par with *musica practica* and *musica theorica*.

magna est distantia. Isti dicunt, illi sciunt, quae componit musica."[8] Of course we cannot forget that Guido was indeed concerned with real *musica instrumentalis*, unlike Boethius. We have unusually specific evidence concerning Guido's activities at Arezzo Cathedral during the early eleventh century as a director and teacher of choirboys. And he was widely credited with developing some of the most important and influential pedagogical aids to help singers learn their craft: staff notation for the accurate reading of neumes, solfège syllables to help learn and memorize chants, and an elementary grammatical taxonomy by which to compose and analyze these chants.[9]

Given the profound influence of Guido's "practical" writings – they were copied and distributed in the Middle Ages more widely than any other musical work save for Boethius's *De institutione musica*[10] – we are clearly entering a new period with new expectations for the *musicus*. For all that musicians of the early Middle Ages may have revered the authority of the Greek and Hellenistic writers – or at least what they gleaned through Boethius and Martianus Capella – they were also committed to another authority: that of the church and its sacred chant repertoire. Thus, as Joseph Smits van Waesberghe has pointed out, there was a pronounced tension between the *auctoritas ecclesiastica* and the *auctoritas greca* (although some theorists such as Hucbald strove mightily to reconcile the two).[11] No longer could a true musician remain aloof from musical practice and lead the contemplative life of the *bios theoretikos* (if indeed that was ever possible outside of Boethius's lonely prison cell, where he composed the *Consolatio philosophiae* shortly before his execution). Given that virtually all musical writers in the Middle Ages were associated in some way with the church, it would have been incredible for them not to have been concerned about the *musica instrumentalis* they would have heard and chanted in their daily offices of worship – the *opus Dei*. With the pressing need for Carolingian authorities to bring some kind of order to a burgeoning but chaotic chant practice, choir directors were pressed to think of means for classifying, notating, and teaching singers a stabilized chant repertoire. Aurelian's modest tract, *Musica disciplina*, from the late ninth century, was only the first such propaedeutic textbook of *musica plana* (although Aurelian still included generous coverage of more speculative topics rooted in *ars musica*; see **Chapter 11, pp. 314–15**). And as more complex performance problems arose with the introduction of improvised organum and discant singing, new pedagogical demands faced the *cantor* – above all, that of mensuration. (It was arguably not so much issues of modal identity or dissonance regulation that offered the most intractable problem to medieval musicians with the rise of contrapuntal

8 Indeed, Guido at one point compared the singer who did not understand music to an animal ("bestia"). For the complete quotation, see **Chapter 5, p. 163** of the present volume. For a masterly survey of the musicus–cantor dichotomy in medieval thought, see the entry "Musicus-Cantor" by Erich Reimer in *HmT* (1978).

9 Waesberghe, *Musikerziehung*, p. 23. Ironically, the pedagogical aid for which his name is probably best known – the Guidonian hand – was one for which he almost certainly had no responsibility.

10 Bernhard, "Das musikalische Fachschrifttum im lateinischen Mittelalter," p. 72.

11 Waesberghe, *Musikerziehung*, p. 19.

singing as it was the conceptualization and notation of a hierarchy of rhythmic values by which to coordinate the voices of *musica mensurabilis*.)

With the transmission into the West of many of Aristotle's most important writings by Arab writers beginning in the twelfth century, musicians finally were provided with an unimpeachable authority by which to legitimize the kinds of propaedeutic writings of Aurelian and Guido – or, as musical *praktike* was rendered by the twelfth-century translators of al-Fārābī, "musica activa." To be sure, as the venerable curriculum of the "studium generale" migrated from the Cathedral and monastic schools to the newly formed universities of Bologna, Paris, and Oxford, scholars continued to study and offer their own glosses of *musica speculativa* in the Boethian paradigm.[12] Much more vigorous, though, was the industry of music instructors (*praeceptores*) who attempted to offer regulation and codification for the various parameters of rapidly changing musical practice through the textbook genre of the *eisagoge*.[13] And even when speculative topics were taught, they were often done so within a treatise having largely practical aims.[14] Hundreds of music treatises were penned and copied throughout the Middle Ages that offered more or less practical guidance on every possible problem of singing and composition (the boundaries between the two hardly recognized). Even as scholastic rhetoric became increasingly conspicuous during the thirteenth and fourteenth centuries, musicians trained in the newly flourishing universities devoted most of their energies to issues of *musica activa*. While it is perhaps an exaggeration for Albrecht Riethmüller to say that music entered the Middle Ages as theory and left it as practice, there is no question that the prestige of music theory was now declining precipitously as a philosophical and scientific discipline.[15]

But it would be wrong to see this process simply as one of an invigorated pedagogy of *musica practica* evermore encroaching upon the territory of an enfeebled *musica speculativa*, of *usus* triumphing over *ars*. Rather, it was more a case of music theory being refocused, its principles reconfigured so as to accommodate better the domain of *musica instrumentalis*. Lawrence Gushee has remarked that theory and practice emerge

12 Carpenter, *Music in the Medieval and Renaissance Universities*, pp. 32ff. Properly speaking, we might note that the term *theoria* was never used in the Middle Ages to designate writings on music, even for the most speculative genre of harmonics. With the spread of Aristotelian thought in the thirteenth century, however, a number of scholastically trained musical writers did start to employ the Latin cognates *theoria* and *practica* in their writings, including the likes of Franco of Cologne, Jehan des Murs, Walter of Odington, and Johannes Grocheo. But as Jacques of Liège noted, there was already a perfectly good Latin translation for the Greek word *theoria*: *speculum* (*Compendium de musica* 1.1; *Speculum musicae* 5.13). Hence, whereas earlier medieval writers would refer to the *scientia* of music with regard to its philosophical study, later medieval writers employed the term *speculatio* (as in Jacques's eponymous *summa* of musical knowledge). It was only in the later fifteenth century that some Italian humanists (above all, Franchino Gaffurio) explicitly entitled their musical writings "theoria."

13 Waesberghe, *Musikerziehung*, pp. 24ff.

14 So works as early as the *Musica enchiriadis* and *Scolica enchiriadis*, texts from the late ninth century, can be read as both theoretical and practical, each containing Boethian discussions of musical arithmetic in addition to practical guides for notating, classifying, and singing chant and organum.

15 Riethmüller, "Probleme der spekulativen Musiktheorie im Mittelalter," p. 177.

in the Middle Ages not so much as distinct epistemological genres but more as a mix of intellectual styles, social functions, and musical contexts – features that may be differently combined in any given treatise.[16] Most treatises of "speculative" music theory in the late Middle Ages had dropped any serious discussion of celestial harmony (or at least, tempered it by a healthy dose of Aristotelian skepticism).[17] Instead, the authors of these treatises – mostly scholastic writers of encyclopedic *Summae* of comprehensive musical knowledge such as Jehan des Murs, Jacques of Liège, Walter of Odington, Marchetto of Padua, or Jerome of Moravia – took many of the received quantitative topics of classical harmonics – the tetrachord, octave species, calculations of interval ratios, etc. – and adapted them with various degrees of success to issues of contemporary musical practice. Problems of pitch material (scales, intervals, mode, and solfège) were grouped under the rubric of *musica plana*; that of rhythm and mensural theory (really a kind of advanced counterpoint) under the rubric of *musica mensurabilis*. Even that venerated tool of speculative canonics – the monochord – was now used in a highly practical way by teachers: as a musical instrument to establish pitches and scales for singers. The task of the music theorist was now that of the practical pedagogue: to teach the elements of music to be applied by the would-be performer or composer, while conversely helping to discipline that practice through the establishment of regulative rules. This is by no means to say that "speculative" knowledge of music was in complete disrepute; such knowledge was valued, but mainly to the extent that it could be of value to *musica practica*. The true *musicus* of the later Middle Ages was now the "cantor peritus et perfectus" – one who not only knew, but could do, to turn Guido's aphorism on its head.[18]

With the humanistic revival of ancient Greek thought in the latter half of the fifteenth century, we find some renewed interest in the Boethian paradigm of cosmic harmonics. Indeed, among many Italian humanists, we witness a veritable "mania for music theory," as Knud Jeppesen has so aptly put it.[19] Questions of interval calculation and tuning were attacked with a vigor not seen since the mysterious group of "harmonicists" reported by Aristoxenus almost 2,000 years earlier. Franchino Gaffurio (1451–1522) was one such individual. It is not without significance that his major incunabulum of 1492, the *Theorica musice*, explicitly resurrected the Greek appellation *theoria*.[20] In the scramble to find and translate any ancient text concerning musical

16 Gushee, "Questions of Genre," p. 388.

17 Again another terminological clarification is in order. No late medieval writer would call such philosophical writings on music "speculative theory," since it was understood that any properly "theoretical " discussion of music was "speculative" in the original, Platonic sense of the word. Albrecht Riethmüller has thus made the amusing point that the modern locution "speculative music theory" would have been doubly redundant for a medieval writer, since the original concept of *musica* as a quadrivial science already entailed the concepts of both *speculatio* and *theoria*. Riethmüller, "Probleme der spekulativen Musiktheorie im Mittelalter," p. 174.

18 Gushee, "Questions of Genre," p. 408.

19 Quoted in Palisca, *Humanism in Italian Renaissance Musical Thought*, p. 8.

20 *Theorica musice* (Milan, 1492). Gaffurio had actually published a shorter version of this treatise in 1480 entitled *Theoricum opus musicae disciplinae*.

topics, scholars of the late *Quattrocento* made the first real inroads in understanding Greek music theory.[21] The resulting publications of music theory – such as Gaffurio's – constituted a heady mix of antiquarian topics: the ancient Greek *tonoi* and genres, monochord calculations based on Euclid and Ptolemy, and reflections upon the cathartic and magical powers of music. Yet it is noteworthy that Gaffurio did not see himself restricted as a writer to the ancient parameters of *musica theorica*, for in his next major treatise, he dealt head on with practical issues of counterpoint, mode, and mensuration. His *Practica musice* of 1496 was conceived not so much in opposition to the text that preceded it, but rather as a logical and necessary complement to it, upon the foundation of which it builds. It is worth noting that of the most important treatises of speculative music theory that would be penned over the following centuries by Zarlino, Salinas, Cerone, Mersenne, and Rameau, all were paired with complementing treatises of *musica practica* – all indeed bound within the covers of the same volume. As Bartolomeo Ramis de Pareia (c. 1440–91) put it poetically, the new integration of theory and practice was as if "mouse and elephant can swim together; Daedalus and Icarus can fly together."[22]

The increasingly close dialectic that constituted Renaissance *theoria* and *practica* is paradigmatically evident in the area of tuning. As composers were increasingly employing tertian sonorities in their compositions by the fifteenth century, the received Pythagorean tuning of the ditone (81 : 64) was proving unsustainable. But the theoretical argument for tuning the major third to a just superparticular ratio (5 : 4) required considerable effort in the face of tenacious canonist traditions. The extended and passionate arguments waged on behalf of the justly tuned major third by Ramis de Pareia and his allies show vividly how traditional *musica theorica* was being bent in the service of practice.[23] Conversely, tuning became an area of speculative thought in the Renaissance that was in many ways far ahead of practice, contrary to the widespread notion that theory must necessarily lag behind. The various proposals for enharmonic or quasi-equal temperaments by the likes of Vincenzo Galilei, Nicola Vicentino, and Simon Stevin far outpaced the practice of their contemporaries and would have to wait at least another hundred years before enjoying wider acceptance and application by musicians.

An even more striking change in the fortunes of music theory, however, occurred in the late sixteenth and early seventeenth centuries at the advent of the so-called "scientific revolution." Many of the hitherto classical problems of musical harmonics – in particular the generation and ranking of consonances – were newly treated by scientists as problems of acoustical mechanics. This shift toward mechanics did not in fact dislodge music theory as a quantitative science. (One merely substituted proportions measured by vibrational frequency for those plotted out on a monochord.) But the shift did change much of the metaphysical grounding by which consonance was understood. No longer evaluated by numerological constructs (such as Zarlino's *senario*),

21 A story brilliantly told in Palisca's study, *Humanism in Italian Renaissance Musical Thought.*
22 *Musica practica* (1482) (Miller trans., p. 42).
23 Palisca, *Humanism in Italian Renaissance Musical Thought*, pp. 235–44.

consonance could be seen as a purely physiological consequence of coincidental vibrational frequencies; hence the boundary between consonance and dissonance could now be a continuum that shifted according to context and taste.[24]

Music theory thus seemed to have suffered a double loss by the end of the seventeenth century. On the one hand, it gradually receded from its Boethian heights through the robust growth of *musica practica* as a discipline. More and more energy seemed to be devoted to systematizing and regulating the parameters of a rapidly changing musical practice and poetics. On the other hand, many of the most time-honored problems with which music theory was historically identified, such as the measurement and evaluation of consonance, were now being appropriated by disciplines of natural science. (It was in 1701 that the French scientist Joseph Sauveur christened one area of this study as "acoustique.")

"Music theory" continued to be cultivated by a few scholars throughout the Enlightenment in the model of traditional classical canonics. But for the most part, any treatise employing "music theory" in its title presented a limited and by now rather impoverished picture of the venerable discipline, one usually limited to rather pedantic calculations of intervals and tuning systems.[25] To be sure, new mathematical techniques such as logarithms were applied in order to quantify with meticulous precision the various kinds of mean-tone and quasi-equal temperaments thought up by scientists and musicians. But many of these tunings, it should be stressed, were "paper" temperaments with little relevance to the ad hoc practice of most keyboardists.

Thus, by the eighteenth century, music theory had become only a shell of its former glory. (Rameau felt obliged on numerous occasions to defend the honor and dignity of music theory, while at the same time conceding such knowledge might be of little practical use to musicians.) Yet for every defender of music theory – such as Rameau or Lorenz Mizler (1711–78), the founder of the "Corresponding Society of Musical Science" – there were critics such as Johann Mattheson (1681–1764), who would lambaste music *theoria* (or, as he preferred to call it, "musical mathematics") as a discredited remnant of unenlightened prejudice, its advocates as "system builders" blindly – or deafly – constructing their elaborate numerical edifices with no regard to musical reality. With the weapons of empirical philosophy bequeathed by Locke, writers such as Mattheson could militantly hoist the Aristoxenian flag of *sensus* over that of *ratio*. Indeed, for most progressive thinkers of the Enlightenment, theory of almost any sort

24 Palisca, "Scientific Empiricism in Musical Thought," p. 109.

25 A representative sampling of such theory titles is suggestive: Otto Gibel, *Introductio musicae theoreticae didacticae. . . cum primis vero mathematica* (Bremen, 1660); Thomas Salmon, "The Theory of Musick Reduced to Arithmetical and Geometric Proportions" (1705); Leonhard Euler, *Tentamen novae theoriae musicae* (St. Petersburg, 1739); Friederich Wilhelm Marpurg, *Anfangsgründe der theoretischen Musik* (Leipzig, 1757); Giovanni Battista Martini, *Compendio della teoria de' numeri per uso del musico* (Bologna, 1769). Jean-Philippe Rameau's *Nouveau système de musique théorique* of 1726 is also in the tradition, it being "new" only in the sense that it substituted an acoustical principle – the *corps sonore* – as the origin of musical proportions rather than the traditional canonist origin in string divisions (as was proposed in his *Traité de l'harmonie* four years earlier).

was viewed suspiciously in comparison to the measured empiricism of inductive reasoning drawn from practice. (The French philosophes would contrast this as the *esprit de système* versus the *esprit systématique*.)

Perhaps because music theory had been so emptied of its traditional prestige and content, then, it was ripe to be rehabilitated with new empirical sobriety. By reconceiving theory as a systematic program of popular philosophy and pedagogy, Johann Georg Sulzer (1720–79) could appropriate the term in his ambitious encyclopedia of aesthetics, the *Allgemeine Theorie der schönen Künste* (1771–74). For Sulzer, theory was not so much an abstracted foundation of a given science from which are deduced empirical axioms in geometric fashion as it was a general process of reasoning by which the empirical and metaphysical components of a science were systematically itemized and coordinated (although it would not be until the end of the century that Kant completed Sulzer's great rescue project by rigorously working out the epistemological basis upon which valid theoretical reasoning may be conducted). Thus, in Sulzer's program, "theory" would necessarily encompass those "practical" elements of taxonomy and regulation necessary to the instruction of any art in addition to its more abstracted, normative principles. But while Sulzer's encyclopedia may have sketched out what such a program of music might entail (in the various articles written by Johann Kirnberger and his student J. A. P. Schulz), it was Johann Forkel (1749–1818), the famed music lexicographer, historian, organist, and music director at the university of Göttingen, who first – in 1777 – proposed a systematic program of study he called "Theorie der Musik" that seemed to fulfill Sulzer's plan.[26]

Far from restricting music theory to a rarefied science of interval calculations and tuning, Forkel redefines it as a broad pedagogical discipline of musical study "insofar as it is necessary and useful to amateurs and connoisseurs." Specifically, Forkel includes five parts within his program of music theory: 1. Physics; 2. Mathematics; 3. Grammar; 4. Rhetoric; 5. Criticism. Parts 1 and 2, roughly speaking, cover the traditional speculative domain of *musica theorica*, albeit updated with new scientific knowledge and languages. Parts 3 and 4 cover the traditional regulative functions of *musica practica* and poetics: systems of scales, keys, harmony, and meter, as well as their application by composers in terms of phrasing, genre, and rhetoric. Finally, part 5 foretokens a new concern that will play an increasingly important role in music-theoretical discussions: critical analysis. Here the theorist is concerned with such elusive qualities as the "inner character" of a musical work.[27] Forkel's program constitutes an extraordinary change in the meaning of music theory by radically expanding its domain in relation to practical pedagogy and criticism. No longer was music theory a preliminary or metaphysical foundation to practice. On the contrary, it was practical pedagogy that was now a subset of theory.

26 Forkel, "Über die Theorie der Musik" (1777).

27 Forkel's program is discussed in more detail by Leslie Blasius in the present volume, Chapter 1, pp. 39–40.

With the advent of the nineteenth century and the founding of the many music conservatories and schools throughout Europe that would institutionalize the training of the next generations of performers, composers, and conductors, music theory fractured into a number of competing disciplinary paradigms that elude easy synthesis. On the one hand, the utilitarian turn of music theory evidenced in Forkel's program was taken up by a few nineteenth-century theorists in whose works theory was colloquially understood as a general program of music pedagogy. Characteristic is Gottfried Weber's comprehensive *Kompositionslehre*, the *Versuch einer geordneten Theorie der Tonsetzkunst* (Mainz, 1817–21). Yet in its tendentious empiricism, Weber's "Systematically Arranged Theory of Composition" hardly would be recognized as a theory of music in any sense by a writer such as Gaffurio – or even Mattheson for that matter.[28] On the other hand, some authors continued to use the term in the area of music in its more traditional sense of speculative foundations (e.g. Moritz Hauptmann in his treatise of pseudo-Hegelian musical dialectics, *Die Natur der Harmonik und Metrik: Zur Theorie der Musik* [Leipzig, 1853]). Still other writers conflated "theory" with the most rudimentary program of music pedagogy, as in the following pocket catechism published in America in 1876: *Palmer's Theory of Music: Being a Practical Guide to the Study of Thorough-Bass, Harmony, Musical Composition and Form* (Cincinnati, 1876).

If there is one element that might tie many of these various configurations of nineteenth-century "music theory" together, it is that authors increasingly relied upon the study of musical works from which they deduced – and illustrated – their teachings. While selected examples of music analysis can be cited as far back as the Middle Ages, it was only in the nineteenth century that theorists would regularly cite musical examples in their texts, more often than not drawn from a rapidly coalescing canon of "classical" masterworks. The aim in most cases was not – as with earlier theories – to look at individual works in order to derive normative patterns of compositional practice; rather, analysis was employed to gain insight into and understanding of the individuating particulars of the artwork, the analysis often being couched in the rhetoric of biological organicism. For the most ardent Romanticists, in fact, masterworks were defined precisely by their uniqueness, their status as sublime creations of genius that we might only begin to comprehend – though never replicate – through profound and prolonged contemplation.[29] (Thus then does the activity of music analysis curl back and connect with the original Platonic occupation of the *theoros*.)

By the beginning of the twentieth century, a sharp reaction to music theory as a pedagogical discipline had set in. Partly in response to the grand theoretical projects of

28 It is not surprising that at least in German-speaking countries, *Musiktheorie* never caught on as a broad disciplinary appellation, being superseded at the end of the nineteenth century by the program of *systematische Musikwissenschaft* articulated by Guido Adler. And to this day, *Musiktheorie* is mostly equated in Germany with practical skills in musicianship, found primarily in the music conservatories or *Hochschulen* rather than the univerisities.

29 Ian Bent's *Musical Analysis in the Nineteenth Century* (see p. xxiii) offers a valuable survey of some of this literature, with insightful commentary and lucid translations.

scholars such as Hugo Riemann (who, ironically, never actually entitled any of his works as theoretical),[30] writers such as Arnold Schoenberg would castigate the pretensions and conservatism of academic music theorists; indeed, the whole preface to the third edition of Schoenberg's own *Harmonielehre* (1921) opens with a blistering assault on the hidebound discipline of "Musiktheorie" and its stultified pedantry.[31] Heinrich Schenker's own *bêtes noires* were the "concert guides" of musical hermeneutics penned by the likes of Hermann Kretzschmar. Pointedly, Schenker entitled his own rehabilitation project "*New* Musical Theories and Fantasies" in clear contradistinction to the impressionistic poetical readings of Kretzschmar and his company.

Polemics aside, the twentieth century witnessed an unprecedented explosion of music theory. Not since the late fifteenth century was there such a fermentation of theoretical thought in all its various guises: speculative, practical, and analytical. Certainly one explanation can be posited: the loss of a common language of harmonic tonality. In the case of Schoenberg, of course, this entailed the formulation of an entirely new compositional system of serialism "using twelve tones related to one another" that he believed was the natural and inevitable successor of harmonic tonality. For Heinrich Schenker, on the other hand, this entailed a defensive, almost reactionary music theory that sought to rescue and validate a waning tonal tradition of which he believed himself to be a guardian and expositor. The two theoretical paradigms that Schoenberg and Schenker bequeathed – those of compositional (prescriptive) serial theory and of analytical (descriptive) tonal theory, respectively – proved to be two of the most resilient and resonant in the twentieth century.

Another remarkable development of twentieth-century music theory was its broad professionalization as it became increasingly institutionalized within university programs. Like its medieval precursor, the modern university, particularly in North America, has offered a congenial home to the dedicated music theorist. This professionalization of music theory may be credited to a number of factors. There was of course the growth of musicology itself as an academic discipline, in which the scholarly study of music and musical documents (including those of historical music theory) was cultivated. There was also a favorable intellectual climate, particularly at mid-century, in which "positivistic" sciences were widely cultivated, and music analysis was a beneficiary – or at least certain styles of more "formalistic" analysis (of which Schenker's, ironically, became a prime example).[32] Finally, there was a growing sense that the practical subject matter of music theory pedagogy (historically considered the domain of *musica practica*, as we have seen) demanded specialists for its teaching.

30 His very first publication, a series of articles which appeared in 1872 under the title "Musikalische Logik: Ein Beitrag zur Theorie der Musik," is the exception that proves the point.

31 Yet it is as ironic as it is indicative that the English translation of Schoenberg's treatise published sixty years later would bear a title that would surely have its author turning in his grave: *Theory of Harmony*.

32 For an insightful narrative of the intellectual origins of contemporary American music theory, see McCreless, "Rethinking Contemporary Music Theory."

Thus, by the 1950s, we find the first academic appointments of music theory in several American music departments and the foundation of advanced degree programs in music theory. (The Yale University Department of Music, under the leadership of Paul Hindemith, seems to have been the first academic institution to establish a music theory degree in the modern era.[33]) Significant, too, was the founding of several scholarly journals devoted to music theory, including the *Journal of Music Theory* (1957) and *Perspectives of New Music* (1962). The former journal was associated appropriately enough with the Yale program, the latter with the music department at Princeton University, where a combined program of composition and theory was developed under the leadership of Milton Babbitt. Noteworthy, too, was the founding of the Society for Music Theory in 1977, the first scholarly society devoted to the discipline of music theory since Mizler's organization some two hundred years earlier. And while this professionalization of music theory was initially limited to North American universities, in more recent years it has become broadly international in scope, with new courses of study, degree programs, conferences, and publications devoted to music theory springing up around the world each year.

At the opening of the twenty-first century, then, there seems little doubt that music theory has once again firmly found its place in the scholarly study of music. To be sure, there remain many of the same disciplinary tensions we have witnessed in previous centuries between practical and speculative strains of musical study, between descriptive and prescriptive methods of inquiry. And music theory has continued to suffer its share of criticisms in the wake of the general rise of postmodern malaise at the close of the twentieth century. In particular, a number of musicologists have faulted theorists for cleaving to a perceived modernist mentality innocent of questions concerning cultural or social context. Certainly among music theorists themselves, there have been spirited debates and some anxious hand-wringing concerning the identity and methods of music theory. But as we enter a new millennium in the now two and a half millennia old discipline of music theory, a new sense of confidence and energy seems to be animating the work of theorists. One of the most remarkable signs of this new vitalization is seen in the recent resurgence of unabashed speculative theorizing among a number of scholars. For instance, under the general rubric of "neo-Riemannian" theory, a group of theorists led by David Lewin, Richard Cohn, and John Clough have sought to extend imaginatively some ideas drawn from Hugo Riemann's theory of harmonic functions using advanced tools of algebraic group theory.[34] Their aim is not so much to deduce insight analytically from musical practice, or to regulate music peda-

33 Ironically, Yale had established an endowed chair in the Theory of Music as early as 1890. (The first appointment was of Jakob Stoeckel, by then a senior music instructor at the Yale School of Music.) But the real florescence of scholarly music theory came to Yale only with Hindemith's arrival in 1940 in the newly consitituted Department of Music (Forte, "Paul Hindemith's Contribution to Music Theory in the United States," p. 6).

34 A useful introduction to the work of these theorists is provided in Richard Cohn's essay, "Introduction to Neo-Riemannian Theory: A Survey and a Historical Perspective."

gogically. Rather, they aim for a most traditional goal: to explore the universe of tonal *materia* in order to understand its boundless properties and potential. This resuscitation of the seemingly dormant tradition of speculative harmonics constitutes a remarkable chapter in the long history of music theory and suggests that the venerable study of *ars musica* as envisioned almost 1,500 years ago by Boethius may yet have the capacity to animate the imagination of musicians.

II

I have offered this abbreviated – and obviously highly selective – survey of the disciplinary peregrinations of music theory as it vividly opens up one of the fundamental difficulties facing the present volume in defining its proper subject matter. The problem is not simply one of vicissitudes of labels and lexical taxonomies; rather, it goes to the fundamental ontological changes of meaning concerning *musica theorica*. To return to Dahlhaus's challenge raised at the beginning of this introduction, we can see how the writing of a "history of music theory" poses any number of formidable paradoxes. To be at all meaningful, such a history would have to be both prospective and retrospective; it would need to look forward to the changes and ruptures of meaning that *theoria* underwent from its earliest conceptions – its migration into the emerging fields of acoustics and analysis, for example – as well as look backwards and reconstruct an idealized discipline of music theory containing topics that were not originally considered to be part of its program of study, such as the propaedeutic writings of the Middle Ages or many of the treatises of musical poetics and performance from the Baroque and Classical eras. Put simply, a comprehensive history of "music theory" must include a prodigious quantity of topics and problems that were at differing times not properly considered to be part of it.

Such a history of music theory is only conceivable, then, if we abandon any fixed definition of theory and allow instead for a flexible network of meanings. Dahlhaus has proposed one way to do this by distinguishing various "traditions" of music theory.[35] For Dahlhaus, the "speculative" and "practical" tensions we have just analyzed constitute two discrete traditions of "theorizing" that need to be kept conceptually separate, however entangled they may appear within any given text. The "speculative" tradition he characterizes as the "ontological contemplation of tone systems." This would encompass, then, not only the traditional programs of classical harmonics and canonics but much research in the areas of acoustics and tuning theory during the seventeenth and eighteenth centuries and tone psychology in the nineteenth and twentieth centuries. The second "practical" tradition is characterized by Dahlhaus as the "regulation" and "coordination" of these tone systems applied to compositional

35 Dahlhaus, *Grundzüge einer Systematik*, pp. 6–9.

practice. As a regulatory discipline, such music "theory" seeks to draw from practice normative rules of syntax and models of structure, while at the same time disciplining that practice through pedagogical strictures. Here we would have an even more expansive category of pedagogical writings crossing the centuries and touching on just about every parameter of music: counterpoint, harmony, rhythm, meter, melody, form, genre, and style. Dahlhaus adds a third theoretical tradition to his outline, one that really only rose to prominence in the nineteenth century, although it was foretokened, as we have seen, by Forkel: music analysis. Here, the music analyst studies individual musical works not so much to derive normative patterns of compositional practice, as to gain understanding of the individuating particulars of the artwork.

Dahlhaus calls each of these theoretical traditions "paradigms" (borrowing from the historian of science Thomas Kuhn).[36] It should be obvious from our brief historical overview that the boundaries among these three traditions are porous. Many theories and theorists mix them dialectically in often quite intricate ways. (For example, it would hardly be an effortless task to disentangle those elements of Schenker's theory that are regulative from those that are analytic – let alone even speculative.) Still, these three traditions can be useful heuristics in sorting out the diversity of theoretical "styles" we find throughout history. By thinking of music theory less as epistemology than as a conceptual attitude, perhaps it is possible to map out a kind of historical evolution of musical thought while at the same time accounting for divergences and diversity within this thought.

It goes without saying that the writing of such a history entails potential pitfalls. We need only glance backwards at a few of the attempts to construct a history of music theory to see what some of these might be. Perhaps the first such attempt was by François Joseph Fétis (1784–1871), who published his *Esquisse de l'histoire de l'harmonie, considérée comme art et comme science systématique* in 1840 as a monograph to preface his famous treatise on harmony. (In fact, the *Esquisse* was subsequently revised and included as the fourth and concluding section of Fétis's oft-reprinted *Traité de l'harmonie*.) In a desultory survey of theoretical writings that begins in the Middle Ages, Fétis attempted to chronicle the evolution of harmonic thought culminating in his own formulation of *tonalité*. Inspired by Hegel's philosophy of history, Fétis saw music theorists as vessels of an emerging tonal consciousness scrolling across time, and he was therefore not slow to either praise or censure any given writer depending upon how closely the writer was able to give voice to this tonal spirit.[37] But clearly, Fétis's myopic teleology coupled with an almost pathological orientalist prejudice severely constricted the value of his survey, one further marred by his notoriously sloppy scholarship.[38]

36 Dahlhaus, "Was heisst 'Geschichte der Musiktheorie'?," p. 29.

37 Christensen, "Fétis and Emerging Tonal Consciousness."

38 A sort of "follow up" history to Fétis's that has received far less attention but is certainly valuable for its bibliographic expanse, is Chevaillier, "Les Théories harmoniques."

Of far greater scholarly value and breadth, although perhaps no less lacking in historicist audacity, is the *Geschichte der Musiktheorie* first published in 1898 by Hugo Riemann (1849– 1919). Riemann was able to offer a far more detailed study than Fétis of historical music theory since the Middle Ages, drawing upon the fruits of the first generation of German musicology (to which he was himself an active contributor). Broadening his survey to include problems of mensural theory, counterpoint, mode, tuning, acoustics, and what he termed (borrowing from Forkel) "musical logic," Riemann produced a stunning historical synthesis of materials that can still be profitably – if cautiously – consulted by scholars today. Tellingly, Riemann's work has been translated into English, and until the present volume, has constituted the only such history to be published in English. Still, like Fétis's, Riemann's history is crippled by an almost fatal Whiggism, one in which past harmonic theories are measured by the extent to which they are seen as adumbrating Riemann's own controversial view of harmonic functionality and dualism.[39] And given the vast increase of musicological knowledge in the century since Riemann's history was published, there is scarcely a paragraph in it that does not stand in need of some correction or qualification.

As I noted earlier, the twentieth century has seen impressive advances in the study of historical music theory. The editions of Gerbert and Coussemaker of the most important medieval theory treatises have been supplemented by vastly more accurate scholarly editions.[40] Virtually the entire surviving corpus of Greek musical writings is now available in meticulously annotated translations (and accessible to any scholar for comparison and study through electronic databases). And important monographs now exist that shed light on the lives and works of many of the most important music theorists, including Rameau, Riemann, Schoenberg, and Schenker.[41]

One recent scholarly project related to historical music theory, however, does stand out from the rest and deserves special mention here. Beginning in 1977, a group of German musicologists under the leadership of Frieder Zaminer at the Berlin Staatliches Institut für Musikforschung undertook to produce a new history of music theory that aimed to be as expansive in coverage as it was detailed in its treatment of subject matter. Eventually to constitute fifteen volumes, the Berlin *Geschichte der Musiktheorie* promises to offer the most scholarly survey yet published on topics of historical music theory. (As of this date of writing, ten of the fifteen planned volumes have appeared in print; see the bibliography on **pp. xxii–xxiii**.) It can already be said that many of the lengthy chapters in this project – most of which are substantial monographs in themselves – are already classical sources to which all future scholars will

39 Burnham, "Method and Motivation in Hugo Riemann's History of Harmonic Theory."

40 See Huglo, "Bibliographie des éditions et études relatives à la théorie musicale du Moyen Âge (1972–1987)."

41 A good starting point into this literature is the indispensable bibliography compiled by David Damschroder and David Russell Williams (*Music Theory from Zarlino to Schenker*), even though their work is limited–as its title would suggest – roughly to theorists active from the late sixteenth to the early twentieth century.

need to turn. Indeed, readers will find many references to these studies in the present volume (and including this introduction). But for all its indispensable scholarly value, the Zaminer project still can be an unwieldy – and not always uniform – resource, with great fluctuation in coverage among the individual contributors. And for the reader lacking fluency in the German language, the work will obviously be of limited value.

It is to meet the needs of English-speaking scholars, then, that the *Cambridge History of Western Music Theory* was conceived. We have set for ourselves two ambitious – and not always consonant – goals. First, we seek to provide a comprehensive, broad historical survey of the vast and varied historical terrain of music theory we have outlined above that draws upon the prodigious amount of scholarly research produced over the past decades. Second, we seek to do so in the most synthetic manner possible. If I may use a relevant analogy: we aim for the expansive, observational overview of the *theoros*, with the empirical sobriety and pragmatic efficiency of *praktike*.

To this end, thirty-two experts in the area of historical music theory were commissioned to contribute to this project. Following Dahlhaus's suggestion, we have imposed a tripartite conceptual division, comprising the speculative, regulatory and analytic traditions he has outlined.[42] Within these three broad categories, readers will quickly see that we have employed a variety of historiographical approaches involving both diacronic (chronologically delimited) and synchronic (broadly thematic) approaches. As a principal aim of this project was to provide English-speaking readers with a practical research tool, we felt it necessary to limit the size of each chapter. Each author was thus encouraged to come up with an organizational strategy by which the key issues of the chapter could be efficiently treated, perhaps using only a few representative topics or authors as nodal points around which others may be clustered or refracted. The *Cambridge History of Western Music Theory*, it should be stressed, aims to be more a resource for scholars and students than a source itself. To aid in this goal, we have been generous in our use of musical examples, graphs, tables, textual "windows" and other illustrative material. At the same time, multiple cross-citations have been provided to guide the reader to related discussions in other chapters, as well as to underscore the thematic unity of the volume (these cross-references are indicated in boldface type within the text and in the footnotes). Finally, each chapter is provided with its own bibliographies of important primary and secondary sources to which the reader will be guided for further information (commonly cited sources are abbreviated, however, according to the list on pp. xxii–xxiii).

It should go without saying, although I will nonetheless do so here, that the resulting thirty-one essays cannot possibly presume comprehensive coverage over such a vast intellectual and creative domain. As replete as we have tried to make this volume, there will obviously be gaps and omissions. Most crucially, we decided early on that the

42 It is ironic that the *Geschichte der Musiktheorie* project discussed above does not betray much evidence of Dahlhaus's conceptual organization, despite that the very essay in which he outlined his ideas served as a kind of prolegomenon of the whole project.

many distinguished non-Western traditions of music theorizing could not be given any responsible coverage within the modest scope of the present project. But even within the Western domain, many authors, theoretical concepts, and national traditions must remain unmentioned. At the same time, there has been some unavoidable duplication in the treatment of certain prominent theorists. In particular, names like Aristoxenus, Zarlino, Rameau, Riemann, and Schenker will be frequently encountered in the chapters of this volume, their writings raked over from a number of different directions. Yet by this means, we hope precisely to indicate the complex – and interdependent – nature of the music-theoretical enterprise. Although we cannot promise exhaustive coverage of our topics, we do modestly hope that within our thirty-one chapters, most of the major issues of Western music theory are mapped out, the principal theoretical problems, personalities, and publications discussed, and varying social functions, intellectual influences, and historical contexts given due consideration.

III

To help the reader more efficiently navigate this volume, the following discussion is provided as an organizational orientation. We begin Part I with a triad of "meta-historical" essays that set out to explore some of the conceptual problems involved in defining music theory from a historical perspective – most of which expand upon issues that have been touched upon in this introduction. Thus, Leslie Blasius opens up our volume appropriately enough by analyzing the ontological problem of organizing and "mapping out" the conceptual geographies of music theory through a number of case studies. The tension between music theory and practice that I have already sounded as a Leitmotiv in this introduction receives further treatment in Robert Wason's panoptic essay on "practical" music theory pedagogy (Chapter 2). Finally, Nicholas Cook attempts to inventory and analyze many of the intricate epistemological claims made by music theorists over the ages, some of them explicitly articulated, others only covertly so (Chapter 3).

Under Part II, "Speculative Traditions," we group together seven essays concerning those currents of musical thought that may be affiliated to the original ontological conception of *musica theorica* discussed above. This includes, naturally, detailed consideration of Greek musical harmonics (Chapter 4 by Thomas Mathiesen) and its dissemination and reception in the early Middle Ages (Chapter 5 by Calvin Bower). But as Bower's chapter makes clear, in the very earliest medieval writings the dialectical tension with musical practice comes to the fore. In a suggestive poetic image, Bower likens this tectonic collision of musical epistemologies to that of a voice-leading suspension: the dissonant clash of *musica practica* in the early tenth century against the sustained tone of traditional speculative theory is ultimately resolved in the course of the Middle Ages to the discipline we can call "music theory." This synthesis is made more concrete in the following chapter by Jan Herlinger (Chapter 6). The medieval science of dividing the monochord – "canonics" – seems obviously related to the quadrivial tradition of *musica theorica*. Yet the ever-enlarging pitch gamuts that resulted from these divisions during the thirteenth through fifteenth centuries, as well as their reconfiguration through tuning, were ultimately motivated by changes of musical practice. Rudolf Rasch continues the unfolding story of tuning and temperament theory into the eighteenth century (Chapter 7) where we find some of the most brilliant scientific minds of the time attempting to reconcile the musical preference for justly tuned consonances with the practical needs of a tempered twelve-note keyboard gamut.

Of more secure affiliation to the tradition of ancient harmonics is the subject matter of Chapter 8 by Penelope Gouk, although it is a topic that is not likely to be familiar to most musicians today. During the period we now call the "scientific revolution," spanning the "long" seventeenth century, ancient cosmological harmonics provided an ordered – and quantitative – model of the universe that inspired scientists such as Galileo, Kepler, and Newton in their own searches to discover the mathematical laws regulating the motions of the planets. Yet not all of the scientific work during this period can properly be ascribed to harmonics. In Chapter 9, co-authored by Burdette Green and David Butler, we are shown how many of the traditional problems of speculative music theory – understanding the nature of sound, or evaluations of consonance and dissonance – were absorbed into the research paradigm of physical acoustics, eventually developing into the nineteenth-century field of tone psychology. Finally, we have attempted to document the continued vigor – and perhaps even rejuvenation – of speculative music theory by considering the role mathematics continued to play in much twentieth-century scholarship (Chapter 10 by Catherine Nolan).

Given the overwhelming importance practical pedagogy has historically enjoyed in the work of most music theorists, the tradition of "regulative" music theory covered in Part III not surprisingly comprises the bulk of this volume. In the opening chapters that will constitute Section IIIA, four authors will consider the problem of "tonal space" as conceptualized by theorists at key historical moments. This has traditionally constituted one of the most important and challenging tasks of music theory. We will see in David E. Cohen's contribution (Chapter 11) how the very notion of a pitch space – and indeed, of pitch itself – proved a difficult ontological conundrum for Carolingian theorists, and the resultant struggle this entailed in their attempts to conceive, parse, and notate this space. For subsequent generations of theorists, challenges lay in accommodating and articulating these concepts of tonal space in the light of ever-changing compositional languages, whether that of an elusive Renaissance modal taxonomy (Chapter 12 by Cristle Collins Judd), the emergence of a transposable major/minor key system in the seventeenth century (Chapter 13 by Gregory Barnett), or finally, a chromatic tonal space in the nineteenth century in which new models of transpositional relations and dualist properties could be imaged (Chapter 14 by Henry Klumpenhouwer).

The propaedeutic demands of compositional pedagogy that increasingly encroached upon the domain of *musica theorica* beginning in the Middle Ages constitutes the heart of the chapters in Section IIIB. Five case studies are presented: medieval organum and discant practice (Chapter 15 by Sarah Fuller), Renaissance contrapuntal pedagogy (Chapter 16 by Peter Schubert), species counterpoint as a compositional disciplinary matrix (Chapter 18 by Ian Bent), and systems of serial composition conceived early in the twentieth century (Chapter 19 by John Covach) accounting for four of them. In all of these chapters, a constant epistemological tension will again be observed in the theorists' attempt to be both descriptive and prescriptive: to account analytically for some empirical component of compositional practice while at the same time regulating and codifying that very practice through the systematization of prescriptive rules and heuristic taxonomies. Although the topic of Chapter 17 by Albert Cohen might seem out of place here – it concerns the improvisation guidelines offered to instrumentalists in many Baroque music treatises – it too constitutes a theory of "compositional" poetics.

The three chapters of Section IIIC concern another important parameter of musical practice that is historically entangled with music theory: musical time. Here, perhaps more than in any other topic, we see how porous the borders can be between theory and practice, for many of the developments and advances of composers in exploring the temporal parameters of music are directly contingent upon music theory for conceptual clarification, notation, and pedagogy. Whether we consider problems of medieval mensural notation (Chapter 20 by Anna Maria Busse Berger), classical metrical theories (Chapter 21 by William Caplin), or twentieth-century concepts of time and rhythm (Chapter 22 by Justin London), theories of rhythm and meter have always constituted real metaphysical challenges; implicit behind the many "practical" problems of notating rhythm and meter lurk intractable philosophical issues about the ontology and phenomenology of musical temporality.

Section IIID, which we have cautiously called "tonality," marks another precarious slippage in theory's epistemology from the empirical to the metaphysical. Tonality, as Brian Hyer shows us in Chapter 23, is one of the most elusive conceptual categories of music theory, burdened with weighty rhetorical, ideological, and historiographical baggage. Yet it also seems to be an indispensable concept. The subsequent three chapters offer more framed case studies of this concept as represented through the harmonic theories of arguably its three most influential advocates: Rameau (Chapter 24 by Joel Lester), Riemann (Chapter 25 by David W. Bernstein), and Schenker (Chapter 26 by William Drabkin). While numerous other theorists are considered in each of these chapters, the triumvirate of Rameau, Riemann, and Schenker certainly constitutes the three most important thinkers grappling with the problem of tonality: their systems of the fundamental bass, harmonic functionality, and the *Ursatz* offer three of the most compelling theories ever conceived for modeling this tonality.

As I have already mentioned, the rationale for grouping all of the chapters in Part III together is that, in the broadest sense, each chapter deals with some problem of "practical" theory. Each considers pedagogical formulations that result from an inductive process whereby empirical observations of musical practice become the starting point for generalized descriptions and compositional regulations. The fourth and final part of this volume contains five essays that instead remain within the general paradigm of "music analysis" whereby the theorist's concern is upon the individual structure or experience of a piece of music. (Nicholas Cook has called this "performative" music theory: see **Chapter 3, pp. 91–99.**) Again, it cannot be emphasized enough that this stands in a dialectical relation with the regulatory traditions dealt with in Part III. Nonetheless, in Section IVA, we are provided with three chapters that attempt to explore historically significant paradigms of musical analysis as independent traditions. In what is arguably the earliest such tradition of analysis, Patrick McCreless considers in Chapter 27 the use of rhetoric through the seventeenth and eighteenth centuries as an analytic taxonomy for musical structure and compositional process. In Chapter 28, Scott Burnham turns to the nineteenth-century topic of *Formenlehre* and considers the prototypical construct of "sonata form" as a synecdoche to the broader problem of inferring and ossifying formal models of musical structure. The isolation and comparison of motives, which constitute such a significant aspect of most analytic methods, is explored by Jonathan Dunsby in Chapter 29 from three completely differing models relying upon contrasting intellectual sources: Schoenberg's theory of developing variation and its roots in Goethean organicism, structural semiotics and its derivation from generative linguistics, and pitch-class set theory and its intersections with mathematical group theory.

We have included the last two chapters on music psychology of Section IVB under the general rubric of "analytic" theories, in that the kinds of questions asked there are those that often relate to the experience of some musical piece, not unlike that of analytical theory. That is, both the music analyst and music psychologist can be seen as concerned with the empirical musical work and its reception – in the latter case by a sentient, cognitive being. Concern with the psychological effects of music, as Lee Rothfarb shows in Chapter 30, goes back a long way; since antiquity, musicians have relied upon an assortment of "energeticist" metaphors to describe the musical experience. It was only at the turn of the twentieth century, though, that it became the central concern of a remarkable group of German-speaking theorists. And it was not until later in the twentieth century, as Robert Gjerdingen shows us in Chapter 31, that systematic theories of musical cognition were first worked out by which the phenomenological experience of music could be more empirically analyzed.

IV

Given the diversity of approaches taken by the authors in this volume, the attentive reader will note some mild dissonances between chapters. Assessments of the importance of certain theorists and their legacy are not always uniform; interpretations of many theoretical concepts vary slightly from chapter to chapter. The editor has felt it incumbent upon himself not to intercede in all cases and attempt to resolve such discrepancies. Rather, all authors have been encouraged to find their own vantage point, to express their own opinions without polemic. In every case, we have attempted to verify facts when we can. But ultimately, the stories that unfold over the following pages are ones told by many voices.

If there is one unifying theme to the stories that emerge from all these chapters, perhaps, it is in the perplexing and never-ending dilemmas music theory engenders: a discipline that seems to stand apart from practice yet is inextricably tied to that practice; a discipline that claims to transcend history yet is through and through historical. Ultimately, I believe, none of these tensions can be – or should be – resolved. Rather, each can be seen as helping to provide the energy and impetus of the music-theoretical enterprise. For theory is not just a set of observational tools; these tools also tell us something about those who use them. If we recall that the Latin root of "theory" – *speculum* – also means "mirror," we can begin to understand how historical music theories act as a mirror of past musical intellectual cultures, ones in which the theorist too is reflected as an observer. For the very act of reflection must necessarily put the interlocutor in a recursive relation with the object under scrutiny. There is ultimately no transcendental point of observation, given that such reflection must always take place at a given position in culture and in time. A true theory of music, then, reflects in both directions, telling us as much about the individual theorist as it does about the musical problem under consideration. At the same time, we as historians enter into this optical nexus, with our own reflections upon the past shining back in our own faces, revealing something about our own position in this labyrinth of historical hermeneutics.

This reflexivity of music theory was already understood in the eighteenth century by an insightful – though today little-known – music pedagogue named Johann Kessel (c. 1766–1823). Inspired by the historicist theories of his contemporary Johann Gottfried Herder, Kessel recognized that the evolution of music theory – like musical art itself – could offer a revealing window to our understanding of past musical cultures:

> Since music itself is always changing and will continue to change, so must from time to time new theories of composition be developed that can explain and justify these new changes . . . Whoever wishes to penetrate the spirit of an entire nation and an age or the history of mankind should perhaps give attention to musical artworks and their theories in order to gain deeper understanding . . . [43]

The shifting configurations of music theory over the centuries, then, far from undermining any epistemic claims to transcendence or logical coherence, in fact endow the discipline with cultural vitality and relevance. The differing questions posed as well as the differing tools and languages used to answer these questions constitute windows through which the historian may look and glimpse a view of past musical cultures,

43 Kessel, *Unterricht im Generalbasse zum Gebrauche für Lehrer und Lernende*, Preface.

thereby allowing us to see what problems of music theory were considered most pressing to solve, what topics of pedagogy the most critical for students to master. In short, a theory text may be itself a *speculum* of intellectual and spiritual values as we observe the struggle of theorists to answer anew the age-old question of the scholastics: "Quid sit musica?"[44]

Grau, teurer Freund, ist alle Theorie,
grün des Lebens goldener Baum . . .

"Grey, dear friend, is all theory" – Goethe's Mephisto famously warns Faust. And from the perspective of the author of the *Farbenlehre*, the systematic theorizing of Newton's mechanical universe might have indeed seemed dishearteningly monochromatic in comparison to the living colors of the "golden tree of life." Yet theories of music, whether lying low to the empirical ground, or soaring high into the rarefied air of speculation and abstraction have nonetheless always possessed the capacity to instruct and inspire. Far from finding theory only an etiolating agent of impoverishment, countless generations of musicians have on the contrary found the intellectual contemplation of music to be enriching and ennobling, one that endows the musical experience with increased pleasure and profounder meaning.

It has been a crooked journey since Pythagoras first stumbled into the blacksmith's forge and contemplated the numerical ratios that underlay the harmonious sounds he had heard. But as long as we continue to contemplate that delightful phenomenon which so enchants our ears, engages our minds, agitates our emotions, and lifts our souls, there will always be those who pursue the intellectual quest. They will wish to engage in that ethical speculation of music, to assume the venerable and honorable occupation that is the true *theoros* of music.

44 I have elaborated this hermeneutic thesis further in my essay, "Music Theory and its Histories."

Bibliography

Ball, T. "On the Unity and Autonomy of Theory and Practice," in *Political Theory and Praxis: New Perspectives*, ed. T. Ball, Minneapolis, University of Minnesota Press, 1977, pp. 13–27

Bernhard, M. "Das musikalische Fachschrifttum im lateinischen Mittelalter,' in *Rezeption des Antiken Fachs im Mittelalter*, *GMt* 3 (1990), pp. 37–104

Burnham, S. "Method and Motivation in Hugo Riemann's History of Harmonic Theory," *MTS* 14 (1992), pp. 1–14

Carpenter, N. C. *Music in the Medieval and Renaissance Universities*, Norman, University of Oklahoma Press, 1958; New York, Da Capo, 1972

Chevaillier, L. "Les Théories harmoniques," in *Encyclopédie de la musique et Dictionnaire du*

Conservatoire, 4 vols., ed. A. Lavignac and L. de la Laurencie, Paris, Delagrave, 1925, vol. II, pp. 519–90

Christensen, T. "Fétis and Emerging Tonal Consciousness," in *Music Theory in the Age of Romanticism*, ed. I. Bent, Cambridge University Press, 1996, pp. 37–56

"Music Theory and its Histories," in *Music Theory and the Exploration of the Past*, ed. C. Hatch and D. W. Bernstein, University of Chicago Press, 1993, pp. 9–39

Cohn, R. "Introduction to Neo-Riemannian Theory: A Survey and a Historical Perspective," *JMT* 42 (1998), pp. 167–80

Dahlhaus, C. "Was heisst 'Geschichte des Musiktheorie'?," in *Ideen zu einer Geschichte der Musiktheorie*, *GMt* 1 (1985), pp. 8–39

Die Musiktheorie im 18. Und 19. Jahrhundert: Grundzüge einer Systematik, *GMt* 10 (1984)

Damschroder, D. and D. R. Williams, *Music Theory from Zarlino to Schenker: A Bibliography and Guide*, Stuyvesant, NY, Pendragon Press, 1990

Farmer, H. G. "Al-Fārābī's Arabic-Latin Writings on Music" (1965), in *Studies in Oriental Music*, vol. I, Frankfurt am Main, 1997, pp. 467–526

Forkel, J. "Über die Theorie der Musik" (1777), reprinted in C. F. Cramer, *Magazin der Musik* 1 (1785), pp. 855–912

Forte, A. "Paul Hindemith's Contribution to Music Theory in the United States," *JMT* 42 (1998), pp. 1–14

Gushee, L. A. "Questions of Genre in Medieval Treatises on Music," in *Gattungen der Musik in Einzeldarstellungen. Gedenkschrift Leo Schrade*, ed. W. Arlt et al., Bern, Francke, 1973, pp. 365–433

Huglo, M. "Bibliographie des éditions et études relatives à la théorie musicale du Moyen Âge (1972–1987)," *Acta* 60 (1988), pp. 229–72

Kessel, J. C. *Unterricht im Generalbasse zum Gebrauche für Lehrer und Lernende*, Leipzig, Hertel, 1790

Lobkowicz, N. *Theory and Practice: History of a Concept from Aristotle to Marx*, South Bend, University of Notre Dame Press, 1967

McCreless, P. "Rethinking Contemporary Music Theory," in *Keeping Score: Music, Disciplinarity, Culture*, ed. A. Kassabian and D. Schwarz, Charlottesville, University of Virginia Press, 1997, pp. 13–53

Palisca, C. V. *Humanism in Italian Renaissance Musical Thought*, New Haven, Yale University Press, 1985

"Scientific Empiricism in Musical Thought," in *Seventeenth Century Science and the Arts*, ed. H. Rhys, Princeton University Press, 1961, pp. 91–137

Riethmüller, A. "Probleme der spekulativen Musiktheorie im Mittelalter," in *Rezeption des Antiken Fachs im Mittelalter*, *GMt* 3 (1990), pp. 165–201

Schoenberg, A. *Harmonielehre*, 3rd edn., Vienna, Universal, 1922; trans. R. Carter as *Theory of Harmony*, Berkeley, University of California Press, 1978

Waesberghe, J. S. van, *Musikerziehung: Lehre und Theorie der Musik im Mittelalter*, vol. III/3 of *Musikgeschichte in Bildern*, ed. H. Besseler and W. Bachmann, Leipzig, VEB Deutscher Verlag für Musik, 1969

Wolf, J. "Die Musiklehre des Johannes de Grocheo," *Sammelbände der Internationalen Musikgesellschaft* 1 (1899–1900), pp. 65–130

· PART I ·

DISCIPLINING MUSIC THEORY

· 1 ·

Mapping the terrain

LESLIE BLASIUS

Every musical culture possesses its own representation of what constitutes its music theory, a "map" of the domains of inquiry or precept and the relations between these domains, thus providing a degree of completeness and coherence to the discipline. The works of some theorists contain explicit and comprehensive mappings: this is particularly the case in music theory of the sixteenth and early seventeenth centuries. Yet there also are implicit mappings of music theory, which are to some degree recoverable by the historian. Often, the appearance of new theoretical constructs is symptomatic of an underlying remapping of the realm of theory. Particularly after the middle of the seventeenth century explicit mappings of theory come to have a metatheoretical and disciplinary function, often seeming to be attempts to stabilize a discourse perceived as being on the verge of fragmentation.[1] For the purposes of this exposition, we will distinguish three broad historical cartographies, the first governing music theory through the sixteenth century, the second governing seventeenth- and eighteenth-century theory, and the last governing theory after the turn of the nineteenth century.

Architectures and harmonizations

The most basic representation of music theory is the *schema*, an attempt to analyze or systematize a body of knowledge through its division into idealized categories. As such, it is akin to classification, with the distinction that the latter pertains to autonomous data (harmonies, pieces, styles, etc.). A simple phenomenal schema of music might hypothetically distinguish the attributes of pitch and temporality, and indeed, theoretical schemas often do involve such binary discriminations. Except as a pedagogical or philosophical device, however, no schema which attempts to accommodate the complexity of musical events or practices can ever be so simple. Thus, in addition to phenomenal schemas, there are schemas of function and of form, the first distinguishing, for example, between "theoretical" and "practical" discourses or between

1 Given that much of current intellectual history has focused on the notion of the reorderings of disciplines and the often sudden birth of new domains of inquiry, the idea of intellectual maps has taken on a new importance. This is particularly the case in the work of Michel Foucault, whose ideas are of importance to the latter part of this chapter. See Foucault, *The Order of Things*.

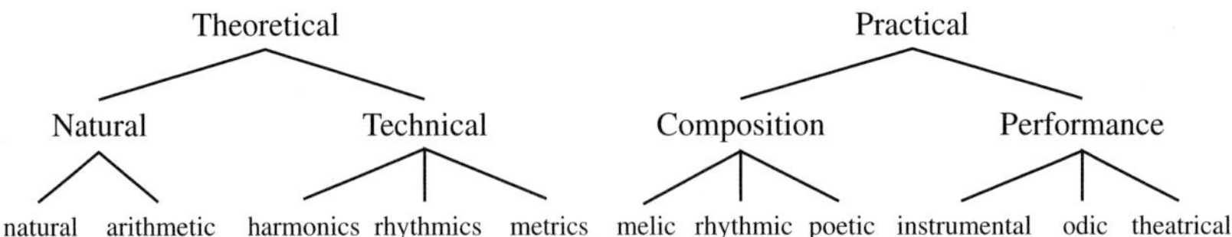

Figure 1.1 Architecture of music theory in Aristides Quintilianus, *On Music*

theorizations of sacred and secular musics, the second, for example, between theorizations of composition and reception, or between constitutions of "ideal" and "phenomenal" musics. So while a schema has the virtue of enforcing comprehensiveness and coherence, it also tends to be multiplicative, imposing upon differing musical domains conceptual architectures which are to a high degree arbitrary and often dependent on extrinsic justification.

The schematization of music theory in the Western traditions comes into being as a natural extension of Aristotelian systematics. The first substantive if incompletely surviving body of music theory, that of Aristoxenus of Tarentum (c. 375/360 BCE), presents itself as a comprehensive rationalization of music theory.[2] It partitions music into three domains (pitch, rhythmics, and melodics) and grounds the study of these domains phenomenally in the observation of musical practice. In doing this, Aristoxenus reifies the empirical phenomenon of sounding music over the disparate discourses of Pythagorean speculation and traditional metrics respectively, and thus creates an autonomous music theory subordinated only to a general systematics (see also Chapter 4, pp. 120–29).

A more complete, complex, and elegant architecture of music theory is only to be found much later in Aristides Quintilianus's three-volume *On Music* (early fourth century CE).[3] Within this ambitious and comprehensive text, Aristides presents a relatively straightforward mapping of topics (Figure 1.1).

As is easily seen, Aristides' conception is multidimensional, superimposing schemas of feature, function, and form. What is most interesting is the function of this structure within the treatise. Aristides does not use it as an agenda, exhausting each of the domains and subdomains in turn. Indeed, it serves as a foil against which develops a sophisticated middle-Platonic argument. It is not presented until after an extended proem, and after music is tellingly defined as "the knowledge of things seemly in bodies and motions." The first volume transits between the technical domain of theory and the domain of composition. Harmonics, rhythm, and meter are commensurably developed in terms of systems of seven categories: the study of harmonics defines the constructs of note, interval, scale, genus, topos, modulation, and melic composition;

2 See Barker, *Greek Musical Writings*, vol. II, pp. 119–25. Also see Mathiesen, *Apollo's Lyre*, pp. 321–22.
3 Aristides Quintilianus, *On Music*.

the study of rhythmics likewise defines seven constructs beginning with the *chronus protus* and closing with compositional considerations; and the study of meter does likewise beginning with the definition of the phoneme. The second volume returns to this material from a different perspective, drawing in the expressive or performative domain of the practical, dealing first with the ethical dimension of music, then developing a theory of the affective correlates of the various theoretical constructs of the first volume, and finally addressing instruments, their power over the soul, the notion of musical sympathies, and the sympathies of the natural world. The third volume draws in the natural portion of the theoretical, speaking of number, proportion, consonance, and the numerical correlations between musical constructs and the natural world.

Little music theory for the next thousand years approaches this sort of sophistication. Indeed, the Platonic bifurcation between ideal and mundane music which animates Aristides Quintilianus tends in late-Hellenistic and Christian writers to discourage any ambitious remapping of theory, and gives rise only to a simple schematics (Boethius's division of music into the celestial, the human, and the instrumental being the principal example).[4] None the less, by the early Middle Ages, two simple schemas of great import become well established: the division of theory between the pragmatics of the cantorial school and the speculations of the university and the division of musical composition into monophony and polyphony – *musica plana* and *musica mensurabilis*.[5]

With the pragmatic nominalism of the fourteenth century, however, several fresh and sophisticated architectures of music are conceived. For example, Marchetto of Padua, in the *Lucidarium* (1309–18) constructs a mapping little indebted to its predecessors (Figure 1.2). Marchetto makes use of the mechanics of Aristotelian systematics, speaking of genus and species, yet in a radically different manner than that of the earlier systematists. Within the genus of music, or modulated sound, the species of the *harmonic* is defined by the sounds of men and of animals (specifically sounds which are articulate and notatable), the *organic* by the sounds produced by the movement of air through instruments, and the *rhythmic* by instrumental sounds which are not the product of moving air. This schema is then superimposed on one distinguishing unmeasured and measured musics (the latter to be covered in his *Pomerium*). Likewise, the genus of performed music moves through the same species, and superimposes on this the three subspecies of the diatonic, chromatic, and enharmonic, a schema which gives rise to Marchetto's famous division of the tone into five parts (see **Chapter 6, pp. 186–87**).

4 In part, the inability to construct larger schemas may stem from the fact that early medieval theoretical writing is in truth an unstable collection of different discursive genres. See Gushee, "Questions of Genre in Medieval Treatises on Music," pp. 365–433. For further discussion of Boethius, see **Chapter 5, pp. 141–47**.

5 The division between cantorial and speculative music theory is discussed in **Chapter 5, p. 152**. For the distinction between *musica plana* and *musica mensurabilis*, see **Chapter 12, p. 485**.

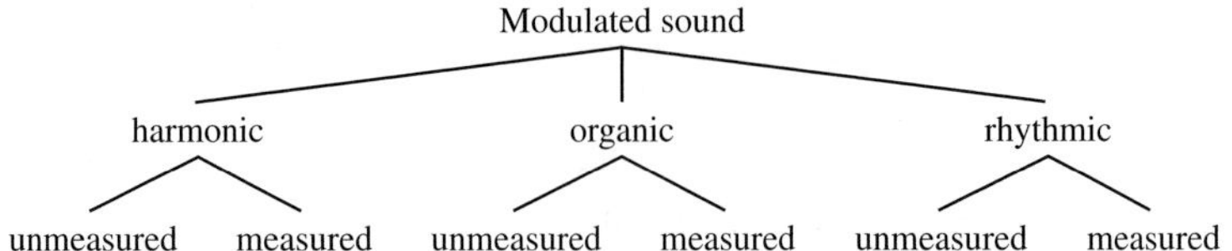

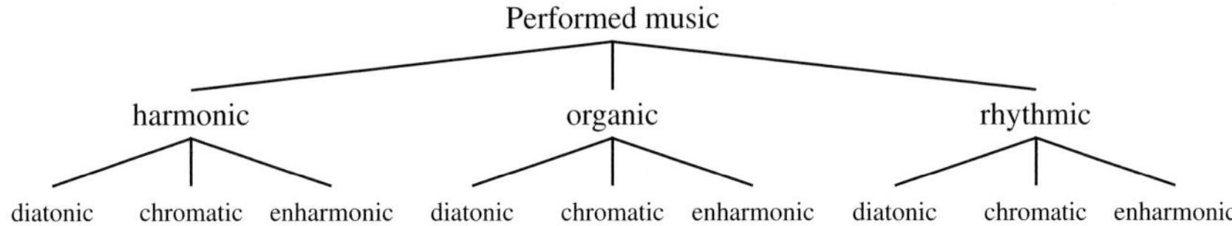

Figure 1.2 Architecture of music theory in Marchetto of Padua, *Lucidarium* (1309–18)

What is most striking about this architecture is its reliance on exclusively phenomenal criteria, a consistency characteristic of the scholasticism of the fourteenth century. What is also striking, though, is the way in which this consistency makes visible the limitations of the schema. Music theory is by nature and necessity a conservative discipline. It seems the destiny of any theoretical construct to become fixed as a topic: even when Aristoxenus or Aristides Quintilianus conceive their projects in terms of a systematics, their procedure is more often than not a way of rationalizing inherited topics. The best compilations of music theory in the fourteenth and fifteenth centuries – Marchetto, Jacques of Liège, Tinctoris – reconceive the architecture of music theory in fresh ways. Yet their modes of organization seem to become overwhelmed by the diversity of topics covered: remnants of Hellenic theory, Boethian canonics, monophonic modal classification, Guidonian hexachord theory, discant and contrapunctus practice, rhythmic notation and mensural theory, and even organology. Thus, in the works of the sixteenth century, where the received schemas are for the most part vestigial, where an important part of the theoretical effort involves the recuperation of Hellenic texts and doctrines, and where a reborn Platonism displaces the scholastic systematics of the fourteenth and fifteenth centuries, a different conception of mapping comes into being.

In the simplest of terms, the task of mapping in the sixteenth century is reconceived as synthetic rather than analytical. The organization of diverse topics is no longer a preliminary to theorizing but rather a mode of theorizing in itself. Thus, sixteenth-century theory can see itself ideally as exhaustive, with all knowledge of music (even with the traditional schemas of music) having some – and often multiple – places within the whole. It aspires to almost an organic unity in which seemingly disparate parts both give evidence of, and gain resonance from, a universally transcendent order.

An early manifestation of this remapping is seen in the music theory of the Milanese choirmaster Franchino Gaffurio (1451–1522). His three major works, the *Theorica musice* (1480, revised 1492), the *Practica musice* (1496), and *De harmonia musicorum instrumentorum opus* (1518, although probably written around 1500), were intended to form a whole, this intention being signaled by a series of internal citations, and also iconically by the reprinting of the frontispiece of the *Theorica musice* at the close of *De harmonia* (see Plate 1.1).

The contents of the three treatises may be summarized as follows:

Theorica musice
I. The traditional schemas of music
II. The mathematical foundations of proportion
III. The doctrine of proportion
IV. The derivation of musical interval from proportion
V. The generation of the tetrachords and the different species of imperfect consonance

Practica musice
I. The species of perfect consonances and their determinations of the eight modes
II. The terminology and mechanics of mensural music
III. The elements of counterpoint
IV. Additional material on the mathematics of proportion

De harmonia
I. Interval
II. The species of tetrachord, their mutations and retunings
III. Species of interval division
IV. Mode and the correlation of music with the universal order

Two features of this compilation bear remarking. First, as indicated by the titles of the initial two treatises, Gaffurio holds to the traditional distinction between theory and practice, which is to say, between *musicus* and *cantor*. This schematic division of the practical from the properly theoretical stands as perhaps the strongest heritage of medieval theory: indeed, its recalcitrance may be seen as the major disability of fourteenth- and fifteenth-century theory. Gaffurio, however, dissolves this distinction in a striking fashion in the last treatise. Whereas the *Theorica musice* constitutes the most ambitious attempt among any musical humanist of the Italian Renaissance to subsume and synthesize Boethian harmonics and its few Hellenistic predecessors known to Gaffurio, the *Practica musice* makes extensive and almost exclusive reference to issues of contemporary composition. *De harmonia*, however, benefiting from access to the writings of Aristoxenus, Aristides Quintilianus, and most importantly Claudius Ptolemy, locates a new discursive ground. Moving beyond the medieval orthodoxies of Pythagorean proportions, it reorients the doctrine of modes and the concomitant notion of pitch

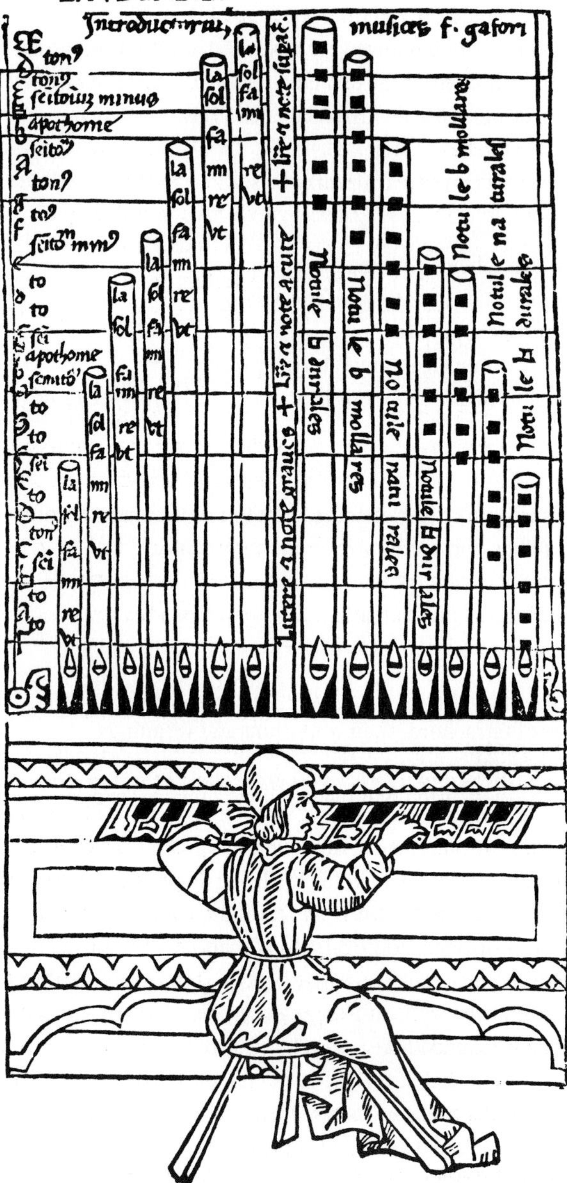

Plate 1.1 Frontispiece to Franchino Gaffurio, *Theorica musice* (1492)

space, and in doing so creates a new theoretical topic – temperament – which mediates or harmonizes the musical constructions of ancients and moderns, and, perhaps more importantly, musical practice and musical theory.[6]

The second feature worth remarking is a formal conceit of Gaffurio. Each of the five books of the *Theorica musice* contains eight chapters, each of the four books of the *Practica musice* fifteen, while the four books of *De harmonia musicorum instrumentorum opus* contain, respectively, an introduction and twenty-three chapters (i.e., twenty-four sections), forty chapters, twelve chapters, and twenty chapters. The regularity of the divisions make possible an explicit analogy with contemporary cartography. In the later fifteenth century, consequent to the recirculation of the same Claudius Ptolemy's *Geography*, with its system of meridians and parallels and its exposition of the mathematics of conic and circular projections, a new cartography is born, whose culmination arrives in Mercator's famous global projection of 1567. While eschewing the simple grouping of physical features characteristic of earlier maps, this cartography harmonizes such features as compass headings and distance in terms of a suprasensible order. The curious divisions of Gaffurio's trilogy might be seen to perform the same function. The relations holding between these three treatises are of a different substance than the schematic or architectural relations of earlier theorists: the projection of proportions in the structure of the treatises creates an abstract and synthetic discursive space, one different from the argumentative and analytical space of genus and species. Gaffurio's disposition of topics signals a resonance between domains, a suprasensible order of knowledge, a harmonization.

Thus, we might conceive of the music theory of the sixteenth century as involving the harmonization of the musical discourse in both sensible and suprasensible domains.[7] In the former the new project of music theory revolves around the construction of an unbounded and homogeneous pitch space to replace the schematized note-collection of the medieval treatise (notably in Ramis de Pareia's *Musica practica* [1482], wherein the sixth is displaced as the modular interval by the octave and the octave is divided into twelve semitones, dissolving the distinction between *vera* and *ficta* pitches; and in Vicentino's *L'antica musica ridotta alla moderna prattica* [1555], wherein the three classical genera are systematized within a single temperament). This harmonization of pitch space has ramifications in the pragmatics of composition (notably in Aaron's *Trattato della natura et cognitione di tutti gli tuoni di canto figurato* [1525], wherein the modal system is extended to govern polyphony; in the same author's *Toscanello in musica* [1523], wherein the successive composition of musical lines gives way to the notion of simultaneous composition; and in Zarlino's *Le istitutioni harmoniche* [1556],

6 See the Introduction to Clement Miller's translation of *De Harmonia*.

7 Most of the authors and topics raised in this paragraph will be found discussed in greater detail in Chapters 7, 12, and 15. See also, however, Lowinsky, "The Concept of Physical and Musical Space in the Renaissance," and Walker, *Studies in Musical Science in the late Renaissance*.

wherein counterpoint is redefined as the phenomenal whole of a musical passage rather than as the simple placement of note against note). Yet also, it is authorized by its sympathy with the domain of the suprasensible. Gaffurio's *De harmonia* closes with the resonances of musical systems with the virtues, the senses, and the cosmological structure of the world, resonances reflected in the structure and disposition of his treatises. Hence, the great synthetic project of music theory is equally dependent on the sanction of neo-Platonic idealism.

Moreover, given that as in cartography any harmonization is a privileging of one possible "projection," theoretical topics gain a new plasticity. While most sixteenth-century treatises offer some acknowledgement of the traditional schemas of music, their subsequent ordering and distribution of topics is characteristically unique, and hence important. (This concern with ordering is often signaled by the rhetorical adoption of the *mos geometricus*, the practice of presenting material under the rubrics of theorems and propositions.) Gioseffo Zarlino's *Le istitutioni harmoniche* (1556) divides elegantly into four books, the first dealing with proportion, the second with the mathematics of consonance, the third with composition, and the fourth with mode. Nicola Vicentino's *L'antica musica ridotta alla moderna prattica* (1555) disposes quickly of the traditional "theoretical" topics before moving through five lengthy books on "practical" topics, the first introducing melodic intervals through the three genera, the second extending this introduction to their determination of vertical sonorities, the third projecting the diatonic modal system on the other genera, the fourth giving the rules of counterpoint in the different genera, and the fifth presenting the comprehensive keyboard of the *arcicembalo*. Lodovico Zacconi's *Prattica di musica* (1592/1622) falls into two parts, the four books of the first volume covering respectively the knowledge of notation and embellishment necessary to the singer, problems of rhythm, problems of proportion, and the theory of mode and register, and the four books of the second volume elaborating the practice of improvised counterpoint. Zarlino, Vicentino, and Zacconi necessarily have much material in common. Yet each approaches the topics of music theory from a different vantage point, each harmonizes music theory according to a different projection or perspective.

Taxonomies and mechanics

One of the most vivid illustrations of an implicit remapping of music theory is gained by comparing two slightly later treatises, the *Harmonie universelle* (1636–37) of the French savant Marin Mersenne and the *Musurgia universalis* (1650) of the Jesuit Athanasius Kircher. They cover much of the same material (with Kircher drawing at times on Mersenne) yet suppose two very different mappings of the musical terrain. Kircher presents an extreme version of the previous century's harmonization, and Mersenne anticipates the new science of the eighteenth century.

Kircher's compendium unfolds through two great divisions of respectively seven and three books:

I The nature of sound and voice
II The music (both ancient and modern) of the Hebrews and Greeks
III The basic mathematics of harmony
IV The divisions of the monochord
V The elements of composition
VI Musical instruments
VII Style (both ancient and modern), affect, and the relations of poetry and music

VIII Combinatorics and is application to the composition of music
IX The magic of consonance and dissonance
X The correspondence of *musica mundana* to the harmonies of nature, the spirits, and the universe

While the succession of topics as given in this table has a certain logic, a close reading of the *Musurgia* reveals more. The first book closes with a series of short essays on the sounds produced by animals, birds, and insects. In particular, these essays focus on the treatments of these subjects in classical myth – which itself leads gently into Kircher's account of ancient music in the second book. This sort of thematic contiguity governs the progression between each of the books. Yet at a more local level it can take on a startling form. In the latter portion of the ninth book, a discussion of prodigious sounds (great bells, the trumpets at the walls of Jericho) and the miracles attributed to them leads to a discussion of echo and architectural acoustics, which leads in turn to the construction of mechanical instruments, which then leads to a discussion of musical codes. Most interesting is the contiguity of these subjects: prodigious sounds often do their miraculous work at a distance, when the source of the sound is unknown; echo likewise is a sound without bodily source, one whose ghostly presence can be conjured by the right architectural construction; mechanical instruments are a source of music without obvious human presence; and finally, in so far as echo has often been taken for the voices of spirits, and spirits are known to communicate over distances without sound, musical cryptography constitutes a mundane analogy to this ghostly communication. The harmonization of musical topics is taken to an extreme: the theorist, sensitive to the subtlest of resonances, uncovers long chains of similitudes which link topic to topic, any of which can recur at various places in various chains. (The subject of mode makes five separate appearances in the *Musurgia*.) The task of the theorist is slowly to uncover the relations between musical facts, to gradually expand the harmonization of musical discourse by bringing even the most remote evidence into some sort of projection: thus the theoretical treatise cannot but culminate in the exposition of the contiguities of music, of number, of astronomy, of angels – contiguities strikingly illustrated in the frontispiece to the *Musurgia* (see Plate 1.2).

Plate 1.2 Frontispiece to Athanasius Kircher, *Musurgia universalis* (1650)

Mersenne's treatise is suggestively different in argument and organization. Its nineteen books group as follows:

I–V	The physics of sound, the mechanics of motion, and the physiology of the voice
VI–XI	The nature of song, the doctrines of theory, the mechanics of composition and performance
XII–XVIII	The physics and construction of all manner of instruments
XIX	Arguments for a universal harmony

What is absent in Mersenne is the obsession with similitudes, with the associative links characterizing Kircher. What is striking is an obsession with the mechanics of motion (harking back to Aristides Quintilianus's definition of music as "what is seemly in bodies and motions"), and beyond, an obsession with phenomena. Still to be found are legendary reports and anecdotes, yet of more interest to Mersenne is the accumulation of detail: the sounds of different alloys in varying environments, the construction of organ pipes, multiple systems of temperament. In both activities (the return to mechanics and the collection of facts) the task of the theorist is not the harmonization of given topics but rather the generation of new knowledge. In discarding the associative links and similitudes which govern Kircher's world, a new order takes shape, one which organizes itself not simply to distribute knowledge or harmonize theoretical topics, but to open out knowledge so that its gaps become visible. To again draw an analogy to cartography, this opening out reflects the sort of map which comes to the fore in the seventeenth and eighteenth centuries – the military or topographic map – in which the focus of the mapmaker turns to the area between landmarks.

Implicit in Mersenne's topography are the two dominant epistemologies of the seventeenth and eighteenth centuries, rationalism and empiricism. The first posits a synthesis, in which simple primitives are subsumed in a calculus or mechanics whose product is a complex (and usually phenomenal) whole. (In some ways, it may be seen as a rigorous successor to the *mos geometricus* – the organization of material in terms of propositions and theorems – which is characteristic of the sixteenth-century musical treatise.) Musically, this rationalism reaches its apogee in the harmonic calculus found in Leonhard Euler's *Tentamen novae theoriae musicae* (1739), yet it is in a different guise to be found in the various reconstructions of the origin of music popular in the later eighteenth century. The second (empirical) epistemology abstracts criteria by which a range of distinct and commensurable areas can be ordered taxonomically on some sort of series through decomposition or analysis. This ordering of musical knowledge is observable as early as the tabulations of musical figures in the works of the *musica poetica* tradition at the beginning of the seventeenth century. Most tellingly, it makes possible an alternative to the notion of a comprehensive mapping of the discipline. With the expansion of musical information and its differentiation, the ideal of the comprehensive treatise becomes increasingly less plausible. Hence, we find a turn to a taxonomy which can encompass all knowledge (although at the cost of any analytical function): the musical dictionary or encyclopedia of the later eighteenth century.

While the dictionary or encyclopedia would seem to usurp the organizing function of any explicit mapping of the musical discourse, an implicit mapping is very much still in place in the seventeenth and eighteenth centuries, one which at every locale subsumes both the mechanistic and the taxonomic methods, and articulates the musical discourse. (As will be seen to be the case, the dictionary or encyclopedia in actuality restores its metatheoretical function to the explicit mapping.) Johann Mattheson, one of the last authors of a comprehensive treatise in the early eighteenth century, argues in the foreword to *Der vollkommene Capellmeister* (1739) against the subsumption of music theory within mathematics (by which he means the mathematical synthesis of the sort found in Zarlino or Kircher) by postulating a system of four sorts of musical relationships – "natural," "moral," "rhetorical," and "mathematical."[8] Mattheson's systems of relationships may be conceived as specifying four musical functions, and hence four discrete domains of study: (1) the "natural" – the domain of acoustics (the phenomenal basis of sound); (2) the "moral" – the domain of affect and style (the particular psychology of music); (3) the "rhetorical" – the domain wherein are studied the performative and grammatical aspects of musical composition (as in the *musica poetica* tradition or in the later treatises on performance itself); and (4) the "mathematical" – the traditional theorization of musical material.

Given this system of four functions, and the analysis or decomposition of the Renaissance synthesis, music can be located (in the later seventeenth and eighteenth centuries) within any one of four discrete systems of perspective. At one level, these systems are governed by shared epistemologies. The task of both harmonic theory and the theory of musical affect involves the construction of taxonomies. Even more, though, the sorts of theorizations most peculiar to this period come into being as examinations of relations between each of these four perspectives. Euler's system of harmony, wherein any musical moment is defined by an index of consonance, derives from whole-number acoustics through an ingenious calculus, and Rameau correspondingly generates his harmony from the natural acoustics of the *corps sonore*. The study of harmony and affect gives rise to the science of aesthetics, a generalization of the notions of proportion, commensurability, and balance. The study of affect and style in concert with the codifications of performance practice and musical rhetoric opens ground for the later eighteenth-century study of phrase structure and the dispositions of musical form. Similarly, natural acoustics and notions of musical rhetoric combine to give the empirical evidence for the genealogy of music, and the mechanistic reconstruction of its common origins with language and dance.

8 See Mattheson's *Der vollkommene Capellmeister* (Harriss trans., Section VI: "On the Mathematics of Music," p. 46). Mattheson later in this section draws an analogy between the theorist and a navigator, the mathematical foundations of theory standing as a necessary set of coordinates.

Histories and psychologies

As noted, the explicit mapping of musical discourse in the Enlightenment is not abandoned, but rather assumes a more explicitly metatheoretical function. Just prior to the turn of the nineteenth century, Johann Nicolaus Forkel gives the following schema of musical studies in his *Allgemeine Geschichte der Musik* (1792):[9]

Musical grammar
I Tones, scales, keys, modes, and melodic patterns
II Harmony
III Rhythm (including prosody, accent, meter, and phrase)

Musical rhetoric
I Periodic structures (rhythmic, logical, homophonic, polyphonic)
II Musical style as determined by function (church, chamber, deriving from particular affects)
III Musical species as determined by function (church, chamber, theatrical)
IV The ordering of musical ideas by content or character (argumentative schemas, rhetorical ordering)
V Performance (vocal, instrumental, combined)
VI Musical criticism (the necessity of rules, notions of beauty, personal and national taste)

Though Forkel's mapping bears a kinship to that of previous eighteenth-century writers, it is abstracted through an explicit analogy to language. The necessity for this abstraction is obvious, given Forkel's need to construct a theoretical framework – a collection of descriptive criteria – against which to write the history of music. Yet moreover, this framework itself is subject to strong internal tensions. While Forkel's schema seems to mark an expansion of the scope and power of music theory at the close of the eighteenth century, bringing under its sway phrase rhythm, argumentative structure, style, and aesthetics, it also gives evidence of a compensatory impoverishment: most notably, harmony and the construction of scales and modes have lost their grounding in acoustics, and thus change status, serving no longer as representations of nature but rather as particular grammatical conventions which (among a finite number of other conventions) govern particular phenomenal features of music.[10] It is under this system that the various analyses of musical rhetoric come to being. Yet whereas the analyses of musical grammar are finite, fixed, and commensurable, the analyses of musical rhetoric are potentially infinite, contingent, and incommensurable. Although Forkel's list

9 Forkel's schema is derived from his earlier essay, "Über Musik Theorie" (1777). See also in the present volume, the **Introduction, p. 9**.
10 Forkel had, in fact, incorporated acoustics into "Über Musik Theorie", and its absence in the *Allgemeine Geschichte* is telling. See Duckles, "Johann Nicolaus Forkel."

includes the traditional eighteenth-century topics of musical rhetoric, his distribution could easily have been reworked into something much different. Even as it is, rhetoric threatens to overwhelm the cohesion of his musical grammar.

Forkel's schema anticipates a final general remapping of music theory which occurs at the opening of the nineteenth century. The agency motivating this remapping is the newly pregnant notion of history. Paradoxically, the most compelling evidence for the importance of the history of music is a complete cessation of musical historiography through the first three decades of the century, after which, in place of the exemplary biographies which constituted music history in the seventeenth and eighteenth centuries, through the great age of Burney and Hawkins, a new and newly self-reflective historiography arises which is concerned with the evolution of music itself.[11] Almost too obviously this new discipline juxtaposes theory with history. Yet this discursive economy is not so simply conceived as Forkel would imagine. In fact, the engagement between theory and history is profoundly reciprocal. François-Joseph Fétis, abandoning the naturalist epistemology of Rameau, reconceives music in terms of scales, distributing harmony along a temporal axis through its progression from "unitonic" to "transitonic" to "pluritonic" to "omnitonic" musics, and thus implicitly arguing that a historically contingent notion of music theory becomes necessary to the task of stylistic description and the construction of musical genealogies (see **Chapter 22, p. 748**). More abstractly, the Hegelian construction of the dialectic grounds both Moritz Hauptmann's conception of triadic formation and Adolph Bernhard Marx's conception of sonata form in a powerful temporality. For Hauptmann, the justification of the triad is historical rather than acoustic. And although the later eighteenth century had seen attempts to codify the rules of musical succession, Marx's projection of the dialectic across the breadth of the sonata movement reconceives musical form as the crystallization of temporal forces (see **Chapter 27, pp. 887–89**). At an even deeper and less explicit level, a conception of the "history of music" as mandating not simply the situation of individual musical artifacts within a temporal continuity, but conversely the location of temporal continuity within the musical artifact, leads to two of the theoretical constructs which most immediately characterize the early nineteenth century: the "canon" and the critical (and eventually analytical) study of the individual piece; and if by analogy the musical individual is awarded a "history," this leads to a third construct, the rationalization of musical pedagogy.

The notion of a "canon" of great instrumental works (first adumbrated in E. T. A. Hoffmann) comes into being as a consequence of a conscious step over a historical divide. Likewise, criticism (of which analysis stands as a later reconciliation with theory) from its inceptions concerns itself deeply with the temporality of the canonical artifact, with the temporality of the compositional process, and even, in so far as it embodies the hermeneutics of the early nineteenth century, the temporality of the

11 See Allen, *Philosophies of Music History*.

process of understanding itself. Finally, the rationalizations of music theory pedagogy at the turn of the nineteenth century, both those of the newly founded conservatories with their simplified harmony texts and those of the educational theorists such as Johann Friedrich Herbart and Johann Heinrich Pestolozzi, are inconceivable without the projection of a developmental history onto music theory. In fact, it is this sort of developmental history which makes possible the last great tradition of summatory theoretical treatises, the *Kompositionlehren* of the mid to late nineteenth century.

When extrapolated, the historicization of theory has striking consequences, mandating a radically diachronic atomism of music (characteristic of some theorists of the latter half of the twentieth century) wherein any individual piece of music (or even musical passage) can be taken as the product of a unique, ad hoc "theory of music," and wherein even the notion of theory as a concatenation of contingent "covering laws" governing "styles of music" is viewed with particular suspicion. Similarly, theory itself, in the conception of some musicologists, exists exclusively as a historical phenomenon, the only analytical interpretation of any validity being that which draws on an empirically established theory of music contemporaneous with the work in question. But the historicism of music theory in the nineteenth and twentieth centuries has itself always carried with it a counter-argument. The critical or analytical discourse and the new pedagogies of the early nineteenth century engage at some basic level the epistemology of sensation and association inherited from the eighteenth century. This prefigures an engagement with more powerful constructions of mental experience, the first of these, of course, being Hermann Helmholtz's physiological acoustics of the mid nineteenth century. Later it includes in succession the systematic empirical introspection of the late nineteenth-century psychological laboratory, the post-introspective perceptual studies of the Gestalt psychologists, structural linguistics, and contemporary theories of cognition.[12]

Thus, the music theory of the past two centuries can be seen to be caught between the two paradigms of historicization and psychologism. Yet music theory's situation is more complex. The nature of these paradigms, and the nature of theory's appeal to them, has changed over time. The idealist historicization of music theory common in the nineteenth and early twentieth centuries (for example, Fétis's progressive tonalities, or "the emancipation of the dissonance" and the "objectification of the musically subjective" in Theodor Adorno) has lost ground to a modernist notion of the dispersal of different theoretical discourses along historic and cultural axes. And, as noted, the conception of innate musical sensibilities has undergone a whole series of epistemological reconceptions. More importantly, though, these paradigms reveal a range or depth of empiricisms: Helmholtz's physiological acoustics of the mid nineteenth century, with its quantitative biases, is more empirical than Noam Chomsky's transformation grammar of the mid twentieth century (both of which have occasioned theories of music); and the musicological science of the German universities at the turn of

12 These latter developments are discussed, respectively, in Chapters 9, 30, and 31.

the twentieth century, with its array of paleographic and archival methodologies, is likewise more empirical than the stylistic historiography which was its predecessor. Yet while such empirical methodologies are conceivable for musical historiographies and musical psychologies, they are not so conceivable for music theory. One cannot assert with certainty what constitutes the basic ontological data of music theory in the same way that one might assert a particular historical fact or the result of some perceptual or cognitive trial; at various times, this data has been differently conceived: to be the notation itself, or the perception of music, or various definable receptions of music, or constructions such as harmonies, phrases, or lines.

Thus, for the first time, the map of music theory is not coterminous with the map of musical studies. In fact, the region between the empiricisms in which music theory unfolds may be seen to be transcendental. For example, let us take the notion of "consonance." The historian may problematize consonance by arguing that it is variably constructed across a range of cultures, historical or anthropological; consonance, as such, does not admit a stable definition, only instances of definition (which can be empirically substantiated). The psychoacoustician, correspondingly, may locate the boundary between consonance as a contextual phenomenon and consonance as a perceptual or cognitive *a priori*. For the theorist of the past two centuries, however, consonance is at once empirically unproblematized yet productively contingent. It may be pragmatized (as in Fétis's substitution of the scale for the chord as the basis of tonality), naturalized (as in the later nineteenth century's recourse to the overtone series), or idealized (as in Hauptmann's triad, or Heinrich Schenker's "chord of nature"). While the idealization of consonance may be dismissed as a rhetorical strategy, none of these cases endows consonance with true empirical reality. Yet all three allow its use as a primitive in some formal or quasi-formal system, and in the best of theorists the play or tension between the transcendental nature of theory and the empiricism of psychoacoustics or historiography is conceived with great sophistication: Hugo Riemann's mature amalgamation of psychoacoustics with his idealist harmonic theory is elaborated with great subtlety and nuance in his theory of tonal imagination, while Theodor Adorno's construction of an ontology and morphogenesis of music by relation to historical structures stands as one of the monuments of twentieth-century music theory.

The domain of the transcendental might further be parsed into two mirroring regions, one prescriptive and *a priori* and the second descriptive and *a posteriori*, both of which admit a constellation of theoretical constructions. The first (*a priori*) kind of prescriptive theory admits such music theories as derive from constructivist formalism. For an example, the equally tempered diatonic collection can be characterized by a specific property; after Milton Babbitt, it can be said to exhibit a unique multiplicity of interval classes.[13] Given this fact, one might generalize a sequence of axioms and theorems revealing further properties, and possible compositional uses for these

13 Babbitt, "The Structure and Function of Music Theory," p. 54.

properties. Yet this analysis stands before any particular empirically accessible mechanisms of perception, or any historical or cultural theorization or compositional manifestation of the diatonic collection.

The most influential exemplar of the second (*a posteriori*) sort of descriptive theory is given in the mature work of the early twentieth-century music theorist Heinrich Schenker. Schenker's early theoretical work concentrates on the affectual psychology of harmony and counterpoint: the latter, in particular, comes to be seen as a pedagogical laboratory within which the affect of music can be studied. Out of this is born the notion of counterpoint as a sort of affectual shorthand. In Schenker's later work this reconstruction of counterpoint is synthesized with a consistent narrative of the history of music, one which sees a unique conflation of contrapuntal and diminutional techniques in the works of the German instrumental masters. Hence the command of musical psychology and the plotting of a particular historical trajectory produce between them the analysis of the transcendental masterwork.

Given this complex situation, any explicit mapping of music theory (or of music theory within the discursive economy of musical studies as a whole) might seem implausible. Yet at a critical moment in the formation of the modern study of music, just such an explicit mapping of musical studies is given in Guido Adler's "Umfang, Methode und Ziel der Musikwissenschaft" (1885), one in which the various undercurrents of musical thought are frozen (if but for a moment):

I The historical field
- A Musical notation
- B Historical categories (groupings of musical forms)
- C Historical succession of musical laws (as given in composition, by theorists, and as appearing in practice)
- D Historical organology

II The systematic field
- A Investigation of musical laws (harmonic, temporal, and melic)
- B Aesthetics of music (reception, notions of musical beauty, the complex relation of ideas)
- C Musical pedagogy (basic theory, harmony, counterpoint, composition, orchestration, practical methods)
- D Musicology (ethnographic and folkloristic studies)

Adler's schema is a disciplinary map, one in which the commensurability of each of the constituent domains is maintained through the aid of a collection of auxiliary disciplines – on the historical side, such methodologies as archival science, liturgical history, biography; on the systematic side, acoustics and mathematics, physiology, psychology, logic, grammatics, metrics, poetics, aesthetics. In other words, the disciplinary locations on the map come into being as focuses for the auxiliary disciplines, auxiliary disciplines which variously construct differing empiricisms. Adler's schema rectifies the tensions and imbalances inherent in Forkel's project by incorporating the historiography of music into the mapping, thus configuring the whole of the traditional discourse of music as the synchronic division of a now-enlarged science of music (a "Musikwissenschaft").

Forkel's two domains of music, the grammatical and the rhetorical, survive as the respective investigations of the laws and the aesthetics of music. However, Adler's pedagogical component of music theory (its policing function) is distinguished as an independent domain, and this whole structure is further extended to cover extra-European music through the discipline of systematic musicology. This dispersal serves to redistribute the tensions inherent to Forkel's structure. Adler's mapping, though, goes further in this regard. The four domains of the systematic field are subtly bound to the corresponding domains of the historical field, notation depending on some notion of musical laws, musical form and genre likewise constituting a projection of musical aesthetics, the succession of musical laws mirroring the successions of musical pedagogies, and historical organology constituting a sort of record of non-notated musical cultures.

In this way, Adler's projection has its own underlying architecture. Moreover, his project is one which is aware of its own historical contingency, and thus can resonate with earlier mappings. Like those mappings of the eighteenth century, it constructs an analytical grid (here defined by diachronic and synchronic axes) upon which new investigations can arise in those spaces which are blank; and like those mappings of the eighteenth century, it rules out the comprehensive treatment of music in a single treatise. But as with the mappings of the sixteenth century, it harmonizes and synthesizes existing disciplines (in fact, accommodating all that has been said about music), allowing for a whole range of resonances or sympathies between topics treated in different domains. The author himself, though, explicitly draws a comparison between his schema and that of Aristides Quintilianus (presenting both as tables, Adler above Aristides Quintilianus on a double page), thus ideologically linking his project with the first complete mapping of the musical domain to survive. Both achieve the most important goal of the map maker: not to discipline what is said about music, but rather to create a new musical discourse.

Bibliography

Adler, G. "Umfang, Methode und Ziel der Musikwissenschaft," *Vierteljahrschrift für Musikwissenschaft* 5/1, Leipzig, Brietkopf und Härtel, 1885

Aristides Quintilianus, *On Music, in Three Books*, trans. and ed. T. Mathiesen, New Haven, Yale University Press, 1983

Barker, A. *Greek Musical Writings*, 2 vols., Cambridge University Press, 1984–89

Duckles, V. "Johann Nicolaus Forkel: The Beginning of Music Historiography," *Eighteenth-Century Studies* 1 (1968) pp. 277–90

Euler, L. *Tentamen novae theoriae musicae*, St. Petersburg, Academiae Scientiarum, 1739; facs. New York, Broude, 1968

Forkel, J. N. *Allgemeine Geschichte der Musik*, Göttingen, Schwickert, 1788; facs. Graz, Akademische Druck- und Verlagsanstalt, 1967

Foucault, M. *The Order of Things: An Archaeology of the Human Sciences*, New York, Pantheon, 1971

Gaffurio, F. *De harmonia musicorum instrumentorum opus*, Milan, G. Pontanus, 1518; facs. Bologna, Forni, 1972 and New York, Broude, 1979; trans. C. Miller, *MSD* 33 (1977)

Practica musice, Milan, G. Le Signerre 1496; facs. Bologna, Forni, 1972 and New York, Broude, 1979; trans. C. Miller as *Practica musicae*, *MSD* 20 (1968); trans. I. Young as *The "Practica musicae" of Franchinus Gafurius*, Madison, University of Wisconsin Press, 1969

Theorica musice, Milan, P. Mantegatius, 1492; facs. New York, Broude, 1967 and Bologna, Forni, 1969; trans. W. Kreyzig, ed. C. Palisca as *The Theory of Music*, New Haven, Yale University Press, 1993

Gushee, L. A. "Questions of Genre in Medieval Treatises on Music," in *Gattungen der Musik in Einzeldarstellung. Gedenkschrift Leo Schrade*, ed. W. Arlt et al., Bern, Francke, 1973, pp. 365–433

Kircher, A. *Musurgia universalis*, Rome, F. Corbelletti, 1650; facs. Hildesheim, G. Olms, 1970

Lowinsky, E. E. "The Concept of Physical and Musical Space in the Renaissance: A Preliminary Sketch," in *Music in the Culture of the Renaissance and other Essays*, vol. I, ed. B. Blackburn, University of Chicago Press, 1989, pp. 6–18

Marchetto of Padua, *The Lucidarium of Marchetto of Padua*, trans. and ed. J. Herlinger, University of Chicago Press, 1985

Mattheson, J. *Der vollkommene Capellmeister*, Hamburg, C. Herold, 1739; facs. Kassel, Bärenreiter, 1954; trans. and ed. E. Harriss as *Johann Mattheson's "Der Vollkommene Capellmeister"*, Ann Arbor, UMI Research Press, 1981

Mersenne, M. *Harmonie universelle*, Paris, S. Cramoisy, 1636–37; facs. Paris, Centre national de la recherche scientifique, 1963 and 1986

Vicentino, N. *L'antica musica ridotta alla moderna prattica*, Rome, A. Barre, 1555; trans. M. Maniates, ed. C. V. Palisca as *Ancient Music Adapted to Modern Practice*, New Haven, Yale University Press, 1996

Walker, D. P. *Studies in Musical Science in the Late Renaissance*, London, Warburg Institute/University of London, 1978

Zacconi, L. *Prattica di musica utile et necessaria*, Venice, G. Polo, 1592; facs. Hildesheim, G. Olms, 1982

Zarlino, G. *Le istitutione harmoniche*, Venice, Franceschi, 1558; facs. New York, Broude, 1965

· 2 ·

Musica practica: music theory as pedagogy

ROBERT W. WASON

One of the most consequential developments in the long history of music theory has been its gradual integration with the discipline of *musica practica*, a discipline that until at least the eighteenth century was considered largely distinct from the rarefied concerns of classical *musica theorica*.[1] In the present chapter, we will attempt to look at some traditions of "practical" music theory in more detail. We will begin first with a brief discussion of the difficulties in defining "practical" theory and assessing its relation to functions of music pedagogy. We will then proceed to a broad survey of some of the major contributions to practical music instruction from the Middle Ages to the present day. Needless to say, this constitutes a vast quantity of writings that cannot be analyzed comprehensively here. But by focusing upon a few selected examples at historically significant moments, we hope to illustrate the principal parameters – structural, stylistic and institutional – which have together helped shape the discipline of "practical" music theory.

Praxis and pedagogy

The notions of "pedagogy" and "practice" have historically been closely linked, although they are by no means synonymous. In ancient Greece, the pedagogue was the "leader" or "teacher" of boys (usually the slave assigned to transport the boys from one schoolmaster to another). Today, the term "pedagogue" often carries with it negative connotations of pedantry and dogmatism, although in music, the term has perhaps a somewhat more benign association related to the teaching of basic skills. As pointed out in the Introduction to this volume, the origin of the dialectical juxtaposition of theory with practice may be traced to Aristotle (see **p. 2**). There was never any necessary connection between the "pedagogical" and the "practical," however. (*Theoria* was as much a subject of pedagogy in the Lyceum as was *praxis* – indeed perhaps more so.)

The first writer to apply the Aristotelian division of knowledge to musical study

1 The history of the tensions between *musica practica* and *musica theorica* is addressed in numerous chapters in the present volume. But see, especially, the **Introduction, pp. 2–13** and **Chapter 5, pp. 158–64**.

seems to have been Aristides Quintilianus, who divided all knowledge of music into the "theoretical, [which] coordinates technical rules and natural causes[,] while the practical embraces the application of musical science and its different genres."[2] Aristides further subdivided the "practical" into two branches, one of which "directs the use in melodic, rhythmic and poetic composition of structures that have already been technically analyzed; the second concerns their proper modes of expression in instrumental performance, singing and acting."[3] This seems to suggest that Aristides had some sort of musical repertoire in mind. Still, the *content* of his "practical theory" is very different from anything that we would recognize as such today. But this is hardly surprising, for the notion of practical theory has changed continually throughout history. There has never been a consensus among musical pedagogues as to the exact function of *musica practica* or its precise relation to *musica theorica*. A glance at a few selected medieval treatises will suggest the scope of the problem.

Medieval musical pedagogy

It is important to realize that Aristides' scheme was not universally adopted – or even known – in the Middle Ages. One early attempt to classify medieval theory treatises calls them "occasional writings, in the best sense of the word," and emphasizes the fragmented, "special-interest" nature of the medieval readership.[4] In his comprehensive survey of medieval theory treatises, Lawrence Gushee concedes that "a good many music-theoretical writings of the Middle Ages are distinguished by lack of adherence to clear-cut genre."[5] Indeed, most of the sources are eclectic with regard to theoretical content and equivocal with regard to purpose. Thus, the opposition of "speculative" and "practical" theory as general categories is problematic, at least in the earlier Middle Ages. Still, a putative division between practice and theory in music may be implicit in the distinction widely invoked by medieval authors between *musicus* and *cantor*. As defined by the ninth-century writer Aurelian of Réôme, for example, the former was a "scientist" knowledgeable in ancient Greek musical theory (*musica*) as transmitted by Boethius, while the latter was a musical practitioner, a singer of chant in the church.[6] Yet the treatises surviving from Carolingian times suggest how difficult it was to maintain a strict distinction between the two. Hucbald, working in the middle of the tenth century, is an example of a theorist who strove mightily to reconcile current chant practice with

2 See Mathiesen's Introduction to his translation of Aristides Quintilianus, *On Music*, p. 17. Also see Chapter 1, pp. 28–29. 3 Barker, ed., *Greek Musical Writings*, p. 392.
4 Pietzsch, *Die Klassifikation der Musik*, p. 4. Pietzsch classifies treatises as *musica practica* (which he divides into what might be called "instructional works" vs. "specialized monographs"), *musica theorica* (which he divides further by level of comprehensiveness), or combinations of both (pp. 6ff.).
5 Gushee, "Questions of Genre," p. 367.
6 Aurelian, *Musica disciplina*. For a more extensive discussion of the musicus–cantor opposition, see Chapter 5, p. 163.

Greek music theory – or at least that Greek music theory which he could derive from Ptolemy and Boethius (see **Chapter 5, p. 159**). An even earlier example of medieval pedagogical synthesis is found in the ninth-century treatise *Musica enchiriadis* and its companion treatise, *Scolica enchiriadis*. As among the first Western writings to offer fixed-pitch notation (despite the awkward Daseian nomenclature), descriptions of polyphonic singing, and a technical discussion of modal theory based on the finals and ambitus of a chant, the *enchiriadis* texts clearly betray highly practical intentions. At the same time, the authors of these texts rely upon ancient (Latin) authorities for much of their terminology. Yet how thorough the integration of received theory and contemporary practice is remains open to question given that the two most substantial discussions of ancient musical thought seem to come at the ends of each of these treatises almost as an afterthought (concerning, respectively, the Orpheus myth and the affective qualities of music – Chapter 19 of the *Musica enchiriadis*; and a substantial gloss of Boethian harmonics – end of Part II, and Part III of the *Scolica enchiriadis*).[7]

Guido of Arezzo

Whatever tension there may be in the Carolingian sources between practice and pedagogy, there is little dispute as to the major milestone of medieval pedagogical theory: the writings of the eleventh-century Italian monk Guido, active for most of his life in the cathedral of Arezzo. While it is not in every case possible to disentangle an authentic corpus of writings authored by Guido from ideas attributed to him, it is clear that his primary interest was in the teaching of music theory for practical ends. Even the classical instrument of ancient canonics – the monochord – was used by Guido with a most practical end: as a pedagogical device to teach a secure sense of pitch. He boasted: "Some [students], trained by imitating the [steps of the mono]chord, with the practice of our notation, were within the space of a month singing so securely at first sight chants they had not seen or heard, that it was the greatest wonder to many people."[8]

Three brilliant pedagogical ideas have traditionally been attributed to Guido, earning him his honored place in the history of music pedagogy: staff notation, the system of hexachords, and his "classroom visual aid" for sight-singing performance, the "Guidonian Hand." Unfortunately, his extant works – primarily the "Micrologus" – do not prove beyond a shadow of a doubt that they were his invention, and his posthumous reputation assumed such legendary proportions that some skepticism is warranted. Josef Smits van Waesberghe has shown that the basic innovation in his notation was "construction in thirds of parallel lines of definite pitch."[9] Guido himself demonstrates the abstraction of a C hexachord from a chant committed to memory (*Ut queant laxis*),

7 And indeed, it has been questioned whether each of these sections are a part of the original texts. See the discussion by Raymond Erickson in his English translation: *Musica enchiriadis and Scolica enchiriadis*, pp. xxvi–xxvii. 8 Prologue to *Micrologus* (Babb trans.), p. 58.
9 Waesberghe, "Musical Notation of Guido," p. 49.

and its use as a means to help a singer notate an unknown melody, or produce sound from notation at sight.[10] But there is no mention of transpositions of a "natural hexachord," or of the principle of "hexachord mutation," and the hexachord in general is absent from the "Micrologus." Whether or not Guido was the first to assign pitch-letters to parts of the hand (curiously, the mnemonic is not actually found in his works), we do know that the use of the hand as an aid to memory predates Guido.[11]

These three innovations are so towering, that it is less often noted that the "Micrologus," besides being in effect an early sight-singing manual, is also one of the very first in another long line of music-pedagogical genres: the treatise on composition. Approximately one quarter of the work (the last five of twenty chapters) deals with the composition first of monophonic melody, and then "diaphony" (organum). In discussing melody, Guido points out analogies between the structure of speech and melodic phraseology, thus pioneering a grammatical correspondence that would have a long history in subsequent music-theoretical writings.

Musical study in the medieval university

Despite their frequent citations of classical sources, the works just discussed all reflect the Carolingian emphasis upon practicality and utility. This is not surprising given that they were written by authors active in cathedral or monastic schools charged with instructing young singers. However, the cultural and intellectual developments sometimes called the "Renaissance of the Twelfth Century" brought about great changes in musical study. During this period, there was a marked decline of the monastic schools, and the beginnings of the *studium generale*, which grew out of the various cathedral schools, eventually evolving into the *universitas*.[12] The earliest musical curriculum of the medieval universities drew heavily upon Boethius and his program of the seven liberal arts, in which music was included as one of the quadrivial sciences.[13] As one would expect, this study had little to do with any practical considerations of music, and was concerned entirely with classical problems of musical harmonics as transmitted by Boethius. But in the course of the twelfth and thirteenth centuries, a new intellectual influence becomes strongly in evidence in the universities that greatly weakened the quadrivial paradigm: Aristotle.[14]

10 Guido, *Epistola de ignoto cantu* (see **Example 11.1, p. 343**). The text of the chant predates Guido, but the melody as Guido gives it seems to have been unknown before his time, leading to speculation that he composed it or altered an extant tune to satisfy his pedagogical purposes.

11 Waesberghe, *Guidone Aretino*; also see his *Musikerziehung*, pp. 120ff. Examples of a Guidonian hand may be seen in **Plate 11.1, p. 345** and **Plate 12.1, p. 369**. Further information on Guido and the Guidonian solfège tradition is found in **Chapter 11, pp. 341–43**.

12 Carpenter, *Music in Medieval and Renaissance Universities*. Also see the first part of her article "Education" in *NG*, vol. VI, pp. 1–15.

13 Huglo, "Study of Ancient Sources," p. 172.

14 Yudkin, "Influence of Aristotle," p. 179.

Aristotle's works had for some time been the subject of study by Arab scholars, and it was through their translations that most of Aristotle's writings became known in the West beginning in the twelfth century. The influence of Aristotle's thought on music was apparent in the influential writings of the Arab polymath, Al-Fārābī (d. 950), who divided the pursuit of music into theoretical and practical parts. (Al-Fārābī's Latin term for the Greek *praktike* was *activa* – the applied activity of performing music.) The "theoretical" study of music, on the other hand, was to be divided into five sections: (1) principles and fundamentals; (2) rudiments ("derivation of the notes, and the knowledge of the constitution of the notes . . . and how many their species"); (3) instruments; (4) rhythm; and finally, (5) "composition of the melodies in general; then about the composition of the perfect melodies – and they are those set in poetical speech . . ."[15] Al-Fārābī's analysis of musical study, which in some respects recalls that of Aristides, proved highly influential after Latin translations began circulating in the twelfth century.

One of the most characteristic signs of scholastic Aristotelianism in music writings during the later Middle Ages was the rise of the encyclopedic *summa* typically used as a textbook in the universities. Throughout the thirteenth and fourteenth centuries, numerous authors penned comprehensive *summae* that attempted to deal systematically with all aspects of music, both theoretical and practical, including Johannes de Muris (Jehan des Murs), Walter of Odington, Marchetto of Padua, and Jacques of Liège. While the writings of each of these authors typically contained learned discussions of classical Boethian harmonics, there were also substantial – and in certain cases, ground-breaking – instructions concerning contemporaneous practical music, including detailed consideration of mensuration, counterpoint, and genre. While some of these writers seemed to make attempts at describing faithfully the musical practice they may have heard around them, occasionally their writings betray a more creative spirit in conceiving and prescribing notational or stylistic innovations not yet in common practice, especially in the area of mensuration (see **Chapter 20, pp. 628ff.**). On the other hand, a few of these authors – particularly Jacques – were notoriously conservative in their views, and highly critical of the mensural innovations associated with the music of the *ars nova*. In any event, these encyclopedic writings of the Middle Ages represent a high-water mark in the history of music theory in which both speculative and practical concerns seem to have achieved a balance. With the advent of Renaissance musical culture in the fifteenth century, however, an important new turn in the teaching of music may be seen to begin.

Renaissance compositional pedagogy

With the combined changes wrought by Renaissance humanism and the ever more ambitious and sophisticated genres tested by composers, the nature of compositional

15 *Al-Fārābī's Arabic-Latin Writings on Music*, ed. and trans. Farmer, pp. 14–16.

pedagogy in the late fifteenth century changed markedly. It can by no means be presumed that extant treatises on musical composition provide a perfectly faithful picture of contemporaneous musical practice. For one thing, musical practice was changing with unprecedented speed at this time, and there were great variations between various national traditions and compositional genres. For another, the published treatises may not well reflect the kinds of flexible, ad hoc oral instruction that a student might receive at the hands of a master. The testimony of the German composer Adrianus Petit Coclico is telling:

> My teacher Josquin . . . never gave a lecture on music or wrote a theoretical work, and yet he was able in a short time to form complete musicians, because he did not keep back his pupils with long and useless instructions but taught them the rules in a few words, through practical application in the course of singing . . . If he discovered . . . pupils with an ingenious mind and promising disposition, then he would teach these in a few words the rules of three-part and later four-, five-, six-part, etc. writing, always providing them with examples to imitate.[16]

Fortunately, though, most of the monuments of Renaissance *musica practica* were the creation of active composers who were well regarded in their own time, and thus can be read by us today without undue suspicion.[17]

In the late fifteenth century, the first of these composers, Johannes Tinctoris, "exhausted current knowledge of musical practice" in a series of twelve treatises.[18] Personal acquaintance with Tinctoris inspired Franchino Gaffurio in a similar direction. The advent of printing effectively made Gaffurio's *Theorica musice* (1492) and *Practica musice* (1496) the models of their respective genres for a much larger reading public.[19] The *Practica* gathers together in one volume material on topics of musical practice on which Tinctoris and the earlier university writers had written separate treatises.[20] Pietro Aaron's thoroughly practical *Toscanello in Musica* (1523) appeared early in the next century, the first attempt to teach the harmonic combinations usable in four-voice, simultaneous composition, and a work that was conceived and published in Italian – not Latin.[21]

Zarlino. The culmination of this development is certainly *Le istitutioni harmoniche* (1558) by Gioseffo Zarlino (1517–90). Written in his native tongue, the *Istitutioni* for the first time combines the genres of *musica theorica* and *musica practica* into a single

16 Owens, *Composers at Work*, p. 11.

17 See **Chapter 16, pp. 503–28** for a more in-depth discussion of one aspect of Renaissance music pedagogy – that of counterpoint – largely drawing upon the treatises of active composers.

18 Palisca, "Theory, theorists" in *NG2*, vol. xxv, pp. 355–89.

19 Between 1494 and 1499 Gaffurio also held a chair in music at the University of Pavia – the only certain example of such a position in an Italian university.

20 Book I is on plainchant, Book II on mensuration, Book III on counterpoint, and Book IV on proportions. In fact, the four books were originally conceived as separate works; Gaffurio's humanistic studies led to significant revisions of the manuscript version (Miller, "Gaffurius's *Practica Musicae*," pp. 105–28). Very likely that revision process as well as the possibility of publication in print led to their compilation into one volume.

21 Aaron, *Toscanello in Musica*, pp. 35–42.

treatise in a manner that would be influential well into the eighteenth century. This work, of four parts and more than four hundred pages, divides almost in half. After beginning in the manner of the classical *protreptikos* (a hortation offering praises of music, speculations on its origins, definitions, etc.) the bulk of Part I deals with the study of numbers, proportions, and their manipulation in generating the consonant intervals (their "formal cause"). Part II presents a more empirical side of Boethian canonics; here, the abstractions of the earlier discussion are realized on an instrument (their "material cause"), but outside of any compositional practice. During the course of both parts, Zarlino substitutes his *senario* for the Greek *tetraktys* (that had been passed on by Boethius), legitimizing the consonances of imperfect thirds and sixths as primitives, rather than as derivatives of fifths (see **Figure 10.2, p. 277**). Part III, "the first part of the second [half], which is called *Pratica*," is the definitive contemporaneous discussion of *prima prattica* compositional technique, while Part IV on modes presents (uncredited) Glarean's dodecaphonic modal system (see **Chapter 12, pp. 389–98**). Both the latter two parts provide extensive prescriptive advice to the young composer along with numerous examples composed by Zarlino to illustrate his instructions.

As can be discovered by any careful reading of the latter two parts, however, the practical nature of their content is not always self-evident. It cannot be assumed, for instance, that his rather conservative rules of counterpoint and strictures concerning modal classification that are illustrated in his own examples are an undistorted mirror of the practice of his contemporaries. Just as the first two "theoretical" parts of the *Istitutioni* betray obvious evidence of contemporary practice (especially in the reification of the *senario*, reflecting the predilection of singers for justly tuned imperfect consonances), the last two parts clearly show the more speculative, classically oriented side of their author's personality (rationalization of counterpoint rules, justifications for reordering and renaming the modes, etc.). In short, the dialectical tension – and symbiosis – that characterizes the relation of *theoria* and *practica* comes strongly to the fore between the covers of Zarlino's *Le istitutioni harmoniche*. It is this quality, perhaps more than any specific rule of counterpoint or theory of mode, that constitutes the legacy of Zarlino, and would continue to cast such a shadow over music theory for the next 200 years.

German *Lateinschule* texts. In Germany, *musica practica* was concerned primarily with performance, for books of this period were strongly influenced by the Lutheran Reformation, which made musical performance an important component of elementary education.[22] From at least the time of Listenius's *Rudimenta musicae* (1533), the curriculum of rhetorical study strongly influenced German music theory, leading to a third division of musical study dedicated to the art of musical composition: *musica*

22 See Butt, *Music education* – in particular Chapters 2 and 3, "The Role of Practical Music in Education c. 1600–1750," and "The Contents, Layout and Style of Instruction Books."

poetica. A broad range of German pedagogical texts appeared in the sixteenth and seventeenth centuries designed for the rank-and-file Latin schools (*Lateinschulen*). Among such elementary texts are Heinrich Faber's *Compendiolum musicae pro incipientibus* (1545 – and reprinted in a further forty-six editions through the early seventeenth century) and J. T. Freig's *Paedagogus* (1582). While often borrowing material from more learned authors such as Glarean (Freig's teacher), such Latin school texts presented only the basic rudiments of music necessary for the singing and reading of music. (Sometimes – as with Freig – such fundamentals were taught in the venerable dialogue form of the catechism.) Still, the elementary nature of this text – and dozens like it – should not obscure the importance of music in the Lutheran school curriculum. (The timetable at the beginning of Freig's book shows that by the fourth year, more time was spent studying music than any other subject.[23]) Nor should we underestimate the importance of these texts for stabilizing – and indeed helping to institute – important reforms of notation and theory in Reformation Germany, particularly with regard to mode.[24]

Baroque music theory

Music in the seventeenth and early eighteenth centuries (the "Baroque" period as it has invidiously come to be called by music historians) is confoundingly rich in its diversity of genres, styles, and tonal languages. During the same time period, Western intellectual thought was undergoing a profound transformation stimulated by revolutionary upheavals in science and philosophy. Not surprisingly, the music-theoretical literature of this time reflects a commensurate complexity. Didactic literature ranging from the most speculative and encyclopedic to the most mundane and utilitarian can be found in unprecedented quantities. As much of this literature is treated elsewhere in this volume in greater depth (*inter alia*, **Chapters 9, 13, and 17**), it will not be necessary to review it in detail here. Suffice it to say that the profound changes in musical style brought on by the *seconda prattica* entailed a radical reorientation of pedagogical literature, one in which the boundaries between pedagogy and practice became particularly blurred.

But perhaps more consequential to the history of music theory than any innovations of style introduced by the *seconda prattica* (as profound and far-reaching as they may be) was the rise of instrumental music. For it was through Baroque instrumental practice – and particularly that of the keyboard – that the emergence of a major/minor transposable key system most clearly is to be seen. And this emerging harmonic tonality finds its most explicit articulation and rationalization in the concomitant pedagogical

23 Livingstone has shown that music occupied a central place in the school curriculum; see his *Theory and Practice of Protestant School Music*.

24 On the importance of the *Lateinschule* texts for the question of mode in Germany during the fifteenth and sixteenth centuries, see Lester, *Between Modes and Keys*, pp. 68–76.

literature. The most important such literature possessing the most far-reaching consequences was the "figured-bass" or "thorough-bass" manual.

Figured-bass texts were written as attempts to solve a very practical problem: teaching keyboardists (though sometimes also performers of the lute, theorbo, or guitar) to provide a harmonic "foundation" for a piece of music as part of the *basso continuo* ensemble. For the most part, the harmonies that such a performer was required to supply consisted of consonant triads. But given the increasing complexity of the harmonic language of *seconda prattica* music, the figured-bass performer was faced with a plethora of more complex chord ciphers to learn. The cataloging and ordering of such "figures" in instructional manuals seemed to be an inscrutable assemblage of minutiae.

The earliest figured-bass instructional books were "practical" in the least imaginative sense of the word.[25] Often consisting of little more than mechanical rules for realizing a given figure by the memorization of certain stock formulae, these manuals presumed little "theoretical" understanding on the part of the performer. Charles Masson, for example, the author of one of the more interesting ones, would claim that "in this treatise, one will find neither curiosities, nor difficult and embarrassing terms of the Ancients, but only that which is useful in practice."[26] (Masson's view was reflective of a wider reaction against speculative *musica theorica* characteristic of French music pedagogy in the second half of the seventeenth century.) Yet it was through problems posed by the thorough bass – the structure of chords, the succession of these chords over a bass line – that theorists eventually were able to rationalize the system of harmonic tonality. This is most clearly to be seen in the work of Rameau.

Rameau. Today, Jean-Philippe Rameau (1683–1764) is celebrated as one of the most historically important music theorists. His theory of the *basse fondamentale* offered a revolutionary reconceptualization of tonal harmony that has continued to influence music theory to this day. (See **Chapter 24, pp. 759–72** for a comprehensive discussion of Rameau's theory of harmony.) But Rameau was hardly oblivious to the practical application of his ideas. Indeed, the utility of the fundamental bass to the pedagogies of keyboard accompaniment (thorough bass) and composition was a dominant theme in most of his writings. Unfortunately, the intensive (although not necessarily extensive) speculative arguments of Rameau have tended to obscure for many observers the truly practical roots of his pedagogy. (See also **Chapter 3, p. 84**.)

The four "Books" of the *Traité* divide, as Zarlino's work did, into "theory" and "practice":[27] the first two books deal with ratios and proportions and "the Nature and Properties of Chords," while the last two are on composition and accompaniment – the

25 See Arnold, *Art of Accompaniment*, Chapter 1, for a complete survey. Also see **Chapter 17, pp. 540–43**.
26 Masson, *Nouveau Traité*, "Avertissement."
27 Christensen believes it unlikely that Rameau knew enough Italian to have gained a sophisticated understanding of Zarlino (Christensen, *Rameau*, p. 23); still, the structure of Zarlino's treatises and his ideas on tuning (clearly presented in figures) would have been apparent to him.

two principal genres of *musica practica*. In comparison to Zarlino's work, however, Rameau's synthesis shows a decisive shift toward contemporary practice with its attention to problems of the through bass. Indeed, the fundamental bass is in many respects but a theory of the thorough bass, codifying and rationalizing the chords and harmonic progressions performed by a continuo ensemble or written down by a composer.

Rameau's attempt to affect musical pedagogy began with his first work, and continued throughout his career. In a sequence of publications that invites comparison with Riemann (see below), Rameau seems to alternate between "practical" and "theoretical" works, although in most of them, there was a mixture of the two. An account we have of Rameau's first "theoretical" writings (the now-lost "Clermont Notes" dating from before his move to Paris in 1722) shows him working toward the theory of the fundamental bass, "which seems to have originated in his mind as a pedagogical tool."[28] Ten years after the appearance of the *Traité*, he attempted to simplify pedagogy further in his *Dissertation sur les différentes méthodes d'accompagnement* (1732), in which he mixes his theory with ideas for a mechanical "system" by which to realize figured basses, requiring no musical notation; here Rameau attempts to teach amateurs (a growing market in the eighteenth century for such instructional books) the chord connections of figured bass as movements of hand and finger positions on the keyboard.[29] "L'Art de la basse fondamentale," a manuscript probably written by Rameau between 1738 and 1745, and unknown until recently, very likely was used by Rameau in his own teaching of composition; "its systematic attention to the fundamental bass arguably earns it the honor of being the first real harmony textbook in the modern sense."[30] Finally, the keystone to Rameau's pedagogical writing is the *Code de musique pratique* (1760), in which he takes on all music pedagogy, dividing it somewhat eclectically into "seven methods": (1) rudiments; (2) hand position for harpsichord and organ; (3) vocal production; (4) thorough bass; (5) composition; (6) unfigured bass; and (7) improvising a prelude. Here, Rameau brings together a lifetime's work on pedagogical matters, attempting to demonstrate that his concept of the fundamental bass offers a way to unite the conceptual rigor of music theory with the practical training of an instrumental and vocal student. For Rameau, it was practice which drove his theory, not the other way around. Always sensitive and honest concerning the correlation of his theoretical arguments to empirical practice, Rameau found himself again and again revising his ideas, admitting licenses to his rules, and generally acknowledging the epistemological limitations of his theory.[31]

Unfortunately, Rameau's intense interest in pedagogical musical theory was largely forgotten with his death. He has been primarily remembered as a speculative and learned theorist (and not always in the most flattering terms). Matters were not helped

28 Ibid., p. 24. 29 See Hayes, "Rameau's 'Nouvelle Méthode.'"

30 Christensen, *Rameau*, p. 286.

31 Christensen discusses in detail Rameau's efforts to reconcile theory and practice in his many publications. See especially Chapter 2 of *Rameau*, pp. 21–42.

any in that later generations learned their Rameau mainly through redactions of his theory by writers who were not always skilled in conveying its subtleties and pragmatic pliability: d'Alembert in the *Elemens de musique théorique et pratique* (1751; German translation by Marpurg, 1757), and Rousseau's music articles for the *Encyclopédie* (1751–65; later taken over in Rousseau's *Dictionnaire de la Musique*, 1768).[32]

Fux. Despite the success of Rameau's accomplishments, a harmonic paradigm of musical pedagogy was not everywhere dominant in the eighteenth century. In Vienna, the liturgical court composer Johann-Joseph Fux (1660–1741) reformed and systematized a model of contrapuntal pedagogy that would be as long-lasting and influential as Rameau's harmonic pedagogy. Published just three years after Rameau's *Traité*, Fux's *Gradus ad Parnassum* became arguably the single most influential and widely studied textbook of *musica practica* in the modern era.[33] Since Fux's *Gradus* is the subject of an entire chapter in this volume (see **Chapter 18, pp. 554–602**), a discussion of its contents will not be undertaken in this chapter. It only remains to emphasize that the *Gradus* is both a speculative and a practical work (the former qualities being often overlooked by English readers who know only the partial English translation). While the musical language of Fux's text was a conservative one for the eighteenth century, the principles and techniques that underlie it were recognized by generations of subsequent musicians as possessing incalculable educational value.

Heinichen. If Rameau's theory of the fundamental bass and Fux's species counterpoint offered the two most dominant compositional pedagogies in the eighteenth century, a third, less systematic model, was cultivated in Germany through the skills of chorale harmonization and figured-bass diminution. This pedagogical model was neatly described by C. P. E. Bach in his account of his father's musical atelier:

> In composition he started his pupils right in with what was practical, and omitted all the *dry species* of counterpoint that are given in Fux and others. His pupils had to begin their studies by learning pure four-part thorough bass. From this he went to chorales; first he added the basses to them himself, and they had to invent the alto and tenor. Then he taught them to devise the basses themselves . . .[34]

The chorale, for German pedagogues like Bach, became a microcosm of compositional techniques. By combining the efficient harmonic scaffolding of the chorale with the elaborative diminution techniques of the through bass, a student could learn a variety of compositional techniques that could be adapted to any number of genres and styles. We find such a method of "thorough-bass composition" already in a treatise that we know Bach admired and copied from: Friedrich Niedt's *Musicalische Handleitung*

32 Ibid., Chapter 9, pp. 252–90. 33 Mann, "Fux's Theoretical Writings," p. 57.
34 David and Mendel, eds., *The Bach Reader*, p. 279.

(1700–17). But the *summa* of the thorough-bass composition text is undoubtedly the 960-page *Der General-Bass in der Composition* of Bach's contemporary Johann David Heinichen (1683–1729), published in 1728 – six years after Rameau's *Traité* and three years after Fux's *Gradus*.

Far more than a guide for deciphering figured-bass signatures (as the seventeenth-century thorough-bass manuals had been), Heinichen's massive work is a complete compositional text, showing the keyboardist how a variety of styles and musical genres (including advanced "theatrical" styles of dissonance treatment) may be mastered through the thorough bass. With a rich assortment of musical compositions quoted and analyzed, Heinichen's text is a truly "practical" one reflecting a living musical tradition, albeit one that was probably only useful to a musician already possessing considerable experience and skills. In Example 17.1 (**p. 543**), we can see an illustration of Heinichen's thorough-bass method of compositional elaboration. There Heinichen takes a basic harmonic realization of a figured-bass line and shows how a skilled keyboardist might elaborate the figure to produce a variety of different textures – in the present case, in "cantabile" style. Like the treatises of both Rameau and Fux, Heinichen's text is a truly practical one reflecting the rich experience and knowledge of a seasoned composer.

Music theory in the "Classical" era

During the second half of the eighteenth century, compositional pedagogy evolved in remarkable ways. While numerous pedagogues continued to teach exclusively from contrapuntal and harmonic perspectives, respectively (the former frequently through adaptations of Fux's strict species approach, the latter through some adaptation of Rameau's fundamental bass or Bach's thorough-bass model), a number of theorists in Germany began to integrate these approaches within their own treatises. Johann Philipp Kirnberger's *Kunst des reinen Satzes in der Musik* (1771–79) presents probably the most successful such synthesis (see **Chapter 24, p. 772**). But a new element of compositional instruction also emerged that reflected the concomitant shifts of compositional style characteristic of the so-called "Classical" era: phrase and melody.

Koch. While discussions of phrase and melody are found in numerous treatises earlier in the century (primarily by Mattheson and Riepel), it was in the *Versuch einer Anleitung zur Komposition* (1782–93) of Heinrich Christoph Koch (1749–1816) that we find the most systematic attempt to offer a true method of melodic composition.[35] The most

35 The recent partial translation by Nancy Baker reflects this interest by beginning late in volume II (p. 342) and continuing through the complete volume III – essentially all of the material on phrase and formal structure. See Koch, *Introductory Essay*.

imposing and comprehensive presentation of pedagogical music theory of the Classical era, the treatise appeared in three volumes, in 1782, 1787, and 1793.[36]

Musica theorica survives in "Part I, Section I" (vol. I, pp. 15–50), which serves primarily to generate the tonal material – chords and keys – for a practical course in composition. Section II (pp. 51–120) puts the material generated in Section I into practice, beginning with a relatively brief treatment of "consonant combinations of tones" (Chapter 1) and then moving on to "dissonant combinations of tones" (Chapter 2, pp. 68–120). Section III (pp. 121–228), titled "Strict composition, or the correct use of chords and their intervals," resembles outwardly the version of "Strict Composition" that Kirnberger presents in Part I of *Kunst*, though the two differ profoundly in theoretical content. Just as Kirnberger had, Koch discusses submetrical elaboration of a four-part sketch at the end of the figured-bass course (pp. 213–28), and then procedes to a course in counterpoint in Part II (vol. I, pp. 231–374).

In the second volume of Koch's treatise, we move from the lessons in harmony and counterpoint found in the previous volume to lessons in composition, and it is immediately clear that "melody" will become the focus of study. (He emphasizes, for example, the melodic character of voice-leading taught in volume I.) Koch continues by outlining a compositional strategy he has derived from Sulzer, though it might be found in other rhetorically based compositional pedagogies: the composer should begin with a "plan" (*Anlage*), and continue with its "realization" (*Ausführung*), finally moving on to its "elaboration" (*Ausarbeitung*) (vol. II, p. 52). Urging the composer to "conceive melody harmonically" (vol. II, p. 87), Koch moves on to a lengthy and highly original discussion of modulation (vol. II, pp. 137–269), the purpose of which is to open up melodic choice to "non-diatonic" pitches, and sensitize the student to melodic movements that imply modulation, temporary or longer-lasting. Many of the examples of modulation consist only of single-line melodies, and it is clear that Koch sees "modulation" as a way of conceiving of more extended melodies. Subsequent discussion of musical meter (vol. II, pp. 288–341) concludes the preparation for composing melodies.

Koch makes it clear that the "inner nature" of melody is not something that can be taught. (It can only be understood by those musicians possessing these old standbys, "genius" and "good taste.") But the "outer nature" of melody is subject to a series of "mechanical rules." Thus, he titles the whole of Part II of vol. II (pp. 135–464) "On the Mechanical Rules of Melody," though most of it turns out to be introductory to the composing of melodies, until Section III.

It is here that Koch moves beyond the abstract comparisons of music and speech that were to be found in so many earlier rhetorically oriented treatises, and establishes a

36 Study of the treatise's organization is greatly facilitated by the table of contents for the work as a whole thoughtfully provided in the English translation as an Appendix (absent in Koch's treatise as it was in Kirnberger's); the work is far more comprehensive than English-language discussion of it might seem to indicate.

more empirical working vocabulary for the analysis and composition of melody, albeit a vocabulary still heavily indebted to grammar and rhetoric. Starting with the idea of punctuation and resting points in speech, Koch turns to the topic of melody: "Just as in speech, the melody of a composition can be broken up into periods by means of analogous resting points, and these, again, into single phrases (*Sätze*) and melodic segments (*Theile*)" (*Introductory Essay*, p. 1). The end of a period is effected by both melodic and harmonic punctuation: harmonic cadence-types align with melodic closure and help articulate rhythmic structure. Phrase-types are defined by this cadential ending, but also by their length (their "rhythmic nature" [*rhythmische Beschaffenheit*]). Thus, phrases that divide periods may be inconclusive (called by Koch an *Absatz*) or a "closing phrase" (*Schlussatz*), depending on their cadences. Phrases divide further into "segments" or "incises" (*Einschnitte*), which we might today call "half-phrases" or "phrase-members." Balance and periodicity are essential to Koch, who, like so many subsequent analysts, shows a predilection for the four-measure phrase as the basic model, viewing longer melodic entities as "extended" (*erweitert*) or "compound" (*zusammengeschobene*) phrases. Indeed, later in his treatise, Koch shows how to extend a period so as to create an entire movement of a larger work, and ultimately to the formation of multi-movement works.[37] Of particular interest in Koch's treatise are the many musical examples he cites to illustrate his ideas. While many of these musical examples are of his own creation, a large number of them originate from the works of his contemporaries, including Joseph Haydn.

"Musique pratique" in the era of the conservatory

By the end of the eighteenth century, the hitherto distinct national traditions of music theory – French fundamental bass, Italian species counterpoint, and German thorough bass – had begun to blend together in such varying configurations that it is difficult to speak any more of specific national traditions. But one element of music pedagogy did remain constant during the eighteenth century through all the momentous shifts of theoretical thought we have witnessed: most advanced musical instruction seems to have been designed principally for the single student, whether working through the material with a teacher, or perhaps alone reading a text. Class instruction in practical music theory, geared as it was to the skills of composition and accompaniment, was the exception (although Rameau taught "classes" of composition in the 1740s using his "textbook" *L'Art de la basse fondamentale*).[38] Theory instruction after the French Revolution would change markedly in this respect, bringing about new genres of practical music theory. For in the course of the nineteenth century, numerous educational institutions – particularly those of the music "conservatory" – were established

37 See Lester, *Compositional Theory in the Eighteenth Century*, pp. 290–93 for an illustration of Koch's method of melodic expansion. 38 Christensen, *Rameau*, pp. 309–10.

throughout Europe, in which formal instruction on topics of applied music were given that had hitherto been the province of private music instructors. This new institutionalization of music pedagogy would have profound influence on the development of music theory.

Paris

While the origin of conservatories of music can be traced back to well before the French Revolution (particularly in Italy), the modern European conservatories are largely a product of the post-revolutionary period – a government response to the music-educational demands of an emerging middle class. After a protracted period of gestation, the Conservatoire National de Musique et de Déclamation was established in Paris in 1795, followed by the state-sponsored conservatories in Prague (1811), Graz (1813), and Vienna (1817). In various parts of what would eventually be a unified Germany, the famous Leipzig Conservatory opened in 1843, directed by Mendelssohn, followed soon thereafter by conservatories in Munich (1846) and Berlin (1850). By the 1860s, the conservatory movement had spread east to Russia, and would eventually gain a foothold in America as well.

In Paris, a major center of nineteenth-century musical "progress," the post-revolutionary era brought with it a cosmopolitan environment for musical study: an international faculty from various musical backgrounds staffed the Conservatoire, which drew a diverse lot of students hoping for musical careers. Consensus on a curriculum of study was elusive, however, and the debate within the committee entrusted with producing the theory curriculum was forceful, though the committee met its charge: beginning with a *Principes élémentaires de musique* (1799), it produced five *livres de solfège*, a *Traité d'harmonie* and numerous pedagogical works for voice, piano, and orchestral instruments within the next ten years. The theory curriculum was divided into *composition théorique* and *composition pratique*, the former constituting courses in elementary voice-leading and figured bass called *harmonie*, the latter instructions in counterpoint and fugue (and much later on, also instrumentation).[39] It is not possible in this chapter to trace the development of the entire music curriculum in Paris and elsewhere. Instead, we will concentrate on one component of this curriculum, albeit probably the most critical: harmony. Despite the profusion of other skills taught, harmony was – and remains largely to this day – the core element of any music pedagogy.

The "official" Conservatoire harmony text of *composition théorique* was the brief (eighty-page) *Traité d'harmonie* (1804) written by Charles-Simon Catel (1773–1830), one of the founding members of the Conservatoire. Adopted unanimously by the committee, it was reissued numerous times until the aftermath of the Congress of Vienna,

39 Groth, *Die französische Kompositionslehre*, p. 14. The table on p. 17 demonstrates the evolution of the theory curriculum throughout the century.

and the reorganization of the Conservatoire in 1815–16. According to Fétis, Rameau's theory of harmony was the dominant paradigm for French music teachers when Catel wrote his treatise.[40] The theory promulgated by those teachers was really a parody of Rameau's system, with an emphasis upon chordal generation by mechanical third-stacking.[41] Not surprisingly, the theory of third-stacking eventually garnered opposition by a number of younger committee members.

Catel attempted to avoid the arbitrariness of such ad hoc manipulations of the *corps sonore* by positing a single ninth chord (either natural or flat) as the source of all harmony. There was no "natural" justification for this construct by appeals to acoustics or numerology. It was simply a practical heuristic. Chords extractable from this construct are *harmonie simple ou naturelle*. The remaining chordal vocabulary falls into the category of *harmonie composée ou artificielle*; these chords are constructed by suspending tones from previous chords.[42] Although Catel's category of *harmonie composée ou artificielle* is arguably too broad (admitting combinations of submetric dissonance, chordal dissonance, and apparently consonant "chords"), his intention is clear enough: the ninth chord can furnish a "natural" vocabulary of chords, while voice-leading is invoked to explain "modifications" of these natural chords. In fact, lessons in voice-leading form an important component of Catel's book, though they are largely lessons by example, not verbal explanation: chord progressions are always demonstrated in four written-out parts (with no analytical "shorthand" other than figured-bass symbols), and many are subsequently "elaborated" in shorter note values in the manner of Kirnberger (or Fux). Catel scrupulously preserves Rameau's terminology for cadential types, but he never uses Rameau's fundamental bass theory as a means of teaching "preferred" chord progression.

With the end of the Catel era, other texts were published that continued the spirit of Catel's pragmatic approach. For example, Anton Reicha (1770–1836), a member of the original committee who had been educated in Vienna, published a harmony course that he had certainly taught in the classroom: *Cours de composition musicale, ou traité complet et raisonné d'harmonie pratique* (1816–18). "There are only thirteen chords in our musical system," Reicha claimed, and he proceeded to present a list of frequently occurring "harmonies" from contemporary music with little consistent theoretical thread to hold them together.[43] Such a work could only appear to Fétis as "a most deplorable return to the empiricism of old methods from the beginning of the eighteenth century": evidently the pedagogical ordering of the chordal vocabulary was once again thrown into question with the new music of the early nineteenth century.[44] Catel was

40 Wagner, *Die Harmonielehre*, p. 62; also see Gessele, *Institutionalization*.

41 Groth, *Die französische Kompositionslehre*, pp. 26–30. As shown in **Chapter 24, pp. 760–61**, the theory of third-stacking was in fact a relatively minor – and ultimately negligible – element of Rameau's system, although it received exaggerated emphasis by "followers" such as Marpurg, d'Alembert, and Roussier.

42 "*Harmonie composée* is based upon *harmonie simple*; it is formed by retarding one or more parts, which prolong one or more sounds from a chord into the following chord" (Groth, quoting Catel, *Die französische Kompositionslehre*, p. 31).

43 Ibid., p. 42. See **Chapter 18, p. 586** for a listing of Reicha's fundamental harmonies.

44 Quoted in Groth, *Die französische Kompositionslehre*, p. 41.

the ultimate victor, however, for Reicha seems to have had no followers, and it was Catel's system that formed the basis of Fétis's *Traité complet de la théorie et de la pratique de l'harmonie* (1844), the best-known French harmony book of the nineteenth century.[45]

Vienna

Music theory in Vienna was altogether a different matter. Vienna was no revolutionary city: indeed, much was unchanged since the eighteenth century. The traditional figured-bass manual remained the basis of theory pedagogy for much of the first half of the century; often called *Generalbaßlehre-Harmonielehre*, the title was more frequently reversed by the 1840s.[46] By contrast with Paris, where the Conservatoire was the music-pedagogical center throughout the century and beyond, and royal patronage had all but dried up, in Vienna, the Imperial Court continued to offer employment to musicians, and the Catholic Church continued as an important sponsor of music and music education, as it had well back into the Middle Ages.

Vienna's most famous theory pedagogue of the nineteenth century, Simon Sechter (1788–1867), began his career very much in the eighteenth-century tradition as a private instructor (the circumstances under which he gave one counterpoint lesson to Schubert).[47] Sechter published his first text, a *Generalbaßlehre*, in 1830 in the midst of a flood of such books by fellow organist-pedagogues. But his crowning achievement was his *Grundsätze der musikalischen Komposition* (1853–54), published, as Fux's *Gradus* had been, when the author was sixty-five (though certainly Sechter had been teaching much of this material at the newly established Conservatory since the 1830s). Like Fux, his illustrious predecessor in Vienna, Sechter was essentially a liturgical composer, and, also like Fux, his reputation and financial support, at least early in his career, were due in part to his position at the Imperial Court.[48] In later life when the *Grundsätze* was published, his fame as a pedagogue had grown considerably, capped apparently when the insecure Anton Bruckner came to him for composition lessons. Bruckner was in fact forbidden by Sechter to compose anything original in his lessons. Instead, he was obliged to write out a seemingly endless stream of abstract counterpoint and harmony exercises, preserved to this day in Vienna. Bruckner's faith in Sechter's authority was apparently never shaken, and there may well be some "Sechter-influence" on his music, though that remains controversial. However, Bruckner's famous one-liner, "Look Gentlemen, this is the rule, but I don't compose that way," is indicative of how far pedagogical theory had moved from compositional practice – at least pedagogical theory as he learned and taught it.[49]

45 For more on Fétis's *Traité*, see **Chapter 30, pp. 934–35**.
46 U. Thomson, *Voraussetzungen*; see Wason, *Viennese Harmonic Theory* for a more wide-ranging study.
47 Mann, *Theory and Practice*, pp. 79–85 and 143–48.
48 Ibid., pp. 80–85. Also see Tittel, *Die Wiener Musikhochschule*.
49 Sechter's own theory of harmony is discussed and illustrated in **Chapter 25, pp. 788–91**.

Germany

In Germany, early nineteenth-century pedagogues responded to a growing middle-class market of educated music *Liebhaber*. The run of "general music texts" (*Allgemeine Musiklehren*) directed at this public began early in the century with books by Gottfried Weber (1779–1839) and Adolph Bernhard Marx. In both cases, they were abstracted from much larger treatises on composition. Most of Weber's *Allgemeine Musiklehre zum Selbstunterricht für Lehrer und Lernende* (1822) was extracted from his *Versuch einer geordneten Theorie der Tonsetzkunst* (1817).[50] Oddly, though, the prominence given harmony in the larger *Versuch* is absent in the far more rudimentary *Allgemeine Musiklehre*, where the subject is folded into a single short chapter entitled "Harmony, Melody, Key, and Scale" (Chapter 3).

The *Allgemeine Musiklehre* (1839) of Adolph Bernhard Marx (1795–1866) is if anything even more elementary in technical coverage of harmony, perhaps because the author was far more concerned with certain aesthetic and pedagogical issues. The seven chapters of Marx's catechism cover (1) basic pitch material; (2) rhythm; (3) the human voice and study of instruments; (4) elementary formal structure; (5) theory of form in art-music; (6) artistic performance, with an appendix on playing from score; and (7) music education and music instruction.[51] This author's iconoclastic approach is even more evident in his *Die Lehre von der musikalischen Komposition, praktisch-theoretisch* (1837–47). Marx completely ignores the traditional division into individual disciplines (e.g., harmony and counterpoint), distinguishing merely between a sort of Aristotelian *pure* and *applied* theory of composition. The first two volumes of the work deal with the "pure" theory, presenting an integrated discussion of rhythm, melody, harmony, form, and counterpoint, together with work in motivic development and symmetrical period construction. Marx's "pure" theory holds true for all instrumental genres and stylistic idioms, and it is always compositional in orientation: rather than learning techniques of "harmony" in isolation, students prepare small compositions from the first lesson on. Applied composition (covered in vols. III and IV) concerns advanced vocal and instrumental forms. In Marx's view, the point of theory pedagogy is not so much to impart "knowledge," but to stimulate creative activity.

Marx undoubtedly taught material from his *Kompositionslehre* in Berlin, where he had been named University Music Director in 1833, and his progressive views on education, inspired very likely by the Swiss pedagogue Johann Heinrich Pestalozzi, "were very much in line with the pedagogical mandate of the University of Berlin."[52] But Marx's

50 For information on Weber's music theory, see **Chapter 25, pp. 782–88**.

51 Hahn, "Die Anfänge der Allgemeinen Musiklehre," p. 65.

52 Marx, *Musical Form* (Burnham trans., pp. 6–7). In Rainbow's view, "it was Pestalozzi's achievement to demonstrate that a child's education depended less upon memorizing facts than on the provision of opportunities to make factual discoveries for himself" (*Music in Educational Thought and Practice*, p. 135). This is precisely what Marx was trying to do.

ideas were evidently not as popular or influential everywhere in Berlin. The harmony textbook of Siegried Dehn (*Theoretisch-praktische Harmonielehre*, 1840) offered serious competition to Marx, being adopted as the official music theory text in Prussia. Dehn was a rather conservative pedagogue who eschewed what he considered to be Marx's highly metaphysical approach to music; instead Dehn believed musical instruction should be based upon a more empirical, sober study of Classical norms of practice.[53]

When the Leipzig Conservatory got underway in 1843, Mendelssohn and Spohr recommended Moritz Hauptmann (1792–1868) as professor of music theory. A thinker regarded by one commentator as responsible for "returning music theory to the universal significance it had in the middle ages,"[54] Hauptmann was nevertheless interested in the more mundane, pedagogical application of his ideas. Indeed, he left a torso of a harmony book (completed by his student Oscar Paul) that presents most of the topics that would be more fully developed in Part I of his major work: *Die Natur der Harmonik und der Metrik: Zur Theorie der Musik* (1853).[55] The Leipzig Conservatory was also the point of origin of two works that went through many editions, continuing to be the standard harmony books almost everywhere that European classical music was studied through the rest of the century: the *Lehrbuch der Harmonie* (1853) by Ernst Friedrich Richter; and the *Musikalische Kompositionslehre* (1883–84) of Salomon Jadassohn.[56] Richter's book turned Gottfried Weber's critical empiricism into textbook dogma, popularizing his use of roman numerals and other notational innovations. Jadassohn's *Harmonielehre* (which constituted one part of his comprehensive *Kompositionslehre*) is hardly distinguishable from Richter's, except that it deals more extensively with chromatic chord-progression owing to the author's aesthetic proclivities and the work's later publication date. (Jadassohn was actually Richter's successor at the Conservatory.) The fact that these books went into edition after edition is symptomatic of the dearth of new ideas, and the irrelevance that pedagogical theory was falling into: despite attempts at reform by the likes of A. B. Marx, neither a theory nor a pedagogy of "Nineteenth-Century Harmony" ever really seemed to get underway.

Riemann. The towering pedagogical figure in Germany of the latter part of the century, Hugo Riemann (1849–1919), did his best to move the pedagogy of theory beyond this impasse. A student of Jadassohn's at the Conservatory and the University of Leipzig, he went on to take a doctorate in Göttingen, returning briefly to the University of Leipzig in 1878 to begin his academic career. After positions in Hamburg

53 See Eicke, *Der Streit*, p. 15. Dehn's book is divided into *musica theorica* vs. *musica practica*, though the former begins to look at times more like an acoustics manual. Footnotes trace ideas back to eighteenth-century sources (Dehn was one of the first historians of theory). Dehn's system of chord classification contained in the second practical part recalls Marpurg, but comes directly from his teacher, Bernhard Klein. 54 Rummenhöller, "Hauptmann," p. 11.

55 On Hauptmann's Theory of harmony, see **Chapter 14, pp. 459–62**.

56 Richter's book was the first volume of a three-volume set entitled *Die praktischen Studien zur Theorie der Musik*; the first volume was translated into at least eight European languages (see Thomson, *History of Harmonic Theory*, p. 17). Jadassohn likewise produced a three-volume pedagogical work called *Die Lehre vom reinen Satze*, which first appeared in 1884.

and Wiesbaden, among other places, he returned to Leipzig in 1895 for the rest of his professional life. If Rameau had attempted to "formalize" the figured-bass practice of the early eighteenth century, Riemann undertook a similar agenda with respect to harmonic practice of the middle to late nineteenth century (although one might argue that the harmonic practice Riemann sought to formalize in 1882 at the beginning of his career – when he dedicated his *Handbuch der Harmonielehre* to Liszt – is not the same one that he formalized in his mature harmonic theory, where his tastes seem to have become more conservative with age). Like Rameau, Riemann understood the importance of speculative music theory as a source of intellectual renewal for practical theory: thus, his career also alternated between "speculative" and "practical" works, and also like Rameau, theoretical advances might well occur in the midst of overtly pedagogical works, such as his mature harmonic theory *Vereinfachte Harmonielehre; oder, Die Lehre von den tonalen Funktionen der Akkorde* (1893), which has clear pedagogical aspirations.[57] The "theory of tonal functions of chords," as the book was subtitled, is clearly Riemann's chief original contribution to the central pedagogical discipline, and the one which continued to influence a line of theorists.[58] Riemann also published tirelessly on many other pedagogical topics, including fugal and vocal composition, figured bass, piano-playing, instrumentation, score-reading, and rhythmic agogics. Moreover, he produced editions of the *Kompositionslehren* of Marx and Lobe, making these pedagogical works available to a later generation, and published a collection of analyses of all of the Beethoven Piano Sonatas and Bach's *Well-Tempered Clavier* intended for piano teachers and students.[59] (This is not to mention, of course, his even more voluminous output in more "scholarly" areas of systematic music theory, psychology, and historical musicology.) But clearly, the practical theory curriculum of the nineteenth-century conservatory was central to his interests. No writer from the nineteenth century exerted such a profound influence upon musical pedagogy as did Riemann, or has continued (at least in many European countries) to exert such a marked presence.

England and North America

Translations of the major French and German pedagogical treatises had appeared in England throughout the eighteenth and into the nineteenth century. There was little indigenous music pedagogy from England from this time, however. Perhaps the first truly original voice of English music theory came with the *Treatise on Harmony* by Alfred Day, which appeared in 1845. The author, a physician by vocation, presented all chords as derived from seven-note third-stacks modeled on the harmonic series ("9th, 11th and 13th chords") over tonic, dominant, and supertonic, and attempted to promote a new "figured bass" notation that specified precisely the relationship of the

57 See the table of publications given by Seidel in "Die Harmonielehre Hugo Riemanns."

58 See Imig, *Systeme der Funktionsbezeichnung*. For further discussion on Riemann's theories, see Chapter 25, pp. 796–800.

59 Riemann, *L. van Beethovens sämtliche Klaviersolosonaten* (1917–19); *Katechismus der Fugen-Komposition* (1890).

bass to the root of the chord. This idiosyncratic development of post-Rameauian theory by an author outside of the pedagogical mainstream would likely have had little influence had it not been taken up by Day's friend, the prolific composer and influential teacher George Macfarren.[60] In fact, espousal of Day's system led to Macfarren's resignation from the Royal Academy of Music in 1847, though he was recalled to his position in 1851. Day's ideas were also taught by Sir F. A. Gore Ouseley, professor of music at Oxford from 1855 until his death in 1889,[61] and ultimately by Ebenezer Prout, whose numerous music texts were the most widely used in Victorian Britain.[62]

Prout's treatises became also important in North America, where they were often reprinted. To be sure, a number of earlier continental music theorists had been imported to North America in English translation. First, Catel's *Traité* was translated by the pioneering American music educator Lowell Mason.[63] It was followed by James Warner's abridged translation of Weber's *Versuch*, while a translation of Marx's *Kompositionslehre* offered his unique view of pedagogy to an English-speaking readership.[64] By the 1860s, the American conservatory movement had produced new and voracious consumers of imported pedagogical material. Richter's simplification of Weber appeared, followed by a translation of Sechter's volume I; even the Hauptmann–Paul harmony book was translated by another pioneer of American music education, Theodore Baker.[65] One of the only indigenous American pedagogues of the time was Percy Goetschius (1853–1943) American born, but German trained.[66] Pedagogical theory in America at the turn of the twentieth century, then, was a melange of stultified ideas drawn from the principal European works of the genre. With few exceptions, the beginnings of institutional music theory in the New World coincided with a period of its decline in the Old World, for pedagogical music theory in Europe had lost touch with the way in which theory and composition were taught in the eighteenth century, while, on the other hand, largely ignoring the newer compositional developments of the nineteenth century.

Twentieth-century educational reforms

Perhaps the one credible attempt at the turn of the twentieth century to write a text of harmony that actually took into serious account contemporaneous musical practice was

60 Macfarren, *The Rudiments of Harmony*; *Six Lectures on Harmony*. 61 Ouseley, *Treatise on Harmony*.
62 Prout, *Harmony*. Prout's influence is also apparent in Foote and Spaulding, *Modern Harmony*.
63 Mason, *A Treatise by Catel*. 64 Weber, *Theory of Musical Composition*; Marx, *Musical Composition*.
65 Richter, *A Manual of Harmony*; Sechter, *The Correct Order*; Hauptmann, *Manual of Harmony*.
66 Goetschius studied in Stuttgart with Immanuel Faisst, a founder of the Stuttgart Conservatory. *The Material Used in Musical Composition* is reputedly Goethschius's adaptation of Faisst's (unpublished) system of harmony designed for English-speaking students at the Conservatory. With the publication of this work, Goetschius returned to the United States, and to a long teaching career, beginning at Syracuse University, and then the New England Conservatory. With the founding of the "Institute of Musical Art" in New York in 1905 (later to become the Juilliard School in 1923), he became head of theory and composition, teaching there until his retirement in 1925.

the *Harmonielehre* of Rudolf Louis and Ludwig Thuille (1906). The quality of instruction in Munich had already shone forth in a slim, but interesting *Harmonielehre* (1900) by the young Munich-trained composer and critic August Halm. Louis and Thuille went well beyond this, however, devoting half of their own *Harmonielehre* to an exploration of "chromatic harmony" and other progressive compositional techniques. The book was the product of a number of fortunate circumstances. The method and many of the musical examples were by Thuille, an experienced pedagogue and talented composer, while Louis, a composer and music critic (who had taken a doctorate in Vienna), brought both aesthetic and theoretical erudition to the project. Finally, the core repertoire of the book was music of the "Munich School," whose most important international exponent was Richard Strauss. The notion that this repertoire emanated from a "school" of composition, current in the music-critical literature of the time and in subsequent musicological writing, pointed to its relatively unified cultural and aesthetic origins, and endowed the work with stylistic and technical consistency. Thuille had studied with Josef Pembauer (a Bruckner student) in Innsbruck before working with Rheinberger in Munich, and Louis certainly knew Bruckner's teaching at the University of Vienna; thus it is not surprising that the book synthesized features of the Sechter–Bruckner step theory with Riemann's function theory. Despite the extraordinary musical change that would occur in the years to follow, the book remained the most frequently cited harmony text in a survey of German conservatories dating from the early 1960s.[67]

Almost everywhere else, however, the "Golden Age" of *musica practica* was a distant memory. The composer Vincent d'Indy, studying at the Paris Conservatoire in the 1870s, found only César Franck's organ classes to have had any value, the lessons of the Belgian master having become "the veritable center of composition study." The three courses in "advanced composition," on the other hand, were taught by a "composer of comic operas who had no notion of the symphony." D'Indy's experience as a student eventually turned him into an educational reformer. Inspired by his experience with Franck, whose lessons were "founded on Bach and Beethoven, but admitted all of the new ideas and initiatives," d'Indy advocated a return to classicism as an antidote to the Conservatoire's academicism. Unable to realize his reform at the Conservatoire, he co-founded and directed a new kind of educational institution in 1900: the Schola Cantorum. In his opening address, he proclaimed loudly "Art is not a trade" ("L'Art n'est pas un métier"), thereby declaring war on the unimaginative theory instruction of the Conservatoire pedants.[68] Echoing Marx's earlier renewal attempt, d'Indy regarded the study of compositional craft as essential preparation for the creative act of composition, not an end in itself.

67 Förster, "Heutige Praktiken im Harmonielehreunterricht," in *Beiträge*, ed. Vogel, p. 259.
68 D'Indy's *Cours de composition musicale* is a comprehensive treatise (recalling Marx, in some respects) that includes considerable study of a broad range of styles, and much work in early music. However, many anecdotes testify to d'Indy's conservative tastes with respect to music of his own time, a conservatism that grew more pronounced in the 1920s.

Schoenberg and Schenker. Music theory instruction at the Vienna Akademie (later renamed the Hochschule) had already run into criticism during Sechter's last years, and by 1910, an "exposé" painted a dismal picture.[69] Both Heinrich Schenker and Arnold Schoenberg were considered as potential rescuers of theory instruction. Schoenberg eventually received the appointment, and it seems clear that the writing of his *Harmonielehre* (1911) was designed to provide the pedagogical authority he lacked in the absence of an academic degree. Schenker, on the other hand, had already published a *Harmonielehre* in 1906, the opening volume of what he called "New Musical Theories and Fantasies of an Artist" – another attempt to reconnect theory instruction with the larger concerns of Art, and a reform effort that was in part a reaction against his own studies with the notoriously pedantic Anton Bruckner at the Akademie. Though "conservative" in the sense that it too was a return to the canonical music of the Viennese Classical composers, Schenker's *Harmonielehre* radically revised the discipline by banishing the study of voice-leading to the volumes on counterpoint he was then writing; "harmony" became, in effect, the first step to analysis rather than composition. Schoenberg's pedagogy of harmony, on the other hand, remained a preparation for composition. He had little use for "theorists" and their theories; his focus remained upon the teaching of compositional craft in the clearest and most efficient way. Indeed, Schoenberg's pedagogy departs little from convention – at least until the chapter on "Non-Harmonic Tones," anyway. There, he voices strong skepticism of this concept. It becomes clear that Schoenberg is attempting to revise the traditional theory to help make it account for his own musical language of the time – which had just turned to atonality.

Schenker's own teaching was limited (he never held an academic appointment), and his influence on pedagogy was essentially posthumous, occurring after the emigration of a handful of his disciples to America in the late 1930s, and the reemergence of his ideas in an entirely different musical culture in the latter half of the century. Schoenberg's pedagogical influence, on the other hand, began early (Berg and Webern studied with him right after the turn of the century), and was strong throughout the first half of the century. The Viennese Classical composers (particularly Beethoven) loomed large in his teaching from the beginning, and apparently this focus became even sharper in his teaching in California in the 1930s, to judge by the pedagogical manuals dating from that period.[70] Ironically, his twelve-tone theory – the source of so much of Schoenberg's fame and notoriety – remained primarily within his private compositional workshop (see **Chapter 20, pp. 609–13**). But despite their radically different interpretations of the music of their Viennese predecessors, Schoenberg and Schenker were of one mind with regard to its hallowed place in their curricula.

69 Violin, *Zustände*; also see Simms, "Schoenberg."

70 For examples of Schoenberg's pedagogy, see *Structural Functions*; *Preliminary Exercises*; *Fundamentals*; *Models*. Also see the discussion in **Chapter 25, pp. 802–06**.

Hindemith. If Schoenberg's tonal theory can be seen to have been strongly influenced by his own compositional work, the same can be said even more emphatically of another prominent composer-theorist from the early twentieth century: Paul Hindemith (1895–1963). Having reached considerable prominence as a composer and performer of new music, Hindemith, like Schoenberg, without an academic degree, was appointed to a teaching position at the prestigious Berlin Musikhochschule in 1927. Even before his move to Berlin, Hindemith had expressed definite ideas on the shape a theory/composition curriculum should take. But his experience of actually teaching composition convinced him of the need for a firmer theoretical framework. Accordingly, Hindemith began to study the theoretical literature, teaching himself Latin so that he could read medieval and Renaissance treatises. Numerous sources testify to his prodigious knowledge of historical music theory. In 1933, a commission for a series of musical "handbooks" occasioned a manuscript Hindemith called "Composition and Its Teaching" (*Komposition und Kompositionslehre*). Though this work never reached publication (owing to the worsening political climate that would force his emigration to America six years later), much of the substance of that work was taken over into his major theoretical project, collectively entitled in English *The Craft of Musical Composition* and published in several installments between 1935 and 1942. (A third, unfinished section of the *Craft* was eventually published posthumously in 1970.)

Hindemith's major innovation as a theorist of harmony was to obviate distinctions between diatonicism and chromaticism by invoking various continuums of tonal relations based upon acoustical grounds. With few exceptions, all chords have "roots" (determined by the root of their lowest, most "consonant" interval), and a Hindemithian analysis would notate the succession of these roots (thus updating the venerable "fundamental bass"), as well as indicate the chord group (which, in turn, shows the level of consonance or dissonance in each chord). This reading of "harmonic fluctuation," as Hindemith called these analyses, was flexible enough to have implications for composers working in many styles, including jazz, and this theory enjoyed unprecedented popularity in America for a period in the mid-twentieth century.

But times quickly changed. In 1952, Hindemith left Yale to return to Europe, where he taught at the University of Zurich, and the English-language criticism of his pedagogical project began in earnest.[71] Most consequentially, perhaps, a strong alternative to Hindemith's theory was gaining a foothold in American soil. In the same year Hindemith left Yale, Felix Salzer published his *Structural Hearing*, the first large-scale analytical study to apply the theories of Heinrich Schenker to the same broad repertoire that had interested Hindemith – early polyphony to twentieth-century "tonal" music. And through the following decades, Schenkerian theory gained an increased

71 Cazden, "Hindemith and Nature"; Landau, "Hindemith the System Builder"; Thomson, "Hindemith's Contribution."

following such that Hindemith's pedagogical program soon became little more than a historical curiosity.

Boulanger. While all of the modern music pedagogues whose "theories" we have considered in this essay published works in which their ideas were developed and explained, we should keep in mind that not all theory pedagogy is necessarily so systematically articulated. (Recall Coclico's description of Josquin's compositional pedagogy cited above.) If we judge the effectiveness of teachers by the quality and esteem of their students, then no teacher of composition and analysis was probably more venerated in the twentieth century than Nadia Boulanger (1887–1979). Although trained as a composer by Widor and Fauré, Boulanger abandoned composition early on to dedicate herself to the teaching of other composers. Rather than attempting to critique the compositional submissions of her students, though, her lessons seemed to have centered more on the careful analysis of music by certain "Classical" composers in addition to selected new works of composers that she held in high regard (such as Fauré and Stravinsky). In addition, Boulanger demanded of her students the full mastery of traditional practical skills of score-reading, solfège, and figured-bass realization. While it is not possible to speak of any codified theoretical or compositional doctrines that Boulanger propagated, the fierce integrity and profound musicality with which she undertook the study of musical scores proved to be a lasting inspiration for her dozens of important students.

Music theory in the academy

At the close of the Hindemith era, two important developments got underway that would have a significant impact on the pedagogy of music theory in North America. The more short-lived of these was the so-called Contemporary Music Project (CMP), sponsored by grants from the Ford Foundation, which began its activities in this area by funding residencies for composers in the public schools in 1959. In July 1963, CMP was established formally, seeking "to modernize and broaden the quality and scope of music education at all levels."[72] The increasing gulf between contemporary music and the broader public was one of the main concerns of the CMP project. To that effect, it inaugurated a series of seminars and workshops on contemporary music in many universities that brought together composers and musical scholars from a number of disciplines to discuss "comprehensive musicianship," yet another attempt to rescue a theory curriculum that had lost touch with music of its own day. Thus, an important theme was "restructuring the existing courses in theory and history – not only to devote adequate time to consideration of contemporary music, but even more importantly, to

72 *Comprehensive Musicianship*, p. 3.

consider all musical traditions in terms of our present-day vantage point."[73] The "comprehensive" part of the program (echoing Pestalozzi, A. B. Marx, and other educational reformers of the nineteenth century) attempted to address the perennial complaint that "a synthesis rarely occurs between courses within the general area of musicianship or between musicianship courses and professional studies; the student receives very little opportunity to develop a comprehensive view of his entire field."[74] The impact of CMP was felt on the pedagogy of music theory throughout the late 1960s and 70s: the traditional categories of "harmony," "counterpoint," and "aural skills" were effaced as many of the textbooks of this era combined these pedagogical genres. As for organizational schemes, some writers did indeed focus on contemporary music first (Cogan, *Sonic Design*), or perhaps attempted to move across repertoires according to theoretical "topics" (Christ, DeLone, and Kliewer, *Materials and Structures of Music*), or took a purely "historical" approach (Ultan, *Music Theory: Problems and Practices*). CMP also inspired legendary pedagogues (e.g., Robert Trotter of the University of Oregon) whose curricula never reached published form. Thus the late 1960s and 1970s in American pedagogy of theory were years of experimentation in curriculum design and content.

The second development that would have the most far-reaching impact on theory teaching in North America was the professionalization of music theory as an independent academic discipline. Perhaps ironically, it was Hindemith who seems to have been the prime mover behind this idea. While teaching at Yale, Hindemith founded the first professional degree program (at a Master's level) in music theory that focused heavily upon the study of historical documents of music theory as well as the analysis of contemporary music. While he was opposed bitterly by a number of faculty, it was he "who insisted that theory should be offered as a separate major and not combined with composition . . ."[75] Indeed, of the forty-four graduates educated under Hindemith at Yale, thirty-four of those were majors in theory. Moreover, the founding, in the 1950s, of the *Yale Music Theory Translation Series* and the *Journal of Music Theory* (with its strong interest in the history of theory) can be seen as legacies of Hindemith's work at Yale. Nor were his interests purely academic; he sought to bring his studies of music history and theory to life through the Collegium Musicum that he founded and conducted – one of the first such organizations in an American university.

Whatever Hindemith's larger design for theory study at Yale may have been, after his departure it developed in ways that might have surprised him. When he stopped teaching "The History of the Theory of Music" and it was taken over by one of his students, David Kraehenbuehl (the founding editor of the *Journal of Music Theory*), the Collegium concerts stopped. And the Ph.D. that evolved from the M.Mus. in the early 1960s did so not in the School of Music, but in the Department of Music of Yale College (and the Graduate School of Arts and Sciences), where it became allied with studies in historical musicology.

73 Ibid. 74 Ibid., p. 5. 75 Forte, "Hindemith's Contribution," p. 10.

At about the same time, the composer Milton Babbitt was helping to establish a Ph.D. program in theory and composition at Princeton University, along with a professional journal – *Perspectives of New Music* – devoted to the ideal of the composer-theorist, thus offering a competing model for doctoral-level theory study. By contrast with the "Yale model," theory was taught in Princeton not solely as an independent historical and analytical program, but rather as a component of applied compositional pedagogy, one that emphasized original research into issues of serialism and electronic music.

But ultimately, it was the Yale model of the academic music theorist that seems to have taken root during the heady expansion of North American university programs in the 1960s and 70s. The teaching of practical music theory to students – hitherto the domain of composers and performers in most conservatories and universities – was increasingly taken over by scholars who were trained within the growing number of Ph.D. programs where degrees in music theory were offered. The reader of the present volume will find little precedent in the past for this occupation.[76]

This turn of events has brought with it a number of benefits for the pedagogy of theory. Above all, the influence of Heinrich Schenker, which had grown gradually through the 1950s in North America, began to permeate undergraduate theory instruction with the most wholesome consequences. Schenker's sensitivity to the combined functions of voice-leading and harmony in tonal music led to a healthy integration of the two in numerous American college textbooks, and clarified a relationship that was too often obscured in previous theoretical taxonomies.[77] It also led to an interest in the historical music pedagogies of the eighteenth century, including a renewed emphasis upon species counterpoint and thorough-bass theory. But its very success also led to a narrowing of focus in undergraduate curricula; only the select "masterworks" that Schenker's theory addresses best tend to be taught. The attempts by Felix Salzer and other "reformed" Schenkerians to broaden the domain of Schenkerian theory to a more diverse repertoire (including both pre- and post-tonal music) have met with considerable resistance.[78]

Meanwhile, there was an extraordinary development of "atonal" theory, inspired by the seminal writings of Milton Babbitt and Allen Forte. While much of this theoretical work lies beyond the normal pedagogical curriculum of most music students, attempts have been made to simplify the analysis of much post-tonal music using tools of pitch-class set theory and serialism, and even to develop pedagogies of post-tonal aural skills. A final aspect of theoretical research that has had implications for music pedagogy lies in the burgeoning field of music psychology. For pedagogy, this plays out in attempts to refine pedagogical strategies through empirical studies of musical cognition. All of these developments have improved theory instruction immeasurably.

76 McCreless ("Rethinking") considers many of the ramifications of the refocusing of the music-theory profession in this thought-provoking essay.

77 One of the most widely used such Schenker-influenced text books in North America is Aldwell and Schachter's *Harmony and Voice Leading*.

78 See Chapter 26, pp. 835–38.

But there has also been a serious loss with the dedicated study of theory: the connection with musical composition as a living, evolving entity seems to have been cut, once and for all. From our vantage point at the end of this essay, we might say that the history of pedagogical music theory began with composers of standing teaching their craft, and reached its zenith with the great treatises of the Renaissance and Baroque eras, almost all of which were penned by composers who attempted to convey a contemporaneous and living language to their students. The intimate connection between theory pedagogy and musical composition began to weaken in the nineteenth century with conservatory epigones teaching the compositional craft. And despite a few exceptions, in the twentieth century this connection was largely severed. Given the loss of a common language of harmonic tonality in the twentieth century, and the flux of competing musical styles and languages that rushed in to fill the vacuum, it is little wonder that the music taught to students was by and large made up of a historical canon of musical artworks; no longer did music teachers convey a living, vibrant language, let alone contribute to this language themselves as composers. Perhaps the plethora of co-existing musical styles that characterizes our contemporary scene – Leonard Meyer's "dynamic steady-state" – makes such a coupling between contemporary composition and theory instruction no longer a practical reality.[79] If this is so, though, the status of the professional music theory instructor seems to have ironically returned at least in part to that of the speculative *musicus* of medieval lore – who is a "knower" but not necessarily a "doer". To that extent, the academization of music theory may be seen to have come at a cost.

79 Meyer, *Music, the Arts, and Ideas*, Chapter 9.

Bibliography

Primary sources

Aaron, P. *Toscanello in musica* (1523), trans. P. Bergquist, Colorado Springs, Colorado College Music Press, 1970

Aldwell, E. and C. Schachter, *Harmony and Voice Leading*, 2nd edn., New York, Harcourt Brace Jovanovich, 1989

Aristides Quintilianus, *On Music, in Three Books*, trans. and ed. T. Mathiesen, New Haven, Yale University Press, 1983

Aurelian of Réôme, *Musica disciplina*, ed. L. Gushee as *Aureliani Reomensis Musica Disciplina*, *CSM* 21 (1975); trans. J. Ponte as *Aurelian of Réôme: "The Discipline of Music"*, Colorado Springs, Colorado College Music Press, 1968

Barker, A. *Greek Musical Writings*, 2 vols., Cambridge University Press, 1984–89

Catel, C.-S. *Traité d'harmonie*, Paris, Janet et Cotelle, 1804, trans. C. Clarke as *A Treatise on Harmony*, ed. L. Mason, Boston, J. Loring, 1832

Christ, W. *Materials and Structures of Music*, 3rd edn., Englewood Cliffs, NJ, Prentice-Hall, 1980

Cogan, R. *Sonic Design; The Nature of Sound and Music*, Englewood Cliffs, NJ, Prentice-Hall, 1976

Comprehensive Musicianship; the Foundation for College Education in Music, Washington, D.C., CMP/MENC, 1965

Dehn, S. *Theoretisch-praktische Harmonielehre*, Berlin, Thome, 1840

D'Indy, V. *Cours de Composition Musicale*, 3 vols. (in 4 books), Paris, Durand, 1912

Farmer, H. G. "Al-Fārābī's Arabic-Latin Writings on Music" (1965), in *Studies in Oriental Music*, vol. 1, Frankfurt am Main, 1997, pp. 467–526

Fétis, F.-J. *Traité complet de la théorie et de la pratique de l'harmonie*, Paris, Schlesinger, 1844

Foote, A. and W. Spaulding, *Modern Harmony in its Theory and Practice*, Boston, A. P. Schmidt, 1905

Freig, J. T. *Paedagogus: the Chapter on Music* (1582), trans. and ed. J. Yudkin, *MSD* 38 (1983)

Fux, J. J. *Gradus ad Parnassum*, Vienna, J. P. Van Ghelen, 1725; facs. New York, Broude, 1966

Goetschius, P. *The Material Used in Musical Composition*, New York, G. Schirmer, 1889

Guido of Arezzo, *Epistle Concerning an Unknown Chant*, trans. O. Strunk in *SR*, pp. 214–18

Micrologus, trans. W. Babb, ed. C. V. Palisca in *Hucbald, Guido and John on Music; Three Medieval Treatises*, New Haven, Yale University Press, 1978

Heinichen, J. D. *Der General-bass in der Komposition*, Dresden, Heinichen, 1728; facs. Hildesheim, G. Olms, 1969 and 1994; trans. and ed. G. Buelow as *Figured Bass According to Johann David Heinichen*, rev. edn., University of California Press, 1986 and 1992

Hindemith, P. *The Craft of Musical Composition*, 2 vols. (1937–39), trans. A. Mendel, New York, Associated Music Publishers, London, Schott, 1942

"Methods of Music Theory," *Musical Quarterly* 30 (1944), pp. 20–28

Jadassohn, S. *Lehrbuch der Harmonie*, 12th edn., Leipzig, Breitkopf und Härtel, 1910

Kirnberger, J. P. *Die Kunst des reinen Satzes*, 2 vols., Decker und Hartung, 1771–79; facs. Hildesheim, G. Olms, 1968 and 1988; trans. D. Beach and J. Thym as *The Art of Strict Musical Composition*, New Haven, Yale University Press, 1982

Grundsätze des Generalbasses, Berlin, Decker und Hartung, 1781; facs. Hildesheim, G. Olms, 1999

Koch, H. C. *Versuch einer Anleitung zur Composition*, 3 vols., Leipzig, A. F. Böhme, 1782–93; facs. Hildesheim, G. Olms, 1969 and 2000; Partial trans. N. Baker as *Introductory Essay on Composition*, New Haven, Yale University Press, 1983

Louis, R. and L. Thuille, *Harmonielehre*, Stuttgart, C. Grüninger, 1906

Macfarren, G. *The Rudiments of Harmony*, London, J. B. Cramer, 1860

Six Lectures on Harmony, London, Longmans et al., 1867

Marx, A. B. *Musical Form in the Age of Beethoven; Selected Writings on Theory and Method*, trans. and ed. S. Burnham, Cambridge University Press, 1997

Die Lehre von der musikalischen Komposition, praktisch-theoretisch, 4 vols., Leipzig, Breitkopf und Härtel, 1837–47; trans. H. Saroni as *The Theory and Practice of Musical Composition*, NY, Huntington, Mason and Law, 1851

Masson, C. *Nouveau Traité des regles pour la Composition de la Musique*, Paris, C. Ballard, 1699; facs. New York, Da Capo, 1976

Morley, T. *A Plain and Easy Introduction to Practical Music* (1597), ed. A. Harman, New York, Norton, 1973

Musica enchiriadis and *Scolica enchiriadis*, trans. R. Erickson, ed. C. V. Palisca, New Haven, Yale Univ. Press, 1995

Niedt, F. *The Musical Guide*, 3 parts (1700–21), trans. P. Poulin and I. Taylor, Oxford, Clarendon Press, 1988
Ouseley, Sir F. A. Gore, *Treatise on Harmony*, Oxford, Clarendon Press, 1868
Prout, E. *Harmony: Its Theory and Practice*, London, Augener, 1889
Richter, E. F. *Lehrbuch der Harmonie*, Leipzig, Breitkopf und Härtel, 1853; trans. J. Morgan as *Richter's Manual of Harmony*, New York, G. Schirmer, 1867
Reimann, H. L. *van Beethovens sämtliche Klaviersolosonaten: ästhetische und formaltechnische Analyse*, 3 vols., Berlin, M. Hesse, 1917–19
Katechismus der Fugen-Komposition, Leipzig, M. Hesse, 1890
Vereinfachte Harmonielehre, oder die Lehre von den tonalen Funktionen der Akkorde, London, Augener, 1893; trans. H. Bewerung as *Harmony Simplified*, London, Augener, 1896
Schenker, H. *Harmony* (1906), trans. E. M. Borgese, ed. O. Jonas, University of Chicago Press, 1954
Schoenberg, A. *Harmonielehre* (1911), 3rd edn., Vienna, Universal, 1922; trans. R. Carter as *Theory of Harmony*, Berkeley, University of California Press, 1978
Structural Functions of Harmony, ed. H. Searle, New York, Norton, 1954; rev. ed. L. Stein, New York, Norton, 1969
Preliminary Exercises in Counterpoint, ed. L. Stein, New York, St. Martin's Press, 1964
Fundamentals of Musical Composition, ed. G. Strang and L. Stein, New York, St. Martin's Press, 1967
Models for Beginners in Composition, rev. ed. L. Stein, Los Angeles, Belmont, 1972
Sechter, S. *Grundsätze der musikalischen Komposition*, 3 vols., Leipzig, Breitkopf und Härtel, 1853–54; vol. 1 trans. and ed. C. Müller as *The Correct Order of Fundamental Harmonies: A Treatise on Fundamental Basses, and Their Inversions and Substitutes*, New York, W. A. Pond, 1871
Practische Generalbass-Schule, Vienna, J. Czerny-Witzendorf, 1830
Weber, G. *Versuch einer geordneten Theorie der Tonsetzkunst* (1817–21), 3rd edn., 3 vols., Mainz, B. Schott, 1830–32; trans. J. Warner as *Theory of Musical Compostion*, Boston, Ditson, 1842; trans. Warner, ed. J. Bishop, London, Cocks, 1851
Zarlino, G. *The Art of Counterpoint; Part Three of "Le Istitutioni Harmoniche, 1558"*, trans. G. Marco, ed. C. Palisca, New Haven, Yale University Press, 1968
On the Modes; Part Four of "Le Istitutioni Harmoniche, 1558", trans. V. Cohen, ed. C. Palisca, New Haven, Yale University Press, 1983

Secondary sources

Apfel, E. *Geschichte der Kompositionslehre von den Anfängen bis gegen 1700*, 3 vols., Wilhelmshaven, Heinrichshofen, 1981
Arnold, F. T. *The Art of Accompaniment from a Thoroughbass*, London, Holland, 1931; reprint New York, Dover, 1965
Butt, J. *Music Education and the Art of Performance in the German Baroque*, Cambridge University Press, 1994
Carpenter, N. C., *Music in the Medieval and Renaissance Universities*, Norman, University of Oklahoma Press, 1958; New York, Da Capo, 1972
Cazden, N. "Hindemith and Nature," *Music Review* 25 (1954), pp. 288–306

Christensen, T. *Rameau and Musical Thought in the Enlightenment*, Cambridge University Press, 1993

David, H. and A. Mendel (eds.), *The Bach Reader*, New York, Norton, 1945

Eicke, K.-E. *Der Streit zwischen Adolph Bernhard Marx und Gottfried Wilhelm Fink um die Kompositionslehre*, Regensburg, Bosse, 1966

Förster, W. "Heutige Praktiken im Harmonielehreunterricht," in *Beiträge zur Musiktheorie des 19. Jahrhunderts*, ed. M. Vogel, Regensburg, Bosse, 1966, pp. 259–80

Forte, A. "Paul Hindemith's Contribution to Music Theory in the United States," *JMT* 42 (1998), pp. 1–14

Gessele, C. "The Institutionalization of Music Theory in France: 1764–1802," Ph.D. diss., Princeton University (1989)

Groth, R. *Die französische Kompositionslehre des 19. Jahrhunderts*, Wiesbaden, Steiner, 1983

Gushee, L. "Questions of Genre in Medieval Treatises on Music," in *Gattungen der Musik in Einzeldarstellungen; Gedenkschrift Leo Schrade*, ed. W. Arlt et al., Bern, Francke, 1973, pp. 365–433

Hahn, K. "Die Anfänge der allgemeinen Musiklehre: Gottfried Weber – Adolf Bernhard Marx," in *Musikalische Zeitfragen*, vol. ix, *Die vielspältige Musik und die allgemeine Musiklehre*, ed. W. Wiora, Kassel, Bärenreiter, 1960

Hayes, D. "Rameau's 'Nouvelle Méthode'," *JAMS* 27 (1974), pp. 61–74

Huglo, M. "The Study of Ancient Sources of Music Theory in the Medieval University," in *Music Theory and Its Sources*, ed. A. Barbera, South Bend, University of Notre Dame Press, 1990, pp. 150–72

Imig, R. *Systeme der Funktionsbezeichnung in den Harmonielehren seit Hugo Riemann*, Düsseldorf, Gesellschaft zur Förderung der systematischen Musikwissenschaft, 1970

Landau, V. "Hindemith the System Builder: a Critique of his Theory of Harmony," *Music Review* 22 (1961), pp. 136–51

Lester, J. *Compositional Theory in the Eighteenth Century*, Cambridge, MA, Harvard University Press, 1992

Livingstone, E. "The Theory and Practice of Protestant School Music as seen through the Collection of Abraham Urinsus (c. 1600)," Ph.D. diss., Eastman School of Music, 1962

Mann, A. *Theory and Practice; The Great Composer as Student and Teacher*, New York, Norton, 1987

"Johann Joseph Fux's theoretical writings: a classical legacy," in *Johann Joseph Fux and the Music of the Austro-Italian Baroque*, ed. H. White, Aldershot, England, Scholar Press, 1991

McCreless, P. "Rethinking Contemporary Music Theory," in *Keeping Score: Music, Disciplinarity, Culture*, ed. D. Schwarz and A. Kassabian, Charlottesville, University of Virginia Press, 1997, pp. 13–53

Meyer, L. B. *Music, the Arts, and Ideas*, University of Chicago Press, 1967

Miller, C. "Gaffurius's *Practica Musicae*: Origin and Contents," *Musica Disciplina* 22 (1968), pp. 105–28

Owens, J. A. *Composers at Work*, New York, Oxford University Press, 1997

Palisca, C. V. *Humanism in Italian Renaissance Musical Thought*, New Haven, Yale University Press, 1985

Pietzsch, G. *Die Klassifikation der Musik von Boetius bis Ugolino von Orvieto*, Halle, Niemeyer, 1929

Rainbow, B. *Music in Educational Thought and Practice*, Aberystwyth, Wales, Boethius Press, 1989

Rummenhöller, P. "Moritz Hauptmann, der Begründer einer transzendental-dialektischen Musiktheorie," in *Beiträge zur Musiktheorie des 19. Jahrhunderts*, ed. M. Vogel, Regensburg, Bosse, 1966

Schneider, H. *Die französische Kompositionslehre in der ersten Hälfte des 17. Jahrhunderts*, Tutzing, H. Schneider, 1972

Seidel, E. "Die Harmonielehre Hugo Riemanns," in *Beiträge zur Musiktheorie des 19. Jahrhunderts*, ed. M. Vogel, Regensburg, Bosse, 1966, pp. 39–92

Simms, B. review of "Arnold Schoenberg, *Theory of Harmony*, translated by Roy E. Carter," *MTS* 4 (1982), pp. 155–62

Thompson, D. *History of Harmonic Theory in the United States*, Kent, OH, Kent State University Press, 1980

Thomson, U. *Voraussetzungen und Artungen der österreichischen Generalbasslehre zwischen Albrechtsberger und Sechter*, Tutzing, H. Schneider, 1978

Thomson, W. "Hindemith's Contribution to Music Theory," *JMT* 9 (1965), pp. 52–71

Tittel, E. *Die Wiener Musikhochschule*, Vienna, E. Lafite, 1967

Violin, M. *Die Zustände an der k. und k. Akademie*, Vienna, 1912

Waesberghe, J. S. van, *De musico-pedagogico et theoretico Guidone Aretino*, Florence, L. Olschki, 1953

"The Musical Notation of Guido of Arezzo," *Musica Disciplina* 5 (1951), pp. 15–53

Musikerziehung: Lehre und Theorie der Musik im Mittelalter, vol. III/3 of *Musikgeschichte in Bildern*, ed. H. Besseler and W. Bachmann, Leipzig, VEB Deutscher Verlag für Musik, 1969

Wagner, M. *Die Harmonielehre des ersten Hälfte des 19. Jahrhunderts*, Regensburg, Bosse, 1973

Wason, R. *Viennese Harmonic Theory from Albrechtsberger to Schenker and Schoenberg*, Ann Arbor, UMI Research Press, 1985; University of Rochester Press, 1995

Yudkin, J. "The Influence of Aristotle on French University Music Texts," in *Music Theory and Its Sources*, ed. A. Barbera, South Bend, University of Notre Dame Press, 1990, pp. 173–89

· 3 ·

Epistemologies of music theory

NICHOLAS COOK

"The epistemological underpinnings of Schenker's theory," writes Leslie Blasius, "are far from obvious."[1] Such a statement might well give his readers pause. After all, Blasius is talking about what must be the most widespread approach to the advanced analysis of the common-practice repertory today, and the doubt he is expressing goes to the heart of what Schenkerian analysis tells us: what sort of knowledge of music it gives us, what sort of truth it aspires to. And this of a theorist who devoted considerable attention to the underpinnings of his theory, for instance by carefully distinguishing those elements of music that he saw as given in nature from those that resulted from artifice, and thereby demarcating the province of the scientist from that of the music theorist. Most music-theoretical writing betrays few of Schenker's epistemological qualms; Allen Forte's *The Structure of Atonal Music*, to cite an example more or less at random, plunges straight into its topic in the same spirit of epistemological self-evidence that characterized the contemporary scientific writing on which Forte modeled both his literary and his theoretical approach. Like scientists, perhaps, music theorists address epistemological issues only when the truth-value of their work no longer seems self-evident to them. And if this is the case – if music-theoretical concern with epistemology is at root an expression of anxiety – then we have a fundamental problem in trying to unravel the epistemological underpinnings of music theory: when theorists are confident of the epistemological status of their work they will say nothing about it, whereas when they *do* talk about it we can deduce they are not quite sure about what they are saying.

Carl Dahlhaus saw the issue of self-evidence as a crucial one for the historiography of music theory, stressing the extent to which "music theory in the 18th and 19th centuries was burdened . . . with problems that lay concealed in apparent self-evidence."[2] Nothing, perhaps, is as likely to appear self-evident in theory as the epistemological status of what is being talked about, and accordingly as likely to create problems of understanding for the modern reader. You can easily find yourself asking, without any clear sense of what the answer might be: is this theory about acoustic events or percep-

My thanks to William Drabkin and Aaron Ridley for their comments on a draft version of this chapter.

1 Blasius, *Schenker's Argument*, p. xv.

2 Dahlhaus, *Musiktheorie*, p. vii; translation from Thomas Christensen's review (p. 131). In the absence of an English translation, this review offers a concise summary and critique of Dahlhaus's monograph.

tions, about notational traces or ideal content? Sometimes one and sometimes another? Or several at once? (Sometimes the work of the same theorist suggests different answers at different times; the classic example is Rameau's concept of the *corps sonore*, the sounding body from the multiple vibrations of which he sought to derive the basic principles of harmony, and which variously appears in his writings as a Cartesian first principle, a natural phenomenon open to empirical investigation, and a Lockeian sense impression.[3]) But there is a more particular way in which questions of epistemology impinge on the study of music theory from the late eighteenth century onwards. This is the result of the influence upon it of philosophical aesthetics, defined by what is in essence an epistemological question: what is the nature of the non-propositional knowledge acquired through the perception of art, and what are the criteria of adequacy or inadequacy, truth or untruth, that apply to it? To the extent that Romantic and modernist theories of music revolved round the concept of the "purely musical" experience, they might be seen as attempting to answer questions the motivation of which was as much philosophical as musical.

It would not do, though, to assimilate music theory to any one philosophical stance; indeed theory resists any such generalization, for throughout history it has been undertaken for a wide variety of aims and motivations. It is not one cultural practice but many, given a largely spurious unity by virtue of its singular appellation. It may serve purposes of cultural legitimation (on the first page of his *Traité*, Rameau wrote that "through the exposition of an evident principle, from which we can then draw just and certain conclusions, we can show that our music has attained the last degree and that the Ancients were far from this perfection"),[4] or even of personal credibility: Rameau's successive recastings of the *corps sonore*, reflecting each new scientific fashion, were a condition of his being taken seriously by the scientific establishment of the day. Again, it may be invoked as a means of underwriting national traditions, as in the cases of Riemann and Schenker. It may bolster claims for the aesthetic value of individual musical works, or support agendas of social and educational reform (as in the cases of Marx, Kurth, or Halm).[5] It may be directed at the training of composers or at enhancing the pleasure of musical listeners. It may aim at logical proof or at persuasion, in the manner of aesthetic criticism. Or it may be pursued for its own reward in terms of intellectual verve or speculative pleasure. Under such conditions there can be no reasonable expectation of discovering a unified epistemology of music theory, or of reducing its historical unfolding to a coherent plan. More modestly, then, this chapter aims to identify some of the epistemological options available to the music theorist, to place them in broad historical contexts, and to locate some of the points of epistemological slippage that characterize the history of music theory.

3 Christensen, *Rameau*, p. 235; my discussion of Rameau draws frequently on this book. On Rameau's acoustical principle of the *corps sonore* see **Chapters 9 (p. 253) and 24 (pp. 770–72).**
4 Rameau, *Treatise*, p. xxxiii.
5 Marx, *Musical Form*; Rothfarb, "The 'New Education'" (for Kurth and Halm).

Historical frameworks and epistemological options

For the broadest-brush historical interpretation of music theory, one premised on its epistemological underpinnings, we have to turn again to Dahlhaus, who in his *Die Musiktheorie im 18. und 19. Jahrhundert* distinguishes three basic traditions of theory.[6] The first tradition, dominant up to the end of the Renaissance, is characterized by a focus on abstract intervallic and scalar structures. Speculative in nature, such theory may incorporate empirical as well as mathematical elements, but they are encompassed within a theological epistemology: the theorist aims to display the design of the universe as manifested in music. (Clear traces of this ontology are to be found in later writers drawing on this tradition, among them Schenker and Schoenberg.[7]) The second and more practically oriented tradition, particularly influential during the seventeenth and eighteenth centuries, is concerned primarily with codification and classification, culminating in the grand semiotic projects of the Enlightenment; seen in this light, Rameau's harmonic theory might be seen as falling within the same epistemological ambit as the *Logique du Port-Royal.* Finally, from the late eighteenth century onwards, there is a turn away from the construction of generalized systems and towards what is sometimes termed particularism:[8] the focus on individual musical works, now seen as the ultimate repository of musical signification. This in turn brings with it an epistemological shift towards interpretation based on individual experience; theoretical systems are invoked as an aid in the interpretation of individual works, rather than the other way round.

It is worth noting that we have already drawn a distinction between method (for example, recourse to empirical observation) and its epistemological underpinnings: as I have already suggested, what is characteristic of music theory falling within the first of Dahlhaus's traditions is not that it excludes the empirical as such, but that it embraces it within a theological rather than a scientific epistemology. Michel Foucault has made the same point in relation to the comparative illustrations of human and bird skeletons which Pierre Belon published in 1555; the scientific accuracy of these illustrations does not make them comparative anatomy, Foucault comments, "except to an eye armed with nineteenth-century knowledge. It is merely that the grid through which we permit the figures of resemblance to enter our knowledge happens to coincide at this point (and at almost no other) with that which sixteenth-century learning had laid over things."[9] In the domain of music theory, much the same kind of interplay between empirical observation and shifting epistemological frameworks can be

6 See also Thomas Christensen's Introduction to the present volume for a further discussion of Dahlhaus's schema, pp. 13–14.

7 See Dahlhaus, "Schoenberg's Aesthetic Ideology," trans. in *Schoenberg*, pp. 81–93. Much of what Dahlhaus says about Schoenberg translates readily to Schenker.

8 See, eg., Brown and Dempster, "Scientific Image," p. 82.

9 Foucault, *Order of Things*, p. 22.

observed in the extended controversies that took place between Fludd, Kepler, and Mersenne in the early decades of the seventeenth century – at a time, that is to say, when Dahlhaus's first and second traditions were fighting for dominance.[10]

Foucault has put forward a historical scheme of his own, expressed in terms of what he calls "epistemes" rather than periods, which is intended to apply to the broadest field of cultural practice but has some resonance with Dahlhaus's framework for music theory. As Foucault sees it, the episteme which remained dominant until the early years of the seventeenth century was characterized as much by natural magic as by theology, predicated as it was on principles of similitude; the ubiquitous image of the "great chain of being"[11] is only the most overt expression of the unbroken signification that links the divine, the human, and the natural worlds. Seen in such a context, as Foucault puts it, "language is not an arbitrary system; it has been set down in the world and forms a part of it."[12] By contrast, under the rationalist or Classical episteme (which largely coincides with Dahlhaus's second tradition), language is seen as separable from that which it represents – as, in a word, transparent. In the same way, Foucault says, "Similitude is no longer the form of knowledge but rather the occasion of error . . . From now on, every resemblance must be subjected to proof by comparison, that is, it will not be accepted until its identity and the series of its differences have been discovered by means of measurement with a common unit."[13] But it is when we come to Dahlhaus's third tradition that the comparison with Foucault becomes most interesting. For Foucault, the nineteenth and twentieth centuries represent an age of epistemological pluralism. On the one hand, the rationalist episteme has continued in science and in other areas of social, economic, and political practice. On the other, in the field of literature there has been a recrudescence of the earlier episteme: in Foucault's words, literature "separated itself from all other language with a deep scission, only by forming a sort of 'counter-discourse' and by finding its way back from the representative or signifying function of language to this raw being that had been forgotten since the sixteenth century."[14]

Foucault's characterization of literature transfers readily to the methodologies for its study. One can distinguish two epistemological frameworks running side by side: on the one hand source-based criticism adopting rationalist methods for the purposes of discovering a truth which lies outside the text and, on the other, broadly hermeneutical approaches directed at a truth which lies, so to speak, within it. Given that the study of literary texts has long constituted not just a parallel to but a model for that of music, it comes as no surprise that music theory too has found itself caught between two distinct and largely incommensurable epistemological traditions. Of course much

10 Ammann, "Musical Theory of Fludd," pp. 210–19. The emphasis on epistemological framework rather than empirical observation *per se* would permit an extension of Dahlhaus's first period well into the seventeenth century.

11 The classic account is Lovejoy, *Great Chain*.

12 Foucault, *Order of Things*, p. 35.

13 Ibid., pp. 51, 55.

14 Ibid., p. 44.

the same might be said of musicology in general; my distinction between pursuing a truth that lies outside the text and one that lies within it maps easily enough onto Dahlhaus's diagnosis of the tension between the narrative and aesthetic impulses in musical historiography.[15] But the situation is more uncomfortable in the case of music theory, because it is that much harder to make a confident distinction between the theory and the reality that it purports to represent. As we shall see, the issue finally resolves into one of how far music-theoretical language is to be understood as a mode of representation at all, as against the extent to which it is to be understood in performative terms.

So far I have been concerned with broad historical frameworks within which music theory may be located, and the extent to which they reflect ultimately epistemological values. But we can go further by attempting to correlate these historical frameworks with what I called the epistemological options available to music theory. It is conventional to characterize the opposite poles of what might be seen as an epistemological continuum as coherentism (or holism) and foundationalism, and at first sight these positions map rather straightforwardly onto Foucault's epistemic scheme, with elements from both coexisting within the pluralist epistemic structure of the modern period (by which I mean the nineteenth and twentieth centuries). According to coherentism, then, one is justified in a particular belief if it is consistent with one's other beliefs, or in changing one's beliefs when the result is a higher degree of consistency between them. Of course consistency is a desirable quality within any epistemology. But coherentism, at least in its "strong" form, goes further in claiming that optimal coherence is the *only* justification for belief. And this means that there is a strongly historical element in any coherentist epistemology; each new candidate for belief is measured against existing beliefs. This is precisely the manner in which Foucault characterizes his first epistemic period, with its filtering of observation against established authority; commentary, endlessly reiterated, is accorded the same epistemological status as empirical observation, and the result is what Foucault calls "a non-distinction between what is seen and what is heard, between observation and relation."[16] It follows that knowledge proceeds by a process of accumulation, through the laying down of successive layers of belief.

Remote from present-day values as such a world view might seem, it is one that resonates with surprising strength in much twentieth-century theory (and that, of course, underlines the pertinence of Foucault's pluralist episteme); Schillinger, for instance, stands anachronistically in the tradition of Pythagorean thought that played so prominent a role in music theory up to the seventeenth century. But the same applies to writers closer to the theoretical mainstream, such as Réti, the persuasive value (such as it is) of whose brand of motivicism depends on the piling up of resemblance upon resemblance rather than on a plausible theory of either composition or perception.

15 See, e.g., Dahlhaus, *Foundations*, Chapter 2.

16 Foucault, *Order of Things*, p. 39.

Recourse is made neither to empirical verification (indeed Réti specifically rules out the relevance of perceptual realization)[17] nor to statistical demonstration. Instead Réti encourages the reader to marvel at the unity he discovers in music's diversity in a manner that would hardly have been out of place four centuries earlier.[18] More recent writers associated with hard-edged analysis display comparable qualms about invoking empirical verification; an example is Jonathan Dunsby, who writes in his significantly named "Criteria of correctness in music theory and analysis" (remember what I previously said about anxiety) that "if I think a particular music theory is wrong . . . I ought to be able to fault it purely theoretically, without reference to any opinion of analytical results which calls for empirical evidence."[19] The dangers of such an approach are precisely those which attend all forms of coherentism: theory, increasingly self-sustaining, becomes a filter through which observation has to pass in order to be accepted. Under such circumstances, as Robert Gjerdingen has sourly expressed it, "The self-stabilizing, corroborating effect of interdependent premises precludes fundamental revisions, major discoveries, or even accidental breakthroughs."[20]

After he has outlined what he sees as the sixteenth-century episteme, Foucault delivers a devastating critique of it, referring to

> the plethoric yet absolutely poverty-stricken character of this knowledge. Plethoric because it is limitless. Resemblance never remains stable within itself; it can be fixed only if it refers back to another similitude, which then, in turn, refers to others; each resemblance, therefore, has value only from the accumulation of all the others, and the whole world must be explored if even the slightest of analogies is to be justified and finally take on the appearance of certainty. It is therefore a knowledge that can, and must, proceed by the infinite accumulations of confirmations all dependent on one another. And for this reason, from its very foundations, this knowledge will be a thing of sand.[21]

This is the circularity which foundationalism attempts once and for all to cut through. The transition from a theological to a scientific epistemology that took place during the seventeenth and eighteenth centuries tends to be seen as the subordination

17 Réti states that it is not necessary that a motivic relationship "be heard and understood as a motivic utterance by the listener. The unnoticeable influence that it may exert on the listener as a passing subconscious recollection – in fact, *its theoretical existence in the piece* – suffices" (*Thematic Process*, p. 47, Réti's italics). For a discussion of this statement see Cook, *Guide*, pp. 113–14. Also see **Chapter 29, pp. 911–15**.

18 Given that the aesthetic model of "unity in diversity" is generally associated with the pre-classical era, in contrast to the organicist model that came to prominence in the second half of the eighteenth century (see e.g. Bent, ed., *Music Analysis*, vol. 1, pp. 12–13), it is remarkable how many twentieth-century music theorists specifically refer to it – among them not only Schoenberg's followers (Keller and Walker as well as Réti) but also Schenker, as most notably expressed in the motto "semper idem sed non eodem modo" (always the same, but not in the same way) displayed between divisions in the second volume of *Kontrapunkt* and on the title page of *Der freie Satz*.

19 Dunsby, "Criteria," p. 79. Dunsby is referring specifically to what he terms instances of theoretical over- or underdetermination (essentially, mismatches between theoretical descriptions and perceptual experience), but he generalizes his statement on the next page, asking whether it does not amount to eliminating "the dirty but exciting world of real-life music" (and answering with a qualified yes).

20 Gjerdingen, "Experimental Music Theory?," p. 162.

21 Foucault, *Order of Things*, p. 30.

of book learning (Foucault's endlessly reiterated commentary) to a direct, unmediated observation that takes nothing for granted; this is what Schoenberg evokes when near the beginning of his *Harmonielehre* he calls on us to get away from established theory and "again and again to begin at the beginning; again and again to examine anew for ourselves and attempt to organize anew for ourselves. Regarding nothing as given but the phenomena."[22] The concept of unmediated perception is of course a problematic one, but in any case classical empiricism – Lockeian sense-data theory, for instance – is only one variety of foundationalism. What characterizes foundationalism as such is the impulse which Schoenberg vividly expresses to sweep away sedimented knowledge and start with a clean slate, admitting as knowledge only that which can be regarded as certain. The different varieties of foundationalism arise from different ways in which certainty might be established. Cartesian first principles represent one such: basic beliefs which cannot admit of rational doubt (the *cogito* representing the most famous of these). And in the formulation of his theory of harmony, Rameau consciously aspired to achieve certainty through an analogue of the Cartesian method; as he tells us, "Enlightened by the *Méthode* of Descartes which I had fortunately read and had been impressed by, I . . . placed myself as well as I could into the state of a man who had neither sung nor heard singing, promising myself even to resort to extraneous experiments whenever I suspected that habit . . . might influence me despite myself."[23] Small wonder, then, that Charles Lalo described Rameau's theory as predicated on an *audio*.[24]

Rameau's avowed purpose of recovering the native perception that underlies sedimented knowledge emphasizes the continuity between the Cartesian project and the empiricism which reached its zenith in France during the mid-eighteenth century (his invocation of someone who has never experienced singing is reminiscent of the lively scientific interest at this time in so-called wolf children). It becomes easier to see how Rameau could transform the concept of the *corps sonore* from a Cartesian first principle to a Lockeian sense impression. But it is Rameau's promising himself "*even* to resort to extraneous experiments" (my italics) that underlines the difference between foundationalism *per se* and empiricism; Descartes's method was in essence deductive and it was only in the course of the eighteenth century, and particularly through the influence of Newton, that inductive and deductive approaches were integrated within an effectively unified scientific methodology. No such unified methodology is to be found in Rameau's work; as Thomas Christensen says, "At times he insists upon the need to rely upon musical experience and the empirical judgement of one's ear in formulating any theory, while at other times he emphasizes the absolute necessity of reason and mathematical demonstration."[25] And Christensen goes on to draw a comparison between Rameau and d'Alembert, who successfully systematized Rameau's theory in

22 Schoenberg, *Theory of Harmony*, p. 8.
23 Rameau, *Démonstration*, pp. 8–12; trans. in Christensen, *Rameau*, p. 12.
24 Quoted (from Lalo's *Eléments d'une esthétique musicale scientifique*) in Christensen, *Rameau*, p. 32.
25 Christensen, *Rameau*, p. 31.

the sense of reducing it to a small number of principles from which the rules of harmony could be more or less rigorously deduced. What makes the comparison illuminating is the way in which, to achieve this systematization, d'Alembert had to ride roughshod over the musical intuitions and sensitive contextualizations which, in the end, justify Rameau's theory in the eyes of musicians. The tension between musically veridical description and a systematization which may be variously seen as premature or inappropriate is a recurrent theme in the history of theory; if Rameau performed a kind of epistemological balancing act, adopting the rhetoric of foundationalism but in reality synthesizing received knowledge within a more or less unified framework, then he was setting the pattern for most subsequent theory. For this reason the problems attendant on reconciling empirical observation with the demands of systematic coherence represent a short cut to some of the most central issues of music-theoretical epistemology, and in the following section I examine these problems in relation to the historically shifting and contested boundary between the art of music and the emerging science of acoustics.

Between art and nature

"As to the eleventh and thirteenth [partials]," wrote Momigny, "they elude everybody's ear, and it is less *de auditu* that I posit them than by analogy and reasoning, although I believe myself to have heard them several times."[26] It is of course an established phenomenon that empirical observation may follow theoretical prediction, although even that hardly gives grounds for crediting Sauveur's claim that with sufficient attention it is possible to hear up to the 128th partial.[27] And the image of Momigny and Sauveur straining to detect something that lies at (if not beyond) the margins of audibility might be said to represent empiricism with a vengeance. But what exactly did their efforts have to do with music theory? As I have already suggested, empiricism as a method requires a framework of epistemological regulation, and this is what has frequently been lacking or at best tenuous in the theoretical no-man's-land between musical art and nature.

Rameau developed the essential principles of his theory before being introduced, through Louis-Bertrand Castel, to the concept of the *corps sonore*: in the *Traité de l'harmonie* he explained the fundamental consonances in terms of the monochord. But the successive reformulations of his theory did not entail wholesale rethinking of its operational principles (and in particular the principle of the fundamental bass). In one sense this is not surprising; the mathematical relationships derived from the division of a string and from the measurement of its overtones are commensurable. And yet the new

26 Momigny, *Cours Complet*, p. 639; translation and commentary in Bent, "Momigny," p. 336.
27 Christensen, *Rameau*, p. 137.

foundation involves a subtle change in conceptualization. True to the Pythagorean tradition, the canonists (monochord theorists) understood music as a play of mathematical relationships motivated by the striving of imperfect consonances (that is, ones involving higher integer ratios) towards a state of perfection; the continuum from imperfection to perfection was an expression of the great chain of being to which I have already referred. But to see the material of music as deriving from the *corps sonore* is to understand it as an ultimately physical phenomenon,[28] which immediately problematizes the issue of what I referred to as motivation; it turns the notion of intervals striving towards perfection into what Philip Gossett, in the introduction to his translation of the *Traité*, dismisses as "fanciful metaphors about notes returning to their source."[29] The result is an epistemological stand-off between Rameau and his translator: "Since the time of Rameau," says Gossett, "it has gradually become evident that tonal music as a whole is not based on natural principles and cannot be reduced to natural principles."[30] Rameau, by contrast, devotes a great deal of intellectual energy to demonstrating the opposite (even though he warns the reader of the *Traité* that Book I, the one concerned with the acoustical underpinnings of harmony, "will not be much use in practice"),[31] and the language of return to the source pervades much later theory – conspicuously that of Schenker, who for a long time had similar problems with his editors and translators.

Problematic though Gossett's approach may be in terms of achieving a historical understanding of his subject, it is easy to sympathize with his exasperation at Rameau's attempts to demonstrate the natural origins of music. One might say that the very impossibility of the demonstration is the best evidence of the importance that Rameau, and at least some of his contemporary readers, attached to it. Despite his constant reformulation of the acoustical underpinnings of his theory in light of scientific developments, the principal problems which Rameau faced were familiar to a line of theorists from Zarlino to Schenker. The most obvious is the need to reconcile the continuum of values yielded by both canonist and overtone theory with the binary distinction between consonance and dissonance that remained more or less unquestioned by theorists until the beginning of the twentieth century; more specifically, it was necessary to cut off the derivation of musical intervals from their acoustical origin before the out-of-tune seventh partial. Zarlino achieved this by reciting the magical properties of the number six; Schenker, who adopted an alternative derivation for the minor third 5:6 and consequently had no need for the sixth partial, recited the magical properties of the number five.[32] (In this case Rameau simply followed Zarlino.) As for Rameau's other problems, we can say by way of generalization that they can be assigned to one

28 Christensen traces this shift back to Descartes's reinterpretation of the canonist model (ibid., p. 77).

29 Rameau, *Treatise*, p. xxii. 30 Ibid., pp. xxi–ii. 31 Ibid., p. xxxvii.

32 Schenker, *Harmony*, pp. 25–26, 30; his remarks occasion embarrassed footnotes by his editor, Oswald Jonas. For a recent analysis of the pervasive role of the number five in Schenker's thought see Clark, "Schenker's Mysterious Five." Schoenberg's acid comment was that "The number five is . . . no less mysterious than all other numbers, nor is it any more mysterious" (Schoenberg, *Harmony*, p. 318).

of two causes: they result either from the discrepancies between incompatible theoretical models that he is trying to combine, or else from discrepancies between the theoretical model and empirical observation.

The latter category is of particular interest, not only because it gives the lie to Rameau's reputation (already under construction in his own lifetime, and reinforced in the following generation by Momigny)[33] as a rigidly deductive thinker, but also because it illustrates how a pursuit of systematic coherence at all costs would have resulted in a fundamentally different theory. Two related illustrations are provided by Rameau's various derivations of the minor triad. In the *Traité* (1722), having carefully derived each interval in sequence from the fundamental, he suddenly announces that different thirds are interchangeable, effectively establishing the minor triad as equivalent to the major; in the *Nouveau système* (1726) he adds "At least this is what the ear decides, and no further proof is necessary."[34] What is striking is not just the peremptory and final appeal to the ear, but the fact that if the principle of interchangeability is to be taken seriously then much of the apparatus of generation becomes redundant (and as we shall see, this is the basis of Schenker's simplification of Rameau's generative approach). By the time of the *Génération harmonique* (1737), however, Rameau has a new explanation, which Christensen calls "sympathetic resonance theory,"[35] according to which a vibrating string gives rise to frequencies an octave, perfect twelfth, and major seventeenth below the fundamental; these become the direct source of the minor triad, but only at the expense of seeing the fifth rather than the fundamental of the triad as its generator. This is both counter-intuitive and contradictory to other components of Rameau's harmonic theory (particularly as regards the progression of the fundamental bass). So Rameau resorts again to the ear as the final court of appeal, stating that "the lowest and predominating sound of a *corps sonore* is always, in the judgment of the ear, the fundamental sound."[36] And we know what would have happened had he decided at this point to give priority to systematic coherence rather than musical intuition: he would have ended up with something resembling the theory of harmonic dualism developed by Hauptmann and Oettingen but most closely associated with Riemann, which was widely criticized as being contrary to the evidence of the ear.[37]

33 See Bent, ed, *Music Analysis*, vol. 1, pp. 1–5.

34 Rameau, *Treatise*, p. 15; *Nouveau Système*, p. 21; see Christensen, *Rameau*, p. 96.

35 See Christensen, *Rameau*, pp. 148–49, 162–64. Recognizing the problems in this derivation, Rameau subsequently developed a third model, that of "co-generation" (Christensen, pp. 165–67).

36 Rameau, *Génération harmonique*, p. 37, trans. in Christensen, *Rameau*, p. 164. Christensen comments that "Rameau is thus forced to sever the connection he had earlier made between chord generation and root attribution; but since it is precisely the point of his theory that these should be identical, he finds himself in an untenable position."

37 See, eg., Bernstein, "Symmetry," pp. 386–88; Bernstein suggests that the symmetrical principles underlying dualistic harmony eventually found compositional expression in serialism. For another example of the tension between theoretical consistency and empirical observation in Rameau's writings, see Burnham, "Musical and Intellectual Values," pp. 79–83. On dualism, see **Chapter 14, pp. 456 ff.**

In this way Rameau's theory treads a fine line between art and nature; as demonstrated by the contrast with d'Alembert's rationalized version, its musical value depends on the firm and sometimes apparently arbitrary limits he imposes on systematization. In fact some of his deepest insights seem to depend on what might be called setting nature against itself. An example is his reduction of dissonant chords to a single prototype, namely the dominant seventh (and in connection with this we should remember that Dahlhaus saw the role Rameau accorded to dissonances as the most important feature of his theory).[38] This idea was unprecedented, and not surprisingly, because it runs counter to the entire project of deriving dissonances from the fundamental via the consonances; as Christensen puts it, "After all, if dissonance was indeed a product of consonance, how can any dissonant structure be considered fundamental?"[39] It only becomes logical if you think not in terms of generation, but in terms of its reciprocal, *reduction* (a term whose anatomical connotations in eighteenth- and nineteenth-century writings have been explored by Ian Bent, but which could be profitably traced back to the Renaissance culture of dissection):[40] for if you can reduce consonances to a prototype, then why not dissonances? At the same time, the source of Rameau's frequent theoretical embarrassments (and of Gossett's exasperation) lies in the lack of any principled basis for theorizing, so to speak, against nature. What Rameau lacks is, in a nutshell, the concept of arbitrary signification that plays a central role in the general theory of signs developed by French thinkers during the eighteenth century and expressed, in particular, in the *Logique du Port-Royal.* As explained by Foucault, this involves the exact inversion of an earlier concept of the sign: in sixteenth-century thought "artificial signs owed their power only to their fidelity to natural signs," whereas by the eighteenth century "a sign is no more than an element selected from the world of things and constituted as a sign by our knowledge."[41] The sign belongs, in short, not to nature but to artifice.

Foucault's formulation accurately locates the terrain in dispute during subsequent negotiations of the boundary between musical art and nature, and we can trace these developments without entering into too much detail. It is perhaps only to be expected that the definitive separation of the two domains should come from the scientist Hermann Helmholtz, who established what remains in essence the accepted theory of acoustic consonance. (In brief, whereas Rameau and his contemporaries understood consonance as resulting from the relationship of only the fundamentals of the respective tones, Helmholtz modeled it as the interaction of their harmonics.) On the one hand Helmholtz complained that "everything that has been taught so far about the scientific foundation of harmony has been empty talk," and claimed that "Music stands

38 Dahlhaus, *Studies*, p. 23. 39 Christensen, *Rameau*, p. 98.

40 Bent, ed, *Music Analysis*, vol. 1, pp. 7–8, 21–23; Sawday, *Body Emblazoned*. Particularly suggestive aspects of the Renaissance culture of dissection include the problematic nature of the relationship between theory and practice, and the practice of public demonstration whose legacy survives in the term "operating theatre." 41 Foucault, *Order of Things*, p. 61.

in a much closer connection with pure sensation than any of the other arts."[42] But on the other hand he distinguished the sensation of tones in isolation from their effect within a musical context, writing at the beginning of the third section of his *On the Sensations of Tone* that

> Because in this third part of our enquiry we turn primarily to music . . . we tread on new ground, which is no longer purely natural-scientific . . . When we spoke previously, in the theory of consonance, of the agreeable and the disagreeable, we considered only the immediate impression made on the senses when an isolated combination of sounds strikes the ear, without regard to artistic contrasts and means of expression: we considered only sensuous pleasure, not aesthetic beauty. The two must be kept strictly apart, even if the first is an important means for attaining the second.[43]

And he went on to conclude that scales, modes, harmonies, and other elements of musical construction did not reflect immutable, natural laws but were subject to historical change.

Schenker, who had at least some acquaintance with Helmholtz's work,[44] would of course have summarily rejected this last conclusion. Nevertheless his reinterpretation, in *Harmonielehre*, of Rameau's derivation of musical art from nature is based on precisely Helmholtz's distinction of "means" from what he elsewhere refers to as "goals."[45] Like Helmholtz, Schenker clearly separates the provinces of art and nature, maintaining that while the acoustician knows exactly how to describe the perception of tones, "He gets onto slippery ground . . . as soon as he applies this knowledge to an understanding of art and the practice of the artist."[46] Accordingly, while the overtone series indeed provides the basis – the means – of music, "Nature's help to music consisted of nothing but a hint, a counsel forever mute, whose perception and interpretation were fraught with the gravest difficulties."[47] He characterizes the major scale system as "natural," but explains how it nevertheless "abbreviates" nature through the compression of the first five partials into the close-position triad, and incorporates the fourth scale-step through an artificial inversion of the fifth. By contrast, the minor scale system is artificial through and through, constructed after the model of the major scale. In this way Schenker cuts at a stroke through the problems that beset Rameau in the derivation of the minor triad, and he does this not by virtue of new derivational techniques (the ideas of inversion and imitation are to be found in Rameau) but simply because he is not committed to an exclusively naturalistic epistemology for music. In short, he is prepared to see music as "a compromise between Nature and art."[48]

42 Helmholtz, letter to Friedrich Vieweg, November 21, 1861, translated in Vogel, "Sensation of Tone," p. 270; Helmholtz, *On the Sensations of Tone*, p. 2. See also **Chapter 9, pp. 257–62**.

43 Helmholtz, *On the Sensations of Tone*, translated in Hatfield, "Helmholtz and Classicism," p. 542 (cf. p. 234 of Ellis's translation).

44 Schenker cites Helmholtz in *Counterpoint*, vol. 1, p. 29.

45 Dahlhaus, *Studies*, p. 60.

46 Schenker, *Harmony*, p. 21.

47 Ibid., p. 20.

48 Ibid., p. 44. A vestige of earlier thinking based on intervallic perfection nevertheless remains in his remark that the natural origin of the major mode makes it "no doubt superior" to the minor (p. 48).

Schenker might be accused of not following through the consequences of his own principle. If the overtone series does no more than hint at the means, then it cannot be regarded as circumscribing the goal; music may represent a realization of the potential present within the natural tone system, but the specific form of that realization is determined historically. And yet the whole drift of Schenker's theory, especially his later writings, was to deny the element of historical freedom, insisting that the music of the Germanic masters represented the fulfillment of a destiny that assumed the status of a natural law. When Schoenberg published his own *Harmonielehre*, five years after Schenker's, this was the point at which he parted company with Schenker. Schoenberg's discussion of the underpinnings of music in the overtone series carries further the process of simplification and abbreviation: he builds on Schenker's principle that the fourth scale step represents an inversion of the fifth (there is of course a common origin for this in the work of nineteenth-century German theorists such as Hauptmann and Riemann), and derives the notes of the scale from the overtones of the first, fourth, and fifth scale-degrees. Having done this, he feels free to permutate them at will, so that the problem of the minor triad simply disappears. More telling than these technicalities, however, is Schoenberg's view of the relationship between art and nature. For him, the major-minor tonal system is no more than "a formal possibility that emerges from the nature of the tonal material,"[49] and as such merely one of an indefinite number of such possibilities. In short, it is a product of history, and as such subject to historical change; the major scale "is not the last word, the ultimate goal of music, but rather a provisional stopping place."[50] Like any other human activity, music must work within the constraints that are set by nature, but once this condition has been satisfied it belongs unambiguously to the province of art.

I am not going to trace the continuation of this story through the twentieth century, except to mention one late recrudescence of the derivation from nature of permanent musical laws: the once influential system set out by Hindemith in his *Craft of Musical Composition*, which first appeared (in German) in 1937. Both the rhetoric of natural origins and the drawing from them of universal and unchangeable criteria of value resonate strongly with the ideologies of German conservatism that came to a head in National Socialism (it seems unlikely that the last word has yet been said on the extent of Hindemith's sympathies with the Nazi regime).[51] And this forms the background to the extreme version of Schoenbergian historicism characteristic of American music theory in the decades following the Second World War (and reflected in Gossett's strictures concerning Rameau). In 1965, Milton Babbitt recited what he dubbed the "comedy of methodological errors" through which theorists have sought to ground

49 Schoenberg, *Harmony*, p. 27.

50 Ibid., p. 25, echoing Hanslick's assertion that "our tonal system . . . will undergo extension and alteration in the course of time" (*On the Musically Beautiful*, p. 71); for Hanslick, "Nature does not give us the artistic materials for a complete, ready-made tonal system but only the raw physical materials which *we* make subservient to music" (p. 72).

51 For a critical discussion see Taylor-Jay, "Politics and the Ideology of the Artist," Chapter 4.

major-minor tonality in nature, arguing that the consonance or dissonance of any interval depends entirely on its musical context;[52] nature, in short, has no purchase on music. He was practically quoting from an article published in the immediate aftermath of the war by Norman Cazden, who put forward the same arguments and concluded that the tonal system, even the "chord of nature" itself, "has no basis in the nature of tone."[53] Taken literally, this statement is plain wrong; subsequent experimentation has shown that contextual effects of consonance and dissonance – effects of harmonic direction, of progression towards cadences – do not obtain when synthesized tones with inharmonic spectra are substituted for "natural" ones.[54] But in a way this misses the point, for the motivation for this programmatically anti-naturalist stance was less empirical than ideological. It was part and parcel of a general reaction against Nazi abuses of supposed natural laws, most obviously as applied to racial inheritance. There was, so to speak, a single if extended chain of cause and effect linking Belsen and Princeton. And this single example must stand for a phenomenon that would otherwise seem to fall outside the scope of this chapter: the extent to which the perceived adequacy of a music theory depends not on its epistemological underpinnings, but on the web of deeply held beliefs which it both reflects and contributes to.

A performative turn

More than any other theorist, it is Rameau who established the discursive space within which music theory has operated ever since. As we have seen, there is in Rameau's theory of music, as in practically every other, a tension between induction and deduction, between the demands of veridical description and of theoretical adequacy. Rameau makes use of a number of terminological get-out clauses to ease this tension, ranging from technical terms like supposition to such frankly extra-theoretical concepts as *notes de goût* and *jeu de doigts*. (Concepts playing a comparable role in the work of other theorists include Schenkerian implied notes and the recourse of Schoenberg's followers to the idea of unconscious perception.) Nevertheless it is clear that Rameau's aim is to do justice to the phenomena while at the same time reducing them to the operation of a relatively small number of general principles; in this his explanatory model conforms to what Brown and Dempster term "law-like generalization"[55] and to what epistemologists call inference to the best explanation. And the theory is intended to explain the actual practice of music, demonstrating the principles to which composers have historically adhered even though they were unaware of them. Rameau explains what Lully

52 Babbitt, "Structure and Function," p. 19. 53 Cazden, "Musical Consonance," p. 5.

54 See Pierce, *Musical Sound*, pp. 87–101. On the basis of experiments using tones with "stretched" partials, Pierce concludes that "the coincidence or near-coincidence of partials we find for normal (harmonic partials) musical sounds and for consonant intervals (with frequency ratios in the ratio of small integers) is a necessary condition for Western harmonic effects" (p. 92, typographical error corrected).

55 Brown and Dempster, "Scientific Image," p. 68.

achieved through the mere exercise of good taste, just as Schenker demonstrates the authentic tonal principles that govern the "Heiliger Dankgesang" from Op. 132, even though Beethoven himself "was sure he was composing in the Lydian mode."[56] Equally, the theory explains unconscious or autonomic processes that give rise to conscious perceptions, resulting in the ubiquitous rhetorical invocations of "the ear," as if the organ of hearing could be separated from the individual who listens. In this way a privileged domain of knowledge is constructed; subjective experience is explained through being derived from a reality that is cognitively inaccessible to the individual.

But how was this model of theoretical explanation affected by the steady process of retrenchment that I charted in the previous section, through which music was seen less and less as a phenomenon of nature, and more and more as one of art? We can answer this question by tracing a general development in intellectual history before considering its application to music theory, and the answer comes in two parts. The first has to do with the epistemological status of the reality that is invoked in the act of explanation, the source of the privileged domain of knowledge to which I referred. I have already referred to the work of Newton, which provided a model for scientific explanation throughout the eighteenth century, and the principles of which were understood as having an objective existence even when (as in the case of the First Law of Motion) it was by definition impossible to establish their validity through experimental means.[57] Similarly, during the early part of his career, Helmholtz believed that the business of the scientist was to deduce the operation of real though unobservable forces from observable phenomena: "Since we can never perceive the forces per se but only their effects," he wrote, "we have to leave the realm of the senses in every explanation of natural phenomena and [instead] turn to unobservable objects that are determined only by concepts."[58] Towards the end of his life, however, Helmholtz began to think of these forces as law-like relationships among observables, that is to say as cognitive constructions rather than hidden realities.[59] And this is consistent with a general pattern of epistemological retrenchment in both the physical and the social sciences, highlights of which include Dewey's characterization of natural laws as "intellectual instrumentalities"[60] and Wittgenstein's interpretation of psychoanalysis as based on the creation of fictive (but therapeutically efficacious) narratives rather than the recovery of biographically accurate information.[61]

The second part of the answer concerns the formal structure, so to speak, of explanation. Common to Cartesian philosophy and classical science is the principle of

56 Schenker, *Harmony*, p. 61. 57 See the discussion in Harré, *Laws of Nature*, pp. 22–29.

58 From Helmholtz's "Über Goethe's naturwissenchftliche Arbeiten," trans. in Heidelberger, "Force," p. 465. 59 Cahan, "Introduction," p. 11; see also Heidelberger, "Force," p. 495.

60 Quoted (from Dewey's *The Quest for Certainty*) and discussed in Dancy and Sosa, eds, *Epistemology*, p. 355.

61 A critical account may be found in MacIntyre, *The Unconscious*. For a brief discussion of "anti-realism" in relation to music theory, centred on Bas van Frassen, see Brown and Dempster, "Scientific Image," p. 98.

explaining phenomena by deriving them from a domain of knowledge to which ontological priority is ascribed. And during the nineteenth century this explanatory structure was extended to encompass historical phenomena, on both a geological scale (Darwinian evolution) and a human one (for instance, in the philological derivation of existing languages from hypothetical ancestors which became a model for text criticism in both literature and music). As is well known, however, this development provoked a widespread reaction in the latter part of the century, which was expressed through the drawing of a distinction between the natural and the historical sciences – a distinction generally associated with Dilthey's philosophical hermeneutics, though advanced as early as 1862 by Helmholtz.[62] The distinction was made partly in terms of the object of study: whereas the scientist aimed to proceed from certain principles to the explanation of individual phenomena, the inevitable reflexivity of the human sciences meant that there could be no absolute starting point and no absolute certainty. The appropriate objective for the human sciences is therefore not certainty but understanding, and the means by which it is to be achieved is not explanation but elucidation. But there was also a structural aspect to the distinction between the natural and human sciences. As Bent expresses it, "Whereas the natural scientist was seen as accounting for the particular *linearly* in terms of the general, the human scientist was left to account *circularly* for the relation between the part and the whole."[63] And this, of course, is the origin of the so-called hermeneutic circle, better described as a process of oscillation or shuttling back and forth between opposites (part and whole, text and context, subject and object), the purpose of which is to converge upon an integrated understanding of the phenomenon in question.

How might all this apply to music theory? Writing in 1887, Hartmann reflected the prevailing sense of disenchantment with positivist methods: "The enthusiastic hopes for swift advances in forming a theory of music which I as a youngster pinned on Helmholtz's discoveries . . . have not so far been realized. On the contrary, no progress of any kind has been made."[64] Many writers in the last years of the nineteenth century and the first years of the twentieth turned away from any recognizably theoretical engagement with music; Kretzschmar would be a representative example (though the extent to which he can reasonably be regarded as conforming to Dilthey's model of hermeneutics is a matter of controversy).[65] Others, like Kurth, developed models based on hypothetical natural forces which were designed to represent the qualities of musical experience rather than to be amenable to experimental verification. But the examples of Schoenberg and Schenker are perhaps the most revealing, because they both attempted to reconcile the new thinking with traditional theoretical concerns.

62 For a summary history of the term *Geisteswissenschaften* see Hatfield, "Helmholtz and Classicism," p. 544.

63 Bent, ed., *Music Analysis*, vol. II, p. 9; Bent offers an illuminating account of this whole development, including an exposition of the hermeneutic method.

64 From Hartmann's *Philosophie des Schönen*, translated in Bujić, ed., *Music in European Thought*, p. 166.

65 See Bent, ed., *Music Analysis*, vol. II, pp. 22–25 and Bujić, ed., *Music in European Thought*, p. 367, n. 6.

One symptom of this is Schenker's conspicuous use of the term "elucidation" (*Erläuterung*) in his *Erläuterungsausgaben* of music by Bach and Beethoven, although Bent has demonstrated that the usage was not a new one.[66] More suggestive, if debatable, is the parallel Bent draws between the hermeneutic method as represented in the writings of Friedrich Schleiermacher and Schenkerian analysis:[67] a typical *Meisterwerk* analysis shuttles back and forth between part and whole, converging on a unified conception of the work. Bent points out that, unlike Schleiermacher's, Schenker's conclusion is always determined in advance so that "the initial presentation is authoritative,"[68] but that is really a matter of presentation: the *process* of Schenkerian analysis is certainly one of oscillating between the notated surface and the emerging underlying structure, between a bottom-up approach and a top-down one.

At the same time, Schenker retained a belief in musical laws which are the exact analogue of the natural laws of classical science, insofar as they are immutable and admit of no exceptions; hence his scoffing at his teacher Bruckner's suggestion that the regular laws of harmony might not apply to the composer of genius.[69] It is precisely because he saw the theoretical principles that he developed for the common-practice style as natural laws, or at least as firmly embedded in natural laws, that Schenker dismissed the music of other times and places as more or less valueless. An alternative would have been to draw a sharp line between natural law on the one hand and pedagogic rules or guidelines on the other, and this is the distinction that Schoenberg repeatedly emphasizes in his *Harmonielehre*. Schoenberg is not such a radical historicist as to deny the existence of immutable and exception-free natural laws. On the contrary, he writes that "A real system should have, above all, principles that embrace all the facts. Ideally, just as many facts as there actually are, no more, no less. Such principles are natural laws. And only such principles, which are not qualified by exceptions, would have the right to be regarded as generally valid."[70] But now comes the bad news: up to now, nobody has ever discovered such laws. Schoenberg continues:

> Nor have *I* been able to discover such principles, either; and I believe they will not be discovered very soon. Attempts to explain artistic matters exclusively on natural grounds will continue to founder for a long time to come. Efforts to discover laws of art can then, at best, produce results something like those of a good comparison: that is, they can influence the way in which the sense organ of the subject, the observer, orients itself to the attributes of the object observed. In making a comparison we bring closer what is too distant, thereby enlarging details, and remove to some distance what is too close, thereby gaining perspective. No greater worth than something of this sort can, at present, be ascribed to laws of art. Yet that is already quite a lot.[71]

66 Bent, ed., *Music Analysis*, vol. II, pp. 31–34. It should also be borne in mind that the term *Erläuterung* is more common in German than "elucidation" in English. 67 Ibid., pp. 12–13.

68 Ibid., vol. II, p. 13. 69 Schenker, *Harmony*, pp. 177–8 (n. 2).

70 Schoenberg, *Harmony*, p. 10.

71 Ibid., pp. 10–11. I have discussed the implications of this passage in Cook, "Music and 'Good Comparison'," pp. 124–26.

And in this way, he concludes, what we can sensibly aspire to is a "system of presentation – a system . . . whose clarity is simply clarity of presentation, a system that does not pretend to clarify the ultimate nature of the things presented."

In this passage Schoenberg spells out, cautiously and even apologetically, the epistemological premise of a great deal of twentieth-century music theory. Of particular interest is the suggestion that analysis should aim not to replicate, in some veridical manner, but rather to complement the immediately perceptible and thus self-evident qualities of the music. (That of course is implicit, though rarely recognized as such, in the familiar trope of analysis reading "through" the musical surface to an underlying structure – an epistemological model that dates back to the rationalist suspicion of resemblance to which I have already referred.)[72] Most important, however, is the idea that analysis is performative, in the sense that it is designed to modify the perception of music – which in turn implies that its value subsists in the altered experience to which it gives rise.[73] Indeed this provides what is in many ways a more fitting epistemological basis for understanding Schenker than his own recourse to putative natural laws; Joseph Dubiel has argued tellingly that Schenker characteristically presents as universal statements of truth and inevitability (it had to be precisely as it is) what are better thought of as performative injunctions (hear it *this* way!).[74] Similarly, Robert Snarrenberg has drawn attention to the way in which Schenker constantly invites his reader's participation in the aesthetic act, thereby "poetically co-creating" the musical effect[75] (which incidentally explains his otherwise puzzling statement that "*my theory . . . is and must remain itself art*").[76] And this in itself is enough to answer the arguments of critics like Joseph Kerman who have complained that Schenkerian analysis "repeatedly slights salient features in the music,"[77] for (to take Kerman's own example) Schenker's graph of the "Ode to Joy" tune precisely "remove[s] to some distance what is too close, thereby gaining perspective," as Schoenberg put it, so appealing to a recreative experience in which the salient features of the music emerge through the contrast with Schenker's essentialized, flattened-out scheme.[78] But we can push

72 See Foucault, *Order of Things*, p. 51.

73 For a general discussion of analysis and performativity see Cook, "Analysing Performance."

74 Dubiel, "'When You Are a Beethoven,'" p. 307 and *passim*. Much has recently been made of Schenker's initial training as a lawyer, arguably instilling in him a conception of law as based on precedent and aiming at persuasion (ongoing research by Wayne Alpern); if such a conception left its mark on his analytical practice, however, it was never properly assimilated into his theory.

75 From Federhofer, *Heinrich Schenker als Essayist und Kritiker* (p. 99), quoted and discussed by Snarrenberg, *Interpretive Practice*, p. 143. Snarrenberg's book further develops the approach outlined in Dubiel's "'When You Are a Beethoven.'"

76 Schenker, *Masterwork*, vol. III, p. 8 (Schenker's italics); see Snarrenberg, *Interpretive Practice*, p. 144.

77 Kerman, *Musicology*, p. 82.

78 I have set out this argument in greater detail in "Music and 'Good Comparison,'" pp. 131–34; for a complementary argument, turning on the distinction between salience ("importance") and syntax, see Lewin, "Music Theory," pp. 362–66. Either argument casts doubt on the recent tendency (noted in Clark, "Schenker's Mysterious Five," pp. 99–101 and illustrated by Smith, "Musical Form") for Schenkerian theorists to absorb striking features of the musical surface into the remote midleground or background, a strategy based on seeing the relationship of surface and underlying structure in terms of replication.

Schenker's invocation of the experiential properties of music a bit further than this. Indeed, if his theory is to be compared to Schleiermacher's or Dilthey's hermeneutics, it might just as well be compared to another intellectual movement of the same pedigree, though one that became influential in the field of aesthetics only in the 1920s: phenomenology. Schenker's foundationalist appeals for the setting aside of sedimented knowledge, as well as his reductive method, bear more than a passing resemblance to the Husserlian *epoché*, though it has to be admitted that the area where a genuine phenomenology might have developed would be better described in Schenker's theory as an overlay of psychologism and metaphysics.[79]

Though espoused by a number of more or less influential theorists since Schenker's time (among them Victor Zuckerkandl, Thomas Clifton, and Judith Lochhead), phenomenology can be said to have slipped into the theoretical mainstream only in 1986 with David Lewin's article "Music theory, phenomenology, and modes of perception." But the article makes a convenient vantage point from which to survey the development of what I am calling a performative turn in music-theoretical epistemology. Its specifically phenomenological aspect consists in a critique, in the tradition of Husserlian reduction, of the sedimented influence of musical notation on our characterization of listening experiences: "Our fallacious sense of one object at a unique spatial location," Lewin says, "is prompted by the unique vertical coordinate for the B flat notehead-point on the Euclidean/Cartesian score-plane . . . And so we begin trying to deny and suppress various of our perceptual phenomena [sic], not realizing that our conceptual tools are inadequate for the analytical task at hand."[80] But he develops this into a more general attack on the framing of music theory in exclusively perceptual terms, on the grounds that "'music' is something you *do*, and not just something you *perceive* (or understand)"; it follows that "a theory of music cannot be developed fully from a theory of musical perception."[81] This also means that "music theories of all kinds can be useful beyond analysis and perception as goads to musical action, ways of suggesting what *might* be done, beyond ways of regarding what *has* been done."[82] Here, then, Lewin draws on the performative principle which Schoenberg enunciated: theory doesn't just register how things are but seeks to change them. But he also adds something else: the idea that a music theory might be justified because it is *useful*. And this, too, is prefigured by Schoenberg, who wrote that "whenever I theorize, it is less important whether these theories be right than whether they be useful as comparisons to clarify the object and to give the study perspective."[83]

79 For a rather more negative, though brief, assessment of the parallel between Schenker's theory and phenomenology see Blasius, *Schenker's Argument*, pp. 35, 133. Mention should be made in this context of Riemann's "Ideas for a Study 'On the Imagination of Tone,'" which dates from 1914 and anticipates, at some points startlingly, the musical phenomenology of (in particular) Alfred Schutz (trans. in Wason and West, "Riemann's 'Ideen'").

80 Lewin, "Music Theory," p. 360; the [sic] is in the original.

81 Ibid., p. 377. At this point Lewin makes the memorable comment, coming from a Harvard professor of music theory, that "Actually, I am not very sure what a 'theory of music' might be."

82 Ibid. 83 Schoenberg, *Harmony*, p. 19.

Lewin's frank profession of pragmatism is particularly striking in view of his position as the leading contemporary exponent of a formalized approach to music that would appear, more than any other, to embody the strictly scientific epistemology that Babbitt adumbrated in 1961: "there is but one kind of language, one kind of method for the verbal formulation of 'concepts,' whether in music theory or in anything else: 'scientific' language and 'scientific' method."[84] Four years later, however, in the same article in which he recited the "comedy of errors" concerning the acoustical origins of music, Babbitt himself made a profession of pragmatism almost as frank as Lewin's or Schoenberg's: "the relation between a formal theory and its empirical interpretation is not merely that of the relation of validity to truth (in some sense of verifiability), but of the whole area of the criteria of useful, useable, relevant, or significant characterization."[85] Already in 1952 Babbitt had offered an explicitly performative account of Schenkerian (or at any rate Salzerian) analysis when he characterized its "validity" in terms of its ability not only to "codify" the reader's hearing of the music, but also to "extend and enrich his perceptive powers by . . . granting additional significance to all degrees of musical phenomena."[86] All this becomes less surprising, however, when we recall that Babbitt was writing as not only a theorist but also a composer for whom, as he put it, "every musical composition justifiably may be regarded as an experiment, the embodiment of hypotheses as to certain specific conditions of musical coherence."[87] Babbitt's distinctive blend of theorizing and composing gave rise to that uniquely American identity of the post-war period, the composer/theorist, epitomized in Dubiel's statement that "To me . . . wanting to write music has always involved wanting to explore ideas about how I write it and how it is heard, and I honestly cannot think of any theoretical work that I've ever done or encountered that seemed valid 'as theory' yet irrelevant to composition."[88] Or to put it more concisely, there is no theoretical knowledge that is not at the same time a way of hearing things and even of deciding what there is to hear.

And the same approach can be applied to existing music. Both Lewin and, more recently, Guck have offered examples of explicitly performative analysis in which (to quote Guck's version of the pragmatist principle) "Truth is replaced by the plausibility of the narrative."[89] Lewin "coaches" his reader in how to play the role of "F♯/G♭" in the first movement of Beethoven's Fifth Symphony, adopting the metaphor of dramatic production or operatic direction.[90] More extravagantly, Guck likens the repeated incursions of C♭ in the second movement of Mozart's Symphony No. 40 to the story of an immigrant who gradually becomes naturalized to an alien culture.[91]

84 Babbitt, "Past and Present Concepts," p. 3.

85 Babbitt, "Structure and Function," p. 14. Babbitt's pragmatism is however qualified by the word "merely": analysis should be useful, relevant, etc., but it should be true (verifiable) as well.

86 Quoted (from a 1952 review of Salzer's *Structural Hearing*) in Guck, "Rehabilitating the Incorrigible," p. 62.

87 Babbitt, "Twelve-tone Rhythmic Structure," p. 148.

88 Dubiel, "Composer, Theorist," p. 262.

89 Guck, "Rehabilitating the Incorrigible," p. 72.

90 Lewin, "Music Theory," pp. 389–90; cf. his discussion of the First Act Trio from Mozart's *Le Nozze di Figaro* in "Musical Analysis."

91 Guck, "Rehabilitating the Incorrigible," pp. 67–73.

Guck's narrative is openly fictional, of course; there is no suggestion that Mozart's symphony is "really" about immigration. What is invoked, then, is not the ontologically privileged domain from which a natural-law explanation might be derived, but simply a metaphorical construction that highlights certain properties of Mozart's music, filters out others, and gives rise to new properties through the blending of source and target domains.[92] And yet the discursive structure of a natural-law explanation and of Guck's narrative fiction is essentially the same: music is assimilated to a generalized model within some kind of regulatory framework. A specific example may help to clarify this. From Rameau and Capellen to Fétis, Schoenberg, Hindemith, and Lerdahl, theorists have likened aspects of tonal structure to gravity.[93] In so doing, they have suggested that elements of music are subject to forces of attraction that may operate even at a distance, that music occupies a kind of force-field in which up is qualitatively different from down, and that these forces are somehow conveyed to or experienced by the listener. But have they intended their descriptions as scientific ones? In the case of Rameau and Hindemith the answer is probably yes; Hindemith specifically calls tonality "a natural law, like gravity." Schoenberg, by contrast, is consciously invoking a metaphor (the relationship of dominant to tonic "may be considered like the force of a man hanging by his hands from a beam"). As for Capellen and Lerdahl, it is hard to say one way or the other. The epistemological underpinnings of these descriptions, in other words, are certainly variable and in some cases perhaps undecidable. But their performative effect, their impact on perception or belief, remains the same.

And what about the regulatory framework to which I referred? Natural-law explanations are regulated by established principles of inference and verification as well as by the specific properties of the theoretical model. A performative epistemology, by contrast, might be construed as a kind of epistemological throwing in of the towel, a submission to the unbridled subjectivity that it was the purpose of the epistemological project to avoid. (Certainly it might be argued that an analytical approach which appeals only to its readers' sense of satisfaction is incapable of offering the kind of critique of established aesthetic frameworks at which Adorno, for one, aimed.) On the other hand, the Wittgensteinian argument might be made that Schoenberg was being too apologetic in offering his "system of representation" as a kind of theoretical stopgap, to be retained only until the real laws of music are discovered, for it is precisely through such "perspicuous representation" (as Wittgenstein termed it) that we come to have knowledge at all. Seen this way, the validity of any theory is underwrit-

92 In describing Guck's analysis this way I am assimilating it to the theory of "cognitive blending" first outlined (though not under that name) by George Lakoff and Mark Johnson, and elaborated by Mark Turner and Gilles Fauconnier; for applications of this approach to music theory, with references, see Saslaw, "Forces, Containers, and Paths"; Zbikowski, "Conceptual Models."

93 See, respectively, Christensen, *Rameau*, pp. 40, 131–32; Bernstein, "Symmetry," p. 388; Schoenberg, *Theory of Harmony*, pp. 23–24; Hindemith, *Craft of Musical Composition*, vol. 1, p. 152; Lerdahl, "Calculating Tonal Tension," *passim*.

ten not by its objective truth (a concept that has lost its apparent self-evidence even in the natural sciences) but by intersubjectivity: that is, by the possibility of one theorist replicating what Guck refers to as the "(thought) experiments" of another.[94] It would hardly be going too far to define the established methods of music theory as means, above all else, of regulating the empirical resistance that distinguishes analysis from unfettered speculation, and of communicating the resulting insights to others.

Conclusion: plural epistemologies

The story I have told in this chapter could be construed as one of consistent epistemological transition from the outer world to the inner: from natural science to psychology and on to phenomenology. But at a deeper level it is a story of retrenchment from the claims implicit in traditional epistemological debate. I have focused on the performative turn in music theory partly because it is a relatively coherent thread within a highly variegated practice, and partly because it is through its performative effect rather than its epistemological underpinnings that any music theory achieves its cash value. And I have put forward, though not developed, the suggestion that a performative approach – that is, one that asks of any theory what interpretive or cultural work it transacts and in what or whose interests – might be seen as something more than an evasion or deferral of the demands of epistemology. (Seen thus, the ideological context of Babbitt's anti-naturalism turns out not to fall outside the scope of this chapter after all.) In this way it seems to be definitive of music theory, at least from Rameau onwards, that it is caught between Foucault's incommensurable epistemes, so that the coexistence of different epistemologies represents, so to speak, a permanent condition for the time being. Trying to unravel the resulting epistemological web within present-day music-theoretical practice is more than can be accomplished within the space of this chapter (or any other space, maybe). But it might be worth at least briefly illustrating it through the example of Lerdahl, whose writings draw on a wide variety of methodological sources and resonate with a variety of epistemological traditions.

The generative theory of tonal music (GTTM) that Lerdahl developed with Ray Jackendoff drew primarily on two music-theoretical traditions and one extramusical one. First there is Schenkerian theory, which in its original form was located at the intersection of psychology, phenomenonology, and metaphysics, but after crossing the Atlantic became assimilated within the post-war formalist tradition (itself underwritten, as we have seen, by a performative epistemology).[95] Then there is the approach to rhythmic analysis developed during the 1950s by Meyer and Cooper, heavily influenced by Gestalt psychology though without the empirical control that one would expect of an explicitly psychological theory. The third element is structural linguistics,

94 Guck, "Rehabilitating the Incorrigible," p. 62.

95 The classic account of the Americanization of Schenker is Rothstein's article of that name.

which provided not only certain key features of the theoretical model (in particular its formulation in terms of rules) but also its epistemological orientation: GTTM was to explicate the intuitions of musically "experienced" listeners through constructing "an explicit formal musical grammar that models the listener's connection between the presented musical surface of a piece and the structure he attributes to the piece."[96] So did that mean GTTM was a scientific theory, open to empirical verification? The parallel with structural linguistics is enough to indicate that there is not going to be an easy answer to this question.[97] The paradigm case of structural linguistics, Chomsky's generative grammar (again dating from the 1950s), was formulated as a theory of "competence," which is to say of the knowledge that underlies "performance" or actual language use. You can subject performance to empirical investigation, but not competence; at most, you can deduce competence indirectly from the analysis of performance. But you can never refute a theory of competence, because any counter-indications can be put down to performative factors (limitations of memory, say). And while the application of the competence/performance distinction to GTTM is itself less than straightforward, Lerdahl and Jackendoff were quite clear that their theory represented an "idealization" of real life. It would be easy to conclude that GTTM was a formalist theory disguised as a psychological one.

This conclusion would be not exactly wrong but certainly over-simplified. In its original (1983) form GTTM was presented without empirical support and its formulations were not fully operationalized (that is, you could not have directly implemented them on a computer). Moreover, like the earlier music theories on which it drew, it implied assumptions regarding the perceptual reality of large-scale tonal structure which seemed implausible to some of its original readers and which subsequent experimentation has failed to substantiate.[98] But music psychologists rapidly set to work on formulating aspects of the theory in empirically testable form, and GTTM became one of the principal agents of the convergence between music theory and psychological research that took place during the 1980s and 90s. And as Lerdahl developed and extended the theory, he himself recast it so as to render it both more explicit and more quantifiable. A good example is the "stability conditions" of GTTM, which embody the intuition that a structural interpretation involving closely related pitches will be favored over one involving distantly related pitches. In the 1983 version of the theory there was no formal definition of what "closely" and "distantly" might mean. And so, in an article published five years later,[99] Lerdahl incorporated within it a spatial model of tonal relations that in its essentials goes back to Oettingen and Riemann but is best

96 Lerdahl and Jackendoff, *Generative Theory*, p. 3.

97 The remainder of this paragraph is condensed from Cook, "Perception," pp. 70–71, 76–78.

98 Burton Rosner expressed such misgivings about the perceptibility of large-scale tonal structures in his review of *Generative Theory* (pp. 289–90), and confirmed them in experiments published jointly with Meyer (Rosner and Meyer, "Perceptual Roles"). For experiments with comparable results see Cook, "Large-scale Tonal Structure"; Tillmann and Bigand, "Formal Musical Structure."

99 Lerdahl, "Tonal Pitch Space."

known to music theorists through its adoption by Schoenberg.[100] There is a further source, however, for Lerdahl's assimilation of this model: a series of experiments conducted during the 1970s and 80s by Carol Krumhansl and others, the aim of which was to find out how closely the notes of the diatonic and chromatic scales are perceived to relate to one another, and the results of which were presented by means of diagrams broadly corresponding to Schoenberg's.[101] The originally informal definition of "stability conditions" was now not only rendered quantifiable through the spatial model, but also supported by experimental evidence. And Lerdahl has gone on to develop, on this basis, a fully elaborated model for the calculation of tonal tension that assigns specific values to the processes of tensing and relaxation represented by the tree diagrams of GTTM.[102]

The incorporation within GTTM of this spatial model – itself based on the principal consonances of canonist theory, the third and fifth – might be regarded as (to date) the final stage in the story of theorizing music between art and nature which I recounted earlier in this chapter; the basic idea is the same as Schenker's "hint" or Schoenberg's "formal possibility," but it is now formulated in an empirically testable form.[103] That does not however mean that the theory as a whole can be regarded as unproblematically assimilated to the domain of psychological explanation. For one thing, there is the outstanding issue of large-scale tonal structure: if listeners do not and under at least some circumstances cannot perceive tonal closure at the highest levels at which eighteenth- and nineteenth-century composers employed it, such as the structure of an entire movement, then from a psychological point of view we must conclude that there is no such phenomenon as large-scale tonal closure. Yet, for the music theorist, the indication that classical composers routinely organized their music in this way, as it were conceptualizing large-scale tonal form on the model of what on the small scale is directly perceptible, is just as significant as any experimentally demonstrable proposition about musical structure; seen this way, the model of large-scale tonal organization codified by GTTM (and largely borrowed from Schenker) represents a valuable historical insight. And of course, there is the possibility that through the process of analysis

100 Bernstein, "Symmetry," p. 383 (for further references, going as far back as the eighteenth-century physicist Leonhard Euler, see p. 405, n. 23); Schoenberg, *Structural Functions*, p. 20 (discussed in Carpenter, "Tonality," pp. 104–11).

101 Krumhansl, *Cognitive Foundations*, Figs 2.8, 7.4. A minor but telling historical narrative might be appended. Krumhansl originally sought to explain her results in terms of tonal consonance, but discrepancies in the case of the minor scale led her to abandon this explanation in favor of one based on frequency of ocurrence and resultant exposure. Her difficulties with the minor scale exactly replicate those of Rameau and other "generation" theorists, while the exposure hypothesis was itself put forward in eighteenth-century France (Mairan and Diderot, see Christensen, *Rameau*, pp. 141, 216). Subsequent research has rehabilitated the tonal consonance explanation (see Smith, "'Cumulative' method").

102 Lerdahl, "Calculating Tonal Tension."

103 More specifically, it might be described in terms of J. J. Gibson's concept of affordance, defined by Harré as "whatever a physical system can do in response to some human requirement" (*Laws of Nature*, p. 46); music becomes an affordance of the overtone series and other relevant psychoacoustic factors. This in turn would be compatible with the "dispositional" model of natural laws (ibid., pp. 44–48).

you might come to hear a level of tonal closure that you otherwise would not, and that this would in its own way contribute to a more satisfying hearing of the music.

GTTM draws for its performative effect, then, upon what might be termed multiple epistemological registers: it says how things are, it suggests how you might hear things, it recaptures historical conceptions, and each register merges imperceptibly into the next. The domains of the theory's application are equally varied. Much of Lerdahl's writing falls within the genre of the scientific paper, presenting itself as a contribution to psychological or more broadly theoretical debate. But then, his theory is equally linked to his ongoing (though less widely publicized) activities as a composer. And sometimes the performative dimension spills over into his literary output, most conspicuously in a 1988 article in which Lerdahl applied his theory as a criterion of aesthetic value. He based his argument on the premise that "The best music utilizes the full potential of our cognitive resources,"[104] a condition that is satisfied when its structure is neither too primitive to be interesting nor too complex to be perceptible. However his concept of "the best music" is not controlled by any empirical measure, for instance record sales, and indeed one of the casualties of his approach is rock music (which "fails on grounds of insufficient complexity").[105] The argument is incapable of empirical verification or refutation, so becoming perfectly circular: the best music uses the full potential of our cognitive resources (as defined by GTTM) because that is what "best" means. To be sure, Lerdahl's model of musical value could be transformed into an empirically testable one (for instance by adopting the criterion of aesthetic value I suggested, and developing a more adequate model of complexity for rock music). The point I want to make, however, is simply that Lerdahl did not see fit to do so, and that the kind of slippage from the descriptive to the prescriptive which psychologists conscientiously avoid is part and parcel of the music theorist's stock-in-trade. Lerdahl's theory, like most if not all music theory of the modern period, derives its performative effect from a multiplicity of models of truth or justifiability. In other words, epistemological pluralism is the condition of its signification. And under such conditions Occam's razor loses its edge as an instrument of historical understanding. Epistemological slippage becomes not so much a defect in music theory as one of its defining characteristics.

104 Lerdahl, "Cognitive Constraints," p. 256. 105 Ibid.

Bibliography

Ammann, P. J. "The Musical Theory and Philosophy of Robert Fludd," *Journal of the Warburg and Cortauld Institutes* 13 (1967), pp. 198–227

Babbitt, M. "Past and Present Concepts of the Nature and Limits of Music," in *Perspectives on Contemporary Music Theory*, ed. B. Boretz and E. Cone, New York, Norton, 1972, pp. 3–9

"The Structure and Function of Musical Theory," in *Perspectives on Contemporary Music Theory*, ed. B. Boretz and E. Cone, New York, Norton, 1972, pp. 10–21

"Twelve-tone Rhythmic Structure and the Electronic Medium," in *Perspectives on Contemporary Music Theory*, ed. B. Boretz and E. Cone, New York, Norton, 1972, pp. 148–79

Bent, I. "Momigny's *Type de la Musique* and a Treatise in the Making," in *Music Theory and the Exploration of the Past*, ed. C. Hatch and D. Bernstein, University of Chicago Press, 1993, pp. 309–40

Bernstein, D. W. "Symmetry and Symmetrical Inversion in Turn-of-the-Century Theory and Practice," in *Music Theory and the Exploration of the Past*, ed. C. Hatch and D. W. Bernstein, University of Chicago Press, 1993, pp. 377–407

Blasius, L. D. *Schenker's Argument and the Claims of Music Theory*, Cambridge University Press, 1996

Brown, M. and D. J. Dempster, "The Scientific Image of Music Theory," *JMT* 33 (1989), pp. 65–106

Bujić, B., ed., *Music in European Thought 1851–1912*, Cambridge University Press, 1988

Burnham, S. "Musical and Intellectual Values: Interpreting the History of Tonal Theory," *Current Musicology* 53 (1993), pp. 76–88

Cahan, D. "Introduction: Helmholtz at the Borders of Science," in *Hermann von Helmholtz and the Foundations of Nineteenth-Century Science*, ed. D. Cahan, Berkeley, University of California Press, 1993, pp. 1–13

Carpenter, P. "Tonality: A Conflict of Forces," in *Music Theory in Concept and Practice*, ed. J. M. Baker, D. W. Beach, and J. W. Bernard, University of Rochester Press, 1997, pp. 97–129

Cazden, N. "Musical Consonance and Dissonance: A Cultural Criterion," *Journal of Aesthetics and Art Criticism* 4 (1945–46), pp. 3–11

Christensen, T. review of *Die Musiktheorie im 18. und 19. Jahrhundert: Grundzüge eine Systematik* by C. Dahlhaus, *MTS* 10 (1988), pp. 127–37

Rameau and Musical Thought in the Enlightenment, Cambridge University Press, 1993

Clark, S. "Schenker's Mysterious Five," *19th-Century Music* 23 (1999), pp. 84–102

Cook, N. *A Guide to Musical Analysis*, London, Dent, 1987

"The Perception of Large-scale Tonal Closure," *MP* 5 (1987), pp. 197–205

"Music Theory and 'Good Comparison': A Viennese Perspective," *JMT* 33 (1989), pp. 117–41

"Perception: A Perspective from Music Theory," in *Musical Perceptions*, ed. R. Aiello, New York, Oxford University Press, 1994, pp. 64–95

"Analysing Performance and Performing Analysis," in *Rethinking Music*, ed. N. Cook and M. Everist, Oxford University Press, 1999, pp. 239–61

Dahlhaus, C. *Schoenberg and the New Music*, trans. D. Puffett and A. Clayton, Cambridge University Press, 1987

Foundations of Music History, trans. J. B. Robinson, Cambridge University Press, 1983

Die Musiktheorie im 18. und 19. Jahrhundert: Grundzüge eine Systematik, *GMt* 10 (1984)

Studies on the Origin of Harmonic Tonality, trans. R. Gjerdingen, Princeton University Press, 1990

Dancy, J. and E. Sosa, *A Companion to Epistemology*, Oxford, Blackwell, 1992

Dubiel, J. "'When You Are a Beethoven': Kinds of Rules in Schenker's *Counterpoint*," *JMT* 34 (1990), pp. 291–340

"Composer, Theorist, Composer/Theorist," in *Rethinking Music*, ed. N. Cook and M. Everist, Oxford University Press, 1999, pp. 262–83

Dunsby, J. "Criteria of Correctness in Music Theory and Analysis," in *Theory, Analysis and Meaning in Music*, ed. A. Pople, Cambridge University Press, 1994, pp. 77–85

Federhofer, H. *Heinrich Schenker als Essayer und Kritiker: Gesammelte Aufsätze, Rezensionen und kleinere Berichte aus den Jahren 1891–1901*, Hildesheim, G. Olms, 1985

Foucault, M. *The Order of Things: An Archaeology of the Human Sciences*, trans. anon., London, Tavistock, 1970

Gjerdingen, R. O. "An Experimental Music Theory?," in *Rethinking Music*, ed. N. Cook and M. Everist, Oxford University Press, 1999, pp. 161–70

Guck, M. "Rehabilitating the Incorrigible," in *Theory, Analysis and Meaning in Music*, ed. A. Pople, Cambridge University Press, 1994, pp. 57–73

Hanslick, E. *On the Musically Beautiful: A Contribution towards the Revision of the Aesthetics of Music*, 8th edn. (1891), trans. G. Payzant, Indianapolis, Hackett, 1986

Harré, R. *Laws of Nature*, London, Duckworth, 1993

Hatfield, G. "Helmholtz and Classicism: the Science of Aesthetics and Aesthetic of Science," in *Hermann von Helmholtz and the Foundations of Nineteenth-Century Science*, ed. D. Cahan, Berkeley, University of California Press, 1993, pp. 522–58

Heidelberger, M. "Force, Law, and Experiment: The Evolution of Hemholtz's Philosophy of Science," in *Hermann von Helmholtz and the Foundations of Nineteenth-Century Science*, ed. D. Cahan, Berkeley, University of California Press, 1993, pp. 461–97

Helmholtz, H. *On the Sensations of Tone as a Physiological Basis for the Theory of Music*, (4th edn., 1877), trans. A. J. Ellis, New York, Dover, 1954

Hindemith, P. *The Craft of Musical Composition*, 2 vols. (1937–39), trans. A. Mendel, London, Schott, 1942

Kerman, J. *Musicology*, London, Fontana, 1985; American edn. *Contemplating Music*, Cambridge, MA, Harvard University Press, 1985

Krumhansl, C. *Cognitive Foundations of Musical Pitch*, New York, Oxford University Press, 1990

Lerdahl, F. "Tonal Pitch Space," *MP* 5 (1988), pp. 315–49

"Cognitive Constraints on Compositional Systems," in *Generative Processes in Music: the Psychology of Performance, Improvisation, and Composition*, ed. J. Sloboda, Oxford University Press, 1988, pp. 231–59

"Calculating Tonal Tension," *MP* 13 (1996), pp. 319–63

Lerdahl, F. and R. Jackendoff, *A Generative Theory of Tonal Music*, Cambridge, MA, MIT Press, 1983

Lewin, D. "Music Theory, Phenomenology, and Modes of Perception," *MP* 3 (1986), pp. 327–92

"Musical Analysis as Stage Direction," in *Music and Text: Critical Inquiries*, ed. S. Scher, Cambridge University Press, 1992, pp. 177–92

Lovejoy, A. O. *The Great Chain of Being: A Study of the History of an Idea*, Cambridge, MA, Harvard University Press, 1948

MacIntyre, A. C. *The Unconscious: A Conceptual Analysis*, London, Routledge and K. Paul, 1958

Marx, A. B. *Musical Form in the Age of Beethoven: Selected Writings on Theory and Method*, ed. and trans. S. Burnham, Cambridge University Press, 1997

Momigny, J.-J. de, *Cours complet d'harmonie et de composition*, 3 vols., Paris, Momigny and Bailleul, 1803–06

Pierce, J. R. *The Science of Musical Sound*, rev. edn., New York, W. H. Freeman, 1992

Rameau, J.-P. *Treatise on Harmony* (1722), trans. P. Gossett, New York, Dover, 1971

Nouveau système de musique théorique, Paris, Ballard, 1726

Démonstration du principe de l'harmonie, Paris, Durand and Pissot, 1750

Réti, R. *The Thematic Process in Music*, New York, Macmillan, 1951

Rosner, B. review of *A Generative Theory of Tonal Music* by F. Lerdahl and R. Jackendoff, *MP* 2 (1984), pp. 275–90

Rosner, B. and L. B. Meyer, "The Perceptual Roles of Melodic Process, Contour, and Form," *MP* 4 (1986), pp. 1–39

Rothfarb, L. A. "The 'New Education' and Music Theory, 1900–1925," in *Music Theory and the Exploration of the Past*, ed. C. Hatch and D. W. Bernstein, University of Chicago Press, 1993, pp. 449–71

Rothstein, W. "The Americanization of Schenker," in *Schenker Studies*, ed. H Siegel, Cambridge University Press, 1990, pp. 193–203

Saslaw, J. K. "Forces, Containers, and Paths: The Role of Body-Derived Image Schemas in the Conceptualization of Music," *JMT* 40 (1996), pp. 217–43

Sawday, J. *The Body Emblazoned: Dissection and the Human Body in Renaissance Culture*, London, Routledge, 1995

Schenker, H. *Harmony* (1906), trans. E. M. Borgese, ed. O. Jonas, University of Chicago Press, 1954

Counterpoint, 2 vols. (1910–22), ed. and trans. J. Rothgeb and J. Thym, New York, Schirmer, 1987

Schoenberg, A. *Theory of Harmony*, 3rd edn. (1922), trans. R. Carter, London, Faber, 1978

Smith, A. B. "A 'Cumulative' Method of Quantifying Tonal Consonance in Musical Key Contexts," *MP* 15 (1997), pp. 175–88

Smith, C. J. "Musical Form and Fundamental Structure: An Investigation of Schenker's *Formenlehre*," *Music Analysis* 15 (1996), pp. 191–297

Snarrenberg, R. *Schenker's Interpretive Practice*, Cambridge University Press, 1997

Taylor-Jay, C. "Politics and the Ideology of the Artist in the *Künstleropern* of Pfitzner, Krenek and Hindemith," Ph.D. diss., University of Southampton (2000)

Tillmann, B. and E. Bigand, "Does Formal Musical Structure Affect Perception of Musical Expressiveness?," *Psychology of Music* 24 (1996), pp. 3–17

Vogel, S. "Sensation of Tone, Perception of Sound, and Empiricism: Helmholtz's Psychological Acoustics," in *Hermann von Helmholtz and the Foundations of Nineteenth-Century Science*, ed. D. Cahan, Berkeley, University of California Press, 1993, pp. 259–87

Wason, R. W. and E. W. Marvin, "Riemann's 'Ideen zu einer "Lehre von Tonvorstellungen"': An Annotated Translation," *JMT* 36 (1992), pp. 69–117

Zbikowski, L. M. "Conceptual Models and Cross-domain Mapping: New Perspectives on Theories of Music and Hierarchy," *JMT* 41 (1997), pp. 193–225

PART II

SPECULATIVE TRADITIONS

·4·

Greek music theory

THOMAS J. MATHIESEN

Introduction

In the history of Western music theory, technical works written in Greek on the general subjects of "music" (μουσική) and "harmonics" (ἁρμονικά) play an anomalous role. On the one hand, they are not "Western," especially in the linguistic and geographic senses reinforced in the Middle Ages by the gradual schism between Eastern and Western Christendom. On the other hand, the tradition never ceased to exert an influence during this period, not only because some parts of it were carried over into the West by authors writing in Latin, but also because the early church readily acknowledged and accepted – though not without reservations – the ancient power of music and its centrality to human existence. This combination of causes was sufficient to sustain an interest in early writings on music, especially those in Greek, throughout the Middle Ages. Thus, unlike other early Eastern traditions, the tradition represented by Greek works on music and harmonics assumed a prominence in the West even as it acquired a sense of the esoteric and foreign, a duality of character it retains in the modern conception of "ancient Greek music theory."[1]

Prior to the Middle Ages, the tradition of writing technical works in Greek "on music" (περὶ μουσικῆς), on the subject of "harmonics" (ἁρμονικά), or as a general introduction (εἰσαγωγή) to one or both subjects was extraordinarily resilient, extending easily over eight centuries. But by the collapse of Rome in the fifth century CE, the tradition had become moribund, though certainly not entirely forgotten. Martianus Capella, for instance, remembered enough of it to appropriate substantial sections of Aristides Quintilianus's treatise for Book IX of his *De nuptiis Philologiae et Mercurii* with no indication of his debt to the earlier author. A fair amount of technical detail can be gleaned from Martianus Capella's great work, but it is doubtful whether he intended the material to be read for its technical content. In the early sixth century, Cassiodorus still knew (or knew of) the treatises of Gaudentius, Claudius Ptolemy, Alypius, and Euclid (perhaps actually Cleonides), though his summary in section 5 of Book II of the *Institutiones* presents only a few bits and pieces of the fading tradition. Boethius, by contrast, had a much fuller knowledge of the treatises of Nicomachus and Ptolemy, which formed the groundwork for his *De institutione musica*. In the seventh

1 Much of this chapter appears in a somewhat different form in my article "Greece," in *NG2*; both have been adapted from my book *Apollo's Lyre*.

century, Isidore of Seville clearly regarded the Greek musical traditions as an important heritage to be preserved from a vanishing past in his *Etymologiae*, but his connection with original Greek sources is tenuous at best. From this point until the West experienced a rebirth of interest in ancient Greek science in the fourteenth and fifteenth centuries, the traditions of Greek music theory were known only in a highly refracted form through a complex stream of adaptations and paraphrases in the new tradition of medieval Latin musicography.

When ostensibly complete and authoritative versions of the Greek musical writings began to be rediscovered in the West in the thirteenth, fourteenth, and especially fifteenth centuries, they were greeted by receptive readers, anxious to shine the light of reason on forgotten or misunderstood texts and perhaps rediscover techniques that could once again come to life in the music of their own time. Humanists such as Pietro d'Abano (1250–1315), Niccolò Niccoli (1363–1437), Giovanni Pico della Mirandola (1463–94), Giorgio Valla (1447–99), and Carlo Valgulio collected manuscripts, published translations, and wrote commentaries, all of which greatly advanced knowledge of the tradition, while at the same time uncovering apparent contradictions and inconsistencies.

By the end of the fifteenth century and on into the sixteenth, so many of the treatises – not to mention general collections of musical lore such as Athenaeus's *Dinner-Table Philosophers* – had become available, either in Greek or in Latin translation, that authors such as Franchino Gaffurio (1451–1522), Girolamo Mei (1519–94), Vincenzo Galilei (1520s–91), Lodovico Fogliano (d. c. 1539), and Gioseffo Zarlino (1517–90) could construct elaborate treatments of Greek theories of tuning, modal theory, modulation, and the influence of music on behavior. Nevertheless, it was only the privileged few who had access to the original Greek texts in manuscript or to Latin translations, most of which remained unpublished. Readers in general had to rely on secondary sources for their knowledge of the music and music theory of the ancient Greeks.[2]

The humanists quite naturally favored those treatises that seemed to provide answers to the questions in which they were most interested, and a hierarchy of authority among the texts began to develop accordingly, regardless of the actual authority of the treatise in its own time – a difficult matter to determine in any event.

In the seventeenth and eighteenth centuries, many of the writings that speak of ancient Greek music began to be circulated in published form. The most important publication was Marcus Meibom's *Antiquae musicae auctores septem*, an edition of seven Greek treatises with parallel translations in Latin, a book of some 800 pages published in 1652 when Meibom was only twenty-two years old.[3] Meibom's edition complemented Athanasius Kircher's famous *Musurgia universalis*, published in 1650, and both

2 For an excellent survey of the musical humanists, see Palisca, *Humanism*.

3 Meibom, ed., *Antiquae musicae auctores septem* The collection includes the *Division of the Canon* (attributed to Euclid) and the treatises of Aristoxenus, Cleonides (attributed to Euclid), Nicomachus, Alypius, Gaudentius, Bacchius, and Aristides Quintilianus, as well as Book IX of Martianus Capella's *De nuptiis Philologiae et Mercurii*.

of these influenced John Wallis's 1682 and 1699 editions of two treatises Meibom had not included in his collection: the *Harmonics* of Claudius Ptolemy and Porphyrius's commentary.[4] These substantial and highly technical publications provided eighteenth-century scholars with a wealth of material appealing to their antiquarian and historical interests while also offering them positions from which they could advance arguments about the purpose and meaning of music. Lorenz Christoph Mizler (1711–78) and Johann Mattheson (1681–1764), for example, drew on ostensibly divergent trends in the Greek sources to bolster their own aesthetic differences, while historians such as F. W. Marpurg (1718–95), G. B. Martini (1706–84), and Sir John Hawkins (1719–89) tried to develop coherent historical surveys.[5] Thus, a certain body of texts began to be codified as representing a tradition of "ancient Greek music theory," even though the content and method of the texts varied widely and relatively little was known about many of the authors.

In the nineteenth and twentieth centuries, still greater control of the literary sources was accomplished, and a fair amount of actual music notated on stone and papyrus and in manuscripts began to be discovered. Meibom's collection was updated (and in some senses expanded) by Karl von Jan's *Musici scriptores graeci* of 1895, which, while not including any translations, did include an edition and transcription of the musical fragments then known, and by J. F. Bellermann's *Anonymi scriptio de musica*.[6] The discovery of actual pieces of music excited scholars and musicians with the prospect of understanding the legendary powers of Greek music, heightening an enthusiasm for the subject that had been growing throughout the nineteenth century. Friedrich Nietzsche's Basel lecture "Das griechische Musikdrama,"[7] for example, found a receptive audience in Richard Wagner, whose conception of *Der Ring des Nibelungen* was profoundly influenced by his understanding of Greek *music drama*. Twentieth-century scholars have continued to build on these earlier foundations with the publication of new critical texts, catalogues of manuscripts, and an enormous quantity of critical studies.

4 A. Kircher, SJ, *Musurgia universalis*, 2 vols. (Rome: Corbelletti 1650); John Wallis, ed., *Harmonicorum libri tres*; reprinted with a Latin translation in Wallis's *Operum mathematicorum*, 3 vols. (Oxford: Sheldonian Theatre, 1699), vol. III, pp. i–xii, 1–152. This latter publication also includes (vol. III, pp. 185–355) his text and translation for Porphyrius: "*Πορφυρίου εἰς τὰ ἁρμονικὰ Πτολεμαίου ὑπόμνημα*. Nunc primum ex codd. mss. (Graece et Latine) editus."

5 Mattheson allied himself with the progressives by using the pseudonym "Aristoxenus the Younger" in his *Phthongologia systematica* (Hamburg: Martini, 1748). On the conflict between Mattheson and Mizler, see L Richter, "'Psellus' Treatise on Music' in Mizler's 'Bibliothek,'" in *Studies in Eastern Chant*, vol. II, ed. M. Velimirović (London: Oxford University Press, 1971), pp. 112–28. Major sections on ancient Greek music appear in Marpurg's *Kritische Einleitung in die Geschichte und Lehrsätze der alten und neuen Musik* (Berlin: G. A. Lange, 1759); Martini's *Storia della musica*, 3 vols. (Bologna: Lelio della Volpe, 1757–81); and Hawkins's *A General History of the Science and Practice of Music*, 5 vols. (London: T. Payne and Son, 1776).

6 See full citations in the Bibliography, p. 130.

7 The lecture was originally delivered at the University of Basel on January 18, 1870; Nietzsche read the lecture to Wagner during a visit to his home on June 11, 1870 See M. Gregor-Dellin and D. Mack, eds., *Cosima Wagner's Diaries*, vol. I: *1869–1877*, trans. G. Skelton (New York: Harcourt Brace Jovanovich, 1978), pp. 231–32. See also R. Günther, "Richard Wagner und die Antike," *Neue Jahrbücher* 16 (1913), pp. 323–37.

The corpus of Greek music theory

A significant body of Greek literature can properly be considered music theory, although some works are known only as titles mentioned in passing or as brief quotations in the works of Athenaeus and similar sorts of writers. Nevertheless, a substantial portion of Greek music theory does survive, extending over a wide period from the fourth century BCE to the fourth century CE, or even later (see Table 4.1). These later works, however, should be considered representatives of the transmission of ancient Greek music theory rather than parts of its primary corpus (and, as those written in the Middle Ages in Greek and Arabic are not "Western" in the commonly accepted sense of the term, they fall outside the scope of this chapter).

Of the earlier treatises, some are technical manuals detailing the Greeks' musical system, including notation, the function and placement of notes in a scale, characteristics of consonance and dissonance, rhythm, and types of musical composition. This group includes the *Division of the Canon* (sometimes but erroneously attributed to Euclid); Cleonides, *Introduction to Harmonics*; Nicomachus of Gerasa, *Manual of Harmonics*; Theon of Smyrna, *On Mathematics Useful for the Understanding of Plato*; Gaudentius, *Harmonic Introduction*; Alypius, *Introduction to Music*; Bacchius, *Introduction to the Art of Music*; the so-called Bellermann's Anonymous; and others. By contrast, some of the treatises are elaborate and systematic books exploring the ways in which *μουσική* reveals universal patterns of order, leading to the highest levels of knowledge and understanding. Authors of these longer books include such well-known figures of antiquity as Aristoxenus, Claudius Ptolemy, and Porphyry.

While this literature has come to be known as "ancient Greek music theory," the phrase is not especially apt. First, the majority of the surviving texts are not ancient in the sense of having been written before the first or second centuries BCE. With the exception of quotations in later literature, the earliest surviving independent theoretical works are Aristoxenus's *Harmonic Elements* and *Rhythmic Elements*, both of which are fragmentary. At least some parts of the *Division of the Canon* are perhaps nearly contemporary, but all the other treatises date from the end of the first century CE or later. Second, the modern conceptual meaning of the phrase "music theory" is foreign to these writings. With the possible exception of the rather late writer Alypius, it is quite unlikely that any of the authors intended his work for practicing musicians or was concerned with actual pieces of music. Ancient Greek music theory was not interested in the descriptive or analytical study of pieces of music, nor was it concerned with explaining compositional or performance practice. Still, as long as the imperfections of the phrase are understood, "ancient Greek music theory" does provide a useful label for collective reference to the specialized literature ranging from the Pythagorean excerpts quoted in various sources to the treatises of Porphyrius, Aristides Quintilianus, Alypius, and Bacchius written in the third and fourth centuries CE.

The nature of the sources themselves is problematic. Of the independent theoretical works, only Aristoxenus's *Rhythmic Elements* survives in any medium older than the

Table 4.1 *Primary Greek treatises*

Aristoxenus	375/360 BCE – after 320 BCE	*Harmonic Elements* (Ἁρμονικὰ στοιχεῖα) and *Rhythmic Elements* (Ῥυθμικὰ στοιχεῖα)
Anonymous (attr. to Euclid in some sources)	4th–3rd century BCE	*Division of the Canon* (Κατατομὴ κανόνος)
Cleonides	2nd century CE	*Introduction to Harmonics* (Εἰσαγωγὴ ἁρμονική)
Nicomachus of Gerasa	fl. 100–50 CE	*Manual of Harmonics* (Ἁρμονικὸν ἐγχειρίδιον)
Theon of Smyrna	fl. 115–40 CE	*On Mathematics Useful for the Understanding of Plato* (Τῶν κατὰ τὸ μαθηματικὸν χρησίμων εἰς τὴν Πλάτωνος ἀνάγνωσιν)
Claudius Ptolemy	fl. 127–48 CE	*Harmonics* (Ἁρμονικά)
Gaudentius	3rd or 4th century CE	*Harmonic introduction* (Ἁρμονικὴ εἰσαγωγή)
Porphyrius	232/3 – c. 305 CE	*On Ptolemy's Harmonics* (Εἰς τὰ ἁρμονικὰ Πτολεμαίου ὑπόμνημα)
Aristides Quintilianus	late 3rd – mid 4th century CE	*On Music* (Περὶ μουσικῆς)
Bacchius Geron	4th century CE or later	*Introduction to the Art of Music* (Εἰσαγωγὴ τέχνης μουσικῆς)
Alypius	4th–5th century CE	*Introduction to Music* (Εἰσαγωγὴ μουσική)

eleventh century CE, and with a few exceptions, even those quoted in other sources exist only in manuscripts of this period or later. The extent to which these later copies preserve the form and content of any of the treatises is, in general, impossible to determine, nor can one be certain whether the titles or even the authors assigned to the treatises in the manuscripts represent the actual author and title of the treatise when it was first composed. It is also uncertain whether the earliest treatises on ancient Greek music theory were "composed" (in the modern sense of the term) by an individual author or whether they were later assembled by disciples or from tradition. In rare cases, it is possible to see the way in which a treatise "grows," even to the extent of changing its entire method of argumentation, as it is transmitted across the centuries.[8] Of course, similar problems exist for other Greek literary remains, and there is no special reason to distrust the authenticity of the independent treatises and fragments now taken as comprising the corpus of ancient Greek music theory. Nevertheless, the inherent limitations of the form in which it exists must be recognized.

8 Barbera, "Reconstructing Lost Byzantine Sources," pp. 38–67; Barbera, ed. and trans., *Euclidean Division.*

Problems notwithstanding, the tradition of scholarship on ancient Greek music theory underscores an importance that goes beyond the evidence these texts may supply about the Greeks' own music; the theory is also significant as an intellectual monument that exerted a marked influence on later Latin, Byzantine, and Arabic musical writings. As such, its significance resides in later writers' use and understanding of the literature at least as much as in the genuine evidence it may provide of ancient Greek music and music theory.

The traditions of ancient Greek music theory

The corpus of ancient Greek music theory comprises three basic traditions: the Pythagorean tradition (including later manifestations in Platonism and neo-Platonism) primarily concerned with number theory and the relationships between music and the cosmos (pertaining as well to the influence of music on behavior); a related scientific tradition of harmonics associated with a group known as "Harmonicists"; and an Aristoxenian tradition based on Aristotelian principles. Some of the treatises represent a single tradition, while others combine the traditions.[9] The characteristics of the individual traditions can be generalized (insofar as music is concerned), although for the most part, no single treatise provides a comprehensive treatment of any of the traditions.[10]

The Pythagoreans

The Pythagoreans were particularly interested in the paradigmatic and mimetic characteristics of music, which they saw as underlying its power in human life. In general, Pythagoreans were not concerned with deducing musical science from musical phenomena because the imperfection of temporal things precluded them from conveying anything beyond a reflection of higher reality. The important truths about music were to be found instead in its harmonious reflection of number, which was ultimate reality. As a mere temporal manifestation, the employment of this harmonious structure in actual pieces of music was of decidedly secondary interest.

The scientific side of Pythagoreanism, and particularly the part of it concerned with musical science, is primarily known first through the *Division of the Canon* and the writings of Plato, Aristotle, Plutarch (and the treatise *On Music* attributed to Pseudo-Plutarch), Nicomachus of Gerasa, Theon of Smyrna, and Claudius Ptolemy, and later

9 For discussions of each individual theorist, see the respective article in *NG2*.

10 Although the Pythagorean and Harmonicist traditions are certainly older than the Aristoxenian, it is the Aristoxenian tradition that has supplied to modern scholarship the basic definitions of general terms and concepts essential to understanding the differences among the positions. If these general terms and concepts are unfamiliar, the reader is advised to read the section on the Aristoxenian tradition first and then return to the sections on the Pythagoreans and Harmonicists

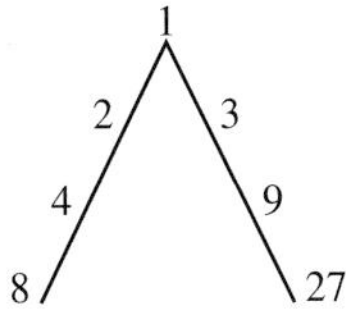

As a series of ratios, the numbers on the left represent such musical intervals as the octave (2 : 1), double octave (4 : 1), and triple octave (8 : 1), while the numbers on the right represent the octave and a fifth (3 : 1), the triple octave and a tone (9 : 1), and the quadruple octave and a major sixth (27 : 1). Aristides Quintilianus paraphrases this material in *On Music* iii.24, developing it with various neo-Platonic interpretations of the numbers and mathematical processes.

Figure 4.1 The Pythagorean lambda

– when merged with neo-Platonism – through the writings of Porphyrius, Aristides Quintilianus, Iamblichus, and later writers.

In the *Republic*, the *Laws*, and the *Timaeus*, Plato was especially influenced by the Pythagorean tradition in his treatments of music and his concern with regulating its use. *Republic* x.13–16 provides a general description of the "harmony of the spheres," but in the *Timaeus* (34b–37c), Plato presents a much more detailed model for the creation of the soul of the universe embodying characteristic Pythagorean ratios and means, which produce a kind of musical shape, as illustrated in Figure 4.1.[11]

Many of these same numbers and ratios appear in the *Division of the Canon*, which applies Pythagorean mathematics to such musical topics as consonance, the magnitudes of certain consonant intervals, the location of movable notes in an enharmonic tetrachord, and the location of the notes of the Immutable System on a monochord. The Introduction to the *Division* defines the physical basis of sound as a series of motions; by producing a percussion (πληγή) of air, motion creates sound: denser motion is associated with greater string tension and higher pitch, sparser motion with lesser string tension and lower pitch. Since pitches are related to the number of motions of a string, the pitches of notes are comprised of certain numbers of parts; thus, they can be described and compared in numerical terms and ratios. Notes are related to one another in one of three numerical ratios: multiple, superparticular, and superpartient; the relationship of notes consonant by definition (i.e., those spanning the fourth, fifth, octave, twelfth, and fifteenth) can be expressed in a superparticular or a multiple ratio (i.e., 4:3, 3:2, 2:1, 3:1, and 4:1) formed only of the numbers of the *tetractys* (τετρακτύς) of the decad (i.e., 1, 2, 3, 4, the sum of which equals 10), although the *Division* does not explicitly refer to this famous Pythagorean *tetractys*.[12]

The Pythagoreans were also concerned with the measurement of intervals smaller than the fourth, which they identified through mathematical processes. The tone, for

11 For a translation of this passage, see *SR*, pp. 19–23.

12 For a detailed study and translation of this treatise, see Barbera, ed. and trans., *Euclidean Division*.

Mean	Formula (x>y>z)	
arithmetic	$y = z + \left(\frac{x-z}{2}\right)$	or
	$y = \frac{x}{2} + \frac{z}{2}$	or
	$y = \frac{x+z}{2}$	
harmonic	$y = z + \frac{z(x-z)}{x+z}$	

In prose terms, the arithmetic mean is usually described as (1) a number exceeding the lesser extreme by the same amount as it is exceeded by the greater extreme (e.g., 12:9:6), (2) a number that if squared will exceed the product of the extremes by the square of the difference between the terms (e.g., $9^2 = 81$, $6 \times 12 = 72$, $81 - 72 = 9$ [i.e., 3^2]); or (3) a number equal to half the sum of the extremes (e.g., $12 + 6 = 18$; $18 \div 2 = 9$). The harmonic mean is usually described as (1) a number exceeding and being exceeded by the same part of the extremes (e.g., 12:8:6 [8 exceeds 6 by one-third of 6 and 12 exceeds 8 by one-third of 12]); (2) a number that divides the difference between the extremes so that the two excesses are in the same ratio as the extremes (e.g., $12 - 8 = 4$, $8 - 6 = 2$, $12:6 = 4:2$); or (3) a number that when multiplied by the sum of the extremes produces a number equal to twice the product of the extremes (e.g., $12 + 6 = 18$, $8 \times 18 = 144$; $12 \times 6 = 72$, $2 \times 72 = 144$). The formulas are derived from Theon of Smyrna, *On mathmatics useful for the understanding of Plato*, §61.

Figure 4.2 Formulas for the arithmetic and harmonic means

instance, was shown to be the difference (9:8) between the fifth (3:2) and the fourth (4:3), and various sizes of "semitones" were identified, such as 256:243 (the *limma* [λεῖμμα]), 2,187:2,048 (the *apotome* [ἀποτομή]), and additional "semitones" created by proportioning the ratio 9:8 to produce any number of small subdivisions (e.g., 18:17:16 or 36:35:34:33:32 and so on). The size of the semitone and the addition of tones and semitones to create fourths, fifths, and octaves eventually became a subject of heated controversy between the Pythagoreans, with their fundamentally arithmetic approach, and the Aristoxenians, who adopted a geometric approach to the measurement of musical space – a controversy that extended into the Renaissance and beyond. (For more details on Pythagorean music theory, see **Chapter 10, pp. 273–76.**)

The mathematical background for the *Division of the Canon* and other Pythagorean treatments of music is explained in Nicomachus's *Introduction to Arithmetic* (Ἀριθμητικὴ εἰσαγωγή) and Theon of Smyrna's *On Mathematics Useful for the Understanding of Plato* (especially the sections "On music"). Likewise, Nicomachus's *Manual of Harmonics* (§§6 and 8–9) includes a discussion of the basic Pythagorean

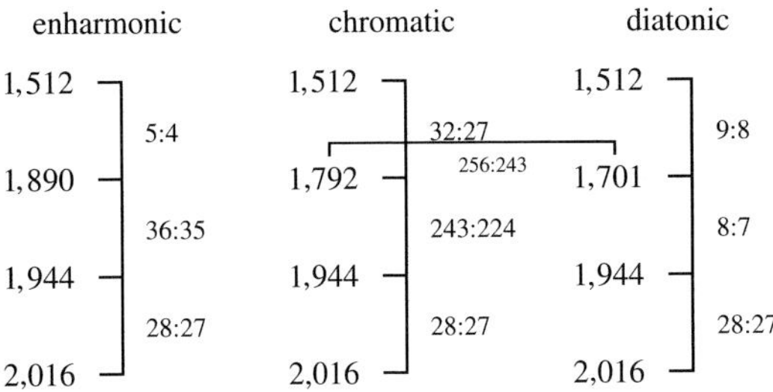

Archytas did not provide any integers to demonstrate these ratios, but Ptolemy proposed a set of smallest integers by way of demonstration.

Figure 4.3 The three genera of Archytas

consonances (including the famous story of Pythagoras's discovery of them, which also appears in a somewhat different version in Gaudentius's *Harmonic Introduction*, §11); the two means, harmonic and arithmetic (see Figure 4.2), described by Archytas and employed by Plato in the *Timaeus* to construct his musical soul of the universe; and the scale of Philolaus.[13] A group of excerpts attributed to Nicomachus in some manuscripts preserves further observations about the relationships between the twenty-eight musical notes and the *harmonia* of the cosmos.[14]

Both Gaudentius's *Harmonic Introduction*, §§15–16, and Ptolemy's *Harmonics* provide examples of the application of Pythagorean music theory to the construction of musical genera and scales also known in the other theoretical traditions. In *Harmonics* i.13, Ptolemy describes Archytas's measurement of the three genera[15] of the tetrachord (see Figure 4.3) and in *Harmonics* ii.14, he provides an extensive collection of measurements of the three genera expressed in terms of Pythagorean mathematics, attributed to Archytas, Eratosthenes, Didymus, and himself.

Because the Pythagorean tradition was fundamentally abstract and idealized, it could not provide a way of addressing the observable phenomena of musical practice. The Harmonicists, no doubt thoroughly familiar with Pythagorean mathematics, attempted to apply mathematical principles to the description of at least some parts of musical practice. In doing so, they might seem to represent a link between the Pythagorean and Aristoxenian traditions, although the precise historical relationships among the three traditions remain elusive.

The Harmonicists

The Harmonicists are primarily known through Aristoxenus's negative assessment of them in his *Harmonic Elements*, at the beginning of which he defines the study of

13 For translations, see Levin, trans., *Manual of Harmonics of Nicomachus*, pp. 83–139; and *SR*, pp. 74–75.
14 Edited in *Musici scriptores graeci*, 266.2–282.18.
15 A fuller discussion of the three genera is provided by the Aristoxenians (see below).

nete hyperbolaion	10,368
diatonic paranete hyperbolaion	11,664
chromatic paranete hyperbolaion	12,288
trite hyperbolaion	13,122
nete diezeugmenon	13,824
diatonic paranete diezeugmenon (= nete synemmenon)	15,552
chromatic paranete diezeugmenon	16,384
trite diezeugmenon (= diatonic paranete synemmenon)	17,496
paramese	18,432
trite synemmenon	19,683
mese	20,736
diatonic lichanos meson	23,328
chromatic lichanos meson	24,576
parhypate meson	26,244
hypate meson	27,648
diatonic lichanos hypaton	31,104
[chromatic lichanos hypaton (note not specified by Thrasyllus)]	32,768
parhypate hypaton	34,992
hypate hypaton	36,864
proslambanomenos	41,472

Figure 4.4 Thrasyllus's division of the monochord

harmonics as pertaining to the theory of scales and *tonoi* (τόνοι).[16] Earlier authors, identified by him as "the Harmonicists" (οἱ ἁρμονικοί), had based their theory on a single genus in the range of an octave, which they had represented in a series of diagrams. The precise nature of the Harmonicists' diagrams cannot be determined, but they may have been something like the diagrams that form the final two sections of the *Division of the Canon*, the monochord division of Thrasyllus preserved in §36 of Theon of Smyrna's *On Mathematics Useful for the Understanding of Plato* (see Figure 4.4), or the "diagram of modes" in Aristides Quintilianus's *On Music* i.11.[17]

16 A fuller discussion of the *tonoi* is provided by the Aristoxenians (see below). For a text of Aristoxenus's *Harmonic Elements*, see da Rios, ed., *Aristoxeni Elementa harmonica*. Full English translations appear in Macran, ed. and trans., *Harmonics of Aristoxenus*; and Barker, trans., *Greek Musical Writings*, vol. II, pp. 119–84.

17 Thrasyllus turns to number as a way of facilitating visualization of the relationship of all these notes, but he provides only the initial number that is to be assigned to the nete hyperbolaion: 10,368. The successive numbers, he says, can easily be computed by anyone who has followed the ratios already described, and in fact, 10,368 is the smallest common denominator that will accommodate all the ratios over the two octaves from nete hyperbolaion to proslambanomenos. For the diagrams in the *Division of the canon*, see Barbera, ed. and trans., *Euclidean Division*, pp. 178–87; for Aristides Quintilianus's "diagram of modes," see *SR*, p. 64.

Diagrams of this sort show the "close-packing" (καταπύκνωσις) of intervals that Aristoxenus describes as a feature of the Harmonicists' diagrams, and since they are intended to illustrate all the locations where pitches might be found rather than any genuine musical scale, they also fail to show, as Aristoxenus noted, anything about actual scales or *tonoi*. Aristoxenus refers to "close-packing" in only a few places in the treatise: first (i.7 [da Rios 12.8–12]), where he observes that there is a close relationship among scales, "positions of the voice," and the *tonoi*, a relationship that must be examined not by close-packing, but rather in the reciprocal melodic relationships of the scales themselves; second (i.27–28 [da Rios 35.9–37.4]), where he contrasts continuity (συνέχεια) and consecution (ἑξῆς) as he observes that musical continuity is a matter of musical logic, or synthesis (σύνθεσις), not a series of consecutive notes closely packed together on a chart with the smallest possible interval separating one from another.

Contrasting his concept of synthesis with the misguided notions of the Harmonicists, Aristoxenus notes that the Harmonicist Eratocles (fl. fifth century BCE) was primarily interested in the possible cyclic orderings of the intervals in an octave, which led him to observe seven species. Aristoxenus derides such mechanical manipulation, which was apparently typical of the Harmonicist approach, because it does not take into account the possible species of the fifth and fourth and the various musical syntheses, which would produce many more than seven species.

In treating the *tonoi*, some of the Harmonicists arranged them in the ascending order of Hypodorian, Mixolydian, Dorian, Phrygian, and Lydian, with the first three separated from each other by a half-tone and the final three by a tone, while others, basing their assumptions on the aulos, thought that the ascending order should be Hypophrygian, Hypodorian, Dorian, Phrygian, Lydian, and Mixolydian, with the first three separated from each other by three dieses (i.e., approximately three quartertones), the Dorian and the Phrygian by a tone, and the last three once again by three dieses. In another reference to close-packing, Aristoxenus (ii.37–38 [da Rios 46.17–47.16]) objected that this identification of a series of *tonoi* separated by some small interval resulted merely in a closely packed diagram and not in any useful understanding of musical phenomena.

The characteristics of the aulos and musical notation were two apparent preoccupations of the Harmonicists, but Aristoxenus dismisses both of these as unscientific. In his view, the Harmonicists "have it backwards when they think that placing some apparent thing is the end of comprehension, for comprehension is the end of every visible thing" (ii.41 [da Rios 51.10–13]); by concentrating on the "subject of judgment" rather than on judgment itself, the Harmonicists "miss the truth" (ii.41 [da Rios 52.1–4]).

Though it clearly represents the Pythagorean tradition, the *Division of the Canon* also exhibits precisely the sort of limited diagrammatic view of music theory attributed by Aristoxenus to the Harmonicists. The two final sections of the *Division* may not have been part of its earliest form,[18] but the structure of the demonstrations and the

18 Barbera, ed. and trans., *Euclidean Division*, pp. 40–44.

division of the monochord itself are nevertheless expressed in diagrammatic terms. Moreover, the *Division* says nothing at all about the ways in which one note might or might not move to another; makes no specific reference to the various genera, although the enharmonic genus is certainly produced by the demonstrations of propositions 17–18; and is limited to a single two-octave display. Likewise, the *Introduction to Music* of Alypius, devoted almost entirely to a series of notational tables, might be seen as growing out of the Harmonicist tradition, although its late date would make such a classification largely irrelevant.

The Harmonicists would seem to have represented an attempt to systematize musical space in the most efficient and rational manner. They shared some affinities with the Pythagorean tradition in relying on number to define particular intervals and arrange them sequentially in a composite diagram, but they differed from the Pythagorean tradition in their interest in actual musical phenomena. By acknowledging the importance of the phenomena, the Harmonicists anticipated Aristoxenus. Nevertheless, from the Aristoxenian point of view, they erred in employing a reductive process rather than developing an inductive scheme that could encompass the endlessly variable nature of musical sound.

The Aristoxenian tradition

The most systematic discussion of ostensibly musical phenomena is found in the fragmentary *Harmonic Elements* of Aristoxenus and later treatises based on its principles (especially the Aristoxenian epitome by Cleonides and parts of the treatises of Gaudentius, Bacchius, Ptolemy, and Aristides Quintilianus). Aristoxenus himself was concerned with the philosophical definitions and categories necessary to establish a complete and correct view of the musical reality of scales and *tonoi*, two primary elements of musical composition, and in the first part of his treatise, he introduces and discusses such subjects as motion of the voice (ἡ τῆς φωνῆς κίνησις), pitch (τάσις), compass (ἡ τοῦ βαρέος τε καὶ ὀξέος διάτασις), intervals (διαστήματα), consonance and dissonance, scales (συστήματα), melos (μέλος), continuity and consecution (συνέχεια, ἑξῆς), genera (γένη), synthesis (σύνθεσις), mixing of genera (μιγνύμενος τῶν γενῶν), notes (φθόγγοι), and position of the voice (ὁ τῆς φωνῆς τόπος). From these, he develops a set of seven categories (genera, intervals, notes, scales, *tonoi*, modulation [μεταβολή], and melic composition [μελοποιΐα]), framed by two additional categories: first, hearing and intellect (ἀκοή διάνοια), and last, comprehension (ξύνεσις). As the later Aristoxenian tradition did not share Aristoxenus's broader philosophical interests, the framing categories and much of the subtlety of language and argument largely disappeared, while the seven "technical" categories (especially the first three) were rearranged and expanded to include additional technical details – such as the names of the individual notes – that Aristoxenus took for granted. The surviving portions of Aristoxenus's treatise do not contain his explanations of each category, but the tradition as a whole may be summarized as follows.

Notes. Aristoxenus's definition is both economical and sophisticated: "a falling of the voice on one pitch is a note; then, it appears to be a note as such because it is ordered in a melos and stands harmonically on a single pitch" (i.15 [da Rios 20.16–19]). This subtle definition distinguishes among a voice, which is articulate sound; a single pitch, which is a position of a voice; and a note, which is a production of sound at a single relative ordered position within a musical composition, a melos. In the treatise of Cleonides, this becomes: "A note is the musical falling of the voice on one pitch" (Jan 179.9–10); while Gaudentius preserves much of the original: "a note is the falling of the voice upon one pitch; pitch is a tarrying and standing of the voice; whenever the voice seems to stop on one pitch, we say that the voice is a note that can be ordered in melos" (Jan 329.7–11).[19] Aristoxenus did not name or define all the notes (since they were "so well known to the adherents of music" [i.22 (da Rios 29.1–2)]), nor do the surviving portions of his treatise describe the full array of notes and tetrachords (groups of four notes) that came to be known as the Greater and Lesser Perfect Systems. Later theorists, however, present and characterize them as shown in Table 4.2.[20]

The tetrachord was regarded by Aristoxenus as the basic musical unit, and all but three of the note names indicate the tetrachord (hypaton, meson, synemmenon, diezeugmenon, and hyperbolaion) to which they belong. The proslambanomenos ("added note") was not considered a part of any tetrachord; the mese formed the upper limit of the meson and the paramese the lower limit of the diezeugmenon.

Intervals. Intervals are defined as bounded by two notes of differing pitch, distinguished by magnitude, by consonance or dissonance, as rational or irrational, by genus, and as simple or compound (the first four distinctions also apply to scales). For Aristoxenus, the fourth and the fifth, not the octave, were the primary scalar components of music and music theory. In order to be musical, he required that intervals be combined in a certain way; thus the study of intervals was not just a matter of measurement, as it had been for the Pythagoreans and the Harmonicists, but a matter of understanding "synthesis," the coherent musical arrangement of intervals (i.27 [da Rios 35.10–36.1]). Once again, Cleonides simplifies the definition to: "an interval is

19 All translations are those of the author. For full English translations of the treatises of Cleonides and Gaudentius, see *SR*, pp. 35–46 and 66–85; for Aristoxenus, see n. 16 above. 20 In the table, the pitches are purely conventional, intended only to show the intervallic pattern (an asterisk indicates an enharmonic diesis, i.e., a microtonal sharp); various classifications pertaining to the genera are given in parentheses: immovable notes are marked "im" (all other notes are movable), notes not part of a *pycnon* (i.e., a cluster of three notes at the bottom of a tetrachord; a fuller discussion of this term appears below) are marked "ap," and notes that form the bottom, middle, or top of a *pycnon* are marked "bp," "mp," and "tp."

Table 4.2 *The Greek Greater and Lesser Perfect Systems*

	Greater Perfect System (GPS)		Lesser Perfect System (LPS)		
	Proslambanomenos (im, ap)	[a]	Proslambanomenos (im, ap)	[a]	
	Hypate hypaton (im, bp)	[b]	Hypate hypaton (im, bp)	[b]	
	Parhypate hypaton (mp)	[c^1]	Parhypate hypaton (mp)	[c^1]	
1	[or, if enharmonic, b*]		[or, if enharmonic, b*]		
	Enharmonic lichanos hypaton (tp)	[c^1]	Enharmonic lichanos hypaton (tp)	[c^1]	1
	Chromatic lichanos hypaton (tp)	[$c\sharp^1$]	Chromatic lichanos hypaton (tp)	[$c\sharp^1$]	
	Diatonic lichanos hypaton (ap)	[d^1]	Diatonic lichanos hypaton (ap)	[d^1]	
	Hypate meson (im, bp)	[e^1]	Hypate meson (im, bp)	[e^1]	
	Parhypate meson (mp)	[f^1]	Parhypate meson (mp)	[f^1]	
	[or, if enharmonic, e^{*1}]		[or, if enharmonic, e^{*1}]		
2	Enharmonic lichanos meson (tp)	[f^1]	Enharmonic lichanos meson (tp)	[f^1]	2
	Chromatic lichanos meson (tp)	[$f\sharp^1$]	Chromatic lichanos meson (tp)	[$f\sharp^1$]	
	Diatonic lichanos meson (ap)	[g^1]	Diatonic lichanos meson (ap)	[g^1]	
	Mese (im, bp)	[a^1]	Mese (im, bp)	[a^1]	
	Paramese (im, bp)	[b^1]	Trite synnemmenon (mp)	[$b\flat^1$]	
	Trite diezeugmenon (mp)	[c^2]	[or, if enharmonic, a^{*1}]		
	[or, if enharmonic, b^{*1}]		Enharmonic paranete		
	Enharmonic paranete		synemmenon (tp)	[$b\flat^1$]	
3	diezeugmenon (tp)	[c^2]	Chromatic paranete		5
	Chromatic paranete		synemmenon (tp)	[b^1]	
	diezeugmenon (tp)	[$c\sharp^2$]	Diatonic paranete		
	Diatonic paranete		synemmenon (ap)	[c^2]	
	diezeugmenon (ap)	[d^2]	Nete synemmenon (im, ap)	[d^2]	
	Nete diezeugmenon (im, bp)	[e^2]			
	Trite hyperbolaion (mp)	[f^2]			
	[or, if enharmonic, e^{*2}]				
	Enharmonic paranete				
	hyperbolaion (tp)	[f^2]			
4	Chromatic paranete				
	hyperbolaion (tp)	[$f\sharp^2$]			
	Diatonic paranete				
	hyperbolaion (ap)	[g^2]			
	Nete hyperbolaion (im, ap)	[a^2]			

Note: (The brackets show the possible notes in each tetrachord, depending on the genus; no single tetrachord would ever include all these notes. Tetrachord 1 is the hypaton; 2, the meson; 3, the diezeugmenon; 4, the hyperbolaion; and 5, the synemmenon. A tone of disjunction follows the proslambanomenos in both systems and the mese in the GPS. In both systems, tetrachords 1 and 2 are conjunct; in the GPS, tetrachords 3 and 4 are conjunct; and in the LPS, tetrachords 2 and 5 are conjunct.)

bounded by two notes, dissimilar in height and depth" (Jan 179.11–12), although he does provide (§5) a rather comprehensive summary of the five Aristoxenian distinctions. Theorists readily accepted the possibility that intervals could be of infinite magnitude but in general restricted their interest to the range between the smallest enharmonic diesis (approximately a quarter-tone) and the double-octave-and-a-fifth, identified by Aristoxenus as the practical range of the human voice or a musical instrument. The consonant intervals were at least the fourth, fifth, octave, twelfth, and double octave; the Aristoxenians tended to include the eleventh (or indeed any consonant interval compounded with the octave), while the Pythagoreans rejected this interval since it could not be represented by a multiple or a superparticular ratio. Intervals were simple if bounded by musically consecutive notes (an implicit rejection of Harmonicist "close-packing"), otherwise they were compound; thus an interval of the same magnitude might be simple or compound depending on the context. In clear contradistinction to the Pythagorean sense, intervals were rational if they were known and employed in music (e.g., the tone, semitone, ditone), irrational if they varied from the defined forms. For Pythagoreans, of course, rationality was a matter of expressible numerical relationships (e.g., 3:2, 4:3, 2:1, etc.): intervals that cannot be expressed in such a relationship are irrational, even though they may be employed in practice. Additional distinctions such as "paraphonic" and "antiphonic" are also developed by later theorists such as Theon of Smyrna, Gaudentius, and Bacchius.[21]

Genera. Aristoxenus recognized three basic genera of tetrachords: the enharmonic (also known as *harmonia* [ἁρμονία]), the chromatic (also known as *color* [χρῶμα]), and the diatonic; the last two of which exhibited various shades (χρόαι). The intonations were created by the two middle notes of the tetrachord, which were "movable" (κινούμενοι), in relation to the two outer notes of the tetrachord, which were "immovable" (ἑστῶτες). To describe these intonations, Aristoxenus posited (i.21–27 [da Rios 28.3–35.8]) a tetrachord of two-and-a-half tones, with the tone itself comprised of half-tones, third-tones, and quarter-tones. He avoided specific numerical terms because his descriptions are intended to be approximations; the shades are not actually fixed but infinitely variable within their regions (i.23 [da Rios 30.14–16]). The character of the genera is perceived not in a particular order of specific intervals arranged sequentially in a static scale but rather in characteristic dynamic progressions of intervals, or "roads" (ὁδοί), that differ in ascent and descent (iii.66–72 [da Rios 83–89]). These progressions are readily recognizable, even though the exact sizes of the intervals may vary from piece to piece. In order to convey the characteristic quality of the genera, the theorist needs to specify not every possible note and interval but rather the relative sizes of intervals and their typical patterns of succession. So, Aristoxenus was able to reduce the infinite number of possible arrangements to a manageable series of archetypal genera.

21 See *SR*, p. 73.

Harmonia	3+3+24
Mild color	4+4+22
Hemiolic color	4½+4½+21
Whole-tone color	6+6+18
Mild diatonic	6+9+15
Intense diatonic	6+12+12

Figure 4.5 Cleonides' shades of the tetrachord genera

In the later Aristoxenian treatises, only the static descriptions of the genera survive. Cleonides deduces a tetrachord of thirty units on which the genera and shades are projected in specific numbers, as shown in Figure 4.5.

The three notes bounding the two small intervals were known as a *pycnon* (πυκνόν) if their composite interval was smaller than the remaining interval in the tetrachord, as is the case in the first four shades. Later theorists expand the division of the tetrachord into sixty parts, express the divisions in terms of ratios instead of parts, or provide somewhat different names, but the basic Aristoxenian design remains the standard for all subsequent theorists who concern themselves with the subject of genera.

Scales. Aristoxenus rejected the closely packed scales of the Harmonicists because by ignoring the principles of synthesis and continuity and consecution, they failed to accord with musical logic. Scales, Aristoxenus asserts, must always follow "the nature of *melos*" (ἡ τοῦ μέλους φύσις): an infinite number of notes cannot simply be strung together; and if a melos ascends or descends, the intervals formed by notes separated by four or five consecutive degrees in the scale must form the consonant intervals of a fourth or a fifth. Scales larger than the tetrachord are assembled by combining tetrachords, either by conjunction (συναφή) (e.g., e^1–f^1–g^1–a^1 and a^1–b^1–c^2–d^2) or disjunction (διάζευξις) (e.g., e^1–f^1–g^1–a^1 and b^1–c^2–d^2–e^2). Relying on the aforestated principles, Aristoxenus (iii.63–74 [da Rios 78.13–92.5]) formulates a detailed set of possible progressions.

The later Aristoxenians expand this discussion to include consideration of the ways in which the tetrachords are combined to produce the Greater and Lesser Perfect Systems, but they are also concerned with the classification of scales according to four of the distinctions applied to intervals, to which are added distinctions between gapped or continuous, conjunct or disjunct, and modulating or non-modulating scales. They also explore the various species (εἴδη) or forms (σχήματα) of the fourth, fifth, and octave, perhaps building on Aristoxenus's own description of the species of the fourth, which appears at the very end of the surviving portion of his *Harmonic Elements*. Of these, the octave species are the most important because of their apparent relationship to the *tonoi*; they are commonly described and named as shown in Figure 4.6.

hypate hypaton–paramese [b–b′]	Mixolydian
parhypate hypaton–trite diezeugmenon [c′–c″]	Lydian
lichanos hypaton–paranete diezeugmenon [d′–d″]	Phrygian
hypate meson–nete diezeugmenon [e′–e″]	Dorian
parhypate meson–trite hyperbolaion [f′–f″]	Hypolydian
lichanos meson–paranete hyperbolaion [g′–g″]	Hypophrygian
mese–nete hyperbolaion [a′–a″]	Common, Locrian, and Hypodorian

Figure 4.6 The Aristoxenian octave species

The association of ethnic names with the octave species probably does not come from Aristoxenus himself, who criticizes (ii.37–38 [da Rios 46.17–47.16]) their application to the *tonoi* by the Harmonicists.

The final distinction of scales as modulating or non-modulating pertains to the number of "functional" mesai. According to Aristoxenus, "function" (δύναμις) is a matter of context; Cleonides, the Aristotelian *Problems*, and especially Ptolemy (*Harmonics* ii) elaborate on the term, making it clear that the "function" of notes involved their relationship in a specific sequence of intervals typical of any one of the genera. The mese, in particular, played an important role because of its strategic position at a point from which a scale could proceed either by conjunction or by disjunction.

Tonoi and harmoniai. The section of the *Harmonic Elements* in which Aristoxenus discussed the *tonoi* has not survived, but it is clear from other sections of the treatise that Aristoxenus associated the *tonoi* with "positions of the voice." This feature is preserved in Cleonides' later definition (Jan 202.6–8), which states that the term *tonos* can refer to a note, an interval, a position of the voice, and a pitch. Cleonides attributes to Aristoxenus thirteen *tonoi*, with the proslambanomenoi advancing by semitone over the range of an octave between the Hypodorian and the Hypermixolydian; Aristides Quintilianus (*On Music* i.10) observes that the "younger theorists" (νεώτεροι) added two additional *tonoi*, and in fact just such a set of fifteen *tonoi* is preserved in the notational tables of Alypius. The full set may be displayed as in Figure 4.7 (as always, the pitches are purely conventional). Cleonides probably borrowed his arrangement from an earlier "Aristoxenian" treatise or inadvertently conflated material from the Harmonicist and Aristoxenian traditions. It is doubtful that the left column of the figure is an accurate representation of Aristoxenus's own treatment, inasmuch as he derides a rather similar arrangement of the *tonoi* by the Harmonicists.

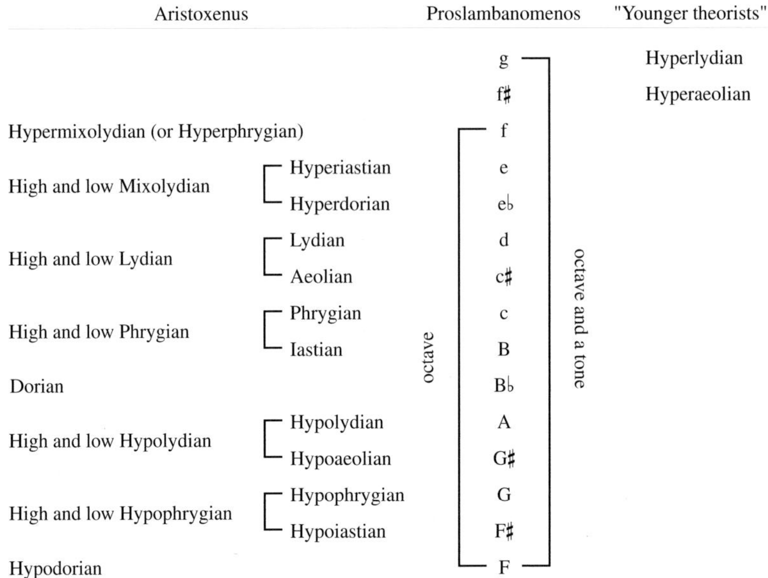

Figure 4.7 The *tonoi* attributed to Aristoxenus and the "younger theorists"

Claudius Ptolemy presents (*Harmonics*, especially ii.3–11) a different conception of the *tonoi*, based on the seven octave species; this is not strictly a part of the Aristoxenian tradition but is related to it. In Ptolemy's view, since the seven octave species might be replicated within a single range of so-called "thetic" notes, with the dynamic function of the various notes determined by the mese (which is itself partly determined by the intervals that surround it), there need only be seven *tonoi* (see Figure 4.8).

Ptolemy's conception is unobjectionable as a logical system, but it is unlikely that it represents either a historical view of the *tonoi* or a description of contemporary practice. Aristoxenus specifically repudiated such figures as Eratocles for limiting their view to a mechanical manipulation of the seven octave species or other intervallic patterns and the Harmonicists in general for basing their theory on a single genus in the range of an octave, which they had represented in a series of diagrams. Moreover, even the musical fragments dated to a period more or less contemporary with Ptolemy tend to exhibit a much wider range of *tonoi* and distribution of relative pitch than Ptolemy's characteristic octave would suggest. His system did, however, have a profound impact on later theorists, who appreciated its inherent logic.

Many of the ethnic names applied to the *tonoi* are also applied to *harmoniai* described by Plato (especially *Republic* iii), Aristotle (especially *Politics* viii), other philosophers, and some of the music theorists. Aristides Quintilianus, for instance, preserves (i.9) in Alypian notation six scales, which he says Plato "calls to mind" (μνημονεύει) in his discussion of the character of the *harmoniai* (the pitches are, as always, purely conven-

thetic	Mixolydian	Lydian	Phrygian	Dorian	Hypolydian	Hypophrygian	Hypodorian
	dynamic						
nd	e″ (pm)	e″ (td)	e″ (pnd)	e″ (nd)	e″ (th)	e″ (pnh)	e″ (nh)
pnd	d″ (m)	d♯″ (pm)	d″ (td)	d″ (pnd)	d♯″ (nd)	d″ (th)	d″ (pnh)
td	c″ (lm)	c♯″ (m)	c♯″ (pm)	c″ (td)	c♯″ (pnd)	c♯″ (nd)	c″ (th)
pm	b♭′ (phm)	b′ (lm)	b′ (m)	b′ (pm)	b′ (td)	b′ (pnd)	b′ (nd)
m	a′ (hm)	a′ (phm)	a′ (lm)	a′ (m)	a♯′ (pm)	a′ (td)	a′ (pnd)
lm	g′ (lh)	g♯′ (hm)	g′ (phm)	g′ (lm)	g♯′ (m)	g♯′ (pm)	g′ (td)
phm	f′ (phh)	f♯′ (lh)	f♯′ (hm)	f′ (phm)	f♯′ (lm)	f♯′ (m)	f♯′ (pm)
hm	e′ (hh)	e′ (phh)	e′ (lh)	e′ (hm)	e′ (phm)	e′ (lm)	e′ (m)

Abbreviations for the names of notes:

proslambanomenos (=pl)
hypate hypaton (=hh)
parhypate hypaton (=phh)
lichanos hypaton (=lh)
hypate meson (=hm)
parhypate meson (=phm)
lichanos meson (=lm)
mese (=m)
paramese (=pm)
trite diezeugmenon (=td)
paranete diezeugmenon (=pnd)
nete diezeugmenon (=nd)
trite hyperbolaion (=th)
paranete hyperbolaion (=pnh)
nete hyperbolaion (=nh)

Figure 4.8 Ptolemy's *tonoi*

tional and are intended only to show the intervallic pattern [an asterisk indicates a diesis])[22] (see Figure 4.9).

These scales may indeed be early, and with their unusual gapped character, they are reminiscent of the Spondeion scale described in Pseudo-Plutarch's *On Music* (1135a–b). It is also noteworthy that one of the earliest surviving fragments of ancient Greek music, which preserves a few lines from Euripides' *Orestes*, exhibits in its notation either the Dorian or Phrygian *harmonia* as presented by Aristides Quintilianus.[23]

Both Plato and Aristotle considered that the *harmoniai* could have an impact on human character, but in their use of the term, they are almost certainly referring to a full complex of musical elements, including a particular type of scale, range and register, characteristic rhythmic pattern, textual subject, and so on. In terms of Greek music

22 Ibid., p. 59.
23 See Egert Pöhlmann, *Denkmäler altgriechischer Musik*, Erlanger Beiträge zur Sprach- und Kunstwissenschaft, vol. XXXI (Nuremberg: Hans Carl, 1970), pp. 78–82.

Lydian	e*	f	a	b	b*	c'	e'	e*'	
Dorian	g	a	a*	a#	d'	e'	e*'	f	a'
Phrygian	g	a	a*	a#	d'	e'	e*'	f'	g'
Iastian	e	e*	f	a	c'	d'			
Mixolydian	e	e*	f	g	a	a*	a#	e'	
Intense Lydian	e	e*	f	a	c'				

Figure 4.9 Aristides Quintilianus's six early *harmoniai*

theory, references to particular *harmoniai* would normally subsume the corresponding *tonos*, but the converse would not necessarily be true.[24]

Modulation. Since the functions of the notes in a scale would change in the course of a modulation, a full comprehension of musical logic would be impossible without determining the nature of a modulation. Aristoxenus's discussion of modulation is not preserved in the fragments of the *Harmonic elements*, but Cleonides articulates four types of modulation: in scale, genus, *tonos*, and melic composition. Scalar modulation is based on the number of potential "functional" mesai within a scale, and shifts of this sort could be used to change from one *tonos* to another. Modulations involving shifts of a consonant interval or a whole-tone were considered more musical because, as Cleonides states, "it is necessary that for every modulation, a certain common note or interval or scale be present" (Jan 205.18–19). The importance of the mese in establishing a modulation is confirmed by the Aristotelian *Problems* xix.20 (919a13–28), which observes that all good *mele* use the mese more frequently than any of the other notes, adding that the mese – like the grammatical conjunction "and" – is a kind of musical conjunction. *Problems* xix.36 (920b7–15) further hypothesizes that the mese is so important because all the other strings of the instrument are tuned to it. Both statements are reasonable: the mese is not only an immovable note – and therefore well suited to govern the tuning of an instrument – but also the "pivot" note from which the scale may ascend either through a conjunct tetrachord – the synemmenon – or across the tone of disjunction and into the diezeugmenon tetrachord. Several notes might function as mese, depending on the placement of whole-tones and semitones in a scale and its range. In fact, such shifts of mesai can be seen in a number of the musical fragments; these would presumably fit Cleonides' definition of "modulating" scales.

Ptolemy's *Harmonics* (i.16 and ii.16) actually demonstrates a series of tunings that would enable the performer to modulate among several *tonoi*, while Aristides Quintilianus (i.11) describes a "diagram of the modes akin to a wing" (πτέρυγι δὲ τὸ διάγραμμα τῶν τρόπων γίνεται παραπλήσιον), which demonstrates the various

24 Thomas J Mathiesen, "Problems of Terminology in Ancient Greek Theory: ἉΡΜΟΝΙΑ," in *Festival Essays for Pauline Alderman*, ed. B. Karson (Provo, UT: Brigham Young University Press, 1976), pp. 3–17; Mathiesen, "Harmonia and Ethos in Ancient Greek Music," *Journal of Musicology* 3 (1984), pp. 264–79.

common points among the *tonoi*, at which a modulation might presumably take place.[25]

Melic composition. This subject, Aristoxenus's final category, remains obscure in the surviving treatises. Aristides Quintilianus (i.12) refers to choice (λῆψις), mixing (μίξις), and usage (χρῆσις) as the three parts of melic (and rhythmic) composition. Choice is a matter of deciding upon the proper scale and position of the voice; mixing involves the arrangement of notes, positions of the voice, genera, and scales; and usage pertains to three types of musical gestures: sequence (ἀγωγή), succession (πλοκή), and repetition (πεττεία) (Cleonides adds a fourth, prolongation [τονή]). In sequence, the melody moves up or down by successive notes (a revolving [περιφερής] sequence involves shifting between conjunct and disjunct tetrachords); in succession, the notes outline a sequence of parallel intervals moving up or down (e.g., c–e–d–f–e–g–f–a or c–f–d–g–e–a or other comparable patterns); repetition is a matter of knowing which notes should be used (and how often) and which not; and prolongation pertains to sustaining particular notes. Additional melodic figures are described in the Byzantine treatise known as Bellermann's Anonymous, but these may pertain more to Byzantine than to ancient Greek music.

Aristides Quintilianus remarks that the particular notes used will indicate the ethos of the composition. Cleonides identified (Jan 206.3–18) three types: diastaltic (διασταλτικόν), or elevating, which conveyed a sense of magnificence, manly elevation of the soul, and heroic deeds, especially appropriate to tragedy; systaltic (συσταλτικόν), or depressing, which expressed dejection and unmanliness, suitable to lamentation and eroticism; and hesychastic (ἡσυχαστικόν), or soothing, which evoked quietude and peacefulness, suitable to hymns and paeans. Aristides Quintilianus, who identifies a similar triad, calls the hesychastic "medial," and much of Books II and III is devoted to an explanation of musical ethos.

Because the Aristoxenian tradition lent itself to the construction of musical "rules," it came to be viewed as a practical tradition, distinct from the ideal or purely theoretical traditions of the Pythagoreans and the Harmonicists. Yet this is a misleading and simplistic dichotomy. While Aristoxenus's followers may often have failed to grasp his larger epistemological concerns, it is clear that he was trying to develop an idealized phenomenology of music, based not on the abstraction of number but rather on a careful definition of the separable elements of musical sound that became music only when they combined to create something the intellect would comprehend. It is one of the ironies of history that the Aristoxenian tradition, especially as it was adopted and adapted by later Western theorists, forgot the interests of its founder and instead became mired in fruitless practical controversies, especially in the areas of tuning.

25 See *SR*, p. 64.

Conclusion

By the end of the fourth century CE, ancient Greek music theory was merely part of the residue of an ancient civilization and the distinctions among the traditions were blurred or forgotten. It remained for writers such as Martianus Capella, Boethius, and Cassiodorus – all of whom relied on relatively late sources – to preserve and transmit the little that remained to the Latin readers of the Middle Ages. Thus, later Greek writers such as Nicomachus, Ptolemy, Gaudentius, and Aristides Quintilianus represent both the final stages of Greek music theory in antiquity and, as filtered through their Latin interpreters, the first stages of ancient Greek music theory as it came to be known in the Middle Ages.

Bibliography

The following bibliography is highly selective, with an emphasis on current literature.

Manuscripts

Mathiesen, T. J. *Ancient Greek Music Theory: A Catalogue raisonné of Manuscripts*, RISM BXI, Munich, Henle, 1988

Greek authors: texts, translations, and commentaries

Collections

Barker, A. *Greek Musical Writings*, 2 vols., Cambridge University Press, 1984–89

Jan, K. von. *Musici scriptores graeci. Aristoteles. Euclides. Nicomachus. Bacchius. Gaudentius. Alypius et melodiarum veterum quidquid exstat; Supplementum, melodiarum reliquiae*, Leipzig, Teubner, 1895–99; facs. Hildesheim, G. Olms, 1962

Mathiesen, T. J., ed., "Greek Views of Music," Part I of *SR*, pp. 1–109

Meibom, M. *Antiquae musicae auctores septem, Graece et Latine*, 2 vols., Amsterdam, Elzevir, 1652; facs. New York, Broude, 1977

Zanoncelli, L. *La manualistica musicale greca: [Euclide]. Cleonide. Nicomaco. Excerpta Nicomachi. Bacchio il Vecchio. Gaudenzio. Alipio. Excerpta Neapolitana*, Milan, Guerini, 1990

Separate authors (selective list), not including editions and translations in the collections above

Alypius, ed. and Fr. trans. C.-E. Ruelle as *Alypius et Gaudence . . . Bacchius l'Ancien*, Paris, Firmin-Didot, 1895

Anonymous (Bellermann's), ed. and trans. D. Najock as *Anonyma de musica scripta Bellermanniana*, Leipzig, Teubner, 1975

Aristides Quintilianus, ed. R. P. Winnington-Ingram as *Aristidis Quintiliani De musica libri tres*, Leipzig, Teubner, 1963; trans. and ed. T. J. Mathiesen as *On Music in Three Books*, New Haven, Yale University Press, 1983

Aristotle [Pseudo], ed. and Fr. trans. C.-E. Ruelle as *Problèmes musicaux d'Aristote*, Paris, Firmin-Didot, 1891; ed. and trans. F. Gevaert and J. Vollgraff as *Problèmes musicaux d'Aristote*, Ghent, Hoste, 1903; reprint Osnabrück, Biblio, 1977; trans. W. Hett as *Problems, Books I–XXXVIII*, vols. xv–xvi of *Aristotle in Twenty-Three Volumes*, Loeb Classical Library, Cambridge, MA, Harvard University Press, 1926–37, rev. 1965–70

Aristoxenus, ed. and Fr. trans. C.-E. Ruelle as *Eléments harmoniques d'Aristoxène*, Paris, P. de la Laine, 1871; ed. and Ger. trans. R. Westphal as *Aristoxenos von Tarent, Melik und Rhythmik des classischen Hellenentums*, 2 vols., Leipzig, Abel, 1883–89; facs. Hildesheim, G. Olms, 1965; ed. and trans. H. S. Macran as *The Harmonics of Aristoxenus*, Oxford, Clarendon, 1902; facs. Hildesheim, G. Olms, 1974; ed. and It. trans. R. da Rios as *Aristoxeni elementa harmonica*, Rome, Typis publicae officinae polygraphicae, 1954; ed. and trans. L. Pearson as *Elementa rhythmica: The Fragment of Book II and the Additional Evidence for Aristoxenian Rhythmic Theory*, Oxford, Clarendon, 1990; L. Rowell "Aristoxenus on Rhythm," *JMT* 23 (1979), pp. 63–79

Athenaeus, ed. G. Kaibel as *Athenaei Naucratitae Dipnosophistarum libri XV*, 3 vols., Leipzig, Teubner, 1887–90; facs. Stuttgart, Teubner, 1965–66; ed. and trans. C. B. Gulick as *Deipnosophistae*, 7 vols., Loeb Classical Library, Cambridge, MA, Harvard University Press, 1927–41, rev. 1957–63

Bacchius, ed. and trans K. von Jan as *Die Eisagoge des Bacchius*, 2 vols., Strassburg, Strassburger Druckerei und Verlagsanstalt, 1890–91; trans. O. Steinmayer, as "Bacchius Geron's *Introduction to the Art of Music*," *JMT* 29 (1985), pp. 271–98

Cleonides, ed. and Fr. trans. C.-E. Ruelle as *L'Introduction harmonique de Cléonide. La division du canon d'Euclide le géomètre. Canons harmoniques de Florence*, Paris, Firmin-Didot, 1884; ed. and trans. J. Solomon as "Cleonides: *ΕΙΣΑΓΩΓΗ ΑΡΜΟΝΙΚΗ*; Critical Edition, Translation, and Commentary," Ph.D. diss., Univ. of North Carolina – Chapel Hill (1980)

Dionysius, ed. J. F. Bellermann as "*Εἰσαγωγὴ τέχνης μουσικῆς Βακχείου τοῦ γέροντος*," in *Anonymi scriptio de musica*, Berlin, Förstner, 1841, pp. 101–08; trans. A. J. H. Vincent as "Introduction à l'art musical par Bacchius l'ancien," in *Notice sur trois manuscrits grecs relatifs à la musique, avec une traduction française et des commentaires*, Paris, Imprimerie royale, 1847, pp. 64–72

[Euclid], trans. T. J. Mathiesen as "An Annotated Translation of Euclid's Division of a Monochord," *JMT* 19 (1975), pp. 236–58; ed. and trans. A. Barbera as *The Euclidean Division of the Canon: Greek and Latin Sources*, Lincoln, University of Nebraska Press, 1991

Gaudentius, see Alypius; and Mathiesen, "Greek Views," above

Nicomachus, ed. and Fr. trans. C.-E. Ruelle as *Nicomaque de Gérase. Manuel d'harmonique et autres textes relatifs à la musique*, Paris, Baur, 1881; trans. F. R. Levin as *The Manual of Harmonics of Nicomachus the Pythagorean*, Grand Rapids, MI, Phanes, 1994

Philodemus, in G. M. Rispoli, "Filodemo sulla musica," *Cronache Ercolanesi* 4 (1974), pp. 57–84; ed. and Ger. trans. A. J. Neubecker as *Philodemus, Über die Musik IV*, Naples, Bibliopolis, 1986; Fr. trans. D. Delattre as "Philodème, de la musique: livre IV," *Cronache Ercolanesi* 19 (1989), pp. 49–143

Plato, ed. J. Burnet as *Platonis opera*, Oxford, Clarendon, 1900–07; ed. and trans. H. N. Fowler, W. R. M. Lamb, P. Shorey, and R. G. Bury as *Plato in Twelve Volumes*, Loeb Classical Library, Cambridge, MA, Harvard University Press, 1914–35

Plutarch [Pseudo], ed. and trans. H. Weil and T. Reinach as *Plutarque de la musique*, Paris, Leroux, 1900; ed. K. Ziegler as *Plutarchi Moralia VI 3*, Leipzig, Teubner, 1966; ed. and trans. B. Einarson and P. H. de Lacy as "On Music," in *Plutarch's Moralia*, vol. xiv, Loeb Classical Library, Cambridge, MA, Harvard University Press, 1967; ed. and Fr. trans. F. Lasserre as *Plutarque, De la musique*, Olten and Lausanne, URS Graf, 1954; It. trans. L. Gamberini as *Plutarco "della musica"*, Florence, Olschki, 1979

Porphyry, ed. I. Düring as *Porphyrios Kommentar zur Harmonielehre des Ptolemaios*, Göteborg, Elanders, 1932; reprint New York, Garland, 1980; Ger. trans. I. Düring as *Ptolemaios und Porphyrios über die Musik*, Göteborg, Elanders, 1934; facs. New York, Garland, 1980

Ptolemy, Claudius, ed. J. Wallis as *Κλαυδίου Πτολεμαίου ἁρμονικῶν βιβλία γ. Harmonicorum libri tres. Ex Codd. MSS. undecim, nunc primum Graece editus*, Oxonii, e Theatro Sheldoniano, 1682; facs. New York, Broude Brothers, 1977; ed. I. Düring in *Die Harmonielehre des Klaudios Ptolemaios*, Göteborg, Elanders, 1930; facs. New York, Garland, 1980; Ger. trans. I. Düring in *Ptolemaios und Porphyrios über die Musik*, Göteborg, Elanders, 1934; facs. New York, Garland, 1980

Sextus Empiricus, ed. and Fr. trans. C.-E. Ruelle as *Contre les musiciens (Livre VI du traité contre les savants)*, Paris, Firmin-Didot, 1898; trans. R. G. Bury as "Against the Musicians," in vol. iv of *Sextus Empiricus in Four Volumes*, Loeb Classical Library, Cambridge, MA, Harvard University Press, 1933–49, pp. 372–405; ed. J. Mau, *Sexti Empirici opera*, 4 vols., Leipzig, Teubner, 1954–62; ed. and trans. D. D. Greaves as *Against the Musicians (Adversus musicos)*, Lincoln, University of Nebraska Press, 1986

Theon of Smyrna, ed. E. Hiller, *Theonis Smyrnaei philosophi Platonici, Expositio rerum mathematicarum ad legendum Platonem utilium*, Leipzig, Teubner, 1878; facs. New York, Garland, 1987; Fr. trans. J. Dupuis as *Théon de Smyrne philosophe platonicien exposition des connaissances mathématiques utiles pour la lecture de Platon*, Paris, Hachette, 1892; facs. Brussels, Culture et Civilisation, 1966; trans. R. and D. Lawlor from J. Dupuis as *Mathematics Useful for Understanding Plato*, San Diego, CA, Wizards Bookshelf, 1979

General accounts

Anderson, W. D. *Music and Musicians in Ancient Greece*, Ithaca, Cornell University Press, 1994

Bélis, A. *Les Musiciens dans l'antiquité*, Paris, Hachette, 1999

Chailley, J. *La Musique grecque antique*, Paris, Belles Lettres, 1979

Comotti, G. *Music in Greek and Roman Culture*, trans. R. V. Munson, Baltimore, Johns Hopkins University Press, 1989

Gentili, B., and R. Pretagostini, eds., *La musica in Grecia*, Rome and Bari, Laterza, 1988

Gevaert, F. A. *Histoire et théorie de la musique de l'antiquité*, 2 vols., Ghent, Annoot-Braeckman, 1875–81

Henderson, I. "Ancient Greek Music," in *Ancient and Oriental Music*, ed. E. Wellesz, London, Oxford University Press, 1957, pp. 336–403

Mathiesen, T. J. *Apollo's Lyre: Greek Music and Music Theory in Antiquity and the Middle Ages*, Lincoln, University of Nebraska Press, 1999

Neubecker, A. J. *Altgriechische Musik: Eine Einführung*, Darmstadt, Wissenschaftliche Buchgesellschaft, 1977
Riethmüller, A., and F. Zaminer, eds., *Die Musik des Altertums*, Laaber, Laaber Verlag, 1989
Rossbach, A., and R. Westphal, *Theorie der musischen Künste der Hellenen*, 4 vols. in 3, Leipzig, Teubner, 1885–89; facs. Hildesheim, G. Olms, 1966
Wegner, M. *Das Musikleben der Griechen*, Berlin, W. de Gruyter, 1949
West, M. L. *Ancient Greek Music*, Oxford, Clarendon, 1992

Pythagorean theory and the harmony of the spheres

Barbera, A. "The Consonant Eleventh and the Expansion of the Musical Tetraktys," *JMT* 28 (1984), pp. 191–224
"The Persistence of Pythagorean Mathematics in Ancient Musical Thought," Ph.D. diss., University of North Carolina – Chapel Hill (1980)
"Placing *Sectio canonis* in Historical and Philosophical Contexts," *Journal of Hellenic Studies* 104 (1984), pp. 157–61
"*Republic* 530c–531c: Another Look at Plato and the Pythagoreans," *American Journal of Philology* 102 (1981), pp. 395–410
Barker, A. "Ptolemy's Pythagoreans, Archytas, and Plato's Conception of Mathematics," *Phronesis* 39 (1994), pp. 113–35
Bowen, A. C. "Euclid's *sectio canonis* and the History of Pythagoreanism," in *Science and Philosophy in Classical Greece*, ed. A. C. Bowen, New York, Garland, 1991, pp. 164–87
"The Foundations of Early Pythagorean Harmonic Science: Archytas, Fragment 1," *Ancient Philosophy* 2 (1982), pp. 79–104
Burkert, W. *Lore and Science in Ancient Pythagoreanism*, trans. E. L. Minar, Jr., Cambridge, MA, Harvard University Press, 1972
Crocker, R. "Pythagorean Mathematics and Music," *Journal of Aesthetics and Art Criticism* 22 (1963–1964), pp. 189–98, 325–35
Haase, R. *Geschichte des harmonikalen Pythagoreismus*, Vienna, E. Lafite, 1969
Jahoda, G. "Die Tonleiter des *Timaios* – Bild und Abbild," in *Festschrift Rudolf Haase*, ed. W. Schulze, Eisenstadt, Elfriede Rötzer, 1980, pp. 43–80
Levin, F. R. *The Harmonics of Nicomachus and the Pythagorean Tradition*, University Park, PA, American Philological Association, 1975
McClain, E. G. "Plato's Musical Cosmology," *Main Currents in Modern Thought* 30 (1973), pp. 34–42
"A New Look at Plato's *Timaeus*," *Music and Man* 1 (1975), pp. 341–60
The Pythagorean Plato: Prelude to the Song Itself, Stony Brook, NY, N. Hays, 1978
Zaminer, F. "Pythagoras und die Anfänge des musiktheoretischen Denkens bei den Griechen," *Jahrbuch des Staatlichen Instituts für Musikforschung* (1979–80), pp. 203–11

Aristoxenus, Aristoxenians, and harmonicist theory

Auda, A. *Les Gammes musicales. Essai historique sur les modes et sur les tons de la musique depuis l'antiquité jusqu'à l'époque moderne*, Woluwé-St.-Pierre, Edition nationale belge, 1947

Barbera, A. "Octave Species," *JM* 3 (1984), pp. 229–41

Barker, A. "Aristoxenus' Harmonics and Aristotle's Theory of Science," in *Science and Philosophy in Classical Greece*, ed. A. C. Bowen, New York, Garland, 1991, pp. 188–226

"Aristoxenus' Theorems and the Foundations of Harmonic Science," *Ancient Philosophy* 4 (1984), pp. 23–64

"*OI ΚΑΛΟΥΜΕΝΟΙ ἉΡΜΟΝΙΚΟΙ*: The Predecessors of Aristoxenus," *Proceedings of the Cambridge Philological Society* 24 (1978), pp. 1–21

"Music and Perception: A Study in Aristoxenus," *Journal of Hellenic Studies* 98 (1978), pp. 9–16

Bélis, A. *Aristoxène de Tarente et Aristote: Le Traité d'harmonique*, Paris, Klincksieck, 1986

Chailley, J. *L'Imbroglio des modes*, Paris, Leduc, 1960

"Nicomaque, Aristote et Terpandre devant la transformation de l'heptacorde grec en octocorde," *Yuval* 1 (1968), pp. 132–54

Crocker, R. "Aristoxenus and Greek Mathematics," in *Aspects of Medieval and Renaissance Music: A Birthday Offering to Gustave Reese*, ed. J. LaRue, New York, Norton, 1966, pp. 96–110

Levin, F. R. "*Synesis* in Aristoxenian Theory," *Transactions of the American Philological Association* 103 (1972), pp. 211–34

Litchfield, M. "Aristoxenus and Empiricism: A Reevaluation Based on His Theories," *JMT* 32 (1988), pp. 51–73

Richter, L. "Die Aufgaben der Musiklehre nach Aristoxenos und Klaudios Ptolemaios," *AfMw* 15 (1958), pp. 209–29

Solomon, J. "Towards a History of *Tonoi*," *JM* 3 (1984), pp. 242–51

Winnington-Ingram, R. P. "Aristoxenus and the Intervals of Greek Music," *Classical Quarterly* 26 (1932), pp. 195–208

Mode in Ancient Greek Music, Cambridge University Press, 1936; reprint Amsterdam, Hakkert, 1968

Influence and history of scholarship

Barbera, A. "Reconstructing Lost Byzantine Sources for MSS Vat. BAV gr. 2338 and Ven. BNM gr. VI.3: What Is an Ancient Treatise?," in *Music Theory and Its Sources: Antiquity and the Middle Ages*, ed. A. Barbera, South Bend, Notre Dame University Press, 1990, pp. 38–67

Düring, I. "Impact of Greek Music on Western Civilization," in *Proceedings of the Second International Congress of Classical Studies* (1954), Copenhagen, E. Munksgaard, 1958, pp. 169–84

Fellerer, K. G. "Zur Erforschung der antiken Musik im 16.–18. Jahrhundert," *Jahrbuch der Musikbibliothek Peters* 42 (1936), pp. 84–95

Holbrook, A. "The Concept of Musical Consonance in Greek Antiquity and Its Application in the Earliest Medieval Descriptions of Polyphony," Ph.D. diss., University of Washington (1983)

Mathiesen, T. J. "Aristides Quintilianus and the *Harmonics* of Manuel Bryennius: A Study in Byzantine Music Theory," *JMT* 27 (1983), pp. 31–47

"*Ars critica* and *fata libellorum*: The Significance of Codicology to Text Critical Theory," in

Music Theory and Its Sources: Antiquity and the Middle Ages, ed. A. Barbera, South Bend, Notre Dame University Press, 1990, pp. 19–37

"Hermes or Clio? The Transmission of Ancient Greek Music Theory," in *Musical Humanism and Its Legacy: Essays in Honor of Claude V. Palisca*, ed. B. R. Hanning and N. K. Baker, Stuyvesant, NY, Pendragon, 1992, pp. 3–35

Moyer, A. E. *Musica scientia: Musical Scholarship in the Italian Renaissance*, Ithaca, Cornell University Press, 1992

Palisca, C. V. *Humanism in Italian Renaissance Musical Thought*, New Haven, Yale University Press, 1985

Pöhlmann, E. "Antikenverständnis und Antikenmißverständnis in der Operntheorie der Florentiner Camerata," *Die Musikforschung* 22 (1969), pp. 5–13

Richter, L. "Antike Überlieferungen in der byzantinischen Musiktheorie," *Deutsches Jahrbuch der Musikwissenschaft* 6 (1962), pp. 75–115

Turrell, F. B. "Modulation: An Outline of Its Prehistory from Aristoxenus to Henry Glarean," Ph.D. diss., University of Southern California (1956)

Zaminer, F. "Griechische Musiktheorie und das Problem ihrer Rezeption," in *Über Musiktheorie. Referate der Arbeitstagung 1970 in Berlin*, ed. F. Zaminer, Cologne, Arno Volk, 1970, pp. 9–14

·5·

The transmission of ancient music theory into the Middle Ages

CALVIN M. BOWER

The chronicle of musical thought in the Latin world from the beginning of the Common Era through the first millennium of European history presents a metamorphosis of various intellectual traditions into what we today call "music theory." The adjectives "middle" and "dark" hardly apply to these ages when one is writing the history of musical thought, for these centuries witness the beginning – indeed the birth – of that Western discipline which attempts to reflect systematically about given musical phenomena and apply these reflections to the analysis and composition of musical repertoires. While one might speak of *a* tradition of musical thought during the early Middle Ages, the integrity of that tradition is achieved not by any continuous thread that runs through the whole, but by a number of overlapping strands that give strength to a broad tradition. Often these strands forming the very core of musical thought draw their character from traditions other than music, and the continuity of musical reflections must be viewed from proximate perspectives.

While the first millennium saw the birth of Christianity and the flourishing musical liturgy built principally around psalmody,[1] in the first centuries of the new millennium the study of music theory as a technical discipline remained largely isolated from the fresh artistic tradition. The development of musical learning in the Latin West basically grew from the technical subject formulated by the ancient Greeks, namely *musica* (*μουσική*) or *harmonica* (*ἁρμονικά*). (see also **Chapter 4, pp. 109–35**). Hence in the early sections of this chapter, music theory as a general discipline will be referred to as *musica* to distinguish it from "music," which would imply the totality of musical experience, practical and theoretical, or from "music theory," which would imply some relation between a repertoire and systematic reflections concerning music.

Since the transmission of ancient thought into these ages was both limited and enriched by the intellectual and spiritual contexts in which it was received, the history of *musica* in the early Middle Ages cannot be separated from the history of education, of philosophy, and of learning in general. The first part of this chapter, therefore, must describe the broad intellectual stage on which *musica* first appeared. Yet *musica* could not remain unmoved by the vital, contemporaneous culture of liturgical chant, particularly

1 For a lucid discussion of the rise of music in Christian worship, particularly as part of the Mass, see James McKinnon, *The Advent Project: The Later Seventh-Century Creation of the Roman Mass Proper* (Berkeley, Los Angeles, London: University of California Press, 2000).

as that movement gained momentum in the ninth and tenth centuries; hence the second section of this chapter will address the initial interaction between *musica* and *cantus*, and the intellectual and artistic synthesis that represents the beginnings of "music theory." The brush strokes in this history covering more than a thousand years are of necessity broad, and many important details are never introduced into the narrative. Nevertheless the six sections of this two-part chapter may serve as a multi-focal lens through which one can gain a view of the intellectual and artistic forces that shaped musical thought during the first millennium of the Common Era.[2]

Musica in the late Roman and early medieval worlds

Musica *in the Roman rhetorical tradition*

Musica first appeared in Roman education as a discipline fundamental to the formation of the orator – that Roman patrician who was expected to lead and shape his society through eloquence and persuasion. Certain disciplines (*artes*) were considered essential to the training of the person born free of servile and commercial obligations (the *homo liber*), and these disciplines came to be known as the *artes liberales*, or the "free" or "liberal arts." The great Roman encyclopedist Marcus Terentius Varro (first century BCE), had written a seminal work on the disciplines appropriate to the education of the free man, *Nine Books on the Disciplines* (*Disciplinarum libri IX*), a work (now lost) that offered introductions to nine disciplines: grammar, dialectic, rhetoric, geometry, arithmetic, astrology, music, medicine, and architecture. Traces of the Roman hortatory tradition of the study of the arts can be found in the *Fundamentals of Oratory* (*Institutio oratoria*) of Quintilian and in Vitruvius's *On Architecture* (*De architectura*).[3]

Music and the other arts were hardly considered fields worthy of study for any noble end among the Roman orators. The principal goal for learning *musica* seemed to have been mastering a repertoire of facts and references that might be dropped in a speech at an appropriate moment, thereby making a favorable impression and giving the orator more credibility. The content of the brief sections on music among these

2 While the present narrative of music theory during the early Middle Ages is in many ways different from that of Michael Bernhard, I must express my debt at the beginning of this essay to the survey of ancient and medieval theory offered by my colleague in "Überlieferung und Fortleben der antiken lateinischen Musiktheorie im Mittelalter" and "Das musikalische Fachschrifttum im lateinischen Mittelalter." These two essays are fundamental to any history of medieval theory, and could be cited in virtually every paragraph that follows.

3 For a general introduction to the role of music in the Roman world, see Günther Wille, *Musica romana. Die Bedeutung der Musik im Leben der Römer* (Amsterdam: P. Schippers, 1967), and *Einführung in das römische Musikleben* (Darmstadt: Wissenschaftliche Buchgesellschaft, 1977); the lost work of Varro is placed in historical context in William Harris Stahl, Richard Johnson, and E. L. Burge, *Martianus Capella and the Seven Liberal Arts*, vol. 1, *The Quadrivium of Martianus Capella, Latin Traditions in the Mathematical Sciences, 50 B.C.–A.D.1250* (New York and London: Columbia University Press, 1971), pp. 96–97 and *passim*.

Table 5.1 *Late Roman and early medieval authors and texts*

Cicero (d. 43 BCE)	*De re publica*
Varro (d. 27 BCE)	*Displinarum libri IX*
Vitruvius (d. before 27 BCE)	*De architectura*
Quintilian (d. c. 100 CE)	*Institutio oratoria*
Censorinus	*De die natali* (238 CE)
Calcidius (4th c.)	*Timaeus . . . translatus commentarioque instructus*
Macrobius (c. 400)	*Commentarii in somnium Scipionis*
Martianus Capella (before 439)	*De nuptiis Philologiae et Mercurii*
Augustine (354–430)	*De musica* (387–89) *De ordine* *De doctrina christiana*
Favonius Eulogius (5th c.)	*Disputatio in somnium Scipionis*
Boethius (early 6th c.)	*De institutione arithmetica* *De institutione musica*
Cassiodorus (after 540)	*Institutiones*
Isidore (d. 636)	*Etymologiae*

authors reflects a superficial understanding of Greek tonal systems, enumerates notable persons from Greek antiquity who were inventors of musical instruments or able performers, and repeats various myths and accounts of the affective potential of instrumental and vocal music.

The arts designated as "liberal" were by no means a canon among ancient Latin authors, and the number of arts seems to have varied to fit the occasion. Thus it is remarkable that music is invariably counted among the disciplines worthy of the free man among ancient authors (see Table 5.2).

The figure who seems to have been instrumental in establishing the number of arts at seven – and indeed in establishing the canon of the arts for the later Middle Ages – was the North African writer Martianus Capella.[4] While writing in the early fifth century, Martianus clearly reflects several aspects of the Roman rhetorical tradition: the order of the arts (excluding medicine and architecture) is similar to that of Varro; the chapters on the individual arts are relatively brief and represent little more than basic introductions to the disciplines; and the treatment of the last four arts – arithmetic, geometry, astronomy, and music – shows little grasp of the underlying mathematical principles developed by earlier Greek authors.

4 Concerning Martianus Capella, see James A Willis, "Martianus Capella and His Early Commentators" (Ph.D. diss., University of London, 1952); Stahl, Johnson, and Burge, *Martianus Capella*; Danuta Schanzer, "Three Textual Problems in Martianus Capella," *Classical Philology* 79 (1984), pp. 142–45; and *A Philosophical and Literary Commentary on Martianus Capella's De Nuptiis Philologiae et Mercurii Book I* (Berkeley, Los Angeles, London: University of California Press, 1986).

Table 5.2 *The place of* musica *in the liberal arts*

	Varro (1st c. BCE)	Martianus (5th c. CE)	Boethius (6th c. CE)	Cassiodorus (6th c. CE)	Isisdore (7th c. CE)
i	Grammar	Grammar		Grammar	Grammar
ii	Dialectic	Dialectic		Rhetoric	Rhetoric
iii	Rhetoric	Rhetoric		Dialectic	Dialectic
iv	Geometry	Geometry	Arithmetic	Arithmetic	Arithmetic
v	Arithmetic	Arithmetic	Music	Music	Geometry
vi	Astrology	Astronomy	Geometry	Geometry	Music
vii	Music	Harmony	Astronomy	Astronomy	Astronomy
viii	Medicine				Medicine
ix	Architecture				

Yet the tone of Martianus's presentation is strikingly different from that of the earlier Roman patricians. Martianus's treatise is entitled *The Marriage of Philology and Mercury* (*De nuptiis Philologiae et Mercurii*); Philology and Mercury symbolize human and divine intellect, and their wedding represents the union of the human intellect with that of the gods. The arts in Martianus's allegory are wedding gifts personified as maidens, and each of the maidens represents an art by which the human intellect may rise to the level of the divine. The arts of medicine and architecture are rejected because they deal with mortal matters and their skills are mundane.[5]

Throughout Martianus's allegory harmony (or *musica*) holds a unique position, for the order of the cosmos itself is set out according to harmonic principles, and music, unlike some of the other arts, is treated in the first two books that set the stage for the allegory as well as the last book that reveals *Harmonia* herself: in the final book she is presented as a bridesmaid particularly cherished in the heavenly realm.[6]

Thus Martianus transformed the Roman rhetorical tradition of the arts as evidence of humane erudition into a tradition in which the arts were intellectual disciplines that enabled the human mind to rise to the level of divine intellect. This new status of music and the other arts resonated well with an essentially Platonic exposition of music and the other mathematical disciplines that had developed in the time between Varro's introduction to the *artes liberales* and Martianus's allegory.[7]

Musica *and the late Latin Platonists*

In the first century BCE, Marcus Tullius Cicero concluded his philosophical treatise *The Republic* (*De re publica*) with a moving account of the ascent of the soul to

5 *De nuptiis* 339, 3–7; all textual references to Martianus follow the page and line numbers in the Willis edition 6 Ibid. 339, 7–10.

7 Concerning the place of Martianus in medieval Platonism, see Stephen Gersh, *Middle Platonism and Neoplatonism: The Latin Tradition* (Notre Dame: University of Notre Dame Press, 1986), pp. 597–646.

knowledge of its own immortality; Cicero's narrative is known as the *Dream of Scipio* (*Somnium Scipionis*). When viewing the marvels of the cosmos, Cicero's soul inquires concerning the nature of the wondrous sound filling its ears, and is told that the harmony results from the motion of the spheres that are spaced according to musical ratios. Only souls who search for truth, along with certain musicians who can imitate the heavenly order in their playing and singing, are able to hear these celestial tones.[8]

To ancient and medieval scholars in the Platonic[9] tradition – to which Cicero's philosophical works belong[10] – the ratios that governed the highest order of the physical universe and the metaphysical world itself were those that determined musical concord, and the degree to which sensual music was shaped by these ratios, was the degree to which the soul was led away from rank sensuality to contemplate eternal truths. The most important source for a narrative of the creator's application of arithmetic ratios and musical intervals was found in Plato's account in *Timaeus* of the creation of the world soul.[11] In the fourth century, Calcidius translated this section of *Timaeus* into Latin, replete with arithmetic and musical commentary and diagrams concerning the ratios and intervals.[12] Early medieval scholars sensed the resonance between Cicero's *Somnium Scipionis* and Plato's *Timaeus*; Macrobius (c. 400) and Favonius Eulogius (fifth century) both wrote commentaries on Cicero's text that emphasized the mathematical ratios and musical intervals, and that discussed at length the ratios Plato's demiurge applied in creating the world soul.[13]

The figure of Augustine, the famous saint of North Africa and bishop of Hippo, was a dominating force in the intellectual history of the Middle Ages, and, albeit indirectly, a powerful influence on musical thought during that formative period. Augustine's much celebrated conversion in 387 marked the major turning point in his intellectual as well as his spiritual life, and more than one modern scholar has suggested that the conversion was as much to neo-Platonism as to Christianity.[14] In the months and years immediately

8 See *De re publica* vi.17–18 (Keyes edn., pp. 272–73).

9 In this essay I use the term "Platonist" very broadly to embrace both pure Platonism (if there is such a thing) and the neo-Platonism of the early common era; properly speaking, most of the authors treated in this chapter would be termed "neo-Platonists."

10 Concerning Cicero's place among Platonists, see Gersh, *Middle Platonism and Neoplatonism*, pp. 55–154.

11 See Francis M. Cornford, *Plato's Cosmology, The* Timaeus *of Plato Translated with a Running Commentary* (New York: The Liberal Arts Press, 1957); Jacques Handschin, "The Timaeus Scale," *Musica disciplina* 4 (1950), pp. 3–42.

12 For a concise summary of Calcidius, see Thomas J. Mathiesen, *Apollo's Lyre: Greek Music and Music Theory in Antiquity and the Middle Ages* (Lincoln, NB and London: University of Nebraska Press, 1999), pp. 616–19.

13 For a general discussion of Macrobius, see Introduction to Stahl trans.; See also Mathiesen, *Apollo's Lyre*, pp. 617–18.

14 Concerning the role of Platonism in the Christian formation of the young Augustine, see especially John J. O'Meara, *The Young Augustine: The Growth of St. Augustine's Mind up to his Conversion* (Staten Island: Alba House, 1965), esp. pp. 131–155; see also Dominic J. O'Meara, "The Neoplatonism of Saint Augustine," in *Neoplatonism and Christian Thought*, ed. D. J. O'Meara (Norfolk: International Society of Neoplatonic Studies, 1982), pp. 34–41. For a broader study of Augustine, see Peter Brown, *Augustine of Hippo: A Biography*, new edn. with an epilogue (Berkeley and Los Angeles: University of California Press, 2000).

following the famous scene in the garden of Milan, Augustine surrounded himself with austere and high-minded Christian scholars, and during these years he wrote a series of works that are distinctly philosophical in character. One was a treatise on music.

In his *On Music* (*De musica*) Augustine allies himself with the Pythagorean tradition of ancient Greek musical thought and the Platonic philosophical tradition. The matter of musical discipline is number, specifically the ratios that govern musical consonances. The first five books of Augustine's treatise apply the theory of ratios not to musical pitch or consonances, but to quantitative verse, that is, to the metrics of the corpus of Latin poetry beloved and taught by the young Augustine. The final book of *On Music*, on the other hand, uses number and ratios as a way to lead the reader away from the corporeal world of sound; for the ratios first encountered in poetic meters can lead the soul to appreciate harmony as abstract truth, and thence to philosophical knowledge, indeed to knowledge of God.[15]

While music as a manifestation of beauty appears repeatedly in the works of Augustine, and while he was obviously moved by song,[16] his chief role in the development of musical theory lies in his establishing two traditions within early Christian thought: (1) in *On Christian Doctrine* (*De doctrina christiana*) and *Order in the Universe* (*De ordine*) – as well as in several other works – Augustine justified secular learning, in particular the liberal arts, as integral to the proper formation of the Christian; (2) in these works, and more specifically in his *De musica*, he set forth the principle that music was one of the disciplines that enabled the mind to transcend sensual reality and rise to a knowledge of rational truth, to a knowledge of the divine. In a civilization that could have all too easily taken a turn toward the suppression of secular learning, Augustine's episcopal and spiritual authority became a crucial apology for preserving and cultivating ancient knowledge concerning the arts, particularly *musica*.

Anicius Manlius Severinus Boethius (480-525/26) was the most prolific and the most influential scholar in the Platonic tradition of the early Middle Ages.[17] Greatly influenced by Greek writers such as Nicomachus, Ptolemy, Euclid, Plato, and Aristotle, the young Boethius set out to write works treating arithmetic, music, geometry, and astronomy as disciplines that lead the soul to its first encounter with incorporeal knowledge. He expressed little interest in the Roman liberal arts of grammar, rhetoric, and dialectic;[18] in the introduction to his *De arithmetica*, however, he defined an educational program in the mathematical disciplines that influenced the study of *musica* for over a millennium. Boethius, following Pythagorean and neo-Platonic

15 For a general survey of Augustine's view of music, see Herbert M Schueller, *The Idea of Music: An Introduction to Musical Aesthetics in Antiquity and the Middle Ages* (Kalamazoo: Medieval Institute Publications, Western Michigan University, 1998), esp. pp. 239–56.

16 See, for example, the famous passage from the *Confessions* x.33, trans. James McKinnon in *SR*, pp. 132–33.

17 For a thorough examination of Boethius's thought, see Henry Chadwick, *Boethius: The Consolations of Music, Logic, Theology, and Philosophy* (Oxford: Clarendon Press, 1981).

18 I imply not that Boethius was not interested in logic, but that logic was not merely an art of elocution for Boethius as it was for earlier Roman writers; indeed, Boethius's translations of Aristotle's Prior and Posterior Analytics testify to Boethius's view of logic's position in philosophy.

	(1)		(2)		(3)		(4)
	256	:	243	:	216	:	192
			= 9	:	8 *and* 9	:	8
e.g.	E		F		G		A

Figure 5.1 The Pythagorean tetrachord

authors before him, held that quantity was divided into two basic genera: discrete quantity – or multitude; and continuous quantity – or magnitude. The *monad*, or unity, was the source of discrete quantity, and this genus could increase into infinite multitude; yet its basic element, unity, remained indivisible. Magnitude, or continuous quantity, might be represented by the line or a shape, which was delimited with respect to increasing and growth, but could be infinitely divided. The two basic genera of quantity were, in turn, subdivided into two species: multitude is best represented by number, and every number can be considered in and of itself (even, odd, perfect, square, cube, etc), or it can be considered in relation to another (in ratios and proportions – e.g., 2:1, 3:2, or 6:4:2); magnitude is best represented by shapes, and some shapes are fixed and immobile (e.g., a line, a triangle, a cube), while others are in motion (e.g., the sun, the moon, the heavenly spheres). Four areas of study were thus defined by the very nature of quantity: *arithmetic* pursued number in and of itself; *music* examined number in ratios and proportions; *geometry* considered immobile magnitudes; *astronomy* investigated magnitudes in motion. Boethius described these four disciplines as the *quadrivium*, the fourfold path by which the soul was led from the slavery of sensual knowledge to the mastery of knowing immutable essences. *Musica* thus became a necessary prerequisite to the study of philosophy.[19]

Boethius opens his *Fundamentals of Music* (*De institutione musica*) with a grand juxtaposition of sensual experience and reasoned truth that is worthy of the Roman rhetorical tradition. Of all the mathematical disciplines, music is unique; for music is the most sensual of the arts, and can thus influence behavior, can determine character. Boethius proceeded to develop a theory of sound that was quantitative, and argued that the rational person must cultivate a music structured according to principles that were themselves rational, principles that reflected the most consonant essences found in that species of quantity expressed in beautiful ratios and proportions. For Boethius – and indeed for the Pythagoreans and neo-Platonists – those essences were discovered neither by rational deduction nor by induction from sensual experience; they were revealed truths. The following account represents a condensed paraphrase of the myth from *Fundamentals of Music* i.10:

> Pythagoras had long sought the rational criteria that determined musical consonances. One day, by divine guidance, he passed a smithy from which the sounds of musical harmonies emerged. He approached the place with amazement, for pitches sounding consonant with each other seemed to come from the hammers. He examined the weights of

19 See *De institutione arithmetica* i.1; *De institutione musica* ii.3.

> the hammers and discovered that one weighed 12 pounds, a second 9 pounds, a third 8 pounds, and a fourth 6 pounds. The hammers of 12 and 6 pounds sounded the octave – that interval in which the two pitches were most identical. The hammers of 12 and 8 pounds, as well as those of 9 and 6 pounds, sounded the fifth – an interval which, next to the octave, was most beautiful. The hammers of 12 and 9 pounds, as well as those of 8 and 6 pounds, sounded the fourth – that interval which seemed to be the smallest consonance. In this manner Pythagoras discovered the ratios – the immutable essences – of musical harmonies: the octave lay in the ratio of 2 : 1; the fifth was determined by the ratio of 3 : 2; and the fourth was found in the ratio of 4 : 3. Moreover, since the basic building block of music, the tone, was the difference between a fourth and a fifth, the ratio of that interval was the difference between 3 : 2 (or 12 : 8) and 4 : 3 (or 12 : 9), thus 9 : 8.[20]

The roots of this myth so fundamental to the history of Western musical thought are buried within ancient values and archetypes that can never be fully fathomed. The empirical data offered in the myth is wholly specious, for hammers of comparable weights would not sound the musical intervals presented in the story.[21] However, the myths and dreams of a civilization are judged not by their empirical truth or falsity, but by the expression of intellectual and spiritual complexes they reveal within a culture. Given the four mathematical values revealed in the myth of the hammers, and given the position that sound was quantitative and that musical intervals could be scientifically measured only by ratios, the Pythagoreans and Platonists unfolded the musical cosmos of the diatonic scale and developed an arithmetic apparatus that presented some of the most rigorous mathematical reckoning known in antiquity and the Middle Ages.

The fundamental building block of the Pythagorean scale was the tetrachord, four notes – three intervals – defined by the fourth. The diatonic tetrachord contained two tones (each 9:8) plus a remainder (limma), which was called the "semitone" – not because it was half of a tone, but because it was less than a whole tone (see also **Chapter 4, pp. 115–16**). The ratio of the remainder, the semitone, was 256:243, a measure defended as the legitimate interval of the semitone at excessive length by Boethius following other Pythagoreans. In keeping with traditional Greek tetrachordal structures, the semitone was the lowest interval of a tetrachord (Figure 5.1).

Boethius offered a "history" of the Greek tonal system (i.20) that is as mythic in tone as the "history" of Pythagoras and the smithy – but myth had been established by Plato himself as a primary vehicle for leading the reader toward philosophical truths. Two fundamental collections of pitches unfold built on the principle of conjunct and disjunct tetrachords: (1) a two-octave, "disjunct" system, and (2) an octave-plus-fourth, "conjunct" system (Table 5.3).[22]

20 For the Latin text of this myth, see Friedlein edn., 19616–198.8; for complete text in English see Bower trans., pp. 17–19. Also see **Chapter 10, p. 272**.

21 See Claude V. Palisca, "Scientific Empiricism in Musical Thought," in *Seventeenth-Century Science and the Arts*, ed. H. H. Rhys (Princeton: Princeton University Press, 1961), pp. 127–29; see also Walter Burkert, *Lore and Science in Ancient Pythagoreanism*, trans. E. L. Minar, Jr. (Cambridge, MA: Harvard University Press, 1972), pp. 374–77.

22 For the Latin text of this mythic history see Friedlein ed., 205.27–212.22; for English text, see Bower trans., pp. 29–39.

Table 5.3 *Disjunct and conjunct systems from* Fundamentals of Music

Two-octave system (systema teleion) Names: of notes	of tetrachords	Octave-plus-fourth system (systema synemmenon) Names: of notes	of tetrachords	Letters for pitches: iv.6–11	iv.14	iv.18	Modern pitches
Proslambanomenos		Proslambanomenos		A		P	A
	(disjunct)		(disjunct)				
Hypate	hypaton	Hypate	hypaton	B	A	O	B
Parhypate		Parhypate		C	B	N	C
Lichanos		Lichanos		E	C	M	D
Hypate	meson (conjunct)	Hypate	meson (conj.)	H	D	L	E
Parhypate		Parhypate		I	E	K	F
Lichanos		Lichanos		M	F	I	G

Mese		Mese	(conj.)	O		G	H	a
	(disjunct)	Trite	synemmenon		Q			b♭
Paramese	diezeugmenon			X		H	G	b
Trite		Paranete		Y	T	K	R	c
Paranete		Nete		CC	V	L	E	d
Nete	hyperboleon (conjunct)			DD		M	D	e
Paranete				FF		N	C	f
Trite				KK		X	B	g
Nete				LL		O	A	a^1

After all mathematical essences had been exhaustively examined in the course of the first three books of his treatise, Boethius took up the division of the musical ruler (division of the canon), a line divided geometrically over which a string can be placed and "notes" may be tested by positioning a movable bridge at points of division (see also Chapter 6, pp. 168–69). Boethius undertakes this division (1) to demonstrate how the Pythagorean arithmetic and geometric apparatus can shape a whole musical system and (2) to confirm the veracity of the ratios to the sense of hearing.[23] In the course of the monochord division Boethius uses ancient Greek notation, a notation he takes up again when discussing the ancient Greek modes; but equally significant – indeed more significant – to the history of music theory, Boethius employs various letters to represent geometric points in the division of the ruler, points which in turn designate and represent specific "strings" or "notes." A single pitch within a collection could thus be assigned a discrete symbol, and could be "noted" by that symbol in subsequent discussions of functions within the collection.[24] While Boethius had no intention of using these letters as any form of "notation," the abbreviated, objective representation of a function within a set of pitches clearly becomes possible; a basic step in the development of "noting" pitches within a collection had been taken.

In the opening chapters of his treatise, Boethius developed his threefold division of music: cosmic music (*musica mundana*), which was subdivided into the harmony of the spheres, the concord of the elements, and the consonance of the seasons; human music (*musica humana*), which was subdivided into the harmony of the soul and the body, the consonance of the parts of the soul, and the concord of the parts of the body; and instrumental music (*musica in instrumentis constituta*), which is subdivided into string, wind, and percussion instruments.[25] In the closing chapter of the first book, Boethius elaborated his threefold division of those who might be named "musicians": instrumentalists (or performers), poets (or composers), and those who adjudicate performers and composers; only the last class is a true musician, according to Boethius, for only this class is concerned with knowing, through reason, the fundamental essences which determine the value of performances and compositions.[26]

Boethius's justly famous divisions of music and musicians link him most closely with the Platonic tradition of musical thought: the essences expressed in ratios pervade every level of being, and by coming to know these essences – even in the corporeal world of sound – the mind is able to transcend cursory sensory experience and rise to a higher level of knowing; it is reminded of these essences as it comes to know its own

23 While divisions of the chromatic and enharmonic genera are appended to this diatonic division, they are merely ancillary: the diatonic division clearly holds primary position in the theoretical consciousness of the Pythagorean, and the intervals necessary for these divisions (the second semitone and the quarter tone) are derived from diatonic intervals.

24 For Boethius's exposition of Greek notation, see *De institutione musica* iv.3–4 (Friedlein edn., 308–14; Bower trans., pp. 122–27). Boethius employs Latin letters to represent pitches throughout the work, but develops this aspect of theory very extensively in Book IV.

25 See Friedlein edn., 187.20–189.12; Bower trans. pp. 9–10.

26 Ibid., 224.25–225.15; p. 51.

being and as it studies nature and the cosmos. The goal of learning *musica* is to ascend to the level of reason. The fundamental principle motivating Platonic music theory is *knowing*, the acquisition of pure knowledge, and Boethius's threefold division of music and three classes of musicians resonate consistently with that principle. Every legitimate facet of *musica* was subject to quantification by Boethius: every function in the collection of pitches was calculated with a point on the ruler, was assigned a discrete number, and was noted with a geometric symbol (a letter); even basic elements in the theory of ancient tonality (the *tonoi* and the *harmonia*) were reduced to expositions of species of fourth, fifth, and octave – quantitative reductions that reveal little of musical function or effect. The beauty of this theoretical system – if one may so speak – lies in its internal consistency and its congruence with Platonic ontology and epistemology.

Yet the limitations of quantification in ancient musical thought must be recognized. The values that the Boethian *musicus* applied in his judgments were *a priori* principles grounded in abstract thought, not principles grounded in experience of actual music. The diatonic system derived from a limited number of ratios was computed with little – indeed *no* – reference to a musical repertoire. The names of the notes and tetrachords obviously had some functional correspondence in their origins, yet in the Latin theoretical tradition of the early Middle Ages no musical function or character is ascribed to any note; the construct exists as an abstract entity determined by arithmetic principles. While the Platonists – including Boethius – cannot be described as philosophical puritans taking no pleasure in song, they can be accused of abstracting values and principles from sound and moving ever upwards toward pure reason, thereby never returning to describe and analyze the structures and functions that dwelt in the sonorous matter of the music that, in the beginning, had so moved them.

Musica *and the early medieval encyclopedists*

Two writers occupy a crucial position in the transmission of ancient musical thought in the later Middle Ages, not because of the originality or significance of their thought, but because of the particular intellectual tradition within Western Christendom that they cultivated with respect to *musica*. Cassiodorus (c. 485–580) and Isidore (c. 570–636) were Christian intellectuals deeply influenced by the tradition of Christian humanism formulated by Augustine in such works as *De ordine* and *De doctrina christiana*. Each in his own way set out to pass secular learning on to his community and to posterity.

Cassiodorus had originally intended to found a Christian university in Rome, but following the decline and conquest of Rome around the middle of the sixth century, he retired to his native estate in the south of Italy and established a monastery where he compiled a great library of sacred and secular learning. Cassiodorus wrote a great two-volume encyclopedic work for his community, the *Introduction to Divine and Human Readings*. His first book examined Biblical and patristic scholarship, while his second book discussed secular learning. The seven liberal arts represented the organization of secular learning for Cassiodorus (see Table 5.2); his extended treatment of the first three arts – grammar, rhetoric, and dialectic – links his program of secular learning to the Roman rhetorical tradition. Yet he describes the arts of Boethius's quadrivium as *mathematica*, and, while their treatment is much more cursory than the arts of elocution, their sequence and organization reflect elements of the Platonic and neo-Pythagorean tradition.[27]

Isidore, an influential secular bishop residing in Seville, compiled his *Etymologies* in the early seventh century, and this encyclopedic work became one of the most universally known books of the Middle Ages. The *Etymologies* commences with a treatment of the liberal arts. And while Isidore obviously owes a great debt to the work of Cassiodorus, his order and treatment of the arts is rather distinctive: *musica* is given the rather unusual position of the sixth art, placed between geometry and astronomy (see Table 5.2).[28]

Both Cassiodorus and Isidore were leaders of Christian groups who wrote principally as a means of establishing an intellectual tradition within their respective communities – a monastery for the former, a diocese for the latter. Because of their offices and their spiritual characters, they introduced two new dimensions into reflections concerning music: (1) the presence of music in Biblical literature and (2) the centrality of singing in Christian worship. Both writers draw on Biblical passages to demonstrate the power of music, thereby supplementing pagan myth with Judeo-Christian narratives. Both authors are clearly moved by the singing of psalms in the liturgy, and begin to integrate the spheres of secular learning concerning *musica* with the sacred tradition of singing in worship. Cassiodorus considers the discipline of music essential to the study of the psalms, particularly since they make reference to so many musical instruments; moreover he discerns the active presence of musical concord in the singing of psalms, active both in the harmony immediately present in singing and the harmony achieved between the soul and God brought about through prayer and praise.[29] Isidore recognizes the ecclesiastical office of *cantor*, and seems so influenced by the practical activity of singing that subtle but fundamental changes in basic definitions are found in his writings: music is defined as skill (*peritia*) rather than knowledge (*scientia*),[30] and *musica* is said to consist in "songs and chants."[31] These authors thus began to break

27 Concerning Cassiodorus, see Günter Ludwig, *Cassiodor: Über den Ursprung der abendländischen Schule* (Frankfurt, 1967); James O'Donnell, *Cassiodorus* (Berkeley, Los Angeles, and London: University of California Press, 1979); Jacques Fontaine, "Cassiodore et Isidore: L'évolution de l'encyclopédisme latin du VIe au VIIe siècle," in *Atti della settimana di studi su Flavio Magno Aurelio Cassiodoro (Cosenza-Squillace 19–24 settembre 1983)*, ed. S. Leanza (Catanzaro: Soveria Mannelli, 1986), pp. 72–91; Ubaldo Pizzani, "Cassiodoro e le discipline del quadrivio," in ibid., pp. 49–71.

28 Concerning Isidore, see Jacques Fontaine, *Isidore de Séville et la culture classique dans l'Espagne Wisigothique*, 2nd rev. edn., 3 vols (Paris: Etudes Augustiniennes, 1983), esp. vol. I, pp. 413–40.

29 See *Expositio psalmorum*, ed M. Adriaen, Corpus Christianorum (1958), Series latina 98, p. 881.

30 *Etymologies* III.15: "musica est peritia modulationis sono cantuque consistens."

31 Ibid., I.2: "musica quae in carminibus cantibusque consistit."

down the boundaries that isolated the ancient discipline of *musica* – that collection of facts known by the orator and that Platonic sphere of learning leading to abstract knowledge – from the practice of music that was rapidly becoming an ever more significant part of the liturgy. They also played a crucial role in cultivating the tradition established by Augustine that secular learning, particularly the liberal arts, was an integral part of Christian education.

Formation of a medieval theoretical tradition in the Carolingian and post-Carolingian eras

The reception of ancient theory in the ninth and early tenth centuries

In the closing years of the eighth century and the opening decade of the ninth, Europe achieved a degree of cultural and political unity under Charlemagne (d. 814) that remains exceptional in the entire history of the West. Every aspect of culture – clerical and secular education, the Latin language, theology, the liturgy and the chant sung therein, scriptural texts, even the script employed in copying manuscripts – was subject to the Carolingian principle of unification through established order and style. Alcuin of York (d. 804), one of the leading scholars brought into educational reforms by Charlemagne, set both the intellectual tone and the program of study for his age when he compared the seven liberal arts with the seven pillars of Salomon's temple, and described them as seven steps leading to wisdom.[32] Thus Alcuin grounded Carolingian intellectual and spiritual formation in both the Roman rhetorical tradition and the Platonic tradition of the early Middle Ages, and gave *musica* an important place in that program.

The acquisition of manuscripts formed an important part of Charlemagne's conquests, and scholars such as Alcuin and Theodulf of Orléans (d. 821) encouraged the transport of manuscripts from remote boundaries of the new empire to Aachen, the intellectual and geographical center of the Carolingian court. The court library itself drew more scholars to the court, and the scholars in turn brought additional texts with them that became part of the library.[33] An important textual movement referred to by scholars as the Δ (Delta) tradition was introduced to the Carolingian court through the second book of Cassiodorus's *Introduction to Divine and Human Readings*.[34] This tradition brought together the justification for secular learning formulated by Cassiodorus,

32 *De vera philosophie* (*PL* 101, 849–54), 852B–853B.

33 On manuscript culture in the Carolingian period, see Bernhard Bischoff, "Manuscripts in the Age of Charlemagne," in *Manuscripts and Libraries in the Age of Charlemagne*, trans. and ed. Michael Gorman (Cambridge: Cambridge University Press, 1994), pp. 20–55; and "The Court Library of Charlemagne," in ibid., pp. 56–75.

34 Concerning the Δ tradition, see Bischoff, "The Court Library of Charlemagne," p. 62.

Table 5.4 *Authors and texts in Carolingian and post-Carolingian eras*

	Glossa maior in musicam Boethius
Johannes Scotus Eriugena (c. 810–c. 877)	*Annotationes in Marcianum*
Remigius of Auxerre (c. 841–c. 908)	*Commentum in Martianum Capellam*
Aurelian of Réôme	*Musica disciplina* (lost half of 9th c.)
Regino of Prüm (c. 840–915)	*Epistola de harmonica institutione* (c. 900)
	Musica et Scolica enchiriadis (late 9th c.)
Hucbald of Saint-Amand (c. 840–930)	*Musica* (c. 900)
Berno of Reichenau (c. 978–1048)	*Prologus in tonarium* (after 1021)
Hermanus Contractus (1013–54)	*Musica* (before 1054)
Wilhelmus of Hirsau (d. 1091)	*Musica* (before 1069)
Theogerus of Metz (d. 1120)	*Musica* (before 1120)
[Pseudo-Odo]	*Dialogus de musica* (c. 1000)
Guido of Arezzo (c. 900–c. 1050)	*Prologus in antiphonarium* (before 1025)
	Micrologus (1025/26)
	Regule rhythmice (1025/26)
	Epistola ad Michahelem (after 1028)

a number of excerpts from Augustine emphasizing the value of education (from *On Music*, *On Christian Doctrine*, *The Order of the Universe*, *The City of God*, and *First Meanings in Genesis*), and a précis of Boethius's *Fundamentals of Arithmetic*. Thus the principle of including secular learning – specifically the liberal arts – in Christian education established by Augustine and developed by Cassiodorus was taken up by scholars surrounding Charlemagne, and the liberal arts were given a privileged position in Carolingian learning.

Two works that were particularly significant in the tradition of *musica* began to be copied in and around the court of Charlemagne and dispersed throughout the empire: Martianus Capella's *Marriage of Mercury and Philology* and Boethius's *Fundamentals of Music*. An explicit reference to Boethius's musical treatise is even found among the texts brought together in the textual tradition of Cassiodorus used in the royal library. From these works early Carolingian scholars learned basic elements of Greek musical theory within the context of liberal learning. But both of these works were transcendent in tone rather than practical, and in their early reception they did little to focus the scholar's attention on the vital tradition of liturgical chant that was as integral to Carolingian civilization as the liberal arts.

The nature of the early ninth-century reception of *musica* can be traced using the extensive commentary copied into the margins and between the lines of manuscripts containing Martianus's and Boethius's treatises. The writers of these glosses were obviously scholars and philosophers, not musicians; for their primary concerns were

(1) explanation of Greek proper names and places using medieval principles of etymology, (2) definitions and explanations of technical terms inherited from the Greeks, (3) discussion of basic elements of Greek music theory – particularly the basic building blocks of the Greek musical systems, and (4) relating the whole of the discipline of music to the broader issues of philosophy. These scholars were particularly attracted to the advanced mathematical problems discussed in Boethius's text, and wrote numerous commentaries on the semitone, the apotome (2,187 : 2,048), and the Pythagorean comma (531,441 : 524,288). Their interest in ratios led them to an obsession with musical pitch, with the consequence that other parameters of music were largely ignored. Conspicuously absent from the early ninth-century commentaries on classical musical texts is any extended discussion of practical music.[35]

As the Carolingian kingdom was divided among his sons following the death of Charlemagne, and as the political unity of Europe waxed and waned during the course of the ninth century as kingdoms were repeatedly divided and unified, the vital culture that had originally been associated with the court moved into monasteries. The manuscript traditions originally associated with scholars not necessarily attached to a given location became established in monastic centers such as Corbie, Saint-Riquier, Saint-Denis, Fleury, Tours, Saint-Amand, and Ferrières. While monastic scholars were by nature drawn to theories of transcendence set forth in the Platonic tradition of *musica*, the singing of the liturgy played such a central role in their daily lives that they were unable or unwilling to divorce musical speculation from liturgical practice. Thus in the marginal commentaries on Boethius's musical treatise formulated in the late ninth century, musical intervals defined by ratios are likewise exemplified by musical examples taken from chant.[36] Pythagoras's discovery of the four ratios governing musical consonances is allegorized to represent the four tonal (or modal) qualities of liturgical chant: *protus*, *deuterus*, *tritus*, and *tetrardus*.[37] In short, monastic scholars began to connect concrete musical practice with abstract musical thought, and the synthesis that was to become medieval musical theory had begun.

The closing decades of the ninth century and the opening decade of the tenth also witness the beginnings of "writing" music theory; for two "theorists" from these years may be cited: Aurelian of Réôme and Regino of Prüm. Yet while "treatises" have been preserved associated with the names of these two monastic scholars, the nature of the texts associated with their names resembles more a centonization of musical thought than the purposeful writing of systematic theory. The textual traditions of treatises

35 On the nature of these commentaries, see Calvin M. Bower, "Die Wechselwirkung von philosophie, mathematica und musica in der karolingischen Rezeption der 'Institutio musica' von Boethius," in *Musik und die Geschichte der Philosophie und Naturwissenschaften im Mittelalter*, ed. Frank Hentschel (Leiden, Boston, Cologne: Brill, 1998), pp. 163–83; and Mariken Teeuwen, "Harmony and the Music of the Spheres: *Ars musica* in Ninth-century Commentaries on Martianus Capella" (Ph.D. diss., University of Utrecht, 2000). While no references to practical music are found among the glosses on Boethius, Teeuwen has found references to organum and *sequentia* among ninth-century glosses on Martianus; nevertheless no systematic discussion of practical music is found in any of the early glosses.

36 See, e.g., *Glossa maior in musicam Boethii* 1,3,150.

37 Ibid., 1,10,143; 1,10,146; 1,10,151; 1,10,153.

attributed to these authors is extremely complex, for many shorter sections of their texts have been preserved as fragments in other texts independent of the "treatises" as a whole. Moreover, fragments from commentary on Martianus Capella and Boethius, as well as excerpts from Cassiodorus and Isidore, are taken into these treatises with little or no acknowledgment of their sources. The texts associated with Aurelian and Regino thus reflect the active reception of *musica* in late ninth-century monastic circles, and the conscious association of *musica* with the musical practice of liturgical chant. Ultimately the act of music-theoretical texts being copied and circulated from one monastic center to another is more critical to the formation of a tradition of music theory than the fact of various texts being compiled by a single agent or "author."

Nevertheless important first steps in the development of a mainstream of later medieval theory are taken in the texts associated with Aurelian and Regino. A fundamental emphasis of these treatises is *knowing* the unchanging essences of Pythagorean ratios. The myth of Pythagoras as transmitted by Boethius is repeated in both treatises, and each develops the basic theory of ratios as a fundamental element in the theory of *musica*. The texts assembled by Aurelian[38] introduce the important distinction between *musicus* and *cantor*; following Boethius's definition of *musicus*, the text argues that the true musician knows music as a speculative discipline, while the cantor merely applies basic skills.[39] Yet the concept of "cantor" does not appear in the Boethian text, and the dichotomy between *musicus* and *cantor* reveals the degree to which the philosophical discipline of *musica* is being assimilated into the practical musical world of the ninth-century abbey.

Regino, like Aurelian, draws heavily on the Platonic tradition of early *musica*, but does so in a manner original and appropriate to ninth-century monastic spirituality and practice. While the treatise attributed to Regino pulls together virtually every thread of early medieval musical thought – including an explication of the Greek musical system – it offers a musical ontology that rationalizes the systematic study of chant as well as the ancient discipline of *musica*. Music exists on two levels: natural music and artificial music. Natural music (*musica naturalis*) is defined as that music sung by the human voice in divine praises[40] and that music which governs the celestial spheres; artificial music (*musica artificialis*) is defined as that music performed through human artifice, namely instrumental music.[41] Four *tones* (*toni*) form the origins of natural music, the four fundamental pitches (*principia*) that govern the tonal structure

38 Concerning Aurelian, see Lawrence Gushee, "The *Musica disciplina* of Aurelian of Réôme: A Critical Text and Commentary" (PhD. diss., Yale University, 1962); but see also Michael Bernhard, "Textkritisches zu Aurelianus Reomensis," *Musica disciplina* 40 (1986), pp. 49–61. I follow Bernhard's revised (later) dating of the texts assembled under Aurelian's name. In a recent study Barbara Haggh argues for placing the origins of Aurelian's treatise as early as 843 and 856, with revisions of the treatise continuing into the next two decades; see "Traktat 'Musica disciplina' Aureliana Reomensis. Proweniencja I Datowanie," *Muzyka* 2 (2000), pp. 25–77 (with English summary pp. 78–98). Finally, see the discussion in Chapter 11, pp. 313–15.

39 Aurelian, *Musica disciplina*, Chapter 7 (Gushee edn., p. 77).

40 Regino, *Epistola de harmonica institutione*, III,1 (Bernhard edn., p. 42); V,5 (Bernhard edn., p. 45).

41 Ibid., V,91–93; p. 51.

of chant: *protus*, *deuterus*, *tritus*, and *tetrardus*; the four tones are described as "fountains," from which eight *tones* flow, four *authentic* and four *plagal*.[42] Five tones and two semitones, on the other hand, govern artificial music, the intervals that form the basic content of *musica*, and one comes to know these intervals through instrumental music and through the study of arithmetic theory, i.e., through the liberal art of *musica*.[43] But these two levels of being are not independent of each other: the experience of artificial music through instruments and the study of *musica* as a liberal art are basic to the knowledge of natural music, for musical knowledge begins with the artificial and rises to the natural. Natural music is "proved" by the artificial; things invisible are demonstrated by the visible.[44]

Fundamental to both of these early medieval theoretical treatises are the eight modes as tonal principles organizing music. Both treatises are associated with *tonaries*, extended catalogues of individual chants organized according to the four primary *tones* (*protus*, *deuterus*, *tritus*, and *tetrardus*) that are in turn subdivided into plagal and authentic species. Independent tonaries and catalogues of chants combined with musical treatises played a very significant role in the manuscript culture of *cantus* and *musica* during the Carolingian period, and they remained practical and theoretical tools for the *cantor* and *musicus* until the end of the Middle Ages.[45]

The modes of liturgical music form a crucial new element in the systematic study of music in the ninth century, for they were unknown to the treatises discussed in the first section of this chapter. The introduction of the modes as a subject of systematic musical reflection is obviously an answer to the practical as well as theoretical needs of monastic culture in the ninth century, and the cross-fertilization between the philosophical tradition of *musica* and the practical tradition of chant defines a new chapter in the study of music theory. But before the initial phases of the new chapter can be traced, the four tones – *protus*, *deuterus*, *tritus*, and *tetrardus* – must be examined as fundamental parts of a musical system independent of *musica*.

The special place of Musica enchiriadis *and the four qualities*

Paths of transmission and reception have been easy to trace to this point in the history of music theory in the early Middle Ages; for, even if some textual transmissions are complex, the footprints of earlier texts, authors, and intellectual traditions have been easily identifiable. The case of a complex of texts and treatises that might be named the *enchiriadis* tradition is strikingly different. The name "enchiriadis" is taken from the musical treatise *Musica enchiriadis*, the musical text that was copied more than any other theoretical text during the ninth and tenth centuries. This treatise, the author of which

42 Ibid., III, 2–4; p. 42. 43 Ibid., IV, 2–6; p. 43.

44 Ibid., V, 98–99; p. 51. Concerning the philosophical background of natural and artificial music, see Calvin M. Bower, "Natural and Artificial Music: The Origins and Development of an Aesthetic Concept," *Musica Disciplina* 25 (1971), pp. 17–33.

45 See Michel Huglo, *Les Tonaires: inventaire, analyse, comparaison* (Paris: Société Française de Musicologie, 1971).

remains unknown, presents an almost insurmountable task to any editor of Latin texts: on the one hand, the text of the "treatise" itself is extremely complex, and, on the other hand, a multiplicity of texts clearly associated with *Musica enchiriadis* are scattered in manuscripts throughout Europe. Hans Schmid, the scholar who finally succeeded in bringing some order to this difficult textual tradition, had to publish a collection of texts along with the central treatise in order to present accurately and completely the complex theoretical tradition of *Musica enchiriadis*.[46]

It is highly unlikely that the *enchiriadis* tradition was created *ex nihilo* by Western European scholars in the ninth century. The treatises of the tradition reveal a knowledge of ancient literature, for Censorinus, Calcidius, Augustine, Fulgentius, Boethius, and Cassiodorus are cited and/or quoted within the texts. Yet the essential "theory" of the treatises appears with little precedent. The terminology that lies at the basis of the *enchiriadis* texts – as well as the character of the title itself – is Greek rather than Latin, the basic terminology has roots deep in musical practice of the Roman liturgy, and the basic set of four tones become a tetrachord that is developed into a functional and flexible musical system; these facts coupled with the complexity of the textual tradition seem to posit a long-lived tradition rather than a single, highly imaginative invention. Nevertheless the sources for the basic terminology and the system can be traced back only to the earlier Middle Ages. In the late eighth and ninth centuries we repeatedly discover the basic terminology (*protus*, *deuterus*, etc.) used in describing and organizing chant – in marginal commentary on Boethius and Martianus, in early treatises, and in particular in tonaries. Yet these "footprints" seem to emerge from the darkness, and we lose any trail if we try to follow them back further than around 800.

If the *enchiriadis* tradition is difficult to trace into periods before its appearance, it emerges in the tenth and eleventh centuries as one of the most widely copied and dispersed treatises of the Middle Ages. Until the eleventh century *Musica enchiriadis* was copied more than any treatise other than Boethius's *Fundamentals of Music*, and even in the eleventh and twelfth centuries it is outnumbered only by manuscripts containing the *Dialogus* attributed to Odo and Guido's *Micrologus*. Thus the music theory of the *enchiriadis* tradition must be viewed as lying right in the center of theoretical developments in the post-Carolingian era.

The terms *protus*, *deuterus*, *tritus*, and *tetrardus* have been introduced in the previous

46 The most complete and authoritative study of the *enchiriadis* tradition is found in Nancy Catherine Phillips, "*Musica* and *Scolica enchiriadis*: The Literary, Theoretical, and Musical Sources" (Ph.D. diss., New York University, 1984); Phillips's thorough discussion of Schmid's edition is also indispensable: Review of Hans Schmid, ed., *Musica et Scolica enchiriadis una cum aliquibus tractatulis adiunctis*, *JAMS* 36 (1983), pp. 129–43. Erikson's lucid introduction to his translation offers crucial perspectives. Two recent studies by Dieter Torkewitz add important discussion concerning the origins of the treatises: "Zur Entstehung der *Musica* und *Scolica Enchiriadis*," *Acta Musicologica* 69 (1997), pp. 156–81; and "Das älteste Dokument zur Entstehung der abendländischen Mehrstimmigkeit, eine Handschrift aus Werden an der Ruhr: Das Düsseldorfer Fragment," *Beihefte zum Archiv für Musikwissenschaft* 44 (Stuttgart: Franz Steiner Verlag, 1999). Two classical studies in the history of medieval theory should also be noted: Philipp Spitta, "Die *Musica enchiriadis* und ihr Zeitalter," *Vierteljahrschrift für Musikwissenschaft* 5 (1889), pp. 443–82; and Heinrich Sowa, "Textvariationen zur *Musica Enchiriadis*," *Zeitschrift für Musikwissenschaft* 17 (1935), pp. 194–207.

	protus		deuterus		tritus		tetrardus
		tone		semitone		tone	
e.g.	D		E		F		G

Figure 5.2 The *enchiriadis* tetrachord

section of this essay as tonal centers governing the modes. These terms form the very foundation of texts in the *enchiriadis* tradition, for here they form the names of pitches and functions within basic tetrachords used to build a musical system. The tenor of *enchiriadis* texts stands in striking contrast to the texts belonging to the traditions of the liberal arts, the medieval Platonists, and the encyclopedists; for in the *enchiriadis* texts the chant of the liturgy lies at the center of all musical reflection, and, at least in the most ancient layers of texts, the quantitative dimension of the other traditions is markedly absent. Two further aspects of the *enchiriadis* tradition contribute to its unique character: (1) a type of "Daseian" notation – based on the four pitches forming the foundation of these texts – is shared by the treatises and texts recording the tradition; (2) the earliest systematic discussions of polyphonic music (organum) appear in some of the treatises of the tradition. Nevertheless in this chapter the structure and character of the pitch collection and the general character of the treatise will serve as primary focus.

With no reference to ratios or any other objective measurement of intervals, *Musica enchiriadis* introduces the four pitches, *protus*, *deuterus*, *tritus*, and *tetrardus*. The pitches are defined simply as "qualities," and the intervallic relations among the four basic pitches determine their individual characters. From *protus* to *deuterus* is described as a tone, from *deuterus* to *tritus* a semitone, and from tritus to *tetrardus* again a tone – yet no objective measure determines these intervals.[47] Thus the basic building block of music according to the *enchiriadis* texts is a tetrachord with semitone in the middle position, a tetrachord essentially different from that of the ancient Greek tradition with the semitone in the first and lowest position, the tetrachord found (or implied) in all texts examined to this point (see Figure 5.2).

A series of *enchiriadis* tetrachords are thus joined together to form a collection of eighteen pitches, but rather than alternating conjunct and disjunct tetrachords, all tetrachords are disjunct. The tetrachords are given names *according to their function in chant*: low pitches (*graves*), final pitches (*finales*), high pitches (*superiores*), upper pitches (*excellentes*).[48]

When describing the functions of pitches in this collection, the *Musica enchiriadis* and other treatises in this tradition portray pitches in terms of function and character rather than calculate them with mathematical precision: a pitch has a corresponding pitch *of the same quality* a fifth higher or a fifth lower,[49] and pitches standing a ninth apart share the same quality (Chapter 11).[50] Indeed both the name

47 *Musica enchiriadis* I (Schmid edn., pp. 2–3).
48 Ibid., I, p. 5. For a full illustration of the *enchiriadis* scale and its Daseian notation, see **Figure 11.5, p. 324**.
49 Ibid., VI, p. 10.
50 Ibid., XI, pp. 33–34.

and intervallic disposition of pitches in the collection are identical at the fifth and at the ninth.[51]

The consistent disposition of tones and semitones – the ratios of which remain undefined – forms the basis of melodic qualities that unfold within this system, and the four basic qualities are unequivocally those of the four modes of chant. Yet a remarkable degree of flexibility is possible within the *enchiriadis* pitch collection, for each *deuterus* pitch may be lowered a semitone, each *tritus* pitch may be raised a semitone, thereby producing further subtleties of melodic quality. These minor alterations are described as melodic defects or imperfections (*vitia*) – a kind of dissonance in melody – and their use in melodies is compared with the appearance of barbarisms or solecisms in prose and poetry.[52]

The congruence of the *enchiriadis* pitch collection with liturgical chant becomes even clearer when the four basic qualities of melodies (i.e., the four modes) are explicated, for each of the four basic melodic qualities is exemplified by two antiphons (Chapter 8).[53] Throughout the textual tradition associated with *Musica enchiriadis*, the close association of theoretical apparatus and that repertoire of chant generally known as "Gregorian" is a given; musical repertoire and theoretical construct are essentially inseparable in this tradition. Even perimeters of composition other than pitch are addressed; for basic phrase-structure and functions of phrases, sub-phrases, and melodic gestures are analyzed and described using vocabulary borrowed largely from grammar (e.g., comma, colon, and period).[54]

The most obvious peculiarity of the *enchiriadis* pitch collection lies in the fact that this text seems oblivious to the lack of periodicity at the octave (and double octave); augmented octaves occur between the tritus of the lower pitches (B♭) and the deuterus of the high pitches (b), between the tritus of the final pitches (f) and the deuterus of the upper pitches (f♯), and between the tritus of the high pitches (c) and the deuterus of the residual pitches (c♯) (see **Figure 11.5, p. 324**). This aspect of the *enchiriadis* tradition must have strained the credulity of a scholar steeped in the mathematical tradition of Carolingian Platonism. Yet it is specifically at this moment that the quantitative theory of Boethius is drawn into the text of *Musica enchiriadis*.

While *Musica enchiriadis* remains essentially a theoretical treatise setting out the tonal foundation for liturgical chant, it also offers one of the earliest discussions on singing organum. The principal interval employed is the fourth, and a basic rule for avoiding the tritone is formulated for singing organum in the *enchiriadis* pitch collection.[55] Polyphony may be sung as simple organum (with two voices), or as compound organum (with doublings of the two voices at the octave). When introducing the octave in simultaneous singing, the author of *Musica enchiriadis* introduces a new wrinkle into this

51 The qualitative identity of pitches at the fifth and the ninth is even more obvious given the notational system of the *enchiriadis* tradition, for different versions of the same notational symbols occur at these same intervals.

52 *Scolica enchiriadis*, Part I (Schmid edn., pp. 65–73).

53 *Musica enchiriadis* VIII (Schmid edn., pp. 16–20).

54 Ibid., IX, pp. 22–23; *Scolica enchiriadis*, Part I (Schmid edn., pp. 86–89).

55 See especially *Musica enchiriadis* XVIII (Schmid edn., pp. 53–56). See also **Chapter 15, pp. 481–82**.

theory, a theory (*ratio*) which he describes as "astonishing" (*mira*); for when singing at the eighth degree, a new series of pitches (i.e., qualities of pitches) begins.[56] One finds a literal quotation of Ptolemy's theory of the octave taken from Boethius associated with this passage: the octave is like the number 10; for, unlike other numbers, when any number (less than 10) is added to 10, the identity of 10 is preserved; similarly the octave preserves its consonant quality when another interval is added to it.[57] Thus while in strict singing (*absolute canendo*) all fifths and ninths share the same quality (and name), when singing consonances in organum the eighth degree – the octave – becomes the same quality *through a miraculous mutation* (*mutatione mirabili*).[58] While the duple ratio and the octave lie as a first principle in Pythagorean theorizing, in the *enchiriadis* tradition it is brought into consideration only to describe a *miraculous mutation* that occurs in a pitch collection in which the octave is rather insignificant except when singing polyphony.

Theory of a quantitative nature appears in other sections of the text of *Musica* and *Scolica enchiriadis*, yet it often seems like an element appropriated into a tradition within which it does not really fit. The essence of the *enchiriadis* tradition lies in singing rather than in knowing, yet the fundamentals of singing (pitch- and phrase-structure) are treated with a theoretical rigor comparable to the mathematical theory of Boethius and his Carolingian commentators. While the myth of Pythagoras is notably absent from the *enchiriadis* tradition, another myth taken from Fulgentius's *Mythologies* serves to paint the aesthetic tone of this tradition, so different from that of the earlier Platonists. The following paraphrase of the myth is based on the concluding chapter of *Musica enchiriadis*:

> Aristeus loved the nymph Eurydice, the wife of Orpheus. In this allegory the names are understood as follows: Aristeus represents the "good man" (*vir bonus*), Eurydice "profound understanding" (*profunda diiudicatio*), and Orpheus "most excellent voice" (*optima vox*), that is, what we experience in beautiful sound when a skillful cantor performs. When Good Man, out of love, pursues Profound Understanding, he is hindered by divine providence from possessing her – the snake, as it were, removes her. Most Excellent Voice, through the sound of his song, is capable of calling her from the underworld – from her hidden places – into the ears of this life. Yet just when she seems to be seen, she is taken away. For among those things which we now know only in part and through a glass darkly,[59] even the discipline of music cannot offer a theory that explains all things fully in the present life.[60]

56 Ibid., XI, p. 33. 57 Ibid., XVI, pp. 43–47; based on *De institutione musica* V,10.

58 *Musica enchiriadis* XI (Schmid edn., pp. 33–34).

59 The resonance with 1 Corinthians 12, 9–12 is unmistakable.

60 *Musica enchiriadis* XIX (Schmid edn., p. 57); for a complete translation of the passage, see Erickson trans., p. 31. The first appearance of this version of the Orpheus myth is found in Fulgentius, *Mithologiae* III.10 (see *Opera; accedunt Fabii Claudii Goridiani Fulgentii De aetatibus mundi et hominis et S. Fulgentii episcopi Super Thebaiden*, ed. Rudolfus Helm [1898], revised by Jean Préaux, Bibliotheca scriptorum Graecorum et Romanorum Teubneriana [Leipzig: Teubner, 1970]; and *Fulgentius the Mythographer*, trans. and intro. Leslie George Whitbread [Columbus, Ohio: Ohio State University Press, 1971]). For a survey of iterations of the myth and a review of secondary scholarship, see Susan Boynton, "The Sources and Significance of the Orpheus Myth in *Musica enchiriadis* and Regino of Prüm's *Epistola de harmonica institutione*," *Early Music History* 18 (1999), pp. 47–74.

While the transcendent nature of song in this myth may be understood in Platonic terms, the essence of the narrative lies in the importance of *singing* beautiful song rather than in *knowing* quantities abstracted from sensual reality. In contrast to the myth of Pythagoras – in which divine providence likewise had a role – the highest good in this Orpheus myth appears in the fleeting glimpse of musical reality we perceive when an able cantor sings. The musical structures themselves perceived by the ears in the performance, not mathematical ratios, offer direct, albeit partial, knowledge of a higher reality, a reality that will be known in full only when one exists at a higher level of being. Thus the discipline of music should be directed toward gaining some understanding – albeit incomplete – of the sonorous revelation of a higher order reflected in the cantor's song.

The resolution to a musical *theory in the tenth and eleventh centuries*

The flowering of ancient musical thought and the emergence of the *enchiriadis* tradition during the Carolingian intellectual revival and the decades immediately following precipitated a striking discord in musical thought. The ancient, quantitative tradition – holding that intervals are determined and expressed as ratios, that pitch collections are shaped by the ancient Greek tetrachord and principles of conjunction and disjunction, that theorizing takes place with little or no reference to repertoire, and that the purpose of studying *musica* is to take the first steps in knowing abstract truths – may be viewed as the *preparation* for the discord. The *enchiriadis* tradition – holding that pitches are qualities determined by their intervallic disposition, that pitch collections are formed by bringing together tetrachords structured according to four qualities, that qualities and collections and every other parameter of musical thinking are considered with reference to a repertoire of liturgical chant, and that the purpose of studying music is to gain some fleeting knowledge of beautiful song through the experience of musical performance – may be viewed as the *dissonance* sounding against the tradition of antiquity. As in the resolution of a suspension, the preparation remained essentially unchanged, while the dissonance resolved to the nearest position from which it could itself persevere in consonance with the prior element. Ultimately both elements were transformed by the resolution.

Secular learning established in the disciplines of the *trivium* and *quadrivium* had become a fundamental principle of Christian formation during the late ninth and tenth centuries, particularly in the monastic communities that were now the intellectual and cultural centers of Europe. After all, the liberal arts – particularly the *quadrivium* – constituted the means by which the student and scholar were prepared for the ascent to philosophy and theology, to knowledge of the divine. The monk studying the discipline of music in the tenth and eleventh centuries, whether detached scholar or practicing cantor, could not escape exposure to the quantitative arguments and arithmetical reductions found in *musica*, particularly as articulated by the most authoritative Boethius. *Knowing* was ultimately a value superior to *singing* – even in the monastery where hours of each day were devoted to singing – and that basic judgment had inevitable implications for both music theory and singing. The ratios were presumed knowledge in *musica*, and the intervals determined by the Pythagorean ratios inexorably unfolded a diatonic system with octave periodicity and very little flexibility. Thus the task of the scholar of the late ninth and tenth centuries was to adapt the discipline of singing – particularly in light of the basic concepts known through the *enchiriadis* tradition – to the quantitative values and pitch collection of Boethius. Yet no organic, no *artistic*, relationship existed between *theory* and *practice*, between the musical system exemplified in Boethius and the repertoire of chant sung daily in the liturgy. The monastic theorists were forced to adapt the four *qualities* of pitch inherent in chant to the Pythagorean tonal structure.

The tenth century seems to have been a period of ferment, for comparatively few theoretical texts can be found that were written between the flowering of the *enchiriadis* tradition in the late ninth century and the numerous theorists and texts that arise in the eleventh century. Hucbald, who wrote in the monastery of Saint-Amand around the turn of the tenth century, is almost alone in revealing some of the difficult problems facing the tenth-century monastic scholar. Hucbald was clearly well schooled in both Boethius and chant, and one of the principal tasks of his highly original treatise was to explain chant in terms and concepts consistent with the theory found in Boethius – the theory shaped by numbers.[61] Thus – and he cites seventy-one different chants as examples – specific musical intervals are illustrated with examples from chant;[62] small segments of chants are shown to fit within the Pythagorean diatonic system;[63] four notes from the ancient system (lichanos hypaton [d], hypate meson [e], parhypate meson [f], and lichanos meson [g]) are compared to the four qualities of chant (*protus*, *deuterus*, *tritus*, and *tetrardus*) and designated as the finals (*finales*), the pitches on which chants end;[64] and a significant collection of chants, organized according to their finals, are demonstrated to begin and unfold on notes within the diatonic system.[65] (For more on Hucbald, see **Chapter 11, pp. 318–23**.)

One early tenth-century text, the so-called *Alia musica*, attempts to combine elements of tonaries with mathematical and musical elements of *musica*; passages in this complex collection of texts, like Hucbald, relate the modal finals to specific pitches in the Pythagorean system and even introduce the notion of species of consonances into the discussion of modes.[66]

Hucbald's treatise along with *Alia musica* represents a beginning to the resolution,

61 Hucbald, *Musica* 25 (Chartier edn., p. 164). 62 Ibid., 5–8, pp. 140–44.
63 Ibid., 21–22, p. 160. 64 Ibid., 49, p. 200. 65 Ibid., 50–55, pp. 202–12.
66 The complex textual history of *Alia musica* is yet to be disentangled, thus I hesitate to call the text a "treatise." The standard edition of the text (that of Chailley) is to be used with caution. One layer of text present in *Alia musica* has been edited by Michael Bernhard as an independent treatise: *Anonymi saeculi decimi vel undecimi tractatus de musica: "Dulce ingenium musicae"*, Bayerische Akademie der Wissenschaften, Veröffentlichungen der Musikhistorischen Kommission, vol. VI (Munich: Verlag der Bayerischen Akademie der Wissenschaften, 1987). See also Edmund Heard, "'Alia musica': A Chapter in the History of Medieval Music Theory" (Ph.D. diss., University of Wisconsin, 1966). A fuller discussion of the *Alia musica* texts is found in **Chapter 11, pp. 331–39**.

but the manuscript tradition of Hucbald is relatively limited and specific influences of this scholar are difficult to trace, while the textual tradition of *Alia musica* is too complex to unravel in any lucid perspective. Nevertheless in Hucbald and such texts as *Alia musica* we witness the fundamental task that faced scholars in the tenth century: the reconciling of liturgical chant to the Pythagorean diatonic system. While four pitches in the Greek Greater Perfect System – as identified by Hucbald – could serve as the four finals, significant incongruencies between pitch collection and practice persisted. Many chants that end on the protus quality (D) required a major third below the final (i.e., B♭) – for example, the Easter gradual *Haec dies* – but such an interval was not possible below the lichanos hypaton in the ancient system. Some chants ending on the protus also required intervals of both a tone and a semitone above the final (again the Easter gradual *Haec dies*, for example), but such chromatic alteration was foreign to the ancient system. While these simple melodic gestures were easily accommodated in the *enchiriadis* system based on the four qualities, they represent only two examples of many discords between the established and extensive repertoire of liturgical chant and the authoritative, quantitative theoretical system.

The theorists of the tenth century thus faced two basic problems: (1) how to "fit" chants of given melodic qualities into the quantitative system, and (2) how to accommodate the chromatic alterations – the melodic imperfections (*vitia*) – necessary in the performance of numerous chants. The first problem was solved by recognizing that the four pitches identified by Hucbald would not serve as universal finals, that is, as the tetrachord of final pitches had in the *enchiriadis* tradition; thus chants were transposed to various positions within the Greater Perfect System in order to preserve the intervallic structure of the melody as integrally as possible. The monochord with letters designating specific pitches in the collection – a musical tool known through Boethius – became a fundamental means for theorists to conceive, test, and objectively represent ("notate") various transpositions.[67] For example, if *Haec dies* were begun on the mese (a) rather than on the lichanos hypaton (D), the notes immediately above this "final" would be qualitatively identical, but the note a third below the final, the parhypate meson (F), functioned as the required major third.

The second problem was solved by using the synemmenon (or conjunct) system in a manner in which it was never intended to be used, but nevertheless in a manner that ingeniously combined practice with authority. Two pitch collections had been handed down by Boethius: a two-octave (disjunct) collection, and an octave-plus-fourth (conjunct) collection. The lower octave of both systems was identical (see Table 5.3, pp. 144–45 above), but a *disjunct* tetrachord followed the mese (a) in the two-octave collection (a | b c d e), while a *conjunct* tetrachord followed the mese (a) in the octave-plus-

67 Latin texts for divisions of the monochord have been collected and edited by Christian Meyer in *Mensura monochordi: La division du monochorde (IXe–XVe siècle)* (Paris: Editions Klincksieck, 1996). One regrets the absence of a chronological tables in this otherwise indispensable collection. (See also Chapter 6, esp. pp. 168–71.)

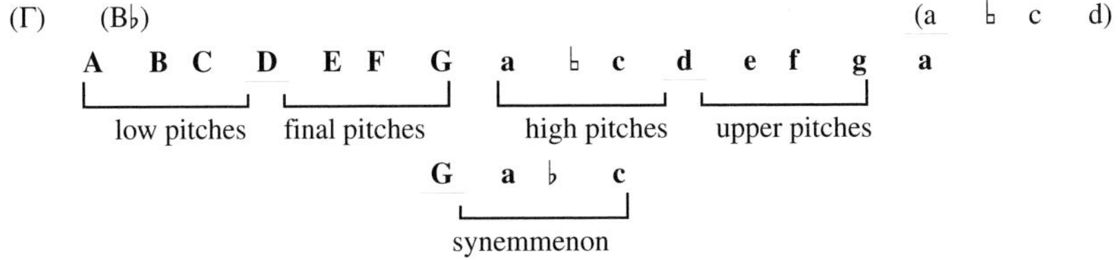

Figure 5.3 Pitch collection of the South German school (pitches underlined with a solid line indicate conjunction of two tetrachords)

fourth collection (a b♭ c d). The musical function within these two systems in antiquity is by no means clear, but it is certain that they were never meant to be combined or superimposed. Yet when these two collections are computed together on a monochord, the only point of division – the only specific note – that is different between them lies in the b♭, the trite synemmenon. This conjunct note became the b-molle, while the disjunct note became the b-durum, and the ancient system was made to accommodate one chromatic alteration without major compromise in the structure of the ancient system. Thus both the semitone and tone of *Haec dies* could be sung when the mese became the final, for the *conjunct* note yielded the semitone, the *disjunct* note the tone (see **Figure 11.2, p. 320**).

A learned and long-lived theoretical tradition flourished in South Germany during the eleventh and twelfth centuries that exemplifies an astute resolution to the discord set in play between *musica* and musical practice. The tradition originated with Berno of Reichenau, and continued in the works of Hermannus Contractus,[68] Wilhelmus of Hirsau, and Theogerus of Metz.[69] These German theorists treat Boethius with considerable deference, and hold rather conservatively to the basic tonal system (monochord division) set out by the ancient authority. Yet they offer a new concept of the tetrachordal structure within the collection of pitches, a concept which combines the ancient principles of conjunction and disjunction with a tetrachord based on the four qualities of the *enchiriadis* tradition (Figure 5.3).

Berno also enumerates a fifth tetrachord, the synemmenon, which is superimposed in the middle of these, thereby achieving the b♭, the "accidental" necessary for chromatic alterations.[70] Wilhelmus and Theogerus, under the influence of the Italian tradition (see below), augment the collection with the low G, i.e., the gamma, and

68 For a study of Berno and Hermannus, see Hans Oesch, *Berno und Hermann von Reichenau als Musiktheoretiker*, Publikationen der Schweizerischen Musikforschenden Gesellschaft, series II, vol. IX (Bern: Verlag Paul Haupt, 1961); Fabian Lochner's "Dieter (Theogerus) of Metz and his *Musica*" (Ph.D. diss., University of Notre Dame, 1995) adds musical and cultural perspective to Oesch's monograph.
69 While Theogerus (or Dietger) carried the title of bishop of Metz, he never functioned in that office, and spent most of his productive life in the abbey of Hirsau; see Lochner, "Dieter (Theogerus) of Metz and his *Musica*."
70 For Berno's exposition of "*enchiriadis* tetrachords" in the context of Boethius's system, see *Prologus* 1–1–7 (Rausch edn., pp. 32–33).

Γ A B C D E F G a ♭ ♮ c d e f g a/a ♭/♮ c/c

Figure 5.4 Pitch collection of *Dialogus de musica* and Guido

additional pitches above. Theogerus even adds a low B♭,[71] described as *synemmenon grave*, to accommodate chants of the *Haec dies* type.

The South German tradition pays careful attention to both the quantitative bases of ancient theory and the qualitative nature of musical practice. The species of consonances – an essentially quantitative concept used by Boethius in his discussion of the ancient *tonoi* – is taken up by the German theorists as a means of defining and describing the eight modes confronted in singing chant. Various tonal structures in chant are described and analyzed as combinations of the three species of the fourth and the four species of the fifth, which in turn form the seven species of the octave – species all defined in Boethius's treatise. Yet the quantitative reduction never seems to compromise the qualitative subtleties evident in the melodic tradition, and the two traditions are made consonant with one another.

A considerably more practical (and pedagogical) approach to the resolution of the discord between *musica* and *cantus* is taken by two widely circulated treatises that originated in Italy during the first half of the eleventh century: the *Dialogus de musica* (falsely attributed to Odo)[72] and Guido's *Micrologus*, two treatises that are found in more extant manuscripts than any other musical treatise with the exception of Boethius.[73] Their all-pervasive influence in the subsequent history of musical thought is evident at every turn.[74] Both begin with a monochord division, that is, with the assumption that the Pythagorean ratios determine the intervallic structure of the pitch collection; both derive a collection that is, at its core, identical with the ancient system; and both signify notes on the monochord only with letters that articulate the underlying principle of octave periodicity (when justifying the principle of octave periodicity Guido cites Boethius and criticizes *Musica enchiriadis*).[75]

The collection from the ancient system is underlined in this table (Figure 5.4), while the expansions on either end represent the new additions. The addition of the lower G

71 Also the monochord division *Cum primum a G ad finem novem passibus* (Meyer edn., pp. 154–55).

72 For a thorough inquiry concerning the origins of this treatise, see Michel Huglo, "L'Auteur du 'Dialogue sur la musique' attribué a Odon," *Revue de Musicologie* 55 (1969), pp. 121–71; and "Der Prolog des Odo zugeschriebenen 'Dialogus de Musica,'" *AfMW* 28 (1971), pp. 134–46.

73 See Bernhard, "Das musikalische Fachschrifttum im lateinischen Mittelalter," pp. 72–73.

74 For a study of common theoretical concepts shared by pseudo-Odo and Guido, see Hans Oesch, *Guido von Arezzo: Biographisches und Theoretisches unter besonderer Berücksichtigung der sogenannten odonischen Traktate*, Publikationen der Schweizerischen Musikforschenden Gesellschaft, series II, vol. IX (Bern: P. Haupt, 1954). Joseph Smits van Waesberghe's *De musico-paedagogico et theoretico Guidone Aretino eiusque vita et moribus* (Florence: L. S. Olschki, 1953) remains fundamental to the study of Guido; the "Introduction" by Claude V. Palisca in *Hucbald, Guido, and John on Music*, pp. 49–56, and the "Introduction" by Dolores Pesce in *Guido d'Arezzo's* Regule Rithmice, pp. 1–38, also represent significant contributions to the study of this crucial theorist.

75 Guido, *Micrologus* 5, ll. 19–20 (Waesberghe edn., pp. 112–13). See **Chapter 11, pp. 339–51**.

– the gamma – makes the fifth degree below the final necessary for plagal chants available, and incorporates an element from the *enchiriadis* tradition into the ancient collection. The notes added at the high end vary according to the treatise, but again resonate with the "residual notes" of the *enchiriadis* tradition.

While D, E, F, and G are identified as the notes on which chants end, no use of the ancient names of notes, no theory of tetrachords, and no theory of conjunction and disjunction are offered in these Italian treatises. The building blocks of the ancient system are ignored, and the qualitative functions of the *enchiriadis* tradition are suppressed. Nevertheless the qualitative nature of the pitch collection is stressed by pointing out pitches that share *affinity* at intervals of fifths and fourths from a given note,[76] and the qualitative nature of the modes is unfolded in relation to the doctrine of affinities.[77] In his theory of the hexachord, Guido creates a qualitative matrix with which he can navigate the multivalent functions reduced to a series of letters.[78] At the heart of the Guidonian hexachord – the central four pitches – lies the qualitative tetrachord of the *enchiriadis* tradition.

While much of the mathematical apparatus central to *musica* as presented in Boethius is never mentioned by Guido, when he arrives at the close of *Micrologus* he repeats the myth of Pythagoras and the hammers, and he even assigns letters to the hammers representing four pitches from his collection (A, D, E, a).[79] Following the narrative of the myth, Guido cites Boethius as the great expositor of music who explained the difficult problems of this art through numerical ratios.[80] Thus the epistemological emphasis of *musica* – one of its central and defining characteristics – remains even after the discipline has been transformed into a means of theorizing about chant. The dichotomy between *musicus* and *cantor* – first encountered in Aurelian – is given more articulate form by Guido in the famous lines from *Regule rithmice*:

> Musicorum et cantorum, magna est distantia
> isti dicunt, illi sciunt, quae componit musica.
> Nam qui facit quod non sapit, diffinitur bestia.[81]
>
> Great is the difference between musicians and singers,
> The latter *say*, the former *know* what music comprises.
> And he who does what he does not know is defined as a beast.

These lines will be repeated *ad infinitum* by music theorists in the centuries to come, and the diatonic pitch collection tempered according to the Pythagorean ratios will likewise remain the old skin into which new melodies are poured. Essential elements of Pythagorean musical thought transmitted by Boethius have been preserved.

76 Ibid., 7–8, pp. 117–29. 77 Ibid., 10–13, pp. 133–57. Also see Dolores Pesce, *The Affinities and Medieval Transposition* (Bloomington and Indianapolis: Indiana University Press, 1987).

78 Guido's hexachord theory is found in the *Epistola ad Michahelem*.

79 Guido, *Micrologus* 20 (Waesberghe edn., pp. 228–32). 80 Ibid., p. 233.

81 Guido, *Regule rithmice* ll. 8–10 (Pesce edn., pp. 330–32); the translation is my own.

What of the ancient tradition has been lost in the resolution? What new has been achieved? While the new reflections about music treat chants of the divine liturgy, little consideration of the transcendent nature of liturgical song or of music itself is preserved, and thus much of the Platonic tone of musical thought is lost. The new matter of music theory is hardly preparation for the study of philosophy, and thus the place of music in the *quadrivium* is substantially compromised. In the final lines of his *Letter to Michael*, Guido again cites Boethius as the model according to which he has fashioned his musical system, but he closes with the remark that Boethius's book, useful only to philosophers, is useless for cantors.[82] Yet, at the same time, a discipline has been reformulated: while it maintains its roots deep in the matter of Pythagorean arithmetic and unfolds its pitches and intervals with the absolute security of mathematical ratios, its principal subject has become actual contemporaneous music. The subjects of music theory have become the character of liturgical chants, the pitches and intervals that determine their character, the modes into which they fall, the structures of their subphrases and phrases, and even the basic techniques of polyphonic singing. *Musica* and *cantus* have been synthesized into *music theory*.

82 Guido, *Epistola ad Michahelem* ll. 385–88 (Pesce edn., p. 530).

Bibliography

Texts and translations

"Musica" in the late Roman and early medieval worlds

Augustine, *De musica*, ed. J. P. Migne as "Sancti Aurelii Augustini Hipponensis Episcopi de musica libri sex," in *Patrologia cursus completus, series latina*, Paris, 1844–1894; ed. and trans. G. Marzi as *Aurelii Augustini de musica*, Florence, Sansoni, 1969; ed. and trans. L. Schopp as "On Music," in *The Writings of Saint Augustine*, ed. Schopp, New York, Cima, 1947

Boethius, A. M. S. *De institutione musica*, ed. G. Friedlein as *Anicii Manlii Torquati Severini Boetii De institutione arithmetica libri duo, De institutione musica libri quinque, accedit Geometria quae fertur Boetii*, Leipzig, Teubner, 1867; reprint Frankfurt, Minerva, 1966; trans. C. Bower, ed. C. Palisca as *Fundamentals of Music*, New Haven, Yale University Press, 1989

De arithmetica, ed. H. Oosthout and J. Schilling in *Anicii Manlii Severini Boethii Opera pars II*, Turnhout, Brepols, 1999; trans. M. Masi as *Boethian Number Theory: A Translation of the "De Institutione Arithmetica"*, Amsterdam, Editions Rodopi B.V., 1983

Calcidius, *Timaeus a Calcidio translatus commentarioque instructus*, ed. J. Waszink, London, Warburg Institute, 1962

Cassiodorus, *Institutiones divinarum et saecularium litterarum*, ed. R. Mynors as *Cassiodori Senatoris Institutiones*, Oxford, Clarendon Press, 1937; trans. and ed. L. W. Jones as *An*

Introduction to Divine and Human Readings, New York, Octagon Books, 1946; Book V trans. W. and O. Strunk as "Of Music" in *SR*, pp. 143–48

Censorinus, *Liber de die natali*, ed. N. Sallmann as *Censorini De die natali liber ad Q. Caerellium: accedit anonymi cuiusdam epitoma disciplinarum (fragmentum Censorini)*, Leipzig, Teubner, 1983

Cicero, M. Tullius, *De re publica. De legibus*, with Eng. trans. by C. W. Keyes, Loeb Classical Library, no. 213, Cambridge, MA, Harvard University Press, 1928

Favonius Eulogius, *Disputatio de somnio Scipionis*, ed. L. Scarpa as *Favonii Eulogii Disputatio de somnio Scipionis*, Padua, Accademia Patavina di Scienze Lettere ed Arti, 1974

Isidore of Seville, *Etymologiarum sive Originum libri XX*, ed. W. M. Lindsay as *Isidori Hispalensis episcopi Etymologiarum sive originum libri XX*, Oxford, Clarendon, 1911; Book III trans. W. and O. Strunk in *SR*, pp. 149–55

Macrobius, *In somnium Scipionis*, ed. J. Willis as *Ambrosii Theodosii Macrobii Commentarii in somnium Scipionis*, Leipzig, Teubner, 1963, 2nd edn., 1970; trans. and ed. W. H. Stahl as *Macrobius, Commentary on the Dream of Scipio*, New York, Columbia University Press, 1952

Martianus Capella, *De nuptiis Philologiae e Mercurii*, ed. J. Willis, Leipzig, Teubner, 1983; trans. W. H. Stahl and R. Johnson as *Martianus Capella and the Seven Liberal Arts*, 2 vols., New York, Columbia University Press, 1971–77

Pollio, M. Vitruvius, *On Architecture*, ed. and trans. F. Granger, Loeb Classical Library, nos. 251 and 280, Cambridge, MA, Harvard University Press, 1931–34

Quintilianus, M. Fabius, *Institutionis oratoriae libri duodecim*, ed. M. Winterbottom, Oxford University Press, 1970; trans. H. E. Butler as *The Institutio Oratoria of Quintilian*, Loeb Classical Library, nos. 124–27. Cambridge, MA, Harvard University Press, 1921

Formation of a medieval theoretical tradition in the Carolingian and post-Carolingian eras

Alia Musica, ed. and Fr. trans J. Chailley, Paris, Centre de documentation universitaire, 1965; partial trans. J. McKinnon in *SR*, pp. 196–98

Berno of Reichenau, *Musica* ed. A. Rausch as *Die Musiktraktate des Abtes Bern von Reichenau*, Tutzing, H. Schneider, 1999

Dialogus de musica, in *GS* 1 (1784), pp. 25–59, 263–64; trans. W. and O. Strunk as *Dialogue on Music* in *SR*, pp. 198–210

Glossa maior in institutionem musicam Boethii, ed. M. Bernhard and C. Bower, Munich, Bayerische Akademie der Wissenschaften, 1993

Guido of Arezzo, *Epistola de ignoto cantu (ad Michahelem)*, in *GS* 2 (1784), pp. 42–46, 50; trans. O. Strunk as *Epistle Concerning an Unknown Chant*, in *SR*, pp. 214–18; trans. D. Pesce in *Guido d'Arezzo's "Regule rithmice," "Prologus in antiphonarium," and "Epistola ad Michahelem": A Critical Text and Translation*, Ottawa, Institute of Medieval Music, 1999

Micrologus, ed. J. S. van Waesberghe as *Guidonis Aretini Micrologus*, *CSM* 4 (1955); trans. W. Babb, ed. C. Palisca in *Hucbald, Guido, and John on Music: Three Medieval Treatises*, New Haven, Yale University Press, 1978, pp. 57–83

Prologus in antiphonarium, ed. J. S. van Waesberghe as *Guidonis Prologus in Antiphonarium*, Buren, F. Knuf, 1975; trans. O. Strunk as *Prologue to His Antiphoner*, in *SR*, pp. 211–14; trans. and ed. D. Pesce in *Guido d'Arezzo's "Regule rithmice," "Prologus in antiphonarium," and "Epistola ad Michahelem": A Critical Text and Translation*, Ottawa, Institute of Medieval Music, 1999

Regule rithmice, in *GS* 2 (1784), pp. 25–34; ed. J. S. van Waesberghe in *Guidonis Prologus in Antiphonarium*, Buren, F. Knuf, 1975; trans. and ed. D. Pesce in *Guido d'Arezzo's "Regule rithmice," "Prologus in antiphonarium," and "Epistola ad Michahelem": A Critical Text and Translation*, Ottawa, Institute of Medieval Music, 1999

Hermannus Contractus, *Musica*, in *GS* 2 (1784), pp. 124–53; ed. and trans. L. Ellingwood as *Musica Hermanni Contracti*, Rochester, NY, Eastman School of Music, 1936

Hucbald of Saint-Amand, *De harmonica institutione*, ed. with Fr. trans. by Y. Chartier in *L'Œuvre musicale d'Hucbald de Saint-Amand: Les compositions et le traité de musique*, Bellarmin Editions Bellarmin, 1995; ed. with Ger. trans. by A. Traub, Regensburg, G. Bosse, 1989; Eng. trans. W. Babb, ed. C. Palisca in *Hucbald, Guido, and John on Music: Three Medieval Treatises*, New Haven, Yale University Press, 1978, pp. 13–46; cf. review of *Hucbald, Guido, and John on Music: Three Medieval Treatises* by C. Bower, *JAMS* 35 (1982), pp. 155–67

Johannes Scottus, *Annotationes in Marcianum*, ed. C. Lutz, Cambridge, MA, Mediaeval Academy of America, 1939

Musica, Scolica enchiriadis, ed. H. Schmid as *Musica et scolica enchiriadis una cum aliquibus tractatulis adiunctis*, Munich, Bayerische Akademie der Wissenschaften, 1981; trans. R. Erickson, ed. C. Palisca as *"Musica enchiriadis" and "Scolica enchiriadis." Translated, with Introduction and Notes*, New Haven, Yale University Press, 1995

Regino of Prüm, *De harmonica institutione*, ed Michael Bernhard as *Clavis Gerberti: Eine Revision von Martin Gerbert's Scriptores ecclesiastici de musica sacra potissimum (St. Blasien 1784)*, Munich, Bayerische Akademie der Wissenschaften, 1989, Part I, vol. VII, pp. 39–73

Remi of Auxerre, *Commentum in Martianum Capellam*, ed. C. Lutz as *Remigii Autissiodorensis commentum in Martianum Capellam*, 2 vols., Leiden, E. J. Brill, 1962–65

Teeuwen, M. "Harmony and the Music of the Spheres: *Ars Musica* in Ninth-century Commentaries on Martianus Capella," Ph.D. diss., University of Utrecht (2000)

Theogerus of Metz, *Musica*, in *GS* 2 (1784), pp. 182–96; ed. and trans. F. C. Lochner in "Dieter (Theogerus) of Metz and his *Musica*," Ph.D. diss., University of Notre Dame (1995)

Wilhelmus of Hirsau, *Musica*, ed. D. Harbinson as *Willehelmi Hirsavgensis Mvsica*, *CSM* 23 (1975)

Secondary sources

The following books and articles are of a general nature, and, with exception of the two essays by Michael Bernhard and Thomas Mathiesen's monograph, are not cited in any notes. These studies nevertheless form the scholarly foundation of the history of music theory found in this essay.

Atkinson, C. M. "Modus," in *HmT* 24 (1996)

Bellingham, J. "The Development of Musical Thought in the Medieval West from Late Antiquity to the Mid-Ninth Century," Ph.D. diss., Oxford University (1998)

Bernhard, M. *Studien zur Epistola de armonica institutione des Regino von Prüm*, Munich, Bayerische Akademie der Wissenschaften, 1979

"Überlieferung und Fortleben der antiken lateinischen Musiktheorie im Mittelalter," in *GMt* 3 (1990), pp. 7–36

"Das musikalische Fachschrifttum im lateinischen Mittelalter," in *GMt* 3 (1990), pp. 37–103

Bower, C. M. "The Role of Boethius' *De institutione musica* in the Speculative Tradition of Western Musical Thought," in *Boethius and the Liberal Arts: A Collection of Essays*, ed. M. Masi, Bern, P. Lang, 1981, pp. 157–74

Gushee, L. A. "Questions of Genre in Medieval Treatises on Music," in *Gattungen der Musik in Einzeldarstellungen*, ed. W. Arlt et al., Bern, Francke, 1973, pp. 365–433

Handschin, J. "Die Musikanschauung des Johannes Scotus (Erigena)," *Deutsche Vierteljahresschrift für Literaturwissenschaft und Geistesgeschichte* 5 (1927), pp. 316–41

Der Toncharakter, Zurich, Atlantis, 1948

Huglo, M. "Le Développement du vocabulaire de l'Ars Musica à l'époque carolingienne," *Latomus* 34 (1975), pp. 131–51

"Bibliographie des éditions et études relatives à la théorie musicale du moyen âge (1972–1987)," *Acta* 60 (1988), pp. 229–72

Markovits, M. *Das Tonsystem der abendländischen Musik im frühen Mittelalter*, Bern, P. Haupt, 1977

Mathiesen, T. J. *Apollo's Lyre: Greek Music and Music Theory in Antiquity and the Middle Ages*, Lincoln, University of Nebraska Press, 1999

Phillips, N. "Classical and Late Latin Sources for Ninth-Century Treatises on Music," in *Music Theory and Its Sources: Antiquity and the Middle Ages*, ed. A. Barbera, South Bend, University of Notre Dame Press, 1990, pp. 100–35

Sachs, K.-J. "Musikalische Elementarlehre im Mittelalter," *GMt* 3 (1990), pp. 105–61

Vetter, E. "Concentrische Cirkels: Modus, Affect, Sfeer en Tijd en een Middeleeuws Muziektheoretisch Gedicht," Ph.D. diss., University of Utrecht (1999)

Waesberghe, J. S. van, "La Place exceptionelle de l'ars musica dans le développement des sciences au siècle des Carolingiens," *Revue Grégorienne* 31 (1952), pp. 81–104

Muziekgeschiedenis der Middeleeuwen, Tilburg, Bergmans, 1936–42

Musikerziehung: Lehre und Theorie der Musik im Mittelalter, vol. III/3 of *Musikgeschichte in Bildern*, Leipzig, VEB Deutscher Verlag, 1969

·6·

Medieval canonics

JAN HERLINGER

The "canon" is the monochord, a single-stringed instrument suited for the production of musical pitches and the comparative measurement of the lengths of the string segments that produce them. In Plate 6.1, from Lodovico Fogliano's *Musica theorica* of 1529,[1] the monochordist has placed two movable bridges "about three fingers apart" at points marked A and B (the letters do not indicate the names of pitches, but designate points as in a geometric diagram); he has marked equal segments AC, CD, DE, EF, and BG, and placed bridges under points F and G. By moving the bridge he holds in his right hand, the monochordist can demonstrate that string segment DF, twice the length of BG, produces a pitch an octave (*diapason*) below that of BG; that CF, three times the length of BG, produces a pitch a twelfth (*diapasondiapente*) below that of BG; that AF, four times the length of BG, produces a pitch two octaves (*bisdiapason*) below that of BG.

In a systematic division of the monochord, a musician defines a number of pitches successively, at each step specifying the ratio between the length of the string segment that produces one pitch and that of the string segment that produces some other. The end results of such a monochord division are an array of pitches (which can be arranged in a scale) and a set of intervallic relationships between them specifically defined by numeric ratios (a tuning system). Canonics is the study of such pitch arrays and intervals and the ratios through which they are defined.

Ancient Greek music theory developed canonics to a sophisticated degree, describing ditones, trihemitones, tones, semitones, and dieses (i.e., intervals smaller than semitones) in a variety of sizes, organized into diatonic, chromatic, and enharmonic tetrachords (i.e., tetrachords of the types semitone–tone–tone, semitone – semitone–trihemitone, and diesis–diesis–ditone respectively.)[2] The *De institutione musica* (early sixth century) of Boethius transmitted a number of these tunings to the Latin Middle Ages, along with techniques for obtaining them on the monochord. Western musicians and scholars devoted a great deal of attention to *De institutione musica* from the ninth century at the latest, and from about the year 1000 divisions of the monochord proliferated in Latin music theory. The extant corpus of texts dealing with canonics written

1 Fogliano, *Musica theorica*, fol. 12v.

2 Barbour, *Tuning and Temperament*, Chapter 2 lists a number of such tunings. See also **Chapter 4, p. 117, p. 124.**

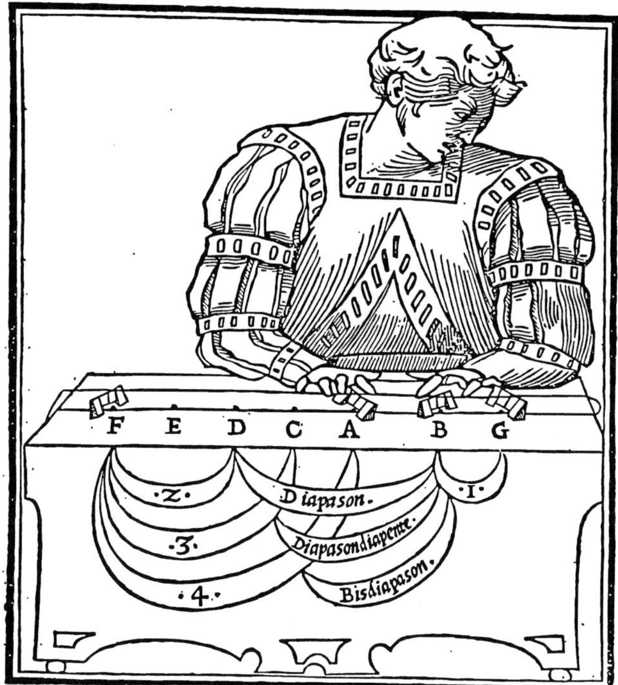

Plate 6.1 A monochordist at work. L. Fogliano, *Musica theorica*, fol. 12v

in the West between c. 1000 and c. 1500 runs to about 150 items;[3] and the authors of any number of other medieval treatises presupposed a knowledge of canonics on the part of their readers.

The profusion of monochord divisions in medieval music theory of course indicates the medievals' great interest in tuning: comparison of measured string lengths was the only means they had for representing the tunings of intervals accurately. Though they knew that higher pitches were associated with faster motions and greater tensions,[4] they had no way of measuring the frequencies of bodies vibrating quickly enough to produce pitches, and they could not have measured tension with anything like the precision string lengths afforded.

But the profusion of monochord divisions also indicates the importance of Pythagorean doctrine to medieval scholars. Pythagoreanism may be defined as the belief that all reality – including music – inheres in numbers and their relationships. When Marchetto of Padua stated in his *Lucidarium* of 1317/18 that "truth in music lies

3 Meyer includes 143 in his *Mensura Monochordi*.
4 See Boethius, *De institutione musica* 1.3; (Bower trans., pp. 11–12). For the first acoustical measurements of string frequency, see Chapter 9, p. 249.

in the numbers of ratios," he was glossing a much broader statement of Remi of Auxerre: "Truth is contained in numbers."[5] Indeed, medieval scholars found the same numeric ratios that represented musical intervals also in musical rhythms, the quantitative patterns of poetic meters, the design of baptismal fonts, the proportions of cathedrals, the harmonic structure of the cosmos, and the harmonious relationships that obtain in the human microcosm – the last two specifically called *musica mundana* and *musica humana*.[6] Thus one must sometimes ask whether a medieval music theorist discussing a monochord tuning was describing observed musical practice or attesting to a harmonic relationship that *ought* to be observable.

In any case, the large corpus of medieval treatises on the subject of canonics that we will consider in this chapter stems from a long tradition of speculative *musica theorica* treatises that frequently push against the boundaries of *musica practica*. While a few theorists after the fifteenth century continued to sustain the tradition of canonics, by and large it fell into disuse, usurped by the more practical exigencies of calculating various temperaments, whose irrational expressions (surds) are not easily derived through monochord divisions. (A slightly more robust interest in cosmological harmonics was maintained in the sixteenth and seventeenth centuries, and is discussed in **Chapter 8, passim.**) Only in the twentieth century has interest been revived in the proper subject of canonics among historical musicologists, commencing principally with Wantzloeben's pioneering study *Das Monochord als Instrument und als System* (1911). Smits van Waesberghe (*De Guidone Aretino*, 1953), Adkins ("Theory and Practice of the Monochord," 1963), and Markovits (*Tonsystem der abendländischen Musik*, 1977) developed taxonomies for monochord divisions;[7] Sachs (*Mensura Fistularum*, 1970–80) and Bröcker (*Drehleier*, 1977) studied related tuning systems for the organ and the hurdy-gurdy. Finally, Meyer's exhaustive *Mensura Monochordi* surveys the entire corpus of monochord divisions from about 1000 to about 1500, presenting complete transcriptions of their texts.[8] In the following survey, we will consider the many medieval monochord treatises grouped into three basic categories: those that involve entirely diatonic divisions using Pythagorean tuning, those that involve diatonic divisions using just tunings, and those that involve calculations of chromatic and enharmonic divisions.

5 Marchetto, *Lucidarium* 1.4.5 (Herlinger trans., pp. 84–85); Remi, *Commentum in Martianum Capellam* 46.8 (Lutz edn., vol. 1, p. 153).

6 On Pythagoreanism, see Robertson, *Preface to Chaucer*, and Heninger, *Touches of Sweet Harmony*. Also see the discussion in **Chapter 4, pp. 114–17; Chapter 5, pp. 142–43.**

7 Of these, Adkins's dissertation is the most comprehensive, surveying treatments of the monochord from ancient times through textbooks of the 1950s. Wantzloeben's 130-page monograph covers ancient times through about 1500; Smits's devotes one chapter to monochord treatments from Boethius through the twelfth century; Markovits devotes one chapter to the monochord from Euclid to about 1100, and includes chapters on the tuning of organs and bells as well.

8 Or almost the entire corpus; he seems to have missed the monochord treatise of Ugolino of Orvieto (discussed below, p. 186).

A medieval monochord division, from *Magadis in utraque parte* (by c. 1100)

Regular division of the monochord in the diatonic genus

To produce a scale like that in Table 6.1, the author first divides the monochord string into quarters, takes the last quarter as the string length that will produce his highest pitch, and derives the pitches of the top two tetrachords:

> Divide the entire length [of the monochord] . . . into four equal parts . . . Take the fourth quarter . . . as the shortest string segment, which is called the nete hyperboleon. Then divide the third quarter . . . by eight, and add a ninth [to the fourth quarter] to produce the next string segment; this is called the paranete hyperboleon, which lies distant from the previous degree by a tone. Divide this segment by eight, and adjoin a ninth [such part] to produce the next string segment; this is termed the trite hyperboleon. You will be delighted to find two tones. Thereupon divide the first nete hyperboleon by three, add a fourth [such part], and you will find the nete diezeugmenon, which lies distant from the trite hyperboleon by a semitone. Thus you will be pleased to have finished the hyperboleon tetrachord.
>
> Then you can find the paranete diezeugmenon either by dividing the nete hyperboleon by two, the paranete hyperboleon by three, or the nete diezeugmenon by eight, [always adding one additional such part]. After this you will be able to search out the trite diezeugmenon either by dividing the paranete diezeugmenon by eight, the trite hyperboleon by three, or the paranete hyperboleon by two. Then seek the following degree, the paramese, by dividing the nete diezeugmenon by three. You will recognize that the diezeugmenon tetrachord is complete . . .

The author derives the remaining tetrachords in similar fashion.

Meyer, *Mensura Monochordi*, pp. 13–14.

Diatonic monochords with Pythagorean tuning

The monochord division *Magadis in utraque parte* (by c. 1100)[9] demonstrates clearly its roots in ancient Greek theory: it represents the Greek scale (the four tetrachords of the Greater Perfect System plus the synemmenon tetrachord) in a diatonic tuning (see Table 6.1 and the window above). It may serve as an introduction to the workings of a monochord division.

In this division, the length of the entire string produces the proslambanomenos; division of the string into four parts (as the author clarifies in a passage not included in the window) yields the lichanos hypaton, the mese, and the nete hyperboleon. The proslambanomenos is distant from these three other pitches by a perfect fourth, an octave, and a double octave respectively; the string length producing the proslambanomenos is related to the string lengths producing the other pitches by the ratios 4 : 3, 2 : 1, and 4 : 1. In the course of the division, each of the remaining degrees of the scale is approached, through a single operation, by a tone (ratio 9 : 8), a fourth (4 : 3), a fifth (3 : 2), or an octave (2 : 1) from a higher degree already established. The result is a system in which every tone

9 Meyer, *Mensura Monochordi*, pp. 13–14. Rubrics of monochord divisions are those assigned by Meyer.

Table 6.1 *The Greek scale as represented in the text* Magadis in utraque parte *(by c. 1100)*

Tetrachord	Interval	Note	Note	Interval	Tetrachord
hyperboleon tetrachord		nete hyperboleon			
	9:8				
		paranete hyperboleon			
	9:8				
		trite hyperboleon			
	256:243				
diezeugmenon tetrachord		nete diezeugmenon			
	9:8				
		paranete diezeugmenon	nete synemmenon		synemmenon tetrachord
	9:8			9:8	
		trite diezeugmenon	paranete synemmenon		
	256:243				
		paramese		9:8	
		2,187:2,048	trite synemmenon		
	9:8			256:243	
meson tetrachord		mese	mese		
	9:8				
		lichanos meson			
	9:8				
		parhypate meson			
	256:243				
hypaton tetrachord		hypate meson			
	9:8				
		lichanos hypaton			
	9:8				
		parhypate hypaton			
	256:243				
		hypate hypaton			
	9:8				
		proslambanomenos			

Source: Meyer, *Mensura Monochordi*, pp. 13–14.

has the ratio 9:8, every semitone within a tetrachord (the difference between a fourth and two tones) the ratio 256:243, and the interval between the paramese and the trite synemmenon (the difference between the tone and that semitone) the ratio 2,187:2,048. Since this division traces the scale tetrachord by tetrachord from top to bottom, the structure of the five identical tetrachords and of their composite is made clear. (C.f. **Table 7.1, p. 197**; and **Figure 11.2, p. 320**).

Not every Greek diatonic tuning used tones exclusively with the ratio 9:8.[10] But this

10 For a list of other diatonic tunings, see Barbour, *Tuning and Temperament*, Chapter 2.

is the tuning that took hold in the medieval West and is the basis of the vast majority of medieval monochord divisions; it has come to be called "Pythagorean" tuning. However, the medieval monochord divisions that preserve this tuning trace various routes through the degrees of the scale. The *Dialogus de musica*,[11] a North Italian treatise of c. 1000 (often attributed to a certain Odo) begins by calling the degree produced by the entire string gamma (i.e., G); its monochord division proceeds by producing ascending whole tones to A and B through successive nine-part divisions; it finds the other degrees, each through a single operation, by fourth, fifth, or octave from a lower degree already established. Thus it may be seen as an obverse of the previous division, proceeding upwards from the lowest pitch instead of downward from the highest. Table 6.2 shows the scale of the *Dialogus*; note that except for the "new" low degree, G, the degrees of the scale and the intervals between them match those of the Greek scale in Table 6.1 in number, size, and ratio; only the Greek names of the degrees have been replaced by Latin letters A through G, reduplicated for the upper register. Even the paramese and trite synemmenon of the intersecting diezeugmenon and synemmenon tetrachords are replaced by b♮ and b♭.

The *Dialogus de musica*, incidentally, is the earliest extant treatise to present the letter names of the notes as we still know them today. There were many systems of letter notation during the early Middle Ages, some showing reduplication at the octave, some not.[12]

The low G quickly became an established degree in the medieval scale, and retained its position as the lowest legitimate note of the system well into the Renaissance, though the occasional treatise (and many musical compositions) included lower notes. During the eleventh century especially, many monochord divisions that start with G end with g^1 rather than a^1. But the upper limit in monochord divisions rose over time – to c^2 in the *Micrologus* of Guido d'Arezzo (usually dated to the 1020s);[13] to d^2 in the *De musica* of c. 1100 attributed to the John often called "Cotton" or "of Afflighem";[14] to e^2 with the Paris version of the *De plana musica* sometimes attributed to John of Garland (mid-thirteenth century);[15] to f^2 with the Vatican version of the same treatise, a version formerly known as the *Ars nova* of Philippe de Vitry;[16] to g^2 with the treatise *Medietas lineae*,[17] transmitted in a manuscript from the second half of the fifteenth century.

11 Latin text in *GS* 1, pp. 251–64. English translation in *SR*, pp. 198–210; the chapter in question, pp. 201–02. On the date and provenance, see Huglo, "L'Auteur du *Dialogue sur la musique* attribué a Odon." Also see **Chapter 11, p. 339**.
12 Alma Colk Browne, "Medieval Letter Notations: A Survey of the Sources."
13 Though the description of the scale in *Micrologus* 2 extends to d^2, the monochord division of *Micrologus* 3 (Smits edn., pp. 96–102; Babb trans., pp. 60–61) does not unequivocally go past c^2.
14 On the identity of John, see Palisca, introduction to "John on Music (*De musica*)," in Babb, *Hucbald, Guido, and John on Music*, pp. 87–91.
15 *Si aliqua linea*, in Meyer, *Mensura Monochordi*, pp. 117–20; Gwee, "*De plana musica*," pp. 181–83.
16 Philippe de Vitry, *Ars nova*, p. 17. On the misattribution, see Fuller, "Phantom Treatise."
17 Meyer, *Mensura Monochordi*, p. 143.

Table 6.2 *The scale of the* Dialogus de musica

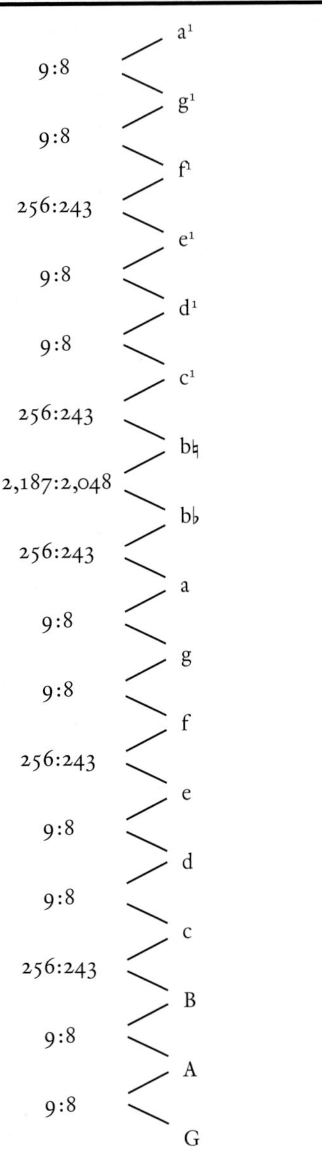

Interval	Note
	a^{1}
9:8	
	g^{1}
9:8	
	f^{1}
256:243	
	e^{1}
9:8	
	d^{1}
9:8	
	c^{1}
256:243	
	b♮
2,187:2,048	
	b♭
256:243	
	a
9:8	
	g
9:8	
	f
256:243	
	e
9:8	
	d
9:8	
	c
256:243	
	B
9:8	
	A
9:8	
	G

Source: GS 1, p. 253; *SR*, pp. 201–02.

Guido not only reported the upward extension of the monochord to c^2; he also described a simpler method of division. The methods reported in *Magadis in utraque parte* and the *Dialogus de musica* require a great many divisions of the string: the former requires thirteen divisions to construct the fifteen pitches above the proslambanomenos, the latter sixteen divisions for the sixteen pitches above G (to a^1). Guido's division – actually the second of two divisions in his *Micrologus*, Chapter 3 – produces pitches from G up to c^2 unequivocally (his words make it unclear how much further he might have assumed it could climb) with only five divisions of the string. First, he divided the entire string into ninths, locating A, d, a, d^1, and a^1 at the first, third, fifth, sixth, and seventh points marking ninth-divisions; second, he divided the string segment from the point marking A into ninths, locating B, e, b, e^1, and b^1 at the first, third, fifth, sixth, and seventh points marking ninth-divisions from A; third, he divided the entire string into fourths, locating C, g, and g^1 at the first, second, and third points marking fourths of the string; fourth, he divided the string segment from the point marking C into fourths, locating f, c^1, and c^2 at the points marking fourths of the string segment from C; finally, he divided the string segment from the point marking f into fourths, locating b♭ and f^1 at the first and second points marking fourths of the string from f. Guido characterized this method as "harder to memorize, but by it the monochord is more quickly divided";[18] and many later divisions adopted simplifications like his.[19]

The internal makeup of the scales of early monochord divisions occasionally varied somewhat from the norm (naturals plus b♭ in the second register): some divisions (especially, during the eleventh and twelfth centuries, German ones) included B♭ in the lowest register as well;[20] others omitted the b♭ in the second register. (Monochord divisions with additional chromatically altered notes will be dealt with later.) As the upper limit climbed past a^1, some divisions included b♭^{1} in the third register, others did not.

By the late fourteenth century, one particular scale had become the norm: the array of notes from G to e^2, including only naturals plus b♭ and b♭^{1} (though not B♭). The normalization of this scale was undoubtedly bolstered by the development of a series of interlocking hexachords spanning that range and including precisely those notes (see **Table 11.8, p. 342**). In time these notes came to be referred to collectively as *musica recta* or *vera* (regular or true music), in contrast to the other notes called *musica ficta* or *falsa* (fictive or false music).[21]

Musica ficta notes gradually made their way into Pythagorean monochord divisions.

18 Guido, *Micrologus* 3; trans. in Babb, *Hucbald, Guido, and John on Music*, p. 60.
19 Guido of Arezzo, who wrote the *Micrologus* and three shorter treatises during the third or fourth decade of the eleventh century, is undoubtedly the most influential theorist of the Middle Ages. In addition to the scale and the monochord he discussed modal theory, polyphony, and the melodic structure we call the hexachord; he also seems to have been first to describe the staff. For further information on Guido, see **Chapter 2, pp. 48–49**; and **Chapter 11, pp. 339–46**.
20 E.g. *Primum divide monochordum*, in Meyer, *Mensura Monochordi*, pp. 24–25, transmitted in a MS of the eleventh century.
21 Bent, "*Musica recta* and *musica ficta*."

The *Enchiriadis* treatises of the ninth century had described a scale including the notes G A B♭ c d e f g a b c^1 d^1 e^1 f^1 g^1 a^1 b^1 c♯^{2}.[22] These treatises were widely disseminated, so it is not surprising that the earliest extant monochord divisions that include sharps present them in the context of this scale (they are always derived from previously established notes through fourths, fifths, or seconds), and that several of these include the low B♭ as well.[23] The sharps were extended through the Gs and the flats through the Es by the time of the *De plana musica* attributed to John of Garland; this monochord division, then, includes twelve degrees to the octave and, as its putative author lived in the mid-thirteenth century and was associated with Paris, it may reflect the taste for sharps and flats evident in some pieces of the so-called "Notre Dame" repertory. The treatise *Sequitur de synemmenis*, from about the same time as *De plana musica*, includes sharps on Fs, Cs, Gs, Ds, and As and flats on Es, As, Ds, and Gs (as well as Bs; the *musica recta* system was presupposed). The same arrays of sharps and flats, but with the *musica recta* system explicitly derived, appeared in Prosdocimo's *Parvus tractatulus* (1413); this latter was reduplicated by Ugolino of Orvieto, probably in the 1430s.[24] In systems like these last three, the sharps are higher than the flats to which they would be enharmonically equivalent in equal temperament by the "Pythagorean" comma, 23 cents, with the ratio 531,441 : 524,288.

In Pythagorean tuning, perfect octaves and fifths are acoustically pure; all other intervals are derived from them. Table 6.3 shows the derivation of the intervals of the Pythagorean system and how they compare to their equally tempered and acoustically pure ("just") counterparts. The Pythagorean perfect fifth and fourth differ from those of equal temperament by only 2 cents.[25] But that difference is compounded in the major second, which is 4 cents wider than that of equal temperament, and compounded yet again in the major third, 8 cents larger than that of equal temperament. More significantly, the Pythagorean major third is 22 cents – the "syntonic" comma, more than a fifth of a semitone – wider than the acoustically pure major third; consequently it is quite dissonant, as is any major triad that contains it. The Pythagorean minor second, as the difference between the perfect fourth and the wide major third, is narrow, measuring just 90 cents.

What are the implications of Pythagorean tuning for musical practice? With its acoustically pure octaves, fifths, and fourths, it is admirably suited to parallel organum employing these intervals. It is also apt for repertoires, like most Western repertoires through the thirteenth century and into the fourteenth, in which these intervals

22 This so-called "Daseian" scale consists of four disjunct T–S–T tetrachords respectively termed *graves* (G–c), *finales* (d–g), *superiores* (a–d^1), and *excellentes* (e^1–a^1) plus two additional notes termed *residui* or *remanentes* (b^1, c♯^{2}). See **Figure 11.5, p. 324.**

23 E.g., *Si vis mensurare monocordum* (c. 1100), in Meyer, *Mensura monochordi*, p. 197.

24 See also **Chapter 11, p. 356.**

25 A cent is $^1/_{100}$ of the equally tempered semitone. For tables showing sizes of intervals in various tunings in cents, and for rules for converting ratios to cents, see Helmholtz, *Sensations of Tone*, pp. 446–57; see also **Chapter 7, p. 210.**

Table 6.3 *Same Pythagorean intervals in relation to corresponding intervals in equal temperament and just tuning*

	Pythagorean tuning				Equal temperament	Just tuning	
Interval	Ratio	Derivation of interval	Derivation of ratio	Size in cents	Size in cents	Size in cents	Ratio
P8	2:1	–	–	1,200	1,200	1,200	2:1
P5	3:2	–	–	702	700	702	3:2
P4	4:3	P8 – P5	2:1 / 3:2	498	500	498	4:3
M3	81:64	2 × M2	$(9:8)^2$	408	400	386	5:4
m3	32:27	P5 – M3	3:2 / 81:64	294	300	316	6:5
M2	9:8	P5 – P4	3:2 / 4:3	204	200	204 or 182	9:8 or 10:9
m2	256:243	P4 – M3	4:3 / 81:64	90	100	112*	16:15*
Apotome	2,187:2,048	M2 – m2	9:8 / 256:243	114	100	92*	135:128*
Comma	531,441:524,288	Ap – m2	2,187:2,048 / 256:243	23	–	–	–

Note: *may vary

Example 6.1 Archetypical medieval cadence

are treated as consonances but thirds and sixths (and their triadic combinations) as dissonances. Indeed, the dissonance of the penultimate major triad in the archetypical medieval ("double-leading-tone") cadence actually enhances its drive toward the final fifth–octave combination, as does the narrowness of the melodic minor seconds involved (see Example 6.1) . But the increasing use of triads in the late fourteenth century, and especially their pervasiveness in music of the fifteenth, demanded mitigation of the harshness of Pythagorean thirds and sixths. This new preference for consonant triads is reflected in some fifteenth-century monochord divisions that vary toward just tuning.

Diatonic monochords with just tuning

A tuning that varies from Pythagorean by introducing pure thirds is called a "just" tuning. The best known of early just monochord tunings is that of the Spaniard Bartolomeo Ramis de Pareia, presented in the incomplete treatise *Musica practica* (1.1.2) that he published in Bologna in 1482. Ramis's stated purpose was to present a monochord division that was simpler than the traditional one:

> A standard monochord has been subtly divided by Boethius in numbers and measurement. But still, although it is useful and pleasing to theorists, it is laborious and difficult for singers to understand. But since we promised to satisfy everyone, we will present a very easy division of the standard monochord, which let no one believe we discovered without great labor, for we found it with toil by reading in many nightly vigils the precepts of early writers, and by avoiding the errors of modern writers.[26]

Ramis built a scale whose notes correspond in number and intervallic relationship (but not tuning) to that of the ancient Greek scale (Table 6.1): it extends from A to a^2, employing b♭ alongside b♮. His tuning employs two sequences of pure fifths, D–A–E–B and B♭–F–C–G; but since he tunes F, C, and G up from D, A, and E respectively by pure minor thirds with the ratio 6 : 5 – wider than Pythagorean minor thirds by the syntonic comma, 22 cents – notes of the B♭–F–C–G sequence are a syntonic comma higher than they would be in Pythagorean tuning, and hence correspondingly high with respect to the notes of the other sequence. In Figure 6.1, which illustrates Ramis's tuning, the superscript numbers reflect these discrepancies. Perfect fifths (all

26 Ramis de Pareia, *Musica practica* 1.1.2 (Wolf edn., pp. 4–5; Miller trans., pp. 46–47).

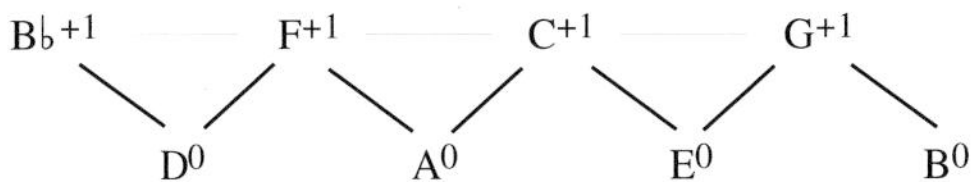

Figure 6.1 Ramis's monochord division in *Musica practica* 1.1.2

horizontal contiguities) are pure when both their notes have the same superscript number; major thirds (all contiguities from upper left to lower right) are pure when the superscript of the lower-sounding note is 1 greater than that of the higher-sounding note; minor thirds (all contiguities from lower left to upper right) are pure when the superscript of the lower-sounding note is 1 less than that of the higher-sounding note. In Ramis's tuning, all thirds are pure except B–D and G–B♭; seen another way, his tuning yields pure major triads on B♭, F, and C, and a pure major third as well on G.

But a price is paid for these euphonious triads and thirds. The G–D fifth, 22 cents narrower than the pure fifth, is not usable; and in the scale that results from this tuning (Figure 6.2) whole tones alternate in size between 204 and 182 cents (with ratios of 9:8 and 10:9 respectively) and the semitones E–F, A–B♭, and B–C are wide at 112 cents (16:15), a circumstance that compromises the ability of Es, As, and Bs to function effectively as leading tones.

Later in the *Musica practica* (1.2.5) Ramis proposed the construction on F and A of arrays similar to the normal array extending from G to e^2 (with naturals plus b♭ and $b♭^1$). But as his discussion implies duplication of common notes from the normal array, he in effect extended the two sequences of fifths to include F♯ and C♯ in the one case and E♭ and A♭ in the other (Figure 6.3), an extension that yielded no additional pure thirds or triads – though the interval C♯–A♭, only two cents smaller than the pure fifth, would be usable.

In addition to the just monochord, the *Musica practica* included a reform of solmization based on eight syllables (*Psal-li-tur per vo-ces is-tas*; "it is sung through these syllables") in an array similar to our major scale instead of the (in his view) outmoded Guidonian hexachord; the treatise sparked a firestorm of protest from defenders of the Pythagorean standard and the Guidonian tradition.[27] The English Carmelite John Hothby (died 1487), who taught for many years in Italy, wrote three treatises attacking Ramis; in his *Excitatio* he presented excerpts from Ramis's writings alongside his own refutations, explicitly declaring Ramis's ratios incorrect for the g–d^1 fifth (40:27, 680 cents), c–e major third (5:4, 386 cents), c–d and g–a major seconds (10:9, 182 cents), B–c and e–f minor seconds (16:15, 112 cents), and b♭–b♮ augmented second (135:128, 92 cents), among others.[28] The disagreement hinges on differences between

27 It is perhaps because of the strongly negative reception that Ramis left Bologna for Rome "almost in a rage," where, according to a famous letter written by his pupil Giovanni Spataro, he eventually died "because of his lascivious lifestyle." Blackburn et al., *Correspondence of Renaissance Musicians*, pp. 463–65. Translations are mine.

28 *Johannis Octobi tres tractatuli*, ed. Seay, pp. 17–21.

ratios:		10:9		9:8		16:15		9:8		10:9		16:15		135:128		16:15	
	C		D		E		F		G		A		B♭		B♮		C
cents:		182		204		112		204		182		112		92		112	

Figure 6.2 The scale resulting from Ramis's monochord division in *Musica practica* 1.1.2

Pythagorean and just tunings: in Pythagorean tuning, the minor semitone of 90 cents is the one used for diatonic progressions (minor seconds), the major semitone, 114 cents, the one used for chromatic progressions (augmented primes); in just tunings, like Ramis's, the situation is reversed, with the major semitones used in diatonic progressions, the minor semitones in chromatic progressions.

The Italian theorist Nicolò Burzio, who served for a time as rector of the university of Bologna, denounced Ramis in the preface of his *Musices opusculum* (or *Florum libellus*) of 1487:

> This man wrote a little book on the study of music in which, when he wanted to explain what Boethius meant in his five books, he was very clearly confused and thus subverted every arrangement of value and principle. . .
>
> The ignorance of the man, the conceit of the man! For at the beginning of his work, where he examines the division of a monochord (which is complete confusion), he says that he had read thoroughly the teachings of the ancients in many vigils and with considerable labor, since he wished in this way to avoid the errors of modern writers.
>
> Do you not see, I ask, how worthless, how arrogant, how impudent, is the criticism of this man? Where is Boethius, the monarch of musicians, who shows such a division with the most excellent ratios? Where is the very common division of Guido. . . ?[29]

Burzio's own monochord (3.20–21) is in Pythagorean tuning. He first constructed the naturals from A to a², giving them the corresponding Greek names, then constructed five additional notes per octave that he said would be produced on the black keys of an organ. The first of these lies a whole tone below c (i.e., B♭); the others are derived from it successively by fifths or fourths (e♭, a♭, d♭, g♭ and their octaves), though Burzio did not give the letter names. Burzio pointed out (correctly) that each of these intermediate notes divides a whole tone into a minor semitone below (256:243, 90 cents) and a major semitone (2,187:2,048, 114 cents) above.

In his *Bartolomei Ramis honesta defensio in Nicolai Burtii parmensis opusculum* (1491), Ramis's Bolognese pupil Giovanni Spataro (d. 1541) defended his teacher by presenting twenty-seven passages from the *Musices opusculum* in Italian translation, pointing out the errors in each. The last of these he devoted to Burzio's monochord:

> You state that according to this division the minor semitone always precedes [the major], and that the major semitone is called the apotome, and is a very discordant sound. But I wish to prove to you that, *according to you*, the major semitone is that which

29 Burzio, *Musices opusculum*, trans. Miller, pp. 25–26.

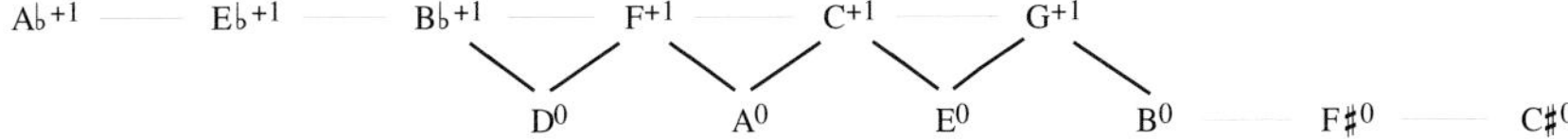

Figure 6.3 Ramis's monochord division extended as suggested in *Musica practica* 1.2.5

is sung and not the minor; as appears when the tenor descends f–e–d and the organum uses the high d¹–c¹–d¹, with the c¹ produced by the black key between c¹ and d¹. Because you state that from the c¹ to that black key is a minor semitone, it follows that from that black key to the d¹ is a major semitone; and that is the one we sing.[30]

Indeed, Burzio had stumbled into an area where theoretical and practical considerations collided: though he had criticized Ramis's monochord, whose diatonic semitones are major, and though he himself had divided a monochord using strictly Pythagorean procedures designed to yield diatonic semitones that were minor, Spataro was able to cite a common contrapuntal procedure that, when played on an instrument tuned to Burzio's monochord, yielded diatonic semitones that were major.[31]

Tensions between theory and practice lie at the heart of the controversy surrounding Ramis's monochord. While conceding in his *Practica musice* (1496) that organs of the time were tempered by having their fifths reduced by a small amount he called *partecipatio*, Franchino Gaffurio (1451–1522), who was choirmaster at the Cathedral of Milan, never abandoned the traditional Pythagorean monochord divisions, from his earliest treatises down to the *Apologia adversus Ioannem Spatarium et complices musicos bononienses* of 1520. In this treatise, Gaffurio explicitly rejected the ratios 5:4 and 6:5 for the major and minor thirds and of 10:9 for the whole tone (which he pointed out were Ramis's ratios), and presented in their stead a traditional monochord with thirds measured by the Pythagorean ratios 81:64 and 32:27 along with the 9:8 whole tone; this monochord divides all whole tones between natural notes, producing B♭s, F♯s, and C♯s, and double notes in the positions e♭ /d♯, a♭/g♯, and e♭¹/d♯¹ – an arrangement Gaffurio called *genus permixtum*.[32] Gaffurio's *Apologia* was published on April 20, 1520, and on July 20 of that year Spataro wrote to his colleague Giovanni del Lago affirming 16:15 as the ratio of the semitone used in "active" music (*el semitonio in la activa musica usitato* – "active" being his term for music as actually practiced), 5:4 as that of the ditone used in practice (*ditono in practica exercitato*); he reaffirmed as much in his *Errori*

30 *Honesta defensio*, fol. 47r.

31 Lindley has pointed out that Pythagorean monochord divisions such as Burzio's yield major triads in which the thirds differ from pure thirds by only two cents, and has argued that, during the fifteenth and early sixteenth centuries, such Pythagorean monochord divisions "whetted that Renaissance appetite for sonorous triads which only meantone temperaments could fully satisfy on keyboard instruments" (see Lindley, "Pythagorean Intonation and the Rise of the Triad"). Meantone temperaments are like just tuning in that their major thirds are small and their diatonic semitones large. For a more detailed description of meantone tuning, see **Chapter 7, pp. 201–04**.

32 *Apologia*, fols. Aiii v, Aiiii r.

de Franchino Gafurio published the following year. On the other hand (as Blackburn points out), when Spataro wrote of purely theoretical matters in the correspondence he carried on with Cavazzoni, del Lago, and Aaron, he used Pythagorean terminology; so it appears that Spataro recognized the dichotomy between theory and practice that inheres in the monochord controversy.[33]

In the final chapter of *Musica practica*, Ramis discussed which intervals were usable and which unusable. Lindley has shown that Ramis's comments here, which seem to refer to the musical practice of his time, are incompatible with the just monochord he had presented earlier (Ramis here calls all fifths good except that from c♯ to a♭, whereas in earlier chapters his g–d^1 was the unusable interval of 680 cents, and c♯/a♭ was the usable interval of 700 cents) but compatible with both Pythagorean tuning and meantone temperament. On the basis of historical context, Lindley determines that the former is virtually impossible for Ramis and the latter highly likely; he thus takes Ramis's final chapter as evidence of the use of meantone temperament as early as the 1470s.[34]

Why did Gaffurio cling so tenaciously to Pythagorean tuning while acknowledging the use of keyboard temperament in practice? Could it have been the traditional association of Pythagorean tuning with the structure of the cosmos, and with the harmony of the human microcosm? There is no question that Gaffurio was acquainted with this tradition, as he wrote about it in *Theoricum opus* (1480), *Theorica musice* (1492), and *De harmonia musicorum instrumentorum opus* (1518); moreover, he began the *Practica musice* – ostensibly concerning the practice rather than the theory of music – with a woodcut that coordinates the tones of the scale (and the modes) with the heavenly spheres (see Plate 6.2).

Despite the furor it called forth, Ramis's monochord was by no means the only fifteenth-century monochord division with just tuning, nor was it the first. *Incipiendo primum*, appearing in a Bohemian manuscript from the end of the fifteenth century, describes a monochord similar to Ramis's, but with the sequences of fifths divided not between G and D (as Ramis had it) but between D and A (see Figure 6.4); this monochord has pure major triads on F, C, and G, and a pure major third D/F♯.[35] *Divide per quatuor a primo byduro*, also transmitted in a fifteenth-century manuscript (this one German), presents a monochord with the sequence of fifths A♭–E♭–B♭–F–C–G–D, the sequence of fifths A–E–B–F♯ tuned a syntonic comma low in comparison to the first sequence, and the note D♭ tuned a syntonic comma high in comparison to the first sequence (see Figure 6.5); this monochord has pure major triads on F, C, and G, and

33 Introduction to Blackburn, Lowinsky, and Miller, eds., *Correspondence of Renaissance Musicians*, pp. 67–68. For Spataro's letter of July 20, 1520, see pp. 217–31. On the Gafurio–Ramis–Spataro exchange, see also Palisca, *Humanism in Italian Renaissance Musical Thought*, pp. 232–35.

34 Lindley, "Fifteenth-Century Evidence for Meantone Temperament."

35 Meyer, *Mensura Monochordi*, pp. cxvii, 228. A rubric indicates that the division is appropriate for a keyboard instrument.

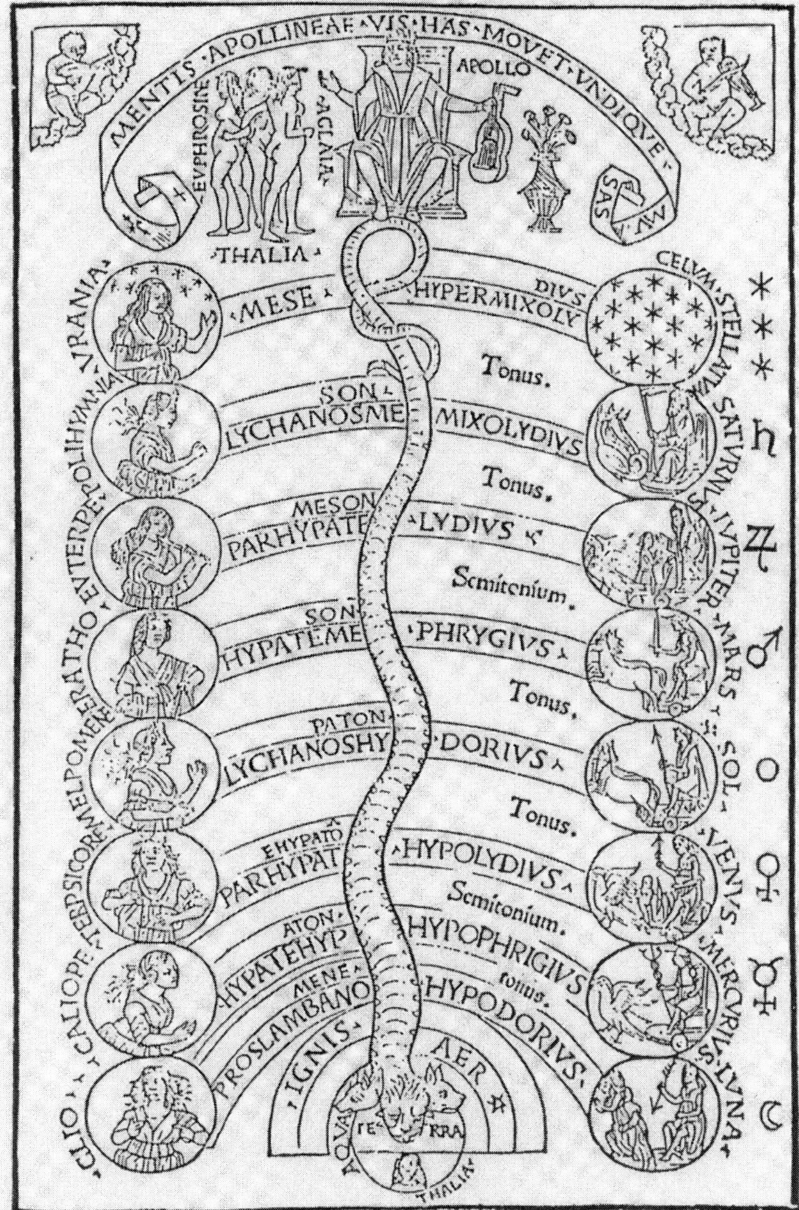

Plate 6.2 Gaffurio, *Practica musice* (1496), fol. $\Gamma 1^r$. Miller trans., p. 8; Young trans., p. 1.

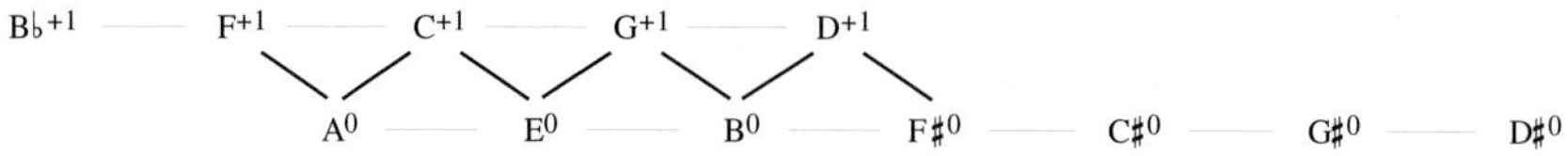

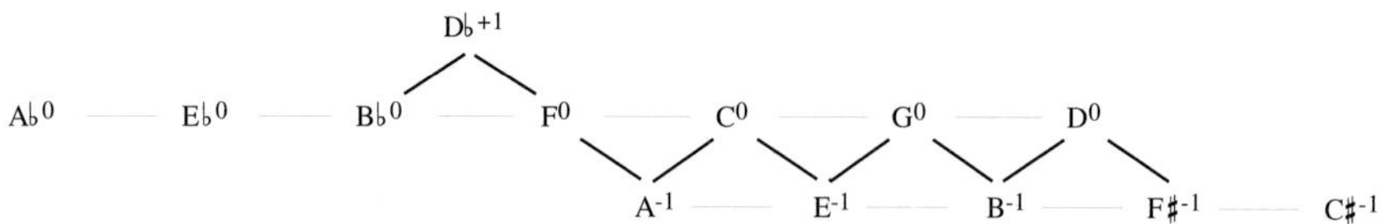

Figure 6.4 The monochord division of *Incipiendo primum*

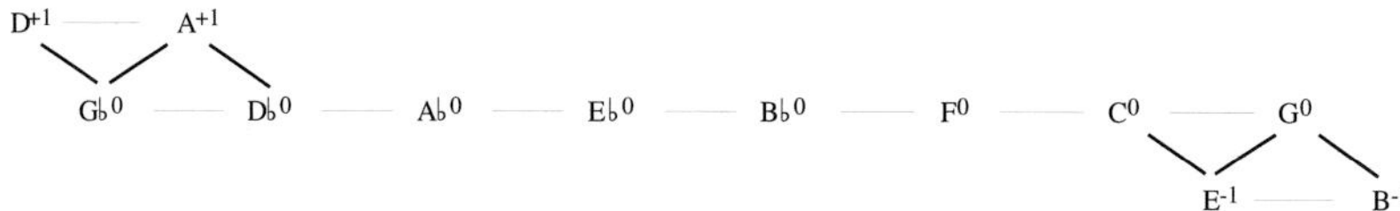

Figure 6.5 The monochord division of *Divide per quatuor a primo byduro*

D+1 A+1
G♭0 D♭0 A♭0 E♭0 B♭0 F0 C0 G0
E-1 B-1

Figure 6.6 The monochord division of *Divide primo*

pure major thirds D♭/F and D/F♯.[36] *Divide primo*, transmitted in a German manuscript from the first quarter of the fifteenth century, contains a monochord division with the sequence of fifths G♭–D♭–A♭–E♭–B♭–F–C–G, the fifth pair D–A a comma high, and the fifth pair E–B a comma low (see Figure 6.6),[37] producing pure major triads on C and D, and the pure major thirds G–B and A–D♭.

Chromatic and enharmonic monochords

Although the overwhelming majority of medieval monochord divisions were diatonic, a significant fraction of them – thirteen of the 143 monochord divisions that Meyer presents – include chromatic and/or enharmonic tunings.[38] Eleven of the thirteen present divisions similar to one reported by Boethius in *De institutione musica* 4.6; typical of these is the treatise *In primis divide* (first documented in a manuscript from the early twelfth century).[39] After presenting the pitches of the ancient Greek scale in Pythagorean

36 Ibid., pp. lxxvi, 226. A similar division appears in the German MS Erlangen, Universitätsbibliothek, 554, fols. 202v–203r (Meyer, *Mensura Monochordi*, pp. 227, 274, under the rubric *Tali a principio*).
37 Meyer, *Mensura Monochordi* , pp. lxxvi, 224. Barbour knew a similar division from a manuscript in Erlangen (*Tuning and Temperament*, pp. 92–93).
38 Listed and discussed in Meyer, *Mensura Monochordi*, pp. xxxiv–xxxvii.
39 Ibid., pp. 5–7. For the tuning in Boethius, see Book IV, Chapter 6 (Bower trans., pp. 131–34).

In primis divide, chromatic and enharmonic divisions

On the division of the chromatic genus

If you wish to find the chromatic division, return to the nete hyperboleon, and divide the space between it and the paranete hyperboleon in half; and when this amount has been added [to the length of the string producing the paranete hyperboleon] you constitute the paranete hyperboleon in the chromatic genus, and it will be a trihemitone [with the nete hyperboleon]. The trite hyperboleon and the nete diezeugmenon in the chromatic genus are the same as in the diatonic genus.

On the enharmonic genus

If you should want to find [this] tetrachord in the enharmonic genus, leave as much space between the nete and the paranete hyperboleon as there is in the chromatic genus between the nete hyperboleon and the trite hyperboleon. The nete diezeugmenon is the same in the enharmonic as it is in the other genera, and you will have a semitone from the nete diezeugmenon to the paranete hyperboleon. Divide [the space between the points marking] this semitone in half, and place the trite hyperboleon in the middle. In this way you have one tetrachord of the enharmonic genus.

Meyer, *Mensura Monochordi*, p. 6

tuning (a division yielding the same pitches in the same intervallic relations as the *Magadis in utraque parte* given above, p. 171), the author turns to the chromatic and enharmonic divisions of the hyperboleon tetrachord; see the window directly above.

In *In primis divide*, halving the string segment between the points marking the nete hyperboleon and the paranete hyperboleon and adding a similar length to the segment between the point marking the paranete hyperboleon and the end of the string yields a chromatic tetrachord with pitches we might call e^1–f^1–$f\sharp^1$–a^1 enclosing the 256:243 semitone (90 cents), an 81:76 semitone (110 cents), and a 19:16 trihemitone (298 cents); placing the paranete hyperboleon where the nete hyperboleon lies in the diatonic genus and halving the segment between the points marking it and the nete diezeugmenon yields an enharmonic tetrachord with pitches we might call e^1–$e+^1$–f^1–a^1 ($e+^1$ representing a quarter tone between e^1 and f^1) enclosing two dieses in the ratios 512:499 and 499:486 (in ascending order; somewhat less and somewhat more than 45 cents respectively) and the Pythagorean ditone 81:64 (408 cents). Of the other divisions in this group of eleven, some divide the b–e^1, e–a, and B–e tetrachords chromatically (producing f♯s and c♯s in one or both registers) or enharmonically (producing e+s and b+s); two (one is that of the eleventh-century theorist Berno of Reichenau) even divide the synemmenon (a-d^1) tetrachord enharmonically as well (producing a+). Some use Greek names for the pitches, some Latin letters.

The two remaining of the thirteen divisions differ in procedure. *In primis censeo*[40]

40 Ibid., pp. 29–31.

achieves f♯^{1} and c♯^{1} in both registers by halving the string lengths between points marking f^1 and g^1 and between points marking c^1 and d^1, then doubling string lengths from the end for f♯ and c♯, producing chromatic tetrachords e^1–f^1–f♯^{1}–a^1, b–c^1–c♯^{1}–e^1, e–f–f♯–a, and B–c–c♯–e, each enclosing the Pythagorean semitone 256:243 (90 cents), an 18:17 semitone (99 cents), and a trihemitone of 153:128 (309 cents). The treatise also describes enharmonic divisions (like those discussed above) producing the tetrachords e^1–e+^{1}–f^1–a^1, b–b+–c^1–e^1, e–e+–f–a, and B–B+–c–e.[41]

Finally, an interpolation that appears as part of Guido's *Micrologus*[42] in nine of its almost eighty sources divides the b–c^1, e^1–f^1, and b^1–c^2 semitones by placing notes between them equal to $^6/_7$ and $^3/_7$ the length of the string from a to the end, $^6/_7$ the length of the string from d^1 to the end, yielding dieses in the ratios 28:27 and 64:63 (about 63 and 27 cents).

Are these chromatic and enharmonic divisions manifestations of an antiquarian interest in obsolete tunings? Or are they, as Meyer surmised, evidence of a practical interest in micro-intervals that flourished in the eleventh and twelfth centuries but vanished with the advent of staff notation and the normalization of diatonic tunings? Ferreira has studied the question in detail, and, after surveying medieval references to singing in chromatic and enharmonic genera, analyzing the *Micrologus* interpolation in detail, and studying neumes (in the Dijon Tonary and other practical sources) that may represent microtonal inflections, concludes that the evidence does indeed support the existence, in eleventh- and twelfth-century practice, of microtonal singing. While Ferreira describes his conclusions as provisional, he certainly has thrown down the gauntlet for anyone seeking to argue the other side of the question.[43]

The terms diatonic, chromatic, and enharmonic reappear in the *Lucidarium* (1317/18) of the theorist, composer, and choirmaster Marchetto of Padua, not as varieties of tetrachords but of semitones. Marchetto proposed dividing the whole tone into fifths, yielding a system with four intervals smaller that the tone: the diesis, $^1/_5$ tone; the "enharmonic" semitone, $^2/_5$ tone; the "diatonic" semitone, $^3/_5$ tone; and the "chromatic" semitone, $^4/_5$ tone.[44] Thus a tone would be divided either into enharmonic and diatonic semitones or into a chromatic semitone and a diesis. The latter division was to be used in polyphony when an imperfect consonance (i.e., third, sixth, or tenth – and in Marchetto's terminology a "tolerable dissonance") moved to a perfect one (fifth or octave) by stepwise contrary motion; in other cases the former division was expected. Example 6.2 illustrates their use: In Example 6.2a, enharmonic semitones lie between

41 Similarly, after constructing a traditional Pythagorean monochord with five flats and five sharps in addition to the natural notes (modeled on Prosdocimo's), Ugolino of Orvieto inserted a point midway between those marking E and F, from which he derived other points midway between e and f, B and c, b and c,^{1} and b^1 and c^2, thus creating the possibility of enharmonic tetrachords built on B, e, b, e^1, and b^1; he noted that these were used by ancients, but are not by moderns (*Tractatus monochordi* 10.55–65; Seay edn., pp. 252–53). 42 Meyer, *Mensura Monochordi*, p. 235.

43 Ferreira, "Music at Cluny," esp. pp. 160–289.

44 Marchetto, *Lucidarium* 2.5–8 (Herlinger edn., pp. 130–57).

Example 6.2 Progressions from Marchetto, *Lucidarium* 2.7, 8; Herlinger, *Lucidarium of Marchetto of Padua*, pp. 145, 151

a and b♭ and between b♮ and c¹, the diatonic semitone between b♭ and b♮; in Example 6.2b, chromatic semitones lie between c¹ and c♯¹, f¹ and f♯¹, g and g♯, dieses between c♯¹ and d¹, f♯¹and g¹, g♯ and a. As Marchetto interchanges the terms "enharmonic semitone," "minor semitone," and "limma" (on the one hand) and "diatonic semitone," "major semitone," and "apotome" (on the other), it seems likely that he intended his enharmonic and diatonic semitones to represent the minor and major semitones (90 and 114 cents respectively) of the standard Pythagorean system; I have argued elsewhere that, given the extreme highness notes like those sharped in Example 6.2b would have if Marchetto's division into $^4/_5$ and $^1/_5$ tone were taken literally (the chromatic semitone and diesis would have 163 and 41 cents respectively), Marchetto must have had in mind a division differing from the standard one much less drastically.[45] The wide major thirds and sixths of Pythagorean tuning are already dissonant, as noted above (p. 176); even a slight increase in their sizes renders them remarkably pungent.[46]

There is another link (other than the terminological) between Marchetto's system and chromatic and enharmonic monochord divisions: Marchetto claimed that in the monochord "the nature of these semitones is clearly recognized when the space of the whole tone is divided into five parts" – words that seem to refer to the division into fifths of the string segment between two points marking pitches a whole tone apart, and that clearly recall the procedures for fractional divisions of string segments for chromatic and enharmonic monochords in texts such as *In primis divide* and *In primis censeo*. Although dividing the space of the whole tone into fifths does not yield five precisely equal intervals, the string lengths involved (from each of the points marking the

45 Herlinger, "Marchetto's Division of the Whole Tone."

46 Christopher Page has described eloquently the "almost fierce beauty" of such widened major thirds and sixths, especially in alternation with perfect consonances; he observes that although Marchetto's precepts for dividing the tone cannot be taken literally, they "required imperfect consonances to be widened in certain cadential positions beyond all modern expectations" ("Polyphony before 1400," pp. 79–82).

fifth-divisions to the end of the string) are so close in size that each of the intervals differs from the next by only about one cent.[47] What is really surprising is how close the intervals resulting from division of the space of the whole tone into $^3/_5$ and $^2/_5$ are to the Pythagorean major and minor semitones, especially when the former is placed below the latter (as when the b♭–c¹ tone is divided by b): they are slightly more than 119 and slightly less than 85 cents respectively, differing from the correct Pythagorean values 114 and 90 by only about 5 cents (when the minor semitone is below the major – as when the a–b tone is divided by b♭ – the values are about 5 cents further off). The closeness of approximation strengthens the hypothesis that Marchetto's "diatonic" and "enharmonic" semitones are representations of the Pythagorean major and minor semitones.

Is it conceivable that chromatic or enharmonic monochord divisions such as the thirteen Meyer discusses could have influenced Marchetto? Although all but one of these appear in manuscripts dating from as early as the eleventh or twelfth century, five of them survive as well in fourteenth- or fifteenth-century copies, a circumstance showing that interest in them persisted into (or revived during) the later Middle Ages. Indeed, two of the texts – the *Micrologus* interpolation (along with the entire treatise) and *Monocordum divisurus*[48] – are found in a fourteenth-century manuscript in Milan, the earliest source for Marchetto's treatises and a source that has been linked to Marchetto's Angevin milieu.[49]

At any rate, Marchetto's system is the first viable medieval proposal for division of the tone – at least conceptually – into some number of fractional parts, and as such represents a crucial advance in music theory. Traditionally, division of the Pythagorean whole tone into halves, fifths, or any number of equal parts was considered impossible, as the arithmetic involved required the insertion, between the terms of the superparticular ratio 9:8, of irrational numbers, which were beyond the scope of Pythagorean arithmetic.[50] This is precisely the point made by the bitterest of Marchetto's critics, the physician and professor of arts (and fellow Paduan citizen) Prosdocimo de' Beldomandi, who wrote in his *Tractatus musice speculative* of 1425 that

> the whole tone . . . is not divisible into any number of equal parts: neither into two halves nor three thirds nor four fourths nor five fifths nor six sixths, and so forth. For no superparticular ratio is divisible into equal parts; therefore the sesquioctave ratio [9:8] is not so divisible and, consequently, neither is the whole tone.[51]

Thus a tradition-minded theorist took Marchetto to task, much as other tradition-minded theorists would take Ramis to task a few decades later. But the theories of both survived; and Marchetto's five-part division of the tone appears to converge with

47 Their ratios are respectively 45:44, 44:43, 43:42, 42:41, and 41:40.
48 Meyer, *Mensura Monochordi*, pp. 39–43.
49 Herlinger, introduction to *The Lucidarium of Marchetto of Padua*, p. 23.
50 Crocker, "Pythagorean Mathematics and Music."
51 Baralli and Torri, "*Trattato* di Prosdocimo," p. 743.

Ramis's description of just tuning and his implied reference to meantone temperament in Nicola Vicentino's 31-step division of the octave, which consists of five whole tones (each divided into five dieses) and two major diatonic semitones each divided into three dieses.[52] Certainly Marchetto and Vicentino represent important milestones along the road that led to equal temperament, as proposed eventually by Vincenzo Galilei (1581).[53]

52 Vicentino, *L'antica musica*, fols. 17v–20v. Barbour calls Vicentino's system "a clever method for extending the usual meantone temperament of $^1/_4$ comma until it formed practically a closed system," and links it to Marchetto's (*Tuning and Temperament*, pp. 117–20). Maniates, however, claims that Vicentino must have known Marchetto's theory only through an intermediary like Fogliano, Gaffurio, or Aaron (introduction to Vicentino, *L'antica musica*, p. xxxvi).

53 In his *Dialogo della musica antica de moderna* (1581) the lutenist and theorist Vincenzo Galilei (father of Galileo Galilei) proposed placing the frets of string instruments by successive 18:17 ratios, thus obtaining semitones of 99 cents, indistinguishable from the 100-cent semitones of equal temperament. See Barbour, *Tuning and Temperament*, pp. 57–64. For more on equal temperament, see **Chapter** 7, **pp.** 204–09.

Bibliography

Primary sources

Blackburn, B. J., E. E. Lowinsky, and C. A. Miller (eds.), *A Correspondence of Renaissance Musicians*, Oxford, Clarendon Press, 1991

Boethius, A. M. S. *De institutione musica*, ed. G. Friedlein as *Anicii Manlii Torquati Severini Boetii De institutione arithmetica libri duo, De institutione musica libri quinque; accedit Geometria quae fertur Boetii*, Leipzig, Teubner, 1867; reprint Frankfurt, Minerva, 1966; trans. C. Bower, ed. C. Palisca as *Fundamentals of Music*, New Haven, Yale University Press, 1989

Burzio, N. *Musices opusculum*, ed. G. Massera as *Nicolai Burtii parmensis florum libellus*, Florence, L. Olschki, 1975; trans. C. Miller as N. Burtius, *Musices opusculum*, *MSD* 37 (1983)

Dialogus de musica, *GS* 1, pp. 251–64; trans. W. and O. Strunk as *Dialogue on Music* in *SR*, pp. 198–210

Divide per quatuor a primo byduro, in Meyer, *Mensura Monochordi*, p. 226

Divide primo, in Meyer, *Mensura Monochordi*, p. 224

Fogliano, L. *Musica theorica*, Venice, J. Antonius, 1529; facs. Bologna, Forni, 1970

Gaffurio, F. *Apologia Franchini Gafurii adversus Ioannem Spatarium et complices musicos bononienses*, Turin, A. de Vicomercato, 1520; facs. New York, Broude, 1979

De harmonia musicorum instrumentorum opus, Milan, G. Pontanus, 1518; facs. Bologna, Forni, 1972 and New York, Broude, 1979; trans. C. Miller, *MSD* 33 (1977)

Practica musice, Milan, G. Le Signerre 1496; facs. Bologna, Forni, 1972 and New York, Broude, 1979; trans. C. Miller as *Practica musicae*, *MSD* 20 (1968); trans. I. Young as *The "Practica musicae" of Franchinus Gafurius*, Madison, University of Wisconsin Press, 1969

Theorica musice, Milan, P. Mantegatius, 1492; facs. New York, Broude, 1967 and Bologna, Forni, 1969; trans. W. Kreyszig, ed. C. Palisca as *The Theory of Music*, New Haven, Yale University Press, 1993

Theoricum opus musice discipline, Naples, Dino, 1480; facs. Lucca, Libreria musicale italiana, 1996

Guido of Arezzo, *Micrologus*, ed. J. S. van Waesberghe as *Guidonis Aretini micrologus*, *CSM* 4 (1955); trans. W. Babb, ed. C. Palisca in *Hucbald, Guido, and John on Music: Three Medieval Treatises*, New Haven, Yale University Press, 1978, pp. 49–83

Hothby, Johannes, *Excitatio quaedam musicae artis per refutationem*, ed. A. Seay in *Johannis Octobi tres tractatuli contra Bartholomeum Ramum*, *CSM* 10 (1964), pp. 17–57

Incipiendo primum, in Meyer, *Mensura Monochordi*, p. 228

In primis censeo, in Meyer, *Mensura Monochordi*, pp. 29–31

In primis divide, in Meyer, *Mensura Monochordi*, pp. 5–7

John of Afflighem (Cotton), *De musica*, ed. J. S. van Waesberghe as *Johannis Affligemensis de musica cum tonario*, *CSM* no. 1 (1950); trans. W. Babb, ed. C. Palisca in *Hucbald, Guido, and John on Music: Three Medieval Treatises*, New Haven, Yale University Press, 1978, pp. 87–190

John of Garland, *De plana musica*, trans. N. Gwee as "*De plana musica* and *Introductio musice*: a Critical Edition and Translation, with Commentary, of Two Treatises Attributed to Johannes de Garlandia," Ph.D. diss., Louisiana State University (1996)

Magadis in utraque parte, in Meyer, *Mensura Monochordi*, pp. 13–14

Marchetto of Padua, *Lucidarium in arte musicae planae*, trans. and ed. J. Herlinger as *The Lucidarium of Marchetto of Padua: a Critical Edition, Translation, and Commentary*, University of Chicago Press, 1985

Medietas lineae, in Meyer, *Mensura Monochordi*, p. 143

Meyer, C. *Mensura Monochordi: la division du monocorde (IXe–XVe siècles)*, Paris, Klincksieck, 1996

Musica, Scolica enchiriadis, ed. H. Schmid as *Musica et scolica enchiriadis una cum aliquibus tractatulis adiunctis*, Munich, Bayerische Akademie der Wissenschaften, 1981; trans. R. Erickson, ed. C. Palisca as *"Musica enchiriadis" and "Scolica enchiriadis"*, New Haven, Yale University Press, 1995

Philippe de Vitry, *Ars nova*, ed. G. Reaney, A. Gilles, and J. Maillard as *Philippi de Vitriaco ars nova*, *CSM* 8 (1964); trans. L. Plantinga as "Philippe de Vitry's *Ars nova*: A Translation," *JMT* 5 (1961), pp. 204–23

Primum divide monochordum, in Meyer, *Mensura Monochordi*, pp. 24–25

Prosdocimo de' Beldomandi, *"Brevis summula proportionum quantum ad musicam pertinet" and "Parvus tractatulus de modo monacordi dividendi"*, trans. and ed. J. Herlinger, Lincoln, University of Nebraska Press, 1987

Tractatus musice speculative, Ital. trans. D. Baralli and L. Torri in "Il *Trattato* di Prosdocimo de' Beldomandi contro il *Lucidario* di Marchetto de Padova," *Rivista musicale italiana* 20 (1913), pp. 707–62

Ramis de Pareia, B. *Musica practica*, Bologna, B. de Hiriberia, 1482; ed. J. Wolf as *Musica practica Bartolomei Rami de Pareja Bononiae*, Leipzig, Breitkopf und Härtel, 1901; trans. C. Miller, *MSD* 44 (1993)

Remi of Auxerre, *Commentum in Martianum Capellam*, ed. C. Lutz as *Remigii Autissiodorensis commentum in Martianum Capellam*, 2 vols., Leiden, E. Brill, 1962–65

Sequitur de synemmenis, in Prosdocimo, *"Parvus tractatulus"*, pp. 126–35, and Meyer, *Mensura Monochordi*, pp. 185–87

Si aliqua linea, in Meyer, *Mensura Monochordi*, pp. 117–20

Si vis mensurare monocordum, in Meyer, *Mensura Monochordi*, p. 197

Spataro, G. *Bartolomei Ramis honesta defensio*, Bologna, P. de Benedecti, 1491; facs. ed. G. Vecchi as *Johannis Spatarii opera omnia I: Bartolomei Ramis honesta defensio in Nicolai Burtii parmensis opusculum*, Università degli studi di Bologna, 1967

Errori de Franchino Gafurio da Lodi, Bologna, B. Hectoris, 1521

Tali a principio, in Meyer, *Mensura Monochordi*, p. 227

Ugolino of Orvieto, *Tractatus monochordi*, ed. A. Seay in *Ugolini Urbevetani declaratio musicae disciplinae*, *CSM* 7/3 (1962), pp. 227–53

Vicentino, N. *L'antica musica ridotta alla moderna prattica*. Rome, A. Barre, 1555; facs. Kassel, Bärenreiter, 1959; trans. M. Maniates, ed. C. Palisca as *Ancient Music Adapted to Modern Practice*, New Haven, Yale University Press, 1996

Secondary sources

Adkins, C. D. "The Theory and Practice of the Monochord," Ph.D. diss., State University of Iowa (1963)

Barbour, J. M. *Tuning and Temperament: A Historical Survey*, East Lansing, Michigan State College Press, 1953

Bent, M. "Musica Recta and Musica Ficta," *Musica Disciplina* 26 (1972), pp. 73–100

Bröcker, M. *Die Drehleier: ihr Bau und ihre Geschichte*, 2 vols., Bonn-Bad Godesberg, Verlag für Systematische Musikwissenschaft, 1977

Browne, A. C. "Medieval Letter Notations: A Survey of the Sources," Ph.D. diss., University of Illinois (1979)

Crocker, R. L. "Pythagorean Mathematics and Music," *Journal of Aesthetics and Art Criticism* 22 (1963–64), pp. 189–98, 325–35

Ferreira, M. P. R. "Music at Cluny: The Tradition of Gregorian Chant for the Proper of the Mass – Melodic Variants and Microtonal Nuances," Ph.D. diss., Princeton University (1997)

Fuller, S. "A Phantom Treatise of the Fourteenth Century? the *Ars nova*," *JM* 4 (1985), pp. 23–50

Helmholtz, H., *On the Sensations of Tone as a Physiological Basis for the Theory of Music*, 4th edn. (1877), trans. A. Ellis, New York, Dover, 1954

Heninger, S. K. *Touches of Sweet Harmony: Pythagorean Cosmology and Renaissance Poetics*, San Marino, Huntington Library, 1974

Herlinger, J. W. "Marchetto's Division of the Whole Tone," *JAMS* 35 (1981), pp. 193–21

Huglo, M. "L'Auteur du *Dialogue sur la musique* attribué à Odon," *Revue de musicologie* 55 (1969), pp. 121–71.

Lindley, M. "Fifteenth-Century Evidence for Meantone Temperament," *Proceedings of the Royal Musical Association* 102 (1975–76), pp. 37–51

"Pythagorean Intonation and the Rise of the Triad," *Royal Musical Association Research Chronicle* 16 (1980), pp. 4–61

Markovits, M. *Das Tonsystem der abendländischen Musik im frühen Mittelalter*, Bern, P. Haupt, 1977

Page, C. "Polyphony before 1400," in *Performance Practice: Music before 1600*, ed. H. M. Brown and S. Sadie, New York, Norton, 1989, pp. 79–104

Palisca, C. V. *Humanism in Italian Renaissance Musical Thought*, New Haven, Yale University Press, 1985

Robertson, D. W. *A Preface to Chaucer: Studies in Medieval Perspectives*, Princeton University Press, 1963

Sachs, K.-J. *Mensura Fistularum: die Mensurierung der Orgelpfeifen im Mittelalter*, 2 vols., Stuttgart, Musikwissenschaftliche Verlags-Gesellschaft, 1970–80

Waesberghe, J. Smits van, *De Musico-Paedagogico et Theoretico Guidone Aretino, eiusque Vita et Moribus*, Florence, L. Olschki, 1953

Wantzloeben, S. *Das Monochord als Instrument und als System*, Halle, Niemeyer, 1911

·7·

Tuning and temperament

RUDOLF RASCH

The tuning of musical instruments has kept music theorists busy since antiquity. It is a commonplace – although no less true for that – to say that each period in the history of music has had its own theory of tuning in order to meet its own musical needs. Likewise, the quantitative language used to calculate and represent these various tuning systems has changed. In the medieval and Renaissance periods, theories of tuning were usually formulated in terms of relative string lengths on a monochord, to be calculated by arithmetic methods.

From the end of the sixteenth century, until around 1800, string lengths remained in use by theorists, but their calculations were often refined by the use of mathematical tools such as root extraction. With root extraction, the various equal and unequal temperaments that dominated theory and practice from the sixteenth century onwards could be adequately described. Musically, this meant that intervals of any size could be divided into equal parts. (This was possible with arithmetic methods in exceptional cases only.) At some point in the seventeenth century, logarithmic measures of pitch were added to the common string-length values, by which a psychologically more realistic picture of the relations among pitches could be presented. Logarithms facilitated the description and calculation of virtually any tuning system conceivable.

Tuning and temperament theory was especially developed by eighteenth-century German authors. They used a variety a methods to describe a great number of tuning systems, both equal and unequal. From about 1800, string lengths were progressively replaced by frequency values to indicate pitches, making it possible to establish empirically the relations between theory and practice. During the nineteenth century, when an expanded chromatic/enharmonic tonal system had become the frame of reference for musical composition, generalized theories of musical tunings were developed.[1] The twentieth century, finally, saw the rise of the study of tuning in a historical perspective, which made possible combinations of the various historical tunings and temperaments mentioned above, and to be described in more detail below.

The literature on tuning – both historical and current – is enormous in size and bewildering in variety. There are practical tuning instructions without a single

1 Drobisch, "Ueber musikalische Tonbestimmung"; Bosanquet, "An Elementary Treatise."

technical term, table or figure. At the other end, there are mathematical treatises not comprehensible without a sound formal training in mathematical calculus and analysis. Works on tuning have been written by a great diversity of people: not only by musicians and music theorists, but also by mathematicians, scientists, and even amateur enthusiasts. Whereas sometimes these writings belong squarely within a certain coherent tradition (such as Renaissance just intonation theory or eighteenth-century German temperament theory), in other cases there is an overlap in the traditions with regard to terminology, representations, or goals.

Because of the varying approaches apparent in the history of the subject, it is not easy to synthesize the theory of tuning and temperament within a single chapter of limited size. One has to be highly selective in the choice of theorists to discuss on the one hand, and quite economical in the choice of concepts and terms to describe their theories on the other. To meet the first requirement, a selection has been made of about a dozen theories from the sixteenth to the eighteenth century, which together seem to constitute a representative cross-section of various tuning and temperament systems. In many cases, the theory chosen represents the first – or the first major – use of a certain approach. For the second requirement we will try to make use of a more or less standardized set of terms and symbols in order to make possible cross-comparisons (for example the measuring unit of "cents," which was actually only first worked out in the nineteenth century; see below, p. 210 for an explanation of cents).

The basic modern text on tuning and temperament is still, despite its many (and sometimes serious) shortcomings, James Murray Barbour's *Tuning and Temperament: A Historical Survey* of 1951. This work delineates various problems of tuning and temperament, partitions the tuning systems described in the literature into a small number of well-chosen categories, presents a standard method of comparison (by comparing them all to equal temperament) and pays attention to the relation between theory and practice. All later works on the subject (including mine) pay tribute to Barbour's indispensable book. Many books on the subject have appeared since Barbour's, but they seem only to have been able to revise or to refine sections of his study, not to replace it as a whole.[2]

In this chapter, I will roughly follow a historical chronology, starting in the middle of the sixteenth century and ending at the end of the eighteenth. Throughout this period of some two and a half centuries, the time-honored monochord remained in use as the basic tool of tuning and temperament theory. Glarean's description of Pythagorean tuning will serve to explain both the use of the monochord at that time and the Pythagorean system. The sixteenth century saw the rise of two new concepts: that of just intonation (from the introduction of the just major third) and that of temperament

2 Among the most important recent scholarship on the history of tuning and temperament that can also be recommended are Dupont, *Geschichte der musikalischen Temperatur*; Jorgensen, *Tuning the Historical Temperaments by Ear*; and *Tuning*; Lindley, "Stimmung und Temperatur"; Devie, *Le tempérament musical*; Ratte, *Die Temperatur der Clavierinstrumente*; Lindley and Turner-Smith, *Mathematical Models.*

(in order to acknowledge the practical use of intervals deviating from their just values). As illustrations, we will consider Salinas's exposition of just intonation and Zarlino's treatment of temperament. Around 1600 theorists extended the use of the monochord, by first calculating more complicated kinds of theoretical string lengths (for example, by root extractions), then rounding them off and finally applying them in practice. With this "equipment," equal temperament and meantone temperament could be successfully plotted on the monochord. For equal temperament, we follow Stevin's description (however flawed), for meantone temperament, that of Stevin's opponent Jacobus Verheyden.

Logarithmic transformations of the numerical values used to define a tuning system were introduced in musical calculations during the seventeenth century, first to facilitate the calculation of string lengths in complicated cases, later to calculate any string length. They have the property that their values correspond better to our perceptions of tonal space and tonal systems than either string lengths or frequencies do. Owing to the availability of logarithmic calculation, many fine varieties of tuning could be calculated rather quickly.

A final tool was contributed to the field by Andreas Werckmeister and Johann Georg Neidhardt: they realized that little was lost when complicated geometric divisions of intervals (such as the comma) were replaced by arithmetic divisions. This substitution was of importance both when the goal was to provide a series of figures to describe a tuning and when the tuning had to be plotted on a monochord.

Pythagorean tuning: Glarean (1547)

The monochord is the traditional instrument used to illustrate tuning systems both visually and aurally. It has a tradition that dates back, via Boethius, to antiquity. (see **Chapter 6, pp. 168–70**). Most authors writing on tuning and temperament from the fifteenth century until the end of the eighteenth century used the monochord to explain intervals and to define tuning systems. A monochord division may be presented either graphically, in the form of a drawing or engraving, or as a series of numbers, which represent string lengths expressed in an arbitrary unit of length (for examples of the former, see **Plate 6.1, p. 169**; and **Plate 8.1, p. 230**). The total length of the string is usually chosen in such a way that it is either a round number (2,000, 5,000, 10,000, etc.) or a product, which ensures that most if not all of the divisions produce integer numbers (such as Glarean's $11{,}664 = 2^4 \times 3^6$). The larger the number is, the finer the shades of pitch that can be represented. Smaller numbers are of course easier to work with, but numbers which are too small may require too much rounding to represent the intended system well enough. The treatment of the monochord by Henrich Glarean (1488–1563) in his famous *Dodecachordon* (1547) is a good example of Pythagorean tuning in that it merely uses octaves with string-length ratios 1:2 and fifths with string-length ratios 2:3.[3] (We will write ratios always with the smaller number first.) By restricting himself to intervals defined by factors not greater than 3, Glarean faithfully adhered to time-honored Pythagorean principles of interval theory. In the construction of his monochord, he proceeds entirely by division into two, three, four, and nine parts. Let us have a look at his procedure (see Table 7.1).

The entire string with length 11,664 (marked γγ) represents the note FF. The string is divided into nine parts. Eight-ninths of the string, 10,368, provides the note GG (marked Γ), $^8/_9$ of 10,368 the note AA: 9,216. Two-thirds of the string length for FF (11,664) gives the length for C (7,776), 2/3 of the length for GG (10,368) that for D (6,912), 2/3 of the length for AA (9,216) that for E (6,144). $^2/_3$ of the length for E gives that for B (4,096). Thus all the diatonic notes have their place on the string.

The chromatic notes are less elegantly treated. BB♭ is found by dividing the string length of FF (11,664) into four parts, and taking $^3/_4$ of the original lengths (8,748). E♭ is similarly derived from B♭, and A♭ from E♭. But E♭ and A♭ are included in the list of note names simply as "Semitone" and no string lengths are provided. Sharps do not have a place in Glarean's monochord.

Some chromatic degrees are, however, introduced via the chromatic tetrachord. For the notes of this tetrachord, Glarean retains the names of the diatonic notes, for example, E–F–G–A. In the chromatic tetrachord, the pitch of the G is lowered to correspond to G♭. In the tetrachord B–C–D–E, the D is lowered to D♭ in the chromatic version. A similar procedure is followed for the enharmonic tetrachords: in the given example the pitch of the F is lowered by half a semitone, the pitch of the G is lowered a full tone (to become identical to the diatonic F).

For the new chromatic and enharmonic pitches numerical values have been provided, albeit without rationale. The chromatic lowering of the second higher note of a tetrachord appears to be carried out by dividing the whole tone 8:9 arithmetically into two unequal portions, so that the compound ratio is 72:76:81 (72:81 = 8:9). The enharmonic lowering of the second lower note of a tetrachord is carried out by averaging arithmetically the semitone around it. If the semitone BB–C is 8,192:7,776, an enharmonic pitch between BB and C is formed by (8,192 + 7,776)/2 = 7,984.

Apart from the "chromatic" and "enharmonic" values, Glarean's monochord represents what is now generally called a *Pythagorean tuning*. The fifths are just; the major thirds are formed as the sum of four fifths minus two octaves, which leads to a ratio of 64:81 (or 407.820 cents), definitely larger than the "true" ratio of the major third, 64:80 or 4:5 (or 386.314 cents). The difference is the interval with the ratio 80:81, an interval known as the *syntonic comma*. It has the logarithmic size of 21.506 cents, about one-fifth of a tempered semitone. Major thirds which are too large by a syntonic comma are not really acceptable in keyboard tuning. Pythagorean minor thirds have the ratio 27:32 (or 294.135 cents), which is less than the true ratio 5:6 (or 315.614

3 Glarean, *Dodecachordon*, pp. 50ff.

Table 7.1 *Pythagorean tuning according to Heinrich Glarean,* Dodecachordon *(Basel, 1547), p. 55*

Notes	Diatonic notes	Chromatic notes	Enharmonic notes	String lengths (Glarean)	Cents (C = 0 cents)
FF	γγ		Γ	11,664	
GG♭		Γ		10,944	
GG	Γ			10,368	
AA	A	A	A	9,216	
BB♭	B			8,748	
BB	H	H	H	8,192	
C≃			C	7,984	
C	C	C	D	7,776	0
D♭		D		7,296	110.307
D	D			6,912	203.910
E♭	Semitone			[6,561]	294.135
E	E	E	E	6,144	407.820
F≃			F	5,988	452.345
F	F	F	G	5,832	498.045
G♭		G		5,472	605.352
G	G			5,184	701.955
A♭	Semitone			[4,920.75]	792.180
A	a	a	a	4,608	905.865
B♭	b			4,374	996.090
B	h	h	h	4,096	1,109.775
c≃			c	3,992	1,200
c	c	c	d	3,888	
d♭		d		3,648	
d	d			3,456	
e♭	Semitone			[3,280.5]	
e	e	e	e	3,072	
f≃			f	2,994	
f	f	f	g	2,916	
g♭		g		2,736	
g	g			2,592	
a♭	Semitone			[2,460.375]	
a	Aa	Aa	Aa	2,304	
b♭	Bb			2,187	
b	Hh	Hh	Hh	2,048	
c^1	Cc	Cc	Dd	1,944	
$d♭^1$		Dd		1,824	
d^1	Dd			1,728	
$e♭^1$	Semitone			[1,640.25]	
e^1	Ee	Ee	Ee	1,536	

Notes: The first column includes modern note names (the enharmonic pitch between B and C has been named C≃; that between E and F, F≃). The columns marked "Diatonic notes," "Chromatic notes," and "Enharmonic notes" are Glarean's names.

cents) by a syntonic comma. Apart from the poor thirds (and sixths), Pythagorean tuning has yet another shortcoming, which is that the circle of fifths cannot be closed. If eleven fifths are just, the twelfth one (technically a diminished sixth – for example, G♯-E♭, 678.495 cents), is too small by the amount of a *ditonic comma*, an interval with a ratio of 524,288 : 531,441 and a logarithmic size of 23.460 cents. It is 2 cents larger than the syntonic comma (more precisely 1.954 cents, an interval known as a schisma), but should not be confused with it or interchanged with it (although some theorists have equated the two commas for simplicity's sake).

Pythagorean tuning is thought to represent the tuning of instruments in medieval times, when the fifths were still the predominant consonant intervals and the thirds only of secondary importance, so that their poor tuning could be accepted. (See the discussion in **Chapter 6, pp. 176–78**.) Much later in history – from the nineteenth century onwards – one of the characteristics of Pythagorean tuning, high sharps and low flats (a consequence of the wide major thirds and the narrow minor thirds), became the underlying principle in melodic intonation, since it strengthens the leading-note and stresses the major–minor opposition in nineteenth-century harmony. But from the sixteenth through the eighteenth centuries, the need for better-tuned thirds and sixths necessitated the development of other tuning systems.

Just intonation: Salinas (1577)

Already before the end of the fifteenth century a new type of monochord division was becoming popular, namely divisions based on both the just fifth (2 : 3) and the just major third (4 : 5 or 386.314 cents). Such monochords are now generally called *just-intonation monochords*. Many theorists from this and later periods provide examples of such monochords (see also **Chapter 6, pp. 178–84**). As an example, the one given by the Spanish theorist Francisco Salinas (1513–90) in his *De musica libri septem* (1577) will be discussed here (see Table 7.2).[4]

Although just-intonation monochords are characterized by just fifths and just major thirds, their construction usually begins with the melodic diatonic scale, in which as many just intervals are to be realized as possible. So Salinas's discussion started with the following scale between E and e:

E – [sem] – F [maj] – G [min] – a [maj] – b [sem] – c [maj] – dj – [comma] ds – [min] e

The interval between any adjacent tones (given between square brackets) was either a syntonic comma (80 : 81), a just diatonic semitone ([sem]; 15 : 16 or 111.731 cents), a minor whole tone ([min]; 9 : 10 or 182.404 cents) or a major whole tone ([maj]; 8 : 9 or 203.910 cents). The D is present twice, once as a "lower D" (dj = D inferior), once as a "higher D" (ds = D superior). This double presence is necessary to provide the required

4 Salinas, *De musica libri septem*, pp. 110ff.

Table 7.2 *Just intonation according to Francisco Salinas,* De musica libri septem *(Salamanca, 1577), p. 122*

Note	Diatonic notes	Chromatic notes	Enharmonic notes	Cents (C = 0 cents)
E	57,600			386.314
E♯			55,296	456.986
F	54,000			498.045
F♯j		51,840		568.717
F♯s		51,200		590.224
G♭j			50,625	609.776
G♭s			50,000	631.283
G	48,000			701.955
G♯		46,080		772.627
a♭			45,000	813.686
a	43,200			884.359
a♯j			41,472	955.031
a♯s			40,960	976.537
bj		40,500		996.090
bs		40,000		1,017.596
h	38,400			1,088.269
h♯			36,864	1,158.941
c	36,000			1,200 = 0
c♯		34,560		70.672
d♭			33,750	111.731
dj	32,400			182.404
ds	32,000			203.910
d♯			30,720	274.582
e♭		30,000		315.641
e	28,800			386.314

Note: The suffixes -j and -s distinguish between pairs of notes with the same name, but at a comma distance (21.506 cents) of one another.

just relations to other tones, as becomes clear from the following diagram, in which horizontal connections represent just fifths, vertical ones just major thirds:

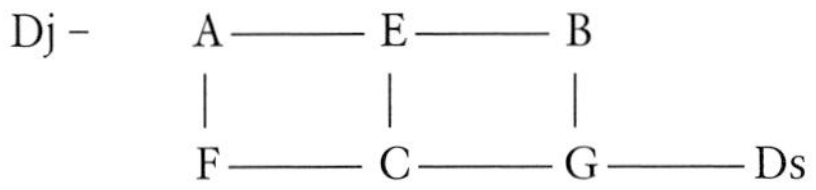

```
Dj –    A——— E——— B
        |     |     |
        F——— C——— G——— Ds
```

Just as Glarean had done, Salinas expanded his monochord by the inclusion of the chromatic and enharmonic genera, but here they have entirely different meanings. The chromatic notes are generated by the division of the whole tone (either major or minor) into two semitones, one minor or chromatic (24:25 or 70.672 cents), the other one

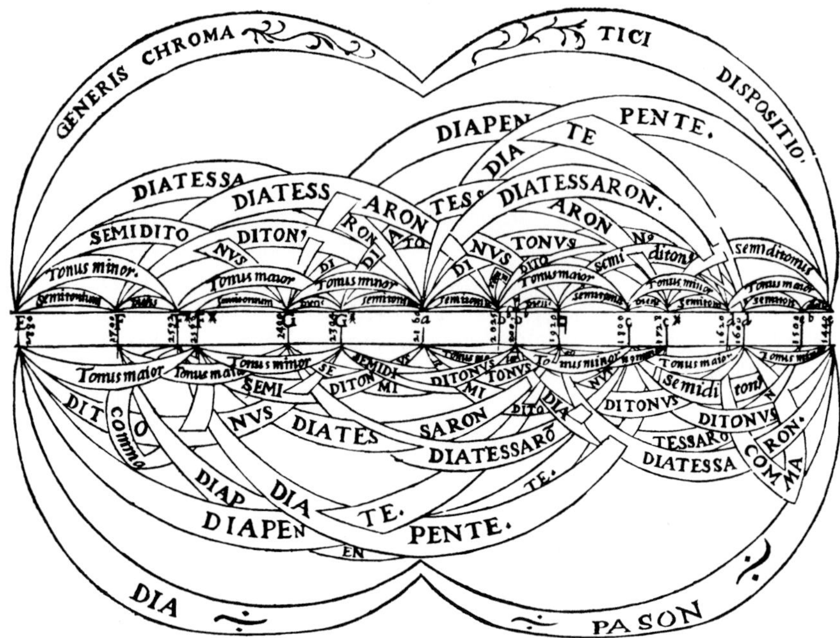

Plate 7.1 Chromatic just-intonation monochord by Francisco Salinas, *De musica libri septem* (1577), p. 119

major or diatonic (15 : 16 or 111.731 cents). These two semitones together make up a minor whole tone (9 : 10). If the whole tone is a major whole tone (8 : 9), though, it is divided into the two semitones plus a syntonic comma in the middle. By these procedures the diatonic scale is converted into a chromatic scale, containing, in addition, a number of pairs of notes with the same names at the distance of a syntonic comma.

Salinas's enharmonic notes are generated by the division of the diatonic semitones of 15 : 16 into a chromatic semitone (in this context also called the chromatic diesis; 24 : 25) and an enharmonic diesis (125 : 128 or 41,059 cents). The latter interval would lie enharmonically between equivalent sharps and flats in just intonation. Salinas presented his monochords in woodcuts, which count among the most beautiful illustrations in Western books about music theory of all times (see Plate 7.1).

Just intonations play an important role in nearly every book on music theory from the sixteenth century onwards. They provide the framework for any further discussion of the musical scale, be it in terms of tuning or in terms of interval or chord theory. Just intonations were appealing to many Renaissance musicians owing to their rich palette of "natural" perfect and imperfect consonances. But if no double pitches (such as Dj and Ds) are allowed, there are also many fifths off by a syntonic comma (680.449 cents) and major thirds off by a minor diesis (427.373 cents), a property that stands in the way of nearly every practical application. Just tuning can only imperfectly be used on twelve-tone keyboards. On such keyboards, the raised ("black") keys will inevitably have to be used in multiple functions: the key between D and E, for example, may be required to provide a major third above B (it is then D♯) or a major third below G (it is then E♭). In a just intonation, only one of these functions is possible. What is needed is a compromise between the two just-intonation values for a raised key.

Temperament: Zarlino (1558)

Despite its high theoretical prestige in the sixteenth century, just intonation was already known to be inappropriate as a tuning system for keyboards. A solution to the problem inevitably involved altering or *tempering* certain intervals. (It should be kept in mind that, technically speaking, "tuning" refers to the pitching of only just intervals [made up of whole ratios], while "temperament" refers to the slight alteration of these just tunings [involving irrational ratios].) All tempered intervals deviate somewhat from just values. They may be either wider or narrower. We will consider tempered intervals as the sum of a just interval plus or minus its *tempering*. In this view the tempering is a small interval added or subtracted from the just interval to change it into the tempered interval.

A characteristic of tempering in general is that, when the intervals to which it applies are ordered into circles, the total amount of tempering in a circle is constant and equal to a given value. This means that if one tries to keep certain intervals just or close to just, inevitably other intervals will be further removed from their just sizes. As an example let us look at the circle of major thirds C–E–G♯/A♭–B♯/C (the pairs of notes refer to the one pitch, as if we do want to use that pitch enharmonically for both note names). Since three major thirds is a little less than an octave (namely a minor diesis), at least one of the three major thirds in the circle has to be altered (enlarged) to let the sum be equal to an octave. One could enlarge all three major thirds by the same amount (then we may speak of equal temperament), or one could enlarge one or two major thirds more than the remaining one(s), as long as the sum total of the tempering equals the minor diesis.

Not only do the intervals in a circle influence the other intervals in the same circle, the fifth and the major third are connected to one another in such a way that their temperings interact. If one tries to tune the fifths just or nearly so, the major thirds will be of poor quality (namely, too wide). If one tries to tune the major thirds just or nearly so, than the fifths will be unsatisfactory (namely, too small). This is due to the simple rule connecting the sizes of the just fifth and the just major third:

$$(5/4) = (3/2)^4 \,/\, (2/1)^2 \,/\, (81/80).$$

The right-hand part of the equation shows that the sum of four fifths minus two octaves provides a major third that has to be diminished by the amount of a *syntonic comma* (of 80 : 81) in order to be equal to a just-intonation major third. That means that either the fifths have to be narrowed or the major third has to be left wider than just, or both. The decision is basically a musical one: which interval needs to be kept just or as just as possible: the fifth or the major third? During the sixteenth and seventeenth centuries the priority was given to the major third. One may assume that the most important factor in this choice was the fact that just major thirds lead to moderately tempered, if still acceptable, fifths, whereas just fifths lead to overly wide and quite unusable major thirds. The temperament in which the fifths were diminished by one quarter of a syntonic comma (in order to produce just major thirds) was from the eighteenth century onward called *meantone temperament*. Its history, however, dates back to the sixteenth century, if not earlier.

The first temperament ever described in systematic terms was, however, not meantone temperament, but a system which does not seem to have had any practical significance. It is the system in which the fifths are diminished by 2/7 of a syntonic comma, as described by Gioseffo Zarlino in *Le istitutioni harmoniche* (1558).[5] Since the tempering of the fifths is larger than $^1/_4$ of a comma, the major thirds turn out to be *smaller* than just, by the amount of $^1/_7$ of a comma. The minor thirds are diminished by the same amount. It is not clear why Zarlino chose this system for further elaboration: perhaps the equal amounts of tempering of the major and minor thirds played a role in his decision. The calculation of the string lengths corresponding to the tones which make up tempered fifths, major and minor thirds was not so easy: it required 7th-power roots and Zarlino was unable to do that. He could not go further than graphically indicate the pitches on the monochord (see Plate 7.2). Zarlino did work out a meantone temperament in his *Dimostrationi armoniche* (1571).[6] As in the case of the $^2/_7$-comma temperament, however, no calculated values of string lengths were given. In his re-edition of the *Istitutioni harmoniche* in 1573, Zarlino repeated his description of the $^2/_7$-comma temperament, again mentioned meantone temperament, and referred to a third variety, namely the $^1/_3$-comma temperament (see Plate 7.2).[7]

If Zarlino's description of meantone temperament is the first exact one, it is already implied in the informal tuning instructions given by Pietro Aaron (c. 1480 – c. 1550) in his *Toscanello in musica* (1523).[8] There, the general rule is to tune the fifths as narrow as the ear will permit and then check if, after four of those fifths, one arrives at a major third which is practically just. Even the tuning instructions for organ by Arnolt Schlick (c. 1450 – c. 1525) in his *Spiegel der Orgelmacher und Organisten* (1511) may refer to meantone tuning: there is no explicit remark about the just major thirds, but the fifths have to be narrowed as much as the ear may permit. After Zarlino, meantone temperament is probably the most commonly described single tuning system until well into the eighteenth century. Its ubiquity in the literature suggests a rather general application on keyboard instruments throughout this period.

5 Zarlino, *Istitutioni*, Part II, pp. 125ff. 6 Zarlino, *Dimostrationi*, Part II, pp. 283ff.
7 Zarlino, *Istitutioni*, Part II, p. 145. The system with fifths tempered by $^1/_3$ of a comma had been worked out by Salinas, *De musica*, pp. 145ff., where also the $^2/_7$- and $^1/_4$-comma temperaments were described.
8 Aaron, *Toscanello in musica*, Chapter 41.

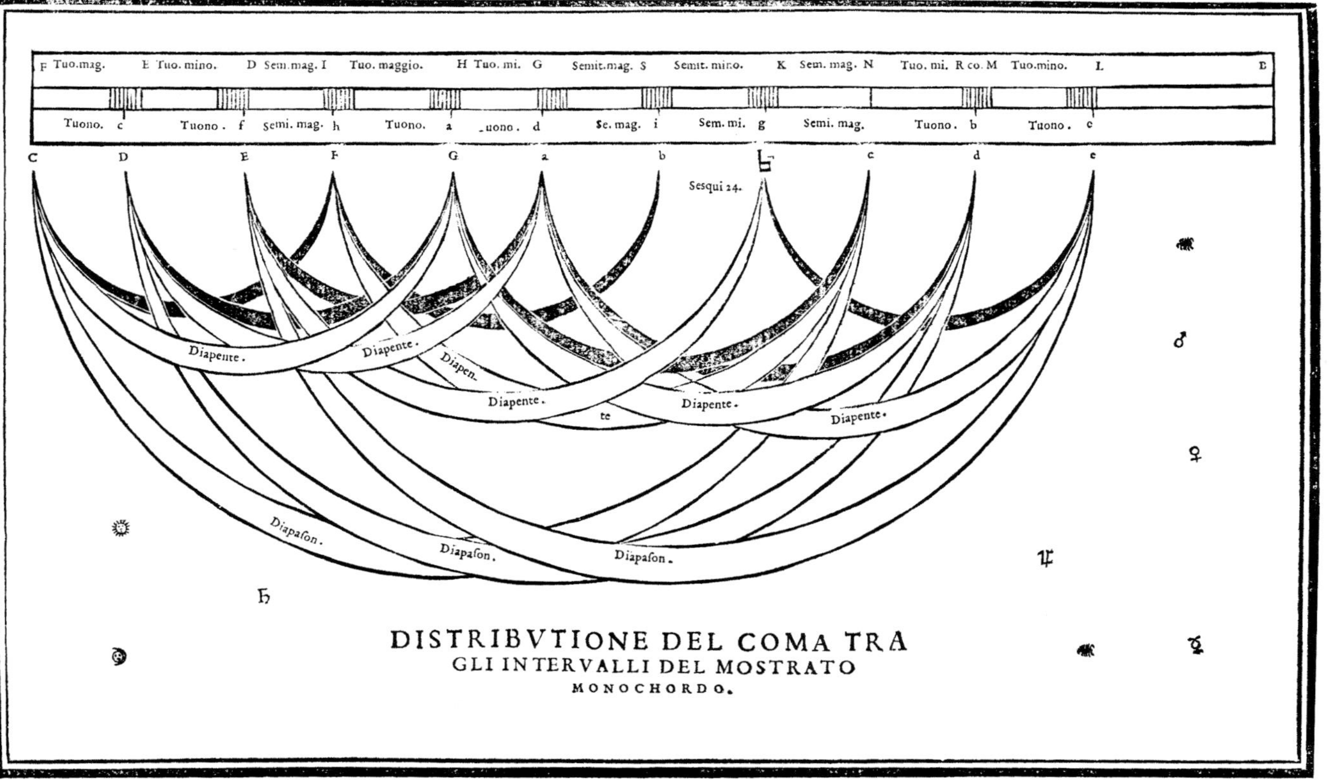

Plate 7.2 Zarlino's monochord for 2/7-comma temperament, *Le istitutioni harmoniche* (1558), p. 130

As noted, the most characteristic feature of meantone temperament is its just major thirds. The fifths are on the small side, but acceptable. Like Pythagorean tuning, it has an unusable "wolf fifth" between G♯ and E♭ (737.637 cents) if one tries to close the circle of fifths. As in Pythagorean tuning, raised keys can only be used in one function, either as sharp or as flat. Usually C♯, E♭, F♯, G♯ and B♭ are chosen; sometimes there is D♯ instead of E♭, and there are a number of instruments (mostly from the seventeenth century) constructed with split keys (most often D♯–E♭ and G♯–A♭) to widen the set of usable intervals. Whereas in Pythagorean tuning the chromatic semitone is the larger one and the diatonic the smaller one, in meantone temperament the chromatic semitone (76.849 cents) is the smaller one, the diatonic semitone (117.108 cents) the larger one, a property which it shares with just intonation.

It was not the tuning itself, but the limitations set by the singular use of the raised keys which eventually led to the development of new methods of tuning at the expense of meantone tuning. The simplest way to overcome these limitations was to narrow the fifths *less* than in meantone tuning. This improved the fifths and only slightly worsened the major thirds. Most importantly, it made the "enharmonic intervals" (for example, G♯–C, which has to function as A♭–C) less problematic. A number of these "compromise tunings" were proposed during the seventeenth and eighteenth centuries,[9] the most significant being, of course, equal temperament, in which the comma is divided equally among all (twelve) fifths. But calculating these minute temperaments on the monochord proved to be a challenge.

Equal temperament

Root extraction methods became known among mathematicians during the sixteenth century. As a matter of fact, they are indispensable tools when one wants to calculate string lengths for notes which divide an interval into geometrically equal parts (that is, parts with the same ratios). If two notes with string lengths x_o and x_N are given, and the interval between them has to be divided into N equal parts, N−1 new notes in between them are created, of which the string lengths are defined by:

$$x_i = \sqrt[N]{(x_o)^{N-i}(x_N)^i}$$

In mathematical terms the quantities x_i are called the *mean proportionals* between x_o and x_N. The powers under the root sign were easy enough to calculate; the mathematical bottle-neck is the Nth-power root needed for a division into N parts. So, for the division of the comma into seven parts, one had to know how to extract the 7th-power root, for the division into three parts the 3rd-power or cube root, for the division into four parts the 4th-power root. The latter root can be found by twice applying the

9 The most important ones are those in which the fifths are tempered by $^1/_5$ or $^1/_6$ of a syntonic comma or 1/6 of a ditonic comma.

square root. The calculation of tempered intervals was first performed towards the end of the sixteenth century by the Dutch mathematician and engineer Simon Stevin for the calculation of equal temperament.

Although basically a scientist, Simon Stevin (1548–1620) wrote about many subjects belonging to the humanities or the social sciences. His treatise on music, entitled "De spiegheling der singconst," was drafted in the 1580s, subsequently rewritten during the 1610s, but was eventually left unpublished at the author's death in 1620. In it, Stevin rejected the inequality of the chromatic and the diatonic semitones, a rejection that led automatically toward what is called today equal temperament.[10] We must realize, however, that for Stevin, this was properly not a temperament, since in his eyes the "equal-tempered" intervals were in effect the true intervals, whereas the small-integer-ratio intervals were to him misconceptions lying near the more complicated truth. As a mathematician, Stevin realized that the string lengths of an equal-tempered monochord required root extraction for their calculation. In principle it was the 12th-power root which was needed. He recognized how this root could be either resolved into a combination of one cube root and two square roots, or simplified in relation to the powers underneath the root sign. Actually, quite a number of formulations in terms of various roots were possible, which, of course, all boiled down to the same result.

Since the calculation of roots by hand was, and is, a rather cumbersome process, Stevin combined it in the actual process of calculation with another arithmetical rule, the one known as the *rule of three* (regola di tre), which essentially translates as: if $a:b=c:x$, then $x=bc/a$. Maximum efficiency is reached when only one square and one cube root had to be calculated. Stevin followed this principle when, for his octave from C (string length 10,000) to c (5,000), he first calculated E as mean proportional in the series C–E–G♯–c, thereby needing one cube root: $E = \sqrt[3]{(10{,}000)^2(5{,}000)} = 7{,}937$. E♭ was calculated as mean proportional in the series C–E♭–F♯–A–c, needing two square roots: $E\flat = \sqrt[4]{(10{,}000)^3(5{,}000)} = 8{,}409$. By comparison with the 10,000 for the full string, these numbers provided the ratios of the major and minor third. The ratio of the lengths for E and E♭ provides the ratio for the semitone. The string length for C♯ can then easily be found by the rule of three: $10{,}000 : x = 8{,}409 : 7{,}937$ or $x = 10{,}000$ $7{,}937\ /\ 8{,}409 = 9{,}439$. By similar calculations lengths for all the other notes could be calculated (See Table 7.3).[11]

Stevin's equal-tempered monochord, however ingeniously calculated for its time, is of rather poor quality. Many figures are one or two units off what they should be. (These are indicated in the right-hand columns under the rubric "better figures.") The problem appears to be Stevin's sometimes rather reckless rounding of digits after the decimal period, which are often truncated rather than rounded. Since his calculations

10 Bierens de Haan, *Simon Stevin*, pp. 54ff.

11 A related use of the "rule of three" in medieval mensural theory is described and illustrated in Chapter 20, pp. 650–53.

Table 7.3 *Equal temperament according to Simon Stevin*, De spiegheling der singconst *(c. 1585, c. 1615)*

Notes	Intervals	Root expressions (1)	Alternate Root expressions (2)	Resulting String lengths (3)	Resulting Cents	Better figures	Cents (equal temp.)
C	Unison	1:1	12√(1):1	10,000	0		0
D♭	Minor second	12√(1/2):1	12√(1/2):1	9,438	100.136	9,439	100
D	Major second	6√(1/2):1	12√(1/4):1	8,909 (1)	199.998	8,909	200
				8,908 (2)	200.192		
E♭	Minor third	4√(1/2):1	12√(1/8):1	8,408	300.192	8,409	300
E	Major third	3√(1/2):1	12√(1/16):1	7,937 (1)	400.001	7,937	400
				7,936 (2)	400.219		
F	Fourth	12√(1/32):1	12√(1/32):1	7,491	500.124	7,492	500
F♯	Tritone	2√(1/2):1	12√(1/64):1	7,071	600.017		600
G	Fifth	12√(1/128):1	12√(1/128):1	6,674	700.052		700
A♭	Minor sixth	3√(1/4):1	12√(1/256):1	6,298	800.441		800
A	Major sixth	4√(1/8):1	12√(1/512):1	5,944	900.593	5,946	900
B♭	Minor seventh	6√(1/32):1	12√(1/1,024):1	5,611	1,000.404		1,000
B	Major seventh	12√(1/2,048):1	12√(1/2,048):1	5,296	1,100.430	5,297	1,100
c	Octave	2:1	12√(1/4,096):1	5,000	1,200		1,200

Note: If two figures are given, one is from the early version, one from the later. The first column, with note names, is an editorial addition, since Stevin's descriptions are entirely in terms of interval names.

Source: Bierens de Haan, "Stevin", pp. 25–29 and 68–72.

include a number of repeated applications of the rule of three, rounding errors may aggravate with each application. Nevertheless, Stevin's monochord deserves appreciation as being the first calculation of equal temperament as well as the first application of roots to the calculation of string lengths of tempered intervals.

A generation later, Marin Mersenne (1588–1648) presented in his *Harmonie universelle* (Paris 1636–37) figures for equal-tempered string lengths that were both worse and better than Stevin, most often with many more digits. Actually, the *Harmonie* contains several tables with figures for equal-temperament monochords, given to him by scientists in his milieu, such as Jean Beaugrand (c. 1595–1640),[12] Ismaël Bouillaud (1605–91),[13] and Jean Gallé.[14] The first two tables were certainly calculated with help of root extraction, the third one probably so. Beaugrand's and Bouillaud's tables are no better than Stevin's, but Gallé's table is exact to one-thousandth of a cent, except for one clear typographical error (see Table 7.4).

During the sixteenth and seventeenth centuries, equal temperament was well known among theorists, but its practical application was probably limited. Early, informal descriptions had already been given by Zarlino, Salinas, and Vincenzo Galilei (c. 1530–1591).[15] (Galilei published the earliest practical means for deriving equal temperament on fretted instruments in 1581, using the ratio 17 : 18 as an approximation of the equal-tempered semitone.) Some sort of equal temperament was certainly essential for the placement of frets on the fingerboards of viols, lutes, and related instruments, since any unequal placement of frets could lead to many false octaves.[16] It may have been applied to keyboard tuning as well: the names of John Bull and Girolamo Frescobaldi have been mentioned in this connection. During the eighteenth century, the rise of equal temperament as the most prominent tuning for keyboard instruments could not be halted. This rise cannot, of course, be separated from the free use of all twenty-four major or minor keys that was becoming the standard in musical composition.[17]

Stevin's early advocacy of equal temperament was read in manuscript by a few individuals during the early seventeenth century, among them Jacobus Verheyden (c. 1570–1619), an organist in Nijmegen in the Dutch Republic. Verheyden disagreed with Stevin concerning the validity of equal temperament for the tuning of keyboard instruments of the time.[18] He rightly remarked that the instruments he knew had their major thirds pure and beatless, their fifths "beating downwards" a bit, and indeed with a marked difference between the chromatic and the diatonic semitones, the former noticeably narrower than the latter. This is of course meantone temperament as described before him by Zarlino and others. It is to Verheyden's credit that he

12 Mersenne, *Harmonie universelle*, "Livre deuxième de dissonances," p. 132; "Livre quatrème des instruments," p. 199.

13 Ibid., "Livre sixième des instruments," p. 385.

14 Ibid, "Nouvelles observations," p. 21.

15 Salinas, *De musica*, pp. 166 ff.; Galilei, *Dialogo della musica*, p. 49; Zarlino, *Sopplimenti musicali*, pp. 197ff.

16 Lindley, *Lutes, Viols and Temperaments*.

17 See Rasch, "The Musical Circle" Also see Chapter 13, pp. 426–35, p. 445.

18 Bierens de Haan, *Simon Stevin*, pp. 87ff.

Table 7.4 *Equal temperament after Marin Mersenne,* Harmonie universelle *(Paris, 1636–37)*

Note	Beaugrand	Bouillaud		Gallé
	Lengths	Lengths	Cents	Lengths
C	200,000	14,400	100	100,000,000,000
C♯	188,700+(4+)	13,580 (92)	101.503	94,387,431,198
D	178,171+	12,822 (29)	200.802	89,090,418,365*
E♭	168,178+(9+)	12,110 (09)	299.844	84,089,641,454
E	158,740+	11,405 (29)	403.683	79,370,052,622
F	149,829+	10,772 (88)	502.539	74,915,353,818
F♯	141,421+	10,179 (82)	600.568	70,710,678,109
G	133,480+	9,605 (11)	701.053	66,741,992,715
G♯	125,992+	9,072 (71)	799.891	62,996,052,457
A	118,920+	8,553 (62)	901.880	59,460,355.690
B♭	112,245+	8,092 (82)	997.800	56,123,102,370
B	105,945+	7,632 (28)	1,099.123	52,973,154,575
c	100,000	7,200	1,200	50,000,000,000

Note: In Beaugrand's table, "188,700+" means that the intended value is between that figure and the next higher. In cases where better figures are available, they have been added in parentheses. The figures in parentheses in Bouillaud's table are also more accurate last digits. Gallé's table is accurate to one thousandth of a cent, except for the asterisked figure, whose first eight digits should read 89,089,871.

succeeded in providing a mathematical definition of this temperament, and that he was able to calculate string lengths in accordance with this mathematical definition. In one respect, his task was easier than Stevin's: since in meantone temperament the comma is divided into *four* equal parts, the calculations include only square roots, and no cube roots. Verheyden wrote out a table of mathematical expressions (of the type $\sqrt{\sqrt{78{,}125 : 16}}$, for the chromatic semitone; $\sqrt{\sqrt{}}$ is Verheyden's notation for the 4th-power root) for the ratios of twenty-four intervals; thirteen of these ratios (those for an octave from F to f inclusive on a keyboard) were worked out into numerical ratios (such as 10,000 : 9,570 for the chromatic semitone). Verheyden's calculations were never published, and remained unknown in the seventeenth century (see Table 7.5).[19]

In general, calculations for meantone monochords are relatively rare. Most of the mathematically inclined authors directed their attention to equal temperament, and once the required mathematical tools had been made *easily* applicable (namely, in the eighteenth century), meantone tuning became obsolete.

19 Verheyden's calculations are provided in a letter he wrote to Stevin, now extant among a number of papers from Stevin's estate in the Royal Library in The Hague, MS KA 47.

Table 7.5 *Meantone tuning according to Jacobus Verheyden (?1618)*

Interval	Expressions	Ratios	Cents
Unison	1:1	10,000:10,000	0
Chromatic semitone	$\sqrt{\sqrt{78{,}125}}:16$	10,000:9,570	76.049
Diatonic semitone	$8:\sqrt{\sqrt{3{,}125}}$		117.108
Whole tone	$\sqrt{5}:2$	10,000:8,944	193.157
Diminished third	$64:\sqrt{3{,}125}$		234.216
Augmented second	$\sqrt{\sqrt{1{,}953{,}125}}:32$	10,000:8,560	269.206
Minor third	$4:\sqrt{\sqrt{125}}$		310.265
Major third	5:4	10,000:8,000	386.314
Diminished fourth	32:25		427.373
Augmented third	$\sqrt{\sqrt{48{,}828{,}125}}:64$		462.367
Fourth	$2:\sqrt{\sqrt{5}}$	10,000:7,477	503.427
Augmented fourth	$\sqrt{125}:8$	10,000:7,155	579.471
Diminished fifth	$16:\sqrt{125}$		620.529
Fifth	$\sqrt{\sqrt{5}}:1$	10,000:6,687	696.578
Dimished sixth	$128:\sqrt{\sqrt{48{,}828{,}125}}$		737.637
Augmented fifth	25:16	10,000:6,400	772.627
Minor sixth	8:5		813.686
Major sixth	$\sqrt{\sqrt{125}}:2$	10,000:5,981	889.735
Diminished seventh	$64:\sqrt{\sqrt{1{,}953{,}125}}$		930.794
Augmented sixth	$\sqrt{3{,}125}:32$		965.784
Minor seventh	$4:\sqrt{5}$	10,000:5,590	1,006.843
Major seventh	$\sqrt{\sqrt{3{,}125}}:4$	10,000:5,350	1,082.892
Diminished octave	$32:\sqrt{\sqrt{78{,}125}}$		1,123.951
Octave	2:1	10,000:5,000	1,200

Source: Bierens de Haan, "Stevin," pp. 93–97.

Among the appendices of Verheyden's letter there is a little table, with various ratios which may be used for the tuning of the fifths on organs and harpsichords.[20] There are four such ratios: $\sqrt[3]{10}:\sqrt[3]{3}$, $\sqrt[4]{5}:1$, $\sqrt[5]{15}:\sqrt[5]{2}$, and $\sqrt[7]{50}:\sqrt[7]{3}$. If one calculates the temperings of the fifth which is implied in these ratios, one finds $^1/_3$ of a comma, $^1/_4$, $^1/_5$ and $^2/_7$, respectively. Two things are remarkable: the calculation of these ratios themselves, because they show a profound insight in the subject, and the $^1/_5$-comma temperament which had not yet been described before by any theorist.

The calculation of square and cube roots remained in use as a method for calculating the string-lengths of temperament throughout the seventeenth and eighteenth centuries (and later). But it was soon joined and later superseded by another mathematical method, namely the application of logarithms.

20 Bierens de Haan, *Simon Stevin*, p. 95.

Cents

The measurement of interval size in cents was introduced by the nineteenth-century English scholar Alexander John Ellis, especially to be able to express intonations used in non-Western music that could not be well represented by normal notation. It is a logarithmic measure, which means that interval sizes can be added and subtracted just as one can do in musical terms (such as saying that a minor third equals a major second plus a minor second). The size in cents of an interval is given by the formula $I = 1{,}200 \times {}_2\log i$, where I is the size in cents and i the size in terms of frequency or string-length ratio. On a pocket calculator it is most easily calculated as [(log i) / (log2)] 1200, where the logarithm can be of any base. So, if we take the fifth, with the ratio 2:3 or $^3/_2$ =1.5, than its size in cents is [(log 1.5) / (log2)] × 1,200 = 701.955. Values in cents are easy to evaluate: the octave contains 1,200 cents, each equal-tempered semitone 100 cents (hence its name).

Logarithms

When notes are positioned on the string of a monochord, they have the annoying property that distances among them become smaller and smaller if one goes higher up on the string. If the full string is 10,000 units, the first octave is reached after 5,000 units, the second one after 2,500 additional units, the third one after 1,250 additional units, and so on. In other words, the representation of pitch on a monochord does not conform to our internal or psychological representation of that quality, which presupposes constant distances for the same interval, irrespective of the pitch level. This flaw can be repaired when actual string lengths are replaced by logarithmic transformations, of the form $F = \log f$, where f is a linear measure of pitch (such as string length or frequency), log is a logarithmic function of any base, and F is the logarithmic measure of pitch. In the same vein, frequency ratios of intervals can be transformed by the formula $I = \log i$, where i is the linear ratio (of string lengths or frequencies) and I the logarithmic measure. Each chosen base sets a different scale for the transformations, all scales being simple linear transformations among themselves. The most often chosen base today is $2^{1/1{,}200}$ (or $\sqrt[1{,}200]{2}$), which results in an octave of 1,200 units. This measure was devised in the nineteenth century by Alexander John Ellis; its units are usually called *cents*, because 100 units make up an equal-tempered semitone.

The logarithmic transformation of linear pitch values and ratios dates back to the seventeenth century. However, it was proposed not to provide a better representation of the pitch continuum, but as a mathematical tool to bypass the forbidding square and cube (and possibly other) root calculations needed for equal and other temperaments. When one is treating linear quantities, multiplication is performed by the addition of their logarithmic counterparts, division by subtraction. The raising to a power of linear quantities is performed by the multiplication of logarithmic quantities and, what is most important, the extraction of roots of linear quantities is attained by the simple division of logarithmic quantities. In the calculation of temperaments, logarithms serve especially well in the geometrical division of intervals, where they replace root extraction by division. To give an example of the latter process: assuming X_0 and X_N to be the logarithmic transformations of two string lengths x_0 and x_N, the notes X_i in between them and forming equal-sized intervals among them (mean proportionals), are found by dividing $X_0 - X_N$ into N parts and adding the ($^1/_N$)th part of the difference repeatedly to the smaller value. The values found are logarithmic values and can be converted into linear values with the help of a table of logarithms. Therefore, the availability of such tables is of paramount importance in the procedure. Tables of logarithms were published from about the late 1620s, and from that time onwards we see the application of logarithms to the calculation of temperament. The application of logarithms to the calculation of monochord string lengths evidently was so obvious that at least five scholars tried it independently of one another.

The first calculation of equal temperament with logarithms seems to have been produced by the German engineer Johann Faulhaber (1580–1635). In his *Ingenieurs-Schul* (1630) he presented a table of differences between the linear values of adjacent notes.[21] Faulhaber did not explain his method, but since the same book contains logarithmic tables, we may assume that he used them for this calculation as well.

A particularly remarkable use of logarithms was made by William Brouncker (c. 1620–84) in his *Animadversions*, published as an appendix to his English translation of René Descartes's *Compendium musicae* (London 1653).[22] Brouncker insightfully described the nature of hearing as "geometrical." Hence, he believed that the division of intervals also should be geometrical. He then presented three such divisions, calculated with decimal logarithms. The first one is the division of the interval $(3-\sqrt{5})/2:1$ (or 1:2.618034 or 1666.180 cents, roughly an octave plus a fourth) into seventeen equal semitones (of 1:1.058 or 98 cents); the second was the division of 1:2 into twelve equal semitones (equal temperament); and the third the division of the interval $(\sqrt{2}-1):1$ (or 1:2.414214 or 1525.864 cents, roughly an octave plus a minor third) into fifteen equal semitones (of 1.065 or 102 cents).

At least three other scholars in the early seventeenth century also tried their hands at applying logarithms to musical temperament, including the Italian scientist Lemme Rossi (c. 1600–73)[23] and the polyhistorian Juan Caramuel de Lobkowitz (1606–82), of Spanish descent but active most of his life in Vienna and Italy.[24] But it was the

21 Faulhaber, *Ingenieurs-Schul*, vol. I, p. 167.

22 Brouncker, *Animadversions*, pp. 84ff.

23 Rossi, *Sistema musico*. See also Barbour, *Tuning and Temperament*, p. 30.

24 Lobkowitz applied "musical logarithms" liberally in his *Musica*, a giant manuscript encyclopedia of music, compiled probably during the 1670s. See Sabaino, *Il Rinascimento*, for further information on Lobkowitz.

renowned Dutch scientist Christiaan Huygens (1629–95) who was without doubt the most important and influential of these early logarithmic "pioneers."

In a manuscript treatise entitled "Divisio monochordi" (1661), Huygens described the string lengths of meantone tuning in terms of algebraic expressions.[25] In a notebook of the same time tables are found which provide the corresponding string lengths; his accompanying calculations make clear that the figures in the table were found with help of logarithms.[26] About the same time Huygens discovered that the pitches of meantone tuning could well be described as a subset of the tones of an octave divided into thirty-one equal parts or steps. The size of each step is $1:\sqrt[31]{2}$ or 1:1.022611 or 38.710 cents. The chromatic semitone would then correspond to an interval equal to two such steps, the diatonic semitone to three, the whole tone to five, the minor third to eight, the major third to ten, etc. The correspondence (of course, a very good approximation only) could easily be shown with the help of the logarithmic calculation of interval width.[27] The relation between the meantone system and the division of the octave into thirty-one equal parts is also the major topic of Huygens's *Lettre touchant le cycle harmonique*, published much later, in 1691 (see Plate 7.3).[28]

So, during the seventeenth century, the feasibility of logarithms for musical calculations was picked up, seemingly independently by five different researchers. But their work was rather poorly publicized. In the end, the description by Christiaan Huygens became best known, being published in French in a relatively widely disseminated publication. Lobkowitz's calculations remained in manuscript, Faulhaber's book was in German and not aimed at musicians or musical scientists, while Brouncker's and Rossi's calculations were in publications primarily available to English and Italian readerships respectively.

The first wide-ranging application of the logarithmic method in print was provided by the French scientist Joseph Sauveur (1653–1716), who had first explained his ideas in a manuscript treatise dated 1697 entitled "Traité de la théorie de la musique," probably reflecting his lectures at the Collège Royal in Paris.[29] Roughly the same materials appeared a few years later in his "Système général des intervalles des sons," published in the *Mémoires* of the French Royal Academy of Sciences for the year 1701.[30]

In his application of logarithmic interval sizes, Sauveur made use of an interesting property of ${}_{10}\log 2 = 0.301$. When multiplied by 1,000, this equals 301 or 7×43. Sauveur first divided the octave into forty-three equal parts, which he called *merides*;

25 Huygens, *Œuvres complètes*, vol. xx, pp. 49–56. English translation in Rasch, *Christiaan Huygens*, pp. 121–27. 26 Leiden, University Library, MS Hugeniani, 13, p. 27 and MS 27, fol. 6v, respectively.

27 The correspondence had already been informally noted before Huygens by, among others, Nicola Vicentino, in his *L'antica musica ridotta alla moderna prattica* of 1555.

28 Huygens, "Lettre touchant le cycle harmonique."

29 Paris, Bibliothèque Nationale, MS Nouv. Acqu. Fr. 4674. (For more on Sauveur, see Chapter 9, pp. 252–53.) 30 Sauveur, "Système général des intervalles des sons."

Division de l'Octave en 31 parties égales.				*Division de l'Octave suivant le Temperament ordinaire.*	
I.	II.	III.	IV.	V.	VI.
N 97106450					
4,6989700043	50000	Ut 2	C 2	50000	4,6989700043
4,7086806493	51131				
4,7183912943	52278				
4,7281019393	53469	Si	Bx	53499	4,7283474859
4,7378125843	54678				
4,7475232293	55914	Sa	B	55902	4,7474250108
4,7572338743	57179	*	*	57243	4,7577249574
4,7669445193	58471				
4,7766551643	59794	La	A	59814	4,7768024824
4,7863658093	61146				
4,7960764543	62528	*	*	62500	4,7958800173
4,8057870993	63942	Sol x	Gx	64000	4,8061799740
4,8154977443	65388				
4,8252083893	66866	Sol	G	66874	4,8252574989
4,8349190343	68378				
4,8446296793	69924				
4,8543403243	71506	Fa x	Fx	71554	4,8546349804
4,8640509693	73122				
4,8737616143	74776	Fa	F	74767	4,8737125054
4,8834722593	76467				
4,8931829043	78196				
4,9028935493	79964	Mi	E	80000	4,9030899870
4,9126041943	81772				
4,9223148393	83621	Ma	Eb	83592	3,9221675119
4,9320254843	85512	*	*	85599	4,9324674685
4,9417361293	87445				
4,9514467743	89422	Re	D	89443	4,9515449935
4,9611574193	91444				
4,9708680643	93512	*	*	93459	4,9706225184
4,9805787093	95627	Ut x	Cx	95702	4,9809224750
4,9902893543	97789				
4,9999999993	100000	Ut	C	100000	5,0000000000

Plate 7.3 Christiaan Huygens's table with the comparison of the 31-tone system and meantone tuning, in *Lettre touchant le cycle harmonique* (1691), opposite p. 85. Columns I and VI contain logarithmic values, II and V string lengths.

each meride was then divided into seven *eptamerides*, so that the octave contained 301 eptamerides. That meant that if an interval had the ratio of 1:i, the number of eptamerides that equals that interval is 1,000 × $_{10}$log i. The division of the octave into forty-three merides is particularly practical since the notes created may contain all traditional intervals in it, in the same way as the division into thirty-one parts included the primary intervals of meantone tuning within it. If the octave is divided into forty-three merides, the chromatic semitone can be set at 3 merides, the diatonic semitone at 4 merides, the whole tone at 7, the minor third at 11, the major third at 14, the perfect fifth at 25, and so on. By doing so, the sizes of these intervals are very nearly equal to the sizes they would take in a temperament where the fifths are narrowed by $^1/_5$ of a syntonic comma, a tuning system described repeatedly during the seventeenth and eighteenth centuries, and first hinted at by Verheyden at the beginning of the seventeenth century.

The logarithmic method is outstandingly useful for the calculations of notes in multiple divisions of the octave. If the octave is divided into N steps, the logarithmic pitches of the notes $F_0, F_1, F_2, \ldots, F_i, \ldots, F_N$ are equal to:

$$F_i = F_o + (F_N - F_o)/N$$

Of course, not all divisions of the octave lead to musically sensible systems. In a later paper, published in the *Mémoires* of the French Royal Academy of Sciences in 1707, Sauveur defined the comma as the difference between the chromatic and the diatonic semitones and set the comma to one or two steps in the system.[31] By an ingenious reasoning he concluded that the logarithmic size of the chromatic semitone should be no less than $^{12}/_7$ times that of the comma, and no more than $^{33}/_7$. This point of departure leads to chromatic semitones consisting of two, three, or four steps for a one-step comma (so that the diatonic semitone contains three, four, or five steps, respectively), and of four to nine steps for a two-step comma (implying diatonic semitones of six to eleven steps). The resulting systems have 31, 43, or 55 notes per octave for a one-step comma, and 62, 74, 86, 98, 110, or 122 notes per octave for a two-step comma, respectively. These systems indeed have interval sizes that fall well into acceptable ranges. The second group, however, has too many notes to be of practical value. The first group, consisting of systems with 31, 43, or 55 notes per octave, is impractical, too, but the systems are of importance because their interval sizes very nearly approach those of "classical" temperaments with fifths narrowed by $^1/_4$, $^1/_5$, or $^1/_6$ of a syntonic comma, respectively. It is no wonder that these systems play the most important roles in discussions of multiple divisions during the eighteenth century and beyond.

31 Sauveur, "Méthode générale pour former les systêmes tempérés de musique." (A step, it will be recalled, is the interval that arises by dividing an octave into an arbitrary number of equal intervals.)

Concentric tuning: Werckmeister (1691)

German theory on tuning and temperament of the eighteenth century would take entirely different routes than did French or Italian theory. The first in a long string of German publications on the subject was Andreas Werckmeister's (1645–1706) *Musicalische Temperatur*, published in 1691 in the Saxon town of Quedlinburg where he worked most of his life as an organist.[32] The musical repertoire that Werckmeister played more and more required the arbitrary use of raised keys for sharps and flats, but not yet in such a rigorous way that equal temperament would have been the only solution. The major challenge to the tuner was to see that in principle all twelve keys of the keyboard were usable in all functions, but that the most often occurring intervals (those in the "central" keys with no or few sharps or flats in the signature) were better (that is, less tempered) than the ones less often used (those in "peripheral" keys with many sharps or flats). These conditions are met when one considers the twelve fifths of a twelve-tone keyboard as forming a circle and then narrows the "central" fifths more or less as in meantone temperament ($^1/_4$ comma or a little less), but leaves the "peripheral" fifths just (as in Pythagorean tuning) or occasionally wider. Since these tunings concentrate on the central fifths, they will be called *concentric tunings*. The concept more or less coincides with earlier concepts introduced by Barbour under the term *"good" temperaments* and Jorgensen as *well-temperaments*.[33]

During the period from about 1690 to about 1790, a great number of proposals for concentric tunings were published, mainly in Germany. After Werckmeister, Johann Georg Neidhardt, Georg Andreas Sorge and Friedrich Wilhelm Marpurg were the most important authors.[34] All their proposals were based on the circle of fifths: a number of these fifths were left in their just form, the others tempered by certain amounts. One rule connects them all: the total tempering of the circle of fifths sums up to the ditonic comma. So the challenge facing these theorists can be stated simply as a problem of dividing the ditonic comma into various parts serving as temperings for various fifths. To give an example: in Werckmeister's famous tuning no. III, the ditonic comma is divided into four parts, and four "central" fifths are tempered by $^1/_4$ comma: C–G, G–D, D–A and B–F♯. In Werckmeister's system no. IV, the comma is divided into three parts. Now, the fifths B♭-F, C–G, D–A, E–B and F♯–C♯ are each narrowed by $^1/_3$ of a comma; G♯–D♯ and E♭–B♭ are widened by the same amount (so that the sum is still the ditonic comma). Other descriptions, by later authors, involve $^1/_2$, $^1/_5$, $^1/_6$, $^1/_7$, $^1/_8$ and $^1/_{12}$ parts of a comma (this last division resulting, of course, in an equal temperament).

32 Werckmeister, *Musicalische Temperatur*. The gist of his theories, including the two systems labeled nos. III and IV, can already be found his his *Orgel-Probe* of ten years earlier.

33 Barbour, *Tuning and Temperament*, pp. 178ff.; Jorgensen, *Tuning the Historical Temperaments*, pp. 245ff.

34 Neidhardt, *Sectio canonis monochordi*; Sorge, *Anweisung zur Stimmung und Temperatur*; Marpurg, *Versuch über die musikalische Temperatur*; and *Neue Methode allerley Arten von Temperaturen*.

There were also numerous "compound" temperaments proposed, such as $^{2}/_{5}$, $^{2}/_{7}$, etc. There is an infinity of possibilities. But they all have the property – at least when the central fifths are tempered more clearly than the peripheral ones – that the central keys are less tempered than the peripheral keys,[35] while all keys are of acceptable quality.

Not only was Werckmeister the originator of this class of tuning, he also devised a clever method to show them on the monochord. In principle, the division of the comma into equal parts implies the use of root extractions or of tables of logarithms. Werckmeister realized – as had several authors before him, incidentally – that not much is lost if the true, geometric division of a comma is replaced by an arithmetic division. Take, for example, the syntonic comma, which is 80 : 81 or 320 : 324. A geometric division with mean proportionals leads to the series 320 : 320.995 : 321.994 : 322.995 : 324. The arithmetic division 320 : 321 : 322 : 323 : 324 really comes so close that in all practical situations it may replace the geometric division. By substituting geometric with arithmetic division, every comma division is calculated within a few minutes' time without further tools.

In a way, Werckmeister was simply extending the graphic method of Zarlino. Every tempered value of a note lies between two untempered or just values. In the case of divisions of the ditonic comma, the two untempered values are Pythagorean values. For example, if C is taken as the point of departure in equal temperament, the G in equal temperament has the Pythagorean value lowered by $^{1}/_{12}$ of a ditonic comma. A ditonic comma lower than Pythagorean G is Pythagorean A♭♭, and although it will take some time, its string length is not difficult to compute. Having established both values (G and A♭♭), the difference can be divided by 12 and eleven "pitches" between G and A♭♭ can be inserted, each at 1/12 comma distance (accepting approximation by arithmetic division). In this way, the string-length values of tempered tones are not only very easy to calculate, they can with equal ease be plotted on a monochord: just put the two untempered values first, then divide the space between them in twelve equal parts.

It must be admitted that Werckmeister himself did not apply this method in any consistent way. On his monochord, he created a number of pairs of notes at the distance of a comma, but the comma in question often was the syntonic comma (or sometimes of a diaschisma only), and this led to a slight deviation from the theoretical model since it is the ditonic comma that has to be divided. The difference between the commas is slight – they form approximately a ratio of 11 : 12 – so that in practical situations it may be neglected. Certainly when a monochord with a string of at most 50 cm is marked, the difference between the syntonic and the ditonic commas cannot be realized. Werckmeister's monochord (reproduced as Plate 7.4) contains six tuning systems: a

35 While most keys are of acceptable quality in such unequal keyboard temperaments, certain of them would project unique tonal qualities based upon the particular tuning used. These qualities might have suggested to theorists of the time certain affective characteristics to each key that were then generalized in the tables of key characteristics one finds in some eighteenth-century theory treatises (Mattheson, Rameau, Rousseau, etc.). Far from being considered a defect, then, the various differences in sound quality between keys resulting from unequal temperament could be considered resources of tonal color and expression that might be exploited by composers. See Rita Steblin, *A History of Key Characteristics*.

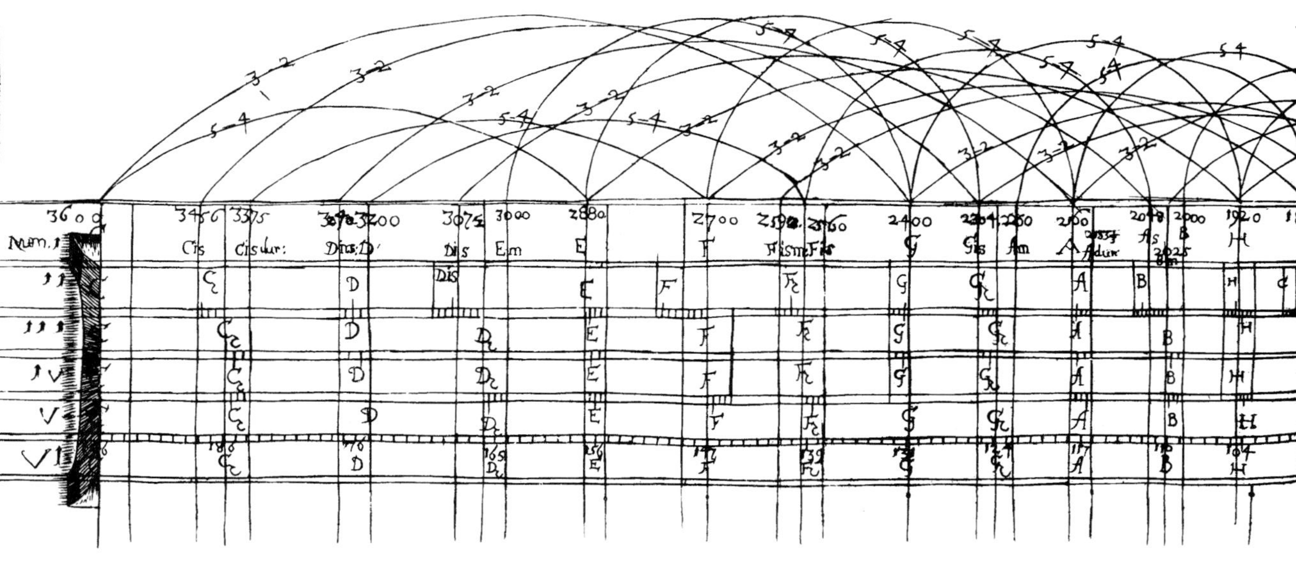

Plate 7.4 Andreas Werckmeister's monochord, in the engraving belonging to his *Musicalische Temperatur* (1691)

Table 7.6 *Unequal temperaments according to Neidhart (1724), pp. 16–18*

	First temperament "for a village"		Second temperament "for a town"		Third temperament "for a city"	
Note	Lengths	Cents	Lengths	Cents	Lengths	Cents
C	2,000.00	0	2,000.00	0	2,000.00	0
C♯	1,894.15	94.139	1,892.01	96.096	1,892.01	96.096
D	1,785.82	196.096	1,785.82	196.096	1,785.82	196.096
D♯	1,685.59	296.096	1,683.68	298.058	1,683.68	298.058
E	1,594.58	392.188	1,592.78	394.144	1,592.78	394.144
F	1,500.00	498.045	1,498.30	500.008	1,500.00	498.045
F♯	1,420.61	592.931	1,417.40	596.104	1,417.40	596.104
G	1,336.34	698.055	1,336.34	698.055	1,336.34	698.055
G♯	1,262.76	796.103	1,262.76	796.103	1,262.76	796.103
A	1,193.23	894.153	1,193.23	894.153	1,193.23	894.153
B	1,125.00	996.090	1,122.45	1,000.019	1,123.72	998.061
H	1,064.25	1,092.195	1,061.85	1,096.104	1,061.85	1,096.104
c	1,000.00	1,200	1,000.00	1,200	1,000.00	1,200

multi-tone just intonation (to generate the tones at comma distances), meantone tuning, three unequal temperaments of the concentric type (his nos. III, IV, V) and one simply defined by string-length numbers without explanation.

Johann Georg Neidhardt (1685–1739) applied Werckmeister's method in order to plot equal temperament on the monochord in his *Beste und leichteste Temperatur des Monochordi* (1706). Since he copied Werckmeister's standard commas (instead of observing the difference between the two commas), his result is an approximation only (one beyond those discrepancies inherent in the method of arithmetic division). In his *Sectio canonis harmonici* (1724) Neidhardt repaired this shortcoming by using pairs of Pythagorean tones as a basis to divide the ditonic comma. He applied his method to four temperaments, which are ordered from unequal to equal. It is interesting to note that he considered the first temperament, the most unequal of all, fit for a village, the second one, less unequal, for a town, the third one, only slightly unequal, for a city, and the fourth and last one, equal temperament, for the court (see Tables 7.6 and 7.7). Although unequal temperaments were still widely prescribed, equal temperament little by little was becoming first in prestige among all temperaments.

Conclusion: Marpurg

The many works on tuning and temperament by Friedrich Wilhelm Marpurg (1718–95) represent, in a way, the culmination of the historical theory of tuning and

Table 7.7 *Equal temperaments according to Neidhart (1724), p. 19*

	Arithmetic division of the ditonic comma		Geometric division of the ditonic comma	
Note	Lengths	Cents	Lengths	Cents
C	2,000.00	0	2,000.00	0
C♯	1,887.79	99.962	1,887.74	100.008
D	1,781.82	199.978	1,781.79	200.007
D♯	1,681.82	299.972	1,681.78	300.013
E	1,587.43	399.968	1,587.39	400.012
F	1,498.31	499.997	1,498.30	500.008
F♯	1,414.24	599.968	1,414.20	600.017
G	1,334.84	700.000	1,334.83	700.013
G♯	1,259.94	799.974	1,259.91	800.015
A	1,189.22	899.981	1,189.20	900.010
B	1,122.47	999.988	1,122.45	1,000.019
H	1,059.48	1,099.972	1,059.45	1,100.021
c	1,000.00	1,200	1,000.00	1,200

Note: Although the figures produced by the geometric division of the ditonic comma come closer to true equal temperament than those found with an arithmetic division, they are systematically one digit too low, probably owing to rounding errors.

temperament.[36] In his works, a great diversity of methodological approaches can be encountered, which are applied to a great number of different tuning and temperament systems. His three major works on the subject were the *Anfangsgründe der theoretischen Musik* (1757), the *Versuch über die musikalischen Temperatur* (1776) and *Neue Methode allerley Arten von Temperaturen dem Claviere aufs bequemste mitzutheilen* (1790). Despite the great variety of unequal temperaments described, Marpurg basically adhered to equal temperament. It is rather as if he described the unequal temperaments only to show his knowledge of the subject and thereby to strengthen his case in favor of equal temperament. His position drew him into a polemic with Johann Philipp Kirnberger (1721–83), the only late eighteenth-century author who published an unequal temperament in an authoritative book on music theory: *Die Kunst des reinen Satzes in der Musik* (1771). This temperament (today mostly known as Kirnberger II) therefore became the prototype of unequal temperament at that time. It is a concentric tuning in which the tempering of a syntonic comma is divided over only two fifths (D–A, A–E); the fifth F♯–C♯ is tempered by a schisma to make the tempering of the circle of fifths complete. It seems a rather impractical tuning and one

36 Frosztega, "Friedrich Wilhelm Marpurg."

wonders whether it really had ever been put into practice. Nevertheless, from 1773 up to 1809, about a dozen authors – among them Sorge (1773), Marpurg (1776) and Daniel Gottlob Türk (1808) – brought a variety of arguments to the fore, either in favor of Kirnberger's unequal temperament or against it. The controversy was never really settled, but rather faded away into insignificance. By the end of the eighteenth century, most unequal temperaments had precipitously declined in popularity (with some notable exceptions, especially in Britain) and equal temperament reigned supreme.[37]

37 It should be noted, however, that some church organists continued to tune their instruments well into the nineteenth century in various forms of meantone temperament. For evidence concerning the persistence of meantone tuning in England during the nineteenth century, see Alexander J. Ellis's appendix to his translation of Helmholtz, *On the Sensations of Tone*, p. 549. In addition, a number of scientists interested in questions of music theory strongly advocated just tuning, among them Hermann von Helmholtz and Arthur von Oettingen.

Bibliography

Primary sources

Aaron, P. *Toscanello in musica*, Venice, M. Vitali, 1523, and M. Sessa, 1539; facs. Kassel, Bärenreiter-Verlag, 1970

Brouncker, W. "Animadversions upon the Musick-Compendium of Renat. Descartes," appendix to Descartes, *Excellent Compendium of Musick*, trans. W. Brouncker, London, H. Moseley, 1653

Faulhaber, J. *Ingenieurs Schul*, Frankfurt, J. N. Stoltzenbergern 1630

Galilei, V. *Dialogo della musica antica e della moderna*. Florence, G. Marescotti, 1581; facs. New York, Broude, 1967

Glarean, H. *Dodekachordon*, Basel, H. Petri, 1547; facs. Hildesheim, G. Olms, 1969

Helmholtz, H., *On the Sensations of Tone as a Physiological Basis for the Theory of Music*, 4th edn. (1877), trans. A. Ellis, New York, Dover, 1954

Huygens, C. "Lettre touchant le cycle harmonique," in *Histoire des Ouvrages de Sçavans*, October 1691, pp. 78–88; facs. and trans. R. Rasch in *Christiaan Huygens: Le cycle harmonique (Rotterdam 1691)*, Utrecht, Diapason, 1986

Kirnberger, J. P. *Die Kunst des reinen Satzes*, 2 vols., Berlin, Decker und Hartung, 1771–79; facs. Hildesheim, G. Olms, 1968 and 1988

Lobkowitz, Juan Caramuel, <*musica*>, MS. Archivio Capitolare della Diocesi, Fondo Caramuel, Vigerano, Italy

Marpurg, F. W. *Anfangsgründe der theoretischen Musik*, Leipzig, J. G. Immanuel, 1757; facs. New York, Broude, 1966

Versuch über die musikalische Temperatur, Breslau, J. F. Korn, 1776

Neue Methode allerley Arten von Temperaturen dem Claviere aufs bequemste mitzutheilen, Berlin, G. A. Lange, 1790; facs. Hildesheim, G. Olms, 1970

Mersenne, M. *Harmonie universelle*, Paris, S. Cramoisy, 1636–37; facs. Paris, Centre National de la Recherche Scientifique, 1963 and 1986

Neidhardt, J. G. *Beste und leichteste Temperatur des Monochordi*, Jena, J. Bielcke, 1706

Sectio canonis monochordi, Königsberg, C. G. Eckart, 1724

Rossi, L. *Sistema musico, overo Musica speculativa*, Perugia, Angelo Laurenzi, 1666

Salinas, F. *De musica libri septem*, Salamanca, M. Gastius, 1577; facs. Kassel, Bärenreiter-Verlag, 1958

Sauveur, J. "Système général des intervalles des sons, et de son application à tous les systèmes et à tous les instrumens de musique," in *Histoire de l'Académie Royale des Sciences, Année MDCCI, avec les Mémoires de Mathématique et de Physique pour la même année*, Paris, 1704, pp. 297–364; facs. in Rasch, *Joseph Sauveur: Collected Writings on Musical Acoustics (Paris 1700–1713)*, Utrecht, Diapason Press, 1984, pp. 99–166

"Méthode générale pour former les systêmes tempérés de musique, et du choix de celui qu'on doit suivre," in *Histoire de l'Académie Royale des Sciences, Année MDCCVII, avec les Mémoires de Mathématique et de Physique pour la même année*, Paris, 1708, pp. 203–22; facs. in Rasch, *Joseph Sauveur: Collected Writings on Musical Acoustics (Paris 1700–1713)*, Utrecht, Diapason Press, 1984, pp. 199–218

Schlick, A. *Spiegel der Orgelmacher und Organisten*, Speyer, P. Drach, 1511; facs. Mainz, Rheingold-Verlag, 1959

Sorge, G. A. *Anweisung zur Stimmung und Temperatur*, Hamburg, Sorge, 1744

Ausführliche und deutliche Anweisung zur Rational-Rechnung, Lobenstein, Sorge, 1749

Der in der Rechen- und Messkunst wohlerfahrne Orgelbaumeister, Lobenstein, Sorge, 1773

Stevin, S. *Vande spiegeling der singkonst et Vande molens*, D. Bierens de Haan, Amsterdam, 1884

Türk, D. G. *Anleitung zu Temperaturberechnungen*, Halle, Schimmelpfennig, 1808

Vicentino, N. *L'antica musica ridotta alla moderna prattica*, Rome, A. Barre, 1555; facs. Kassel, Bärenreiter, 1959

Werckmeister, A. *Orgel-Probe*, Quedlinburg, T. P. Calvisius, 1681

Musicalische Temperatur, Quedlinburg, T. P. Calvisius, 1691; reprint ed. R. Rasch, Utrecht, Diapason Press, 1983

Zarlino, G. *Le istitutioni harmoniche*, Venice, Franceschi, 1558; facs. New York, Broude, 1965

Le istitutioni harmoniche, rev. edn., Venice, Franceschi, 1573; facs. Ridgewood, NJ, Gregg, 1966

Dimostrationi armoniche, Venice, 1571; facs. New York, Broude, 1965 and Ridgewood, NJ, Gregg, 1966

Sopplimenti musicali. Venice, 1588; facs. Ridgewood, NJ, Gregg, 1966, and New York, Broude, 1979

Secondary sources

Barbieri, P. *Acustica, accordatura e temperamento nell'Illuminismo veneto*, Rome, Torre d'Orfeo, 1987

Barbour, M. J. *Tuning and Temperament: An Historical Approach*, East Lansing, Michigan State College Press, 1951; reprint New York, Da Capo Press, 1972

Bosanquet, R. H. M. *An Elementary Treatise on Musical Intervals and Temperament*, London, Macmillan, 1876; reprint Utrecht, Diapason Press, 1987

Devie, D. *Le Tempérament musical: Philosophie, histoire, théorie et pratique*, Béziers, Société de Musicologie de Languedoc, 1990

Drobisch, M. "Ueber musikalische Tonbestimmung und Temperatur", *Abhandlungen der Mathematisch-Physischen Classe der Königlichen Sächsischen Gesellschaft der Wissenschaften* 2 (1855), pp. 1–120

Dupont, W. *Geschichte der musikalischen Temperatur*, Kassel, Bärenreiter, 1935

Frosztega, A. "Friedrich Wilhelm Marpurg and Musical Temperament in Late Eighteenth-century Germany," Ph.D. diss., University of Utrecht (1999)

Huygens, C. *Œuvres complètes . . . Tome vingtième*, The Hague, Nijhoff, 1940

Jorgensen, O. *Tuning the Historical Temperaments by Ear*, Marquette, Northern Michigan University Press, 1977

Tuning: Containing the Perfection of Eighteenth-century Temperament, the Lost Art of Nineteenth-century Temperament, and the Science of Equal Temperament, East Lansing, Michigan State University Press, 1991

Lindley, M. *Lutes, Viols and Temperament*, Cambridge University Press, 1984

"Stimmung und Temperatur," in *GMt* 6 (1987), pp. 109–331

Lindley, M. and R. Turner-Smith, *Mathematical Models of Musical Scales: A New Approach*, Bonn, Verlag für Systematische Musikwissenschaft, 1993

Rasch, R. "Description of Regular Twelve-tone Musical Tunings," *Journal of the Acoustical Society of America* 73 (1983), pp. 1023–35

Joseph Sauveur: Collected Writings on Musical Acoustics (Paris 1700–1713), Utrecht, Diapason Press, 1984

Christiaan Huygens: Le cycle harmonique (Rotterdam 1691), Utrecht, Diapason Press, 1986

"The musical circle," *Tijdschrift voor Muziektheorie* 2 (1997), pp. 1–17, 110–33; 4 (1999), pp. 23–39, 206–13

Ratte, F. J. *Die Temperatur der Clavierinstrumente*, Kassel, Bärenreiter, 1991

Sabaino, D. *Il rinascimento dopo il Rinascimento: Scientia musicae e musica scientiae nella "Musica" di Juan Caramuel Lobkowitz*, paper given at symposium "Musique et mathématique à la Renaissance," Tours, 17–19 February 2000

·8·

The role of harmonics in the scientific revolution

PENELOPE GOUK

This chapter aims to highlight the influential role that harmonics played in the "scientific revolution," which historians of science see taking place in Western thinking between the sixteenth and early eighteenth centuries.[1] Between the publication of Nicolaus Copernicus's *De revolutionibus* in 1543 and Isaac Newton's *Principia mathematica* in 1687, a profound transformation took place in understanding about the laws governing the universe and man's place within it. Why harmonics should have been relevant to this process may require some explanation, especially since music itself is now classified among the arts rather than the sciences, and harmonics is no longer recognised as a viable scientific discipline.[2]

In its narrowest sense, harmonics has been understood since the Greeks as the study of the mathematical relations (*harmonia*) underlying the structure of audible music. This branch of mathematics was also known as "canonics," a term recalling Euclid's *Sectio canonis* (fourth to third century BCE), in which the propositions of harmonics are demonstrated as mathematical theorems. Greek harmonic writings which focused on musical organization and structure characteristically fell into one of two categories, following respectively the "Pythagorean" and the "Aristoxenian" schools of thought.[3] There was a traditional component of physical explanations for these mathematical relationships (e.g., the weights of Pythagoras's hammers), but this was only put on a sound experimental footing in the seventeenth century, by which time the field had been redefined as acoustics.[4]

Beyond this realm of practical harmonics, however, was an altogether broader conception of harmonics that had its roots in Pythagorean and neo-Platonic philosophy.[5] As will be explained below in the context of Boethius's *Fundamentals of Music* (sixth

1 Henry, *Scientific Revolution*, pp. 1–7; Cohen, *Quantifying Music*, pp. 7–10.

2 For a discussion of how the terms "art" and "science" have changed their meanings over time, see Gouk, *Music, Science and Natural Magic*, pp. 9–10, 24–27.

3 Barker, *Greek Musical Writings II*, pp. 3–8; Gozza, *Number to Sound*, pp. 1–9. A third tradition of Greek music theory standing somewhat between the Phythagorean and Aristoxenian schools called "harmonicist" can also be identified. See Chapter 4, pp. 117–20.

4 Acoustics, the science of sound, first took shape as a recognizably independent branch of natural philosophy in the seventeenth century For an account of this development, see Chapter 9, pp. 246 ff.

5 For further details see Gozza's introduction to *Number to Sound*; Kassler, "Music as a Model in Early Science"; also Isherwood, *Music in the Service of the King*, pp. 4–16.

century CE), this speculative tradition assumed that audible music is a tangible expression of the underlying principles which govern the harmonious relations between the elements of all significant structures in the cosmos. An important early source for this tradition was Ptolemy's *Harmonics* (second century CE). This work demonstrates that the structures found in music have their analogues in the soul and in the heavens, and therefore astrology and music are intimately related.[6]

The scientific revolution and occult philosophy

With this broad conception of harmonics in mind, we can begin to see why it should have played a significant role in the scientific revolution, a period in which leading mathematicians, natural philosophers and medical theorists advanced their knowledge and control of the natural world, most notably through the mathematization of physics. Today the manipulation of natural objects and processes and the application of mathematics to the physical world are seen as hallmarks of the scientific method, but before the seventeenth century they were seen as part of natural magic.[7] From around 1600, however, the occult phenomenon of sympathy (i.e. resonance between bodies at a distance), which played a central role in the theory of magical operations, became an integral part of the new experimental philosophy.[8] The scientific revolution marks the period when the most powerful aspects of this occult tradition were absorbed into mainstream natural philosophy, above all in the experimental physics of Isaac Newton and his contemporaries in the Royal Society.[9] Within this newly defined field, musical sympathy especially came to serve as a model for other hidden forces in nature, most notably gravity and magnetism. Yet even as Enlightenment philosophers supposedly banished all traces of the occult from the natural world, sympathy also remained a defining attribute of the magical tradition, one which has continued to flourish in a variety of forms down to the twentieth century.[10]

6 For a translation and commentary see Barker, *Greek Musical Writings II*, pp. 270–391.

7 Natural magic can be defined as the art of bringing about amazing effects by harnessing occult but natural, or spiritual forces (as opposed to demonic magic which relies on the intervention of demons, i.e., intelligent but immaterial beings). For a general discussion see Henry, *Scientific Revolution*, Chapter 3, "Magic and the origins of modern science."

8 Apart from its general meaning of "hidden," the term "occult" in this period was also used in a specific technical sense. In Aristotelian natural philosophy "occult" qualities included anything which could not be explained in elemental terms, and was therefore excluded from physics. See Henry, *Scientific Revolution*; also Gouk, *Music, Science and Natural Magic*, esp. pp. 11–14.

9 Gouk, *Music, Science and Natural Magic*, Chapters 5–7. "Natural philosophy" was the term most often used before the nineteenth century to denote systematic understandings of the natural world, a usage closely corresponding to popular understandings of "science" today.

10 For further details of the occult tradition and its relationship with music theory after the seventeenth century see Godwin, *Harmonies of Heaven and Earth*; *Music and the Occult*.

Harmonics: the classical background

The impact that the rediscovery of ancient harmonic texts from Aristoxenus to Ptolemy had on Renaissance musical thought is familiar to musicologists, chiefly through the work of D. P. Walker and Claude Palisca.[11] Several chapters in the present volume also describe the key ancient and medieval sources on harmonic doctrine, of which the most important by far was Boethius's *Fundamentals of Music* (see, especially, **Chapter 5, pp. 141–47**). The wider intellectual significance of this work beyond purely musical considerations deserves emphasis here. The *Fundamentals of Music* became established as the university set text for music as early as the twelfth century, and remained part of the liberal arts curriculum into the eighteenth century and beyond, notably in the universities of Oxford and Cambridge.[12]

If Boethius's text was of little relevance to most practicing musicians by the sixteenth century, his Pythagorean conception of music remained of vital interest to university scholars, mathematicians, and philosophers. Within this conceptual framework, music was classified as one of the seven liberal arts, which were regarded as essential grounding for training in the higher faculties of philosophy and theology. It was Boethius himself who first coined the term *quadrivium* to designate the mathematical disciplines of arithmetic, geometry, astronomy, and music (by analogy the *trivium* denoted the verbal disciplines of grammar, rhetoric, and logic).

Within this Boethian view of music, performance was regarded as ancillary to acquiring speculative knowledge about the world, which is achieved primarily through an understanding of harmony. This emphasis is enshrined in Boethius's famous tripartate classification of music, which in ascending order of importance comprises singing and instrumental performance (*musica instrumentalis*), the harmony of the body and soul (*musica humana*), and the harmony of the universe (*musica mundana*). Musicians are correspondingly classified into three distinct groups: the most lowly perform on instruments, the middle category compose songs, while members of the third group are "true musicians," namely philosophers with a capacity for judging instrumental performance and songs.[13]

Underpinning this hierarchical division is the fundamental belief that cosmic music embodies "true" music – or rather harmony – while instrumental music merely offers an imperfect approximation of these divine and unchanging proportions. By the early seventeenth century however, this hierarchy had become completely destabilized. Philosophers, not just practicing musicians, disagreed about the true harmonic laws governing the universe as well as the natural foundations of musical practice. As a

11 See Walker, *Spiritual and Demonic Magic*; *Studies in Musical Science*; and *Music, Spirit and Language*; also Palisca, "Scientific Empiricism"; and *Humanism in Italian Renaissance Musical Thought.*

12 Carpenter, *Music in Medieval and Renaissance Universities*, pp. 153–210.

13 Boethius, *Fundamentals of Music*, pp. 50–1; Gozza, *Number to Sound*, pp. 17–19. See also **Chapter 5, p. 146**.

means of resolving these issues, scholars typically appealed to ancient and Arab authorities which appeared to offer new and exciting alternatives to the static Boethian model of cosmic harmony. Works which had been unknown to medieval scholars and were now becoming more available fundamentally transformed the way natural philosophers thought about the structure of the heavens, as well as man's ability to control the hidden forces operating throughout nature. Many of these texts were not just about harmonics, but were also recognized as part of an ancient magical tradition embracing alchemy, astrology, and other occult arts. This dangerous and even forbidden kind of knowledge was thought to have come out of post-diluvian Egypt, and was accessible to only a few chosen initiates.[14]

A central figure in the transmission and interpretation of this esoteric wisdom was Marsilio Ficino (1433–99), one of the leading members of the Florentine Platonic Academy. Commissioned by his patron Cosimo de' Medici, Ficino first translated the *Corpus Hermeticum* (pub. 1463), a body of texts thought to be by Hermes Trismegistus, an ancient Egyptian magus whose learning predated that of Moses and also the Greeks (in fact the material dates from the second century CE). Ficino then went on to produce a complete edition of Plato's works, including the *Timaeus* and *Republic* (1484), as well as Plotinus's *Enneads* (1492), the classic text of neo-Platonic philosophy. In 1489 Ficino published his own *De vita comparanda*, or *Three Books on Life*. The work not only gave a systematic explanation of astrological influences on the earth, but also became the *locus classicus* for sixteenth- and seventeenth-century discussions of music's effects.[15] The linkage between musical modes, bodily temperaments, and planetary harmonies had already been suggested by the music theorist Bartolomeo Ramis de Pareia in his *Musica practica* (1482), but it was chiefly through Ficino's work that it became widely known.[16]

During the course of the sixteenth century Ficino's editions of Plato and his followers became increasingly accessible, and his theory of music and *spiritus* was popularized through Heinrich Cornelius Agrippa's *De occulta philosphia* or *Occult Philosophy* (1533), a highly influential handbook on astrological medicine. In the middle of Book II, which deals with the mathematical arts and their use in magical operations, Agrippa explains how music affects the passions of the mind via the "aerious spirit of the hearer, which is the bond of soul and body" and in successive chapters discusses the composition and harmony of the body and soul.[17] Drawing on the same neo-Platonic sources as Agrippa (but without direct reference to him), Gioseffo Zarlino similarly reflected on the link

14 Walker, *Ancient Theology*, pp. 1–21; Godwin, *Athanasius Kircher*, pp. 15–24; Gouk, *Music, Science and Natural Magic*, pp. 102–03.

15 Voss, "Marsilio Ficino"; Walker, *Spiritual and Demonic Magic*, pp. 36–44, 75–84; Isherwood, *Music in the Service of the King*, pp. 16–32; Tomlinson, *Music in Renaissance Magic*, pp. 84–89, 101–45; Gouk, *Music, Science and Natural Magic*, pp. 5–7, 70; Boccadoro, "Marsilio Ficino."

16 Tomlinson, *Music in Renaissance Magic*, pp. 78–84. **Plate 6.2, p. 183** shows one illustration of the Renaissance correspondence between musical modes and planetary harmonies.

17 Agrippa, *Occult Philosophy*, Book II, Chapters 24–28, quotation from English 1651 translation p. 259. For his sources see Tomlinson, *Music in Renaissance Magic*, pp. 45–52.

between musical modes and bodily temperaments in the first book of his *Istitutioni harmoniche* (1558). Given the strong affinity between music and the emotions, Zarlino claimed that physicians as well as musicians ought to understand the fundamental principles of harmony in order to investigate properly music's effects on the body and soul.[18]

Doctors do not seem to have taken this suggestion at all seriously until the eighteenth century, when a few medical men began to try to analyze the effects of music on the body.[19] In the sixteenth century it was composers and musicians who were most interested in exploring the relationship between the humors and the modes, between the human spirit and musical air, with a view to arousing particular effects in their audiences. In the last quarter of the century, however, a coherent system of "occult philosophy" began to be articulated in European courtly circles in which musical harmony figured prominently. A major reason for this prominence was that a number of high-ranking patrons such as the Landgrave Moritz of Hesse were skilled amateur musicians as well as supporters of the occult arts.[20] Based on the harmonies operating at all levels of existence, the occult philosophy provided a theoretical underpinning for a wide range of experimental activities that not only embraced the production of spectacular mechanical, chemical, and physical effects by engineers and alchemists, for example, but also included the manipulation of human emotions. Ficino's doctrine was particularly associated with the masques and festivities which were commissioned for dynastic weddings and other royal occasions (e.g., the Florentine *intermedi* staged at the wedding of Grand Duke Ferdinando de' Medici and Christine of Lorraine in 1589). These productions deployed complex machinery for in the creation of visual and aural effects that astonished and moved their audiences even while affirming princely power. Such courtly experiments gave concrete expression to the Platonic belief that music is an embodiment of cosmic as well as social relations, a means of tempering passions and restoring order, but also a source of disruption, disease, and disorder if not properly controlled.[21]

The value that philosophers were still placing on universal harmony in the early seventeenth century is indicated by the publication of four geographically dispersed treatises on the subject over this period: Robert Fludd's *Utriusque cosmi majoris scilicet et minoris metaphysica, physica atque technica historia* or *History of the Macrocosm and Microcosm* (1617–21); Johannes Kepler's *Harmonices mundi libri quinque* (1619), Marin

18 Zarlino, *Le istitutioni harmoniche*, Part I, Chapters 2, 4, 7; see also Carapetyan, "Music and Medicine"; Palisca, "Moving the Affections through Music," esp. pp. 295–96.

19 Prominent examples include Richard Browne, *Medicina Musica: or a Mechanical Essay on the Effects of Singing, Music, and Dancing* (London, 1729) and Louis Roger's *Tentamen de vi soni et musices in corpus humanum* (Avignon, 1758); see Carapetyan, "Music and Medicine," and Gouk, "Music, Melancholy and Medical Spirits."

20 Moran, *Alchemical World of the German Court*, pp. 11–24, 107–11; Gouk, *Music, Science and Natural Magic*, pp. 12–13, 263–64.

21 Yates, *French Academies*, pp. 77–94; Isherwood, *Music in the Service of the King*, pp. 55–67; Gouk, *Music, Science and Natural Magic*, pp. 31–33.

Mersenne's *Harmonie universelle* (1636–37), and Athanasius Kircher's *Musurgia universalis* (1650). It is significant that all these men had received a university training in theology, although on different sides of the Protestant–Catholic divide. Also, it was the possession of higher academic degrees in philosophy and theology, rather than any practical training in performance, that qualified them to write authoritatively on music theory. The occupational identities of these men also deserves emphasis: Kepler had originally intended to become a Lutheran pastor, but ended up as imperial mathematician and court astrologer. Fludd took a degree in divinity at Christ Church, Oxford, but eventually became a successful Paracelsian physician in London. Both of the Catholics were priests in holy orders: Mersenne was a Minim friar, while Kircher was a Jesuit.[22]

Although sharing a belief in the harmonic structure of God's creation, these individuals held rather different views on the true relationship between cosmic, human, and instrumental music. Not all their disagreements can be ascribed to a simple doctrinal divide, however. In several crucial respects Fludd and Kircher (likewise Kepler and Mersenne) appear to have had more in common with each other than their religious commitments might suggest. Thus, for example, Fludd's encyclopedic history of the macrocosm and microcosm (which used Boethius's tripartite division of music as its organizing principle) was roundly condemned by both Kepler and Mersenne. Their grounds for rejecting Fludd's musical schema (i.e., that it had no foundation in empirical data) seem to have been vindicated by later natural philosophers, whose demand for empirically demonstrable laws have become the cornerstone of modern science. Similar objections were later raised against Kircher's *Musurgia*, which like Fludd's work is conceptualized in terms of neo-Platonic and occult doctrines of sympathy and the macrocosm–microcosm correspondence.[23]

Since the rejection of magic is supposedly one of the defining features of the scientific revolution, it is perhaps not surprising to find that occult harmonies are less frequently alluded to in the latter part of the century. Thus while Kepler framed his astronomy in terms of universal harmonies, Newton took mathematical physics as his ultimate frame of reference. This shift in thinking appears to correspond with wider cultural trends in the period. As is well known through the writings of Shakespeare and Milton, for example, the affective powers of music and its links to the heavens were exceptionally prominent tropes in early seventeenth-century poetic and literary discourse. But according to some scholars, at least, by the end of the century the notion of heavenly harmonies was no longer popular, having largely given way to acoustical studies based on the joint development of classical physics and mathematical analysis,

22 Apart from relevant entries in *NG2*, consult the following works for further information: Stephenson, *Harmony of the Heavens* (Kepler); Godwin, *Robert Fludd*; Dear, *Mersenne*; Godwin, *Athanasius Kircher*.

23 For these debates, see articles in Vickers, ed., *Occult and Scientific Mentalities*, especially Westman, "Nature, Art, and Psyche"; see also Godwin, *Harmonies of Heaven and Earth*, pp. 143–52, 171–76; and Gouk, *Music, Science and Natural Magic*, Chapter 3.

and the harmonies of the heavens had fallen silent.[24] Enlightenment *philosophes* themselves certainly claimed to have removed the need for occult principles in nature.[25]

Closer examination suggests a more complex picture, in which neo-Platonic and occult ideas were not so much rejected as simply taken over by mathematicians and natural philosophers – indeed, it is clear that Newton saw himself as a latter-day Pythagorean.[26] To show this continuity in thinking, but also to identify what was different about the new experimental philosophy, the next section summarizes the key features of neo-Platonic doctrine as portrayed by Fludd in two of his best-known visualizations of cosmic and human harmonies. The remainder of the chapter looks at how these features were reworked and transformed in the seventeenth and early eighteenth centuries. We will see how astronomers such as Kepler and Newton incorporated musical models into their mathematical physics, while "Human harmonies" focuses on how physicians such as Thomas Willis and William Cheyne used musical models to conceptualize the hidden workings of the body. In each case we will see that the properties of musical instruments, most notably those of vibrating strings (especially resonance), were crucial to the development of new forms of scientific explanation.

Robert Fludd: visualizing hidden harmonies

Taken from the first book of Fludd's *History*, which considers *musica mundana*, Plate 8.1 portrays God's divine monochord and encapsulates the neo-Platonic assumption that the universe is constructed according to mathematical harmonies which can be expressed in musical ratios.[27] The box represents mind, the formal principle, the string represents body, the material principle, its life being set in motion by the divine tuner, the efficient principle. The picture also offers a realization of the story told by Plato and his followers about Pythagoras's discovery of these cosmic harmonies and his invention of the musical canon or monochord. This instrument could demonstrate the arithmetic ratios governing musical consonance, the structure of the heavens, as well as the soul of man. These legends were notably recounted in Franchino Gaffurio's *Theorica musice* (1492), which together with Francesco Giorgi's *De harmonia mundi* (1525) and Agrippa's *De occulta philosphia* (1533) served as Fludd's main source of musical doctrine.[28]

Fludd's picture shows a finite, geocentric, and static cosmos divided into a series of

24 See, e.g., Hollander, *Untuning of the Sky*, esp. pp. 381–90.

25 On definitions of Enlightenment thought, see Christensen, *Rameau and Musical Thought*, pp. 1–20.

26 Gouk, *Music, Science and Natural Magic*, Chapter 7, esp. pp. 254–57.

27 For further examples of Fludd's monochord diagrams, with explanations, see Godwin, *Robert Fludd*, pp. 42–53. It is interesting to compare Plate 8.1 with **Plate 1.2, p. 36**, a related depiction of cosmic *harmonia*.

28 In addition to ibid, see also Amman, "Music Theory and Philosophy of Robert Fludd."

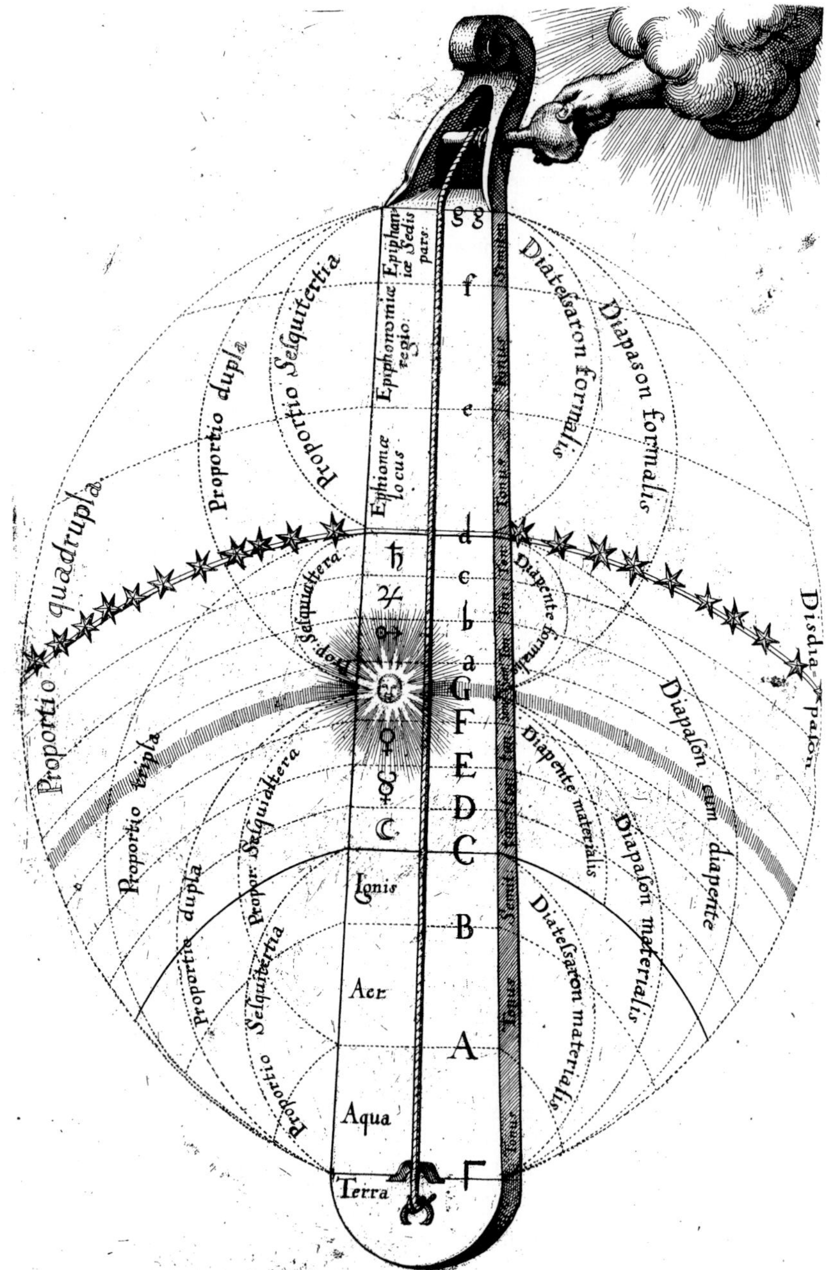

Plate 8.1 The "Divine monochord," from Robert Fludd, *Utriusque cosmi . . . historia* (1617), p. 90

realms emanating from a transcendent One. Three levels of existence (empyrean, ethereal, elemental) are set out along a monochord which shows the musical scale with its proportions in Pythagorean intonation. The ethereal realm of the zodiac between the moon and the fixed stars is bounded by the octave D–d, and each of the planets is assigned a tone: moon D, Mercury E, Venus F, sun G, Mars a, Jupiter b, Saturn c (in other words the tones get higher further away from the earth). Critics such as Kepler and Mersenne were quick to point out the errors in this picture even if it were judged on its own terms (e.g., the F should be sharp for the tones and semitones to be correct). More seriously, they disparaged Fludd's apparent indifference to both astronomical and musical experience (compare Kepler's treatment of the same concepts below).

Such details aside, this neo-Platonic image of the universe as a stringed instrument proved a potent one for early modern natural philosophers, even though their understanding of its harmony was different from that of the ancients. In particular, the claim that all parts of the universe are sympathetically interrelated, and that an action carried out in one part (e.g., on earth) can have an effect in another (e.g., in the heavens), was especially easy to grasp in musical terms. The concept of sympathy, or "action at a distance" could be demonstrated by anyone who had a couple of lutes at their disposal: a string plucked on one instrument could set in vibration a string tuned to the same pitch on a neighboring instrument. Although this experiment originated in the context of natural magic, by the end of the seventeenth century it had become incorporated into the new experimental philosophy as a means of picturing other kinds of hidden but natural vibrations.[29]

If the correspondence between microcosm and macrocosm is assumed, the human body, like the cosmic body, can also be conceived of as a musical instrument whose sounds are produced by the action of the musician (i.e., the mind, soul, or God). For example, the mysterious link between mind, brain, and nerves can be pictured in terms of sympathetic resonance between strings or other vibrating musical bodies (e.g., bells).[30] This musical conception of the body was a commonplace for university-educated physicians like Fludd because the basic principle, although not worked out in detail, was found in the writings of Galen (second century CE). Newly translated and edited by medical humanists in the early sixteenth century, these texts remained an essential part of the university curriculum for the next three hundred years.

Within the Galenic system, health can be construed as a balance or harmony of opposites within the body, maintained through *tonos* or sympathy. At the same time the relationship between different parts of the body can be understood in terms of how particular instruments are played. Apart from stringed instruments, the other kind of instruments most commonly invoked to explain bodily functions (e.g., respiration) was wind instruments. As we shall see in the section on "Human harmonies," far from

29 Gouk, *Music, Science and Natural Magic*, pp. 214–23.
30 Ibid., pp. 216–19, 221; Kassler, *Inner Music*, pp. 16–48, 139–59.

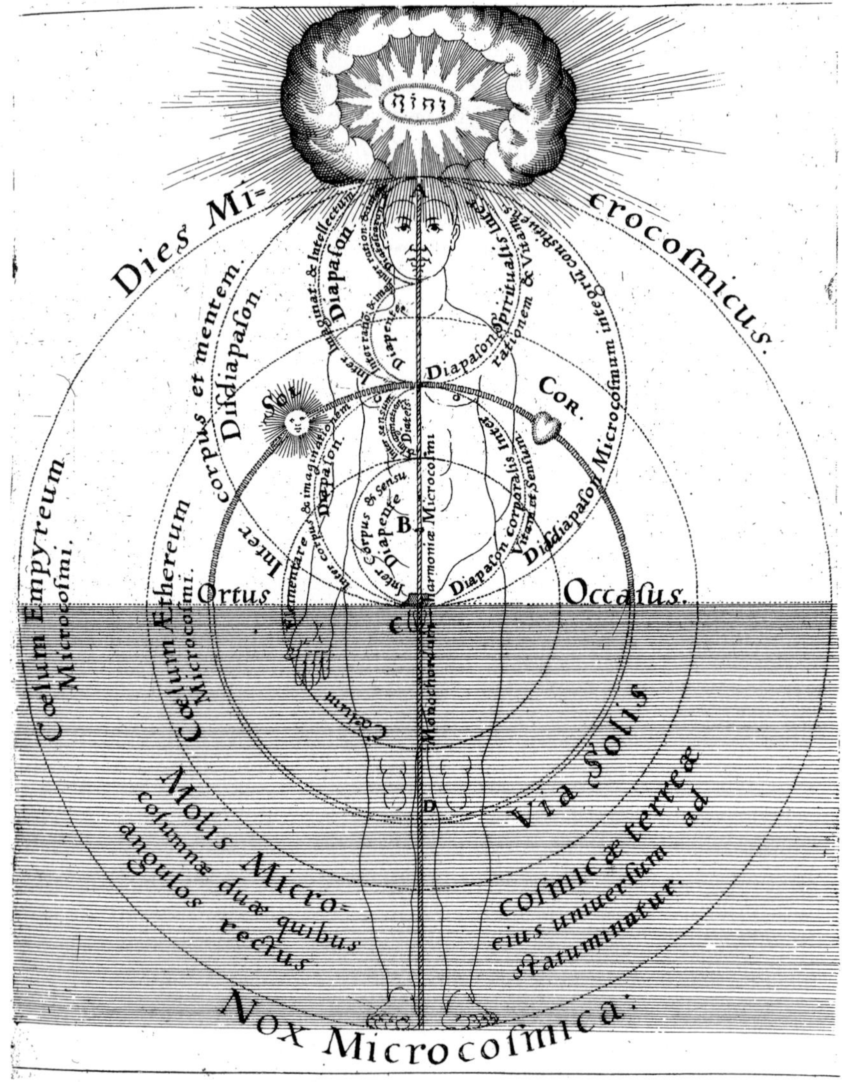

Plate 8.2 "Man the microcosm," from Robert Fludd, *Utriusque cosmi . . . historia* II (1619), p. 274

losing their potency, these kinds of instrumental models became increasingly important in the course of the seventeenth century as the laws of musical vibration became amenable to mathematical analysis.

In the neo-Platonic universe, sympathy – that is, the interaction and affinity of different parts of the cosmos – is maintained by *tonos*, or tension, a dynamic property of the *spiritus*, or world soul, which is represented in Plate 8.2 by Fludd as a musical string. *Spiritus*, or *pneuma*, was thought to be an extremely fine and active substance which mediates between God and His creation. It acted as the principal medium for planetary influences on the earth, and also intermingled with earthly matter, bringing about changes in its form; hence it was the medium of alchemical operations. *Spiritus* was also important for those seeking to understand the hidden (i.e., occult) workings of the human body, and the harmonious relations between its parts. This vital substance was thought to be analogous to, but not necessarily identical with, the medical spirits that link the immaterial soul to the body.[31]

Johannes Kepler: planetary music and polyphonic practice

At first glance, the difference between Fludd's occult vision of cosmic harmony and the planetary laws discovered by Kepler and Newton seems overwhelming. Yet Kepler and Newton also devoted their lives to uncovering the hidden harmonies of the macrocosm and microcosm. Kepler's prominence in the history of astronomy arises from his three planetary laws.[32] These laws were based on his revolutionary hypothesis that there is a force emanating from the sun governing the motion of the planets, which he assumed was inversely proportional to distance. They represent the culmination of Kepler's lifelong search for the laws of harmony governing nature, a search which was profoundly shaped by his belief that musical experience, especially polyphonic practice, validated his discovery of planetary harmonies.

In Book V of *Harmonices mundi* Kepler offers the fullest account of the musical harmonies that are embodied in the angular motion of the planets as seen from the sun. In these apparent motions are found the system of the notes of the musical scale, as well as the major and minor modes. Although the concept of planetary music was ancient, Kepler's cosmic harmonies differed from earlier examples in several fundamental respects. First, the harmonies are real but soundless; second, they are perceived from the sun rather than the earth; third, they are polyphonic, i.e., harmonies in the modern sense of the word; and fourth, they follow the proportions of just intonation, which in Kepler's time was a system known as Ptolemy's syntonic diatonic.[33]

In his *Mysterium cosmographicum* (1596) Kepler first attempted to link the six

31 Walker, "Medical Spirits in Philosophy and Theology"; Isherwood, *Music in the Service of the King*, pp. 19–23; Gouk, "Music, Melancholy and Medical Spirits."

32 Kepler's first law states that planets move in elliptical paths, with the sun at one focus of the ellipse. The second law states during a given time a line from the sun to any planet sweeps out an equal area anywhere along its path. The third law (known as the harmonic law) is that the ratio between the periodic times for any of planets is the $^3/_2$ power of the ratio of their mean distances. The first two laws were expounded in the *Epitome Astronomiae Copernicae* (1618–21), while the third appears for the first time in *Harmonices Mundi libri V* (1619). For further details, see Stephenson, *The Music of the Heavens* and works cited in the following footnote.

33 Walker, "Kepler's Celestial Music"; Cohen, *Quantifying Music*, pp. 13–34; Gingerich, "Kepler, Galilei, and the Harmony of the World"; Gozza, *Number to Sound*, pp. 42–50, pp. 173–88 (this last section is a translation of Chapter 2 of M. Dickreiter, *Der Musiktheoretiker Johannes Kepler* [Bern and Munich, Francke Verlag, 1973], pp. 49–61).

C		D		E		F		G		A		B		C
	$\frac{9}{8}$		$\frac{9}{8}$		$\frac{256}{243}$		$\frac{9}{8}$		$\frac{9}{8}$		$\frac{9}{8}$		$\frac{256}{243}$	

Figure 8.1 Proportions of the Pythagorean diatonic scale

planets and their relative distances from the sun with the relationships between the five so-called Platonic solids. (According to the principles of Euclidean geometry, there are only five polyhedra that have identical polygons for each face: tetrahedron, cube, octahedron, dodecahedron, and icosahedron.) In the course of his search, Kepler began to consider whether musical harmonies are also grounded in geometry (rather than arithmetic as Boethius claimed), and tried unsuccessfully to show that all the musical ratios could be found in the same geometric calculations he had made for the planets. The important point about this stage of Kepler's search is that if he had recognized Pythagorean intonation as the correct theoretical basis for musical practice, his calculations would have worked. Had he been alive in Copernicus's lifetime, he almost certainly would have taken this Pythagorean path. Up to the middle of the sixteenth century, the explanation given in Gaffurio's *Theorica musice* (1492) of how Pythagoras had discovered the arithmetic foundations of harmony in the numbers 1 to 4 was still generally accepted by elite musicians as the correct theoretical underpinning of their art. Within this system, consonances are limited to the octave (1:2), fifth (2:3) and fourth (3:4) and their octaves; all other intervals, including thirds and sixths, are classified as dissonances. The diatonic scale as shown in Figure 8.1 consists of five whole tones (8:9) and two semitones (243:256). (See also **Chapter 6, pp. 171–78**; and **Chapter 7, pp. 195–98**.

By the time that Kepler wrote his *Mysterium cosmographicum* in the 1590s, the multi-textured harmonies of polyphonic music constituted a thoroughly natural part of the world he inhabited. Kepler could not accept a Pythagorean solution to his search for the relationship between musical and planetary harmony because he knew through his own experience that musicians were using thirds and sixths consonantly in practice, even while Pythagorean theory claimed them to be dissonances. As yet, however, he was unable to provide a satisfactory alternative.

Almost twenty-five years later Kepler was at last able to announce in the *Harmonices mundi* (1619) that all the musical intervals of the scale were expressed in the elliptical motions of the planets as they orbited around the sun. Rather than relying on actual speeds, his calculations were instead based on the minimal and maximal orbital velocities of each planet as they would appear from the sun. As Plate 8.3 shows, each planet "sings" a range of notes depending on its rate of acceleration and deceleration. Although the pitches shown here are discrete, if the planets actually emitted sounds (which Kepler explains they do not because of lack of air) their continuous pitches would rise and fall like a siren.

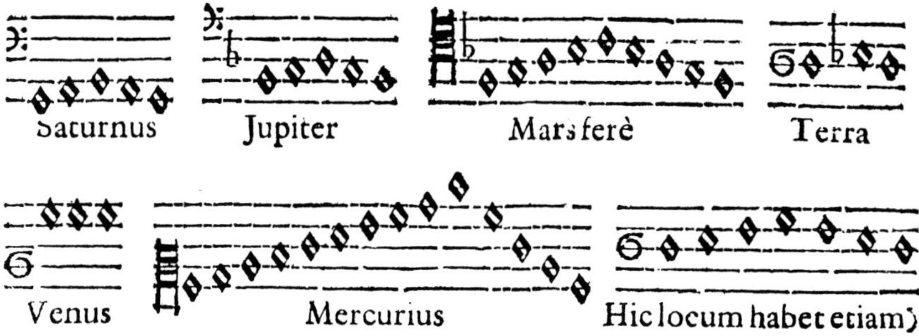

Plate 8.3 Planetary scales, from Johannes Kepler, *Harmonices mundi* (1619), p. 207

The ratios of the scale which Kepler found in the planetary orbits were those of the syntonic diatonic, or in modern terms, the just intonation scale shown in Figure 8.2. The proportions of this scale were already mentioned in Ptolemy's *Harmonics*, an important ancient source for Kepler's harmonic thinking, but the theorist who successfully proved them to be the foundation of modern polyphonic practice was Zarlino. As Kepler had now discovered from reading *Le istitutioni harmoniche*, Zarlino legimitated this new scale not only with the *senario*, the first six integers which Plato described as perfect numbers, but also with appeal to the judgment of the senses (see **Chapter 7, pp. 201–04** and also **Plate 10.2, p. 277**). Although Kepler agreed with these experimental findings, he did not accept Zarlino's arithmetic explanation for the perfection of the musical consonances, preferring instead his own geometric theory.[34]

Isaac Newton: harmonic laws and the new physics

While Kepler construed his planetary laws in terms of harmonics, Newton situated his inverse square law of universal gravitation within the broader framework of a new mathematical physics.[35] And in contrast to Kepler, who took pleasure in music, Newton seems to have had little or no interest in its performance. Nevertheless, music theory contributed positively to Newton's work in three crucial areas: in the development of his theory of color (the realm of optics), in his analysis of wave propagation in

34 Another important feature of Kepler's theory was its historical dimension, informed chiefly by Sethus Calvisius's *De initio et progressu musices* (1600), an account of musical theory and practice from the Flood to the present day. In Book III of the *Harmonices mundi*, Kepler argues for a progressive model of human achievement in both music and astronomy. He believed that the development of polyphony is directly comparable to the Copernican revolution in that both are based on eternal principles of nature, but both were unknown to the Greeks because they did not stay close enough to empirically established facts. These revolutions would not have been so long in coming had the ancients been prepared to trust the judgment of their ears, rather than turning too quickly toward numerical speculation.

35 Newton proved that the forces acting on each planet must obey an inverse square law. For further details of what follows, see Chapter 7 of Gouk, *Music, Science and Natural Magic.*

C		D		E		F		G		A		B		C
	$\frac{9}{8}$		$\frac{10}{9}$		$\frac{16}{15}$		$\frac{9}{8}$		$\frac{10}{9}$		$\frac{9}{8}$		$\frac{16}{15}$	

Figure 8.2 Proportions of just intonation (Ptolemy's syntonic diatonic)

the *Principia* (dynamics), and, finally, in his law of universal gravitational attraction, the achievement which built so effectively on Kepler's work already described.

From his earliest years as a Cambridge undergraduate, Newton studied the mathematical and physical foundations of music. From the outset he seems to have taken for granted what historians call the coincidence theory of consonance. This theory, first elaborated by Mersenne in the *Harmonie universelle* (1636), was based on his discovery of the laws governing the vibration of musical strings, namely that the length, thickness, and tension of a string govern the frequency of its harmonic motion.[36] From this Mersenne argued (in fact wrongly!) that the pleasing effects of musical consonance result from the relative frequency of the pulses or vibrations produced by strings striking the ear: the more often their pulses coincide, the more harmonious the interval. (For further discussion of the "coincidence theory" of consonance, see **Chapter 9, pp. 247–49**.) Because it was possible to show a direct correspondence between musical vibration and the perception of consonance, this theory played an important role in the thinking of mechanical philosophers such as Descartes and Hobbes, who sought to explain all physical phenomena in terms of matter and motion, expressed in mathematical laws.[37]

This mechanistic way of thinking proved an important influence on Newton's intellectual development. He first began to search for an adequate mechanical explanation for the phenomenon of colors in 1666 when he pioneered his prism experiments. Following Descartes's example, he tried to develop a mathematical theory in which colors of bodies were reduced to kinematic laws of elastic collision. This theory first appeared in 1672, following his discovery of the composite nature of white light. At this stage his aim was simply to describe the behavior of colored light in terms of momentum change, rather than to explain how color is actually caused or perceived. The number of colors in the spectrum was not yet significant (two and five colors are referred to, but not seven).

The Royal Society's Curator of Experiments, Robert Hooke, was the first natural philosopher to raise objections to Newton's corpuscular theory of colors. Hooke himself thought that light was not corpuscular, but, like sound, was a pulse-like motion propagated through a fine ethereal medium. He believed that his theory was

36 Mersenne's laws can be summarized mathematically in the following expression:

$$\text{pitch} \propto \frac{\sqrt{(\text{tension})}}{\text{length} \times (\text{diameter})^2}$$

37 Cohen, *Quantifying Music*, pp. 97–114, 161–79.

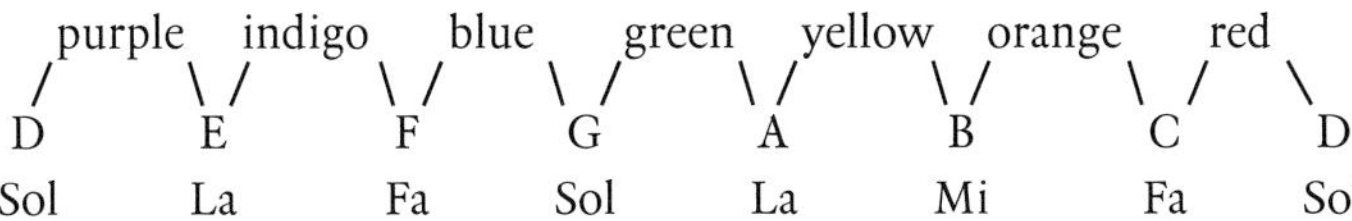

Figure 8.3 Newton's color scale

better than Newton's because it fitted into his matter theory more generally, at the heart of which was musical vibration.[38] Hooke's criticisms made a significant impression on Newton, who now began to develop an alternative physical model of light which was drawn from the alchemical sources he was studying at this time. In his "Hypothesis explaining the properties of light" (1675), Newton postulates the existence of a universal ether or *spiritus*, an extremely rarefied, active substance which vivifies matter and connects the planets to the earth. As we have seen in connection with Fludd's striking images, the ability to harness the power of *spiritus* was central to both alchemical and astrological operations, and was a core feature of the natural magic tradition.[39]

In the "Hypothesis" Newton now explained all optical phenomena by the interaction between light corpuscles of varying size or mass and an extremely fine material ether. Pursuing the "analogy of Nature," Newton suggested that the sensations of different colors are produced in a similar way to musical tones, that the harmony or dissonance between certain colors is a result of the proportion (or lack of it) between ethereal vibrations. The proportions that Newton now "discovered" in the spectrum were those of the syntonic diatonic, in the Dorian mode (i.e., equivalent to the white notes of a piano from D to d). What matters about this particular scale is not its musical value, but its symmetry, which closely corresponds to the distribution of colors (which he now numbered as seven, not five or two) Newton found in the spectrum.[40] (See Figure 8.3)

Newton was keenly aware that his two physical models of light were contradictory, and this was one reason why his *Opticks* was only finally published in 1704. The appearance of this work prompted a lively debate over the color–sound analogy among eighteenth-century natural philosophers, notably Rousseau, Diderot, Castel (the inventor of the ocular harpsichord), and Goethe.[41] In the meantime, however, musical vibration went on to play an important role in the development of Newton's physics. In the *Principia* Newton was the first to offer a coherent mathematical explanation connecting the properties of musical strings and other elastic vibrating bodies. In the section dealing with the mechanics of fluids, Newton gives a mathematical and physical analysis of waves in a compressible elastic medium, from which he is able to derive the

38 On Hooke's theory of universal vibration and its relationship to experimental philosophy, see Gouk, *Music, Science and Natural Magic*, Chapter 6.

39 For further details, see Henry, "Newton, Matter and Magic."

40 The solfège mutation used by Newton is discussed in **Chapter 13, pp. 435–38**.

41 Christensen, *Rameau and Musical Thought*, pp. 109, 142–47; Godwin, *Music and the Occult*, pp. 10–17.

speed of sound. What is of interest here is the physical model which enabled him to mathematize the problem. Newton's method was to make an analogy between the motion of a pendulum and the particles of fluid. On the basis of Boyle's law he was able to assume that the length of a "segment" of fluid changes periodically, and that this length is inversely proportional to its elastic force. In other words, he visualized the air as being made up of particles which oscillate backwards and forwards like tiny pendulums or strings, each one obeying the laws of simple harmonic motion.

Newton's calculations marked a new phase in mathematical thought. The isochronous properties of vibrating strings and pendulums had been discovered in the course of the sixteenth and seventeenth centuries through experiments which crucially relied on the judgment of the ear, as well as the eye, for their confirmation. Yet once the laws of simple harmonic motion were established, their empirical foundations receded in importance. From around 1675 these abstract mathematical relationships took on an independent mode of existence with an explanatory force of their own. While earlier understandings of harmonic motion had been embodied in the motion of the pendulum and vibrating string, these were now replaced, not by another physical instance, but by a mathematical relation. Eighteenth-century mathematicians such as Euler and d'Alembert could take Newton's laws as the point of departure for their investigations into different branches of the physical sciences.[42]

The last musical model in Newton's cosmology to be considered here is his radical interpretation of the ancient concept of the harmony of the spheres.[43] While Kepler regarded heliocentrism as an advance on ancient geocentric astronomy, Newton saw his own system of celestial mechanics as a recovery of Adamic wisdom, lost since the Fall of mankind to all but a few wise men. He first began to develop his ideas about this lost pristine natural philosophy during the late 1670s, a period when he was intensively studying patristic theology, gnostic texts, and pagan mythology as sources of historical and allegorical truths. In 1683 Newton began writing the "Philosophical Origins of Gentile Philosophy," in which he suggested that the heliocentric, vacuist system was known to the ancients and expressed symbolically through Vestal temple ceremonies and the Jewish tabernacle, a building which embodied the harmonic proportions of the universe. Transmitted via the early magi, these truths became known to Pythagoras, who expressed them in his musical allegories, above all in the myth of the harmony of the spheres. Corruption set in when such symbols were misinterpreted later by gentile philosophers such as Eudoxus and Ptolemy.

A similar account appears in material that Newton wrote about 1694 for a projected second edition of the *Principia*, which was never published. Nevertheless, it is clear that he regarded such ideas as essential justification for his own cosmological system. In the Scholia in the section of Book III on universal gravitation, Newton asserts that

42 See Cannon and Dostrovsky, *The Evolution of Dynamics*; also Christensen, *Rameau and Musical Thought*, pp. 150–59, 264–69. 43 Gouk, *Music, Science and Natural Magic*, pp. 251–54.

Pythagoras had already known the inverse square law theory, but that this knowledge was hidden allegorically in the story of Pythagoras's discovery at the blacksmith of the numerical laws governing musical consonance. Ironically, it was this very legend which had demonstrated to Kepler, via his reading of Vincenzo Galilei, the limitations of Pythagorean science. A further irony is that Newton actually misrepresented the ancient tradition by claiming that the proportions of the planetary scale corresponded to the those of his own spectrum scale – that is, of the syntonic diatonic. In taking this line he followed Kepler, the first mathematician to discover the proportions of this scale in planetary harmony.

Human harmonies: new conceptions of the body and soul

Newton's success in ("re")discovering the mathematical laws governing the entire system of the world inspired others to apply the principles of classical mechanics to the hidden forces at work in human bodies. We have already seen from Fludd's picture of "man the microcosm" how neo-Platonic ideas about bodily harmony were commonplace in the early seventeenth century. Of these the most important were that the body and soul are constructed according to the same harmonic principles, that they are also connected by a vital medium or spirit, and that musical instruments can be used as analogies for body parts and systems. The way that these core principles of *musica humana* were simply translated into the language of experimental philosophy can be illustrated with reference to three seventeenth-century figures who revolutionized medical understandings of the body. William Harvey, René Descartes, and Thomas Willis all used musical analogies for conceptualizing the hidden workings of the body and its relationship to the soul. In his anatomical lectures of 1616, for example, William Harvey (1578–1657) divided the body into musical proportions and briefly compared some of its parts to particular musical instruments. More interestingly, Harvey's 1627 lectures on animal motion compared the brain to a choir-master regulating the actions of muscles (actors, singers, and dancers) and nerves (which acted as time-keepers).[44]

This line of thinking was fruitfully extended by Descartes in his highly influential *Traité de l'Homme* or *Treatise on Man* (1632, published 1662). Here all bodily functions are to be explained in mechanical terms, the body being subject to the same laws which govern the actions of machines. At one point Descartes compares the vascular system to the pneumatic organ: the heart and arteries act as bellows, while external objects act as the organist's fingers on the keyboard. In another instance he likens the nervous system to a carillon (i.e., a set of tuned bells hung in a tower and activated from a keyboard).[45] After Descartes popularized the concept of using automatic instruments as a

44 Kassler, *Inner Music*, pp. 36–37. 45 Ibid., pp. 43–48.

means of understanding bodily functions these kinds of musical models became commonplace.

The explanatory potential of such models is illustrated most clearly in the work of Thomas Willis (1621–75), who coined the term "neurology" and is therefore celebrated as the founder of the neurological sciences. In his *De anima brutorum* (1672) Willis postulated the existence of two souls in man: the incorporeal soul, whose seat is the brain, and the corporeal soul, located in the medical spirits. These chemical substances take the form of vital spirits in the blood and the more refined animal spirits in the cortex, which he identified as the immediate organ of neuromuscular function. Like Descartes, Willis used a keyboard instrument as a model for understanding mind–body interaction, but with a far greater degree of rigor. In Willis's model involuntary muscular motions are likened to the action of a hydraulic organ whose barrel has been pre-programmed to play the keys in a set order. Voluntary actions, by contrast, involve the cerebrum, and "fingering" by the "musician": that is, the mind or soul. Willis gives a detailed account of how, once activated, the nerves carry spirits to the different parts of the brain, flowing like the wind in organ pipes.[46]

Willis himself did not attempt to quantify the motion of the nervous spirits, and although he assumed they were distilled out of the blood he was not able to analyze their chemical composition. In the eighteenth century, however, medical theorists tried to apply their experimental knowledge of hydraulics and chemistry to the body more systematically, at the same time as invoking the principles of Newtonian dynamics. The Leiden medical educator Herman Boerhaave (1668–1738), for example, saw the body as reducible to two primary components, namely fluids (humors) and solids (fibers), whose motions could be expressed in simple mechanical terms.

Yet although the language of mechanics was fashionable in Enlightenment discourse on the body, the neo-Platonic concepts of universal harmony, *spiritus*, and the macrocosm–microcosm analogy did not entirely disappear. Their continuing importance is shown, for example, in the vitalist theories of the Scottish medical practitioner and popular author William Cheyne (1671–1743). In his *Essay on Health and Long Life* (1724) Cheyne implicitly follows Willis by asserting that the soul resides in the brain, "where all the Nervous fibres terminate inwardly, like a *Musician* by a well-tuned *Instrument*."[47] On the basis of this analogy he says that if the organ of the human body is in tune, its "music" will be distinct and harmonious, but if it is spoiled or "broken," it will not yield "true Harmony." Cheyne continues the analogy by suggesting that men who have "springy, lively and elastic fibres" for nerves have the quickest sensations, and "generally excel in the faculty of imagination," while those with rigid and unyielding fibres are dull but healthy. In his *English Malady: Or a Treatise of Nervous Diseases* (1733) he suggests that this elasticity might be due to an extremely fine and active spirit which "may make the cement between the human Soul and Body, and may be . . . the same . . . with

46 Ibid., pp. 188–92. 47 Cheyne, *Essay*, p. 144.

Sir Isaac Newton's infinitely fine and elastic fluid or Spirit."[48] The affinity between the *spiritus mundi* and medical spirits (which we see illustrated in Fludd's diagram) is given scientific authority here through reference to Newton.

Few of Cheyne's medical contemporaries admitted to sharing his vitalist and mystical beliefs. Yet most agreed with his musical model of nervous action, believing that the nerves "are the principal instruments of our sensations and motion" and that the limits of health are bound by their "tone" or tension. This doctrine leads to a "scale of health" whereby nerves stretched too tightly mean a person is highly strung, while nerves that are too loose mean a slackness of imagination. Authors were, however, divided on the means by which nerves worked. The majority conceived of them in Galenic terms as pipes through which an extremely fine liquor flowed, a medium which served as the "principal instrument which the mind makes use of to influence the actions of the body." A minority claimed that nerves were like solid strings which communicated their impulses by vibration. Despite these differences, both camps implicitly relied on their understanding of the way musical instruments worked for their grasp of mind–body interaction, just as as Fludd had done a hundred years previously (and Ficino more than a century before that). The chief difference was that in the interim natural philosophers had succeeded in translating the vibration of musical strings and the dynamics of wave motion into abstract mathematical relationships.[49]

Conclusion

This brief overview has shown the central role that harmonics played in the scientific revolution, and just how important musical models were in seventeenth-century philosophical and scientific thought. By contrast, harmonics appears to have lost its intellectual status in the eighteenth century, even as Enlightenment philosophers tried to banish occult harmonies from the realms of scientific discourse. There are three main reasons why music and natural philosophy seemed more remote from each other around 1750 than they had been in 1600.

First, music suffered a loss of status because it no longer functioned as an important intellectual model. For over a century after Zarlino's *Le istitutioni harmoniche* first appeared, practical harmonics offered a paradigm for a new kind of mathematico-experimental science that philosophers and mathematicians believed could be fruitfully applied to other physical phenomena. We have seen, for example, how practical music theory provided Kepler with a key to understanding the mechanisms of heavenly harmony. After the *Principia* appeared, however, Newtonianism rapidly became the dominant paradigm for proper scientific method. In this work, Newton succeeded

48 Cheyne, *English Malady*, p. 87.

49 For further details, see Gouk, "Music, Melancholy and Medical Spirits."

in expanding the symbolic realm of mathematics by unifying the mathematical principles that underlay manifest mechanical actions and occult attractive forces. Only a generation or so earlier, the ability to conceptualize the laws of nature in this way was almost unimaginable, and certainly considered magical. The properties of musical strings provided one of the most tangible links between the mathematical and physical realms, which had traditionally been distinct from each other. Mersenne's laws were among the few physical laws to have been experimentally established by the mid-seventeenth century, and they were clearly essential to the development of Newtonian dynamics. After Newton, however, the abstract formula expressing harmonic motion took on an independent life of its own, and became detached from the instrumental context in which it had been generated. For Enlightenment philosophers, music theory did not have the same kind of explanatory power that it offered Kepler and his contemporaries.[50]

The second reason for music's apparent decline can be found in the contrast between the marginal status of experimental philosophy around 1600 and its successful institutionalization by the 1700s. In the early seventeenth century experimental philosophy was an unstable category whose supporters drew on more established arts and sciences for defining its boundaries. At a time when many elite patrons valued both music and magic, the epistemological status of both these arts was correspondingly high. Music theory played a signficant part in the informal "training" of some of the most influential natural philosophers of the period, who in their quest to uncover the hidden secrets of the universe also drew on the resources of natural magic. By the middle of the eighteenth century, however, experimental philosophy was formally established as a means of advancing scientific knowledge, while magic had been correspondingly discredited. National and regional academies of science were created across Europe, together with new university chairs in the mathematical and physical sciences. Within this institutional framework what had once comprised the domain of speculative harmonics was now fragmented across new disciplines such as acoustics and rational mechanics, and these in turn claimed to provide the philosophical grounds and principles of harmony (See **Chapter 9, passim**).

These institutional transformations are mirrored in Denis Diderot's *Encyclopédie* (begun in 1751), which adopts Bacon's tripartite arrangement of knowledge under the main headings of history, poetry, and philosophy/theology. These conceptual divisions correspond to the mental faculties of memory, imagination, and reason, which are in turn assigned respectively to the *érudits*, *beaux esprits*, and *philosophes*. Within this overall framework it is significant that both music and magic are linked to the imagination, which means that they are effectively denied philosophical status. Music is not

50 Although in at least one case, it was the methodology of empirical music theory that proved influential to an eighteenth-century scientist – in this instance, Rameau's music theory inspiring the rationalist epistemology of the scientist, Jean Le Rond d'Alembert. See Christensen, *Rameau and Musical Thought*, Chapter 9, esp. pp. 266–69.

seen as providing a rational means of knowing the world, and harmony has no serious ontological or epistemological role to play. (See also **Chapter 1, pp. 38–39**.)

This leads us to the third main reason for music's increasing separation from science at this time: that is, its growing recognition as one of the fine arts along with painting and sculpture. Crucially, it was not just philosophers and scientists who saw music as lying outside their domain. Composers and music theorists celebrated the power music exercised over the imagination, and especially its capacity to represent and move the emotions. Instead of emphasizing their mathematical and technical mastery of compositional skills, practitioners now preferred to see themselves as divinely inspired manipulators of the passions. Within this aesthetic there was little to be gained in linking music with the natural sciences.

Throughout Western history, the making of music and the making of scientific knowledge have always been intertwined. At certain junctures, however, music theory seems particularly valuable to mathematicians, philosophers and scientists, and the links between their conceptual universe and that of music are manifest and direct. The period between 1550 and 1700, known as the scientific revolution, was one such epoch. By focusing on harmonics, and especially the properties of vibrating strings, we have seen how seventeenth-century experimental philosophy simply took over many of the harmonies and correspondences that were fundamental to magical operations. And although music continued to play an important role in the occult and mystical traditions, these were now firmly outside the mainstream of Western thought.

Bibliography

Primary sources

Agrippa, H. C. *Three Books of Occult Philosophy*, trans. J. French, London, G. Moule, 1651

Boethius, A. M. S. *Fundamentals of Music*, trans. C. Bower, ed. C. Palisca, New Haven, Yale University Press, 1989

Ficino, M. *Three Books on Life*, ed. and trans. C. Kaske and J. Clark, Binghamton, Medieval and Renaissance Texts and Studies, 1989

Fludd, R., *Utriusque cosmi majoris scilicet et minoris metaphysica, physica atque technica historia*, 2 vols. Oppenheim, J. T. De Bry, 1617–21

Gaffurio, F. *Theorica musice*, Milan, P. Mantegatius, 1492; facs. New York, Broude, 1967 and Bologna, Forni, 1969; trans. W. Kreyzig, ed. C. Palisca as *The Theory of Music*, New Haven, Yale University Press, 1993

Kepler, J. *Harmonices mundi libri V*, Linz, G. Tampachius, 1619; facs. Bologna, Forni, 1969

Kircher, A. *Musurgia universalis, sive ars magna consoni et dissoni*, 2 vols., Rome, F. Corbelletti, 1650

Mersenne, M. *Harmonie universelle*, Paris, S. Cramoisy, 1636–37; facs. Paris, Centre National de la Recherche Scientifique, 1963 and 1986

Newton, I. *Isaac Newton's "Philosophiae naturalis principia mathematica": The Third Edition (1726) With Variant Readings*, ed. A. Koyré and I. B. Cohen, 2 vols., Cambridge University Press, 1972

Opticks, London, n.p., 1704

Zarlino, G. *Le istitutioni harmoniche* Venice, Franceschi, 1558; facs. New York, Broude, 1965

Secondary sources

Amman, P. J. "The Music Theory and Philosophy of Robert Fludd," *Journal of the Warburg and Courtauld Institutes* 30 (1967), pp. 198–227

Barker, A. *Greek Musical Writings*, 2 vols., Cambridge University Press, 1984–89

Boccadoro, B. "Marsilio Ficino: The Soul and the Body of Counterpoint," in *Number to Sound*, ed. P. Gozza, Dordrecht, Kluwer, 2000, pp. 99–134

Cannon, J. T. and S. Dostrovsky, *The Evolution of Dynamics: Vibration Theory from 1687 to 1742*, New York, Springer, 1981

Carapetyan, A. "Music and Medicine in the Renaissance and in the 17th and 18th Centuries," in *Music and Medicine*, ed. D. M. Schullian and M. Schoen, New York, H. Schuman, 1948, pp. 117–57

Carpenter, N. C. *Music in the Medieval and Renaissance Universities*, Norman, University of Oklahoma Press, 1958

Christensen, T. *Rameau and Musical Thought in the Enlightenment*, Cambridge University Press, 1993

Cohen, A. *Music in the French Royal Academy of Sciences: A Study in the Evolution of Musical Thought*, Princeton University Press, 1981

Cohen, H. F. *Quantifying Music: The Science of Music at the First Stage of the Scientific Revolution, 1580–1650*, Dordrecht, D. Reidel, 1984

Dear, P. R. *Mersenne and the Language of the Schools*, Ithaca, Cornell University Press, 1988

Gingerich, O. "Kepler, Galilei, and the Harmony of the World," in *Music and Science in the Age of Galileo*, ed. V. Coelho, Dordrecht, Kluwer, 1992, pp. 45–63

Godwin, J. *Robert Fludd: Hermetic Philosopher and Surveyor of Two Worlds*, London, Thames and Hudson, 1979

Athanasius Kircher: A Renaissance Man and the Quest for Lost Knowledge, London, Thames and Hudson, 1979

Harmonies of Heaven and Earth: The Spiritual Dimension of Music from Antiquity to the Avant-garde, London, Thames and Hudson, 1987

Music and the Occult: French Musical Philosophies, 1750–1950, New York, University of Rochester Press, 1995

Gouk, P. M. *Music, Science and Natural Magic in Seventeenth-Century England*, New Haven, Yale University Press, 1999

"Music, Melancholy and Medical Spirits in Early Modern Thought," In *Music as Medicine*, ed. P. Horden, Aldershot, Ashgate, 2000, pp. 173–94

Gozza, P., ed., *Number to Sound: the Musical Way to the Scientific Revolution*, Dordrecht, Kluwer, 2000

Henry, J. "Newton, Matter and Magic," in *Let Newton Be! A New Perspective on His Life and Works*, ed. J. Fauvel et al., Oxford University Press, 1988, pp. 127–45

The Scientific Revolution and the Origins of Modern Science, Houndsmills and London, Macmillan Press, 1997

Hollander, J. *The Untuning of the Sky: Ideas of Music in English Poetry 1500–1700*, Princeton University Press, 1961

Isherwood, R. M. *Music in the Service of the King: France in the Seventeenth Century*, Ithaca, Cornell University Press, 1973

Kassler, J. C. "Music as a Model in Early Science," *History of Science* 20 (1982), pp. 103–39

Inner Music: Hobbes, Hooke and North on Internal Character, London, Athlone Press, 1995

Moran, B. T. *The Alchemical World of the German Court: Occult Philosophy and Chemical Medicine in the Circle of Moritz of Hessen, 1572–1632*, Stuttgart, H. Steiner, 1991

Palisca, C. V. *Humanism in Italian Renaissance Musical Thought*, New Haven, Yale University Press, 1985

"Scientific Empiricism in Musical Thought," in *Seventeenth-Century Science and the Arts*, ed. H. H. Rhys, Princeton University Press, 1961, pp. 91–137

"Moving the Affections through Music: Pre-Cartesian Psycho-Physiological Theories," in *Number to Sound*, ed. P. Gozza, Dordrecht, Kluwer, 2000, pp. 289–308

Stephenson, B. *The Music of the Heavens: Kepler's Harmonic Astronomy*, Princeton University Press, 1994

Tomlinson, G. *Music in Renaissance Magic: Toward a Historiography of Others*, University of Chicago Press, 1993

Vickers, B., ed., *Occult and Scientific Mentalities in the Renaissance*, Cambridge University Press, 1984

Voss, A. "Marsilio Ficino, the Second Orpheus," in *Music as Medicine*, ed. P. Horden, Aldershot, Ashgate, 2000, pp. 154–72

Walker, D. P. *The Ancient Theology: Studies in Christian Platonism from the Fifteenth to the Eighteenth Century*, London, Duckworth, 1972

Spiritual and Demonic Magic from Ficino to Campanella, London, Warburg Institute, 1958

"Kepler's Celestial Music," in *Studies in Musical Science in the Late Renaissance*, ed. D. P. Walker, London, Brill, 1978, pp. 34–62

Music, Spirit and Language in the Renaissance, London, Variorum, 1985

"Medical Spirits in Philosophy and Theology from Ficino to Newton," in *Arts du spectacle et histoire des ideés*, Tours, Centre d'Etudes Supérieures de la Renaissance, 1984, pp. 287–300

Westman, R. S. "Nature, Art, and Psyche: Jung, Pauli, and the Kepler–Fludd Polemic," in *Occult and Scientific Mentalities in the Renaissance*, ed. B. Vickers, Cambridge University Press, 1984, pp. 177–229

Yates, F. A. *The French Academies of the Sixteenth Century*, London, Warburg Institute, 1947

·9·

From acoustics to *Tonpsychologie*

BURDETTE GREEN AND DAVID BUTLER

The rise of *Tonpsychologie* as a scientific discipline in the nineteenth century was a key moment in the history of music theory. It revived topics hitherto situated in the venerable, although largely enfeebled, study of speculative harmonics, and at the same time prefigured future directions for research in music perception. In the final third of the century, this research field underwent two major epistemological shifts that revolved around the German polymaths Hermann von Helmholtz (1821–94) and Carl Stumpf (1848–1936). Both of these scientists were accomplished amateur musicians; both were avidly interested in music theory. Using experimental methods to study pitch organization and the physiology of hearing, they tried to answer age-old ontological questions of *musica theorica*: what are the origins and nature of musical sound, consonance, harmony, and scales? In so doing, they offered fresh perspectives that can be appreciated only by distinguishing their individual viewpoints and by reviewing the long prehistory of their work.

The scientific revolution of the seventeenth century gave birth to the experimental/empirical methods of natural science and stirred interest in the physical basis of pitch organization. Physical acoustics fascinated investigators from Mersenne to Helmholtz and largely replaced the dominating mode of speculative, numerical inquiry. Questions about harmony and about consonance and dissonance were now evaluated acoustically rather than by reference to canonics.[1] By the middle of the nineteenth century it became apparent that experimental methods could be applied not only to the physics of music but also to the physiology of hearing and the psychology of perception. Helmholtz, the empiricist, advanced physical and physiological acoustics; Stumpf, the mentalist, established a psychological frame of reference – *Tonpsychologie* (the psychology of musical sound). These moves from the physical to the physiological and then to the psychological represented substantially different conceptual models in that they shifted the focus of inquiry from exterior to interior aspects of the perceptual process. Helmholtz modified the traditional "outside to inside" model by drawing attention to the anatomy of the ear and the sensory phase of perception – a step toward attending to the "inside." Stumpf shifted the emphasis from

1 For a discussion of these early canonic traditions, see **Chapter 4, pp. 114–17, Chapter 6, passim,** and the **Introduction, pp. 3–5**.

anatomy to mental activity, thereby opening the possibility of the "inside to outside" model that figured prominently in later research.[2]

The specific contributions of both Helmholtz and Stumpf to the field of tone physiology and psychology are so wide-ranging as to preclude adequate summary in a single chapter. We will instead limit the focus of this chapter to a single golden thread that runs through their work: the consonance/dissonance problem. Their work on consonance and dissonance formed the very center of the empirical support structure they erected for their musical theories, and an investigation of this work provides clear insight into their fresh approaches to musical science.

Acoustical foundations

Before considering the contributions of Helmholtz and Stumpf, it is first necessary to understand the historical knowledge upon which each built in the field of acoustics. Research on five key acoustical phenomena – sympathetic resonance, complex tones, the harmonic series, beats, and combination tones – provided a base of axiomatic knowledge for nineteenth-century researchers. For the sake of clarity, these acoustical topics and certain physiological discoveries will receive individual historical accounts, concentrating on the seventeenth and eighteenth centuries, the period in which the most significant advances in the new science of acoustics took place.[3] Following some reflections on laboratory-based standards of scientific experimentation, the narrative will return to Helmholtz and Stumpf and their theories of consonance and dissonance and will conclude with an assessment of the legacy of these great pioneers.

Sympathetic resonance

Knowledge of sympathetic resonance, also called sympathetic vibration, can be traced to antiquity. Like the magnetic attraction of iron shavings to a lodestone, the sympathetic response of one sonorous vibrator to the sound of another was a natural mystery that defied easy explanation. Many thought that occult affinities and antipathies were operating (see **Chapter 8, p. 224**). To explain sympathetic resonance, natural philosophers had to describe the mechanics of vibrators and specify the relation of vibrational frequency to the sensation of pitch.

2 For a review of the mind/body problem see Fancher, *Pioneers of Psychology*, pp. 87–125; Ash, *Gestalt Psychology*, pp. 51–67.
3 Useful surveys of seventeenth- and eighteenth-century acoustics include Truesdell, *Rational Mechanics* (1960); Palisca, "Scientific Empiricism" (1961); Lindsay, "Story of Acoustics" (1966); Dostrovsky, "Origins of Vibration Theory" (1969); Cannon and Dostrovsky, *Evolution of Dynamics* (1981); H. F. Cohen, *Quantifying Music* (1984); and Hunt, *Origins in Acoustics* (1978).

Sympathetic vibration is a special type of resonance in which sound waves, traveling in air, transmit energy from one sonorous vibrator to another. The second vibrator must possess the same natural frequency (a specific number of vibrations per unit of time), or have a frequency that is an integral multiple of that natural frequency. The repetitive pressure waves of tones find an analogue in the pendulum, whose motion remains nominally constant (isochronic) regardless of the amplitude or amount of energy involved – the arc, large or small, has a fixed period. In sympathetic resonance the responding vibrator moves because its natural period is excited at exactly the right intervals of time by the sound waves from the first vibrator. Sympathetic resonance is possible even at a considerable distance, but, because the energy carried by sound waves is weak, conditions must be ideal if the second vibrator is to produce an audible response rather than a mere trembling. To be heard, both vibrators must be attached to resonators. Historically, the best results were obtained from steady-sounding, high-energy sources such as musical instruments that are bowed or blown.[4]

Although sympathetic resonance stirred philosophical interest in ancient China and in the Greco-Roman world, both the written accounts and the history of musical instruments suggest that experience was limited to resonance at the unison or octave. Investigations of sympathetic resonance by Renaissance Italians such as Leonardo da Vinci (1452–1519), Girolamo Fracastoro (1483–1553), and G. B. Benedetti (1530–90) contributed to the physical understanding of sound and set the stage for the mechanical explanation of the harmonic series, which as we shall see is the key to understanding the relation of resonance to musical consonance.[5] By then it was evident that in sound the rate of vibration is independent of the speed of propagation. Moreover, the idea that sonorous vibrators have natural oscillatory periods had begun to crystalize. These points were clearly defined and validated by observation in the acoustically productive seventeenth century.

Working independently, Isaac Beeckman (1588–1637) and Galileo Galilei (1564–1642) realized that the sensation of pitch depends somehow on the frequency of vibrations of the sounding object, and that, as with pendulums, the vibrations of stretched strings are periodic. By linking frequency of vibration with "equal intervals of time," they clarified an assumption left unexpressed in the writings of Fracastoro and Benedetti.[6] The concept of regular, repetitive motion enabled Beeckman to improve on the mechanical description of resonance at unison frequencies and encouraged him to speculate about resonance at the octave and the twelfth.[7] Unfortunately Beeckman's findings circulated only in a manuscript journal. Galileo's published and

4 On the history of applications of sympathetic resonance, see Green, "Harmonic Series," pp. 98–151.

5 Leonardo, *Codice Atlantico*, fol. 242v; Fracastoro, *De sympathia et antipathia rerum* (1546), Book I, Chapter 1; Benedetti, *De intervallis musicis* (1585), pp. 277–87. Excerpts are translated in Truesdell, *Rational Mechanics*, pp. 19–23.

6 Beeckman, "Journal" (c. 1618), fol. 102r. Excerpt translated in Green, "Harmonic Series," p. 138.

7 Truesdell, *Rational Mechanics*, p. 27.

widely distributed observations covered much the same ground, but his inquiry dealt primarily with the resonance of unison frequencies.[8] Marin Mersenne (1588–1648) quantified the effects of length, tension, and mass on the vibration rates of stretched strings, and these considerations supported the notion that frequency of vibration is the determining factor of pitch.[9] Robert Hooke (1635–1703) provided a physical demonstration of the pitch–frequency relationship by means of a twirling ratchet wheel – the faster it engaged the lingua, the higher the pitch rose. Two wheels on the same spindle could verify the frequency ratios of intervals such as the fourth or fifth.[10] Hooke's ratchet anticipated the principle of Savart's wheel (1830).[11]

In 1638 René Descartes (1596–1650) reported that a blind bellmaster at Utrecht, Jacob van Eyck, had demonstrated how partial tones of a bell could be made to resound by softly singing their respective pitches near the rim. Apparently he could elicit five or six partial tones in this manner.[12] Early in the eighteenth century, Joseph Sauveur (1653–1716) investigated resonance in detail and recognized that an upper partial (i.e., overtone) of one string can induce the resonance of an upper partial in another string. He accurately identified the responding pitch as that of the lowest tone partial common to both strings.[13]

The widespread interest in sympathetic resonance can be credited, in part, to instruments fitted with sympathetic strings, a novelty that had been introduced into Europe about 1600 (see below, p. 252). Indeed, had it not been for late Renaissance innovations in instrument design inspired by the musician's quest to extend ranges and enlarge the tonal palette, natural philosophers would have lacked the elegant sound sources needed to study and test vibrational theory.[14]

Complex tones and tone partials

The mechanical properties of complex tones are difficult to describe because their sound waves are exceedingly intricate and their cyclic waveforms are subject to changes in spectral characteristics across time. These waveforms (i.e., the patterns of pressure fluctuation in one wave cycle) are best described as quasi-periodic because a host of physical anomalies introduce transient effects. Few vibrating bodies behave as perfectly flexible jump ropes could, with the smooth and simple motion of a pendulum. While most investigators agree that strong correlations exist between wave frequency and

8 Galileo, *Two New Sciences* (1638), pp. 99–100. See H. F. Cohen, *Music Quantified*, pp. 134–39, for a discussion of the resonance–consonant interval relation.
9 Mersenne, *Harmonie universelle* (1636–37), vol. I, pp. 174–75.
10 See North, *Lives of the Norths* (1740), vol. II, pp. 206–09.
11 Savart, "Sensibilité de l'ouïe" (1830); trans. in Lindsay, *Acoustics*, pp. 202–09.
12 Letter from Descartes to Mersenne dated August 23, 1638 in *Correspondance du P. Mersenne*, vol. VIII, pp. 57–58.
13 Sauveur, "Système générale" (1701), p. 354.
14 On the relation of musical instruments and acoustic discovery, see Green, "Harmonic Series," pp. 152–311.

perceived pitch and between wave amplitude and perceived intensity, the correlation between waveform and perceived timbre must be regarded as considerably less than a one-to-one match. Musical sound sources produce a complex amalgam of partial tones that perceptually coalesce as a single tone having a fundamental pitch and a specific timbre, or tone color. The timbre of a complex tone is affected by the number, the frequencies, and the amplitudes of these partial tones; moreover, the timbre is significantly affected by their transient characteristics. Timbre, even more than pitch, is vulnerable to simplistic description because its physical and perceptual attributes are acoustically more complex and the correspondences of these attributes are not as direct.[15]

Awareness of overtones in musical sounds was not new to the seventeenth century – consider the trade secrets of Renaissance organ makers and bell founders – but Mersenne (1636) was the first to investigate the phenomenon in detail.[16] Within a century, Rameau and others were enlisting the knowledge of complex tones and partial tones to support their harmonic theories.

To understand complex tones, investigators had to sort out the mechanics of sound propagation, the dynamics of compound modes of vibration, and the harmonic series principle. The quest began with attempts to describe the acoustical properties of organ pipes, trumpets, tower bells, and bowed stringed instruments. As early as 1623, Mersenne observed partial tones in the sounds of bells and other musical sources.[17] The partials of bell tones, though distinct, are artificially regulated by the founders to achieve certain consonant relationships because bells, plates, and rods inherently produce inharmonic partials.[18] As an acoustic specimen, the bell's clang was rather like the siren's song luring her victims astray. Mersenne and his contemporaries wisely concentrated on the vibrational properties of stretched strings because they tended to be more uniform and they could also be analyzed visually.

The problem of how a string produces a simultaneous cluster of pitches elicited some curious theories of sound propagation. Instead of relating the *sons extraordinaires* to the segmented motion of the vibrating string, Mersenne adopted the commonsense view that the string's single movement as a whole causes the surrounding air to vibrate in diverse, consonantly related modes.[19] But do the multiple vibrations originate in the air or in the string? Theories of both kinds were offered but none was considered convincing until, in 1677, the mathematician and astronomer John Wallis (1616–1703) reported the presence of nodes and antinodes in the string's vibration. By means of sympathetic resonance, he induced a string to vibrate in aliquot (whole number) segments delimited by points of no motion that could be located and

15 Butler, *Guide to Perception*, pp. 129–42.

16 For a possible early reference to harmonic partials, see the Aristotelian *Problemata*, XIX, 8. For a critique, see Barker, *Greek Musical Writings*, vol. II, p. 92, n. 45.

17 Mersenne, *Quaestiones celeberrimae* (1623), col. 1699b. Excerpt translated in Green, "Harmonic Series," p. 327.

18 Benade, *Musical Acoustics*, pp. 124–47.

19 Mersenne, *Harmonie universelle*, vol. III, p. 210 (Chapman trans., p. 269).

observed by applying paper riders.[20] The French pioneer of scientific "acoustique," Joseph Sauveur (1653–1716), conducted similar experiments, and, in his first memoir on acoustics (1701), he coined the terms node (*nœud*) and loop (*ventre*) to describe the string's action.[21] The discovery of nodes had important consequences: it caused investigators to conclude that the source of partial tones resides in the string itself, not in the air, and it led them to calculate correctly the ratios of the "overtone series" (i.e., the ascending partials above the fundamental).

While Sauveur realized that a stretched string vibrates in a complex manner, he offered no theoretical explanation for its spectrum of frequencies. Nevertheless, he saw clearly the connection between partial tones and partial vibrations. He observed (despite an apparent hearing defect!) that sliding a light obstacle along a sounding string causes a "twittering" of harmonics to be heard as the object passes from one nodal point to another.[22] The mathematical solution to the vibrating string problem – the superposition of oscillators – awaited the initial analyses of Brooke Taylor (1685–1731), Daniel Bernoulli (1700–82), and Jean Le Rond d'Alembert (1717–83), and the definitive formulation by Leonhard Euler (1707–83).[23] The work of these mathematicians also led to the realization that some sound sources emitted inharmonic upper partials. The acoustician Ernst Chladni (1756–1827) cleverly demonstrated harmonic and inharmonic modes of vibration by means of sand patterns on bow-activated elastic plates.[24]

The harmonic series and ratios of consonant intervals

For natural philosophers who were convinced that nature conforms to the "rule of consonance," the rigidity of the harmonic series presented a formidable barrier, since there are many natural ratios to be found among its upper partials that are completely unusable in any just tuning system. Mersenne, as we have seen, was fascinated by the phenomenon of overtones, but was unable to find a coherent use for them in his own system, hampered as he was by a lack of knowledge of nodes, a mistrust of sympathetic resonance due to its occult reputation, and the assumption of a universal harmony exemplified by the intervals of the just scale. By studying overblown partials (trumpet notes) and flageolet tones (string "harmonics") using the trumpet and its ersatz cousin, the trumpet marine, Mersenne arrived at a clever approximation of the harmonic series. His natural pitch series constituted an interrupted arithmetic progression. He

20 Wallis, "A New Musical Discovery" (1677), pp. 839–42.

21 Sauveur, "Système générale" pp. 301, 352–53. 22 Ibid, p. 355.

23 For a review of eighteenth-century vibrational theory, see Christensen, *Rameau and Musical Thought*, pp. 150–59; also see Cannon and Dostrovsky, *Evolution of Dynamics*, pp. 123–76, which includes translations of Daniel Bernoulli's papers (1732–35).

24 Excerpts from Chladni, *Entdeckungen über die Theorie des Klanges* (1787) are trans. in Lindsay, *Acoustics*, pp. 156–65. See *Sensations of Tone*, pp. 70–74, for Helmholtz's discussion of Chladni's inharmonic partials.

envisioned a monochord model that successively divides the string in halves, thirds, fourths, and fifths, and then subdivides these segments in halves, thirds, fourths, and fifths. With these constraints, all terms of his natural pitch series formed consonant ratios with the fundamental or with a prior term in the series. In addition his scheme avoided the troublesome seventh partial in the third octave and achieved a just, diatonic scale in the fourth octave.[25]

In 1692, another English experimental scientist, Francis Roberts (c. 1650–1718), identified the true succession of tones in the natural series of the trumpet and the trumpet marine. Roberts asserted that the tones conform to an infinite sequence of aliquot divisions, and that some tones conform to the tunings of the just (syntonic diatonic) scale while others do not. By assuming a monochord measured in 720 units, he showed that partials 7, 13, and 14 are flat and 11 sharp in comparison to their counterparts in the just scale.[26] His monochord measures give the approximate deviations of the out-of-tune partials and thereby illustrate how easily these variants could have gone unnoticed by earlier investigators of the trumpet marine. For example, the deviation of the eleventh partial is about two units, which in terms of the trumpet marine's 5-foot string is about one-sixth of an inch.

The trumpet was an unreliable source for demonstrating the harmonic series because players could skip the fundamental and partials 7 and 14; they could add "privileged notes" in the second octave; and they could "favor" the pitch of out-of-tune notes to make them approximate the just scale. The trumpet marine – a bowed monochord played with flageolet tones amplified by a rattling bridge mechanism – was a more reliable source because no pitch adjustments could be made.[27] As early as 1667, J.-B. Prin, a virtuoso performer, added sympathetic strings inside the long sound box of the trumpet marine to obtain resonating chordal effects. He thereby designed the first instrument capable of producing a four-octave series of resonating partials: each of its "trumpet notes" excited the corresponding partials of the unison-tuned sympathetic strings.[28] Here was an instrument that could demonstrate the successive and the concurrent manifestations of the harmonic series through flageolet tones and resonance, respectively.

The notion that the sounding string simultaneously oscillates in many vibrational modes helped Sauveur to understand in 1701 the physical basis of the harmonic series. Ultimately, however, he determined the pitch relationships of the *sons harmoniques* by observing their successive and simultaneous manifestations: the natural series of flageolet tones; the natural series of overblown partials; the sympathetic resonance of partials; and the clang of overtones. Sauveur was the first to recognize that a single

25 Mersenne, *Harmonie universelle*, vol. III, pp. 250–53 (Chapman, trans. pp. 321–24). On Werckmeister's (1687) similar view that the trumpet series is a source of musical proportions, see Christensen, *Rameau and Musical Thought*, pp. 87–89.

26 Roberts, "Musical Notes of the Trumpet" (1692), pp. 559–63.

27 For an accurate description of the trumpet marine, see North, *Cursory Notes* (c. 1698–1703), pp. 113–15.

28 Galpin, "Prin and his Trumpet Marine," pp. 18–29.

principle underlies the pitch characteristics of all these phenomena.[29] In 1702, he went on to suggest that the same principle should apply to timbre synthesis in specially voiced organ pipes, and certain pitch mixtures in organ stops such as the *cornet*.[30] This suggestion was perhaps his greatest contribution to musical practice; by drawing a direct connection between the harmonic series and the artificial mixture of pitches, he took a step beyond Mersenne's reach. Yet, Sauveur could not realize the full potential of his construct because he, like Mersenne, lacked the requisite knowledge of the relationship between the spectrum of upper partials and timbre perception.

To appreciate the difficulties the harmonic series posed, one must consider the limitations of applying it to harmonic theory. Although monochord divisions – sometimes called "sonorous numbers" – provided physical as well as mathematical evidence, they required no fixed recipe or procedure to demonstrate the ratios of intervals; all ratios of rational numbers produced on the monochord (strictly speaking) had equal validity, since monochord theorists were not obliged to follow a sequence of divisions by halves, thirds, fourths, fifths, sixths, sevenths, and so forth. In the harmonic series, however, a fixed ratio order is confirmed both by concurrent and successive phenomena. Savants wishing to place music on a scientific basis found this new physical evidence convincing, but, as a source of the conventional intervals, it proved less fruitful than they anticipated. As Roberts and Sauveur showed, the harmonic series generates out-of-tune intervals with harmonics 7, 11, 13, and 14, and so forth. Moreover, it cannot generate directly from the fundamental the fourth scale degree, or constructs such as the perfect fourth, minor third, major sixth, minor sixth, or minor triad. Yet, the thought that many simple ratios exist in the vibration patterns of most musical tones is almost irresistible, even though it forces one to pick and choose particular ratios from an infinite set simply because of traditional norms.

Some theorists, notably Rameau (prior to 1760), chose to limit the harmonic influence of overtones to a senary series.[31] The distinction between the *senario* idea and a senary series is subtle but important. The *senario* was a system of six "sounding numbers" (1 to 6) nominally of equal validity; senary division, on the other hand, implies that segments must always be compared to the whole as halves, thirds, fourths, and so forth. Senary division has a Platonic appeal because of the constant reference to unity and a tidy hierarchy, but at a price. In *senario* theory, ratios *may* be compared to unity, as in Zarlino's *harmonia perfetta*;[32] in senary division theory the ratios *must* be compared to unity. Thus, explaining the nature of the perfect fourth and the

29 For an assessment of the contributions of Sauveur and of his reviewer, Bernard de Fontenelle (1657–1757), see Christensen, *Rameau and Musical Thought*, pp. 137–38; Green, "Harmonic Series," pp. 403–26; Rasch, ed., *Sauveur's Collected Writings*, pp. 25–53. See also **Chapter 7, pp. 212–14**.

30 Sauveur, "Application des sons harmoniques" (1702), p. 328.

31 For a discussion of Rameau's evolving conception of the *corps sonore* see Christensen, *Rameau and Musical Thought*, pp. 133–68, and in this volume, **Chapter 24, pp. 770–72**; on Schenker's similar abbreviation of the harmonic series, see Clark, "Schenker's Mysterious Five," pp. 84–102.

32 Zarlino, *Le istitutioni harmoniche* (1558), Part I, p. 25. See also **Chapter 24, p. 754** and **Chapter 10, p. 277**.

derivation of the minor triad was more bothersome for Rameau than for Zarlino. Fundamentally, Zarlino's system permitted a measure of leeway in the combination of consonant intervals (*harmonia*) in polyphony.

The theoretical shift to the harmonic series, truncated or not, was forced by the relationships discovered in acoustic phenomena. Descartes tempered his discussion of the *senario* by discussing relationships observed in the sympathetic resonance of lute strings,[33] while Mersenne, for his part, saw importance in the natural series of the trumpet.[34] Both Descartes and Mersenne considered the twelfth (3 : 1) and the major seventeenth (5 : 1) to be more nearly perfect than the fifth (3 : 2) and the major third (5 : 4), respectively, not only because the ratios of the former pairs were "simpler" than the latter, but also because each partook of unity (1) – an aesthetic desideratum of great Platonic importance. The mathematicians Leonhard Euler[35] and Robert Smith (1689–1768)[36] reached similar conclusions but on the basis of ratio elegance. Euler, drawing upon Leibniz, believed that the mind unconsciously calculates the ratios of vibrations: the simpler the ratio, the greater the degree of consonance.[37]

Harmonic-series and senary division theories can be distinguished from each other only when terms beyond the sixth, such as the natural seventh (7 : 4) – proposed for use by Sorge in 1747 – are introduced.[38] Moreover, once the implications of the harmonic series were realized, no one could assume that nature generates only consonances. Only around 1760 did Rameau finally conclude that both consonances and dissonances must stem from the same derivation.[39] As a source of musical intervals, consonant or dissonant, the harmonic series is quite restrictive, but to many eighteenth-century musicians the newly discovered natural basis was enticing.[40]

Beats and combination tones

Acoustic beats have been known to organists and organ builders since the Renaissance. In 1511 the German organist Arnolt Schlick (c. 1450 – c. 1525) alluded to their use as

33 Descartes, *Compendium musicae* (1650), pp. 102–03 (Robert trans., p. 21).

34 Mersenne, *Harmonie universelle*, vol. III, p. 250 (Chapman trans., pp. 321–22). For Mersenne's views on the importance of the trumpet series, see Green, "Harmonic Series," pp. 368–75.

35 For discussions of Euler's consonance/dissonance theory in *Tentamen novae theoriae musicae* (1739), see Chapter 10, pp. 278–79; C. S. Smith, "Translation and Commentary," pp. 6–19; and Bailey, "Music and Mathematics: Writings of Euler," pp. 30–76. For a discussion of Johann Mattheson's objections to Euler's consonance theory, see Christensen, "Sensus, Ratio, and Phthongos," pp. 1–22.

36 For a critique of Smith's *Harmonics* (1749), see Barbour's "Introduction," pp. v–xi.

37 For Helmholtz's review of Euler's theory of consonance, see *Sensations of Tone*, pp. 229–32. The "coincidence theory" of consonance reflected in Euler's theory is discussed extensively in Cohen, *Quantifying Music*.

38 Partch, *Genesis of Music*, pp. 90–104, offers a history of "consonant" extensions beyond the ratios of the *senario*. It should be noted, though, that Sorge regarded the natural seventh as dissonant, whereas Tartini, Kirnberger, and Euler regarded it as consonant.

39 Rameau, "Réflexions sur le principe sonore" appended to *Code de musique pratique* (1760), pp. 202–03. Excerpt trans. in Green, "Harmonic Series," p. 478.

40 Hall, *Musical Acoustics*, pp. 441–44.

a way to achieve a tempered tuning.[41] A century later Beeckman and Mersenne discussed the usefulness of beats in tuning harpsichord strings and organ pipes.[42] In simple terms, first-order beats are perceived as regular fluctuations in loudness resulting from the acoustic interference of two near-unison tones. The rate of the beating is equal to the difference of the two fundamental frequencies; the greater the discrepancy, the faster the beating. In addition, beats can also occur between the harmonic partials of the two tones. Second-order beats are perceived when tones of "just" intervals stand in near-consonant relation. Fourths, fifths, and octaves that are beatless (i.e., pure or "just") have long been used in tuning. By introducing beats to pure fourths and fifths, temperaments can be approximated. In the midrange of the piano, beats of about one per second tell tuners that they have sufficiently diminished pure fifths to approximate equal-tempered fifths. Sauveur claimed he used beats to determine the absolute frequencies of two organ pipes. By tuning them a minor semitone apart (i.e., the ratio of 25 : 24) and using a pendulum as a metronome, he could estimate their fundamental frequencies by counting the acoustic beats.[43]

Combination tones are a class of subjective tones that include difference tones and summation tones. The difference tone, whose perceived pitch frequency equals the frequency difference of two stimulus tones, is the most audible species of combination tone. Summation tones – tones with frequencies equivalent to the sums of the stimulus frequencies – are audible only to some listeners. The discovery of difference tones is usually credited to the violin virtuoso and composer Giuseppe Tartini (1692–1770), who claimed to have used the *terzo suono* for tuning the violin starting in 1714, though he did not discuss the phenomenon in print until 1754. By then, J.-A. Serre (1704–88), J.-B. Romieu (1723–66), and G. A. Sorge (1703–78) had also published accounts of difference tones.[44] Summation tones were first reported a century later by Helmholtz.

Although difference tones were regarded as "beat-tones" by J. L. Lagrange (1736–1813) and Thomas Young (1773–1829), most sources now agree with Helmholtz's judgment that beats and combination tones as a class are different in kind.[45] Combination tones are subjective tones that reside entirely within the perception of listeners; they are commonly thought to originate in the cochlea and/or in the central nervous system. By contrast, beats are measurable changes in the intensity level

41 Schlick, *Spiegel der Orgelmacher* (1511), Chapter 8, n.p. (Barber trans., pp. 73–89).

42 Beeckman, "Journal" (c. 1618), vol. I, fol. 310; Mersenne, *Harmonie universelle*, vol. III, Book VI, prop. 28, pp. 362–63 and prop. 30, pp. 366–68 (Chapman trans., pp. 445–46, 450–51). For a discussion of these accounts of beats, see H. F. Cohen, *Quantifying Music*, pp. 103, 143–46.

43 Sauveur, "Système générale" pp. 360–61. For a discussion of this method, see Dostrovsky, "Origins of Vibration Theory," pp. 255–56.

44 On the early history of difference tones and their use in harmonic theory, see Lester, *Theory in the Eighteenth Century*, pp. 198–200. Also see Maley, "The Theory of Beats and Combination Tones"; and Chapter 24, p. 771.

45 On the beat-tone theory, see Wever and Lawrence, *Physiological Acoustics*, pp. 132–33.

of a sound. Unlike beats, combination tones are perceptible only when the stimulus signals are sufficiently loud.[46]

Physiology and experimental models

Having reviewed some of the most important advances in musical acoustics made during the seventeenth and eighteenth centuries, we now turn to consider briefly the work of some scientists in the early nineteenth century in the areas of physiology and experimental methods that, together with the earlier acoustical advances, would provide the foundation for Helmholtz's influential synthesis at mid-century. While studying the flow of heat, the mathematician J. B. J. Fourier (1768–1830) developed, in 1822, the theorem that any complex periodic vibration may be resolved into a number of simple harmonic vibrations.[47] In 1843, the physicist Georg Ohm (1787–1854) hypothesized that musical sounds are characterized by the distribution of energies among the harmonics in accordance with Fourier analysis and that the distribution *pattern* is the source of timbre perception. Ohm's law motivated Helmholtz to demonstrate experimentally that, in effect, the ear itself performs a Fourier analysis on a complex sound wave, discerning each partial tone in the frequency spectrum.[48] This model depended on physiologist Johannes Müller's law of specific nerve energies (1837). Müller held that each sensory nerve fiber can give rise to but one specific sensation.[49] As we shall see, these ideas supported Helmholtz's mechanistic explanation of how the ear discriminates clusters of pitches.

Resonance theories of hearing based on sympathetic vibration between the sound stimulus and receptors in the ear were not new to the mid-nineteenth century: Dortous de Mairan (1678–1771),[50] Albrecht von Haller (1708–77),[51] and Charles Bell (1774–1842)[52] had proposed such theories but without supporting experimental evidence. Convincing evidence became available only in the 1830s when researchers could take advantage of the newly improved compound microscope to investigate the anatomy of the ear. Between 1835 and 1851, anatomists such as Huschke, Reissner,

46 Butler, *Guide to Perception*, pp. 68–69.

47 On Fourier's theorem, see Rayleigh, *Theory of Sound*, vol. I, pp. 24–25, 202–03; and Klein, *Mathematics in Western Culture*, pp. 287–303. Helmholtz presents the theorem in *Sensations of Tone*, p. 34.

48 Excerpts of Ohm's *Über die Definition des Tones* (1843) are trans. in Lindsay, *Acoustics*, pp. 242–47. See Boring, *Sensation and Perception*, pp. 326–28. Helmholtz presents Ohm's law in *Sensations of Tone*, p. 33.

49 Müller, "Specific Energies of Nerves" (1838), trans. by Braly in Dennis, *Readings in Psychology*, pp. 157–68. Also see Boring, *Sensation and Perception*, pp. 68–73.

50 On Mairan's *Discours sur la propagation du son* (1737), see Christensen, "Eighteenth-Century Science," pp. 26–28.

51 For discussion of Haller's auditory theory in *Elementa physiologiae* (1763), see Boring, *Sensation and Perception*, pp. 400–01; and Wever and Lawrence, *Physiological Acoustics*, p. 10.

52 Bell's auditory theory in *Anatomy of the Human Body* (1809) is discussed in Boring, *Sensation and Perception*, pp. 402–03.

and Corti used the device to detail the intricate anatomical structure of the basilar membrane.[53]

Another aspect of early nineteenth-century science relevant to Helmholtz's work that we should consider concerned the rise and rigorous control of experimental methods. Prior to the systematizing efforts of J. S. Mill (1806–73),[54] Johannes Müller (1801–58),[55] and others, the methodology of science was more a matter of fortuitous observation than of controlled experiment. The idea of designing controlled experiments to test hypotheses was more quickly accepted in the realm of acoustics than in the discipline that came to be called the psychology of music, in which it was widely thought that mental operations are beyond that grasp of science and belong entirely in the domain of philosophy.[56] Indeed, the history of music theory since Aristoxenus has never been far from the question of whether music is within or beyond the realm of quantitative analysis – a question that pervaded nineteenth-century thought and that still lives on.[57] The sort of experimental methodology espoused by nineteenth-century scientists derives from the physical sciences and is fundamentally reductionistic; it measures simple, discrete segments of complicated physical events or objects, and of complicated mental activities. Rigor is determined largely by the degree to which the experimenter controls the stimuli, the test environment, and the responses of the subjects. Ideally, controlled experimental procedures produce sterile stimuli in regulated laboratory environments supported by solicited responses uncontaminated by the subjects' prior knowledge.[58] This amount of reduction had little appeal for many who, like Goethe, an impassioned critic of laboratory experiments, sought answers to complex musical issues.[59]

Hermann von Helmholtz

The son of a teacher at the Potsdam Gymnasium, Helmholtz, began his career rather modestly as an army surgeon and ended it as one of Germany's most esteemed citizens.[60]

53 Wever and Lawrence, *Physiological Acoustics*, p. 10.
54 On the importance of Mill's *System of Logic* (1843) see Boring, *Sensation and Perception*, pp. 227–33.
55 For discussions of Müller's *Handbuch der Physiologie* (1833–40), see Murphy and Kovach, *Modern Psychology*, pp. 88–91; and Schultz and Schultz, *History of Modern Psychology*, pp. 54–55.
56 Surveys of the history of music psychology include Heidbreder, *Seven Psychologies* (1933); Boring, *Sensation and Perception* (1942); and *History of Experimental Psychology* (1950); Murphy and Kovach, *Modern Psychology* (1972); Spender and Shuter-Dyson, "Psychology of Music" (1980); Murray, *History of Western Psychology* (1988); Schultz and Schultz, *History of Modern Psychology* (1992).
57 Butler, "Nineteenth-Century Music Psychology Literature," pp. 9–163.
58 Butler, *Guide to Perception*, pp. 4–13.
59 Warren, "Helmholtz's Continuing Influence," p. 256.
60 For Helmholtz's intellectual biography, see Boring, *History of Experimental Psychology*, pp. 297–315; Turner, "Helmholtz," pp. 241–53; Warren and Warren, *Helmholtz on Perception*, pp. 3–23; Cohen and Elkana, *Helmholtz's Epistemological Writings*, pp. ix–xxviii; and Stumpf, "Helmholtz and the New Psychology," pp. 1–12.

By Imperial decree he was elevated to the status of the nobility in recognition of his remarkable contribution to science. University study in Berlin in medicine, chemistry, physics, and physiology led to his M.D. degree at age twenty-one. Following his military commitment he held professorships in Königsberg, Bonn, Heidelberg, and Berlin. At Heidelberg and Berlin he established laboratories that were models for later researchers such as Wundt and Stumpf. His broad training and his talent for the invention of experimental apparatus explain in part the vast range of his scientific achievement.

Helmholtz's deep commitment to empirical methodology was due partly to his study with the great physiologist Johannes Müller and partly to an admiration for Newton's mathematical/experimental approach to sensory issues. Helmholtz believed that living organisms – including humans –are not excluded from the laws of physics, and agreed with British associationists that the mind develops through individual experience. Since he regarded psychology as essentially physiological, and physiology as essentially physical, his goal was to apply the methods of physics to at least the physiological aspects of perception.[61]

Helmholtz's invention, at age thirty, of the ophthalmoloscope (a device to examine the interior of the eye) brought him international fame and stimulated further work on the senses and perception during the next two decades. His determination in 1852 that the velocity of nerve impulses is not immeasurably fast but surprisingly slow – about 90 feet per second according to his calculation[62] – supported his mechanistic view that external stimuli are mediated by the sensory organs independently of volition. With the recently perfected compound microscope and other inventions of his own making, he discovered design flaws in the eyes of vertebrates that cause visual aberrations. From this he realized that sensation was not a direct process; our sensations do not enable us to perceive directly the outside world. Furthermore, he discovered that visual sensations in the optic nerve can be caused by pressure on the nerve as well as by the stimulus of light waves. His work on neural impulses and responses (the theory of specific fiber energies) suggested to him that "inductive inference" (unconscious mental activity that interprets the input) based on experience and conditioning accounts for the sensory "signs" that represent external objects. In other words, sensory mechanisms add supplemental data not found in the stimulus, and these additions accrue to perception through the experience and learning of the individual. He reported his work on optics in his great three-volume classic, *Handbuch der physiologischen Optik* (1856–67). As we shall see, his work in optics influenced his subsequent work in acoustics, and his theory of vision found parallels in his theory of hearing.

61 See Boring, *History of Experimental Psychology*, pp. 299–308. (For a comment on the significance of Boring's pioneering history, see **Chapter 31, p. 959, fn. 5**.)

62 See Boring, *Sensation and Perception*, pp. 41–45; cf. Helmholtz, "Rate of Transmission of the Nerve Impulse" (1850), trans. Dietze in Dennis, *Readings in Psychology*, pp. 197–98.

Physiological acoustics

While working on optical problems, Helmholtz turned to acoustics in a published lecture, *Über die physiologischen Ursachen der musikalischen Harmonie* (1857). In it, he detailed the physical attributes of musical sound and, to isolate the role of the ear, delineated a new point of view, "physiological acoustics."[63] After dividing acoustics into the physical and the physiological, he discussed the sensation of tone, the operation of resonance in the ear, compound waveforms, the harmonic series, acoustic beats, dissonance, combination tones, and organ stop mixtures. He supported his description of sound propagation by the water wave analogy and his explanation of phenomena by demonstrations using devices such as sirens, tuning forks, resonators, and plucked and bowed strings.[64]

In *Die Lehre von den Tonempfindungen* (1863), Helmholtz presented a formal exposition of the sensation of tone, but in the context of a broader purpose. He not only defined physical and physiological acoustics, he also engaged aesthetics and music theory. Thus, after summarizing the state of research in physical acoustics, he turned to the physiology of hearing and to the history of music theory and musical styles. His goal was twofold: to advance the knowledge of hearing and sensation, and to provide a physical explanation of the tonal system of Western music. He acknowledged the influence of artistic invention and cultural preferences, even though his harmonic conception was fundamentally a deterministic theory based on the just scale.[65] Basically his aesthetics followed Hanslick's structuralism; his music theory followed Rameau's harmonic system, primarily as transmitted by d'Alembert.

Die Lehre von den Tonempfindungen appeared in four editions (1863, 1865, 1870, 1877) and in two English editions (1875, 1885) translated by Alexander Ellis (1814–90). The early appearance of Ellis's brilliant translation with appended studies of his own stimulated interest and research in Britain and the United States. Tyndall and Rayleigh were notably influenced by Helmholtz's work, as were numerous music theorists who have – to this day – cited Helmholtz's magnum opus to support their various claims regarding the scientific basis of musical consonance, harmony, and tonality.

Consonance and dissonance

To understand Helmholtz's work on the consonance/dissonance issue, one must examine his theory of hearing and his ideas about timbre perception. With anatomical evidence disclosed by use of the compound microscope and with the explanatory

63 Helmholtz, *On the Physiological Causes of Harmony in Music*, pp. 27–58.

64 For detailed descriptions of Helmholtz's acoustic apparatus, see *Sensations of Tone*, Parts I and II, and Appendices 1, 2, 4, 8, and 13; cf. Tyndall, *Sound* (1903 [1867]) for a contemporary description of apparatus and demonstration. For a history of acoustic apparatus, see Boring, *Sensation and Perception*, pp. 328–32.

65 Helmholtz, *Sensations of Tone*, pp. 364–65.

theories of Fourier, Ohm, and Müller, Helmholtz formulated a sophisticated theory of hearing, asserting that elastic appendages to the nerves in the basilar membrane respond to particular frequencies by means of sympathetic vibration.[66] Helmholtz believed that sympathetic vibration is the only natural analogue to the resolution of compound into simple vibrations by the ear.

As in all his conceptions about pitch relations, Helmholtz's ideas about timbre were formed on the basis of the harmonic series. While he recognized that some tones contain inharmonic partials as shown earlier by Chladni and others, he argued that the most pleasing musical timbres are those that emphasize only the first six harmonic partials.[67] He clarified the relation of timbre to the spectrum of harmonics by devising accurately tuned resonators to aid the ear in detecting the presence and strength of specific partials. With these resonators he was able to isolate all the partials up to the sixteenth in the sound of long metal strings.[68] Furthermore, using amplified tuning forks, he synthesized the timbres of vowel sounds to demonstrate their spectral components.[69] This sort of experimental documentation set his work apart from that of earlier investigators.

Believing that the ear itself is the sole locus of sensation, Helmholtz endeavored to show that the ear, like the eye, introduces aberrations; it not only senses complex vibrations in the air, it also introduces distortion owing to the nonlinearity of the cochlea. Moreover, in the case of pure tones, the ear may even supply subjective harmonics, otherwise known as "aural harmonics."[70] It appears that Helmholtz thought these subjective harmonics were identical to combination tones.[71]

Fourier analysis and the hypothesis of a nonlinear receptor enabled Helmholtz to develop plausible explanations for all of the physical phenomena discussed in previous sections. Major questions that Helmholtz failed to answer are why we hear complex tones as unanalyzed, and how the ear mechanism by itself can support the isomorphism of his specific nerve energies model.[72]

Helmholtz conceived of consonance as a sensory response caused by two factors, the affinity of the upper partials of two or more tones (*Klangverwandtschaft*) and the absence of acoustic beats among these partials. The affinity factor owes much to earlier coincidence theories. The simpler the vibrational ratio of the interval, the greater is the number of coinciding harmonic partials of the component tones. Dissonance, in his view, is caused by a lack of such affinity and by the presence of beats. In technical terms, he conceived of dissonance as a sensation of roughness caused by the interference patterns of the sound waves.[73] Helmholtz argued that audible beats are caused only when

66 Ibid., pp. 140–51. 67 Ibid., pp. 45, 182–84, 188. 68 Ibid., p. 47.
69 Ibid., pp. 120–24. 70 Ibid., pp. 158–59. 71 Boring, *Sensation and Perception*, p. 359.
72 On the isomorphism problem, see ibid., pp. 83–5, 90, 404–08; Spender, "Psychology of Music," pp. 389–90.
73 Helmholtz, *Sensations of Tone*, pp. 185–96. For earlier coincidence-of-vibrations theories of consonance, see Palisca, "Scientific Empiricism," pp. 106–10, on Benedetti (1585); H. F. Cohen, *Quantifying Music*, pp. 90–97, 103–11, 166–70, 199–201, on Galileo (1638), Descartes (1633), and Mersenne (1636–37);

frequencies near to each other induce the same elastic appendages of the nerves to vibrate sympathetically. Since beats can be caused both by upper partials and by the fundamental, pure intervals beyond the unison can be sensed to beat. Moreover, beats can be caused by combination tones. He concluded that beating at 33 Hz (cycles per second) is the roughest sounding; beating at less than 6 Hz is tolerable and at more than 132 Hz is imperceptible.[74] Although he reasoned that no clear physiological dividing line separates consonance and dissonance, his harmonic theory accepts the traditional *senario*-based categorization. Major problems for his "roughness" theory of dissonance include its failure to sort out the distinction between dissonant intervals and out-of-tune intervals, and its failure to square with his fixed beat findings the varying limmata that characterize different auditory ranges.[75]

Helmholtz believed that a theory of harmony based on scientific fact need not resort to metaphysics. For him, consonance and dissonance were intrinsic properties of tone. He thought he had been more successful than mathematicians, such as Euler, in answering the questions surrounding Pythagorean notions of consonance. Helmholtz moved the consonance argument from the realm of number theory to that of physiology, but he ended up with a harmonic theory that has all of the limitations of a harmonic-series-based system: his theory was hobbled by reliance on the just scale with its inability to support modulation,[76] and he had no solid basis for the minor chord, the minor scale, or the subdominant harmonic function. Drawing upon his acoustical criteria, Helmholtz decided that the minor triad was "inferior" to the major triad, since "the relation of all the parts of a minor chord to the fundamental note is not so immediate as that for the major chord." He concluded from this that the minor key was likewise "inferior" to the major key, citing the predominance of major-mode works in both popular and classical repertories in support of his argument.

Helmholtz's views about harmonic theory were largely mechanistic, but obviously the product of careful study.[77] From Rameau he took the idea of the *Klang* (*corps sonore*) as the source of consonance, the major triad, and the native intervals (octave and fifth). He offered two explanations of the minor triad, one resembling Rameau's double root theory, the other original: the faintness of the *Klang*'s fifth partial – the major seventeenth above the fundamental – permits its modification from major to minor. Likewise, he offered two explanations for the origins of the dominant seventh chord, one resembling Moritz Hauptmann's (1792–1868) overlapping triads

Christensen, *Rameau and Musical Thought*, pp. 244–46, on Estève (1751) and Euler (1739). For an earlier no-beats theory of consonance, see Fontenelle [Sauveur], "Determination d'un son fixe" (1700), p. 143.

74 Helmholtz, *Sensations of Tone*, pp. 166–73, 191–92.

75 On the limma problem, see Pierce, *Science of Musical Sound*, pp. 78–86.

76 In *Sensations of Tone*, pp. 320–21, Helmholtz admitted the need for tempered tuning in modern instrumental music.

77 For Helmholtz's harmonic theory, see ibid., pp. 290–362; on the two derivations of the minor triad, p. 294; on the superiority of the major mode, p. 301; on seventh chords as overlapping triads, pp. 341–44; on the dominant seventh chord with natural seventh (4:7), p. 347.

theory,[78] the other resembling Sorge's idea that it essentially stems from harmonics 4, 5, 6, and 7.[79] Helmholtz rather conservatively advocated just tuning because it fit his theory of hearing and his acoustic basis for consonance and dissonance; on the other hand, he took the idea of a scale-based tonality from F.-J. Fétis (1784–1871) and developed it into a well-reasoned description of the major-minor key system.[80] At bottom, the harmonic series is Helmholtz's building block. It shaped his entire theory of hearing, his explanation of consonance and dissonance, and ultimately his theory of harmony and tonality. Although he expressed the idea indirectly, Helmholtz was perhaps history's most persuasive advocate for the "physicalist" view that the harmonic series is the fundamental natural force that shaped the Western pitch system. Unlike many earlier advocates of this position, however (such as Rameau), Helmholtz was original by focusing less on the "external" acoustical phenomenon than upon its operations within the ear itself.

Carl Stumpf

Circumstances in Stumpf's life brought him into contact with an intellectual stream rather different from the Helmholtzian tradition. Coming from a family of physicians, he was able early on to prepare himself for an academic career – although his first desire was to pursue the study of music. His university training at Würzburg and Göttingen brought him into contact with the philosopher-psychologists Franz Brentano (1838–1917) and Hermann Lotze (1817–81). Following studies in physics, physiology, philosophy, and theology, he held professorships at Würzburg, Prague, Halle, Munich, and Berlin. At Berlin he expanded a small psychological laboratory founded by Hermann Ebbinghaus (1850–1909) into a full-blown institute. It soon competed with the Leipzig laboratory founded earlier by his influential rival Wilhelm Wundt (1832–1920), the architect of experimental psychology. Interestingly, it was only in 1894, when Stumpf accepted the Berlin post, that he became personally acquainted with Helmholtz, by then terminally ill and in the last months of life.

Stumpf followed the phenomenological path of his mentor Franz Brentano. Brentano's "act psychology" claimed to deal with pure consciousness; it stressed systematic observation more than experimentation and examined the mental act –

78 For Hauptmann's theory of seventh chords in *Harmonik und Metrik* (1853), see Heathcote trans., pp. 55–64. Shirlaw, *Theory of Harmony*, pp. 363–65, provides a commentary. Also see the discussion in **Chapter 14, pp. 459–61**.

79 For Sorge's derivation of the dominant seventh chord in *Vorgemach der musicalischen Composition* (1745–47), see Reilly, "Translation and Commentary," pp. 81–84, 494–99.

80 Helmholtz, *Sensations of Tone*, p. 240. See also Warren, "Helmholtz's Continuing Influence," pp. 263–64. On Fétis, see **Chapter 23, pp. 747–49**.

judging, imagining, experiencing – more than the "content" of the experience. Stumpf's focus was similar, but his personal methodology relied on expert introspective observation supported by experiment and demonstration.[81] Stumpf was interested in the mental aspects of perception and in group differences, which, in his music research, translated into investigations of musical apperception, issues of musicality, and music of other cultures. Wundt, who had been an assistant to Helmholtz for thirteen years, studied the elements of immediate experience as the key to higher-level states of consciousness; he valued experimental design and rigorous laboratory control. Stumpf's holistic perspective and reliance on expert judgment stood in sharp contrast and fueled the acrimonious Stumpf–Wundt debate over methodology.[82] Fundamentally, Stumpf's position was this: if the findings of sterile laboratory experiments contradict expert introspective judgments, the experiments are probably faulty.

Tone psychology

Like Helmholtz, Stumpf turned to issues of musical perception during his thirties and forties. He spent fifteen years writing his monumental, two-volume *Tonpsychologie* (1883, 1890). Stumpf coined the term *Tonpsychologie* to designate a new discipline that placed musical acoustics and physiology in the service of psychology. Tone psychology may be viewed as a philosophically oriented phase of music psychology whose scope was limited to psychoacoustics and the experiential aspects of elementary tonal organization. Under the mounting pressure of Behaviorism and Gestalt psychology, the label and viewpoint fell into disuse after Géza Révész's *Zur Grundlegung der Tonpsychologie* (1913).

While much of Stumpf's output was directed rather narrowly toward musical issues, the broader implications of his theoretical stance were not lost on his students. His renowned student Edmund Husserl (1859–1938) formulated a philosophy of phenomenology that, in its early version, prefigured Gestalt psychology.[83] All three of the founding figures of the Gestalt school of psychology – Max Wertheimer (1880–1943), Wolfgang Köhler (1887–1967), and Kurt Koffka (1886–1941) – were Stumpf's students at the University of Berlin, and both Köhler and Wertheimer taught there as they articulated and developed their theories.[84]

81 Discussions of the orientation of Brentano and Stumpf include "Carl Stumpf," pp. 40–57; Heidbreder, *Seven Psychologies*, pp. 98–101; Boring, *History of Experimental Psychology*, pp. 356–71; Rothfarb, "Beginnings of Music Psychology," pp. 10–17; Ash, *Gestalt Psychology*, pp. 28–38.

82 On the Stumpf–Wundt debate see Blumenthal, "Shaping a Tradition," p. 59; Boring, *History of Experimental Psychology*, p. 365. Also see **Chapter 31, pp. 960–61**.

83 On Husserl's relation to Gestalt psychology, see Boring, *History of Experimental Psychology*, pp. 367–68.

84 See Ash, *Gestalt Psychology*, pp. 38–41.

Tonal fusion

Stumpf's assessment of the consonance/dissonance problem shows how far he departed from Helmholtz's theoretical stance. More an Aristoxenian than a Pythagorean, Stumpf based his investigation on his own perceptual judgments and on the judgments of other listeners. He was mainly interested in the mental processes underlying music.

Stumpf argued that intervals formed from pure (sinusoidal) tones can, like complex tones, be judged consonant or dissonant – and thus the phenomenon must be independent of both the coincidence and the beating of the partials of complex tones.[85] He proposed instead that consonance is the perceptual result of tonal fusion (*Tonverschmelzung*) – the phenomenon of two tones blending to the extent that they are sensed to be "unitary."[86] Stumpf deemed this characteristic to be an unanalyzable percept of the mind. The tonal fusion of dyads, he asserted, is entirely a function of the ratios of the fundamental frequencies of the tones – even if slightly mistuned – and is independent of timbre, loudness, or register. The epistemological foundation of Stumpf's *Tonverschmelzung* theory was psychological, rather than physical or physiological, and the evidence he used to bolster it was a mix of empiricism and mentalism.[87]

Following pilot studies conducted in Würzburg and Prague, he undertook a formal study of tonal fusion at the University of Halle, where he asked listeners of differing levels of musical experience to report their perceptions when they heard various dyads. Musically naive listeners would misperceive two different tones as a single tonal percept (i.e., report tonal fusion) quite often, and levels of these misperceptions varied systematically across five gradations such that the octave was most often misperceived as a single tone – that is, perceived as fused. The perfect fifth had the second highest level of perceptual fusion, followed by the perfect fourth, the major and minor thirds (and their octave complements), and then the major and minor seconds (and complements) and the tritone. Fusion levels for octave compounds of these intervals tended to follow the same pattern. Thus the sequence of intervals in this spectrum of consonance and dissonance resembles that described by Helmholtz, but the evidentiary basis of Stumpf's sequence was very different. Where Helmholtz had held that beats among upper partials of complex tones generate dissonance, Stumpf asserted instead that dissonance is a psychological response: the perception of lack of tonal fusion of two tones. The tones could themselves lack upper partials (and even be presented to separate ears) and still be judged dissonant. Stumpf even argued that neither the physical stimulus nor the physiological experience is a necessary condition of consonance: the mental

85 Stumpf, *Tonpsychologie*, vol. II, pp. 206–08.

86 Stumpf's coverage of fusion theory appears in ibid., pp. 127–219.

87 See Boring, *History of Experimental Psychology*, pp. 368–71.

images (*Phantasievorstellungen*) of the tones can be judged, through introspective "listening," as either consonant or dissonant.[88]

Stumpf's early work on consonance and dissonance was limited to the perceptual fusion or non-fusion of dyadic tonal combinations. Hugo Riemann (1849–1919) – perhaps motivated by Stumpf's refutation of the theory of undertones[89] – criticized the theory of tonal fusion as too limited because it failed to describe, let alone explain, consonance and dissonance of combinations of three or more tones.[90] Stumpf revisited the issue in 1911.[91] He held that additional tones have no effect on judgments of consonance and dissonance, which are immediate (unmediated) sensations. By stating that tonal fusion results from perceiving irreducible wholes rather than sums of components of the physical stimulus, Stumpf seemed to approach the Gestaltist position but stop short: the irreducible wholes that he described still constituted musical elements. To describe the perceptual characteristics of chordal structures, Stumpf used the alternative terms concordance and discordance, which he proposed are percepts based on reflection and interpretation; he realized that chordal effects are very context-dependent. But this attempt did not diffuse the criticism that his theory of tonal fusion is too elemental to be useful to musicians.[92]

The legacy of Helmholtz and Stumpf

Before the twentieth century, concepts such as "native" intervals, "natural" scales, and "laws" of consonance were accepted as self-evident. Today, the truth of such terms stands in doubt. Even basic notions of consonance and dissonance have been encumbered with multiple, often contradictory, meanings.[93] For musicians these constructs depend on musical contexts that are subject to the stylistic norms of the culture. In functional harmony, verticalities exhibit levels of tendency or attraction, stability or instability; in color harmony the identical structures are generally devoid of these characteristics but instead exhibit levels of color tension. Such fluid characteristics seem far removed from the scientist's neatly defined notions of fusion, sensory consonance (euphony), or sensory dissonance (roughness). Sweet, salt, sour, bitter – all are agreeable sensations to the chef when judiciously used. Similar comparative judgments apply in music. While interesting to contemplate, theory-bound classifications of

88 For a more ample discussion of Stumpf's fusion theory, see Boring, *Sensation and Perception*, pp. 360–63; Davies, *Psychology of Music*, pp. 160–62.
89 Stumpf refutes the undertone idea in *Tonpsychologie*, vol. II, pp. 264–67.
90 For a discussion of Riemann's "Zur Theorie der Konsonanz und Dissonanz" (1901), see Mickelsen, *Riemann's Theory of Harmony*, pp. 57–59.
91 Stumpf, "Konsonanz und Konkordanz" (1911). For a synopsis of this work, see Rothfarb, *Kurth: Selected Writings*, pp. 42–43.
92 See Rothfarb, "Beginnings of Music Psychology," pp. 20–30, on Kurth's critique of Stumpf's tone psychology. On Kurth, see Chapter 30, pp. 939–44.
93 See Butler, *Guide to Perception*, pp. 118–22.

pleasant/unpleasant, euphonious/rough – vestiges of the clockwork universe – seem to most musicians to miss the target.[94] Neither Helmholtz nor Stumpf seemed to anticipate this assessment.

To music theorists contemplating the radical style changes in Western music during the past two centuries, the allure of Helmholtzian natural-law theories of music has faded. To be sure, Helmholtz's laboratory study of the properties of raw sound has spurred investigators to continue the exploration. After all, any work in music cognition requires an accurate understanding of the physical components of the process.[95] Helmholtz's lasting contribution to music theory was not his tradition-bound harmonic system but rather his vision that, despite Immanuel Kant's reservations about the analyzability of psychic processes,[96] experimental methodology can be applied to aspects of music perception.

Stumpf's legacy to music theory rests more on viewpoint than discovery. His theory of tonal fusion appears to have had little influence, to judge from the scant number of discussions of *Tonverschmelzung* by leading music theorists of the twentieth century. Perhaps tonal fusion is such an apparent sensory attribute that his elementary findings inspired little comment. Stumpf's indirect influence on perceptual theories of music may be considered his most important contribution – a contribution found not so much in his theories as in the way he gathered evidence to support them. He was convinced that the perception of musical relationships is necessarily guided by musically informed judgment – learned perceptual skills. He realized that declarations – physical or physiological – about the consonant or dissonant value of tonal combinations have no musical meaning unless actual listeners say they sound consonant or dissonant.

Clearly Stumpf found Helmholtz's sensory-level data insufficient to explain higher-level perceptual judgments of music. Much of his research effort was directed at correcting Helmholtz's conclusions about the consonance/dissonance problem. But, despite their very different scientific orientations, Stumpf acknowledged Helmholtz's eminence as a spokesman for mechanistic research. Shortly after Helmholtz's death, Stumpf expressed his esteem in this magnanimous eulogy:

> Since the death of Darwin, the loss of no one in the scientific world has made such a deep impression as that of Helmholtz . . . From the early beginning of his career, from the time of the anatomical and chemical studies of his youth, all his researches were directed towards high ends, and were crowned with great success. Whenever he smote the rock of nature, there gushed forth the living waters of knowledge.[97]

94 For critiques of the consonance/dissonance problem, see Butler, *Guide to Perception*, pp. 118–22; Davies, *Psychology of Music*, pp. 156–75; Farnsworth, *Social Psychology of Music*, pp. 42–46; Lundin, *Objective Psychology of Music*, pp. 82–92; Pierce, *Science of Musical Sound*, pp. 78–101.

95 For discussions of on-going research in the Helmholtz tradition, see Rasch and Plomp, "Perception of Musical Tones," pp. 1–24; Risset and Wessel, "Exploration of Timbre," pp. 25–58; Terhardt, "Concept of Musical Consonance," pp. 276–95.

96 On the Kantian legacy, see Gardner, *Mind's New Science*, pp. 98–102.

97 Stumpf, "Helmholtz and the New Psychology," p. 1.

Bibliography

Primary sources

Barker, A. *Greek Musical Writings*, 2 vols., Cambridge University Press, 1984–89

Chladni, E. F. F. *Entdeckungen über die Theorie des Klanges* (1787), trans. R. B. Lindsay in *Acoustics: Historical and Philosophical Development*, ed. Lindsay, Stroudsburg, PA, Dowden, Hutchinson and Ross, 1973, pp. 156–65

Descartes, R. *Compendium musicae*, Utrecht, G. Zijll and T. ab Ackersdijck, 1650; in *Œuvres de Descartes*, vol. x, ed. C. Adam and P. Tannery, Paris, L. Cerf, 1908; facs. Strasbourg, Heitz, 1965 and New York, Broude, 1968; trans W. Robert as *Compendium of Music*, American Institute of Musicology, 1961

Euler, L. *Tentamen novae theoriae musicae*, St. Petersburg, Academiae Scientarium, 1739; facs. New York, Broude, 1968

"Letter to Joseph Louis Lagrange, from Berlin" (1759), trans. R. B. Lindsay in *Acoustics: Historical and Philosophical Development*, ed. Lindsay, Stroudsburg, A. Dowden, Hutchinson and Ross, 1973, pp. 131–35

Fontenelle, B. de, "Sur la determination d'un son fixe" (1700), in *Joseph Sauveur, Collected Writings on Musical Acoustics (Paris 1700–1713)*, ed. R. Rasch, Utrecht, Diapason Press, 1984

Galileo, G. *Two New Sciences; including Centers of Gravity and Force of Percussion* (1638), trans. S. Drake, Madison, University of Wisconsin Press, 1974

Hauptmann, M. *Die Natur der Harmonik und der Metrik*, Leipzig, Breitkopf und Härtel, 1853; trans. W. E. Heathcote as *The Nature of Harmony and Metre*, London, S. Sonnenschein, 1888

Helmholtz, H. *Handbuch der physiologischen Optik*, 3 vols., Hamburg and Leipzig, L. Voss, 1856–67, 3rd edn., 1909–11; trans. J. P. C. Southall as *Treatise on Physiological Optics*, 3 vols., Rochester, NY, Optical Society of America, 1924–25; reprint New York, Dover, 1962

Die Lehre von den Tonempfindungen als physiologischer Grundlage für die Theorie der Musik (1863), 4th edn., Braunschweig, F. Vieweg, 1877; trans. A. J. Ellis as *On the Sensations of Tone as a Physiological Basis for the Theory of Music*, 2nd edn., London, Longman and Green, 1885; reprint New York, Dover, 1954

"On the Physiological Causes of Harmony in Music" (1857), in *Helmholtz on Perception: Its Physiology and Development*, ed. R. M. Warren and R. P. Warren, New York, J. Wiley, 1968, pp. 27–58

"On the Rate of Transmission of the Nerve Impulse" (1850), trans. A. G. Dietze in *Readings in the History of Psychology*, ed. W. Dennis, New York, Appleton-Century-Crofts, 1948, pp. 197–98

Kirnberger, J. P. *Die Kunst des reinen Satzes*, Berlin, 1771–79; partial trans. D. Beach and J. Thym as *The Art of Strict Musical Composition*, New Haven, Yale University Press, 1982

Mersenne, M. *Quaestiones celeberrimae in Genesim*, Paris, S. Cramoisy, 1623

Harmonie universelle, Paris, Cramoisy, 1636–37; facs. Paris, Centre National de la Recherche Scientifique, 1963 and 1986; Book IV trans. R. E. Chapman as *Harmonie universelle: The Books on Instruments*, The Hague, M. Nijhoff, 1957

Correspondance du P. Marin Mersenne, ed. C. de Waard et al., 10 vols., Paris, Centre National de la Recherche Scientifique, 1945–67

Müller, J. "The Specific Energies of Nerves" (1838), trans. W. Braly in *Readings in the History of Psychology*, ed. W. Dennis, New York, Appleton-Century-Crofts, 1948, pp. 157–68

North, R. *Cursory Notes of Musicke (c. 1698–1703): A Physical, Psychological and Critical Theory*, ed. M. Chan and J. C. Kassler, Kensington, Australia, Unisearch Limited, University of New South Wales, 1986

The Lives of the Norths (1740), 2nd edn., 3 vols., London, H. Colbur, 1826

Ohm, G. S. "On the Definition of a Tone with the Associated Theory of the Siren and Similar Sound Producing Devices" (1843), trans. R. B. Lindsay in *Acoustics: Historical and Philosophical Development*, ed. Lindsay, Stroudsburg, PA. Dowden, Hutchinson and Ross, 1973, pp. 243–47

Rameau, J.-P. *Code de musique pratique*, Paris, Imprimerie royale, 1760; facs. New York, Broude, 1965

Rayleigh, J. W. S. *The Theory of Sound*, 2 vols. (2nd edn., 1894), New York, Dover, 1945

Révész, G. *Zur Grundlegung der Tonpsychologie*, Leipzig, Veit, 1913

Riemann, H. "Zur Theorie der Konsonanz und Dissonanz" (1901), in *Präludien und Studien*, vol. III, Leipzig, H. Seemann, 1901; facs. Hildesheim, G. Olms, 1967

Roberts, F. "A Discourse concerning the Musical Notes on the Trumpet, and the Trumpet Marine, and of the Defects of the Same," *Philosophical Transcriptions of the Royal Society of London* 16 (1692), pp. 559–63

Sauveur, J. "Système général des intervalles des sons, et son application à tous les systèmes et à tous les instrumens de musique" (1701), in *Joseph Sauveur: Collected Writings on Musical Acoustics (Paris 1700–1713)*, ed. R. Rasch, Utrecht, Diapason Press, 1984

"Application des sons harmoniques à la composition des jeux d'orgues" (1702), in *Joseph Sauveur: Collected Writings on Musical Acoustics (Paris 1700–1713)*, ed. R. Rasch, Utrecht, Diapason Press, 1984

Savart, F. "Sensibilité de l'ouïe" (1830), trans. R. B. Lindsay in *Acoustics: Historical and Philosophical Development*, ed. Lindsay, Stroudsburg, PA, Dowden, Hutchinson and Ross, 1973, pp. 202–09

Schlick, A. *Spiegel der Orgelmacher und Organisten*, Mainz, P. Schöffer, 1511; facs. with trans. by E. Barber, Buren, Netherlands, F. Knuf, 1980

Smith, R. *Harmonics or the Philosophy of Musical Sounds* (1749), facs. New York, Da Capo Press, 1966

Stumpf, C. *Tonpsychologie*, 2 vols., Leipzig, S. Hirzel, 1883–90; reprint Hilversum, F. Knuf, 1965

"Hermann von Helmholtz and the New Psychology," trans. J. G. Hibben in *Psychological Review* 2 (1895), pp. 1–12

"Konsonanz und Konkordanz," in *Beiträge zur Akustik und Musikwissenschaft*, vol. VI, ed. C. Stumpf, Leipzig, J. A. Barth, 1911, pp. 116–50

"Carl Stumpf," in *Die Philosophie der Gegenwart in Selbstdarstellungen*, ed. R. Schmidt, Leipzig, F. Meiner, 1924, pp. 205–65

Tyndall, J. *Sound*, 3rd. edn., New York, Appleton, 1903; reprint New York, Greenwood, 1969

Wallis, J. "Dr Wallis's Letter to the Publisher, concerning a new Musical Discovery," *Philosophical Transcriptions of the Royal Society of London* 12 (1677), pp. 839–42
Zarlino, G. *Le istitutioni harmoniche*, Venice, Franceschi, 1558; facs., New York, Broude, 1965

Secondary sources

Ash, M. G. *Gestalt Psychology in German Culture, 1890–1976; Holism and the Quest for Objectivity*, Cambridge University Press, 1995
Bailey, R. L. "Music and Mathematics: An Interface in the Writings of Leonhard Euler," Ph.D. diss., State University of New York at Buffalo (1980)
Barbour, J. M. Introduction to R. Smith, *Harmonics or the Philosophy of Musical Sounds* (1749), facs. New York, Da Capo Press, 1966, pp. v–xi
Benade, A. H. *Fundamentals of Musical Acoustics*, New York, Dover, 1976
Blumenthal, A. L. "Shaping a Tradition: Experimentalism Begins," in *Points of View in the Modern History of Psychology*, ed. C. E. Buxton, Orlando, Academic Press, 1985, pp. 51–83
Boring, E. G. *Sensation and Perception in the History of Experimental Psychology*, New York, Appleton-Century-Crofts, 1942
A History of Experimental Psychology, 2nd edn., New York, Appleton-Century-Crofts, 1950
Butler, D. M. "An Historical Investigation and Bibliography of Nineteenth Century Music Psychology Literature," Ph.D. diss., Ohio State University (1973)
"Describing the Perception of Tonality in Music: A Proposal for a Theory of Intervallic Rivalry," *MP* 6 (1989), pp. 219–41
The Musician's Guide to Perception and Cognition, New York, Schirmer, 1992
Cannon, J. T. and S. Dostrovsky, *The Evolution of Dynamics: Vibration Theory from 1687 to 1742*, New York, Springer-Verlag, 1981
Cazden, N. "Sensory Theories of Musical Consonance," *Journal of Aesthetics and Art Criticism* 20 (1962), pp. 301–19
Christensen, T. "Science and Music Theory in the Enlightenment: d'Alembert's Critique of Rameau," Ph.D. diss., Yale University (1985)
"Eighteenth-Century Science and the *Corps Sonore*: The Scientific Background to Rameau's Principle of Harmony," *JMT* 31 (1987), pp. 23–50
Rameau and Musical Thought in the Enlightenment, Cambridge University Press, 1993
"Sensus, Ratio, and Phthongos: Mattheson's Theory of Tone Perception," in *Musical Transformation and Musical Intuition*, ed. R. Atlas and M. Cherlin, Boston, Ovenbird Press, 1994, pp. 1–16
Clark, S. "Schenker's Mysterious Five," *Nineteenth Century Music* 23 (1999), pp. 84–102
Cohen, H. F. *Quantifying Music: The Science of Music at the First Stage of the Scientific Revolution, 1580–1650*, Dordrecht, D. Reidel, 1984
Cohen, R. S. and Y. Elkana, "Introduction: Helmholtz in the History of Scientific Method," in *Hermann von Helmholtz: Epistemological Writings*, ed. Cohen and Elkana, Dordrecht, Reidel, 1977, pp. ix–xxviii
Davies, J. B. *The Psychology of Music*, Stanford University Press, 1978
Dostrovsky, S. "The Origins of Vibration Theory: The Scientific Revolution and the Nature of Music," Ph.D. diss., Princeton University (1969)

Fancher, R. E. *Pioneers of Psychology*, New York, Norton, 1979

Farnsworth, P. R. *Social Psychology of Music*, 2nd edn., Ames, Iowa State University Press, 1969

Galpin, F. W. "Monsieur Prin and his Trumpet Marine," *Music and Letters* 14 (1933), pp. 18–29

Gardner, H. *The Mind's New Science: A History of the Cognitive Revolution*, New York, Basic Books, 1985

Gouk, P. *Music, Science and Natural Magic in Seventeenth-Century England*, New Haven, Yale University Press, 1999

Green, B. L. "The Harmonic Series from Mersenne to Rameau: An Historical Study of Circumstances Leading to Its Recognition," Ph.D. diss., Ohio State University (1969)

Hall, D. E. *Musical Acoustics: An Introduction*, Belmont, CA, Wadsworth, 1980

Handel, S. *Listening, An Introduction to the Perception of Auditory Events*, Cambridge, MA, MIT Press, 1989

Heidbreder, E. *Seven Psychologies*, New York, Appleton-Century-Crofts, 1933

Hunt, F. V. *Origins in Acoustics: The Science of Sound from Antiquity to the Age of Newton*, Yale University Press, 1978

Jones, A. T. "The Discovery of Difference Tones," *American Physics Teacher* 3 (1935), pp. 49–51

Klein, M. *Mathematics in Western Culture*, Oxford University Press, 1953

Lester, J. *Compositional Theory in The Eighteenth Century*, Cambridge, MA, Harvard University Press, 1992

Lindsay, R. B. "The Story of Acoustics," *The Journal of the Acoustical Society of America* 39 (1966), pp. 629–44

Ludwig, H. *Marin Mersenne und seine Musiklehre*, Halle, Buchhandlung des Waisenhauses, 1935

Lundin, R. W. *An Objective Psychology of Music*, New York, Ronald Press, 1953

Maley, C. V. "The Theory of Beats and Combination Tones, 1700–1863," Ph.D. diss., Harvard University (1990)

Mickelsen, W. C. *Hugo Riemann's Theory of Harmony: A Study and History of Music Theory*, Lincoln, University of Nebraska Press, 1977

Murphy, G. and J. K. Kovach, *Historical Introduction to Modern Psychology*, 3rd edn., New York, Harcourt Brace Jovanovich, 1972

Murray, D. J. *A History of Western Psychology*, 2nd edn., Englewood Cliffs, Prentice Hall, 1988

Palisca, C. V. "Scientific Empiricism," in *Seventeenth Century Science in the Arts*, ed. H. H. Rhys, Princeton University Press, 1961, pp. 91–137

Palisca, C. V. and N. Spender, "Consonance" in *NG2*, vol. VI, pp. 325–28

Partch, H. *Genesis of a Music*, 2nd edn., New York, Da Capo Press, 1974

Pierce, J. R. *The Science of Musical Sound*, rev. edn., New York, Freeman, 1992

Rasch, R. A. Introduction to *Joseph Sauveur: Collected Writings on Musical Acoustics (Paris 1700–1713)*, ed. R. A. Rasch, Utrecht, Diapason Press, 1984, pp. 8–56

Rasch, R. A. and R. Plomp, "The Perception of Musical Tones," in *The Psychology of Music*, ed. D. Deutsch, San Diego, Academic Press, 1982, pp. 1–24

Reilly, A. D. "Georg Andreas Sorge's Vorgemach der Musicalischen Composition: A Translation and Commentary," 2 vols., Ph.D. diss., Northwestern University (1980)

Risset, J.-C. and D. L. Wessel, "Exploration of Timbre by Analysis and Synthesis," in *The Psychology of Music*, ed. D. Deutsch, San Diego, Academic Press, 1982, pp. 25–58

Rothfarb, L. A. "Ernst Kurth's *Die Voraussetzungen der theoretischen Harmonik* and the Beginnings of Music Psychology," *Theoria* 4 (1989), pp. 10–33
Rothfarb, L. A. (ed.), *Ernst Kurth: Selected Writings*, Cambridge University Press, 1991
Schultz, D. P. and S. L. Schultz, *A History of Modern Psychology*, 5th edn., New York, Harcourt Brace Jovanovich, 1992
Shirlaw, M. *The Theory of Harmony*, 2nd edn., Dekalb, IL, B. Coar, 1955
Smith, C. S. "Leonhard Euler's *Tentamen novae theoriae musicae*: A Translation and Commentary," Ph.D. diss., Indiana University (1960)
Spender, N. and R. Shuter-Dyson, "Psychology of Music" in *NG2*, vol. xx, pp. 527–62
Terhardt, E. "Concept of Musical Consonance: A Link between Music and Psychoacoustics," *MP* 1 (1984), pp. 276–95
Truesdell, C. "The Rational Mechanics of Flexible or Elastic Bodies, 1638–1788," in *Leonhardi Euleri Opera Omnia*, Ser. 2/x–xi, Zurich, O. Füssli, 1960
Turner, R. S. "Helmholtz, Hermann von" in *Dictionary of Scientific Biography*, vol. VI, ed. C. C. Gillispie (1972), pp. 241–53
Vogel, S. "Sensation of Tone, Perception of Sound, and Empiricism; Helmholtz's Physiological Acoustics," in *Hermann von Helmholtz and the Foundation of Nineteenth-Century Science*, ed. D. Cahan, Berkeley, University of California Press, 1993
Warren, R. M. "Helmholtz and His Continuing Influence," *MP* 1 (1984), pp. 95–124
Wever, E. G. and M. Lawrence, *Physiological Acoustics*, Princeton University Press, 1954

· 10 ·

Music theory and mathematics

CATHERINE NOLAN

In Chapter 6 of *The Manual of Harmonics* (early second century CE), Nicomachus of Gerasa narrates the legendary story of Pythagoras passing by the blacksmith's shop, during which in an epiphany of sonorous revelation, he discovered the correlation of sounding intervals and their numerical ratios. According to Nicomachus, Pythagoras perceived from the striking of the hammers on the anvils the consonant intervals of the octave, fifth, and fourth, and the dissonant interval of the whole tone separating the fifth and fourth. Experimenting in the smithy with various factors that might have influenced the interval differences he heard (force of the hammer blows, shape of the hammer, material being cast), he concluded that it was the relative weight of the hammers that engendered the differences in the sounding intervals, and he attempted to verify his conclusion by comparing the sounds of plucked strings of equal tension and lengths, proportionally weighted according to the ratios of the intervals.[1]

Physical and logical incongruities or misrepresentations in Nicomachus's narrative aside, the parable became a fixture of neo-Pythagorean discourse because of its metaphoric resonance: it encapsulated the essence of Pythagorean understanding of number as material or corporeal, and it venerated Pythagoras as the discoverer of the mathematical ratios underlying the science of harmonics. The parable also established a frame of reference in music-theoretical thought in the association between music and number, or more accurately, music theory and mathematical models, since it is not through number alone but through the more fundamental notions of universality and truth embedded in Pythagorean and Platonic mathematics and philosophy that one can best begin to apprehend the broad range of interrelationships between music theory and mathematics.

Following an overview of the legacies of Pythagorean arithmetic that forged the tenacious bond between mathematics and music theory, I explore the association of music theory and mathematics from several perspectives: numerical models, geometric imagery, combinatorics, set theory and group theory, and transformational theory. Collectively, these perspectives encompass the most fertile interconnections of music theory and mathematics from the Middle Ages to the late twentieth century. I conclude with some reflections on prescriptive applications of mathematics in twentieth-century music-theoretical thought.

1 Levin, *The Manual of Harmonics*, pp. 83–97. A related version of the Pythagorean Myth is narrated in Chapter 5, pp. 142–43.

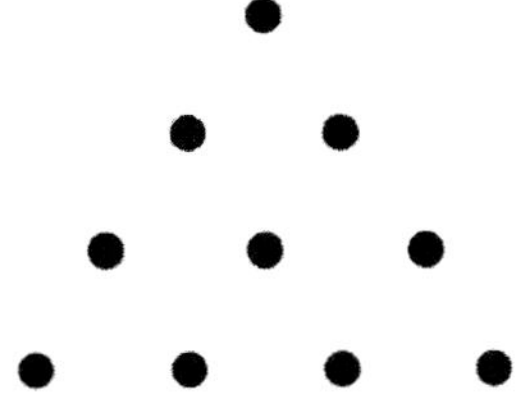

Figure 10.1 The Pythagorean *tetractys*

Pythagorean legacies: an overview

The two most fundamental tenets of the syncretic intellectual force known as Pythagoreanism are: (1) that numbers are constituent elements of reality; and (2) that numbers and their ratios provide the key to explaining the order of nature and the universe.[2] These tenets epitomize the central doctrine of Pythagorean philosophy and science: the metaphysical significance of numbers transcends their computational utility. Pythagorean mathematician-philosophers grouped together the subjects that Boethius later called the *quadrivium* – arithmetic, geometry, music (harmonics), and astronomy – through the conformity of number and observation they revealed.[3] Mathematics permeates the quadrivial sciences, whose cosmological aspirations imbue certain numbers and ratios with mystical or symbolic meaning. One of the most potent Pythagorean symbols was the *tetractys* of the decad (see Figure 10.1). The *tetractys* is an arrangement of points in the shape of a triangle, and represents the first four natural numbers, whose sum is 10 ($1+2+3+4=10$).[4] The number 4 possessed various symbolic, if eclectic associations, such as the number of elements (earth, water, air, and fire), the number of seasons, and the number of points or vertices needed to construct a tetrahedron (pyramid), the simplest regular polyhedron. The number 10 represented the basis of the numeration system (units, tens, hundreds, etc.) and the concomitant principle of cyclical renewal, another manifestation of the unity of mathematical, natural, and cosmological elements. From the integral constituents of the Pythagorean *tetractys* arise the ratios of the harmonious intervals or consonances: the unison (1:1), the octave (2:1), the fifth (3:2), and the fourth (4:3). The cosmological order expressed by these simple proportions corresponds to

2 Lippman, *Musical Thought*, pp. 2–44. Numbers in Pythagorean mathematics refer to the natural numbers (the positive integers beginning with 1, also called the counting numbers) and fractions or ratios formed of those numbers. See Barker, *Greek Musical Writings*, pp. 5–11, 28–51; see also James, *The Music of the Spheres*, pp. 20–40. Also see **Chapter 4, pp. 114–17**.

3 Lippman, *Musical Thought*, p. 155; Wagner, "The Seven Liberal Arts," pp. 2–9. Also see **Chapter 5, p. 142**.

4 The number 10 is a triangular number, a species of figurate numbers, which can be represented as geometric figures (triangles, squares, etc.) constructed by arrangements of points. See Gullberg, *Mathematics*, pp. 289–92; Mariarz and Greenwood, *Greek Mathematical Philosophy*, pp. 24–29; Crocker, "Pythagorean Mathematics and Music," pp. 190–91.

the harmonic consonances, which were demonstrated empirically in the ratios of the lengths of vibrating strings.[5]

Pythagorean mathematics included a theory of ratio (the relation of two quantities) and a theory of proportion (the relation of two or more ratios). Ratios were classified exhaustively into six categories: equal, superparticular (or epimere), superpartient (or epimore), multiple, multiple-superparticular, and multiple-superpartient.[6] Proportions of three terms were identified as arithmetic, geometric, and harmonic progressions, the middle term being the mean.[7] String lengths of 12, 9, 8, and 6 embody the ratios of the consonances (12:6=2:1, 12:8=9:6=3:2, 8:6=4:3) and the Pythagorean whole tone (9:8), as well as the arithmetic and harmonic means (12:9:6 and 12:8:6 respectively). (see **Figure 10.3, p. 281.**)

Explaining musical intervals through ratios and combinations of ratios became the defining feature of the Pythagorean tradition of inquiry in music theory and acoustical science. Ratios of (as opposed to differences between) string lengths or vibration frequencies yield universally valid quantification of intervals, independent of the actual pitches involved. Arithmetic operations were used to calculate combinations of intervals: the addition of intervals was computed by multiplication of their ratios, while the subtraction of intervals was computed by their division. Thus, the terms of the ratios involved in the formation of the octave by the addition of the fifth and the fourth (3:2×4:3=2:1) reinforce the integrity of the *tetractys*, and dissonant intervals were computed in relation to the consonances. The interval representing the difference between a fifth and a fourth, the Pythagorean whole tone, expresses the ratio 9:8 (3:2÷4:3=9:8), while the interval remaining when two whole tones are subtracted from a fourth, the Pythagorean diatonic semitone, expresses the ratio 256:243 ((4:3÷9:8)÷9:8=256:243).[8] The consonant intervals form a fixed intervallic framework, in which the octave is subdivided into two fourths separated by a whole tone (4:3×9:8×4:3=144:72=2:1); the disjunct fourths form the fixed boundaries of two tetrachords, whose movable interior pitches could be tuned in various ratios prescribed by theorists in their determinations of the intervals characteristic of the three genera (diatonic, chromatic, and enharmonic). The formally simple mathematics underlying the Pythagorean system established a later standard for comparison with other tuning systems.[9]

5 For consistency, ratios of intervals in this essay are given in terms of vibration frequencies rather than string lengths, despite the resultant anachronism with respect to Pythagorean mathematics. The two ratios are inversely proportional; that is, the ratio 2:1 represents the relation between frequencies, while 1:2 represents the relation between string lengths of octave-related pitches.

6 See Crocker, "Pythagorean Mathematics," pp. 191–92. In algebraic terms, the six ratio classes in their lowest terms can be represented as follows: equal (x:x); superparticular (x+1:x); superpartient (x+m:x, where m is not a factor of x); multiple (nx:x); multiple-superparticular (nx+1:x); and multiple-superpartient (nx+m:x, where m is not a factor of x).

7 The theory of proportion in ancient Greek mathematics is clearly explained in Mariarz and Greenwood, *Greek Mathematical Philosophy*, pp. 30–36. See also **Figure 4.2, p. 116.**

8 Barker, *Greek Musical Writings*, vol. I, pp. 3–52; Lippman, *Musical Thought*, pp. 13–19.

9 For more on Pythagorean tuning see **Chapter 7, pp. 195–98.**

Notwithstanding the monumental position of the Pythagorean tradition in speculative music theory, Pythagoras holds an even greater place of honor in Western civilization. His importance as a mathematician rests largely on his celebrated theorem about the relationships of the sides of all right triangles.[10] His (later reconstructed) proof of the theorem established the timeless methodology of mathematical proof by deduction from a set of axioms,[11] and the deductive method was propounded by Greek mathematicians and philosophers as the only certain means to obtain universal truths. The thirteen books of Euclid's *Elements*, for example, present a logically organized compendium of ancient knowledge in plane and solid geometry and number theory through a series of definitions, postulates or axioms, and propositions or theorems, and is still regarded as the ideal model of deductive reasoning. The quintessential rationalism of deduction in Greek mathematics formed the bedrock of mathematical formulation, and vitalized the discipline by fostering continual inquiry into its first principles.[12] Later reevaluations of Euclidean standards of universality, particularly those arising in the seventeenth and nineteenth centuries from the invention of new algebraic and geometric rules or axioms upon which to build deductive systems, ultimately led to revised conceptions of truth in mathematics, and opened up vast new areas of mathematical and philosophical inquiry, some of which had a profound impact on speculative music theory.

Post-Pythagorean mathematical achievements offered intellectual stimulation in both scientific and humanistic disciplines as the conceptual scope of European mathematics expanded in response to scientific discoveries, cultural developments, and technological accomplishments. The sixteenth-century coalescence of humanism in the rediscovery of ancient Greek texts and scientific empiricism in the early experimental tradition eroded the cornerstone of Pythagoreanism, and the process of undermining Pythagorean and neo-Platonic mysticism set the stage for new types of engagement between the disciplines of music theory and mathematics. The seventeenth century marked a watershed in musical science, as the analysis of sound shifted from its Pythagorean foundation in number to a scientific foundation in physics, and empirical experimentation began to claim partnership with mathematics.[13] The scope of mathematics, which in the Pythagorean tradition was concerned with the qualities of magnitude and multitude, dramatically expanded in and after the seventeenth century to embrace temporal, spatial, and logical conceptualizations of objects, qualities, and relations. The efflorescence of new branches of mathematics in the seventeenth

10 The square of the hypotenuse (h) is equal to the sum of the squares of the other two sides (a and b): that is, $h^2 = a^2 + b^2$.

11 Pythagoras's proof appears in Singh, *Fermat's Enigma*, pp. 287–88. See also Rotman, *Journey into Mathematics*, pp. 47–51.

12 Aaboe, *Episodes*, pp. 46–53; Mariarz and Greenwood, *Greek Mathematical Philosophy*, pp. 233–41; Tiles, *Mathematics and the Image of Reason*, pp. 1–32.

13 For contrasting, but complementary, perspectives on music theory and science in the seventeenth century see Palisca, *Humanism*; Cohen, *Quantifying Music*. Also see Chapter 8, pp. 223–24 and Chapter 9, pp. 246–47.

century (analytic geometry, combinatorics and probability theory, and calculus) and in the nineteenth century (modular arithmetic, non-Euclidean geometries, group theory, and set theory) brought new dimensions – literally and figuratively – to both algebra and geometry, and strengthened the already firm association of mathematics and music theory by introducing novel mathematical models.

Numerical models in music theory

The rich implications of Pythagorean and Platonic philosophy and mathematics, ratios and magnitudes and their geometric representation, governed the science of music from the Middle Ages to the Renaissance. Ratio and proportion, understood today in algebraic terms, were conceived in Greek mathematics in terms of a close association of arithmetic and geometry epitomized by proportional relations of the lengths of vibrating strings. Geometric primitives – lengths, areas, angles – were expressed exclusively as numbers and fractions or ratios. Numbers themselves could be represented as geometric figures, while mathematical properties of figurate numbers were demonstrated with arithmetic.[14] Until the fifteenth century, the ratios of Pythagorean diatonic tuning remained virtually unchallenged in speculative music theory, even as the inventory of consonances expanded in contrapuntal practice and practical treatises to embrace thirds and sixths as imperfect consonances.[15] In the early Renaissance, the disunion of theory and practice became an important issue when new speculations on tuning focused on the imperfect consonances. The Pythagorean major third (81:64) and minor third (32:27) were apprehended as too large and too small respectively, and were replaced where possible by the mathematically simpler, just ratios 5:4 and 6:5 by Bartolomeo Ramis de Pareia (*Musica practica*, 1482), who articulated the principle of just intonation based on maximizing the number of pure fifths and thirds in a scale.[16] The theoretical ideal of just intonation was bolstered by its advocates through appeal to the authority of Ptolemy's syntonic diatonic tuning. Lodovico Fogliano (*Musica theorica*, 1529) defended the ratios of the just thirds (5:4 and 6:5) by invoking the Pythagorean classes of ratios; the ratios of the just major and minor thirds, like those of the four Pythagorean consonances, are superparticular, while the major and minor sixths, 5:3 and 8:5 respectively, belong to the superpartient class of ratios.[17]

14 See note 4 above. The intimate alliance of arithmetic and geometry was not even broken by the crisis of Pythagorean mathematics over the existence of irrational numbers.
15 See **Chapter 6, pp. 178–84.**
16 The ratios of the successive intervals within an octave in most representations of just intonation (corresponding to the major scale) are: 9:8, 10:9, 16:15, 9:8, 10:9, 9:8, 16:15. (See Backus, *Acoustical Foundations*, p. 125.) Barbour discusses the history of just intonation from Ramis to Kepler, Mersenne, Marpurg, and Euler in *Tuning and Temperament*, pp. 89–105. Also see **Chapter 7, pp. 198–201** and **Figure 8.2, p. 236.**
17 Palisca, *Humanism*, pp. 235–44. See also Barbour, *Tuning and Temperament*, pp. 16–24, 93–96.

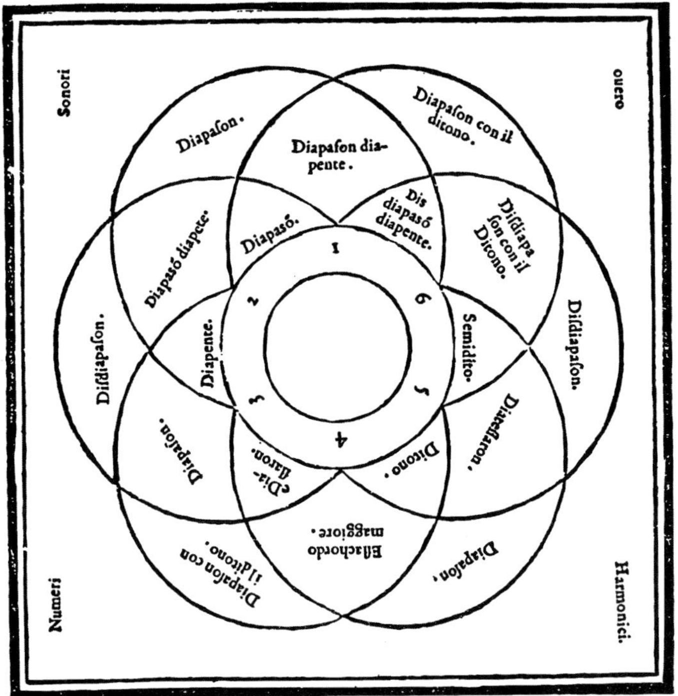

Figure 10.2 Zarlino's *senario*, *Le istitutioni harmoniche*, Part I, p. 25

Zarlino (*Le istitutioni harmoniche*, 1558) appealed to neo-Platonic number theory for theoretical justification of the imperfect consonances with his construction of the *senario*, a conceptual extension of the Pythagorean *tetractys*, comprising the integers from 1 to 6 (see Figure 10.2). Like the *tetractys*, Zarlino's *senario* affirms the association of number and the cosmos, possesses a special numerical property, and embodies the ratios of the consonances, extended to include the just major third (5:4), minor third (6:5), and major sixth (5:3). (The ratio of the just minor sixth [8:5] falls outside the *senario*, but Zarlino explains its consonant status through its adjoining of the fourth and minor third with the shared term 6 – 8:6 and 6:5.)[18] The symbolic importance of 6 is that it is the first perfect number; that is, 6 is the sum of all its factors except itself (1 + 2 + 3 = 6). All ratios of terms from 1 to 6 form consonances (in just intonation) or their octave compounds. Zarlino's diagram of the "sonorous numbers" shows the numbers 1 to 6 distributed equidistantly in the center ring. Ratios between all pairs of terms are identified in three concentric levels: those between adjacent terms in the first

18 Zarlino could not extend the *senario* to 8 to accommodate the 8:5 ratio of the minor sixth, because that would have forced the inclusion of ratios involving the term 7 as consonances (Palisca, *Humanism*, pp. 247–50). See also Cohen, *Quantifying Music*, pp. 3–6; and Chapter 24, pp. 754–55.

level, those between terms which differ by 2 in the middle level, and those between terms which differ by 3 in the outermost level.

Zarlino's conception of the *senario* was challenged not long after its publication by authors seeking a physical, rather than numerical, explanation for consonance (e.g., Vincenzo Galilei, *Discorso intorno all'opere di messer Gioseffo Zarlino*, 1589); their empirical methods marked the early stages of the scientific revolution. Marin Mersenne's *Harmonie universelle* (1636–37) refers to a number of important early scientific investigations (e.g., by Benedetti, Galileo Galilei, and Beeckman) on the acoustical propagation of sound.[19] Number continued to govern the assessment of consonance through comparison of the relative simplicity of frequency ratios, and the monochord continued to be used to represent intervals by string lengths as late as Rameau's *Traité de l'harmonie* (1722), but a revisionist attitude had nevertheless taken hold in musical science.[20] Certain seventeenth- and eighteenth-century speculative theorists – including Mersenne, Werckmeister, Huygens, and Sauveur – who were simultaneously physicists and mathematicians, wrote prolifically on systems of temperament for keyboard and fretted instruments. The ratios of Pythagorean or just intonation were adjusted according to a variety of mathematical schemes to avoid the disequilibrium of the octave upon successive concatenations of consonances. Pitch was determined through physical measurement of vibration frequencies, and mathematics, loosened from neo-Platonic mysticism, served as a companion to physics, a means to quantify relationships and to structure arguments and proofs.

The numerical approach to the problem of ranking intervals, however, continued to find expression in the arithmetic and geometric solutions of Kepler, Tartini, and Euler. Kepler (*Harmonice mundi*, 1619) utilized the diameter of a circle and inscribed regular polygons (equilateral triangle, square, pentagon, hexagon, and octagon) to explain the consonances of the *senario* (including the minor sixth, 8 : 5).[21] Tartini (*Trattato di musica secondo la vera scienza dell'armonica*, 1754) attempted imaginatively, if faultily, to derive the intervals of major and minor harmony from a hierarchy of relationships based on harmonic, arithmetic, and geometric proportions between the circumference, diameter, and sines of a circle.[22] Instead of measuring consonance or dissonance in absolute terms, Euler (*Tentamen novae theoriae musicae*, 1739) devised an index with which to measure the degree of agreeableness (*gradus suavitatis*) of each interval; his method involved taking the prime factors of the terms of the interval's ratio, subtracting 1 from each factor, and adding 1 to the subtotal to arrive at a *gradus suavitatis* – the smaller the

19 See Dostrovsky, "Early Vibration Theory." See also **Chapter 9, p. 250**.

20 Christensen presents an illuminating discussion of the incursion of empirical science into speculative music theory during the period following Zarlino to Rameau's *Traité* in *Rameau and Musical Thought*, pp. 71–90.

21 Walker, *Studies in Musical Science*, pp. 44–54; Cohen, *Quantifying Music*, pp. 16–23. See also **Chapter 8, pp. 233–35**.

22 The musical theory of Tartini, including a discussion of its mathematical shortcomings, is discussed in depth by Walker, *Studies in Music*, pp. 123–70. Tartini's mathematical errors are discussed in Planchart, "Theories of Giuseppe Tartini," pp. 40–47.

total, the higher the degree of suavity. Euler, evidently undeterred by the anomalies arising within his rankings, extended the mathematical ranking process to configurations of multiple intervals (chords).[23]

New mathematical discoveries and inventions were swiftly adopted by scientists and theorists of music during the sixteenth and seventeenth centuries. The late sixteenth-century innovation of decimal fractions and the early seventeenth-century invention of logarithms (the exponent to which a base must be raised to yield a given number) further facilitated comparison of intervals. Logarithms, by transmuting interval ratios to exponents, simplified the comparison of intervals, even those with complex ratios. The relatively cumbersome operations of multiplication or division of ratios were converted to simple addition or subtraction. Logarithms also consummately reflected the geometric progression of frequencies from a fundamental, and provided close approximations of irrational quantities.[24] Joseph Sauveur explained his use of common logarithms (to base 10) as a computational aid in his unpublished *Traité de la théorie de la musique* (1697); each term of the ratio is expressed as a logarithmic value, and the smaller value is then simply subtracted from the larger.[25] Logarithms to base 2, expedient for measuring intervals because they reflect the primacy of the octave ($\log_2 2 = 1$), were employed by Juan Caramuel de Lobkowitz (*Mathesis nova*, 1670), Euler (*Tentamen novae theorae musicae*, 1739), and later by Riemann ("Über das musikalische Hören," 1873).[26]

Although the practice of equal temperament dates back at least to the mid-sixteenth century, the theory engendered its most spirited technical and aesthetic debate beginning with Rameau's *Génération harmonique* (1737).[27] Regular and irregular mean-tone temperaments continued actively to be employed in practice, while just intonation and equal temperament competed for preeminence in nineteenth-century theoretical writings. The authoritative figures of Simon Sechter, Moritz Hauptmann, and Hermann Helmholtz strongly favored just intonation, claiming its natural foundation

23 See Lindley, *Mathematical Models*, pp. 234–39. Mooney, in "The 'Table of Relations,'" pp. 10–21, discusses the mathematical processes and problems of Euler's *gradus suavitatis* and rankings of chordal consonance.

24 The invention of logarithms is attributed to the Scottish mathematician John Napier (1550–1617); Henry Briggs (1561–1630) introduced the common logarithm, the logarithm to base 10. See Barbour, "Musical Logarithms," for a study of the history and utility of logarithmic measures of musical intervals. See also Walker, *Studies in Musical Science*, p. 10.

25 A thorough discussion of the adoption of logarithms by Sauveur and several earlier scientists in the area of acoustics is found in **Chapter 7, pp. 210–14**. See also Semmens, "Joseph Sauveur's Treatise," pp. 23–25; Barbour, "Musical Logarithms," pp. 26–27; and *Tuning and Temperament*, pp. 77–79.

26 The first use of logarithms to calculate equal temperament seems actually to have been done in 1630 by a German engineer named Johann Faulhaber. (See **Chapter 7, p. 211**.) Semmens, in "Sauveur," pp. 36–40, discusses Sauveur's representation of octaves by powers of 2 in his 1713 *Mémoires de l'académie royale des sciences*, a pronounced change from his earlier representations in terms of powers of 10. Mooney, "The 'Table of Relations,'" pp. 153–56, discusses Riemann's use of logarithms to base 2 in calculations of relative frequencies.

27 Christensen reflects on the mathematical and theoretical implications of Rameau's abrupt shift in support from mean-tone to equal temperament in *Rameau and Musical Thought*, pp. 201–08. See also Lindley, *Mathematical Models*, pp. 246–48; and **Chapter 7, pp. 204–09**.

and universality. The logarithmic unit of the cent, comprising $^1/_{100}$ of an equal-tempered semitone, was developed by Alexander Ellis, known for his translation of Helmholtz's *Die Lehre von den Tonempfindungen* (1877). From the frequency ratio of an interval of n cents, $2^{n/1200}$, the number of cents in an interval is calculated using logarithms (to base 10).[28] Although devised with equal temperament as its point of reference, the unit of the cent has become an international standard for comparison of intervals in any system of tuning or temperament.

Analogous to the longstanding geometric division of harmonic space, geometric division of time became systematized in thirteenth- and fourteenth-century treatises on discant and polyphony. Perhaps more than coincidentally, it was during this period that the growing practice of algorism (the Arabic system of numeration and computation used in commercial and lay applications) began to be reflected, gradually, in treatises on music.[29] This development, while not revolutionary, was significant, for it reflected a release from Pythagorean hegemony, growing freedom and imagination in recognizing the compatibility of mathematics and music theory, and a turn to more pragmatic mathematics, which played a crucial role in the evolution of the conception and notation of temporal and other relations in music.

Geometric imagery in music theory

While the representation of musical intervals through numbers has undoubtedly been most important to music theory, other kinds of mathematical models have also been adopted. In particular, geometric images as heuristic devices have been affiliated with speculative music theory throughout its history. In practical terms, they may supplement a text with illustrative material, clarifying complex ideas by reducing them to their essentials; they may delineate abstract relations; or they may serve as icons for whole complexes of relations. Moreover, beyond its heuristic value, geometric imagery conceptually telescopes the full range of historical associations of music theory and mathematics from number and proportion to logical and spatial representations of relations.

For example, Boethius and his successors in the Pythagorean tradition utilized geometric figures – ideal, universal shapes constructed mainly of lines, circles, and arcs – to illustrate harmonic ratios and divisions of the monochord.[30] Figure 10.3 shows a

28 Ellis's ingenious invention appears in an appendix to his translation of Helmholtz's *On the Sensations of Tone* (2nd English edn., 1885), pp. 446–51. See also Backus, *Acoustical Foundations*, pp. 292–93. For a short explanation of cents and their calculation, see **Chapter 7, p. 210**.

29 Page, *Discarding Images*, pp. 124–37. See also Eves, *History of Mathematics*, pp. 23–24; and **Chapter 20, pp. 642–45**.

30 See Aaboe, *Episodes*, "Construction of Regular Polygons," pp. 81–85. See also Seebass, "The Illustration of Music Theory," pp. 211–14. Seebass points out that to illustrate schemes of proportions in medieval treatises did not require great graphic or artistic skill, in contrast to other types of manuscript illumination, but such illustrations were important for visualizing the content of a text.

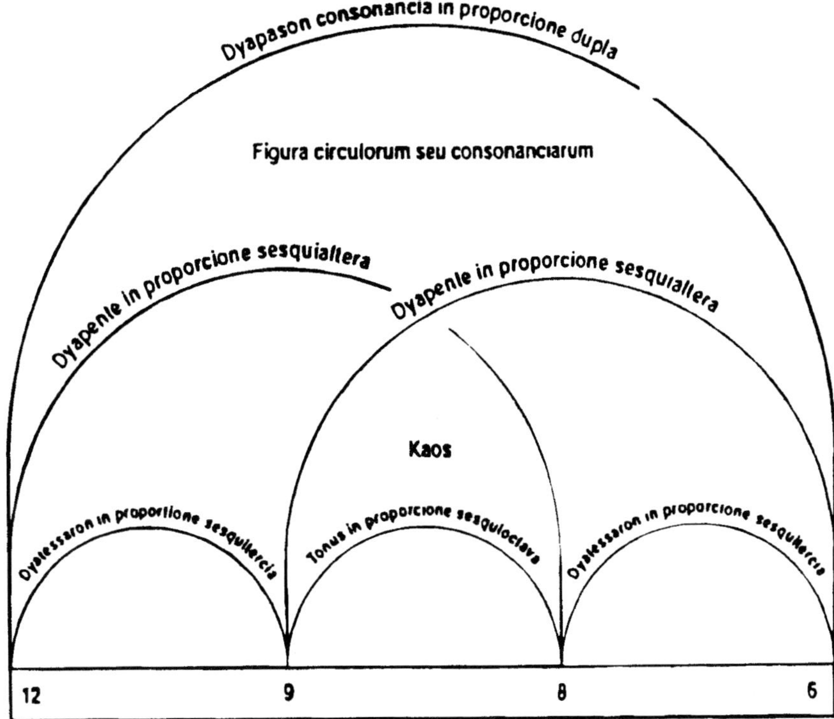

Figure 10.3 Des Murs's representation of the Pythagorean consonances from *Musica <speculativa>*, p. 56

transcription of a diagram from Jehan des Murs's *Musica <speculativa>* (1325) representing the Pythagorean consonances; the diagram illustrates the ratios between all terms of the tetrad 12, 9, 8, and 6, connecting them with semicircular arcs. The symmetric disposition of the consonant ratios (12 : 8 = 4 : 3 and 8 : 6 = 3 : 2) around the ratio of the central tone (9 : 8) brings the dissonant interval into relief as the quiescent adumbration of disorder latent within the order of the consonant ratios. In this way, the example, intended to illustrate the Pythagorean consonances, introduces an interpretive dimension independent of Boethius.[31]

Des Murs's illustration reveals the potential of geometric diagrams to capture through their design non-numerical or qualitative rather than simply quantitative relations. Even earlier, in Guido's *Micrologus* (c. 1026), for example, reticulate patterns of

31 Des Murs, *Musica*, p. 56. It is instructive to compare this illustration with the "Pythagorean lambda" shown in Figure 4.6, p. 115.

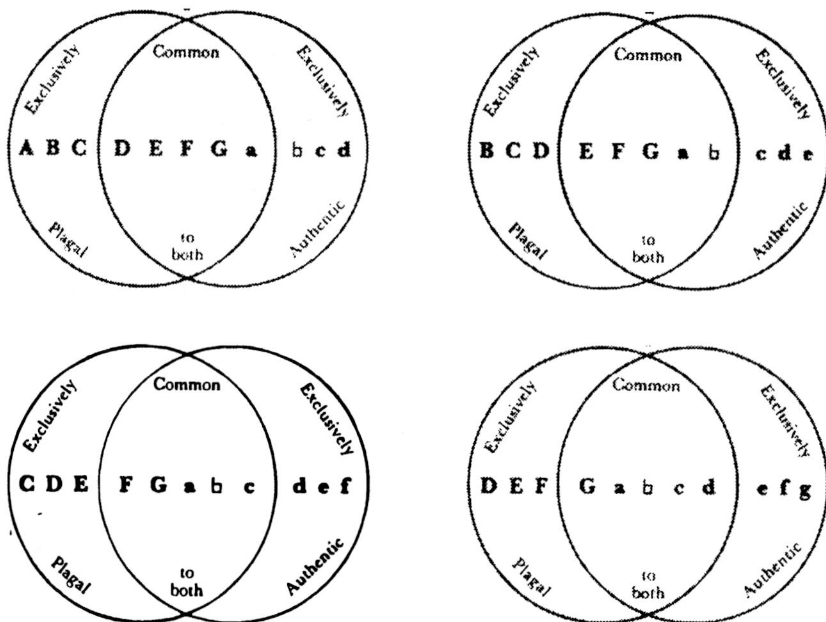

Figure 10.4 John of Afflighem, plagal and authentic modes from *De Musica*, p. 124

connecting and intersecting lines appear in two diagrams modeling the principles of modal affinities and distinctions; recurring patterns in the intervals surrounding a modal final and its upper fifth or lower fourth permitted chants in three of the four modes (*protus*, *deuterus*, and *tritus*) to conclude not only on the modal final, but also on the cofinal.[32] The connecting lines in Guido's diagrams link the letter names representing the pitches which bear the affinitive relation, indicating a recurrence of an intervallic pattern, even though that pattern does not appear in the illustration. A remarkable image in the treatise *De musica* (c. 1100) of John of Afflighem shows four pairs of intersecting circles representing the ranges of the authentic and plagal modes, distinguishing shared and unshared notes in each pair (see Figure 10.4.).[33] The circles portray what in modern parlance would be called the intersection of sets, anticipating by some 800 years the spatial representations of classes of objects named after John Venn (1834–1923) that appear in modern mathematics textbooks. By objectifying a particular relation within a larger concept, and rendering it in a simplified, abstract form, these medieval images convey information and meaning independently of the language and rhetoric of the text they accompany.

Music theory has a long tradition extending back to Boethius and early medieval models of monochord tunings of engaging geometric space to represent harmonic

32 Guido of Arezzo, *Micrologus*, pp. 64–65. See Pesce, *The Affinities and Medieval Transposition*, pp. 18–22. See also **Chapter 11, pp. 348–50.** 33 John of Afflighem, *De Musica*, p. 124.

space.[34] In the seventeenth century, Descartes's revolutionary formulation of the coordinate system and analytical geometry in *La géométrie*, originally an appendix to his monumental philosophical work *Discours de la méthode* (1637), introduced a new method for geometric representation of abstract algebraic relations. His intention was to demonstrate through the coordinate system his new philosophical method, which was based not on authority or received knowledge, but on reason alone.[35] In the coordinate system, the basic geometric unit, the point, represents an ordered pair of real numbers or coordinates: the first number (the abscissa) measures the distance of the point from the horizontal axis, while the second number (the ordinate) measures the distance of the point from the vertical axis. Geometric objects – points, lines, rectilinear figures, and curves – can then be expressed by algebraic equations in which variables are represented by coordinates on a graph.

Cartesian rationalism is evident in representations of tonal relations between pitches or keys identified by positions in a planar space. A familiar example is the archetypal figure of the circle, richly symbolic of completeness and modularity, which was adopted by a number of eighteenth-century theorists to display relations of proximity and remoteness in the system of twenty-four major and minor keys. The musical circles of Heinichen (*Neu erfundene und gründliche Anweisung*, 1711), Mattheson (*Kleine General-Bass Schule*, 1735), and Sorge (*Vorgemach der musicalischen Composition*, 1745–47) were essentially practical devices intended to reveal patterns and associations between keys related by fifth (and relative major and minor keys).[36] Lippius's "circular scale" (*Synopsis musicae novae*, 1612) and Descartes's representation of the octave partitioned into complementary consonant intervals (*Compendium musicae*, 1618) demonstrate the effectiveness of the circle for exemplifying the novel concept of intervallic inversion through complementation within the octave.[37]

A potent two-dimensional image composed of a grid or lattice of parallel horizontal and vertical lines and nodes was employed by Arthur von Oettingen (*Harmoniesystem in dualer Entwicklung*, 1866) and later by Hugo Riemann ("Über das musikalische Hören," 1873, "Die Natur der Harmonik," 1882, and later works) to model intervallic relations between fifth- and third-related chords and keys. The *Tonnetz* displays successive fifths along the rows, major thirds along the columns, and, consequently, minor thirds along the northwest–southeast diagonals.[38] (For examples of a *Tonnetz*, see **Plate 23.1, p. 737 and Plate 25.1, p. 786.**) The spatial representation of the consonant intervals and the

34 See **Chapter 6, passim.** 35 Tiles, *Mathematics and the Image of Reason*, pp. 13–24.

36 Lester, *Between Modes and Keys*, p. 108. See also Neveling, "Geometrische Modelle in der Musiktheorie," pp. 108–20. For an illustration of Heinichen's circle, see **Plate 13.1, p. 445.**

37 Descartes, *Compendium musicae*, p. 22. A transcription of Lippius's "circular scale" is given in Rivera, *German Music Theory*, p. 91.

38 Oettingen's *Tonnetz* and his description of its geometric properties appear in *Harmoniesystem in dualer Entwicklung*, pp. 15–17. Two-dimensional networks of intervals along the horizontal and vertical axes in a two-dimensional space can be back traced to Euler. See Mooney, "The 'Table of Relations'" for a comprehensive study of the history of the *Tonnetz*. See also Busch, *Leonhard Eulers Beitrag*; Lindley, *Mathematical Models*, p. 237. Richard Cohn, in "Neo-Riemannian Operations," generalizes the algebraic structure of the *Tonnetz*.

delineation of the consonant triads as triangles within the *Tonnetz* agreed well with Oettingen's and Riemann's dual system of harmony. Euclidean transformations (translation and reflection) of the triangles, representing triads, modeled harmonic relations.

Combinatorics

Combinatorics, the branch of mathematics concerned with numeration, groupings, and arrangements of elements in finite collections or sets, can be traced back thousands of years to the *I Ching*, the ancient Chinese *Book of Changes*, but entered Western mathematics in the effusive expansion of knowledge in the seventeenth century, and has become an essential part of numerous branches of modern mathematics.[39] Combinatorial processes were incorporated into music theory almost immediately upon their appearance in formal mathematical discourse by Mersenne. Mersenne's zeal for new techniques of computing all possible permutations (ordered arrangements) and combinations (unordered arrangements) of any number of elements almost leaps from the pages of *Harmonie universelle* (1636–37). In the treatise on melody, he tabulates the number of permutations of diatonic melodic units from 1 to 22 pitches over a range of three octaves. The last figure is a colossal number of 22 digits. (see Figure 10.5). He follows this table with not one but two exhaustive tabulations of all 720 permutations of six objects: first the six solmization syllables, then the notated pitches of the diatonic hexachord. The latter tabulation occupies twelve full pages of the treatise, giving an indication of the enormous number of pages that would be required to notate all the melodic permutations of up to 22 notes. The tabulations of solmization syllables and notated pitches correspond to each other in the order of the permutations, though only in the second are the permutations enumerated from 1 to 720. Using state-of-the-art combinatorial formulas, Mersenne carried out rigorous calculations of combinations of elements selected from larger collections of elements (notated pitches, solmization syllables, linguistic symbols including letters and syllables), with and without repetitions.[40]

Through the seventeenth and eighteenth centuries, mathematical *ars combinatoria* inspired numerous discourses on rational methods of musical composition by a variety of authors of theoretical treatises and practical manuals: Kircher (*Musurgia*

39 Combinatorics (today usually called combinatorial mathematics, combinatorial analysis, or combinatorial theory) and probability theory are especially closely interconnected, both historically and conceptually. The distinguished mathematicians Blaise Pascal (1623–62) and Pierre de Fermat (1601–65) recognized the potential for combinatorics to reveal underlying laws of chance, and collaboratively developed theorems for some of the classical combinatorial formulas. (See Edwards, *Pascal's Arithmetical Triangle*, pp. 138–50.)

40 Following are some classical combinatorial formulas used by Mersenne: the number of permutations of n objects, $n! = n \times (n-1) \times (n-2) \ldots 2 \times 1$; the number of permutations, P, of n objects taken k at a time, $P(n, k) = n! / (n-k)!$; the number of combinations, C, of n objects taken r at a time, $C(n, r) = n! / r!(n-r)!$.

1	1
2	2
3	6
4	24
5	120
6	720
7	5040
8	40320
9	362880
10	3628800
11	39916800
12	479001600
13	6227020800
14	87178291200
15	1307674368000
16	20922789888000
17	355687428096000
18	6402373705728000
19	121645100408832000
20	2432902008176640000
21	51090942171709440000
22	1124000727777607680000

Figure 10.5 Mersenne's table of the number of possible melodies (permutations) from 1 to 22 notes (range of the three-octave diatonic gamut), *Harmonie universelle*, Book II, "Livre second de chants," p. 108

universalis, 1650), Printz (*Phrynis Mytilenaeus oder Satyrischer Componist*, 1696), Heinichen (*Der General-bass in der Composition*, 1728), Mattheson (*Der vollkommene Capellmeister*, 1739), Riepel (*Grundregeln zur Tonordnung insgemein*, 1755), Kirnberger (*Der allezeit fertige Menuetten- und Polonoisenkomponist*, 1757), and others.[41] These writings describe compositional decision-making by selection, using chance procedures, from the total compilation of permutations of a given unit such as a melodic or rhythmic figure (or both together) or a two-part melodic-harmonic module. Such parodic treatments of the compositional process, regardless of how removed they may be from the practices of master composers and from their mathematical underpinnings, reveal a cognizance of the finite order of musical materials under specified conditions, the range of possibilities for harmonic or melodic substitution, and of musical rhetoric. Systematic exhaustion of all permutations or combinations of a musical module inevitably leads to some results that transcend normative harmonic or melodic syntax. Riepel, for example, appears, like Mersenne, to have been enraptured by

41 Ratner, "Ars combinatoria," pp. 343–54.

combinatorial possibilities,[42] and in *Grundregeln zur Tonordnung insgemein* tabulates all 120 permutations of the five keys related diatonically to C, exhausting all orderings of interior cadences on diatonic scale degrees.[43]

The science of combinatorics proved to be of inestimable importance in the nineteenth and twentieth centuries in advancing harmonic theories that defy traditional limits. Beginning in the second half of the nineteenth century, a small number of little-known theorists working independently in Austria, France, and the United States – Heinrich Vincent, Anatole Loquin, and Ernst Bacon – adventurously adopted combinatorial principles and processes to quantify methodically the finite resources of the tonal system outside the familiar rubrics (fundamental bass theory, *Stufentheorie*, harmonic dualism, Riemannian functions). Modular arithmetic, that important contribution to number theory codified by the great mathematician Carl Friedrich Gauss (1777–1855) at the turn of the nineteenth century,[44] and equal temperament were accepted by these progressive theorists as axiomatic within a system of twelve congruent classes of pitches.[45]

Vincent. In *Die Einheit in der Tonwelt* (1862), the Austrian music theorist Heinrich Vincent (1819–1901) (pen name for Heinrich Joseph Winzenhörlein) represented the compatibility of the diatonic (major) scale with the chromatic system of twelve pitch classes by mapping each integer from 1 to 12, representing intervals measured in semitones, onto a unique symbol from the set of integers from 1 to 7, enriched where required with the addition of a sharp or flat. The symmetry and modularity of the system of twelve pitch classes were displayed geometrically by inscribing triads and seventh chords as polygons (triangles and rectangles) within circles whose circumference is marked off with twelve nodes representing the twelve pitch classes; the shapes of the inscribed figures can then be compared for similarity or equivalence of their component intervals.[46] In *Ist unsere Harmonielehre wirklich eine Theorie?* [1894], Vincent explicitly adopted arithmetic modulo 12, using the integers (residue classes) from 0 to 11, where 0 represents the tonal center.[47]

42 Riepel, *Grundregeln*, p. 26, includes a table of the number of permutations of from 1 to 40 elements.

43 Ratner, "Ars combinatoria," p. 354.

44 Gauss formulated the algebra of modular arithmetic in *Disquisitiones arithmeticae* (1801) as a means for manipulating large integers in terms of a finite universe of smaller integers through his theory of congruences: two integers a and b are congruent modulo n if and only if n divides the absolute value of the difference a – b, symbolized as $a \equiv b \pmod{n}$. Gauss, *Disquisitiones arithmeticae*, pp. 1–4. See Eves, *History of Mathematics*, p. 523.

45 These theorists did not use the term pitch class, of course, but their conception of twelve equivalence classes of pitches based on octave and enharmonic equivalence and a system of theoretically identical semitones is indubitable. See Wason, "Progressive Harmonic Theory," pp. 58–61, on equal temperament and just intonation in nineteenth-century music theory. Also see **Chapter 14, p. 457**.

46 Vincent, *Die Einheit*, pp. 23–54.

47 No date of publication appears on this short work. (The date 1894 appears in *Baker's Biographical Dictionary of Musicians*, 5th edn., and is inscribed on the back cover of the copy in the Staatsbibliothek zu Berlin.) See Wason, "Progressive Harmonic Theory," pp. 62–65.

Loquin. With evident mathematical training, the French music theorist Anatole Loquin (1834–1903) listed 562 *effets harmoniques* or harmonies of cardinalities 1 to 5 (containing 1 to 5 distinct notes), in *Tableau de tous les effets harmoniques* (1873). Loquin regarded harmonies (or *effets*) of more than five distinct notes (pitch classes) impractical for composition, so he did not enumerate these possibilities, but he created a table giving the number of harmonies of cardinalities 1 to 12.[48] For assistance in deriving specific harmonies, he provided a 12 × 12 matrix whose rows and columns model the twelve pitch classes (see Figure 10.6).[49] In the matrix, the seven diatonic notes are identified by the conventional French *solfège* syllables, and the interstitial notes are identified by their distance (in semitones) from Ut (or C). From a fixed note selected from the first column, the remaining notes of the harmony are selected from the corresponding row. Each harmony of up to five unique notes formed this way is found on the sorted list of 562 harmonies of cardinalities 1 to 5. In his last publication, *L'harmonie rendue claire* (1895), Loquin identifies species (*espèces*) of harmonies of all cardinalities from 1 to 12, effectively grouping them into equivalence classes based on transpositional equivalence.[50] Loquin's ideas, inspired by the rational, combinatorial model afforded by mathematics, were transcendent of the harmonic practice of his time.

Bacon. As a young American piano student in Chicago, Ernst Bacon (1898–1990) employed combinatorial methods to account for all classes of harmonies equivalent under transposition in an unusual monograph entitled "Our Musical Idiom," published in 1917.[51] Bacon's methodology evinces certain similarities with Loquin's, but Bacon's combinatorial processes are more formal and explicit, leading directly to the equivalence classes (based on transpositional equivalence).[52] Bacon's remarkable

48 Loquin, *Tableau de tous les effets* (1873). The table, a refashioning of Pascal's arithmetical triangle, first appeared in Loquin's *Aperçu* (1871), and reappeared in his *Algèbre de l'harmonie* (1884). Loquin calculates 2,048 harmonies of up to 12 notes, exactly half of 4,096 (2^{12}), the number of subsets of the twelve-pitch-class aggregate. Loquin's total of 2,048($=2^{11}$) combinations results from computing the number of combinations of eleven pitch classes (taken 1 to 11 at a time), and joining each combination to a non-duplicating referential pitch class.

49 Figure 10.6 is a reconstruction of the matrix as it appears in *Tableau de tous les effets*, p. 3.

50 Loquin, *L'Harmonie rendu claire*, p. 137. Loquin's calculations were not entirely accurate, but his methodology for recognizing duplications among the cyclic permutations of transpositionally symmetric collections was sophisticated and forward-looking.

51 Bacon, "Our Musical Idiom," pp. 22–44. Bernard discusses some aspects of Bacon's essay in relation to modern pitch-class set theory in "Chord, Collection, and Set," pp. 21–23. See also Baron, "At the Cutting Edge."

52 The universe of 4,096 pitch-class sets may be partitioned into equivalence classes using a variety of criteria. Equivalence under the operations of transposition or inversion is generally assumed in contemporary music theory unless otherwise specified, because of the interval-class-preserving property shared by the two operations. There are 352 classes of pitch-class sets of cardinalities 0 to 12 equivalent under transposition alone and 224 classes equivalent under transposition or inversion. See Morris, *Composition with Pitch-Classes*, pp. 78–81; and Rahn, *Basic Atonal Theory*, pp. 74–75. See also Morris, "Set Groups, Complementation, and Mappings."

	1	2	3	4	5	6	7	8	9	10	11	12	
1	UT	2e son	RÉ	4e son	MI	FA	7e son	SOL	9e son	LA	11e son	SI	1
2	2e son	RÉ	4e son	MI	FA	7e son	SOL	9e son	LA	11e son	SI	UT	2
3	RÉ	4e son	MI	FA	7e son	SOL	9e son	LA	11e son	SI	UT	2e son	3
4	4e son	MI	FA	7e son	SOL	9e son	LA	11e son	SI	UT	2e son	RÉ	4
5	MI	FA	7e son	SOL	9e son	LA	11e son	SI	UT	2e son	RÉ	4e son	5
6	FA	7e son	SOL	9e son	LA	11e son	SI	UT	2e son	RÉ	4e son	MI	6
7	7e son	SOL	9e son	LA	11e son	SI	UT	2e son	RÉ	4e son	MI	FA	7
8	SOL	9e son	LA	11e son	SI	UT	2e son	RÉ	4e son	MI	FA	7e son	8
9	9e son	LA	11e son	SI	UT	2e son	RÉ	4e son	MI	FA	7e son	SOL	9
10	LA	11e son	SI	UT	2e son	RÉ	4e son	MI	FA	7e son	SOL	9e son	10
11	11e son	SI	UT	2e son	RÉ	4e son	MI	FA	7e son	SOL	9e son	LA	11
12	SI	UT	2e son	RÉ	4e son	MI	FA	7e son	SOL	9e son	LA	11e son	12
	1	2	3	4	5	6	7	8	9	10	11	12	

Figure 10.6 Loquin's 12 × 12 matrix in *Tableau de tous les effets harmoniques*, p. 3

achievement was to calculate accurately all classes of transpositionally equivalent pitch-class sets using an elegant and simple procedure: first, interval successions of from two to twelve notes are shown to sum to 12 by analogy using points along the circumference of a circle (including the complementary interval that returns to the point of origin), reducing any combination to the compass of an octave; cyclic permutations (rotations) of interval successions are eliminated, leaving one representative of each harmony; finally, sets of non-cyclic permutations of addends summing to 12 are grouped together as interval combinations. For example, the four five-note harmonies formed by the interval successions <1–1–1–4–5>, <1–1–1–5–4>, <1–1–4–1–5>, and <1–1–5–1–4> are unique, but belong to the same interval combination because they share the same addends that sum to 12; any other permutation of these addends is a (clockwise) cyclic permutation of one of the four interval successions.[53] Bacon summarized his computations in a series of tables, one for each cardinality, and provided the combinatorial formula for each computation.

The three authors just discussed – Vincent, Loquin, and Bacon – have remained almost unknown to the wider music-theoretical community. Their classificatory designs shed little light on harmonic syntax, but through mathematical abstraction, their independent explorations of combinational relations within the system of twelve pitch classes crossed national and music-stylistic boundaries – a reminder of the universality of mathematical relations. Their work exemplified the taxonomic impulse so prevalent in the work of numerous authors in the twentieth century, such as Joseph Matthias Hauer and Paul Hindemith, who attempted to classify pitch materials systematically in the context of a rapidly changing harmonic language. The science of combinatorics also supplies the algorithmic protocol that underlies many of the powerful relations expressed with the aid of the mathematical theories of sets and groups, to which we now turn.

Set theory and group theory

Abstraction, intrinsic overall to mathematics, is especially intrinsic to the theory of sets, since the concept of a set itself is unconstrained. A set, a collection of well-defined objects, is resolutely non-numerical in essence, and thereby endowed with great versatility in terms of the elements that can be amassed as a set, and power in terms of the formal logic of set-theoretic relations. While the capacity of algebra to model deductive reasoning dates back to Descartes and Leibniz, the power of set theory was first articulated in the mid-nineteenth century by George Boole (1815–64), who captured the structure of Aristotle's syllogistic logic using algebraic methods in *An Investigation of the Laws of Thought on Which are Founded the Mathematical Theories of Logic and Possibility* (1854).[54] Boole translated the logical patterns of the syllogism into algebraic statements, revolutionizing algebra by emancipating it from its numerical foundation (a process analogous to the emancipation of geometry from its Euclidean space in the non-Euclidean geometries developed during the nineteenth century); Boole's work also laid the foundation for the study of symbolic or formal logic. In Boolean logic, variables can have only two values – 0 (false) or 1 (true); the logical operations of union (AND), intersection (OR), and negation (NOT) are modeled as algebraic operations.

53 The interval successions of the given combination yield inversionally related members of set classes 5–5 [0,1,2,3,7] and 5–7 [0,1,2,6,7] See Forte, *Structure*, and Morris, *Composition with Pitch-Classes*.

54 Georg Cantor (1845–1918) is usually cited as the founder of mathematical set theory because of his systematic studies of infinite sets of (real) numbers, but the fundamental logical concepts were anticipated by Boole. See Devlin, *Mathematics*, pp. 42–46. See also Eves, *Foundations and Fundamental Concepts of Mathematics*, pp. 243–49.

Babbitt. Interdependencies of mathematics, philosophy, and logic, understood since the time of Plato, were formalized in the programs of analytic philosophy and logical positivism, particularly in the writings of Bertrand Russell (1872–1970) and Rudolf Carnap (1891–1970). During the 1960s and 1970s a group of young music theorists and composers taught by Milton Babbitt (1916–) at Princeton University (including Benjamin Boretz, Michael Kassler, John Rahn, and Godfrey Winham) were guided by principles of analytic philosophy, predicate calculus, and scientism in their endeavors to demonstrate the epistemological foundations of musical structure using the language of formal systems.[55] The thrust of their work was meta-theoretical: to secure a fresh foundation for music theory emphasizing methodological rigor and emulating the scientific method. Some members of the Princeton school, notably Milton Babbitt, in addition to theorizing about the epistemological foundations of music theory, also embraced a rigorously mathematical compositional theory manifesting aggregate-completing arrays.

In a series of three profoundly influential articles published between 1955 and 1961, Babbitt documented the mathematical foundations of the system of twelve pitch classes using the vehicles of set theory and finite group theory.[56] In this seminal body of work, Babbitt generalizes properties of the system of twelve pitch classes exemplified in the twelve-tone works of Schoenberg and Webern, and unveils the foundational principle that the four serial operations (prime or transposition, inversion, retrograde, and retrograde-inversion) form a transformation group.[57] He reveals the systemic basis for invariance, row derivation, and combinatoriality, and generalizes these relations beyond the practice of the Viennese composers, offering insight into his own compositional techniques and a groundbreaking model of pitch relations rooted in contemporary mathematics. Babbitt drew a fundamental distinction between permutational and combinational systems of pitch classes: a permutational system (such as twelve-tone serialism) defines relations on the permutations of all the system's elements, whereas a combinational system (such as the traditional tonal system), defines relations on subsets of the system's totality of elements, which are identified only by their content. The powerful algebraic structures of set theory and group theory interact within and inform both combinational and permutational systems.

55 The following writings epitomize the theoretical and compositional philosophy of the Princeton school of the 1960s and 1970s: Babbitt, "Past and Present Concepts"; Boretz, "Meta-variations"; Kassler, "A Sketch of the Use of Formalized Languages"; Winham, "Composition with Arrays"; Rahn, "Aspects of Musical Explanation"; and "Relating Sets." See also Blasius, *The Music Theory of Godfrey Winham*. For the epistemological underpinnings of music-theoretical positivism, see **Chapter 3, pp. 85–91**.

56 See Babbitt, "Some Aspects" (1955); "Twelve-Tone Invariants" (1960); and "Set Structure" (1961). See also **Chapter 19, pp. 622–24**.

57 Babbitt, "Twelve-Tone Invariants." The concept of a mathematical group was first articulated by Evariste Galois (1811–32), who discovered regular, symmetrical properties among the roots of polynomial equations. Galois's discovery of algebra's underlying rational design inaugurated a new branch of mathematics that was generalized, refined, and extended by a succession of nineteenth-century mathematicians, eventually finding expression in virtually all branches of mathematics and other fields. See Devlin, *Mathematics*, pp. 146–52, and Eves, *History of Mathematics*, pp. 489–93.

Forte. Unordered sets or collections of pitch classes, differentiated by content alone with members represented by the integers from 0 to 11 (with C arbitrarily assigned integer 0, C♯ integer 1, etc.), form the basic unit of pitch-class set theory, formalized by Allen Forte (1926–) in *The Structure of Atonal Music* (1973). In addition to the algebraic set-theoretic relations (union, intersection, complementation, inclusion), algorithms from combinatorics and algebraic structures from group theory inform the relations affiliated with pitch-class set theory. In this way, several mathematical models cooperate in the formulation of the theory of pitch-class sets. The 4,096 (2^{12}) unique pitch-class sets are partitioned into equivalence classes – set classes – whose members are mutually related under the operations of transposition (T_n) and/or inversion (T_nI).[58] The set of twenty-four T_n and T_nI operators fulfill the conditions, listed below, of a mathematical group, where the group operation, represented as "*," is a composition of operators:

property of closure: if operators q and r are members of the set, then $q * r$ is a member of the set;
property of associativity: for all operators q, r, and s, $(q * r) * s = q * (r * s)$;
existence of an *identity* operator, e, such that, for any operator q, $q * e = q$;
for each operator q, the existence of an *inverse* operator, q^{-1}, such that $q * q^{-1} = e$.[59]

Each class of equivalent sets is identified or represented by one of its members, known as the prime form or normal-form representative. In Forte's practice, each set class is further assigned a label consisting of the cardinal number and an ordinal number representing the location of the prime form on a list sorted by the entries in the interval-class vector, a 6-place vector whose entries give, in succession, the number of occurrences of each interval class (from 1 to 6). The interval-class vector catalogues the total interval content of each member of a set class, but cannot serve to identify the set class, because it is possible for the membership of certain discrete pairs of set classes to share the same total interval-class content. This relation is called by Forte the Z-relation, exemplified by set classes 4-Z15 and 4-Z29, 5-Z12 and 5-Z36, 5-Z17 and 5-Z37, 5-Z18 and 5-Z38, and fifteen pairs of hexachordal set classes (out of the total of 50–60 percent of all hexachordal classes).[60]

An example of a set-theoretic segmentation of a short movement is provided below, Forte's 1973 analysis of Webern's *Four Pieces for Violin and Piano*, Op. 7, No. 3 (see Figure 10.7).[61] The analysis consists of a pitch reduction of the score (all markings indicating non-pitch parameters, i.e., rhythmic values, dynamic and articulation markings, etc.,

58 See Morris, *Composition with Pitch-Classes*, pp. 81–84.
59 This summary of the conditions for a mathematical group is adapted from Eves, *Foundations and Fundamental Concepts of Mathematics*, p. 140.
60 Tables showing the prime forms, set names, interval-class vectors, and other information can be found in Forte, *Structure*, pp. 179–81; Morris, *Composition with Pitch-Classes*, pp. 315–20; Rahn, *Basic Atonal Theory*, pp. 140–43; and Straus, *Introduction*, pp. 180–83.
61 Forte, *Structure*, p. 127. Also see **Chapter 3, pp. 82–84** for consideration of the epistemological underpinnings – and implications – of the kind of set segmentation seen in Figure 10.7.

are removed), formal sections (A, B, C, D), and a segmentation of the pitch material into configurations identified with set-labels. The bracket labeled with set-name 6–Z6 below the staves in section A, for example, indicates that the discrete pitch classes of the section, (8,9,10,1,2,3) in normal order, belong to set class 6–Z6, whose prime form is [0,1,2,5,6,7]. Other segments are shown by solid-line and occasionally dashed-line enclosures, the former indicating primary, the latter indicating composite segments, and additional segmentations in sections B and C are shown on the separate single staff.

Forte's segmentation exemplifies the basic set-theoretic relations: equivalence, union, intersection, complementation, and inclusion.[62] Equivalent pitch-class sets are easily recognized by recurring set-labels, such as 4-9, 4-18, 5-7, 5-19, 6-Z13. For example, the 6-Z13 set in the C section, comprising all pitches except the lowest A♯, in normal order (8,9,11,0,2,3), is a transposition by T_8 of the 6-Z13 set that comprises the entire D section, in normal order (0,1,3,4,6,7); the two 4-18 sets in the supplementary segmentation below the staves in section B, (5,6,11,2) and (2,3,6,9) in normal order, are inversionally related to each other under T_8I. Certain set-theoretic relations may be described as either literal (where the relation obtains between specific pitch-class sets) or abstract (where the relation obtains between set classes). Relations of literal union and intersection of sets are apparent through the union or intersection of the enclosures surrounding sets identified in the analysis. No example of literal complementation (the relation by which the union of one set with another exhausts the aggregate) appears in this segmentation, but the relation of abstract complementation obtains between three pairs of set classes, 4-Z15 and 8-Z15, 5-6 and 7-6, and 6-Z6 and 6-Z38; that is, within the complementary pairs, each set is equivalent (under some value(s) of T_n and/or T_nI) to the other's literal complement. (The complementation relation is easily recognized by the identical ordinal number in pairs of sets of complementary cardinalities.) The complementary set pair 4–Z15 and 8–Z15 identified in section B exhibits an embedded complement relation; that is, the smaller set (4–Z15) is literally included within the larger (8–Z15). The more general relation of literal inclusion is also self-evident in the segmentation; for example, in section C, the 6–Z13 and 4-9 sets identified are literally contained within the larger 7-4 set, and in section B, the 8–Z15 set is a superset of all the smaller sets identified within it. Many examples of abstract inclusion relations, whereby any member of a set class represented in the segmentation includes or is included in one or more members of another set class represented, obtain in this segmentation. For example, 8–Z15 bears the abstract inclusion relation with fourteen of the nineteen identified set classes, and 4-8 bears the relation with ten.

As this informal overview of set-theoretic relations in Forte's segmentation suggests, the basic algebraic operations of pitch-class set theory are relatively simple. As a means to model relations governing harmonic or pitch organization in complete

62 Formal explanations of the relations described in this paragraph can be found in the works cited in note 60 above.

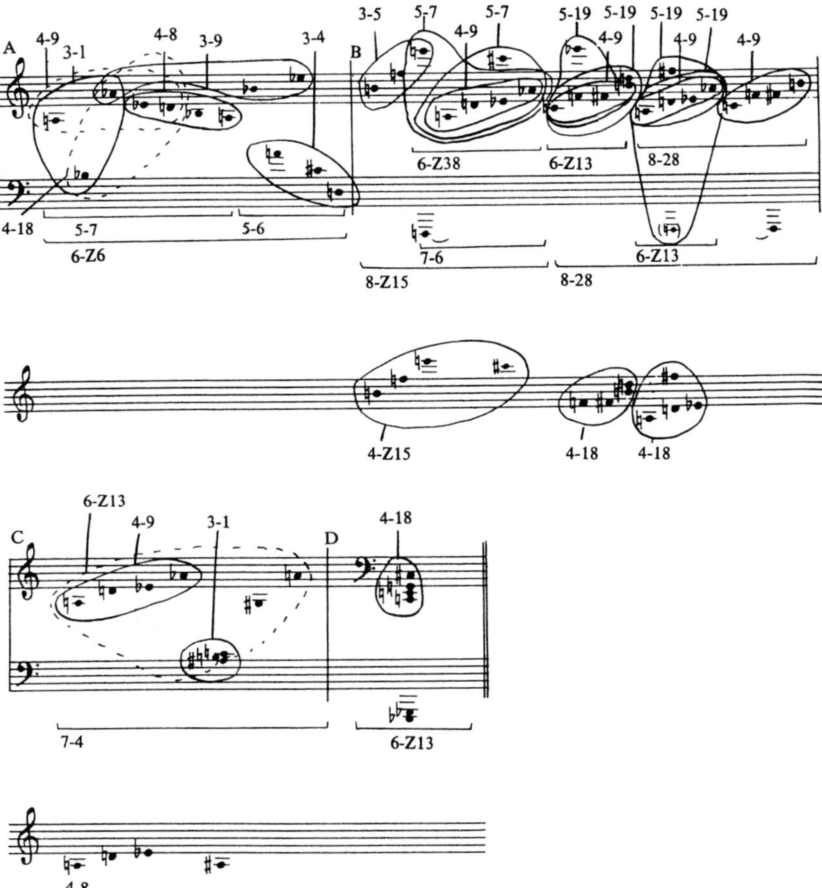

Figure 10.7 Forte's analytical segmentation of Webern, Op. 7, No. 3, *The Structure of Atonal Music*, p. 127

formal units or compositions, Forte developed a theory of set-complexes, which extends the relations of inclusion and complementation to congregate cohesive families of set classes.[63] A K complex comprises a nexus pair of complementary set classes and all set classes bearing an abstract inclusion relation with either member of the nexus pair; the more exclusive Kh subcomplex comprises all set classes bearing an abstract inclusion relation with both members of the nexus pair. More recently, Forte advanced an alternate methodology for congregating families of set classes (non-exclusively) into twelve *genera* (and four supragenera); while some set classes belong to more than one genus, each genus as whole models a distinctive membership of set classes that

63 Forte, *Structure*, pp. 93–100.

is evocative of general intervallic characteristics originating in its progenitor trichord(s). The genera are determined by a systematic process beginning with one or two trichordal progenitors (identified by unique patterns of interval distribution), from which certain rules, based on inclusion relations and complementation to guarantee internal consistency and symmetry within the genus, determine the set-class membership of each genus.[64]

Some concepts associated with pitch-class set theory have been explored by other theorists isolated for various reasons from the mainstream developments initiated by Babbitt and Forte. Howard Hanson (*Harmonic Materials of Modern Music*, 1960), for example, formulated a construct to represent the total interval content of a set using categories corresponding to the six interval classes, and produced, as was his objective, a complete inventory of all (220) classes of sets of cardinalities 2 to 10 equivalent under the operations of transposition or inversion. Despite this achievement and other flashes of insight, Hanson did not explicate clearly the eclectic methodology and all the premises behind his taxonomy; nor did he articulate any analytical applications and only vaguely suggested compositional applications. Not surprisingly, his work remains only of historical interest.[65]

The Romanian composer and theorist Anatol Vieru (*The Book of Modes*, 1993), by contrast, independently of North American theoretical developments, evolved a theory of pitch-class sets, which he calls modes, in which transpositionally related equivalence classes are determined on the basis of identity of the interval successions of their members.[66] After setting forth the algebraic foundation of the system in arithmetic modulo 12 and revealing the group-theoretic properties that underlie the system, Vieru outlines the classical set-theoretic relations, illustrating concepts with musical examples from a wide range of historical periods, genres, and composers such as Beethoven, Chopin, Debussy, Messiaen, and Scriabin, as well as himself and other Romanian composers. With its foundation in rigorously logical, combinatorial processes, the theory is presented by Vieru as universal, well suited to the mathematical orientation of late twentieth-century theoretical thought, but serving to model musical relations of any age or culture.

The algebraic structures of set theory and group theory, which initially inspired music theories designed to explain harmonic innovations in the refractory repertoire of post-tonal music, have been extended to theoretical studies of other musical parameters and harmonic languages or systems. Marvin and Laprade, for example, employ set-theoretic procedures to classify melodic and other contour relations by formulating

64 Forte, "Pitch-Class Set Genera."

65 Bernard, "Chord, Collection, and Set," pp. 45–49, discusses Hanson's work in light of Forte's set theory.

66 Some features of Vieru's theories are presented in his article "Modalism – A 'Third World'" See also Chrisman, "Describing Structural Aspects of Pitch-Class Sets Using Successive Interval Arrays."

equivalence classes of "contour segments" based on defined canonical operations and relations founded in group theory.[67] A growing number of mathematicians and theorists continue to explore and generalize the algebraic structure of the diatonic system, and scales or tonal systems of disparate origins, ranging from diatonic or microtonal scale systems to medieval or non-Western modal systems.[68]

As previously noted, the group-theoretic infrastructure of the system of twelve pitch classes has been comprehensively disclosed by Robert Morris, whose work demonstrates formally that the canonical twelve-tone operators of pitch-class set theory form a mathematical group, irrespective of the size of the set or segment to which they are applied.[69] This important point reveals the power of group theory to model deep-seated systemic relations disengaged from the characteristics of a specific harmonic language or musical style. The powerful model of the finite mathematical group encloses the network of relations within a system, making all relations synchronously apprehensible, and suggests the metaphor of space traversed by the relations or operations of the system. The spaces in a system of musical objects may represent ranges or distances in pitch frequencies, registral positions, temporal units or spans, or any parameter in which shifts may be measured. While the spatial metaphor is not exclusive to the mathematical group (i.e., not all musical spaces are groups), the interaction of objects and relations embedded in the group concept offers a particularly compelling facility through which to form a mental image of musical space.

Transformation theory

The metaphor of space lies at the heart of David Lewin's profound treatise *Generalized Musical Intervals and Transformations* (1987), in which he uses formal mathematics to develop two models of unconstrained abstraction: the GIS (generalized interval system) and the transformation network. A GIS delineates a formal space consisting of three elements: (1) a set of musical objects (e.g., pitches, rhythmic durations, time spans, or time points); (2) a mathematical group of generalized intervals (any measurable distance, span, or motion between a pair of objects in the system); (3) a function that maps all possible pairs of objects in the system (its Cartesian product) into the group of intervals.[70] Lewin provides numerous examples of GISs, including the diatonic hexachord under

67 Marvin and Laprade, "Relating Musical Contours."

68 For example: Clough, "Aspects of Diatonic Sets"; "Diatonic Interval Sets"; and "Diatonic Interval Cycles"; Clough and Myerson, "Variety and Multiplicity in Diatonic Systems"; Clough, Engebretsen, and Kochavi, "Scales, Sets, and Interval Cycles"; Balzano, "The Group-Theoretic Description"; Agmon, "A Mathematical Model"; and "Coherent Tone Systems"; Carey and Clampitt, "Aspects of Well-Formed Scales"; and "Regions."

69 Morris, *Composition with Pitch-Classes*. Many of the group-theoretic properties of the canonical operators were demonstrated by Morris in earlier writings, including "Set Groups, Complementation, and Mappings" and "Combinatoriality without the Aggregate."

70 Lewin, *Generalized Musical Intervals*, pp. 16–30.

addition modulo 6, the diatonic collection of pitch classes under addition modulo 7, the twelve pitch classes under addition modulo 12, and the infinite set of pitches derivable under addition in just intonation, as well as temporal examples in which the system's objects are time points or durations and the intervals are differences or ratios.

A transformation network recasts the role of generalized intervals, modeling actions upon or motions between objects, rather than the extensions that join them.[71] A GIS reflects the relative positions of objects in the system, in Cartesian fashion, by tracing the extensions between them. In a transformation network, the gesture which moves or transports one object to another within the system appropriates the role of the intervals in a GIS. Motion in a transformation network is not – or at least not necessarily – temporal, but spatial. A transformation network defines the objects of a system kinetically in terms of the transformations upon them: objects and their transformations are joined as two aspects of the same entity. Lewin's models of the GIS and transformation networks suggest an uncountable number of conceivable musical spaces, limited only by the imaginations and conceptual faculties of music theorists.

An apparent outpouring of music-theoretical writings inspired by Lewin's pioneering work in transformation theory – by authors such as Robert Morris, Richard Cohn, Brian Hyer, John Clough, Henry Klumpenhouwer, and Norman Carey and David Clampitt – attests to the fertility of the concept to model both familiar and unexplored relations between musical objects and classes of objects.[72] The work of these theorists – much of it presented under the rubric of "neo-Riemannian" theory – concerns such diverse topics as nineteenth-century harmonic practice, twentieth-century harmonic and voice-leading practice, and the transformational properties of diatonic and other scale systems.[73] These writings demonstrate not only the power of mathematics to formalize relations of interest to music theorists, but also the necessity for mathematical rigor in order to arrive at the level of abstraction and generality required to portray complex, spatial conceptions in words, symbols, and geometric images.

Prescriptive applications

Music theory in the twentieth century came to be characterized in large part by its association with mathematics. Modernist attitudes toward harmonic language, rhythm,

71 Ibid., pp. 157–74. See also **Chapter 14, pp. 465–73** for a more detailed account of transformation networks. 72 See Cohn, "Introduction to Neo-Riemannian Theory."

73 The following is a partial list of some recent writings invoking the formalism of the transformation groups or networks in three areas: (1) studies of nineteenth-century harmonic practice – Hyer, "Reimag(in)ing Riemann"; Cohn, "Maximally Smooth Cycles"; and "Neo-Riemannian Operations"; (2) studies of twentieth-century harmonic and voice-leading practice – Morris, "Compositional Spaces and Other Territories"; and "Voice-Leading Spaces"; Lewin, "Cohn Functions"; and "Some Ideas About Voice-Leading"; (3) studies of transformational properties of diatonic and other scale systems – Carey and Clampitt, "Aspects of Well-Formed Scales"; "Clough, "Diatonic Interval Sets and Transformational Structures"; and "Diatonic Interval Cycles and Hierarchical Structure."

and form that characterize much European and American music of the first half of the twentieth century are also evident in the many prescriptive writings whose authors sought to refashion traditional theoretical formulations or to reform the ways in which they were taught. A conspicuous number of such authors invoked mathematics, with varying degrees of rigor and practical, theoretical, or analytical consequence. Some, such as Alois Hába (*Neue Harmonielehre*, 1927) and Joseph Yasser (*A Theory of Evolving Tonality*, 1932), proposed new microtonal tuning systems that divide the octave equally or unequally into a number of intervals greater than twelve. Joseph Schillinger's hubristic two-volume tome (*The Schillinger System of Musical Composition*, 1946) purports to classify conventional resources of musical composition – rhythm, scales, melody, harmony, counterpoint, variation techniques – in algebraic and geometric terms; his philosophical work (*The Mathematical Basis of the Arts*, 1948) attempts to develop a general theory of artistic production based on the scientific method and mathematical principles. While Schillinger's work has been largely discredited for intrinsic and extrinsic methodological flaws, his recourse to mathematics as a means to reevaluate traditional theories of music is most symptomatic of its time.[74] In a sympathetic vein, Henry Cowell (*New Musical Resources*, 1930) reconceives temporal relations in music (rhythm, meter, and tempo) by rendering as durational spans the ratios of overtones to their fundamentals.

Some early twentieth-century authors took a less evolutionary theoretical approach to reinvigorating musical resources, adopting a transformational attitude toward musical materials. Bernhard Ziehn (*Five- and Six-Part Harmonies*, 1911, and *Canonical Studies*, 1912), for example, reconceived melodic inversion as a geometric transformation in which pitches and gestures are reflected around an axial pitch, and exact (not generic) intervallic distances between successive notes are preserved, regardless of the effects on tonal syntax; he extended the notion of geometric transformation to musical texture, inverting all pitch constituents around a defined axis of symmetry. Serge Taneiev (*Convertible Counterpoint in the Strict Style*, 1909) drew on the precision of algebraic symbols and equations to calculate and classify transformations of voices in invertible counterpoint, both spatially (vertically) and temporally (horizontally). In contrast to Ziehn, whose writings are dominated by musical examples and minimal explanatory text, Taneiev outlines his mathematical approach at the outset and concludes his treatise by explaining that its underlying objective has been to develop powers of reason as a basis for revitalizing what he perceives as the stagnant state of musical composition.[75]

In the second half of the twentieth century, as we have just seen, music theory became characterized by its remarkable integration of rigorous and sophisticated formulations from modern mathematics, specifically the logical, algebraic, and geometric

74 Backus, "Pseudo-Science in Music." Schillinger's writings, and those of his compatriot, Nicolas Slonimsky, insofar as they relate to theories of scale and chord construction, are discussed in Bernard, "Chord, Collection, and Set," pp. 32–38.

75 Taneiev, *Convertible Counterpoint*, p. 301.

apparatus of set theory and group theory. Developments in computer technology beginning in the 1950s allowed for unprecedented accuracy and speed in complex numerical calculation, providing theorists and composers with the technology to achieve emancipatory objectives articulated earlier in the century. Composers of electronic music, such as Herbert Eimert and Karlheinz Stockhausen, exploited the mathematical resources of the digital computer to reconfigure artificially the generation, structure, and acoustic production of sound itself. Computer technology also inspired attempts to formulate theories of music from the mathematical model of information theory, which used probability functions to measure information and redundancy in order to quantify assessments of musical syntax or style.[76] While the information theory model proved unable to make profound or long-lasting contributions to music theory, its influence endures in expectancy-based theories of music cognition and perception. In terms of speculative music theory since the 1960s, computer technology has played and continues to play an important part in the work of Forte, Morris, Clough, and others discussed earlier, in calculating and sorting the often complex results of mathematical algorithms.

The twentieth-century intensification of the bond between music theory and mathematics may have originated in response to developments in compositional technique that demanded new paradigms for theorizing about pitch materials and their organization, but the generalizing power of mathematics pervades speculative music theory independent of compositional practice.[77] The dual mathematical principles of methodological rigor and epistemological conviction cannot be overestimated in the shaping of the discipline of music theory in the second half of the twentieth century. Formal mathematical apparatus stemming from combinatorics, set theory, and group theory (and hence also from logic and graph theory) permits a level of clarity and exactitude that can yield solutions, insights, and discoveries inaccessible through other means.

Mathematics brings to music theory not only the technical means to perform measurements and computations, and the statistical means to correlate data, but also the conceptual means, symbols, and vocabulary needed in order to model musical relations of various kinds and to delineate levels of abstraction. Mathematics – conceived broadly as the study of quantities, magnitudes, shapes, motions, and relations – has historically provided a dynamic frame of reference for speculative thought in music theory. As the scope and techniques of mathematics have evolved, its influence upon music theory has escalated emphatically through the twentieth century, embracing more recently formulated branches of modern mathematics. The extraordinary association of mathematics and music has inspired music theory throughout its history, and shows no signs of dissipation at the dawn of the new millennium.

76 See Cohen, "Information Theory and Music."

77 For example, Morris's *Composition with Pitch-Classes* is a text that can serve both music theorists and composers seeking to study the mathematical foundations of pitch and pitch-class materials.

Bibliography

Aaboe, A. *Episodes from the Early History of Mathematics*, New York, Random House, 1964

Agmon, E. "A Mathematical Model of the Diatonic System," *JMT* 33 (1989), pp. 1–25

"Coherent Tone Systems: A Study in the Theory of Diatonicism," *JMT* 40 (1996), pp. 39–59

Babbitt, M. "Some Aspects of Twelve-Tone Composition," *The Score and I.M.A. Magazine* 12 (1955), pp. 53–61

"Twelve-Tone Invariants as Compositional Determinants," *Musical Quarterly* 46 (1960), pp. 246–59

"Set Structure as a Compositional Determinant," *JMT* 5 (1961), pp. 72–94; reprint in *Perspectives on Contemporary Music Theory*, ed. B. Boretz and E. Cone, New York, Norton, 1972, pp. 129–47

"Past and Present Concepts of the Nature and Limits of Music," in *Perspectives on Contemporary Music Theory*, ed. B. Boretz and E. Cone, New York, Norton, 1972, pp. 3–9

Backus, J. "Pseudo-Science in Music," *JMT* 4 (1960), pp. 221–32

The Acoustical Foundations of Music, 2nd edn., New York, Norton, 1977

Bacon, E. "Our Musical Idiom," *The Monist* 27 (1917), pp. 560–607

Baeumer-Mertens, D. "Gedanken zu einem Ansatzpunkt in der Beziehung von Musik und Mathematik," in *Colloquium: Festschrift Martin Vogel zum 65. Geburtstag*, ed. H. Schröder, Bad Honnef, G. Schröder, 1988, pp. 9–10

Balzano, G. "The Group-Theoretic Description of 12-Fold and Microtonal Pitch Systems," *Computer Music Journal* 40 (1980), pp. 66–84

Barbera, A., ed., *Music Theory and Its Sources*, South Bend, University of Notre Dame Press, 1990

Barbour, J. M. "Musical Logarithms," *Scripta Mathematica* 7 (1943), pp. 21–31

Tuning and Temperament: A Historical Survey, East Lansing, Michigan State College Press, 1953

Barker, A. *Greek Musical Writings*, 2 vols., Cambridge University Press, 1984–89

Baron, C., K., "At the Cutting Edge: Three American Theorists at the End of the Nineteenth Century," *International Journal of Musicology* 2 (1993), pp. 193–247

Berger, A. M. Busse, *Mensuration and Proportion Signs*, Oxford University Press, 1993

Bernard, J. "Chord, Collection, and Set in Twentieth-Century Theory," in *Music Theory in Concept and Practice*, ed. J. Baker, D. Beach, and J. Bernard, University of Rochester Press, 1997, pp. 11–51

Blasius, L. *The Music Theory of Godfrey Winham*, Princeton University Press, 1997

Boethius, A. *Fundamentals of Music*, trans. C. Bower, ed. C. Palisca, New Haven, Yale University Press, 1989

Bogart, K. *Introductory Combinatorics*, Boston, Pitman, 1983

Boretz, B. "Metavariations: Studies in the Foundations of Musical Thought," *Perspectives of New Music* 8 (1969), pp. 1–74; 8 (1970), pp. 49–111; 9 (1970), pp. 23–42; 9–10 (1971), pp. 232–70; 11/1 (1972), pp. 146–223; 11/2 (1973), pp. 156–203

Brown, M. and D. Dempster, "The Scientific Image of Music Theory," *JMT* 33 (1989), pp. 65–106

Budden, F. *The Fascination of Groups*, Cambridge University Press, 1972

Burkert, W. *Lore and Science in Ancient Pythagoreanism*, trans. E. Minar, Jr., Cambridge, MA, Harvard University Press, 1972

Busch, H. *Leonhard Eulers Beitrag zur Musiktheorie*, Regensburg, G. Bosse, 1970

Cameron, P. *Combinatorics: Topics, Techniques, Algorithms*, Cambridge University Press, 1994

Carey, N. and D. Clampitt, "Aspects of Well-Formed Scales," *MTS* 11 (1989), pp. 187–206

"Regions: A Theory of Tonal Spaces in Early Medieval Treatises," *JMT* 40 (1996), pp. 113–47

Chrisman, R. "Describing Structural Aspects of Pitch-Class Sets Using Successive Interval Arrays," *JMT* 21 (1977), pp. 1–28

Christensen, T. *Rameau and Musical Thought in the Enlightenment*, Cambridge University Press, 1993

Clough, J. "Aspects of Diatonic Sets," *JMT* 23 (1979), pp. 45–61

"Diatonic Interval Sets and Transformational Structures," *Perspectives of New Music* 18 (1979–80), pp. 461–82

review of *Generalized Musical Intervals and Transformations*, by D. Lewin, *MTS* 11 (1989), pp. 226–31

"Diatonic Interval Cycles and Hierarchical Structure," *Perspectives of New Music* 32 (1994), pp. 228–53

Clough, J., N. Engebretsen, and J. Kochavi, "Scales, Set, and Interval Cycles: A Taxonomy," *MTS* 21 (1999), pp. 74–104

Clough, J. and G. Myerson, "Variety and Multiplicity in Diatonic Systems," *JMT* 29 (1985), pp. 249–70

Cohen, H. *Quantifying Music: The Science of Music at the First Stage of the Scientific Revolution, 1580–1650*, Dordrecht, D. Reidel, 1984

Cohen, J. "Information Theory and Music," *Behavioral Science* 7 (1962), pp. 137–63

Cohn, R. "Maximally Smooth Cycles, Hexatonic Systems, and the Analysis of Late Nineteenth-Century Triadic Progressions," *MA* 15 (1996), pp. 22–40

"Neo-Riemannian Operations, Parsimonious Trichords, and Their *Tonnetz* Representations," *JMT* 41 (1997), pp. 1–66

"Introduction to Neo-Riemannian Theory: A Survey and Historical Perspective," *JMT* 42 (1998), pp. 167–80

Cowell, H. *New Musical Resources* (1930), New York, Something Else Press, 1969

Crocker, R. "Pythagorean Mathematics and Music," *Journal of Aesthetics and Art Criticism* 22/23 (1963–64), pp. 189–98, 325–35

Descartes, R. *Compendium of Music* (1650), trans. W. Robert, American Institute of Musicology, 1961

Devlin, K. *Mathematics: The Science of Patterns*, New York, Scientific American Library, 1997

Dostrovsky, S. "Early Vibration Theory: Physics and Music in the Seventeenth Century," *Archive for History of Exact Sciences* 14 (1974), 169–218

Edwards, A. *Pascal's Arithmetical Triangle*, London, C. Griffin, 1987

Euler, L. *Tentamen novae theoriae musicae*, St. Petersburg, Academiae Scientiarum, 1739; facs. New York, Broude, 1968

Eves, H. *An Introduction to the History of Mathematics*, 6th edn., Philadelphia, Saunders College Publishing, 1990

Eves, H. and C. Newsom, *An Introduction to the Foundations and Fundamental Concepts of Mathematics*, rev. edn., New York, Holt, Rinehart and Winston, 1965

Faber, R. *Foundations of Euclidean and Non-Euclidean Geometry*, New York, M. Dekker, 1983

Forte, A. *The Structure of Atonal Music*, New Haven, Yale University Press, 1973

"Pitch-Class Set Genera and the Origin of Modern Harmonic Species," *JMT* 32 (1988), pp. 187–271

Gans, D. *Transformations and Geometries*, New York, Appleton-Century-Crofts, 1969

Gauss, C. *Disquisitiones arithmeticae*, Leipzig, G. Fleischer, 1801; trans. of 2nd edn. (1870) by A. Clark, New Haven, Yale University Press, 1966

Greenberg, M. *Euclidean and Non-Euclidean Geometries: Development and History*, 3rd edn., New York, W. H. Freeman, 1993

Grossman, I. and W. Magnus, *Groups and their Graphs*, New York, Random House, 1964

Gullberg, J. *Mathematics: From the Birth of Number*, New York, Norton, 1997

Hába, A. *Neue Harmonielehre des diatonischen, chromatischen, Viertel-, Drittel-, Sechstel-, und Zwölftel-Tonsystems*, Leipzig, Kistner and Siegel, 1927

Hanson, H. *Harmonic Materials of Modern Music: Resources of the Tempered Scale*, New York, Appleton-Century-Crofts, 1960

Helmholtz, H. *On the Sensations of Tone as a Physiological Basis for the Theory of Music* (4th edn., 1877), trans. A. J. Ellis, 2nd edn., London, Longman and Green, 1885; reprint New York, Dover, 1954

Howe, H. "Some Combinational Properties of Pitch Structures," *Perspectives of New Music* 4 (1965), pp. 45–61

Hyer, B. "Reimag(in)ing Riemann,' *JMT* 39 (1995), pp. 1–38

James, J. *The Music of the Spheres: Music, Science, and the Natural Order of the Universe*, New York, Grove Press, 1993

John of Afflighem, *De musica*, trans. W. Babb, ed. C. Palisca as *On Music*, in *Hucbald, Guido, and John on Music: Three Medieval Treatises*, New Haven, Yale University Press, 1978, pp. 87–190

Kassler, M. "A Sketch of the Use of Formalized Languages for the Assertion of Music," *Perspectives of New Music* 1 (1963), pp. 83–94

Kirnberger, J. *Der allezeit fertige Polonoisen und Menuettencomponist*, Berlin, G. Ludewig Winter, 1757

Kline, M. *Mathematics for the Nonmathematician*, New York, Dover, 1967

Mathematics: The Loss of Certainty, Oxford University Press, 1980

Lasserre, F. *The Birth of Mathematics in the Age of Plato*, London, Hutchison, 1964

Lester, J. *Between Modes and Keys: German Theory 1592–1802*, Stuyvesant, NY, Pendragon Press, 1989

Compositional Theory in the Eighteenth Century, Cambridge, MA, Harvard University Press, 1992

Levin, F., tr., *The Manual of Harmonics of Nicomachus the Pythagorean*, Grand Rapids, MI, Phanes Press, 1994

The Harmonics of Nicomachus and the Pythagorean Tradition, The American Philological Association, 1975

Lewin, D. *Generalized Musical Intervals and Transformations*, New Haven, Yale University Press, 1987

"Cohn Functions," *JMT* 40 (1996), pp. 181–216

"Some Ideas about Voice-Leading Between Pc-sets," *JMT* 42 (1998), pp. 15–72

Lindley, M. *Lutes, Viols and Temperaments*, Cambridge University Press, 1984

Lindley, M. and R. Turner-Smith, *Mathematical Models of Musical Scales: A New Approach*, Bonn, Verlag für systematische Musikwissenschaft, 1993

"An Algebraic Approach to Mathematical Models of Scales," *Music Theory Online* 0/3 (1993)

Lippman, E. *Musical Thought in Ancient Greece*, New York, Columbia University Press, 1964

Loquin, A. *Aperçu sur la possibilité d'établir une notation représentant d'une manière à la fois exacte et suffisamment abréviative les successions harmoniques*, Bordeaux, Féret et fils, 1871

Tableau de tous les effets harmoniques: de une à cinq notes inclusivement au nombre de cinq cent soixantedeux, Bordeaux, Féret et fils, 1873

Algèbre de l'harmonie, traité complet d'harmonie moderne, Paris, Richault, 1884

L'Harmonie rendue claire et mise à la portée de tous les musiciens, Paris, Richault, 1895

Mariarz, E. and T. Greenwood, *Greek Mathematical Philosophy*, New York, F. Ungar, 1968

Martino, D. "The Source Set and its Aggregate Formations," *JMT* 5 (1961), pp. 224–73

Marvin, E. and P. Laprade, "Relating Musical Contours: Extensions of a Theory for Contour," *JMT* 31 (1987), pp. 225–67

Mattheson, J. *Kleine General-Bass Schule*, Hamburg, J. C. Kißner, 1735

McClain, E. *The Pythagorean Plato: Prelude to the Song Itself*, Stony Brook, NY, N. Hays, 1978

Mersenne, M. *Harmonie universelle*, Paris, S. Cramoisy, 1636–37; facs. Paris, Centre National de la Recherche Scientifique, 1963 and 1986

Mooney, K. "The 'Table of Relations' and Music Psychology in Hugo Riemann's Harmonic Theory," Ph.D. diss., Columbia University (1996)

Morris, R. "Set Groups, Complementation, and Mappings among Pitch-Class Sets," *JMT* 26 (1982), pp. 101–44

"Combinatoriality Without the Aggregate," *Perspectives of New Music* 21 (1982–83), pp. 432–86

Composition with Pitch-Classes: A Theory of Compositional Design, New Haven, Yale University Press, 1987

"Compositional Spaces and Other Territories," *Perspectives of New Music* 33 (1995), pp. 328–58

"Voice-Leading Spaces," *MTS* 20 (1998), pp.175–208

Murs, J. de, ed. S. Fast, as Johannes de Muris, '*musica <speculativa>*', Ottawa, Institute of Medieval Music, 1994

Neveling, A. "Geometrische Modelle in der Musiktheorie: *Mos geometricus* und Quintenzirkel," in *Colloquium: Festschrift Martin Vogel zum 65. Geburtstag*, ed. H. Schröder, Bad Honnef, G. Schröder, 1988, pp. 103–20

Oettingen, A. von. *Harmoniesystem in dualer Entwicklung: Studien zur Theorie der Musik*, Dorpat and Leipzig, W. Gläser, 1866

Page, C. *Discarding Images: Reflections on Music and Culture in Medieval France*, Oxford, Clarendon Press, 1993

Palisca, C. V. "Scientific Empiricism in Musical Thought," in *Seventeenth Century Science and the Arts*, ed. H. Rhys, Princeton University Press, 1961, pp. 91–137

Humanism in Italian Renaissance Musical Thought, New Haven, Yale University Press, 1985

Pesce, D. *The Affinities and Medieval Transposition*, Bloomington, Indiana University Press, 1987

Planchart, A. "A Study of the Theories of Giuseppe Tartini," *JMT* 4 (1960), pp. 32–61

Rahn, J. "Aspects of Musical Explanation," *Perspectives of New Music* 17 (1979), pp. 204–24

"Logic, Set Theory, Music Theory," *College Music Symposium* 19 (1979), pp. 114–27

"Relating Sets," *Perspectives of New Music* 18 (1980), pp. 483–502
Basic Atonal Theory, New York, Longman, 1980
Rameau, J.-P. *Treatise on Harmony* (1722), trans. P. Gossett, New York, Dover, 1971
Ratner, L. "*Ars Combinatoria*: Chance and Choice in Eighteenth-Century Music," in *Studies in Eighteenth-Century Music*, ed. H. Landon and R. Chapman, London, G. Allen and Unwin, 1970, pp. 343–60
Riepel, J. *Grundregeln zur Tonordung insgemein*, Frankfurt, C. Wagner, 1755
Riordan, J. *An Introduction to Combinatorial Analysis*, New York, Wiley, 1958 and 1967; Princeton University Press, 1978
Rivera, B. *German Music Theory in the Early 17th Century: The Treatises of Johannes Lippius*, Ann Arbor, UMI Research Press, 1980
Roeder, J. "A Geometric Representation of Pitch-Class Series," *Perspectives of New Music* 25 (1987), pp. 362–409
Rothgeb, "Some Uses of Mathematical Concepts in Theories of Music," *JMT* 10 (1966), pp. 200–15
Rotman, J. *Journey into Mathematics: An Introduction to Proofs*, Englewood Cliffs, NJ, Prentice Hall, 1998
Schillinger, J. *The Schillinger System of Musical Composition*, New York, C. Fisher, 1946
The Mathematical Basis of the Arts, New York, Philosophical Library, 1948
Seebass, T. "The Illustration of Music Theory in the Late Middle Ages: Some Thoughts on Its Principles and a Few Examples," in *Music Theory and Its Sources: Antiquity and the Middle Ages*, ed. A. Barbera, South Bend, University of Notre Dame Press, 1990
Semmens, R. *Joseph Sauveur's "Treatise on the Theory of Music": A Study, Diplomatic Transcription and Annotated Translation*, London, Ontario, University of Western Ontario, 1987
"Sauveur and the Absolute Frequency of Pitch," *Theoria* 5 (1990–91), pp. 1–41
Singh, S. *Fermat's Enigma: The Epic Quest to Solve the World's Greatest Mathematical Problem*, Toronto, Penguin, 1997
Smith, C. "Leonhard Euler's *Tentamen novae theoriae musicae*: A Translation and Commentary," Ph.D. diss., Indiana University (1960)
Starr, D. "Sets, Invariance and Partitions," *JMT* 22 (1978), pp. 1–42
Straus, J. N. *Introduction to Post-Tonal Theory*, 2nd edn., Englewood Cliffs, NJ, Prentice Hall, 1999
Taneiev, S. *Convertible Counterpoint in the Strict Style* (1909), trans. C. Brower, Boston, B. Humphries, 1962
Tarski, A. *Introduction to Logic and to the Methodology of Deductive Sciences*, trans. O. Helmer, 3rd edn., New York, Oxford University Press, 1965
Tiles, M. *The Philosophy of Set Theory: An Introduction to Cantor's Paradise*, Oxford, B. Blackwell, 1989
Mathematics and the Image of Reason, London, Routledge, 1991
Vieru, A. "Modalism – A 'Third World,'" *Perspectives of New Music* 24 (1985), pp. 62–71
Book of Modes, vol. I: From Modes to a Model of the Intervallic Musical Thought, trans. Y. Petrescu, Bucharest, Editura muzicala, 1993
Vincent, H. *Die Einheit in der Tonwelt: Ein kurzgefasstes Lehrbuch für Musiker und Dilettanten zum Selbstudium*, Leipzig, H. Matthes, 1862
Ist unsere Harmonielehre wirklich eine Theorie?, Vienna, Rörich, [1894]

Wagner, D. "The Seven Liberal Arts and Classical Scholarship," in *The Seven Liberal Arts in the Middle Ages*, ed. D. Wagner, Indiana University Press, 1983, pp. 2–25

Walker, D. *Studies in Musical Science in the Late Renaissance*, London, Warburg Institute, 1978

Wason, R. "Progressive Harmonic Theory in the Mid-Nineteenth Century," *Journal of Musicological Research* 8 (1988), pp. 55–90

Winham, G. "Composition with Arrays," in *Perspectives on Contemporary Music Theory*, ed. B. Boretz and E. Cone, New York, Norton, 1972, pp. 261–85

Yasser, J. *A Theory of Evolving Tonality*, reprint of 1932 edition, New York, Da Capo Press, 1975

Zarlino, G. *Le istitutioni harmoniche*, 2nd edn., Venice, Franceschi, 1561; facs. Bologna, A. Forni, 1999

Ziehn, B. *Five- and Six-Part Harmonies: How to Use Them*, Milwaukee, Kaun, 1911

Canonical Studies, Milwaulkee, Kaun, 1912

· PART III ·

REGULATIVE TRADITIONS

· 11 ·

Notes, scales, and modes in the earlier Middle Ages

DAVID E. COHEN

Introduction

The basis of most musical instruction, thought, and activity in the Western world is a particular conceptualization of pitch. We understand musical pitches as distinct sonic entities ("discrete pitch"), specifiable by name, and we mentally represent them as a series of points occupying higher or lower, intervallically defined positions on an imaginary, quasi-spatial, vertically aligned two-dimensional continuum – or basic "pitch space." (We may also conceive the positions as defined by *absolute* pitch, determined by vibrational frequencies; this modern concept will not be considered here.) The pitches, or as I shall usually call them, "notes,"[1] constitute a system defined by various intervallic and other relationships and comprising a multitude of specific structures, including our familiar major, minor, and chromatic scales. These conceptualizations of discrete pitch, pitch space, and pitch-intervallic scalar system have their ultimate origins in the music theory of Greek antiquity. But the particular scale system we use is the result of a long historical evolution, in which the most crucial developments occurred in the ninth and eleventh centuries. Sections I and II of this chapter, respectively, will provide a fairly detailed examination of those developments, together with others to which they are closely connected, especially those concerning the early stages of pitch notation, solmization, and the theoretical systematization of the church modes.[2] Section III, a brief *postscriptum*, will indicate some of the developments of the later Middle Ages and early Renaissance, to c. 1500.

In brief, the reader will find here an account of the establishment and development

1 Since no single English word precisely and unambiguously denotes the concept of musical pitch defined above, I use here the word "note." A possible objection to it – that it properly denotes a written symbol rather than a sound event – seems less serious, for our present purposes, than the disadvantages of the two other candidates, "pitch" and "tone": "pitch" is an acoustical, rather than a musical, concept which properly denotes an (essential) *property* of a note, while "tone," as we shall see, has a number of other meanings that would make its use for this purpose particularly confusing here. "Note," in normal English usage, frequently designates precisely the concept we need. (When the concept of "note" as written symbol is intended, but is not immediately clear from the context, I shall specify "written note" or use some other locution.)

2 The historical development of medieval modal theory is surveyed in Hiley, *Western Plainchant*, pp. 454–77. See further Powers et al., "Mode," pp. 776–96; Hiley et al., "Modus"; Meyer, "Tonartenlehre."

of two basic features of the theoretical conceptualization of music that has fundamentally shaped our own musical culture and remained with us to this day: an abstract background scale system, and the intervallic analysis of pitch structures.

I Rediscoveries and innovations: the ninth century

The musical developments of this period, which were part of the broader cultural movement known as the Carolingian "Renaissance" or *renovatio*, are fundamental to the entire subsequent history of Western music.[3] They include the "final shaping" of the Gregorian chant dialect and the invention of neumatic notation, the chief precursor to staff notation, and with these, the laying of the foundation of Western music theory.[4] It was this period that saw the establishment of a scale system and the development of a systematic or "scientific" modal theory based upon that system. These were results of a complex process which is still only imperfectly understood, but which clearly involved the integration of several disparate elements. One was the still evolving repertory of Gregorian chant melodies – the concrete actuality of the liturgical song (*cantus*) that was the constant touchstone and ultimate object of all theory construction. The second was the system of eight "tones" or "modes" used by the church to classify and organize those melodies, a system that in its organization, nomenclature, and procedures bore the marks of its origin in Byzantine liturgical practices. (These two together may be called "the *cantus* tradition.") And finally, the third comprised a number of concepts, constructions, and procedures of analysis adapted from ancient Greek harmonics, the scientific study of the pitch components of music (pitch itself, notes, intervals, scales, "modes," etc.), as transmitted to the Carolingians by a number of late Roman and earlier medieval writers.[5] This body of knowledge, called in Latin the "science" or "art" of music (*ars musica*), may be called "the harmonics tradition."

The Carolingian cantors and scholars took it as their task to integrate all of these, using each to illuminate the others. There was a practical motivation for doing so: the awareness that a more systematic and rationalized understanding of the *cantus* tradition would promote the liturgical uniformity that was always an ideal of the Carolingian monarchs and higher clergy, by securing more accurate transmission of the traditional, sacred melodies, and more disciplined, uniform performance of them.

3 See especially **Chapter 5, pp. 149–50**; Brown, "Introduction: The Carolingian Renaissance," pp. 1–51; and Rankin, "Carolingian Music," pp. 274–316, in McKitterick, ed., *Carolingian Culture*. See also McKinnon, "Emergence"; Reckow, "Zur Formung."

4 For introductions to the difficult and controversial questions regarding the origins and transmission of "Gregorian" chant, see Levy et al., "Plainchant," pp. 827–31; McKinnon, "Emergence"; Hiley, *Western Plainchant*, pp. 514–21, 560–62; Phillips, "Notationen," pp. 529–31; see further the studies cited in n. 23 below. For neumes, see below, n. 33.

5 Phillips, "Classical and Late Latin Sources"; Bernhard, "Überlieferung und Fortleben"; Huglo, "Grundlagen," pp. 25–51. Detailed summaries of essentially all pre-Carolingian Latin musical texts are found in Wille, *Musica Romana*.

In their attempts to integrate the *cantus* and harmonics traditions, Carolingian cantors and scholars forged a new way of understanding the concrete actualities of liturgical song, with new ways of conceptualizing musical entities and events that had formerly been grasped only (or primarily) empirically, ways which were truly "theoretical" in that they involved intellectual acts of abstraction and system construction, and which formed the foundation for all subsequent western music-theoretical thought.

In view of the foundational importance of the developments of this period, and the difficulties they present, the major portion (section I) of this chapter is devoted to them, in addition to the necessarily broader coverage to be found in **Chapter 5** of this volume (**pp.** 136–67).

The situation up to the mid-to-late ninth century

In the late ninth century, the set of melodic categories – the eight "modes" or "tones" (*toni*) – used by the church to classify and organize the melodies of plainchant became linked to the structure of the newly established scale system, in a development that was crucial to the subsequent histories of both. Prior to that time we find a situation which is difficult to reconstruct with any degree of certainty, but which must be considered since it constituted the background and starting point for all further developments. In so doing, we shall review some essential matters regarding the modal system and its nomenclature in their earliest known form.

The modal system and its nomenclature in the earliest extant documents. By c. 800, it seems, a set of eight melodic categories, called *toni*, had been superimposed by Frankish cantors upon the repertory of Gregorian chant melodies.[6] They functioned primarily as a classificatory system, used to ensure, in certain genres of plainchant, a smooth, "euphonious" melodic connection between the end of the psalm tone (a simple, formulaic melodic pattern used for chanting psalm verses) and the beginning of the main melody (the antiphon) upon its return after the psalm tone, by providing, on the basis of the melodic qualities of the antiphons, a set of categories – the modes (*toni*) – whereby any antiphon could be matched up with the most appropriate psalm tone.[7] In its "standard" form the system provided a psalm tone for each of the eight modal categories.[8] An additional level of classification was provided by the use of several alternative cadence formulas or terminations, usually called "differences"

6 See Hucke, "Karolingische Renaissance"; Powers et al., "Mode," pp. 781–2.

7 On psalm tones, see Hiley, *Western Plainchant*, pp. 58–68.

8 The use, in at least some places, of a set of four (or six) additional psalm tones (later called *parapteres*, *medii toni*, etc.) for antiphon melodies not well served by any of the standard eight is attested in a number of earlier medieval sources beginning with Aurelian of Réôme's *Musica disciplina*, Chapter 8 (ed. Gushee, *Aureliani*, pp. 82.41–83.46). See Hiley, *Western Plainchant*, p. 62–63; Atkinson, "The *Parapteres*"; Bailey, "*De Modis Musicis*."

(*differentiae*), for some of the psalm tones, to accommodate the various ways in which antiphons belonging to the corresponding modes might begin.

This system is first attested in the earliest extant tonaries (lists of chants arranged by modal assignment) and modal treatises. Of the many extant tonaries, two are thought to date from the period prior to c. 850: the "St.-Riquier Tonary," dated to c. 800, and the "Carolingian Tonary of Metz," whose archetype has been dated to c. 825–55.[9] Treatises on the modes often occur in conjunction with a tonary and probably originated as collections of glosses on the modal terminology used in tonaries; their basic purpose is to lay out the system of the eight *toni* and explicate their nomenclature.[10] Two such treatises, both very brief, are associated with the tonary of Metz, and several other very early ones are extant as well.[11] The most important of these is the text *De octo tonis* ("On the eight modes"), which circulated in several versions, both as an independent treatise attributed to Alcuin, and as the first part of Chapter 8 of Aurelian of Réôme's *Musica disciplina* (ninth century); its original version may perhaps date back as far as the late eighth century.[12]

None of these brief, early modal treatises provides anything approaching a theoretical explanation of the modal categories themselves. Instead, they exemplify the modes by citing conventionalized "intonation formulas," and they explain the modal terminology by providing literal definitions of the verbal terms employed, most of which are Latinized Greek.

The presence of this Greek terminology in the earliest extant modal documents is part of the evidence that the Carolingian *toni* were adapted from a system known as the *oktoechos*, used by the Byzantine clergy since at least the seventh century for the classification of their liturgical melodies into eight categories (called *echoi*).[13] In both systems there are four main categories, called "authentic" in the West, each of which

9 Regarding tonaries, see Hiley, *Western Plainchant*, pp. 325–31; Huglo, "Tonary"; *Les Tonaires*; and "Grundlagen." The "Carolingian Tonary of Metz" is edited in Lipphardt, *Karolingische Tonar*, pp. 12–63; regarding its date, see ibid., p. 200, and Huglo, *Tonaires*, pp. 30–31. The fragmentary and anomalous "St.-Riquier Tonary," dated by Huglo to c. 795–800, is edited and discussed in Huglo, "Un tonaire," and *Les Tonaires*, pp. 25–29. Updated discussions of both tonaries are in Huglo, "Grundlagen," pp. 81–88.

10 Other aspects of Carolingian musical thought are reflected in the glosses on late Roman texts, especially those of Boethius and Martianus Capella; see **Chapter 5, pp. 139–47**.

11 Some of these are edited and discussed by Huglo, *Les Tonaires*, pp. 46–56, but see also Möller, "Zur Frage," pp. 278–79. For the Metz treatises, see Lipphardt, *Karolingische Tonar*, pp. 12–13, 62–63.

12 The version attributed to Alcuin is edited in *GS* 1, pp. 26–27. The version in *Musica disciplina* is edited in Gushee, *Aureliani*, pp. 78.1–79.21. The texts' sources, variants, and possible origins are discussed by Gushee, ibid., pp. 21, 39–40; and "The *Musica disciplina*," pp. 138–48; Huglo, *Les Tonaires*, pp. 47–56; Bernhard, "Textkritisches zu Aurelianus," p. 54; Möller, "Zur Frage." Aurelian of Réôme's *Musica disciplina* is discussed below, **pp. 314–17**.

13 On the *oktoechos*, see Jeffery, "Oktōēchos"; Hiley, *Western Plainchant*, pp. 454, 459–60; and "Modus," cols. 406–07; Wellesz, *A History of Byzantine Music*, pp. 69–71, 300–03; Gombosi, "Studien" (esp. Parts II–III); Strunk, "Tonal System"; Huglo, "Développement"; "Comparaison"; and "Grundlagen," pp. 59–69; Atkinson, "Interpretation," pp. 486–88; Markovits, *Tonsystem*, pp. 75–79, 97–102, 108–12.

Table 11.1 *The earliest known Western modal system*

I. Protus: authentic, plagal
II. Deuterus: authentic, plagal
III. Tritus: authentic, plagal
IV. Tetrardus: authentic, plagal

has a related "plagal" category (although their ordering and relationships are different in the two systems). The four main categories were named by the Greek ordinal numbers *protus*, *deuterus*, *tritus*, and *tetrardus* ("first," "second," etc.), and the two subclasses by Latinized forms of the Greek words *authentes* or *authentikos* ("having authority or power") and *plagios* ("oblique," "collateral," hence "derived," "subordinate"): in Latin, *aut(h)ent(ic)us* and *pla(g)i(us)* (later *plagalis*), or – in literal translation rather than transliteration – *auctoralis* and *lateralis*. The resulting four pairs were ordered as shown in Table 11.1. This is, in effect, already the eight-fold system of later medieval theory, shown in Table 11.2. The *protus* pair of authentic and plagal modes was the one to which the note equivalent to our D would soon be assigned as its final. The *deuterus* pair would similarly be assigned the final E; and so on. At the earliest stage, however, there is no mention of finals, or indeed of any criterion distinguishing the four main categories from each other; these are developments first seen in the later ninth-century treaties that we shall consider below.

Authentic and plagal, on the other hand, are already distinguished on the basis of range, although in ways that are different from and less precise than those found in later treatises. The latter usually define the range (*ambitus*) of each mode as essentially comprising an octave (with one or two notes added above and below the modal octave), and distinguish the authentic and plagal *ambitus* of each modal pair in terms of their positions with respect to their common final; the two ranges overlap, with the basic modal octave of the plagal lying a perfect fourth below that of the authentic. (See **Figure 10.4, p. 282** for an eleventh-century representation of the overlapping octave ranges of each pair of modes.) By contrast, in the earliest modal documents the ranges are not yet defined in terms of the final (which is not mentioned at all), and are not specified in any precise way. Plagal melodies are regarded simply as having a "smaller" and "lower" (*inferiores*) range than the melodies belonging to the corresponding authentic mode, which are "higher" (*altiores*); the plagal range is equivalent to the lower "part" of the authentic range, and is included within it. Their relationship is often expressed by saying that the authentic mode is the "master" (*magister*), the plagal its "pupil" or "disciple" (*discipulus*), which "lies beneath" and "to the side of" its paired authentic.

The key term *tonus* itself (pl. *toni*), used to denote the eight melodic categories, remains ill-defined in this early period. The second treatise attached to the tonary of

Table 11.2 *The eight-mode system*

	Final	Authentic modes	Plagal modes
[I. Protus]	D	1	2
[II. Deuterus]	E	3	4
[III. Tritus]	F	5	6
[IV. Tetrardus]	G	7	8

Metz tells us that *tonus* is that which both regulates and lends coherence to melodies,[14] and *De octo tonis* begins by stating that "there are eight *toni* in music, by means of which every melody (*modulatio*) seems to hold together as though with a sort of glue,"[15] again emphasizing the idea of melodic coherence. Yet no explanations of this "regulation" and "coherence" are offered, and indeed, no extant text of this period explains exactly how *tonus*, in its modal significance, was conceived at this time.

This is doubtless due, at least in part, to the fact that, in the Middle Ages, *tonus* had a number of additional meanings: (1) the interval of the whole tone (Gr. *tonos*), conceived in the harmonics tradition as a precisely determined pitch-relationship or "space" between two adjacent notes – a concept crucial for the developments to be discussed below;[16] (2) a single pitched musical sound (what we would call a note), for which the more usual terms were *sonus* or *sonitus*, the Greek *phthongos* (often corrupted to *ptongos*), and *vox*;[17] (3) in grammar, a verbal accent – also called *accentus* and *tenor* – often understood as a variation in pitch, as in Greek;[18] (4) one of Boethius's terms for the "transposition keys" (*tonoi*) of ancient Greek theory, whereby the entire Greater Perfect System was shifted up or down in pitch. (Although Boethius's preferred term for these is *modus* [mode], in one crucial passage he states that they are also called *toni* and *tropi*.[19])

The treatise *De octo tonis*, in its attempt to provide a definition of *tonus* as the term denoting mode, conflates all of these (except the first) with each other and with vague

14 "Every kind of melody is justly [said to be] regulated and bound together (*regulatur ac perstringitur*) by the eight *toni* . . . " (*Karolingische Tonar*, ed. Lipphardt, p. 63.8–10).
15 *GS* 1, p. 26; new edn. in Möller, "Zur Frage," p. 276. This is the text version bearing the attribution to Alcuin (see above, n. 12).
16 See Duchez, "Jean-Scot Erigene," p. 186; Cohen, "Boethius and the *Enchiriadis* Theory," pp. 137–40.
17 Most of these were also used in grammar to denote various aspects of speech sound. The sense of *tonus* as "pitched sound" or "musical note" probably came from the Latin verb *tono*, *-are* ("to thunder, to make a loud sound"), rather than from the occasional use of the Greek *tonos* to mean a "note" (see Mathiesen, *Apollo's Lyre*, p. 384).
18 Duchez, "Déscription grammaticale," pp. 572–73; Gushee, "The *Musica disciplina*," pp. 188–95.
19 *De institutione musica*, IV.15 (Friedlein edn., p. 341.19–21; trans. Bower, *Fundamentals of Music*, p. 153); Atkinson, "Modus," p. 11, discusses this passage. For explanations of the Greek Greater Perfect System and the *tonoi*, see above, **Chapter 4, pp. 122, 125–28**; Barker, *Greek Musical Writings*, vol. II, pp. 11–27; West, *Ancient Greek Music*, Chapters 6 and 8. Exhaustive coverage of Greek music theory is found in Mathiesen, *Apollo's Lyre*.

hints at the idea of mode as a regulatory principle governing melodies.[20] The resulting diffusion of meaning contributes to the passage's failure to communicate clearly the relevant sense of the term.

It was presumably to rectify this confused state of affairs that treatises of the later ninth century introduced the words *modus* and *tropus* as the proper designations for what was usually called *tonus*, that is, mode, as part of their attempt to clarify this concept by virtue of a new, more "scientific" way of understanding it. (Their authority was doubtless the Boethius passage mentioned above under point 4.) *Musica enchiriadis*, in so doing (Chapter 8), asserts that the traditional term *tonus* was used "improperly" (*abusive*) in this sense, a dictum repeated by many subsequent theorists.[21] Nevertheless, *tonus* long remained a standard term for "mode."

A further important aspect of early discussions of the modes is the use of intonation formulas (*echemata*, in later Byzantine terminology). These were melodies of brief or moderate length sung to successions of syllables such as *Nonanoeane* and *Noeagis*, cited in tonaries and treatises as exemplars of the modes and apparently designed for this purpose. Our first Western witnesses for this device, which was almost certainly adapted from Byzantine practice, are modal treatises of the ninth century, although the use of such melodic formulas, from about the tenth century sung to Latin texts such as "Primus tonus sic incipit" ("The first mode begins thus") and "model antiphons" like "Primum quaerite regnum Dei" ("First seek the Kingdom of God"), continued long past that time.[22]

Mode, pitch, and melodic description in Aurelian's *Musica disciplina*. Carolingian tonaries and modal treatises of the period before c. 850–900 provide no criteria for the assignments of melodies to modal categories, which they take as a given. Indeed, they make no use of, and no reference to, the basic theoretical concepts and structures which are taught and applied in analytical discussions of mode from the later ninth century on and which to us seem required for any technical analysis of melodies in structural terms – the note, the interval, a background scale of some kind – and therefore make no use of, or reference to, the notion of the final, which soon after became so important to modal theory. This, and other points such as the use of intonation formulas, suggests that the initial modal classification was carried out on the basis of the kinds of similarities among melodies called by modern scholars

20 *De octo tonis*, ed. *GS* 1, p. 26; Möller, "Zur Frage," p. 276; different version in Aurelian, *Musica disciplina*, Chapter 8 (ed. Gushee, *Aureliani*, p. 78.2–4; trans. Ponte, *Aurelian*). For discussion, see Gushee, "The *Musica disciplina*," pp. 193–95, also p. 145.

21 See Atkinson, "Interpretation"; "*Harmonia*"; and "Modus," pp. 14–22. The word *modus* too, even as a technical term in medieval music theory, had a number of distinct meanings, including "interval"; see Powers et al., "Mode," pp. 775–76; Atkinson, "Modus"; Hiley et al., "Modus."

22 On the intonation formulas, both Western and Byzantine, see Hiley, *Western Plainchant*, pp. 331–33; Hiley, in Hiley et al., "Modus," cols. 410–11; Huglo, "L'Introduction"; "Tonary"; and "Grundlagen," pp. 69–75; Bailey, *Intonation Formulas*; and "*De modis musicis*"; Strunk, "Intonations and Signatures"; Raasted, *Intonation Formulas*.

"melodic formulas" and "melody types" or "melodic families."[23] Yet the possibility remains that theoretical constructs such as the one-octave scale represented in some Spanish diagrams of the seventh or eighth century might have played a role.[24] This difficult question must remain open.[25]

Aurelian's *Musica disciplina*, in any case, shows that singers had other ways of understanding and discussing melodies – ways that did not rely on theoretical concepts such as notes, intervals, and scale, but which instead employed a qualitative, metaphorical language, comprising words and phrases expressing direction (up and down) and vocal effort or tension, to give the singer a sense of what his voice was to do in singing one or another part of a melody. Much of this vocabulary was derived from grammar, in particular the names and descriptions of the verbal accents (acute, grave, circumflex) of Greek, called *accentus*, *tenor*, or *tonus*.[26] Although mutual exchange of terms between grammar and music theory goes back to the pre-classical Greeks, the systematic borrowing of grammatical terms in the Middle Ages, beginning with the Carolingians, was of crucial importance for the history of western music theory.[27] Grammatical discussions of such matters as the nature of the voice, the elements of language, the articulation of a text by means of punctuation and pauses, the correct rendering of verbal accents and syllabic quantities, and the correct writing of the graphic symbols for accents provided the Carolingian cantors with a variety of terms and verbal strategies for the description of melodic events.

It is this kind of qualitative, metaphorical, often grammatically influenced description that we find in the earliest modally oriented discussion of specific plainchant melodies, in Chapters 10–20 of *Musica disciplina*, a compilation of texts attributed to one Aurelian of Réôme and customarily dated to the 840s, although this dating is now in question.[28] Chapters 1–7, possibly based on an already existing "general introduction to the art of music" (Gushee, "The *Musica disciplina*," p. 149), cover some of the typical

23 On these concepts and related issues in plainchant scholarship, see Treitler, "Homer and Gregory"; "'Centonate Chant'"; "The 'Unwritten' and 'Written' Transmission"; and "Sinners and Singers," esp. pp. 162–65; Hucke, "Toward a New Historical View"; Nowacki, "Syntactical Analysis"; "Studies"; and "The Gregorian Office Antiphons"; Karp, *Aspects of Orality and Formularity*.

24 The diagram, which appears as an interpolation in some Spanish manuscripts of Isidore of Seville's *Etymologiae* written c. 700, is reproduced and discussed in Huglo, "Grundlagen," pp. 42–46. It shows a scale with the interval series T–S–T–T–T–S–T, equivalent to D–E–F–G–A–B–C–D; the notes are labeled with the Latin letters A to h, and the intervals are labeled and related to numerical ratios.

25 For discussion of points relevant to this question, see Bielitz, *Musik und Grammatik*; Crocker, "Hermann's Major Sixth"; Duchez, "Déscription grammaticale."

26 See above, p. 312; Duchez, "La Représentation."

27 See Duchez, "Déscription grammaticale," and "La Représentation"; Bower, "The Grammatical Model"; Bielitz, *Musik und Grammatik*; Law, "The Study of Grammar."

28 For edition and translation, see the Bibliography, p. 357. Subsequent page citations are of the edition by Gushee, *Aureliani*. For introductory discussions, see Chapter 5, p. 152 and Hiley, *Western Plainchant*, pp. 456–58. Regarding the title, the author, and the dating in the 840s, see Gushee, *Aureliani*, pp. 13–16; his arguments, and those for a later date in Bernhard, "Textkritisches zu Aurelianus," pp. 60–61, are reported and critiqued by Phillips, "Notationen," pp. 544–58, who urges the view that the compilation had no single point and date of origin (see, however, n. 38, p. 152). Gushee's interpretive remarks concerning the treatise in his "Questions of Genre," pp. 383–93 are of interest.

topics of the ancient *ars musica*, including its mathematical character and basis, by means of extracts drawn from such authorities as Boethius, Cassiodorus, and Isidore. Included here is one of the earliest known attempts to bring this harmonics tradition into connection with the contemporary *cantus* tradition: in Chapter 2 the basic intervals of the octave, perfect fifth and fourth, and whole tone are exemplified with citations of plainchant melodies; less justifiably, the author also links these four intervals with the four authentic modes.[29]

Chapter 8 begins the second main section of the text, concerned with aspects of the *cantus* tradition, including the modes; its opening sentences are a version of the text *De octo tonis*, whose unsuccessful attempt to explain the basic concept of *tonus* was mentioned above (pp. 312–13).

Chapters 10–17 consist largely of detailed descriptions of the melodic events that occur at the junctures between antiphons and psalm tones ("versicles"); while they may be primarily oriented to "details of performance practice and . . . esthetic questions" rather than modal classification per se (Gushee, "Questions of Genre," p. 389), they proceed by cataloguing and differentiating the various ways in which these melodic junctures (called *varietates*, *differentiae*, *divisiones*, and *definitiones*) occur in each of the modes. The descriptions use a varied, metaphorical, non-pitch-specific vocabulary that addresses not only melodic motion and contour but also tempo and vocal timbre.[30] Grammatical terms, especially those denoting the three kinds of verbal accent (acute, grave, circumflex), are frequent in Chapter 19, which provides syllable-by-syllable descriptions of the psalm tones. These accentual terms and phrases do not indicate specific melodic events in any consistent way (Gushee, "The *Musica disciplina*," pp. 216–21). Neither here nor elsewhere is there any attempt to provide precise, intervallically determined instructions, much less a translation of melodies into notes.[31]

Also noteworthy is Aurelian's use of language indicative of a spatial, vertically oriented mental representation of relative pitch in terms of "height."[32] As already mentioned, other early modal treatises say that the authentic modes are "higher" (*altiores*) and the plagal modes "lower" (*inferiores*). Yet this familiar spatial image or metaphor, which we take for granted, seems to have been absent or merely inchoate in the conceptualization of music until about this time. The technical terms in ancient Greek and Roman music-theoretical writings for what we call "high" and "low" pitch were, instead, "acute," that is, "sharp" or "pointed" (Gr. *oxeia*, Lat. *acuta*), and "grave," that is, "heavy" (Gr. *bareia*, Lat. *gravis*). These were also the standard grammatical terms for

29 Gushee, *Aureliani*, pp. 62–63; cf. Ponte, *Aurelian*, p. 16; Meyer, "Die Tonartenlehre," pp. 142–43.

30 Examples and discussion in Hiley, *Western Plainchant*, pp. 456–7; Gushee, "The *Musica disciplina*," pp. 211–14; Duchez, "Déscription grammaticale," esp. pp. 564–65.

31 Chapter 19 does use, on four occasions (pp. 123.48, 126.66, 126.70, 127.81), two Greek terms which in Chapter 6 are taken to be designations of pitches (pp. 75.29, 76.43); their use in Chapter 19, however, is imprecise (cf. Chapter 5, pp. 69.9–12 and ff.). See Phillips, "Notationen," pp. 340–42.

32 The topic of this paragraph receives fuller discussion in Duchez, "Représentation."

the two basic types of verbal prosodic accent, the acute (´) and the grave (`), and grammarians' discussion of these accents may have played a role in establishing the Western spatial image of pitch.[33] In Aurelian, however, as in the other very early modal treatises, this image remains vague. The assignment of specific positions along the vertical axis to notes separated by precisely determined intervallic distances came only with the later ninth-century theorists. The traditional Latin terms *acuta* and *gravis*, however, remained standard throughout the Middle Ages and beyond. (Indeed, the metaphor "sharp" is still with us, albeit with a changed – but similar – meaning.)

As to the key concept, *tonus* itself, this remains elusive throughout Aurelian's text. Nowhere is there a clear account of what a *tonus* actually is, or of what it means to say that a melody is "of" a particular *tonus*. The term's meaning is fixed neither by definition (as we have seen above) nor by usage, since the author uses it to denote a number of distinct things.[34] Still, it is clear that at least sometimes he understands by *tonus* that property of melodies which we would call their "modality." In several passages this seems to be conceived as a regulatory property of melodies that is both inherent and pervasive in them,[35] although we are also told that it is chiefly at the juncture between psalm tone and antiphon that the *tonus* of a chant melody is to be sought: not at the melody's end, but either at its beginning, or at the close of the conjoined psalm tone, or both.[36] The later doctrine that a melody's modality is most definitively determined or recognized by its last note, its "final," is notably absent.

In short, it seems that in *Musica disciplina* a *tonus* is not yet conceived in terms of generalized abstract features such as final, ambitus, and intervallic structure which require a mapping of melodies onto a background scale. Instead, *tonus* is an intrinsic but undefined property of each melody in the family of melodies of a given *tonus*, a property that is recognized empirically by the way in which the melody of the psalm verse ends and/or that of the antiphon begins. Yet these melodic junctures serve to differentiate, not the *toni* themselves, but their *varietates* or *differentiae*. Why the latter are "varieties," melodic sub-types, of a single *tonus* rather than distinct *toni* themselves remains unclear, since the specific properties distinguishing any given *tonus* from the rest are never stated. For Aurelian the modal classification of any melody is simply given by tradition; criteria for that classification are absent (Gushee, "The *Musica Disciplina*," p. 200). The attempt to state such criteria, and to do so in a systematic, "scientific" way, required an epistemological shift to a more abstract concept of mode, one in which the

33 Duchez, "Représentation," p. 65. It has long been argued that the early, adiastematic neumes also derive from these prosodic accent signs, although this is far from proven. On neumes and the theories as to their origin, see Hiley, *Western Plainchant*, pp. 340–92; Levy, "Origin"; Phillips, "Notationen," pp. 347–548.

34 Examples and discussion in Gushee, "The *Musica disciplina*," pp. 187–204.

35 Most clearly in the Preface, which states that the work will explain "certain rules of melodies (*quibusdam regulis modulationum*) that are called *toni* or *tenores*" (p. 53.3). Cf. Chapter 10, p. 86.11: "As already stated, every melody (*modulatio*) winds its way (*vergit*) according to these *toni* . . ."

36 See especially Chapter 10 (p. 89.30) and, for discussion, Gushee, "The *Musica disciplina*," pp. 195–98; Hiley, *Western Plainchant*, pp. 457–58.

essential features of a mode were identified with the way melodies map onto a background scale system – a shift which represents the next, and defining, stage in its history, and the inauguration of modal theory as we know it.

Systems of scale and mode in the later ninth and tenth centuries

In several treatises of the later ninth (and/or early tenth) century, and owing to Carolingian rediscoveries in the field of ancient Greco-Roman harmonics, the qualitative, empirical concept of mode found in *Musica disciplina* begins to give way to a new, systematic concept of mode as *a priori* system, the object of systematic theoretical explanation and elaboration: mode as the pre-given set of organized pitch and intervallic relationships that determines the character of any given chant melody. This new, more "theoretical" conception of mode presupposes the availability of an abstract, intervallically determined system of notes – a scale system – because its basic method is the structural analysis and comparison, in terms of intervallic patterns, of the scale itself with the melodies known to be "of" each of the modes: the mapping of chant melodies onto the scale system, such that the specific location of a melody upon the known intervallic structure of the scale somehow accounts for its perceived modal character or quality. These intervallic structures and their specific scalar locations eventually become the structural definition of that mode itself.

Although this concept is already discernible in at least some of the writings to be discussed in this section (the *Enchiriadis* treatises and the later layers of *Alia musica*), the more immediate task was the establishment of the scale system itself. The efforts toward the establishment and structural analysis of such systems in the early Middle Ages clearly reflect their authors' recognition that such a system, by providing the means for far more precise transcription and analysis of melodies, would support two related goals: more accurate transmission and performance of the chant melodies, and a clearer definition of the principles of their modal assignments. In fact, the late ninth century produced several scale systems, one of which, Hucbald's adaptation of the scale system of Greek antiquity, is essentially the one that became standard in the later Middle Ages. But all of the texts discussed in this section demonstrably draw upon the harmonics tradition's vast array of related theoretical terms and concepts as transmitted by Boethius, Martianus Capella, and other late Roman writers on the ancient *ars musica*. The Carolingian authors treated these inherited theoretical materials selectively, choosing and adapting those concepts, structures, and procedures that they recognized as applicable to their own, largely pragmatic ends. The offspring of this marriage of ancient theory and medieval practice was the first truly Western medieval music theory.

There are three main sources of such systematizing music theory that can be dated to the later ninth and/or tenth centuries. Their exact dates of composition are unknown. I shall discuss them in an order determined by methodological, not chronological, considerations. Requirements of space demand that our treatment be limited to points directly pertinent to the topic of this chapter.

Hucbald. The earliest extant account of a scale system essentially like that of the later Middle Ages is found in the *Musica*, generally known as *De harmonica institutione* (its title in *GS* I), composed by Hucbald of Saint-Amand, probably in the years 870–900.[37] Along with the establishment of the scale itself, Hucbald presents a pitch-specific letter notation for the transcription of chant melodies, and applies both of these to issues of modality. Throughout, he employs an aurally based pedagogical method well suited to the needs and prior training of his monastic readers. For example, he (like *Musica enchiriadis*) uses no numerical interval ratios or monochord division. Instead, the scale, and the intervals that structure it, are taught empirically by means of concrete examples drawn from the plainchant melodies and intonation formulas of the *cantus* tradition, demonstrating by direct experience the connection between the two. This characteristically Carolingian pragmatic approach is evident throughout in Hucbald's continual citation of specific chant melodies to exemplify theoretical concepts. The concepts themselves, however, are adapted from late Roman writings on the ancient *ars musica*, especially Boethius's *De institutione musica*.

Beginning with the basic distinction between equal and unequal pitch, Hucbald proceeds to the nine melodic intervals of chant (called *spatia*, *intervalla*, *modi*, *species*). The first two intervals, the semitone (*semitonium*) and the whole tone (*tonus*), are the basic constituents or "elements" of all the others, and are the "spaces" by which the adjacent notes of the scale are separated; although these "spaces" are defined empirically, they are nonetheless clearly understood to be precisely determined in "size" and invariable (pp. 136.1–160.22; Babb, pp. 13–23). They are exemplified by means of a diagram (see Figure 11.1) in which a melody with the range of a major sixth is mapped onto a set of six lines representing the strings of a *cithara* tuned to pitches separated by the intervals T, T, S, T, T (pp. 160.21–22; Babb, pp. 22–23). The resemblance of this intervallic structure to the later Guidonian hexachord is striking, and perhaps not entirely coincidental (see Crocker, "Hermann's Major Sixth"). This is not staff notation: only the lines, which actually represent the strings of an instrument, signify notes; the spaces represent only intervals. It is therefore closer to being an iconic representation of an instrument than it is to the more purely symbolic semiotic system of the staff. Similar "string" diagrams in Boethius's *De institutione musica* were probably the inspiration for this and other diagrams of the kind in the *Enchiriadis* treatises, which in turn were an important precursor to staff notation (see below, pp. 329–30, 344–46).

A similar sense of innovation accompanies Hucbald's careful introduction of the

37 For editions and translations see the Bibliography, p. 358. Chartier's edition of the *Musica* in his *L'Œuvre musicale d'Hucbald* is cited here, by page and section numbers. Babb's translation is cited as "Babb." The most thorough study of Hucbald's life, musical works, and treatise is in Chartier, *L'Œuvre*. See also Palisca's "Introduction" to Hucbald, in Babb, pp. 3–11; Weakland, "Hucbald as Musician and Theorist"; Hiley, *Western Plainchant*, pp. 448–52; Gushee, "Questions," pp. 395–98.

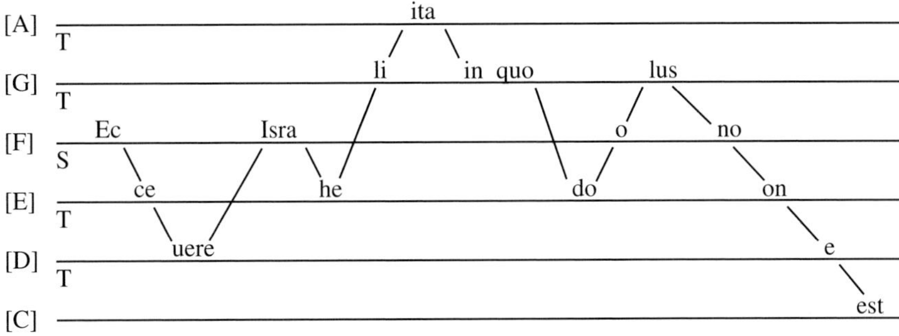

Figure 11.1 Hucbald: String diagram (up to final melisma). Modern note names supplied in brackets. (See Hiley, *Western Plainchant*, p. 449, Example V.3, for final melisma and transcription into staff notation.)

crucial, fundamental conceptual basis for any scalar system: the individual, discretely pitched musical note (*ptongus*, *sonus*) as the "element" of melody, a concept that Hucbald backs with the authority of the ancient *ars musica* (pp. 152.15–154.17; Babb, pp. 20–21). These elementary musical entities, the "most sure foundations of all song," are specifically "those sounds distinct [in pitch from each other] and determined by calculable quantities, and which [therefore] stood forth as suitable for melody" (ibid.). They have the same status and perform the same function in music as letters (that is, speech sounds) in language. A definition, taken from Boethius, defines the note (*sonus*) as "an incidence of the voice brought forth at one pitch, suitable for melody."[38] Each note is thus a distinct entity, and "like a flight of stairs (*in modum scalarum*), they ascend and descend, each set apart from the other by the quantity of its proper interval (*proprii spatii quantitate discreta*)" (p. 154.17; Babb, p. 21). This very early use of the "scale" analogy and the reference to determinate intervallic positions bear witness to a more sharply focused conception of the vertically oriented spatial image of "high" and "low" pitches that first appears, in an undefined and imprecise way, in our earlier sources (see above, pp. 315–16).

Having established these "elementary" components, Hucbald now proceeds to the scale system itself and its application to the modes. In effect, he proposes an adaptation of the diatonic form of the Greek Greater Perfect System (GPS).[39] After presenting the latter in its traditional form, he observes that, instead of ↓T–T–S tetrachords starting

38 "Sonus est vocis casus emmeles, id est, melo aptus, una intensione productus" (p. 152.16); Babb's translation of the sentence (p. 21) is inaccurate and misses its relationship to its source. Cf. Boethius, *De inst. mus.*, I.8 (Friedlein edn., p. 195.2–3; trans. Bower, *Fundamentals*, p. 16). The definition goes back to Aristoxenus (*Elementa harmonica*, I.15).

39 Chartier edn., pp. 162.23–192.43; Babb, pp. 23–35. On the Greek scale systems, see Chapter 4, pp. 124–25. On the combination of the GPS with the *synemmenon* tetrachord, see below, p. 341. Hucbald's source here is Boethius, *De inst. mus.*, I.20–25 (diatonic genus only). He also discusses briefly an alternative diatonic scale, with an intervallic structure like that of the major scale from C (pp. 164.25–166.27; Babb, pp. 24–25), and explains the principle of octave equivalence (pp. 150.14, 166.28; Babb, pp. 19, 25).

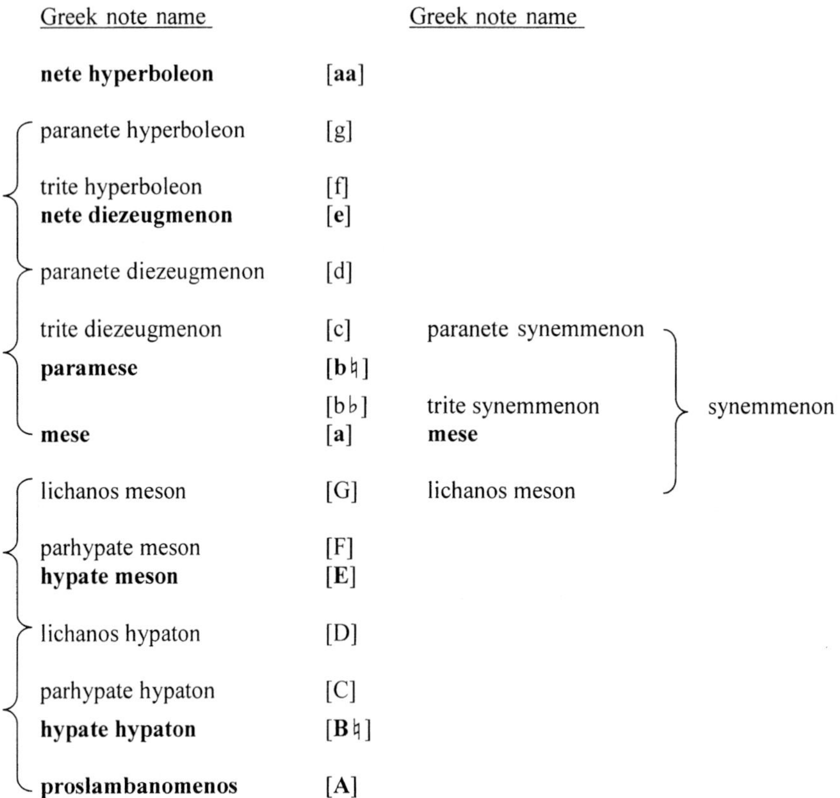

Figure 11.2 Hucbald's adapted GPS-plus-*synemmenon* scale system, with T–S–T tetrachords. Equivalent notes in the later medieval gamut are shown in brackets. Spacing indicates whole tones and semitones. The boundary tones of the hexachords in the ancient Greek system are shown in boldface, to facilitate comparison.

at the top, the system can be conceived in terms of ↓T–S–T tetrachords starting at the bottom, with *proslambanomenos* (A) as the first note of the lowest tetrachord. (See the left-hand column of Figure 11.2.) Hucbald then adds the *synemmenon* tetrachord, adapted from the Lesser Perfect System (LPS) in the same way, to arrive at a system of five T–S–T tetrachords constituting a two-octave diatonic scale plus one alternative note, the *trite synemmenon* (b♭), a semitone above *mese*, which in many melodies occurs alternatively to the note *paramese* (b♮). The complete scale is shown in Figure 11.2.

Hucbald's scale (minus the *synemmenon* tetrachord) is identical, with regard to intervallic series and tetrachordal organization, to the one shown in Figure 11.3, which may have been the scale underlying the Byzantine *oktoechos*.[40] (In both, moreover, the

40 See Jeffery, "Oktōēchos"; Strunk, "Tonal System"; Markovits, *Tonsystem*, pp. 97–99.

						α'		β'		γ'		δ'		α'		β'		γ'		δ'								
	t		s		t		t		s		t		T		t		s		t		t		s		t		T	
[A		B		C		D		E		F		G		a		b		c		d		e		f		g		a]

Figure 11.3 Reconstructed Byzantine tetrachordal scale (after Markovits, *Tonsystem*, p. 98): "t" = whole tone; "s" = semitone; "T" = the central disjunctive whole tone that separates the two t–s–t tetrachords of the central octave. Modern note equivalents in brackets. The Greek characters α', β', γ', δ' in the top row (representing the numbers 1, 2, 3, 4) signify the notes *protus*, *deuterus*, *tritus*, and *tetrardus* in the two central tetrachords.

central octave is identical to the "Spanish" scale mentioned above; see n. 24.) The T–S–T tetrachord that serves as the organizational module in both of these scale systems is also the basis of the *Enchiriadis* scale system (see below, p. 324), and indeed from this time on remained the standard type of tetrachord in Western medieval scalar systems; it is discernible as the nucleus of the Guidonian hexachord as well. It must be stressed, however, that the scale shown in Figure 11.3 represents a hypothetical reconstruction based on later Byzantine sources, the earliest of which postdates our period by centuries, and that no influence in either direction can be demonstrated.

Hucbald next proposes a pitch-specific alphabetic notation (pp. 194.44–198.47; Babb, pp. 35–37). The sixteen notes of distinct pitch are represented by graphic signs – for all but one, Greek capital letters sometimes slightly modified. The one exception is the sign for *proslambanomenos* (A), which is the grammatical symbol *daseia* or *tau jacens* (⊢), used in grammar to indicate an aspirated "h." As Hucbald tells us, he has drawn these notational signs from the list of such signs found in Boethius,[41] and he urges that they be used in conjunction with neumes (which at this time were adiastematic) to provide what the latter do not: a precise indication of a melody's notes and intervals.

Although Hucbald's signs seem not to have been much used, they are related in principle to other alphabetic pitch-notational systems of the Middle Ages, such as the Daseian system used by the *Enchiriadis* treatises (to which Hucbald's is linked by his own use of the *daseia* sign), and the Latin-letter system of the eleventh century, both of which are briefly discussed below (pp. 326–28, 331, 340–41).

The reason for Hucbald's alternative tetrachordal organization of the scale emerges when he reaches the point "toward which from the outset everything looked forward" (Babb, p. 37): the application of the scale system to issues concerning the modes (pp.

41 Hucbald's signs are a selection from the vocal and instrumental signs for the Lydian mode transmitted in Boethius, *De inst. mus.*, IV.3, IV.15–16. Regarding these, see Bower, *Fundamentals*, pp. 122–27, 153–56, 194–95. For complete tables of Hucbald's notational signs, see Babb, p. 38, Fig. 16; Hiley, *Western Plainchant*, p. 393; Chartier, *L'Œuvre*, p. 198; Phillips, "Notationen," p. 331. Regarding alphabetic notations, including Hucbald's, see Hiley, *Western Plainchant*, pp. 386–88, 392–95; Crocker, "Alphabet Notations"; Phillips, "Notationen" (for Hucbald, pp. 327–39).

200.48–212.55; Babb, pp. 37–44). The link between them is provided by the modal finals, which Hucbald identifies (by their Greek names) as the notes equivalent to our D, E, F, and G, and which (he says)

> are suited to the completion of the four modes or tropes, that is, the *protus*, *deuterus*, *tritus*, and *tetrardus*, which are nowadays called "tones," in such a way that each of these four notes governs, as its subjects, a pair of tropes: a principal, which is called "authentic," and a collateral, called "plagal." . . . Thus every melody . . . is necessarily led back to one of these same four [notes]. Therefore they are called "finals," because anything that is sung finds its ending (*finem*) in [one of] them.[42]

This concept of the final, so basic to modal theory from this time on, is (as we have seen) absent from the earliest modal texts. Hucbald and the *Enchiriadis* treatises are the first known sources to define and use the concept of modal finals, and to locate them as specific notes within a scale.

Further, as Hucbald points out, the modal finals constitute the second-lowest of the T–S–T tetrachords in his adapted scale system (p. 202.50), which is thus equivalent in all but name to the "tetrachord of the finals" of the *Enchiriadis* scale system and many later theorists. Hucbald, to be sure, never explicitly says that his alternative scheme is to replace the traditional one, nor does he assign names to its tetrachords. Still, his alternative tetrachordal organization is an important adaptation of the traditional Greek scale system to its new application as a background scale for the modes, and was the basis for certain influential developments in modal theory of the eleventh century (see below, p. 351).

Hucbald concludes by using his scale system to clarify the ways in which melodies relate to the modes at two important points: their endings, and their beginnings (pp. 202.50–212.55). With regard to endings, Hucbald provides our earliest discussion of what is later termed modal "affinity," which he calls *socialitas*: the recurrence of modal quality in notes a perfect fifth or fourth apart. Each final, he observes, has "a certain union of connection" to the note five steps higher (omitting the *synemmenon* tetrachord), such that "many melodies are found to end in them as if by rule (*quasi regulariter*) . . . and to run their course perfectly according to the same mode or trope [as that of the true final]" (p. 202.50; cf. Babb, p. 39). He finds an "equal" (*par*) relationship between the finals and the notes four (and in one case five) steps *below* the final as well – although these pertain, he says, not to endings, but to beginnings (p. 202.51; Babb, p. 39). The notes related in this "bond of fellowship" (*socialitas*) are shown in Figure 11.4. We shall have much more to say about these relationships of *socialitas* – or, as they are later called, "affinities" – in section II.[43]

The topic of beginnings having been raised, the treatise concludes with an examination of the possible starting notes for melodies in each mode: these are restricted in all

42 Chartier edn., p. 200.49; cf. Babb, pp. 38–39.

43 Below, pp. 326, 346–51, 355. The most thorough study of the subject is Pesce, *Affinities*; see pp. 6–8 for Hucbald.

Tetrachords	Note Names	Protus	Deuterus	Tritus	Tetrardus
	nete hyperboleon [a]				
	paranete hyperboleon [g]				
	trite hyperboleon [f]				
	nete diezeugmenenon [e]				
	paranete diezeugmen. [d]				[d]
	trite diezeugmenon [c]			[c]	
	paramese [b♮]		[b♮]		
	mese [a]	[a]			
	lichanos meson [G]				**[G]**
	parhypate meson [F]			**[F]**	
(Finals)	**hypate meson [E]**		**[E]**		
	lichanos hypaton [D]	**[D]**			[D]
	parhypate hypaton [C]			[C]	[C]
	hypate hypaton [B♮]		[B♮] ('rarely')		
	proslambanomenos [A]	[A]			

Figure 11.4 Hucbald's modal *socialitas*. The finals are shown in boldface.

cases to the "eight or nine" notes between the fifth step above and below the final (p. 202.51). The point is demonstrated by a long series of examples that employ vertically oriented diagrams (showing the relevant scalar segments), Greek note names, Hucbald's alphabetic notation, and the letters "t" and "s" to indicate the positions of whole tones and semitones (pp. 204.51–210.54; Babb, p. 40–44). For its time it would have been an impressive demonstration of Hucbald's primary thesis: the power of the theoretical concepts and constructs of the ancient *ars musica* to illuminate the principles of modality.

The *Enchiriadis* treatises. The treatises that we call *Musica enchiriadis* and *Scolica enchiriadis* (hereafter *ME* and *SE*) are widely known for containing the earliest extant descriptions of actual procedures for singing organum.[44] Their origins and relationship to each other remain obscure. Although they are clearly "sister" treatises, they do not appear to be the work of the same author; nor is *SE* a commentary (*scholia*) on *ME*, as previously thought.[45] As for the dates of composition, most scholars now agree on the period c. 850–c. 900; others favor a dating in the tenth century.

44 See the Bibliography, p. 358, for edition and translation. Schmid's edition is cited by page and (where appropriate) line numbers; Erickson's translation in his *Musica enchiriadis and Scolica enchiriadis* is cited simply as "trans."; his "Introduction" thereto as *Musica enchiriadis*. See Chapter 5, pp. 153–57 and Chapter 15, pp. 480–82, for a brief account of the *Enchiriadis* teachings, including those concerning organum. The most detailed study of the treatises is Phillips, "*Musica* and *Scolica Enchiriadis*" (hereafter cited as "*Musica*").

45 An introduction to these questions is Erickson, *Musica enchiriadis*, pp. xxi–xxiv. More detailed discussions are found in Phillips, "*Musica*," esp. pp. 5–16, 377–419; "Notationen," pp. 302–05; Müller, *Hucbalds echte und unechte Schriften*, disproved an early and erroneous attribution to Hucbald. Gushee's remarks in "Questions of Genre," pp. 398–402 have been fundamental in shaping subsequent research. The latest theory as to the treatises' origins is found in Torkewitz, "Zur Entstehung"; *Das älteste Dokument.*

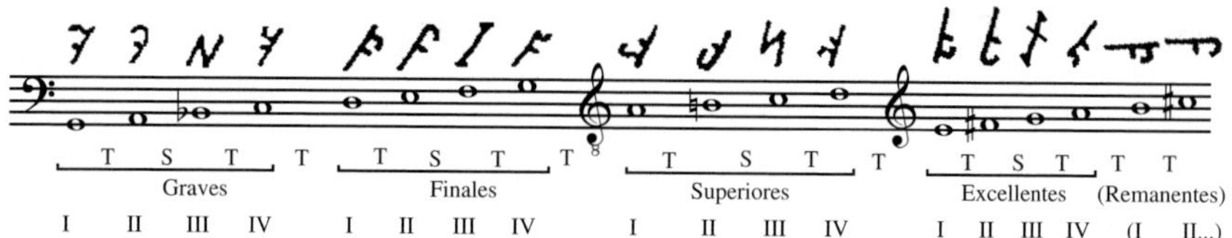

Figure 11.5 The *Enchiriadis* scale system and Daseian notation (I = *protus*, II = *deuterus*, III = *tritus*, IV = *tetrardus*)

Both treatises teach the same idiosyncratic scale and notational systems, using these as the basis for essentially similar accounts of the principles of modality and the practice of organum. Yet their styles and organization differ, the topics covered are not exactly the same, and they offer different (although usually compatible) explanations of certain points.[46] The account offered here draws on both treatises; it is intended to supplement the discussion of the *Enchiriadis* treatises found in Chapter 5 of the present volume by addressing in greater detail certain points of interest or controversy with regard to the scalar system and its relationship to the modes.[47]

The scalar system comprises a series of T–S–T tetrachords (like Hucbald's), whose notes are named by the series of Greek ordinal numbers traditionally used to denote the four basic modal categories: *protus*, *deuterus*, *tritus*, and *tetrardus* (see Figure 11.5). Four such tetrachords (plus the first two notes of a fifth) are deployed, and are given names reflecting their functional roles in chant melodies: *graves*, *finales*, *superiores*, and *excellentes* ("low," "finals," "higher," and "highest").[48] Most unusually, however, each of these tetrachords is disjunct (separated by a whole step) from both of its neighbouring tetrachords. As a result, the system is periodic at the fifth rather than at the octave; that is, precisely the same pattern of whole tones and semitones recurs at every fifth step (in either direction), rather than at every eighth step as in octave-based systems. Consequently, augmented octaves occur at three points, between the *tritus* of any tetrachord and the *deuterus* eight steps higher.

Despite certain shared features, the system is obviously very different both in structure and nomenclature from Hucbald's, which maintains the octave periodicity and ancient Greek note names of its Hellenistic model. And although Hucbald's tetrachordal re-organization of that system may point to a possible Byzantine forebear (see

46 One significant difference between the two is that *SE*, unlike *ME*, teaches interval ratios, in a lengthy disquisition on Pythagorean-Platonic harmonics (pp. 106–47; trans., pp. 65–89); this culminates in a monochord division (the only one in the late Carolingian treatises discussed here) that produces a two-octave scale equivalent to C–c[1], also mentioned by Hucbald as the scale used on instruments such as the organ (see above, n. {39}). It is worth noting that this scale differs sharply from the *Enchiriadis* scale used everywhere else in *ME* and *SE*.

47 See **Chapter 5, pp. 153–57**. The following account of the *Enchiriadis* scale system is based on the interpretation of Spitta ("Die Musica enchiriadis und ihr Zeitalter"), which is almost universally accepted by modern scholars. A sharply divergent interpretation is proposed in Hebborn, *Die Dasia-Notation*.

48 The series of notes and tetrachords is, in principle, infinitely extensible in both directions; the limitation to eighteen notes (four complete tetrachords plus two *residui*) is explained in *ME*, Chapter 2; see also *SE* (Schmid, p. 63; trans., p. 36).

above, pp. 320–21), the *Enchiriadis* scale, which is so different from every other Western scale, seems even more likely to have had such an origin.[49] If the naming of the notes with the borrowed Byzantine modal names *protus–tetrardus* is not necessarily further evidence of this, it certainly betrays the system's intimate connection with the Carolingian liturgical *cantus* tradition (which is in any case unmistakable in all of these treatises). Yet the influence of Boethius and the ancient *ars musica* is much in evidence as well,[50] and the *Enchiriadis* treatises apply, to both the scale itself and the modes, techniques of intervallic structural analysis that are in some ways more advanced than anything we find in Hucbald. Indeed, the *Enchiriadis* treatises are our earliest witnesses to the sort of the structural analysis of scale and mode that later became standard practice among theorists, and their analyses provide the best explanation and justification for their own idiosyncratic scale by demonstrating its crucial role in what amounts to the first theoretical *explanation* of modality as a quality of melodies.[51]

The basic assumption of that explanation is that there are just four modal "qualities" (*protus*, *deuterus*, etc.), corresponding to the four chief modal categories, which are called "modes" or "tropes," and that every melody possesses one of those four modal qualities and therefore belongs to one of those four modes or tropes. The explanation itself is based on the principle that the modal quality of a melody is due to the pattern of intervals (the ordered disposition of whole tones and semitone) it exhibits with respect to the melody's final. Each final has its own intervallic pattern owing to its location within the tetrachordal matrix, and this pattern determines the modal quality (*qualitas*, *proprietas*) of that final, which it bestows on any melody that ends on it (*ME*, Chapter 8). As we have seen, the modal quality also constitutes the *identity* of the final that possesses it.

The scale's periodicity at the fifth, however, means that the intervallic pattern of each final, and indeed of each note, recurs without alteration every five steps – that is, between notes occupying analogous positions in neighbouring tetrachords – and is thus effectively limited to that range. *SE* therefore sometimes analyzes these patterns in terms of the pentachords lying between such analogously positioned notes. For example, the pentachord from any *protus* to the *protus* in the adjacent higher tetrachord has the interval series T–S–T–T (Schmid, pp. 64–65; trans., p. 36). Each final has its own pentachordal pattern. But these are necessarily shared by all the analogously positioned notes in the other tetrachords, and these replications of intervallic pattern mean that the modal qualities of the finals are replicated as well in the other tetrachords: the

49 As Gombosi ("Studien," Part II, pp. 129–30) points out, this scale structure resembles the Byzantine *Rad* (*trochos*: "wheel")-system, shown in Tardo, *L'antica melurgia*, p. 159. On the question of the system's Byzantine origins, see Erickson, *Musica enchiriadis*, pp. xxxix–xli; Atkinson "*Harmonia*," p. 488; and "Tonsystem," pp. 115–17.

50 See Phillips, "*Musica*"; Erickson, *Musica enchiriadis*, pp. xli–xlvi.

51 It is often said that the scale system is designed to accommodate the parallel organum in perfect fifths taught by the treatises; organum at the fourth, however, is at least as important a topic and this, like the doublings of organal voices at the octave, is not particularly well served by the system's periodicity at the fifth. For other explanations of the reason for this peculiar scale, see Phillips, "Notationen," pp. 311–14; "The Dasia Notation"; and "*Musica*," Chapter 11 (cf. Erickson, *Musica enchiriadis*, p. xxxi); Hebborn, *Die Dasia-Notation*.

first note of each and every tetrachord has the same modal quality (*protus*), and thus the same name (*protus*), and so too for the other three notes. That is, since there are only four different tetrachordal positions, each of which creates (by its pattern) one of the four basic modal qualities by which the notes are identified, there are, in a sense, really only four "truly different" notes, all the others being replications of these at higher and lower levels of pitch, separated by perfect fifths. (In a similar way, the octave periodicity of our modern system makes it possible to operate with pitch classes.) Every note – not just the finals – is thus conceived as a pitch embodying the "quality" of one of the four basic modal categories; the names of the latter, which heretofore had merely denoted classes of melodies, now become the names of all the individual notes as well, each of which, since it is identified purely in terms of its modal quality, is either a *protus*, a *deuterus*, a *tritus*, or a *tetrardus*.

The tetrachord of the finals, then, is simply the one containing the specific note on which a given melody ends, and the others are disposed and named with respect to it, in a way that reflects modal *ambitus*, which is a secondary feature with respect to the four modes themselves. Both the authentic and the plagal *ambitus* of any mode extend to the fifth below the final (hence the need for the *graves* tetrachord) and to the fifth above it (hence the *superiores*), while the authentic *ambitus* extends beyond that to the ninth above the final (hence the *excellentes*) (*SE*, Schmid, pp. 84–85; trans., pp. 49–50).

The reduction of the scale to a series of replications of the same four modal qualities at intervals of the fifth reflects an extreme commitment to the principle of modal affinity or, as both Hucbald and *SE* call it, *socialitas*.[52] Octave-based systems differ from this one in two ways: first, in the interval of periodicity – the point at which note "qualities" recur – which in octave-based systems coincides with the most acoustically pure interval; and second, in that the recurring "qualities" of the *Enchiriadis* system are specifically modal. Whatever else may be true of it, the system clearly reflects a theoretical agenda: to explain the modal qualities of melodies in terms of the scale system and its inherent intervallic structure. Indeed, the system represents the closest possible integration of the scalar and modal systems, for it posits a total identification of tetrachordal position, intervallic pattern, modal quality, and note identity.

ME, in Chapter 12, shows graphically how the modal quality of a melody is determined by the tetrachordal position of its final: shifting the position of the melody up by successive steps with respect to the background tetrachordal matrix causes it to change mode, from its original *protus* to *deuterus* to *tritus* to *tetrardus*, and finally back to *protus* again, at which point the new final and the original one are of the same quality (pp. 35–36; trans., pp. 19–21). (See Figure 11.6.) The point is made with even greater clarity by *SE* (pp. 76.201–82.317; trans., pp. 44–48).

The Daseian notation, shown in Figure 11.5, directly reflects all this. It uses

52 *SE*, pp. 73.162, 82.323 (trans., pp. 43, 48). See above, p. 322 for Hucbald's *socialitas*; below, section II, for the "affinities." Regarding the question of the possible applications of these relationships of *socialitas* in *ME* and *SE*, see Pesce, *Affinities*, pp. 9–11.

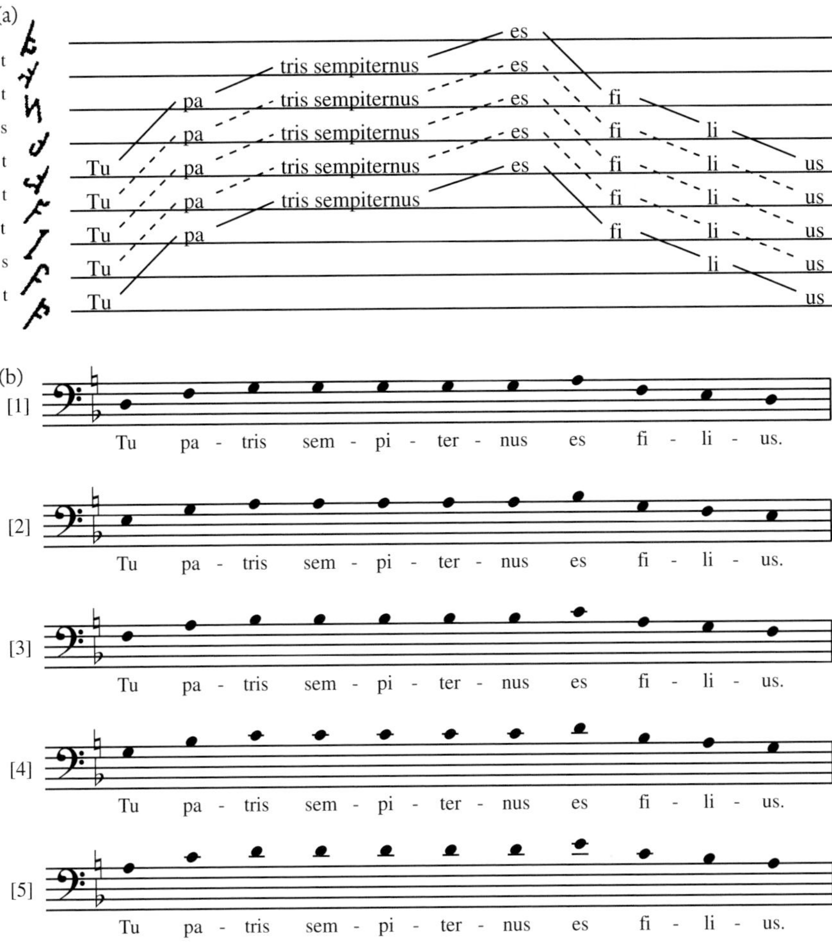

Figure 11.6 *Musica enchiriadis*: Modal alteration of a melody by shift of position in the scale
(a) Schmid, *Musica et Scolica enchiriadis*, Chapter XII, descr. 2, p. 36
(b) Erickson, *Musica enchiriadis*, Fig. 12.2, p. 20

variations of just four truly distinct graphic signs, one for *protus*, one for *deuterus*, and so on. These appear in their basic forms in the tetrachord of the finals. The signs for *protus*, *deuterus*, and *tetrardus* are all derived from the *daseia* or *tau jacens* (⊢) symbol, used by grammarians to indicate an aspirated "h." (Hucbald's alphabetic notation also uses this sign; see above, p. 321.) The symbol is tilted to the right, and three different kinds of curved lines are added to it at the top to distinguish *protus*, *deuterus*, and *tetrardus*. The same symbols, rotated in various ways, represent the analogously positioned notes in the other tetrachords. The remaining signs, for *tritus*, are different from all the rest, as can be seen in Figure 11.5. This visual differentiation of *tritus* is significant: it marks the location of the central semitone in the tetrachord, and it is the semitones that define the intervallic patterns of the tetrachordal matrix, which in turn are directly responsible for the modal qualities, and thus the identities, of the notes. (See especially *SE*, pp, 148–154; trans., pp. 89–92.)[53]

Semitone placement is the crucial issue in *SE*'s discussion of what we may call, for the sake of convenience, "chromatic alterations." This topic arises early in *SE*, in connection with its admonishment that the singer avoid various kinds of "faults" or "blemishes" (*vitia*) that "disfigure" or "corrupt" melodies by altering the "natural qualities" of the notes, creating what the author calls *absonia* (literally, "off-sound") and *dissonantia* (pp. 61–62; trans., p. 34). The first such *vitium* is simply singing out of tune. The others occur when, as *SE* puts it, "a note is measured incorrectly from another note, that is, [when] one [is sung] instead of another" (p. 61.25–26; trans., p. 34). This refers to singing a note a semitone higher or lower than it would normally be in the scale. The author's explanation clearly reflects the basic principles explained above, according to which any sung pitch must be identified as one of just four kinds of note, *protus*, *deuterus*, *tritus*, or *tetrardus*, depending on its position within the ordered T–S–T–/–T–/ series of the tetrachordal matrix. In this series, as we have seen, the location of the semitone, which always falls between *deuterus* and *tritus*, is the crucial factor. Since the notes' identities are completely determined by their positions in this fixed intervallic series, singing a note higher or lower by a semitone has the effect of shifting the location of the *deuterus–tritus* semitone, and with it, the whole intervallic series and therefore the qualitative identities of all the other notes as well.

Fig. 11.7 reproduces the first example of such a *vitium* in *SE*. The lambda-shaped diagram on the left shows ascent and descent through a pentachordal scale segment bounded by *tetrardus* (IV) notes, with the pentachord ↑T–T–S–T (equivalent to C–D–E–F–G). The diagram on the right shows the alteration of this pattern, in two stages. Its left leg shows ascent from the lower *tetrardus* note (IV = C); after the whole-tone step up from that note to the *protus* note (I = D) there *should* be another ascending whole-tone step to *deuterus* (E), but the latter is instead sung a semitone lower. This turns it into a *tritus* note (III = E♭), and the rest of the ascent continues with *tetrardus* (IV = F) and *protus* (I = G). The right leg of this second diagram then shows a descent through the pentachord, demonstrating the consequences of this "chromatic alteration" for the lower notes of the pentachord: below the newly defined *tritus* (E♭) come a *deuterus* (II = D) and a *protus* (I = C). The pentachord has thus become ↑T–S–T–T (equivalent to C–D–E♭–F–G), which is, indeed, the pentachord found above any *protus* note. The "chromatic alteration" of a single note, by changing the sequence of whole tones and semitones relative to the starting point, inevitably causes the modal qualities

53 More detailed discussion in Phillips, "The Dasia Notation"; "*Musica*," pp. 163–82; "Notationen," pp. 305–11. Hebborn, *Die Dasia-Notation*, offers a new explanation of the symbols.

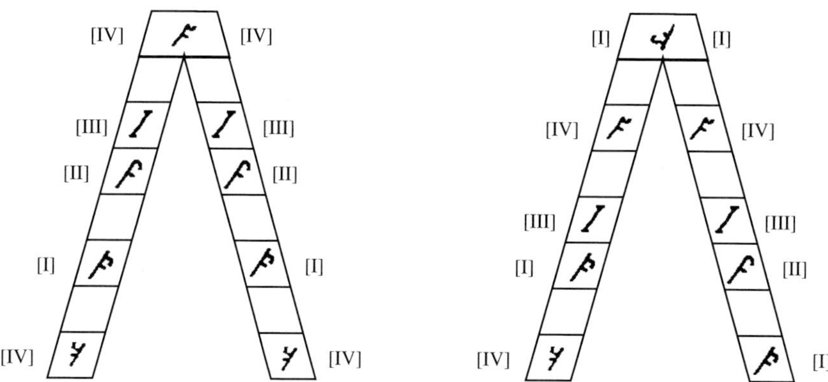

Figure 11.7 Chromatic alteration in *Scolica enchiriadis*: "block" diagrams (roman numerals added)

and identities of *all* the notes in the series to change, even those whose pitch remains unaffected. (A series of further examples shows additional possibilities.)[54] This disturbance of the "natural qualities" of the notes clearly offends the author's sense of theoretical propriety. Yet despite his evident discomfort with such *vitia*, he does seem, reluctantly, to admit them, presumably for the sake of accommodating pitches that occurred in chant melodies but were not in the regular scale.[55]

The block diagrams used by *SE* in its discussion of this issue, such as the one reproduced in Figure 11.7, are designed to represent graphically the all-important location of the semitone.[56] More common in the *Enchiriadis* treatises, however, are other kinds of notational diagrams, such as the one shown in Figure 11.6a, in which the pitch levels of notes are represented by horizontal lines (with higher notes at the top). As in Hucbald's *cithara* diagram (Fig. 11.1), only the lines (which actually represent strings) signify notes, usually identified with Daseian signs; the intervening spaces represent, but do not differentiate, the intervening whole tones and semitones (although these are often indicated with the letters "t" and "s"). These line diagrams, like Hucbald's, derive from diagrams in Boethius's *De institutione musica*, and were an important

54 *SE*, pp. 61.25–62.29, 65.86–72.149 (trans., pp. 34, 37–42). See Jacobsthal, *Die chromatische Alteration*, pp. 274–354, for extensive discussion of these examples.

55 *SE*, p. 70.132–35 (trans., p. 41). See Atkinson, "From 'Vitium' to 'Tonus acquisitus.'" As Phillips points out, however, this procedure is only workable in "block" diagrams such as these which explicitly show the shift in the position of the semitone, and it occurs only in *SE*'s discussion of *vitia* ("Notationen," pp. 322–23).

56 These block diagrams occur in *SE* on pp. 67–72, 150, 152 (trans., pp. 39, 90–91). Erickson transcribes them into modern notation, but reproduces only the first and last two diagrams as such; in his notes to pp. 39–40, however, he points out three places in Schmid's diplomatic transcriptions where the *tritus* symbol is misplaced. The various diagrams and notational systems used in the *Enchiriadis* treatises receive detailed discussion in Phillips, "Notationen," pp. 305–27. On the importance of such visual representations for music theory, see **Chapter 10, pp. 280–84**.

precursor to staff notation (see below, pp. 344–46). They also shed light on the final topic to be discussed in connection with the *Enchiriadis* system.

This is a problem arising from the conflict between the system's periodicity at the fifth and the acoustical consonance of the octave. In the *Enchiriadis* system, as have seen, recurrence of the modal qualities and identities of notes is found at every fifth step. The number of steps between notes related in this way in two *non-adjacent* tetrachords (for example, *protus gravium* [G] and *protus superiorium* [a]) is therefore nine, not eight. (Two perfect fifths sum to a ninth, not an octave.) Yet singers routinely doubled melodies, and vocal lines in organum, at the octave, and whenever they did so, notes separated at the eighth step clearly shared the same modal quality.

The dilemma, and its solution, are evident in the line diagrams used (especially in *SE*) to represent the intervallic relations among the voices in compound organum.[57] In these, the Daseian signs placed alongside the lines to identify the notes of the octave-doubling voices are not those of the tetrachords in which they would be located were the system being followed strictly. Instead, exactly the same Daseian signs are used for the notes of the doubling voice as for those of its primary voice, merely re-writing them eight lines higher (or lower) so as to represent the octave relationship between the voices. In effect, an octave-based pitch-set is assumed and superimposed, as it were, on the treatises' normative fifth-based system.

The treatises' explanations of this, although different, both amount to saying that the octave, the most "perfect" of the consonances, produces its own set of qualitative replications, different from those of the scale system and independent of it, but not superseding it except for specific purposes. *SE* in addition uses its highly developed concept of modal intervallic pattern to provide a very clear explanation of the underlying cause of the problem.[58] *ME* says little about this, placing greater emphasis on the unique character of the octave itself. Notes in octave relationship "can be said to be not so much 'sounding well together' (*consonae*) as 'equal-sounding' (*aequisonae*), for in this *symphonia* [the same] note recurs anew (*denuo innovatur*)."[59] The sequence of notes is therefore reiterated every eight steps; the contradiction between this and the scalar structure is resolved by invoking the "wondrous change" (*mutatio mirabilis*) wrought by the perfection of the octave (Chapter 11, pp. 33–34; trans., pp. 18–19).

57 See Schmid, pp. 93–101, for this series of diagrams pertaining to compound organum; a similar diagram, but showing simple octave doublings of a single melody, is at ibid., p. 91. (Erickson's transcriptions of these diagrams, pp. 54, 56–63, do not show the use of the Daseian signs.) *ME* says much less about compound organum than does *SE*, and its pertinent diagrams do not employ the device discussed here; see Schmid, pp. 39 and 42 (trans., pp. 22, 24); and Chapter 15, pp. 482–83.

58 *SE*, pp. 148–56 (trans., pp. 89–93). Most of this explanation concerns the system's lack of periodicity at the perfect fourth, which is an important issue in the *Enchiriadis* treatises' teaching of organum, and which, like the system's lack of periodicity at the octave, is due to its periodicity at the perfect fifth (see Fuller, "Theoretical Foundations," pp. 55–57; Cohen, "Boethius and the *Enchiriadis* Theory," esp. pp. 10–16, 205–29).

59 *ME*, Chapter 10, p. 26 (trans., p. 15). The source here is ultimately Ptolemy, but as transmitted by Boethius in *De inst. mus.*, v.9–11 (trans. Bower, *Fundamentals*, pp. 169–72). See also *ME*, Chapters 11, 14, 16, and 17.

It is also in regard to the octave that *ME*, in Chapters 10 and 11, has diagrams that use Latin letters instead of (or in addition to) Daseian signs to represent – although not to identify or name – pitches; they constitute, not a true alphabetic notation, but rather a special device for displaying octave relationships in diagrams designed for that purpose.[60] The use of the recurring series of letters A–G, A–G + A to represent octave-related pitches, seen in the diagrams of Chapter 11, appears to be a Frankish innovation, with no earlier extant medieval witness than *ME*.[61] Its occurrences there foreshadow the letter notation introduced in the *Dialogus de musica* of c. 1000 (discussed below, pp. 340–41), which is the direct ancestor of the letter names we still use today.

The *Enchiriadis* treatises provide our earliest extant statements of an approach that was to be fundamental for all subsequent Western modal theory: the modal character and identity of a melody is determined by, and identified with, the pattern of intervals exhibited by that melody with respect to its final, in relation to a background scale system. With this radical change in the conception of its nature, mode becomes, at least in principle, a scientifically definable property.

The *Alia musica*. The compilation of texts known collectively as *Alia musica* (hereafter *AM*) introduces several ideas that would become important aspects of modal theory from the eleventh century on.[62] This "treatise" comprises at least three textual layers, the number and relations of which remain a matter of dispute, as do their individual dates, relative chronology, and the date of the compilation as a whole – although it is generally accepted that they probably fall within the later ninth and/or earlier tenth centuries. According to Chailley's widely accepted analysis, *AM* consists of three distinct and successive layers (intermingled in the text itself), of which the second is described by Chailley as "the principal treatise" (*Traité principale*) – the *Alia musica* "proper" – and the third a "new exposition" (*Nova expositio*), by three distinct authors, all anonymous.[63] For the sake of convenience I follow his analysis here, calling his three authors simply Authors 1, 2, and 3.

60 See pp. 27, 29, 32 (trans., pp. 16–18). Erickson gives the first and last of these only in modern transcription, but comments on the use of letters in his notes 27 and 29, ibid. Two rather different uses of Latin letters in diagrams occur in *SE*, on pp. 91 and 147 (trans., pp. 54, 89).
61 Boethius uses continuous series of Latin letters (A–G–O and A–G–P) to represent notes or pitches in *De inst. mus.*, IV.14 and 17; in IV.6–11 he uses the series A–O–LL to mark points in monochord divisions. See Crocker, "Alphabet Notations"; Phillips, "Notationen," pp. 549–51.
62 For citations see the Bibliography, p. 357. For accounts of the treatise, see Hiley, *Western Plainchant*, pp. 461–62; Meyer, "Tonartenlehre," pp. 149–53; Chailley, *Alia musica*, "Introduction." Chailley's edition and its introduction are henceforth cited simply by page and (for the edition only) section numbers.
63 Regarding the specific contributions of each, the relations of these to each other, and their distribution in the text as we have it, see Chailley, pp. 3–27; Heard, "*Alia musica*," p. 2–23. Chailley's edition is organized according to his textual analysis: it presents the three layers separately rather than in the sequence of material in the manuscripts, in which they are intermingled; his section numbers, however, reflect the latter ordering.

The text assigned by Chailley to Author 1 (pp. 85.181–97.156) is an attempt to define and distinguish the eight modes by purely mathematical means – numerical ratios representing intervals as produced on a monochord – which we may pass over here.[64] Author 1 neither teaches a scale system nor refers to notes in any way other than by these numbers, or by letters that represent the numbers themselves, not notes. Each *tonus* is identified by the syllables of its intonation formula (e.g., "Nonanoeane") and by the traditional Greek-derived names (*autentus protus*, etc.); antiphons are cited as examples of each.

The text ascribed to Author 2, the "principal treatise" (pp. 99.1–179.180) is, in Chailley's view, largely a commentary on the text of Author 1, supplementing the latter with material drawn mainly from Boethius. Author 2 increases the clarity and concreteness of the latter's discussion by occasionally using the ancient Greek note names (*proslambanomenos*, etc.) to designate specific notes, which Author 1 had designated only by numbers.[65] But the principal treatise's chief contributions consist in its importation into western modal theory of two doctrines of ancient Greek harmonics, adapted from Boethius: the species of the octave, and the Greek topical or ethnic names – "Dorian," "Phrygian," and so on – of the *tonoi*, the transposition keys of Greek theory. Both the ethnic names and a particular enumeration of the species of the octave figure conspicuously in Boethius's account of the *tonoi*, which Boethius calls "modes," "tropes," and "tones" (*modi*, *tropi*, *toni*), and which "arise from the species of the octave."[66]

"Species" in this context means a particular ordering of the intervals between the consecutive notes contained within one of the consonances of the perfect fourth (*diatessaron*), fifth (*diapente*), and octave (*diapason*).[67] In the diatonic genus – the only one used by the medieval theorists – these inter-step intervals are always whole tones and semitones. The distinct species of any consonance are always fewer by one than the number of notes comprised inclusively by that consonance. Thus there are three species of fourth, each with two whole tones and one semitone; four species of fifth, each with three whole tones and one semitone; and seven species of octave, each with five whole tones and two semitones. The species are, properly speaking, simply the various distinct orderings of these inter-step intervals, which can be numbered in any way desired. Typically, however, the species are taught by selecting successively higher

64 See Chailley, pp. 14–20; Meyer, "Tonartenlehre," pp. 149–52.

65 See, e.g., pp. 135.62–141.72. In just one passage the Byzantine ordinal numbers (*protos*, etc.) are used, as they are in the *Enchiriadis* treatises, to designate individual notes (p. 138.68).

66 *De inst. mus.*, IV.15. Regarding this passage and the Greek *tonoi*, see above, p. 312 and n. 19. Boethius's discussion of the species and the "modes" is in *De inst. mus.*, IV.14–17; see Bower, *Fundamentals*, pp. 148–60, with notes. For further discussion of these topics, see Barbera, "Octave Species"; Bower, "The Modes of Boethius"; Markovits, *Tonsystem*, pp. 81–93.

67 Medieval theorists referred to these intervals by their Greek names: *diatessaron*, *diapente*, and *diapason* (respectively). The familiar English names will be used in this chapter, however, for the sake of convenience. Note that, in this context, "fourth," "fifth," and "octave" always denote the "perfect" forms of those intervals.

or lower appropriately sized segments of a background scale; the resulting different sequences of whole tones and semitones between the different pairs of segmental boundary notes are the different species of the consonance. (Usually these scale segments are adjacent.) For example, the three species of fourth can be mapped consecutively onto a diatonic scale in several ways, one of which would be to define the first species of fourth as S–T–T, located between B and E; the second species as T–T–S, between C and F; and the third as T–S–T, between D and G.

Boethius provides two distinct enumerations of the species of all three consonances (*De institutione musica*, IV.14). His first enumeration of the species of the octave (Friedlein, p. 339.4–10; trans. Bower, p. 150) is the one he employs in his subsequent discussion of the "modes" (ibid., Chapters 15–17). In it, the octave species are listed in descending order: the first octave species is at the top of scale, between *nete hyperbolaion* (aa) and *mese* (a), and the seventh octave species occurs seven steps lower, between *paramese* (b) and *hypate hypaton* (B). See Table 11.3, left side. (The eighth octave species will be explained shortly.)

Boethius's "modes" (*modi*, *toni*, *tropi*) are equivalent to the Greek *tonoi* in that they are different transpositional levels of the complete double-octave scale. They "arise from the species of the octave" in the sense that the sequence of *descending* intervals (↓T–T–S–T–T–S–T) between the starting notes of the octave species (aa, g, f, e, d, c, b, a) determines the intervals of *upward* transposition between the "modes": the order of the intervals is the same, but their direction is reversed.[68] The octave species and the modes are quite different things, which stand in a subtly inverse and, in a sense, causal relationship.[69]

It is to these transpositional "modes," and not to the octave species themselves, that Boethius applies the ancient Greek ethnic names ("Dorian," etc.). Further, Boethius, erroneously citing Ptolemy in support, also includes an eighth "mode," the "Hypermixolydian," whose associated "eighth" octave species is in fact simply the first octave species an octave lower.[70] See again the left-hand side of Table 11.3.

It is on the basis of a misreading of this complicated, utterly alien system that our

68 As Bower puts it, the octave species form an "intervallic matrix" that determines the successive upward transpositions of the scale ("Modes of Boethius," p. 261).

69 Powers's explanation of Boethius's "modes" ("Mode," pp. 777–78) provides a rationale for the system, adapted from Ptolemy's explanation of his own system of *tonoi* in *Harmonics*, II.11 (trans. Barker, *Greek Musical Writings*, vol. II, pp. 338–40): the upward transpositions of the scale, by tones and semitones whose sequence is determined by the descending series of octave species, generate those same octave species, successively and in order, at a fixed level of pitch equivalent to the octave between *nete diezeugmenon* (e) and *hypate meson* (E) in the central, Dorian *tonos*. (See further Barker, ibid., pp. 14–27; Mathiesen, *Apollo's Lyre*, pp. 458–66, 634.) Certain basic resemblances between Ptolemy's and Boethius's systems make it plausible that this or something like it was the underlying reason for Boethius's "modes," but Boethius himself says nothing to indicate that he was even aware of it.

70 *De inst. mus.*, IV.17 (Friedlein edn., pp. 347.18–348.3; trans. Bower, *Fundamentals*, pp. 159–60). Ptolemy had in fact explicitly rejected the notion of an eighth *tonos*, since for him the number of *tonoi* is determined by the number of distinct octave species, that is, seven; see Ptolemy, *Harmonics*, II.9; trans. Barker, *Greek Musical Writings*, vol. II, pp. 334–36; Mathiesen, *Apollo's Lyre*, pp. 463–64.

Table 11.3 *Modes and octave species in Boethius and* Alia musica *(principal treatise)*

Boethius	Alia musica	
Octave species → Mode (tonos)	Octave species = mode (tonus)	
1. aa–a (↓ t–t–s–t–t–s–t) → Hypodorian	1. A–a	= Hypodorian
2. g–G (↓ t–s–t–t–s–t–t) → Hypophrygian	2. B–b	= Hypophrygian
3. f–F (↓ s–t–t–s–t–t–t) → Hypolydian	3. C–c	= Hypolydian
4. e–E (↓ t–t–s–t–t–t–s) → Dorian	4. D–d	= Dorian
5. d–D (↓ t–s–t–t–t–s–t) → Phrygian	5. E–d	= Phrygian
6. c–C (↓ s–t–t–t–s–t–t) → Lydian	6. F–f	= Lydian
7. b–B (↓ t–t–t–s–t–t–s) → Mixolydian	7. G–g	= Mixolydian
8. a–A (↓ t–t–s–t–t–s–t) → Hypermixolydian	8. a–aa	= Hypermixolydian

Notes: The boundary notes of Boethius's octave species (left-most column) are represented by their equivalents in the Western diatonic scale, expressed in medieval letter notation. The symbols → and = represent the different relationships between the modes and the octave species in the two systems, as discussed in the text.

Author 2 imports the octave species and the ethnic Greek names into the system of the ecclesiastical *toni* (the church modes), resulting in what Chailley calls the "baptism" of the latter with the names "Dorian." "Phrygian," and so on (pp. 28–56; p. 40).[71] He begins from the basic misunderstanding that Boethius's *modi* or *toni* must be the same things as the eight *toni* of ecclesiastical chant – a misprision made almost inevitable by Boethius's statement that the terms *modus*, *tropus*, and *tonus* all refer to the same thing, and by the fact that Boethius's set of "modes," like the *toni* of the church, are eight in number. On this basis, he – like Hucbald and *Musica enchiriadis* – adopts the terms *modus* and *tropus* (especially the latter) as the proper designations for those things traditionally called *toni* (p. 105.13). Yet the church modes were more than mere scales: certain notes, especially the finals, had special significance, and the melodies of each mode shared common melodic characteristics (Hiley, "Modus," p. 402).

With this, however, our author's errors have only begun. (See now the right-hand side of Table 11.3.) Where Boethius's system had the octave species and the modes in a subtle causal and structurally inverse relationship, our Author 2 simply equates the two, creating a set of modes conceived as octave scales ("modal octaves"), each associated with an octave species and mapped onto an octave segment of the background scale (pp. 32–46). And where Boethius's octave species proceeded in descending sequence, our author has them in ascending order, with the first species running

71 *AM*'s Author 2 also lists the species of fourth and fifth (pp. 107.16–110.18), just *after* the species of the octave; unlike the latter, however, they play no role in his modal theory. It should also be noted that these Greek names ("Dorian," etc.) are also occasionally applied to the modes in texts of the *Enchiriadis* group; see, e.g., *ME*, Chapter 9 (Schmid, p. 22.20; trans., p. 12).

Table 11.4 Alia musica *(principal treatise): octave species, modes (first enumeration), and ethnic names*

Octave species/mode	Ethnic name	Boundary notes	Intervallic pattern (↑)
8	Hypermixolydian	a–aa	t–s–t–t–s–t–t
7	Mixolydian	G–g	t–t–s–t–t–s–t
6	Lydian	F–f	t–t–t–s–t–t–s
5	Phrygian	E–e	s–t–t–t–s–t–t
4	Dorian	D–d	t–s–t–t–t–s–t
3	Hypolydian	C–c	t–t–s–t–t–t–s
2	Hypophrygian	B–b	s–t–t–s–t–t–t
1	Hypodorian	A–a	t–s–t–t–s–t–t

between the lowest note of the scale, *proslambanomenos* (A), and *mese* (a).[72] Yet in making this reversal in the ordering of the species themselves he keeps the association between their ordinal numbers and the Greek ethnic names the same: his first octave species is still called "Hypodorian," although it is actually the one associated with the last of Boethius's eight modes, the "Hypermixolydian," and so on for the rest. Finally, our author has no choice but to assign the number and name of this eighth mode, the Hypermixolydian, along with the octave species he has assigned to it (a–aa), to the eighth church mode, the plagal *tetrardus* (p. 107.16), despite the fact that this octave species is inappropriate for that mode, as we shall see shortly.

As a result of these various distortions of Boethius's "modes," our author is convinced that a set of eight octave species, in ascending order from the bottom of the scale, are to be identified with the eight ecclesiastical *toni* (which he calls *modi* or *tropi*), creating a series of modal octaves which he therefore feels justified in designating by the eight ethnic names ("Dorian," etc.) that Boethius had used for his eight "modes."[73] The resulting system is summarized in Table 11.4. As Tables 11.3 and 11.4 show, because Boethius here counted his octave species down from the top of the scale, while our author counts them up from the bottom, the latter symmetrically inverts the ordered series of octave species around the two middle ones, the octaves on E and D, which switch places, while the correlation of the ordinal numbers and the ethnic names remains unchanged. Thus Boethius's fourth octave species (counting from the top), E–e, which is associated (indirectly) with the mode he called "Dorian," appears in *AM* as the fifth one (from the bottom), and is directly identified with a mode named "Phrygian." Precisely the converse is true of Boethius's fifth octave species, D–d, and its mode, "Phrygian": in *AM* this species is the fourth one, and is identified with the

72 Unlike Hucbald's re-structuring of the tetrachords of the GPS (above, pp. 319–22), this seems to be simply an error, not a conscious adaptation; see Chailley, pp. 46–49.
73 Chailley, p. 107.15. The passage is translated in *SR*, p. 197.

Table 11.5 Alia musica *(principal treatise): modal octaves and traditional enumeration of the church modes*

Octave species	Ethnic name	Mode	Final	Ambitus
8. a–aa (!?)	Hypermixolydian	8	G	Plagal (!?)
7. G–g	Mixolydian	7	G	Authentic
6. F–f	Lydian	5	F	Authentic
5. E–e	Phrygian	3	E	Authentic
4. D–d	Dorian	1	D	Authentic
3. C–c	Hypolydian	6	F	Plagal
2. B–b	Hypophrygian	4	E	Plagal
1. A–a	Hypodorian	2	D	Plagal

"Dorian" mode. The same inversion occurs between the pairs numbered 3 and 6 (Hypolydian and Lydian), 2 and 7 (Hypophrygian and Phrygian), and 1 and 8 (Hypodorian and Hypermixolydian).[74]

For Modes 1–6 the results are satisfactory: the two modes of each of the first three pairs have similar octave species, and the plagal or "Hypo-" mode in each pair is located a fourth *below* its partner (*hypo* means "below") (p. 111.20). The eighth mode, on the other hand, whose very name, "Hypermixolydian," suggests a range *above* Mode 7 (Mixolydian), was anomalous, as can be seen in Table 11.5, in which the modes with their new ethnic names are arranged in order of octave species and grouped by authentic or plagal ambitus. The obvious problems with the eighth mode, including its discrepant relationship with Mode 7, result directly from our author's assumption that the eighth church mode must be identical to an eighth octave species that simply replicates the first species, one octave higher (a–aa). Subsequently, when he switches from ordering by octave species to the traditional ordering of *toni* by final and ambitus (pp. 121.30ff.), our author avoids stating that this octave species belongs to the eighth mode, although he continues to call this mode "Hypermixolydian," as shown in Table 11.6.

The problem of the eighth mode was solved in two stages, the first of which was accomplished in *AM*'s *Nova expositio*, by Author 3. The latter text (pp. 180–204), in Chailley's analysis, consists of a series of interpolations into the already compound text of Authors 1 and 2. In addition to further concretizing their discussions by regular use of note names,[75] these interpolations present for the first time one of the crucial con-

74 See Gollin, "From *Tonoi* to *Modi*," for further discussion of these inversional relationships.

75 Like Author 2, Author 3 employs the GPS plus *synemmenon* tetrachord. In addition to the ancient Greek note names and the Byzantine-derived modal nomenclature (*protus*, etc.), he also designates notes with the series of Latin letters – (A–O–LL) used in Boethius's main monochord division (*De inst. mus.*, IV.6–11); see Phillips, "Notationen," pp. 549–54. (Chailley's discussion of this notation, pp. 180–82, is unreliable.)

Table 11.6 Alia musica *(principal treatise): Same system as in Table 11.5, but with modes ordered by authentic–plagal pairs*

Mode	Final	Ambitus	Ethnic name	Octave species	
7	G	Authentic	Mixolydian		7. G–g
8	G	Plagal	Hypermixolydian	(8. a–aa?)	
5	F	Authentic	Lydian		6. F–f
6	F	Plagal	Hypolydian	3. C–c	
3	E	Authentic	Phrygian		5. E–e
4	E	Plagal	Hypophrygian	2. B–b	
1	D	Authentic	Dorian		4. D–d
2	D	Plagal	Hypodorian	1. A–a	

ceptual developments in Western medieval modal theory: the division of the modal octaves into their constituent perfect fourths and fifths as a means of distinguishing the authentic and plagal modes with the same final. The result is the first (and more important) step in the solution of the problem of the eighth mode.

This solution (pp. 196.133ff.) is represented in Figure 11.8. Its key is the positing of regular divisions of the modal octaves, different for authentics and plagals, and a mapping of these onto a background scalar system. The authentic modes are bounded at the bottom by a set of four notes called *inferiores*, which are identified as the finals, and divided by the *superiores*, which act as their "middle notes" (*mediae chordae*), into a perfect fifth below a perfect fourth. The plagals, conversely, are bounded at the top by the notes a perfect fifth above the finals (the *superiores*), and are divided by their finals into a perfect fourth below a perfect fifth.[76] Modes 1 through 7 have the same octave species as in Author 2's account. But the last plagal, Mode 8 (the "Hypermixolydian"), no longer has the latter author's eighth octave species. This mode has been shifted to a new location and now runs between D and d. This makes it consistent with the other plagals: like them, it now lies a fourth below its authentic partner, Mode 7 (Mixolydian), with its final, G, at the fourth step from the bottom. The fourth-species octave, D–d, is thus assigned to both Mode 8 and Mode 1. Yet the two are different, Author 3 explains, because they divide their common octave differently: "the former has the *media chorda G* as the guardian of its quality (*suae qualitatis custodem*), while the latter [has in this role] a, under the name *protus*" (p. 202.143). The author does not explicitly say that G is the final of the eighth mode; he calls it instead the "middle note" (*media chorda*), the same term he applies to the note a in the first mode. Yet his earlier statement that "each plagal has a perfect fifth above, and a perfect fourth below, its final"

76 See especially p. 200.140. Author 3 goes on to give the numerical proportions corresponding to these divisions of the octave (fifth below, fourth above = 12:8:6; the converse = 12:9:6). Such proportions (the harmonic and the arithmetic, respectively) had already been discussed by Author 2 (pp. 99.1–104.12), following Boethius's *De institutione arithmetica*, II.48, 49, 54.

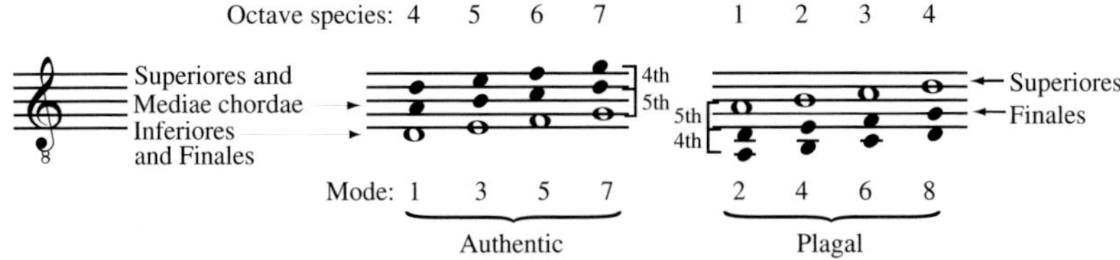

Figure 11.8 *Alia musica, Nova expositio*: authentic and plagal modes distinguished by division of modal octave (after Chailley, *Alia musica*, p. 199)

(p. 201.140), and the designation of G as the "guardian of [the mode's] quality" here, at least imply that Author 3 did indeed understand G to be the final.

This was, in effect, the basic solution to the problem of the eighth mode that was to become standard in medieval theory from the first half of the eleventh century on. The theorists of both the North Italian and South German "schools" discussed in section II below assign to Mode 8 the same modal octave (D–d) as Mode 1, but a different final, G. Clarification of the difference between Modes 1 and 8 is particularly important in the writings of the south German theorists, especially Hermannus Contractus, who also seems to have been the first to replace the term "Hypermixolydian" with "Hypomixolydian" (see *GS* II, pp. 132a, 134), thus bringing Mode 8 completely into line with the other plagals and completing the familiar set of Greek modal names and correspondent church modes occasionally used by subsequent medieval theorists.

Each of the later ninth-century treatises discussed in this chapter testifies, in its own way, to the later Carolingians' realization that two of their goals – more accurate transmission and performance of chant melodies, and more precise and consistent definition of the properties of the eight modes, to facilitate modal classification of melodies – could be brought much closer to full realization by the adaptation and application of music-theoretical concepts and constructs found in the writers of antiquity, especially Boethius. The result was a new, "scientific" concept of mode, far more abstract than that of the earlier Carolingian period, but also, and for just that reason, capable of far more precise definition and general application: mode as a particular series of identifiable notes, comprising a set of specifiable intervallic relations, occupying a specific set of positions on a background scale system. Indeed, the evidence suggests that it was precisely the Carolingians' rediscovery, in their ancient sources, of the idea of a scale system, and of its elementary components, notes and intervals, that made this new conception of mode possible. With it, the melodies of plainchant became objects of precise, systematic structural analysis, and the medieval West, building on foundations laid down in antiquity, inaugurated a new tradition of music theory.[77]

77 Calvin Bower presents a complementary assessment in Chapter 5, pp. 158–64.

II The eleventh-century syntheses

Starting about the year 1000, theorists, combining elements selected from the disparate approaches of the Carolingians with new ideas of their own, produced new theoretical syntheses that incorporated, or formed the basis for, further developments in pedagogy and systematizing theory in the eleventh and later centuries. Among these were a new use of the monochord and the creation of the standard medieval scale system (the Guidonian "gamut"), hexachordal solmization and the "Guidonian Hand," and staff notation, along with significant contributions to the theory of the modes. It was at this time, too, that the method of intervallic analysis – of melodies, of the modes, and of the structure of the scale itself – became firmly established, in two distinct and ultimately compatible doctrines of modal theory: the "affinities" and *modi vocum*, and the modal species of the consonances. These doctrines were, respectively, the creations of the two main eleventh-century "schools" of music theory: the Northern Italian school of Guido of Arezzo and his important predecessor, Pseudo-Odo, and the South German school that originated with Berno of Reichenau and Hermannus Contractus.

Italian pedagogy c. 1000–1032: the Dialogus de musica *and Guido of Arezzo*

Guido of Arezzo, the most influential music theorist and pedagogue of the Middle Ages, was the author of four extant musical texts, all composed c. 1026 – c. 1033.[78] The scholarly literature on Guido is, of course, considerable.[79]

Guido's teachings represent the culmination of a Northern Italian school of music theory and pedagogy, the most important representative of which (apart from Guido himself) is the *Dialogus de musica*, also known as *Enchiridion musices* ("Handbook of Music").[80] Formerly attributed to the Abbot Odo of Cluny (d. 942), it was compiled c. 1000 by an anonymous Lombard monk now known as "Pseudo-Odo." The *Dialogus* is a source for much of Guido's teaching, particularly in his principal treatise, the *Micrologus*.

These and other texts in this Italian tradition share a common inclination to downplay the speculative aspects of music theory in favor of a more pragmatically pedagogical approach oriented to the needs of the *cantor* and the schoolmaster. Yet at

78 Full citations of titles, editions and translations are found in the Bibliography, pp. 357–58, under "Guido." For the *Micrologus*, the translation in Babb, *Hucbald, Guido, and John* is cited here (as "Babb"). For the "Epistola" and the "Prologus," the translations in *SR* are cited here (as "trans.").

79 See, e.g., Palisca, "Guido of Arezzo"; and "Introduction" to the *Micrologus* in Babb, *Hucbald, Guido and John*, pp. 49–56; Hiley, *Western Plainchant*, pp. 466–70; Pesce's "Introduction" to her *Guido d'Arezzo's Regulae*, pp. 1–38; Atkinson, "Tonsystem," pp. 124–33; Meyer, "Tonartenlehre," pp. 155–71; Gushee, "Questions," pp. 407–10; Oesch, *Guido von Arezzo*.

80 Ed. *GS* 1, pp. 251–64. Partial translation in *SR*, pp. 198–210 (cited hereafter as "trans."). For discussion of the text's origins, context, and contents, see ibid., pp. 198–99; Hiley, *Western Plainchant*, pp. 463–66; Atkinson, "Tonsystem," pp. 120–24; Meyer, "Tonartenlehre," pp. 155–71; Huglo, "Odo"; "L'Auteur"; and "Prolog"; Gushee, "Questions," pp. 404–07; Oesch, *Guido von Arezzo*.

the same time they carry forward, in new ways, a theoretical agenda begun by the *Enchiriadis* treatises: structural analysis of the scale as the basis for structural definition of the modes.

Monochord divisions, scale systems, and letter notation. Pseudo-Odo's *Dialogus* and Guido's *Micrologus* both begin with the monochord – its use as a didactic tool, and easy ways of dividing its string to produce the notes of the scale.[81] Both thus immediately exemplify a new pedagogical approach that would be widespread from the eleventh century on. In antiquity and in Carolingian times, the monochord had been used as an instrument for "demonstrating" interval ratios in the science of harmonics, the *ars musica*. (This is its function in its only appearances in the late Carolingian treatises.)[82] From about the year 1000, however, it is frequently used as a didactic tool, taught as a way of laying out the scale and training the ear in the correct sounds of its intervals. For Pseudo-Odo, and for Guido in the *Micrologus*, this use of the monochord is an essential first step in a new method designed to teach student singers how to learn new melodies by singing them at sight from letter notation.[83]

The scale produced by Pseudo-Odo's monochord division is essentially that of the GPS-plus-*synemmenon* (see below) used by Hucbald (A–aa, with b♭ in the upper octave), but without any tetrachordal subdivision, and with an additional low G, named *gamma* (written Γ), below the scale's official "first step," A, to accommodate those plagal *protus* melodies that reach the fifth below the final. The notes b♭ and b♮ in the second octave are, respectively, the "first" and "second ninth steps." Pseudo-Odo names these notes (except for *gamma*) with the same octave-based series of Latin letters that we still use today (A–G). He also introduces two graphic conventions that remained in use well beyond the end of the Middle Ages: the use of capital, lower-case, and doubled lower-case letters to differentiate octave related notes (A–G, a–g, aa); and the use of two forms of the letter "b" for the two pitches available as alternative forms of the "ninth step": the "square b" (*b quadratum*), written ♮, as the symbol for "hard b" (*b durum*), our "b-natural," and "round b" (*b rotundum*), written ♭, as the symbol for "soft b" (*b molle*), our "b-flat." (The modern symbols for "flat," "natural," and "sharp" derive from these.) See Table 11.7. Guido keeps all of this, and adds four more notes above aa, notated as ♮♮/♭♭, cc, and dd. The note ee was later added to complete a hexachord on g (see below).

Neither Pseudo-Odo nor Guido divides the scale into tetrachords. Instead, each points out its division into octave segments, and stresses the concept of octave equivalence, which results both from the acoustical consonance of the octave itself and the recurrence of identical intervallic patterns around notes eight steps apart (*Micrologus*,

81 Regarding monochord divisions, see **Chapter 6, pp. 168–92**; Adkins, "Theory and Practice"; Meyer, *Mensura monochordi*; Sachs, "Elementarlehre," pp. 152–61; Brockett, Jr., "Comparison."
82 See above, n. 46 and pp. 318, 322. On the concept and use of the monochord as "a precision instrument for scientific demonstration," see Reckow, "Organum-Begriff."
83 See *Dialogus*, trans., pp. 199–204; *Micrologus*, Prologue (Babb, p. 58).

Table 11.7 *The scale of Pseudo-Odo's* Dialogus (*GS* I, p. 253; Trans. *SR*, p. 202)

"Step":		1	2	3	4	5	6	7	8	9	9	10	11	12	13	14	15
	Γ	A	B	C	D	E	F	G	a	♭	♮	c	d	e	f	g	aa
		t	t	s	t	t	s	t	t	s		s	t	t	s	t	t

Chapters 5–6, 9). Guido further emphasizes the scale's octave-based structure with a new set of names for its subsegments: *graves* for the notes from the low A to G; *acutae* for the notes a–g; and *superacutae* for aa–dd (and later ee) (ibid., Chapter 2). The resulting scale – the Guidonian gamut – is shown at the left of Table 11.8.

The scale in this form remained standard throughout the Middle Ages, although for some time there was disagreement about the status of the note b♭. Its presence in the otherwise purely diatonic system was due to a possibility of the ancient Greek scalar systems that provided the basis for the gamut: the addition of the *synemmenon* tetrachord, properly part of the Lesser Perfect System (LPS), to the four tetrachords of the Greater Perfect System (GPS) to form the so-called "Immutable System" (*systema ametabolon*). The latter's five tetrachords comprised eighteen notes but only sixteen distinct pitches: the fifteen of the GPS plus the *trite synemmenon*, the note equivalent to b♭, which the medievals often simply called "the *synemmenon*." This was the scale system that Hucbald had reorganized into T–S–T tetrachords in ascending order from the lowest note, *proslambanomenos* (A). The note b♭ was for centuries seen by most theorists as an additional, extraneous element, not a fully fledged member of the scale; Guido himself was particularly adamant on this point. Others, however, especially German theorists writing c. 1100, were less suspicious of the b♭, and even urged the inclusion of a low B♭, a *synemmenon grave*, as well.

Optional extensions and additions to the gamut began to appear by the later fourteenth century (see below, **p. 356** and also **Chapter 6, p. 173**). The Latin letter names for the notes are, of course, still with us to this day.

Hexachords and the "Hand"; solmization and mutation; staff notation. The right-hand portion of Table 11.8 shows the system of hexachords that developed from one of Guido's most celebrated and influential innovations, solmization, which Guido presents (in the *Epistola de ignoto cantu*) as a new and more efficient method of learning how to sing at sight and transcribe by ear an unfamiliar melody.

The basis of Guido's method was to have the student singer learn to recognize and produce the notes of the scale by associating each with a melodic phrase that starts with that note and thus provides a mnemonic for the intervallic relations of that note to the notes around it. He used for this purpose the hymn *Ut queant laxis*, each of whose first six short phrases begins with a different note, in ascending order by step, starting from C. (See Example 11.1, p. 343.)

Table 11.8 *The Guidonian gamut and hexachords*

	ee							la
	dd						la	sol
superacutae	cc						sol	fa
	♭♭/♮♮						fa	mi
	aa					la	mi	re
	g					sol	re	ut
	f					fa	ut	
	e				la	mi		
acutae	d			la	sol	re		
	c			sol	fa	ut		
	♭ / ♮			fa	mi			
	a		la	mi	re			
	G		sol	re	ut			
	F		fa	ut				
	E	la	mi					
graves	D	sol	re					
	C	fa	ut					
	B	mi						
	A	re						
	Γ	ut						

The result (not stated explicitly by Guido) is a scale segment of six notes, C–D–E–F–G–A, with the interval series T–T–S–T–T, sung to the initial syllables of the first six phrases of the hymn: *Ut*, *Re*, *Mi*, *Fa*, *Sol*, *La*.[84] Guido's method was quickly adopted, elaborated, and formalized by subsequent teachers and theorists of the later eleventh and twelfth centuries into the system shown in the right-hand portion of Table 11.8, an explanation of which now follows.

Guido's six-note segment comprises, in effect, a T–S–T tetrachord plus the notes a whole tone above and below; its size, a major sixth, and its symmetrical intervallic structure make position finding with respect to the central semitone easy. Placed at all seven of its possible locations in the gamut, it acts as a basic scalar module: the "hexachord" (as we call it). The six notes of any hexachord, regardless of its location, are sung to the syllables *ut*, *re*, *mi*, *fa*, *sol*, *la*, which act as vocables for solmization, or as the medievals called them, *voces* (singular: *vox*), and also embody the intervallic relationships of each note to the others. The semitone, crucial for position finding, is always located between the two middle notes, *mi* and *fa*.

The intervallic structure of the gamut is such that this hexachord is the largest scale segment whose internal series of tones and semitones replicates itself at intervals other than the octave, namely, the perfect fourth and fifth. This allows the hexachord to be

84 For a fuller discussion of Guido's method, see Pesce, *Guido d'Arezzo's Regulae*, pp. 19–20.

Example 11.1 The hymn "Ut queant laxis" (*Liber usualis*, p. 1504) in Odonian letter notation. From Guido of Arezzo, *Epistola de ignoto cantu*, trans. *SR*, p. 217

C D F D–E D
Ut que – ant la – xis

D D C D E E
Re – so – na – re fi – bris

E–F–G E D E–C D
Mi – ra ges – to – rum

F G a G F–D D
Fa – mu – li tu – o – rum

G–A–G F–E F G D
Sol – ve pol – lu – ti

a G a F G–a a
La – bi – i re – a – tum

G–F E–D C E D
Sanc – te Jo – an – nes

(Translation: "That your servants may be able freely to proclaim the wonders of your deeds, absolve the guilt of their unclean lips, O holy John.")

located with *ut* on any C, G, or (by using b♭) F. These constituted three basic types or species of hexachord: the "hard" (*durum*), G–E, with "hard b" as *mi*; the "soft" (*molle*), F–D, with "soft b" as *fa*; and the "natural" (*naturale*), C–A, with neither form of b. The theorists referred to each of these as a "song" (*cantus*) or (from the thirteenth century) a "property" (*proprietas*). See Table 11.9. Placing each of these at all its possible locations in the gamut results in the complete system of seven overlapping hexachords – or *deductiones*, as they were called – shown in Table 11.8.

The Latin letter name of each note (its *littera* or *clavis*) was combined with its solmization syllable (*vox*) or syllables (*voces*) in a composite note name; thus the lowest note, for example, was called *gamma-ut* (written Γ-*ut*) – whence the name "gamut." Because the seven hexachords overlap at various points, most pitches in the system have two or three different *voces* in their composite name; for example, the middle G of the system

Table 11.9 *The three hexachordal* proprietates

	Ut	*Re*	*Mi*	*Fa*	*Sol*	*La*
"Hard"	G (t)	A (t)	B (s)	C (t)	D (t)	E
"Natural"	C (t)	D (t)	E (s)	F (t)	G (t)	A
"Soft"	F (t)	G (t)	A (s)	B♭ (t)	C (t)	D

was called G-*sol-re-ut*. The note b in the upper two octaves is always named (in this system of nomenclature) b *fa b mi*; in this case, however, the two *voces* denote two distinct pitches. (A note's specific registral location was often made completely explicit by including the word *gravis*, *acutus*, or *superacutus*.) Each of these composite names constitutes a "place" (*locus*) in the system.

Moving through the scale beyond the range of a single hexachord required the singer to make a "mutation" at an appropriate *locus*, that is, to treat one of the notes with two or three *voces* as a pivot point, shifting from one of its *voces* to the other so as to accommodate the direction and range of the melodic phrase being sung: mutating from a higher *vox* in one hexachord to a lower one in another hexachord (for example, from *sol* to *re* or *ut* on G-*sol-re-ut*) facilitates upward motion beyond the top note of the first hexachord, and conversely for downward motion. Mutation was not permitted between b *fa* and b *mi*, however, since these represented different pitches.[85]

Closely associated with hexachordal solmization is another, equally celebrated pedagogical device that was universally attributed to Guido, although no extant text by him mentions it: the Guidonian "hand" (*manus*). Each "place" of the gamut (the *littera* plus *vox* or *voces* for each note) was visualized as occupying a position on one of the joints or fingertips of the left hand (see Plate 11.1 for a seventeenth-century rendition). The importance of this device in pedagogy led in time to the habit of referring to the gamut as "the Hand."[86] From the later thirteenth century on, hexachordal solmization and modal theory were brought into increasingly close connection; see below, p. 355.

Finally we must mention the most important of all the innovations ascribed to Guido, and one in which he certainly played an early and significant role: staff notation.[87] In his *Prologue to an Antiphoner*, Guido explains the principles of staff notation,

85 The procedures of solmization and mutation are taught in countless elementary texts from the thirteenth through the sixteenth century and beyond. (See, for example, the discussion in Chapter 13, pp. 408–13.) A particularly exhaustive discussion of these topics occurs in Johannes Aegidius de Zamora, *Ars musica* (c. 1300), Chapters 5–8 (ed./trans. cit., pp. 62–77).

86 For more detailed discussion of solmization and its subsequent development, see Hughes, "Solmization"; Berger, *Musica Ficta*, pp. 2–55; Atkinson, "Tonsystem," pp. 126–33. Regarding the Hand, see further Waesberghe, *Musikerziehung*, pp. 118–43 with plates 57–84; Berger, "The Hand and the Art of Memory." Another illustration of the "Hand" is found in Plate 12.1, p. 369.

87 Regarding Guido's staff notation, its precursors and its development, see Pesce, *Guido d'Arezzo's Regulae*, pp. 17–19; Phillips, "Notationen," pp. 581–85, 602–23; Smits van Waesberghe, "The Musical Notation of Guido"; and *Musikerziehung*, pp. 110–11.

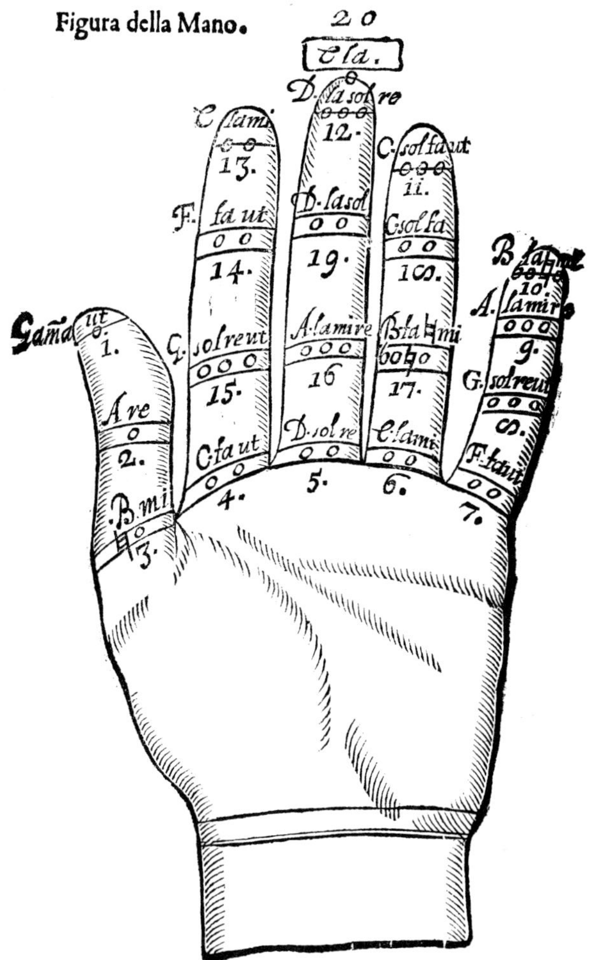

Plate 11.1 The Guidonian Hand from L. Penna, *Li primi albori musicali* (1672), p. 9

the really revolutionary feature of which is that not only the lines, but also the spaces between them, represent notes. Some of the lines or spaces are labeled, at the left margin, with the appropriate letter (*littera*), which indirectly indicates the identities of the rest (hence the practice of calling the letters *claves*, that is, "keys" to the staff). Guido mentions specifically in this regard the notes F and C (each of which borders a semitone), and adds that the lines or spaces representing these notes are to be marked with colored ink: red for F, yellow for C. (Guido did not specify how many lines should be used; multiple-line staves are found in practical sources from the mid-eleventh century, and the four-line staff had become standard by the thirteenth. The use of

Table 11.10 *Pseudo-Odo,* Dialogus*: The "form" of Mode 1 and Mode 2 (after GS I, p. 259). "to." = whole tone, "sem." = semitone*

Mode 1: C to. D to. E sem. F to. G to. a sem. ♭ ♮ sem. C to. d
Mode 2: Γ to. A to. B sem. C to. D to. E sem. F to. G to. a [sem.] ♭

colors was gradually abandoned during the thirteenth century. The use of letters, especially F and C, as "keys" to the staff continued, and is the origin of our modern clefs.) Superimposed on the resulting series of horizontal lines and spaces are neumes, which thereby acquire the power of communicating specific information about the notes and intervals of the melody.

Medieval staff notation thus combines neumatic notation, used in practical sources for the transmission of repertoire, with the horizontal-line diagrams found in theoretical and didactic texts such as the *Enchiriadis* treatises (see pp. 329–30), but with the crucial difference that now it is the spaces as well as the lines that signify notes. These diagrams, which trace their lineage back to Boethius, were, as we have seen, really iconic representations of instruments, in so far as the lines actually represent strings. The new idea of using the interlinear spaces, although it may well have been motivated by circumstantial factors such as the desire to save parchment, thus represents a crucial shift to a more purely symbolic mode of semiosis.

Modal theory: modal affinities, Guido's *modi vocum*, and transposition. Pseudo-Odo and Guido both advanced the structural analysis of the scale and modal systems, within an understanding of mode that focused primarily on the functional significance of particular notes (chiefly the final) or scalar segments.[88] For both (as for the *Enchiriadis* treatises), it is the scalar pattern of intervals – the ordered series of whole tones and semitones – with respect to the final that ultimately determines the mode both of the final itself and of the melodies ending on it. The result is summed up in their doctrine that a melody's mode is determined, above all, by its final.[89] Pseudo-Odo defines each of the eight modes in terms of its final, ambitus, and the complete series of tones and semitones within its ambitus, which is then located on the background scale in a diagram giving the "form" (*forma*) of each mode.[90] (The diagrams for the first two of these "forms" of the modes are reproduced in Table 11.10.) The standard doctrine of ambitus, enunciated by Guido, extends Odo's ranges a bit at the high end: mel-

88 Regarding the modal-functional notes other than the final (the initial note of the melody, the initial and terminal notes of its internal phrases or *distinctiones*, and the "tenor"), see Powers et al., "Mode," pp. 783–86.

89 In Pseudo-Odo's famous formulation (*Dialogus*, Chapter 8): "A mode (*Tonus vel modus*) is a rule (*regula*) that distinguishes (*diiudicat*) each melody on the [basis of its] final" (*GS* 1, p. 257b; cf. trans., p. 207). Cf. *Micrologus*, Chapter 11.

90 Pseudo-Odo, *Dialogus*, Chapter 11–18; *GS* 1, pp. 259–63. (These chapters are omitted from the translation in *SR*.)

Table 11.11 *Modal "likenesses of the notes"* (similitudines vocum) *in Pseudo-Odo's* Dialogus *(after GS I, p. 264; trans. SR*, p. 210)

VII	I		V	I	III	V	VII	I		V	I	III	V	VII	I
Γ	A	B	C	D	E	F	G	a	♮	c	d	e	f	g	aa
VIII	II	IV	VI	II	IV	VI	VIII	II	IV	VI	II	IV	VI	VIII	II
								III		VIII					

Note: Roman numerals represent the modal qualities of Modes 1–8 assigned to the various notes. The additional modal qualities listed for the notes a (III) and c (VIII) result from the use of the "first ninth step," b♭, which does not appear in the diagram.

odies in the authentic modes can go one step below the final and up to nine (or even ten steps) above it; plagal melodies can descend to the fifth below the final (for *tritus*, the fourth below: C), and ascend to the sixth (or even the seventh) above it. For post-Guidonian theorists there is typically a simpler structure underlying these practical ranges: modal octaves composed of the fifth above the final plus a fourth either above that, for authentics, or below it, for plagals (thus for mode 1: D–a–d; for mode 2: A–D–a); see Figure 11.10 below (p. 354).

The practice, by this time standard, of counting each of the authentic and plagal modes separately, making eight modes or "tones" (numbered as in Table 11.2 above) is reflected in Pseudo-Odo's enumeration of eight distinct modal "forms." Nevertheless, the emphasis on the final makes the authentic–plagal distinction a secondary feature, resulting from subdivision of the four chief modal categories – *protus*, *deuterus*, *tritus*, *tetrardus*. For Guido, especially, and for many subsequent theorists, it is the latter that are primary. I shall refer to them henceforth as the four *maneriae*.[91]

Both theorists also address the recurrence of modal qualities among the notes. Hucbald in the ninth century had commented upon this phenomenon, which he called *socialitas*, and the *Enchiriadis* authors, who seem to have taken it as the organizational principle of their idiosyncratic scale system, had provided an explanation for it: the recurrence of identical intervallic configurations around pairs of notes located five steps apart (see above, pp. 322–23, 326).

Pseudo-Odo, in taking up this topic, also explains such "likenesses of notes" (*similitudines vocum*), as he calls them, in terms of recurrent intervallic patterns, assigning each note of his scale (except b♭) to one, two, or three modes. See Table 11.11. The *Dialogus* does not, however, grapple with the question of whether there might be some larger pattern or principle controlling the occurrence of these modal "likenesses"

91 The term *maneria*, used with this meaning, was introduced in the idiosyncratic modal theory developed by the Cistercian Order in the twelfth century, regarding which see Fuller, "An Anonymous Treatise"; Meyer, "Tonartenlehre," pp. 183–96; Maître, *La réforme cistercienne*; see also Hiley, *Western Plainchant*, pp. 608–11.

within the octave-based, mainly diatonic system that Pseudo-Odo adopted. The first attempt to solve this important problem was made by Guido, in Chapters 7–9 of the *Micrologus*.

There Guido discusses the "qualities" (*qualitates*) and the "affinities" (*affinitates*) of the notes, explaining these in terms of intervallic patterns that he calls *modi vocum* ("modes of notes"); the phrase denotes the idea that the particular intervallic configuration in the vicinity around any note causes it to be of a certain "kind" or "type" (*modus*), which is equivalent to its having a certain "quality." For example, the first *modus vocum* consists of a whole tone *below* some starting note, and the ascending series T–S–T–T *above* it, a configuration found around the notes A and D (*Micrologus*, Chapter 7). These intervallic "modes" are not the same as the church modes, although they do seem clearly to be related to them, as we shall see.[92]

In his discussion of these matters, Guido first emphasizes that, because octave equivalence reduces the number of truly distinct notes to seven (A–G), there can *at most* be only seven note-qualities. In fact, it turns out, there are only four: three pairs of notes (A/D, B/E, C/F) share the same quality due to their having the same *modus vocum*, and thus have "affinity" with each other, while the seventh note (G) stands alone, with its own quality and *modus vocum*, without affinity to any other note.[93] See Table 11.12.

As Table 11.12 shows, the shared *modi vocum* of the first three note-pairs (A/D, B/E, C/F) all occupy the same two, identically structured six-note scale segments, Γ–E and C–a, which are substantively (although not functionally) identical to the hard and natural hexachords.[94] Guido goes on to say that all such affinities occur at the intervals of the perfect fourth and fifth, and adds as three more affinities to the notes D, E, and F the notes a fifth above them (a, ♮, c); these, and their six-note module, G–e, are shown in brackets in Table 11.12. The seventh note, G, however, has no such affinities, because its *modus vocum*, as Guido defines it, is not replicated at the lower fourth or upper fifth (D, d).[95]

Although Guido does not say so, it seems clear that these note qualities and affinities

92 A similar account occurs in the *Epistola*; see Pesce, *Guido d'Arezzo's Regulae*, pp. 490–95. For discussion of these doctrines, see Pesce, ibid., pp. 20–29; Pesce, *Affinities*, pp. 18–22; Crocker, "Hermann's Major Sixth"; Meyer, "Tonartenlehre," pp. 161–63.

93 Guido clearly found G problematical. In the *Epistola* he extends its pattern down to C, that is, down to the lower boundary of one of his regular six-note segments, while continuing to give it the same ascending pattern that it has here (Pesce, *Guido d'Arezzo's Regulae*, p. 495). In *Micrologus*, Chapter 8, where he is discussing further affinities at the upper *fourth* (and lower fifth), he mentions that G has partial affinities with both D and C, in that G and C both have above them the series T–T–S, while G and D share the descending series T–S (Babb, p. 64). (In both cases the series could have been extended by two more whole tones, but this would have muddled the seemingly neat distinctions Guido makes here.)

94 Regarding the later relationship established, via these six-note segments, between hexachordal solmization and the modes, see below, p. 355. Although Guido himself says nothing of this, some scholars believe that it may have been in Guido's mind as well; see Pesce, *Guido d'Arezzo's Regulae*, pp. 27–28; and "B-Flat"; Crocker, "Hermann's Major Sixth."

95 Guido does not explain why he assigns to G a *modus vocum* so different from those of the other six notes. Various reasons have been proposed; see the studies cited in n. 92 above.

Table 11.12 *Guido's* modi vocum *and "affinities"*

																	c
																s	
																	b
																t	
		E	a	[e]			E	a	[e]			E	a	[e]			a
	t					t					t					t	
		D	G	[d]			D	G	[d]			D	G	[d]	IV.		G
	t					t					t					t	
		C	F	[c]			C	F	[c]	III.		C	F	[c]			F
	s					s					s						
		B	E	[♮]	II.		B	E	[♮]			B	E	[♮]			
	t					t					t						
I.		A	D	[a]			A	D	[a]			A	D	[A]			
	t					t					t						
		Γ	C	[G]			Γ	C	[G]			Γ	C	[G]			

and intervallic patterns have modal significance; they were certainly so understood by later theorists. One of his six-note segments (C–a) comprises the finals plus the notes a whole tone above and below them; the others replicate this one at the fourth below and fifth above. The affinities among the sets of notes A/D/a, B/E/♮, and C/F/c, created by their shared *modi vocum* within the identically structured six-note segments related at the fourth and fifth, amount to an explanation of why the modal quality or "property" (*proprietas*) of each of these three finals recurs at the notes a fourth below and a fifth above, while the absence of such affinities explains why the modal quality of the fourth final, G, does not recur elsewhere. Remarks in *Micrologus*, Chapters 8 and 9, suggest that Guido sees all of this as having relevance to a long-standing problem of chant theory and (notational) practice: finding the best location for a given melody with respect to the background scale. In this regard it is the three upper-fifth affinities, a, ♮, and c, that are of particular importance because these were the most commonly used alternative ending notes, or "cofinals," for chant melodies in the *protus*, *deuterus*, and *tritus* modes.

Such cofinals (called *affinales* or *confinales* by later theorists) were the most common solution to various conflicts between the scale and the implicit pitch content of a number of traditional plainchant melodies (as determined by their intervallic series) – conflicts due to the fact that those melodies pre-dated the modal and scalar systems later imposed on the repertory, and hence were unconstrained by the structural "requirements" of those systems.

The kind of conflict most relevant to the present topic was the need, in some melodies, for pitches not provided by the scale, especially those equivalent to low B♭, E♭, and F♯(f♯). While some theorists advocated (and some practical sources used) the low B♭ as a regular note of the scale, this was never a very common solution; moreover, lack of the concept of "chromatic alteration" or "accidentals" in this period rendered pitches such as E♭ and F♯ even more problematical.[96] Instead, for such melodies, the usual solution was use of the cofinals via transposition to the fifth above, where the structure of the gamut, with both b♭ and b♮, often made the requisite pitches and intervals available.[97]

In Chapter 8 Guido mentions several further instances of affinity, these at the fourth above the finals, some involving the use of b♭. Guido himself, however, clearly disapproves of the use of b♭ in this context (even the one among the *acutae*, which is included in his gamut) because it creates "a certain confusion and transformation" in the established modal qualities of the notes: in the scale segment g–a–b♭–c, the g assumes *protus* quality, the a becomes *deuterus*, and the c becomes *tetrardus*, while the b♭ itself would count as a *tritus* note. Guido does his best here to minimize its presence, which is implicit in transpositions to the upper fourth. Use of such affinities at the upper fourth (called "transformation") did find some acceptance among other theorists of the time, however, although they were always much less common than "transposition" to the normal cofinals at the upper fifth, as long as the music in question was plainchant. From the thirteenth century on, however, they are increasingly accepted, especially by theorists of the late fifteenth and sixteenth centuries who are discussing mode in polyphony.[98]

Guido's doctrines of *affinitas* and *modus vocum* bear witness to an on-going theoretical project in which the problem of finding the "best" place to locate a chant melody on the scale (necessary both for theoretical reasons and for the practical purposes of notation) was addressed by means of structural analyses of the scale itself in its relation to mode: the discovery of those scalar segments in which the intervallic patterns characteristic of the modal finals are replicated at other pitch levels. It was Guido, indeed, who discovered the two intra-octave segments of the diatonic scale (G–E and C–A) with the longest identical series of intervals (T–T–S–T–T), and applied this discovery both to the elementary pedagogy of sight singing and to the explanation of recurrent (modal) qualities ("affinities") among certain sets of fourth- and fifth-related notes. In effect, Guido here defined (or hinted at the definition of) each *maneria* in terms of a "modal nucleus" (Pesce, *Affinities*, p. 21): a scale segment smaller than an octave that encircles the final and determines the latter's modal quality by its intervallic configuration, which (except in the case of *tetrardus*) is replicated at the notes four steps lower

96 See below, pp. 356–57. However, see **Chapter 6, pp. 184–86**, for a few examples of late medieval scale divisions entailing such chromatics.

97 For explanation of this procedure in connection with the Easter Gradual "Haec dies" (*Liber usualis*, pp. 778–79), see **Chapter 5, pp. 160–61**. For discussion of the various problems raised by specific chant melodies, and the medieval theorists' solutions to them, see Pesce, *Affinities* (passim), and "B-Flat"; Atkinson, "From 'Vitium' to 'Tonus acquisitus'"; and "Tonsystem," pp. 128–33; Meyer, "Tonartenlehre," pp. 200–03, 208–10; Phillips, "Notationen," pp. 591–602. For Guido's own position with respect to this issue, see Pesce, "Affinities," pp. 18–22; *Guido d'Arezzo's Regulae*, pp. 20–29.

98 See Meyer, "Tonartenlehre," pp. 169–71, and the studies cited in n. 97 above, and below, pp. 355–56.

and five steps higher, causing them to have "affinity" with the final.

The links, left largely implicit by Guido himself, between this insight and the modes and between both of these and the hexachord as a module for solmization would be further explored and elaborated by subsequent generations of theorists. Many of them would do so by means of an old theoretical approach to the modes that reappears in the theorists to be discussed next: the species of the consonances.

The South German school: the species of the consonances and the modes

During the eleventh century, a succession of theorists in Southern Germany – Berno of Reichenau, Hermannus Contractus of Reichenau, Wilhelm of Hirsau, and others – developed a style of modal theory largely concerned with rationalistic system construction based on structural analysis of the scale system itself.[99] The scale used was the Hucbaldian two-octave scale (A–aa with b♭), with Hucbald's division into T–S–T tetrachords, which are given the functional names of the *Enchiriadis* tradition: *graves* (A–B–C–D), *finales* (D–E–F–G), *superiores* (a–♮–c–d) and *excellentes* (d–e–f–g). (The low *gamma* introduced by the Italian school was later added by Hermannus.) The tetrachordal organization was of great importance to Hermannus and his followers.

Among the most important contributions of this school were the establishment of the doctrine of the "species of the consonances," in particular the species of the perfect fourth and fifth, as an instrument for the structural analysis and definition of the modes,[100] and Hermannus Contractus's doctrine of the *sedes troporum*.

Modal species. As we have seen, the "principal treatise" of *Alia musica* was the first text to bring the church modes into connection with the ancient harmonics doctrine of the species of the consonances – more precisely, the species of the octave (above, pp. 332–38). The use of the species of fourth and fifth, in a new format designed for application to the medieval church modes, was first carried out, and then further developed, in the texts of the eleventh-century South German school. This occurred in three stages, of which I summarize here the middle one, which is the one most directly related to the modal species as taught by later theorists. See Table 11.13.[101]

99 See the Bibliography pp. 357–58 for editions and translations. The basic study is Oesch, *Berno und Hermann von Reichenau*. An introductory summary is found in Chapter 5, pp. 161–62. See also Hiley, *Western Plainchant*, pp. 470–75. Gushee's discussion of this "school" in "Questions," pp. 412–21 is of interest. Further secondary literature is cited in notes 101 and 107 below.

100 The "species of the consequences" are explained above, pp. 332–33.

101 The first stage of medieval species theory is found in the short text *Cita et vera divisio monochordi* attributed to one "Bernelinus" (*GS* 1, pp. 312–14), probably of c. 1000 and perhaps of South German origin, and in the genuine part of Chapter 5 of Berno's *Prologus* (*GS* 2, p. 67a–b), composed c. 1021–36. The second stage occurs in the subsequent passages of Berno's *Prologus* and its interpolations (*GS* 2, pp. 67b–72a), and in the related text *Duo semispheria* ("Anonymous I," *GS* 1, pp. 330–38). For discussion of the relations among the texts involved in stages 1 and 2, with accounts of the species theory in each, see Powers et al., "Mode," pp. 786–87; Warburton, "Questions of Attribution"; see also Rausch, *Musiktraktate*, esp. pp. 117–27. Regarding the third stage, see below, p. 353.

Table 11.13 *Species of perfect fourth and perfect fifth in Berno,* Prologus *(interpolation after Chapter 5, GS* II, pp. 67b–68b; Rausch, *Musik Traktate*, pp. 43–44*). (Odonian letter notation is used for clarity.)*

Species of fourth			Species of fifth			
1	2	3	1	2	3	4
						d
						t
					c	c
					s	s
				♮	♮	♮
				t	t	t
			a	a	a	a
			t	t	t	t
			G	G	G	G
			t	t	t	
		F	F	F	F	
		s	s	s		
	E	E	E	E		
	t	t	t			
D	D	D	D			
t	t	t				
C	C	C				
s	s					
B	B					
t						
A						

As Table 11.13 shows, in this second stage of the theory, the three species of fourth and the four species of fifth are listed in a continuous ascending series.[102] Thus the first species of fourth (T–S–T) runs A–B–C–D; the second species (S–T–T), B–C–D–E; and so on. Each species, however, recurs at all other scalar segments having the appropriate intervallic series.

The species of fifths and fourths are applied to the modes as shown in Figure 11.9.[103] The *protus* modes are both structured by the first species of fifth and fourth, the *deuterus* modes by the second, and the *tritus* by the third. This neat pattern of numerical correspondence breaks down, however, with the *tetrardus* modes, which have the

102 In the first stage of the theory, the species of fifths were derived from the species of fourths by the addition of a fifth note a whole tone above or below the fourth; the two sets of species thus occupied (at least implicitly) the same scalar region; see Powers, "Mode," p. 387; Warburton, "Questions of Attribution." A similar derivation occurs in the later Italian species theory discussed below.
103 *GS* 2, Chapter 7, pp. 69a–70a; Rausch edn., Chapter <6>, pp. 44–46 (main text).

fourth species of fifth with the *first* species of fourth (since there *is* no fourth species of fourth), at alternative positions on at D–G and d–g. (The fourth *maneria* thus once again stands apart from the other three.) Figure 11.9 also exhibits a fundamental principle of modal species theory: "Every plagal mode has the same [species of] fifth and fourth as its authentic; they differ, however, in that the authentic has its perfect fourth above its perfect fifth, while the plagal has it below."[104] That is, the *species* of fifth and fourth determine modal *quality* (as one of the four *maneriae*), while their relative positions reflect *ambitus*.

The conjunction of the species of fifths and fourths results in a series of "modal octaves" (as they are now called), shown in Figure 11.9, the structure of which is determined by the principles just stated. These modal octaves are idealized, theoretical constructs; as we have seen, the practical ranges assigned individually to the authentic and plagal modes were wider by one or two notes at each end.[105]

The modal species provide a new explanation of the difference between Modes 1 and 8. Although the modal octave of each runs from D to d (the fourth species of octave), it is structured differently in each case. In Mode 1, D is the final, and the octave is divided into the first species of fifth below the first species of fourth. In Mode 8, G is the final, and the division is into the first species of fourth below the fourth species of fifth.

The system presented above – the "second stage" of modal species theory – is already present in Berno's *Prologus* and its interpolations. In this form, the application of the species of fifths and fourths to the differentiation of the modes, at the level both of *maneria* (final) and ambitus, was widely adopted. Enjoying particular success in Italy in the fourteenth and fifteenth centuries, the species of the consonances became a common component of modal theory throughout Western Europe by the sixteenth century. (See further below, p. 355.)

The third stage of species theory is deeply imbricated within the highly rationalized systems and constructions of Berno's younger colleague at Reichenau, Hermannus Contractus (*Musica*, c. 1050). It has little discernible influence beyond his followers, the later representatives of the South German school.[106] But the theory's elegant symmetries make it a rewarding study, and its doctrine of the four *sedes troporum* (a reconceptualization of Guido's *modi vocum* in the terms of Hermannus's system) seems to have played some part in shaping the thinking of subsequent theorists.[107]

104 *Cita et vera divisio*, ed. *GS* 1, p. 313b; Berno, *Prologus*, Chapter 7, ed. *GS* 2, p. 70a; Rausch edn., p. 46.15–16.

105 The set of octave species 1–7, in the order and numbering established by *Alia musica* (above, pp. 334–35), also appears in the treatises, but plays little role as such.

106 These include Wilhelm of Hirsau, Aribo Scholasticus, Frutolf of Michelsberg at Bamberg, and Theogerus of Metz, all of the later eleventh to the early twelfth century. See the Bibliography, for the titles and editions of their principal treatises.

107 For more detailed accounts, see first Powers et al., "Mode," pp. 787–88; also, Meyer, "Tonartenlehre," pp. 172–82. See also the interesting (but in part highly speculative) observations regarding the *sedes troporum* in relation to Guido's *modi vocum* and hexachord solmization in Crocker, "Hermann's Major Sixth."

Protus

Mode 1 (Authentic) **D** E F G a ♮ c d
t s t t | t s t
5^1 4^1

Mode 2 (Plagal) A B C **D** E F G a
t s t | t s t t
4^1 5^1

Deuterus

Mode 3 (Authentic) **E** F G a ♮ c d e
s t t t | s t t
5^2 4^2

Mode 4 (Plagal) B C D **E** F G a ♮
s t t | s t t t
4^2 5^2

Tritus

Mode 5 (Authentic) **F** G a ♮ c d e f
t t t s | t t s
5^3 4^3

Mode 6 (Plagal) C D E **F** G a ♮ c
t t s | t t t s
4^3 5^3

Tetrardus

Mode 7 (Authentic) **G** a ♮ c d e f g
t t s t | t s t
5^4 4^1

Mode 8 (Plagal) D E F **G** a ♮ c d
t s t | t t s t
4^1 5^4

Figure 11.9 Species of fifths and fourths and modal octaves in Berno, *Prologus*. (Finals are shown in boldface. Superscript indicates the number of the species, e.g., 4^2 = second species of fourth.)

III Postscript: developments of the later Middle Ages and Renaissance

Brief indications of some further developments of the later Middle Ages and early Renaissance will conclude this survey.[108]

(1) The development of rhythmic notation in the late twelfth and thirteenth centuries led to a new categorial distinction in music theory and pedagogy: *Musica mensurabilis* (or *mensurata*) dealt with the advanced and specialized knowledge involved in written, mensural polyphony (*cantus mensurabilis*), especially the notation of rhythm (note shapes, ligatures, the rhythmic modes, etc.). It was "subaltern" to *musica plana*, which comprised the fundamental and general principles of all music, both mensural polyphony and plainchant (*cantus planus*). These included, along with quadrivial topics, the topics discussed in the present chapter – the notes and the scale, staff notation, hexachordal solmization and the Hand, and the modes – which were now relegated to the elementary level of musical instruction.[109]

(2) The structural identities between the solmization hexachords and the six-note intervallic modules of the *modi vocum* led theorists, beginning in the late thirteenth century with Jerome (Hieronymus) of Moravia (*Tractatus de musica*, c. 1272–1304), to incorporate the hexachord syllables into modal theory, lending them a significance as markers of modal qualities and affinities that they had previously lacked. Most basically, for the first three *maneriae*, the syllables *re*, *mi*, and *fa* in the natural and hard hexachords indicated, respectively, both the finals (D, E, F) and the cofinals (a, ♮, c), while *sol* (G) in the natural hexachord was the final for *tetrardus*. From the early fourteenth century, theorists increasingly admitted as well the "transformative" transpositions at the upper fourth, involving use of the soft hexachord with b♭, in which, for example, the *protus* modes were situated on G as *re*, and the *deuterus* modes on a as *mi*.[110]

(3) Species theory became increasingly widely known and applied in the later Middle Ages and Renaissance, particularly with regard to polyphony, and helped to validate the transpositions of the modes to the upper fourth with b♭, since this preserves the modal species for all four *maneriae* exactly, while the upper-fifth cofinals do not. A highly elaborated version of species theory, which appears alongside an expanded set of categories for classifying the *ambitus* of chant melodies, is found in Marchetto of Padua's *Lucidarium* (1317/18). Both aspects of Marchetto's modal theory were passed on in other Italian treatises, such as the *Liber de natura et proprietate tonorum* of Johannes Tinctoris (1476). By the mid-sixteenth century, species theory was a commonplace throughout much of the continent.[111] A growing conviction among many theorists

108 The reader is urged to consult the sources cited in the following notes for more thorough accounts of the topics summarily sketched in the following pages.
109 See Gushee, "Question of Genre," pp. 426–27.
110 See Powers et al., "Mode," pp. 790–91; Meyer, "Tonartenlehre," pp. 200–03; Pesce, *Affinities*, pp. 50–79; and "B-Flat."
111 See Powers et al., "Mode," pp. 791–95; Meyer, "Tonartenlehre," pp. 203–15; Pesce, *Affinities*, pp. 98–132.

that the mediated octave species formed by the conjunction of species of fifths and fourths were the true determinants of mode led to dissatisfaction with the traditional upper-fifth cofinals, culminating in Glarean's rejection of these and his promotion, in *Dodecachordon* (Basel, 1547), of the notes c and a to the status of regular finals of their own distinct modes (Aeolian and Hypoaeolian; Ionian and Hypoionian, respectively).

(4) Tinctoris's treatise on the modes is explicitly concerned with applying modal theory to polyphony as well as plainchant. This was a theoretical project with few precedents (owing perhaps in part to the categorial distinction mentioned in point 1 above), but destined to undergo very considerable development in the sixteenth century and beyond.[112]

(5) Use of flat signatures in polyphonic works to indicate systematic preference of B♭ over B♮ throughout a piece or vocal part led, by about 1500, to the division of the traditional Guidonian gamut into two distinct and basic scales, called *cantus durus* (or *scala ♮-duralis*) and *cantus mollis* (or *scala ♭-mollaris*). The former, used in pieces without a flat signature, comprised the natural and hard hexachords and used B♮ (in various octaves); the other, for pieces with a one-flat signature, comprised the natural and soft hexachords and used B♭s. Some theorists also recognized a third scale, *cantus fictus*, with a two-flat signature, which used the soft hexachord together with a "fictive" hexachord whose *ut* lay on B♭ (in various octaves) and included e♭ as *fa*. These practices, combined with the use of species theory, led many theorists to a complete acceptance by c. 1500 of the "transformative" transpositions of the modes to the upper fourth with b♭. (The *tritus* modes, however, used B♭ regularly in their untransposed position on F, so for them it was not *cantus mollis* that signified transposition, but *cantus durus*, which placed the *tritus* final at the traditional upper-fifth cofinal, c, or an octave lower on C.) *Cantus fictus* indicated transposition by a further upward fourth (or downward fifth), such that C, solmizated as *re* in the fictive hexachord on B♭, could serve as an "irregular" final for *protus*.[113]

(6) Beginning in the late fourteenth century, the Guidonian gamut began to undergo expansion in two ways; both occurred primarily in connection with polyphony. On the one hand, new notes below *gamma-ut* and above ee-*la* were added. On the other hand, what we would call the "chromatic" pitch content of the gamut was supplemented by the recognition of pitches located between the notes of the Hand, for example, between C and D, D and E, F and G, G and A (in various octaves). (See **Chapter 6, pp. 186–89** for illustrations.) These additional, interstitial pitches, lacking proper "places" and names in the Hand, were understood under the concepts of *musica ficta* or *coniuncta*, both of which involved the imagining (or "feigning") of hexachords with *ut* located on notes other than C, G, and F, so as to produce the desired pitch as one of the members of a "fictive" *mi–fa* semitone. This, indeed, was the primary meaning of the notational signs used to indicate the use of *musica ficta*, which were actually the signs for "hard b"

112 See **Chapter 12, pp. 376–77**; Hiley et al., "Modus," cols. 421–25.
113 See Powers et al., "Mode," pp. 795–96.

(♮ or ♯) and "soft b" (♭), placed on whatever line or space was appropriate: they indicated that one should sing (or conceptualize) a note as a *mi* or a *fa*, respectively; although this usually resulted in alteration of that note's pitch by a semitone (up or down, respectively), there were instances in which it would not. Theorists provided simple "rules" or guidelines as to the musical circumstances in which it was deemed appropriate or necessary to employ *musica ficta*. Their application in specific cases has been much debated by those (editors, performers, historians, analysts) concerned to established the exact pitch content of late-medieval and Renaissance polyphonic works.[114]

114 The most thorough study of theorists' dicta on the subject is Berger, *Musica Ficta*. See also Bent and Silbiger, "Musica Ficta"; Seay, "The 15th-Century Coniuncta"; Ellsworth, "Origin"; Atkinson, "From 'Vitium' to 'Tonus Acquisitus'"; "Tonsystem," pp. 128–33.

Bibliography

Primary sorces

Alia Musica (ninth century), ed. and Fr. trans. J. Chailley, Paris, Centre de documentation universitaire, 1965; trans. E. Heard as "*Alia musica*: A Chapter in the History of Music Theory," Ph.D. diss., University of Wisconsin-Madison (1966); partial trans. J. McKinnon in *SR*, pp. 196–98

Aribo Scholasticus, *De musica*, in *GS* 2 (1784), pp. 197–230; ed. J. S. van Waesberghe as *Aribonis de musica*, *CSM* 2 (1951)

Aurelian of Réôme, *Musica disciplina*, ed. L. Gushee as *Aureliani Reomensis Musica Disciplina*, *CSM* 21 (1975); trans. J. Ponte as *Aurelian of Réome: "The Discipline of Music"*, Colorado Springs, Colorado College Music Press, 1968

Berno of Reichenau, *Musica*, ed. A. Rausch as *Die Musiktraktate des Abtes Bern von Reichenau*, Tutzing, H. Schneider, 1999

Boethius, A. M. S. *De institutione musica*, ed. G. Friedlein as *Anicii Manlii Torquati Severini Boetii De institutione arithmetica libri duo, De institutione musica libri quinque, accedit Geometria quae fertur Boetii*, Leipzig, Teubner, 1867; reprint Frankfurt, Minerva, 1966; trans. C. Bower, ed. C. Palisca, as *Fundamentals of Music*, New Haven, Yale University Press, 1989

Cita et vera divisio monochordi in diatonico genere, *GS* 1 (1784), pp. 312–14

Dialogus de musica, in *CS* 1, pp. 25–59, 263–64; trans. W. and O. Strunk as *Dialogue on Music* in *SR*, pp. 198–210

Frutolf of Michelsberg, *Breviarum de musica et Tonarius*, ed. C. Vivell, Vienna, Akademie der Wissenschaften, 1919

Guido of Arezzo, *Epistola de ignoto cantu (ad Michahelem)*, in *GS* 2 (1784), pp. 42–46, 50; trans. O. Strunk as *Epistle Concerning an Unknown Chant*, in *SR*, pp. 214–18; trans. D. Pesce in *Guido d'Arezzo's "Regule rithmice," "Prologus in antiphonarium," and "Epistola ad Michahelem": A Critical Text and Translation*, Ottawa, Institute of Medieval Music, 1999

Micrologus, ed. J. S. van Waesberghe as *Guidonis Aretini Micrologus*, CSM 4 (1955); trans. W.

Babb, ed. C. Palisca in *Hucbald, Guido, and John on Music: Three Medieval Treatises*, New Haven, Yale University Press, 1978, pp. 57–83

Prologus in antiphonarium, in *GS* 2 (1784) pp. 34–42; ed. J. S. van Waesberghe as *Guidonis Prologus in Antiphonarium*, Buren, F. Knuf, 1975; trans. O. Strunk as *Prologue to His Antiphoner*, in *SR*, pp. 211–14; trans. and ed. D. Pesce in *Guido d'Arezzo's "Regule rithmice," "Prologus in antiphonarium," and "Epistola ad Michahelem": A Critical Text and Translation*, Ottawa, Institute of Medieval Music, 1999

Regule rithmice, in *GS* 2 (1784), pp. 25–34; ed. J. S. van Waesberghe as *Guidonis Prologus in Antiphonarium*, Buren, F. Knuf, 1975; trans. and ed. D. Pesce in *Guido d'Arezzo's "Regule rithmice," "Prologus in antiphonarium," and "Epistola ad Michahelem": A Critical Text and Translation*, Ottawa, Institute of Medieval Music, 1999

Hermannus Contractus, *Musica*, in *GS* 2 (1784), pp. 124–53; ed. and trans. L. Ellingwood as *Musica Hermanni Contracti*, Rochester, NY, Eastman School of Music, 1936

Hucbald of Saint-Amand, *De harmonica institutione*, ed. with Fr. trans. by Y. Chartier in *L'Œuvre musicale d'Hucbald de Saint-Amand: Les compositions et le traité de musique*, Bellarmin, Editions Bellarmin, 1995; ed. with Ger. trans. by A. Traub, Regensburg, G. Bosse, 1989; Eng. trans. W. Babb, ed. C. Palisca in *Hucbald, Guido, and John on Music: Three Medieval Treatises*, New Haven, Yale University Press, 1978, pp. 13–46

Jerome of Moravia, *Tractatus de musica*, ed. S. M. Cserba O.P. in *Discantus positio vulgaris, Hieronymus de Moravia O.P. Tractatus de Musica*, Regensburg, F. Pustet, 1935

Johannes Aegidius de Zamora, *Ars musica*, ed. and Fr. trans. M. Robert-Tissot, *CSM* 20 (1974)

Marchetto of Padua, *Lucidarium in arte Musicae planae*, trans. and ed. J. Herlinger as *The Lucidarium of Marchetto of Padua: A Critical Edition, Translation, and Commentary*, University of Chicago Press, 1985

Musica, Scolica enchiriadis, ed. H. Schmid as *Musica et scolica enchiriadis una cum aliquibus tractatulis adiunctis*, Munich, Bayerische Akademie der Wissenschaften, 1981; trans. R. Erickson, ed. C. Palisca as *"Musica enchiriadis" and "Scolica enchiriadis": Translated, with Introduction and Notes*, New Haven, Yale University Press, 1995

Theogerus of Metz, *Musica*, in *GS* 2 (1784), pp. 182–96; ed. and trans. F. C. Lochner in "Dieter (Theogerus) of Metz and his *Musica*," Ph.D. diss., University of Notre Dame (1995)

Tinctoris, J. *de natura et proprietate tonorum*, (1476) ed. A. Seay, CSM 22/1 (1975), pp. 59–104; trans. A. Seay as *Concerning the Nature and Propriety of Tones*, Colorado Springs, Colorado College Music Press, 1976

Wilhelmus of Hirsau, *Musica*, ed. D. Harbinson as *Willehelmi Hirsavgensis Mvsica*, *CSM* 23 (1975)

Secondary sources

Adkins, C. "The Theory and Practice of the Monochord," Ph.D. diss., University of Iowa (1963)

Atkinson, C. "Das Tonsystem des Chorals im Spiegel mittelalterlicher Musiktraktate," in *GMt* 4 (2000), pp. 103–33

"From 'Vitium' to 'Tonus acquisitus': On the Evolution of the Notational Matrix of Medieval Chant," *Cantus Planus* (1990), pp. 181–97

"*Harmonia* and the *Modi, quos abusive tonos dicimus*," in *Atti del XIV Congresso della Società Internazionale di Musicologia* (1987), 3 vols., ed. A. Pompilio et al., Turin, EDT, 1990, pp. 485–500
"Modus," *HmT* (1996)
"Parapter," *HmT* (1979)
"On the Interpretation of *Modi, quos abusive tonos dicimus*," in *Hermeneutics and Medieval Culture*, ed. P. Gallacher and H. Damico, Albany, State University of New York, 1989, pp. 147–61
"The *Parapteres*: *Nothi* or Not?," *Musical Quarterly* 68 (1982), pp. 32–59
Babb, W., trans., and C. V. Palisca, ed., *Hucbald, Guido, and John on Music: Three Medieval Treatises*, New Haven, Yale University Press, 1978
Bailey, T. "*De modis musicis*: A New Edition and Explanation," *Kirchenmusikalishes Jahrbuch* 61–62 (1977–78), pp. 47–60
The Intonation Formulas of Western Chant, Toronto, Pontifical Institute of Medieval Studies, 1974
Barbera, A. "Octave Species," *JM* 3 (1984), pp. 229–41
Barbera, A., ed., *Music Theory and Its Sources: Antiquity and the Middle Ages*, South Bend, University of Notre Dame Press, 1990
Barker, A. *Greek Musical Writings*, 2 vols., Cambridge University Press, 1984–89
Bent, M. and Silbiger, A., "Musica ficta," *NG2*, vol. XVII, pp. 441–53
Berger, K. "The Hand and the Art of Memory," *Musica disciplina* 35 (1981), pp. 117–24
Musica Ficta: Theories of Accidental Inflections in Vocal Polyphony from Marchetto da Padova to Gioseffo Zarlino, Cambridge University Press, 1987
Bernhard, M. "Das musikalische Fachschrifttum im lateinischen Mittelalter," in *GMt* 3 (1990), pp. 37–103
"Textkritisches zu Aurelianus Reomensis," *Musica Disciplina* 40 (1986), pp. 49–61
"Überlieferung und Fortleben der antiken lateinischen Musiktheorie im Mittelalter," in *GMt* 3 (1990), pp. 7–35
Bielitz, M. *Musik und Grammatik. Studien zur mittelalterlichen Musiklehre*, Munich, Katzbichler, 1977
Bower, C. "The Modes of Boethius," *JM* 3 (1984), pp. 252–63
"The Grammatical Model of Musical Understanding in the Middle Ages," in *Hermeneutics and Medieval Culture*, ed. P. Gallacher and H. Damico, Albany, State University of New York, 1989, pp. 133–45
Bower, C., ed. and trans., *The Fundamentals of Music*, by A. M. S. Boethius, New Haven, Yale University Press, 1989
Brockett, Jr., C. "A comparison of the five monochords of Guido of Arezzo," *Current Musicology* 32 (1981), pp. 29–42
Chartier, Y. *L'Œuvre musicale d'Hucbald de Saint-Amand: Les compositions et le traité de musique*, Saint-Laurent Bellarmin, 1995
Cohen, D. E. "Boethius and the *Enchiriadis* Theory: The Metaphysics of Consonance and the Concept of Organum," Ph.D. diss., Brandeis University (1993)
Crocker, R. "Alphabet Notations for Early Medieval Music," in *Saints, Scholars and Heroes: Studies in Honor of Charles W. Jones*, ed. M. King and W. Stevens, Collegeville, MN, Saint John's Abbey and University, 1979, pp. 79–104; reprint in Crocker, *Studies in Medieval Music Theory and the Early Sequence*, Aldershot, VT, Variorum, 1997

"Hermann's Major Sixth," *JAMS* 25 (1972), pp. 19–37
Studies in Medieval Music Theory and the Early Sequence, Aldershot, VT, Variorum, 1997
Duchez, M.-E. "Jean-Scot Erigène premier lecteur du *De institutione musica* de Boèce?," in *Eriugena: Studien zu seinen Quellen. Vorträge des III. Internationalen Eriugena-Colloquiums, Freiburg-im-Breisgau, 27.–30. August 1979*, ed. W. Beierwaltes, Heidelberg, Universitäts Verlag, 1980, pp. 165–87
"Déscription grammaticale et déscription arithmétique des phénomènes musicaux: le tournant du IXe siècle," in *Sprache und Erkenntniss im Mittelalter. Akten des VI. Internationalen Kongresses für mittelalterliche Philosophie der Société Internationale pour l'Etude de la Philosophie Médiévale. Bonn, 1977*, Berlin, 1981, pp. 561–79
"La représentation spatio-verticale du caractère musical grave-aigu et l'élaboration de la notion de hauteur de son dans la conscience musicale occidentale," *Acta* 51 (1979), pp. 54–73
"L'émergence acoustico-musicale de terme 'sonus' dans les commentaires carolingiens de Martianus Capella," *Documents pour l'histoire du vocabulaire scientifique* 7 (1985), pp. 97–149
Ellsworth, O. "The Origin of the Coniuncta: a Reappraisal," *JMT* 17 (1973), pp. 86–109
Erickson, R., trans., and C. V. Palisca, ed., *Musica enchiriadis and Scolica enchiriadis*, New Haven, Yale University Press, 1995
Fuller, S. "An Anonymous Treatise *dictus de Sanco Martiale*: A New Source for Cistercian Music Theory," *Musica Disciplina* 31 (1977), pp. 5–30
"Theoretical Foundations of Early Organum Theory," *Acta* 53 (1981), pp. 52–84
Gallacher, P. J. and H. Damico, eds., *Hermeneutics and Medieval Culture*, Albany, State University of New York, 1989
Gollin, E. "From *Tonoi* to *Modi*: A Set-Transformational Approach to Reception History," paper presented at meeting of Music Theory Society of New York, 20–21 April, 2001
Gombosi, O. "Studien zur Tonartenlehre des frühen Mittelalters," 3 parts, *Acta* 10 (1938), pp. 149–74; 11 (1939), pp. 28–39; 12 (1940), pp. 21–52
Gushee, L. A. "The *Musica disciplina* of Aurelian of Réôme: A Critical Text and Commentary", 2 vols., Ph.D. diss., Yale University (1962)
"Questions of Genre in Medieval Treatises on Music," in *Gattungen der Musik in Einzeldarstellungen*, ed. W. Arlt et al., Bern, Francke, 1973, pp. 365–433
Gushee, L. A., ed., *Aureliani Reomensis Musica disciplina*, *CSM* 21 (1975)
Heard, E. B. "*Alia musica*: A Chapter in the History of Music Theory," Ph.D. diss., University of Wisconsin-Madison (1966)
Hebborn, B. *Die Dasia-Notation*, Bonn, Orpheus, 1995
Hiley, D. *Western Plainchant: A Handbook*, Oxford University Press, 1993
Hiley, D. et al., "Modus," *MGG2*, vol. VI, col. 397–435
Hucke, H. "Karolingische Renaissance und Gregorianischer Gesang," *Die Musikforschung* 28 (1975), pp. 4–18
"Towards a New Historical View of Gregorian Chant," *JAMS* 33 (1980), pp. 437–67
Hughes, A. "Solmization," *NG2*, vol. XXIII, pp. 644–49
Huglo, M. "L'Auteur de 'Dialogue sur la musique' attribué à Odon," *Revue de musicologie* 55 (1969), pp. 119–71
"Comparaison de la terminologie modale en orient et en occident," *International Musicological Society: Report of the Eleventh Congress, Copenhagen 1972*, vol. II, Copenhagen, 1974, pp. 758–61

"Le Développement du vocabulaire de l'Ars Musica à l'époque carolingienne," *Latomus* 34 (1975), pp. 131–51

"Grundlagen und Ansätze der mittelalterlichen Musiktheorie von der Spätantike bis zur Ottonischen Zeit," in *GMt* 4 (2000), pp. 17–101

"L'Introduction en occident des formules Byzantines d'intonation," *Studies in Eastern Chant* 3 (1973), pp. 81–90

"Der Prolog des Odo zugeschriebene *Dialogus de musica*," *AfMw* 27 (1971), pp. 134ff.

"Tonary," *NG2*, vol. xxv, pp. 594–98

"Un tonaire du graduel de la fin du VIIIe siècle (Paris, B.N. lat. 15139)," *Revue grégorienne* 31 (1952), pp. 176–86, 224–33

Les Tonaires: inventaire, analyse, comparaison, Paris, Société Française de Musicologie, 1971

Huglo, M. and C. Brockett, "Odo," *NG2*, vol. xviii, pp. 337–39

Jacobsthal, G. *Die chromatische Alteration im liturgischen Gesang der abendländischen Kirche*. Berlin, J. Springer, 1897; facs. Hildesheim, G. Olms, 1970

Jeffery, P. "Oktōēchos," *NG2*, vol. xviii, pp. 370–73

Karp, T. *Aspects of Orality and Formularity in Gregorian Chant*. Evanston, IL, Northwestern University Press, 1998

Law, V. "The Study of Grammar," in *Carolingian Culture: Emulation and Innovation.*, ed. R. McKitterick, Cambridge University Press, 1994, pp. 88–110

Levy, K. "On the Origin of Neumes," *Early Music History* 7 (1987), pp. 59–90; reprint in *Gregorian Chant and the Carolingians*, ed. Levy, Princeton University Press, 1998, pp. 109–40

Levy, K., Emerson, J. and Hiley, D. "Plainchant," *NG2*, vol. xix, pp. 825–86

Lipphardt, W. *Der karolingische Tonar von Metz*, Münster, Aschendorff, 1965

Maître, C. *La Réforme cistercienne du plainchant. Étude d'un traité theorique*, Cîteaux, Brecht, 1995

Markovits, M. *Das Tonsystem der abendländischen Musik im frühen Mittelalter*, Bern, P. Haupt, 1977

Mathiesen, T. J. *Apollo's Lyre: Greek Music and Music Theory in Antiquity and the Middle Ages*, Lincoln, University of Nebraska Press, 1999

McKinnon, J. "The Emergence of Gregorian Chant in the Carolingian Era," in *Antiquity and the Middle Ages*, ed. J. McKinnon, London: MacMillan, 1990, pp. 88–119.

McKitterick, R., ed., *Carolingian Culture: Emulation and Innovation*, Cambridge University Press, 1994

Meyer, C. *Mensura Monochordi: la division du monocorde (IXe–XVe siècle)*, Paris, Klincksieck, 1996

"Die Tonartenlehre im Mittelalter," in *GMt* 4 (2000) pp. 135–215

Möller, H. "Zur Frage der musikgeschichtlichen Bedeutung der Akadamie Karls des Grossen: Die *Musica Albini*," in *Akademie und Musik: Erscheinungsweisen und Wirkungen des Akademiegedankens in Kultur- und Musikgeschichte*, ed. W. Frobenius et al., Saarbrücken, Saarbrücker Druckerei und Verlag, 1993

Müller, H. *Hucbalds echte und unechte Schriften über Musik*, Leipzig, B. G. Teubner, 1884; facs. New York, Broude, 1960

Nowacki, E. "The Gregorian Office Antiphons and the Comparative Method," *JM* 4 (1985–86), pp. 243–75

"Studies on the Office Antiphons of the Old Roman Manuscripts," 2 vols., Ph.D. diss., Brandeis University (1980)

"The Syntactical Analysis of Plainchant," in *International Musicological Society, Report of the Twelfth Congress, Berkeley 1977*, Basel, Bärenreiter, 1981, pp. 191–201
Oesch, H. *Guido von Arezzo*. Bern, P. Haupt, 1954
Berno und Hermann von Reichenau als Musiktheoretiker, Bern, P. Haupt, 1961
Pesce, D. *The Affinities and Medieval Transposition*, Bloomington, Indiana University Press, 1987
"B Flat: Transposition or Transformation?," *JM* 4 (1986), pp. 330–49
Pesce, D., ed. and trans., *Guido d'Arezzo's "Regule rithmice," "Prologus in antiphonarium," and "Epistola ad Michahelem": A Critical Text and Translation*, Ottawa, Institute of Medieval Music, 1999
Phillips, N. C. "Classical and Late Latin Sources for Ninth-Century Treatises on Music," in *Music Theory and Its Sources: Antiquity and the Middle Ages*, ed. A. Barbera, South Bend, University of Notre Dame Press, 1990, pp. 100–35
"The Dasia Notation and Its Manuscript Tradition," In *Musicologie médiévale: notations et séquences*, Paris, Librairie Honoré Champion, 1987, pp. 157–73
"*Musica* and *Scolica Enchiriadis*: The Literary, Theoretical, and Musical Sources," Ph.D. diss., New York University (1984)
"Notationen und Notationslehren von Boethius bis zum 12. Jahrhundert," in *GMt* 4 (2000), pp. 293–623
Ponte, J. "Aureliani Reomensis, *Musica disciplina*: A Revised Text, Translation and Commentary," 3 vols., Ph.D. diss., Brandeis University (1961)
Ponte, J., trans., *Aurelian of Réome: "The Discipline of Music"*, Colorado Springs, Colorado College Music Press, 1968
Powers, H., et al. "Mode," *NG2*, vol. XVI, pp. 775–860
Raasted, J. *Intonation Formulas and Modal Signatures in Byzantine Musical Manuscripts*, Copenhagen, E. Munksgaard, 1966
Rankin, S. "Carolingian Music," in *Carolingian Culture: Emulation and Innovation*, ed. R. McKitterick, Cambridge University Press, 1994, pp. 274–316
Rausch, A. *Die Musiktraktate des Abtes Bern von Reichenau. Edition und Interpretation*, Tutzing, H. Schneider, 1999
Reckow, F. "Organum-Begriff und frühe Mehrstimmigkeit. Zugleich ein Beitrag zur Bedeutung des 'instrumentalen' in der spätantiken und mittelalterlichen Musiktheorie," in *Forum Musicologicum* 1, ed. H. Oesch and W. Arlt, Bern, Francke, 1975, pp. 31–167
"Zur Formung einer europäischen musikalischen Kultur im Mittelalter. Kriterien und Faktoren ihrer Geschichtlichkeit," in *Gesellschaft für Musikforschung, Bericht über den internationalen musikwissenschaftlichen Kongress Bayreuth 1981*, ed. C.-H. Nahling and S. Wiesmann, Kassel, Bärenreiter, 1985, pp. 12–29
Sachs, K.-J. "Musikalische Elementarlehre im Mittelalter," in *GMt* 3 (1990), pp. 105–61
Seay, A. "The 15th-Century Coniuncta: A Preliminary Study," in *Aspects of Medieval and Renaissance Music: A Birthday Offering to Gustave Reese*, ed. J. La Rue, New York, Norton, 1966, pp. 723–37
Spitta, P. "Die *Musica enchiriadis* und ihr Zeitalter," *Vierteljahrsschrift für Musikwissenschaft* 5 (1889), pp. 443–82
Strunk, O. *Essays on Music in the Byzantine World*, New York, Norton, 1977
"The Tonal System of Byzantine Music," *Musical Quarterly* 28 (1942), pp. 190–204;

reprint in *Essays on Music in the Byzantine World*, ed. Strunk, New York, Norton 1977, pp. 3–18

"Intonations and Signatures of Byzantine Music," *Musical Quarterly* 31 (1945), pp. 339–55; reprint in *Essays on Music in the Byzantine World*, ed. Strunk, New York, Norton, 1977, pp. 15–36

Traub, A. "Hucbald von St. Amand. *De harmonica institutione*," *Beiträge zur Gregorianik* 7 (1989), pp. 3–101

Treitler, L. "'Centonate' Chant: 'Übles Flickwerk' or *E Pluribus Unum?*,'" *JAMS* 28 (1975), pp. 1–23

"Homer and Gregory: The Transmission of Epic Poetry and Plainchant," *Musical Quarterly* 60 (1974), pp. 333–72

"Sinners and Singers: A Morality Tale," *JAMS* 47 (1994), pp. 137–71

"The 'Unwritten' and 'Written' Transmission of Medieval Chant and the Start-Up of Musical Notation," *JM* 10 (1992), pp. 131–91

Waesberghe, J. S. van, "The Musical Notation of Guido of Arezzo," *Musica Disciplina* 5 (1951), pp. 15–53

Musikerziehung: Lehre und Theorie der Musik im Mittelalter, vol. III/3 of *Musikgeschichte in Bildern*, ed. H. Besseler and W. Bachmann, Leipzig, VEB Deutscher Verlag für Musik, 1969

Warburton, J. "Questions of Attribution and Chronology in Three Medieval Texts on Species Theory," *MTS* 22 (2000), pp. 225–35

Weakland, R. "Hucbald as Musician and Theorist," *Musical Quarterly* 42 (1942), pp. 93–99

Wellesz, E. *A History of Byzantine Music and Hymnography*, 2nd edn., Oxford University Press, 1961

West, M. L. *Ancient Greek Music*, Oxford, Clarendon Press, 1992

Wille, G. *Musica Romana. Die Bedeutung der Musik im Leben der Römer*, Amsterdam, P. Schippers, 1967

Renaissance modal theory: theoretical, compositional, and editorial perspectives

CRISTLE COLLINS JUDD

The word "mode" is one of the most richly textured and problematic terms of Renaissance discourse about music. The difficulties associated with interpreting modal theory are hardly recent creations: sixteenth-century writers frequently framed their discussion of modal theory with assertions that they intended to clarify a difficult concept that earlier writers had not fully grasped. Thus Pietro Aaron claimed in 1525:

> And knowing [an explanation of the modes in polyphony] to be exacting and strange, I judge that it was abandoned by the celebrated musicians . . . not through ignorance but merely because it proved otherwise troublesome and exacting at the time. For it is clear that no writers of our age have explained how the many different modes are to be recognized . . . I show briefly what I know to be necessary, for I see that many are deceived about the true understanding, and regarding this I hope in some measure to satisfy them.[1]

The central problem – a problem that Aaron appears to have been the first to articulate explicitly – hinges on the nature of the relationship to polyphony of a theory intimately tied to monophonic music in its origins. If anything, twentieth-century attempts to recover, explain, and in some cases extend, modal theory have become even more subject to contention than their sixteenth-century antecedents. Several facets of the tradition, history, and reception of the body of writings generally known as "modal theory" contribute to these difficulties. Discussions of mode appear in wide-ranging contexts that reflect antecedents in classical and ecclesiastical traditions as well as a complex, and at times contradictory, network of concepts associated with the term. In modern English usage, "mode" is usually appropriated as an umbrella term that stands for a conflation of fifteenth- and sixteenth-century Latin and Italian terms. These terms – namely, *modus/tonus* and *modo/tuono*, but also including *tropus* – are sometimes used interchangeably in Renaissance writing, sometimes with distinct meanings, and always intertwined with practical, theoretical, and even philosophical associations.[2] Sixteenth-century writers conflated these terms in

1 Aaron, *Trattato*; trans. *SR*, p. 417.

2 On the associations of "modus" and "tonus," see Wiering, "Language of the Modes," pp. 101–41. Confusion of terminology was even more pronounced, of course, in the Middle Ages. See **Chapter 11, esp. pp. 312–13**.

ways that fundamentally altered the meaning of earlier modal theory while retaining its existing nomenclature.

From a modern perspective, these many changes in modal thought result in tensions that are reflected in sixteenth-century theoretical writing, musical composition, and editorial practice: most notably, the relationship of mode to polyphonic music as well as plainchant; the applicability of modal theory to secular as well as sacred genres; and the understanding of mode as an *a priori* compositional construct versus an *a posteriori* analytical deduction. At a more detailed level of examination, questions arise about the nature of modal classification in relation to the consideration of species versus final as determinants; the relevance of authentic and plagal distinctions for polyphony; the mode of individual voices versus that of an entire complex; and the audibility of modal determinants. Issues such as these prompted Harold Powers, one of the most prominent scholars of the history of mode, to pose the question "Is Mode Real?"[3] Powers's provocative title was not simply a rhetorical gesture but rather the culmination of a scholarly career which consistently hammered away at modern notions of "modality" as an inherent property of music of the Renaissance, analogous to, yet distinct from, common-practice "tonality."

Sixteenth-century modal theory drew upon and often synthesized diverse theoretical traditions that posited mode in radically different ways. In what may be loosely described as the ecclesiastical tradition, mode had developed first and foremost as a practical means of classifying and relating antiphons and psalm-tones. More broadly extended to the corpus of plainchant, it was, in essence, a scheme of classification that relied on final, ambitus, and beginnings. At its core was a definition that Frans Wiering has labeled the "omnis cantus" definition: a mode is the rule by which every song is to be judged.[4] The final served as the source of that rule. This final-dominated view formed a nearly unchanged stable core of modal theory in the most practical strain of the tradition associated with plainsong. But it was both modified by and contrasted with "pseudo-classical" species theory.[5] From Boethius, seven octave species were associated with eight modes. With Marchetto, the species approach was subjugated to the governance of the final. This, itself, was not new – it can be traced to the eleventh-century theorist Hermannus Contractus (see **Chapter 11, pp. 351–54**) – but it found its most lasting expression in the writings of Marchetto. A species of fifth and a species of fourth were added together to comprise two modes: one in which the mode was arranged above the final (fifth plus fourth) and the other in which the species surrounded the final (fourth below and fifth above). Although these species of consonances were tied to a final, they also represented a specific ordered pattern of tones and semitones. Thus the first species of fifth consisted of tone–semitone–tone–tone and the first species of fourth of tone–semitone–tone. These intervallic relationships were

3 Powers, "Is Mode Real?" 4 Wiering, "Language of the Modes," pp. 118–21.

5 Meier, *The Modes*, pp. 34–46, outlines the distinction of ecclesiastical and pseudo-classical theory.

usually represented by solmization syllables, e.g., re–mi–fa–sol–la for the first species of fifth, and in shorthand by the boundary pitches as re–la. Thus modal and hexachordal relationships beyond those of the final and ambitus became explicitly associated with modal theory.[6] In the nineteenth and twentieth centuries, "modality" came to be viewed in some quarters as an all-encompassing, systematic, and even expressive means of pitch organization – the Renaissance equivalent in some sense of the "tonality" of common-practice music. Bernhard Meier may be cited as perhaps the most passionate advocate of this view of mode as a powerful explanatory and analytical tool of Renaissance vocal and instrumental polyphony.[7]

The present essay will not attempt an exhaustive account of Renaissance theorists' discussions of mode (available in Powers's magisterial *New Grove* essay in any case, and now supplemented by the recent surveys by Schmidt-Beste and Wiering, along with the terminological essay by Atkinson).[8] Nor will it offer an analytical survey of repertory (illustrated most persuasively in Meier's work). Rather this chapter provides a localized study of modal theory in mid-century Venice. It centers round the compositions and theoretical writings of Gioseffo Zarlino (1517–90), without doubt the most famous theorist of the sixteenth century. The purpose of such a specialized study in the context of the present volume is to illustrate in detail the way many discrete facets of modal theory came together in the writings of one author, describing antecedents as well as subsequent influences. Zarlino's approach to mode thus supplies a fixed point of refraction by which to consider broader issues common to theories and practice of mode in the Renaissance.

Zarlino's interaction with Italian humanistic learning, musical theory, composition, and print culture makes this window on modal theory particularly revealing. Most notable among his achievements was *Le istitutioni harmoniche*, a treatise that has remained a primary theoretical source since its first publication in 1558. Zarlino also held the prestigious position of *maestro di cappella* at the Venetian basilica of San Marco during some of its most glorious musical years – from 1565 until his death in 1590.[9] For the purposes of this essay, I will begin with an exploration of a relatively little-known period in Zarlino's life: the decade immediately after his arrival in Venice, a formative period that preceded the publication of his treatises and his

6 From this intersection of modal and hexachordal representations, it is possible to imply hierarchical relationships to pitches beyond those explicitly described in modal theory. See Judd, "Modal Types," pp. 437–41. 7 Meier, *The Modes*.

8 Powers, "Mode"; Wiering, "Language of the Modes"; Schmidt-Beste, "Modus"; Atkinson, "Modus."

9 Modern accounts of Zarlino's biography rely for the most part on anecdotal evidence provided in Zarlino's treatises: Baldi's account ("Vite inedite di matematici italiani"), written shortly after Zarlino's death; and Caffi, *Della vita*. For a summary, see Palisca, "Zarlino, Gioseffo"; on Zarlino's compositions, see Flury, *Gioseffo Zarlino*; on the intellectual and musical culture of mid-century Venice, see Feldman, *City Culture*; on Zarlino and the *Accademia Veneziana*, as well as his interaction with print culture see Judd, *Reading Renaissance Music Theory*, pp. 181–98.

increasing renown as a music theorist. Taking the young Zarlino – rather than the authority represented by his mature writings – as a point of departure offers a unique vantage point from which to explore the extraordinary range of meanings, traditions, and applications associated with the theoretical concept of mode in the mid-sixteenth century.

What could one routinely expect an Italian musician and budding humanist such as Zarlino to have known of modal theory in the 1540s? Several strands of evidence suggest a wide range of possibilities: the background of an inherited ecclesiastical tradition; the descriptions provided in theory treatises; humanist attention to the writings of antiquity; a trend among publishers to arrange publications by features that could serve as modal markers; and compositional interest in large-scale, modally ordered motet and madrigal cycles. While these are not mutually exclusive concerns, they often suggest very different perspectives on what constituted modal theory, its most significant aspects, and its applicability in a variety of musical and literary contexts. Zarlino explored all these perspectives wearing his various hats as student, composer, associate of Antonio Gardano (a Venetian music printer), theorist, and humanist. They come together in remarkable ways in his first publication, a book of five-voice motets that appeared in 1549. One motet from this collection, *Ego veni in hortum meum*, offers a focal point in this chapter for the consideration of eight versus twelve mode systems, the relationship of tonal types and modal categories, and the impetus for (and significance of) modally ordered compositions. To approach that motet requires sketching first a theoretical background.

Theory treatises

The range and types of theoretical writing that in some way touch on the question of mode reflect the broad readership for whom the concept held some relevance. At one end of an overlapping spectrum of users were clergy who were required to sing the liturgy and thus needed at least a minimal understanding of what modal classification represented. Schoolboys, particularly in the northern humanist *Lateinschulen*, similarly encountered mode in relation to the plainchant that they were required to sing in church. Mode also figured in the more speculative study of music as a liberal art in school and university curricula.[10] Didactic treatises of a different sort were aimed specifically at composers and performers of polyphony. In a still different vein were books for the humanist *literati*: these focused on mode in the context of *musica speculativa* and the recovery of the ancient Greek modes. Finally, the sixteenth century also saw the rise of treatises aimed specifically at patrons and amateurs in which at least an elementary

10 See the discussion of Cochlaeus and Heyden in Judd, *Reading Renaissance Music Theory*, pp. 84–94.

explanation of the modes figured as knowledge with which any musician should familiarize himself. Each of these categories will be represented in the following discussion by a range of treatises that formed the background to Zarlino's own concept of mode in his own writing.

The most practical and basic of all music books in the sixteenth century was the instructional manual known generically as a cantorinus. These books provided rudimentary instruction to those – primarily priests but also choirboys – who required it in order to sing the liturgy. Such a book may well have been part of Zarlino's musical education as a choirboy in Chioggia. Distillations of the principles of modal theory were enumerated solely as an aid to singing chant. Providing the most elementary of explanations, a cantorinus usually begins with the principles of solmization illustrated via the Guidonian hand, as in the title page of the anonymous cantorinus from 1513 reproduced in Plate 12.1. From there, the tract moved to simple formulas for mutations and a minimal explanation of the intervals, the *diapente* and *diatessaron* (species of fifths and fourths), and modal ambitus. A manual of basic chants and recitation formulae usually followed. Normally in pocket-sized format, these slim manuals were often hardly more than pamphlets of a few folios in the early part of the century.[11] Frequently reprinted throughout the sixteenth century and into the seventeenth, they were occasionally integrated with more substantial theoretical trappings, culminating in works such as Adriano Banchieri's *Cantorino* of 1622. Unlike the earlier works, Banchieri's treatise was neither anonymous nor unpretentious; nevertheless it remained tied to the basic function of a cantorinus: teaching clergy to sing the liturgy. This function prescribed the nature and presentation of modal theory as it figured in the treatise.

The appearance of the modes in books of this sort serves as a useful reminder that modal theory, first and foremost, retained its practical association with the chant repertory of the Roman Catholic Church throughout the early sixteenth century. This elementary knowledge of the modes had remained essentially unchanged since its medieval formulation and provided the point of departure for sixteenth-century discussions of mode that in any way considered or related to the ecclesiastical tradition. Under the umbrella of modal theory were a number of categories of pitch organization related to specific chant types: modes (*toni* or, less frequently in this practical tradition, *modi*), psalm tones, magnificat tones, gospel tones, and so forth. While modes, psalm tones, and other recitation formulas share a number of features, it is important to realize that they also represent discrete entities, as Powers has amply demonstrated.[12]

11 For a discussion of the publication history of one cantorinus (the anonymous *Compendium musices*), see Crawford, "Chant Manual."

12 See especially Powers, "From Psalmody to Tonality," p. 289 and passim; see also Judd, "Josquin's Gospel Motets and Chant-Based Tonality," pp. 118, 145.

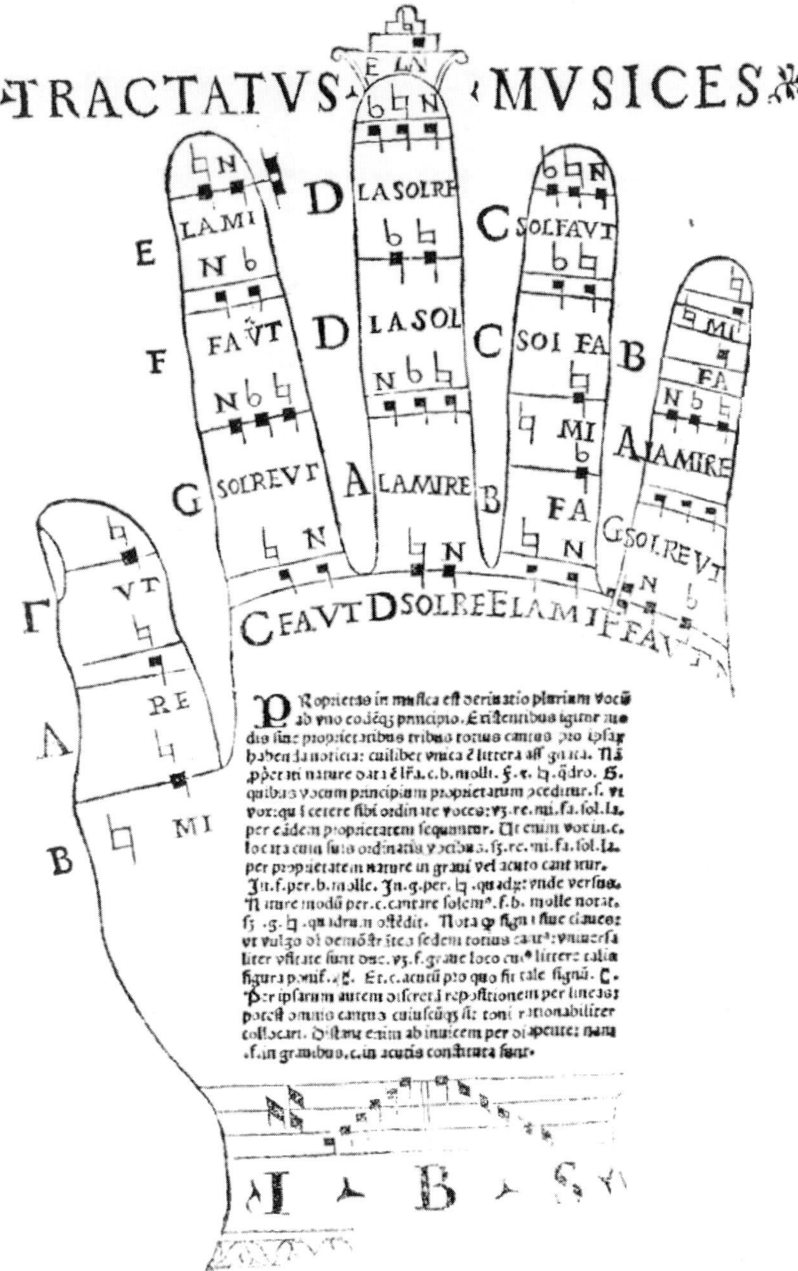

Plate 12.1 Title page, anon., *Tractatus musices* (Venice, c. 1513)

Side by side with the cantorinus tradition are didactic works aimed at somewhat more musically sophisticated audiences. On the one hand, we find humanist textbooks, usually in question-and-answer format, composed for schoolboys and university students, such as Johannes Cochlaeus's *Tetrachordum musices*. While the books provide the necessary means for students to obtain the required abilities to fulfill their obligations to provide plainsong and polyphony for the church, they also enable the serious student to benefit from music-making in the Ciceronian sense that held up the study and practice of music as a refreshment for the mind. They are neither aimed directly at the cleric, nor couched specifically in the service of singing chant.[13]

Other didactic works more explicitly counted the potential performer and composer among their audience, as well as appealing to a burgeoning market of amateur musicians. Shortly after his arrival in Venice, Zarlino apparently obtained just such a treatise: Steffano Vanneus's *Recanetum de musica aurea* (Rome, 1533).[14] This volume offers a means for exploring modal theory as it might have been known in mid-century by a more educated reader with different aims than the user of the cantorinus or the schoolboys' textbook. In Zarlino's case, the reader was in his early twenties, an ordained priest, a trained singer and organist, a student of Hebrew, Latin, and Greek, and perhaps already a pupil of the most revered musician of his day, Adrian Willaert. Vanneus's treatise is rarely cited in modern study of modal theory – a reflection of its lack of obvious innovations. Yet just this lack of innovation makes the *Recanetum* a particularly useful touchstone for laying out generally accepted practical tenets of modal theory in the 1530s and 40s. As in many such essentially practical treatises, mode appears in the *Recanetum* under the topic of plainsong, in the last chapters of Book I (Chapters 47–64). These chapters follow discussions of the definitions of music, the *voces* and *litterae*, mutation, and the species of consonances. The book concludes with a discussion of *musica ficta* and an explanation of the three genera: diatonic, chromatic, and enharmonic. Book II covers mensural theory and the proportions while Book III considers counterpoint.[15]

The treatment of mode in this theoretical tradition belongs to the exposition of plainchant and its precepts as outlined by Johannes Tinctoris in his *Liber de natura et proprietate tonorum* (1476). Tinctoris's treatise, in turn, presented an exposition based on Marchetto's *Lucidarium* that was also influenced by the Western ecclesiastical modal

13 For a more detailed discussion of such texts, see Judd, *Reading Renaissance Music Theory*, pp. 84–90. See also Lester, *Between Mode and Keys*, pp. 68–76, and Chapter 2, pp. 52–53.

14 The copy, in the Newberry Library, Chicago, is cited in Cohen, *On the Modes*, p. 47 n. 7. Although minimally annotated, the work contains three pages of Latin manuscript at the end thought to be in Zarlino's hand. Although this has generally been presumed to be the start of a treatise in Latin by Zarlino, I have identified a large section as an extended quotation from Guillaume Guerson, *Utilissime musicales regule* (Paris: Michel Thouloze [c. 1495]). According to a note on the flyleaf in a nineteenth-century hand, the *Recanetum* was originally bound with Zarlino's copy of Boethius.

15 This represents the "standard" order of such a treatise.

tradition while incorporating aspects of species theory.[16] In general terms, the understanding of modes that a sixteenth-century musician might hold in this tradition could be summarized under three headings: (1) the species; (2) modal finals and the appropriate tones for beginnings and endings; and (3) ambitus, mixture, and commixture. (Mixed modes are those encompassing the composite ambitus of a plagal and authentic mode that share the same final, while commixed modes join together the species of fifth and species of fourth from modes that do not share a final.) These are the same areas that receive treatment in a cantorinus, but the nature of the discussion differs in its depth and perspective.

Vanneus's definition of mode, based on Gaffurio's *Practica Musice* (1496), falls into Wiering's "omnis cantus" category, placing the understanding of mode presented in this treatise firmly in the ecclesiastical tradition.[17]

Tonus regula dicitur, quae per ascensum	A tone [i.e., "mode"] is called a rule that distinguishes
et descensum omnes descriptas ac etiam	in their final all written or indeed writable melodies
pernotabiles modulationes in fine diiudicat. (Vanneus, fol. 29v)	by means of their ascent and descent.

Vanneus provides a convenient summary of the species and finals in the diagram reproduced in Plate 12.2. The four conventional finals are listed by *vox* and *littera* across the center of the diagram: D *sol re*, E *la mi*, F *fa ut*, and G *sol re ut*.[18] The four categories of modes (*maneriae*) associated with these finals and the distribution of the species in relation to final appear at the top and bottom of the page: *protus*, *deuterus*, *tritus*, and *tetrardus*. The odd-numbered authentic modes are indicated on the top half of the diagram, their even-numbered plagal partners mirrored on the bottom. Following this overview, the modes are discussed in plagal and authentic pairs, with a summary of their composition (i.e., the species of which they are constituted) followed by a list of chants – antiphons, responsories, and occasionally introits – that illustrate the modes and the various tones for beginnings.

From there, the discussion moves to psalm tones, including a solmization mnemonic for recognizing the tones that had been known since at least the fourteenth century:

16 This tradition is discussed in Powers, "Mode," pp. 392–96; see also Niemöller, "Tonus-Lehre"; Wiering, "Language of the Modes," pp. 95–100.
17 Wiering, "Language of the Modes," pp. 118ff. Wiering refers to the "omnis cantus" definition as one in which the function of a mode is the categorization of "all songs" and outlines an extended tradition for this formulation.
18 Finals are always indicated by a combination of *vox* and *littera*. See Chapter 11, pp. 341–46 for an explanation and illustration of these concepts.

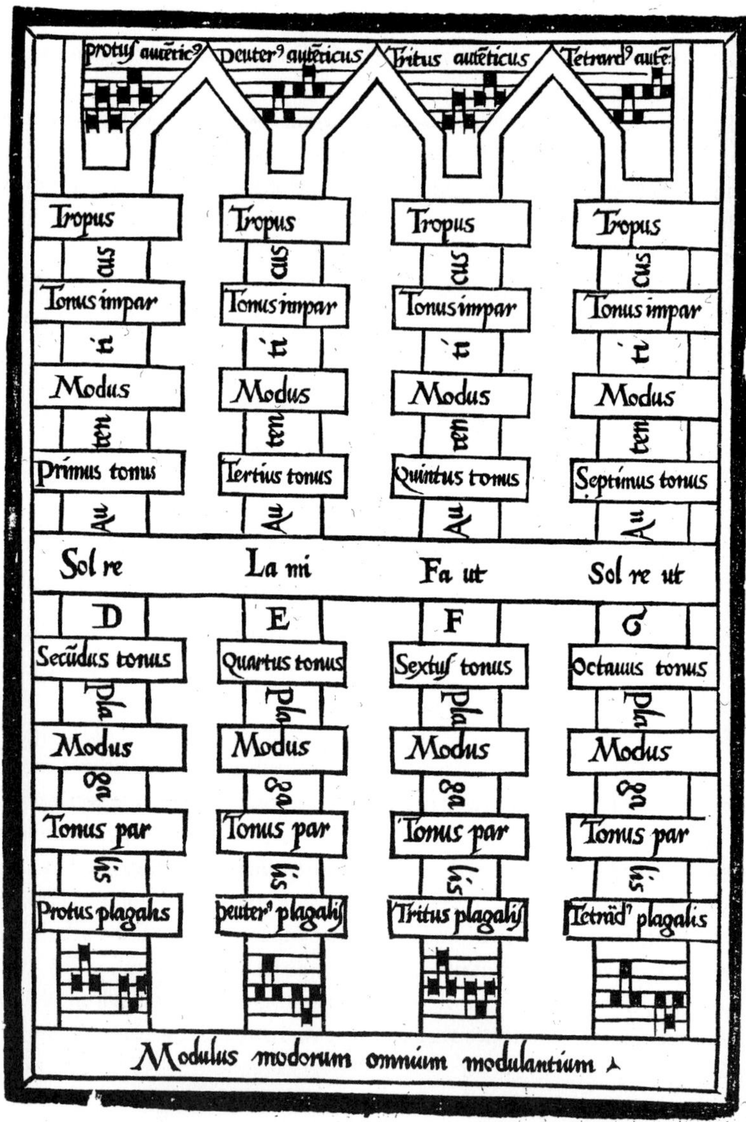

Plate 12.2 Vanneus, *Recanetum* (Rome, 1533), fol. 30r, diagram of the modes

Primus cum sexto fa sol la semper habebunt,	First and sixth shall always have fa sol la,
Tercius octavus ut re fa, sicque secundus,	Third and eighth ut re fa, and so the second,
La sol la quartus, ut mi sol sit tibi quintus,	La sol la you have for the fourth, ut mi sol for the fifth
Septimus fa mi fa sol, sic omnis esse recordor.	For the seventh fa mi fa sol; and so I remember all to be.

(Vanneus, fol. 36v)[19]

This mnemonic supplies a generic intonation for each psalm, implicitly indicating the reciting tone as well. Knowledge of the just-discussed finals is assumed in the mnemonic.[20]

Tone 1 (final D), initial: f–g–a, reciting tone: a;
Tone 2 (final D); initial: c–d–f; reciting tone: f;
Tone 3 (final E); initial: g–a–c^1; reciting tone: c^1;
Tone 4 (final E); initial: a–g–a; reciting tone: a;
Tone 5 (final F); initial: f–a–c^1; reciting tone: c^1; (the solmization implies a B♭; later versions of this mnemonic in "pseudo-classical" traditions employ a B♮ with the solmization of f–a–c^1 as "fa–re–fa")
Tone 6 (final F); initial: f–g–a; reciting tone: a;
Tone 7 (final G); initial: c^1–b–c^1–d^1; reciting tone: d^1;
Tone 8 (final G); initial: g–a–c^1; reciting tone: c^1.

Vanneus then provides examples of the psalm tones and a variety of intonations, along with instructions for recognizing the modes of introits and the *gloria patri*. His examples are eminently practical. The musician must be able to recognize the modes and tones in order to make the appropriate connections between the various parts of the liturgy: antiphons with psalm tones, and so forth.

The exact nature of the relevance of modal theory such as this – essentially ecclesiastical chant theory following in the tradition of Tinctoris – to polyphony in the years 1475–1525 remains hotly debated among modern scholars. Writings on the modes from the late fifteenth century on do regularly make mention of polyphony and the necessity for composers to be thoroughly acquainted with the modes, but as a matter of convention the presentation of modal theory occurs in books or sections of treatises

19 Translation after Wiering, "Language of the Modes," p. 68. On the various occurrences of this mnemonic from 1375 to 1622, see ibid.
20 Another similar mnemonic relies not on the intonation formulas, but on the interval between final and recitation tone (the "repercussio"): Tone 1: *re–la*; Tone 2: *re–fa*; Tone 3: *mi–fa* (e–c^1); Tone 4: *mi–la*; Tone 5: *fa–sol*; Tone 6: *fa–la*; Tone 7: *ut–sol*; and Tone 8: *ut–fa*. See, for example, Cochlaeus, *Tetrachordum musices*, fol. Ciii r.

on plainchant, as it does in the *Recanetum*. The scant attention accorded mode in sections of treatises dealing specifically with mensural music and the precepts of counterpoint leaves the exact nature of the relationship open to question, even if such placement reflects the traditional organization of such treatises. When, for example, Tinctoris does talk about a polyphonic example in *Liber de natura et proprietate tonorum* (Dufay's *Le Serviteur*) he discusses the mode of each individual voice, not the polyphonic complex as a whole. Similarly, Vanneus brings mode into the counterpoint book of his treatise only peripherally: in the discussion of cadences (Book III, Chapter 35, fol. 89v) which he assigns to appropriate modes. He also supplies a list of modal affects (see window on p. 375.)[21] As is often the case with such summaries of modal ethos, Vanneus asserts that composers need to be familiar with this aspect of modal theory because

> These are things that should least escape the notice of a good composer, so that he will know how to join same with same and like with like. And if you should scorn them, you will be a laughing-stock to the learned, and will be regarded as an unmusical musician by all. So watch yourself![22]

From Tinctoris's *Liber de natura* (1476), it was a commonplace for theorists to stress the relevance of modal knowledge to those wishing to compose not only plainchant, but, by extension, polyphony, even if the invocation occurred in the context of a discussion focused solely on plainchant. With its nod toward that tradition, Vanneus's treatise provides a reminder of a separate strand of modal theory that was increasingly (and with varying degrees of success) interwoven with that of the ecclesiastical modes: the discussions of the modes of classical antiquity and the philosophical tradition which defined modes via the species (as opposed to the final).

The Greek modes as described by Boethius in *De institutione musica* had long been associated with the eight-mode plainchant system.[23] In this long-standing tradition Boethius was paraphrased or repeated verbatim, and classical nomenclature (Dorian, Phrygian, etc.) was mapped onto the numbered modes of chant theory and the authentic–plagal relationships of the *maneriae*. The writings of Franchino Gaffurio mark the beginning of an explicitly humanist attempt to flesh out Boethius through study of the writings of the ancients. In relation to modal theory, this is most pronounced in

21 To compare with other theorists, see Beebe's summary of modal affect in Tinctoris, Cochlaeus, Aaron, Heyden, Coclico, Bermudo, Finck, Zarlino, and Glarean: "Mode, Structure, and Text Expression," pp. 434–44. Also see Palisca, "Mode Ethos."

22 "Haec sunt quae bonum Compositorem minime latere debent, ut sciret paria paribus, et similia similibus copulare. Quae si Contempseris, eris doctis ludibrio, Musicusque non Musicus, ab omnibus habeberis, tibi igitur consule" (fol. 93r).

23 Boethius's *De institutione musica* was first printed at the end of the fifteenth century and subsequent editions appeared throughout the sixteenth century. For a discussion of the differences between the Greek modes and the modes of chant theory, see Palisca, "Mode Ethos." (Also see Chapter 11, pp. 332–38.) Zarlino's copy of Boethius was apparently originally bound with the *Recanetum*; see Judd, *Reading Renaissance Music Theory*, p. 182, n. 9.

Vanneus's listing of the affects associated with each mode

Mode	Summary	Description
1	The first tone is cheerful.	Since, then, the first tone, an Authentic, is naturally tuneful, jocund, cheerful, and especially apt to excite the emotions of the soul, this mode demands that words, either in the vernacular or in Latin, be coupled with it; and since it is adaptable to these words, it is called by musicians the adaptable tone.
2	The second tone is woeful.	Words that carry with them sadness, weeping, cares, woes, captivity, and all sorts of miseries agree with the second tone, the first of the Plagals, which by its nature is tearful, serious, and humble, and for that very reason is called by musicians the humble and deprecatory.
3	The third tone is sharp and harsh.	The third tone, second in the series of Authentics, is considered sharp, vehement, blazing, provocative of anger and bile, spirited, harsh, and cruel. For that reason it properly embraces bellicose, threatening words, and other things of that sort like itself, and it has for that reason been given the name harsh.
4	The fourth tone is given to love and adulation.	The fourth tone, second among the Plagals, is completely unlike the third that precedes it, wherefore all words either of love, leisure, rest, tranquility, adulation, deceit, and detraction can properly be fitted to it, and from this effect it is called the adulatory mode.
5	The fifth tone is moderate.	The fifth tone, third of the Authentics, when sung brings delight, moderation, and joy, relieves the soul of every trouble, and matters that concern victory particularly become this mode; hence it is deservedly called jocund, moderate, and delightful.
6	The sixth mode is pious and devoted.	The sixth mode, the third of the Plagals, is most suitably given all words of piety that move [one] to tears, especially from devotion, or from pity and joy, and not without justice do musicians call it the devoted, tearful, and most pious mode, in distinction to the second mode, which we have called the dirgelike and grief-stricken.
7	The seventh mode is mixed and with complaint.	The seventh tone, fourth in the complement of the Authentics, is especially suited to lascivious words mixed in with moderate and pleasant ones, but then also to excited, angry, and threatening ones; and for this reason it is called the querulous mode.
8	The eighth mode is mild and sweet.	The eighth, the last of all modes, affects all who hear it with joy, pleasure, and sweetness, and it is completely alien to lasciviousness and to every vice. To it by right musicians have dedicated speech that is mild, unhurried, serious, that contains profound matter, or philosophical, or theological, since they concern heavenly happiness and glory; nor do words shrink from this mode that are attempted for the sake of asking favor. Its name follows the facts, since it is called sweet and mild.

Gaffurio's final treatise, *De harmonia musicorum instrumentorum opus* (1518). There he applied ancient erudition to the modes of plainchant, supplying information about the structure of the modes, the octave species, and ancient nomenclature, all of which became the basis of much subsequent writing on the modes. In particular, his discussion of the history of the modes, their ethos, and cosmic analogies, moved them from the realm of compositional or practical theory into the world of *musica speculativa* (see **Plate 6.2, p. 183**). As Palisca has shown, Gaffurio's writing was a product of a humanist revival of interest in modal theory and it stimulated a modal consciousness in a number of subsequent authors.[24]

In the period 1525–45, side by side with the traditional viewpoint articulated by Vanneus and the influence of humanistic interest in Greek modal theory as represented by the writings of Gaffurio, clear evidence surfaces of overt compositional, theoretical, and editorial association of traditional eight-mode theory with polyphonic composition. Yet the understanding of mode in relationship to polyphony from each of these perspectives – compositional, theoretical, editorial – was hardly a unified one. Two treatises published in Venice associate mode with polyphony more specifically than any that had preceded them: Pietro Aaron's *Trattato della natura et cognitione di tutti gli tuoni di canto figurato* (1525) and Giovanni Del Lago's *Breve introduttione di musica misurata* (1540). Strikingly, both are in Italian, not Latin, and Del Lago was well acquainted with Aaron and his work, as is attested in the so-called "Spataro correspondence."[25] Both treatises appear to be aimed at least in part – on the evidence of their language and contents – toward a different audience than that of the *Recanetum*. Both seem to satisfy particularly the needs of amateurs as well as would-be composers. Aaron's *Trattato* boldly proclaims the novelty of its undertaking:

> For it is clear that no writers of our age have explained how the many different modes are to be recognized, although to their greater credit they have treated of matters which can be readily understood.[26]

But the undertaking is striking not so much for its new or ingenious theoretical formulations – Powers has shown the indebtedness of Aaron's theoretical writing to earlier traditions – but for its assimilation of a polyphonic repertory as instantiations of that theory.[27] As Powers demonstrated, the assimilation is primarily that of a repertory to a theory, and not the other way around. Aaron's priorities for adducing the mode of the examples he cites reflect a hierarchical interrelationship that proceeds

24 For a concise overview of Gaffurio's interaction with Greek sources, see Palisca, "Gaffurio as a Humanist," Chapter 9, *Humanism in Italian Renaissance Musical Thought* On the relationship of Greek writings to modal theory of the sixteenth century, see Chapter 11 of the same work: "Greek Tonality and Western Modality."

25 Blackburn et al., *Correspondence*.

26 Aaron, *Trattato*; trans. *SR*, p. 417.

27 Powers, "Is Mode Real?" pp. 22–23; Judd, "Reading Aron Reading Petrucci."

from the mode of the tenor or pre-existing melody to a consideration of final, species, and *processo*. His single concession to the difficulty of describing the tenors of the repertory of Petrucci prints to which he refers in modal terms is his invocation of the *differentiae* to explain apparently unconventional finals, theoretically a dubious innovation, at best. The *differentiae* are normally understood as melodic formulae for ending psalm tones chosen to accommodate the return to the antiphon. In Aaron's usage however, the term represents not a formula but a specific pitch that may function as an alternative to the final and in addition to the cofinal as the place of termination of the tenor voice. It is a strategy that ultimately proved deeply problematic to Aaron's later readers, stirring together as it does aspects of modal theory, psalmodic conventions, and secular genres. Further, since Aaron's citations of polyphony come only in the first seven chapters of the *Trattato*, the relationship of the rest of the treatise to polyphonic composition has been the source of much debate.[28]

Giovanni Del Lago's *Breve introduttione* (1540) takes up mode in the context of an introductory text on polyphony. The second part begins with a technical treatment of the eight modes, now explicitly in the context of a book on counterpoint and a treatise on mensural music; there is no section on plainchant. Like Vanneus, Del Lago concludes with a discussion of modal affect in the context of choosing and expressing texts.

Printed music collections

At roughly the same time that Del Lago published his treatise, one can see a general trend among music printers toward ordering publications of vocal polyphony in partbooks by "tonal types," which have been defined by Harold Powers, following Siegfried Hermelink, as in combination of ambitus (represented by clef combinations: "normal" low clefs ranging from c1 to f4 versus the so-called *chiavette* or "high" clefs ranging from g2 to c4), some combination of system (*cantus durus* or *cantus mollis* as represented respectively by the absence or presence of a flat signature), and final.[29] For example, the nineteen motets of Zarlino's first printed anthology (*Musica Quinque Vocum*, Venice: Antonio Gardano, 1549) have clearly been grouped on the basis of signature and final, as shown in Table 12.1. While such editorial decisions might reflect an interest in modal theory, more often than not they appear to be the result of pragmatic considerations on the part of publishers, particularly obvious in the case of Gardano, rather than a reflection of interest in abstract theoretical speculation.[30]

28 Perkins, "Mode and Structure" and "Modal Species"; Bergquist, "Mode and Polyphony"; Powers, "Is Mode Real?"; Judd, "Modal Types" and "Reading Aron"; Meier, *The Modes* and *Alte Tonarten*.
29 Powers, "Tonal Types." Tonal types are usually represented by an expression consisting of the clef of the superius, the signature, and the concluding note of the bass voice, as in g2–♭–G.
30 Bernstein, *Scotto*, pp. 162–63; Lewis, *Gardano*, pp. 123–49.

Table 12.1 *Tonal types in Gioseffo Zarlino,* Musica Quinque Vocum *(Venice: Gardano, 1549)*

Number	Title	Clef	System	Final
1	*Veni Sancte Spiritus*	g2–c2–c3–c3–f3	♭	G
2	*O beatum pontificem*	g2–c2–c3–c3–f3	♭	G
3	*Nemo potest venire*	c1–c3–c4–c4–f4	♭	F
4	*Ave regina celorum*	c3–c4–f3–f3–f4	♭	F
5	*Osculetur me*	c1–c3–c4–c4–f4	–	D
6	*Nigra sum*	c1–c3–c4–c4–f4	–	D
7	*Ecce tu pulchra es*	c1–c3–c4–c4–f4	–	D
8	*Ego veni in hortum meum*	g2–c2–c3–c3–f3	♭	F
9	*Confitebor tibi (a voce pari)*	c2–c2–c3–c4–f3	♭	F
10	*Beatissimus marcus*	c2–c2–c3–c4–f3	♭	F
11	*O sacrum convivium*	c2–c3–c3–c4–f3	♭	F
12	*Si bona suscepimus*	c2–c3–c4–c3–f3	♭	D
13	*Clodia quem genuit*	g2–c2–c3–c3–f3	♭	A
14	*Ferculum fecit sibi*	c1–c3–c4–c4–f4	–	E
15	*In lectulo meo*	c1–c3–c4–c4–f4	–	E
16	*Ego rosa saron*	c1–c3–c4–c1–f4	♭	G
17	*Aptabo cythare modos*	c1–c3–c4–c4–f4	♭	G
18	*Capite nobis*	c1–c3–c4–c1–f4	♭	G
19	*Pater noster (a7)*	c1–c3–c4–c2–c3–c4–f4	♭/♭♭	G

Yet there are also music prints which overtly draw attention to the modality of their contents, either through the inclusion of modal labels in indices or individual parts, or in the ordering of their contents. The earliest of these are most often publications of madrigals, confirming the broad applicability of the concept of mode to all repertories at mid-century despite its liturgical origins and continuing liturgical associations. Among the first such prints are Girolamo Scotto's two books of madrigals for two and three voices from 1541 in which the pieces are identified and grouped according to genre and mode.[31] While the madrigals are given modal labels (e.g., *primi toni*), the collections themselves are not arranged according to modal order, nor are all eight modes represented. With two exceptions in the second print labeled "quarti toni," only authentic modes are represented (e.g., *primi*, *tertii*, *quinti*, and *septimi toni*).

What appears to be the first fully ordered modal collection was issued by the same

31 Bernstein, *Scotto*, pp. 270–74.

Table 12.2 *Tonal types in Cipriano de Rore's first book of madrigals (1542), after Powers, "Tonal Types," p. 444*

No.	Clef	System	Final	Mode
1	g2–c2–c3–c3–f3	♭	G	1
2	g2–c2–c3–c3–f3	♭	G	1
3	g2–c2–c3–c3–f3	♭	G	1
4	c1–c3–c4–c4–f4	♭	G	2
5	c1–c3–c4–c4–f4	♭	G	2
6	c1–c3–c4–c4–f4	–	E	3
7	c1–c3–c4–c4–f4	–	E	3
8	c1–c3–c4–c4–f4	–	E	3
9	c2–c4–c4–f3–f5	–	E	4
10	g2–c2–c3–c3–f3	♭	F	5
11	g2–c2–c3–c3–f3	♭	F	5
12	c1–c3–c4–c4–f4	♭	F	6
13	c1–c3–c4–c4–f4	♭	F	6
14	g2–c2–c3–c3–f3	–	G	7
15	g2–c2–c3–c3–f3	–	G	7
16	c1–c3–c4–c4–f4	–	G	8
17	c1–c3–c4–c4–f4	–	G	8
18	g2–c2–c3–c3–f3	♭	D	(1)
19	c1–c3–c4–c4–f4	♭	G	(2)
20	c1–c3–c4–c4–f4	–	E	(3)

printer a year later: Cipriano de Rore's *Madrigali a cinque voci*. As Bernhard Meier has shown, the first seventeen madrigals follow the order of the eight modes.[32] Although the impetus for such ordering might have come from Scotto, the appearance of an ordered print of Rore's motets in 1545 from Gardano's press suggests that the arrangement came from the composer himself.[33] Indeed, as Bernstein documents, the many subsequent editions of these madrigals retain neither the content nor the order of the first print. Rore's collection along with such later publications as the Susato motet anthologies and a number of works by Lasso and Palestrina provide the principal evidence by which Harold Powers articulated his theory of tonal types. Powers's tonal types are

32 Meier, ed., Cipriano de Rore, *Opera omnia*, vol. II, p. iii; Bernstein, *Scotto*, pp. 280–81; Powers, "Tonal Types," pp. 443–44. On "modal ethos" in Rore's cycle, see Palisca, "Mode Ethos," pp. 133–37.

33 Wiering, "Language of the Modes," pp. 154–56. For a discussion of earlier editorially ordered collections, see Brown, "Attaignant."

based on the same markers that editors and publishers such as Susato, Scotto, and Gardano appear to have used in ordering their collections. Central to Powers's argument is an assertion of a varied and not necessarily causal relationship of twenty-four possible tonal types to systems of eight or twelve modes. While tonal types may serve as a compositional means of representing (or editorial means of classifying) mode, they need not do so. A clear distinction is drawn between those polyphonic works which were intentionally written "in the modes" and those which may be assigned to modes after the fact.[34] Powers was able to summarize the plan of Rore's twenty madrigals as shown in Table 12.2. This position is in sharp contradistinction to one that relies on melodic features, articulation of species, and the characteristic use of the repercussion as modal determinants: features outlined to a greater or lesser degree in chant theory and applied by analogy to the individual voices of a polyphonic complex.[35] This latter stance was articulated most extensively in recent years in Bernhard Meier's work.[36] Meier posited modality as an inherent property of sixteenth-century polyphony – thus, by definition, all music from the period is "in the modes" – and argued an expressive theory derived from theoretical statements about melodic features of modes and modal ethos as well as empirical observation from this basis of a wide range of repertory.

Willaert and his circle seem to have had a particular preoccupation with the possibilities afforded by modal ordering, and Anne Smith has offered two different interpretations of the modality of Willaert's first books of motets, published by Scotto in 1539 and reprinted by Gardano in 1545.[37] The difficulty lies in ascertaining the distinction between those prints in which the process was one of *a posteriori* classification – i.e., a means of organizing a printed publication, as appears to be the case with these Willaert prints – and those in which modal theory played a generative role, as it apparently did in the Rore prints. The distinction may reside, in part, in the nature of the printed collection: between anthologies (where the ordering was at the behest of the publisher); the increasingly popular individual prints (in which the composer might exert a degree of control over the order in which his works were presented); and large-scale textual cycles in which mode provided a compositional means of overarching, if abstract, musical organization. Best-known among such large-scale cycles are the Palestrina offertories, discussed at length by Meier, Dahlhaus, and Powers, and Palestrina's *Song of Songs* motets, examined by Owens. Wiering provides a comprehensive listing of some 400 modal cycles, including Magnificat cycles.[38]

34 Powers, "Mode"; "Tonal Types"; "Modal Representation"; "Is Mode Real?"; and "Anomalous Modalities"; Hermelink, *Dispositiones modorum*.

35 The reciting tone of a mode, similar to the tenor of a psalm tone, is frequently labeled the "repercussion." In the later sixteenth century, the term encompasses more broadly the interval from the final to the reciting tone as a characteristic melodic pattern.

36 Most notably, Meier, *The Modes*; *Alte Tonarten*. See also Perkins, "Modal Species." For an overview of Meier's work, see Wiering, "Language of the Modes," pp. 31–46.

37 Smith, "Willaert Motets."

38 Meier, *The Modes*; Dahlhaus, *Studies*; Powers, "Modal Representation"; Owens, "Palestrina as Reader"; Wiering, "Language of the Modes," Appendices C and D.

MUSIC THEORY AND PRINT CULTURE

The advent of printed polyphonic music at the beginning of the sixteenth century betokened an irreversible change in the ways in which music treatises were conceived, presented, and exemplified. It also signaled a newly defined relationship between a shared, printed image and a theorist and his audience. Nowhere was this trend more evident than in the writing of modal theory, with its long tradition of instantiation. Just as monophonic modal theory was intimately tied to a corpus of chant, so sixteenth-century treatises were tied to specific polyphonic repertories. More often than not, they were repertories that were defined primarily by the printed sources in which they appeared. Indeed, the modal theory of Aaron, Glarean, and Zarlino is unimaginable without the access to music afforded by printed sources. The different circles in which these theorists moved, as well as rapid changes in the burgeoning music print culture and the growth of a musically literate public in the first half of the sixteenth century, meant that the specific nature of the relationships between theoretical writing, ways of reading, and printed sources takes a different shape in each of their treatises. (For a detailed examination of the relationship of music theory and print culture in the Renaissance, see Judd, *Reading Renaissance Music Theory* pp. 3–33.)

At his death, the inventory of Zarlino's house recorded his ownership of some 1,141 books. This is an extraordinary number of books for someone of his status to have owned, but the quantity is not altogether surprising given the obvious breadth of reading reflected in his citations of both classical and post-classical authors. There is tantalizing evidence, albeit of a circumstantial nature, that Zarlino's involvement in book culture extended not just to traditional pursuits of collection, consumption (reading), and production (writing), but to aspects of physical production and design, as well as the author's financial stake in his publications that went hand in hand with book production in the sixteenth century. With remarkable canniness, Zarlino masterfully and meticulously manipulated his public image through the medium of print over a forty-year period beginning with his first book of motets in 1549.

Part IV of the *Istitutioni*, the section on the modes, offers a vivid demonstration of the intertwining of print culture and music theorizing. Zarlino's citations are normally presented in an order that moves from "ancient" to "modern," concluding with examples chosen from his own works. While the ancient/modern distinction may seem mere formality, for Zarlino, it was defined by two printed sources: Grimm and Wyrsyng's *Liber Selectarum Cantionum* of 1520, a beautifully printed large folio choirbook, supplies the examples of the "ancients" while Willaert's *Musica Nova* of 1559, an equally prestigious print, supplies the "moderns." These two publications, along with his own motet prints, are responsible for the majority of Zarlino's nearly eighty citations in Part IV of the *Istitutioni*. Whether or not his readers had access to the music cited, these examples supplied an authoritative instantiation of Zarlino's claims while implicitly connecting Zarlino's theory to the whole of the polyphonic repertory. Such a gesture was unfathomable without the availability of printed music.

A number of single-composer editions from the 1540s reflected the impetus toward modal ordering. For example, Gabriele Martinengo's 1544 *Madrigali a quatro voce a misura di breve* stated on the title page that he had composed and arranged his madrigals according to their modal order. The specific attention drawn here to "composing" according to modal order highlights the important possibility not just that individual compositions were "in the modes," but that "modal composition" made possible the structuring of cycles of texts.

Zarlino's eight-mode Song of Songs motets

Zarlino embarked on just such a cycle in the 1540s: an unprecedented eight-mode motet setting of the *Song of Songs*.[39] Zarlino's *Canticum Canticorum* sets the Biblical text, not the more usual centonate liturgical texts derived from it, and deliberately drew a parallel between the eight chapters that comprised the book of *Song of Songs* and the eight modes. Thus, Chapter 1 is set as four motets with the same cleffing, signature, and final, representing Mode 1 on D; Chapter 2 as Mode 2, Chapter 3 as Mode 3. Such a textually ordered cycle suggests that affective associations of the modes could have played at best a minimal role in the pre-compositional decision to set the *Song of Songs* as an eight-mode cycle, despite the standard injunction to composers to set texts with due consideration for modal ethos. Rather, modal order offered an abstract musical means of creating narrative continuity while at the same time implicitly providing a theological statement about the primacy of the eight modes of ecclesiastical chant in these freely composed motets. Yet, with one important exception, Zarlino appears to have ceased work on the projected cycle at the conclusion of Chapter 3 (= Mode 3). For reasons to be discussed below, Zarlino removed and reordered motets from the cycle in 1549, spreading them across three prints and obscuring the cyclic origins of individual motets.

Ego veni in hortum meum, the text of the beginning of Chapter 5 of the *Song of Songs*, appears to mark the end of Zarlino's work on this cycle. By any of the criteria outlined above, its associations with the fifth mode are easily recognized. Its tonal type (g2–♭–C,F) is the same as that used by Rore in his 1542 madrigal publication (compare Table 12.2). The opening point of imitation signals Mode 5 with the *soggetto*'s emphasis on C and F as boundary points of melodic lines, and the modified "tonal" imitation (see Example 12.1). Similarly, the opening of the *secunda pars* unequivocally suggests Mode 5 in its melodic and cadential material, as illustrated in Example 12.2. The vocal ranges of superius, tenor, and quintus are overtly those associated with authentic Mode 5, while those of the altus and bassus less obviously reflect the kind of plagal/authentic voice pairing sometimes seen in adjacent voices (see Example 12.3).[40]

Zarlino's contrapuntal style is remarkably free from cadential articulation, but one senses a self-conscious restriction, even compositional reliance, in this particular motet on adhering to theoretical descriptions of the modes in an almost textbook manner. F, without doubt, functions as the primary choice for cadences, with C taking a secondary role in this motet. Yet, to examine the pitch content of the *soggetto* of the opening tenor and soprano is to encounter immediately the long-standing

39 This previously unrecognized cycle and its origins are discussed in detail in Judd, "A Newly Recovered Eight-Mode Motet Cycle."

40 For contrasting opinions on the validity of the authentic–plagal distinction, see Dahlhaus, *Studies*, pp. 189–90; Meier, *The Modes*, pp. 47–88; Powers, "Tonal Types" and "Modal Representation," pp. 59–80.

"problem" of Mode 5: the *diapente* here is not the third species of fifth proper to the *tritus* modal pair. The *cantus mollis* system of the motet with its B♭ signature has transformed the *diapente* to that proper to Modes 7 and 8. Such a transformation had long been accepted by theorists from the necessity to avoid the tritone inherent in the third species of *diapente*. Thus, Vanneus's generic representation of the form of tones for Mode 5 (Example 12.4) includes a B♭ signature, even though the only B that appears in the example (in the termination formula) would not create any melodic difficulties were it sung as B-mi proper to the species, rather than the B-fa dictated by the signature.[41] Yet while such anomalies partook of a long theoretical tradition, the renewed scrutiny accorded modal theory from the humanist perspective led to a new model of modality: the dodecachordal system.

Glarean's twelve-mode theory

Although the Swiss humanist Heinrich Glarean (1488–1563) hinted at his dissatisfaction with traditonal modal theory in his *Isagoge* (1516), it was only with his *Dodecachordon* (1547) that he rejected the received eight-mode system in favor of a theory of twelve modes. He was at pains to connect this theory with classical antecedents while simultaneously authenticating it with the chants of the church.[42] The *Dodecachordon* in aim, content, and presentation is quite unlike the treatises discussed thus far in this chapter. A luxurious folio volume of 470 pages, it includes numerous polyphonic examples in choirbook format.[43] The treatise begins with a discussion of the elements of music followed by an exposition of monophonic modal theory. After a basic introduction to mensural music, the polyphonic modal examples are presented. There is no book on counterpoint, or a *theorica* in the usual sense.

The essence of Glarean's theory was its derivation of the modes not from the usual addition of *diapente* and *diatessaron*, but from the division of the *diapason* (octave species). In this, Glarean saw himself following the in footsteps of Boethius and Gaffurio and a recovery of the modes of ancient Greek theory, although as Palisca has shown, Glarean got his Greek modal theory terribly wrong.[44] How closely he attempted to follow Gaffurio and Boethius in deriving his modal theories is evident from his heavily annotated copies of Boethius's *De institutione musica* and *De arithmetica* and Gaffurio's *De harmonia* and *Practica musice*.[45] So, for example, one sees in

41 Similarly, Modes 1 and 2 frequently admitted B♭, by means of a *fa-supra-la* rationale in relation to the first species of *diapente* (d–a/re–la).

42 Fuller, "Defending the *Dodecachordon*."

43 On Glarean's examples, see Judd, "Musical Commonplace Books"; *Reading Renaissance Music Theory*, Chapters 5–6.

44 Palisca, "Mode Ethos," pp. 129–30. For a later synopsis of the dodecachordal modal system, see Table 13.2, p. 416.

45 Glarean's annotations of various printed books are discussed in Judd, *Reading Renaissance Music Theory*, Chapters 5 and 6.

Example 12.1 Zarlino, *Ego veni*, *prima pars*, mm. 1–16

Example 12.1 (*cont.*)

Example 12.2 Zarlino, *Ego veni, secunda pars*, mm. 1–15

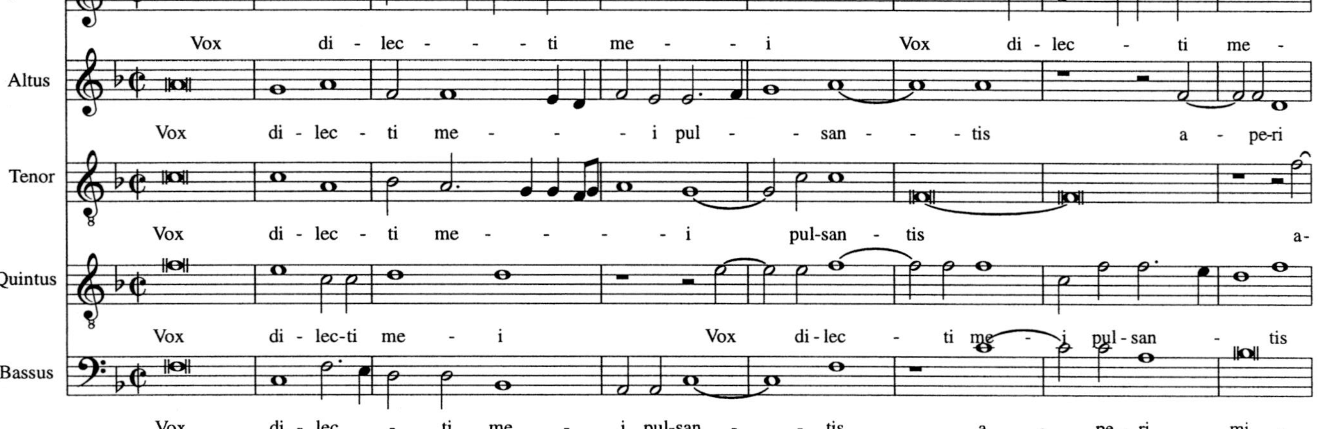

Example 12.2 (*cont.*)

Example 12.3 *Ego veni*, vocal ranges

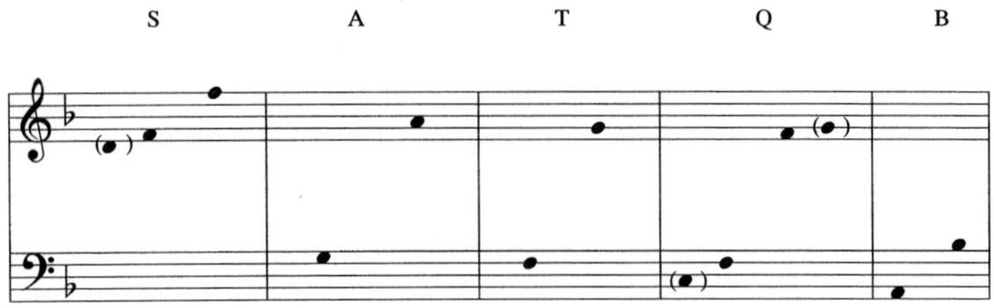

Example 12.4 Vanneus's generic representation of the form of tones for Mode 5

Glarean's annotations to Gaffurio's *De harmonia* his focus on the seven octave species and the names he supplied for the modal pairs derived from them. Glarean adds the letter names of the scala to Gaffurio's diagram (Plate 12.3a), and his notes in the upper right hand corner of the diagram refer to other Greek sources. When the diagram reappears in the *Dodecachordon*, it is as two versions on facing pages (Plate 12.3b). The relationship of octave species and modes is also summarized in relation to the final (Plate 12.3c). The two modes derived from the octave species on B were ultimately rejected because of its false fifth. Glarean's system now neatly covered the possibilities framed by the diatonic system with twelve modes comprising six modal pairs that he claimed represented the modes of classical antiquity. Like Aaron, he provided instantiations from the polyphonic repertory. Most of the work on the treatise had been completed by 1539, and many of the examples had been compiled as early as 1527, making for a decidedly antiquated repertory by the time the treatise was actually published in 1547. Unlike Aaron, Glarean actually included the music to which he referred with commentary. Further, Glarean was at pains to authenticate the theory he propagated (and implicitly its classical origins) with the ecclesiastical authority of chant. In its specifics, this may be seen as the gesture of a northern Catholic humanist in the face of the Reformation. Unlike Aaron, Del Lago, and Zarlino, Glarean was neither priest, nor singer, nor organist, nor in the employ of the church. He was an itinerant scholar and university professor. Yet whereas Aaron's choice of repertory attests to universalizing tendencies, Glarean elucidated his theory almost entirely with Latin-texted examples on sacred subjects.

The first known application of Glarean's dodecachordal system appears in the Zarlino motet print already discussed: the *Musici Quinque Vocum* of 1549. In addition to Gardano's grouping of motets in the print by tonal type, as illustrated in Table 12.1, the tenor (and occasionally quintus) partbook includes printed modal attributions (see Table 12.3).[46] As can be seen from the classifications, Zarlino adopted Glarean's nomenclature, including the new Aeolian and Ionian modes. Thus *Ego veni*, composed as a representation of Mode 5 in the putative eight-mode *Song of Songs* cycle, was now classified as Ionian. Zarlino's encounter with, and apparent acceptance of, Glarean's theory sometime after the publication of the *Dodecachordon* in 1547 undermined the very premise of the largest-scale compositional endeavor he is known to have undertaken. Zarlino appears to have used parts of the cycle shorn of their original purposes in the service of his publication ambitions.[47] Obviously in this instance, the dodecachordal labels represent the categorization of a pre-existing repertory, at least some of which had been composed within a different theoretical framework.

Zarlino's theoretical writings on mode

Zarlino's gradual assimilation of dodecachordal theory continued across his theoretical publications for the next twenty-five years in two editions of *Le istitutioni harmoniche* (1558 and 1573) and the intervening *Dimostrationi harmoniche* (1571). Magisterial in scope, the *Istitutioni* stands as one of the best-known treatises of the sixteenth century. It draws together in a single book areas of music study that had always before merited not just discrete sections, but separate and distinctly defined volumes in the *speculativa* and *practica* traditions. (See also **Chapter 2, pp. 51–52.**) Both the format and intellectual framework of the *Istitutioni* place it firmly within the particularly rich humanistic environment of mid-century Venice. Martha Feldman has persuasively argued that the *Istitutioni* reflects the influence of Pietro Bembo's theory of imitation, pointing to the obvious Ciceronian gesture of its title page.[48] Zarlino's decision to write in Italian rather than Latin also reflects a specifically Bembist impulse from the 1530s that argued for Italian as a language in its own right. The publication of the *Istitutioni* positioned Zarlino as Willaert's successor by overt references to the composer and his teaching as well as by tying the work specifically to the contents of Willaert's *Musica nova* and Zarlino's own motet prints.[49]

46 Plates from Zarlino's 1549 print on which these attributions may be seen are reproduced in Lewis, "Zarlino's Theories," p. 245; see also Judd, "A Newly Recovered Eight-Mode Motet Cycle"; and *Reading Renaissance Music Theory*, pp. 210, 215.

47 For a more detailed discussion of Zarlino's reasons for stopping work on the *Song of Songs* cycle, see Judd, "A Newly Recovered Eight-Mode Motet Cycle." On Zarlino's publication ambitions, see Judd, *Reading Renaissance Music Theory*, Chapters 7–8.

48 Feldman, *City Culture*, p. 172.

49 Judd, *Reading Renaissance Music Theory*, pp. 234ff.

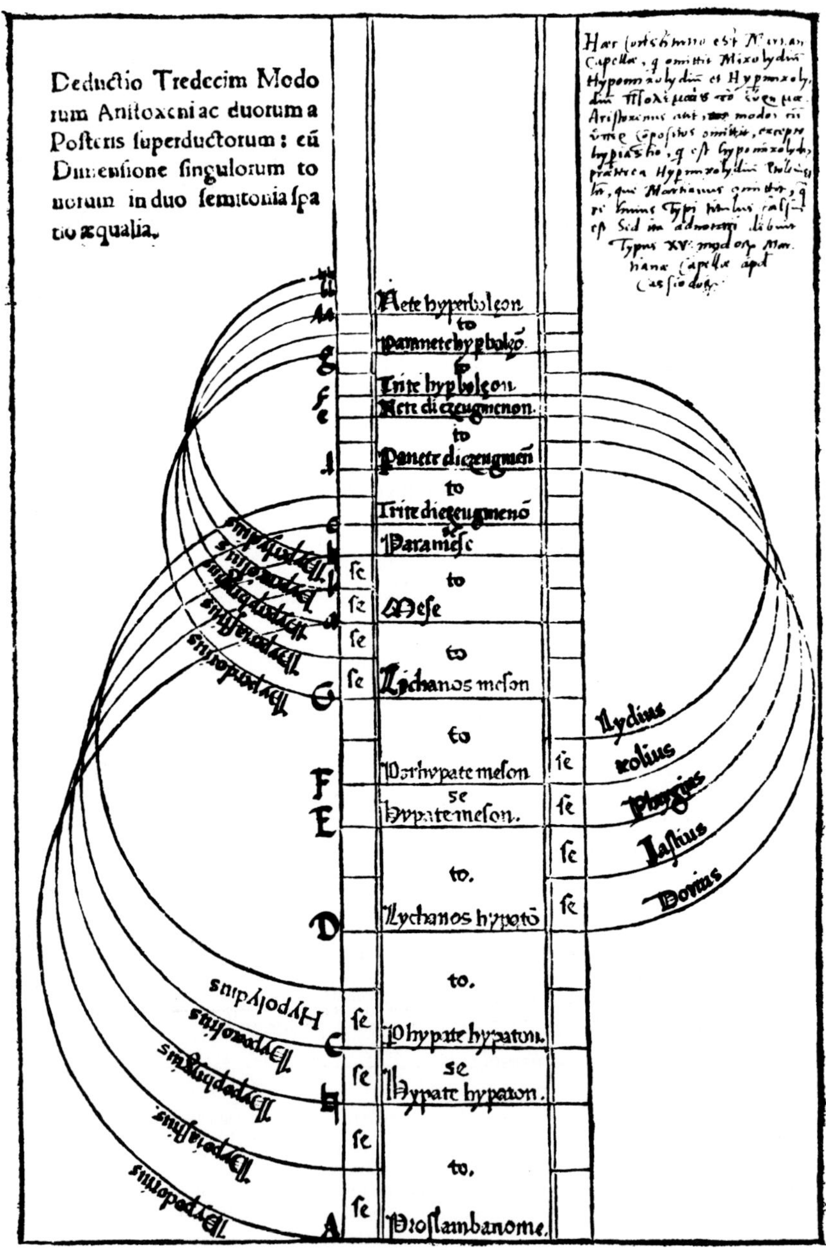

Plate 12.3a Octave species of Gaffurio, *De harmonia* with Glarean's annotation

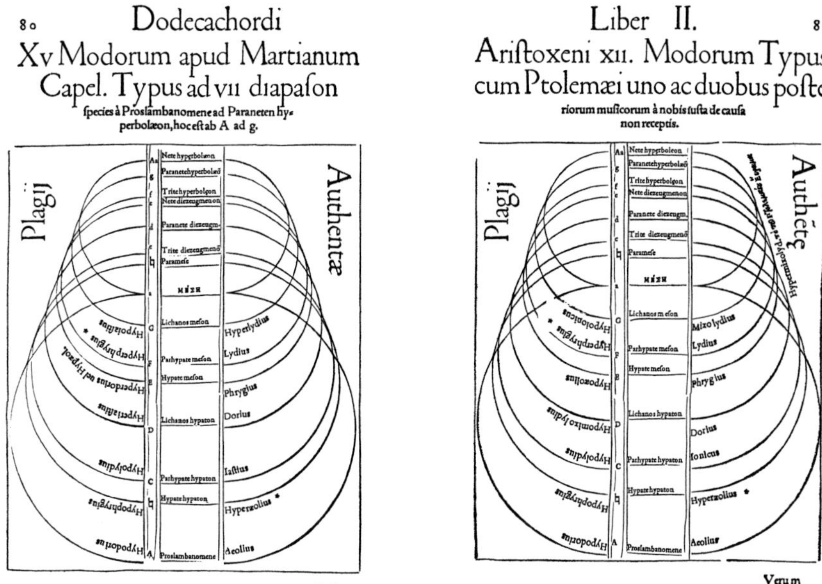

Plate 12.3b Octave species from Glarean, *Dodecachordon*, pp. 80–81

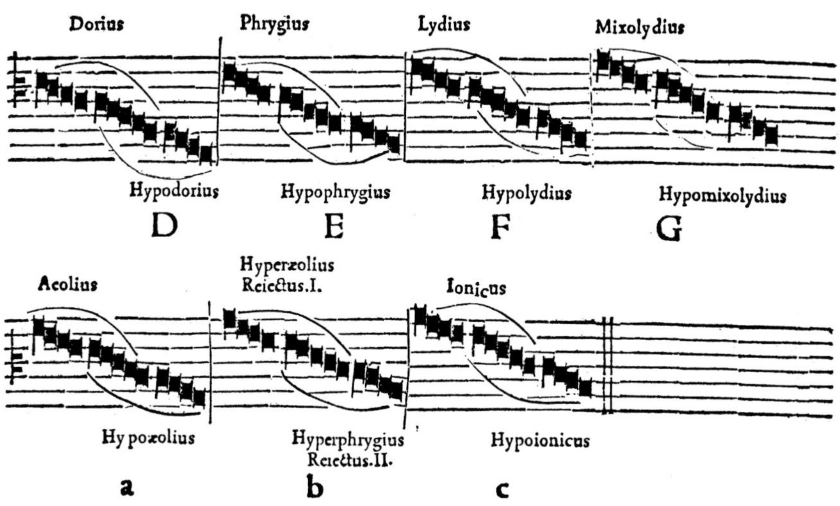

Plate 12.3c The twelve modes from Glarean, *Dodecachordon*, p. 140

Table 12.3 *Modal attributions in Gioseffo Zarlino,* Musica Quinque Vocum *(Venice: Gardano, 1549)*

Number	Title	Mode
1	*Veni Sancte Spiritus*	Dorian
2	*O beatum pontificem*	Dorian
3	*Nemo potest venire*	Hypoionian
4	*Ave regina celorum*	Hypoionian
5	*Osculetur me*	Dorian
6	*Nigra sum*	Dorian
7	*Ecce tu pulchra es*	Dorian
8	*Ego veni in hortum meum*	Ionian
9	*Confitebor tibi (a voce pari)*	Ionian
10	*Beatissimus marcus*	Ionian
11	*O sacrum convivium*	Ionian
12	*Si bona suscepimus*	Aeolian
13	*Clodia quem genuit*	Hypophrygian
14	*Ferculum fecit sibi*	Phrygian
15	*In lectulo meo*	Phrygian
16	*Ego rosa saron*	Hypodorian
17	*Aptabo cythare modos*	Hypodorian
18	*Capite nobis*	Hypodorian
19	*Pater noster (a7)*	[Hypodorian]

In the fourth part, on mode, Zarlino draws on three strands of argument: (1) the discourse of traditional modal theory as mediated by Glarean's dodecachordal theory in a presentation of the species and appropriate cadences; (2) the specifically Venetian strand of modal theory exemplified by Aaron's *Trattato*, with its instantiations from contemporary printed polyphonic repertories; and (3) the *musica practica* tradition that forms the basis of the counterpoint section of the *Istitutioni*. Although Zarlino is openly contemptuous of the works of his Italian predecessors, including Vanneus and Aaron, dismissing them as the "sophists of their time," the influence of both may be seen in the modal section of the *Istitutioni*. On the other hand, the system expounded here is that of twelve modes, and Glarean's presence is strongly felt in these chapters although never explicitly acknowledged.[50] Along with his citations of repertory,

50 The most detailed examination of Zarlino's borrowing from Glarean is found in Meier, "Heinrich Loriti Glareanus." Zarlino borrows most heavily and directly from Glarean in his description of the "new" modes, Modes 5 and 6, and 9 and 10.

Zarlino's most original contribution to the continuing modal discourse is the inclusion of newly composed duos representing each mode. Their appearance corresponds to the numerous didactic examples of the counterpoint book of the treatise and they also serve as illustrations of the contrapuntal devices discussed earlier in the book. Thus they move the discussion from a classificatory status like Aaron's toward didactic compositional prescriptions. The substance of Glarean's modal theory is placed in a new context that renders the twelve modes recognizable in name only. While Zarlino adopted Glarean's "classical" modal nomenclature in his 1549 motet print – including the "new" Aeolian and Ionian designations – he abandons these names in the course of Part IV of the *Istitutioni* in favor of simple numerals when he actually comes to discuss individual modes. Palisca has suggested that this points to Zarlino's recognition of the incompatibility of Glarean's nomenclature with his newly acquired understanding of Ptolemy.[51] Certainly, Zarlino is at pains to illustrate his recognition of the disjunction between the ancient Greek modes and those he is describing.

Each of the chapters on individual modes in the *Istitutioni* follows a standard format that begins by outlining the species of the mode, as can be seen from the opening of the discussion of the eleventh mode:

> The eleventh mode comes into being from the third species of diapason, C to c, mediated harmonically by the note G. Practitioners say that this mode is composed of the fourth species of diapente, C to G, placed below, and the third species of diatessaron, G to c, placed above.

Thus the more "learned" octave species identification is coupled immediately with the *diapente* plus *diatessaron* formula, which is overtly linked to practical theory. Mention and explanation of traditional associations of modal ethos follow. Because this is one of Zarlino's "new" modes, he is careful to explain the relationship of this mode to its counterpart in the traditional eight-mode system:

> The eleventh mode is by its nature very suitable for dances and *balli*, and therefore we find that most *balli* heard in Italy are played in this mode. Hence it has happened that some have called it a lascivious mode.
>
> There are many chants in the eleventh mode in the sacred choirbooks, such as the Mass called *De Angelis* and the antiphons *Alma redemptoris mater* and *Regina coeli laetare Haleluiah*. This mode is so much in use and so loved by the moderns that, induced by its sweetness and beauty, they have changed many compositions written in the fifth mode into the eleventh mode by putting the note b♭ in place of the note b♮.

Like the other discussions of the "new" modes, Zarlino here appears to feel obliged to cite chant examples. While he allows in his text that the fifth mode is transposed into

51 Palisca, Introduction to Cohen, trans., *On the Modes*, pp. x–xii

Example 12.5 Kyrie I, Missa de Angelis (*Liber usualis* 37)

the eleventh by the addition of B♭, all three chants would have traditionally and unproblematically been assigned to Mode 5. All, like the Kyrie that opens the *Missa De Angelis* (see Example 12.5), clearly mark the ambitus F to f, divided at C with signed B♭s. Although Zarlino often used Glarean's chant examples, he has chosen his own here. By contrast, Glarean was at pains to include two chants that used C as finals and whose modal classification might therefore have been more problematic in the eight-mode system.

Each of the chapters lists the appropriate initials and cadences for the mode, always with an emphasis on the final, third, and fifth of the mode:[52]

> The regular initial tones of the eleventh mode are placed on C, E, G, and c, and so are its cadences. Its irregular initial tones and cadences are placed on the other notes.

To this point, the areas covered – species, ethos, beginnings and endings – are recognizable as the topics a theorist such as Tinctoris addressed in his book on the modes more than half a century before. Yet aspects of the substance of the discussion have changed dramatically. Zarlino is, of course, outlining not an eight-mode but a twelve-mode system. His lists of possible beginnings and cadences is aimed not at chant but explicitly at polyphony. Endings are determined not in relation to psalm-tones but in a systematic fashion across the modes. This regularization extends further the consistent framework of the species that was the hallmark of Glarean's twelve-mode theory. Yet even when Zarlino baldly, and without acknowledgment, relies on direct translation of Glarean's text, Glarean's words cannot hold the same meaning in the very different context in which they now serve. Breaking clearly from the earlier eight-mode ecclesiastical tradition, but writing in a very different intellectual and musical framework than that of the *Dodecachordon*, Zarlino moves from these traditional topics toward his instantiations of the modes through citations of polyphonic compositions in a manner reminiscent of Pietro Aaron's *Trattato*:

> Musicians have written many compositions in this mode, among them *Stabat mater dolorosa* by Josquin for five voices, *O salutaris hostia*, *Alma redemptoris mater*, and *Pien d'un*

52 This aspect of Zarlino's theory was often cited by writers in the early part of the twentieth century in support of an interpretation of Zarlino as a theorist on the cusp of tonal understanding, e.g., Riemann and Shirlaw. See Chapter 14, pp. 461–62.

> *vago pensier* by Adriano, and *Descendi in [h]ortum meum* by Jacquet, all composed for six voices, as well as the motet *Audi filia et vide* for five voices by Gombert, and the motet *Ego veni in hortum meum*, also for five voices, which I myself composed many years ago. There are innumerable other compositions in this mode, and it would take a long time to list them.

All of the polyphonic examples cited in the chapter share the tonal type of Zarlino's *Ego veni* discussed above: g2–♭-C,F. Yet in the didactic duo provided for this chapter (see Example 12.6) Zarlino demonstrates the mode with C as final, illustrating the cadence tones he enumerates (C, E, and G). As in all of his duos in these chapters on the modes, the first cadence is to the final (m. 9), followed by an elided cadence (m. 13). A single cadence to the third is included (m. 19); cadences to the fifth (mm. 21, 33) and final (mm. 25 [evaded], 30) follow, with a cadence to the final marking the end of the schematic example. Zarlino does not discuss melodic procedures and offers no real equivalent for the concept Glarean termed *phrasis*. Nevertheless, the diapason of the mode and its articulation as a combination of *diapente* and *diatessaron* is always obvious from the opening point of imitation, appearing to demonstrate something akin to the phenomenon Aaron described as *processo*.

The chapter concludes with an explanation of the "irregularities" associated with the mode:

> The eleventh mode is transposed away from its natural notes, up by a diatessaron or down by a diapente, with the help of the note b♭, proceeding through the notes of the tetrachord Synemmenon.[53]

Thus Zarlino here offers two distinct ways of understanding modality. His citations represent *descriptive* accommodation of existing repertories to his twelve-mode categories. These works fulfill to a greater or lesser degree those features of mode enumerated in the chapter and the process is not so different from Pietro Aaron's, although the criteria appear to be different. In Zarlino's own eight-mode motets, for example, it is clear that tonal types are being used compositionally to represent modes; cadences follow the scheme outlined in the *Istitutioni* in only the most general sense. By contrast, Zarlino's duos illustrating each of the modes function as a twelve-mode cycle of sorts, offering a *prescriptive* guide for how one ought to compose. In these didactic examples, *soggetti*, cadences, and intervals of imitation are all a reflection of the contrapuntal theory of Part III of the *Istitutioni* and the modal theory of Part IV.

The publication of the *Dimostrationi harmoniche* in 1571 marked Zarlino's move into a different literary genre, the dialogue, and a different intellectual domain, that of

53 Translations of the preceeding excerpts are taken from Cohen, *On the Modes*, pp. 85–86 with slight modifications.

Example 12.6 Zarlino, Duo illustrating Mode 11

"demonstration."[54] The dialogue is set in April 1562 as a conversation among Zarlino, Willaert, Claudio Merulo, Francesco dalla Viola, and a nobleman from Pavia named "Desiderio" who initiates the discussion by his questions. Even though it was published in 1571, the fictional setting of the dialogue could be no later than 1562, the year of Willaert's death. Most pertinent in the present context, although not the central focus of the treatise, is Zarlino's renumbering of the modes. Crocker has illustrated that Zarlino's renumbering served the function of correlating the order of hexachordal syllables with the modal finals and establishing the superiority of harmonic division over arithmetic.[55] The modes are now ordered from C to a, with no gap in finals (for the discarded diapason on B). The former "Ionian" mode becomes Mode 1, the "Hypoionian," Mode 2, and so on (see Plate 12.4). In both rationale and ordering, Zarlino's dodecachordal system was thus further distanced from its origins in Glarean's treatise. Zarlino was also motivated by an attempt to align the Greek modes with an order of finals that reflected what he understood of ancient descriptions. Thus new Mode 1 (with C final) is equated with Dorian, Mode 3 (D final) with Phrygian, and so forth. In addition, the context of the *Dimostrationi* places modal theory firmly in the world of *speculativa* and away from the *practica* environment it occupies in the *Istitutioni*, even if Willaert's blessing on Zarlino's new modal order proceeds from that of the practical musician.

The renumbering of the modes is responsible for the primary revisions in content that occur in Part IV of the 1573 edition of *Le istitutioni harmoniche*. Thus *Ego veni* – which Zarlino had composed as a representation of Mode 5, labeled as "Ionian" in his 1549 motet print, and used as an example of Mode 11 in the 1558 edition of *Le Istitutioni harmoniche* – now instantiated Mode 1 (presumably "Dorian," although Zarlino retains his use of number rather than name in identifying modes). In the revised treatise, Zarlino also acknowledged more obviously the distinction between his composed duo, with its final on C, and the examples he cited with their g2–♭-F tonal types, adding at the end of the chapter an explanation that all of his examples illustrate the transposition of the mode to F.

Zarlino's citations are taken almost entirely from a few printed collections whose contents appear almost without exception to represent an eight-mode conception, in so far as the works within them were written "in the modes."[56] Indeed, there are few, if any, pieces that might be construed as representing this mode in its untransposed form with a C final amongst the madrigals and motets he surveyed. This may be responsible for Zarlino's mention of the *balli* as a genre that frequently used this mode, along with his assertion about the frequency with which the mode is used by modern composers.

54 On the methodology of the treatise, see Kelleher, "Zarlino's 'Dimostrationi Harmoniche.'"
55 Crocker, "Perchè Zarlino?" 56 Judd, *Reading Renaissance Music Theory*, pp. 240–42.

ORDINE NATVRALE DE TVTTI LI MODI.

		PRIMO MODO PRINCIPALE	SECONDO MODO NONPRINCIPALE	TERZO MODO PRINCIPALE	QVARTO MODO PRINCIPALE	QVINTO MODO PRINCIPALE	SESTO MODO NONPRINCIPALE	SETTIMO MODO PRINCIPALE	OTTAVO MODO NONPRINCIPALE	NONO MODO PRINCIPALE	DECIMO MODO NONPRINCIPALE	VNDECIMO MODO PRINCIPALE	DVODECIMO MODO NON PRINCIPALE
Γ.	Hypoproslābanomenos.		Γ.										
A.	Proslambanomenos.				A.								
♮.	Hypate hypaton.						♮.						
C.	Parhypatehypaton.	C.	C.						C.				
D.	Lychanos hyp aton.			D.	D.						D.		
E.	Hypate meſon.					E.	E.						E.
F.	Parhypate meſon.							F.	F.				
G.	Lychanos meſon.	G.	G.							G.	G.		
a.	Meſe.			a.	a.							a.	a.
♮.	Parameſe.					♮.	♮.						
c.	Tritediezeugmenon.	c.						c.	c.				
P.	Paranete diezeugmenon.			d.						d.	d.		
e.	Netediezeugmenon.					e.						e.	e.
f.	Tritehyperboleon.							f.					
g.	Paranete hyperboleon.									g.			
aa.	Netehyperboleon.											aa.	

Plate 12.4 Octave species and order of the modes from Zarlino, *Dimostrationi harmoniche*, p. 306

After Zarlino

The myriad possibilities of modal categorization for the motet *Ego veni* – mode 1, 5, 11, Ionian, or even potentially Dorian – depending on whether an eight- or twelve-mode system was considered, what numbering scheme was invoked, and what naming conventions were applied – is a fair representation of the multi-faceted situation that held sway from the 1570s well into the seventeenth century. While Glarean's dodecachordal theory and Zarlino's adaptation of it gained advocates, it by no means replaced traditional eight-mode theory. Treatises such as Dressler's *Practica modorum explicatio* (1561) and Aiguino's *La illuminata de tutti i tuoni di canto fermo* (1562) continued to advocate the eight-mode system, even though both were clearly aware of the twelve-mode alternative. Indeed, Aiguino explicitly refuted not only twelve-, but also fourteen-mode systems in his revision of the treatise in 1581. *La illuminata*, like Vanneus's *Recanetum*, stands firmly in the ecclesiastical chant tradition. Dressler's lecture notes, with their explicit information on the modal disposition of cadences and imitative subjects, provided a central text for later scholars intent on describing the musical nature of modality in relation to polyphony. Cerreto, too, retained the eight-mode system in his *Della prattica musica vocale* (1601) and *Dialoghi harmonici* (1626), offering a pointed refutation of the twelve-mode system and supplying polyphonic settings of antiphons for each mode. Similar approaches may be found throughout the seventeenth century. Testimony to the staying power of the eight-mode tradition, theoretical arguments to its insufficiency notwithstanding, are the many eight-mode cyclic compositions, most notably those by Palestrina and Lasso from the second half of the century.

The most direct transmission of Glarean's teaching in the German *Lateinschule* tradition is found in Hoffmann's *Doctrina de tonis* (1582). As mediated by Zarlino's 1558 publication, dodecachordal theory was transmitted in a number of Italian theoretical sources, among them Artusi (1586), Tigrini (1588), and Cerone (1613).[57] Musical cycles in the twelve modes are most often instrumental cycles of ricercars or toccatas by composers such as Merulo, Gabrieli, Luzzaschi, and Frescobaldi. In many cases, the composers (e.g. Merulo and Gabrieli) had Venetian connections with Zarlino or had studied with someone linked to Zarlino – Luzzaschi was a pupil of Francesco dalla Viola, one of the participants in the dialogue of the *Dimostrationi*. Theoretical works directed at keyboard players, such as Banchieri's treatises, often include the eight- and twelve-mode systems side by side, using the eight modes specifically in reference to chant and relating them to the psalm tones (the so-called "church keys") and using the traditional numbering of the twelve modes, with a nodding reference to Zarlino's

57 See Wiering, "Language of the Modes," pp. 221–43 for a detailed discussion of the reception of Zarlino's theories.

renumbering.[58] In France, Zarlino's new scheme was adopted in a number of Claude Le Jeune's cycles, while in England the influence of continental modal theory during the sixteenth century appears to have been minimal at best.[59]

Postscript: modal theory and the analysis of sixteenth-century polyphony

Much of the controversy that has surrounded interpretations of modal theory of the Renaissance in recent years has been generated by the potential mode holds for the analysis of Renaissance polyphony. At the beginning of this chapter, I suggested that mode had been a problematic concept for the sixteenth as well as the twentieth century, but the nature and cause of difficulty in the discourse of the two centuries stems from different sources. The 1960s and 70s saw a growing movement which decried as anachronistic the tonal analyses that underpinned the work of scholars such as Besseler and Lowinsky. In response, musicologists increasingly looked to sixteenth-century theorists for an explanation of how "pre-tonal" polyphony worked.[60] Thus when Lewis Lockwood began an examination of Josquin's *Missa Hercules dux Ferrarie*, he observed that a systematic interpretation of the work would consider "the basic tone-system of the period, as we find it expounded by the best-informed and most authoritative theorists of Josquin's time, especially Tinctoris."[61] Self-evident though such a statement may appear to be, understanding the "modality" of works by the Josquin generation has proved difficult. In fact, most historians have looked not to Tinctoris, but to the far more specific pronouncements of Pietro Aaron. The association remains problematic nevertheless. Aaron's connection of mode and polyphony has been the subject of a wide variety of historical and theoretical interpretations. Perkins based a study of the masses of Josquin on principles derived from Aaron's *Trattato*, while Bergquist argued that Aaron's classifications were essentially irrelevant for polyphony, despite the claims of the treatise.[62] Powers showed that Aaron's concern extended only to the tenor parts of the compositions he adduced in support of his theory and thus raised a fundamental question about the relationship of mode and polyphony.[63] Krantz's dissertation started from the premise that Josquin's motets were modal; however, he based his discussion not on the writings of a single theorist, but on Meier's codification of modal theory.[64] My own hypothetical classification of Josquin's motets based on Aaron's criteria sug-

58 On keyboard cycles, see Meier, *Alte Tonarten*; Robert Judd, "Notational Formats at the Keyboard." Also see Chapter 13, pp. 414–15.

59 Owens, "Concepts of Pitch," pp. 184–91

60 Most recently, see Bent, "Grammar."

61 Lockwood, *Music in Renaissance Ferrara*, p. 241.

62 Perkins, "Mode and Structure"; Bergquist, "Mode and Polyphony."

63 Powers, "Is mode real?"

64 Krantz, "Rhetorical and Structural Functions of Mode."

gested how uneasily the repertory sat with the theory. An invocation of the repercussion, other voices, and appropriate cadence tones – concepts Aaron does not discuss in the chapters in which he categorizes polyphony – does not ease the fit, nor does recourse to later twelve-mode theory.[65] In response to this difficulty, I suggested that elements of hexachordal position and pitch of the final, melodic characteristics, contrapuntal procedures, and the registral conventions of a voice ensemble might usefully be employed as a composite in a theory of three basic tonal systems described as "ut, re, mi" tonalities.[66] These elements were essentially distinct in the minds of fifteenth- and sixteenth-century theorists, but intimately related in polyphonic composition. Although the elements united in this theory would all be familiar to earlier writers, the way in which they are associated is a modern analytical construction.

The situation with polyphony from mid-century has been equally problematic, despite the demonstrable concern of composers and editors with the concept of mode. Jessie Ann Owens has shown the pervasive superimposition in twentieth-century writing of a "neo-modal" system derived from a modern understanding of scale types broadly conflated with medieval and Renaissance modal theory.[67] The result is a series of transposable scales which function in some sense as keys: hence the neologisms "G-Dorian," "B♭-Ionian," and so forth. Yet scale type, in the modern sense of ordered pattern of pitch-classes (in contrast to a Boethian or Guidonian understanding of *scala*), is at best a resultant from earlier models of generating modes, certainly not a defining feature.

The most thorough-going and persuasive attempt to demonstrate the relevance of modal theory for Renaissance polyphony was undoubtedly Bernhard Meier's *The Modes of Classical Vocal Polyphony*. A penetrating study of the evolution of Meier's work is available in Wiering.[68] The heart of Meier's work rested in an attempt to study the theoretical sources for polyphonic modality and apply them to a discussion of the music. One cannot but be impressed by his vast knowledge of both repertory and theoretical sources. Enlightening and influential though Meier's work was, it has nevertheless been subjected to fierce criticism. On the one hand, *The Modes* represented the culmination of an on-going polemic with Carl Dahlhaus that centered on the recognition of authentic and plagal modes in polyphony. While Dahlhaus argued for the convergence of complementary modal pairs as *Gesamtmodi*,[69] Meier attempted to demonstrate the distinction of authentic and

65 Judd, "Modal Types," pp. 431–37.

66 The notion of three tonal systems receives some belated support from Glarean's observation that "The same men teach in this way concerning the ending of songs in all modes: every song ends either on *re* or on *mi* or on *ut*." For further instances of Glarean's teaching on "ut, re, mi," see Judd, "Modal Types," p. 437.

67 Owens, "Concepts of Pitch," p. 186.

68 Wiering, *The Language of the Modes*, pp. 31–46.

69 Dahlhaus, *Studies*, pp. 195–96.

plagal modes in polyphony. Both bolstered their arguments with examples from Palestrina's offertory cycle.[70] On the other hand, Meier often used sources in what appears to be an uncritical manner, ever ready to attach expressive interpretation to his understanding of modal theory. While a number of articles followed Meier's lead, a series of increasingly skeptical articles by Powers attempted to demonstrate the artificiality of the modal–tonal dichotomy enshrined in this debate. Despite Powers's remonstrances, new studies continue to explore aspects of modal theory in discussing repertories for which no better analytical models appear to exist.[71] So, too, "neo-modal" terminology remains a familiar part of undergraduate textbooks, while analyses inspired by Meier's approach continue to proliferate. That such diversity of understanding should hold sway is hardly surprising in light of the extraordinary wealth of opinion shaping the concept of mode for a cross-section of sixteenth-century society that included priests, schoolboys, singers, composers, theorists, music publishers, humanists, musical amateurs, and patrons.

70 Powers demonstrated that both extremes suffered from shortcomings, refuting Dahlhaus's claim that a distinction could not be made between the Mode 3 and Mode 4 offertories while showing that the criteria by which Palestrina made the distinction were not primarily those to which Meier referred (Powers, "Modal Representation").

71 See, for example, the essays by Wiering, Judd, Owens, Powers, and Dodds in *Tonal Structures in Early Music.*

Bibliography

Primary sources

Aaron, P. *Trattato della natura et cognitione di tutti gli tuoni di canto figurato*, Venice, B. Vitali, 1525; facs. Bologna, Forni, 1970 and Utrecht, Joachimsthal, 1966

Aiguino, I. *La Illuminata de tutti i tuoni di canto fermo*, Venice, A. Gardano, 1562

Il tesoro illuminato di tutti i tuoni di canto figurato, Venice, G. Varisco, 1581

Artusi, G. M. T. *L'arte del contraponto*, Venice, G. Vicenti and R. Amadino, 1586; facs. Bologna, Forni, 1980

Banchieri, A. *L'organo suonarino opera ventesimaquinta*, Venice, R. Amadino, 1611; facs. Bologna, Forni, 1978

Cartella musicale nel canto figurato Fermo, & Contrapunto, Venice, G. Vincenti, 1614; facs. Bologna, Forni, 1968

Cantorino utile a novizzi, e Chierici Secolari, e Regolari principianti del canto fermo alla Romana, Bologna, B. Cochi, 1622; facs. Bologna, Forni, 1980

Boethius, A. M. S. *De institutione musica*, ed. G. Friedlein as *Anicii Manlii Torquati Severini Boetii de institutione arithmetica libri duo, de institutione musica libri quinque; accedit geometria quae fertur Boetii*, Leipzig, Teubner, 1867; trans. C. Bower, ed. C. Palisca as *Fundamentals of Music*, New Haven, Yale University Press, 1989

Cerone, P. *El melopeo y maestro*, Naples, J. B. Gargano and L. Nucci, 1613

Del Lago, G. *Breve introduttione di musica misurata*, Venice, B. and O. Scotto, 1540; facs. Bologna, Forni, 1969

Dressler, G. *Practica modorum explicatio*, Jena, D. Richtzenhan, 1561

Praecepta musicae Poeticae, ed. B. Engelke in *Geschichts-Blätter für Stadt und Land Magdeburg* 49–50 (1913–15), pp. 214–50

Frescobaldi, G. *Il primo libro delle fantasie a quattro*, Milan, S. Tini and F. Lomazzo, 1608

Recercari, et canzoni franzese fatte sopra diversi oblighi in partitura, Rome, B. Zannetti, 1615

Gabrieli, A. and G. *Intonationi d'organo composte sopra tutti li Dodici Toni della Musica*, Venice, A. Gardano, 1593

Gaffurio, F. *Practica musice*, Milan, G. Le Signerre, 1496; facs. Farnborough, Gregg, 1967, Bologna, Forni, 1972 and New York, Broude, 1979; trans. C. Miller as *Practica musicae*, *MSD* 20 (1968); trans. I. Young as *The "Practica musicae" of Franchinus Gafurius*, Madison, University of Wisconsin Press, 1969

De harmonia musicorum instrumentorum opus, Milan, G. Pontanus, 1518; facs. Bologna, Forni, 1972 and New York, Broude, 1979; trans. C. Miller, *MSD* 33 (1977)

Glarean, H. *Isagoge in musicen*, Basel, Froben, 1516

Dodecachordon, Basel, H. Petri, 1547; facs. Hildesheim, G. Olms, 1969, and New York, Broude, 1967; trans. C. Miller, *MSD* 6 (1965)

Hofmann, E. *Doctrina de tonis seu modis musicis*, Greifswald, A. Ferber, 1582

Le Jeune, C. *Dodecacorde contenant douze pseaumes de David, mis an musique selon les douze modes*, La Rochelle, Haultin, 1598

Luzzaschi, L. *Il Secondo Libro De Ricercari a quattro voci*, MS. Bologna, Convento di S. Francesco; transcribed M. Pascale, Rome, Pro Musica Studium, 1981

Marchetto of Padua, *Lucidarium in arte Musicae planae*, trans. and ed. J. Herlinger as *The Lucidarium of Marchetto of Padua: a Critical Edition, Translation, and Commentary*, University of Chicago Press, 1985

Merulo, C. *Toccate d'intavolature d'organo*. Rome, S. Verovio, 1598

Palestrina, G. *Offertoria totius anni*, Rome, Coattino, 1593

Rore, C. *I madrigali a cinque voci*, Venice, G. Scotto, 1542

Motetta nunc primum summa diligentia in lucem prodita, Venice, A. Gardano, 1545

Scotto, G. *I Madrigali a tre voci*, Venice, G. Scotto, 1541

Il Primo Libro de I Madrigali a doi voci, Venice, G. Scotto, 1541

Susato, T. *Premier livre des Chansons a trois parties*, Antwerp, Susato, 1544

Tigrini, O. *Il compendio della musica nel qualle brevemente si tratta Dell'Arte del Contrapunto*, Venice, R. Amadino, 1588

Tinctoris, J. *de natura et proprietate tonorum*, (1476) ed. A. Seay, *CSM* 22/1 (1975), pp. 59–104; trans. A. Seay as *Concerning the Nature and Propriety of Tones*, Colorado Springs, Colorado College Music Press, 1967 and 1976

Vanneus, S. *Recanetum de musica aurea*, Rome, V. Dorico, 1533; facs. Kassel, Bärenreiter, 1969

Willaert, A. *Il primo libro de motetti a sei*, Venice, A. Gardano, 1542

Musica quatuor vocum, Venice, A. Gardano, 1545

Zarlino, G. *Musici quinque vocum Moduli, Motecta vulgo Nuncupata*, Venice, A. Gardano, 1549

Le istitutioni harmoniche, Venice, Franceschi, 1558; facs. New York, Broude, 1965; trans. of

Part III by G. Marco, ed. C. Palisca as *The Art of Counterpoint*, New Haven, Yale University Press, 1968; trans. of Part IV by V. Cohen, ed. C. Palisca as *On the Modes*, New Haven, Yale University Press, 1983

Le istitutioni harmoniche, rev. edn., Venice, Franceschi, 1573; facs. Ridgewood, NJ, Gregg, 1966; Ger. trans. of Parts I and II by M. Fend in *Theorie des Tonsystems*, Frankfurt, P. Lang, 1989

Dimostrationi harmoniche, Venice, Franceschi, 1571; facs. New York, Broude, 1965 and Ridgewood, NJ, Gregg, 1966

Secondary sources

Atkinson, C. "Modus," *HmT*

Baldi, B. "Vite inedite di matematici italiani," ed. E. Narduci in *Bullettino di bibliografia e storia delle scienze matematiche e fisiche* 19 (1886), pp. 335–406; 437–89; 512–640

Beebe, E. "Mode, Structure, and Text Expression in the Motets of Jacobus Clemens non Papa: A Study of Style in Sacred Music," Ph.D. diss., Yale University (1976)

Bergquist, P. "The Modality of Orlando di Lasso's Compositions in 'A minor,'" in *Orlando di Lasso in der Musikgeschichte*, ed. B. Schmid, Munich, 1996, pp. 7–18

"Mode and Polyphony about 1500: Theory and Practice," *Music Forum* 1 (1967), pp. 99–161

"The Theoretical Writings of Pietro Aaron," Ph.D. diss., Columbia University (1964)

Bernstein, J. *Music Printing in Renaissance Venice: the Scotto Press, 1539–1572*, New York, Oxford University Press, 1998

Blackburn, B. J., E. E. Lowinsky, and C. A. Miller, eds., *A Correspondence of Renaissance Musicians*, Oxford, Clarendon Press, 1991

Bower, C. "The Modes of Boethius," *JM* 3 (1984), pp. 252–63

Brown, H. M. "Theory and Practice in the Sixteenth Century: Preliminary Notes on Attaingnant's Modally Ordered Chansonniers," in *Essays in Musicology*, ed. L Lockwood and E. Roesner, American Musicological Society, 1990, pp. 75–100

Caffi, F. *Della vita e dell'opere del prete Gioseffo Zarlino*, Venice, G. Antonelli, 1856

Crawford, D. "A Chart Manual in Sixteenth-Century Italy," *Musica Disciplina* 36 (1982), pp. 175–90

Crocker, R. "Perchè Zarlino diede una nuova numerazione ai modi?," *Rivista italiana di musicologia* 3 (1968), pp. 49–58

Dahlhaus, C. *Untersuchungen über die Entstehung der harmonischen Tonalität*, Kassel, Bärenreiter, 1968; trans. R. Gjerdingen as *Studies on the Origins of Harmonic Tonality*, Princeton University Press, 1990

Dodds, M. "Tonal Types and Modal Equivalence in Two Keyboard Circles by Murschhauser," in *Tonal Structures in Early Music*, ed. C. Judd, New York, Garland, 1998, pp. 341–72

Feldman, M. *City Culture and the Madrigal at Venice*, Berkeley, University of California Press, 1995

Flury, R. *Gioseffo Zarlino als Komponist*, Winterthur, Keller, 1962

Fuller, S. "Defending the *Dodecachordon*: Ideological Currents in Glarean's Modal Theory," *JAMS* 49 (1996), pp. 191–224

Harrán, D. "The Theorist Giovanni del Lago: A New View of the Man and His Writings," *Musica Disciplina* 27 (1973), pp. 107–51

Hermelink, S. *Dispositiones Modorum: Die Tonarten in der Musik Palestrinas und seiner Zeitgenossen*, Tutzing, Schneider, 1960

Judd, C. "Modal Types and *Ut, Re, Mi* Tonalities: Tonal Coherence in Sacred Vocal Polyphony from about 1500," *JAMS* 45 (1992), pp. 428–67

Reading Renaissance Music Theory: Hearing with the Eyes, Cambridge University Press, 2000

"A Newly Recovered Eight-mode Motet Cycle: Zarlino's *Song of Songs* Motets," in *Theory and Analysis 1540–1650*, ed. A. E. Ceulemans and B. J. Blackburn, forthcoming

"Josquin's Gospel Motets and Chant-Based Tonality," in *Tonal Structures in Early Music*, ed. C. Judd, New York, Garland, 1998, pp. 39–54

"Reading Aron Reading Petrucci," *Early Music History* 14 (1995), pp. 121–52

Judd, R. "The Use of Notational Formats at the Keyboard," Ph.D. diss., Oxford University, (1989)

Kelleher, J. "Zarlino's *Dimostrationi harmoniche* and Demonstrative Methodologies in the Sixteenth Century," Ph.D. diss., Columbia University (1993)

Krantz, S. "Rhetorical and Structure Functions of Mode in Selected Motets of Josquin des Prez," Ph.D. diss., University of Minnesota (1989)

Lester, J. *Between Mode and Keys: German Theory 1592–1802*, Stuyvesant, NY, Pendragon Press, 1989

Lewis, M. "Zarlino's Theories of Text Underlay as Illustrated in his Motet Book of 1549," *MLA* Notes 42 (1985), pp. 239–67

Meier, B. *Alte Tonarten dargestellt an der Instrumentalmusik des 16. und 17. Jahrhunderts*, Kassel, Bärenreiter, 1992

"Heinrich Loriti Glareanus als Musiktheoretiker," in *Aufsätze zur Freiburger Wissenschafts- und Universitätsgeschichte*, ed. C. Bauer, et al., Freiburg im Breisgau, 1960, pp. 65–112

Die Tonarten der klassischen Vokalpolyphonie, nach den Quellen dargestellt, Utrecht, Oosthoek, Scheltema & Holkema, 1974; trans. E. Beebe as *The Modes of Classical Vocal Polyphony*, New York, Broude, 1988

"Zu den 'in mi' fundierten Werken aus Palestrinas Offertoriums-Motettenzyklus," *Die Musikforschung* 37 (1984), pp. 215–20

Niemöller, K. W., "Zur Tonus-Lehre der italienischen Musiktheorie des ausgehenden Mittelalters," *Kirchenmusikalisches Jahrbuch* 40 (1956), pp. 23–32

Owens, J. "Concepts of Pitch in English Music Theory, c. 1560–1640," in *Tonal Structures in Early Music*, ed. C. Judd, New York, Garland, 1998, pp. 183–246

"Mode in the Madrigals of Cipriano de Rore," in *Essays on Italian Music in the Cinquecento*, ed. R. Charteris, Sydney, 1990

"Palestrina as Reader: Motets from the Song of Songs," in *Hearing the Motet*, ed. D. Pesce, New York, Oxford University Press, 1997, pp. 307–28

Palisca, C. V. *Humanism in Italian Renaissance Musical Thought*, New Haven, Yale University Press, 1985

"Mode Ethos in the Renaissance," in *Essays in Musicology*, ed. L. Lockwood and E. Roesner, American Musicological Society, 1990, pp. 126–39

Perkins, L. "Modal Species and Mixtures in a Fifteenth-Century Chanson Repertory," in *Modality in the Music of the Fourteenth and Fifteenth Centuries*, ed. U. Günther, L. Finscher, and J. Dean, American Institute of Musicology, 1996, pp. 177–202

"Mode and Structure in the Masses of Josquin," *JAMS* 26 (1973), pp. 189–239
Powers, H. "Anomalous modalities," in *Orlando di Lasso in der Musikgeschichte*, ed. B. Schmid, Munich, 1996, pp. 221–42
"From Psalmody to Tonality," in *Tonal Structures in Early Music*, ed. C. Judd, New York, Garland, 1998, pp. 275–340
"Is Mode Real? Pietro Aron, the Octenary System, and Polyphony," *Basler Jahrbuch* 16 (1992), pp. 9–53
"Modal Representation in Polyphonic Offertories," *Early Music History* 2 (1982), pp. 43–86
"Mode," *NG*, vol. XII, pp. 376–450.
'Tonal Types and Modal Categories in Renaissance Polyphony," *JAMS* 34 (1981), pp. 428–70
Rivera, B. "Finding the *Soggetto* in Willaert's Free Imitative Counterpoint: A Step in Modal Analysis," in *Music Theory and the Exploration of the Past*, ed. C. Hatch and D. Bernstein, University of Chicago Press, 1993, pp. 73–102
Schubert, P. "Mode and Counterpoint," in *Music Theory and the Exploration of the Past*, ed. C. Hatch and D. Bernstein, University of Chicago Press, 1993, pp. 103–36
Schmidt-Beste, T. "Modus: III ab ca. 1470," *MGG2*, vol. VI, cols. 417–31
Smith, A. "Willaert Motets and Mode," *Basler Jahrbuch* 16 (1992), pp. 117–65
Wiering, F. "The Language of the Modes," Ph.D. diss., University of Amsterdam (1995)
"Internal and External Views of the Modes," in *Tonal Structures in Early Music*, ed. C. Judd, New York, Garland, 1998, pp. 87–107

· 13 ·

Tonal organization in seventeenth-century music theory

GREGORY BARNETT

Otherwise known as the Age of Reason for the scientific undertakings and discoveries it witnessed, the seventeenth century is frequently seen as a period of uncertainty and confusion in the context of musical thought. From our own present perspective, musical thought of this period is overshadowed both by what precedes it and by what follows: the opposing poles of Renaissance modal theory and eighteenth-century harmonic tonality each seem more intelligible than that which we perceive as the transition between the two. Indeed, much of what we find in seventeenth-century theory appears to present a puzzling mix: ideas that accord strikingly well with the precepts of major-minor tonality appear to mingle freely with the teachings and terminology of modal theory. Added to this seeming paradox is the darkened mood of the theorists themselves, many of whom lament the confusion of their age.[1]

And yet, seventeenth-century music treatises paint a clear, if richly detailed, picture of musical thought if we keep in mind that they address widely different purposes: to serve the church singer in a long-standing and relatively stable practice of liturgical chant; to train keyboardists and other chord-playing instrumentalists in the art of extemporizing harmonies over a bass; to educate the well-rounded musician in the established traditions of counterpoint and modal theory; to instruct the rational mind in the scientific bases of tuning systems; and finally, to enlighten the curious on more speculative and imaginative musical topics, such as Pythagoras's fabled discovery of harmony in the sound of hammers at the forge, the Boethian harmonic strata, and the legendary origins of music itself. In short, seventeenth-century theory comprises a rich mixture of myth, scientific research, rules for composition, and basic musical training.

1 Excerpts from a witty but downcast poem by Antonio Maria Abbatini (c. 1609–c. 1679), from his letter to Sig. Bastiano Baldini, c. 1667, Biblioteca Vaticana (MS Chigi L.VI.191), illustrate how this impression may have originated even before the century was ended:

> Wherever is that age, so beautiful,
> when lectures in [the art of] music
> were in use (and this is not a tale)?
>
> Thus the science of composing well
> was truly lit from every side; [compare]
> our own confusion and unhappy state!

Abbatini's poem is quoted in full in English translation by David Bryant in Bianconi, *Music in the Seventeenth Century*, pp. 286–92.

The concern of this chapter lies in seventeenth-century theories of tonal organization that emanate from these various constituents. (Topics of more speculative or scientific thought related to music in the seventeenth century are found in **Chapters** 8 and 9.) For much of the century, the language of tonal organization is that of the modes, as will be seen; but later in the century, conceptions and terms that we now recognize from tonal theory replace the older terminology. How we interpret this change is crucial to our understanding of seventeenth-century musical thought, and fundamental to our interpretation is our awareness of the interdependence of the theorist's objectives and the theory itself. Looking over the entire century, we can see that theorists began speaking in terms of major-minor tonality when their purpose changed from handing down and refining an inherited theoretical tradition to creating a practical construct that most simply and accurately fit the music around them. The two aims engendered substantially different writings on tonal organization. Taken as an undifferentiated body of theory, these writings might suggest a simple evolution from modes to keys in seventeenth-century music, but no such evolution occurred. Instead, at different times within the century and to differing degrees, one set of theoretical concerns and perspectives replaced another, such that the picture of tonal organization described and the very language used to describe it changed almost completely from the early 1600s to the early 1700s.

Solmization

The conception of tonal space during the seventeenth century is founded on an inherited gamut that comprises *litterae*, background letters, and *voces*, hexachordally organized syllables. Solmization according to the system of hexachords remained little changed throughout the century: theorists continued to demonstrate both the graphic model of pitch relationships in the Guidonian hand (see **Plate 11.1, p. 345**)[2] and the system of three overlapping hexachords (the collection of six solmization syllables – *ut*, *re*, *mi*, *fa*, *sol*, *la* – that begin on either c, f, or g), with which one may solmizate the complete gamut (Γ to e^2) (see Table 13.1). Hexachords beginning on c, solmizating from c to a, were referred to as natural; f-hexachords, solmizating from f to d and including b♭, were called "soft" for the soft b (*b-molle*); and g-hexachords, solmizating g to e and including b♮, were called "hard" for the hard or square b (*b-quadro*).

In solmizating a melody a singer would need to "mutate" from one hexachord to another whenever the music exceeded the range of a single hexachord. The rule for mutation simply substitutes the syllable of one hexachord for that of another at specific points in the music, depending on whether the melodic motion is ascending or

2 Another illustration of an earlier Guidonian hand is seen in **Plate 12.1, p. 369**.

Table 13.1 *The gamut and hexachordal deductions, adapted from Zaccaria Tevo,* Il musico testore *(1706)*

	Hard	Natural	Soft	Hard	Natural	Soft	Hard
e^2							LA
d^2						LA	SOL
c^2						SOL	FA
b^1						–	MI
$b\flat^1$						FA	–
a^1					LA	MI	RE
g^1					SOL	RE	UT
f^1					FA	UT	
e^1				LA	MI		
d^1			LA	SOL	RE		
c^1			SOL	FA	UT		
b			–	MI			
b♭			FA	–			
a		LA	MI	RE			
g		SOL	RE	UT			
f		FA	UT				
e	LA	MI					
d	SOL	RE					
c	FA	UT					
B	MI						
A	RE						
Γ (G)	UT						

Example 13.1 Solmization in *cantus durus* and *cantus mollis*

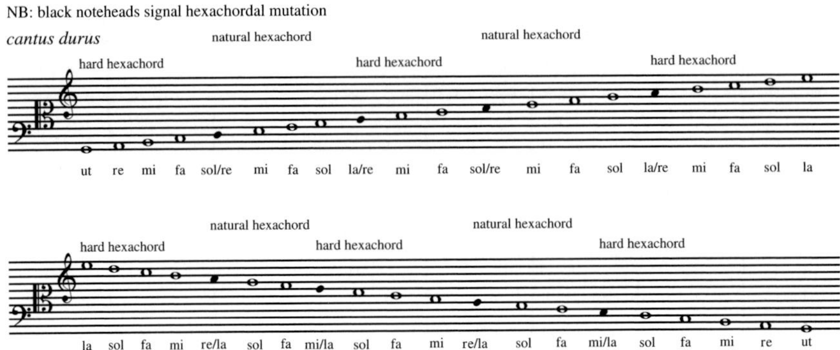

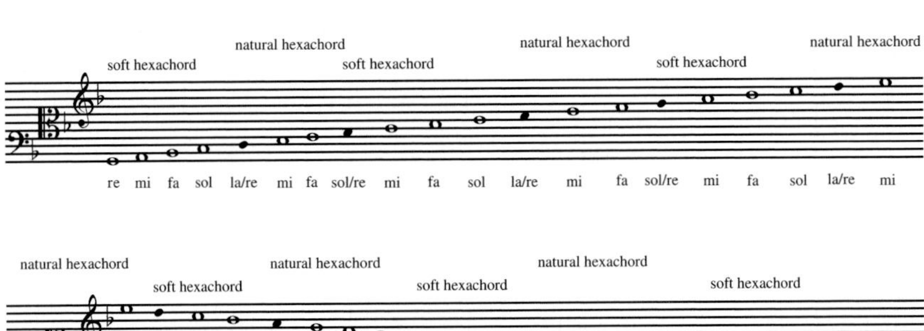

descending and depending on whether the solmizated music uses b♮ or b♭. This latter criterion reveals that the three hexachords were used to solmizate only two scale systems, one that uses b♮ (*cantus durus*) and one that uses b♭ (*cantus mollis*). In *cantus durus* (see Example 13.1),[3] the singer would mutate between the natural and hard hexachords as follows: ascending in *cantus durus*, *la* is changed to *re* at each A, and *sol* is changed to *re* at each D; descending in *cantus durus*, *mi* is changed to *la* at each E, and *re* is changed to *la* at each A. In *cantus mollis*, by contrast, the singer would mutate between the natural and soft hexachords: ascending in *cantus mollis*, *la* is changed to *re* at each D and

3 I have drawn upon illustrations and descriptions from the following sources for Example 13.1: Banchieri, *Cartella musicale*, pp. 12–16; Diruta, *Transilvano*, pp. 2–3; and Penna, *Primi albori*, pp. 21–26. For more on Guido's hexachordal system, see **Chapter 11, pp. 341–46**. Also see **Plate 1.1, p. 32**.

sol to *re* at each G; descending in *cantus mollis*, *mi* is changed to *la* at each A and *re* to *la* at each D.

The Guidonian system of solmizating lasted throughout the seventeenth century and into the next, but seventeenth-century theorists attempted to improve upon it nonetheless. Early in the century, Adriano Banchieri (1614) sought to expand the hexachord to a heptachord, thereby covering a full octave.[4] The added seventh syllable of Banchieri's solmization was of two kinds and accounted for both b♮ and b♭: *ba* (deriving from B-*fa*) would be used for b♭; *bi* (from B-*mi*), for b♮ (see Example 13.2). The addition of a seventh syllable, ostensibly a complication, actually simplifies the Guidonian system by doing away with the need for hexachordal mutations, thus associating each syllable with only a single pitch-class.[5]

Another seven-syllable solmization system – known as bocedization for its non-Guidonian *voces*: *bo*, *ce*, *di*, *ga*, *lo*, *ma*, *ni* – bears mentioning because it further attests the desire of seventeenth-century musicians to improve upon traditional solmization. In this simplified system, possibly the invention of an Amsterdam music teacher and singer, Hubert Waelrant, each syllable corresponds to a single pitch of the octave and each pitch to one syllable.[6] Much of what we know of bocedization may be found in Sethus Calvisius, a strong advocate who praises two qualities of the system: there is no hexachordal mutation, and consequently both upward and downward melodic motion are solmizated in the same way.[7] Like Banchieri's seven-syllable extension of Guidonian solmization, bocedization uses an extra syllable – in this case *pa* for singing the flat seventh degree. Unlike Banchieri's system, however, the entire system of *voces Belgicae* may be transposed down a fifth or up a fourth, thus switching from *cantus durus* to *cantus mollis* (see Example 13.2).

Neither Banchieri's revised solmization nor the Belgian system of bocedization outlined by Calvisius were taken up by other writers; instead, musicians continued to rely on traditional Guidonian principles. Seven-syllable solmization would eventually be taken up through another reform of solmization attributed to Waelrant: the addition of *si* and *ut* for the seventh and eighth degrees above *ut*. And yet, to judge from Continental treatises throughout the seventeenth century, the *ut*–*si* heptachord only slowly gained acceptance. Traditional Guidonian solmization, however, was itself subject to new uses

4 Banchieri, *Cartella musicale*, pp. 18–24.

5 More than a century earlier, Bartolomeo Ramis de Pareia had also advocated a seven-syllable solmization system in his treatise *Musica practica* (Bologna, 1482). See Ramis de Pareia, *Musica practica*, trans. and commentary Clement A. Miller, Musicological Studies and Documents, vol. LXIV (American Institute of Musicology, 1993), pp. 96–99.

6 For a detailed account of bocedization and solmization reform in the early seventeenth century, see Owens, "Waelrant and Bocedization."

7 Calvisius, *Exercitationes musicae duae*, pp. 121–23, gives a description of bocedization and praises its merits over traditional solmization. Referring to the Guidonian hexachord, by contrast, Calvisius points out the frequent mutations it requires and how this problem is avoided in heptachordal solmization (ibid., pp. 121–22).

Example 13.2 Heptachordal solmization

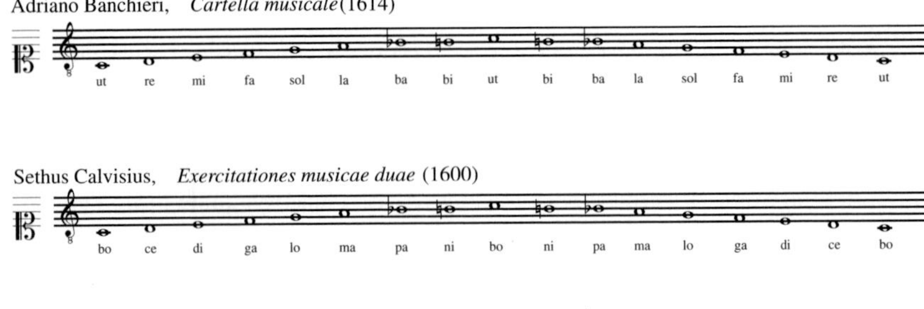

in the singing of music whose key signatures incorporated accidentals beyond the b♭ allowed in Guido's gamut. At the outset of the century, Scipione Cerreto (1601) illustrated hexachordal mutation in music with key signatures of two flats and two sharps: the motivation for doing so came from singing the *chiavi accidentali* ("accidental clefs") that bore such signatures.[8] Cerreto's examples effectively raise and lower the entire pattern of solmization syllables relative to the background *litterae* by a whole step, something not originally intended in Guido's system.

Some forty years earlier, Gioseffo Zarlino had similarly taught transposition, giving examples in two flats and then in two sharps that show a melody transposed up and down by a whole step.[9] Such transpositions, Zarlino explained, furnished the means by which accompanying instrumentalists, particularly organists, could match the pitch-level chosen by singers.[10] Now, in Cerreto's account, singers, too, could read transposed music – or, more accurately, solmizate music with various key signatures – by moving the Guidonian framework of hexachords up and down. Along these lines, Lorenzo Penna (1672) applied traditional hexachordal solmization – including all three hexachords, soft, natural, and hard, but now with the syllable *do* instead of *ut*[11] – to key signatures with up to three sharps and three flats.[12] He points out that "modern composers of nowadays write many compositions in the chromatic style . . .

8 Cerreto, *Pratica musicale*, pp. 30–31 As Cerreto explains (pp. 28–29), accidental clefs – otherwise known as feigned (*finte*) or fictitious (*fitte*) – occur in *musica finta*, which is that music not accounted for in the traditional gamut (*musica vera*). 9 Zarlino, *Le istitutioni harmoniche*, Part IV, pp. 319–20.

10 Ibid., p. 319.

11 Explaining the solmization syllables that beginners should know, Penna (*Primi albori*, p. 16) says: "These are not other than six, that is: UT, or, as is currently used for its being more resonant, DO, RE, MI, FA, SOL, LA . . ." Writing a year later in 1673, Bononcini, *Musico prattico*, p. 35 makes the same comment on the use of *do* in place of *ut* for its greater resonance, but both authors, Penna and Bononcini, retain *ut* in other contexts, such as their explanations of the gamut and illustrations of the Guidonian hand. 12 Penna, *Primi albori*, pp. 26–29.

Example 13.3 Solmization equivalents from Lorenzo Penna, *Li primi albori musicali* (1672)

[I]t is very difficult when one wants to read the notes using the ordinary clef [i. e., without key signatures] . . . and for this reason it is good to read and sing notes of this style according to the scale [i.e., solmization syllables] but in a different location . . ."[13]

To singers trained in Guidonian solmization, the difficulty of doing what Cerreto and Penna advocate undoubtedly presented a challenge comparable to an instrumentalist's transposing a melody on sight. The evidence for this lies in the manner in which singers dealt with "transposed music," that is, key signatures: typically, they mentally made the transposition required to eliminate the sharps and flats of the key signature, thus returning to a conceptual framework wholly within the Guidonian gamut. Penna's treatise, for example, shows where *do* and then subsequent hexachord mutations occur in sixty-three combinations of clefs and key signatures (seven possible key signatures from three flats to three sharps and nine different clefs). The point in showing this wealth of possibilities lies in the fact that all key signatures are reducible to *cantus durus* or *cantus mollis* – the traditional pitch-systems that any singer could easily negotiate – by means of a simple exchange of clefs. Example 13.3, taken from Penna,[14] illustrates the hexachordal equivalence of different pitches in different key signatures: by means of this scheme a singer can imagine a clef substitution that eliminates the accidentals from the key signature without altering the whole- and half-step positions in the melody.[15] A transposition does not actually occur with this exchange; instead the singer imagines one in order to eliminate the accidentals of the key signature.

The rule for imagining a key signature without accidentals would outlast Guidonian solmization itself. By the latter part of the seventeenth century, French musicians had added *si* to the Guidonian hexachord to create a heptachord as Calvisius and Banchieri had earlier advocated. Despite this change, late seventeenth-century French theorists such as Jean Rousseau and Etienne Loulié continued to detail the same method of "naturalizing transposed *tons*" or of "reducing transposed music to a natural key."[16]

13 Ibid., pp. 26–27. 14 Ibid., pp. 28–29.

15 Sabbatini, *Toni ecclesiastici*, pp. 19–20, shows the same equivalencies, indicating that such schemes are designed for beginners.

16 Rousseau, *Methode claire*, p. 23, explains a method "pour naturaliser les tons transposez"; and Loulié, *Eléments ou principes de musique*, p. 29, details a technique "pour reduire la musique transposée à une clef naturelle."

Modal theory and fugal practice

Changes in the familiar Guidonian solmization system inspired little controversy among musicians. No lasting polemics arose over how or how not to solmizate, and no musician is known to have reacted against the notion of transposing Guido's system by means of key signatures beyond a single flat.[17] The proliferation of differing modal theories, by contrast, did provoke intense debate along with a general sense of uncertainty.[18] Theorists writing in the latter half of the century often introduced their remarks on mode with some form of caveat: Giovanni Maria Bononcini (1642–78) warns that "the handling of the *tuoni*, or modes, is a very difficult undertaking given the diversity of opinions as to the number of modes and their name"; Angelo Berardi (c. 1636–1694) laments that "one need not marvel that the modes have been named differently, while [also] identified in various ways and turned upside down from low to high and vice-versa."[19]

One facet of the problem to which Bononcini refers is the question of how many modes existed. Since Heinrich Glarean's introduction of an expanded system of modes, from eight to twelve, musicians had been divided on the question of whether to accept the octonary or the dodecachordal theory of modes.[20] At the beginning of the century, for example, Cerreto railed against dodecachordal theory, devoting a chapter of his treatise to the issue: "Che nella Musica facultà non possono esser più di Otto Modi" (That there cannot be more than eight modes in the discipline of music).[21] Cerreto's argument in support of only eight centers on the limited number of species of fourths and fifths that compose the modes: modes nine through twelve draw upon species that are found in the original eight; therefore, according to Cerreto, the added modes cannot be new, but are instead *modi commisti* (commixed modes) derived from the original eight.[22] Other theorists, by contrast, regarded the twelvefold enumeration of the modes as self-evident: six octave species – not including the B-to-B octave because it cannot be divided into a perfect fifth plus a perfect fourth – serve as the basis for six authentic–plagal pairs of modes, making twelve in all.[23]

The strongest influence in this context is that of Gioseffo Zarlino. Heavily indebted

17 The French theorist Pierre Maillart did, however, raise an eyebrow over the new-fangled seven- and eight-syllable solmization methods that he encountered in late sixteenth-century Antwerp. See Maillart, *Les tons*, p. 61.

18 The Cazzati–Arresti controversy of the 1660s furnishes a well-known debate from this period: while largely concerned with matters of contrapuntal technique, it also touches on modal theory. See Brett, *Music and Ideas*, for a thorough discussion of the issues and a translation of the principal documents that constitute this controversy.

19 Bononcini, *Musico prattico*, p. 121; Berardi, *Miscellanea musicale*, p. 174.

20 Glarean, *Dodecachordon*. The writings of Glarean are summarized in Powers, "Mode," pp. 407–11. See also Chapter 12, pp. 383–89.

21 Cerreto, *Prattica musicale*, p. 95.

22 Ibid., p. 100.

23 Bononcini, *Musico prattico*, for example, includes a chapter arguing the opposing view from that of Cerreto (pp. 148–53): "Che i Tuoni del Canto figurato sono dodici, e non solamente otto, come dicono alcuni" (That the modes of figural music are twelve and not eight as some say).

to Glarean, Zarlino espoused a theory of twelve authentic and plagal modes based on the six finals, D, E, F, G, A, and C, that was perhaps the most widely disseminated of modal doctrines throughout the seventeenth century.[24] For example, Bononcini followed Zarlino closely in his teaching of the modes, which is summarized in Table 13.2 below.[25] As seen, the authentic modes (odd-numbered) combine species of perfect fifth and fourth to form an octave above the modal final.[26] The plagal modes (even-numbered) that share a final with their authentic counterparts differ from them by forming the octave with the species of fourth below the final and the fifth above.[27] The first two modes, for example, share a final on D, but while the ambitus of the authentic spans the octave above D, that of the plagal extends from the A below D to the A above it.

Centuries prior to its application to polyphonic music, modal theory had originated as a system for classifying chants. The idea of analyzing music other than plainchant in terms of modal theory is a Renaissance innovation, the imposition of a long-standing theory upon newer repertories of music. Sixteenth-century theorists such as Pietro Aaron and Gioseffo Zarlino set out detailed and sometimes ingenious methods for applying the tenets of modality to pieces in several voices,[28] and theorists of the seventeenth century readily accepted this recent tradition of ascribing modes to polyphonic compositions if only because no other theory of tonal organization existed.

In particular, the method reported in Zarlino's *Le istitutioni harmoniche* (1558) for applying modal precepts to four-voice polyphony had the greatest impact on seventeenth-century theory. In the fourth part of his treatise, Zarlino sets forth a simple rule for modal-polyphonic composition:[29] the mode of the tenor voice determines the mode of the entire piece; depending on whether the tenor occupies the authentic or plagal ambitus, the bass voice fills the collateral plagal or authentic ambitus because it is pitched approximately a fourth or fifth below the tenor. The soprano, pitched an octave above the tenor, would bear the same authentic or plagal designation, and the alto matches the bass in its individual modal range.

For theorists of the seventeenth century, this parsing of authentic and plagal ambitus between the different voices implied a particular approach toward imitative polyphony in which a subject's fifths are answered by fourths and vice-versa, so that the subject and answer outline the modal octave. Girolamo Diruta, writing in 1609, states this much as a rule for composing or improvising according to the modes:

24 As shown in **Chapter 12, pp. 389–94**. Zarlino first set forth his twelve-mode theory in Part IV of his four-part treatise *Le istitutioni harmoniche* (Venice, 1558). In the 1573 edition of *Le istitutioni harmoniche* he reordered the modes, now beginning on C, so that their rearranged finals correspond to the notes of the natural hexachord. This revised scheme, however, was adopted only by French theorists; in Italian and German theory, the earlier numbering was kept.

25 Table 13.2 draws upon information found in Bononcini, *Musico prattico*, pp. 122–24.

26 Zarlino, *Le istitutioni harmoniche*, Part IV, p. 311.

27 Ibid., pp. 311–12.

28 For a close study of Aaron's approach to modal analysis of polyphonic music, see Powers, "Is mode real?"; and Part I of Meier, *Modes of Classical Vocal Polyphony*. A thorough study of late Renaissance modal theory and its application to polyphonic music. Also see the discussion and cautionary remarks in **Chapter 12, pp. 400–02.**

29 Zarlino, *Le istitutioni harmoniche*, Part IV, pp. 337–38.

Table 13.2 *Giovanni Maria Bononcini,* Musico prattico *(1673), the twelve modes and perfect interval species*

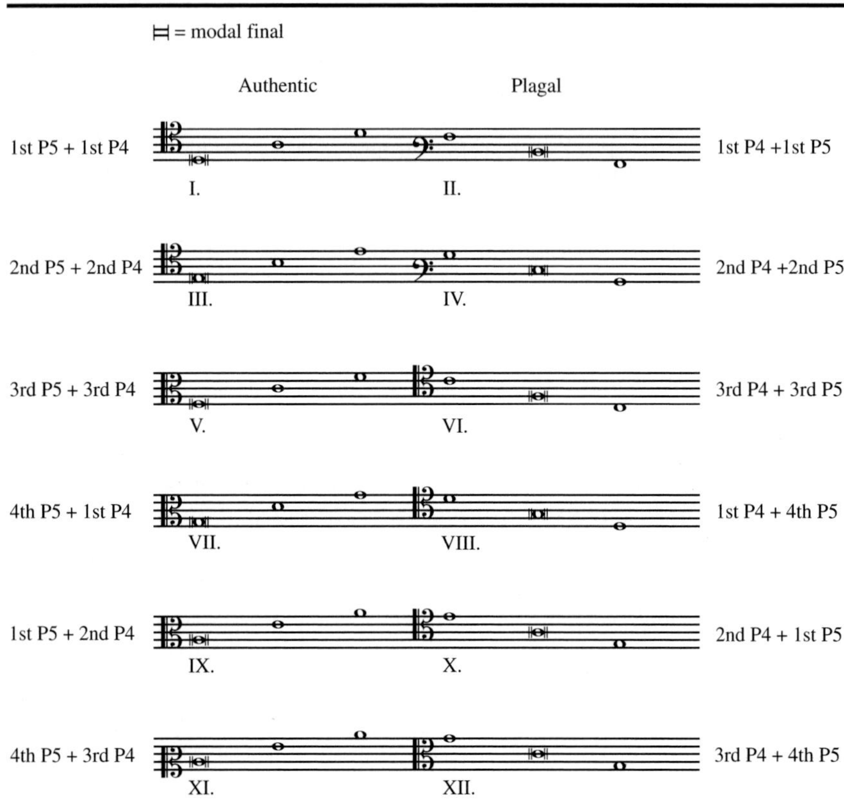

† Interval species

Species	P5	P4
1st	D–A or A–E	A–D or D–G
2nd	E–B	B–E or E–A
3rd	F–C	C–F or G–C
4th	G–D or C–G	–

> You may play the tones with whatever subject you like, as long as the subject is founded on its proper species, namely that one part should have the fifth and the other the fourth. When you wish to improvise or compose other pieces in the first tone, its species are *re la* [d–a] and *re sol* [a–d^1] found between D *la sol re*, A *la mi re*, and D *la sol re* [d–a–d^1]. If the tenor or soprano part has the subject which reads *re la* [d–a] and the bass or alto part reads *re sol* going from A *la mi re* to D *la sol re*, this will be its true formation.[30]

The implications of this association of modal theory with imitative procedure are far-reaching: the authentic–plagal relationship of subject and answer was quickly construed as justification for the modally correct fugue, in which the answer modifies one or more intervals of the subject. In the seventeenth century, exact imitation was therefore seen to contradict modal integrity, and toward the middle of the century the theorist Marco Scacchi emphatically criticized the real answer in compositions on these grounds.[31] Instead he advocated what eventually became known as the tonal answer in modal terms:

> This different division of the octave [i. e. unequally into a fifth plus a fourth or vice versa] constitutes the true ambitus of whatever piece you like, from which no voice, especially in the beginning, ought to step out or stray. Moreover, no mode, whether authentic or plagal, is found which is formed with two fifths or fourths . . .[32]

Demonstrating such precepts, Angelo Berardi (1689) follows Diruta's and Scacchi's guidelines closely in polyphonic examples of each of the twelve modes.[33] Example 13.4 shows the opening measures of Berardi's four-voice fugue in Mode 1: the bass begins with the species of fifth proper to Mode 1 (D–A), and the tenor answers with the proper fourth (A–D); the alto and soprano voices then follow the same procedure. In short, the subject and answer in each pair of voices outline the modal octave of the authentic Mode 1. Conversely, in a plagal mode, the subject outlines the proper species of fourth,

30 Diruta, *Seconda parte del Transilvano*, Book III, p. 12. This translation is taken from Bradshaw and Soehnlen, eds., *The Transylvanian.*

31 Scacchi's conviction on this matter derives in part from the polemical context in which he argued this point: during the 1640s Scacchi and Paul Siefert debated the merits of the tonal answer in fugal composition. Scacchi initiated their dispute with a publication entitled *Cribrum musicum ad triticum Siferticum* ("Musical sieve for the Siefert wheat") attacking Siefert's *Psalmen Davids* (1640) and its real fugal answers. Siefert responded in print with his *Anticribratio musica ad avenam Schachianum* ("Musical unsifting of Scacchi's wild oats"), defending an antiquated style of imitation in which the answering voice and initial subject produce identical hexachordal solmizations. Beyond the admissibility of the tonal answer, at issue was the acceptance of modern Italian style by Northern European composers. Scacchi's teachings would ultimately win out and, to a degree, mark the acceptance of the Italian *seconda prattica* in Northern Europe. For a detailed account of the Scacchi–Siefert polemic, see Walker, "Fugue in German Theory," pp. 226–49. See also Walker, "Theories of Fugue from the Age of Josquin" for a further account of the changing conception of "fugue" in early seventeenth-century theory.

32 Scacchi, *Cribrum musicum*, p. 11. This translation is taken from Walker, "Fugue in German Theory," p. 237. As Walker explains (pp. 235–36), Scacchi uses the term *fuga* to describe points of imitation, and the points of imitation must, according to Scacchi, obey modal criteria.

33 Berardi, *Miscellanea musicale*, pp. 180–93. Berardi was in fact a student of Scacchi.

Example 13.4 Angelo Berardi, *Miscellanea musicale* (1689), "Primo tuono, authentico"

Example 13.5 Angelo Berardi, *Miscellanea musicale* (1689), "Secondo tuono, plagale"

Secondo tuono. plagale

Soprano

Alto

Tenore

Basso

and the answer then responds with the proper fifth. Example 13.5 shows Berardi's unambiguous procedure in this case, his Mode 2 fugue.[34]

The distinctive points of imitation in the authentic and plagal modes obey a further difference between authentic and plagal by linking rising motion with the authentic mode and falling with the plagal. This particular association follows a direct line back to Zarlino, who prescribes no rule, but nonetheless shows the authentic octave species as ascending and the plagal as descending.[35] Diruta, however, explicitly links rising and falling melodic motion with authentic and plagal modes, respectively, and he uses this distinguishing characteristic to explain the differing affects of authentic and plagal modes.[36] Bononcini, too, comments in his treatise on the "lively" and "sad" affects respectively associated with authentic and plagal modes, and he notes that in composing an ascending authentic melody and a descending plagal "one proceeds according to their nature."[37]

So strong was the concept of the correct fugue as composed according to the proper species of the mode that the definitions of "fugue" and "imitation" were reversed from

34 Ibid., pp. 181–82. 35 Zarlino, *Le istitutioni harmoniche*, Part IV, p. 310.

36 Diruta, *Seconda parte del Transilvano*, Book III, p. 11.

37 Bononcini, *Musico prattico*, pp. 123–24 Bononcini, however, also explains that this particular rule is optional (*arbitraria*). In fact, some of the modally designated sonatas from Bononcini's Op. 6 (1672) do not obey this criterion.

what they had been during the late Renaissance. According to Zarlino, *fuga* means intervallically exact imitation at perfect intervals between two or more voices whereas *imitatione* entails close but not exact imitation at both perfect and imperfect intervals.[38] While maintaining the distinction between imitation at perfect intervals and imitation at other intervals as Zarlino had, Zaccaria Tevo, writing nearly a century and a half later (1706), reverses the meanings of *fuga* and *imitatione* in order to accommodate the theory and practice of the intervening time. In Tevo's account,

> fugue occurs at the unison, the fourth, the fifth, the octave, and their compounds [and] with the rule to follow the notes of the *tuono*, or mode. Imitation occurs at the second, the third, the sixth, the seventh, and at their compounds, and for this it is not necessary to observe the *tuono*, or mode. Therefore, not bearing the rigor of touching on the notes of the mode, one may pass from fifth to fifth . . .[39]

In short, what we recognize as the tonal fugue was the very model of a "modal" fugue according to seventeenth-century theorists.

Tuono in the seventeenth century: mode, psalm tone, and church key

During the seventeenth century, the term used for mode or for any conception of tonal organization is *tuono* (also *tono* or *ton*). The term frequently causes modern readers confusion because it comprises several different concepts relating to tonal organization: on the one hand, *tuono* is synonymous with mode, referring to one of the eight or twelve modes discussed above; on the other hand, *tuono* refers to the psalm tones, the set of chants used for the singing of psalms during the Divine Offices of the Catholic liturgy.[40] The problem of competing modal systems, octonary versus dodecachordal, is therefore further complicated by a third system of *tuoni* based, not on the theory of finals and ambitus outlined earlier, but instead on the eight chants of Catholic psalmody known as the psalm tones.[41]

The theoretical and practical significance of this third, psalmodically based system perhaps outweighs any other conception of *tuono* during the seventeenth century. The eight tonalities that arose as accompaniments or substitutes for the eight psalm tones – known as "psalm tone tonalities" or "church keys" by modern scholars[42] – not only form the basis for the early eighteenth-century notion of keys, but also shape tonal practices particular to the seventeenth century far more substantially than did the

38 Zarlino, *The Art of Counterpoint*, pp. 126 and 135; *Le istitutioni harmoniche*, Part III (Venice, 1558).
39 Tevo, *Musico testore*, p. 320.
40 Howell, "Eight Church Tones," explains this very problem (p. 106) in the beginning of his lucid study of the French organ versets and psalm tone transpositions.
41 Atcherson, "Key and Mode," uses the term "pitch-key" to differentiate listings of psalm tone tonalities from listings of traditional modes. Atcherson illustrates numerous instances of such listings from throughout the seventeenth century and well into the eighteenth.
42 Powers, "From Psalmody to Tonality," uses the term "psalm tone tonalities." Lester, *Modes and Keys*, pp. 77–82, uses the term "church keys," based on Adriano Banchieri's term *tuoni ecclesiastici*.

Table 13.3 *Church keys from the late sixteenth through the early eighteenth century*

Tuono (ton, tono)	Anonymous (1598)	Banchieri (1614)	Nivers (1667)	Penna (1672)	Prinner (1677)	Brossard (1703)	Martín y Coll (1706)
1	d –	d –	d –	d –	d –	d –	d –
2	g ♭	g ♭	g ♭	g	g ♭	g ♭	g ♭
3	a –	a –	a –	a –	a –	a –	e –
4	e –	e –	e –	e –	e ♯	e –	e –
5	C –	C –	C –	C –	C –	C –	C –
6	F ♭	F ♭	F ♭	F ♭	F [♭]	F ♭	F ♭
7	d ♭	d ♭	D ♯♯	d ♭	D ♯♯	D ♯♯	d ♭
8	G –	G –	G –	G –	G ♯	G –	G ♯

Sources: Anonymous, *Intavolatura d'organo facilissima accomodata in versetti sopra gli otto tuoni ecclesiastici*, Venice, 1598; Adriano Banchieri, *Cartella musicale*, Venice, 1614; Gabriel-Guillaume Nivers, *Traité de la composition de musique*, Paris, 1667; Lorenzo Penna, *Li primi albori musicali*, Bologna, 1672; J. J. Prinner, *Musikalischer Schlissl*, MS, 1677; Sébastien de Brossard, *Dictionnaire de musique*, "Tuono", Paris, 1703; Antonio Martín y Coll, *Tonos de palacio y canciones comunes*, MS, 1706.

modes. And yet, because seventeenth-century theorists used "tuono" to describe both mode and church key without distinction, considerable confusion surrounds the respective contributions of modal theory and the church keys to tonal organization in seventeenth-century theory and practice.

Table 13.3 shows the finals and key signatures from sets of church keys in treatises whose dates of publication span slightly more than the entire seventeenth century. With some variation from listing to listing, sets of these same tonalities appear in Italian, German, French, and Spanish treatises well into the eighteenth century.[43] An early listing of church keys occurs in Adriano Banchieri's *Cartella musicale* (1614), which furnishes considerable detail on their specific relationship to modal theory and on their particular tonal characteristics. The association of modes and psalm tones lies in Catholic psalmody, which entails the liturgical practice of inserting antiphons – classified according to the eight modes – between psalm verses, which are sung to the psalm tone melodies. Like-numbered modes and psalm tones were thus linked in this practice; for example, Mode 1 antiphons were used with psalms sung in the first psalm tone. Despite this association, the distinction between mode and psalm tone is crucial: modes served as a means for classifying certain chants, antiphons among these, according to final and ambitus; psalm tones, by contrast, are themselves chants – not modal, but also numbered one through eight. In short, modes are abstract categories; psalm tones are actual melodies.

43 Lester, *Modes and Keys*, pp. 80–82, cites several treatises that list the church keys published after those shown in Table 13.3, the latest of which is Heinrich Christoph Koch, *Musikalisches Lexikon* (Frankfurt, 1802).

Practical considerations in the performance of the eight psalm tones largely determine Banchieri's formulation of tonalities based on them. Specifically, some of the psalm tones were transposed in performance in order to limit the range of pitches of the notated chants: untransposed, the psalm tones span an eleventh (c to f^1); their different reciting tones, the pitch at which most of the chant is sung, cover a major sixth (f to d^1). Transposing some of the psalm tones, by contrast, limits their overall range of pitches to just over an octave (c to d^1) and reduces the pitches encompassed by the different reciting tones to a perfect fourth (f^1 to $b\flat^1$).[44] The set of psalm tones given by Banchieri that includes several transpositions, shown in Example 13.6, requires key signatures of only one flat, resulting in a collection of *cantus durus* and *cantus mollis* chants. This particular set of transpositions, moreover, allows for a smooth tonal transition between psalm tones in case one should follow another in the liturgy.[45]

In order to facilitate *alternatim* performances of the psalm tones, the widespread practice in which psalm verses alternate with versets played on the organ,[46] Banchieri formulated finals and cadence points for all eight psalm tones and provided compositions in two voices for each tone so that organists might have a ready-made approach to supplying versets.[47] Two examples show Banchieri's method for creating versets, or compositions based on the psalm tones: shown in Example 13.7 are the points of imitation and principal degrees given by Banchieri for Tones 1 and 4 and then duos that represent those tones. All of his duos are based on the psalm tones in the following way: the key signature reflects the transposition (if any) used for the psalm tone, and the final is taken from the last note of that psalm tone's principal or only *differentia*.[48] The

44 Powers, "From Psalmody to Tonality," Table 4 (pp. 294–95).

45 See Howell, "Eight Church Tones," pp. 109–11, which furnishes a detailed explanation of the tonal implications of the commonly used psalm tone transpositions. Other transpositions that reduce the range of reciting tones even further were known to theorists, but were rejected for not providing smooth transitions between the tones. The practice of adopting the same pitch for all of the reciting tones, known as "singing at the unison," was one of these: Brossard, *Dictionnaire de musique*, explains this method in his entry for "Tuono," wherein the reciting pitch for all of the tones is set at A below middle C. The problem arising from such a practice is the variety of transpositions necessary to bring all of the reciting tones to that pitch. For example, Tone 2 would require an upward transposition by a major third; therefore, a transition from Tone 1, which would need no transposition, to tone 2 would juxtapose a chant in no flats or sharps with one in four sharps.

46 See Van Wye, "Organ in France" for a study of the long history of *alternatim* practice in the Divine Offices and in the Mass.

47 Several sources provide detailed information on *alternatim* practices and their impact on the church keys in various European countries during the seventeenth century: Howell, "Eight Tones"; Bates, "Liturgical Organ Music"; Dodds, "Church Tones"; Nelson, "17th-Century Spain."

48 Some of Banchieri's church keys defy easy explanation: for example, his settings of the fifth and sixth tones are both irregular, but in different ways. It would seem that Tone 5 should use E as its final because that is the last note of the psalm tone *differentia* for the fifth tone transposed down a perfect fourth. But Banchieri uses a C final instead without explanation. Nor does he explain why the transposition of Tone 5 is not indicated by a key signature, but we can surmise that since the transposed chant does not reach b♭, Banchieri felt at liberty to leave it out of the key signature. Tone 6, by contrast, includes a key signature of one flat even though no transposition is used for that tone. Contrary to Tone 5, Tone 6 requires B♭ in order to avoid a melodic progression covering a tritone; therefore, Banchieri added the flat to the signature.

Example 13.6 Adriano Banchieri, *Cartella musicale* (1614), "Trasportato alle compositioni coriste del figurato"

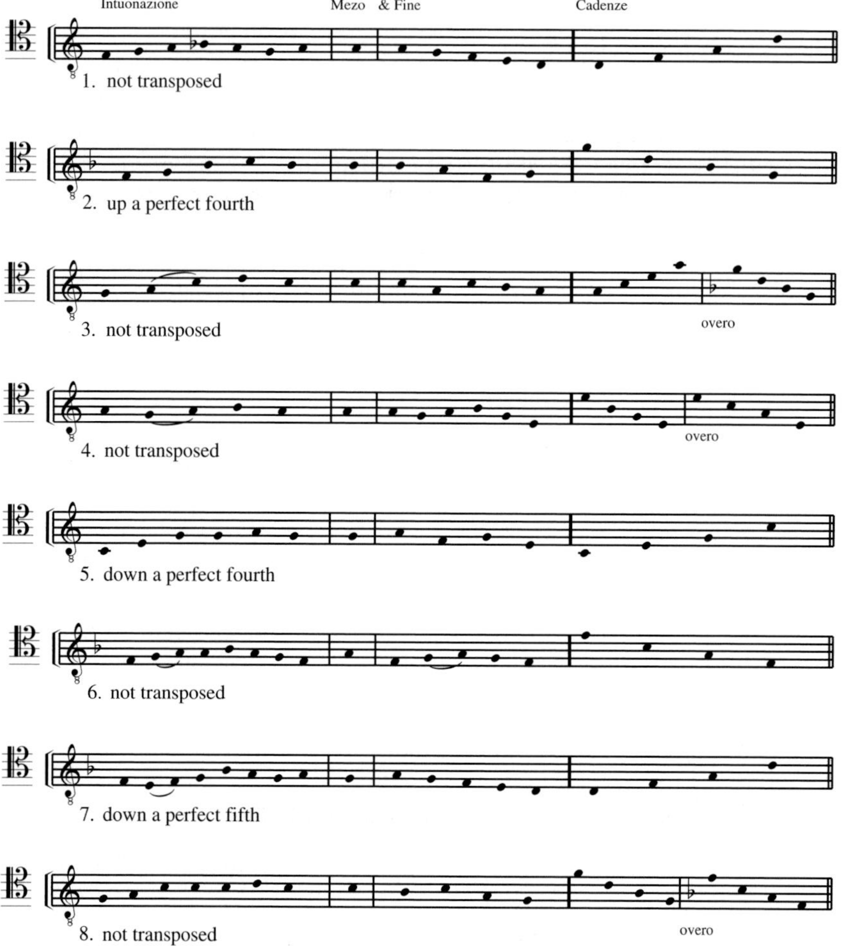

Example 13.7 Adriano Banchieri, *Cartella musicale* (1614), points of imitation, principal degrees, cadences, and example duos for Tones 1 and 4

duos provided by Banchieri and his instructions on points of imitation and cadences for each of the eight psalm tones provide one of the earliest explicit formulations of the church keys.[49]

Other transpositions were used for the psalm tones, and this – in conjunction with the use of modal finals in place of the final note of the psalm tone *differentia* – accounts for the different key signatures and finals that appear in various listings of the church keys.[50] In particular, we may account for the variety of tonalities associated with Tone 7 by examining an alternative transposition used for it, one that is first explained by the French organist and composer Jean Titelouze.[51] In *Le Magnificat* (1626), a collection of psalm settings for the organ, Titelouze explains precisely how he obtains the major-third tonality on D for Tone 7 that later French and German theorists would use in place of the minor-third tonality given by Banchieri:

> The Seventh [Psalm Tone] makes five or six sorts of *differentia*; this is why I have treated it following the principal degrees [the final, in particular] of its Antiphons, which resemble our Ninth Mode [i.e., Mode 7 in Glarean's *Dodecachordon* and in the original edition of Zarlino's *Istitutioni harmoniche*, 1588].[52] Moreover, one must not play it otherwise, the more so in that the Antiphons that precede the Canticle oblige the organ to give to that Canticle its intonation, mediation, and ending. Good composers have done it this way and have finished on *Ut* [G] because the choir would [otherwise] not be able to find its intonation if one did not finish on that degree. I have transposed it a fourth lower for the convenience of the choir.[53]

The downward transposition of a fourth requires F♯s, which Titelouze uses throughout his organ compositions in Tone 7, but does not write into the key signature. The D-final is taken from the mode of the antiphon associated with Tone 7 – that is, G-authentic transposed down to D – which, as Titelouze explains, helps the choir to make the connection between the psalm tone and its associated antiphon. The result of this alternative approach does not change the Tone 7 final – it is still D – but it does change the manner in which that final is derived and the quality of third used above it from minor to major. As seen in Table 13.3 (p. 420), later French and German theorists,

49 Earlier instances of the church keys themselves, however, do exist. An anonymous collection of organ versets, *Intavolatura d'organo* (Venice, 1598), evinces the very tonal characteristics seen in Banchieri and applies the same term to this collection of eight tonalities, "tuoni ecclesiastici."

50 Powers, "From Psalmody to Tonality," gives a full account of both the genesis and the subsequent development of tonalities associated with the psalm tones. Much of the discussion here is indebted to his work.

51 See Bates, "Liturgical Organ Music" for further discussion of French organ versets and of French theoretical discussions of the eight *tons de l'eglise*. In particular, Bates's appendices (pp. 156–264) provide commentaries and translations of selected passages of seventeenth-century French theorists.

52 Glarean had numbered the modes beginning with the authentic and plagal pair on D; thus the order of finals and modes was D (1–2), E (3–4), F (5–6), G (7–8), A (9–10), and C (11–12). As noted in n. 22 above, Zarlino reordered the modes beginning with the authentic/plagal pair on C in the second edition of *Le istitutioni harmoniche* (1573). Titelouze follows this reordered scheme so that Mode 9 refers to the authentic mode on G (known to other theorists as Mode 7).

53 Titelouze, *Le Magnificat*, p. 95.

such as Nivers, Prinner, and Brossard, would follow Titelouze's example in treating Tone 7 as a major-third tonality on D.

Theoretical treatises, particularly later in the seventeenth century, often made no distinction between modes and psalm tones, both known as *tuoni*, but earlier theorists stress their fundamental differences. Zarlino, for example, outlined what he termed "stable" and "varied" modes in Part IV of his *Istitutioni harmoniche* (1558).[54] According to Zarlino, stable *modi* pertain to the psalm tones and canticles, which use specific and unchanging melodies; varied *modi* refer to the modes of the "antiphons, responsories, introits, graduals, and other similar things" that are classifiable according to abstract modal criteria such as final and ambitus.

This distinction between the psalm tones and the modes – between actual melodies and abstract melodic formulas – comes through more emphatically in the work of Pierre Maillart, who devotes a lengthy treatise to modes and psalm tones in 1610. The title, *Les tons, ou discours sur les modes de musique, et les tons de l'eglise, et la distinction entre iceux* ("The tones, or discourse on the musical modes and the church tones, and the difference between them"),[55] conveys his main thesis; and midway through his 380-page discourse, he makes his strongest and most concise argument on the conceptual distinction between psalm tone and mode:

> Well then, is there a difference between the psalm tones and the modes as asserted earlier? Assuredly yes and very great because the above-mentioned modes are such as twelve rules, or twelve categories that beneath them comprise all smaller things. And for this reason [Jacobus] Faber [c. 1455–1537] properly calls them *Harmoniae genera*, because they are twelve greater genres, beneath which are comprised all species and individuals, and all kinds of music that can be imagined . . . But the psalm tones are [themselves] species, which are quite individual and subsumed under the genres given above. They are specific chants invented by men for singing particular things . . .[56]

Both Zarlino and Maillart make clear the distinction between abstract categories and specific instances, but the differences between modes and psalm tones extends to their musical features. The listings of eight tonalities in Table 13.3 clearly defy rationalization according to the modal theory of interval species, ambitus, and final seen in Table 13.2. Nonetheless, musicians and theorists throughout the seventeenth

54 Zarlino, *Le istitutioni harmoniche*, Part IV, Chapter 15, pp. 315–16:

> It must be noted that the modes are considered in two ways: such that there are some modes, under which the Psalms of David and the evangelical canticles are sung; and some under which the antiphons, responsories, introits, graduals, and other similar things are sung. These [latter] may be called varied modes, since there is no one chant and determined form among them for all of the modes, in which one must sing all of the antiphons, responsories, and other similar things in the first mode (to take an example) under a tenor or air, as in the manner in which they sing the psalms and canticles . . . But this does not occur with the former [modes], which we may call stable: such that all of the psalms with their verses of the first mode (and so with the other modes of a tenor or determined chant) are always sung without any mutation, and it is not permitted to vary this tenor, because confusion would follow.

55 Maillart, *Les tons*. 56 Ibid., pp. 194–95.

century merged the two categories because they were so closely intertwined in the daily Catholic liturgy. Theorists, moreover, pursued one of two strategies when addressing the differences between the *tuoni* as modes and the *tuoni* as church keys: either they attempted to reconcile them by viewing the church keys as various transposed and untransposed modes,[57] or they ignored them, recognizing no distinction between *tuono* as mode and *tuono* as psalm tone.[58]

The differing meanings of *tuono* thus engendered competing "modal" theories that proliferated in the latter part of the century. Such was the resulting confusion that Zaccaria Tevo (1706), a theorist with a more encyclopedic approach, simply set down all of the possibilities without any attempt at rationalization or reconciliation: in his treatise, he first lists the traditional eight *tuoni*, that is, authentic and plagal modes on four finals (D, E, F, and G); next he sets forth the twelve *tuoni* of "Henrico Glareano" that extend the original eight by adding two finals (A and C) and thus four modes; and last, he lists the *tuoni delli moderni*, that is, the church keys.[59] Tevo finishes his uniquely comprehensive discussion by citing musicians who recognize only two modes, that with the greater third and that with the lesser.[60]

Over the course of the seventeenth century, the place of the church keys in both theory and practice reveals their startling impact on musical thought: although they originated in psalmody, they came to serve as an organizing formula for compositions outside of psalmody or any sacred context. Collections of sonatas and dances from the latter half of the century testify in two ways to the church keys' more comprehensive role as a widely used system of tonalities: first, the ordering of finals and key signatures used in collections of sonatas agree with those of the church keys; second, cadence points within instrumental compositions further detail this affinity between tonalities commonly practiced and the church keys.[61]

Most significant in this regard is the central position of the church keys in the comprehensive listing of keys by Johann Mattheson in 1713:[62] Table 13.4 shows the finals and key signatures of Mattheson's twenty-four major and minor keys, which Mattheson arranged into three groups of eight, beginning with the church keys. His second group of eight keys appears to comprise upward and downward major-second transpositions of the first eight,[63] and the last eight keys in Mattheson's scheme fill out this list in no particular order. The pattern of Mattheson's twenty-four major and

57 Banchieri, *Cartella musicale*, p. 137; and Bononcini, *Musico prattico*, pp. 137–38, for example, pursue this strategy. 58 See, for example, Penna, *Primi albori*, pp. 128–32.

59 Tevo, *Musico testore*, pp. 262–69. 60 Ibid., p. 269.

61 Barnett, "Modes, Church Keys, and the Sonata," shows how the church keys determine tonal organization in late *Seicento* instrumental music, both in the ordering of tonalities in printed collections and in the tonal features of individual pieces.

62 Mattheson, *Das neu-eröffnete Orchestre*, pp. 60–64.

63 I am indebted to Harold Powers, who first pointed out this relationship in "From Psalmody to Tonality," p. 278. As Powers notes, church keys 1, 2, 5, and 6 transposed down a whole step result in Mattheson's listing of keys 9–12. Church keys 8, 7, 3, and 4 transposed up a whole step, by contrast, result in his keys 13–16.

Table 13.4 *Johann Mattheson's twenty-four keys, from* Das neu-eröffnete Orchestre *(1713)*

(1) d moll	(9) c moll	(17) B dur
(2) g moll	(10) f moll	(18) F♯ dur
(3) a moll	(11) B♭ dur	(19) g♯ moll
(4) e moll	(12) E♭ dur	(20) b♭ moll
(5) C dur	(13) A dur	(21) G♯ dur
(6) F dur	(14) E dur	(22) c♯ moll
(7) D dur	(15) b dur	(23) C♯ dur
(8) G dur	(16) f♯ dur	(24) e♭ moll

minor tonalities thus reveals the centrality of the church keys as a fundamental core, from which other tonalities are derived.

Two distinct aims within seventeenth-century musical thought underlie these various discussions of *tuono*. Those theorists who set forth the abstract principles of modality – the coordination of ambitus, interval species, and final – and the reconciliation of these principles with the phenomenon of church keys reveal a more rationalized approach that details a long-standing, comprehensive, and unified tonal system. Those who put forward the church keys as a de facto system without recourse to traditional means of categorization, by contrast, exemplify a body of theory more concerned with musical practice and basic musicianship. Relative to one another, the modes and church keys represent speculative and practical facets of the theory of tonal organization. The progression from modes to keys in Tevo's account of *tuono* and the emergence of the eight church keys as central to Mattheson's twenty-four thus reveal a shift from speculative to more practical aims among theorists over the course of the century. At any point during the century, moreover, the concept of tonal organization and the terminology used to describe it reflect the relatively practical or speculative orientation of the theorist and not stages in the evolution of musical style.

Transposition and key signature

Transposition as a means for uniformly raising or lowering the pitch of a composition was explained by theorists well before the seventeenth century, as Zarlino's example, mentioned earlier, attests.[64] In the seventeenth century, transpositions were performed not only on compositions, but also on tonalities themselves; thus the church keys could be transposed to suit differing vocal ranges. As seen above, the church keys were designed specifically to accommodate a restricted vocal range, but the vocal range

64 Zarlino, *Le istitutioni harmoniche*, Part IV, pp. 319–20.

Table 13.5 *Church keys and their transpositions, from Giovanni Battista Degli Antonii,* Versetti per tutti li tuoni naturali, come trasportati per l'organo, *Op. 2 (1687)*

Tuono	naturale –		una voce più alta (↑M2)		una voce più bassa (↓M2)	
1	d	–	e	♯	c	♭♭
2	g	♭	a	–	f	♭♭♭
3	a	–	b	♯♯	g	♭
4	e	–	–		–	
5	C	–	D	♯♯	B♭	♭♭
6	F	♭	G	–	E♭	♭♭
7	d	♭	–		–	
8	G	–	A	♯♯	F	♭

in question was that of a male choir. Female and children's choirs would require a different pitch level for the complete set of tonalities. Nivers attests to this in his first *Livre d'orgue* (1665) when he refers to "les voix haultes" in contradistinction to "les voix basses" and provides a table "des Tons de l'Eglise, au naturel et transposez [natural and transposed church keys]" that includes no fewer than four different transposition levels for different types of choir.[65]

Giovanni Battista Degli Antonii's Op. 2 versets (1687), including natural and transposed *tuoni*, substantiate the evidence offered by Nivers and provide written examples in transposed church keys.[66] As seen in Table 13.5, the untransposed (*naturale*) versets follow the church keys as set forth by Banchieri; transposed versets either reuse one of the eight church keys at the appropriate pitch level for the transposition (i.e., a/no signature, the tonality for untransposed Tone 3, is also used for Tone 2 up a whole step), or they draw upon transposed tonalities (i.e. A/two sharps for Tone 8 up a whole step). With two exceptions – e/one sharp and E♭/two flats – Degli Antonii's tonalities comprise only the church keys and their transpositions as shown in Table 13.5.[67]

The significance of this conception of tonalities – natural and transposed – is twofold: first, it provides a seventeenth-century example similar to Mattheson's early eighteenth-century organization of the twenty-four major and minor keys; second, this layout of Degli Antonii's provides a rationale for the so-called incomplete key signatures that proliferated during the seventeenth and early eighteenth centuries. For

65 Nivers, *Livre d'orgue*. His table of contents summarizes this information.

66 Degli Antonii, *Versetti*.

67 The two tonalities – e/one sharp and E♭/two flats – are exceptional in the following manner: they match neither the eight church keys listed in the left-hand column of Table 13.5 nor logical transpositions from those eight (in order to be logical transpositions from Tones 1 and 6 as respectively indicated in Degli Antonii's scheme, e/one sharp would need a second sharp, and E♭/ two flats would need a third flat).

Table 13.6 *Francesco Gasparini's twenty-one keys, from* L'armonico pratico al cimbalo *(1708)*

1.	G	–	9.	d	–	Altri di genere Enarmonico, e Cromatico, che possono cadere nella variazione de Toni		
2.	g	♭	10.	D	♯♯			
3.	a	–	11.	E♭	♭♭			
4.	A	♯♯	12.	e	♯	17.	b♭	♭♭♭♭
5.	B♭	♭	13.	E	♯♯♯	18.	B	♯♯♯♯
6.	b	♯♯	14.	F	♭	19.	c♯	♯♯♯♯
7.	C	–	15.	f	♭♭♭	20.	e♭	♭♭♭[♭?]
8.	c	♭♭	16.	f♯	♯♯♯	21.	F♯	♯♯♯♯

example, c/two flats, A/two sharps in addition to d/no signature, g/one flat, e/no signature, and G/no signature may be properly understood as church keys or their transpositions rather than as incomplete signatures of as yet unrecognized major or minor keys.

By the first decade of the eighteenth century examples of nearly every transposition were included in the more practical manuals such as Francesco Gasparini's *L'armonico pratico al cimbalo* (1708). In the final chapter of his treatise, Gasparini shows the "modo di trasportar per ogni tono" (the manner of transposing to every *tono*), including half-step transpositions that require five sharps or flats.[68] As taught by Gasparini, the skill of making quick and easy transpositions on sight required, not only the mental insertion of key signatures, but also the substitution of a different clef in front of the notes.[69] The complete array of transpositions may be summarized in Gasparini's conspectus of tonalities, shown in Table 13.6. Under the heading "tutti i toni" he provides twenty-one harmonized bass-lines (finals and key signatures are given for each), the last five of which he calls enharmonic and chromatic.[70] Significantly, Gasparini's

68 Gasparini, *L'armonico pratico*, p. 110 The absolute necessity of transposing on sight for any accompanying instrumentalist is emphasized by Rousseau, *Traité*, p. 117, who explains (translation by N. Dolmetsch):

> All those who study the playing of accompaniment, and who like ensemble music, must be able to transpose at sight from all natural and transposed keys; for there is nothing more embarrassing for someone accompanying, than to have to admit before an assembly of people that he does not know how to transpose, and it is a very unpleasant thing for the assembly to be deprived of hearing a fine piece of music because the person who is accompanying does not know how to transpose.

69 Ibid., pp. 110–15. This skill required of the accompanying instrumentalists is nearly similar to that employed by singers, but the motivation for employing it is markedly different. Singers imagine a transposition, but do not effect one in reality, in order to efface a troublesome key signature from the notated music, thus imagining a melody written completely within the Guidonian gamut. Instrumentalists, by contrast, do effect a transposition, possibly necessitating more sharps and flats for the purpose of meeting the pitch requirements dictated by singers or other instrumentalists.

70 Ibid., pp. 83–86.

early eighteenth-century ordering of the keys follows a different pattern from those founded on the church keys. Instead, he arranges them in major and minor pairs on alphabetically ascending finals.[71]

The twelve modes and the *tons de l'eglise* in French theory

Dominante, *mediante*, *majeur*, and *mineur* all ring familiar as terms applied to tonal music; each reflects a particular contribution to tonal theory by French musicians during the seventeenth century.[72] In French musical thought, moreover, we may perceive more immediately than in other theoretical traditions the close relationship between a theorist's objectives, the views put forth, and the terminology used to express these views. French theory experienced a dramatic shift from speculative to practical aims during the mid seventeenth century;[73] concurrent with this change in objectives is the disappearance of the modes in French discussions of tonal organization, replaced by the church keys, the *tons de l'eglise*, and the basic tenets of major/minor tonality. French theory therefore shows modes and keys to be the distinct languages of contrasting pedagogical aims: in the moment that treatises on singing, on playing a specific instrument, or on basic compositional technique displace more broadly conceived volumes whose aim is to pass on a traditional musical education, the modes give way to keys.

Theorists such as Salomon de Caus (*Institution harmonique*, 1615) and Antoine Parran (*Traité de la musique théorique et pratique*, 1639) illustrate the French adaptation of Zarlino's twelve-mode system. This includes Zarlino's revised numbering, mentioned

71 Because the modes are ordered in this fashion, arrangements of tonalities according to the order of their finals is hardly new in the early eighteenth century. Some seventeenth-century collections of music, however, evidence an intermediate step between categorizations either according to church keys or according to the ascending order of finals. The *Pieces de clavessin* (1677) of Nicolas LeBegue, for example, uses all of the church keys in his collection, except for Tone 4; but Le Begue arranges them by pairing major- and minor-third keys that share a final, where possible, while leaving the remaining keys in the order of the church keys.

LeBegue's ordering		*Church keys*	
d	–	d	–
D	♯	g	♭
g	♭	a	–
–		[e	–]
G	–	C	–
a	–	F	♭
C	–	D	♯
F	♭	G	–

72 Seidel, *Französische Musiktheorie*, provides a detailed and comprehensive account of seventeenth-century French music theory, including, among other topics not covered here, a discussion of the *tragédie lyrique*. Cohen, "Seventeenth-Century Music Theory: France" provides a shorter, English-language summary of seventeenth-century French musical thought.
73 Cohen, "Survivals of Renaissance Thought," p. 85, attributes the fundamental change in the nature of French theory to the advent of Jean-Baptiste Lully as a dominant musical force in the 1660s.

in connection with Titelouze, in which the modal finals correspond with the notes of the natural hexachord; therefore, French theorists number the modes beginning with C-authentic and C-plagal as Modes 1 and 2. Caus, in his account of the modes, introduces the *note dominante*, which he defines as a cadence point within the modal octave, one that is secondary to the final.[74] The use of this term evidences a terminological borrowing from psalmody.[75] Since the late Middle Ages, "dominant" served as a synonym for reciting tone, that is, the tone that dominates the psalm tone.[76] *Note dominante* therefore had a long-standing connection with the psalm tones but not with the modes when Caus used it to describe a secondary cadence in each of the twelve modes.[77] His examples illustrate two possible positions for the *note dominante*: in authentic modes it lies at the top of the fifth, that is, a fifth above the final; in plagal modes, at the top of the fourth, which is equivalent to the final itself.[78] Caus's *note dominante* thus lies at the top extreme of the authentic mode's fifth and the plagal mode's fourth. In this way Caus also adds a label to cadences already described by Zarlino, the *chorde estreme della loro diapente e della diatesseron*.[79]

Parran's treatise of a generation later fixes the position of the *note dominante* at a fifth above the final and adds another cadence point, the *mediante*, which accords with Zarlino's *chorda mezzana*, as the note that divides the modal *diapente* (proper species of fifth):

> [I]f we compare the three notes or pitches particular to each mode, one with the other two that are the two nearest consonances (that is, the major third and the fifth as in ut mi sol), then we say that ut is the final, mi the mediant, and sol the dominant . . . [80]

Parran thus formulates cadence points traceable to Zarlino and adopted, not only by French theorists, but also by Germans, beginning with Calvisius (see Table 13.7). The terms *mediante* and *dominante*, however, represent a French contribution. These pitches

74 Caus, *Institution harmonique*, p. 21, "Et quand à la note comprise entre le Diapason dite d'aucuns modernes NOTE DOMINANTE, on la fera ouir souvent, à celle fin de suivre la nature de la Mode, ou ladite note sera." Caus's use of the term *dominante* in connection with the modes is not the earliest, as evidenced by Michel de Menehou's *Nouvelle instruction familière* . . . (1558), which devotes Chapters 14 and 15 to the following topics: (14) *Des huits tons de toute Musique*; (15) *De leurs notes dominantes, & de leur fin.* Menehou, in contrast to Caus, gives the dominants (or reciting tones) of the untransposed eight psalm tones as the *note dominante* for each mode, again illustrating the entangled relationship of modes and psalm tones in sixteenth- and seventeenth-century theory.

75 Serge Gut, "Dominante–Tonika–Subdominante," *HmT*, furnishes a useful summary of the various meanings of the term "dominante" from the sixteenth century on.

76 Nivers, *Livre d'orgue*, states this plainly under the heading *Remarques sur les 8 tons de l'Eglise*: "Note that each tone has two principal pitches or notes, which one calls the dominant and the final. The dominant is that which dominates the most in each tone, and the final is that by which one finishes."

77 Caus, *Institution harmonique*, pp. 21–28; Parran, *Traité de la musique*, p. 128.

78 Caus, *Institution harmonique*, p. 21.

79 Zarlino, *Le istitutioni harmoniche*, pp. 320–36 As Zarlino explains, the cadence points for each mode fall on the extremes of its constituent perfect fifth and perfect fourth and on the middle note that harmonically or arithmetically divides the perfect fifth (the *chorda mezzana*, that is, the third above the final).

80 Parran, *Traité de la musique*, p. 128.

Table 13.7 *Clausulae or cadences appropriate to the modes*

Modal degree	Calvisius (1592)	Burmeister (1601)	Lippius (1612)	Parran (1639)
FINAL	*propria/primaria*	*finis principalis*	*primaria*	*finale*
THIRD	*tertia*	*finis affinalis*	*tertiaria*	*mediante*
FIFTH	*secundaria*	*finus minus principalis*	*secundaria*	*dominant*

Sources: Sethus Calvisius, *Melopoeia*, Erfurt, 1592; Joachim Burmeister, *Musica autoschediastike*, Rostock, 1601; Johannes Lippius, *Synopsis musicae novae*, Strasbourg, 1612; Antoine Parran, *Traité de la musique théorique et pratique*, Paris, 1639.

in addition to the *finale* provide the cadence points for each mode, which, except for the dominant, Parran also describes in terms of where they should occur in a composition:

> The first and most perfect [cadence] is the final, thus called because it is used at the end of the piece rather more than the others . . . The second cadence is called the mediant, or *medieme*, because it is in no way used as a final cadence, but only in the middle . . . The third type of cadence is called dominant, such as a lord or title-holder over the others: for as the mediant is so-named because it holds the middle between the final and the dominant, the dominant similarly takes its name on account of its holding the highest place in comparison with the other two.[81]

In this passage, Parran appears to describe cadences on the modal final and the third and fifth above that final, which would place him squarely in agreement with Zarlino, but Parran's musical examples illustrate something different. The discrepancy between his description and his examples lies largely in the position of the *cadence mediante*, which occurs in a few cases on the third below the final, not above it. In fact, a slight complication of the terminology arises here because *mediante*, according to Parran, has two meanings: first, it may refer to any cadence in the midst of a composition, irrespective of the pitch on which that cadence falls; and second, it may refer to the cadence that ocurs on the mediant pitch between the modal final and the dominant.

Parran appears to draw upon both meanings of *mediante* in his four-part examples. Example 13.8, the cadences of Mode 4 (Mode 2 according to the numbering of Glarean), or D-plagal, demonstrates a *cadence mediante* where we might expect it: on F, the third above the modal final. (Note that Parran reckoned his cadences according to the lowest voice of the texture; were this not so, the cadences of the other three voices from Parran's twelve examples would contradict either the modal final – such as the tenor's A at the end of the example – or other cadence points compatible with dodecachordal theory.) Mode 10, or G-plagal, by contrast, furnishes a case for which *cadence mediante* simply entails a cadence in the midst of the composition: here it falls on the third below

81 Ibid.

Example 13.8 Antoine Parran, *Traité de la musique théorique et pratique* (1639), example cadences, fourth or second modes

Example 13.9 Antoine Parran, *Traité de la musique théorique et pratique* (1639), example cadences, tenth or eighth modes

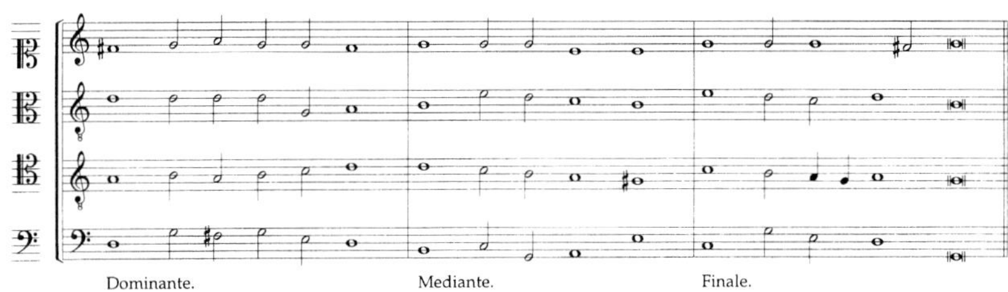

the final, not above it (Example 13.9). Parran's Mode 9 or G-authentic (not shown here) also uses E instead of B for its *cadence mediante*, and an explanation for Parran's preference may lie in the problem of cadences on B: these were discouraged because B has no naturally occurring fifth.[82] Sethus Calvisius (*Exercitatio musica prima*, 1600) and Otto Siegfried Harnisch (*Artis musicae delineatio*, 1608), for example, recommend cadences on A or C instead of B in the E- and G-modes that would otherwise require them.[83]

Despite reservations voiced concerning cadences on B, *dominante* and *mediante* soon attained a permanent place in French musical thought as the third and fifth degrees

82 Parran also uses a lower-third cadence in Mode 1, C-authentic – where there is no possibility of a *cadence mediante* on B – instancing another possibility for the cadences that occur in the midst of a composition (*mediante*), but not necessarily on the third above the final (also *mediante*).
83 This information is taken from Rivera, *German Music Theory*, pp. 208–15, who summarizes the writings of several early seventeenth-century German theorists on proper cadence points within the modes.

above the final, irrespective of what that final might be. Dodecachordal theory, by contrast, disappeared from French musical thought in the latter part of the century. The disappearance of modal theory from French treatises, moreover, signaled a more practical trend among French writers, mentioned earlier.

Authors such as Jean Titelouze (*Le Magnificat*, 1626) and Jean Denis (*Traité de l'accord de l'espinette*, 1650) represent the first wave of practical French theory that came to dominate musical thought later in the century. Like Adriano Banchieri, both Titelouze and Denis address the concerns of the church musician, and both therefore discuss polyphonic settings of the psalm tones – that is, proper transpositions, fugue subjects, and cadences appropriate to each of the eight *tons de l'eglise*. The theorists who followed Titelouze and Denis, even more clearly than their Italian counterparts, conferred a broader role upon these eight tonalities: as seen in the treatises of Nivers (*Traité de la composition de musique*, 1667) and Rousseau (*Méthode claire, certaine et facile pour apprendre à chanter la musique*, 1678), for example, the church keys assumed a status, not simply as settings of the psalm tones, but as a comprehensive set of commonly used tonalities.

The differences between Nivers's and Rousseau's discussions, however, reveal important subtleties in their perspectives. Nivers, a church organist and composer, gives at least passing attention to the twelve modes, postulating an equivalence between the theoretical and practical constructs, that is, between the twelve modes and the eight *tons de l'eglise*, as had Banchieri.[84] Rousseau, a bass violist, reveals a bias more practical than Nivers's: specifically, Rousseau outlines only the most salient features of music as practiced, irrespective of earlier musical thought. The consequence of this approach merits close attention: First, the eight *tons* constitute a central set of tonalities, just as they did for Rousseau's Italian contemporaries; other tonalities are considered transpositions, as summed up by Rousseau's reference to "ces huit tons, et les tons transposez;"[85] Second, his terminology incorporates a major–minor dichotomy: the seminal *huit tons* and other tonalities are named according to the *note finale* (A *mi la*, B *fa si*, C *sol ut*, etc.) and the quality of third over that final, *majeure* or *mineure* – the manner of distinguishing these two types of keys, he explains, rests solely on the third, a ditone or semiditone above the *note finale*.[86] Rousseau thus presents the church keys as major-minor tonalities; in short, he explains the practice of his time in terms of its most essential features.

In the practical vein of treatises, this major-minor conceptualization predates the treatises of both Rousseau and Nivers. Jean Millet, writing in 1666, furnishes a discussion of major and minor that touches only on the cadential embellishments a singer

84 Nivers, *Traité*, p. 19, writes: "The twelve modes of antiquity, both natural and transposed, correspond to these eight tones. Because, for example, the first and second modes in C *sol fa ut* correspond to the fifth tone; the fifth and sixth modes in E *la mi*, to the fourth tone; the seventh and eighth modes in F *fa ut*, to the sixth tone; the ninth and tenth modes in G *sol re ut*, to the eighth tone; the eleventh and twelfth modes in A *la mi re*, to the third tone."

85 Rousseau, *Méthode claire*, p. 85.

86 Ibid., p. 23.

must master; but his thinking, such as Rousseau's, reveals basic concepts that would come to define tonal music:

> it is certain that in all singing, speaking generally, there are but two kinds – all of the others are different by chance [accident] – one I call the cadence of *b. mol*, or of the minor third; the other, cadence of *b. quarré*, or of the major third. That of *b. mol* is formed on all the degrees of the gamut on which one says *re*, and that of *b. quarré* is born of the degrees on which one says *ut.*[87]

Millet's use of *b. mol* and *b. quarré* to differentiate minor and major thirds, tantalizingly similar to later German use of *moll* and *dur* to distinguish major and minor keys, furnishes perhaps the most cogent illustration of the connection between the theorist's pedagogical aims and his perpective on tonal organization. Form in seventeenth-century theory follows function: as diverse as the treatises of Titelouze, Denis, Nivers, Rousseau, and Millet might be, they are all directed toward some facet of music as performed, thus contrasting with the more theoretical writings of Caus and Parran; and this essential difference informs their respective teachings of tonality – tonal in the practical writings and modal in the theoretical. Because practical concerns essentially displaced speculation in French theory over a mere decade or two during the mid seventeenth century, we may see more clearly here than elsewhere that no evolution of musical style or of theoretical approach can adequately account for the emergence of modern tonal theorizing. Instead, one tradition of musical thought supplants another, a newer set of concerns and its attendant perspective of tonal organization simply replaces the older.

Solmization and key in English theory

If French theorists largely turned away from the modes in the mid seventeenth century, German-speaking theorists of Central and Northern Europe held fast to the terminology and ideas of modal theory throughout the century, being similar in this respect to the more conservative Italian theorists.[88] England, by contrast, presents a wholly different case in seventeenth-century musical thought. Far removed from Catholic

87 Millet, *La belle méthode*, p. 38, "il est certain que dans tout le Chant parlant generalement, il n'y en a que de deux sortes, toutes les autres n'estant differentes que par accident, l'une que je nomme Cadence de b mol, ou de Tierce mineure; l'autre Cadence de b. quarré, ou de Tierce majeure: Celle de b. mol est formée sur tous les degrez de la Gamme ou l'on dit Ré, & celle de b. quarré prend sa naissance sur les degrez ou l'on dit Ut."

88 Two sources provide an overview of seventeenth-century German theory: Buelow, "Music Theory: Germany"; and Braun, *Calvisius bis Mattheson*. See also Lester, *Modes and Keys*, for a thorough survey of ideas on tonal organization in German musical thought of the seventeenth and early eighteenth centuries. His Chapter 9, "Epilogue" (pp. 149–61), in particular, discusses the persistence of modal theorizing and the concomitant recognition of major and minor tonalities that characterizes early eighteenth-century German theory.

Europe and its modal traditions, English theory, as evidenced in treatises from Thomas Morley through Christopher Simpson,[89] gives scant attention to the modes.[90] At the end of his treatise, *A plaine & easie introduction to practicall musicke* (1597), Morley briefly discusses the modes: calling them "the ancient 'modi'" and "the Eight Tunes," he describes them only briefly as the means by which churchmen keep the "air" or "key" of a composition.[91] Morley's explanation, however, is confused because he goes on to list the eight psalm tones as examples of these "tunes," thereby conflating psalm tones and modes. In a succinct chapter, "Of the tones of musicke," Thomas Campion (c. 1613) treats "moode" as a synonym for "key" and "tone."[92] Referring only vaguely to "that which many in large and obscure volumes have made fearefull to the idle Reader," Campion proceeds to make the distinction between the authentic and plagal division of the octave, *Modus authentus* and *Modus plagalij*.[93] This, however, is the only recognizably modal element in Campion's discussion, and he immediately moves on to the major and minor triad and never returns to modal precepts.

In the latter half of the seventeenth century, the widely disseminated treatises of John Playford and Christopher Simpson plainly reveal the unimportance of the modes. To Simpson, the modes were simply abstruse and irrelevant. In the second edition of his treatise, *A compendium of practical music* (1667), he mentions them only out of a sense of duty:

> Before we treat of Figurate Descant, I must not omit to say something concerning the Modes or Tones. Not so much for any great use we have of them as to let you know what is meant by them and that I may not appear singular, for you shall scarce meet with any author that has written of music but you will read something concerning them.[94]

Farther along in this dismissive summary Simpson notes Morley's teaching of the matter:

> Mr. Morley upon this subject in his *Introduction to Music*, page 147, his scholar making this query, "Have you no general rule to be given for an instruction for keeping of the key?" answers, "No, for it must proceed only of the judgement of the composer, yet (saith he) the churchmen for keeping of their keys have devised certain notes commonly called the Eight Tunes," etc., of which he only gives examples and so leaves the business.[95]

English solmization, too, differs markedly from that in Continental treatises, although its foundations are similar. In England, theorists taught the Guidonian

89 Cooper, *Englische Musiktheorie* provides brief discussions of the work of numerous English theorists of the seventeenth century and of principal concepts found in English musical thought. A shorter, English-language account of seventeenth-century English theory may be found in Atcherson, "Seventeenth-Century Music Theory: England."

90 John Dowland's translation of an early sixteenth-century treatise by the German theorist Andreas Ornithoparcus, *Andreas Ornithoparcus his Micrologus, or introduction: containing the art of singing* (London, 1609), is exceptional in this regard.

91 Morley, *Plaine and easie introduction*, p. 249.

92 Campion, *Counterpoint*, p. 343.

93 Ibid.

94 Simpson, *Compendium*, p. 57.

95 Ibid., p. 59.

Example 13.10 Solmizations from Adriano Banchieri, *Cartella musicale* (1614), and Christopher Simpson, *A Compendium of practical music* (1667)

Hexachordal solmization (Banchieri, 1614)

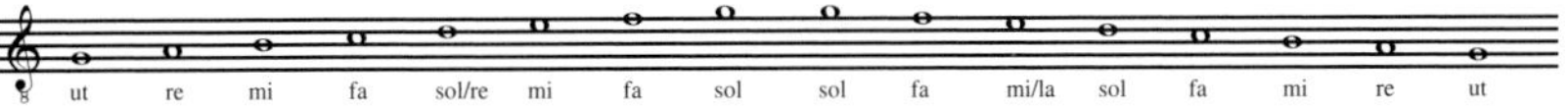

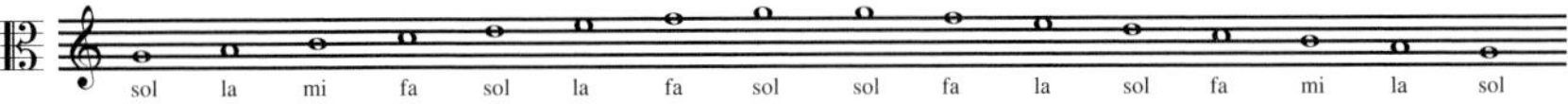

gamut of pitches and recognized the same twofold system of *litterae* and *voces*.[96] Otherwise, English treatises teach solmization in the context of three key signatures – no signature, one flat, and two flats, thus adding a system of two flats to the traditional *cantus durus* and *cantus mollis*.[97] English theorists also adopted a four-syllable system of solmization – *mi*, *fa*, *sol*, *la* – by the latter half of the seventeenth century. For comparison, Example 13.10 shows the same music solmizated first with Guidonian hexachords and then with the English tetrachord: as noted earlier, the point of mutation in hexachordal solmization depends in part on the direction of the melody, up or down;[98] English solmization, by contrast, does not vary according to the melodic motion.[99]

Beyond these basic differences from Continental solmization, subtle variations among individual English theorists also exist: for example, Morley uses *ut* and *re* for the lowest notes of a piece, substituting *sol* and *la* in all other cases;[100] Charles Butler retains *ut* and *re* and adds a syllable, *pha*, where *fa* would occur above *la* in the solmization of an octave, hence the progression from G to G with no key signature: *ut-re-mi-fa-sol-la-pha-ut*.[101] The correspondence between note and syllable is still one-to-one in Butler, but now each different letter name bears a unique syllable name, similar to the heptachordal systems advocated by Calvisius and Banchieri. Table 13.8 compares the solmization of five English theorists; as Playford's treatise points out, all octaves are solmizated equally:

96 See Owens, "Concepts of Pitch," for an insightful reading of English theorists from the late sixteenth through the mid seventeenth century and a detailed account of English solmization. Both Owens and Johnson, "Solmization in English Treatises," emphasize the absence of modal theorizing among English writers.

97 Morley is an exception here; no clear discussion of two-flat solmization emerges from his treatise, although he does give a solmizated example of music in two flats (p. 18).

98 This example draws on the solmization shown in Banchieri, *Cartella musicale*, p. 15.

99 See Simpson, *Compendium*, p. 5.

100 Morley, *Plaine and easie introduction*, p. 15.

101 Butler, *Principles of musick*, p. 12.

Table 13.8 *English solmization*

No signature	G	A	B	C	D	E	F	G
Morley (1597)	ut	re	mi	fa	sol	la	fa	sol
Campion (c. 1618)	sol	la	mi	fa	sol	la	fa	sol
Butler (1636)	ut	re	mi	fa	sol	la	pha	ut
Playford (1674)	sol	la	mi	fa	sol	la	fa	sol
Simpson (1706)	sol	la	mi	fa	sol	la	fa	sol
One flat	G	A	B♭	C	D	E	F	G
Morley (1597)	sol	la	fa	sol	la	mi	fa	sol
Campion (c. 1618)	sol	la	fa	sol	la	mi	fa	sol
Butler (1636)	sol	la	pha	ut	re	mi	fa	sol
Playford (1674)	sol	la	fa	sol	la	mi	fa	sol
Simpson (1706)	sol	la	fa	sol	la	mi	fa	sol
Two flats	G	A	B♭	C	D	E♭	F	G
Morley (1597)	–	–	–	–	–	–	–	–
Campion (c. 1618)	la	mi	fa	sol	la	fa	sol	la
Butler (1636)	re	mi	fa	sol	la	pha	ut	re
Playford (1674)	la	mi	fa	sol	la	fa	sol	la
Simpson (1706)	la	mi	fa	sol	la	fa	sol	la

Sources: Thomas Morley, *A plaine and easie introduction to practicall musicke*, London, 1597; Thomas Campion, *A new way of making fowre parts in counterpoint*, London, c. 1618; Charles Butler, *The principles of musick in singing and setting*, London, 1636; John Playford, *An introduction to the skill of musick*, 7th edn., London, 1674; Christopher Simpson, *A compendium of practical music*, 4th edn., London, 1706.

> If you'll sing true without all blame,
> You call all Eights by the same name.[102]

As little use as they had for modal theory, English theorists gave considerable attention to tonal organization in their music. Throughout the century theorists put forward a consistent idea of "key" (sometimes referred to as "air" or "tune") as the combination of a concluding bass note and the proper cadences related to it. Common to all of these descriptions was the idea of "keeping the key" (i.e., that a composition not end in any key other than that in which it began). Morley, commenting on a brief example that begins on a G major triad and ends on an F major triad, names its fault as

102 Playford, *Skill of musick*, p. 13.

"going out of [the] key, one of the greatest faults which may be committed."[103] He goes on to comment that a composition may make various internal cadences – he names the fourth and fifth degrees as possibilities – but that it must begin and end in the same key. Campion's discussion of tonal organization bears a similar admonition, in which he cites an offending church tune "begun in one key and ended in another, quite contrary to nature."[104] In his correction of the piece, Campion allows that it may begin on the fifth degree relative to the final, that is, begin on D and end on G.[105] Like Morley, Campion allows for internal cadences on various degrees, showing examples of allowable closes (cadences) on all of the first five scale degrees, with preeminence given to the first degree and then, secondly, to the fifth.[106]

Beyond this notion of tonal coherence, English theorists defined keys according to two criteria, the concluding bass note and the quality of third above it. In his discussion of cadences, for example, Campion refers to "the key of G with B flat" and "the key of G with B sharpe."[107] The specific terms, flat and sharp, are significant because theorists of the latter half of the century and beyond would refer to major-third keys as "sharp" and minor-third keys as "flat."[108] The array of keys listed by Simpson, which remained unchanged through the nine editions of his treatise (the last printed c. 1770), constitutes a collection of fourteen major and minor tonalities. In his demonstration of these keys, he shows major and minor triads, signifying "sharp" and "flat" keys built on the following pitches: G, A, B♭, C, D, E, and F.[109] John Playford's *An introduction to the skill of music* – also a long-lived treatise that went through some nineteen editions from 1654 to 1730 and included the work of various authors including Campion (2nd edn.), Simpson (6th edn.) and Henry Purcell (12th edn.) – only slightly modifies Simpson's presentation of keys. The thirteenth edition (1697) lists sixteen major and minor keys, adding B♭ major, E♭ major, and F♯ minor to those listed by Simpson, but not listing B♭ minor as had Simpson.[110]

Playford's names for the keys in most cases uses the same sharp–flat distinction for major and minor as does Simpson, but in several keys Playford introduces added terminology. For example, for keys on A*re* (A minor) and C*faut* (C major) Playford uses the term "the natural key" because no accidentals are needed in the key signature. But Playford's terminology becomes confusing in instances where the use of "flat" or "sharp" in the names of his keys refers, not to the quality of third in the tonic triad, but rather to the name of the tonic note itself: in the case of B♭ major, for example, he terms

103 Morley, *Plaine and easie introduction*, p. 249. 104 Campion, *Counterpoint*, p. 346.
105 Ibid., pp. 347–48.
106 Ibid., p. 344. Campion notes an exception to this general rule as follows: "But if the key should be in G. with B. sharpe [i.e., B♮], then the last close being made in the greater or sharpe third is unproper, and therfore for variety sometime the next key above is joyned with it, which is A and sometimes the fourth key, which is C . . ." 107 Ibid.
108 The treatises of John Playford and Christopher Simpson would use this terminology for as long as they were in print, until 1730 and c. 1770, respectively. 109 Simpson, *Compendium*, p. 23.
110 Playford, *Skill of musick*, pp. 198–204.

Table 13.9 *Charles Butler's tones, from* The principles of musick *(1636)*

Tone/Air	no signature	one flat	two flats
(1) UT	G to G	C to C	F to F
(2) RE	A to A	D to D	G to G
(3) FA	C to C	F to F	B♭ to B♭
(4) SOL	D to D	G to G	C to C
(5) LA	E to E	A to A	D to D
(6) PHA	F to F	B♭ to B♭	E♭ to E♭

it "B*mi* flat," even though it is a major key (i. e., *sharp*). Similarly, Playford's F*faut* sharp (F♯ minor) is a "flat" key according to the quality of third, but the tonic is F♯, which carries over to the name of the key.[111]

A more detailed, if unique, classification of tonalities among English theorists is that of Charles Butler. Contrary to other theorists, Butler does more than simply distinguish major- and minor-third tonalities; nor does he name his tonalities according to the letter name of the tonic. Instead, solmization syllables lie at the heart of Butler's terminology. In his discussion of the "tone" or "air" of a piece, he asserts that the "proper tone of each song is the close-note of the base in his final key."[112] For Butler, "note" refers to solmization syllable; in addition, he uses the term "tone" or "air" to denote a characteristic octave species, each of which is distinguished by one of the solmization syllables (excluding *mi*) that begin and end the octave: *ut*, *re*, *fa*, *sol*, *la*, and *pha*. Drawing upon his method of solmization, the specific octave species indicated by these syllables are shown in Table 13.9.

Each octave species, for Butler, constitutes a particular tonality, or "tone." As signified in the table above, proceeding from *ut* to *ut* (*ut–re–mi–fa–sol–la–pha–ut*) is the solmization for the G-to-G octave species (without flats); the same "tone," *ut* to *ut*, also solmizates the C-to-C octave in a one-flat key signature and the F-to-F octave in two flats. Therefore, each of these is the "*ut* tone" at different transpositions, and more "tones" result from other octave species. According to Butler the *pha* tone (in modern terms, major with a raised fourth) is rare; the *la* tone (otherwise, natural minor with a lowered second), even more rare.[113]

111 As with solmization, the English terminology of keys was passed on to the British Colonies in America and informed music pedagogy there throughout the eighteenth century. Walter, *Grounds and rules of musick*, for example, provides a succinct description of the "sharp" and "flat" keys wholly in agreement with Playford's and Simpson's treatises (pp. 27–28): "If the two Notes above the last Note of your Tune be *whole Notes* [i.e., whole tones], it is upon a *sharp Key*; but if the two Notes above, be one an *whole Note*, and the other an *half Note* [i.e., semitones], then it [is] a *flat Key*."

112 Butler, *Principles of Musick*, p. 80. 113 Ibid., p. 81.

Apart from Butler, English theorists reduced their tonalities to two kinds as many Continental theorists would by the early eighteenth century. It is instructive that English theorists arrived at this conception by the mid seventeenth century: essentially free of the Catholic traditions of modal theory and psalmodic practice, English musicians promoted a two tonality system slightly earlier than all but the most non-liturgically practice-oriented of Continental theorists.

Thorough bass, the "rule of the octave," and the circle of fifths

Over the course of the seventeenth century, tonal style was shaped significantly by the practice, heretofore unmentioned, of realizing accompaniments from figured-bass (or "thorough-bass") notation. Early in the century, when treatises first took account of figured-bass notation, it was explained as a practical and convenient means for accompanying the relatively new *stile recitativo*. Agostino Agazzari, in a concise treatise on basso continuo playing, *Del sonare sopra'l basso . . .* (1607), gives three reasons for the practice: first, for the modern *cantar recitativo*, whose aim is the expression of the text, Agazzari asserts that the performer needs no more than a figured bass and not a full score or tablature; second, figured-bass notation is relatively simple to execute compared to reading from a score or from tablature; and third, the great quantity of music needed to play from scores of ensemble music (*al conserto*) is overly burdensome, and the economizing made possible by figured-bass notation spares the accompanying musician the need of "keeping a library as great as that of a *Dottor di legge*."[114] Apart from these practicalities, the implications for musical style are made clear by Agazzari himself: imitative and fugal music for which figured-bass notation would be a disadvantage was considered inappropriate for the newer style of music – undoubtedly the *seconda prattica* – in which the clarity of the text is of primary importance.[115]

The implications for music theory, although unstated, are no less significant. The reduction of the musical texture and of its tonal properties to a bass line and numbers above that line would fundamentally alter how musicians and theorists conceived tonal organization. Three fundamentals of seventeenth-century thorough-bass practice contributed decisively to the eventual conception of tonal space: (1) the use of the major or minor triad as the basic harmonizing sonority; (2) generalized scale harmonizations that enable the continuo player to realize harmonies where inadequate or no figures are supplied; and (3) the ability to accompany, or harmonize, at any pitch level. On this practice is founded the familiar, eighteenth-century conception of tonal space – one that comprises a set of keys, each of whose member pitches (most conveniently

114 Agazzari, *Del sonare sopra'l basso*, p. 12. For more on the thorough bass in seventeenth- century practice, see Chapter 17, pp. 540–43. 115 Ibid., p. 11.

Example 13.11 Antonio Bruschi, *Regole per il contrapunto e per l'accompagnatura* (1711), "Consonanze per le otto corde del tuono maggiore"

arranged into a scale) are organized into a series of triadic harmonies that gravitate toward a tonic. In this conception, moreover, keys relate to one another in terms of a closed circle: the most closely proximate keys stand a fifth apart, and a progression by fifths from one to the next eventually leads back to the point of departure (see further **Chapter 23, pp. 733–38** and **Chapter 24, pp. 767–69**).

Several features of this comprehensive scheme can be traced to the prescriptions found in thorough-bass treatises from the early seventeenth century, some from even before 1600. Scale harmonizations, although intended simply to provide guidance for continuo players in cases where figures are inadequate or non-existent, organize the pitches of a scale into a series of chords that center on a tonic. Antonio Bruschi's *Regole per il contrapunto e per l'accompagnatura del basso continuo*, published in 1711, furnishes a point of arrival in the context of scale-step harmonizations. Example 13.11 shows Bruschi's harmonization of a major scale on G. Scale degrees $\hat{1}$, $\hat{4}$, and $\hat{5}$ are harmonized as perfect ("root-position") triads, scale degrees $\hat{2}$, $\hat{3}$, $\hat{6}$, and $\hat{7}$ as sixth chords. The purpose of this normative example, as Bruschi asserts, is to establish the key (*tuono*) of a composition through the proper harmonization of each scale degree. According to Bruschi,

> staying in one key does little good in a composition and bores the listener. It is, however, necessary to know that, in whatever key one goes, the same rule of assigning the consonances is to be observed in all of them . . . In the examples given below one will see, first, the consonances that must be given to each of the notes in a major key. Second, the same ordering [is] applied to the minor key; third, [to] diverse variations of keys.[116]

Thus, particular harmonies and their progressions establish the key. Bruschi underscores this point by illustrating in a further example how his *Regola* clarifies the different keys of a modulating passage (see Example 13.12).

The origins of Bruschi's *Regola* lie in the more general instructions for harmonizing a bass. Francesco Bianciardi's *Breve regola per imparar' a sonare sopra il basso con ogni sorte d'istrumento* of 1607, one of the earliest figured-bass treatises, describes the 5/3 triad as the most perfect sonority and stipulates that it be used in all cases, except above bass notes that lack the perfect fifth, which would be B♮ in *cantus durus* and E♮ in *cantus*

116 Bruschi, *Regole per il contrapunto*, p. 36.

Example 13.12 Antonio Bruschi, *Regole per il contrapunto e per l'accompagnatura* (1711), "Variazioni di tuoni"

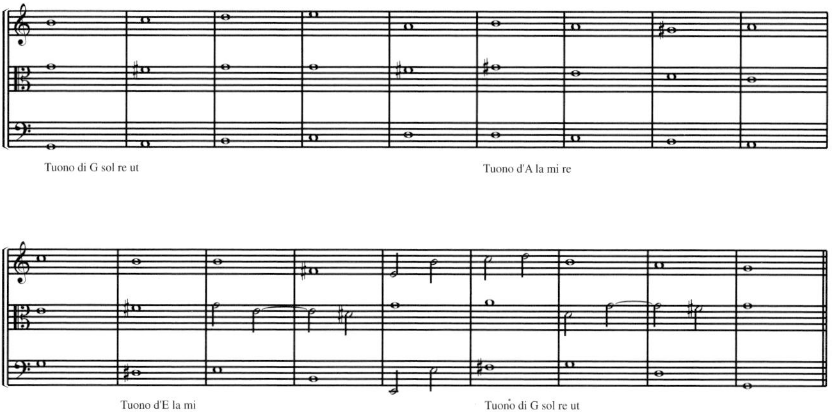

Tuono di G sol re ut

Tuono d'A la mi re

Tuono d'E la mi

Tuono di G sol re ut

mollis.[117] Such cases require a 6/3 harmonization instead. A modified version of this rule that attests its longevity appears in Lorenzo Penna's treatise (*Li primi albori musicali*, 1672).[118] He requires that bass notes read as *mi* be harmonized with a sixth instead of a fifth – these would be E and B in *cantus durus* and A and E in *cantus mollis*. Two significant points separate Bruschi's harmonization of the scale from Bianciardi's and Penna's general rules: first, there is no implication in these earlier works of scale degrees within a tonality, major or minor, or even within an octave; second, were the bass notes arranged as a major scale in one octave, only the third and seventh scale degrees would take sixth chords and not the second and sixth.

In English theory, however, a conception closer to Bruschi's *Regola* emerges well before the end of the century. Matthew Locke (*Melothesia: or, certain general rules for playing upon a continued-bass*, 1673), for example, furnishes a set of harmonization rules that nearly duplicate Bruschi's example: the bass is now conceived as the scale of a "Tone," and scale degree $\hat{6}$, as well as degrees $\hat{3}$ and $\hat{7}$, take sixth chords.[119] Scale harmonizations appear in Italy some time shortly after this point: a set of instructions

117 Bianciardi, *Breve regola*. This brief treatise consists of a single broadsheet in which he sets forth a basic rule of harmonizing a bass line:

> One must observe that music has perfect harmony comprising three elements – that is, in three different notes united together – among which one makes a fifth above the bass, and the other a third; thus one is a perfect consonance, the other imperfect. And one must observe this for all of the bass notes that can take these consonances. But because some notes do not have a [perfect] fifth above, the sixth is used in its place. This occurs in those keys that make different mutations of the fourth, such as when one sings in B♮ from B to F and when one sings in B♭ from E to B♭.

118 Penna, *Primi albori*, p. 146. 119 Locke, *Melothesia*, pp. 5–8.

from an anonymous manuscript dated to the end of the century, *Regole per l'accompagnatura del basso continuo*, essentially replicates Bruschi's instructions as follows:

> The first note of the *tuono* is to be accompanied by the third, fifth, and octave. The second note takes a major sixth. The third note takes a natural sixth. The fourth note takes the third, fifth, and octave, but with the provision that, when the *tuono* is major in its beginning, the accompanying third should be major; if the *tuono* is minor, the accompanying third should be minor even if not indicated by the note or by the key [signature]. The fifth note always takes a major third. The sixth and seventh notes ascending by whole steps are each to be accompanied by the natural sixth.[120]

The significance of this last form of scale harmonization lies in several points: first, we may recognize the distinction between the primary, root-position chords on degrees $\hat{1}$, $\hat{4}$, and $\hat{5}$ and the secondary sixth chords on degrees $\hat{2}$, $\hat{3}$, $\hat{6}$, and $\hat{7}$; second, we may also infer the concept of key in Bruschi's *tuono*, whose varieties are major or minor; and third, the leading-tone is assured by the use of a major third over the fifth degree in both the major and the minor *tuono*. In short, both triadic harmony and tonal harmonic function evolve within these octave harmonizations.

Another cornerstone in the theory of major-minor keys is their relationship by fifths. Extended far enough, a series of major or minor keys whose tonics are separated by a perfect fifth will form a closed circle, allowing for enharmonic equivalence in a tempered system. The first depiction of keys as points a fifth apart on such a circle is Johann David Heinichen's "Musicalischer Circul" found in his treatise on thorough-bass accompaniment at the keyboard, *Neu erfundene und grundliche Anweisung . . . des General-Basses* (1711) (see Plate 13.1).[121] Heinichen attributed his knowledge of the "musical circle" to his study with Johann Kuhnau, who in turn was said to have drawn upon the theories of Athanasius Kircher.[122] The documented roots of the circle of fifths, however, lie in instances of a fully circular pattern of harmonic progressions that predate even Kircher.

The motivation for envisioning a musical circle lies in the need to play chords or chord progressions at all possible pitch levels, which is attested by theorists throughout the century.[123] Early on, for example, Bianciardi notes briefly that the transposition of *tuoni* is required "either for the convenience of the singers or to play in consort with other instruments."[124] The earliest known instance of harmonies arranged about a circle, however, predates the seventeenth century: written sometime in the 1590s, a treatise on *rasgueado* (strummed) guitar accompaniment by Joan Carles Amat (*Guitarra*

120 Anonymous, *Regole per l'accompagnatura*, p. 69. For a later version of the "rule of the octave," see **Example 24.1, p. 757**. For a comprehensive history of the "rule," see Christensen, "The *règle de l'octave*."
121 Heinichen, *Anweisung*, p. 261.
122 Heinichen, *Der General-Bass*, pp. 840–41. Lester, *Modes and Keys*, pp. 108–11, provides a useful summary and assessment of Heinichen's musical circle and its implications for the conception of keys in the early eighteenth century. Also see **Chapter 23, pp. 733–38**. The various kinds of equal and near-equal temperament upon which such cycles of perfect fifths are predicated are discussed in **Chapter 7, pp. 204–20**. 123 See n. 65 above. 124 Bianciardi, *Breve regola*.

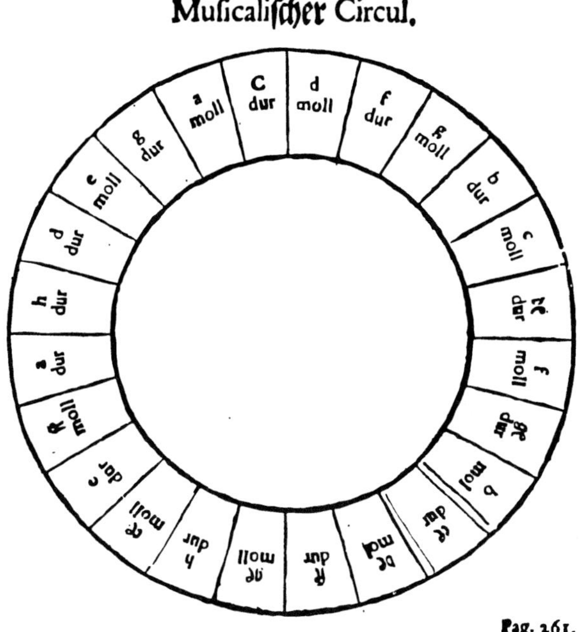

Plate 13.1 Heinichen's musical circle from *Neu erfundene und gründliche Anweisung* (1711), p. 261

española, c. 1596) features a series of tablature chords arranged about a circle.[125] One half of the circle progresses in major triads separated by fifths; the other half in minor. The voicings of the chords accommodate *rasgueado* technique on the five-course guitar so that, in modern terms, both root-position and inverted triads occur.

Amat's intent is clear: he means for the guitarist to be able to play major and minor chords on every chromatic pitch in the octave. Eighty years later, Lorenzo Penna (1672) shows the manner of playing four types of cadence around a complete circle (*circolo, ò ruota delle cadenze*).[126] Example 13.13 shows the first of four types of cadence that Penna uses to navigate the circle of fifths. Twice in his explanation of a circle of cadences Penna alerts the reader to the fact that these cadences may be formed using either the major third or the minor.[127] In these progressions we may see the conception of twenty-four major and minor keys arranged in fifths about a circle, but this is

125 The earliest surviving copy of the *Guitarra española* by Amat (1572–1642) was published in 1626, but Christensen, "Spanish Baroque Guitar," p. 37, n. 10, dates the treatise to 1596 on the basis of remarks made by Amat in his dedication and introduction. Two further studies, one on Amat's treatise and another on the impact of guitar music on tonal style, reflect the little-known influence of popular genres on tonal theory and practice during the seventeenth century: Hall, "Joan Carles Amat"; and Hudson, "Italian Guitar Music." 126 Penna, *Primi albori*, pp. 173–83.
127 Ibid., pp. 178, 182.

Example 13.13 Lorenzo Penna, *Li primi albori musicali* (1672), "Circolo, ò ruota delle cadenze del primo ordine"

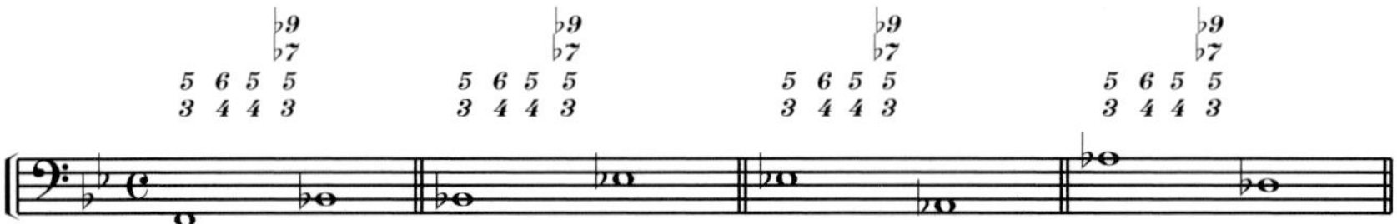

inference only: Penna recognizes the eight *tuoni*, not major and minor keys; he demonstrates a circular progression, but makes no claims of relating keys, or *tuoni*, on a circle; and Penna's aim is to reinforce the accompanist's abilities, not to instill a new conception of tonal space.

At the end of the seventeenth and beginning of the eighteenth century, Werckmeister argued repeatedly for temperaments that allow a closed circular progression of harmonies.[128] For Werckmeister, the advocate of both equal and unequal temperaments that facilitate the use of any tonality, the musical circle connotes one essential feature: it is closed, thus comprising a tempering of intervals in which no wolf fifth exists and thus assuring a continuous progression through all keys. It is therefore Werckmeister who explicitly connects the circular model of tonal space with the use of all conceivable keys and the temperaments that make such keys possible. But the idea of viewing distinct keys around a circle is not articulated before Heinichen in the second decade of the eighteenth century.

128 Werckmeister, *Orgel-Probe*, pp. 78–79. See Werckmeister, *Die nothwendigsten Anmerckungen*, p. 21; and his *Musicalische Paradoxal-Discourse*, pp. 50–51, where he makes similar arguments for tunings that make possible a series of harmonic progressions through a closed circle. Also see Chapter 7, pp. 215–16.

Cadence types and terminology

The cadence proves crucial to the conception of an emerging tonal system late in the century. Put simply, the most immediate means of articulating a final or establishing a key lies in the cadence. Earlier in the century, as seen previously, theorists concentrated on proper cadence positions with respect to the final of a mode or key (see Table 13.7 above). From the mid-century on, theorists also began to devote more attention to specific cadence types. The crucial difference between them, then as now, lies in the degree of finality they achieve. In order to illustrate the nature of various cadences, seventeenth-century theorists frequently draw upon analogies with language in which cadences are likened to punctuation.[129] As Etienne Loulié (1696) points out,

> [t]he cadence is a melodic ending. Now, melodies are related to an air [much in the same manner] as periods and other parts [of speech] are related to an address. The endings of these melodies, or sections of which an air is composed, are related [in speech] sometimes to periods, sometimes to commas, sometimes to question marks, etc., according the different manners in which these melodies conclude.[130]

Unfortunately, Loulié pursues the analogy no further, not mentioning which cadence might be associated with which type of punctuation.

Apart from analogies made with grammatical punctuation, theorists of the seventeenth century lay out the specifics of cadences in terms of either contrapuntal norms or thorough-bass practice. In the context of contrapuntal rules the cadence is described as a particular convergence between two lines of music – a perfect interval (most often an octave or unison) attained through stepwise motion in both voices. Contrapuntal terminology, moreover, heavily influences the terms applied to cadences: analogous to simple and composed counterpoint are simple cadences – note-against-note progressions of consonances only – and composed (*composte*) or diminuted (*diminute*) cadences – progressions containing various rhythmic figures that include dissonances along with consonances.[131] Similarly, the perfection or imperfec-

129 The analogy may be extended in order to make a distinction between cadences and *clausulae*: whereas cadences serve as punctuation, *clausulae* stand as the syntactical unit that is articulated by such punctuation. Berardi's *Il Perché musicale* (pp. 38–43), for example, contains brief musical phrases, called *clausule armoniche* that define each of the twelve modes. Moreover, Berardi, *Miscellanea musicale*, p. 124, implies this distinction between cadence and *clausula* by using them together in the following passage: "La cadenza è il più nobile, & il più vago ornamento, che si trovi nella Musica tuttavia non è lecito usarla, se non quando s'ariva alla clausola, overo periodo della prosa, ò pure del verso . . ." (The cadence is the most noble and charming ornament that one may find in music. All the same, it is not permissible to use it if one has not arrived at the *clausula*, or period of the prose or verse. . . .)

Some theorists, however, do not observe this terminological subtlety: referring to the very same musical phrases that Berardi would use more than half a century later, Parran, *Traité de la musique*, p. 129, simply calls them "cadences en chaque mode."

130 Loulié, *Eléments*, p. 83. (The translation used here is that of Albert Cohen.) Berardi offers a similar definition in his *Miscellanea musicale*, p. 124.

131 Penna, *Primi albori*, p. 132; Bononcini, *Musico prattico*, p. 80; Berardi, *Miscellanea musicale*, pp. 124–25.

tion of a cadence derives from the comparable classification of intervals in contrapuntal theory: a cadence is perfect or imperfect depending on the consonance that results, except that only the octave and unison, and not the fifth, define a perfect cadence; those cadences resulting in a third, fifth, and sixth are considered imperfect.[132]

The continuo player's perspective, in contradistinction to contrapuntal teaching, emerges in descriptions of a cadence either as a characteristic gesture in the bass, or as specific intervals over the bass. Penna's *cadenze del primo ordine* (see Example 13.13) are harmonizations of a bass that leaps down a fifth or up a fourth; his *cadenze del secondo ordine* (cadences of the second order), of a bass that leaps down a fourth or up a fifth; and so on.[133] In a variant on this line of thinking, Berardi categorizes his cadences according to the intervals formed by voices above the bass line. His cadence types include: *cadenza di settima, e sesta ligata* (the cadence of the seventh and tied sixth); *cadenza di quarta rissoluta con la terza* (the cadence of the fourth resolved to the third); and *cadenza . . . di quarta, e terza, e quarta, e settima, sesta, e quinta* (the cadence of the fourth–third–fourth and seventh–sixth–fifth) (the last two are shown in Example 13.14a).[134]

The fact that perspectives associated with contrapuntal terminology or with thorough-bass practice often illustrate two sides of the same coin – two views of a single musical gesture – emerges in a further example given by Berardi. A cadence he labels *all'antica* simply adds a bass line to the fundamental convergence of two voices on a unison or octave (Example 13.14b): this results, to use current terminology, a IV–V–I progression ending with a perfect authentic cadence out of a standard two-voice contrapuntal progression.[135]

And yet, while Berardi's example might seem to reconcile older and newer perspectives on the cadence, a considerable distance separates our own harmonic reductionist perspective from the more multifaceted conception of seventeenth-century theorists. Apparently similar cadences, for example, might be considered separate cases in the seventeenth century: Berardi, for example, treats the two closely similar cadences of Example 13.14a as distinct types because each uses a different set of intervals over the bass. Likewise, La Voye-Mignot places several cadences into a single category that modern theorists might not group together. The three cadences of Example 13.14c, all *cadences parfaites* because they converge on an octave, include only one cadence that we might today label as a perfect authentic cadence. In fact, the third of these is, in modern terms, a Phrygian half cadence.

La Voye-Mignot's discussion of cadences otherwise stands out for the sense of tonal focus it imparts. His three cadences – perfect (*parfaite*), broken (*rompuë*), and waiting (*attendante*) – differ largely in their degree of finality, a point he underscores by notating

132 Bononcini, *Musico prattico*, p. 80. 133 Penna, *Primi albori*, pp. 173, 176.
134 Berardi, *Miscellanea musicale*, pp. 160–61. A full inventory of seventeenth-century cadence types is found in Siegfried Schmalzriedt's entry "Kadenz" in *HmT*.
135 Berardi, *Miscellanea musicale*, p. 161.

Example 13.14 Various seventeenth-century cadence types
(a) Angelo Berardi (1689), third and fourth cadences

(b) Angelo Berardi (1689), cadence "all'antica"

(c) La Voye-Mignot (1656), perfect cadences

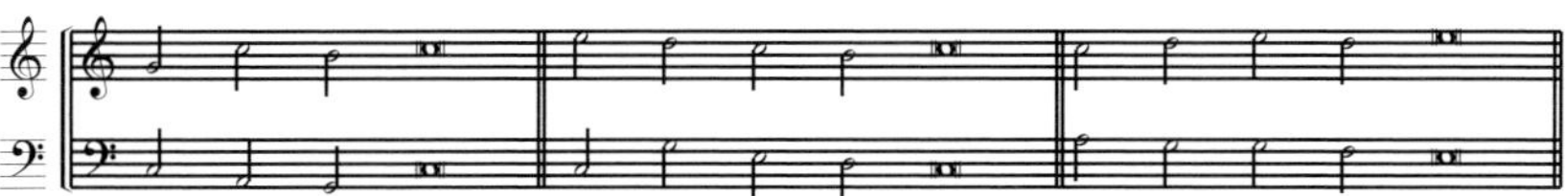

(d) La Voye-Mignot (1656), "cadence rompuë" and "cadence attendante"

less conclusive cadences in shorter note values (Examples 13.14c–d). A clear hierarchy thus informs La Voye-Mignot's cadences: the perfect cadence achieves resolution on an octave or unison; the broken cadence (similar to the deceptive cadence) a deviation from this anticipated resolution; and the waiting cadence an expectation of the octave with a cadence just prior to a resolution (similar to the "half" cadence).

But despite the clarity and logic of La Voye-Mignot's approach to cadences, it is hardly representative. Writing at the end of the century, Charles Masson (1699) sets forth two different criteria by which to distinguish cadences: conjunct or disjunct motion and perfect or imperfect resolution – that is, octave and unison, or otherwise. In contrast to La Voye-Mignot, moreover, Masson's two-voice examples give precedence to those cadences using conjunct motion, reversing La Voye-Mignot's preference for the "authentic" type of perfect cadence, so that Masson prioritizes the second type of cadence seen in Example 13.14c over the first. Perhaps most intriguing in Masson's theory of cadences, however, is its mix of both new and old ideas. As he points out, cadences may occur on the final, mediant, or dominant – a prescription that originates with Zarlino – of the two modes recognized in 1699, major and minor.[136]

Twenty-four major and minor keys organized around a circle of fifths constitutes a fundamental and enduring schematization of tonal space, one that survives to the present day. The beginnings of this conception in the seventeenth century, rather than illustrating the metamorphosis of modes into keys, instead reveal the convergence of several strains firmly rooted in seventeenth-century theoretical and practical traditions: the church keys, originating as psalm tone settings, compose a core set of eight tonalities that were themselves expanded by means of transpositions to a maximum of twenty-four keys; scale harmonizations in figured-bass treatises define the individual keys themselves by establishing the primary and secondary triads centered on a tonic; and the navigation of a complete circle of keys related by fifths shows transposition and modulation extended to their fullest potential, ultimately requiring tunings predicated on a closed circle of fifths.

Such summaries, however, pass too quickly over the particular language in which these ideas are communicated to us. A single example – a brief pronouncement from an anonymous treatise, probably of the early eighteenth century – well attests to the enigma of much seventeenth-century theory. The conception here is crystal clear, but the language with its freight of long-standing connotations nearly obscures the message:

> On the modes: I suppose that the student of music already knows the church modes, of which there are eight, and that upon these eight modes are based the psalms, antiphons, hymns, introits, etc. for singing in the church . . . In our modern music we have modes that are distinct from the above-mentioned church modes . . . But because these [latter modes] have been altered and mixed with one another, I have set down only two: one is authentic, the other plagal. *The authentic has the major third; the plagal has the minor third* [emphasis added].[137]

Seventeenth-century theory thus comprises a body of writings that vividly exemplifies the clash between inherited precepts with their accompanying terminology and new conceptions that strain the existing musical language. Herein lies the greatest fascination and challenge of musical thought from this era. The search for a means of expressing new ideas prior to the creation of an adequate vocabulary characterizes the most enigmatic – but ultimately the most revealing – theory of the period.

136 Masson, *Nouveau traité*, pp. 49–55.

137 *Trattato dell'arte di contrapunto*, p. 75.

Bibliography

Primary sources

Abbatini, A. M. Letter to Sig. Bastiano Baldini, MS c. 1667, Biblioteca Vaticana, Rome, MS Chigi L. VI.191

Agazzari, A. *Del sonare sopra'l basso con tutti li stromenti e dell'uso loro nel conserto*, Siena, Falcini, 1607; facs. Bologna, Forni, 1985

Amat, J. C. *Guitarra española de cinco ordenes*, Lérida, Lorenço, 1627; facs. Barcelona, Edición Facsímil Barcelona, 1956

Angleria, C. *La regola del contraponto*, Milan, Rolla, 1622; facs. Bologna, Forni, 1983

Banchieri, A. *Cartella musicale*, Venice, G. Vincenti, 1614; facs. Bologna, Forni, 1968

Berardi, A. *Il perché musicale*, Bologna, Pier Maria Mont, 1693

Miscellanea musicale, Bologna, G. Monti, 1689

Bianciardi, F. *Breve regola per imparar' a sonar sopra il basso con ogni sorte d'istromento*, Siena, Falcini, 1607

Bismantova, B. *Compendio musicale*, MS, Ferrara, 1694; facs. Florence, Studio per Edizioni Scelte, 1978

Bononcini, G. M. *Musico prattico*, Bologna, G. Monti, Op. 8, 1673; facs. New York, Broude, 1969

Brossard, S. *Dictionnaire de musique*, Paris, Ballard, 1703; facs. Geneva, Minkoff, 1992; trans. A. Gruber as *Dictionary of Music*, Henryville, PA, Institute of Mediaeval Music, 1982

Bruschi, A. *Regole per il contrapunto, e per l'accompagnatura del basso continuo*, Lucca, Venturini, 1711

Burmeister, J. *Musica autoschediastike*, Rostock, C. Reusnerus, 1601

Butler, C. *The principles of musick*, London, Haviland, 1636; facs. New York, Da Capo, 1970

Calvisius, S. *Exercitationes musicae duae*, Leipzig, Apelii, 1600; facs. Hildesheim, G. Olms, 1973

Melopoeia sive melodiae condendae ratio, Erfurt, Baumann, 1592

Campion, T. *A new way of making fowre parts in counterpoint*, London, Snodham, c. 1618; reprint in *Campion's Works*, ed. P. Vivian, Oxford, Clarendon Press, 1909 and 1966, pp. 319–56

Caus, S. *Institution harmonique*, Frankfurt, Norton, 1615; facs. New York, Broude, 1969

Cerreto, S. *Della prattica musica vocale et strumentale*, Naples, Carlino, 1601; facs. Bologna, Forni, 1969

Degli Antonii, G. B. *Versetti per tutti li tuoni naturali, come trasportati per l'organo*, Op. 2, Bologna, Monti, 1687

Denis, J. *Traité de l'accord de l'espinette, auec la comparaison de son clauier à la musique vocale*, Paris, Ballard, 1650; trans. V. Panetta as *Treatise on Harpsichord Tuning by Jean Denis*, Cambridge University Press, 1987

Diruta, G. *Il Transilvano*, 2 vols. Venice, G. and A. Vincenti, 1593–1609; facs. Bologna, Forni, 1969 and 1997; trans. M. Bradshaw and E. Soehnlen as *The Transylvanian*, Henryville, PA, Institute of Mediaeval Music, 1984

Gasparini, F. *L'armonico pratico al cimbalo*, Venice, Bortoli, 1708; facs. New York, Broude, 1967; trans. F. Stillings as *The Practical Harmonist at the Harpsichord*, New Haven, Yale University Press, 1963

Glarean, H. *Dodecachordon*, Basel, H. Petri, 1547; facs. Hildesheim, G. Olms, 1969, and New York, Broude,1967; trans. C. Miller, *MSD* 6 (1965)

Harnisch, O. S. *Artis musicae delineatio*, Frankfurt, Stein, 1608

Heinichen, J. D. *Der General-Bass in der Composition*, Dresden, Heinichen, 1728; facs. Hildesheim, G. Olms, 1994

Neu erfundene und gründliche Anweisung, Hamburg, Schiller, 1711

Herbst, J. *Musica poetica sive compendium melopoëticum*, Nuremberg, Dümler, 1643

Holder, W. *Treatise of the natural grounds and principles of harmony*, London, Heptinstall, 1694; facs. New York, Broude, 1967

Intavolatura d'organo facilissima accomodata in versetti sopra gli otto tuoni ecclesiastici, Venice, Vincenti, 1598; facs. Bologna, Forni, 1970

Janowka, T. *Clavis ad thesaurum magnae artis musicae*, Prague, Labaun, 1701

La Voye-Mignot. *Traité de la musique*, Paris, Ballard, 1656; trans. A. Gruber as *Treatise on Music*, Brooklyn, Institute of Mediaeval Music, 1972

LeBegue, N. *Les pièces de clavessin*, Paris, Baillon, 1677; ed. N. Dufourcq as *Œuvres de clavecin*, Monaco, Oiseau-Lyre, 1956

Lippius, J. *Synopsis musicae novae*, Strassburg, K. Kieffer, 1612; trans. B. Rivera as *Synopsis of New Music*, Colorado Springs, Colorado College Music Press, 1977

Locke, M. *Melothesia: or, certain general rules for playing upon a continued bass*, London, Carr, 1673; facs. New York, Broude, 1975

Loulié, E. *Eléments ou principes de la musique*, Paris, Ballard, 1696; facs. Geneva, Minkoff, 1971; trans. A. Cohen as *Elements or Principles of Music*, New York, Institute of Mediaeval Music, 1965

Maillart, P. *Les tons, ou discours, sur les modes de musique, et les tons de l'eglise, et la distinction en iceux*, Tournai, Martin, 1610; facs. Geneva, Minkoff, 1972

Martín y Coll, A. *Arte de canto llano, y breve resumen de sus principales reglas*, Madrid, García, 1714

Flores de música obras y versos de varios organistas, MS, 1706; transcription, J. Sagasta, *Tonos de palacio canciones comunes*, vol. I. Madrid, Union Musical Española, 1984.

Masson, C. *Nouveau traité des règles pour la composition de la musique*, Paris, Ballard, 1694; facs. New York, Da Capo, 1967

Matteis, N. *The false consonances of musick; or instructions for the playing of a true bass upon the guitarre*, London, 1682; facs. ed. J. Tyler, Monaco, Chanterelle, 1980

Mattheson, J. *Das neu-eröffnete Orchestre*, Hamburg, B. Schiller, 1713; facs. Hildesheim, G. Olms, 1997

Menehou, M. *Nouvelle instruction familière, en laquelle sont contenus les difficultés de la musique, avecques le nombre des concordances, et accords: ensemble la manière d'en user, tant à deux, à trois, à quatres, qu'à cinq parties: nouvellement composée par Michel de Menehou, maistre des enfans de chœur de l'église Sainct Maur des fossez, lez Paris . . .*, Paris, Nicolas du Chemin, 1558.

Mersenne, M. *Harmonie universelle*, Paris, S. Cramoisy, 1636–37; facs. Paris, Centre National de la Recherche Scientifique, 1963 and 1986

Millet, J. *La belle methode, ou l'art de bien chanter*, Lyons, Gregoire, 1666; facs. New York, Da Capo, 1973

Morley, T. *A plaine and easie introduction to practicall musicke*, London, Short, 1597; facs. New York, Da Capo, 1969; ed. Alec Harman as *A Plain and Easy Introduction to Practical Music*, New York, Norton, 1973

Nivers, G. *Livre d'orgue contenant cent pieces de tous les tons de l'eglise*, Paris, Ballard, 1665

Traité de la composition de musique, Paris, Ballard, 1667; trans. A. Cohen as *Treatise on the Composition of Music*, Brooklyn, Institute of Mediaeval Music, 1961

Parran, A. *Traité de la musique théorique et pratique*, Paris, Ballard, 1639

Penna, L. *Li primi albori musicali*, Bologna, Monti, 1672; facs. Bologna, Forni, 1969

Playford, J. *An Introduction to the skill of musick*, 7th edn., London, Playford, 1674; facs. Ridgewood, NJ, Gregg, 1966

Ponzio, P. *Ragionamento di musica*, Parma, Viotto, 1588; facs. Kassel, Bärenreiter, 1959

Regole per l'accompagnatura del basso continuo con un' facil modo per imparare à trasportare in qualsivoglia tuono, MS, late 17th c., Biblioteca del Civico Museo Bibliografico Musicale "G. B. Martini," Bologna, P. 138, no. 3

Rousseau, J. *Méthode claire, certaine et facile pour apprendre à chanter la musique*, Paris, Rousseau, 1683

Traité de la viole, Paris, Ballard, 1687; facs. Amsterdam, Antiqua, 1965; trans. in five parts by N. Dolmetsch as "Jean Rousseau's *Traité de la viole* 1687," *Consort* 33 (1977), pp. 225–36; 34 (1978), pp. 302–11; 36 (1980), pp. 365–70; 37 (1981), pp. 402–05; 38 (1982), pp. 463–66

Sabbatini, G. *Regola facile, e breve per sonare sopra il basso continuo*, Venice, A. Vincenti, 1628

Sabbatini, P. *Toni ecclesiastici colle sue intonationi, all'uso romano. Modo per sonare il basso continuo*, Rome, Grignani, 1650

Scacchi, M. *Cribrum musicum ad triticum Siferticum*, Venice, A. Vincenti, 1643

Siefert, P. *Anticribratio musica ad avenam Schachianam*, Gdansk, Rhetius, 1645

Simpson, C. *A compendium of practical music*, 2nd edn., London, Godbid, 1667; ed. P. Lord, Oxford, Blackwell, 1970

A compendium of practical music, 4th edn., London, Pearson, 1706

Tevo, Z. *Il musico testore*, Venice, Bortoli, 1706; facs. Bologna, Forni, 1969

Titelouze, J. *Le Magnificat ou cantique de la Vierge pour toucher sur l'orgue, suivant les huit tons de l'Eglise*, Paris, Ballard, 1626

Trattato dell'arte di contrapunto d'autore anonimo, MS, early eighteenth century, Biblioteca del Civico Museo Bibliografico Musicale "G. B. Martini," Bologna, P. 120, no. 10

Walter, T. *The grounds and rules of musick explained, or, an introduction to the art of singing by note fitted to the meanest capacities*, Boston, Franklin, 1721

Werckmeister, A. *Die nothwendigsten Anmerckungen und Regeln wie der Bassus Continuus*, Aschersleben, Struntze, 1698; facs. Michaelstein, Kultur- und Forschungsstätte Michaelstein, 1985

Erweiterte und verbesserte Orgel-Probe, Quedlinburg, Calvisius and Sievert, 1698; facs. Kassel, Bärenreiter, 1970

Musicalische Paradoxal-Discourse, Quedlinburg, Calvisius, 1707; facs. Hildesheim, G. Olms, 1972

Zarlino, G. *Le istitutioni harmoniche*, Venice, Franceschi, 1558; facs. New York, Broude, 1965; trans. of Part III by G. Marco as *The Art of Counterpoint*, New Haven, Yale University Press, 1968; trans. of Part IV by V. Cohen as *On the Modes*, New Haven, Yale University Press, 1983

Le istitutioni harmoniche, rev. edn., Venice, Franceschi, 1573; facs. Ridgewood, NJ, Gregg, 1966

Secondary sources

Arnold, F. T. *The Art of Accompaniment from a Thorough-Bass as Practised in the XVIIth & XVIIIth Centuries*, Oxford University Press, 1931

Atcherson, W. T. "Symposium on Seventeenth-Century Music Theory: England," *JMT* 16 (1972), pp. 7–15

"Key and Mode in Seventeenth-Century Music Theory Books," *JMT* 17 (1973), pp. 204–33

Barnett, G. "Modal Theory, Church Keys, and the Sonata at the End of the Seventeenth Century," *JAMS* 51 (1998), pp. 245–81

Bates, R. F. "From Mode to Key: a Study of Seventeenth-Century French Liturgical Organ Music and Music Theory," Ph.D. diss., Stanford University (1986)

Bianconi, L. *Il Seicento*, Turin, Edizioni di Torino, 1982; trans. D. Bryant as *Music in the Seventeenth Century*, Cambridge University Press, 1987

Braun, W. *Deutsche Musiktheorie des 15. bis 17. Jahrhunderts. Zweiter Teil von Calvisius bis Mattheson*, *GMt* 8/2 (1994)

Brett, U. *Music and Ideas in Seventeenth-Century Italy: The Cazzati–Arresti Polemic*, New York, Garland, 1989

Buelow, G. "Symposium on Seventeenth-Century Music Theory: Germany," *JMT* 16 (1972), pp. 36–49

Christensen, T. "The *Règle de l'Octave* in Thorough-bass Theory and Practice," *Acta* 64 (1992), pp. 91–117

"The Spanish Baroque Guitar and Seventeenth-Century Triadic Theory," *JMT* 36 (1992), pp. 1–42

Cohen, A. "Survivals of Renaissance Thought in French Theory 1610–1670: A Bibliographic Study," in *Aspects of Medieval and Renaissance Music: a Birthday Offering to Gustave Reese*, ed. J. LaRue, New York, Norton, 1966, pp. 82–95

"La Supposition and the Changing Concept of Dissonance in Baroque Theory," *JAMS* 24 (1971), pp. 63–84

"Symposium on Seventeenth-Century Music Theory: France," *JMT* 16 (1972), pp. 16–35

Cooper, B. *Englische Musiktheorie im 17. und 18. Jahrhundert*, *GMt* 9 (1986)

Dahlhaus, C. *Untersuchungen über die Entstehung der harmonischen Tonalität*, Kassel, Bärenreiter, 1968; trans. R. Gjerdingen as *Studies on the Origin of Harmonic Tonality*, Princeton University Press, 1990

Damschroder, D. and D. Williams, eds., *Music Theory from Zarlino to Schenker*, Stuyvesant, NY, Pendragon, 1990

Dodds, M. "The Baroque Church Tones in Theory and Practice," Ph.D. diss., University of Rochester (1999)

Federhofer, H. "Eine Musiklehre von J. J. Prinner," in *Festschrift Alfred Orel zum 70. Geburtstag*, ed. Federhofer, Vienna, Rohrer, 1960, pp. 47–58

Gallo, F. A., R. Groth, C. V. Palisca, and F. Rempp, *Italienische Musiktheorie im 16. und 17. Jahrhundert: Antikenrezeption und Satzlehre*, *GMt* 7 (1989)

Hall, M. "The Guitarra Española of Joan Carles Amat," *Early Music* 6 (1978), pp. 362–73

Horsley, I. "Symposium on Seventeenth-Century Music Theory: Italy," *JMT* 16 (1972), pp. 51–61

Howell, A. "French Baroque Organ Music and the Eight Tones," *JAMS* 11 (1958), pp. 106–18

"Symposium on Seventeenth-Century Music Theory: Spain," *JMT*, 16 (1972), pp. 63–71

Hudson, R. "The Concept of Mode in Italian Guitar Music during the First Half of the 17th Century," *Acta* 42 (1970), pp. 163–83

Johnson, T. "Solmization in the English Treatises Around the Turn of the Seventeenth Century: A Break from Modal Theory," *Theoria* 5 (1990), pp. 42–60

Lester, J. *Between Modes and Keys: German Theory, 1592–1802*, Stuyvesant, NY, Pendragon Press, 1989

Meier, B. *Die Tonarten der klassichen Vokalpolyphonie, nach den Quellen dargestellt*, Utrecht, Oosthoek, Scheltema, and Holkema, 1974; trans. E. Beebe as *The Modes of Classical Vocal Polyphony*, New York, Broude, 1988

Nelson, B. "Alternatim Practice in 17th-century Spain," *Early Music* 22 (1994), pp. 239–56

Owens, J. A. "Concepts of Pitch in English Music Theory," in *Tonal Structures in Early Music*, ed. C. Judd, New York, Garland, 1998, pp. 183–246

Powers, H. S. "From Psalmody to Tonality," in *Tonal Structures in Early Music*, ed. C. Judd, New York, Garland, 1998, pp. 275–340

"Is Mode Real? Pietro Aron, the Octenary system, and Polyphony," *Basler Jahrbuch für Historische Musikpraxis*, 16 (1992), pp. 9–52

Rivera, B. *German Music Theory in the Early 17th Century: The Treatises of Johannes Lippius*, Ann Arbor, UMI Research Press, 1974

Seidel, W. *Französische Musiktheorie im 16. und 17. Jahrhundert*, *GMt* 9 (1986)

Tilton, M. "The Influence of Psalm Tone and Mode on the Structure of the Phrygian Toccatas of Claudio Merulo," *Theoria* 4 (1989), pp. 106–22

Tolkoff, L. "French Modal Theory Before Rameau," *JMT* 17 (1973), pp. 150–63

Van Wye, B. "Ritual Use of the Organ in France," *JAMS* 33 (1980), pp. 287–325

Walker, P. "Fugue in German Theory from Dressler to Mattheson," Ph.D. thesis, State University of New York at Buffalo (1987)

"From Renaissance 'Fuga' to Baroque Fugue: The Role of the 'Sweelinck Theory Manuscripts,'" *Schütz-Jahrbuch* 7–8 (1986), pp. 93–104

Theories of Fugue from the Age of Josquin to the Age of Bach, Rochester, NY, University of Rochester Press, 2000.

· 14 ·

Dualist tonal space and transformation in nineteenth-century musical thought

HENRY KLUMPENHOUWER

Introduction: tonal systems without scales

Nineteenth-century music theory in German-speaking countries divides reasonably into two main traditions: thorough-bass styles of music theory and harmonic dualism. The approaches are usually thought of nowadays as scale-degree theory and functionalism, respectively; since the emphasis in the account here is on chord structure and chordal relations as expressions of such structure, the traditions are characterized so as to foreground these particular aspects in their approach.

Interestingly, by the last half of the nineteenth century, the two traditions had become connected to different geo-political formations in Central Europe, such that we may properly speak of thorough-bass theory as Viennese (or more generally, Austrian) and harmonic dualism as Prussian, in the sense that these approaches were developed or extended within the context and dynamic of relevant educational institutions and their corresponding research *ethoi* in those two areas.[1] A third major tradition, the fundamental-bass theory emanating from the work of Rameau, was more international in scope and influence. In spite of obvious dissimilarities, it was considered by harmonic dualists (in particular, Riemann) to form an important early articulation of a number of theoretical concepts basic to their own approach, a judgment shared less positively by Heinrich Schenker, who saw Riemann's approach to tonality as little more than warmed-over Rameau.[2] This particular alignment of approaches seems based entirely on whether one held that the structure-forming relations within chords could withstand registral rearrangement (as both Riemann and Rameau did) or not (as asserted by thorough-bass theorists).

The thorough-bass tradition of music theory has its institutional origins in the late feudal/early modern institution of the Kapellmeister system of central Europe and extends as an identifiable theoretical movement roughly from the work of Heinichen to that of Sechter and late nineteenth-century Viennese theory in general, including

1 A particularly useful examination (in English) of German universities in the nineteenth century is McClelland, *State, Society and University in Germany*. 2 See Chapter 26, pp. 832–33.

Schenker's.[3] The basic tenets of the approach remained generally stable throughout this period, although there were important attempts to update the tradition in the second half of the century, none of which gained even local or partial acceptance. A particularly interesting example is the work of Heinrich Joseph Winzenhörlein (1819–1901), who, under the pen name Heinrich Joseph Vincent, complained about thorough-bass theory's failure to accommodate chromatic music and to take into account the phenomenon of the tonal center's absolute dominance in music. Yet even more importantly for him, the tradition was hopelessly entangled with primitive keyboard temperament schemes. His principal work, *Die Einheit in der Tonwelt*, advances a detailed revision – although Vincent himself saw it as a repudiation – of Sechter's version of thorough-bass theory, a revision that assumes equal temperament and, accordingly, twelve chromatic scales. Vincent furthermore proposes that all figures be calculated from the contextual tonic rather than from the bass pitch of each chord. The former figures represent what he calls "absolute intervals"; the latter, traditional figures are in his view merely "incidental intervals."[4]

As an approach – and this is as true of Vincent as it is of Heinichen or Sechter – thorough-bass theory might reasonably be characterized as principally scale-based, in the sense that it begins by taking as a *donnée* the concept of scale – conceived as a collection of pitch-classes with a corresponding scheme of structural differentiation among its members – and developing from it all other pitch elements, particularly chords, their internal structure, and their interrelations. In effect the scale represents the originary, imaginary topography within which tonal music is to be conceived. The topography or space projected by scales, though unidimensional, is quite clearly derived from the material space of instrumental construction (itself emerging from modal conceptions of melodic systems as well as from acoustic properties of air flowing through metal or wooden pipes).

The second music-theoretical tradition, harmonic dualism, is the starting point for the present chapter. Unlike thorough-bass theorists, almost all of those belonging to this tradition took seriously the Prussian physicist Hermann von Helmholtz's materialist and empiricist research project – established not only in his well-known *Die Lehre von den Tonempfindungen als physiologische Grundlage für die Theorie der Musik* of 1863 (translated as *On the Sensations of Tone as a Physiological Basis for the Theory of Music*) but also in his work on optics and color theory – which involved using physiology (studied according to the research protocols of physics) as a point of departure. If scales appear in the writings of these theorists, they do so not as a foundational concept, but rather as a product of other procedures. Accordingly, the class of theoretical topoi within

3 Discussed in Wason, *Viennese Theory*. Also see **Chapter 25, pp. 788–94**.
4 Wason's "Progressive Harmonic Theory" represents, as far as I can tell, the first treatment of Vincent in English. For more on Vincent, see **Chapter 10, p. 286**.

which such approaches originate is markedly different from the unidimensional locus of pitch(-classes) projected in scale-based theory.

The first major articulation of harmonic dualism as a full-blown theory of music was put forward by yet another Prussian-based physicist, Arthur von Oettingen,[5] who took the results of Helmholtz's work on the physiology and acoustics relevant to music, and synthesized it with features found in the more traditionally articulated harmonic-theoretical work of Moritz Hauptmann;[6] the second major impulse is the more influential work of Hugo Riemann, who repackaged the work of Oettingen for use in the recently established professional programs in conservatories and universities, and whose approach – or at least, aspects of it – dominated continental music theory well into the twentieth century.

This chapter examines the theoretical approaches developed by Hauptmann, Oettingen, and Riemann, with a particular emphasis on the issues of chord structure and chord relations or transformations. In doing so I shall give a sympathetic account of harmonic dualism as a structural premise and as a historical development. An examination of associated topographies of chords, topographies whose dimensions are articulated by transformations, follows.

Klangs: monism and dualism

Almost all tonal theorists have proposed that triadic structure arises from a fundamental, conceptually anterior, constituent pitch – such as *radix*, *son fondamental*, *Grundton*, *Hauptton* – that exerts unity on the collection by means of an array of intervallic relationships sanctioned by Nature (through, say, various properties of string vibrations or harmonic overtones) or, less commonly, by convention or practice, that is, history. (See **Chapter 3, pp. 85–91** for further discussion of this question.) Theorists have disagreed, however, on the factors that could determine the dominant pitch in triads, the intervallic relationships that ought to be privileged, and the manner in which these considerations are deployed in triadic structure.

In classifying this kind of theoretical work, it has become commonplace to established a primary opposition between Rameauian – that is, pertaining to Rameau of the *Traité de l'harmonie* – fundamental-bass procedures and the operations of figured-bass

5 Earlier attempts by Rameau (*Génération harmonique*, 1737) and Goethe in his *Tonlehre* (1815) seem not to have made much impression on their contemporaries or immediate followers. For more on Rameau's proto-functional theories and their progeny in the eighteenth century, see **Chapter 24, pp. 768–70, 774**.

6 It needs to be remembered that however inspirational Oettingen (and Riemann) found Hauptmann's work to be in connection with Helmholtz's research, Hauptmann himself was dismissive of Helmholtz's writing on music, claiming that since Helmholtz failed to account for the role of psychology in the structuration of musical events and musical systems his work did not achieve the status of a proper music theory. Hauptmann's remarks are contained in the form of a letter to Otto Jahn, later published in 1863 ("Ein Brief M. Hauptmann's").

theorists, corresponding conceptually to an opposition between "harmony" and "counterpoint," which are construed in this context more as theoretical *ethoi* rather than properly structural categories. Under this view, the corresponding music-theoretical work of writers such as Oettingen, Hauptmann, and Riemann – all considered harmonic dualists to some degree – constitutes an unsuccessful peripheral tradition. It is safe to say that this view or some reliable variant of it serves as the dominant approach in Anglo-American theoretical circles. In other words, contemporary music-theoretical debate about triadic structure (to the extent that it actually takes place) is framed by a common acceptance – or better, the naturalization – of some variety of harmonic monism. The degree to which figured-bass and fundamental-bass protocols, all of which depend on scales as a point of departure, have been hypostatized by theorists is easily measured by the degree to which active discussion of premises – whether presented in cognitive or in structural categories – are either thoroughly mystified (ironically, by appeals to empiricist themes) or simply avoided altogether. Correspondingly, critiques of harmonic dualism are generally empty of content, and rely either on similar enactments of mystification or on sheer invocation of disciplinary sanction in order to reinforce the predominant orthodoxy of harmonic monism.

Before progressing any further, it is worthwhile clarifying the use of certain terminology. I take "harmonic monism" to represent categories of music-theoretical work that assume the abstract primacy of the major triad, which finds its concrete form in the acoustic structure of the overtone series or in the properties of certain advantaged integer ratios applied to string division; accordingly, the minor triad appears in such theories as a derivative, produced by History, or in the case of Schenker, by the true Subject of History, the Artist. I take "harmonic dualism" to represent categories of music-theoretical work that accept the absolute structural equality of major and minor triads as objects derived from a single, unitary process that structurally contains the potential for twofold, or binary, articulation. There are, of course, other procedures for formalizing a distinction between monist (of some kind) and dualist (of some kind) theories of triadic structure, but they do not engage the particular issues I am concerned with here.

Hauptmann. Moritz Hauptmann (1792–1868) published his most important work, *The Nature of Harmony and Metre*, in 1853. The commonplace characterization of his work as Hegelian and idealist is rather unhelpful, since it encourages an easy dismissal of Hauptmann's significant theoretical insights, in turn distorting a proper understanding of technical development within nineteenth-century North German music theory. Furthermore, singling Hauptmann out as an idealist distracts us from the styles of idealism underlying most approaches to music theory even in its current forms. And while Hauptmann himself regarded his work as Hegelian-dialectical in character, it is difficult to see the relations between his Categories as instantiations of properly dialectical progression, despite the stream of Hegelian code words.

Nevertheless, *The Nature of Harmony and Metre* sought to provide for the first time a natural rather than aesthetic basis for the foundational harmonic and metrical structural categories of music in both their subjective and objective extensions. On Riemann's view, Hauptmann thereby formulated music theory's dominated research project.[7]

In Hauptmann's dualistic model, there are three "functions" assigned to pitches that constitute major and minor triads (or as we will call them, following Hauptmann, "klangs"): unity (*Einheit*); duality or opposition (*Zweiheit*); union (*Verbindung*).[8] The functions or "Moments" (as Hauptmann prefers to call them) are respectively associated with the octave, the perfect fifth, and the major third, whose primacy he derives from string division. Labeling the three functions respectively I, II, and III for reference, Hauptmann assigns them to triad members according to two rules:

1. I and II form a perfect fifth (mod 8ve)
2. I and III form a major third (mod 8ve)[9]

The rules stipulate that only the pitch that acts as I or the *Einheit* participates in both the perfect fifth (mod 8ve) and the major third (mod 8ve) relationships. The octave relation regulates the two structural intervals by allowing them to appear modulo the octave, as inversions or compounds. In turn, the structural assignment of I, II, and III withstands registral rearrangement of triadic members.

Figure 14.1 demonstrates how Hauptmann, following these formulations, distributes the three symbols I, II, and III among the pitches that form a major triad. Figure 14.2 carries out on a minor triad the procedures for assigning the functions I, II, and III. Comparing the assignment of function labels in minor triads and major triads, Hauptmann analyzes the constitutive perfect fifths and major thirds as intervals directed upwards: in major klangs the two intervals extend respectively from I to II and from I to III; in minor klangs the two intervals extend respectively from II to I and from III to I. Furthermore, Hauptmann writes,

> [t]he determination of triadic intervals is . . . taken to proceed from a positive unity, from a fundamental tone, to which the fifth and third relate. They may be considered as opposed. If we express one by saying that a tone *has* a perfect fifth and major third, then we can express the other in the opposite sense that a tone *is* a perfect fifth and major third. Having is an active condition; being, passive. Both determinations in their two meanings relate to Unity which is subject, on one hand, to Having (*Haben*) in the first determination, and, on the other hand, to Being Had (*Gehabt-werden*) in the second. The first corresponds to the major triad; the second, the minor triad.[10]

7 Harrison, *Harmonic Function*, pp. 218–21. Harrison's work is an extremely interesting and thorough recounting of harmonic dualism beginning with an examination of the theorists discussed here, although with a somewhat different focus. For a discussion of Hauptmann's theories on meter and rhythm, see **Chapter 21, pp. 677–82**.

8 Hauptmann's remarks on chord structure appear in *Harmonik und Metrik*, pp. 25–35. *Klang* is technically the German word for "resonance" or "sound," although in this context it refers specifically to the ontological entities of major and minor triads, whether generated acoustically or logically.

9 This discussion is expanded in Klumpenhouwer, "Riemann Transformations," paragraph 9.

10 Hauptmann, *Harmonik und Metrik*, p. 32. My translation.

F	II
D	III
B♭	I

Figure 14.1 Hauptmann's pitch functions assigned to members of a major triad

F	I
D♭	III
B♭	II

Figure 14.2 Hauptmann's pitch functions assigned to members of a minor triad

To foreground these chord-structural issues, we shall represent dualist klangs here as ordered pairs. The first element defines Hauptmann's I-function or *Einheit*. The second element defines the klang's modality: the symbol ↑ (replacing Riemann's and Oettingen's "+") represents a major ("over" or "super") klang, or a "positive" *Einheit* as Hauptmann calls it; the symbol ↓ (replacing Riemann's and Oettingen's "o") represents a minor (or under, or sub) klang, or "negative" *Einheit*. Hence, the klangs in Figures 14.1 and 14.2 are respectively represented as B♭↑ and F↓.

Under Hauptmann's explanation, a dualist model organizes aural sensations in roughly the following way: when listening to a triad, pick out a major third or its inversion, and pick out a perfect fifth or its inversion; when you do, you will become aware that one pitch in the triad is involved in both relationships and thereby seems more prominent than the others. By way of contrast, a fundamental-bass model organizes sensations in roughly the following way: when listening to a triad, reorganize it so that it takes up the smallest registral space and so that only thirds and fifths are formed; assign prominence to the lowest pitch and take note of the quality of the third between that pitch and the next highest. And a figured-bass model organizes aural sensations in roughly the following way: When listening to a triad, concentrate on the lowest-sounding pitch, and assign it prominence; imagine a third and a fifth above the lowest pitch (the qualities of which are determined by a contextual diatonic collection); pitches that do not lie a diatonic third or fifth above the prominent pitch are momentarily displacing the pitches that do.

These scripts for generating monist and dualist structure respectively for major and minor triads from simple elements of structure and the sensations that correspond to them are especially suggestive of Zarlino's well-known discussion of triads in his *Le istitutioni harmoniche*.[11] There, he gauges the character of the third (or tenth) that extends above the lowest-sounding pitch in a triad: "Either this is minor and the resulting harmony is ordered by, or resembles, the arithmetic proportion or mean, or it is

11 Riemann famously mistranslates the passage which enables him to promote Zarlino as a harmonic dualist, work debunked later by others, notably Dahlhaus in "War Zarlino Dualist?"

major and the harmony is ordered by, or resembles, the harmonic."[12] Yet, scarcely a paragraph later he writes:

> But since the extremes of the fifth are invariable and always placed subject to the same proportion, apart from certain cases that are used imperfectly [i.e. "only two parts are heard singing together"], the extremes of the thirds are given different positions. *I do not say different in proportion; I say different in position.* I say different in position for when . . . the major third is placed below, the harmony is made joyful and when it is placed above, the harmony is made mournful. Thus from the different positions of the thirds which are placed in counterpoint between the extremes of the fifth or above the octave, the variety of harmony arises.[13] [Italics mine]

Zarlino's two explanations are particularly striking in the context of the monist and dualist schemes for organizing triadic intervals presented earlier. In fact, using Zarlino's categories, it is possible to characterize monist theory as the view that arises from "listening across position" over against dualist theories that arise from "listening across proportion." Fixing the boundaries of the fifth and concentrating on the major third compels the organization of aural sensations described above with respect to Hauptmann's model, though admittedly it does not address in any way the procedures under which triadic structure is generated. *Those* rather are suggested most strongly by Zarlino's derivations of major and minor triads from harmonic and arithmetic means of the fifth, respectively, since the harmonic mean is obtainable by taking the reciprocals of the terms of an arithmetic series. The point here is not primarily to salvage Riemann's frequently discredited characterization of Zarlino as a dualist, though that issue is a potentially engaging and fruitful enterprise, but rather to foreground in Zarlino's account the possibility of embracing both models as equally conditional and serviceable "modes" of conceptualizing the structure of major and minor triads and their relation to one another, by using relative registral position and diatonic interval size as variables.

Oettingen. The physicist Arthur Joachim von Oettingen (1836–1920) can be seen as the true heir of Hauptmann's dualism, having developed and pursued most rigorously in his *Harmoniesystem in dualer Entwicklung* of 1866 the dualistic framework laid out philosophically by the Leipzig Kantor. But Oettingen could not simply appropriate Hauptmann's thesis uncritically, for an important work had appeared in the years immediately following the publication of Hauptmann's principal treatise that cast considerable doubts upon its dualistic foundation: Hermann von Helmholtz's *Die Lehre von den Tonempfindungen als physiologische Grundlage für die Theorie der Musik*. In this critical work (discussed in more detail in **Chapter 9, pp. 259–62**), Helmholtz had disputed Hauptmann's dualism by showing how the minor harmony was really an inferior and "corrupted" (*getrübt*) form of the major triad by virtue of its having

12 Quoted in *SR*, p. 448.

13 Ibid., **p. 449**. See also the excerpt quoted in **Chapter 24, p. 754**.

$5^m 3^n$

m \ n	-8	-7	-6	-5	-4	-3	-2	-1	0	1	2	3	4	5	6	7	8
2	c	g	d	a	e	b	f♯	c♯	g♯	d♯	a♯	e♯	b♯	f𝄪	c𝄪	g𝄪	d𝄪
1	a♭	e♭	b♭	f	c	g	d	a	e	b	f♯	c♯	g♯	d♯	a♯	e♯	b♯
0	f♭	c♭	g♭	d♭	a♭	e♭	b♭	f	c	g	d	a	e	b	f♯	c♯	g♯
-1	d♭♭	a♭♭	e♭♭	b♭♭	f♭	c♭	g♭	d♭	a♭	e♭	b♭	f	c	g	d	a	e
-2	b♭♭♭	f♭♭	c♭♭	g♭♭	d♭♭	a♭♭	e♭♭	b♭♭	f♭	c♭	g♭	d♭	a♭	e♭	b♭	f	c

Figure 14.3 Oettingen's diagram of tonal space (from *Harmoniesystem*, p. 15)

greater interference among its constituent upper partials. Oettingen attempted to salvage the equal ontological status of the minor triad by showing its generation to be oppositional (*gegensätzlich*) to that of the major triad. If Hauptmann had claimed that the minor triad carries "passive" characteristics because its tones are themselves overtones of various fundamentals, while the tones of a major triad share a common fundamental (*sein* vs. *haben*), for Oettingen, the opposite was true. That is, the notes of a minor triad actively *have* differing fundamentals, while tones in a major triad are passively *being* overtones of the same fundamental. This is the basis of his distinction between *phonicity* and *tonicity* (discussed further below). The point is that Oettingen attempted to reconcile Hauptmann's logical arguments with Helmholtz's acoustical and physiological arguments. The result was the most thorough-going and undiluted doctrine of harmonic dualism articulated in the nineteenth century.

Oettingen takes as a starting point a notion of individual pitches (under just intonation) defined as frequencies expressible as $5^m3^n2^p$, where m, n, and p are integers. According to Oettingen, no matter how much the integers m, n, and p vary, one can never express one pitch in more than one combination, since every number may be analyzed into prime factors in only one way. (This is, of course, untrue if one takes the fifths and major thirds involved to be those developed by equal temperament – measuring 700 and 400 cents, respectively – rather than the pure fifths and major thirds of just intonation, measuring 702 and 386 cents, respectively.)

Such premises lead very naturally to diagrams like the one presented in Figure 14.3, reproduced from Oettingen's *Harmoniesystem in dualer Entwicklung* (1866). Rows are measured in perfect fifths, columns in major thirds. All columns and rows are understood to extend infinitely beyond the limits shown in the diagram. The single and double over- and underlines remind us of the distinctions between pitches of the same letter name but which correspond to different frequency measurements under just intonation.

The diagram aids in calculating the relationship or interval from one pitch to another as powers of major thirds (5/4) and perfect fifths (3/2), as $(5/4)^{m*}(3/2)^n$. As the row headings suggest, moves upwards within columns – that is, moves by increments of a major third – are measured by positive integers, and moves downwards by negative.

And as the column headings suggest, moves to the right within a row – that is moves by increments of a perfect fifth – are measured by positive integers, and moves to the left by negative integers. So, for example, the interval from c^1 in the center of the diagram and b^1 to its upper right corresponds to (5/4)*(3/2), or (15/8).

Oettingen's notion of chord structure may be reasonably described as the application of Helmholtz's discussion of harmonic overtones and undertones to certain broad features of Hauptmann's notion of triadic construction, using non-scale-generated intervals, so that distinctions between, say, major and minor thirds (whose common designation as "thirds" is possible only with reference to the idea of a diatonic scale) are strictly observed.

In *On the Sensations of Tone*, Helmholtz describes the phenomenon of overtones and its corollary concept of undertones.[14] The latter does not – as is often assumed – involve the notion of a series of harmonic partials emitted or extended "downwards" from a fundamental as a direct parallel to the series of harmonic partials emitted or extended upwards from a fundamental.[15] Overtones are an easily observable acoustic feature of tones in general; undertones are not. By overtones, Helmholtz means just that pattern of partials associated with the acoustic *donnée*; by undertones, he means just the patterns of fundamentals associated with a particular partial. The notion can be engaged acoustically, following Helmholtz, by way of a resonator, a hollow sphere of glass with two openings of different sizes, the smaller of which may be sealed with wax and placed in one's ear. If the "proper tone" of the resonator is, say, c^3, that pitch will sound when a nearby musical instrument plays c^2, or f^1, c^1, a♭, f, d, c, and so on. (One could of course repeat the results by silently depressing c^3 on a piano and playing c^2, or f^1, c^1, a♭, f, d, c, and so on.) Accordingly, the concept of undertones is an assertion of no acoustic or psychological phenomenon other than the phenomenon of a tone comprising a fundamental and an associated series of partials. (See also the discussion in Chapter 9, pp. 251–54.)

It is in this connection that Oettingen develops his well-known twin constructs of "tonicity" (*Tonicität*) and "phonicity" (*Phonicität*). Tonicity corresponds to the property of an interval or chord to be grasped as a partial of a fundamental (p. 31). Accordingly under this conception the "tonic" fundamental of the interval c^1–g^1 is c since the pitches that constitute the interval may be understood as partials of c. Phonicity, on the other hand, corresponds to the property of the pitches that constitute an interval or chord to possess common partials. The lowest of all such common partials is called the phonic overtone. Consequently, the phonic overtone of the interval c^1–g^1 is g^2. Under Oettingen's conception, then, each interval or chord possesses both properties and accordingly has both a tonic fundamental and a phonic overtone.

14 Helmholtz's discussion of undertones begins on p. 33 of the English translation.

15 This would be similar to Rameau's "resonance" theory of the minor triad articulated in his *Génération harmonique*, but abandoned soon thereafter (see Chapter 24, p. 771). However, Riemann himself quite clearly attempted to strengthen the concept of undertones along precisely these lines.

So, given the major triad c^2, e^2, g^2 and the minor triad c^2, $e\flat^2$, g^2, Oettingen says the first chord has a tonic fundamental of c and a phonic overtone of b^6, while the second triad has a tonic fundamental of $a\flat_1$ and the phonic overtone of g^4. Furthermore, the tonic fundamental of the major triad is the structural parallel of the phonic overtone of the minor triad: in each case these tones are consonant with their respective chord. On the other hand, the phonic overtone of the major triad and the tonic fundamental of the minor triad are dissonant with their respective chord.

Relating triadic structure to the diagram in Figure 14.3, Oettingen provides a topographic version of major–minor opposition. He writes that "all pure consonant triads stand in the form of right triangles, whose hypotenuses all form a diagonal minor third. In the major klang, the right angle is oriented to the top (of the diagram); in the minor klang, the right angle is oriented to the bottom."[16]

These notions provide Riemann with his theoretical point of departure, and although later on he extends his research agenda to cover an extremely wide array of activities, from phrasing to keyboard technique to more properly music-historical topics, he retains the basic outlines of Oettingen's conception of chord structure and chord relationship, along with the deployment of those structural elements in imaginary topographies. Indeed, it may be appropriate to characterize as Oettingen-Riemannian a theory that involves certain of Oettingen's fundamental conceptions and Riemann's later revision of its details, carried out to integrate the approach more readily with established conservatory theoretical practices.[17] It only remains to say here that Riemann's argumentation on behalf of the undertone series led to any number of unfruitful byways and expended much wasted energy on his part. It was obviously with some regret – but probably also considerable relief – that at the end of his life, he finally abandoned the search for an acoustical proof for the series and instead posited a psychological grounding.[18] It should be emphasized, however, that the heuristic value of Riemann's ontological dualism is by no means dependent upon any natural justification of the undertone series. Its ultimate vindication comes in the logical and revealing network of chord relationships that a dualist perspective affords.

Schritte, Wechsel and topographies

These relationships emerge from the intervals of perfect fifth and major third, the intervallic relations that constitute triads. Moreover, they arise from implementing

16 Oettingen, *Harmoniesystem in dualer Entwicklung*, p. 17. Compare also the related *Tonnetz* by Hostinský, Plate 23.1, p. 737.

17 Riemann's own views on conservatory-style education are particularly interesting in this regard. These views are stated most forcefully in an article entitled "Unsere Konservatorien," published just after he had left the Leipzig Conservatory of Music for a position at The University of Leipzig.

18 Riemann, "Ideen zu einer 'Lehre von den Tonvorstellungen.'" See also the helpful discussion in Harrison, *Harmonic Function*, pp. 261–65.

the dualism immanent in the interaction between the notion of dyadic interval – measuring magnitude alone, as in "major third" or "perfect fifth" – and the notion of directed interval – measuring both magnitude and direction, as in "major third up" or "perfect fifth down": the former defines triads as triads; the latter forms the basis for the distinction between major and minor triads. Since the definition of specific chord relationships in Riemann and Oettingen involves the notion of directed intervals, they possess essential structural features of mathematical "transformations," principally that such relationships are one-to-one: they relate one pitch to only one other pitch. (By contrast, the dyadic notion of interval – a more commonly employed conception – relates one pitch to two others.) This feature is particularly important for us since it serves as the basis of contemporary interest in Riemann's work in contemporary American theoretical circles. In the account of such chord relationships, I shall concentrate on Riemann's simplified version of those first defined by Oettingen.

Riemann establishes two classes of chord relationships or transformations. One, whose elements all have the suffix *Schritt* (step), is analogous but not identical to pitch-class transposition, and preserves the polarity of the klangs to which they are applied. Hence *Schritte* map major klangs onto major klangs, and minor klangs onto minor klangs. Such relationships are termed "homonomic" by Oettingen. The second class of transformations, whose elements all have the suffix *Wechsel* (exchange), is analogous but not identical to pitch-class inversion, and reverses the polarity of the klangs to which they are applied. Hence, *Wechsel* map major klangs onto minor klangs, and minor klangs onto major klangs. Such relationships are termed "antinomic" by Oettingen.

Riemann's catalogue of *Schritte* and *Wechsel* varies considerably from his first "practical" harmony text, *Skizze einer neuen Methode der Harmonielehre* (1880) to its later reworking as *Handbuch der Harmonielehre* (1887), his popular handbooks such as *Handbuch der Harmonie- und Modulationslehre* (1890), and his mature exposition of functional harmony, *Vereinfachte Harmonielehre* (1893). Ultimately, Riemann's purpose is to provide a thorough enough lexicon of relations so that any two klangs could find a relevant transformation within the system, a notion taken up most strikingly by his student Max Reger.[19]

Riemann's interest in these transformations appears within the context of his topographical conception of tonality, which in turn arises from Oettingen's topographical conception of pitch relations regulating the design given earlier in Figure 14.3. Troping Oettingen's diagram, Riemann replaces pitches with klangs, and pitch intervals with klang transformations. Figures 14.4 and 14.5 provide maps of Riemann's

19 In *Harmonic Function* (pp. 296–98), Harrison more thoroughly explores this aspect of Reger's thought.

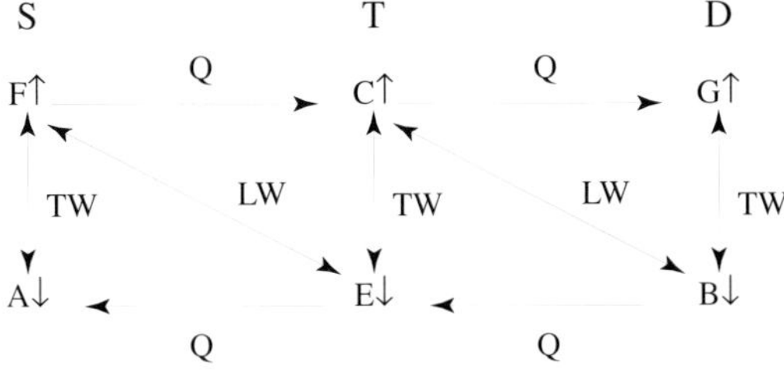

Figure 14.4 A Riemannian map of C major tonality

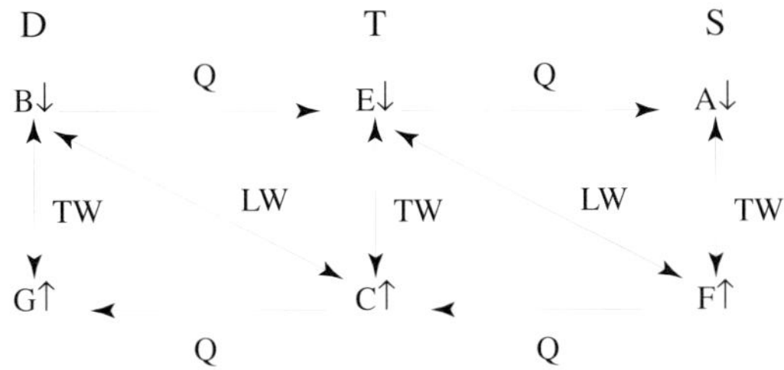

Figure 14.5 A Riemannian map of E minor tonality

major and minor tonalities respectively: the diagrams are developed out of illustrations Riemann presents in *Skizze einer neuen Methode der Harmonielehre* and related diagrams that appear in *Grosse Kompositionslehre*. It is important to stress here that such graphic representations are not simply visual presentations of aspects or features of structure that characterize Riemann transformations. Rather, the topographic models are most fruitfully regarded as representational maps of tonality imagined spatially, and particularly tonality conceived in a space where the distances between the deployed klangs are measured in Riemann's transformational categories. It is only with reference to such maps that Riemannian notions such as chord function and tonality have any concrete relevance.

Each map has two columns of klangs: in place of the perfect fifth, which regulates the horizontal aspect of Oettingen's diagram, Riemann provides *Quintschritt* (abbreviated Q_), a transformation that transposes a klang by the directed interval (mod 8ve) that extends from I to II. In the case of C↑ (C major triad, in standard notation), where C functions as I and G as II, the relevant interval is a perfect fifth up. Accordingly, *Quintschritt* maps C↑ to G↑. In the case of E↓ (A minor in standard notation), where E functions as I and A as II, the relevant interval is a perfect fifth down: hence, *Quintschritt* maps E↓ to A↓ (D minor in standard notation). Alternatively, one could say that

Quintschritt transposes a klang the distance of a *Quint* (perfect fifth) extended in the direction that characterizes the klang in question: up, in the case of major (or over) klangs; down in the case of minor (or under) klangs.

In place of the major third, which regulates the vertical aspect of von Oettingen's diagram, Riemann provides *Terzwechsel* (abbreviated TW), a transformation defined as a composite of *Terzschritt* – which transposes a klang by the interval extending from I to III – followed by *Seitenwechsel* (abbreviated as W), the inversion of a klang around I, which exchanges positive and negative forms of the same *Einheit*, so that it transforms C↑ into C↓, and C↓ into C↑.[20] Taken together, *Terzschritt* and *Seitenwechsel* map C↑ to E↓ via E↑, and E↓ to C↑ via C↓, and are functionally equivalent to what is more commonly called the "relative" relationship.

In each map the top rank of klangs constitute the *Hauptklänge* (primary klangs) of the relevant tonality, the parallel bottom rank the *Nebenklänge* (secondary klangs). The central klang of the primary rank functions as the tonic klang. This function arises from the klang's involvement with both *Quintschritte* in the top rank; accordingly, the function of tonic in this context emerges from the klang's mediation (speaking both visually and dialectically) between the leftmost primary klang (G↑ in Figure 14.4; A↓ in Figure 14.5) and the rightmost primary klang (F↑ in Figure 14.4; B↓ in Figure 14.5). Using Hauptmann's language the tonic both *is* and *has* a *Quintschritt*: its functional centrality is articulated by the two klangs that mark the vertical limits of in each map.

Figures 14.4 and 14.5 include the function labels *S*, *T*, and *D* representing subdominant, tonic, and dominant, respectively. As we have seen, in Riemann's conception of them, these functions have both a dynamic (that is, transformational) and topographical modality. The latter modality on its own is not Riemann's: he himself explicitly traces the origins of this concept of chord function to the work of Fétis.[21] In Riemann's view functions also have a syntactic aspect, since complete harmonic phrases must have the structure T S T D T. Moreover, the syntactical functions may be served not only by the primary klangs in a tonality but also by the secondary klangs (as lexical equivalents) that relate to the primary klangs under *Terzwechsel* or *Leittonwechsel* (abbreviated as LW and defined as a composite of *Leittonschritt* [leading-tone step] – itself the composite of *Quint-* and *Terzschritt* – and *Seitenwechsel*).

Before progressing, it is worthwhile to address an aspect of Riemann's dualism and its interaction with his function theory that has often served as a locus from which to discredit his entire approach. This objection, which, as far as I know, was first articulated around the turn of the twentieth century by the Dutch musicologist Ari Balinfante and revived later on by Carl Dahlhaus, runs something like this, using the

20 *Seitenwechsel* appears in Goetschius's work as "stride relation," defined in his context as "a perfect fifth downward from any major keynote, and upward from any minor keynote, with a change in mode." Goetschius, *Tone-Relations*, p. 114.

21 Riemann, *Harmonielehre*, p. 214.

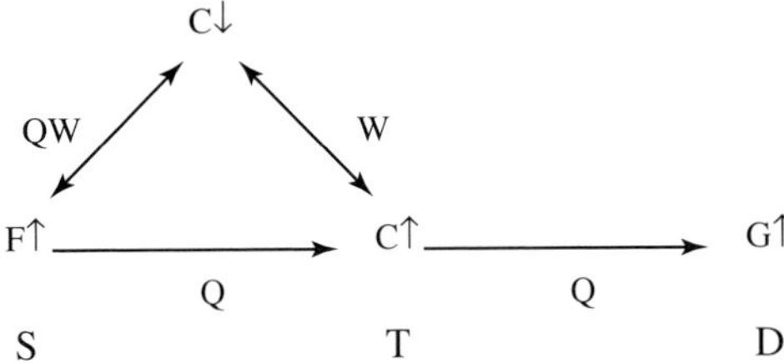

Figure 14.6 A Riemannian map of C major-minor tonality

maps of Figures 14.4 and 14.5 as a context:[22] comparing the two diagrams, one sees that in order to arrange them to match in the terms of harmonic dualism – as the figures certainly do – the deployment of function labels must be reversed. In other words, the argument goes, while Riemann was dualist in chord structure and certain aspects of their interrelations, he was monist in his theory of chord functions. The monist Riemann is the repressed element in this (at least in Balinfante's) account and hence represents Riemann's more basic and fundamental beliefs.

The critique, however, is presumptuous: there is no natural procedure for mapping function assignments onto Riemann's dualist transformations. It still needs to be shown that having function labels and transformation relations line up identically amounts to the proper dualist view. Indeed, it is quite plausible to assert that transformation that maps C↑ onto G↑ – a tonic functioning chord onto dominant functioning chord – *ought* to be the inverse (that is, the structural dual) of the transformation that maps E↓ (as a tonic functioning chord) onto B↓ (a dominant functioning chord) just as the directed interval that extends from I (C) to II (G) in C↑ – namely, a perfect fifth up – is inversely related to the directed interval that extends from I (E) to II (A) in E↓, namely a perfect fifth down. Indeed, such reasoning squares more easily with the dualist klang structure discussed earlier.[23]

Major and minor are just two of the tonal genera defined by Riemann. They may be mixed in systematic ways to produce two further genera, major-minor and minor-major. Figure 14.6 displays the first of these. The primary klangs of the major topography are given and deployed precisely as they are in the (plain) major system. The secondary klangs, which are not provided, are just the secondary klangs of the major

22 Balinfante, "De leer," and Dahlhaus, *Studies*, pp. 51–53. Also see Harrison, *Harmonic Function*, p. 273, n. 37.

23 The Balinfante–Dahlhaus objection to Riemannian dualism interacts suggestively with the more often articulated and less formalized attack generally levelled at Riemann, namely that he sacrificed real musical objects, relations, and experiences in favor of logical consistency. There is a great deal of plain silliness underlying this attack – including anti-intellectualism, and a particularly bone-headed form of empiricism – but in the present context there is an interesting alliance of the concept of "real musical experience" with the concept of function, and coherence and logical consistency with triadic dualism, which are then opposed.

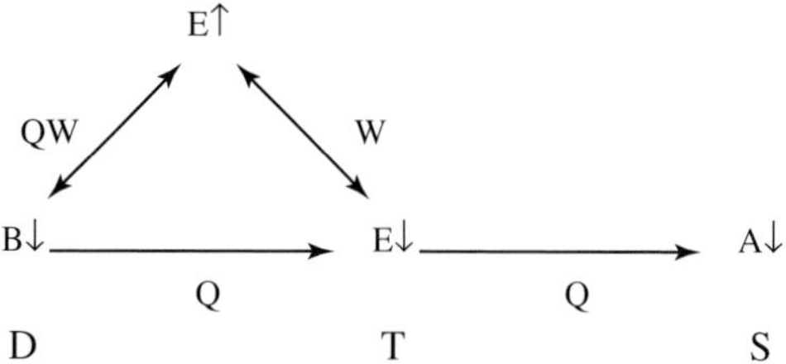

Figure 14.7 A Riemannian map of E minor-major tonality

genus. An additional klang is given in third rank "behind" F↑, namely its *Quintwechsel* relative C↓ (F minor in standard notation), and represents what is commonly called a minor subdominant. The map also measures diagonal distance between C↓ and C↑ as *Seitenwechsel* (W).

Figure 14.7 displays the second genre of Riemann's minor-major tonality. The primary klangs of the minor topography are given and deployed precisely as they are in Figure 14.5. The secondary klangs, which are not provided, are just the secondary klangs of the minor genus. An additional klang is given in third rank "behind" B↓ (E minor in standard notation), namely its *Quintwechsel* relative E↑, and represents what is commonly called harmonic minor. Accordingly, what has changed from major or minor to its relevant mixed genus is the nature of one of the delimiting klangs: F↑ in C major is replaceable by C↓ in C major-minor; B↓ in E minor is replaceable by E↑ in minor-major.

The previous four examples present only a few transformations defined by Riemann. Table 14.1 provides a more complete listing. Since Riemann's own catalogue of transformations changed throughout his publishing career, the table represents a rationalized composite of his various presentations, with an eye to providing enough transformations to map any klang to any other klang.

The top half of the table lists eleven *Schritte*. Each is associated with a particular interval, whose disposition emerges from some internal klang relation or composite of relations. Both major and minor klangs will traverse the same interval under a particular transformation: major klangs will extend that interval upwards, minor klangs downwards. The bottom half of the table lists twelve *Wechsel*. Each is defined as a composite of a *Schritt* defined earlier followed by *Seitenwechsel*. All *Wechsel* are reflexive, which is to say, each serves as its own inverse. Hence, *Quintwechsel* (for instance) maps F↑ to C↓ and C↓ to F↑.

The four tonality maps have two particularly useful and important purposes. First, they each collate the idea of tonal relations as arrangements within imagined geography upon which musical pieces may be seen to traverse. As such, the maps have a direct analytical usefulness when studying pieces with respect to Riemannian transformations. As an example, applying the tonality genus categories to "Im wunderschönen

Table 14.1 *Riemannian Transformations*

I. Schritte

	Transformation	Interval	Klang deployment	Examples
1	*Quintschritt*	P5	I to II	C↑ → G↑; E↓ → A↓
2	*Gegenquintschritt*	P4	II to I	G↑ → C↑; A↓ → E↓
3	*Ganztonschritt*	M2	twice I to II	F↑ → G↑; B↓ → A↓
4	*Gegenganztonschritt*	m7	twice II to I	G↑ → F↑; A↓ → B↓
5	*Terzschritt*	M3	I to III	C↑ → E↑; E↓ → C↓
6	*Sextschritt*	M6	II to III	G↑ → E↑; A↓ → C↓
7	*Leittonschritt*	M7	I to II plus I to III	F↑ → E↑; B↓ → C↓
8	*Gegenleittonschritt*	m2	II to I plus III to I	E↑ → F↑; C↓ → B↓
9	*Gegenterzschritt*	m3	III to II	E↑ → G↑; C↓ → A↓
10	*Gegenterzschritt*	m6	III to I	E↑ → C↑; C↓ → E↓
11	*Tritonusschritt*	d5/a4	twice I to II plus I to III	F↑ → B↑; B↓ → F↓

II. Wechsel

	Transformation	Definition	Examples
12	*Seitenwechsel*	Invert a klang around I	C↑ ↔ C↓
13	*Quintwechsel*	*Quintschritt*, then *Seitenwechsel*	F↑ ↔ C↓
14	*Sextwechsel*	*Sextschritt* then *Seitenwechsel*	G↑ ↔ E↓
15	*Leittonwechsel*	*Leittonscritt* then *Seitenwechsel*	C↑ ↔ B↓
16	*Ganztonwechsel*	*Ganztonschritt*, then *Seitenwechsel*	G↑ ↔ A↓
17	*Terzwechsel*	*Terzschritt*, then *Seitenwechsel*	C↑ ↔ E↓
18	*Tritonuswechsel*	*Tritonusschritt*, then *Seitenwechsel*	F↑ ↔ B↓
19	*Gegenterzwechsel*	*Gegenterzschritt*, then *Seitenwechsel*	C↓ ↔ E↑
20	*Gegenganztonwechsel*	*Gegenganztonschritt*, then *Seitenwechsel*	C↓ ↔ D↑
21	*Gegensextwechsel*	*Gegensextschritt*, then *Seitenwechsel*	E↑ ↔ G↓
22	*Gegenquintwechsel*	*Gegenquintschritt*, then *Seitenwechsel*	G↑ ↔ C↓
23	*Gegenleittonwechsel*	*Gegenleittonschritt*, then *Seitenwechsel*	C↓ ↔ B↑

Monat Mai" from Schumann's *Dichterliebe*, we can assert that the piece presents in turn the following four tonal genera: C♯ minor-major, A major, F♯ minor-major, D major-minor. Moreover, the transformations given in Table 14.1 can be shown to have individual tonal value, by referring them to trajectories on one or more of the topographies.

Secondly, the topographies form the basis from which to understand Riemann's theory of dissonant (non-triadic) events, which derive ultimately from his conceptualization of tonality – that is, his four modes of tonality – along the lines presented in Figures 14.4–14.7.

Dissonant klangs

Dissonance in Riemann's view arises from the "disruption of the unity of klang structure and klang meaning by foreign elements."[24] This disruption is carried out in two ways: the combination of one klang (or its elements) with another; and the alteration of a klang pitch affecting the constituent major third or minor third.

The first of these is of special concern here. Dissonant klangs in this class articulate the tonic or central klang of a particular topography delimiting the relevant topography's boundaries. These chords may usefully be further divided into two categories: dissonant chords that articulate the horizontal boundaries of a topography, which is to say the boundaries within the topographic rows; and chords that articulate the vertical boundaries of a topography, or the extent of the constituent columns. The first of these two classes vary significantly across the four tonal genera; the second does not.

The foremost of these combinations involve the two primary klangs on either side of the tonic klang. These two klangs, the primary dominant and subdominant functioning ones, are all that are needed to provide a sense of the central klang – which mediates the lateral two primary klangs both spatially (or topographically) and transformationally (or dynamically) – as tonic functioning. When the two lateral primary chords are presented as a single, dissonant chord they have the same effect.

In the major and minor topographies presented in Figures 14.4 and 14.5, the relevant dissonant combinations are generated by the transformation *Gegenganztonschritt*, which in each topography maps the leftmost primary klang to the rightmost, and the rightmost secondary klang to the leftmost. In the case of C major, then, *Gegenganztonschritt* adds F↑ to G↑ in the primary rank and B↓ to A↓ in the secondary rank. The same combinations arise within the E minor topography of Figure 14.5. By suppressing various pitches in the combined klangs, Riemann generates a series of non-triadic structures. Accordingly, the combination of [G B D] and [F A C], which articulate the boundaries of the primary rank in C major and the secondary rank in E minor, can yield G^{7}, G^{9}, and B° (in standard, Weberian notation). Correspondingly, the combination of [E G B] and [D F A], which articulates the boundaries of the primary rank in E minor and the secondary rank in C major, can yield $B^{\phi 7}$, G^{9}, and B°.

The boundaries of the primary ranks of the two mixed genera given in Figures 14.6 and 14.7 are defined not by *Gegenganztonschritt* but by *Gegenquintwechsel*: since all *Wechsel* are their own inverses *Gegenquintwechsel* maps both the leftmost klang to the rightmost, and the rightmost to the leftmost. In the case of C major-minor, the transformation combines G↑ and C↓. Accordingly, by suppressing various pitches, the combination of [G B D] and [F Ab C] can yield G^{7}, $G^{7\flat 9}$, $B^{\circ 7}$, $D^{\phi 7}$, $B^{\circ 7\flat 9}$, and $B^{\phi 7}$ (again, in standard, Weberian notation). Correspondingly, the combination of [E G♯ B] and [D F A], the lateral limits of E minor-major, can yield $B^{\phi 7}$, $G\sharp^{\circ 7\flat 9}$, $G\sharp^{\circ 7}$, E^{7}, $E^{7\flat 9}$, and $G\sharp^{\phi 7}$.

24 Riemann, *Harmonielehre*, p. 138.

The vertical limits of the tonal genera are defined, according to Riemann, by *Terzwechsel* and *Leittonwechsel*. Combining *Terzwechsel*-related chords in C major(-minor) yields various "minor seventh" chords: A | C E | G; D | F A | C; and E | G B | D. Combining *Leittonwechsel*-related klangs in those genera produces F major 7 (F | A C | E) and C major 7 (C | E G | B).

The chords discussed here do not exhaust all possible dissonant structures in Riemann's catalogue. But they do constitute the major classes of such chords and illustrate Riemann's and Oettingen's conception of dissonant structures and their role. This approach to seventh chords seems to have become widespread, surviving – to the embarrassment of some – even in Schenker's *Harmonielehre*. In spite of its current discredited status, such an approach to dissonance seems especially suggestive in the context of atonal works of Schoenberg, Webern, Berg, and others, and may provide particularly fruitful access to certain harmonic aspects of that music.

Closing remarks

Almost all of Riemann's theoretical conceits have current advocates. The use of function theory (in some form or another) is widespread. Siegmund Levarie has written on the benefits of harmonic dualism, although leaning much more heavily on Goethe's *Naturwissenschaft* than on Riemann or Oettingen. Daniel Harrison, as already mentioned, has proposed his own revised theory of harmonic dualism (see p. 460 above, n. 7). And David Lewin has revived and further developed – with special reference to group theory – Riemann's transformational categories (see **Chapter 10, pp. 295–96**). However, these three aspects of Riemann's tonal theory are rarely as integrated as they are in Riemann's own thought. Harmonic dualism is altogether evaded in current applications of functionalism and in Lewin's reconstruction of transformational structures; Levarie's harmonic dualism exists outside of the context of functionalism or klang transformations.

A growing number of researchers in North America find themselves engaged in some way or another with some aspects of Lewin's original articulation of transformational Riemannian theory, in particular, Richard Cohn, Brian Hyer, and John Clough. Papers presented at a recent symposium concerning neo-Riemannian theory have appeared in a special issue of the *Journal of Music Theory* (vol. 42, 1999). The work carried out in this symposium is especially broad in scope, and includes Carol Krumhansl's investigations of certain neo-Riemannian conceits along purely music-psychological lines. The recent work of John Clough, Jack Douthett, Norman Carey, and David Clampitt integrates Lewin's and Cohn's work with an already existing tradition of examining the purely structural characteristics of the diatonic collection, the pentatonic collection, set class 3–11, and other tonally meaningful set-classes, as well as extending the discussion from Cohn's three parsimonius transformations to include the entire *Schritt/ Wechsel* group. Others – I have in mind here Edward Gollin, David Kopp, and Michael Mooney – continue to revise and extend neo-Riemannian theory, often with more emphasis on the work of Riemann and Oettingen themselves, and with a particular interest in concrete music-analytical situations.

Bibliography

Primary sources

Hauptmann, M. *Die Natur der Harmonik und der Metrik*, Leipzig, Breitkopf und Härtel, 1853; trans. W. Heathcote as *The Nature of Harmony and Metre*, London, S. Sonnenschein, 1888

"Ein Brief M. Hauptmann's über Helmholtz's 'Tonempfindungen,'" *Allgemeine Musikalische Zeitung* 1/40 (1863), cols. 669–74

Helmholtz, H. *Die Lehre von den Tonempfindungen als physiologischer Grundlage für die Theorie der Musik*, (1863) 4th edn., Braunschweig, F. Vieweg, 1877; trans. A. J. Ellis as *On the Sensations of Tone as a Physiological Basis for the Theory of Music*, 2nd edn., London, Longman and Green, 1885; reprint, New York, Dover, 1954

Oettingen, A. von, *Harmoniesystem in Dualer Entwicklung: Studien zur Theorie der Musik*, Leipzig, W. Gläser, 1866

Riemann, H. *Skizze einer Neuen Methode der Harmonielehre*, Leipzig, Breitkopf und Härtel, 1880

Handbuch der Harmonielehre (1887), 3rd edn., Leipzig, Breitkopf und Härtel, 1898

"Ideen zu einer 'Lehre von den Tonvorstellungen,'" *Jahrbuch der Musikbibliothek Peters* 21 (1914), pp. 1–26; trans. R. Wason and E. West Marvin as "Riemann's 'Ideen zu einer Lehre von den Tonvorstellungen': An Annotated Translation," *JMT* 36 (1992), pp. 69–117

Grosse Kompositionslehre, 2 vols., Berlin, W. Spemann, 1902–03.

"Unsere Konservatorien," in *Präludien und Studien*, vol. I, Leipzig, H. Seemann, 1895, pp. 22–33; facs. Hildesheim, G. Olms, 1967; trans. E. D. Bomberger as "'Our Conservatories,' from *Präludium und Studien* (1895) by Hugo Riemann," *The Bulletin of Historical Research in Music Education* 15 (1994), pp. 220–35

Vereinfachte Harmonielehre, oder die Lehre von den Tonalen Funktionen der Akkorde, London, Augener, 1893; trans. H. Bewerung as *Harmony Simplified*, London, Augener, 1896

Zarlino, G. *Le istitutioni harmoniche*, Venice, Franceschi, 1558

Secondary sources

Balinfante, A. "De leer der tonale functien in conflict met die der polaire tegenstelling," *Orgaan van de Vereeniging van Muziek-Onderwijzers en -Onderwijzeressen* 4/9 (1904), pp. 1–2

Bernstein, D. "Schoenberg contra Riemann: Stufen, Regions, Verwandtschaft, and the Theory of Tonal Function," *Theoria* 6 (1992), pp. 23–53

Burnham, S. "Method and Motivation in History of Harmonic Theory," *MTS* 14 (1992), pp. 1–14

Cohn, R. "Neo-Riemannian Operations, Parsimonious Trichords, and their *Tonnetz* Representations," *JMT* 41 (1997), pp. 1–66

"Maximally Smooth Cycles, Hexatonic Systems, and the Analysis of Late-Romantic Triadic Progressions," *Music Analysis* 15/1 (1996), pp. 9–40

"Introduction to Neo-Riemannian Theory: A Survey and a Historical Perspective," *JMT* 42 (1999), pp. 167–80

Dahlhaus, C. "War Zarlino Dualist?," *Die Musikforschung* (1957), pp. 286–90

Untersuchungen über die Entstehung der harmonischen Tonalität, Kassel, Bärenreiter, 1968; trans. R. Gjerdingen as *Studies on the Origin of Harmonic Tonality*, Princeton University Press, 1990

Goetschius, P. *The Theory and Practice of Tone-Relations*, New York, G. Schirmer, 1917

Gollin, E. "Some Aspects of Three-Dimensional *Tonnetze*," *JMT* 42 (1998), pp. 195–206

Harrison, D. *Harmonic Function in Chromatic Music: A Renewed Dualist Theory and an Account of Its Precedents*, University of Chicago Press, 1994

Hyer, B. "Tonal Intuitions in *Tristan und Isolde*," Ph.D. diss., Yale University (1989)

"Reimag(in)ing Riemann," *JMT* 39 (1995), pp. 101–38

Klumpenhouwer, H. "Some Remarks on the Use of Riemann Transformations," *Music Theory Online* 0/9 (1994)

Kopp, D. "A Comprehensive Theory of Chromatic Mediant Relations in Mid-Nineteenth-Century Music," Ph.D. diss., Brandeis University (1995)

"The Function of Function," *Music Theory Online* 1/3 (1995)

Krumhansl, C. "Perceived Triad Distance: Evidence supporting the Psychological Reality of Neo-Riemannian Transformations," *JMT* 42 (1999), pp. 265–81.

Lerdahl, F. "Tonal Pitch Spaces," *MP* 5 (1988), pp. 315–50

Levarie, S. "Musical Polarity: Major and Minor," *International Journal of Musicology* 1 (1992), pp. 29–45

Lewin, D. "A Formal Theory of Generalized Tonal Functions," *JMT* 26 (1982), pp. 23–60

Generalized Musical Intervals and Transformations, New Haven, Yale University Press, 1987

"Some Notes on Analyzing Wagner: *The Ring* and *Parsifal*," *19th Century Music* 16 (1992), pp. 49–58

Music Form and Transformations: 4 Analytic Essays, New Haven, Yale University Press, 1993

"Cohn Functions," *JMT* 40 (1996), pp. 181–216

Maegaard, J. "Harmonisk analyse af det 19. arhundredes musik: En teoretisk overvejelse," *Musik & Forskning* 15 (1989–90), pp. 79–110; reprint in *Zur harmonischen Analyse der Musik des 19. Jahrhunderts: Eine Theoretische Erwagung*, Wiesbaden, Breitkopf und Härtel, 1990, pp. 61–86

McClelland, C. *State, Society and University in Germany 1700–1914*, Cambridge University Press, 1980

Mooney, M. K. "'Table of Relations' and Music Psychology in Hugo Riemann's Chromatic Theory," Ph.D. diss., Columbia University (1996)

Munnich, R. "Von Entwicklung der Riemannschen Harmonielehre und ihrem Verhältnis zu Oettingen und Stumpf," trans. R. Wason, *Indiana Theory Review* 16 (1995), pp. 197–222

Seidel, W. "Ältere und neuere Musik: Über Hugo Riemanns Bild der Musikgeschichte", in *Alte Musik im 20. Jahrhundert: Wandlungen und Formen ihrer Rezeption*, ed. G. Schubert, Mainz, Schott, 1995, pp. 30–38

Wason, R. W. *Viennese Harmonic Theory from Albrechtsberger to Schenker and Schoenberg*, University of Rochester Press, 1995

"Progressive Harmonic Theory in the Mid-nineteenth Century," *Journal of Musicological Research* 8 (1988), pp. 55–90

Wuensche, G. "Hugo Riemann's Musical Theory," *Studies in Music* 2 (1977), pp. 108–24

IIIB COMPOSITIONAL THEORY

· 15 ·

Organum – *discantus* – *contrapunctus* in the Middle Ages

SARAH FULLER

"Anyone who aspires to understand *contrapunctus* should write down the following matters."[1] So begins a short manual on counterpoint from the early fourteenth century that circulated widely under the authority of Jehan des Murs but is best identified (anonymously) by its incipit "Quilibet affectans." The theorist's remarks are straightforward indeed.[2] *Contrapunctus* observes a strictly note-against-note texture. Only select intervals – some perfect in nature (unisons, fifths, octaves), others imperfect (minor third, major third, and major sixth) – are admitted between the voices, as are their octave compounds. The natural sequel to any authorized interval is that interval from the opposite category closest in size: minor third (imperfect) after unison (perfect); octave (perfect) after major sixth (imperfect). Although characterized as "natural," these contiguous progressions are by no means mandatory. The motion of the cantus, the pre-existent melody to which another line is joined in counterpoint, may well prompt other intervallic successions. Within the latitude this affords, no perfect interval may be reiterated in direct succession, but any imperfect interval may be followed by another, or by several, of the same kind. Aside from such parallels, the two voices ought usually to proceed in contrary directions, so that when the cantus ascends, the new line descends, and vice versa. All *contrapunctus* must begin and end with perfect consonance.

The compact array of precepts set forth in "Quilibet affectans" hardly seems to qualify as theory. It reads as a set of rudimentary guidelines for production of correct note-against-note polyphony in two parts. Yet the opening declaration that the path to understanding *contrapunctus* is to *write* these rules (rather than, say, to sing or to compose model progressions or phrases) does appear to claim some theoretical status for what follows (as does one stray reference to Boethius). Although the implied author neither explains the principles behind the precepts nor defines distinctions such as that between perfect and imperfect intervals, the guidelines do set parameters for grammatical fourteenth-century counterpoint. Little sense of actual participants emerges from this treatise; as necessary, the parts are identified by function as either tenor and cantus,

1 *CS* 3, p. 59.
2 This "theorist" probably represents a teaching tradition rather than an individual author. See remarks on authorship below.

or cantus and *discantus*. A companion treatise, "Cum notum sit omnibus cantoribus," paired with "Quilibet affectans" in several manuscript sources, does specifically invoke singers and their actions in its more extended treatment of *contrapunctus*.[3] Prior to discanting above plainchant, the theorist says, a singer must master the realm of *cantus planus* (which encompasses both theory and practice) and must temper his voice so that it is not too assertive or loud. The nine formal propositions that anchor the treatise include several references to singing, and even the definition of *contrapunctus* as "simply to place (*ponere*) or to make (*facere*) a point or a note against [another] point or note," and as "the foundation of discant" invokes action on the part of the participants or creators.[4] The dual verbs, *ponere vel facere*, and dual nouns, *punctus* and *nota*, of this definition implicitly sweep both extemporaneous singing and notated composition within his field of reference, but the theorist draws no explicit distinction between the two. Like other medieval writings on music in two or more parts, "Cum notum sit" is to be regarded not as a treatise on "composition" but rather as a treatise on "musical production": how to produce another voice or voices upon a given cantus according to conventional stylistic norms and voice-leading constraints.

The two modest early fourteenth-century manuals just reviewed belong to a medieval European tradition of writing on music in two or more parts – polyphony as we have come to call it – that begins in the late ninth century and continues into the late fifteenth century and beyond. Much of this writing is anonymous, and some treatises have such an uncertain pedigree or so complex a transmission history that the individualistic concept of authorship does not appropriately apply to them. They reflect, rather, some (often collective) tradition of instruction. For convenience within this chapter, the term "theorist" is used generically to designate the generator of a theoretical work, whether a teaching tradition or an actual or supposed single author.

The medieval phase of polyphonic theory seems on the surface more rent by discontinuities than bound by common threads. One discontinuity is that of musical idiom: organum in *symphoniae* (perfect consonances of fourth, fifth, and octave) as described in the *Musica* and the *Scolica enchiriadis* is in decided contrast with *musica mensurabilis* cultivated in the thirteenth century, which in turn stands distinctively apart from fourteenth-century *contrapunctus* (simple and elaborated) with its expanded horizons of sonority and (when elaborated) mensuration. These diverse polyphonic idioms, along with various vernacular extempore practices, invite diverse verbal expositions of principle and instructions for production. Another discontinuity is that of theoretical perspective: extant writings range from informal teaching manuals and bare summaries of practical precepts to scholarly treatises concerned with formal examination of principles entailed in pairing one line of melody with another or in proceeding from one interval to another. Although, for example, "Quilibet affectans" and Jacques of Liège's "Speculum musicae" are approximately coeval, a vast gulf separates them in

3 *CS* 3, pp. 60–62. 4 Ibid., p. 60.

terms of the intellectual traditions within which their authors write and the audiences toward which they are directed. (Even to speak of an intellectual tradition for "Quilibet affectans" seems to elevate it unduly.) The differing purposes of theorists reflect multifarious ways (some more intellectual, some more pedagogical or performance oriented) of coming to terms with polyphony. A third complicating rift arises from discrepancies between principles said to govern polyphonic production that are articulated by theorists, and actual characteristics of polyphonic music notated in extant sources. Some discrepancies arguably stem from a theorist's allegiance to established axioms that can be rationally grounded, while others would seem to originate in varied cultural practices that span a continuum from improvised polyphony rendered by generalized rules at one end to notated creations of accomplished composers or singer-composers at the other. Indeed, some theorists make clear that older ways of producing polyphony continued as performance traditions even as newer musical idioms claimed priority in many writings on polyphony. The cleric Elias Salomo describes discanting in parallel fifths, fourths, and octaves as a custom current in the late thirteenth century, while Jacques of Liège, writing in the first quarter of the fourteenth century, begins a chapter on intervals to be used in discant with an example in parallel fourths and fifths.[5] The newer idioms, fraught with complexities that claimed theoretical attention, by no means eliminated customary vernacular practices of improvised polyphonic singing; rather, they constituted challenging frontiers for particularly skilled singers. Some theorists attended to new fashions in polyphony, while others continued to describe traditional ways of generating music in two or more parts. Discontinuities of such magnitude indicate that medieval theorizing about polyphony cannot be said to have followed a uniform path through discrete developmental stages but responded in complex ways to specific cultural practices and intellectual contexts.

Despite such significant discontinuities and complexities, medieval accounts of how multiple strands of sound may legitimately relate to one another do possess certain commonalities. Departing from the premise of a given cantus or a (usually two-note) segment of an imagined cantus, the accounts explain how a second part may be joined to the first. In the process they disclose the controls that govern the added voice and, to varying degrees, the polyphonic complex as a whole. The stipulated controls normally entail:

- designation of intervals permitted between the parts
- indications of how an added voice may move in relation to the pre-existent cantus
- specification of which interval successions are allowed, preferred, or prohibited
- restrictions on intervals allowed or recommended at beginnings or ends of primary temporal units (mensural units, phrases, entire melodies).

5 For Elias Salomo, see *GS* 3, pp. 57–61; for Jacques of Liège, *Speculum musicae*, Book VII, pp. 11–12.

The accounts adopt a level of generality that permits practitioners to respond in standard ways to an infinity of concrete musical situations and that supposes a background of theoretical principle which may or may not be articulated. If additional parts or voices are mentioned, they are subsumed within the same regulative principles as govern the first pair. Controls of the sort outlined above constitute common ground between the anonymous authors of the *Musica enchiriadis* and of "Quilibet affectans," despite a separation of more than five centuries and the very different generating principles and profiles of polyphony rendered from their instructions.

One way of viewing the multi-faceted, fluctuating domain of polyphonic theory in the Middle Ages is to concentrate on three defining phases in its history, phases distinguished in the treatises by the terms organum, *discantus*, and *contrapunctus*. The organum singled out here is not the held-note style of thirteenth-century Parisian polyphony, but the singing-in-*symphoniae* of the earliest Western treatises to describe multi-voice singing. *Discantus* corresponds fairly closely with the idiom of thirteenth-century discant clausulas, conductus, and motets. *Contrapunctus* is the theoretically conceived note-against-note foundation for more elaborate polyphony (motets, cantilenas) in the fourteenth and fifteenth centuries. Indeterminacies in chronology and provenance of the treatises (among other factors) preclude a comprehensive account of these three phases here. The aim is, rather, to portray significant theoretical issues and pedagogical approaches as represented in a few selected treatises and to communicate something of the diversity in intellectual orientations and pedagogical aims evident in the historical record.

Organum (c. 850 – c. 1030)

The earliest theoretical accounts of multi-voiced singing appear in two widely-circulated treatises on music fundamentals, the *Musica* and the *Scolica enchiriadis*, which have been dated to sometime within the last half of the ninth century.[6] Both introduce singing in two or more parts under the rubric of *symphoniae* and their properties and both mention it as a familiar, not a novel, phenomenon. Having defined a class of privileged intervals called *symphoniae* – three simple (fourth, fifth, and octave) and three compound (octave-plus-fourth, octave-plus-fifth, double octave) – the authors explain how the *symphoniae* control simultaneous singing of different pitches "which we call two-voiced (diaphonic) song, or, customarily, organum."[7] The term organum applies particularly to singing at the fourth and the fifth; the other symphonic intervals enter

6 Phillips states circumspectly that "either or both could have been written in the middle of the [ninth] century" ("*Musica* and *Scolica Enchiriadis*," p. 516; discussion pp. 9–18 and 511–16), while Torkewitz inclines to the last quarter of the century, with possible authorship by Abbot Hoger of Werden ("Zur Entstehung"). See also Erickson, *Musica enchiriadis*, pp. xxi–xxii, and in the present volume, **Chapter 5, pp. 153–57**; and **Chapter 11, pp. 323–31**.
7 *Musica enchiriadis*, p. 21. Page numbers here and elsewhere refer to the standard English-language translation by Erickson unless otherwise noted.

in through doublings of the principal or the organal voice, or both, at the octave above or below. The organum described is essentially a special performance practice, a way of elaborating entire chants through duplication (or partial duplication) at a consonant interval below a given melody, the principal voice.[8] The practice is admired, as one of the theorists comments, for its smooth concords and sweet sound.[9] The maximum texture illustrated in *Musica enchiriadis* consists of four lines (the principal and organal voices, plus octave doublings of each) that span two octaves, but the theorist allows up to six simultaneous melodic lines delivered by men's and boys' voices or by a mix of voices and instruments.[10] Because the added voice or voices follow closely the given chant according to a primary interval, this organum is easily extemporized; hence the *Enchiriadis* theorists offer only a few brief illustrations, none longer than a phrase or two, and most on melodies from the daily Offices, not the Mass. Extension of this performance practice to entire chants is assumed.

Given the Daseian notation adopted in the *Enchiriadis* treatises (a notation that replicates a standard tone–semitone–tone tetrachord to form an eighteen-tone pitch system), parallel singing at the fifth (diapente) remains unalterably in the groove of perfect fifths (Example 15.1).[11] Perfect octave doublings are achieved by consonant response in "equal-sounding" pitches.[12] Organum or diaphony at the fourth (diatessaron) is more problematic because the added voice cannot consistently parallel the cantus in perfect fourths without departing from the stipulated pitch system. The *Musica enchiriadis* explains the problem as the "inconsonant" tritone between the *deuterus* pitch of any tetrachord and the *tritus* that lies four notes below it (see **Figure 11.5, p. 324**). Because of this, the organal voice in this type of diaphony may not descend lower than the *tetrardus* pitch situated at or below the end or beginning point of a phrase.[13] Owing to this tritone prohibition, the added voice often sustains a *tetrardus* pitch and so produces intervals of a second or a third against the cantus. It usually then joins the cantus in unison at phrase end (see Example 15.2). The *Scolica enchiriadis* offers a different rationale for irregularities in organum at the fourth: because the organal voice cannot replicate the trope or mode of the principal voice, it cannot parallel that voice rigorously but must follow its own "natural law."[14] The *Scolica* theorist neither specifies the nature of this law nor gives any concrete instructions for behavior of the organal voice (although its examples show sustained tones and unison cadences congruent with the practice reported in the *Musica enchiriadis*). Discrepancy between theoretical explanations for organum at the fourth in these two treatises gives the impression that the writers are trying to integrate an existing practice into a newly framed theoretical universe so as to justify it with principled rationales.

Despite its basis in a *symphonia*, organum at the fourth introduces intervals (unisons,

8 *Musica enchiriadis*, p. 30. 9 Ibid., p. 22. 10 Ibid.
11 On Daseian notation, see **Chapter 11, p. 327–28**.
12 *Musica enchiriadis*, pp. 14–17 and 92–93. Duality between a fifth-based pitch system and an octave-based one is endemic to the *Enchiriadis* treatises (see **Chapter 11, pp. 325–26**). 13 Ibid., p. 27.
14 Ibid., p. 61.

Example 15.1 *Scolica enchiriadis*, composite form of organum at the fifth with organal voice doubled at the octave above

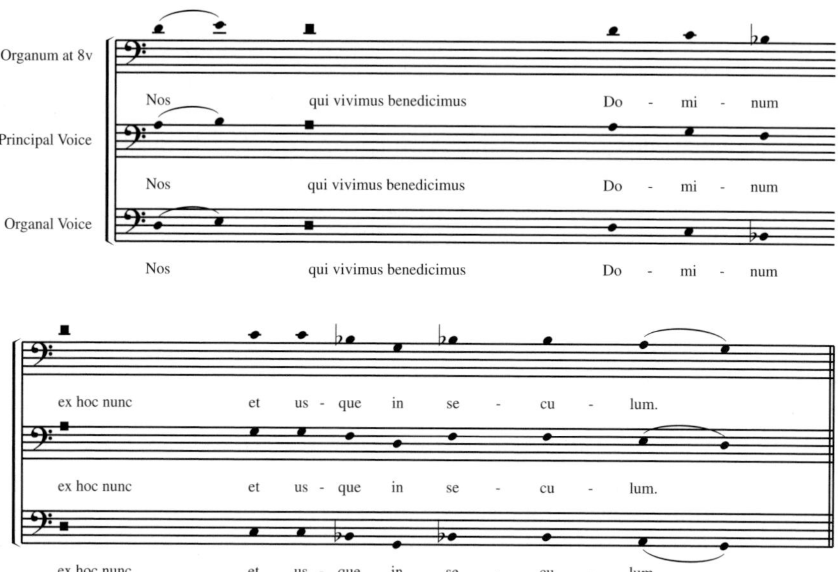

seconds, thirds) that are not *symphoniae*. The *Musica enchiriadis* theorist recognizes the absence of a proper organal response in portions of such organum (e.g., the first three syllables of Example 15.2), but he, like his *Scolica* colleague, holds to the fourth as guarantor of symphonic integrity in this manner of singing. The non-symphonic intervals that occur periodically are rationalized as the byproduct of standard "laws" (avoidance of the tritone, adjustment for the mode). They neither call the prevailing *symphonia* into question nor require individual assessment. As organum changed character, and the organal voice became emancipated from trailing a pre-existent chant in parallel, principled justification for pitch pairings emerged as a challenging theoretical problem.[15]

Guido of Arezzo sidesteps this problem by dispensing with systematic argument and directing his account of diaphony (organum) toward the *usus* or practice familiar to him. In Chapters 18 and 19 of his *Micrologus* (c. 1026–28), he describes two different practices, strict (*durus*) and flexible (*mollis*), that essentially correspond to the two types (at the fifth and at the fourth) known from the *Musica* and *Scolica enchiriadis* to have been practiced at least 125 years earlier. Guido mentions the congenial and smooth blending of symphonic intervals in strict organum, but spends most of his time on the flexible or pleasant kind of diaphony.[16] In contrast to the *Enchiriadis* approach with its emphasis on the *symphoniae* and on underlying principles, his account dwells on prac-

15 On this problem, see Fuller, "Theoretical Foundations."

16 *Micrologus*, pp. 77–82.

Example 15.2 *Musica enchiriadis*, organum at the fourth

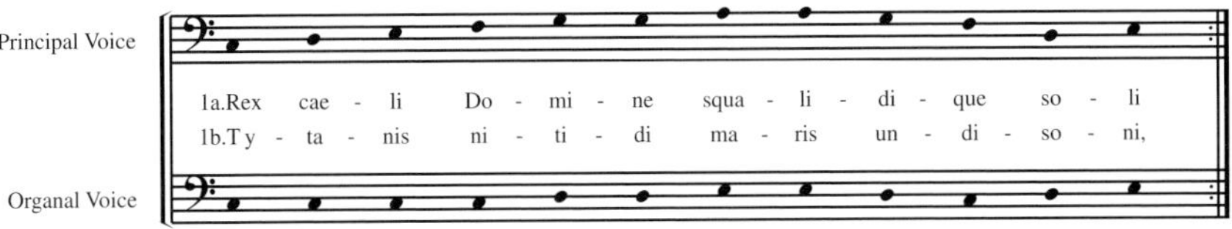

tical rules of execution delivered as axioms. Flexible organum admits only four intervals (fourth, major and minor thirds and whole tone), of which the fourth holds the highest, the minor third the lowest rank. The organal voice, situated below the principal, must never descend below a *tritus* pitch (defined as F or C, possible finals of the *tritus* modes) unless the cantus itself descends to a lower range. In that case it has the option of descending or remaining fixed on *tritus*. At phrase endings the organal voice will often converge to unison with the cantus, a maneuver called *occursus* that is plainly cadential in nature.[17] Guido's diaphonic realization of the Matins antiphon "Ipsi soli" shows prevailing parallel fourths, the *tritus*, C, as boundary tone, and *occursus* only in the first and final phrases (Example 15.3). Guido offers no considered reasons why *tritus* pitches should be boundary tones or why the fourth heads the hierarchy of intervals. His orientation toward instruction of young boys would seem to account on the one hand for his avoidance of ponderous theoretical explanations in the chapters on organum and on the other hand for his precise instructions about acceptable (and unacceptable) procedures.

Given the tendency of the organum theorists (even those as oriented toward local custom as Guido) to prefer orderly, rule-bound accounts of musical practices, it would not be surprising if actual traditions of *symphonic* organum performance diverged from written precepts. We can glimpse such traditions only through the prism of notated music such as the Winchester organa of c. 1000 (the earliest substantial repertory of polyphony to survive in writing) and a few extant shards of continental organa. (The fact that these organa were written down at all already distances them from the sphere of routine improvised practice.) The notated pieces, whose non-staff notation requires

17 Ibid., pp. 78–79. Note that since a unison entails no pitch differentiation between voices, Guido does not consider it to be an "interval," and hence does not itemize it among intervals employed in flexible organum.

Example 15.3 *Micrologus*, phrase endings in diaphony (antiphon "Ipsi soli").

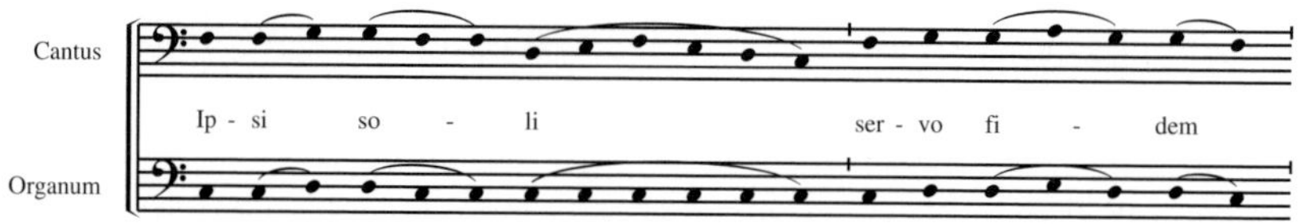

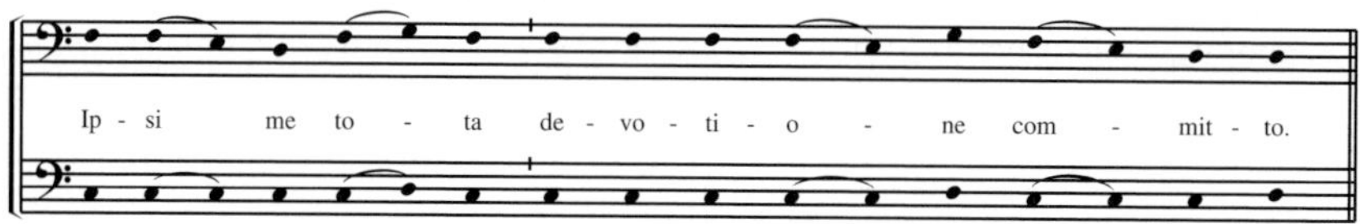

significant decoding, reveal much in common with organum at the fourth, but manifest a wider range of choices for the organal voice than is allowed by the theorists.[18] Taken together, the latitude in the Winchester organa, the revision in some manuscripts of the *Enchiriadis* passages on organum, and Guido's insistence that he is reporting on local usage (*more quo nos utimur*) all suggest that the earliest organum theory we possess presents a somewhat idealized, theoretically coherent version of a performance practice that in actuality was rather more fluid than it is represented to be.[19] But the resemblances are marked, and theorists and the Winchester scribe do seem to share a similar aesthetic – the former viewing organum as a sweet-sounding adornment to chant, the latter characterizing certain organa as *melliflua* (sweet-sounding) and *pulcherrima* (very beautiful).

In the later eleventh and twelfth centuries, polyphonic practice asserts its nature of diaphony – and divergence between voices receives more emphasis in formal definitions. The theorists still describe and illustrate organum in terms of the fourth and fifth as primary intervals, but octave and unison are liberally intermixed. The organal voice moves to a more exposed position above the pre-existent chant, and it inclines to match cantus pitches with varying intervals rather than cleaving to either fourth or fifth as primary. Such changes (particularly the abandonment of parallelism as a guiding principle) forced theorists to come up with new rationales to explain and control polyphonic practice. Much of what modern observers call the "new organum theory" took its point of departure from Guido's *Micrologus* and redirected elements of his theory (such as the doctrine of affinity) in creative ways.[20]

18 On this point, see Fuller, "Early Polyphony," pp. 503–08; Rankin, "Winchester Polyphony."
19 For reworkings of *Enchiriadis* material, see the short treatises in *Musica et Scolica Enchiriadis* (Schmid edn., pp. 205–12, 214–17, 222–23, 229–32).
20 These treatises are collected in *Ad organum faciendum*. For amplification of these remarks see Fuller, "Theoretical Foundations"; Reckow, "Guido's Theory of Organum."

Musica mensurabilis/discantus (1200s)

Perhaps as early as the middle of the thirteenth century, in the region of Paris, learned musicians began using the term *musica mensurabilis* to designate the domain of polyphonic theory and characterize the advanced polyphony of the day.[21] The new term is indicative of instructional innovations that present rhythm and its notation as a central aspect of two-voiced music. Besides detailing durational units and notational figures and explaining how to interpret notational figures in context, the new treatises on polyphony draw distinctions among multi-voiced genres (discant, organum *in speciali*, copula, etc.) based largely on characteristic rhythmic qualities. The focus on issues of duration and notation as essential to discant and basic to generic distinctions within the general sphere of organum (polyphony) gave rise to a distinct dividing line between *musica mensurabilis* and *musica plana* (plainchant and its theory), complementary terms that gained common currency by the last decades of the thirteenth century. An important consequence of this division is that the eight ecclesiastical modes remained under the aegis of *musica plana*. In organum treatises, *modus* referred to rhythmic modes. Among species under the genus organum (discant, copula, and *organum in speciali* for John of Garland), discant receives the major share of attention, for its theory encompasses the system of rhythmic modes as well as notation and vertical relationships between voices.

Prominent in the emerging culture of *musica mensurabilis* is a proclivity for preserving polyphony in notation that is witnessed by a substantial number of manuscripts, including the three great codices that contain the *Magnus liber organi*, and by the presence therein of conductus, discant clausulas, and motets. The advent of specialized notation for rhythmically controlled polyphony spurred theoretical writings oriented toward decoding and understanding that polyphony, whether notated or extemporized. For the Parisian orbit, a key document is *De mensurabili musica*, a treatise attributed to John of Garland in a compilation from the last quarter of the thirteenth century. Its teaching set a pattern for later theorists (Franco of Cologne, the English monk whom Coussemaker published as Anonymous IV, and the St. Emmeram anonymous among others).[22]

In defining discant as "the sounding [together] of diverse melodies according to

21 Just when this occurred cannot be pinpointed owing to uncertainties in dating and tangled transmission histories of extant treatises. For more on the situation, see Haas, "Die Musiklehre im 13. Jahrhundert"; Pinegar, "On Rhythmic Modes."

22 The compilation (made in Paris) is Jerome of Moravia's *Tractatus de musica*. Haas places John of Garland's treatise "after 1250" ("Die Musiklehre," p. 99). Pinegar questions whether John of Garland is responsible for the earliest stages of the theory; she prefers to speak of "Garlandian" theory ("Textual and Conceptual Relationships," pp. 96–102). In the interests of concision, John of Garland will be named as author here without further comment. The most recent attempt to locate John of Garland chronologically (Whitcomb, "Teachers, Booksellers") lends support to Pinegar but argues (plausibly) from circumstance rather than from firm evidence. The writings of John concerning the rhythmic modes are discussed in **Chapter 21, pp. 628–31**.

Concords			Discords		
Perfect	Medial	Imperfect	Imperfect	Medial	Perfect
Unison, octave	fifth, fourth	major third, minor third	major sixth, minor seventh	whole tone, minor sixth	semitone, tritone, major seventh

Figure 15.1 Concord/discord hierarchy from John of Garland, *De mensurabili musica*

[rhythmic] mode and to mutual correspondence in length through concords," John of Garland stresses melodic independence between the voices (*diversi cantus*) which are coordinated through temporal equivalence and intervallic relationships of concord.[23] His remarks on vertical coincidence between parts are proffered not as directions for extempore performance but as declarations of principles on which measured discant is founded. In contrast to prior polyphonic theory, John separates vertical intervals (*consonantia in eodem tempore*) into two categories, concords and discords, which he distinguishes, following Boethius, according to their perceived degree of compatibility.[24] Within each category, he posits a value-laden hierarchy of perfect, imperfect, and medial status. The result is a conspectus of all intervals within the octave distributed according to greater and lesser degrees of concord and discord (Figure 15.1). (Octave compounds are considered equivalent to their simple forms, e.g., minor third = minor tenth.) Theoretical justification for this hierarchy he places in ratios of Boethian authority, with intervals resulting from multiple and superparticular ratios (octave 2:1, fifth 3:2) which "more nearly approach equality" claiming higher status than those deriving from a minor superpartient (major third, 81:64). The explanation is not entirely convincing on numerical grounds (as a superparticular ratio, 9:8, one might expect the whole tone to hold higher status than it does), but in combination with plausible aural perception of blending and with usage in notated discant, John's hierarchy seems a reasonably useful approximation for heuristic purposes. Later theorists do feel free to adjust it, as when Franco of Cologne discards the category of medial discord and consigns the tone to imperfect, the minor sixth to perfect discord status.[25] From the perspectives of both early "symphonic organum" theory and later *contrapunctus* theory, what is remarkable is that John of Garland accepts all intervals within the octave (and by extension their compounds) within the realm of discant. Certain

23 *De mensurabili musica* (Latin edn., pp. 74–75). Compare with "discant responds to its cantus with an equal number of notes and always through some consonance or a unison," a definition from an anonymous twelfth-century treatise that makes no reference to measured durations (Seay, "An Anonymous Treatise," p. 35). The "Discantus positio vulgaris" that is said to precede *De mensurabili musica* speaks of all discant (that is, upper voice) notes as being measured (*Tractatus de musica*, pp. 109–11).

24 *De mensurabili musica* (Latin edn., pp. 67, 71). For the model in Boethius see *Fundamentals of Music*, Book I, Chapter 8, p. 16. The importance of this concept is discussed in Fuller, "Theoretical Foundations," pp. 82–84.

25 *Ars cantus mensurabilis* (Latin edn., pp. 67–68; English trans., p. 239). This unbalances John's threefold division within each category.

intervals enjoy a far higher status of concord and perfection than others, but all are included.

By its theoretical tone, its resonance with Boethius, and its avoidance of practical advice on producing discant, John's treatise projects an intellectual cast that may reflect its role as a specialized sequel to the "Discantus positio vulgaris," a text characterized by the Parisian compiler Jerome of Moravia as the oldest of the discant treatises he knew and the most general or commonly used.[26] Despite its orientation toward "how to understand" rather than "how to do," the treatise does transmit a few casual observations pertinent to the practice of discanting. The firm hierarchy of concords and discords yields before specific musical contexts, for any discord before a perfect or medial concord may be considered equivalent to a medial concord. Furthermore, a rule against the succession discord–imperfect concord may be waived in consideration of melodic structure (*color*) or beauty (*pulchritudo*).[27] The treatise also mandates concords at odd-numbered positions in rhythmic modes 1, 2, or 3 (what Franco later calls the beginnings of perfections).[28] This linkage between stable intervallic quality and the beginning of a primary durational element is a theoretical concept of great moment, for it asserts a role for consonance in articulating mensural units. Melodic/motivic considerations (*color musicae*) may also override this precept, in which case either pitch (even- or odd-numbered) of a pair may concord with the cantus tone.

De mensurabili musica and its descendants constitute a learned tradition oriented toward consonance–dissonance classification, rhythmic paradigms, notational conventions, and genre distinctions. Concurrently, there existed a complementary tradition of practical discant instruction, basic training in the format of standard interval successions to be mastered by any would-be practitioner. (In German, this tradition is known as *Klangschritt-Lehre*.) Interval-succession instruction teaches stock discant responses to the usual diatonic cantus intervals. For every ascending or descending cantus interval (beginning with unison and proceeding to the fifth, sometimes even to the octave), the discantor learns how to move in (mainly) contrary motion from one stable concord (octave, fifth, unison, occasionally fourth) to another. A typical formulation runs: "if the cantus firmus ascends a tone . . . and the discantus is at the octave, it should descend a minor third, through a second, so as to be at a fifth [with the second cantus pitch]. And conversely, the discant should ascend [from a fifth] if the cantus descends a tone."[29] Interval-succession teaching concentrates on perfect consonances as beginning and end points above (and in some instruction manuals also

26 *Tractatus de musica*, p. 189. Jerome characterizes the other four discant treatises in his compilation, including that of John of Garland, as specialized (*speciales*).
27 *De mensurabili musica* (Latin edn., p. 74).
28 Ibid., p. 76. The "Discantus positio vulgaris" anticipates this precept in remarking more generally that the odd-numbered notes in a discant should be either more consonant or less dissonant than the even-numbered ones (Jerome of Moravia, *Tractatus de musica*, p. 191).
29 "Discantus positio vulgaris" (Latin edn., p. 191; English trans., p. 204). See Example 15.4, section 4 on the following page. Most instructions do not mention the middle tone within the third.

Example 15.4 "Discantus positio vulgaris," interval progressions

below) any two-note cantus segment taken as an isolated phenomenon with no reference to mensural context, rhythmic measure, extended cantus phrase, or melodic mode. A complete cycle from the "Discantus positio vulgaris", antecedent to the *De mensurabili musica*, is shown in Example 15.4.[30] That these routines are relevant to organum as well as to discant style is suggested in theorists' designations of the second voice variously as the organum or as the discant. Further documentrary support comes from the Vatican organum treatise that transmits over 340 elaborated upper-voice motions above cantus intervals. It ends with three complete organa that feature elaborated interval progressions in concrete musical situations (a rarity in this type of treatise).[31]

Some interval-succession instructions circulate alone, but some, such as those in the *Discantus positio vulgaris*, occur within texts that include remarks on measured musical notation, musical genres, accidental inflections (*musica falsa)*, or other topics relevant to *musica mensurabilis*. Some authors or compilers assume that the reader/auditor has already learned the principles behind discant and launch into their formulas without a word about governing rationales. Some articulate a few general rules, stipulating contrary motion between the parts or indicating when half-step inflections are needed to

30 Ibid. (Latin edn., pp. 191–92; English trans., pp. 204–05). Like a few other writings, this treatise mixes elements of the learned tradition (such as rhythmic distinctions) with the performative interval-succession tradition. Note that Example 15.4 translates the verbal instructions of the treatise into musical notation. Segments in brackets represent the converse of the principal ascending interval cycle. Cantus notes have descending stems; discant notes ascending stems. Inclusion of cantus leaps as large as a seventh and an octave (which are virtually non-existent in chant melodies) is anomalous in this teaching tradition.

31 See Godt and Rivera,"The Vatican Organum Treatise"; Zaminer, *Der Vatikanische Organum-Traktat.*

secure a perfect consonance. The implied author of the *Discantus positio vulgaris* sees technical knowledge (*ars*) and practice (*usus*) as interrelated, promising that once the standard progressions have been "observed and committed to memory, one will be able to grasp the whole art of discanting through the cognate art of usage."[32] That interval-succession instructions largely abstain from comprehensive theoretical pronouncements can be attributed partly to their function as aural training designed to prepare singers to extemporize a consonant discant against any cantus, and partly to the complementary tradition of scholarly *musica mensurabilis* treatises in which fundamental principles guiding discant were set forth.

Although Klaus-Jürgen Sachs has grouped the undated, anonymous interval-succession treatises according to repertories of progressions and selected linguistic features, the manuscript tradition (which consists largely of fourteenth- and fifteenth-century copies) offers negligible support for his hypothesis that such groups constitute progressive chronological stages.[33] Rather, these practical manuals are best interpreted as traces of diverse aural teaching traditions, for most of them are unica (or survive at most in two copies) and their varied schemes for presenting a common core of material suggest individual, local teaching strategies. Continued transmission of interval succession exercises (sometimes in company with digests of Franconian notation) after the advent of the *ars nova* suggests that this sort of training long remained relevant for ecclesiastical singers, especially those expected to discant spontaneously upon a plainchant cantus as ritual circumstances required. In the thirteenth century, a special subgroup of practical manuals teaches how to "quintare" – to accompany a given chant in parallel fifths with occasional punctuating octaves. Such instructional materials testify to the persistence of a version of the parallel-fifths organum tradition first attested in the ninth-century *Enchiriadis* treatises.[34] The English theorist "Anonymous IV" alludes to such a tradition in identifying "plain singers" or "discantors" (*plani cantores/discantores*) who ascend and descend in step with the plainsong in similar concords. Such singers, he says, are to be distinguished from true discantors who follow an altogether more complex set of conventions and observe contrary motion between parts.[35] Clearly operative here are value judgments on types of polyphonic production, with that entailing the more complex musical reactions and elaborate theoretical apparatus ranking the highest.

32 "Discantus positio vulgaris" (Latin edn., p. 192; English trans., p. 205). The treatise "Quaedam de arte discantandi" refers the student to the *ars discantus* – apparently some learned text such as John's *De mensurabili musica* – for information on which intervals are consonant and which dissonant, and on the nature of *musica falsa* (pp. 290, 294).

33 Sachs, "Zur Tradition der Klangschritt-Lehre."

34 This group of treatises is discussed in Fuller, "Discant and the Theory of Fifthing."

35 Anonymous IV, *Der Musiktraktat* (Latin edn., p. 75; English edn., p. 66). That the theorist also characterizes those who sing in parallel concords as young (*plani et novi*) further suggests that this sort of singing was the first polyphonic training received by boys.

Contrapunctus (1300s–1400s)

By the fourth decade of the fourteenth century, theoretical writing on the making of polyphony had taken a new tack and received a new name, *contrapunctus* or "simple discant" (*simplex discantus*). *Contrapunctus* theory has left a fairly extensive record: Klaus-Jürgen Sachs lists some 185 treatises, of which nine survive in four or more copies.[36] (The highest count goes to "Quilibet affectans" with twelve extant sources, followed by "Cum notum sit"/"De diminutione contrapuncti" with ten.) Those most copied tend to cluster in a northern, Paris-centered strand and a southern, Italian strand that emerges most prominently in the early fifteenth century with the learned musicians Prosdocimo de' Beldomandi (who taught at the University of Padua) and Ugolino of Orvieto. Variety of tone and content within the remaining *contrapunctus* treatises suggests that, as with interval-succession instruction, the written documents stem from a rather informal aural teaching tradition. This is in contrast, for instance, to *musica plana* treatises of the time, whose liberal quotations and paraphrases of such authority figures as Boethius and Guido of Arezzo and citations of chant repertory place them firmly within a literate tradition.

Contrapunctus teaching retains many features of the older discant teaching, but differs significantly in being conceived as strictly note-against-note in texture. In regarding this note-against-note texture as "the foundation of discant" (see quote from "Cum notum sit," p. 478 above), the theorists now distinguish within polyphony a structural level of concords and voice-leading that underpins an elaborated surface of discant. In a favorite metaphor, it acts as a foundation to a building. Except for the generic term "discant" used in the formula "counterpoint is . . . the foundation of discant," the theorists adopt no uniform name for the complex musical creation whose structural support is a *contrapunctus*. Among the terms encountered are *cantus fractabilis* ("Volentibus introduci"), *contrapunctus diminutus* (sequel to "Cum notum sit"), *flores musicae mensurabilis* (Petrus *dictus palma ociosa*), and *voces dividere* (the Parisian theorist of 1375, sometimes called Goscalcus, or author of the Berkeley treatise). These designations emphasize a process of decorating a plain series of intervals through increased melodic activity in the added, contrapuntal voice. In 1412, Prosdocimo de' Beldomandi, a Paduan-educated master, simply distinguished between two understandings of *contrapunctus*, one *communiter sive large* involving many notes against one (which he dismisses as not truly counterpoint) and the other *propria sive stricte*, true counterpoint of one note against another.[37]

Although the *contrapunctus* phase of teaching can be readily distinguished from that of discant on several counts, many of its basic precepts (such as the requirement for contrary motion between parts except in special circumstances) emerge directly from that prior teaching tradition. A few treatises that deal with *contrapunctus*, such as the

36 Sachs, *Der Contrapunctus*, pp. 207–20.

37 Prosdocimo, *Contrapunctus*, pp. 28–29.

Quatuor principalia, also continue the interval-succession tradition with systematic catalogues of moves above set cantus intervals, catalogues that now include vertical thirds and sixths along with fifths, octaves, and unisons.[38] Most simply mention or illustrate the usual sequel to a specific interval. With regard to polyphonic sonorities and voice-leading, early fourteenth-century theorists do not register a sea change in attitude such as that declared in the realm of mensuration through the term *ars nova*. The earliest *dated* treatise in which *contrapunctus* teaching is plainly evident (under the name *simplex discantus*) is the *Compendium de discantu mensurabili* from 1336. Its author/compiler Petrus *dictus palma ociosa* (Peter of the lazy hand) makes no claim to originality, save in his invention of special exercises for florid discant. This is about twenty years after the first ferment of *ars nova* (generally associated with the special *Roman de Fauvel* recension of c. 1316). A few *contrapunctus* treatises of uncertain date did circulate under the names of *ars nova* luminaries such as Philippe de Vitry and Jehan des Murs, but these attributions are tenuous and cannot be reliably used to track the chronology of *contrapunctus* teaching. That the new mensurations and differentiation between quicker and more sedate layers of temporal motion did influence how would-be singers of polyphony were taught their craft can be observed in the exercises offered by Petrus *dictus palma ociosa* and in the "Cum notum sit" sequel, "De diminutione contrapuncti." Both cast their elaborations of a basic *contrapunctus* in terms of the tempus and prolation system.The codification of different durational layers (with a ratio of 81 : 1 from the maximum *longa* to the *minima*) must have encouraged the distinction between a note-against-note *contrapunctus* and a rhythmically elaborated polyphonic surface – the one foundation to the other – but the early fourteenth-century theorists do not make this point.

In a distinctive break from prior interval-succession teaching, *contrapunctus* welcomes imperfect concords (sometimes termed "dissonances") of major and minor third and major sixth along with the established perfect concords (unison, fifth, and octave).[39] The perfect are deemed stable in quality, the imperfect unstable. This language engenders a rhetoric that speaks of imperfect thirds and sixth(s) seeking perfection through progression to a perfect concord. Some texts (such as "Quilibet affectans") adopt a doctrine of natural sequels that has imperfect intervals tending to their most proximate perfect neighbors: minor third to unison, major third to fifth, and major sixth to octave. Although, like older discant teaching, *contrapunctus* instruction prohibits parallel fifths or octaves, it does allow chains of imperfect thirds and sixths, chains that in effect delay resolution. Those texts that stipulate natural motion from a perfect interval to its closest neighboring concord (such as from unison to

38 *Quatuor principalia* (*CS* 4, pp. 282–94; Aluas edn., pp. 469–518; trans., pp. 713–46).

39 The earliest formulations make plain the major form of the sixth in naming it *tonus cum diapente*. In adopting the generic name *sexta* for the interval next above the fifth, other treatises obliterate this distinction, or include *semitonus cum diapente*. This has repercussions for *musica ficta* questions. Note that inclusion of the imperfect concords within practice is in keeping with John of Garland's intellectual scheme of concords and discords.

minor third) typically qualify this with a license for virtually any interval after a stable concord. So "Quilibet affectans" teaches that the fifth "naturally requires after it a ditone or major third . . . but may have some other perfect or imperfect interval, for the reason already stated [variability within the cantus]."[40]

With imperfect consonances accepted as structural components in *contrapunctus*, it becomes necessary to formalize constraints upon them. Whereas ending on any interval other than a unison, fifth, or octave with the cantus would have been unthinkable in thirteenth-century discant, *contrapunctus* teaching needs to specify that a *contrapunctus* must begin and end on a perfect concord. "Cum notum sit" gives insight into the aural perception behind this in commenting: "the reason could be that if the *contrapunctus* were to end on an imperfect [concord], then the mind (*anima*) would remain suspended, nor would it be at peace there since it did not hear a perfect sound; nor, in consequence, would it be indicated that the song ended there."[41] One of the earliest treatises from the Parisian orbit, "Quilibet affectans," specifies that minor thirds should be rendered major if followed by any interval other than unison, and grants only major sixths a place in *contrapunctus*. This treatise does not, however, directly address *musica ficta* or *falsa*, the theory of inflections. That topic was typically integrated into *musica plana* discussions of hexachords, consonances, or melodic neighbor-tone figures (such as sol–fa–sol). The 1375 theorist/compiler from Paris (Goscalcus), for example, deals with *musica ficta* and pitches such as F♯, C♯, E♭, and A♭ in the first section of his treatise, whose topic is pitch and mode, not in the second on discant.[42] Similarly, the Franciscan author of *Quatuor Principalia* (1351) mentions inflections of thirds in discant when reviewing intervals in Tract 3 (not within the section on simple discant, Part 2 of Tract 4), and toward the end of Tract 3 traces to prestigious singers in the chapels of the nobility the modern vogue for making song more delightful by changing tones into semitones.[43] Among northern theorists, Petrus *dictus palma ociosa* most explicitly addresses *musica falsa* within a context of *contrapunctus*, devoting a substantial portion of his treatise to the need for inflections not only to correct fifths and provide an octave below high b♭, but also to provide major-third-to-fifth and major-sixth-to-octave progressions.[44] Some treatises comment that any of the intervals accepted within *contrapunctus* may require "perfection" or that *musica falsa* may be needed, but offer no details.[45]

Marchetto of Padua (fl. 1305–26) is the founding authority for a strong Italian *contrapunctus* tradition that insists upon inflecting imperfect consonances to achieve the closest possible junction with a subsequent perfect consonance.[46] Both Prosdocimo de' Beldomandi (writing c. 1412) and Ugolino of Orvieto (writing c. 1430) favor inflec-

40 *CS* 3, p. 59. For repercussions of such doctrines within notated three-voiced polyphony, see Fuller, "On Sonority." 41 *CS* 3, p. 62.

42 *The Berkeley Manuscript*, pp. 50–67. See also the fifth treatise on division of the tone into semitones, pp. 240–47. 43 *Quatuor principalia* (*CS* 4, pp. 227, 250; Aluas edn., pp. 281–82, 356; trans., pp. 594, 642–43). 44 *Compendium*, pp. 513–16.

45 For example, "Quoniam de arte mensurabili," *CS* 3, p. 36; "Sex sunt species discantus per quas omnis," *GS* 3, p. 307. 46 *Lucidarium*, pp. 206–23. Note that this is a plainchant treatise.

Example 15.5 Ugolino of Orvieto, *Declaratio Musicae Disciplinae*, Book II, second *contrapunctus* example

tion to secure properly directed imperfect intervals and firmly assert rules to ensure the closest possible proximity between an imperfect interval and its perfect sequel.[47] In the model examples he supplies, Ugolino explains the notated *ficta* in terms not only of "coloring" an imperfect interval to achieve proximity but also of achieving pleasant *armonia* (Example 15.5).[48] Although not a *contrapunctus* theorist, Johannes Boen testifies in 1357 to the proliferation of semitone inflections and *musica ficta* in polyphonic music of England and North-western Europe.[49]

Standard *contrapunctus* or simple discant theory takes place in what might be called a neutral zone devoid of either tonal orientation or mensural definition. Specific mensurations are, however, central to most teaching about how to elaborate a *contrapunctus* (the unmeasured *verbulare* formulas of the 1375 Parisian theorist are a notable exception). In dealing with decorations or divisions, treatises such as "De diminutione contrapuncti" and the *Compendium* of Petrus *dictus palma ociosa* offer not instruction in composition, but exercises in how to improvise a decorated contrapuntal voice upon a plain, evenly measured cantus. Petrus states that the routines, or "modes," he has devised will help the young learn techniques of elaboration within *musica mensurabilis*, while the Parisian pedagogue claims that practicing his *verbulae* will facilitate invention of pleasing and refined decorations.[50] Each of Petrus's twelve exercises consists of a cantus in even longs or breves with a second voice in one of the standard mensurations. The series begins with perfect modus, perfect tempus, and major prolation, and proceeds systematically through the possible combinations of modus, tempus, and prolation, ending with a single breve in imperfect tempus, minor prolation.[51] As may be seen in Example 15.6a (his eighth "mode": imperfect modus and tempus, major prolation), the elaborated voice decorates primary consonances with other tones in a variety of rhythms, some animated by rests.[52] In contrast, each example in "De diminutione contrapuncti" reiterates a fixed rhythmic pattern.[53] My *contrapunctus* reduction

47 *Contrapunctus*, pp. 78–87; *Declaratio musicae disciplinae*, pp. 44–53.
48 *Declaratio musicae disciplinae*, 47–48. 49 *Musica*, pp. 67–68, 75–78.
50 *Compendium*, pp. 516–17; *The Berkeley Manuscript*, pp. 146–47.
51 *Compendium*, pp. 518–34. For later incarnations of such a proto-"species" approach, see **Chapter 18, pp. 565–68**, and **Chapter 16, pp. 509–10**.
52 An asterisk over a pitch in Example 15.6a indicates continuation of a preceding accidental inflection.
53 These are printed in Sachs, *Der Contrapunctus*, pp. 146–47.

(Example 15.6b) of Petrus's example adopts the simple premise of taking the first primary consonance in the upper voice for the note-against-note framework. This results in several parallel perfect consonances (a defect according to the Parisian theorist), but most of these are "covered" by connective melodic activity, and some could be finessed by selecting a consonance other than the first. The final cadence is approached through a series of imperfect consonances. Although intended to foster contrapuntal elaboration within a mensural context, the exercises Petrus gives would prepare a singer well for reading complex mensural music, just as prior experience with notated motets and rondeaux would help a singer to master the art of extemporized decoration upon a cantus, as Petrus himself remarks.[54]

Because by definition *contrapunctus* admits only concords, few treatises on the subject concern themselves with discords; but since elaborated *contrapunctus* inevitably introduces dissonant intervals, teaching on that practice usually refers to discords, even if only in a cursory manner. Petrus remarks merely that one should not dwell on dissonances when decorating, but may briefly sound them in moving from one acceptable interval to another. (M. 3 of Example 15.6a with its initial semibreve fourth [whether augmented or adjusted by *ficta*] seems a departure from this precept, as does m. 11 with a major seventh on its last semibreve.) The Parisian theorist of 1375 summarizes what seem to be two schools of teaching: one based on relative duration that requires half or more of the pitches above a cantus tone to be consonant; the other based on position that requires the first pitch to be consonant. In syncopations, he says, a dissonance may equal the consonant pitch(es) in length. Similar precepts are attested some twenty years earlier by Johannes Boen in the fourth section of his treatise *Musica* (1357).[55] The gist of such generalities seems to be that even though singers will and should introduce dissonances in the course of elaboration, those elaborating any *contrapunctus* should preserve its character of consonant relationships.

To judge from the number of treatises on the subject, *contrapunctus* was a widely practiced technique through which able singers could amplify a given cantus with a countermelody in pleasant consonance. More veiled are various vernacular practices in which singers produced commonplace polyphony by applying to a cantus some restricted formula or standard algorithm. Relatively little was written about such practices, perhaps because the traditions were seldom considered dignified enough to deserve theoretical description and explication and so tended to be transmitted by word of mouth from one generation to the next. After spending thirty chapters on standard discant (of the *contrapunctus* variety), the Franciscan monk from Bristol (1351), for example, rather casually mentions another technique of discanting that is "very easy" but is perceived as quite accomplished (*artificiosus*). In this technique, four men sing the cantus at unison, fifth, octave, and twelfth respectively, those doubling it above sometimes embellishing the notes in some mensuration. A fifth man discants,

54 *Compendium*, p. 534. 55 *The Berkeley Manuscript*, pp. 132–33; *Musica*, pp. 68–69.

Example 15.6a Petrus *dictus palma ociosa*, eighth mode of *contrapunctus* elaboration

Example 15.6b *Contrapunctus* reduction of Example 15.6a

using mostly imperfect concords, thirds, sixths, and tenths. In this way, says the monk, "just one person expert in discant . . . can produce a grand song (*magna melodia*) along with others who simply know how to sing."[56] That a significant number of fifteenth-century treatises on ways of improvising polyphony were written in vernacular tongues (English and Italian), suggests that they were directed toward ordinary singers

56 Anonymous, *Quatuor principalia* (*CS* 4, p. 294; Aluas edn., pp. 519–20; trans. pp. 746–47).

who needed to learn elementary techniques and whose command of written (or even spoken) Latin was uncertain, or toward teachers who might favor the local spoken language.

In Italy, several sources attest to a contrapuntal practice organized in four different *gradi*, each corresponding to a hexachord relationship between cantus and contrapuntal voice. The *gradus* system is basically a hexachord-zone practice. The four standard zones of *grado di pari*, *di quarta*, *di quinta*, and *di octava* entail contrapuntal voices that remain respectively within the same hexachord as the cantus, or within the hexachord situated a fourth, fifth, or octave above the cantus. Hexachord-zone teaching follows the same conventions as ordinary *contrapunctus* in terms of limitation to perfect and imperfect consonances, contrary motion except for parallel imperfect consonances, beginnings and endings on perfect consonances (the latter approached by the closest imperfect consonance). Yet it simplifies *contrapunctus* in that a hexachord limit restricts both the intervals and the notes that can be paired with any given cantus pitch. In the *grado di pari*, for example, only four intervals – unison, fifth, third, and sixth – are possible and their availablity is contingent upon specific pitches of the cantus. Against a cantus *ut*, for example, a counterpoint singer may sound unison, third, fifth or sixth above, but against a cantus *mi*, only the unison or the thirds above or below are available. A fifth above is excluded, for that would exceed the hexachord limit. The *grado di quarta* has available for cantus *ut* fifth, sixth, or octave above, and for cantus *sol* unison, third, or fifth above but no intervals below either.[57] At the first level, *gradus* practice has the contrapuntal voice dipping below the cantus more than would be expected in regular *contrapunctus*. At the other three levels, the contrapuntal voice consistently occupies registers above the cantus. The *gradus* system enlists the singer's familiarity with hexachords to train him in a basic, workable counterpoint that could have been a first stage to more advanced training for the more gifted singers.

English musicians developed a method of "sights" to help singers produce a counterpoint upon a plainsong. This teaching is first attested in vernacular treatises from the late fourteenth and early fifteenth centuries, one of which is attributed to the distinguished composer Leonel Power. Power explicitly relates his first instructions to "inform[ing] a child in his counterpoint."[58] Three primary sights are quatreble, treble, and mean. The anonymous "Here folwith a litil tretise" explains that the mean [voice] when beginning a discant will visualize a unison with a chant, but will sing a fifth above, the treble will likewise visualize a unison, but sing an octave above, the quatreble will visualize a unison but sing a twelfth above. Thereafter each voice has a choice of consonant intervals within a certain register above the chant: the mean from unison

57 Hothby, *De arte contrapuncti*, pp. 30–32; *Quatuor tractatuli*, pp. 22–23. Scattolin gives a thorough account of *gradus* teaching and notes that the account attributed to Hothby is not individual to him but conforms to versions of an earlier treatise that circulated anonymously ("La Regola del 'Grado,'" p. 30).
58 Meech, "Three Musical Treatises," pp. 242–58. For the remark quoted, see p. 242. This treatise is also edited in more condensed fashion along with others in Bukofzer, *Geschichte*, pp. 132–36.

to octave, the treble from fifth to twelfth, and the quatreble from octave to fifteenth or double octave. All pitches are, however, sighted or imagined within an octave above or below the chant.[59] The "countertenor" sight explained in this treatise may range from an octave below to an octave above a plainsong: it stays below when the plainsong is in an upper register and moves above when the plainsong descends in register. "Sight" and "voice" coincide for the "countertenor" – that is, the singer produces in register the pitches he envisions. Another sight, the "countir," is a kind of reverse mean, for the singer produces intervals a fifth below the pitches sighted (so a unison sighted with a cantus pitch will sound as a fifth below the cantus). Like the countertenor, the "countir" sight responds to the cantus range, remaining low when the cantus is high and rising when it descends.[60] The practice of sights allows a singer to follow a chant written on a four-line staff and to imagine his part in relation to that chant as situated on the staff, even though the sounds he sings may exist as much as an octave and a fifth (in the case of the quatreble) above a generating cantus pitch. What hexachord zone instruction and sight instruction have in common is attention to registral position of voices in relation to a cantus, a topic hardly touched in standard *contrapunctus* teaching. Both suggest a culture in which separation of voice parts into different registers has taken on considerable significance, a situation that might be inferred from written three- and four-voiced polyphony of the fifteenth century.

Power offers many exercises for producing simple counterpoints upon tenor fragments in treble and quatreble sights. His exercises resemble interval-succession patterns amplified in length and in scope. They involve extended series upon tenors of as many as twelve notes and include imperfect consonances either singly, or in series of two or three among perfect consonances, or intermixed among each other (as sixth with tenth).[61] Several other English treatises explain a common formula for three-part polyphony, one they call faburden. According to "The sight of ffaburden with his a cordis," faburden is "the least [simplest] process of sights, natural and most in use."[62] The basic process is that the treble parallels the plainsong in fourths above while the faburden musician sights thirds and unisons with the plainsong and sings them a fifth lower, producing thirds and fifths (respectively) below the plainsong. (The faburden part thus behaves like the "countir" described in "Here folwith a litil tretise" but with a far more limited scope.) Faburden resembles ordinary *contrapunctus* in requiring octave-and-fifth sonorities as beginnings and ends ("The sight of ffaburden" specifies such closes at ends of words) and in repudiating consecutive perfect consonances. The straightforward and familiar practice of faburden left an impact upon English sacred music. Trowell and others have noted traces of faburden practice in notated mensural

59 Meech, "Three Musical Treatises," pp. 258–59. 60 Bukofzer, *Geschichte*, pp. 150–52.

61 Meech, "Three Musical Treatises," pp. 248–58. He reverses the two musical examples in the middle of p. 249.

62 Trowell, "Faburden and Fauxbourdon," p. 47. Trowell provides both an edition and an extensive commentary on this treatise, pp. 47–52.

music of the Old Hall manuscript, in carols, in hymns, in magnificats and in organ settings from the fifteenth and sixteenth centuries.[63]

In the later fifteenth century, a theorist who identifies himself only as Guilielmus monachus (William the monk) and who seems to have written in Italy takes the trouble to explain the English manner of counterpoint, a practice he calls "faulxbourdon."[64] Although the sonorities rendered in his version of faulxbourdon resemble those of early faburden, the techniques he describes differ markedly from those in "The sight of ffaburden." The technique first discussed entails the plainsong tenor as lowest voice with *suprano* sighting unisons and thirds below which sound as octaves and sixths above and contratenor singing fifths and thirds above the tenor. Both contrapuntal voices are to begin and end on perfect consonances. A subsequent description has the cantus in the *suprano* in triple mensuration, but then reverts to the perspective of intervals above the tenor.[65] What is perhaps most striking about Guilielmus's treatise is that in addition to rehearsing the standard rules for two-voiced *contrapunctus* and listing some common English sights (without using that term), he mentions some five procedures for generating polyphony in three or (in one case) four voices. Insofar as the treatise of this "eminently complete singer" (*cantor integerrimus*, as he describes himself) reflects the training program he offered his students, it shows him transmitting to Northern Italy some specifically English practices and promoting diverse methods of extemporizing more than two voices upon a cantus.

In his attention to extemporizing polyphony upon a cantus firmus, Guilielmus monachus exhibits a mentality distant from that of his approximate contemporary Johannes Tinctoris (1466–1511), a Flemish theorist and composer employed at the court of Naples. Tinctoris's *Liber de arte contrapuncti* from 1477 represents in many ways a culmination of *contrapunctus* theory from the preceding two centuries. The principal topics he addresses are familiar ones: interval successions (an exhaustive inventory, expanded to the triple diapason); eight general rules for counterpoint (standard ones from the past set to a slightly different angle owing to the exceptions allowed); the distinction between simple and decorated counterpoint; regulation of discords in the decorated type (but carried to unprecedented length).[66] What sets Tinctoris decisively apart from his predecessors (and from a figure such as Guilielmus monachus) is his emphasis on notated polypony and on compositions by esteemed composers. This focus appears not in the reams of interval successions but in the (now famous) Prologue where he lauds such *compositores* as Ockeghem, Regis, and Busnois and traces a *compositional* tradition

63 In "Faburden and Fauxbourdon" and in "Faburden – New Sources." For an example of faburden see Chapter 17, p. 536.

64 Scholars regularly distinguish between English faburden (an improvised practice) and fauxbourdon, a method of adding a voice to two written parts which is first attested in notated music See Trowell, "Faburden and Fauxbourdon"; Trumble, *Fauxbourdon*, pp. 13–36.

65 *De preceptis artis musicae*, pp. 29–30, 38–39.

66 Tinctoris's learned treatment takes up forty-nine folios in one manuscript (seventy-nine in another), in comparison to a maximum of four folios for "Cum notum sit"/"De diminutione contrapuncti" in its most ample manuscript version.

between them and Dunstable, Dufay, and Binchois. It also leaps out in the later chapters of Book II where he cites contrapuntal faults in actual pieces by respected composers.[67] His extensive and precise treatment of discords also points toward notated music insofar as he links proper dissonance regulation with specific mensurations. Indeed, Tinctoris famously draws an explicit distinction between an evanescent counterpoint produced mentally "upon the book" (*super librum*) and a more refined written counterpoint that is composed (*res facta*).[68] This echoes an earlier (1412) distinction by the Paduan theorist Prosdocimo de' Beldomandi between a *contrapunctus* that is vocal (*vocalis*) and exists only as a performed event, and one that is written down or notated (*scriptus*).[69] Both theorists (Prosdocimo most specifically) indicate that the general precepts they expound apply to evanescent as well as written *contrapunctus*, but through his opening remarks Tinctoris tips the balance of "the art of counterpoint" markedly toward written polyphony.

Conclusion

In his influential *Geschichte der Musiktheorie im IX.–XIX. Jahrhundert*, Hugo Riemann defined "the task of a theory of art" as "to ground the natural lawfulness that either consciously or unconsciously regulates artistic creations and to expound this in a system of pedagogical statements that cohere logically."[70] Riemann interpreted early theory of polyphony and counterpoint in terms of rules for composition assumed to be universally valid throughout a particular chronological period. But to read even a handful of theorists from the ninth through the fifteenth centuries is to become aware that goals vary, that those who write on procedures for organum, discant, or *contrapunctus* are largely concerned with quite elementary training in the production of many-voiced music, and that the conventions they relay cannot be held universally valid for their time but relate to particular practices in delimited cultural strata and geographical locales. These past theoretical writings on how to combine two or more voices certainly provide guidance on various horizons of awareness musicians brought to polyphony within the period 850–1480 and do relate to changes in stylistic idioms of notated repertories. The practices described in the extant treatises doubtless shaped the basic sensibilities of young musicians some of whom did subsequently create their own polyphony to be preserved in notation; but the sphere of those practices had to do chiefly with oral polyphony and (to varying degrees) theoretical principle and only partially overlapped the sphere of written composition.

67 *The Art of Counterpoint*, Book II, Chapter 29, p. 126; Chapters 32–33, pp. 129–31.
68 *The Art of Counterpoint*, Book II, Chapter 20, pp. 107–10. This chapter is translated and discussed at length in Bent, "*Resfacta* and *Cantare Super Librum*." Sachs offers a somewhat different viewpoint in a postscript to "Arten improvisierter Mehrstimmigkeit," pp. 181–83, as does Blackburn in "On Compositional Process," pp. 248–56. Wegman further pursues the issue in "From Maker to Composer," pp. 439–52. 69 *Contrapunctus*, pp. 32–33.
70 *Geschichte der Musiktheorie*, Book III, Chapter 16, p. 470.

Bibliography

Anonymous IV, ed. F. Reckow as *Der Musiktraktat des Anonymous 4*, 2 vols., Wiesbaden, F. Steiner, 1967; trans. J. Yudkin as *The Music Treatise of Anonymous IV: A New Translation*, *MSD* 41 (1985)

Anonymous of St. Emmeram, *De Musica Mensurata*; trans. and ed. J. Yudkin as *De Musica Mensurata: The Anonymous of St. Emmeram, Complete Critical Edition, Translation, and Commentary*, Bloomington, Indiana University Press, 1990

Arlt, W. "Stylistic Layers in Eleventh-Century Polyphony: How Can the Continental Sources Contribute to our Understanding of the Winchester Organa?," in *Music in the Medieval English Liturgy*, ed. S. Rankin and D. Hiley, Oxford, Clarendon, 1993, pp. 101–41

Bent, M. "*Resfacta* and *Cantare Super Librum*," *JAMS* 36 (1983), pp. 371–91

The Berkeley Manuscript: University of California Music Library, MS.744 (olim Phillipps 4450), ed. O. Ellsworth, Lincoln, University of Nebraska Press, 1984

Blackburn, B. J. "On Compositional Process in the Fifteenth Century," *JAMS* 40 (1987), pp. 210–84

Boen, J. *Johannes Boens Musica und seine Konsonanzenlehre*, ed. W. Frobenius, Stuttgart, Musikwissenschaftliche Verlags-Gesellschaft mbH, 1971

Boethius, A. M. S. *De institutione musica*, ed. G. Friedlein as *Anicii Manlii Torquati Severini Boetii De institutione arithmetica libri duo, De institutione musica libri quinque, accedit Geometria quae fertur Boetii*, Leipzig, Teubner, 1867; reprint Frankfurt-am-Main, Minerva, 1966; trans. C. Bower, ed. C. Palisca as *Fundamentals of Music*, New Haven, Yale University Press, 1989

Bukofzer, M. *Geschichte des englischen Diskants und des Fauxbourdons nach den theoretischen Quellen*, Leipzig, Heitz, 1936

Eggebrecht, H. and F. Zaminer, eds., *Ad Organum Faciendum: Lehrschriften der Mehrstimmigkeit in nachguidonischer Zeit*, Mainz, B. Schotts Söhne, 1970

Franco of Cologne, *Ars cantus mensurabilis*, ed. G. Reaney and A. Gilles as *Franconis de Colonia Ars Cantus Mensurabilis*, *CSM* 18 (1974); trans. O. Strunk in *SR*, pp. 226–45

Fuller, S. "Discant and the Theory of Fifthing," *Acta* 50 (1978), pp. 241–75

"Theoretical Foundations of Early Organum Theory," *Acta* 53 (1981), pp. 52–84

"On Sonority in Fourteenth-Century Polyphony," *JMT* 30 (1986), pp. 35–70

"Early Polyphony," in *The New Oxford History of Music*, vol. II, ed. R. L. Crocker and D. Hiley, Oxford University Press, 1990, pp. 485–556

Godt, I. and B. Rivera, "The Vatican Organum Treatise – A Colour Reproduction, Transcription, and Translation," in *Gordon Athol Anderson (1929–1981) In Memoriam*, Basel Institute of Medieval Music, 1984, pp. 264_{1}–345_{11}

Guido of Arezzo, *Micrologus*, ed. J. Smits van Waesberghe as *Guidonis Aretini Micrologus*, *CSM* 4 (1955); trans. W. Babb, ed. C. Palisca in *Hucbald, Guido, and John On Music: Three Medieval Treatises*, New Haven, Yale University Press, 1978, pp. 57–83

Guilielmus monachus, *De Preceptis Artis Musicae*, ed. A. Seay, *CSM* 11 (1965)

Haas, M. "Die Musiklehre im 13. Jahrhundert von Johannes de Garlandia bis Franco," in *Die Mittelalterliche Lehre von der Mehrstimmigkeit*, *GMt* 5 (1984), pp. 89–158

Hothby, J., *De arte contrapuncti*, ed. G. Reaney, *CSM* 26 (1977)

Jacques of Liège, *Speculum musicae*, ed. R. Bragard, 7 vols., *CSM* 3 (1955–73)

Jerome of Moravia, *Tractatus de musica*, ed. S. M. Cserba O.P. in *Hieronymus de Moravia O.P.*

Tractatus de Musica, Regensburg, F. Pustet, 1935, pp. 189–94; trans. J. Knapp in *JMT* 6 (1962), pp. 201–07

John of Garland, *De mensurabili musica*, ed. E. Reimer, Wiesbaden, F. Steiner, 1972; trans. S. Birnbaum as *Johannes de Garlandia Concerning Measured Music*, Colorado Springs, Colorado College Music Press, 1978

Marchetto of Padua, *Lucidarium in arte Musicae planae*, trans. and ed. J. Herlinger as *The Lucidarium of Marchetto of Padua: A Critical Edition, Translation, and Commentary*, University of Chicago Press, 1985

Meech, S. B. "Three Musical Treatises in English from a Fifteenth-Century Manuscript," *Speculum* 10 (1935), pp. 235–69

Musica Enchiriadis, Scolica Enchiriadis, ed. H. Schmid as *Musica et Scolica Enchiriadis una cum aliquibus tractatulis adiunctis*, Munich, Bayerische Akademie der Wissenschaften, 1981; trans. R. Erickson, ed. C. Palisca as *"Musica enchiriadis" and "Scolica enchiriadis": Translated, with Introduction and Notes*, New Haven, Yale University Press, 1995

Parisian theorist of 1375, see *The Berkeley Manuscript*, above

Petrus *dictus palma ociosa*, *Compendium de discantu mensurabili*, ed. J. Wolf in "Ein Beitrag zur Diskantlehre des 14. Jahrhunderts," *Sammelbände der Internationalem Musikgesellschaft* 15 (1913–14), pp. 504–34

Phillips, N. "*Musica* and *Scolica Enchiriadis*: The Literary, Theoretical, and Musical Sources," Ph.D. diss., New York University (1984)

Pinegar, S. "Textual and Conceptual Relationships among Theoretical Writings on Measurable Music of the Thirteenth and Early Fourteenth Centuries," Ph.D. diss., Columbia University (1991)

"On Rhythmic Modes," *Theoria* 8 (1994), pp. 73–112

Prosdocimo de' Beldomandi, *Contrapunctus* (1942), ed. and trans. J. Herlinger, Lincoln, University of Nebraska Press, 1984

"Quaedam de arte discantandi," ed. C. E. H. de Coussemaker in *Histoire de L'Harmonie au Moyen Age*, Paris, V. Didron, 1852, pp. 274–94; facs. Hildesheim, G. Olms, 1966, pp. 274–94

"Quatuor Principalia Musicae," in *CS* 4 (1876), pp. 201–98; ed. and trans. L. F. Aluas, Ph.D diss., Indiana University (1996)

Quatuor Tractatuli Italici de Contrapuncto, ed. A. Seay, Colorado Springs, Colorado College Music Press, 1977

Rankin, S. "Winchester Polyphony: The Early Theory and Practice of Organum," in *Music in the Medieval English Liturgy*, ed. S. Rankin and D. Hiley, Oxford, Clarendon Press, 1993, pp. 59–99

Reckow, F. "Guido's Theory of Organum after Guido: Transmission–Adaptation–Transformation," in *Essays on Medieval Music in Honor of David G. Hughes*, ed. G. M. Boone, Cambridge, MA, Harvard University Press, 1995, pp. 395–413

Riemann, H. *Geschichte der Musiktheorie im IX.–XIX. Jahrhundert*, reprint of 2nd edn., Hildesheim, G. Olms, 1921; trans. of Riemann, Books I and II, by R. Haggh as *History of Music Theory*, New York, Da Capo, 1966, reprint 1974

Sachs, K.-J. "Zur Tradition der Klangschritt-Lehre: Die Texte mit der Formel 'Si cantus ascendit . . .' und ihre Verwandten," *AfMw* 28 (1971), pp. 233–70

Der Contrapunctus im 14. und 15. Jahrhundert: Untersuchungen zum Terminus, zur Lehre und zu den Quellen, Wiesbaden, F. Steiner, 1974

"Arten improvisierter Mehrstimmigkeit nach Lehrtexten des 14. bis 16. Jahrhunderts," *Basler Jahrbuch für Historische Musikpraxis* 7 (1983), pp. 166–83
"Die Contrapunctus-Lehre im 14. und 15. Jahrhundert," *Die Mittelalterliche Lehre von der Mehrstimmigkeit, GMt* 5 (1984), pp. 161–256
Scattolin, P. P. "La Regola del 'Grado' nella Teoria Medievale del Contrappunto," *Rivista Italiana di Musicologia* 14 (1979), pp. 11–74
Seay, A., ed., "An Anonymous Treatise from St. Martial," *Annales Musicologiques* 5 (1976), pp. 7–42
Tinctoris, J. *Liber de arte contrapuncti* (1477), ed. A. Seay, *CSM* 22/2 (1975), pp. 5–157; trans. A. Seay as *The Art of Counterpoint*, *MSD* 5 (1961)
Torkewitz, D. "Zur Entstehung der Musica und Scolica Enchiriadis," *Acta* 69 (1997), pp. 156–81
Treitler, L. "Der vatikanische Organum-traktat und das Organum von Notre Dame de Paris: Perspektiven der Entwicklung einer schriftlichen Musikkultur in Europa," *Basler Jahrbuch für historische Musikpraxis* 7 (1983), pp. 23–31
Trowell, B. "Faburden and Fauxbourdon," *Musica Disciplina* 13 (1959), pp. 43–78
"Faburden – New Sources, New Evidence: a Preliminary Survey," in *Modern Musical Scholarship*, ed. E. Olleson, Boston, Oriel Press, 1980, pp. 28–78
Trumble, E. *Fauxbourdon: An Historical Survey*, Brooklyn, Institute of Medieval Music, 1959
Ugolino of Orvieto, *Declaratio Musicae Disciplinae*, ed. A. Seay, 3 vols., *CSM* 7 (1959–62)
Wegman, R. "From Maker to Composer: Improvisation and Musical Authorship in the Low Countries, 1450–1500," *JAMS* 49 (1996), pp. 409–79
Whitcomb, P. "Teachers, Booksellers and Taxes: Reinvestigating the Life and Activities of Johannes de Garlandia," *Plainsong and Medieval Music* 8 (1999), pp. 1–13
Zaminer, F. *Der Vatikanische Organum-Traktat (Ottob. lat. 3025): Organum-Praxis der frühen Notre Dame-Schule und ihrer Vorstufen*, Tutzing, H. Schneider, 1959

· 16 ·

Counterpoint pedagogy in the Renaissance

PETER SCHUBERT

How did Renaissance composers learn their craft? They could have learned much of their technique from treatises, especially from those portions devoted to counterpoint. Today, we often think of counterpoint as consisting primarily of rules of voice leading. Such rules, which are found in virtually every music treatise of the time, teach the student to regulate the melodic motions of lines in relation to the simultaneous intervals between them (e.g., conditions for approaching perfect consonances or for preparing and resolving dissonances). They were learned by young singers for the purpose of improvisation, and following them would have been as natural as speaking in grammatically correct sentences.[1] Yet just as the art of oratory consists of more than correct grammar, so musical composition goes far beyond mere voice leading. Composers had to choose between many large-scale contrapuntal techniques involving texture, motivic and structural repetition, and variation. While there has been extensive study by scholars of the rules of voice leading in Renaissance music, less consideration has been given to these more advanced compositional techniques.[2]

In this chapter, then, we will examine some of these compositional techniques by reviewing some two dozen treatises written between the mid-fifteenth and mid-seventeenth centuries. We will see that the real challenge for a Renaissance composer consisted not of employing "correct" contrapuntal voice leading but rather of elaborating primary musical material – sometimes called a *soggetto* – by varying it or combining it with some other melodic material.[3] (As we will see, a *soggetto* need not be

1 Coclico, *Musical Compendium*, pp. 16, 24; Morley, *Plaine and Easie*, p. 120; Montaños, *Arte*, fols. 26v–27r. In some treatises, in fact, the word "counterpoint" refers primarily to improvisation (Bermudo, *Declaracion*, Book V, Chapter 15). See also Garcia's commentary accompanying his translation of Cerone (*Pietro Cerone's "El Melopeo y Maestro,"* pp. 81ff.); Wegman, "From Maker to Composer"; Sachs, "Arten improvisierter Mehrstimmigkeit."

2 For examples of studies of Renaissance voice-leading rules, see Andrews, *The Technique of Byrd's Vocal Polyphony*; Jeppesen, *The Style of Palestrina and the Dissonance*; Sachs, "Counterpoint." See also Rothfarb, "Tinctoris vs. Tinctoris"; Dahlhaus, "On the Treatment of Dissonance." On changing rules toward the end of the century, see Palisca, "The Revision of Counterpoint"; "Vincenzo Galilei's Counterpoint Treatise."

3 According to Harold Powers ("The Modality of Vestiva i colli," p. 31), "the compositional techniques of Palestrina's time are essentially those of elaborating what Zarlino defines as a 'soggetto' . . ."

simply a melodic subject in equal or mixed rhythmic values; it could also be a duo, or, in the case of parody technique, even an entire polyphonic composition.[4]) The resulting contrapuntal combination could be further elaborated by adding more voices or by tacking on varied repetitions of the same combination. Many of these elaborative techniques, such as adding two voices in canon to a cantus firmus or inverting two parts at the tenth, appear to us today as "learned" devices. Yet they were considered routine by most Renaissance composers, and could even be improvised by singers and keyboardists.

In spite of the diversity of musical styles found in the Renaissance, we will see that the principles underlying the elaboration of the *soggetto* were remarkably consistent for nearly two hundred years. Whether you were a Burgundian singer adding a line to a chant, a sixteenth-century Spanish organist eliding two imitative duos at the organ, or a seventeenth-century Italian composer writing a trio on a dance bass, your conceptual framework was fundamentally the same.

Treatises

The major authors whose treatises are the basis of our survey fall into four large groups. The first generation of Renaissance theorists includes Ugolino of Orvieto (*Declaratio musicae disciplinae*, c. 1430), Johannes Tinctoris (*Liber de arte contrapuncti*, 1477), Bartolomeo Ramis de Pareia (*Musica practica*, 1482), and Franchino Gaffurio (*Practica musice*, 1496). These fifteenth-century authors write largely about counterpoint in two parts, divided into simple (note against note) and florid (mixed values) genres. In them we find brief rules combined with more or less exhaustive examples of note-against-note connections.

A second strand of contrapuntal pedagogy begins in the mid-sixteenth century with Gioseffo Zarlino (*Le istitutioni harmoniche*, 1558) and continues with several of his followers: Pietro Pontio (*Ragionamento di musica*, 1588); Orazio Tigrini (*Il compendio della musica*, 1588); Thomas Morley (*A plaine and easie introduction to practicall musicke*, 1597); Giovanni Maria Artusi (*L'arte del contraponto*, 1598); and Scipione Cerreto (*Della prattica musica*, 1601). Zarlino was the first theorist to describe various kinds of *soggetti* in detail, and he offers detailed explanations of how to write or improvise against them. He was also the first to classify types of cadence, types of imitation, and types of double counterpoint. One of his major contributions, not widely recognized nowadays but repeated by his followers, is his setting out conditions for the use of repetition.

A family of Spanish treatises begins roughly at the same time as Zarlino's treatise, but stresses some different principles: Vincenzo Lusitano (*Introduttione facilissima*, 1553) is much more explicit than Zarlino about how to improvise using a repeating

4 For Zarlino's various meanings of *soggetto*, see Rivera, "Finding the *Soggetto* in Willaert's Free Imitative Counterpoint," pp. 99–101.

motive against a cantus firmus, and he offers the earliest example of a "species" approach to counterpoint. Thomas de Sancta Maria (*Libro llamado arte de tañer fantasia*, 1565) and Francisco de Montaños (*Arte de musica theorica y pratica*, 1592) are noteworthy for presenting detailed examples of composing and improvising in four-part imitative texture. Finally, in a brilliant *summa* of counterpoint pedagogy, *El melopeo* (1613), Pietro Cerone expands the work of Montaños and Sancta Maria and integrates it with the work of Zarlino and his followers. (Cerone's is the obvious choice if you can take only one treatise to a desert island!)

Several early seventeenth-century Italian treatises build on Zarlino's work but with different emphases: Adriano Banchieri (*Cartella*, 1614) updates Zarlino's technique of composing a new voice against some pre-existent freely composed line; where Zarlino adds lines to original melodies by Willaert and Josquin, Banchieri elaborates melodies by Lassus and Rore in a more contemporary style. Extensions of Zarlino's discussion of invertible counterpoint (among other topics) are found in Camillo Angleria (*La regola del contraponto*, 1622), Rocco Rodio (*Regole di musica*, 1609), Antonio Brunelli (*Regole et dichiarationi di alcuni contrappunti dopii*, 1610), and Giovanni Chiodino (*Arte pratica latina e volgare*, 1610). Finally, the "chordal" approach of Thomas Campion (*A new way of making fowre parts in counter-point*, c. 1618) will be seen to be as much a direct descendant of fifteenth-century *contrapunctus simplex* concepts (discussed below) as it is a token of the new triadic consciousness animating seventeenth-century musicians.

Simple counterpoint in the fifteenth century

At the end of the fifteenth century, the word "counterpoint" was often synonymous with *contrapunctus simplex*: two lines moving in note-against-note texture, with only consonances allowed between the parts. A counterpoint was constructed by adding notes against some pre-existing monophonic line (the *cantus firmus*, hereafter abbreviated CF). Most fifteenth-century theorists presented six to eight fundamental voice-leading rules to regulate *contrapunctus simplex*.[5] Some of these rules control the most local connections (e.g., how perfect consonances may be approached), and others have to do with permissible opening and closing sonorities. While the rules vary somewhat from one theorist to another, the eight rules of Aaron summarized in **Chapter 18, p. 561** are representative of those found in many counterpoint treatises throughout the sixteenth century.[6]

Theorists typically supplemented these abstract rules with lists of short examples that could run on for many pages. The lengthy itemization of permissible contrapuntal progressions found in many of these treatises, although appearing tediously didactic and uneconomical to us today, were probably intended to provide the singer with a

5 Prosdocimo, Burzio, Ugolino, Ramis de Pareia, Tinctoris, and Gaffurio, for examples.
6 Coclico, Vanneus, Zarlino, and Yssandon, for examples.

Example 16.1 Movements from a sixth from Ugolino and Ramis

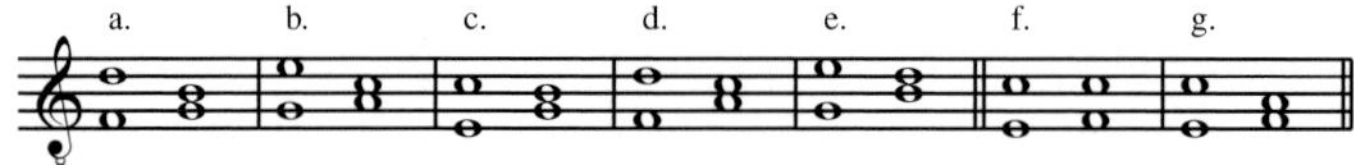

menu of formulas to be memorized that could then be called upon in improvisation. The approach of Ugolino (c. 1430) is typical. Ugolino takes as his initial "givens" the direction of the tenor and the first vertical interval. He then shows for each melodic interval in the tenor how a second vertical interval may follow, determining the motion of the added voice. The voices in most of his examples move by contrary motion, and each one is shown at several transposition levels. Here is one of his rules (expressed in a rhymed couplet): "Seventh rule, [the tenor] ascending from [the vertical interval of] a sixth: a sixth desires a third if it aims above the note" (see Example 16.1a–e).[7]

Ramis cited each of Ugolino's rhymes and examples in his own counterpoint treatise, often adding commentary and counter-examples. In the case of Ugolino's seventh rule, for instance, Ramis noted: "The seventh [rule] is satisfactory; but in fact, if the tenor has e–f, then the other voice might well have c–c, as well as c–a, for from the minor sixth we aim strongly toward the fifth [Example 16.1f–g]."[8] His emendation expresses the so-called "closest approach" principle, a widely taught precept of Renaissance counterpoint which prescribes that one of the notes of a perfect vertical consonance should be approached by semitone.[9] (Thus Ramis would not have illustrated a major sixth moving to a fifth.)

Ugolino's method may be contrasted with that of Tinctoris, who starts not with the first vertical interval and the motion of the tenor, but with a pair of vertical intervals. In Example 16.2, for instance, we see all the ways in which "a sixth above [the tenor] can have a third after it."[10] These examples are ordered by motions of the tenor (shown with open note heads).

7 "Septima regula de sexto ascendendo: Sexta ternam cupit, si supra notam intendit" (*Declaratio musicae disciplinae*, Book II, Chapter 26, p. 34, Ex. II–91). Ugolino shows only two other examples beginning with a sixth, one series in which the tenor descends by step, leading to an octave, and one where it descends a third, leading to a tenth. Presumably, the rules are formulated in rhyme for ease of memorization. 8 Ramis, *Musica practica*, Part II, Tract 1, Chapter 2, p. 126.

9 The "closest approach" rule is first clearly articulated by Marchetto. It is also found discussed by Prosdocimo (*Contrapunctus*, section 5, Chapter 6), Gaffurio (*Practica musice*, Book III, Chapter 3), Vanneus (*Recanetum*, Chapters 14–15), and Zarlino (*Le istitutioni harmoniche*, Part III, Chapter 38). See also the useful commentary by Dahlhaus (*Studies*, pp. 78, 86) and Carpenter ("Tonal Coherence," pp. 50–51).

10 Tinctoris, *Liber de arte contrapuncti*, Book I, Chapter 7, p. 35. Tinctoris is much more thorough than Ugolino. The nineteen chapters of Book I show every possible way two consonances could succeed each other. His examples are exhaustive, providing that no voice can leap more than a fifth, and that similar fifths are not allowed. One reason it takes so many chapters is that Tinctoris does not take the compounding of intervals for granted; the same series of examples given in Chapter 9 is repeated in Chapters 12 and 17, with vertical intervals compounded.

Example 16.2 Movement from a sixth to a third from Tinctoris

Both Ugolino and Tinctoris present examples that are only two notes long. Presumably the singer would consider a tenor CF as a chain of such two-note successions, the second vertical interval in the first two-note segment becoming the first vertical interval in the second segment, and so forth. Each interval succession thus acts as a link to the next. The difference between their examples lies in the relative priority of the horizontal and vertical dimensions. Ugolino's concern with the smooth connection of voices seems to make more sense from the point of view of the improviser, who at a given moment may find himself singing a sixth with the CF, and, looking ahead, sees the CF about to rise. Tinctoris, however, places priority upon the successive vertical intervals before considering the melodic motions that connect them. We may wonder why a composer trained as a young singer to improvise against a CF would think in terms of a succession of vertical intervals, instead of focusing on melodic motion. One factor may have been the association of mode and counterpoint.

Some modal considerations

Mode, we have seen elsewhere, is generally defined in terms of melodic features: ambitus, final, reciting or psalm tone, and characteristic species.[11] While the relation between mode and counterpoint is almost never discussed explicitly in Renaissance treatises, we do find scattered comments by theorists on the modal implications of certain vertical intervals.[12] In one example, Tinctoris says that *musica ficta* added to a line to correct a vertical diminished fifth causes a momentary change of mode (called "commixture"). In regard to the progression shown in Example 16.3, he says that the lower line (the added voice) is of the second mode commixed with the fourth.[13] The modal commixture results from the fact that the B♭ changes the fourth between A and D from what would normally be a first-species fourth into a second-species fourth (semitone-tone-tone, bracketed in the example), which is characteristic of the fourth

11 See **Chapters 11 and 12**, but especially **pp. 311–13** and **pp. 364–66**.

12 The dichotomy in Renaissance treatises between counterpoint and mode has been discussed by Powers in "Modality as a European Cultural Construct," p. 210. Also see **Chapter 12, pp. 400–02**.

13 Tinctoris, *Liber de natura et proprietate tonorum*, Chapter 18, p. 20. Commixture refers to the insertion into a line of species of interval foreign to the governing mode of the line (see Schubert, "The Fourteen-Mode System"; Carpenter "Tonal Coherence").

Example 16.3 Modal comixture from Tinctoris

mode. Presumably, if the composer did not wish commixture, he would have chosen some other note than B to place below the F of the tenor.

For much the same reason, Pietro Aaron objects to placing B♭ in the signature of the bass part to correct an "imperfect fifth" with the tenor F, since the bass will now sing a melodic species different from those sung in the upper voices that lack B♭.[14] Other contrapuntal obligations could also affect mode: Scipione Cerreto, writing as late as 1601, says that the "closest approach" principle is to be used unless accidentals cause the line to leave the mode.[15] For these authors, incidental *musica ficta* can also have modal repercussions.[16]

But it is not only the introduction of accidentals that can destabilize modal identity when adding contrapuntal lines. Sometimes the reiteration of particular notes or the use of certain melodic skips might have modal implications. Ramis criticizes a line added to a Dorian CF because it emphasizes structural tones and leaps associated with the Phrygian mode – in this case, b and a skip from b to e (see Example 16.4a). He then proposes an alternative line using reiterations and leaps more appropriate to the Dorian mode (see Example 16.4b).[17] We can see that the rules of counterpoint might constrain – but do not determine – mode; a singer could conceivably stress a number of differing modes in adding a line to any CF.

In Ramis's improved example, the Ds in the added voice always form perfect vertical intervals with the CF (asterisked), suggesting that these too might have modal significance. This suggestion is corroborated by Tinctoris, who in his fifth rule of counterpoint admonishes that "above absolutely no note . . . should a perfection be taken by which a removal from its mode (*distonatio*) can occur."[18] Thus if the added line sounds an octave against an E in a Dorian CF, *distonatio* will result from the emphasis on E. The word "perfection" can refer to both an octave and a cadence, and Tinctoris's rule foreshadows all the many subsequent treatise strictures concerning

14 Bent, "Accidentals, Counterpoint and Notation in Aaron's *Aggiunta* to the *Toscanello in Musica*," p. 323 and n. 26.

15 Cerreto, *Della prattica musica*, Book IV, Chapter 1, pp. 242–52.

16 Aaron's pupil Illuminato Aiguino even calls into question the *una nota super la* rule because it may cause a change of mode. See Schubert, "The Fourteen-Mode System," p. 181 and n. 21.

17 Horsley, "Fugue and Mode in 16th-Century Vocal Polyphony," p. 410.

18 Tinctoris, *Liber de arte contrapuncti*, Book III, Chapter 5, p. 135.

Example 16.4 Counterpoints emphasizing Phrygian and Dorian modes from Ramis

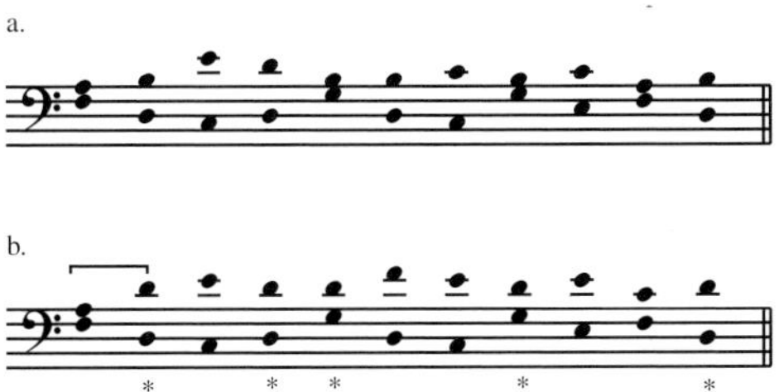

which cadences are appropriate in which modes. These strictures vary from treatise to treatise.

Florid counterpoint

Throughout the Renaissance, theorists normally maintained Tinctoris's distinction between note-against-note (*simplex*) counterpoint and florid (*diminutus*) counterpoint. As late as 1597, Morley defines them as "counterpoint" and "descant," respectively.[19] In florid counterpoint, the added line contains a variety of shorter rhythmic values against a CF sounding in equal values (breves or semibreves). However, beginning with Tinctoris, the rules for the use of dissonance in florid counterpoint tended to be codified even more precisely as to melodic motion and metrical position.[20] This led to a kind of proto-species presentation in which the behavior of each note value was illustrated separately.[21]

Montaños, for instance, shows how different values could be placed against a CF in breves. An added line in breves is called "the first manner" of counterpoint; in semibreves, "the second manner"; in minims, "the third manner" or "the first diminution"; in semiminims, "the second diminution." Montaños gives examples of each one but the last in halved note-values ("tempus imperfectum alla semibreve"), saying that "both are one." He also gives the beginner many short examples of florid lines against pairs of CF notes.[22]

Cerone suggests learning to improvise by practicing first in note-against-note

19 Morley, *Plaine and easie*, p. 93.
20 See Rothfarb, "Tinctoris vs. Tinctoris"; Dahlhaus, "On the Treatment of Dissonance."
21 For examples of the "proto-species" approach, see Lusitano, *Introduttione*, fol. 12; Sancta Maria, *Libro*, Book I, Chapter 20; Cerone, *Il melopeo*, Book IX, Chapter 16, p. 574; Diruta, *Il Transilvano*, Book II, pp. 10–11; Banchieri, *Cartella*, pp. 106–07. (Also see **Chapter 18, pp. 565–66.**) Some earlier (medieval) examples of "species" counterpoint are discussed in **Chapter 15, pp. 493–95**.
22 Montaños, *Arte*, fols. 4r–12v. See also **Figure 18.1, p. 567** for some later (although analogous) schematics of proto-species counterpoint.

texture, then with two minims against a semibreve, then four semiminims, just as in later written species counterpoint.[23] Discussing the question of how to proceed from simple counterpoint to diminished counterpoint, he says:

> We should produce two notes in counterpoint, calling them guides, against two notes of the plainchant. These will serve to establish the two principal positions that are the basis of diminution. Keep these in mind, for if we know the consonant positions where the counterpoint can occur above the plainchant, it will be very easy to fill the space later by subdividing the value of the first note . . .[24]

His "guides" (i.e., two semibreves in note-against-note texture) often contain voice-leading errors that will be corrected when one line is diminished.

Carl Dahlhaus has noted the chasm which seems to separate species counterpoint based upon a CF and the fluid, imitative counterpoint of Renaissance polyphonic practice. The species approach, he points out, is "hardly reconcilable with the historical reality of Palestrina's style, which provides less an example of cantus firmus composition than a way of writing based on pervasive imitation between textually characterized, rhythmically differentiated parts."[25] But this view is based on the erroneous assumption that the improvised activities that prepared the student for composition should themselves resemble finished compositions. Perhaps instead we should consider a CF as a chain of two-note fragments against which additional voices may be improvised, thus providing a vocabulary of consonances underlying all contrapuntal textures and genres. Cerone called vertical intervals *elementos*, saying, "just as we need only 22 letters to make thousands of orations, we only need 22 intervals to make all music."[26] He refers to "the most common" stepwise patterns of semiminims against two-breve CF motions as a "primer" (*Abecedario*).[27] While counterpoint against a complete CF can be an end in itself, for instance in certain liturgical situations, it can also be used as the basis for further elaboration, either through diminutions of one or both lines, or through the addition of other lines.

Contraponto fugato

A notable development in sixteenth-century counterpoint pedagogy concerned the identification of short motives in mixed values (called variously *inventioni*, *riditti*, *punti*, *passaggi*, *passi*, *pertinacie*, or "points") and the establishment of conditions for their repetition against a CF. (These short motives should not be confused with the longer *soggetti* in equal values.) The first author to call attention to motivic repetition was

23 Cerone, *El melopeo*, Book IX, Chapter 18, p. 576. See also Coclico, *Compendium*, p. 23.
24 Cerone, *El melopeo*, Book IX, Chapter 24, p. 587.
25 Dahlhaus, "Counterpoint," p. 845.
26 Cerone, *El melopeo*, Book IX, Chapter 3, p. 565.
27 Ibid., Chapter 23, p. 582.

Tinctoris – albeit in a negative way. In his sixth rule, he wrote: "in singing above a plainchant, we ought to avoid repetitions as much as we can, particularly if some appear in the tenor."[28] By this, Tinctoris means those instances in which the tenor utilizes a repeating melodic pattern, and the added line repeats a motive against that same pattern, causing the whole contrapuntal combination to be duplicated. Zarlino likewise forbade direct repetition of contrapuntal combinations, but allowed for the repetition of a motive in a single voice if it met one of three conditions: (1) if both it and the CF changed pitch level (causing a sequence); (2) if the motive was accompanied by different vertical intervals (i.e., if the CF did not repeat); or (3) if it was varied rhythmically.[29] Zarlino's guidelines were echoed by many theorists, among them Artusi, who expressed them in a wonderful flow chart.[30]

The technique of repeating a motive in quicker values against a CF was called, variously, *contrapunto fugato*, *contraponto con obbligo*, *contraponto per perfidia*, *contraponto per riditta*, *contraponto capriccioso*, *ymitacion*, or "maintaining a point."[31] The term *contrapunto fugato* has its roots in Tinctoris's definition of *fuga*. Although we commonly think of *fuga* as imitation between two voices in "flight," Tinctoris defines it as the repetition of a melodic idea: "*Fuga* is the identity of the parts of a line (*cantus*) as to the value, name, form, and sometimes placement of notes and rests."[32] Thus for him *fuga* could refer to repetitions of a motive within a line, as in the technique of *contrapunto fugato*.

Short melodic motives in mixed values may be freely invented or be drawn from a received source – most commonly the CF. If a voice utilizes motivic fragments taken from a CF, the result is sometimes called *contraponto ad imitatione*. This can exist in note-against-note texture (as when Zarlino adds bits of the CF into the contrapuntal voices, or when Morley writes a first-species canon[33]), but most often fragments of the added line are freely rhythmicized versions of sections of the CF.[34] Whether newly composed or borrowed, the motives can be transposed temporally, displaced, and/or rhythmi-

28 Although Tinctoris tolerates repetition for purposes of text expression. See *Liber de arte contrapuncti*, Book III, Chapter 6, p. 137. See also Meier, *The Modes*, pp. 243ff.

29 Zarlino, *Le istitutioni harmoniche*, Part III, Chapter 55.

30 Artusi, *L'arte del contraponto*, p. 58, transcribed in my *Modal Counterpoint, Renaissance Style*, pp. 104–05. It should be noted, however, that not all composers abided by such strictures. A distributional analysis by Cristle Collins Judd exposes in Josquin's Missa "Hercules Dux Ferrariae" precisely the type of literal motivic repetition forbidden by Zarlino. See her "Josquin des Prez: Salve Regina (à 5)," p. 137.

31 Lusitano, *Introduttione*, fols. 14v–16v; Zarlino, *Le istitutioni harmoniche*, Part III, Chapter 55; Tigrini, *Compendio*, pp. 105–06; Morley, *Plaine and Easie*, pp. 84, 124; Banchieri, *Cartella*, pp. 67, 107; Pontio, *Ragionamento*, p. 90; Cerreto, *Della prattica*, Book IV, Chapter 1, p. 250; Diruta, *Il Transilvano*, Book II, pp. 11–12; Montaños, *Arte* ("Contrapunto"), fols. 13v–15v; Cerone, *El melopeo*, Book IX, Chapter 18, p. 575; Book X, Chapter 1, p. 597; Book XII, Chapter 4, p. 657.

32 Tinctoris, *Diffinitorium*, s.v. "fuga." By "name," Tinctoris means hexachordal solmization syllable; by "form" he means visual notation (single note or ligature); and by "placement" he means pitch class and register.

33 Zarlino, *Le istitutioni harmoniche*, Part III, Chapter 40; Morley, *Plaine and Easie* p. 76.

34 Morley, *Plaine and Easie*, p. 124; Tigrini, *Compendio*, p. 106. For more examples, see my *Modal Counterpoint, Renaissance Style*, Chapter 9.

Example 16.5 *Ymitacion general* from Montaños

cally altered. They may also be used as ostinati, sounded in inversion, in retrograde, or in *fuga d'inganno*.[35]

Many theorists did not make clear distinctions between the technique of imitation between parts and that of repetition within a single part. The confusion is especially pronounced in Montaños, who refers to any repetition as *ymitacion*. He calls harmonic sequence (i.e., the transposition of both the CF and the added part by the same interval) *ymitacion general*, and he distinguishes it from *ymitacion particular*, in which the short motive is repeated with different rhythmic values, and makes different vertical intervals with the CF (as shown in Example 16.5).[36]

Because Montaños does not use the word *soggetto*, it is not clear if the *soggetto* in Example 16.5 is the hexachord of the CF or the bracketed motive in the added voice. Since Zarlino's definition of *soggetto* embraces themes of all sizes, it may be more useful here to invoke Cerone's distinction between a longer, more global theme and a shorter melodic idea that is used briefly and discarded. The former he calls *thema* or *subiecto*, and the latter *passo* (like Lusitano) or *invencione*.[37] Thus in Example 16.5, we could say that Montaños wrote a *subiecto* in the CF against which he repeats a short *passo*.

Contraponto fugato can be a means of giving form to music based upon a CF. Lusitano, the first author to describe this possibility, says that the singer is to "choose a short motive (*passaggio*), and [when it has been] sung once or twice, sing a fast scale (*tirata*) or

35 In *fuga d'inganno* ("deceptive fugue"), the melody is defined not by the pitches sounded, but by solmization syllables (hence the synonymous term *fuga in nomine*); the actual melody sounded changes by virtue of hexachordal mutation. Thus la–sol–fa–re–mi could be sung as A–G–F–D–E or A–G–B♭–G–A or A–G–C–A–B, among other possibilities. The device is found as late as 1731 in John Pepusch's *A Treatise on Harmony*, p. 88. For an inventory and description of such devices, see Agee, "Costanzo Festa's Gradus ad Parnassum," and Newcomb's introduction to *The Ricercars of the Bourdeney Codex*. See also Le Huray, "Some Thoughts about Cantus Firmus Composition."

36 Montaños, *Arte*, "Contrapunto," fols. 13v–15r.

37 Cerone, *El melopeo*, Book XII; compare Chapter 1 (pp. 652ff.) with Chapter 6 (pp. 672ff.). A polyphonic chanson used as the basis for a parody mass would fall into the category of *thema* or *subiecto*.

broad *passo*, ascending or descending, as you like." (Lusitano uses the Italian term *passaggio* and the Spanish term *passo* interchangeably.[38]) In the richest collection of examples of this technique, the *Tratado de canto de organo* (attributed to Lusitano), we find examples in which one *passo* is repeated at the beginning of the CF, another in the middle, and the first again at the end, creating a simple ABA structure.[39] The importance of improvised *contraponto fugato* to Renaissance composition is underlined by the fact that some theorists allowed poor melodic writing and even faulty voice-leading if a more pressing "obligation" was being undertaken.[40] Knowledge of how to repeat a motive in the voice added to a CF without monotony was one of the most essential skills of improvisation and of the compositional craft. The importance to us of Zarlino's three rules for repetition in *contaponto fugato* is that they prove that Renaissance composers were sensitive to the succession of vertical intervals. As we will see below in the section on pairs of duos, the repetition of that succession is a key element of musical structure. However, repetition had to be made acceptable by any of several variation techniques. Those techniques include transposition, harmonic sequence, metric shift, varied countersubjects, and, as we will see below, double counterpoint.

One of the densest kinds of counterpoint that could be added to a CF is a canonic duo. In this popular technique of compositional elaboration, not only must the added lines imitate each other strictly at a given time and pitch interval, they must each work with respect to the CF.[41]

As challenging as this may seem to be, such canons could be improvised by skilled keyboard performers – and singers! Presumably the singer of the guide (the starting part) could look at the CF and know – drawing upon a repertoire of memorized interval patterns – what would work when the consequent voice started at a given time and pitch interval. Perhaps the singer of the consequent could hear the notes sung by the guide and immediately imitate them, even when the time interval was as little as a minim. More likely, though, the guide was probably composed and rehearsed alone, memorized by the singer of the consequent, and finally performed as a canon.

A comprehensive list of pre-composed patterns that could be memorized and then

38 Lusitano, *Introduttione*, fol. 14v. A few of Lusitano's examples are transcribed in Dahlhaus, "Formen improvisierter Mehrstimmigkeit."

39 *Un tratado de canto de organo*, ed. Collet, p. 76 and example 50.

40 Of *contraponto con obbligo* (Zarlino's term for *contraponto fugato*), Zarlino says "Because this style of counterpoint is very difficult, certain liberties are permitted" (*Le istitutioni harmoniche*, Part III, Chapter 55, Marco trans., p. 154). Regarding a case of similar motion to an octave in a note-against-note canon, Morley says "in Fuges we are not so straightlie bound . . . the point excuseth it" (*Plaine and Easie*, pp. 76–77; see also p. 124). And Cerreto says "when the contrapuntist is making a single counterpoint on a *cantus firmus* or other *soggetto*, without obligation of canons, of *perfidie*, or of repetitions," then he must follow the "closest approach" principle; under more difficult conditions he allows the contrapuntist to dispense with the principle (*Della prattica musica*, Book IV, Chapter 1, p. 244).

41 See for instance Lusitano, *Introduttione*, fols. 13–20; Zarlino, *Le istitutioni harmoniche*, Part III, Chapter 63; Tigrini, *Compendio*, Book IV, pp. 12–15; see also discussions in Le Huray, "Some Thoughts about Cantus Firmus composition;" Schubert, *Modal Counterpoint*, pp. 192–97 for examples by Cerreto and Morley; and Collins, "Zarlino and Berardi."

invoked by a singer in order to create a canonic duo is found in the treatise of Lusitano. He first presents segments of a CF line in sequential patterns (e.g., third up, step down, third up . . . , or fourth up, third down, fourth up . . .). By this means, any CF could be interpreted as a succession of segments "borrowed" from these different patterns. Lusitano's canonic duos move mostly in note-against-note texture, at a time interval of one or two minims, and at the interval of a fourth or fifth. The performer presumably is to memorize all of Lusitano's patterns, so that having decided that the consequent was to follow the guide at a fifth above after two minims, and seeing a given CF motion, knows which pattern to employ. Although it would require a good deal of effort to memorize all the possible patterns, the number of different solutions is actually not very large.[42] Still, the results are impressive, with a high proportion of rich, three-pitch-class sonorities.

Double counterpoint

Double (or invertible) counterpoint makes a new combination out of an original by transposing the parts with respect to each other. Such transpositions most often occur at the intervals of an octave, tenth, or twelfth, and constitute one of the most important techniques for varying the repetition of blocks of musical material. The rules for double counterpoint are generally framed as prohibitions of vertical intervals or interval successions. If two voices are to be inverted at the twelfth, for instance, the original combination must contain no sixths in strong metrical positions, because sixths become sevenths in the new combination; if the double counterpoint is at the tenth, the original must contain no parallel thirds or sixths, as they would become parallel octaves or fifths. Thus the technique of double counterpoint imposes more restrictions on the added line than do the basic rules of voice leading.

Double counterpoint may not seem to be a common feature of imitative music. In fact, though, it is quite often employed with imitative textures.[43] And like the canonic duo, it is something that could be improvised, as is made clear from the titles of two 1610 treatises by Brunelli and Chiodino. Tigrini also treats double counterpoint in a discussion of improvised counterpoint,[44] although Lusitano and Morley treat this technique in sections clearly having to do with written composition.[45] In

42 Apparently referring to such methods, Vicentino criticizes singers who repeat the same two or three consonances all the time (*L'antica musica*, Book IV, p. 23). Zarlino invokes the important visual aspect of the art of memory when he says that in improvising a canon on a CF, "the contrapuntist, whether writing or improvising, must always visualize what the consequent will do," adding, "one should not be surprised at occasional lapses from absolute correctness" (*Le istitutioni harmoniche*, Part III, Chapter 63; Marco trans., pp. 217–20). Finally, Rodio says good composers "expect sweetness more than strictness" (*Regole*, Introduction, p. 4).

43 For examples of double counterpoint in an imitative context, see Morley, *Plaine and Easie*, pp. 106–10. Also see Schubert, "A Lesson from Lassus," pp. 14–16.

44 Tigrini, *Compendio*, Book IV, Chapter 11, p. 115.

45 Lusitano, *Introduttione*, fol. 20v, "De la compositione"; Morley, *Plaine and Easie*, "The second part."

either case, a singer would learn to recognize what interval successions would work in invertible counterpoint against a given CF segment. The constraints of double counterpoint, like those of *contraponto fugato*, are quite severe, and sometimes licenses were permitted.[46]

A variation of double counterpoint is to invert both parts melodically and then invert their respective positions. The result ends up being the same succession of vertical intervals. We find this technique first discussed in Zarlino, Brunelli, and Vicentino. Examples 16.6a and b (by Brunelli) offer an illustration.[47] One could further elaborate the original contrapuntal combination by doubling one or both of the parts in parallel tenths. In Example 16.6c, the CF is doubled by Brunelli, adding to the original two-voice combination through invertible counterpoint at the tenth; in Example 16.6d, Brunelli doubles the CF twice, combining inversions at the tenth and twelfth; in Example 16.6e the contrapuntal line is doubled at the tenth below, adding invertible counterpoint at the tenth to the original combination; and finally in Example 16.6f, both the CF and the added line are doubled, so that the original duo (in the tenor and alto) is combined with invertible counterpoint at the tenth (between the soprano and alto and between the tenor and bass) and with invertible counterpoint at the twelfth (between the soprano and bass). To make this composite double counterpoint work, Brunelli had to ensure that the original combination contained no parallel motion. Thus when a singer or composer chooses melodic material, he must have its elaboration already in mind.

Giovanni Chiodino's three-voice examples of invertible counterpoint at the tenth (reprinted by Herbst) suggest successive transpositional stages, like a word ladder in which one letter is changed at each step to make new words (see Example 16.7). In each successive example two voices move down a third (or a tenth) while one of these same voices is replicated with the same pitch classes (at the unison or at the octave). So in Example 16.7b, the original tenor and soprano from Example 16.7a have been transposed down a third to become the bass and tenor, but the tenor is also replicated an octave higher in the soprano, maintaining its original pitch classes (e–d–c). Finally, in Example 16.7c, the soprano and tenor from Example 16.7b are transposed down a tenth, while the bass from Example 16.7b is replicated at the unison in the tenor, making the third combination "the same as the first one" albeit down a third.[48]

Some theorists used double counterpoint at the sixth and third to explain the derivation of lines moving in parallel thirds against another line. Rocco Rodio distinguishes "inverted counterpoints, called double," in which the positions of the parts are switched, from what he calls "inverted counterpoints, without the tenor being

46 Cerone, commenting on various challenging double counterpoints, apologizes for one example, saying "the obligation excuses, and pardons us" (*El melopeo*, p. 602). He adds, "it is a well-known fact that one cannot progress by intervals as beautiful and elegant as when the counterpoint is free of any kind of obligation" (*El melopeo*, p. 604).

47 Zarlino, *Le istitutioni harmoniche*, Part III, Chapter 56, pp. 232–34; Vicentino, *L'antica musica*, Book IV, Chapter 35. Brunelli, *Regole*, "Del contrappunto alla decima con l'osservatione della duodecima" (no page numbers). See also Vicentino, *L'antica musica*, Book IV, Chapter 34.

48 Chiodino, *Arte pratica latina e volgare*, reprinted in Herbst, *Arte prattica*, pp. 39–41.

Example 16.6a–f Examples of double counterpoint by Brunelli

inverted." In the latter case, the relative positions of the parts are not switched; rather, the added part is simply transposed by some small interval (only a third, fourth, fifth or sixth).[49] Angleria uses double counterpoint at the third and sixth to explain the generation of parallel lines against a CF, a typical seventeenth-century texture.[50]

49 Rodio, *Regole*, pp. 36–51. See also Angleria, *La Regola*, p. 94.

50 Angleria, *La Regola*, Chapter 25, pp. 98–100. Much earlier improvisatory techniques of singing in thirds and sixths against a given melody – *faburden* and *fauxbourdon* – are discussed and illustrated in Chapter 17, pp. 535–37.

Example 16.7 Transformational stages of double counterpoint by Chiodino

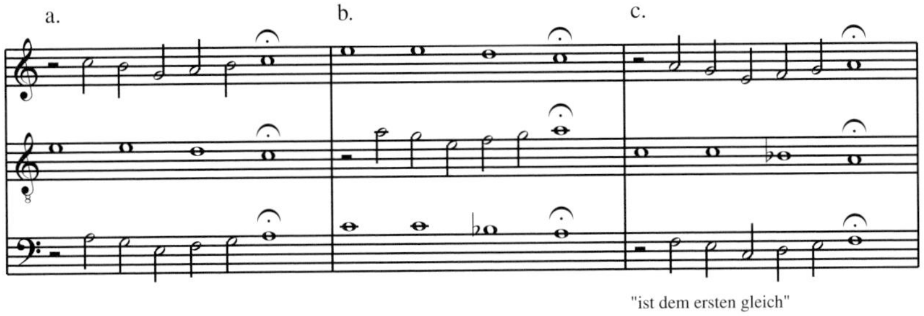

a. b. c.

"ist dem ersten gleich"

Imitation in two parts: the duo

Now we turn from techniques that were taught using a CF *soggetto* to freely invented imitative duos in mixed values. (Later we will consider imitative textures in more than two parts.) Duos typically constituted the first published efforts for beginning composers.[51] The missing links that fill the gap, described by Dahlhaus, between counterpoint against a CF and freely imitative writing with mixed values in both parts are based on the notion of breaking up long notes with embellishing shorter values (diminution). Unfortunately, most authors discussed such ornamentation and diminution in regard to a single line, independent of any contrapuntal context.[52] A few exceptions include Morley's method for writing a canon against a CF, Cerone's embellishments of Pontio's florid examples on a CF, and best of all, some examples by Francisco de Montaños (see the window on p. 518.)

Another link between CF exercises and imitation can be found in a common technique (originally described by Tinctoris) in which the line used as a CF is a melody in mixed values. Such a melody is called a *canto figurato* (so called because the mixed rhythmic values are written with different note shapes or figures). The most common types used as *soggetti* would include chant paraphrases or lines from polyphonic pieces such as chansons. The added line would ideally contain fragmentary imitation. This technique is described by Zarlino, who adds a new line to the soprano line taken from a two-voice motet by his teacher Willaert, imitating bits of the original tune.[53] Banchieri recommends this exercise as well:

> Thus if today's young contrapuntist wants to master the true fundamentals of sweetness, sonority, and propriety, he should choose as a model or for an exercise (*scedula*) a melody by Rore, Lassus, Palestrina, Marenzio, or other similar accepted composers,

51 See Carapezza, *Musiche Rinascimentale Siciliane*, introduction to vol. II.
52 Ortiz, to name just one, in the *Tratado de glosas*, pp. 5–48.
53 Zarlino, *Le istitutioni harmoniche*, Part III, Chapter 43. Montaños also illustrates this technique, but for him the imitations are not based on motives in the given tune; rather, they are repetitions of motives proper to the added voice only, as against a CF in even values (*Arte*, fols. 25v–27r).

A missing link: from first species to free imitation

In the section of his treatise, *Arte de musica theorica y pratica* (1592), called "On Composition," Francisco de Montaños shows how a composer can embellish a strict note-against-note progression in successive stages to arrive at a fully independent duo in mixed values. He writes: "And so that it might be easier, it should be made first only in semibreves, and afterwards the same with diminution, with signs [notes] put in between, and diverse figures [rhythmic values]" (fol. 9v). One of his examples (a) shows a point in semibreves imitating at the fifth below, followed by two embellished versions. The first variation (b) employs repeated notes ("diverse figures") and passing notes ("signs put in between"); the second variation (c) adds other diminutions: consonant skips, a suspension in diminished values, and a lower neighbor. The rhythmic independence of the parts belies their note-against-note origin.

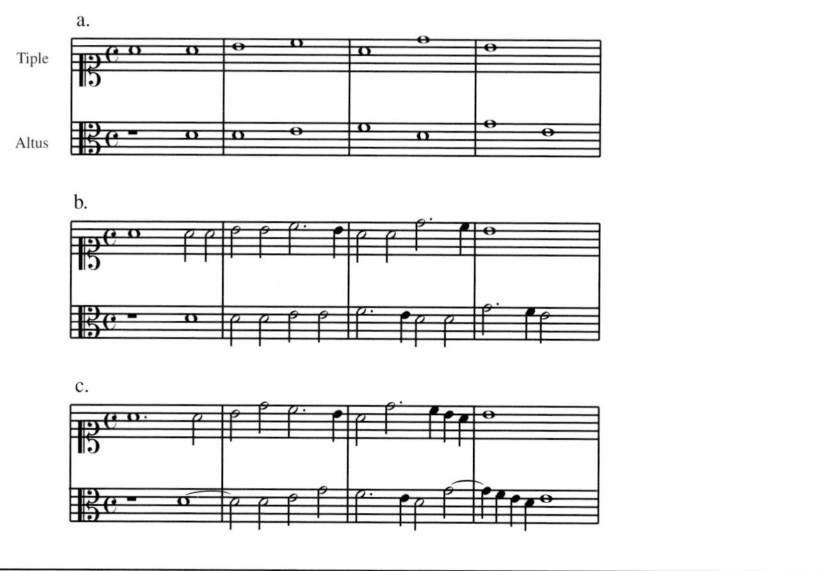

> writing it separately on a *cartella*, and looking either above it or below it for his own imitations (if possible), without looking at the other parts at all.[54]

Banchieri illustrates this in a style he calls the "moderna pratica," adding lines to melodies from sestina settings by Lassus and Rore. He shows how a composer may employ a variety of compositional techniques every few breves: imitation at the sixth, quick repetitions of a tiny motive (*scherzi*), imitation by inversion, "closest approach" motion, evaded cadences, word painting, and anticipatory imitation (*fuga anteveduta*, in which the added voice begins before the given voice). Each technique occurs only very briefly, reinforcing the point that the improviser's training with short interval successions has direct consequences for composition.

At the beginning of this chapter, it was noted that the *soggetto* need not be restricted

54 Banchieri, *Cartella*, p. 166.

to a line in mixed values; it could also be a duo, whether imitative or not (see also the boxed material annotated in Example 16.8, below). The earliest description of writing against a two-voice combination is found in the fifteenth century. Nicolò Burzio, among others, identifies the soprano and tenor as a duo to which a third voice is added, and Gaffurio describes the bass–soprano duo moving in parallel tenths as a duo to which a tenor may be added.[55] (Neither author refers to the original duo as a *soggetto*, however.) Because such a "thicker" *soggetto* often has two different pitch classes sounding simultaneously, there are fewer possibilities for the added line. Still, Zarlino is able to add a third line to a previously composed duo by Josquin, and manage to work in brief imitative fragments. (Cerone might call them *passi.*) Because of the difficult challenge posed by the addition of a third voice, at least when improvised, theorists tended also to tolerate here lapses from correct counterpoint.[56]

Imitation in four parts: pairs of duos

We will now consider imitation in four parts involving a pair of duos. The most thorough discussion of this technique is found in Thomas de Sancta Maria's *Libro llamado arte de tañer fantasia* (1565), the most advanced and informative treatise of large-scale compositional technique at mid-century. Although it addresses organists hoping to learn how to improvise at the keyboard, its ideas, presentation, and examples are valid for any polyphonic medium or genre, and they were picked up by Montaños (1592) and Cerone (1613) with no mention of organs or fantasias. After initiating the student into playing four-part homorhythm (to be discussed in more detail below), Sancta Maria discusses contrapuntal techniques that the composer will need in order to produce four-part fantasias.

First of all, a short subject (*passo*) can be introduced in a duo texture which can be imitative (*en fuga*) or not (*sin fuga*).[57] The *fugas* can be tightly overlapped (*travadas*) in

55 See Burzio, *Musices opusculum*, tractatus secundus, Chapter 5. Gaffurio's method is repeated in Ornithoparchus, and translated a century later by Dowland: "The most famous manner of the Counterpoint, as (saith Franchinus) is, if the Base goe together with the Meane, or any other Voyce, being also distant by a tenth, whilst the Tenor doth goe in Concord to both" (Ornithoparchus/Dowland, *Andreas Ornithoparchus his Micrologus*, Book 4, Chapter 4, p. 82; cf. Gaffurio, *Practica musice*, Book III, Chapter 12). The tenor–soprano duo as a framework has been dubbed by German scholars as *Gerüstsatz*, and now is widely acknowledged as a mark of late medieval polyphony (see Moll, *Counterpoint and Compositional Process in the Time of Dufay*, p. 24). But how late this continues to apply is a matter of debate (see Dahlhaus, *Studies*, pp. 95–96). Because the rules for making a part that can be paralleled in tenths are the same as those for double counterpoint at the tenth, some authors include the three-part technique in discussions of double counterpoint.

56 Zarlino says one "need not adhere strictly to the rules himself" when improvising a third part to a duo (*Le istitutioni harmoniche*, Part III, Chapter 64; Marco trans., p. 222). Artusi says that in order to improvise a third part to a duo, the singer needs to have "practiced at length on a CF . . . A quick and ready ear . . . [and] a good memory without which there is no one who can do anything good or beautiful." He likewise allows some license when adding a third part to a duo or a fourth part to a trio (*L'arte*, p. 66).

57 Sancta Maria, *Libro*, Book II, Chapter 33, fol. 64r.

Example 16.8 A *fuga* by Sancta Maria

①②③ = Sancta Maria's steps of the cadence

⌐——¬ = parts of the duo (hypothetically labeled after Sancta Maria)

stretto, or more loosely combined (*sueltas*). In the former case, the second voice enters before the first has finished (examples show imitation at the minim or semibreve), while in the latter case, the voice that starts the *passo* finishes it before the second voice starts the same *passo*; then, the voice that has finished the *passo* "necessarily has to serve as accompaniment to the other voice."[58] (See Example 16.8.) His example of *fuga suelta* shows imitation at a longer time interval (two breves).[59] This distinction is difficult to make in practice, where melodic functions are elided, and the counter-subject's beginning is obscure. (We have hypothetically labeled the functions in Example 16.8 where imitation is at two semibreves.[60])

In the case of the non-imitative *passo sin fuga*, the two voices start together, each with a different melody. An excerpt in double counterpoint has been boxed in Example 16.9. In practice, it is impossible to decide which of the two voices has the original *passo*, so Sancta Maria recommends at least a little bit of imitation to clarify this.[61] Cerone, on the other hand, prefers the non-imitative duo because it allows the words to be understood more easily.[62]

Sancta Maria continues his survey of presentation types: The *passo* may be played as part of a trio in which the outer voices move in sixths or tenths. But parallel sixths are only to be used in the course of a phrase or piece, never at the beginning or end.[63] The parallel-tenth model from Gaffurio now receives more fine tuning, as Sancta Maria describes other three-note chords (varying the distance between the outer voices) and

58 Ibid., Book II, Chapter 33, fol. 64v. These terms are only distantly related to Zarlino's *fughe legate* and *fughe sciolte*. See Haar, "Zarlino's Definition of Fugue."

59 Sancta Maria, *Libro*, Book II, Chapter 33, fol. 68v.

60 Another good description of an imitative duo comes much later from Lorenzo Penna, who recommends making two pairs of entries, then adding further entries at a closer time interval, finally leading to a cadence (Penna, *Li primi albori*, p. 83). Decreasing the time interval of imitation when approaching the cadence is a general characteristic of Renaissance style.

61 Sancta Maria, *Libro*, Book II, Chapter 33, fols. 68v–69r.

62 Cerone, *El melopeo*, Book XV, p. 813.

63 Sancta Maria, *Libro*, Book II, Chapter 33, fol. 70r.

Example 16.9 A "commonplace" by Montaños

how they may be integrated into the overall parallel-tenth motion. Finally, the *passo* may be played with full-textured four-part chords (called *consonancias*, to be discussed below). He advocates a mixture of these various techniques throughout the piece. The possibilities are summarized in Figure 16.1. Sancta Maria's focus on short segments reminds us that composers must have worked flexibly, adjusting and recomposing their contrapuntal lines as they switched their attention from the tiniest *passo* to the structure of whole points of imitation.[64]

The longest section of Sancta Maria's book now follows (Chapters 35–50), in which imitative duos are built into four-voice openings. He is explicit that four-part music is based on duos, and he shows various deployments of them.[65] He goes on to discuss how the entrance of the second duo may overlap the various parts ("steps") of the suspension figure which characterizes the cadence at the end of the first duo. The three steps of the cadence consist of (1) the consonant preparation of the suspension, (2) the dissonant suspension itself, and (3) the resolution of the dissonance, shown with circled numbers in Example 16.8.

Sancta Maria also gives possibilities for entrances before and after the cadential suspension. Thus a typical chapter title in this section is: "Chapter 45: The method of bringing in the two upper voices on the second step of a cadence formed by the two lower voices."[66] Within the chapter, sections are ordered according to the melodic motions of the entering voices. Sancta Maria runs through many possibilities, although the examples do not illustrate all possible rhythms of the *passo*. Of Example 16.8, he says "When the alto or treble enters with a stepwise ascent during the second cadence step, the cadence . . . must be formed on a note located a second, fifth, or ninth below that of the alto or treble entry."[67] Here the first cadence is formed on a suspended

64 See also Owens, "The Milan Partbooks."

65 "The art of ensemble playing is based on a low duo and another above, and thus the two lower voices and the two upper voices answer each other by turns" (*Libro*, Book II, Chapter 35, fol. 72r–v). He also allows the alto–bass duo to answer the tenor–soprano duo. Montaños stresses pairs of duos, too. "And when there are to be four voices, let the other two enter at their time, an octave below, accompanying them with good intervals, as will be seen at length in the four-voice examples in the Commonplaces" (*Arte*, "De compostura," fol. 11r). Burmeister's example of the steps taken to compose *fuga realis* is based on the same concept of paired duos (*Musical Poetics*, pp. 159–63).

66 Sancta Maria, *Libro*, Book II, Chapter 45, fol. 106v. 67 Ibid., Chapter 45, fol. 107v.

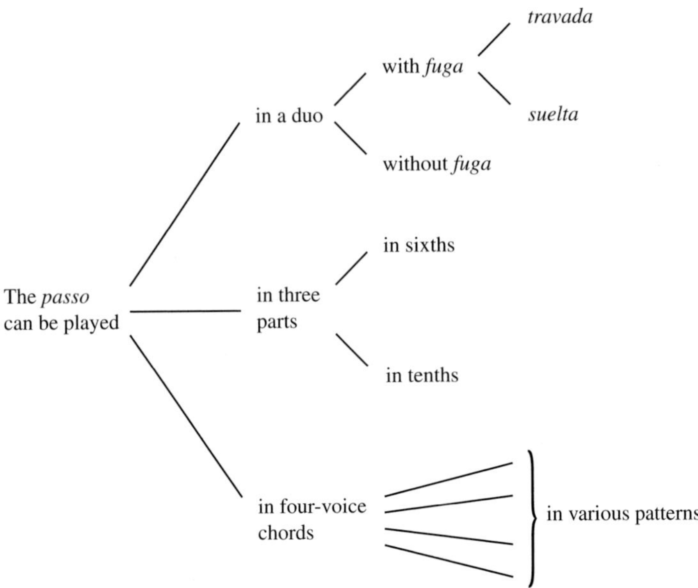

Figure 16.1 Manners of elaborating a *passo* after Sancta Maria

G, a ninth below the soprano entry; the next cadence is formed on a suspended G as well, a fifth below the alto entry.

Sancta Maria's presentation is framed, as in so many treatises, in terms of a series of givens. Given which voice is the third to start, what melodic motion it makes, and on what part of the cadence it is to enter, he tells us what the pitch relation must be between the first note of the *passo* and the cadential goal. It would of course also be possible to consider the members of the cadence as a conventionalized two-voice *soggetto* that must accommodate part of the head motive of the opening *passo*. The duo in the soprano and alto is varied (in Zarlino's terms) by octave transposition and by sounding against the tenor–bass pair.

What is the *soggetto* in an imitative duo? If the opening is long enough, both voices may be considered to constitute a *soggetto*, after Zarlino; if the opening theme is quite short, however, it may be called a *passo*, as Sancta Maria suggests. It is easy to see how training in CF improvisation is relevant to imitative writing. In Example 16.8, the first two notes in the tenor are semibreves, as in a typical CF. When the bass enters with the same notes, the tenor "improvises" a counter-subject in florid counterpoint. The resulting duo becomes a two-voice *soggetto* in its own right; when it appears in the second pair of voices (here soprano and alto, labeled in Example 16.8), the composer will add continuations to the first pair of voices. This should not be so difficult for a composer trained to improvise a third part to a duo, in the manner of Zarlino.

Matching melodic motions with cadences raises yet another modal issue. Just as adding an interval to a tenor had modal implications for Ramis, even more so does adding a line to a cadence, because of the special modal weight given to cadences. In Example 16.8 the cadences to G are "wrong" by Sancta Maria's own criteria: based on the notes of the first two entries, Example 16.8 is unambiguously first or second mode, which should have cadences on D and A, not G, as here.[68] The G cadence comes about because the soprano entry is to be dissonant with the cadential goal. In these examples we are again boxed in by prior decisions: if we want the upper voice to enter with a rising step from the fifth of the mode, creating a second or ninth above the dissonant suspension, we will have a modal irregularity. Again, the composer's thought process might be the reverse of the theorist's presentation: if we want an irregular cadence, and the upper voice has an ascending step, then it would be convenient to enter in the second part of the cadence. These examples merely illustrate a more complex case of Ramis's network of obligations.[69]

Double counterpoint in an imitative context

In most of the paired duos in Sancta Maria's treatise, the two voices of the upper pair are in the same relationship as those in the lower pair. He adds right at the outset that "sometimes the opposite happens," meaning that the voice that was lowest in the first duo is highest in the second. If the voices thus switch their relative positions within the duo while maintaining their temporal relationship, invertible counterpoint comes into play, although he never explicitly illustrates this.[70]

It is Francisco de Montaños who first illustrates invertible counterpoint in the context of four-part imitation. He offers the beginner many sample openings that he calls "commonplaces," a rhetorical term for a quotation that is meant to be memorized and reused at an appropriate occasion. These openings pair duos in the manner of Sancta Maria, both with *fuga* and without. Often, when the voices switch, he uses invertible counterpoint (albeit without comment). Example 16.9 shows a non-imitative duo in which the repetition of the second duo is varied by invertible counterpoint at the tenth; Example 16.10a shows an imitative opening in which invertible counterpoint at the octave is used to vary the opening bass–tenor duo.[71]

In Example 16.10b invertible counterpoint at the twelfth varies the tenor–soprano

68 Ibid., Book I, Chapter 24, fols. 67v. and 70r.

69 In his commentary on Marenzio's "Cruda Amarilli," Ulrich Siegele has shown the effects of transposed voices in a basic two-voice framework on mode, triads, and cadences. See "Wie ist Monteverdis 'seconda pratica' satztechnisch zu verstehen?" pp. 61–62.

70 Sancta Maria, *Libro*, Book II, Chapter 35, fol. 74r. Sancta Maria's relevant example has the entries reversed, but the time relationship between the voices is different, so properly there is no invertible counterpoint.

71 Montaños's examples were reprinted and supplemented by Pietro Cerone. Of Cerone's 106 sample openings, 24 use invertible counterpoint (*El melopeo*, Book XV, pp. 813–72).

Example 16.10a–b Imitative duos using double counterpoint by Montaños

a.

b.

duo when it is repeated in the tenor and alto (in m. 4). That is, the original interval succession between the tenor and soprano (beginning at * in m. 2) is 10–8–10–10; at the alto entry in bar 3 (+), the corresponding alto–tenor intervals are 3–5–3–3, the first duo inverted at the twelfth. Finally, with the bass entry (☆) in bar 4, the corresponding duo between bass and alto is 10–8–10–10. This third duo is the second duo inverted at the twelfth, but the result is the same series of intervals found in the first duo transposed down a fourth.

Invertible counterpoint permits the smooth introduction of thematic material at new transposition levels while a counter-melody retains its old pitch level. In Example 16.10b the counter-melody f–d–f–g is sounded against the principal *passo* both as it first appears (starting on D) and in transposition down a fourth (m. 3). The transpositions of the principal *passo* cause the fifth and sixth bars to lead away from the presumed final, D, and the fifth of the mode, A, to a contrasting sonority on E (which Tinctoris might call *distonatio*). Here we see the same process of transposition in successive steps that we saw in Example 16.7 by Chiodino. Looking back at that example, we may now imagine that Chiodino's series of examples could have occurred in an imitative context, if it had first been pulled apart: perhaps the line in semibreves could be the *passo* and the quicker line the accompaniment.

The idea of breaking down four-part homophonic examples into imitative polyphony is also discussed by Joachim Burmeister. He suggests composing a "short harmonic passage" in four voices and extracting one voice that is "most suited for beginning the composition." When that melody is placed diagonally down the score in all four voices, and the other voices are added to it, the result is a canon at the unison.[72]

72 Burmeister, *Musical Poetics*, pp. 189–95.

Seeing how apparently homophonic examples are potentially imitative, we can appreciate the value of Gabriel Fattorini's hundreds of *accadenze*, some of which are reprinted by Diruta (1608) with marginal commentary. Here a standard melodic cliché is accompanied by various added voices that are, in successive examples, transposed, doubled at various intervals, exchanged, presented in canon, and otherwise made to generate new counterpoints.[73] A Renaissance composer would have known how to "unzip" these phrases, treating any of the lines as a *passo* in an imitative texture.

Four-part sonority

When dealing with compositions in more than two parts, sixteenth-century theorists displayed a distinct preference for triadic sonorities in four voices. This is usually discussed in terms of interval content; Zarlino, for instance, says that vertical sonorities should preferably contain a third and either a fifth or sixth with one of the voices obviously doubled.[74] Throughout the century, authors such as Aaron and Zarlino gave tables or lists of consonances showing interval combinations that we would now call differently voiced chords.[75] These tables take as a given the interval between the tenor and the soprano, and show what alternatives are available for the alto and bass, allowing for unisons and voice crossing. Presumably the composer would construct his *Gerüstsatz*, then look in the tables for possible notes to use for the other parts.[76] But Zarlino's chord tables are not exhaustive, and he does not always articulate criteria for choosing any specific voicing save for a preference for the unmediated intervals of the *senario*.[77]

Only seven years after Zarlino, Sancta Maria approaches sonority quite differently. He starts with a soprano–bass interval (he likens the bass line to the foundation of a building), and classifies four-voice sonorities ("consonances") into groups based on the distance between the outer voices (these are octaves, tenths, twelfths, and thirteenths and their compounds). Within each group he ranks the arrangement of the inner voices into four classes, from the most to the least preferred. The criteria guiding his classification of classes are (1) only one pitch class should be doubled (although he recommends avoiding the unison); (2) the doubled note should not be that of the soprano;

73 Diruta, *Il transilvano*, Book II, pp. 17–23. The process of deriving new *soggetti* from old ones is also described briefly by Artusi in *L'arte*, p. 39.

74 Zarlino, *Le istitutioni harmoniche*, Part III, Chapter 59. See also Artusi, *L'arte*, p. 36; Dahlhaus, *Studies*. p. 92. Also see **Chapter 24, p. 754**.

75 Aaron, *Toscanello*, Book II, Chapter 30. Zarlino's chord tables from *Le istitutioni harmoniche*, Part III, Chapter 58 are reprinted and discussed by Lester, *Between Modes and Keys*, pp. 18–19.

76 Aaron's remarks on considering all four voices at once have led to a vigorous debate among musicologists on whether composers worked from a "simultaneous" or "successive" perspective. See, e.g., Blackburn, "On Compositional Process in the Fifteenth Century"; Lowinsky, "Canon Technique and Simultaneous Conception in Fifteenth-century Music."

77 Zarlino, *Le istitutioni harmoniche*, Part III, Chapter 61; Praetorius also gives priority to certain voicings based on their mathematical proportions: *Syntagma Musicum*, Book III, Part I, Chapter 4, p. 9.

Example 16.11a Four classes of the chord of the tenth by Sancta Maria

a.

Class One Class Two Class Three Class Four

Example 16.11b Examples of class 1 sonorities by Sancta Maria

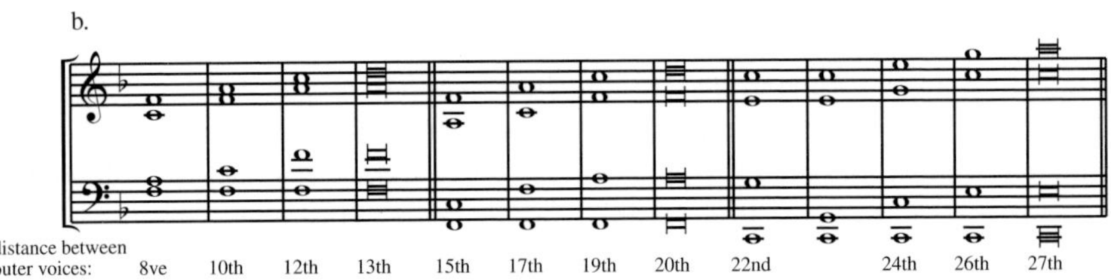

and (3) sixths above the bass are to be used with less frequency. In general, the farther apart the outer voices are, the more "open" the positions of the inner voices.[78] The four classes of the chord "of the tenth" are shown in Example 16.11a.[79] Eventually he calls for the student to memorize all of the preferred class 1 voicings for each outer-voice interval (shown in Example 16.11b).[80]

His examples of four-part note-against-note writing begin with a scale in the soprano as the first given, the position of the first chord (based on the distance between the outer voices) as the second, and a sequence of intervals between the bass and soprano as the third. In one type of progression, the outer voices run in parallel tenths; in another, they alternate octaves and tenths or their compounds; another, shown in Example 16.12, repeats a cycle of three chord types: a class 1 chord of the twelfth, a class 1 chord of the thirteenth, and a class 1 chord of the tenth (compare the third, fourth, and second chords in Example 16.11b).[81] This cycle of class 1 chords repeats until the cadence.

Sancta Maria goes on to consider two-note melodic fragments, starting with a single interval in the soprano and the vertical interval down to the first bass note. The results are several possible bass lines, to which inner voices are added.[82] These examples are the long-lost offspring of Ugolino's two-note interval successions, albeit upside down: the given melody is on top, and the first vertical interval is measured

78 Sancta Maria, *Libro*, Book II, Chapter 7, fol. 15r. 79 Ibid., Chapter 8, fol. 15v.
80 Ibid., Chapter 10, fol. 19v. See also Roig-Francoli, "Playing in Consonances."
81 Sancta Maria, *Libro*, Book II, Chapters 11–12. 82 Ibid., Chapter 13.

Example 16.12 Cycle of class 1 sonorities by Sancta Maria

down from it.[83] The soprano–bass interval is merely thickened by the inner voices, which "serve only as accompaniment and to fill the empty space between the extremes."[84]

The "chord tables" of Campion (c. 1610), like Sancta Maria's progressions of "consonances," can be understood as reinforced consonant interval progressions.[85] But Campion is more restrictive than is Sancta Maria in specifying the disposition and succession of voices in these chord progressions. The first chord of each of his patterns must be a 5/3 triadic sonority, containing a third, fifth, and octave above the bass note (although the order of the upper voices is variable); Campion then applies the "most familiar, and infallible rule," which dictates that when the bass ascends, the octave above the first bass note must go to the fifth above the next bass note, the fifth above the first to the third above the next, and the third above the first to the octave (or unison, depending on the original voicing) above the next. (This is true only for ascending intervals in the bass – for descending intervals, the order of prescribed movements is reversed.) The second chord in any two-note succession presumably then becomes the first chord in the next, just as in Ugolino, resulting in a chain of 5/3 sonorities. Seventeenth-century composers thus may have worked from given basses (dance *ostinati*, freshly composed *passacaglie*, etc.) in the same way that earlier composers worked from chant tenors. In Campion, the positions of the upper voices may be shuffled, but after that there is only one outcome for each motion of the bass because only contrary or oblique motions are acceptable, and all vertical sonorities must be 5/3 chords. Only with Campion may we truly speak of simultaneous composition.

83 Hans Buchner proposes the same method of composing in four parts with two-note successions (*Fundamentum*, p. 22). He also suggests setting a chant as the soprano in homorhythmic note-against-note texture, then enlivening each line with embellishment in diminished values. Buchner is discussed in Owens, *Composers at Work*, pp. 30–32.

84 Sancta Maria, *Libro*, Book II, fol. 13v. The only other author before 1600 to present such a thorough lesson on four-part homorhythmic texture, including commentary on spacing and doubling, is Morley (*Plaine and Easie*, pp. 143–45). His discussion is reprinted in my *Modal Counterpoint, Renaissance Style*, Chapter 17.

85 Campion, *A new way*, pp. 197–202. Similar chord tables by Schonsleder, Herbst, and Coperario are discussed in Dahlhaus (*Studies*, pp. 118ff.).

Conclusion

This brief survey of counterpoint pedagogy in the Renaissance is obviously not exhaustive. For each theorist included here, there is another whose ideas make equally valuable contributions to the picture as a whole, whether in basic concepts, terminology, or examples. No single theorist tells us everything we want to know, and there is little consensus among them. While Zarlino's followers are strong on double counterpoint, they are weak on four-part imitative textures; the Spanish followers of Sancta Maria have the opposite strengths and weaknesses. Yet by synthesizing this information from diverse treatises, we can begin to piece together a picture of Renaissance contrapuntal pedagogy. In short, singers and organists first learned how to deal with a monophonic CF by breaking it down into two-note segments, then adding a second line to it. This created a repertoire of contrapuntal combinations consisting of two vertical and two horizontal intervals, which were then memorized. In the improvised elaboration of a *soggetto*, combinations could be repeated as long as they were legitimately varied; they could be strung together or piled on top of one another to make longer and denser textures, imitative or not. Assembling such fragments – whether Tinctoris's interval successions, Montaños' four-part "commonplaces," or Banchieri's hundred cadences – may seem an unimaginative and mechanical approach to musical creativity. But in the sixteenth century, when rhetoric was a flourishing art and the memorization of stock oratorical formulas was basic to the education of any student, artistic originality was not understood as it is today. The application of pre-composed musical fragments was long considered a legitimate – indeed an essential – element of the composer's craft.[86]

The evolution of Western music can be characterized in terms of a dialectic between acceptable vertical sonorities on the one hand (whether a perfect consonance in Notre Dame polyphony or Schoenberg's famous ninth chord in last inversion), and acceptable melodic motions on the other. Knud Jeppesen writes: "In any style whatsoever, the presence of tension between the horizontal and vertical musical conceptions may be substantiated."[87] Counterpoint study since Jeppesen has focused on the idea of combining beautiful melodies within elaborate polyphonic textures. But Renaissance treatises offer little guidance on how to compose a good melody. For some theorists, it seems that it was counterpoint itself that created beautiful melody. Juan Bermudo went so far as to declare counterpoint the "father of melody."[88] The father of melody! If we are to grasp the implications of this concept, we must radically expand our thinking about Renaissance counterpoint.

86 See Owens, *Composers at Work*, p. 193, n. 55. The use of the verbs "quaerere" (to seek; Ugolino, *Declaratio*, Book II, Chapter 26, p. 33) and "trovare" (to find; Pontio, *Ragionamento*, p. 55) to describe one interval moving to another may not be merely anthropomorphic metaphors; they may come from the discipline of rhetoric to refer to the activity of the singer, who digs up and reuses "bits" that have been memorized. See Carruthers, *The Book of Memory: A Study of Memory in Medieval Culture*.

87 Jeppesen, *The Style of Palestrina*, p. 84.

88 Bermudo, *Declaracion*, Book V, Chapter 15.

Bibliography

Primary sources

Aaron, P. *Toscanello in musica*, Venice, Bernardino and Vitali, 1523; facs. of 1529 edn. Bologna, Forni, 1969; trans. P. Bergquist, Colorado Springs, Colorado College Music Press, 1970

Angleria, C. *La regola del contraponto*, Milan, G. Rolla, 1622; facs. Bologna, Forni, 1983

Artusi, G. M. *L'arte del contraponto*, Venice, G. Vincenti, 1598; facs. Hildesheim, G. Olms, 1969

Banchieri, A. *Cartella musicale*, Venice, G. Vincenti, 1614; facs. Bologna, Forni, 1968

Berardi, A. *Documenti armonici*, Bolgna, G. Monti, 1687; facs. Bologna, Forni, 1970

Bermudo, J. *Comiença el libro llamado declaración de instrumentos musicales*, Seville, J. de Leòn, 1555; facs. Kassel, Bärenreiter, 1957

Brunelli, A. *Regole et dichiaratoni di alcuni contrappunti dopii utili alli studiosi della musica, et maggiormente a quelli che vogliono far contrappunti all'improvviso*, Florence, Marescotti, 1610

Buchner, H. *Fundamentum und Kompositionen der Handschrift Basel FI8a*, vol. I of *Sämtliche Orgelwerke*, ed. J. Schmidt, Frankfurt, H. Litolff, 1974

Burmeister, J. *Musica Poetica*, Rostock, Ruhnke, 1606; trans. B. Rivera, ed. C. Palisca as *Musical Poetics*, New Haven, Yale University Press, 1993

Burzio, N. *Musices opusculum*, ed. G. Massera in *Nicolai Burtii parmensis florum libellus*, Florence, Olschki, 1975; trans. C. Miller as N. Burtius, *Musices opusculum*, *MSD* 37 (1983)

Campion, T. *A new way of making foure parts in counterpoint*, London, Snodham, c. 1618; reprinted in *Campion's Works*, ed. P. Vivian, Oxford, Clarendon Press, 1909 and 1966, pp. 319–56

Cerone, P. *El melopeo*, Naples, Gargano y Nucci, 1613; facs. Bologna, Forni, 1969

Cerreto, S. *Della prattica musica*, Naples, G. J. Carlino, 1601; facs. Bologna, Forni, 1969

Chiodino, G. B. *Arte practica latina e volgare di far contraponto a mente non a penna divisi in 10 libretti*, Venice, R. Amadino, 1610; trans. J. Herbst as *Arte prattica*, Frankfurt, A. Humm, 1653

Coclico, A. *Compendium musices*, Nuremberg, Montanus and Neuber, 1552; facs. Kassel, Bärenreiter, 1954; trans. A. Seay as *Musical Compendium*, Colorado Springs, Colorado College Music Press, 1973

Collet, H., ed., *Un tratado de canto de organo (siglo XVI): Manuscrito en la Biblioteca Nacional de Paris*, Ph.D. diss., Université de Paris (1913)

Diruta, G. *Il Transilvano*, 2 vols., Venice, G. and A. Vincenti, 1593–1622; facs. Bologna, Forni, 1969 and 1997; trans. M. Bradshaw and E. Soehnlen as *The Transylvanian*, Henryville, PA, Institute of Mediaeval Music, 1984

Gaffurio, F. *Practica musice*, Milan, G. Le Signerre, 1496; facs. Farnborough, Gregg, 1967, Bologna, Forni, 1972, and New York, Broude, 1979; trans. C. Miller as *Practica musicae*, *MSD* 20 (1968); trans. I. Young as *The "Practica musicae" of Franchinus Gafurius*, Madison, University of Wisconsin Press, 1969

Herbst, J. A. *Arte prattica et poëtica*, Frankfurt, A. Humm, 1653

Lusitano, V. *Introduttione facilissima, et novissima, di canto fermo, figurato, contraponto semplice, et in concerto*, Venice, A. Blado, 1553, and F. Rampazetto, 1561; facs. of 1561 edn. Rome, Libreria musicale italiana editrice, 1989

Montaños, F. de, *Arte de musica theorica y pratica*, Valladolid, F. de Cordoba, 1592

Morley, T. *A plaine and easie introduction to practicall musicke*, London, P. Short, 1597; facs. New York, Da Capo, 1969; ed. A. Harman as *A Plain and Easy Introduction to Practical Music*, New York, Norton, 1973

Ornithoparchus, A. *Musice active micrologus*, Leipzig, V. Schumann, 1517; trans. J. Dowland as *Andreas Ornithoparchus His Micrologus, or Introduction, Containing the Art of Singing*, London, T. Adams, 1609; facs. ed. G. Reese and S. Ledbetter, New York, Dover, 1973

Ortiz, D. *Tratado de glosas*, Rome, V. Dorico, 1553; trans. and ed. M. Schneider, Kassel, Bärenreiter, 1961

Penna, L. *Li primi albori musicali* (1672), 3 vols., Bologna, G. Monti, 1684; facs. Bologna, Forni, 1969

Pepusch, J. *A Treatise on Harmony*, London, W. Pearson, 1731; reprint, New York, Broude, 1966

Pontio, P. *Ragionamento di musica*, Parma, E. Viotto, 1588; facs. Kassel, Bärenreiter, 1959

Praetorius, M. *Syntagma musicum*, 3 vols., Wolfenbüttel, E. Holwein, 1614–20; facs. Kassel, Bärenreiter, 1958–59

Prosdocimo de' Beldomandi, *Contrapunctus* (1412), ed. and trans. J. Herlinger, Lincoln, University of Nebraska Press, 1984

Ramis de Pareia, B. *Musica practica*, Bologna, B. de Hiriberia, 1482; facs. Bologna, Forni, 1969; ed. J. Wolf as *Musica practica Bartolomei Rami de Pareja Bononiae*, Leipzig, Breitkopf und Härtel, 1901; trans. C. Miller, *MSD* 44 (1993)

Rodio, R. *Regole di musica*, Naples, Vitale, 1609; facs. Bologna, Forni, 1981

Sancta Maria, T. L. de, *Libro llamado arte de tañer fantasia*, Valladolid, F. Fernandez, 1565; facs. Geneva, Minkoff, 1973; trans. A. Howell, Jr. and W. Hultberg as *The Art of Playing the Fantasia*, Pittsburgh, Latin American Literary Review Press, 1991

Tigrini, O. *Il Compendio della musica*, Venice, R. Amadino, 1588; facs. New York, Broude, 1966

Tinctoris, J. *de natura et proprietate tonorum* (1476) ed. A. Seay, *CSM* 22/1 (1975), pp. 59–104; trans. A. Seay as *Concerning the Nature and Propriety of Tones*, Colorado Springs, Colorado College Music Press, 1967 and 1976

Liber de arte contrapuncti (1477), ed. A. Seay, *CSM* 22/2 (1975), pp. 5–157; trans. A. Seay as *The Art of Counterpoint*, *MSD* 5 (1961)

Diffinitorium, Treviso, G. de Lisa, 1495; facs. and Ger. trans. H. Bellermann, Kassel, Bärenreiter, 1983

Ugolino of Orvieto, *Declaratio musicae disciplinae*, ed. A. Seay, 3 vols., *CSM* 7 (1959–62)

Vanneo, S. *Recanetum de musica aurea*, Rome, V. Dorico, 1533; facs. Kassel, Bärenreiter, 1969

Vicentino, N. *L'antica musica ridotta alla moderna prattica* Rome, A. Barre, 1555; facs. Kassel, Bärenreiter, 1959; trans. M. Maniates, ed. C. V. Palisca, as *Ancient Music Adapted to Modern Practica*, New Haven, Yale University Press, 1994

Yssandon, J. *Traité de la musique pratique*, Paris, Le Roy and Ballard, 1582

Zarlino, G. *Le istitutioni harmoniche*, Venice, Franceschi, 1558; facs. New York, Broude, 1965; trans. of Part III by G. Marco, ed. C. V. Palisca as *The Art of Counterpoint*, New Haven, Yale University Press, 1968; trans. of Part IV by V. Cohen, ed. C. V. Palisca as *On the Modes*, New Haven, Yale University Press, 1983

Secondary sources

Agee, R. J. "Constanzo Festa's *Gradus ad Parnassum*," *Early Music History* 15 (1996), pp. 1–58

Aldrich, P. "An Approach to the Analysis of Renaissance Music," *Music Review* 30 (1969), pp. 1–21

Andrews, H. K. *The Technique of Byrd's Vocal Polyphony*, London, Oxford University Press, 1966

Bent, M. "Accidentals, Counterpoint and Notation in Aaron's *Aggiunta* to the *Toscanello in Musica*," *JM* 12 (1994), pp. 306–44

Blackburn, B. J. "On Compositional Process in the Fifteenth Century," *JAMS* 40 (1987), pp. 210–84

Carapezza, P. E., ed., *Scuola Polifonica Siciliana, Musiche Strumentali Didattiche (Musiche Rinascimentali Siciliane II)*, Rome, de Santis, 1971

Carpenter, P. "Tonal Coherence in a Motet of Dufay," *JMT* 17 (1973), pp. 2–65

Carruthers, M. *The Book of Memory: A Study of Memory in Medieval Culture*, Cambridge University Press, 1990

Collins, D. "Zarlino and Berardi as Teachers of Canon," *Theoria* 7 (1993), pp. 103–23

"Fugue, Canon, and Double Counterpoint in Nicole Vicentino's *L'antica musica* (1555)," *Irish Musical Studies* 2 (1993), pp. 276–301

"Canon and Music Pedagogy 1500–1800," *Theoria* 8 (1994), pp. 53–72

Crocker, R. "Discant, Counterpoint, and Harmony," *JAMS* 15 (1962), pp. 1–21

Dahlhaus, C. "On the Treatment of Dissonance in the Motets of Josquin des Prez" *Josquin des Prez Proceedings of the International Josquin Festival-Conference, 1971*, ed. E. Lowinsky, London, Oxford University Press, 1976, pp. 334–44

Untersuchungen über die Entstehung der harmonischen Tonalität, Kassel, Bärenreiter, 1968; trans. R. Gjerdingen as *Studies on the Origin of Harmonic Tonality*, Princeton University Press, 1990

"Formen improvisierter Mehrstimmigkeit im 16. Jahrhundert," *Musica* 13 (1959), pp. 163–67

Ferand, E. T. "Improvised Vocal Counterpoint in the Late Renaissance and Early Baroque," *Annales Musicologiques* 4 (1956), pp. 129–74

Fromson, M. "A. Conjunction of Rhetoric and Music: Structural Modelling in the Italian Counter-Reformation Motet," *Journal of the Royal Musical Association* 117 (1992), pp. 208–46

"Cadential Structure in the Mid-Sixteenth Century: The Analytic Approaches of Bernhard Meier and Karol Berger Compared," *Theory and Practice* 16 (1991), pp. 37–58

Garcia, F. "Pietro Cerone's 'El Melopeo y Maestro,' A Synthesis of Sixteenth-Century Musical Theory," Ph.D. diss., Northwestern University (1978)

Gargiulo, P. "Le regole 'pratiche' e 'utilissime' nei trattati di Antonio Brunelli," *Nuova Rivista Musicale Italiana* 4 (1984), pp. 554–71

Haar, J. "Zarlino's Definition of Fugue and Imitation," *JAMS* 24 (1971), pp. 226–54

Horsley, I. "Fugue and Mode in 16th-Century Vocal Polyphony," in *Aspects of Medieval and Renaissance Music: A Birthday Offering to Gustave Reese*, ed. J. La Rue, Stuyvesant, NY, Pendragon Press, 1978, pp. 406–22

Jeppesen, K. *Counterpoint*, trans. G. Haydon, New York, Prentice-Hall, 1939; reprint New York, Dover, 1992

The Style of Palestrina and the Dissonance, trans. M. Hamerik, London, Oxford University Press, 1946

Judd, C. C. "Some Problems of Pre-Baroque Analysis: An Examination of Josquin's *Ave Maria Virgo Serena*," *Music Analysis* 4 (1985), pp. 201–40

"Josquin des Prez, *Salve Regina* (à5)," in *Music Before 1600*, ed. M. Everist, Oxford, B. Blackwell, 1992, pp. 114–53

Kaufmann, H. W. *The Life and Works of Nicola Vicentino*, *MSD* 11 (1966)

Kerman, J. "Old and New in Byrd's *Cantiones Sacrae*," in *Essays on Opera and English Music*, ed. F. Sternfeld, Oxford, B. Blackwell, 1975, pp. 25–43

"Write All These Down," in *Byrd Studies*, ed. A. Brown and R. Turbet, Cambridge University Press, 1992, pp. 112–28

Le Huray, P. "Some Thoughts about Cantus Firmus Composition; and a Plea for Byrd's *Christus resurgens*," in *Byrd Studies*, ed. A. Brown and R. Turbet, Cambridge University Press, 1992, pp. 1–23

Lester, J. *Between Modes and Keys*, Stuyvesant, NY, Pendragon, 1989

Compositional Theory in the Eighteenth Century, Cambridge, MA, Harvard University Press, 1992

Lowinsky, E. E. *Tonality and Atonality in Sixteenth-Century Music*, Berkeley, University of California Press, 1961; rev. edn. 1962

"Canon Technique and Simultaneous Conception in Fifteenth-century Music: A Comparison of North and South," in *Essays on the Music of J. S. Bach and Other Diverse Subjects: A Tribute to Gerhard Herz*, ed. R. Weaver, University of Louisville Press, 1981, pp. 181–222

Meier, B. *Die Tonarten der klassichen Vokalpolyphonie, nach den Quellen dargestellt*, Utrecht, Oosthoek, Scheltema, and Holkema, 1974; trans. E. Beebe as *The Modes of Classical Vocal Polyphony*, New York, Broude, 1988

"Harmony in the Cantus-Firmus Compositions of the Fifteenth Century," trans. K. Moll in *Counterpoint and Compositional Process in the Time of Dufay, Perspectives from German Musicology*, New York, Garland, 1997, pp. 149–70

Moll, K. N., ed., *Counterpoint and Compositional Process in the Time of Dufay, Perspectives from German Musicology*, New York, Garland, 1997

Newcomb, A., ed., *The Ricercars of the Bourdeney Codex, Recent Researches in the Music of the Renaissance*, vol. LXXXIX, Madison, A-R Editions, 1991

Owens, J. A. "The Milan Partbooks, Evidence of Cipriano de Rore's Compositional Process," *JAMS* 37 (1984), pp. 270–98

Composers at Work, The Craft of Musical Composition 1450–1600, New York, Oxford University Press, 1997

Palisca, C. V. "Vincenzo Galilei's Counterpoint Treatise: A Code for the *Seconda pratica*," *JAMS* 9 (1956), pp. 81–96

"The Revision of Counterpoint and the Embellished Style," in *Studies in the History of Italian Music and Music Theory*, Oxford University Press, 1994, pp. 3–29

Powers, H. S. "The Modality of 'Vestiva i colli,'" in *Studies in Renaissance and Baroque Music in Honor of Arthur Mendel*, ed. R. Marshall, Kassel, Bärenreiter, 1974, pp. 31–46

"Modal Representation in Polyphonic Offertories," *Early Music History* 2 (1982), pp. 43–86

"Modality as a European Cultural Construct," in *Secondo convegno europeo di analisi musicale: atti*, ed. R. Dalmonte and M. Baroni, Trento, Università degli studi di Trento, 1992, pp. 207–19

Quereau, Q. W. "Sixteenth-Century Parody: An Approach to Analysis," *JAMS* 31 (1978), pp. 407–41

Reynolds, C. "Musical Evidence of Compositional Planning in the Renaissance: Josquin's *Plus nulz regretz*," *JAMS* 40 (1987), pp. 53–81

Rivera, B. V. "Harmonic Theory in Musical Treatises of the Late Fifteenth and Early Sixteenth Centuries," *MTS* 1 (1979), pp. 67–79

"The Two-Voice Framework and Its Harmonization in Arcadelt's First Book of Madrigals," *Music Analysis* 6 (1987), pp. 59–88

"Finding the *Soggetto* in Willaert's Free Imitative Counterpoint: A Step in Modal Analysis," in *Music Theory and the Exploration of the Past*, ed. C. Hatch and D. Bernstein, University of Chicago Press, 1993, pp. 73–102

Roig-Francoli, M. "Playing in Consonances: A Spanish Renaissance Technique of Chordal Improvisation," *Early Music* 23 (1995), pp. 461–71

Rothfarb, L. "Tinctoris vs. Tinctoris: Theory and Practice of Dissonance in Counterpoint," *In Theory Only* 9 (1986), pp. 3–32

Sachs, K.-J. "Musikalische 'Struktur' im Spiegel der Kompositionslehre von Pietro Pontios *Ragionamento di musica* (1588)," in *Zeichen und Struktur in der Musik der Renaissance*, ed. K. Hortschansky, Kassel, Bärenreiter, 1989, pp. 141–57

"Counterpoint," parts 1–11, *NG*, vol. IV, pp. 833–43

"Arten improvisierter Mehrstimmigkeit nach Lehrtexten des 14. bis 16. Jahrhunderts," *Basler Jahrbuch für historische Musikpraxis* 7 (1983), pp. 166–83.

Schubert, P. "The Fourteen-Mode System of Illuminato Aiguino," *JMT* 35 (1991), pp. 175–210

"Mode and Counterpoint," in *Music Theory and Exploration of the Past*, ed. C. Hatch and D. Bernstein, University of Chicago Press, 1993, pp. 103–36

"A Lesson from Lassus: Form in the Duos of 1577," *MTS* 17 (1995), pp. 1–26

Siegele, U. "*Cruda Amarilli*, oder, Wie ist Monteverdis 'seconda pratica' satztechnisch zu verstehen?," *Musik-Konzepte* 83 (1994), pp. 31–102

Urquhart, D. M. "Francisco de Montaños' *Arte de musica theorica y pratica*: A Translation and Commentary," Ph.D. diss., Eastman School of Music (1969)

Vendrix, P. "On the Theoretical Expression of Music in France during the Renaissance," *Early Music History* 13 (1994), pp. 249–73

Walker, P. M. "Fugue in German Theory from Dressler to Mattheson," Ph.D. diss., State University of New York at Buffalo (1987)

Wegman, R. "From Maker to Composer: Improvisation and Musical Authorship in the Low Countries, 1450–1500," *JAMS* 49 (1996), pp. 409–79

· 17 ·

Performance theory

ALBERT COHEN

The presumption of a notated musical "score" as the subject for realization by the performer – and the object of analysis by the theorist – has become a foundation of Western musical aesthetics, one whose ontology underlies much of the theory described in the present volume. It is clear, however, that a great deal of music has been based not upon written scores, but rather upon oral transmission and traditions of improvisation. This is most evident, of course, in popular and non-Western repertories. But it is also true of much Western "art" music, particularly during medieval times, when a precise notation had yet to develop. Even after such a notation gradually did evolve, though, a large degree of improvisational freedom continued to be practiced in many different repertories and styles.[1] The result is that the distinction between composer and performer in such music is blurred, if not non-existent. In essence, the musical "work" is the performance.[2]

Improvisational performances are rarely arbitrary. Most genres of music having extempore elements commonly presume guidelines of syntax and style that constrain performers. These guidelines – sometimes explicitly formulated, sometimes informally so – become "theories" that can be understood as historical counterparts to the more formalized prescriptive rules that guide the composition of written scores. Still, the distinction is not always a clear one, and many treatises, particularly in the early modern period, blur the guidelines between written, improvised, and "realized" musics.[3] The resultant theories are often as complex and intricate as are the musical structures for which they purport to account.

The present chapter will offer several contrasting (and obviously highly selective) examples of traditions in performance theory. Emphasis will be placed especially on performance theories from the so-called Baroque era, for it was during this period that perhaps the most vigorous and pervasive practice of improvisational performance was cultivated in Western art music.

1 Concerning this tradition, see Strohm, "Unwritten and Written Music."

2 On this point, see Binkley, "The Work Is not the Performance."

3 Distinctions between "musical practice, practical theory, and the theory of practice" are examined from an ethnomusicological perspective by Blacking, "Performance as a Way of Knowing"; for a view on the theory of improvisation in jazz, see Berliner, *Thinking in Jazz*, pp. 221–22.

Early performance theory

Writers in ancient Greece had already distinguished the practice of music from its theory – the one dealing with performance, composition, and education, and the other with science, technique, and critical intellect. This distinction was codified during Roman times, notably by Aristides Quintilianus, and later transmitted to theorists of the Middle Ages (see **Chapter 1, pp. 27–28** and **Chapter 5, pp. 152–53**). The sixth-century Latin author Boethius defined the difference as one between *cantor* or *poeta* (the performer or composer) and *musicus* (the educated listener capable of critical judgment) – that is, between the maker of music and the philosopher.[4] By the fifteenth century, the distinction was normally expressed as one between *musica practica* (combining performance and composition) and *musica theorica* (or *musica speculativa*). But in the sixteenth century, the terminology *musica poetica* was reintroduced by Listenius to distinguish composition from both performance and theory and, thereby, to identify its mediating role in the creative process.[5]

The earliest medieval treatises on music appeared during Carolingian times; and while they incorporated elements of a largely speculative Greco-Roman theory, their central concern was rather with the practice of music, and with its pedagogy. These works are hardly treatises in a traditional sense, for they were issued primarily as handbooks, prepared by churchmen and monastics, and intended for the training of singers and choirboys to meet the performance requirements of the liturgy (see **Chapter 5, pp. 147–49**). It is not surprising, then, to find in them the first written descriptions of the practice of organum. To be sure, most medieval organum and discant was improvised, and the written descriptions constitute a theory that is little more than the codification of existing principles for extempore elaboration of chant in two or more parts (see **Chapter 15, pp. 484–85**). That there are often notable differences in the description of these principles among the ninth- to twelfth-century treatises where organum is discussed suggests an evolution in its style as well as regional distinctions.

Such is the case also with *faburden*, a technique that emerged in medieval England, and a similar but distinct improvisational practice of continental composers in the fifteenth century termed *fauxbourdon*. The genre is similar to organum, but it is based on an improvisatory style (employing a system of "sights") that favors use of imperfect intervals (thirds and sixths) in the elaboration of chant, elements of which are found as early as the thirteenth century in the English practice of *gymel*. While these interrelated improvisational procedures developed over a period of almost three hundred

4 On the tension between *cantor* and *musicus*, see **Chapter 5, pp. 146–47**.

5 Nikolaus Listenius, *Rudimenta musicae* (1533). The term was quickly adopted by German theorists, notably Heinrich Faber, *Compendiolum musicae* (1545); Gallus Dressler, *Musicae practicae* (1571), Joachim Burmeister, *musica poetica* (1606); and Johannes Lippius, *Synopsis musicae* (1612). See further, Rivera, *German Music Theory*, pp. 24–29.

Fifteenth-century theories of improvisational practice
Gymel – Faburden – Fauxbourdon

gymel – "The English have yet another manner [of discant] which is called gymel. This is sung in two voices, using consonant thirds above and below, and unisons."

(Guilielmus Monachus, *De praeceptis artis musicae* [c. 1480–90], IV–26)

faburden – "Faburden . . . hath but two Sights: a third above the plainsong in Sight, the which is a sixth from the Treble in Voice; and an even [= unison] with the plainsong in Sight, the which is an octave from the Treble in Voice . . . When the Faburdener begins to sing, he should look at [the first note of] the plainsong and imagine the unison with it in Sight; he should then set his Voice a fifth below the plainsong . . . Thereafter, whether the plainsong rises or falls, the Faburdener should always set his Sight on the line or space [of the staff] a third above the plainsong . . . the Faburdener should cadence by moving his Sight down to a unison with the plainsong."

(Anon., British Library, Lansdowne MS 763, fol. 116; quoted in Trowell, "Faburden and Fauxbourdon," pp. 47 and 59)

fauxbourdon – "If you wish a third part, take the notes from the upper one and begin simultaneously, proceeding a fourth below."

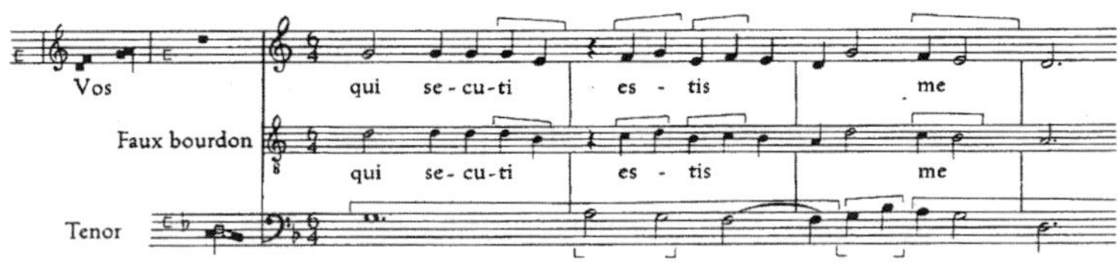

(Verbal canon from G. Dufay's *Missa Sancti Jacobi* (c. 1428), final *Communion*; in Besseler, *Guglielmi Dufay*, pp. XXIII and 44)

years, the written theory that describes them dates only from the fifteenth century, at a time when the practice was already in decline (see the window above).

It was in the fifteenth century, in fact, that theorists first distinguished between improvisational and written polyphony in precise terms. Early in the century (1404), Prosdocimo de' Beldomandi refers to improvised counterpoint as *modus cantandi cantum planum binatim* and mentions that special skills are required of singers in the style.[6] Elsewhere (in 1412), he refers to two different types of counterpoint, vocal and written (*vocalis et scriptus*), adding that "everything that will be said of counterpoint . . . is to be understood to pertain to both."[7] But it is Johannes Tinctoris, later in the century (1477), who makes the clearest distinction between the process of improvisation, which he calls *cantare super librum* ("to sing upon the book"), and written-out music, or *res facta*. He gives detailed and extended rules for their procedures, projecting a tradition of polyphonically embellishing chant through improvisation that was already old by his time. Tinctoris suggests (as had Prosdocimo) that the same rules of counterpoint apply to both written and improvised music. Either one or two voices could be added to a given *cantus prius factus* in improvisation, and there is no restriction placed on maintaining the note-against-note texture that largely characterized earlier practice. (Tinctoris, in fact, admired "diminished" or florid counterpoint by those capable of supplying it.[8]) But improvised pieces were permitted a looser construction and other liberties in performance than normally allowed in *res facta*.[9] Despite differences in their descriptions of improvisatory procedures, almost all theorists underscore an important feature of its performance: rules for improvisation, regardless of medium or musical style, permit the performer a measure of freedom in the realization of a finished work not normally allowed the composer.[10] Further, the larger the improvising group, the more constraints there are in choices made, and the greater the need to coordinate improvisers' roles in performance.

Improvised vocal counterpoint is described by sixteenth-century theorists as well – notably Vicente Lusitano (1553), Nicola Vicentino (1555), and Gioseffo Zarlino (1558)[11] – confirming the admonition of earlier theorists that the basic rules of counterpoint be applied by would-be improvisers. Indeed, Zarlino maintains that the practice (which came to be known as *contrapunto alla mente*)[12] is learned only after the student is a "skilled contrapuntist"; he includes both canons and invertible counterpoint among his examples.[13]

The decoration of notated vocal lines through the application of ornaments and diminutions, although practiced earlier, had special currency during the fifteenth and sixteenth centuries. Specific singing techniques were developed for the practice, which was widely taught during the period, but a theory of ornamentation developed only in the late Renaissance; principles and systematic rules began to appear in treatises from

6 Prosdocimo, *Expositiones*, p. 163. 7 Prosdocimo, *Contrapunctus*, p. 33.

8 Tinctoris, *The Art of Counterpoint*, Book II, Chapter 20, and Book III, Chapter 4.

9 See Haar, "Monophony and the Unwritten Traditions," pp. 258–62.

10 See **Chapter 16, pp. 513–14** for further distinctions between improvised and written counterpoint in the Renaissance.

11 Lusitano, *Introduttione facilissima et novissima*; Vicentino, *L'antica musica ridotta alla moderna prattica*; Zarlino, *Le istitutioni harmoniche*.

12 See Ferand, "Improvised Vocal Counterpoint in the Late Renaissance and Early Baroque," pp. 140–42, for terminology used to signify improvised counterpoint; the study includes a comprehensive list of treatises that deal with the practice, pp. 143–44.

13 Zarlino, *Le istitutioni harmoniche*, Part III, Chapters 63 (expanded in the 1573 edition) and 64.

1535 on, often in works that applied equally to voices and to instruments. Writers catalogued ornamental graces in use, and provided examples of diminutions or passage-work (*passaggi* or *gorgie*) for the performer. Differences between ensemble and solo improvisation lay primarily in the amount and complexity of decoration permitted: solo performers characteristically applied embellishment as virtuosic display.[14]

A written performance tradition came only much later to instruments than it did to voices in the West, and at least at first, it was based largely on vocal practice. The embellishment of existing works was particularly common to instruments on which all parts of a polyphonic texture could be performed, such as keyboard or lute, and a literature of instruction manuals aimed especially towards virtuosic improvisation on these instruments developed during the fifteenth and sixteenth centuries.[15] By the late sixteenth century, however, a new role was assigned to instruments, generally – that of providing harmonic accompaniment to the newly-emerging vocal styles of the time while also reinforcing the emotional and dramatic expression of the music. This led to important changes in instrumental practice, and in the way theorists viewed that practice.

Mersenne consults the performers

The advent of the early modern period in the late sixteenth and early seventeenth centuries witnessed remarkable changes in the nature of Western thought – a revolutionary period that sought new directions in religion, philosophy, science, and the arts. The music spawned in this period (typically, if problematically, called "Baroque" by a later age) assumed a fresh boldness not only in its tonal conception and expression, but also in its performance and social function. And for the first time in Western musical thought, instrumental performance played a dominant role in the formulation of much of the theory of the period, which was characterized generally by a penchant for theoretical systematization and empirical codification.[16]

The decisive changes that took place in the music theory at the time are especially evident in the writings of Marin Mersenne (1588–1648), the French Minim friar whose large and complex body of musical writings lies midway between the works of Zarlino and Rameau. One senses in Mersenne's work the struggle to maintain an equilibrium between music as a mechanistic science and music as an expressive practice. As one of the key figures in the early period of the scientific revolution, Mersenne was extraordinary in his attention to musical questions. While other scientists of the time included music among subjects they investigated (for example, Benedetti, Galileo, Beeckman,

14 See Brown, *Embellishing Sixteenth-Century Music*; McGee, *Medieval and Renaissance Music*; both sources list the principal embellishment treatises of the time.

15 See Horsley et al., "Improvisation," *NG*, vol. IX, pp. 33–34.

16 On this point, see Schulenberg, "Composition Before Rameau," p. 144; Dunsby and Whittall, *Music Analysis in Theory and Practice*, p. 15.

Gassendi, and Descartes), it is Mersenne whose work is acknowledged to constitute what one scholar calls "the first full-fledged application of the experimental method to the science of music."[17] He was, in fact, alone among contemporary scientists, not only to assign a primary role to music in his writings, but also to consider performance along with composition as central to the derivation of its theory.

For Mersenne, these two aspects of the creative process – composition and performance – are by no means distinct from one another. Indeed, as for musicians from earlier generations, the domain of performance and composition frequently overlapped. To be sure, in discussing certain techniques (such as strict imitation or canon), Mersenne most often refers to written composition, but in others (such as free improvisation or embellishment), he alludes to performers who conceive of musical ideas "by whim and by chance . . . in the fancy . . . of their imagination." In these latter cases, he often abandons the term "composer," referring rather to the more neutral "practitioner," "musician," or even "master," as the creative artist.[18]

And while Mersenne consistently invokes the age-old advice to students who seek to produce music, in whatever style, that they "imitate" the work of "the finest masters,"[19] he is careful to warn that the products they so imitate are not necessarily the result of unambiguous rules. In fact, he notes that often the works "of theorists are worthless, when compared with those made by [persons] who know no theory," adding, "Besides, theorists know only what they learn from practitioners, from whom they presume principles and experiences; this is why practice precedes theory."[20] He enjoins performers who invent, but who do not understand the principles that underlie their inventions, "to join theory" to their knowledge, which he believes will result in their creating finer musical works.[21]

While he projected a central role for performance in the formulation of music theory of his time, Mersenne was never able to fully articulate the special nature of that role. Yet he was as open to novel ideas in music and its performance as he was to the new empirical science and the products of its experiments, and he consulted with contemporary musicians on the changing nature of musical style, much as he did with fellow scientists on the evolving character of their scientific investigations. In both cases, the results of his inquiries found their way into his writings.

Mersenne reports on the work of a large roster of performing musicians of his day, most of whom were active in Paris and its environs; he appears to have known many of them personally. Among those who supplied him with musical examples for his publications were the organist Charles Racquet; the lutenists Robert Ballard, René

17 Cohen, *Quantifying Music*, p. 114. See also **Chapter 9, p. 250**.
18 See, for example, Mersenne, *Harmonie universelle*, "Livre Second des Chants," pp. 97–98.
19 Ibid., Livre VI, "L'Art de bien chanter," p. 363. In the general *préface*, Mersenne suggests that to learn "all sorts of simple or figural counterpoint," students should study with "those who are well versed in this practice," many of whom "teach in Paris how to sing as well as how to compose."
20 Mersenne, *Questions harmoniques*, p. 230.
21 Mersenne, *Harmonie universelle*, "Traité des instruments à chordes," *préface*.

Mézangeau, and François de Chancy; the violinist Jehan Henry; and the singers Anthoine Boësset, Etienne Moulinié, Henry du Bailly, and Joseph Chabanceau de La Barre.[22] In addition, Mersenne inserted two short, but complete performance tutors into his *Harmonie universelle* – one a manual on singing supplied by the geometer and amateur musician Girard Désargues, and the other a treatise on playing the lute, commissioned by Mersenne from the lutenist Basset.[23]

Two (overlapping) developments in the performance practice of the music of his day are recognized by Mersenne as especially distinctive and possessing strong implications for music theory: (1) the emergence of thorough-bass practice; and (2) embellishment and improvisation skills for performers. Each of these developments engendered a large literature of pedagogical theory during the period, and will be considered here in more detail.[24]

Thorough-bass practice as theory

Like earlier *contrapunctus* theory that retrospectively codified existing principles of extempore discant performance by singers, the thorough-bass literature of the seventeenth century describes an instrumental practice "in existence since at least the late fifteenth century . . . of providing a simple harmonic accompaniment to a solo singer or ensemble."[25] Sixteenth- and early seventeenth-century precursors of thorough bass, or *basso continuo* (its Italian designation, by which the practice became generally known), included the *partitura*, or open score for organ or lute in support of vocal ensembles, and the *basso seguente*,[26] a line made up of the lowest-sounding bass notes of an ensemble, intended to serve the keyboardist as the basis for providing an accompaniment. The first independent continuo part appeared in Lodovico Viadana's *Cento concerti ecclesiastici . . . con il basso continuo per sonar nel organo* (1602), which also includes the earliest description of the practice (called by the author a "new invention").[27]

22 See the list in Schneider, *Die französische Kompositionslehre*, p. 93, and the musical examples listed in Chapman, *Marin Mersenne*, pp. xi–xii.

23 The treatises by Desargues and Basset are found in *Harmonie universelle*, Livre VI, "L'Art de bien chanter," pp. 332–42, and "Livre Second des Instruments," pp. 76–82, respectively.

24 Selfridge-Field, "Introduction," p. 3, cites these very developments as "central features of Baroque music." While Mersenne devotes large amounts of space in his writings to instruments and to embellishment, he only touches on thorough bass, which he recognizes as largely an Italian practice, not yet fully adopted in France. He describes the practice in both his *Harmonie universelle* ("L'Art de bien chanter," p. 357) and his *Harmonicorum Libri XII* (Lib. VII, prop. XIX, p. 160), and published an example of an unfigured "basse continue" to an air by Boësset in his *Cogitata physico-mathematica*, p. 327.

25 Ashworth and O'Dette, "Overview and Practical Applications," p. 203.

26 The term is found first in Banchieri, *Eclesiastiche sinfonie* (1607). For more on Italian thorough-bass practice, see **Chapter 13, pp. 441–43**.

27 See Ashworth and O'Dette, "Overview and Practical Applications," p. 209.

Agostino Agazzari on thorough bass

"As no definite rule can be given, the player must necessarily rely upon his ear and follow the work and its movements. But if you would have an easy way of avoiding these obstacles and of playing the work exactly, take this one, indicating with figures above the notes of the bass the consonances and dissonances placed there by the composer; for example, if on the first half of a note there is a fifth and then a sixth, or vice versa, or a fourth and then a third, as illustrated."

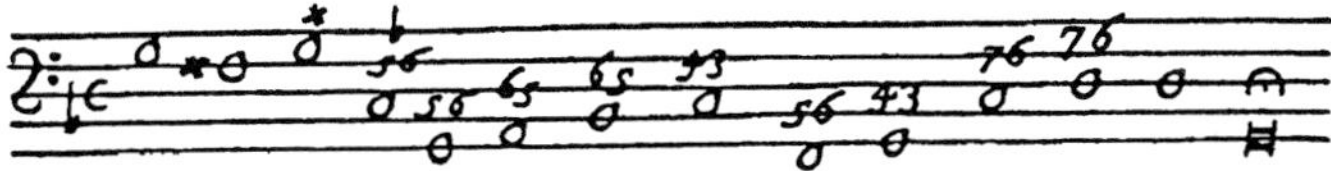

(Agostino Agazzari, *Del sonare sopra'l basso* (1607), p. 5; quoted in Strunk, *SR*, p. 623)

The prevalence – already in the sixteenth century – of homophonic accompaniments and short-score keyboard settings of vocal music (those limited to bass and treble lines) served to highlight a central feature of the new style: chordal thinking as a primary structural force in music. Indeed, along with a preference for families of like instruments rather than for mixed ensembles (as was common in the late Renaissance), there appeared a novel classification for instruments – one based on whether an instrument was capable of providing chordal accompaniment.

Agostino Agazzari (c. 1580–1642), in one of the earliest treatises devoted to thorough-bass performance, *Del sonare sopra'l basso* (1607), suggests that instruments be divided into two basic classes: those "like a foundation," which can supply chordal accompaniment and, thereby, "guide and support the whole body of voices and instruments of the consort" (these are classified as "perfect" instruments); and those "like ornaments," which play rather in a "contrapuntal fashion" and are incapable of providing complete harmonies (these instruments are called "imperfect").[28] Agazzari recommends the use of numerical "signs" to indicate particular harmonic structures above the bass (see the window above), but this notation (already found in music of the time) did not become standard until a later period. Continuo performers were also expected to "realize" a harmonic accompaniment above an unfigured bass line. Thus the many manuals of thorough-bass one finds in the seventeenth and early eighteenth centuries provide guides for realizing both figured and unfigured basses.[29] (The "Rule of the Octave" discussed in **Chapter 13, p. 443** was one of the most common progressions for a continuo player to learn by which to supply harmonies above any unfigured bass.)

28 Translated in *SR*, p. 622.

29 A representative sampling of continuo treatises is listed in Ashworth and O'Dette, "Basso Continuo," p. 289. For a comprehensive review of the sources, see Williams, *Figured Bass Accompaniment*; Arnold, *The Art of Accompaniment from a Thorough-Bass*.

But the guidelines offered still left much for the performer to decide. For the most part, they "are concerned exclusively with getting the chords right and with linking them properly, not with how to play them."[30] Rarely do instructors offer model realizations, or advise on the choice of instruments, or describe stylistic differences between different repertories. Thorough-bass practice thus lies part-way between composed music and improvisation; it supplies the performer with a skeletal structure upon which to create a complete musical work, reflecting conventions of time and place, each performance thus being uniquely different. (It is not surprising, then, that performance of the period has been likened to that of jazz in the modern age.[31])

Because the thorough bass constituted a full replication of the harmonic structure underlying all genres of Baroque music, the ability to realize this harmonic structure extempore was increasingly considered by theorists to be related to the skill of composition. If thorough-bass realization in the seventeenth century was largely a mechanical practice in which the performer was expected to play a suitable chord above a given bass note, by the eighteenth century, a much more refined accompaniment was expected that reflected compositional decisions. That is to say, the performer was faced with improvising the same harmonic structures, voice leading, and textural diminutions consistently throughout a whole piece that a composer would have written out. Conversely, the art of composition was one that was frequently taught through – and identified with – thorough-bass practice. Johann Mattheson (1739) maintained that "composition cannot exist without the thorough bass," while Jean-Philippe Rameau (1760) understood "the principles of composition and accompaniment" to be essentially "the same," and C. P. E. Bach (1753–62) used the thorough bass to explain the construction of the improvised free fantasia.[32] Friedrich Erhardt Niedt (1700–17) – who considered thorough bass to be "the most complete foundation of music"[33] – has been said to demonstrate perhaps "more completely than any other" theorist of the time "the path from learning thorough bass to composing."[34]

But nowhere is the relationship of thorough bass to composition more closely drawn than in *Der General-Bass in der Composition* (1728) by Johann David Heinichen – a relationship emphasized by the very title of the treatise. An encyclopedic manual of

30 Fuller, "The Performer as Composer," p. 122, which includes a list of decisions facing continuo players, pp. 122–23.

31 See, for example, ibid., p. 117. The prevalence of thorough bass practice during the Baroque era later prompted Hugo Riemann, in his *Handbuch der Musikgeschichte* (vol. II/2), to describe the entire period as "the age of the thorough bass" ("das Generalbasszeitalter").

32 Mattheson, *Der vollkommene Capellmeister*, p. 255; Rameau, *Code de musique pratique* (1760), quoted in Christensen, *Rameau and Musical Thought in the Enlightenment*, p. 52; Bach, *Versuch*, Part II, Chapter 7.

33 Niedt, *Die musicalische Handleitung*, 28.

34 Lester, *Compositional Theory in the Eighteenth Century*, p. 66; examples of dance movements derived by Niedt from elaborations of thorough basses are given on p. 67. Also see **Example 17.3, p. 547**.

Example 17.1 Heinichen, different ways of treating a given bass line
(a) Simple accompaniment

(b) *Cantabile* accompaniment

unprecedented scope and detail, Heinichen's treatise opens with an *Einleitung*, setting forth the essence of the work, which begins as follows:

> No music connoisseur will deny that the *Basso Continuo* or so-called thorough-bass is, next to [the art of] composition, one of the most important and most fundamental of the musical sciences. For from what source other than composition itself does it spring forth? And what actually is the playing of a thorough-bass other than to improvise upon a given bass the remaining parts of a full harmony or to compose to [the bass]?[35]

Der General-Bass in der Composition leads the pupil systematically through a study of the realization of figured and unfigured basses at the keyboard, principles of voice leading and dissonance treatment, melodic elaboration, embellishment of harmonic textures, and even questions relating to genre and style (especially of the "theatrical" kind) – all amply illustrated by examples. Particularly revealing are the many illustrations that show different ways of realizing a given bass line. Example 17.1 shows how a "weak-sounding" accompaniment (a) could be made "more elegant" by improvising a *cantabile* melody in the right hand (b); the unusual signs are indications of ornaments (x for appoggiatura, and // for mordent).[36]

35 Buelow, *Thorough-Bass Accompaniment according to Johann David Heinichen*, p. 309.
36 Ibid., derived from Examples 121–23, on pp. 188–90.

Embellishment and diminution

The ever-increasing freedom in performance manifest in thorough-bass realization was perhaps even more pronounced in the approaches employed in the interpretation of solo parts, all in the interests of enhanced expression. This involved several facets: the embellishment of musical lines by the application of numerous ornamental devices, a wide flexibility in rhythmic interpretation of individual passages or entire pieces, and expanded use of elaborative (diminution) techniques in melodies. Large numbers of manuals and tutors in the seventeenth and eighteenth centuries (appearing in many languages and representing different national schools) purport to teach these new practices, all of which were considered indispensable to the performance of music. Mersenne refers to the embellishment of vocal music as an essential requirement of singers, but among the most difficult to learn.[37] He gives examples of embellished airs as taught by Parisian *maîtres* of his day.[38]

While Mersenne discusses embellishment and ornamentation played on musical instruments, he does so largely in terms of techniques borrowed from solo vocal practice. The instruments he mentions as primarily suitable to such practice are the organ, harpsichord, lute, viol, and violin. One of his examples illustrates improvised diminutions played by an ensemble of the twenty-four violinists of the French court orchestra, *les vingt-quatre violons du roy* – one of the earliest permanent orchestras in Europe. Describing the sound produced by the orchestra as "ravishing" and "powerful," Mersenne provides an example of the manner in which orchestral violinists would "customarily elaborate all sorts of songs" (see the window on p. 545), adding that the resultant "beauties and graces . . . have great effect . . . on the passions and affections of the body and soul."[39] It was this very practice, of allowing each of the *dessus* violinists in the orchestra to improvise on a given line at the same time, which Jean-Baptiste Lully (Superintendent of music to Louis XIV) rejected later in the century, thereby "doing away with the custom of adding improvised ornaments."[40]

The many guides to vocal and instrumental performance published through the eighteenth century were mostly written by active performers and virtuosi, almost all of them featuring instruction on improvisation (ornamentation and diminution practice) by which the performer – as in the case of the thorough bass – can be said to help "compose" the piece.[41] Among the most influential manuals to appear were those by the singer Pier Francesco Tosi (*Opinioni de' cantori antichi, e moderni*, 1723), the violinists Francesco Geminiani (*The Art of Playing on the Violin*, 1751) and Leopold Mozart (*Versuch einer gründlichen Violinschule*, 1756), the flutist Johann Joachim Quantz (*Versuch*

37 Mersenne, *Harmonie universelle*, "L'Art de bien chanter," pp. 355–58.

38 The vocal examples of "diminutions" presented by Mersenne are compiled by Ferand, *Improvisation in Nine Centuries of Western Music*, no. 24.

39 Chapman, *Marin Mersenne*, pp. 235, 248.

40 Georg Muffat, in the Foreword to his *Florilegium primum* (1695), describes Lully's rejection of certain "artifices" in performances of his ballet compositions. See the discussion in Boyden, *The History of Violin Playing*, pp. 89, 127, 227.

41 See Brown, *Embellishing Sixteenth-Century Music*, p. 63.

Marin Mersenne, example of instrumental divisions

"In the Fantasy . . . I have given in diminution . . . the treble, so that one sees the method by which the violinists customarily elaborate all sorts of songs."

Fantaiſie à 5. compoſée par le Sieur Henry le Ieune.

(Mersenne, *Harmonie universelle*, "Traité des instruments" (1636–37), pp. 186–89; quoted in Chapman, *Marin Mersenne*, p. 248)

einer Anweisung die Flöte traversiere zu spielen, 1752), the keyboardist Carl Philipp Emanuel Bach (*Versuch über die wahre Art das Clavier zu spielen*, 1753–62), and the viol player Christopher Simpson (*The Division-Violist*, 1659).

An example drawn from Simpson's viol treatise illustrates the common procedure found in these manuals for demonstrating the practice of diminutions or divisions: the presentation of a simple melodic line or figure, followed by a series of possible ways to embellish it. In Example 17.2, the line (here called "The Ground") consists of an ascending octave scale, closed by a downward cadential gesture. Only the first three sets of divisions supplied by Simpson are shown in the example ("The Ground broken"); other, more demanding embellishments include extensive leaps, chordal playing and double-stops.[42]

Diminution techniques were also widely applied by keyboardists. Such a technique, for instance, forms the basis for a "variation" technique described in the *Handleitung* of Niedt, referred to earlier. In Part II of his manual, the author applies diminution practice to the thorough-bass lines of entire compositions. The process is described as providing "variations of the thorough-bass," which he defines as "changing certain slow bass notes (while preserving the intervals of [harmonic] progression) into shorter notes in a such way that the passage maintains its basic character, yet . . . is embellished."[43] Niedt allows "variations" in parts played by both right and left hands, and demonstrates how these altered parts, in turn, can serve as foundations for compositions in

42 Simpson, *The Division-Violist*, p. 39. 43 Niedt, *Die musicalische Handleitung*, p. 74.

Example 17.2 Simpson, divisions on a ground

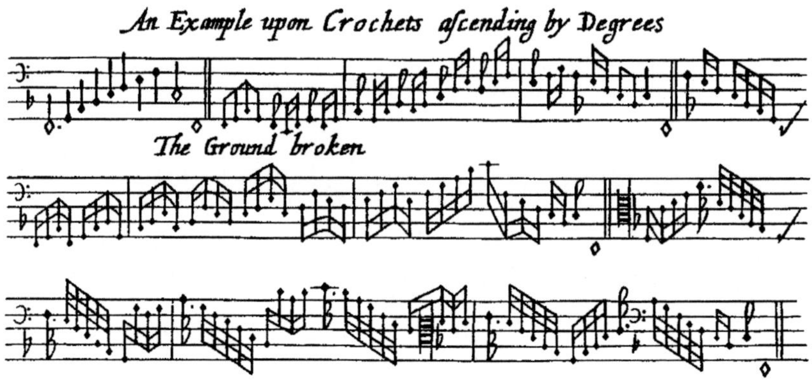

different dance genres. Example 17.3 shows a few of the many "variations" supplied by Niedt of a simple bass line.[44]

The art of improvising complete pieces (especially at the keyboard), although not new to the period, was a display of instrumental virtuosity that reached special heights during the seventeenth and eighteenth centuries. While almost any genre of the time could be so improvised, the most popular were the toccata, the prelude, and the fantasia – all intended primarily for keyboard, in virtuosic, free style. With a few exceptions, these genres shared a number of common features: an expectation of expressive "invention" on the part of the performer/composer, often exploring unusual tonal areas or utilizing distinctive melodic ideas; a sense of freedom in projecting elements of structure, rhythm, meter, and tempo; and a profusion of ornamentation and figuration. The chapter devoted to the "free fantasia" in C. P. E. Bach's *Versuch*, referred to above, has perhaps the best-known discussion of the practice in the eighteenth century. If nineteenth-century pedagogical tutors for keyboard are any guide, the improvisation of preludes and fantasias (often called "preluding") continued to flourish well into mid-century. In 1848, Czerny recommends that composers who would write fantasias, "approximate as closely as possible . . . the freedom of extemporizing." But just one year later, Kalkbrenner lamented: "How many among our best pianists can make [i.e. improvise] a prelude, however unsatisfactory?"[45]

A related species of keyboard improvisation standing halfway between the thorough

44 Ibid., from examples on pp. 90–109.

45 Czerny, *School of Practical Composition*, vol. 1, p. 82; Kalkbrenner, *Traité d'harmonie du pianiste*, p. 1. On characteristics of the "fantasia" style of the Classical period, see Ratner, *Classic Music*, Chapter 18; for "preluding" on non-keyboard instruments, see Mather and Lasocki, *The Art of Preluding, 1700–1830*.

Example 17.3 Niedt, "variations" of a simple bass line

(a) Bass line

(b) "Variation"

(c) "Variations" in the right hand

(d) "Variations" in both hands, "in the form of an echo"

bass and the practice of "preluding" was known as *partimento*. Here, the performer learned to extemporize upon increasingly elaborate (and usually unfigured) bass lines, leading to the improvisation of whole pieces in different styles. Even imitative (fugal) textures were featured in *partimento* treatises. The practice was cultivated as a pedagogical exercise well into the nineteenth century, particularly in Italy.[46]

Written examples of variations on a popular tune or dance bass – a novel improvisatory instrumental style of the Renaissance – were current during the seventeenth century, especially in Italy, Spain, and England. Known by different names (including *partite*, *diferencias*, *glosas*, *doubles*), the style also served for settings of the organ chorale (as versets). It was only in the eighteenth century, however, that theorists began to use the term "variations" (*Variationen*) to describe the style, not only as an extempore technique of embellishment (as found in the treatise of Niedt, discussed above), but increasingly as a formal procedure in composition. Heinrich Koch (1787) was among the first theorists to speak of "theme and variations," calling it "the most appropriate for the first exercises of the beginning composer." From the mid-eighteenth century onward, composed "variations" on popular tunes largely replace examples of the earlier, improvised dance variation.[47]

A special instance of free improvisation developed in the classical cadenza (*cadence*, *Kadenz*, or *fermata*). The term had earlier currency as an ornamental flourish, but by the mid-eighteenth century, it came to mean: "that extempore embellishment created, according to the fancy and pleasure of the performer, by a concertante part at the close of a piece on the penultimate note of the bass, that is, the fifth of the key of the piece."[48] This meaning of the term – as both the closing dominant harmonic progression and an extemporization on the penultimate chord of a concerted work – characterized the classic instrumental cadenza as described in treatises of the time. Rules governing the performance of cadenzas are clearly built on extempore practice of the period, constituting (as it were) "improvised composition."[49]

Performance theory in later times – a postlude

Beginning in the late eighteenth century and extending into the nineteenth, a redefined role for performance and the growing importance given to interpretation of musical scores reduced the practice of performance-based theory. Thorough bass was generally abandoned (outside of pedagogy), and limitations were increasingly placed

46 See Williams, "Partimento"; Christensen, "The *Règle de l'octave* in Thorough-Bass Theory and Practice," pp. 110–15.

47 Koch, *Introductory Essay on Composition*, p. 83; *Musikalisches Lexicon*, cols. 1629–30. See also Türk, *Klavierschule*, p. 392.

48 Quantz, *On Playing the Flute*, p. 179.

49 See, for example, Türk, *Klavierschule*, Chapter 5, section 2; and the discussion by Levin, "Instrumental Ornamentation, Improvisation and Cadenzas," pp. 279–80.

50 Horsley et al., "Improvisation," *NG*, vol. IX, p. 48.

on the "spontaneous creativity" of performers.[50] While a small number of free styles continued to play a part in this literature (principally the prelude, fantasia, and cadenza), they were restricted largely to music for soloists, adapted from eighteenth-century practice.

By the nineteenth century, a more positivist view of musical performance took hold. Partly due to the philological movement in Germany, the notated score reflecting the "intentions" of the composer became the only acceptable guide for performers. Adherents of this position, as noted by Dennis Libby, rejected "a creative collaboration in which the performer added something of his own to the composer's conception"; rather, "the performer was made to feel that his highest calling . . . was to subject himself to the composer's will as the means by which his masterpieces were communicated to the world."[51]

The invention of the phonograph, late in the nineteenth century, was the first of several technological developments that were to challenge the authority of the score. With the widespread availability of competing – and often highly contrasting – performances of the same work for listeners to compare, doubts were sown concerning the viability of the notated score to provide a fixed and infallible guide for acoustical realization by performers. Today, it is generally accepted that scores are only "recipes" for producing music and not the music itself, and that individual performances are but single "options" of the music intended – normally adding features never fully notated by the composer, and often expressing musical conventions or received traditions. Recordings of such performances comprise a repertory of valuable interpretive, critical readings of the score, ones that may be as valuable to an understanding of written works as are theoretical analyses of those works. Certainly, recordings of music either performed or supervised by living composers have come to be considered just as pertinent as notated versions to an understanding of their music.[52]

In the twentieth century, many composers consciously included a creative, contributory role for performers into their music – either through use of aleatoric or chance procedures, or through opportunity for improvisation. Moreover, the growing attraction to traditional and popular musics of all continents – both as areas of ethnomusicological study, and as sources for cross-fertilization with art music – has revived general interest in improvisational practice.[53]

By contrast, electronically produced or computer-generated compositions largely abandon the traditional "author-executant model" characteristic of Western art music for a new model – one in which the composer is the performer, and in which there is but one (recorded) version of the work distributed. In such music, the score is redun-

51 Ibid., p. 49.
52 See further on these issues: Griffiths, "Since 1940," p. 483; Berry, *Musical Structure and Performance*, pp. 217–23; Dunsby, "Performance and Analysis of Music"; Cone, "The Pianist as Critic," pp. 241–43; Philips, *Early Recordings and Musical Style*, p. 230; Lester, "Performance and Analysis," pp. 197–99.
53 See Seeger, "Theory and Method: Ethnography of Music."

dant, having been virtually replaced by the computer program as written representation of the work.[54]

Almost all of these developments have increasingly brought attention to musical performance as a central object of analysis in twentieth-century theory. The one style that combines many of the features noted above, to which the performer's contributions are critical, is jazz. It is a style in which improvisation (both solo and group) plays a principal role, in which the primary documents are not written but recorded, and which has developed a complex, many-layered theory derived from all elements that comprise it – a theory that is, essentially, "performance theory."[55]

54 Griffiths, "Since 1940," pp. 488–89.

55 See Berliner, *Thinking in Jazz*, Chapter 9.

Bibliography

Primary sources

Bach, C. P. E. *Versuch über die wahre Art das Clavier zu spielen*, 2 vols., Berlin, G. L. Winter, 1753–62; trans. W. Mitchell as *Essay on the True Art of Playing Keyboard Instruments*, New York, Norton, 1949

Banchieri, A. *Eclesiastiche sinfonie*, Op. 16, Venice, R. Amadino, 1607

Burmeister, J. *Musica poetica*, Rostock, S. Myliander, 1606

Czerny, C. *School of Practical Composition*, Op. 600, 3 vols., trans. J. Bishop, London, R. Cocks, 1848

Dressler, G. *Musicae practicae*, Magdeburg, Kirchner, 1571

Faber, H. *Compendiolum musicae*, Braunschweig, Montanus and Neuber, 1545

Gasparini, F. *L'armonico pratico al cimbalo*, Venice, A. Bortoli, 1708; facs. New York, Broude, 1967; trans. F. Stillings as *The Practical Harmonist at the Harpsichord*, New Haven, Yale University Press, 1963

Geminiani, F. *The Art of Playing on the Violin*, London, J. Johnson, 1751

Guilielmus Monachus, *De praeceptis artis musicae* (c. 1480–90), ed. A. Seay, *CSM* 2, 1965

Heinichen, J. D. *Der General-Bass in der Composition*, Dresden, Heinichen, 1728; facs. Hildesheim, G. Olms, 1969 and 1994

Kalkbrenner, F. *Traité d'harmonie du pianiste*, Op. 185, Paris, Kalkbrenner, 1849

Koch, H. C. *Musikalisches Lexicon*, Frankfurt am Main, A. Hermann der Jüngere, 1802

Versuch einer Anleitung zur Composition, 3 vols., Leipzig, A. F. Böhme, 1782–93; facs. Hildesheim, G. Olms, 1969 and 2000; partial trans. N. Baker as *Introductory Essay on Composition*, New Haven, Yale University Press, 1983

Lippius, J. *Synopsis musicae novae*, Strassburg, K. Kieffer, 1612; trans. B. Rivera as *Synopsis of New Music*, Colorado Springs, Colorado College Music Press, 1977

Listenius, N. *Rudimenta musicae*, Wittenberg, G. Rhau, 1533

Lusitano, V. *Introduttione facilissima et novissima* (1553), ed. G. Gialdroni, Bologna, Libreria musicale italiana, 1989

Mattheson, J. *Der vollkommene Capellmeister*, Hamburg, C. Herold, 1739; trans. and ed. E.

Harriss as *Johann Mattheson's "Der vollkommene Capellmeister"*, UMI Research Press, Ann Arbor, 1981
Mersenne, M. *Cogitata physico-mathematica*, Paris, A. Bertier, 1644
Harmonicorum Libri XII, Paris, G. Baudry, 1648
Harmonie universelle, Paris, Cramoisy, 1636–37; facs. Paris, Centre National de la Recherche Scientifique, 1963 and 1986
Questions harmoniques, Paris, J. Villery, 1634
Mozart, L. *Versuch einer gründlichen Violinschule*, Augsburg, J. J. Lotter, 1756; trans. E. Knocker as *A Treatise on the Fundamental Principles of Violin Playing*, Oxford University Press, 1948
Muffat, G. *Suavioris harmoniae . . . florilegium primum*, Augsburg, Panneker, 1695
Niedt, F. E. *Die musicalische Handleitung* (3 parts, 1700–21), trans. P. Poulin and I. Taylor as *The Musical Guide*, Oxford, Clarendon Press, 1989
Prosdocimo de' Beldomandi, *Contrapunctus* (1412), ed. and trans. J. Herlinger, Lincoln, University of Nebraska Press, 1984
Expositiones tractatus practice cantus mensurabilis magistri Johannis de Muris (1404), ed. F. Gallo in *Antiquae musicae italicae scriptores*, vol. III, Bologna, Università, Istituto di studi musicali e teatrali, 1966
Quantz, J. J. *Versuch einer Anweisung die Flöte traversiere zu spielen*, Berlin, J. F. Voss, 1752; trans. E. Reilly as *On Playing the Flute*, New York, Free Press, 1966
Simpson, C. *The Division-Violist: or An Introduction to the Playing upon a Ground*, London, W. Godbid, 1659
Tosi, P. F. *Opinioni de' cantori antichi, e moderni*, Bologna, L. dalla Volpe, 1723; trans. J. Galliard as *Observations on the Florid Song*, London, J. Wilcox, 1743
Tinctoris, J. *Liber de arte contrapuncti* (1477), ed. A. Seay in *Opera Theoretica*, *CSM* 22/2 (1975), pp. 5–157; trans. A. Seay as *The Art of Counterpoint*, *MSD* 5 (1961)
Türk, D. G. *Klavierschule*, Leipzig und Halle, Schwickert, 1789; trans. R. Haggh as *School of Clavier Playing*, Lincoln, University of Nebraska Press, 1982
Vicentino, N. *L'antica musica ridotta alla moderna prattica*, Rome, A. Barre, 1555; trans. M. Maniate, ed. C. V. Palisca as *Ancient Music Adapted to Modern Practice*, New Haven, Yale University Press, 1996
Zarlino, G. *Le istitutioni harmoniche*, Venice, Franceschi, 1558; facs. New York, Broude, 1965; trans. of Part III by G. Marco, ed. C. V. Palisca as *The Art of Counterpoint*, New Haven, Yale University Press, 1968

Secondary sources

Arnold, F. T. *The Art of Accompaniment from a Thorough-Bass as Practised in the XVIIth and XVIIIth Centuries*, 2 vols., Oxford University Press, 1931
Ashworth, J., and P. O'Dette, "Basso Continuo," in *A Performer's Guide to Seventeenth-Century Music*, ed. S. Carter, New York, G. Schirmer, 1997, pp. 269–96
"Overview and Practical Applications," in *A Performer's Guide to Renaissance Music*, ed. J. Kite-Powell, New York, Schirmer, 1994, pp. 203–13
Berliner, P. F. *Thinking in Jazz*, University of Chicago Press, 1994
Berry, W. *Musical Structure and Performance*, New Haven, Yale University Press, 1989

Besseler, H., ed., *Guglielmi Dufay, Opera Omnia*, vol. II, Rome, American Institute of Musicology, 1960

Binkley, T. "The Work is not the Performance," in *Companion to Medieval and Renaissance Music*, ed. T. Knighton and D. Fallows, London, Dent, 1992, pp. 36–43

Blacking, J. "Performance as a Way of Knowing," in *Atti del XIV congresso della Società internazionale di musicologia* 1, Turin, Edizioni di Torino, 1990, pp. 214–19

Boyden, D. D. *The History of Violin Playing*, London, Oxford University Press, 1979

Brown, H. M. *Embellishing Sixteenth-Century Music*, Oxford University Press, 1976

Buelow, G. J. *Thorough-Bass Accompaniment according to Johann David Heinichen*, rev. edn., Ann Arbor, UMI Research Press, 1986 and 1992

Chapman, R. E. *Harmonie Universelle: the Books on Instruments*, The Hague, M. Nijhoff, 1957

Christensen, T. *Rameau and Musical Thought in the Enlightenment*, Cambridge University Press, 1993

"The *Règle de l'Octave* in Thorough-Bass Theory and Practice," *Acta* 64 (1992), pp. 91–117

Cohen, H. F. *Quantifying Music*, Dordrecht, Reidel, 1984

Cone, E. T. "The Pianist as Critic," in *The Practice of Performance*, ed. J. Rink, Cambridge University Press, 1995, pp. 241–53

Dunsby, J. "Performance and Analysis of Music," in *MA* 8 (1989), pp. 5–20

Dunsby, J. and A. Whittall, *Music Analysis in Theory and Practice*, London, Faber Music, 1988

Ferand, E. T. *Improvisation in Nine Centuries of Western Music*, Cologne, A. Volk, 1961

"Improvised Vocal Counterpoint in the Late Renaissance and Early Baroque," *Annales Musicologiques* 4 (1956), pp. 129–74

Fuller, D. "The Performer as Composer," in *Performance Practice: Music after 1600*, ed. H. Brown and S. Sadie, London, Macmillan, 1989, pp. 117–46

Griffiths, P. "Since 1940," in *Performance Practice: Music after 1600*, ed. H. Brown and S. Sadie, London, Macmillan, 1989, pp. 483–91

Haar, J. "Monophony and the Unwritten Traditions," in *Performance Practice: Music after 1600*, ed. H. Brown and S. Sadie, London, Macmillan, 1989, pp. 240–66

Lester, J. *Compositional Theory in the Eighteenth Century*, Cambridge, MA, Harvard University Press, 1992

"Performance and Analysis: Interaction and Interpretation," in *The Practice of Performance*, ed. J. Rink, Cambridge University Press, 1995, pp. 197–216

Levin, R. D. "Instrumental Ornamentation, Improvisation and Cadenzas," in *Performance Practice: Music after 1600*, ed. H. Brown and S. Sadie, London, Macmillan, 1989, pp. 267–91

Mather, B. B. and D. Lasocki, *The Art of Preluding, 1700–1830*, New York, McGinnis and Marsh, 1984

McGee, T. J. *Medieval and Renaissance Music: A Performer's Guide*, University of Toronto Press, 1985

Philips, R. T. *Early Recordings and Musical Style*, Cambridge University Press, 1992

Ratner, L. G. *Classic Music: Expression, Form, and Style*, New York, G. Schirmer, 1980

Riemann, H. *Handbuch der Musikgeschichte*, 2 vols., Leipzig, Breitkopf und Härtel, 1920–23

Rivera, B. V. *German Music Theory in the Early Seventeenth Century*, Ann Arbor, UMI Research Press, 1980

Schneider, H. *Die französische Kompositionslehre in der ersten Hälfte des 17. Jahrhunderts*, Tutzing, H. Schneider, 1972

Schulenberg, D. "Composition before Rameau: Harmony, Figured Bass, and Style in the Baroque," *College Music Symposium* 24 (1984), pp. 130–48

Seeger, A. "Theory and Method: Ethnography of Music," in *Ethnomusicology: An Introduction*, ed. H. Myers, New York, Norton, 1992, pp. 88–109

Selfridge-Field, E. "Introduction," in *Performance Practice: Music after 1600*, ed. H. Brown and S. Sadie, London, Macmillan, 1989, pp. 3–19

Strohm, R. "Unwritten and Written Music," in *Companion to Medieval and Renaissance Music*, ed. T. Knighton and D. Fallows, London, Dent, 1992, pp. 228–33

Trowell, B. "Faburden and Fauxbourdon," *Musica Disciplina* 13 (1959), pp. 43–98

Williams, P. *Figured Bass Accompaniment*, Edinburgh University Press, 1970

·18·

Steps to Parnassus: contrapuntal theory in 1725 precursors and successors

IAN BENT

For 250 years, the *Gradus ad Parnassum* of Johann Joseph Fox (1660–1741) has been a *tabula* by-no-means *rasa* on which theorists and pedagogues have written. The remarkable process of accretion and rewriting began within seventeen years of its initial publication, with its first translation – ironically into Fux's own language, German – in 1742. There is no denying that Fux himself had drawn on theorists' writings going back 200 years, indeed back to the Greeks; but the result was no derivative hodgepodge. For all its borrowing and recasting – mostly unacknowledged, in the twentieth-century, positivistic sense – it possesses a sharpness of focus and a singleness of purpose that remain perhaps unrivaled.

"Manuductio ad"...: Virgilian footsteps

The work's title begins:

> *Steps to Parnassus; or, Guide to Musical Composition by the Rules, using a New and Sure Method, never before published in so Methodical an Arrangement*

This title plays in complex ways with the reader's expectations. According to the subtitle, it is a *manuductio* – a "leading by the hand." Like many other treatises before it – for example, Samber's *Manuductio organica* (*Manuductio to the Organ; that is, Thorough and Sure Guide*) (1704), and Niedt's *Musicalische Handleitung* (1700–17) – it offers a certain reassurance that the reader will not be left unaided. As a *-ductio*, the *Gradus* distinguishes itself from theoretical works with such appellations as "Treatise," "Method," "System," "Summa," and "Compendium," all of which offer a formalized statement of a theory or collection of theories. Moreover, it is not merely an *intro*-duction, but a *manu*-duction, recalling Virgil's guidance of Dante through the Inferno and Purgatory ("He laid his hand on mine, and with a face / So joyous that it comforted my quailing, / Into the hidden things he led my ways"[1]). The parallel is strong. In the

For help with aspects of this chapter, my thanks are due to William Drabkin, Cristle Collins Judd, John E Kelleher, Richard Kramer, Maryam Moshaver, Andrea Reiter, Michael Smith, James Webster, James E. G. Zetzel, and the eight graduate students in my Spring 1998 seminar from discussion with whom many of its ideas arose.

1 *Inferno*, Canto 3, lines 19–21 (Sayers trans.).

Divine Comedy, Virgil, as he leads the "modern" medieval poet through the circles of Hell and the terraces and cornices of Purgatory, embodies the ancient classical world; in the *Gradus*, as he leads the "modern" Baroque composer through the species of counterpoint and the realms of free composition, it is Palestrina who embodies the revisited classical world of the Renaissance. Virgil is hailed by Dante as "honour and light of poets all,"[2] Palestrina by Fux as "that most brilliant light of music."[3] (Nor should we altogether discount parallels with Christ – "A light to lighten the Gentiles," Luke 2.32, "light is come into the world, and men loved darkness rather than light," "I am the light," John 3.19, 8.12, etc. – for in giving us his style, Palestrina, Fux seems almost to imply, gave music eternal life.)

But Fux's main title preempts this image. The itinerary of the guided journey is none other than the surmounting of Parnassus, the lofty twin-peaked mountain that Antiquity considered the sacred preserve of Apollo and the Muses. As Fux tells us, "The Muses are said to dwell on a mountain that cannot be reached other than by a precipitous path."[4] Title and subtitle together constitute an oxymoron – an everyman's guide to climbing Everest! Fux's Parnassian image, however, may not be original to him. It perhaps derives from a thesaurus of Horace, Ovid, Virgil, and other classical poets, published variously in Amsterdam, Cologne, London, and Paris in numerous editions between 1688 and the early twentieth century. Edited by the theologian and dramatist Paul Aler (1656–1727), it bore the title *Steps to Parnassus: or, New Treasury of Poetic Synonyms, Epithets, and Phrases*, and claimed to provide "a Poetic Parnassus . . . a Doorway to the Muses" (see Plate 18.1). The work seems originally to have been titled *Treasury of Synonyms and Epithets* (Paris, 1652), author P. Chastillon, and to have acquired its Parnassian lead title only with Aler's editorship. It is notable that Aler was a Jesuit and Fux was brought up by Jesuits; and that the 1721 edition of Aler's work was published with the Caesarean privilege of Charles VI, Holy Roman Emperor 1711–40, Fux's patron, to whom Fux's treatise is dedicated; moreover, five copies of Aler's work were sent to Vienna for approval in 1720.

But no scaling of rockfaces is required: our eye glides across from title-page to frontispiece to see a winding flight of equal-height stone steps cut into the craggy mountainside (see Plate 18.2a). These symbolize Fux's "new method," *certa* – fixed, sure, unerring – and cast *exacto ordine* – in a precise, methodical arrangement or series. While constantly stressing the arduousness of the task ("The ascent to virtue is rugged"),[5] Fux has made it manageable by constructing in Book II a "flight" of equal-sized *lectiones* (lessons, literally "readings"), each in principle traversing the six untransposed modes. These *lectiones* are themselves grouped in fives as *exercitia* ("exercises"), each

2 Canto 1, line 82.

3 *Gradus*, Praefatio, fol.) (2 *recto*; also Exerc. III, Lect. 7, p. 244 "that light of music." The odd-looking pagination used by Fux is correctly cited: it begins with p. 1 at gathering A, the start of the body of the volume. There being no letter preceding A, the printer uses the device ") (" for the two gatherings that precede p. 1, thus ") (2 *recto*" is the third page of gathering)(.

4 Ibid., Lect. 5, p. 139.

5 Ibid., Lect. 1, p. 117.

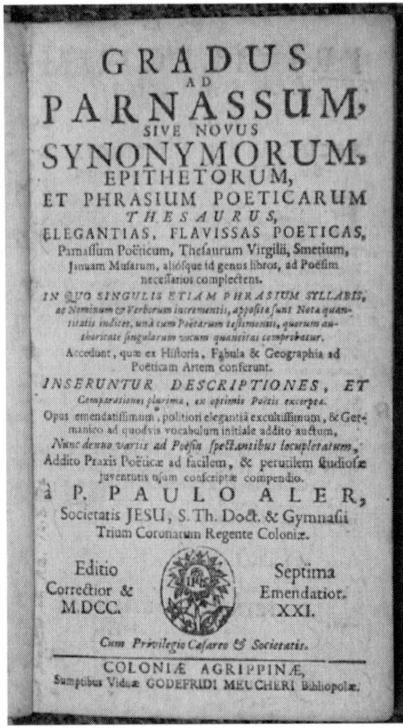

GRADUS
AD
PARNASSUM,
SIVE NOVUS
SYNONYMORUM,
EPITHETORUM,
ET PHRASIUM POETICARUM
THESAURUS,
ELEGANTIAS, FLAVISSAS POETICAS,
Parnassum Poëticum, Thesaurum Virgilii, Smetium,
Januam Musarum, aliósque id genus libros, ad Poësim
necessarios complectens.
IN QUO SINGULIS ETIAM PHRASIUM SYLLABIS,
ac Nominum & Verborum incrementis, apposita sunt Notæ quantitatis indices, unà cum Poëtarum testimoniis, quorum authoritate singularum vocum quantitas comprobatur.
Accedunt, quæ ex Historia, Fabula & Geographia ad
Poëticam Artem conferunt.
INSERUNTUR DESCRIPTIONES, ET
Comparationes plurimæ, ex optimis Poëtis excerptæ.
Opus emendatissimum, politiori elegantiâ excultissimum, & Germanico ad quodvis vocabulum initiale addito auctum,
Nunc denuo variis ad Poësin spectantibus locupletatum,
Addito Praxis Poëticæ ad facilem, & perutilem studiosæ
juventutis usum conscriptæ compendio.
à P. PAULO ALER,
Societatis JESU, S. Th. Doct. & Gymnasii
Trium Coronarum Regente Coloniæ.
Editio Correctior & Septima Emendatior.
M.DCC. XXI.
Cum Privilegio Cæsareo & Societatis.
COLONIÆ AGRIPPINÆ,
Sumptibus Viduæ GODEFRIDI MEUCHERI Bibliopolæ.

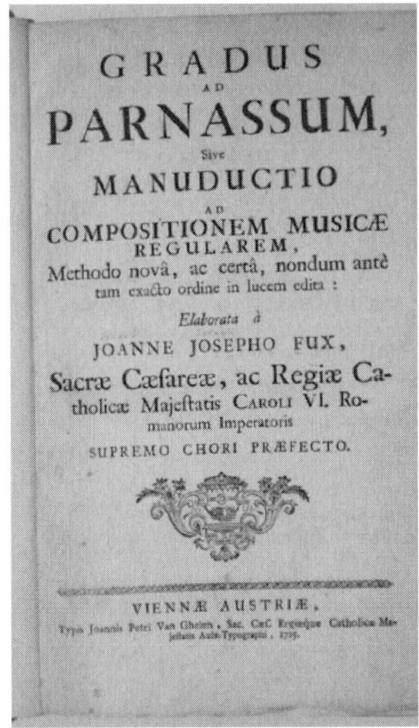

GRADUS
AD
PARNASSUM,
Sive
MANUDUCTIO
AD
COMPOSITIONEM MUSICÆ
REGULAREM,
Methodo novâ, ac certâ, nondum antè
tam exacto ordine in lucem edita:
Elaborata à
JOANNE JOSEPHO FUX,
Sacræ Cæsareæ, ac Regiæ Catholicæ Majestatis CAROLI VI. Romanorum Imperatoris
SUPREMO CHORI PRÆFECTO.
VIENNÆ AUSTRIÆ,
Typis Joannis Petri Van Ghelen, Sac. Cæs. Regiæque Catholicæ Majestatis Aulæ-Typographi, 1725.

Plate 18.1
(a) Title page of Aler, *Gradus ad Parnassum* (1721 edn.)
(b) Title page of Fux, *Gradus ad Parnassum* (1725)

traversing the five species of counterpoint: 6 × 5 = 30. One may speculate that Fux originally had a wholly symmetrical scheme in mind that was undermined by his long years of illness and convalescence.[6] The *Divine Comedy* offers a precursor for such a scheme: 100 cantos divided into three books 34 – 33 – 33, the cantos being of near-equal numbers of lines grouped by rhyme into threes, all lines having eleven syllables.

"I began turning my mind" . . .: three claims

The newness of Fux's method has three stated aspects. First, it is occupied largely with *practical* music, and only very slightly with speculative music. Second, it does not rely on model compositions. Third, designed for easy mastery by beginners, it is based on the elementary reading pedagogy of the day:

6 Flotzinger, "Fux – ein komponierender Theoretiker?", pp. 134–36; *Gradus*, Praefatio, fol.) (2 *recto–verso*; p. 279.

Plate 18.2
(a) Frontispiece of Fux, *Gradus ad Parnassum* (1725)
(b) Frontispiece of Italian translation, *Salita al parnasso* (1761)

by which a child of tender age is taught first to know the letters of the alphabet, after that to pronounce syllables, then to join several syllables together, and finally to read and write.

The resemblance to modern "phonics" is striking. Blaise Pascal (1623–62) evidently devised a method that began with the sounding of individual letters phonetically rather than by letter-name.[7] This method was adopted in the Port-Royal *petites écoles*, probably between 1656 and 1661. Two of the Port-Royalists wrote about the method, notably Claude Lancelot (1615/16–1695), teacher of Racine, who stipulates exactly the process described by Fux: letters → syllables → words.[8] Despite the "small schools" being closed in 1661, their influence was widespread, and long-lasting. Lancelot claimed that he could accomplish in six months what was achieved in three years by conventional methods. Fux makes a similar claim: "in adopting this practice while giving lessons, I observed that zealous students had in a short space of time made miraculous progress."

This analogy works, and on two levels. Narrowly construed, just as phonics refers

7 Letter from Jacqueline Pascal, October 26, 1655; cited in Cadet, *Port-Royal Education*, p. 183.
8 Cadet, *Port-Royal Education*, pp. 183–85, 259–81.

the young reader back to the forty or so phonemes of his language, so Fux's method takes the contrapuntist back to elemental linear motions and sound combinations. But more broadly, the would-be composer who aspires to writing in the latest operatic style must start with the severest, the most rule-bound procedure of all: species counterpoint – a determination that is as much ideological as it is pedagogical, for it represents the conservative theoretical tradition of Pontio and Artusi leading back to Zarlino. Fux makes the connection explicitly:

> These *lectiones* have been devised not for performance (*usus*) but for exercise (*exercitium*), just as pronouncing one's syllables (*Syllabizzatio*) is practiced to acquire the skill of reading, *and nothing more*. In the same manner, the species of counterpoint are prescribed *solely for the purpose of learning*.[9]

The second aspect of Fux's new method is its non-reliance on model compositions: past theorists have, in his words, been "content largely with *paradigmata*" – that is, they have abrogated their responsibilities as teachers. The paradigmatic tradition, which has its roots in antiquity and was developed by northern humanists in the first half of the sixteenth century, involves the systematic collecting, and then ordering, of *exempla* – usually of texts.[10] Classic instances in music are Glarean's *Dodecachordon* (1547), and Cerone's *Il melopeo* (1613), but it is hard to know whom Fux was criticizing. Adriano Banchieri, in his *Cartella musicale* (Musical Writing Tablet) (1614 edition), repeatedly resorts to examples in place of further discussion, either creating the music himself, or taking it over from well-known composers. Plate 18.3a shows the first page of such a paradigm: the soprano part of Cipriano da Rore's sestina *Alla dolce ombra* with a "modern counterpoint" by Banchieri (he does similarly with works by Lassus, Monteverdi, and others), laid out as a duo over twelve pages, with a running commentary of fifty verbal tags, such as "1. The imitation permits entrance on imperfect consonance" and "3. Reiterated second is good." Plate 18.3b shows the same principle at work 160 years later in Martini's *Esemplare* (Examples) (1774), where the three comments are located in footnotes and keyed to the music by numbers. (Analogous examples of such compositional pedagogy are discussed in **Chapter 16, p. 506**.)

By contrast, Fux relies neither on whole compositions nor on short, two-or-three-event examples (though he deploys many of the latter for ancillary purposes). Throughout the section on strict counterpoint, his principal medium is the whole cantus firmus phrase of ten to fourteen notes (generally called *exemplum*, though *paradigma* does occur), worked into counterpoint sometimes by the "master," sometimes by the "pupil"; and in the pupil's case, he often brings depth to the discussion by incorporating corrections by the master, which in turn spark discussion (see Example 18.1). Not until he reaches fugue does he use longer examples; and only in the section on "The *a cappella* Style" does he offer whole, pre-existing works as model compositions.

9 *Gradus*, Exerc. III, Lect. 2, p. 123 (italics added).

10 Judd, *Reading Renaissance Music Theory*, Chapter 5.

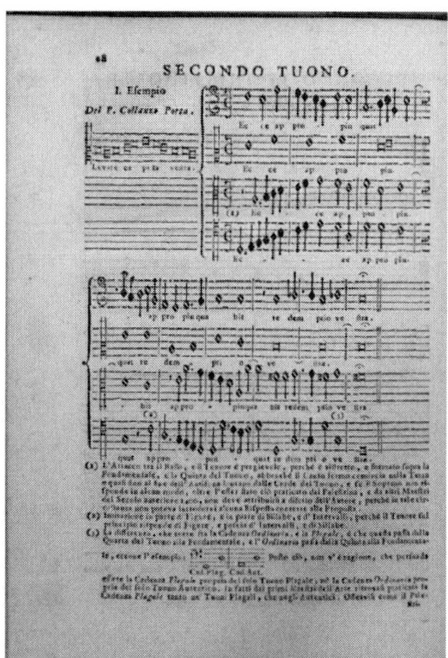

Plate 18.3
(a) Paradigmata from Banchieri, *Cartella musicale*, 1614 edition, p. 189
(b) Paradigmata from Martini, *Esemplare o sia saggio* . . ., vol. I, p. 18

As to the first claim, Fux reiterates at the end of his Preface that "there is very little in this treatise about speculative music; whereas, to musical practice, since it is the greater necessity . . . I have devoted much more attention."[11] He thus locates speculative music (i.e., topics drawn from Aristoxenus, Pythagoras, Ptolemy, Aristides, and other ancient Greek writers, as filtered through the Middle Ages, and revived in the Renaissance) extrinsically. What corresponds in structure and pedagogical method to the description of the treatise in Fux's Preface is Book II, whilst Book I belongs to a different world. Whereas Book II is organized in exercises and lessons, Book I proceeds by chapters; Book II is in dialogue, Book I is a discourse; Book II is graded by difficulty, Book I is a succession of topics; Book I occupies forty-two pages, Book II spreads over 237. With Book I behind him, Fux declares "let us now move forward to the subject proper (*res ipsa*), the second part and step of our work."[12]

Moreover, he actually relocated into Book I topics commonly treated within practical music. Thus, the final chapter, "The Musical System of Today,"[13] expounds the modern diatonic and chromatic scales, describes and tabulates thirty-three major, minor, perfect, diminished, and augmented intervals between the unison and the fifteenth (with solmization syllables), classifies the consonances into perfect and

11 *Gradus*, Praefatio, fol.) (2 *recto*. 12 Ibid., Book I, Chapter 22, p. 42. 13 Ibid., pp. 35–42.

Example 18.1 Fux, *Gradus*, music examples, pp. 47, 53 (top)

imperfect, and then – most significantly – identifies the three types of contrapuntal motion, similar, contrary, and oblique, and articulates his *Regulae cardinales*: the four cardinal rules of progression, concluding: "From these three types of motion, and with correct usage, hang (as the saying goes) all the law and the prophets" (Matthew, 12.40).

"All the law and the prophets . . .": rules of progression

Rules of two-part note-against-note counterpoint feature widely in the practical manuals of the sixteenth and seventeenth centuries. Cochlaeus's popular *Tetrachordum musices* (The Musical Tetrachord) (1511) gives fourteen such rules,[14] Zarlino's *Le istitutioni harmoniche* (1558) twelve (several of them subdivided).[15] From the fifteenth century, they had frequently comprised eight, as for example in Pietro Aaron's *Compendiolo* (Little Compendium) (c. 1545). (See the window on p. 561, contrasting Aaron's eight rules with those of Fux.) The difference between Fux and his predecessors represents not so much an improvement as a veritable *transformation*. To deal with two perfect consonances in succession Aaron requires three rules (2, 3, 7), whilst Fux requires one. Whereas the rules of Cochlaeus, Zarlino, and Aaron deal with surface situations, Fux's four rules operate abstractly, at a high level of generality. True, these do not cover all of the situations addressed by the earlier theorists (e.g. beginning and end, proximate motion), which are left to later discussion in specific contexts; but the four rules cover an infinitely wider range of situations. Taking two classes of consonance

14 Miller trans, pp. 76–79.
15 *Le istitutioni harmoniche*, Part III, Chapters 28–39, pp. 173–91; Marco trans., pp. 55–85.

Rules for two-voice note-against-note counterpoint (summarized): Aaron and Fux

Aaron: *Compendiolo* (c. 1545)	Fux: *Gradus* (1725)
	The three types of motion 1. Parallel 2. Contrary 3. Oblique
Rules for composition	*The four progressions*
1. Begin the piece with whatever cons. pleases.	
2. Two perf cons. in succession, e.g., two fifths, two octaves, ascending or descending, are not permitted.	1. Perf cons. to perf cons.: contrary or oblique.
3. Two perf [identical] cons., e.g., fifths, octaves, twelfths, may occur when one voice ascends and the other descends.	2. Perf cons. to imperf cons.: all three.
4. Ascend and descend consecutively or in alternation as desired.	3. Imperf cons. to perf cons.: contrary or oblique.
5. The counterpoint may not incur *mi* against *fa*, or *fa* against *mi*, unless unavoidable.	4. Imperf cons. to imperf cons.: all three.
6. Several thirds and sixths may be used in succession, ascending or descending.	So long as you take care, oblique motion is permitted in all four progressions.
7. Two perf [non-identical] cons. may be used one after the other in contrary motion, the first ascending, the second descending, and vice versa.	
8. When moving to a [perf] cons. [from an imperf cons.], always adopt the form of the first which is closest.	

"perf" = perfect; "imperf" = imperfect; "cons." = consonance

and mapping them on to three types of movement results in a regulation of great power and memorability.

But we must not attribute the genius of this change to Fux. The real transformation took place a century and a half earlier: The four-rule matrix has as its basis the permutations of two elements (aa, ab, ba, bb), and Artusi diagrammed these, without rules, as early as 1586 (see Plate 18.4a). Girolamo Diruta, in 1609, adumbrated types of motion, while articulating the four rules of progression verbally (see the window on p. 563, cols. A and C).[16] In so doing, he transformed a diffuse set of surface rules into a powerful pedagogical device. His rules are isomorphic with Fux's (Diruta's "contrary" = contrary

16 *Transilvano*, Book II, pp. 1–2; Bradshaw and Soehnlen trans., vol. II, pp. 33–34.

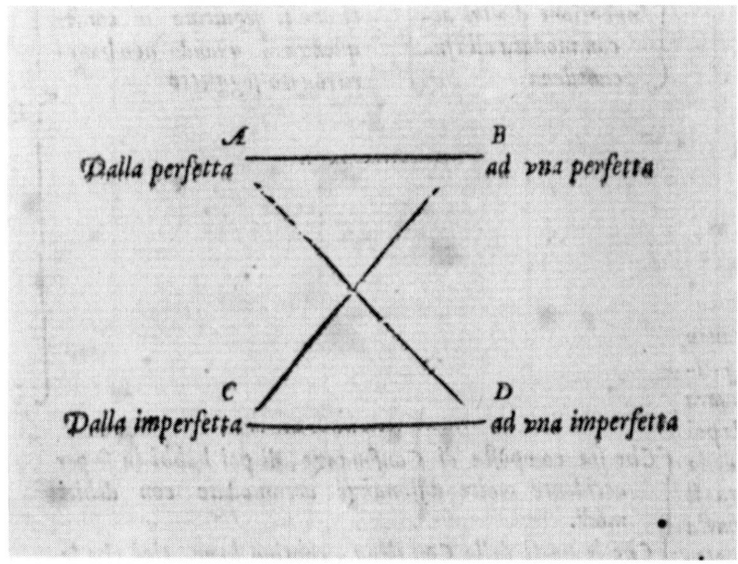

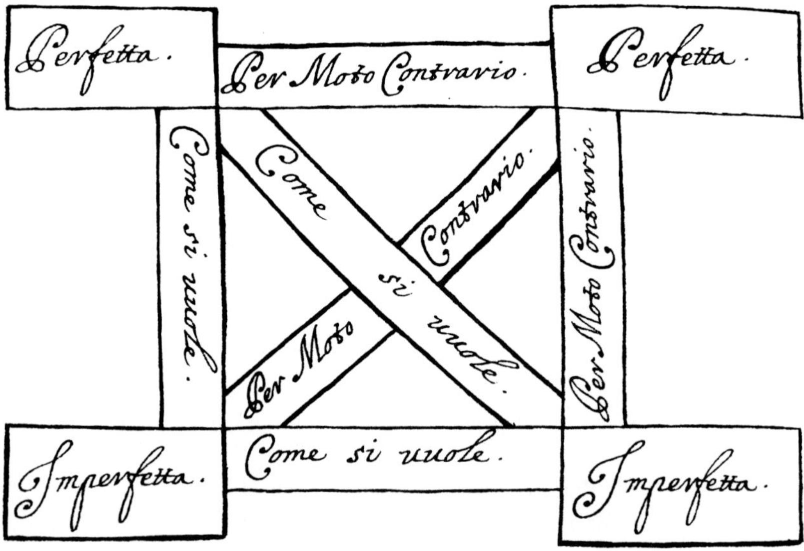

Plate 18.4
(a) Permutation of consonances from Artusi, *L'arte del contraponto* (1586), p. 30
(b) Permutation of consonances from Bismantova, *Compendio musicale* (1677), p. 42

Rules of Diruta, Berardi, and Fux

A: Diruta (1609)	B: Berardi (1689)	C: Fux (1725)
1. Perf → perf : contrary	1. Perf → perf: contrary	1. Perf → perf: contrary or oblique
2. Imperf → imperf: freely	2. Imperf → perf: contrary	2. Perf → imperf: all three
3. Perf → imperf : freely	3. Perf → imperf: freely	3. Imperf → perf: contrary or oblique
4. Imperf → perf : contrary + semitone	4. Imperf → imperf: freely	4. Imperf → imperf: all three So long as you take care, oblique motion is permitted in all four.

and oblique), except for the inclusion of the "semitone" motion. In 1677, Bartolomeo Bismantova mapped the rules, without the semitone provision, on to Artusi's diagram, so exactly equaling Fux's rules (see Plate 18.4b).[17] Not even the specification of three types of motion was original to Fux: Berardi, for example, in 1689, specified *moto retto*, *contrario*, and *obliquo* in terms cognate to those of Fux (*motus rectus*, *contrarius*, and *obliquus*).[18] As to rules of progression, Berardi offers twenty (recalling the Renaissance theorists), but his first four, announced as "the four movements that combine to make good contrapuntal texture," reproduce Diruta's rules almost verbatim (reordered and without semitone provision)[19] (see the window above, col. B). In Berardi, then, the three motions and four rules of progression stand side by side, predating Fux by thirty-six years.

"Steps to . . .": graduated method

Let us return to Fux's image and metaphor of a flight of equal-sized steps, to his exercises and lessons – in short, to his claim of a superior *graduated method* of instruction. To assess what substance there is to it, we might look first at the two-part counterpoint instruction in Part III of Zarlino's *Le institutioni harmoniche*, the overall sequence of which can be seen in **Table 18.1, p. 564**.

Here counterpoint is divided into *simple* – that is, "composed solely of consonances and equal note-values" – and *diminished* – which has "dissonances as well as consonances, and may employ every kind of note-value."[20] Almost twice as much space is allocated to simple as to diminished counterpoint: twenty-two pages, as against twelve. In consequence, Chapters 42–43 plunge the student all at once into writing over each semibreve of the subject "two minims, or four semiminims, or one minim and two semiminims, or similar combinations,"[21] including tied values, and writing

17 *Compendio musicale* (MS), p. 42; from Groth, "Italienische Musiktheorie im 17. Jahrhundert," *GMt*, vol. VII, p. 339. 18 *Miscellanea*, pp. 103–04.
19 Ibid., pp. 104–12; four rules, pp. 104–05; also see *Il Perché musicale* (1693), pp. 8–12.
20 *Le istitutioni harmoniche*, Part III, p. 147; Marco trans., p. 2. 21 Ibid., p. 195; p. 93.

Table 18.1 *Two-part counterpoint: Zarlino (1558)*

Subject matter	Chapters	No. of pp.
Definition of counterpoint: simple and diminished	1–2	2
Basic requirements of two-part counterpoint	26–27	2
Rules for simple two-part counterpoint	28–39	18
Construction of simple two-part counterpoint	40–41	3½
Diminished two-part counterpoint	42–47	12
Measure, syncopation, rests	48–50	5

Table 18.2 *Two-part counterpoint: Fux (1725)*

Subject matter	Lessons	No. of pp.
First species: note-against-note	1	11
Second species: two notes against one	2	8
Third species: four notes against one	3	5½
Fourth species: two notes against one with ties	4	8
Fifth species: combination of species 1–4, with shorter values	5	4½

counterpoint over a subject that is itself diminished. The learning curve of Chapters 42–47 – the mountain slope of Parnassus! – is prodigious.

By contrast, Fux constructs a series of stages of roughly equal length as shown in Table 18.2. The prime concern for Fux is to avoid confusion in the student's mind. This he achieves by holding back information until it is absolutely necessary. Instructions for beginning and ending a composition, given at the outset by earlier theorists but excluded from Fux's "cardinal rules," are now deferred to lesson 1 along with the rule for the penultimate sonority and other rules, thus equipping the student to construct whole miniature compositions of about twelve measures from the start. Other information is introduced at the appropriate point: for example, whereas Zarlino presents beat, measure, syncopation, and meter together *after* he has completed two-part diminished counterpoint, Fux introduces duple and triple meter, upbeat and downbeat, and syncopation precisely *when they are needed*; likewise, he metes out rules for dissonance treatment across Chapters 2–4 as demanded by the rhythmic situation.

The most striking surface change, perhaps, is the application of the term "species" to the ratio of note-values between counterpoint and cantus firmus. Zarlino reminds us of Porphyry's definition of "species" as "that form or figure that contains anything in itself and is contained in a certain genus."[22] This, of course, describes the crux of the taxonomic system that Aristotle developed in his writings on logic and biology.

22 Ibid., p. 151; p. 10.

Table 18.3 *Two-, three-, and four-part counterpoint: Zarlino (1558) and Fux (1725)*

	Zarlino		Fux	
Subject matter	Chapters	No. of pp.	Lessons	No. of pp.
Two-part counterpoint	1–2, 26–47	26	Ex. I, 1–5	36
Three-part counterpoint	59–61	8	Ex. II, 1–5	33
Four-part counterpoint	59, 61	2	Ex. III, 1–5	26

Zarlino uses "species" to describe the seven uninflected intervals from second to octave, all contained in the genus "interval," and each containing itself and its compound intervals. While Fux does use "species" in this sense early in Book I, it is his classification of the types of counterpoint that has gained the term its lasting currency in music. With Fux, the *genera* are two-part, three-part, and four-part composition (and composition in more than four parts, a theory that was planned but never completed[23]), all of which are subalterns of the higher-level genus counterpoint. The *species* "contained in" these genera are (1) note-against-note, (2) two-against-one, (3) four-against-one, (4) syncopated, and (5) florid. In turn, each of these species "contains in itself" the six untransposed modes, on D, E, F, G, A, and C. How smoothly Fux graduates the field overall can be seen by comparing the uneven distribution of Zarlino's categories with that of Fux's (see Table 18.3).

However, neither the classification nor the terminology was original to Fux! In 1609, Girolamo Diruta had categorized six types of strict (*osservato*) counterpoint that superficially resemble Fux's species while not being so called, and free (*commune*) counterpoint in addition:

[A] note-against-note counterpoint in tenor and bass;
[B] three "sorts" (*sorte*) of counterpoint in tenor and soprano: (1) "of untied, undotted minims" (i.e. two-against-one), (2) "of tied consonances," and (3) "of tied dissonances";
[C] "of black notes" (i.e., four/eight/sixteen-against-one) including some imitation;
[D] [mixed values, with ligatures and dots];
[E] "free counterpoint."[24]

These categories do not map directly on to Fux's; they are not through-numbered; nor did Diruta offer sets of rules for each, merely a few words and an example. Four years after this, Banchieri, in 1613, identified six through-numbered counterpoints, (1) "note-against-note," (2) "two minims against one semibreve," (3) "four semiminims against one semibreve," (4) "syncopated," (5) "fugato" (i.e. with imitative

23 *Gradus*, Exerc. V, Lect. 7, sect. 10, p. 279; Mann trans., *Counterpoint*, pp. 138–39; *Fugue*, p. 138.
24 *Transilvano*, Book II, pp. 9–11, 14–15, Bradshaw and Soehnlen trans., vol. II, pp. 48–51, 54–57.

points), and (6) "ostinato" (with repeating figure), all of these set against the Kyrie *Orbis factor*. Here, (1)–(4) map directly on to Fux's species 1–4, and (5)–(6) are special forms of Fux's species 3 and 5. (Banchieri continues with six more, exemplifying double counterpoint at the octave, twelfth, and tenth, and a final example of two-part canon against cantus firmus.[25])

Banchieri used the word "species" only in passing, in connection with "mixed counterpoint"[26] (*misto*, i.e., mixed note-values = *commune*), whereas Ludovico Zacconi's use of it in 1622 was part of a process of extending the Aristotelian classification to counterpoint itself. Overall, he defined three genera of counterpoint, one with the involvement of a composer, the other two performed improvisatorily. He also delineated "four species of counterpoint." Of these, two are for two voices (*semplice voce*), the first species being "note-against-note," the second "with close-packed and diminished motions " (i.e., combining half, quarter, eighth, and sixteenth notes); the other two are with extra voices (*accompagnati*), the third species being created spontaneously "by prior agreement" among the singers and presumably resulting in an essentially note-against-note effect in three or more parts over a cantus firmus, the fourth being created "under the leadership of one singer" and presumably resulting in imitation (*seguitare*), likewise in three or more parts.[27]

Zacconi's classification opens up a space between the first two species: between two-part counterpoint "note-against-note" and "with mixed note-values." This very space Zacconi himself filled out instructively when he remarked (reminiscently of Diruta's three "sorts") that "there are three manners (*manerie*) in which students ought to do exercises: the first is with minims, the second with semiminims, and the third with ties"; each is followed by an example.[28] Bononcini (1673) distinguished "simple" from "compound counterpoint," the former divided into note-against-note and two minims, three minims, and four semiminims against the semibreve; the latter into "mixed" (*sciolto*), "tied," and "fugato."[29] Bononcini reserves the term "species" for fugue, of which he has "free," "strict," "proper," "improper," "authentic," and "plagal," by "regular," "inverse," and "retrograde-inverse" motion.[30] Out of all this, we can trace Fux's own division of labor: in a brilliant synthesis of these counterpoints, sorts, manners, and species, and the various binary categories, he lays out with utmost simplicity five species in a reiterative scheme of "exercises" and "lessons" (see Figure 18.1).

We should not be surprised at the encroachment of Aristotelian classification upon counterpoint. The seventeenth and eighteenth centuries were, after all, the era *par excellence* of taxonomic thinking, the age of Francis Bacon and Comenius, of John Ray

25 *Cartella musicale: Altri documenti* (1613), pp. 106–10. A fourteenth-century example of a graded series of counterpoints ordered by rhythmic mode against a fixed cantus firmus is illustrated and discussed in **Chapter 15, Example 15.6a, p. 495**. Also see **Chapter 16, pp. 509–10.**

26 *Cartella musicale: Moderna prattica musicale* (1613), p. 165.

27 *Prattica di musica*, Part II, Chapter 6, p. 60; Chapter 15, p. 68; see also Chapter 31, p. 81.

28 Ibid., pp. 75–76. 29 *Musico prattico*, pp. 71–76. 30 Ibid., pp. 78–79.

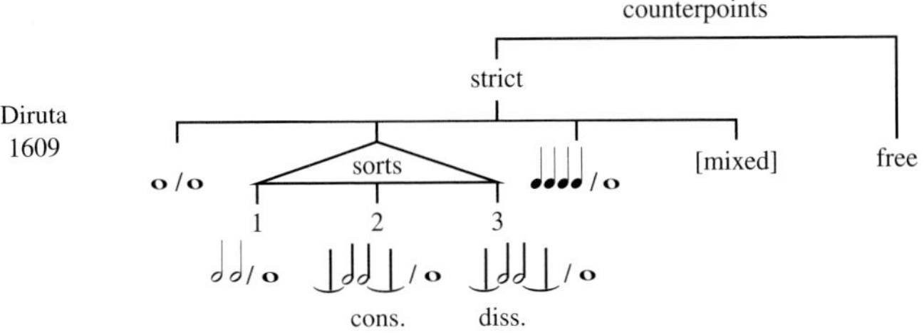

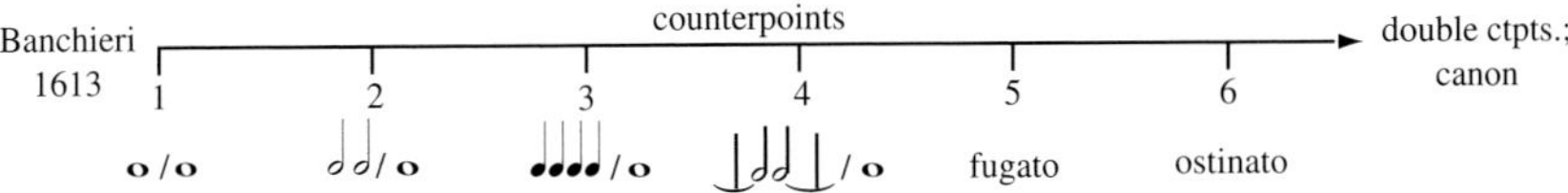

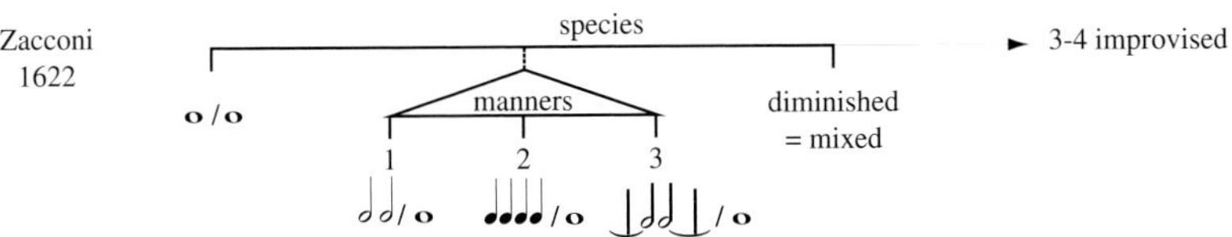

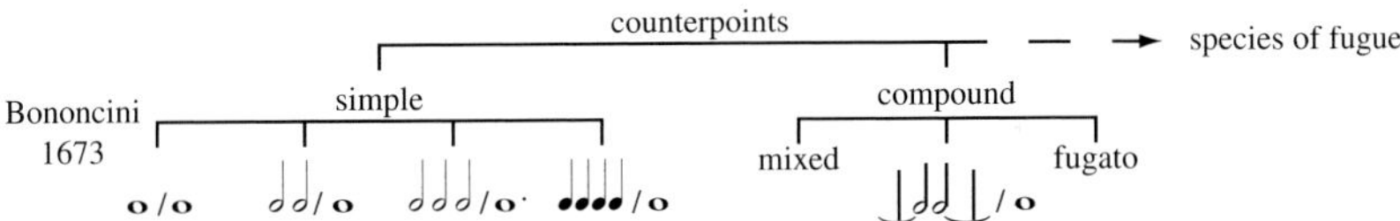

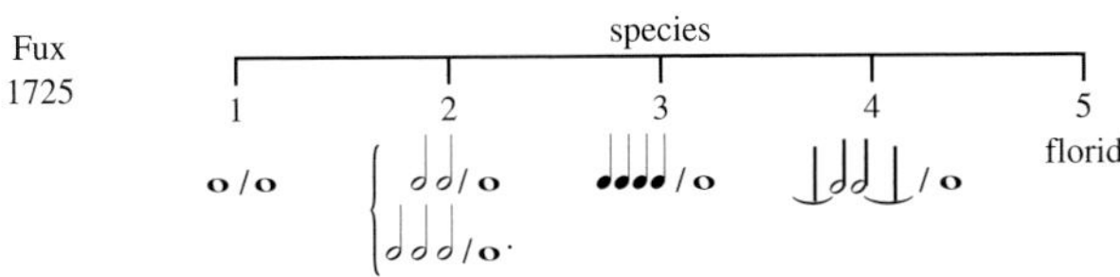

Figure 18.1 Counterpoint taxonomies

and John Wilkins, of classifications of plants, minerals, and animals, of universal languages (Latin playing the preeminent part), and ultimately of Linnaeus, whose classification of families, genera, and species (1735, 1753) holds sway today, and is couched in Latin. The classificatory tendency in music was carried further by Berardi in 1687, when he ranged counterpoints in categories such as *alla zoppa* ("limping" – i.e., short–long–short), *alla diritta* (all conjunct), *saltando* (all by leap), *di perfidia* ("treacherous" – i.e., repeating a rhythmic cell that includes very short values), *d'un sol passo* (repeating a single rhythmic pattern with different notes), and *ostinato*.[31]

"Complete harmony, i.e., third & fifth . . .": triadic theory

Once a third voice entered the prevailing contrapuntal texture, problems of controlling vertical sonority multiplied. It did not suffice (at least by the sixteenth century, and probably not in the later Middle Ages either) for the relationship of each counterpoint on its own to the cantus firmus to conform to the rules for two-part progression (Kurth's notion of latent harmonic implication for this is outlined below, p. 595). The relationship between the two counterpointing voices also required control, and the rules for this did not entirely equate with those for a single counterpoint and cantus firmus. Adding a fourth voice increased the complexity still further, tempting theorists to begin thinking in vertical sound-slices. A common solution was to invoke conditional propositional logic (*if. . ., and if. . ., then. . .*). Zarlino set the logic out in a table, the starting point in each situation being the interval between Tenor (cantus firmus) and Soprano; the logic allowed for more than four voices. For example:

> *If* the Soprano is at the octave with the Tenor
> *and if* the Bass is a third below the Tenor
> *then* the others parts will form a third, fifth, sixth, tenth, twelfth, thirteenth above the Bass.
>
> *Likewise if* [the Bass] is a fifth below the Tenor
> *then* the other parts can make a third above the Bass.
>
> *And if* the Bass is an octave below the Tenor
> *then* the other parts will be a third, fifth, tenth, twelfth above the Bass.
>
> *Lastly if* the Bass is a twelfth below the Tenor
> *then* the other parts will be a tenth or seventeenth above the Bass.[32]

31 *Documenti armonici*, esp pp. 12–23.Further discussion – and examples – of the seventeenth-century classificatory impulse is found in Chapter 1, pp. 34–38.
32 *Le istitutioni harmoniche*, Part III, p. 241; Marco trans., pp. 182–83.

Many theorists set out such relationships in number-tables. (For further instances, see **Examples 16.11** and **16.12, pp. 526, 527.**) Fux, however, turned to a different theoretical tradition for harmonic control, greatly simplifying his treatment. When he arrived at three-part counterpoint, it was his first order of business:

> Three-part counterpoint (*Tricinium*) is the most perfect composition of all because in it the perfect triad of harmony is obtainable without the help of another part, while the addition of a fourth or [even] more parts would be nothing but the repetition of some already-existing part in the harmonic triad (*Trias harmonica*). [33]

The term *Trias harmonica* stems not from an Italian, but from a German theorist, Johannes Lippius (1585–1612), whose *Disputationes* (1609–10) and *Synopsis musicae novae* (1612) first adumbrated the concept of the harmonic triad: a configuration of three pitch-classes yielding three constituent intervals – one framing perfect fifth, subdivided unequally into two thirds, major-minor or vice versa. (See also **Chapter 24, p. 755.**) This phenomenon (the harmonious effect of which Zarlino had lauded in 1558[34]) possessed unity, was capable of octave expansion, doubling, and inversion, and stood as "the greatest, sweetest, and clearest compendium of musical composition."[35] The harmonic triad could be either "more perfect" or "less perfect," i.e., major or minor (terms that Lippius does not use).

As with motions and part progressions, Fux's knack here was to reduce a multifaceted theory to a simple mnemonic: the perfect triad – which he defines as "a complex whole (*sistema*) comprising third and fifth" – "is to be employed in every measure (*tactus*), unless some other consideration weighs against it."[36] The principle applies as much to fugue as to strict counterpoint.[37] The two considerations that may prevent a full triad are (1) avoidance of parallel perfect consonances and (2) fashioning "of a more shapely vocal line." The latter sets up a creative tension between two principles, which refers back to prevailing aesthetic tenets: the composer should strive for "fullness of harmony" (*Harmoniae plenitudo*), but not at the expense of "nature, order, and variety," which Fux identifies with the smooth and varied contouring of all parts.[38] On the other hand, if the second principle is carried to excess an "insatiable lust (*libido*) for variation" can lead to "the ruin of harmony."[39] The tension may even be three-way, for Fux says that the composer when adding a fourth part (*supplementum Harmoniae*) must experiment heuristically to discover which combination of voices will arise, "whether with more harmony, or more grace, or more variety."[40]

Harmony is not to be identified with consonance. Quite the contrary: "the more

33 *Gradus*, Exerc. II, Lect. 1, p. 81.
34 *Le istitutioni harmoniche,* Part III, p. 248; Marco trans., p. 196.
35 Lippius, *Synopsis* (Rivera trans., p. 41). 36 *Gradus*, Exerc. II, Lect. 1, p. 82.
37 Ibid., Exerc. V, Lect. 3, p. 154. 38 Ibid., Exerc. III, Lect. 4, p. 135; Exerc. II, Lect. 1, p. 82.
39 Ibid., Exerc. V, Lect. 7–3, p. 220. 40 Ibid., Exerc. V, Lect. 4, p. 169.

perfect [the consonance], the less the harmony."[41] Moreover, "the more closely packed together the parts, the more perfect the harmony that results."[42] Dissonance "in itself lacks the comeliness of harmony"; and yet in order to ensure that an entering third fugal voice add extra harmony, "one must take pains that it either give rise to a harmonic triad or enter by a tied dissonance (which is the more elegant)."[43]

Thus Fux avails himself of the German triadic tradition; but he does not surrender entirely to the theory. Nowhere, for instance, does he speak of the triad as embodying unity; and yet this lies at the very heart of seventeenth-century triadic theory, with its strong trinitarian parallels. Nor does he fully acknowledge the principle of inversion. Indeed, to use a 6/3 or 8/3 chord in place of a 5/3 constitutes "a triad abandoned." There is some ambivalence here: a 6/3 chord is recognized as a triad with its lowest tone rotated up an octave, but the moment that rotation occurs the triadic entity vanishes and the tone merely makes a sixth with the lowest tone.[44] Finally, Fux adamantly rejects the duality of major and minor triads, and does not even, like Lippius, recognize them as more and less perfect. More broadly, despite being the composer of twenty operas and numerous instrumental works, Fux set his face firmly against the emergent system of twenty-four major and minor keys, and over this he did battle with the new system's keenest advocate, Johann Mattheson, in 1717–18.[45]

"I have opted to conduct Part II as a dialogue . . .": Mode of discourse

"For easier comprehension, and so that the truth may shine forth more fully" – thus Fux declares his reason for switching into dialogue mode after Part I. There are other reasons, too, stated and unstated, but first let us look briefly at the medium itself.

Dialogue – a conversation involving two or more persons, and set down in writing – is a time-honored mode of instruction. It goes back to the early fifth century BCE, and took its canonical form in the dialogues of Plato (early fourth century BCE). In music, it goes back to the fifth century CE. Fux had many precursors in the two centuries prior to the *Gradus*, including Zarlino (1571), Galilei (1581), Diruta (1593, 1609), Bottrigari (1594), Morley (1597), Artusi (1600), Banchieri (1611, 1614), Cerreto (1626), Berardi (1681), and others.

The key to dialogue is disparity: of expertise, of opinion, or of level of knowledge. It is friction between the parties that constitutes the life of dialogue. We might broadly distinguish three types: *catechismic* dialogue, *erotematic* dialogue (*erotema*, Gk.: "question"), and *conversational* dialogue. Just as a bishop may question a child on the articles of faith, so a master (*Magister*: "M.") may question a student (*Discipulus*: "D.") on his knowledge of music. Catechismic dialogue is a long-lived medium in music, going back

41 Ibid., Exerc. II, Lect. 4, p. 106. 42 Ibid., Exerc. III, Lect. 1, p. 117.
43 Ibid., Exerc. II, Lect. 4, p. 106; Exerc. V, Lect. 3, p. 154.
44 Ibid., Exerc. II, Lect. 1, pp. 82–84. 45 Lester: "Fux–Mattheson".

to St. Augustine's *On Music* (c. 400 CE), and epitomized by the exchange "M. What is music? D. The science of regulating properly the movement of sound" (*Scolica enchiriadis*),[46] but continuing into modern times. Thus Johann Christian Lobe's *Katechismus der Compositionslehre* (Catechism of the Theory of Composition), first published around 1862, but remaining on the market until at least 1914:

> *What is meant by theory of composition?*
> The embodiment of those disciplines that develop innate ability as a basis for musical talent.
> *What disciplines belong to the theory of composition?*
> Harmony, melody, rhythm, simple and double counterpoint, fugue, canon, form, writing for instruments, writing for voice.

Where catechismic dialogue is examination, erotematic dialogue is supplication, that is, genuine questioning (pupil) in search of knowledge (master). Henry of Augsburg's *De musica* (eleventh century) offers an early example:[47]

> D. How many simple consonances are there?
> M. It has already been said, though scattered hither and thither; but it is no trouble for me to say it again now: simple are the octave, fifth, and fourth; composite are the twelfth, fifteenth, and eleventh.
> D. How many tones and semitones does the octave comprise?
> M. Five tones and two semitones.

The distinction between catechism and erotema may seem artificial. There are indeed treatises in which no "M." or "D." identifiers appear (e.g., the very *Erotemata of Practical Music*, 1563, itself, in fact, by Luca Lossio), and there are others in which questioning flows back and forth (as in the *Scolica enchiriadis*). Nevertheless, it is useful theoretically to keep in mind the direction in which information is flowing within dialogue.

Whereas these two types of dialogue arise out of different levels of knowledge, and entail a polarity between "authority" and "novitiate," conversational dialogue thrives on differences of viewpoint, often among equals. An early instance is Robert of Handlo's *Rules* (1326), in which the author engages earlier theorists, Franco of Cologne, John of Garland and four others, in fictive, one-at-a-time dialogue. There, information flows from the circumference to the center of a notional circle. The medium became popular in the early sixteenth century with the rediscovery of Plato's dialogues. Often, in Renaissance and early Baroque music treatises, several participants are involved; these may be historical figures, in which case they may bring to the table their established opinions, and the information may flow in any direction: in, out, across, around. The two participants in Galilei's *Dialogue about Ancient and Modern Music* (1581), for example, are members of the Camerata, Piero Strozzi and Count Giovanni Bardi. Zarlino's *Dimostrationi harmoniche* (1571) comprise a conversation

46 Erickson trans., p. 33. (This definition goes back to c. 120 BCE, and is used by many writers.)
47 *De musica*, p. 44.

between the author and the composers Adrian Willaert, Francesco dalla Viola, and Claudio Merulo. Zarlino introduces another figure: a nobleman, classically educated and well read in Greek music theory, who goes by the name of "Desiderio." He has previously read Zarlino's *Le istitutioni harmoniche* (1558), and is now "desirous" of resolving the doubts that it left in his mind. He asks astute questions while at the same time occupying a pupil-like role, and thereby providing the reader with a "window" on to this illustrious conversation. (Bottrigari, in *Il Desiderio* of 1594, expressly revives the latter under the name Gratioso Desiderio.)

Part II of *Steps to Parnassus* falls primarily into the category of erotematic dialogue. However, the initial exchange flows the opposite way – it is a rite of passage in which the would-be pupil must satisfy the master that he is serious, does not count on future riches, and has a natural propensity for music. Catechism over, the questioning turns round. At the same time, these participants are named, and imbued with distinct personalities: Aloys and Joseph. Moreover, "in *Aloys*, the teacher, I see . . . Praenestinus [Palestrina] . . . with the name *Joseph* I designate the pupil." "Aloys" is cognate with Palestrina's second name, Petraloysius = Pierluigi; "Joseph" is Fux's own second name. With two known persons, we have the makings of conversational dialogue: Palestrina, practitioner of the Renaissance *a cappella* style, conversing with Fux, practitioner of the Italian late Baroque style. But there is no doubt of the polarity of authority and novitiate here, and it operates at two levels: Palestrina is master to Fux, Fux (as Joseph) pupil to Palestrina; Fux (as Aloys) is master to Joseph, Joseph pupil to Fux. This situation gives rise to numerous private jokes.[48] Moreover, Joseph is "one who passionately desires to learn the art of music," so is a latter-day Desiderio (the adjective used being more intense: *cupidum*, "longing," even "lustful"). Underlying the whole treatise is the irony that it contains not a note of Palestrina's music! Fux's access to the composer's music must have been severely limited; but then nor does he quote (or even name) any of Palestrina's contemporaries. Instead, he takes a handful of music examples over from Berardi's treatise *Miscellanea musicale* (Musical Miscellany) (1689),[49] but when he recommends Joseph to emulate Palestrina's music, it is his own (Fux's) *Missa vicissitudinis*, Offertories *Ad te domine levavi* and *Ave Maria*, and *Missa in fletu solatium* that he offers.[50]

Fux, then, has cleverly fused the three types of dialogue – most particularly erotematic and conversational. We should not credit him with inventing this fusion, however, for Diruta's *Il Transilvano* (1593, 1609) provides a direct model. Diruta himself and the Prince of Transylvania's musical envoy are both historical figures (as is the Prince), and they engage in a master–pupil dialogue in which the envoy plies the great organist with questions for two long sessions. He then pleads with Diruta to

48 See Wollenberg trans., pp. 210–11.

49 Berardi, *Miscellanea*, pp. 180, 181, 183 = *Gradus*, pp. 228, 229–30.

50 *Gradus*, Exerc. V, Lect. 7, sect. 8, pp. 244–71; Wollenberg trans., pp. 219–35.

publish his teachings, which the latter does, completing it eleven years after the historical envoy has been beheaded, but maintaining the fictive dialogue throughout.

Why would Diruta adopt so elaborate a literary device, at least half of which is fiction? Perhaps the nature of the envoy's mission, coupled with the exotic glamor of the far-off Prince, brought "notability" to his treatise. Perhaps he felt that dialogue added authority to his voice. Undoubtedly, it enabled him to manipulate his student's questions so as to forestall possible criticisms.

Above all, however, it brought a human touch to the proceedings. What might otherwise have been dry rule-giving is lightened by the enthusiasm of the envoy, and by the heady pace at which the instruction proceeds, with moments of hilarity laced with pomposity. Fux takes full advantage of these human properties inherent in dialogue in the *Gradus*. At times, Joseph rushes ahead, and Aloys has to hold him in check ("J. Please may I ask whether the dissonant retardation or ligature is used in ascent? The reasoning behind the next [two] examples seems the same. A. You raise a question more difficult than untying the Gordian knot . . . I shall deal with it later"[51]). At other times Joseph has to slow Aloys down ("J. I implore you not to go ballistic at all the trying little questions I am going to put to you"[52]). Sometimes Aloys does show impatience ("J. I remember your saying earlier . . . A. Best put off your question for now; all will become clear with an example"[53]); sometimes Joseph does ("J. How much longer are you going to go on with your constant variation-writing, venerable master?"[54]). There are moments of great humor in this interplay of characters that alleviate the rigors of the task, and serve other, structural purposes as well.

We can gauge these effects by taking an incident from the chapter on "Double counterpoint at the tenth," and comparing a literal translation of the original Latin with the corresponding passage in the eighteenth-century English translation, which dispenses with dialogue and introduces the whole discussion under the bald heading "Remarks to the foregoing Fugue." Aloys has just worked a four-part fugue as a model for invertible counterpoint, whereupon Joseph raises a string of objections, the last of which is that the model twice breaks a stated rule.

Original Latin:

ALOYS What questions come to mind about points 4 and 5?

JOSEPH I remember your saying on another occasion that after a rest the subject must always be taken up again. This doesn't appear to have been done in these cases.

ALOYS I did indeed say that the subject ought to re-enter, either in its normal form or inverted. Don't you see that the countersubject here is inverted, i.e., upside down . . .

51 Ibid., Exerc. I, Lect. 4, p. 73; cf. note 123 below, and associated text.
52 Ibid., Exerc. V, Lect. 3, p. 157. 53 Ibid., Lect. 2, p. 146. 54 Ibid., Lect. 7, sect. 1, p. 202.

English translation

> At No. 4 and 5. after the Rest the Subject has been introduced by way of Inversion, agreeable to the Rule "that after the Rest the Subject must follow either in a regular way or by Inversion.["][55]

Joseph cries foul here, and in so doing lets the private reader feel that there is room to question the master's word. True, Aloys has invited Joseph's caviling; true, he is generous in his response, rephrasing the rule to fit the situation without contradicting his pupil. However, nothing is as it seems. What Joseph remembers is *his own* first attempt at the rule in an earlier chapter ("I gather that a rest should never be employed except when the subject immediately follows it"), not Aloys's original (much broader) reformulation ("That's right: after a pause, either the old subject *or some new one* must always be introduced").[56] But now we can see that Aloys has himself shifted ground, pretending to repeat his earlier ruling while actually adapting to the new context. From all of this, two distinct personalities emerge, one studious, slightly pert, and craving clear-cut rules, the other kind, learned while not autocratic, yet not above a mild sleight of hand. At one level, all of this is a pedagogical device, stating one rule in four cumulatively different ways, so as to drive it home. At another, the reference backward reinforces the reiterative structure of Fux's design (which is not the case in the English translation, since the earlier passage has been cut). For the rest, it brings to life, it animates, what in the English is merely dry discourse.

"where practical music is concerned . . .": modern practice

Asked about changing taste in contemporary music, Aloys responds: "I by no means disapprove of this cult of novelty, but give it the greatest praise."[57] This answer offers us a timely reminder of Fux's overall purpose in the *Gradus*, namely to bring the student to a command of *modern compositional practice* – the latter being limited to vocal music with Latin text and culminating in the fascinating chapter on the *a cappella* style. But how could the student cope with constantly changing fashion unless he stood on firm ground? The question led Fux to a three-stage trajectory: first the invisible skills of strict counterpoint, then the visible but unchanging skills of imitation, fugue, and invertibility, finally the ever-mutable *practice* of present-day styles (see Table 18.4). The watershed to this final and all-important stage was thus the section on "Taste." We should not blame Fux's principal modern translator, Alfred Mann (who ended his published translations with V/7, s. 2), for our ignorance of the final section.[58] The neglect

55 Ibid., Lect. 6, p. 193; Eng. trans., p. 34. 56 Ibid., Lect. 3, p. 161.
57 Ibid., Lect. 7, sect. 10, p. 278; Wollenberg trans., p. 241.
58 Wollenberg's translation of Exerc. V, Lect. 7, sects. 6–10 (1992) repaired a grievous omission, but we still lack sects.3–5.

Table 18.4 *Sub-sections of Fux's* Gradus

[Non-imitative counterpoint] (140 pp.)	
I–III	Strict counterpoint à2/3/4: 5 species
[Imitative counterpoint] (100 pp.)	
IV/1	Imitation
V/1–4	Fugue à2/3/4
V/5–7, s. 1	Double counterpoint: 3 species
V/7, s.2	Fugue with three subjects
V/7, s. 3	Variation and anticipation
V/7, s. 4	Modes
V/7, s. 5	Various fugue subjects
[Modern musical practice] (40 pp.)	
V/7, s. 6	Taste
V/7, s. 7	Church style
V/7, s. 8	A cappella style
V/7, s. 9	Mixed style
V/7, s. 10	Recitative style

began in around 1768, with the first English translation. It is worth our reviewing the sequence of events.

The printer of the *Gradus* was Johann Peter van Ghelen, of the "printing house of the court of His Catholic Majesty, the Holy Roman Emperor and King, Vienna, Austria, 1725" (see Plate 18.1(b), above). The Emperor "bore the cost," and by his "command it was published."[59] Was Charles VI – a keen music-lover – just giving his trusty Kapellmeister a helping hand? Or was he promulgating Fux's method, Charlemagne-like, throughout his empire? And why the choice of Latin? Fétis suggests that since Fux was born in Styria his German was not up to the task, hence his resort to the classical language he had learned during his Jesuit schooling (Fux invokes the *jus postliminii*: the right to return to one's home).[60] Dittersdorf later described Fux's style as "such dog-Latin that any second grader could understand it."[61] It is at least as likely, however, that Latin was chosen by imperial decree, with an eye to transcending language barriers and giving the work universality. If so, then the Emperor showed sound judgment. The book sold well. Already a year later, van Ghelen reported in the *Wiener Diarium* that "a few copies" were still available.[62] A newspaper in 1728 announced plans by Telemann

59 *Gradus*, Dedication p. *verso*; Mizler, ed., *Neu-eröffnete musikalische Bibliothek*, vol. II, Part IV (1743), p. 119; Walther, *Musikalisches Lexikon*, s.v. "Fux"; *Zeitung von gelehrten Sachen*, December 6, 1725.

60 Fétis, *Biographie universelle des musiciens*, s.v. "Fux"; *Gradus*, Praefatio, p)(2 *recto*.

61 Mann cites *Karl von Dittersdorfs Lebensbeschreibung: seinem Sohne in die Feder diktiert* (1801), ed E. Istel (Leipzig, 1908), p. 68.

62 *Wiener Diarium*, November 27, 1726.

to translate the *Gradus* into German, and a catalogue of his works even quoted its price; but nothing seems to have come of it.[63] In 1743, the German translator, Lorenz Mizler (1711–78), remarked that the original had "very soon found its way to all parts of Europe, such that for some years now it has been unavailable."[64]

Mizler, in 1742, translated both books of the *Gradus* in their entirety, adopting the more compact octavo format and cramming all the music examples into engraved copperplates at the end. Mizler's rationalist mathematical view of music emerges in remarks such as "Where something is ordered and well proportioned, that fact communicates itself to the senses and affords pleasure,"[65] and in the numerous footnotes that flood around the ankles of the text and threaten to engulf it on some pages. While asserting Fux's great gift of "always getting to the heart of the matter," he quibbles with Fux's formulations (e.g., "This is the definition of ratio, not proportion . . ."), updates his scientific knowledge (as in his account of resonating bodies and the physiology of the ear), and disagrees sharply on some issues (he classifies the third as perfect and the fourth and sixth as imperfect consonances, so undermining Fux's rules of progression!).[66] More particularly, he adds a harmonically minded ("All music is nothing but a constant shifting of the harmonic triad") and tonally oriented ("D lasolre is as good as D minor, and G solreut as good as G major") cast to the whole work, recommending his own *Fundamentals of Figured Bass* for further reading.[67]

The Italian translation of 1761, by Alessandro Manfredi, is a magnificent production, with its own Parnassian frontispiece (see Plate 18.2b). A replica of the Latin edition, even down to the mirroring of its typography, it contains all sections, in closely cognate language, using the names "Giuseppe" and "Luigi." We learn elsewhere that the *Gradus* was translated by "Mr. Caffro, Master of Music to the King and Queen of Naples," and that this was "the sole elementary book of composition entrusted to the pupils of the Royal Conservatory there."[68] Niccolò Piccinni, in welcoming the translation, reports that Francesco Durante, the leading Neapolitan composer and teacher of the time, recommended Fux's *Gradus* to him during the period 1741–54.[69] The English translation of 1768 (quoted earlier) eliminates all dialogue and presents Fux's teaching entirely in rules. It omits Book I, and ends with V/7, s. 5 ("Of Some Particular Subjects"); the strict counterpoint sections treat only the D-mode, and with many other cuts the volume comes out at a mere forty-nine pages. Tacked on at the end, however, "as a Specimen of the . . . church Stile" is the Kyrie from Fux's *Missa Vicissitudinis* that Fux gives as an example in V/7, s. 8 ("A cappella style"). The first French translator, Pietro Denis (a mandolin player, who also translated Tartini's *Rules on Playing the Violin*), eliminated all of Book I except the final chapter ("The musical system of today"), which he recast in dialogue form consistent with the rest of the

63 Mann, Preface to *Fux: Sämtliche Werke*, series VII, vol. I, p. XVIII.

64 Mizler, ed., *Neu-eröffnete musikalische Bibliothek*, vol. II, Part IV (1743), pp. 118–19.

65 Mizler trans, fol.)(3 *recto*.

66 Ibid., pp. 85–86 n. 24; p. 4, n. 3; pp. 2–3, n. 2; pp. 60–61, nn. 20, 21.

67 Ibid., p. 87, n.(a); p. 68, n. 23; e.g., p. 87, n. (a); p. 165, n. (b).

68 French trans., vols. I–III, title pages.

69 Letter on unpaginated prelim of Italian trans.

work (the pupil is renamed Theodore). His translation (1773–75), like the English, excludes the sections on modern compositional practice, ending with V/7, s. 3 ("Variation and anticipation").

Fux, as we saw above, embraced the modal system when major-minor tonality had long since taken hold in musical practice. He maintained throughout the *Gradus* that the "authentic" half of the Renaissance twelve-mode system – effectively, the white-note scales on D, E, F, G, A, and C – was adequate for composers' needs: sufficient for strict counterpoint, for fugue, and for unaccompanied *a cappella* free counterpoint. For *a cappella* music accompanied by organ and other instruments, and for the mixed style, the six modes could be transposed to other pitches, permitting "modulation" to what modern ears would call new tonal centers, but what Fux called *Modi affines*.[70] Not even in his chapter on recitative does he invoke major and minor, although he hints at a different type of harmony applicable to secular music[71] – and Fux was no novice in that area, for he had already written seventeen of his operas, including four magnificent "theatrical festivities" culminating in his coronation opera, *Costanza e Fortezza* (1723), the pinnacle of his composing career, by the time he wrote the *Gradus*. Nor is it difficult to see why Fux maintained his position on this issue. It afforded him the best of both worlds: on the one hand, the entire tonal realm, in the C, D, and A modes transposable to all pitches; on the other, the rich and subtle world of the E and F modes – Phrygian and Lydian. In his view, the new tonality was only an impoverishment of the composer's tonal palette; it was incomprehensible that anyone would voluntarily surrender the resources of the modal world.

Mizler, while transmitting the chapter on the modes in 1742 with all its examples, remarked that it was possible at the same time to become versed in the *newer* teachings, "which are more useful, and also derive from the very nature of music itself." As an advocate of Mattheson's teachings, at least as concerned the new 24-major/minor key-system, he found himself in a tricky position, so he compromised with a seven-page footnote explaining the triad, key, major and minor, two forms of the minor scale, key-signatures, and the twelve primary keys with twelve internal permutations yielding 144 keys in all.[72] Fux had discussed the church modes in two places, both retained in the German and Italian translations: summarily in V/1 ("Fugues in General"), then *in extenso* in V/7, s. 4 ("The Modes"). The French and English translations discard the latter, the French retaining just the summary; Pietro Denis adopts the rather arch "modo," thus keeping the treatise modal throughout and explaining awkwardly that "by *modo* is meant [what is] vulgarly called *ton*; thus where one says 'first *ton*,' 'second *ton*,' [etc.], it is better to say *modo*: 'first *modo*,' 'second *modo*,' etc." And at the very end Denis regrets the lack of rules on how to "modulate from one *ton* [clearly "key"] to another," and appends some demonstrations borrowed from the Naples Conservatory. The English translator, on the other hand, sweeps the modal apparatus away alto-

70 *Gradus*, pp. 143–46, 221–31, 243, 265; Mann, trans. *Fugue*, pp. 80–83; Wollenberg trans., pp. 218, 231. 71 *Gradus*, Exerc. V, Lect. 7, sect. 10, p. 276; Wollenberg trans., p. 237.
72 Mizler trans., pp. 165–72, n. (b).

Table 18.5 *Martini's ordering of counterpoint (1774–75)*

Book I: Counterpoint

Elements

Rules of counterpoint

1. Authentic D mode
   à4–à4–à5–à5–à5
2. Plagal D mode
   à4–à4–à5–à6–à6 (5 species)–à6
3. Authentic E mode
   à4–à4–à4–à6–à5–à5–à6
4. Plagal E mode
   à4–à4–à4–à5–à7–à7
5. Authentic F mode
   à4–à4–à5–à5–à5–à6
6. Plagal F mode
   à4–à4–à4–à6–à8
7. Authentic G mode
   à4–à4–à5–à5–à6–à6
8. Plagal G mode
   à4–à4–à5–à5–à5–à6–à6
9. Mixed or irregular mode
   6 exx.: à4 and à5

Book II: Fugue

Rules for composing fugue

Definition of fugue:
subject – continuation – episode – answer – real fugue – canon – tonal fugue – imitation fugue – fugue as a whole – modulation

2-part fugue (8 exx.)
3-part fugue (8 exx.)
4-part fugue (12 exx.)
5-part fugue (8 exx.)
6-part fugue (4 exx.)
7-part fugue (2 exx.)
8-part fugue (4 exx.)

gether, speaking only of "Key" and "Scale," of "Sharp Key" and "Flat Key." Thus even in the orbit of Fux's own text, one sees the erosion of modal content, a process that was to accelerate sharply at the end of the century.

When we find a bastion of the *eight*-mode system contemporary with the English and French translations, it is not surprising that its author was writing near the end of a long career. Padre Giovanni Battista Martini (1706–84), *maestro di cappella* in Bologna and beloved teacher of J. C. Bach, Mozart, and many others, maintained that writing counterpoint on a cantus firmus was still the foundation of all musical training. "Just as the principal elements of a picture are *design* and *coloration*, so the principal elements of music are *counterpoint* . . . and *idea* (or *invention*)." In each volume of his *Esemplare o sia saggio fondamentale pratico di contrappunto* (Examples, or Fundamental Practical Manual of Counterpoint), Part I *Sopra il canto fermo* (On a Cantus Firmus) (1774), Part II *Fugato* (of Fugal Counterpoint) (1775), he adopted an approach maligned by Fux (see Plate 18.3b above), namely the paradigmatic method. He first laid out ten brief rules of composition, then proceeded "to place before the eyes of young men desirous of learning the art of counterpoint [or fugue] a series of examples from the most excellent and authoritative composers."[73] With fugue, his primary order is that of Fux: number of voices. With counterpoint, however, Fux's taxonomy is subverted: the latter's subspecies, mode, is Martini's highest order, his genus, number of voices, Martini's middle order, and his famed species, the backbone of his pedagogy, Martini's lowest order and virtually non-existent. (Martini's five "species" concern texture, but they do not at all correspond with Fux's: while Martini copiously acknowledged and discussed theoretical sources, and is reported by Vogler to have remarked "We have no system other than that of Fux,"[74] he cited the *Gradus* in his *Examples* only scantily, though he owned and annotated a copy.) Mode is front and center of Book I. Each set of full-length paradigms is preceded by an analysis of the mode, showing species of fifth and fourth, and definitions of regular, medial, and final cadence pitches (à4 = in four parts, etc.) (See Table 18.5).

With no counterpoint examples in two or three parts, a yawning gulf separates rules from paradigms. Moreover, while the first example in each series has a cantus firmus in long notes in one voice, with opening intonation that draws attention to it, the remaining examples vary considerably in technique used. How could an elementary student have used this book for private study without personal tuition? Nor are the footnotes accompanying each example elementary; rather, they are sophisticated commentaries on modality, cadences, treatment of cantus firmus, method of imitation, and so forth.[75] The fugue examples are not fugues of the sort that Bach and Handel had written: they include madrigals such as Monteverdi's *Cruda Amarilli*, and Gesualdo's *Moro, e mentre sospiro*, as well as motets, mass movements, canticles, and psalms.

"to publish for the benefit of zealous young men": Fux and Classical composers

Did a chance nine-month overlap have lasting consequences for the course of music history? The eighty-year-old Fux, after forty-three years of "almost continuous

73 *Esemplare*, Book I, p. xiii; rules pp. xix–xxvi. 74 See Mann, "Padre Martini and Fux," p. 253.
75 One from each category of fugue is in Mann trans. *Fugue*, pp. 269–314.

practical musical activity serving three Holy Roman Emperors"[76] (Leopold I, Joseph I, and Charles VI) in Vienna, died on February 13, 1741. The eight-year-old Joseph Haydn, auditioned months earlier by Georg Reutter, Kapellmeister of St. Stephen's Cathedral, arrived in Vienna to become a boy chorister in April or May 1740. Haydn probably did not encounter the ailing Fux (who had himself earlier been Kapellmeister of St. Stephen's), but he must certainly have come to know Fux's mass ordinaries, propers, and motets, and was almost certainly trained with his *Singfundament* (Basics of Singing) for treble voice.[77] What we do know is that in the early 1750s Haydn possessed a copy of the *Gradus*, and scrutinized it minutely, correcting misprints and entering marginal clarifications (in Latin). He probably came to know Mattheson's *Der vollkommene Kapellmeister* around the same time. It is likely that Haydn returned to the *Gradus* again and again in the coming decades, his own music being influenced by it; and that his more searching marginal annotations were made later.[78]

From 1789 there survives, in the hand of Haydn's student F. C. Magnus, an incomplete document entitled *Elementary Book of the Various Species of Counterpoint assembled from the Larger Works of Kapellm. Fux by Joseph Haydn*.[79] Extracted from the last chapter of Book I of the *Gradus* are consonant and dissonant intervals, three motions (with a fourth, "parallel motion," interpolated from Mattheson), and four rules of progression, and passages from the first three lessons of Book II (undialogued, the text shadowing Mizler's translation, pp. 60–79). Many, but not all, of Fux's examples are used, some modified, and new ones added. Conceivably, Haydn had prepared such an abridgment of Fux's counterpoint instruction, and required his students, notably Beethoven whom he taught in 1792–93, to make a fair copy of it for their own use. Haydn also made Beethoven work species exercises in two, three, and four parts systematically in each of the six modes (on cantus firmi clearly derived from Fux's).[80] Mozart put one of his pupils, Thomas Attwood, through a similarly rigorous series of exercises seven years earlier. Over half the exercises are taken from the *Gradus*: sometimes Fux's exercises are transcribed wholesale as models, sometimes the counterpoints of these are modified, and Fux's cantus firmi are used as a basis for other exercises. This course of study, however, continued, first with canon (not represented in the *Gradus*) and then with fugue, in two, three, and four parts (none of Fux's fugue subjects being used). Two things about this study are striking: first, Mozart preceded it with a grounding in chords and inversions, harmonization of figured basses, and free composition; secondly, he co-opted Rameau's concept of *basse fondamentale*.

It is a symbolic moment in the history of theory. As a piece of theoretical eclecticism, it is made all the more blatant by the fact that Attwood's exercise pages are marked

76 *Gradus*, Praefatio, fol.) (*verso*. 77 *Singfundament*, ed E. Badura-Skoda and A. Mann.
78 See Mann, "Haydn's Elementarbuch" and "Haydn and Mozart" for locations of materials discussed in this section. 79 Ed. and trans. Mann, "Haydn's Elementarbuch," pp. 206–37.
80 Nottebohm, "Generalbass und Compositionslehre," pp. 171–72; Mann, "Beethoven's Contrapuntal Studies," pp. 713–19.

with the day of the week and sometimes the date. The harmonic grounding occupied from August 1785 to the end of the year, counterpoint, canon, and fugue the winter (!) months of 1786, free composition resuming in the spring and onward.[81] Fux is, so to speak, put in his place within a broader pedagogical scheme. What we have here is the convergent movement of two huge music-theoretical tectonic plates. On the one hand, Catholic Italian contrapuntal theory – in which strict counterpoint *is itself* a training *in composition* – spread Europe-wide through publication, translation, and personal transmission of Fux's teaching (for example, Georg Wagenseil, a pupil of Fux in 1735–38, taught it to Johann Schenk in 1774, who in turn taught it to Beethoven in 1793; moreover, Attwood's exercises were copied repeatedly in England), like an underground network. On the other hand, a new body of theory, emanating from Protestant Berlin and based on the music not of Palestrina but of J. S. Bach (who repudiated species counterpoint, and started his pupils with four-part figured bass writing[82]), emerged after 1750. This included C. P. E. Bach's *Versuch über die wahre Art das Clavier zu spielen* (Essay on the True Art of Playing Keyboard Instruments) (1753, 1762), Marpurg's *Abhandlung von der Fuge* (Treatise on Fugue) (1753–54), which contrasts sharply with vol. II of Martini's *Esemplare* in representing the late Baroque fugal tradition, and Kirnberger's *Die Kunst des reinen Satzes* (The Art of Strict Composition) (1771–79), which provided a synthesis of figured-bass theory, Rameau's theory of harmony, and simple and double counterpoint (no fugue). We can recognize this convergence of two distinct theoretical traditions already within Haydn, who studied Mattheson and C. P. E. Bach as well as Fux. Indeed, its seeds are present within the *Gradus* itself, which, as we saw earlier, appropriated German triadic theory within Italian contrapuntal method.

At first sight, Albrechtsberger's *Anweisung zur Composition* (Instruction in Composition) (1790) transacts much the same business as Fux. Beginning with the final chapter of Book I (cf. Haydn's *Elementarbuch*), it proceeds (without dialogue, in rule-based form) through species counterpoint ("Strict composition admits the first five species, as seen in this work and in that of Fux"[83]), fugue and double counterpoint, these showing a wholesale shift from Renaissance style to that of the late Baroque, including music examples by J. S. Bach and Handel. It concludes with a section on contemporaneous practice entitled "Church, chamber, and theater style; church music accompanied by instruments." It discards Fux's material on variation (which must have equated in Albrechtsberger's mind with Baroque ornamentation), the modes, and taste. The significant additions are chapters on chorale fugue, five-part counterpoint, and canon, and an appendix on the ranges and characteristics of all instruments in common use.[84]

81 Heartz, "Attwood's Lessons," p. 181.
82 Letter from C. P. E. Bach to Forkel (January 13, 1775). Quoted in Chapter 2, p. 56.
83 *Anweisung*, 2nd edn. (1818), p. 19.
84 Sections on cantus firmus, fugue, and canon, Mann. trans., *Fugue*, pp. 221–62.

A sentence at the beginning of the chapter on first-species two-part counterpoint, however, pulls us up sharp. Let us compare it with the corresponding sentence in Fux, as it reads in Mizler's German translation:

> Fux: The first step in the combining of two voices is, with the help of God, to set down as a basis a cantus firmus, which one either composes (*verfertiget*) oneself, or selects from a plainsong book.
>
> Albrechtsberger: No one can compose (*verfertigen*) one or several voices against a cantus firmus, either newly invented (*erfunden*), or assigned by a teacher, before that cantus firmus has been adequately examined and analyzed in its own right to determine the keys (*Tonarten*) to which it modulates, or the keys of which it is constituted.[85]

The parallels of syntax and vocabulary are plain. But the latter is no mere gloss upon the former; rather, it is (quite apart from other, subtle differences) a cry of *incredulity*! That the mere *act* of writing out a cantus firmus should be sufficient for proceeding to inscribe the second part ("Now one gives to each of these notes its particular consonance, in the upper voice," continues Fux) seems simplistic to Albrechtsberger.

His sentence is literally a defining moment in the history of contrapuntal theory, for it tells us what the Attwood lessons had already practiced: that the student was supposed to think in harmonic terms and be capable of simple harmonic analysis before embarking on counterpoint. Although Albrechtsberger follows Fux by presenting species counterpoint in ascending number of voices, it is clear that he thinks of the contrapuntal process in terms of chordal construction. In spirit, he follows Kirnberger, who in *Die Kunst des reinen Satzes*, Part I (1771), taught chords, progressions, and modulation, and then presented simple counterpoint first in *four*, then *three*, then *two* voices, commenting "Two-part counterpoint is the hardest of all, and cannot be done perfectly before one has a full command of four-part counterpoint."[86] Albrechtsberger teaches two-part counterpoint using examples in three and four parts, so that two-part writing is implicitly a *stripped-down version of full harmony* rather than a combination of two lines governed by what Ernst Kurth would later call "intervallic sociability."

Kirnberger justified his approach in a provocative pamphlet, *Gedanken über die verschiedenen Lehrarten in der Komposition als Vorbereitung zur Fugenkenntis* (Thoughts on the Different Methods of Teaching Composition as a Preparation for Mastering Fugue) (1782), in which he contends that Fux's counterpoint method is "excessively strict," that there are things in the *Gradus* that are "incompatible with art," and makes play with the difference between *strenger* (strict) *Satz* and *reiner* (pure) *Satz*. Inadequately prepared, a Fuxian fugue is "a mere tolling of harmonies" that lacks unity, comparing balefully with its Bachian counterpart. Implicitly eradicating the professed merits of the *Gradus*, he declares: "[Bach's] method is the best, for he proceeds always step by

85 *Gradus*, trans. Mizler, p. 65; *Anweisung*, 2nd edn. (1818), p. 26.

86 *Die Kunst*, Part I, p. 174.

step from easiest to hardest." *Die Kunst des reinen Satzes* is thus an attempt to reduce Bach's unwritten method to its basic principles for all the world to see; and this method involves starting with the bare essentials of thorough-bass.[87]

Albrechtsberger's pupil Ignaz Ritter von Seyfried put the seal on the implied pedagogical master plan c. 1826 when he published what he called *J. G. Albrechtsbergers sämmtliche Schriften über Generalbass, Harmonie-Lehre, und Tonsetzkunst, zum Selbstunterrichte* (J. G. Albrechtberger's Collected Writings on Figured Bass, Harmony, and Counterpoint for Self-instruction), in which he placed the author's later treatise on thorough bass (c. 1791, 1804) *before* the counterpoint treatise, claiming in his preface (Seyfried was, as we will see, notoriously unreliable): "we have exactly followed that which the author himself had found to be most advantageous in the practice of teaching." It was in this combined form that Albrechtsberger's writings (the thorough-bass material contaminated by Seyfried) were widely distributed in Austria and Germany, and then translated into French (refashioned and heavily interpolated by Alexandre Choron, 1830). From thence they were three times translated into English, hence promulgated throughout France, Britain, and North America in a doubly contaminated form, to have lasting influence throughout the nineteenth century.

We noted that Albrechtsberger discarded Fux's chapter on the modes. This is itself a historic coming-to-terms, for whereas Haydn's and Mozart's counterpoint teaching adhered to the six modal cantus firmi that had formed the bedrock of Fux's instruction, Albrechtsberger's replaces them with just two tonal ones, in C major and E minor. Whereas in the fugue chapters Fux had used six fugue subjects, Albrechtsberger uses only two, one in F major, one in D minor, with one concession to the Phrygian mode (see Example 18.2).[88]

Albrechtsberger's importance in the history of theory is enhanced by the knowledge that Haydn recommended him to Beethoven as "the best teacher of composition among all present-day Viennese masters," and that Beethoven took a year of thrice-weekly counterpoint lessons from him (1794–95) – covering the gamut from counterpoint to canon. Ostensibly Seyfried published the exercises from this study in 1832 as the fruit of Beethoven's "two years [!] of apprenticeship under his beloved mentor, Albrechtsberger."[89] However, while a batch of exercises from these lessons covering two-to-four-voice counterpoint in all the species on cantus firmi in F major and D minor does survive in the two men's hands, and also a second batch all on another cantus firmus in F major, Seyfried excluded the first batch altogether, and included the second but omitted Albrechtsberger's comments and Beethoven's inscriptions. Moreover, he inserted completely bogus text as if it were original, failed to distinguish the men's hands, and silently altered many exercises.[90] The resulting 10 pages

87 *Gedanken*, pp. 4–5.
88 *Anweisung*, 2nd edn. (1818), pp. 32–161 *passim*, 248–55, 175–80, 198–208.
89 Seyfried, *Ludwig van Beethoven's Studien*, Foreword, 1st edn.
90 Ibid., Chapter 15; see Nottebohm, "Generalbass und Compositionslehre," pp. 173–75.

Example 18.2 Albrechtsberger, *Anweisung* (1790), cantus firmi and fugue subjects

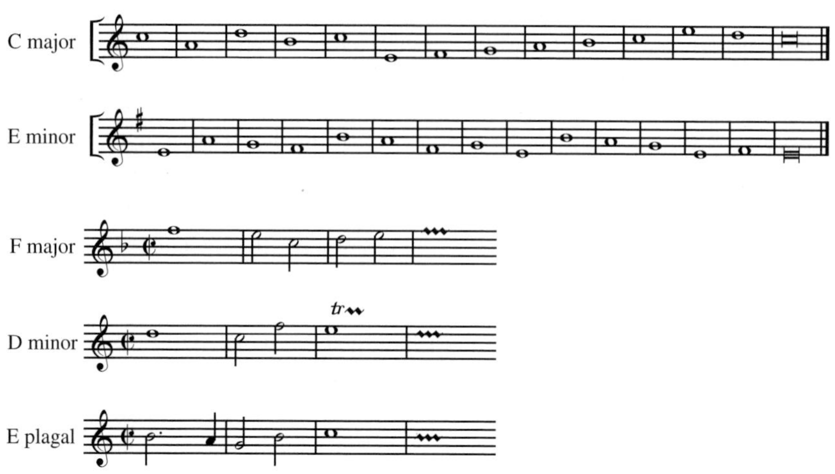

are overshadowed by 129 others culled from the lessons with Haydn, the lessons of an unknown student with Albrechtsberger, an introduction to Fuxian counterpoint prepared by Beethoven himself (how extraordinary that Beethoven would prepare as late as c. 1809, seemingly for one of his own students, a digest of the modal counterpoint material in the *Gradus*!), and other, much later material, all intermingled indiscriminately and without identification. Similar confusion reigns in the materials on imitation, fugue, chorale-fugue, double counterpoint, and canon. According to Nottebohm, Seyfried went about his work "with unbridled recklessness," the result being "counterfeit."[91]

Five years later, Adolf Bernhard Marx was to disparage the apparent influence of Albrechtsberger's teaching on Beethoven – indeed, the influence of traditional theory more generally on Classical composers. In the Foreword to his *Lehre von der musikalischen Komposition, praktisch-theoretisch* (Manual of Musical Composition in Theory and Practice) (1837–47), he remarked of Gluck, Mozart, Beethoven, and Haydn:

> not one of them, or their lofty contemporaries, became what they did by way of the old theory. Rather they became so *despite* it, in finding the right paths early enough by means of their own profundity of thought. And – as the immutable contradiction between their works and the old theoretical principles proves – their spirit rose above all aberrations, impediments and drudgery.[92]

91 Nottebohm, "Generalbass und Compositionslehre," pp. 176–96, 203.
92 *Die Lehre von der musikalischen Komposition*, vol. I (1837), Foreword, p. x.

"the raging torrent that precipitously bursts its banks": Romantic subjectivity

Rameau's theory of harmony, more strongly imprinted than it was in Kirnberger's *Strict Composition*, converged with the Fuxian agenda in the writings of two theorists working in Paris in the early nineteenth century, neither of them French by nationality. Both accepted that the triad and the dominant seventh and ninth chords needed no preparation in modern harmony, both fully assimilated the principle of inversion, and one of them developed a variant of the *basse fondamentale*. The Belgian Jérôme-Joseph de Momigny (1762–1842) affirms Fux's three motions and four rules of progression, and then embarks on two-part writing by Fuxian steps: note-against-note, with and without syncopation, then two, three, and four notes against one, then up to eight against one (calling them "species" on occasion). He then pursues two-part writing on through imitation, fugue, and canon, analyzing examples by Handel, Haydn, and Clementi,[93] overleaping three-part writing and proceeding direct to the string quartet. Later, he takes up double counterpoint, then resumes canon (and then goes on to the symphony).[94] For him, the augmented fourth and diminished fifth could be used unprepared, whereas the perfect fifth, being only a half-consonance, must always be prepared in some fashion.[95] Thus, with characteristic iconoclasm, he takes Fux's first two-part example (see Example 18.1, above, first system) and finds five faults in the first six measures.

The Bohemian Antonín Reicha (1770–1836), who was professor of counterpoint and fugue at the Paris Conservatoire from 1818, pursued his own Fuxian agenda in his *Traité de haute composition musicale* (Treatise on Advanced Musical Composition) (1824–26), which spread over 400 folio pages: (1) the church modes; (2) the "rigorous style," in two to five parts (without species); (3) double-choir writing; (4) double counterpoint, including inversion and retrogression; (5) imitation; (6) canon; (7) fugue, simple and double; (8) accompanied fugue.[96] The modes are presented, however, only for specialist use, and all counterpoint instruction is conducted in the tonal realm and so rests on Reicha's harmony manual *Cours de composition musicale* (Course in Musical Composition) (c. 1816–18). The latter presents the thirteen primary chords of the modern style, of which only *four* are normal usage in the rigorous style, and *six* others can "enrich" that style through suspensions, passing notes, and alterations (see the window on p. 586). As in Albrechtsberger, counterpoint is here seen as creating chordal entities rather than being regulated by intervallic distances between parts. However, a new parsimony of chords is invoked because each one may

93 *Cours complet*, vol. I, pp. 161–79, 262–97; vol. III, Plates 19–21, 27–29.
94 Ibid., vol. II, pp. 544–83; vol. III, Plates 40–45.
95 Ibid., vol. I, pp. 147–58; vol. III, Plates 17G–ZZ.
96 *Traité de haute composition*, vol. I, pp. 1–37, 87–233; vol. II, pp. 1–233.

be represented by any (subject to certain rules) of its inversions. Reicha speaks of the icy depths and harmonic calculuses of the strict style. At the same time, he concedes that it offers pure and celestial harmonic effects that are preferable to the instrumental and theatrical luxuriance then common in churches. Whereas Momigny worked in isolation as a theorist, Reicha was a teacher of influence over many years, his pupils including Berlioz, Liszt, Gounod, Onslow, and Franck, and several important writers; and his books were adopted by other teachers.

If Reicha's treatises exude the world of Haydn and Mozart, Gluck and Cimarosa, they also have a certain erratic, exploratory quality that must have appealed to those burgeoning minds. But it is with Adolf Bernhard Marx (1795–1866) that we find theoretical work that embodies the spirit of Romanticism. Marx's view of the place of counterpoint within the broad scheme of music was a radical one.

In effect, his *Lehre von der musikalischen Komposition* tells, in its four volumes, how music *realizes itself.* It does for music what Hegel's *Phänomenologie des Geistes* (1807) did for the progress of the mind from pure sense-consciousness to full scientific cognition. It recounts music's journey from a simple and singular state to a profusion of forms, genres, and media. Not in historical terms: Marx does not (as Fétis was to do a few years later) begin with plainchant, traverse phases of style, and conclude with the musical world of the 1830s. On the contrary, he conducts the whole process in *modern* terms, showing how the major scale realizes from within itself the complexities of the

Classical-Romantic style, with Beethoven at its center (though frequently with Mendelssohn emerging as the prevailing flavor). What is more, the *Manual*, as a work of pedagogy, causes each pupil in turn to follow this conceptual journey.

According to Marx's telling of it, music grew out of the dualism of *motion* and *rest* (see also **Chapter 30, p. 933**). This dualism manifested itself through tonal rise and fall, and through rate of event-occurrence. Together, these elements constituted the "inexhaustible fount of musical formation."[97] Beginning with the single, fluid line, the sonic arabesque, music acquires identity through the *motive*, and artistic shaping from the extension and compression of that motive. Eventually, however, the single line strives to reach outside of itself. It does so by alternating different octave registers – achieving, we might say, pseudo-polyphony, and ultimately heterophony. But all of this is in vain!

> However hard we try to break away from parallel octave progressions – which is our true purpose – and unfold a true two-part counterpoint in which each voice has its own primary melody, we simply cannot do it. Missing is some other fundamental element that will show us which tones in two independent voices belong together by the higher principle of the very nature of tone itself.[98]

That "other" lies in the realm of acoustics: it is "natural harmony," in the guise of the first twelve tones of the harmonic series (with the low-tuned seventh suppressed – Zarlino's *senario*, extended to include the second and fourth degrees). These tones are sorted into two intersecting "masses" – tonic and dominant-seventh collections – and assembled into whole- and half-cadence formations. All of this constitutes a "substratum (*Grundform*) of two-partness." Now that the single line has reached outside of itself and discovered its "other," it can reintegrate itself (just as in Hegel sense-consciousness reaches out into objectivity and then returns to itself as subjectivity). That is, it becomes self-aware, and can add to itself a second line in accordance with the dictates of harmony. The result resembles more the "duet" of nineteenth-century opera and oratorio than two-part polyphony. It can then add a second duet to the first, so acquiring the possibilities for the antiphonal effects, contrasts, and subgroupings that four lines can offer.[99] Three hundred pages later, it progresses to four-part chorale writing in the church modes and, two whole volumes later still, to choral fugue, motet, and polychoral writing, mostly with texts, and distinctly Protestant rather than Catholic in character.[100] Thus, nothing in the student's journey through counterpoint and fugue smacks of archaism (even the modal chorales relate to contemporary oratorio and cantata writing in the stylistic world of Schumann, Loewe, Mendelssohn, and Marx himself); nothing exists purely for the discipline; the student spends his time within the modern compositional domain. "It is not the task of the artist to peer after

97 *Die Lehre von der musikalischen Komposition*, vol. I (1837), p. 25. 98 Ibid., p. 41.
99 Ibid., pp. 47–61. 100 Ibid., pp. 334–69; vol. III, pp. 442–550.

a now moribund life; his business is living creation." Rather, he must see into the "world of his art's forms . . . and possess it entirely."[101]

Perhaps the most striking feature of Marx's *Lehre*, and the one that makes the starkest contrast with Albrechtsberger's, is the absence – except in matters such as the characteristics of instruments – of prescription and rule-giving. At no point does the theorist assume the mantle of authority. At no point is the composer deemed subject to a higher law. He creates his own laws, he is self-dependent; he composes according to his own will. Marx's student is an artist in the image of the early German Romantics. When he starts to compose, from music's raw material he first fashions the motive – grasps its destiny, one might say – then shapes it and causes it to evolve into a form of which he may have no clear idea at the outset. No wonder, then, that Marx's presentation of musical forms is non-prescriptive, for it is in keeping with a social attitude in which the artist is free to choose both the means and the end.

It is not possible here to pursue further the Romantic reconceptualization of counterpoint. Suffice it to say that such consideration would have to include Johann Christian Lobe's *Lehrbuch der musikalischen Komposition* (Textbook of Musical Composition), in which harmony and elementary counterpoint are fused together in volume I (1850) as a course in writing string quartets and piano genre pieces, and in which fugue, double counterpoint, and canon are taught as a constant cycle of analysis and synthesis in volume III (1860); and above all, Moritz Hauptmann, in whose comprehensive theory of music (1853), profoundly influenced by Hegel, counterpoint is present only implicitly within a theory that overtly concerns harmonic and metrical process.

"whose undying memory I shall never cease to honor . . .": the historicizing of counterpoint

The century that separates Fux's *Gradus* (1725) from Fétis's *Traité du Contre-point et de la fugue* (Treatise on Counterpoint and Fugue) of 1824 and Giuseppe Baini's *Historical and Critical Memoirs of the Life and Work of . . . Palestrina* of 1828 places a distance between writer and subject-matter that had existed for none of the theorists so far reviewed. The sense of existing *within* the Palestrina–Berardi heritage in the case of Fux, Martini, and Albrechtsberger, and that of J. S. Bach with Marpurg and Kirnberger, is of a quite different *quality* from the backwards, objectifying gaze of Fétis and Baini. That difference is pointed up neatly by a comparison: access to the sources of Palestrina's music, the lack of which in part drove Fux to form his idealized image of the composer's style, is precisely what Baini (as archivist in the papal chapel) *did* have, and enabled him to

101 Ibid., vol. I (7/1868), p. 2; Burnham trans., p. 36.

analyze the composer's stylistic development into ten stages.[102] (It was, however, not until Knud Jeppesen's study of Palestrina's dissonance treatment in 1922 that analysis was carried out on the composer's personal style in a critical, positivistic spirit.)

Thus, whereas Albrechtsberger strove to modernize Fux's stylistic terms of reference from within, it was François-Joseph Fétis (1784–1871) who in 1824 was first able to objectify the *Gradus* and treat the Palestrinian style in a historicizing manner. Fétis – later to establish himself as a leading music historian and lexicographer as well as a theorist of lasting importance – already knew not only the treatises of the principal Renaissance writers, but also the music of Monteverdi and the writings of many Baroque theorists, including Zacconi and Berardi, and all the major eighteenth-century theorists. In his counterpoint treatise he adopted Fux's graduated method and broad sequence of topics wholeheartedly while rejecting its reliance on modality. He disputed the placing of fugue before double counterpoint on grounds that the latter was a prerequisite for the former. Having precisely followed Fux on the five species of counterpoint in two, three, and four parts and extended coverage up to eight parts, he then preconditioned the structure of the remainder of his treatise with one simple statement. "There are," he declares, "three main types of imitation: (1) *imitation* proper, which can be interrupted when the progress of the work demands; (2) that with the obligation to continue exact imitation right to the end, namely *canon*; and (3) periodic imitation, namely *fugue*."[103] Thereafter, the discussion of imitation in general is followed by an extended treatment of canon in up to eight parts, then double counterpoint, including that in instrumental style, leading to fugue in up to eight parts, accompanied and instrumental fugue.

Fétis's statement of purpose plots out a far-reaching transformation of Fux's *Steps* and Albrechtsberger's *Instruction*: namely, to bring "the rigor of [their] rules to bear on modern tonalité [a term that Fétis served to establish] while avoiding the temptations of an over-liberal school; classifying the features of each style in orderly fashion; and expounding the precepts in the historical order indicated by the great works of art."[104] He thus included a long and interesting chapter at the end of Part I entitled "The Various Types of Counterpoint on Plainchant, and particularly the Palestrinian style," which surveys the growth of note-against-note composition from fauxbourdon through the sixteenth and seventeenth centuries. He even gave space to Berardi's extended categories of counterpoint *alla diritta*, *saltando*, *perfidiato*, *ostinato*, and *d'un sol passo*, calling them "conditional counterpoints."[105] He achieved a sense of stylistic depth by including full-length examples not only from Palestrina (who "perfected everything while inventing nothing")[106] and Porta, and polychoral works by Valentini, Paolo Agostini, and Benevoli, but also many by J. S. Bach, Perti, Jommelli, Sarti, and Cherubini.

102 Trans in MANC, vol. I, pp. 263–80.
103 Fétis, *Traité du Contre-point*, 1st edn., Part I, p. 71.
104 Ibid., p. VII.
105 Ibid., p. 68.
106 Ibid., p. 129.

Example 18.3 Fux, *Gradus*, C-mode cantus firmus; Fétis, *Traité du Contre-point*, cantus firmus

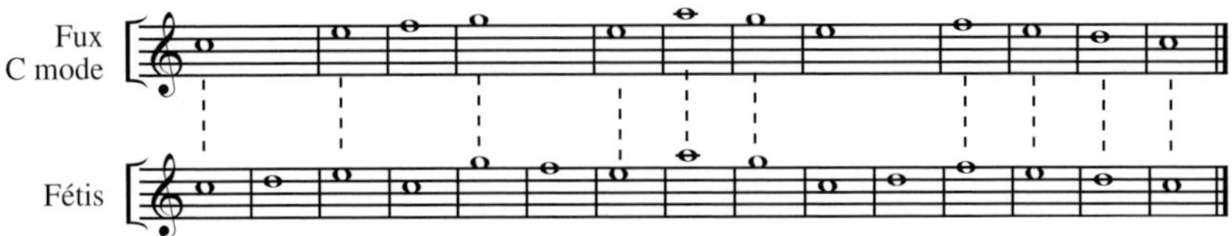

Like Albrechtsberger, and unlike Fux, he illustrated his discourse – which does not use dialogue – with short examples of two to five bars. However, he ended each section with a series of examples working a cantus firmus. Where Albrechtsberger had reduced Fux's six modal cantus firmi to one major and one minor, Fétis went a stage further, employing only one fifteen-measure cantus firmus, which he reworked tirelessly, sometimes as many as sixteen times in succession. Despite its clear C major feel, it has a contour similar to those of Fux, and could indeed be seen as an expansion of the latter's C-mode cantus firmus (see Example 18.3).

The allusion above to an "over-liberal school" is significant. The politics of counterpoint in the Paris Conservatoire around 1824 was intense, Fétis (appointed professor in 1821) attributing "erroneous doctrines" and "arbitrary principles" to teachings of Antonín Reicha, and Luigi Cherubini (who became Director in 1822) seeking to put a stop to the latter's influence for good by commissioning Fétis's counterpoint treatise. The maneuver did not work, so eleven years later, Cherubini was driven to write his own textbook. (Reicha's, Fétis's, and Cherubini's treatises are all folio format, printed by elegant but hard-to-read engraved plates, as if the latter two were exorcisms of the first!). Cherubini's *Cours de contrepoint et de fugue* (Course in Counterpoint and Fugue) (1835) entered into a heated atmosphere in which three professors, a Bohemian, an Italian, and a Belgian, contended – in France – for the minds of their students. As to the first topic of the *Course*, Cherubini was icily clear. It was "rigorous modern counterpoint": "rigorous" (i.e., strict) in limiting itself solely to the consonances and dissonances met with in the earlier theorists; "rigorous" in all senses except the use of "tonality" in place of the medieval modal system. Only in the writing of fugue could the pupil be allowed greater latitude in choice of chords.[107]

The structure of Cherubini's *Course* is virtually a carbon copy of that of Fétis with the exceptions that canon is treated more briefly, and double counterpoint is dealt with not only at the octave, tenth, and twelfth, but also at the ninth, eleventh, thirteenth, and fourteenth, and not in retrograde and retrograde inversion, as it is in Fétis's treatise. The elements of fugal structure (subject, answer, episode, etc.) are handled similarly, but presentation of fugue in two, three, four, and more parts is given in only

107 Cherubini, *Cours de contrepoint et de fugue*, p. 2.

full-length model compositions with detailed on-score annotations, and with almost no separate commentary. Whereas Fétis's weighty two-volume book was merely reprinted in French, that of Cherubini, in one volume, lighter and less than half the price (30fr. as against 66fr. – but then, Reicha's two volumes ran to 80fr.), was immediately translated into German, English (twice each) and Italian, and achieved widespread use for teaching and self-study. (The UK subscription list of 1837 alone comprised 657 people and institutions, including six members of the royal family, and the work was adopted as a textbook by the Royal Academy of Music.)

The price of success was the forfeiture of precisely the historicizing dimension. Fétis's wide range of styles and clear demarcations is replaced by a stylistic never-never-land. Cherubini resorts to many of Fux's music examples, often modified, and this, by a strange twist of fate, brings back into the fold unannounced Fux's modal cantus firmi (history by the back door!). Indeed, Cherubini supplies an appendix of cantus firmi for student exercises, and all six of Fux's modal subjects appear there unmodified save that the E- and F-mode subjects carry one-sharp and one-flat key signatures respectively. Where Fétis's was a treatise, Cherubini's was a textbook.

"the corrupting of our times": theorists cry in the wilderness

There runs in Fux's Preface a vein of pessimism. Composers no longer want to be shackled with rules and prescriptions. With macabre exaggeration, it continues: "at the mention of laws and formal instruction (*schola*), they are filled with dread (*exhorrescunt*), and take on the pallor of death." A century and a quarter later, Siegfried Dehn, in his *Lehre vom Contrapunkt, dem Canon und der Fuge* (Textbook of Counterpoint, Canon, and Fugue) (1869) was to use almost the same verb in complaining that the very word "'counterpoint' causes musical connoisseurs consternation (*zurückschrecken*) as the embodiment of aridity and tedium."[108] Fux refers to "the haters of learning" and "the corrupting of our times." The Preface to Fétis's *Traité du Contre-point* gloomily decries the fact that "learned" and "boring" have now, in 1824, become synonymous. Haydn, Mozart, Sarti, Cimarosa, and Paisiello were learned composers. The world of today is no longer interested in working hard, German composers identify originality with bizarre effect and triviality, and France is suffering an "eruption of musical neologisms," for which Fétis's treatise was to be an antidote.[109]

The Foreword to Heinrich Bellermann's (1832–1903) *Contrapunkt* strikes a similarly alarmist tone in 1862: "The more that is composed nowadays, and the greater the variety, the more rarely does one find that in this, the most important branch of compositional technique, voice-leading, the necessary preliminary studies have been done."[110] What are taught as the "polyphonic forms," including fugue, are no

108 Dehn, *Lehre vom Contrapunkt*, Foreword, p. 1.
109 Fétis, *Traité du Contre-point*, 1st edn., p. vi.
110 Bellermann, *Contrapunkt*, Foreword to 1st edn.

substitute for genuine contrapuntal exercise. The result in many choral-orchestral compositions, the "grasping at mere external effect, so-called 'elegant orchestration' and 'novel tone-colors,'" which mask the lack of flowing lines, is "insufferable to the well-grounded connoisseur." Underlying this, Bellermann felt that the human voice, with its limitations of range and agility, should be the model for all composition. The rise of instrumental music since the late eighteenth century had brought about the "spoliation of vocal music" and the "ruin of the human voice."[111]

Dehn's *Lehre* (1859) and Bellermann's *Contrapunkt* (1862) both uphold the Fuxian tradition. "I divide counterpoint," Dehn declares, "as the ancients divided it," into "equal and unequal," and then into "the five species." While the modern world has "condemned the species and consigned them to the attic," Dehn is unwilling to discard what has proved so valuable for so long.[112] His treatise differs from the *Gradus* mainly in emphasizing canon, in emulating Albrechtsberger's and Cherubini's use of tonal cantus firmi, and in agreeing with Reicha, Fétis, and Cherubini on the one thing on which those three rivals themselves agreed, namely that double counterpoint should be taught before fugue. His historicizing turn of mind shows in the many citations of Zarlino, Berardi, Fux, Mattheson, Mizler, Marpurg and others, and his insistence on layering his treatise with whole-piece examples, from Lassus up to his own time, all attributed.

If Dehn *revived* a flagging tradition, Bellermann saw himself in an act of *restoration.* He replaces Fux's Book I with an introductory chapter providing the necessary rudiments. Rejecting major and minor, he expounds the modes in full, with Greek names; on the other hand, he explains tone and interval in terms of acoustics of moving bodies and aural perception. Bellermann chides recent theorists for making canon a prerequisite for fugue, and placing double counterpoint before simple fugue. Thus, the body of his manual broadly reverts to Fux's original order. Ludwig Bussler increased the number of species to six by interpolating a third species of three notes against one, and rendering fourth species four and six against one in *Der strenge Satz in der musikalischen Compositionslehre* (Strict Counterpoint in Musical Composition) (1877; 2/1905). Preceded by a chapter on monophonic composition, strict counterpoint here operates wholly within the modes (using Greek names), and the book covers also imitation and fugue, followed by double counterpoint, and canon, all exclusively in the strict style. *Contrapunkt und Fuge im freien (modernen) Tonsatz* (Counterpoint and Fugue in Free (Modern) Composition) (1878) then moves to a different stylistic world, dealing with imitation, canon, double counterpoint, and fugue in the late Baroque and Classical period, exemplified copiously from J. S. Bach, Handel, Haydn, Mozart, and Beethoven, with isolated appearances by Meyerbeer, Wagner and others.

The pessimism that we have observed in this section became a veritable jeremiad in the writings of Heinrich Schenker (1868–1935). Not only did the present generation

111 Ibid., Foreword to 2nd edn. (1876). 112 Dehn, *Lehre vom Contrapunkt*, p. 5.

lack musical technique, but also it had lost even the capacity to understand the technique of past composers. Lack of technique "penetrates artists to the core." In light of this situation, he declared in volume I of *Kontrapunkt* (1910): "I invite all true friends of music to examine with me the principles of voice leading. I hope they gain with me the conviction that these principles constitute an inalienable, organic part of all theory and will retain their validity as long as music itself dwells among humans."[113] Speaking of counterpoint theory of the sixteenth and seventeenth centuries, he remarks: "all treatises were superseded in significance finally by a work from the eighteenth century – thus in a sense a posthumous work – the famous *Gradus ad Parnassum* by J. J. Fux from the year 1725." For Schenker, contrary to Bellermann, Fux's adherence to purely vocal polyphony was his greatest shortcoming. Had he not resisted the incursion of instruments into free composition, Fux might have been able to show that the principles of voice leading were "one and the same" in vocal and instrumental context: in short, that voice leading was a universal, that it transcended medium and style. Schenker's purpose in *Kontrapunkt* was to create a new and unified theory of voice leading, first manifest in vocal polyphony, then "revealing its presence in the technique of the thoroughbass, in chorales, and finally in free composition."[114]

Schenker therefore adopted Fux's graduated progression, assigning a chapter to each of the five species respectively for two-, three-, and four-part strict counterpoint, and adding a short chapter on counterpoint in five to eight voices. At this point, however, he stopped. He had no interest in expounding fugue, double counterpoint, and the rest of the topics traditional to the counterpoint manual. His interest lay solely in upholding the laws of part writing as the basis for all free composition – as an immutable foundation of all music. The final section of Book II of *Kontrapunkt* (1922) is entitled "Bridges to Free Composition," in which the combining of the five species together is taught in conjunction with a cantus firmus, until in the last chapter the "eliding" of the cantus firmus voice creates a theoretical transition to free composition.[115] With every topic, Schenker not only took over long passages from Fux's text, but also introduced a bibliographical depth that was quite novel to the pedagogy of his time by conducting reviews of the literature, quoting Albrechtsberger, Cherubini, and Bellermann in turn, and adopting their music examples to meet his purposes. Less frequently, he quoted other authors: notably C. P. E. Bach and Hauptmann with approval, Dehn and Riemann in rebuttal. For all that he used Fux's text and examples, Schenker presented counterpoint in major and minor modes, considering it "insupportable to torture the student . . . with the old modes,"[116] and regarding the church modes as not "real systems."

113 Schenker, *Kontrapunkt*, Book I, Preface; Rothgeb and Thym trans, vol. I, pp. xxii, xxv.
114 Ibid., Book I, Preface; Rothgeb and Thym trans, vol. I, pp. xxvi–xxvii, xxviii, xxx.
115 Ibid., Book II, Part VI; Rothgeb and Thym trans, vol. II, pp. 175–273.
116 Ibid., Book I, Part I, chapter 1, §5; Rothgeb and Thym trans., vol. I, p. 20. Further discussion of Schenker's theory is found in **Chapter 21, pp. 812–43**.

Species counterpoint has been intrinsic to Schenkerian theory in its professionalized form in the United States and elsewhere since the 1930s. Both Salzer, *Structural Hearing* (1952) and Forte and Gilbert, *Introduction to Schenkerian Analysis* (1982), for example, treat it as a pure discipline without reference to harmonic concepts, locating it before harmony in the course of instruction. Salzer and Schachter, *Counterpoint in Composition: The Study of Voice Leading* (1969) devotes its first five chapters to the species, and returns to them in Chapter 9 on the combining of species. Species counterpoint in the Schenkerian context plays two separate but intimately entwined roles. First, it provides an acute training in the hearing of relations between notes, while at the same time enabling the contrapuntal element in almost all kinds of music to be perceived amidst the other elements. Second, *qua* "voice leading" (*Stimmführung*), as distinct from "counterpoint" (*punctus contra punctum*), it paves the way to the underlying diatony that Schenker discerned in his earlier theory, hence to the later concept of *Ursatz*, the two-voice framework, *Urlinie* + *Bassbrechung*. The institutionalizing of Schenkerian theory after World War II removed it from both the socio-political malaise of Germany around the First World War and Schenker's personal disdain for the culture of his times to an era of bright optimism.

A distinct trend in the later nineteenth century was the separation of *counterpoint* from *imitation and fugue*. With the popular growth of choral-orchestral forms, and the resurgence of the organ fugue, fugue became an important technical-formal weapon in the armory of every composer, and afforded insight into the newly reinstated works of Bach and Handel. The separation no doubt also reflected the design of curricula at major European conservatories. Two prominent teachers at the Leipzig Conservatory, for example, adopted this policy. Ernst Friedrich Richter was perhaps the most internationally influential harmony and counterpoint teacher of the nineteenth century. Students flocked from Russia, Scandinavia, Western Europe, and North America to study with him. His *Lehrbuch des einfachen und doppelten Kontrapunkts* (Manual of Simple and Double Counterpoint) (1872) remained in print for fifty years, was translated into Russian, English, and French, and served as a textbook for music courses all over the Western world. It betrays vestiges of the species system, compressed into three stages; but as with Kirnberger, it proceeds from four-part writing (which directly followed study of harmony), to three, then two parts. Imitation and canon are treated as preliminaries within his separate *Lehrbuch der Fuge* (1859). His successor, Salomon Jadassohn, likewise published a *Lehrbuch des einfachen, doppelten, drei- und vierfachen Contrapunkts* (Manual of Simple, Double, Triple, and Quadruple Counterpoint) and separately a *Lehre vom Canon und von der Fuge*, both in 1884. The discipline became even more compartmentalized with Ebenezer Prout, who produced three separate volumes: *Counterpoint, Strict and Free* (1890, which retains the five species), *Double Counterpoint and Canon* (1891), and *Fugue* (1891), with a companion volume to the latter, *Fugal Analysis* (1892).

"Farewell, enjoy, be merciful": Fux's legacy to the twentieth century

Vale, fruere, & indulge. The last of these is probably intended to mean "be indulgent toward *me*," but can equally well mean "indulge yourself [i.e. with this treatise]." Mizler amplifies it to "Farewell, make good use of my work, and make allowances for me [*viz.* my shortcomings]." The twentieth century did indeed make good use of Fux's work, and did not entirely spare the criticism.

Its most stinging critique was perhaps that of the Swiss theorist Ernst Kurth (1886–1946). Writing in *Grundlagen des linearen Kontrapunkts* (Foundations of Linear Counterpoint) (1917), he confirmed the pervasive influence of Fux's *Gradus* at the turn of the century: "it embodies the ideas that underlie counterpoint teaching as generally practiced to this day in the curricula of colleges and professional schools, ideas to which the great majority of commonly used textbooks adhere, regardless of attempts, with varying degrees of effectiveness, at change and modernization." Countless conservatories even cling to church modes, and persist in using the old clefs.[117] Kurth's critique identifies the incompatibility between modally conceived linear formations on the one hand and triadically conceived vertical relations on the other. In "note-against-note writing" (first three species), the added voices are created not linearly but vertically a note at a time: they lack the "inner melodic energy" of genuinely linear invention. Kurth quotes a four-part first-species example from Cherubini as a "lifeless and colorless hermaphrodite product."[118] Fux took what had been *possibilities* in Zarlino and turned them into inanimate *systematizations*. Genuinely linear counterpoint operates by a principle of "intervallic sociability" that is *latently* harmonic but never becomes *actually* so. In the very process of resisting thorough bass, Fux surrendered counterpoint to actual harmonic thought through the rigidity of note-against-note practice. He also failed to articulate the nature of dissonance, or any of the other technical particulars of counterpoint, in anything more than a totally primitive way.[119] On the style-historical front, criticism came from Knud Jeppesen, whose analytical study (1922, subsequently published as *The Style of Palestrina and the Dissonance*, 1923) chided Fux for not crediting his seventeenth-century theoretical sources, and for lack of a sense of style chronology. Jeppesen remarked tartly that Fux's pedagogy "has but slight relation" to Palestrina's style.[120] He produced his own manual of counterpoint (1930), and others who did so in a similar spirit were Springer and Hartmann (1936), and earlier Haller (1891), and Hohn (1918).

Despite such criticisms as these, Fux's method has continued to be the single most influential force in counterpoint teaching through to the beginning of the twenty-first century. Hugo Riemann, for example, at first disparaged it,[121] and followed

117 Kurth, *Grundlagen*, pp. 103, 105–06.
118 Ibid., pp. 108, 110–11, 112n.
119 Ibid., pp. 106, 114–15, 128–29, 131.
120 Jeppesen, *Style of Palestrina*, pp. 2, 5–6.
121 Riemann, *Musiklexikon*, s.v. "Bellermann," "Fux."

Riemann: *Manual of Simple, Double, and Imitative Counterpoint* (1888)

I. Two-part counterpoint

1. note-against-note [= first species]
2. counterpoint *slower than* cantus firmus:
   a: 2 notes (cf) against 1 (cpt)
   b: 3 notes (cf) against 1 (cpt)
   c: 2 notes (cf) in cross-rhythm against 1 (cpt) [hemiola]
3. counterpoint *faster than* cantus firmus:
   a: 2 notes against 1 [= second species]
   b: 3 notes against 1
   c: 4 notes against 1 [= third species]
   d: 6 notes against 1
4. syncopation and cross-rhythm
   a: syncopated [= fourth species]
   b: 3 against 2, and 2 against 3
   c: 4 against 3
   d: 5 against 2
   e: 5 against 3
   f: 5 against 4
5. rhythmically repeating counterpoints (iamb, anapest, etc.)
   a: cf in equal notes, cpt rhythmically repeating
   b: cf rhythmically repeating, cpt in equal notes
   c: cf and cpt both rhythmically repeating
6. Counterpoint in free (i.e. non-repeating) rhythm [= fifth species = florid counterpoint]
7. Maximum freedom: cantus firmus motivically patterned, counterpoint unrestrictedly rhythmicized as a countermelody [free counterpoint]

(II. Three-part counterpoint …)

Hauptmann in collapsing counterpoint into harmony (1883),[122] but subsequently reinstated Fux's species interwoven with a more finely-grained graduation appropriate to Schumann and Brahms, even Bartók (1888: see the window above for Riemann's pedagogical ordering of two-part species). Schoenberg (1936–50) adopted Fux's scheme and order of topics with uncanny closeness, working with major and minor, and forging connections to his concept of tonal "regions." Hindemith (1939), in the context of his acoustically based theory of harmonic relations, traced a Fuxian outline from note-against-note writing to "elaborated melody."

The most deliberate implicit counterblast to Fux has come in what might be called the British "empirical" school, which eschews artificial routines and works at the surface of musical styles. Starting with two- and three-part canzonets by Elizabethan composers, and reduced-scored sections of Palestrina and Byrd, it asks the student to

122 Riemann, *Neue Schule der Melodik*, pp. iii–vi, 35–36.

supply a missing part to complete the texture, and works toward the writing of complete four- or five-voice madrigals and motets in a stipulated style. This "pastiche" approach prepares for historical study or editorial work more than for composition. It can be seen in works by C. H. Kitson (1916; 1924), R. O. Morris (1922), and others, many of them influenced by Jeppesen's work. Those in German-speaking countries who adhered in differing degrees to Fux's procedures include Stöhr (1911), Müller-Blattau (1935), in the Schenkerian tradition Roth (1926), and in the strongest spirit of restoration Tittel (1959). The last of these includes virtually all of Fux's text in a oddly non-dialogue, narrated form: for example, "Fux allows Joseph to raise the question as to whether dissonant suspensions may be used also in ascent, since these [next examples] 'seem to be in essence the same.' The teacher, Aloys, rejects this, explaining . . ."[123] The text, which amounts to a new instructional genre, is furnished with Fux's music examples and interwoven with historical information, and each section concludes with a set of enumerated rules.

Ludwig Bussler (1877) commented that, among writers on the strict style, it was Zarlino who was preeminent in establishing it as an *artistic style*, whereas it was Fux to whom the greatest credit was due for establishing the *method*.[124] There is some truth to this at first surprising formulation. Zarlino wrote from within the horizon of the Renaissance polyphonic style; Fux wrote from outside that horizon with negligible experience of the style itself; thus the *Gradus* was from the outset stylistically profoundly compromised. That what resulted from Fux was a didactic tradition unbroken to the present day is in part due to that very internal contradiction, which takes other forms as well – for example, the choice of Latin, as against the homely manner of the dialogue – and which has seemed to sustain it through decades of contrary opinion. It is probably also in part due to a brilliant – if untraceable – imperial strategy of publication and dissemination. Whatever the causes, however, Fux has proved the most durable of all modern theorists. For a body of music-theoretical work of comparably lasting influence one would have to go back to Boethius, or Guido of Arezzo.

123 Tittel, *Der neue Gradus*, p. 65 = Mizler trans., p. 82 = Mann trans., *Counterpoint*, pp. 59–60; cf. note 51 above, and associated text. 124 Bussler, *Der strenge Satz*, 2nd edn., p. XII.

Bibliography

Primary sources: J. J. Fux

Original edition

Gradus ad Parnassum, sive manuductio ad compositionem musicae regularem, Vienna, Van Ghelen, 1725; facs. New York, Broude, 1966; reprint ed. A. Mann, Kassel and Basel, Bärenreiter and Graz, Akademische Druck und Verlagsanstalt, 1967

Eighteenth-century translations

Ger. trans. L. Mizler as *Gradus ad Parnassum, oder Anführung zur regelmässigen musikalischen Composition*, Leipzig, Mizler, 1742; facs. Hildesheim, G. Olms, 1984

Ital. trans. A. Manfredi as *Salita al Parnasso, o sia Guida alla regolare composizione della musica*, Carpi, Carmignani, 1761

Eng. trans. [J. C. Heck] as *Practical Rules for Learning Composition*, London, J. Preston, c. 1768

Fr. trans. P. Denis as *Traité de composition musicale*, Paris, adresses ordinaires, 1773–75

Twentieth-century translations

Book II, Exerc. I–III, trans. A. Mann with J. St. Edmunds, in *Steps to Parnassus: The Study of Counterpoint*, New York, Norton, 1943; rev. edn., *The Study of Counterpoint from Johann Joseph Fux's "Gradus ad Parnassum"*, New York, Norton, 1965 and 1971

Book II, Exerc. IV, V, Lect. 1–6, 7–1 to 7–2, trans. A. Mann in *The Study of Fugue*, pp. 75–138, New Brunswick, Rutgers University Press, 1958; reprint Westport, Greenwood Press, 1981

Book II, Exerc. V, Lect. 7–6 to 7–10, trans. S. Wollenberg as "*Gradus ad Parnassum* (1725): Concluding Chapters," *Music Analysis* 11 (1992), pp. 209–43 ("On Taste," "On the Ecclesiastical Style," "On the 'Stylus a capella,'" "The Stylus mixtus," "The Stylus recitativus")

Singfundament, MS, ed. E. Badura-Skoda and A. Mann in *Johann Joseph Fux: Sämtliche Werke*, ser. 7, "Theoretische und pädagogische Werke," vol. II, Graz, Akademische Druck und Verlagsanstalt, 1993

Primary sources: other authors

Aaron, P. *Compendiolo di molti dubbi, segreti et sentenze* (c. 1545); facs. New York, Broude, 1974

Albrechtsberger, J. G. *Anweisung zur Composition*, Leipzig, J. Breitkopf, 1790; 2nd edn. c. 1818

J. G. Albrechtsbergers sämmtliche Schriften über Generalbass, Harmonie-Lehre, und Tonsetzkunst, zum Selbstunterrichte, 3 vols., ed. I. Ritter von Seyfried, Vienna, T. Haslinger, c. 1825–26; trans. A.-E. Choron, Paris, Bachelier, 1830; trans. A. Merrick (from Fr.), London, R. Cocks, c. 1834

Attwood, T. *Thomas Attwoods Theorie- und Kompositionsstudien bei Mozart*, ed. D. Heartz and A. Mann, Kassel, Bärenreiter, 1969

Avianus, J. *Isagoge in libros musicae poeticae*, Erfurt, G. Baumannus, 1581; partial reprint and trans. B. Rivera, "The *Isagoge* (1581) of Johannes Avianus: An Early Formulation of Triadic Theory," *JMT* 22 (1978), pp. 43–64

Banchieri, A. *Cartella musicale nel canto figurato*, Venice, G. Vincenti, 1614; facs. Bologna, Forni, 1968; trans. C. A. Cranna, Jr. as "Adriano Banchieri's *Cartella musicale* (1614): Translation and Commentary," Ph.D. diss., Stanford University (1981)

Bellermann, H. *Der Contrapunkt, oder Anleitung zur Stimmführung in der musikalischen Composition*, Berlin, J. Springer, 1862

Berardi, A. *Documenti armonici*, Bologna, G. Monti, 1687
Miscellanea musicale, Bologna, G. Monti, 1689
Il Perché musicale, Bologna, Pier Maria Mont, 1693
Bismantova, B. *Compendio musicale*, MS, Ferrara, 1677, Bibl. Emilio Regg., E. 41; facs. Florence, Studio per edizioni scelte, 1978
Bononcini, G. M. *Musico prattico*, Bologna, G. Monti 1673; facs. Hildesheim, G. Olms, 1969
Burmeister, J. *Musica autoschediastike*, Rostock, C. Reusnerus, 1601
Bussler, L. *Der strenge Satz in der musikalischen Compositionslehre*, Berlin, Habel, 1877, 2nd rev. edn. 1905
Contrapunkt und Fuge im freien (modernen) Tonsatz, Berlin, Habel, 1878
Cherubini, L. *Cours de contrepoint et de fugue*, Paris, M. Schlesinger, 1835
Cochlaeus, J. *Tetrachordum musices* (1511), *MSD* 23 (1970), trans. C. A. Miller
Coclico, A. *Compendium musices*, Nuremberg, Montanus and Neuber, 1552; facs. Kassel, Bärenreiter, 1954; trans. A. Seay as *Musical Compendium*, Colorado Springs, Colorado College Music Press, 1973
Dante Alighieri, *The Divine Comedy*, Cantica I, *Hell (L'Inferno)*, trans. D. L. Sayers, Harmondsworth, Penguin, 1949
Dehn, S. W. *Analysen dreier Fugen aus Joh. Seb. Bach's "wohltemperirtem Clavier" und einer Vocal-Doppelfuge A. M. Bononcini's*, Leipzig, C. F. Peters, 1858
Lehre vom Contrapunkt, dem Canon und der Fuge, posthum, ed. B. Scholz, Berlin, F. Schneider, 1859
Diruta, G. *Il Transilvano: Dialogo sopra il vero modo di sonar organi, et istromenti da penna*, 2 vols., Venice, G. and A. Vincenti, 1593–1622; facs. Bologna, Forni, 1969 and 1997 and Buren, F. Knuf, 1983; trans. M. Bradshaw and E. Soehnlen as *The Transylvanian*, Henryville, PA, Institute of Mediaeval Music, 1984
Fétis, F.-J. *Traité du Contre-point et de la fugue*, Paris, Janet et Cotelle, 1824; rev. edn. 1846
Haller, M. *Kompositionslehre für polyphonen Kirchengesang mit besonderer Rücksicht auf die Meisterwerke des 16. Jahrhunderts*, Regensburg, Coppenrath, 1891
Harnisch, O. S. *Artis musicae delineatio*, Frankfurt, Stein, 1608
Heinrich von Augsburg, *De musica* (11th c.), ed. J. S. van Waesberghe, Buren, F. Knuf, 1977
Hindemith, P. *Unterweisung im Tonsatz*, 3 vols., Mainz, Schott, 1939–70; vol. II, *Übungsbuch für den zweistimmigen Satz*, trans. O. Ortman as *The Craft of Musical Composition 2: Exercises in Two-Part Writing*, New York, Associated Music, 1941
Hohn, W. *Der Kontrapunkt Palestrinas und seiner Zeitgenossen: eine Kontrapunktlehre*, Regensburg, F. Pustet, 1918
Jadassohn, S. *Die Lehre vom reinen Satz*, 3 vols., Leipzig, Breitkopf und Härtel, 1883–84
Erläuterungen zu ausgewählten Fugen aus Johann Sebastian Bach's wohltemperirtem Clavier, Leipzig, F. Leuckart, c. 1887, and Breitkopf und Härtel, 1899
Jeppesen, K. *Counterpoint: The Polyphonic Vocal Style of the Sixteenth Century* (Danish orig. 1931), trans. G. Haydon, Englewood Cliffs, NJ, Prentice Hall, 1939
Kirnberger, J. P. *Die Kunst des reinen Satzes*, 2 vols., Berlin, Decker und Hartung, 1771–79; facs. Hildesheim, G. Olms, 1968 and 1988; trans. D. Beach and J. Thym as *The Art of Strict Musical Composition*, New Haven, Yale University Press, 1982
Gedanken über die verschiedenen Lehrarten in der Komposition als Vorbereitung zur

Fugenkenntnis, Berlin, G. J. Decker, 1782; trans. R. B. Nelson and D. R. Boomgaarden as "Kirnberger's *Thoughts on the Different Methods of Teaching Composition as Preparation for UnderstandingFugue*," *JMT* 30 (1986), pp. 71–94

Kurth, E. *Grundlagen des linearen Kontrapunkts: Bachs melodische Polyphonie*, Bern, M. Drechsel, 1917; 5th edn. Bern, Krompholz, 1956

Lippius, J. *Synopsis musicae novae*, Strassburg, K. Kieffer, 1612; trans. B. Rivera as *Synopsis of New Music*, Colorado Springs, Colorado College Music Press, 1977

Lobe, J. C. *Katechismus der Compositionslehre*, Leipzig, J. J. Weber, c. 1862

Lehrbuch der musikalischen Komposition, 4 vols., Leipzig, Breitkopf und Härtel, 1850–67

Marpurg, F. W. *Abhandlung von der Fuge*, Berlin, A. Haude and J. C. Spener, 1753–54; facs. Hildesheim, G. Olms, 1970

Martini, G. B. *Esemplare o sia saggio fondamentale pratico di contrappunto*, Bologna, L. dalla Volpe, 1774–75; facs. Ridgewood, NJ, Gregg, 1965

Marx, A. B. *Musical Form in the Age of Beethoven: Selected Writings on Theory and Method*, ed. and trans. S. Burnham, Cambridge University Press, 1997

Die Lehre von der musikalischen Komposition, 4 vols., Leipzig, Breitkopf und Härtel, 1837–47; trans. and ed. H. Saroni as *The Theory and Practice of Musical Composition*, New York, Huntington, Mason and Law, 1852

Momigny, J.-J. de, *Cours complet d'harmonie et de composition*, 3 vols., Paris, Momigny and Bailleul, 1803–06

Müller-Blattau, J. *Die Grundlagen des Kontrapunkts*, Potsdam, Athenaion, 1935

Musica, Scolica enchiriadis, ed. H. Schmid as *Musica et scolica enchiriadis una cum aliquibus tractatulis adiunctis*, Munich, Bayerische Akademie der Wissenschaften, 1981; trans. R. Erickson, ed. C. Palisca as *"Musica enchiriadis" and "Scolica enchiriadis": Translated, with Introduction and Notes*, New Haven, Yale University Press, 1995

Prout, E. *Counterpoint: Strict and Free*, London, Augener, 1890

Double Counterpoint and Canon, London, Augener, 1891

Fugue, London, Augener, 1891

Fugal Analysis: A Companion to "Fugue", London, Augener, 1892

Reicha, A. *Cours de composition musicale, ou Traité complet et raisonné d'harmonie pratique*, Paris, Gambaro, c. 1816–18

Traité de haute composition musicale, Paris, Zetter, 1824–26

Richter, E. F. *Lehrbuch der Fuge: Anleitung zur Composition derselben*, Leipzig, Breitkopf und Härtel, 1859

Lehrbuch der Harmonie: Praktische Anleitung, Leipzig, Breitkopf und Härtel, 1853

Lehrbuch des einfachen und doppelten Kontrapunkts: Praktische Anleitung, Leipzig, Breitkopf und Härtel, 1872; trans. J. P. Morgan as *Manual of Simple and Double Counterpoint*, New York, G. Schirmer, 1884

Riemann, H. *Lehrbuch des einfachen, doppelten und imitierenden Kontrapunkts*, Leipzig, Breitkopf und Härtel, 1888

Neue Schule der Melodik: Entwurf einer Lehre des Contrapunkts nach einer gänzlich neuen Methode, Hamburg, K. Grädener and J. F. Richter, 1883

Roth, H. *Elemente der Stimmführung (Der strenge Satz)*, vol. I: *Ein- und Zweistimmigkeit*, Stuttgart, Klett, 1926

Schenker, H. *Kontrapunkt*, 2 vols., Stuttgart, J. G. Cotta, Vienna, Universal Edition,

1910–22; trans. J. Rothgeb and J. Thym as *Counterpoint*, New York, Schirmer Books, 1987

Schoenberg, A. *Preliminary Exercises in Counterpoint* (1936–50), ed. L. Stein, London, Faber and Faber, 1963

Seyfried, I., Ritter von, *Ludwig van Beethoven's Studien im Generalbasse, Contrapuncte und in der Compositions-Lehre*, Vienna, T. Haslinger, 1832; facs. Hildesheim, G. Olms, 1967

Stöhr, R. *Praktischer Leitfaden des Kontrapunkts*, Hamburg, Benjamin, 1911

Tittel, E. *Der neue Gradus: Lehrbuch des strengen Satzes nach Johann Joseph Fux*, Vienna and Munich, Doblinger, 1959

Werckmeister, A. *Harmonologia musica oder kurtze Anleitung zur musikalischen Composition*, Frankfurt, T. P. Calvisius, 1702; facs. Hildesheim, G. Olms, 1970

Zacconi, L. *Prattica di musica*, Venice, Part I, G. Polo, 1592; Part II, A. Vincenti, 1622; facs. Hildesheim, G. Olms, 1982

Zarlino, G. *Dimostrationi harmoniche*, Venice, Franceschi, 1571; facs. New York, Broude, 1965

Le istitutioni harmoniche, Venice, Franceschi, 1558; facs. New York, Broude, 1965; Part III trans. G. Marco, ed. C. V. Palisca as *The Art of Counterpoint*, New Haven, Yale University Press, 1968; reprint New York, Da Capo, 1983

Secondary sources

Cadet, F. *Port-Royal Education: A Sketch of its History with Extracts from its Leading Authors*, Syracuse, NY, C. W. Bardeen, 1899: Lancelot, "Of a New Method of Easily Learning to Read in any Language," pp. 183–85; Guyot, "On Teaching Reading and Writing," pp. 259–81

Federhofer, H. "Fux's *Gradus ad Parnassum* as Viewed by Heinrich Schenker," *MTS* 4 (1982), pp. 66–75

"Johann Joseph Fux und Johann Mattheson im Urteil Lorenz Christoph Mizlers," *Speculum musicae artis: Festgabe für Heinrich Husmann zum 60. Geburtstag am 16. Dezember 1968*, Munich, Fink, 1970, pp. 111–23

Flotzinger, R. "Fux – ein komponierender Theoretiker?," in *J. J. Fux – Symposium Graz '91. Bericht*, ed. R. Flotzinger, Graz, Akademische Druck- und Verlagsanstalt, 1992, pp. 133–40

Groth, R. "Italienische Musiktheorie im 17. Jahrhundert," *GMt* 7 (1989), pp. 307–79

Heartz, D. "Thomas Attwood's Lessons in Composition with Mozart," *Proceedings of the Royal Musical Association* 100 (1973–74), pp. 175–83

Jeppesen, K. *The Style of Palestrina and the Dissonance* (Danish orig. 1922), 2nd rev. edn. Copenhagen, Munksgaard; London, Oxford University Press, 1946

Judd, C. *Reading Renaissance Music Theory: Hearing with the Eyes*, Cambridge University Press, 2000; see Chapter 5, "*Exempla*, Commonplace Books, and Writing Theory"

Köchel, L., Ritter von, *Johann Josef Fux: Hofcompositor und Hofkapellmeister . . .*, Vienna, Hölder, 1872; facs. Hildesheim, G. Olms, 1974

Kramer, R. "*Gradus ad Parnassum*: Beethoven, Schubert, and the Romance of Counterpoint," *19th-century Music* 11 (1987), pp. 107–20

Lester, J. "The Fux–Mattheson Correspondence: An Annotated Translation," *Current Musicology* 24 (1977), pp. 37–62

Between Modes and Keys: German Theory 1592–1802, Stuyvesant, NY, Pendragon Press, 1989

Maniates, M. R. "Bottrigari versus Sigoni: On Vicentino and his Ancient Music Adapted to Modern Practice," in *Musical Humanism and Its Legacy: Essays in Honor of Claude V. Palisca*, ed. N. Baker and B. Hanning, Stuyvesant, NY, Pendragon, 1992, pp. 79–107

"The Cavalier Ercole Bottrigari and his Brickbats: Prolegomena to the Defense of Don Nicola Vicentino against Messer Gandolfo Sigonio," in *Music Theory and the Exploration of the Past*, ed. C. Hatch and D. Bernstein, University of Chicago Press, 1993, pp. 139–89

Mann, A. "Beethoven's Contrapuntal Studies with Haydn," *Musical Quarterly* 66 (1970), pp. 711–26; reprinted in *The Creative World of Beethoven*, ed. P. H. Lang, New York, Norton, 1971, pp. 209–24

"Haydn and Mozart," in *Theory and Practice: The Great Composer as Student and Teacher*, New York, Norton, 1987, pp. 41–54

"Haydn as Student and Critic of Fux," in *Studies in Eighteenth-Century Music: A Tribute to Karl Geiringer*, ed. H. C. Robbins Landon, New York, Oxford University Press, 1970, pp. 323–32

"Haydn's Elementarbuch: A Document of Classic Counterpoint Instruction," *Music Forum* 3 (1973), pp. 197–237

"Padre Martini and Fux," in *Festschrift für Ernst Hermann Meyer zum sechzigsten Geburtstag*, ed. G. Knepler, Leipzig, VEB Deutscher Verlag für Musik, 1973, pp. 253–55

Nottebohm, G. "Generalbass und Compositionslehre betreffende Handschriften Beethoven's und J. R. Seyfried's Buch *Ludwig van Beethoven's Studien im Generalbasse, Contrapuncte u.s.w.*," in *Zweite Beethoveniana*, Leipzig and Winterthur, J. Rieter-Biedermann, 1887, pp. 154–203; reprinted with *Ludwig van Beethoven's Studien*, ed. J. Seyfried, Hildesheim, G. Olms, 1967

Beethoven's Studien, vol. I: *Beethoven's Unterricht bei J. Haydn, Albrechtsberger und Salieri, nach den Original-Manuscripten dargestellt*, Leipzig, J. Rieter-Biedermann, 1873; reprint Niederwalluf, M. Sändig, 1971

Rivera, B. V. *German Music Theory in the Early 17th Century: The Treatises of Johannes Lippius*, Ann Arbor, UMI Research Press, 1974

Salzer, F. and C. Schachter, *Counterpoint in Composition: The Study of Voice Leading*, New York, McGraw-Hill, 1969

Wagner, M. "Johann Joseph Fux als Lehrer kommender Generationen," *J. J. Fux – Symposium Graz '91: Bericht*, ed. R. Flotzinger, Graz, Akademische Druck- und Verlagsanstalt, 1992, pp. 141–49

Wellesz, E. *Fux*, London, Oxford University Press, 1965

Wollenberg, S. "The Unknown 'Gradus,'" *Music & Letters* 51 (1970), pp. 423–34

· 19 ·

Twelve-tone theory

JOHN COVACH

As scholars begin to gain a sense of historical perspective on art music in the twentieth century, it seems clear that the introduction and development of twelve-tone compositional procedures will remain one of the cardinal markers of musical modernism. The careers of Schoenberg, Berg, Webern, Boulez, Stockhausen, Babbitt, and even Stravinsky (among many others) are all at some point intimately bound up with dodecaphonic concerns, as is the course of avant-garde music generally. No matter what one may think of the twelve-tone idea – and it has been the source of considerable controversy almost from the start – understanding dodecaphony and its appeal to several generations of composers in Europe and America will continue to play a central role in understanding twentieth-century music and culture.

The twelve-tone idea has also played a pivotal role in the development of music theory as a professional discipline, especially in the United States during the post-World-War-II period. Indeed, twelve-tone theory and composition are deeply interdependent, and this is in no small measure attributable to the fact that in many cases the theorists involved were also composers. Unlike Schenkerian theory – which along with twelve-tone theory has played an important role in the professional growth of music theory in the second half of this century – twelve-tone theory often seems more prescriptive than descriptive; rather than explicating the structural features of works already established within the canon of Western art music, dodecaphonic theory is frequently speculative, suggesting structural possibilities for pieces yet to be written (or in some cases, pieces just finished by the composer himself). Thus, instead of theory following practice, twelve-tone practice has at times followed theory.

There are at least two approaches available to scholars surveying the history of twelve-tone music and theory, and since theory and practice are so intimately related in this context it will be helpful to consider these. The first approach seeks to focus on the important composers and their works, using twelve-tone theory as a means of explaining the structural features and perhaps the technical concerns that motivate such features; this produces a history of twelve-tone music. The second approach involves tracing the history of twelve-tone theoretical writing and referring to compositions only inasmuch as they clarify theoretical concerns; this produces a history of twelve-tone theory. The current chapter will take the second of these approaches, and will privilege the development of theoretical ideas over establishing a succession of important dodecaphonic works. Despite the obvious interdependence of theory and practice in twelve-tone music, it turns out that many important theoretical documents were not produced by its most important practitioners. And this is the case already at the very beginning of our story.

The early development of twelve-tone theory, 1920–30

Josef Matthias Hauer. The "twelve-tone idea" can be defined as a systematic circulation of all the twelve pitch classes (pcs) in which no pc is repeated before all twelve have been sounded. An early statement of the twelve-tone idea (perhaps the first) may be found in a short monograph published in 1920 by the composer Josef Matthias Hauer (1883–1959).[1] As it does in much early dodecaphonic theory, the constant circulation of the twelve pcs arises in Hauer's writing as a technical solution to a number of music-aesthetic problems with which he was grappling in the late teens and early twenties. It is thus important to understand his *Zwölftongesetz* in this broader music-cultural context. Hauer sets forth his aesthetic positions at various points in *Vom Wesen des Musikalischen*, in a number of articles published early in the 1920s, and especially in his *Deutung des Melos* of 1923. A fundamental premise in Hauer's many arguments is that music, when conceived and perceived in the proper way, is essentially a mental-spiritual (*geistig*) phenomenon. An important distinction must be drawn between music in its pure form, which Hauer maintains is its spiritual form, and music as it occurs in the physical world around us, which constitutes its material form. For Hauer it is essential that in order to raise music to its highest, most spiritual level, the influence of the material world must be suppressed as much as possible.

Consider, for example, the way in which Hauer characterizes the musical event. For Hauer, each musical interval is considered to constitute a type of "gesture" in music, and the character of each interval is thought of as its "color." In its purely spiritual-mental state, a musical gesture resides first in the mind of some musical person, perhaps a composer. In order to share this musical occurrence with some second person, however, this first person must employ the realm of the physical – or some internally imagined physical realm – as a kind of "transmission line." But this physical or material world always alters the pure musical gesture to some extent, distorting it through instrumental noise, poor intonation, and/or other purely physical impediments. It falls then to the receiving mind, in the act of conceptualizing the musical gesture, to improve upon this physical occurrence in an attempt to restore this gesture

1 Hauer, *Vom Wesen des Musikalischen*. This work constitutes an expansion and reworking of the author's earlier *Über die Klangfarbe*, Op. 13 (published in Vienna by the author in 1918) and "Farbenkreis der Temperature, 15 Juli 1917" (manuscript in the Austrian National Library Music Collection). Hauer published a slightly revised version in 1923 as *Lehrbuch der Zwölftontechnik: Vom Wesen des Musikalischen*.

to its original spiritual state. For Hauer, importance is placed on the inner hearing of the two persons involved, and the physically sounding music is reduced to a kind of deficient, yet necessary mode of transmission.[2]

Hauer's aesthetic dualism casts off the material aspect of music wherever possible. This leads Hauer to reject, for example, Schoenberg's notion of *Klangfarbenmelodie*, a technique in which different instruments or instrumental groups of some performing ensemble are juxtaposed in musical succession forming a kind of melody of instrumental timbres. For Hauer, this focuses the musical attention in precisely the wrong way; by relishing the physical timbres and their differences, the listener gets stuck in the physical transmission line itself, and is unable to hear through to the spiritual content of the music. According to Hauer, tone color in music resides in the character of the internally perceived interval, not in the external "noises" of the material means of conveying that inner occurrence.[3] Hauer also downplays the importance of instrumental virtuosity. Here one can again become mired in the admiration of feats of instrumental prowess, and in so doing lose sight of the spiritual content of the music.[4] According to Hauer, one must always work to suppress the attraction to the material, sensual aspect of the musical experience.

Gnostic criticism of musical materialism forms the foundation for Hauer's arguments in favor of the twelve-tone idea. First, Hauer argues for a tempered twelve-note tuning. He begins his discussion by surveying the ways in which one can generate all twelve pitch classes acoustically. Starting from C, Hauer generates the remaining eleven pitches in three ways: up from C in acoustically perfect fifths (2:3); up from C in acoustically perfect fourths (3:4); and up from C in overtones. He then reduces everything down to within an octave and compares the results. The collections of eleven pitches generated from the same starting pitch are in each case different, generating various representatives for each of the other eleven pitch classes. The tempered pitch classes, which are not to be found in nature, offer yet another of twelve pitch classes. Hauer thus asserts that the physical realm is imperfect because it produces no usable chromatic scale. Tempered tuning, on the other hand, does offer a suitable chromatic scale. And since this chromatic scale does not occur in nature, the tempered scale constitutes a kind of spiritualization of musical materials.[5] Thus, by conceptualizing the physical, the mind improves upon it and takes a crucial step toward the spiritual. Hauer compares the fact that the twelve tempered pitch classes do not occur in nature with Goethe's observation in his *Farbenlehre* that the complete color spectrum also cannot be observed in nature. The color circle is thus a creation of the mind, and like the twelve pitch classes, constitutes an enriching of the physical.[6]

2 Hauer, *Vom Wesen des Musikalischen*, p. 5. 3 Ibid., p. 62.

4 In a chapter of *Deutung des Melos* entitled "Musikalische Bildung," Hauer mentions that "true music" never requires virtuosity (pp. 14–15). In another chapter, "Melodie oder Geräusche?," he gives instructions on the proper environment for and approach to the playing of atonal music (pp. 21–23).

5 Hauer, *Vom Wesen des Musikalischen*, p. 23. 6 Ibid., pp. 27–28.

Hauer's argument for the twelve-tone idea depends on his argument in favor of equal temperament. Hauer suggests that one can construct a continuum extending from pure rhythm to pure melody. At the rhythmic end, music is without pitch, and therefore, entirely material; at the melodic end music is without rhythm, and therefore, entirely spiritual. Most music exists between these two poles, because, for example, simply sounding two notes in succession implies some kind of rhythmic component. From this perspective, Hauer argues that tonality, since it involves ultimately subordinating all other pitches to a single pitch, is therefore to be placed closer to the rhythmic pole than atonality. The constant circulation of the twelve pitch classes suppresses this rhythmic component and creates a kind of music that resides closer to the melodic, spiritual end of the continuum. Thus Hauer asserts that atonality supersedes tonality, and the twelve-tone idea is used in the service of raising music to the highest spiritual level possible.[7]

Having briefly explored the aesthetic context that surrounds it, we can now turn to Hauer's 1920 formulation of his *Zwölftongesetz*:

> But in *atonal music*, which arises out of the "totality," only the *intervals* matter. They express musical character, no longer through major or minor or through characteristic instruments (thus through *one* color), but rather directly through the *totality of intervals*, which are best and most purely rendered on an equal-tempered instrument. In atonal music there are no more tonics, dominants, subdominants, scale degress, resolutions, consonances or dissonances, but rather only *the twelve intervals of equal temperament*; their "scale" arises out of the twelve, tempered half steps. In atonal music, both the purely physical, material, and the trivial, sentimental, are, as much as possible, shut out and their "law," their "nomos," is that, within a given tone-series, no tone may be permitted to be repeated or left out (the basic law of melody anyway: in order that no tone acquires physical preponderance [(taking on an) over-riding tonic significance], also so that no scale-degree functions of leading-tone tracks arise. Thus to the player and listener it is solely a matter of the *purely musical phenomenon of the interval*, in its "spiritualization").[8]

In a 1924 exchange of letters in *Die Musik* with Herbert Eimert, Hauer chronicled his August 1919 discovery of the twelve-tone idea, casting himself as desperately searching for some underlying objective principle, not only in his own atonal music up to that time, but also in the atonal music of Webern and Schoenberg. Driven by the hope that such a discovery would vindicate atonality against the criticisms of its many critics in Vienna at the time, he had discovered – or as he put it, "uncovered" (*"entdeckt"*) – an objective and eternal law of music: the notion of constantly circulating the aggregate.[9] The work in which Hauer claims the breakthrough occurred, his piano piece *Nomos*, Op. 19, does indeed begin with five statements of the same twelve-pc series, articulated melodically in units of five pcs creating twelve five-note phases. But

7 Hauer, "Atonale Musik."
8 Hauer, *Vom Wesen des Musikalischen*, p. 53. The translation is mine.
9 Hauer, "Offener Brief."

the piece is not entirely dodecaphonic: twelve-tone sections mark out large-scale formal divisions, but many of the smaller sections seem to experiment with circulating collections of fewer than twelve pcs.

By the early 1920s Hauer's music was entirely twelve-tone, and this turn toward the exclusively dodecaphonic is likely related to his discovery in late 1921 of the forty-four tropes. First mentioned in his 1922 article "Sphärenmusik," the tropes are pairs of complementary hexachords that enabled Hauer to classify any of the 479,001,600 possible twelve-pc melodies into one of these forty-four types. Hauer subsequently discussed the tropes in greater music-technical detail, publishing his *Tropentafel* in 1924, and then again in his two brief books, *Vom Melos zur Pauke* and *Zwölftontechnik*, both of which are filled with musical examples used to illustrate a wide variety of dodecaphonic techniques and procedures.[10] Since Hauer believed that atonal music must always strive toward pure Melos, harmony must derive from melody. Hauer discusses a technique whereby melodic tones are sustained until they are displaced by new melodic tones related by a minor or major second. As a result of this procedure, Hauer in some instances is able to musically project each trope as a vertical ordering: while melodic succession is free within the hexachord, harmonic distribution is fixed according to the structure of the trope. It is important to note, however, that the tropes are a way of viewing twelve-tone materials analytically and are not necessarily prescriptive in a compositional sense. The distinction often made between Hauer and the Schoenberg school – that the former's music is based on unordered hexachords while the latter's is based on an ordered series – is false: while he did write pieces that could be thought of as "trope pieces," much of Hauer's twelve-tone music employs an ordered series.

Herbert Eimert. A 1924 treatise by Herbert Eimert (1897–1972), *Atonale Musiklehre* is a brief but important early text in twelve-tone theory; it consists of thirty-six pages of text into which forty-six musical examples are placed. Eimert was twenty-six years old and still a student when he wrote this theoretical pamphlet, the publication of which – according to Hans Oesch – led to its author leaving the Cologne Conservatory under accusations of being a "frivolous know-nothing."[11] In light of the dispute with Hauer discussed above, it is ironic to note that in his foreword to the pamphlet Eimert credits two major influences on his work: one is his personal acquaintance with Russian émigré composer Jefim Golyscheff and his music, but the other is the writings and compositions of Hauer. Eimert states very clearly that he has not discovered any of what he is writing about; he merely claims to have brought it together and developed it in a systematic manner. It is perhaps interesting to note that Schoenberg and his two famous students are hardly mentioned in the book.

10 Hauer, "Sphärenmusik"; "Die Tropen"; *Vom Melos zur Pauke*; *Zwölftontechnik: Die Lehre von den Tropen*. 11 Oesch, "Pioniere der Zwölftontechnik".

The *Atonale Musiklehre* is rich in musical examples, and Eimert's concerns are set in the pragmatic context of compositional application throughout the theoretical discussions.[12] Eimert divides the book into two major sections: the first is devoted to theoretical and practical aspects of atonality; the second takes up historical and aesthetic concerns. The first, more theoretical section is divided into five chapters. While the first two brief chapters, entitled "General Foundations" and "The Atonal Law of Twelve-Tonality," are at points clearly paraphrases of passages from Hauer's *Vom Wesen des Musikalischen*, Eimert begins to go his own way in the third chapter, entitled "The Atonal Principle of Melody." Eimert's discussion of twelve-tone melody emphasizes the almost infinite number of melodies that can arise when the nearly 500 million possible orderings of the twelve pcs are combined with an unlimited freedom in rhythmic configuration. The only caution he offers is that twelve-tone melodies should avoid creating tonal associations and references. Eimert's twelve-tone melodies can be termed "melodic aggregates"; and while each melodic aggregate could also be thought of as an ordered twelve-tone series, Eimert does not directly invoke the notion of ordering; for Eimert, it is enough that each melodic aggregate circulate all twelve pcs. In one of his examples (No. 15), Eimert seems to come very close to what we would understand as a simple employment of serial technique: because he has set his four-voice example as a canon, the same ordered series is repeated in each voice. However, the second melodic aggregate that follows in each voice is a free reordering of the first and does not conform to the any of the systematic transformations that became standard practice in the Schoenberg circle by the late 1920s. Eimert argues that so long as the music progresses according to melodic aggregates, the harmonic dimension of the music is free from restrictions (except, one might expect, from creating tonal associations).

In Chapter 4, Eimert takes up the "Harmonic Principle of Twelve-Tonality, the 'Complex.'" The complex can be thought of as a "harmonic aggregate" in which the defining feature is that all voices in a texture, when taken together, complete the twelve-pc aggregate. In a four-voice texture, for instance, all four voices taken together unfold a harmonic aggregate even though each voice alone does not unfold a melodic aggregate. In the course of considering the ways in which the harmonic aggregate can be distributed among two or more voices, Eimert calculates the number of possible partitionings per number of distinct voices, prefiguring the discussion of arrays that arose in American twelve-tone theory in the 1960s and 1970s and that finds its most complete formulation in the work of Robert Morris (discussed below). Eimert shows, for instance, that in two voices there are eleven possible partition patterns: these would

12 Hauer's two short twelve-tone books, *Vom Melos zur Pauke* and *Zwölftontechnik*, both appeared in the two years following Eimert's book and are pragmatic in the same way as Eimert's book is; Eimert's book may well have prodded Hauer to give his own theoretical ideas a similar nuts-and-bolts compositional treatment.

be 1 + 11 (one note in one voice, eleven in the other), 2 + 10, and so on, ending with 11 + 1. In three voices there are 55 possible partitionings and in four voices there are 165. He then shows how many different possible orderings there are for each voice based on how many pcs it contains: a voice with eleven pcs, for example, could be reordered almost 40 million ways, but a voice with three pcs can only be reordered six ways. This is all by way of demonstrating that as the number of voices in a partition increases, the number of possible melodic permutations decreases; and as the number of melodic permutations increase, the number of voices in a partition decrease.

This concern with the harmonic and melodic dimensions leads, in Chapter 5, to the consideration of the "Bringing Together of Harmonic and Melodic Principles in Free Composition." Up to this point, Eimert has argued that when the music is unfolding according to melodic aggregates, there is great freedom in the harmonic dimension; when the music is unfolding according to harmonic aggregates (complexes) there is great freedom in the individual voice parts. In Chapter 5, however, Eimert begins to explore ways of coordinating the melodic and harmonic dimensions. Eimert presents a number of examples, including one in which three harmonic aggregates are created by unfolding three melodic aggregates according to a 4+4+4 partitioning scheme (Example 29). If these melodic aggregates were standard serial transformations of one another (which they are not), this would be an example of a simple two-dimensional array based on tetrachordal combinatoriality. As it stands, though, it is at least a noteworthy precursor to this later organizational principle and an important early instance of coordinating the melodic and harmonic dimensions in twelve-tone music.

Unlike that of Hauer, Eimert's consideration of the twelve-tone idea is not driven by spiritual concerns. Instead, Eimert casts his systematic atonalism as a natural development out of chromatic tonality and his focus is clearly on the pragmatic dimension of his ideas. And while Eimert admits he owes a good deal to Hauer's theoretical writing, it is also interesting to note that the future co-editor of *Die Reihe* does not mention an ordered series at any point in his *Atonale Musiklehre*. There is good reason for this: until late 1924 Schoenberg's "method of composing with twelve tones related only to one another" had not been made public outside of the Schoenberg circle in Vienna.

Arnold Schoenberg. While the writings of Hauer and Eimert offer systematic approaches to the constant circulation of the twelve-pc aggregate, these approaches never caught on with other composers to a significant extent. Instead, it is Arnold Schoenberg's (1874–1951) twelve-tone method that has come to define classic twelve-tone practice, with its ordered series and forty-eight row forms based on transposition, inversion, retrograde, and retrograde-inversion. It is thus perhaps surprising that Schoenberg's method was the last to be articulated in print, and when it does appear it is explained not by the composer himself, but rather by one of his students. Erwin Stein's article, "Neue Formprinzipien," appeared in the September 1924 issue of

Musikblätter des Anbruch celebrating Schoenberg's fiftieth birthday.[13] While Schoenberg had lectured his students on his new method already in 1923, Stein's article is the first public articulation of it.

Stein casts Schoenberg's method in the context of the "crisis" of modern composition, by which he means the collapse of tonality and the loss of the form-building potential tonality provides. There is a strong sense of the historical inevitability of the rise of atonality, as chromatic tonality gives way to the free use of the twelve pcs. In what was to become an oft-repeated historical account of the rise of dodecaphony, Stein argues that modern music is turning away from harmony as its principal structural determinant and toward counterpoint, reversing the stylistic change that occurred from Bach to Mozart by returning again to polyphonic thinking. In this context, then, Stein introduces inversion, retrograde, and retrograde-inversion transformations into the discussion. But these arise not as operations on twelve-pc rows – an idea that would figure prominently in Babbitt's writing – but rather more generally as melodic transformations of motives. As elements of Schoenberg's new formal principles, according to Stein, these transformations offer melodic variety in the context of motivic unity (see also **Chapter 29, pp. 911–13**).

The central component holding Schoenberg's new atonal music together is the *Grundgestalt* (basic shape), which, appearing early in a work, is the source of all subsequent musical material. Stein offers a series of often detailed analytical excerpts drawn from Schoenberg's Opp. 23–25 to demonstrate the wide variety of ways in which the composer establishes formal logic and structural unity in these pieces. Since the new works that Stein considers are not all dodecaphonic, the new formal principles have to generalize across both twelve-tone and non-twelve-tone works; this makes it clear that the *Grundgestalt* and the row are not necessarily the same – a *Grundgestalt* need not be twelve-tone. It is important to note then that Stein presents the twelve-tone method not as the only way, but rather as one approach among many. It thus seems that even within his own circle it was not clear that Schoenberg would turn to exclusively twelve-tone composition after his first extended dodecaphonic work, the Wind Quintet, Op. 26 (completed in August 1924). And even when articles by Stein, Felix Greissle, Theodor Adorno, and others began to explore twelve-tone music, it is not clear that these members of the Schoenberg circle ever understood the row as more than a melodic resource; the idea that a row could function as a background context in Schoenberg's music, establishing structural hierarchy and row disposition within a given piece, would have to wait for the later theoretical work of Schoenberg's American exegetes led by Milton Babbitt.

In all of the discussion around Schoenberg's twelve-tone method in the decade after its public introduction by Stein, the composer himself is strangely silent. Schoenberg

13 Stein, "Neue Formprinzipien." Stein's English translation appears in his *Orpheus in New Guises*, pp. 57–77.

had published his *Harmonielehre* in 1911 and prepared a revised and enlarged third edition in 1922; he was thus no stranger to music-theoretical discussion. His most extended treatment of his twelve-tone method appears in his essay "Composition with Twelve Tones," which developed out of a 1934 lecture given at Princeton but was not published until 1950 – a year before the composer's death.[14] Still, by 1925 Hauer and Schoenberg had discussed beginning a school of twelve-tone composition in which Hauer would teach the introductory classes and Schoenberg the more advanced ones; they also considered bringing out a book together, alternating chapters with one another. In 1926 Schoenberg left Vienna for a teaching position in Berlin and these plans to collaborate came to nothing.

In comparing the dodecaphony of Hauer, Eimert, and Schoenberg, certain contrasts and similarities arise. Hauer thought of the twelve pcs as a kind of spiritual universe; thus, twelve-tone composition was a way of communing with the infinite – the structure of any given work was only ever part of a much greater structure that could never be projected in any single piece but was nevertheless already and always present. For Schoenberg, his twelve-tone method provided a means for projecting the *musikalischer Gedanke* of a work, though Stein only hints at this; and while there was nothing especially spiritual about the method itself, the expression of the *Gedanke* was something of a mystical undertaking for Schoenberg. Reflecting on his method some twenty years after he first employed it, Schoenberg likens artistic creation to divine creation (paraphrasing Genesis in the process) and refers his idea of the unity of musical space to Emanuel Swedenborg's characterization of Heaven. Eimert, though influenced by Hauer's writing, seemed unconcerned with the spiritual dimensions of composition or dodecaphony; he focused his efforts instead on the purely technical and pragmatic aspect of twelve-tone composition. The picture of twelve-tone theory that emerges in the first half of the 1920s is thus one of a wide variety of approaches; the dodecaphony of Hauer, Schoenberg, and Eimert are at once contrasting and related, often hitting on similar technical solutions as responses to very different sorts of questions. And there were other approaches as well: in 1925, for instance, Berg's student Fritz Heinrich Klein (1892–1977) published his "Die Grenze der Halbtonwelt," an essay in which he discusses a number of techniques – some of which are twelve-tone – that he employed in his 1921 composition "Die Maschine."[15] Despite the variety of music-theoretical writing on dodecaphony and atonality that appeared in Germany and Austria in the 1920s, however, Schoenberg's serial method became the most widely known. Brief analyses of some early twelve-tone works from the Second Viennese School appeared in music journals and prefaced the published scores, explaining the idea of the row and its transformations, providing a guide to form in these pieces, and introducing many musicians to the technical aspects of dodecaphony.

14 Schoenberg, "Composition with Twelve Tones (1)."
15 Klein, "Die Grenze der Halbtonwelt"; trans. in Headlam, "Fritz Heinrich Klein's 'Die Grenze der Halbtonwelt.'"

Twelve-tone notation

Composers of chromatic music often complain that standard notation makes reading their music more difficult than it needs to be. Shown below are three different approaches to twelve-tone notation that were designed in the early part of the twentieth century to make atonal music easier to read. The first of these is Hauer's *Zwölftonschrift,* which is based on the keyboard: reading like a keyboard standing sideways and going from low to high, the lines stand for the black keys, while the spaces stand for the white ones (the second excerpt is a transcription of the first). A second form of dodecaphonic notation was developed by Jefim Golyscheff (1887–1970): all notes with solid note heads are natural, while all those with an "x" inside the notehead are raised one half step (the example is drawn from Eimert's *Atonale Musiklehre*). The third is from Schoenberg and features three lines, the lowest of which is C, the next highest E, and the top line G♯/A♭. Slanted lines are used to show the notes in between these, with a line above a note indicating a half step above the lower line, a line below indicating a half step below the upper line, and line through the note showing the note a whole step above the lower and below the higher. Schoenberg provides a transcription drawn from his *Pierrot Lunaire*.

A Hauer, *Vom Wesen*, p. 56

B Eimert, *Atonale Musiklehre*, pp. 3, 9

C Schoenberg, "A New Twelve-Tone Notation" (1924), in *Style and Idea*, pp. 356, 359

Further development of twelve-tone theory, 1930–45

While Schoenberg's particular method would come to dominate the public perception of twelve-tone music in the decades that followed its inception in the early 1920s, many composers and theorists devised their own ways of engaging the twelve-tone idea, in some cases appropriating aspects of Schoenberg's method. Numerous essays could be written on the wide variety of idiosyncratic approaches to twelve-tone theory and composition that arose in the 1930s and 1940s, but the rise of twelve-tone modality during this period provides a representative instance of ways in which Schoenberg's method was adapted and extended.

Richard S. Hill. While in many instances the use of modes in music of the first third of the twentieth century is derived from late nineteenth-century musical evocations of folk and exotic styles, the notion of mode when used in the context of counterpoint has clear ties to Western music's pretonal past. Stein had already argued that atonality was a logical successor to chromatic harmony, casting this development in a historical context that suggested that atonality was an inevitable consequence of late nineteenth-century and early twentieth-century extended tonality. While one may question the Hegelian teleology of Stein's position, it is clear nonetheless that he – like many of his generation – evinced a pronounced concern for history. It is perhaps not surprising in this context that some composers and theorists in the 1930s looked to history to provide suggestions for the further development of the twelve-tone idea. If harmony in atonality was an important problem – and many clearly thought it was – perhaps turning to the European music that preceded tonal harmony could provide some answers or suggest some alternative "roads not taken" that could now be explored in the wake of tonality's perceived exhaustion. And among the first theorists to begin working out the consequences of viewing dodecaphony through the lens of modal counterpoint was Richard S. Hill (1901–61).

In his 1936 essay, "Schoenberg's Tone-Rows and the Tonal System of the Future," Hill provides a summary of twelve-tone theory, including the writing of Hauer and Eimert, as well as offering what is probably the most thorough summary of Schoenberg's twelve-tone music up to that point. Hill catalogues in careful and impressive detail the full range of techniques Schoenberg uses for combining, partitioning, and reordering rows in his Opp. 23–35. It is clear from his discussion of the music that Hill had studied these pieces – and the secondary literature surrounding them – very closely. Hill's most important theoretical point about Schoenberg's twelve-tone music, however, is a complaint: according to Hill, Schoenberg's manipulation of the rows in many instances is impossible to discern aurally. While he clearly holds Schoenberg in high regard as a composer, Hill nevertheless believes that a way of employing the twelve-tone idea that renders dodecaphonic processes more vivid aurally must be developed and forwards his notion of twelve-tone modality as a possible solution.

Hill begins his theoretical consideration of modality with a C major scale, pointing out that merely writing an ascending major scale tells us very little about its musical properties. If we were to notate the scale in such a way that we provide not only its content, but also information about the ways in which the elements relate to one another in a musical sense, this would be far more useful and more representative of the aural experience of music in C major. Hill calls this way of construing C a "functional mode," and lists both prime and mirror forms of the C major scale by way of illustration. In the prime form, middle C is followed by the G a fifth above (instead of D), and then by the E a third below G. This suggests that in a functional sense G is more closely related to C than D is, and in the same way that E is more closely related to G than to D is as well. D occurs as the penultimate tone in the functional mode, appearing a major second above the final C (which is an octave above middle C). While one may disagree with Hill's functional ordering, one can still see how such an ordering might provide more useful information than the usual strictly ascending ordering does.

For Hill, simply running off the tones in a twelve-tone row or any of its transformations is the parallel to the standard notation of a scale – it provides content with no sense of functional relationships between the elements. This is why Schoenberg's twelve-tone music is so hard to understand, Hill argues. The rows are used in a motivic way and in practice Schoenberg's disposition of row forms becomes excessively complicated, obscuring motivic relationships. What is needed instead is the development of dodecaphonic modes: "Twelve tone composers . . . would at first manufacture their own rows or functional modes, as they, in fact, are now doing. As time went on, a body of these modes would come to be recognized as superior to the rest. These in turn would probably be whittled down until finally only a chief and a couple of subsidiary modes would be left."[16] Hill then mentions that these new twelve-tone modes might be used to establish contrapuntal lines, "as in medieval times."[17]

Hill was not a composer, and so while he may have thought he could see the promised land of dodecaphonic milk and honey, he could not himself lead twelve-tone music in to it. Instead, it would fall to two composers, Ernst Krenek and his student George Perle, to further develop the notion of twelve-tone modality. Hill's essay sets out the two most important issues to be taken up by Krenek and Perle: the notion that pretonal counterpoint could be used as a model for further development of dodecaphony and the idea that the row can establish a meaningful musical context while not having to appear as an ordered series on the surface of the piece.

Ernst Krenek. Hill's essay had an important impact on Ernst Krenek's (1900–91) thinking about twelve-tone composition. Krenek addressed Hill's writing in his *Music Here and Now*, as well as in his 1940 address "A Study of Cadential Formations in Atonal Music." Hill and Krenek corresponded privately on dodecaphonic concerns, and in the opening paragraphs of his 1943 article, "New Developments of the Twelve-Tone Technique," Krenek acknowledges the influence of Hill's essay and especially his functional modes.[18] Krenek seems to have struggled most with the notion of dodecaphonic functional modes, which Krenek calls "extra-motival" – a term that does not appear in Hill's essay but is used by Perle in his 1941 article discussed below.

Krenek's solution to the question of extra-motival modality was to use the two complementary hexachords of a row to systematically generate a larger collection of hexachords. Thus, beginning with the complementary and ordered hexachords <F, G, A, B♭, D♭, E♭>, <B, C, D, E, F♯, G♯>, and the inversions of each, Krenek performs two kinds of transformation. The first is rotation, which transforms the first ordered hexachord, for instance, to <G, A, B♭, D♭, E♭, F> and then <A, B♭, D♭, E♭, F, G>, and so on until the rotation produces the original hexachord. This process results in six modes Krenek terms "diatonic." In a second type of transformation procedure, Krenek then transposes each of these rotated hexachords obtained in the first procedure such that each hexachord begins on the same pitch class as the first; the first rotated hexachord given above thus becomes <F, G, A♭, C♭, D♭, E♭> and the second <F, F♯, A, B, C♯, D♯>. This second operation produces modes Krenek calls "chromatic." Using these procedures, Krenek forms six diatonic modes each from the original row and its inversion, and six chromatic modes from the row and its inversion, making twenty-four possible modes. Krenek employs these twelve-tone modal materials in his *Lamentatio Jeremiae*

16 Hill, "Schoenberg's Tone-Rows," p. 33. 17 Ibid.
18 A discussion of the Hill–Krenek correspondence may be found in Stewart, *Ernst Krenek*, pp. 224–25.

Prophetae, op. 93 (1941–42), and his 1943 article includes a number of examples drawn from that work to illustrate his application of the modal hexachords.

It is important to note that with his notion of diatonic and chromatic transformations, Krenek introduces the idea of rotation into twelve-tone theory, though the procedure of rotation had been present in the dodecaphonic music of Hauer, Schoenberg, and Berg for over a decade by this time. Far more significant is the way in which the row itself recedes from its role as a motivic entity on the surface to one that generates material from the background – to return to Krenek's language, it is no longer motival, but now extra-motival. The row in its original form need not be literally present in the piece, and the use of chromatic modes even allows the possibility that some passages will not use all twelve tones. This is a clear departure from Krenek's motival approach to twelve-tone composition as it appears in his *Studies in Counterpoint* of 1940, in which the row is subject to the Schoenbergian operations of transposition, inversion, and retrograde. While Krenek's motival and extra-motival approaches each arise from a desire to extend historically validated contrapuntal practices into twelve-tone music, they produce highly contrasting results. While *Studies in Counterpoint* may be grounded in the thinking of Schoenberg's students from the twenties and thirties, Krenek's extra-motival procedures are the ones that most clearly take up Hill's vision of a tonal system of the future.

George Perle. Fascinated especially with the dodecaphonic structure of Berg's *Lyric Suite*, George Perle (1915–) also developed a way of employing the row in an extra-motival context. Perle acknowledged that Hill's article was the first to suggest the notion of twelve-tone functional modes, but he insisted that he was unaware of the essay until after he had worked out his particular version of twelve-tone modality. Perle was also a student of Krenek's at the time the latter was developing his approach, but he may have had more influence on Krenek in this regard than the older composer had on him. In many ways, in fact, Perle's twelve-tone modality is much closer to what Hill proposes than are the diatonic and chromatic modes of Krenek.

Perle understands modality in a very general sense and his theoretical writing makes no attempt to reconfigure elements of modal counterpoint in a dodecaphonic context. He begins with a series of descending fifths – C, F, B♭, E♭, A♭, D♭ – and ascending fifths – C, G, D, A, E, B, F♯ – from which he constructs a row by interleaving the two (allowing for enharmonic notation): C, F, G, B♭, D, E♭, A, G♯, E, C♯, B, F♯. Because of the structure of the row, its transposition beginning on F♯ is identical with the retrograde of original form beginning on C. Since Perle does not consider retrograde forms to be distinct entities in his approach, there are only six discrete transpositions of the row available. Perle does employ inverted forms of the row, and there are likewise six discrete inversion forms available. This row serves as the basis for Perle's system – no others are used – and as a consequence he is able to employ a limited number of possible forms, twelve as opposed to the Schoenbergian forty-eight.

Perle focuses his approach on each tone and its immediate neighbors; the row establishes functional relationships for each pc that the composer may employ freely without regard to the literal serial ordering of the pcs in the twelve available transformations. Perle organizes these clusters of neighbor tones by combining row forms into modes. Inversion forms starting on C and F, G and B♭, and D and E♭ (reflecting the dyads form the first hexachord of the original series) produce neighbor-tone collections of stacked fifths, thirds (minor-minor seventh chords), and fourths respectively, as do transpositions starting on C and G, F and D, and B♭ and A (the dyads from the inverted form). While the manner in which Perle combines his materials may seem complicated, the results produce a palette of possible combinations that are limited in comparison with Schoenbergian procedures (owing in large part to the symmetry of the central row) and match closely Hill's call for a small number of modes that would be superior to the rest. Most importantly, Perle offers a solution to organizing dodecaphony in which the row creates musical context without appearing in any literal way on the surface of the work. Though he insists he was unaware of Hill's article when he developed his approach, Perle ended up addressing Hill's concerns in a very systematic and comprehensive manner. Perle's later articulations of twelve-tone modality did not differ much from the form presented in 1941. The most widely known discussion is probably the one found in his *Serial Composition and Atonality* of 1962, reproduced in subsequent editions of that book until Perle later published an expanded version of his theory – a result of his work with the composer Paul Lansky – in 1977 as *Twelve-Tone Tonality*.

Twelve-tone theory since 1945

The Second World War and the events leading up to it significantly impeded the dissemination of twelve-tone music and theoretical writing. Printed scores of the works of Schoenberg, Berg, and Webern were especially difficult to come by, particularly for those outside Germany and Austria; this prevented the careful study of these works by many interested scholars and composers and greatly attenuated the benefits of the articles one could find, often concerning pieces readers had neither heard nor played. Both Babbitt and Perle have commented on the paucity of scores and information regarding twelve-tone music during this period.[19] Perle even attributes the development of his own dodecaphonic theory to his misunderstanding of Schoenbergian practice.[20] As this chapter has made clear, there was nonetheless some music-technical writing available to readers during wartime: Krenek's *Studies in Counterpoint* or Hill's article in *The Musical Quarterly*, for instance. The period after the war, by contrast, saw the publication and widespread availability of a number of books devoted to twelve-tone music:

19 Babbitt, *Words About Music*, p. 6; Perle, *The Listening Composer*, p. 128.
20 Perle, *The Listening Composer*, pp. 129–34.

Twelve-tone modes

The graphic aspects of the modal systems of Hill, Perle, and Krenek differ at least as much from one another as the systems themselves do. Here Hill opts for standard notation, arranging the notes of a C scale in two inversionally related forms according to their "function" within the major mode. Perle employs a symmetrical row to generate clusters of neighbor tones by combining pairs of inverted transformations of the original row (not shown). Krenek employs a table to show the diatonic (left column) and chromatic (right column) modal transformations that result from his procedure of systematic rotation and transformation within a single twelve-tone row (given as the top pair of hexachords on each column).

A Hill, "Schoenberg's Tone Rows," p. 21

B Perle, "Evolution of the Tone Row," p. 283

C Krenek, "Extents and Limits," p. 74

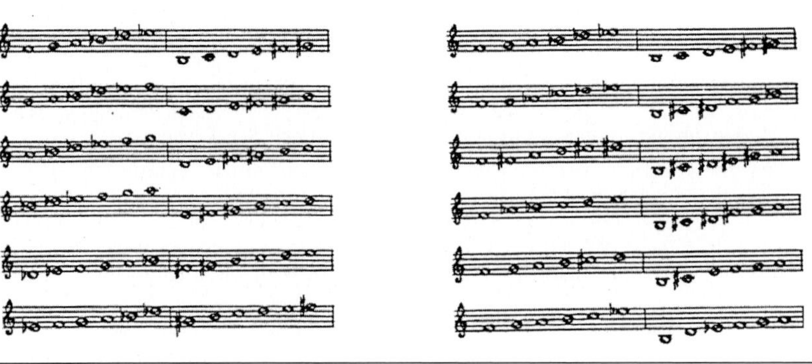

American Karl Eschman's *Changing Forms in Modern Music* appeared in 1945, and from the Schoenberg camp came Josef Rufer's *Komposition mit zwölf Tönen* in 1952, and Schoenberg's own essay, "Composition with Twelve Tones," in 1950. In Paris, composer and conductor René Leibowitz published his theoretical writing on dodecaphony, organized concerts of twelve-tone music, and taught a number of students, some of whom – such as Pierre Boulez – would soon go on to extend the twelve-tone idea, developing a markedly European approach to integral serialism.

René Leibowitz. With his *Schoenberg et son école* in 1947, René Leibowitz (1913–72) offered the first attempt at a comprehensive study of the music of Schoenberg, Berg, and Webern. Following a familiar mode of presentation and arguing his position at some length, Leibowitz casts the three composers in a teleologically driven historical context with Schoenberg as the pivotal figure. According to Leibowitz, the history of polyphony can be seen to focus first on contrapuntal concerns (medieval and Renaissance music) and later on harmonic ones (Classical and Romantic music); only the harmonic counterpoint of Bach seems to hold these two sets of concerns in a perfect, if historically precarious, balance. It thus turns out that counterpoint is mostly a secondary concern in music after 1750, appearing occasionally but almost always subject to harmonic and tonal concerns. It is Schoenberg who "reactivates" polyphonic "evolution" with his turn to atonality, and with his twelve-tone method establishes organizing principles for a "new world of sound." Leibowitz subtitles the section of his book dealing with Schoenberg and his music "The Origins and Foundations of Contemporary Music." The following section devoted to Berg's music is subtitled "The Awareness of the Past in Contemporary Music," while the section on Webern's music runs "The Awareness of the Future in Contemporary Music." Thus with Schoenberg the master at the center of a new era in the development of music, one of his students looks to its rich past while another points the way to the future.

While Leibowitz places tremendous emphasis on the historical importance of the music he discusses, he also devotes a significant amount of attention to the music itself, providing detailed if often fragmentary analyses of dozens of works by the three composers. His next book, *Introduction à la musique de douze sons*, takes Schoenberg's Variations for Orchestra, Op. 31 as its central analytical example; here Leibowitz presents even more detailed analysis, offering at times measure-by-measure, row-by-row accounts of this extended twelve-tone work. While he occasionally hits upon systematic properties in dodecaphony (he notices the consequences of odd and even index numbers under inversion, for instance), his thinking on twelve-tone music remains – to use Perle's term – motival. At the end of his second book, in fact, Leibowitz addresses the Perle and Hill articles discussed above (also briefly mentioning Krenek's writing in *Music Here and Now*). He rejects the notion of establishing the kind of twelve-tone modality Perle describes, calling it "static" and claiming that such ideas have already been left behind by other developments in twelve-tone technique.[21] Whatever developments Leibowitz may have had in mind, it is clear that he finds no value in working toward an extra-motival conception of the row, and it is this claim, along with the reliance on historiographical arguments, that Babbitt will soon attack. The importance of Leibowitz's extensive writing in the mid and late 1940s is that it establishes a kind of post-World War II dodecaphonic orthodoxy, based on the music of the Second Viennese School and focused on the primacy of pitch relationships, against which composers and theorists subsequently would react. In 1949, Leibowitz's *Schoenberg et son école* was published in an English translation by Schoenberg's American student Dika Newlin. Newlin's translation, along with Leibowitz's friendly relations with Schoenberg himself, went a long way toward establishing the credibility of Leibowitz's writing internationally.

European serialism. Before his work was available abroad, Leibowitz's dodecaphonic advocacy was felt first in Paris and then at Darmstadt; and it is likely that his books provide an accurate view of the seminar teaching and compositional instruction in which he was engaged in the late 1940s. But there was another influential approach to modern compositional thinking that affected composers in Paris at the time, as well as at Darmstadt in the early fifties (following Leibowitz's tenure there), and this came from Olivier Messiaen (1908–92).[22] The French composer had published his *Technique de mon langage musical* in 1944 – an important work in twentieth-century theory but one that does not engage twelve-tone composition at all. In the late 1940s Messiaen was fascinated with Stravinsky's use of "personnages rhythmiques" as they could be found in his *Le Sacre du printemps*, and he spent a good deal of time working through this with many of the same students who had attended Leibowitz's sessions. Pierre Boulez (1925–) assumed the role as spokesman for this group of young composers and much of what Messiaen was teaching regarding Stravinsky's rhythmic practice can be found in Boulez's 1948 article, "Propositions"; Boulez later expanded his work on Stravinsky's music with his "Stravinsky demeure" of 1953. The crucial point for Boulez was to establish that rhythm could be separated from pitch, and thus be seen to engage in a kind of counterpoint between domains. This constituted, for Boulez at least, the basis for his strong break with Leibowitz and his more traditional, pitch-based thinking: while some accounts have attributed the rift to Boulez's advocacy of Webern's music over that of Schoenberg – best seen in Boulez's controversial essay, "Schönberg is Dead" of 1952 – the central issue has more to do with what might be called the "emancipation of the rhythmic domain."

In part under the influence of Messiaen's idiosyncratic adaptations of ordering (but not twelve-tone) practices in his *Modes de valeur et d'intensités* (1949), composers at

21 Leibowitz, *La musique*, pp. 274–75.

22 See Vogel's two-volume *Schönberg und die Folgen* for a detailed consideration of European serialism, and especially for an insightful account of the development of Darmstadt in the late 1940s and 50s.

Darmstadt in 1951 began developing an approach to serialism that extended the use of an ordered series to rhythm, dynamics, and timbre.[23] The logic behind this extension of the twelve-tone idea to non-pitch domains is spelled out initially by Boulez in his "Eventuellement..." of 1952. According to Boulez, Schoenberg's twelve-tone method constitutes a tremendous advance in modern composition, but it is innovative only in the pitch domain; in regard to rhythm, timbre, and form it is still hopelessly mired in the past. Stravinsky's music has demonstrated that rhythm can be an independent component in musical composition. It thus makes sense to bring these two practices together, treating rhythm with as much serial consideration as has been reserved traditionally for pitch. Boulez goes on to cite examples from his own *Polyphonie X* (1951) and *Structures*, Book 1 (1951–52) to illustrate his recent practice of employing rhythmic series of both twelve and less than twelve values.

Toward the end of his essay Boulez refers to the new possibilities for the control of duration and timbre that tape composition offers, a topic he takes up in more detail in his "An der Grenze der Fruchtlandes (Paul Klee)" – his contribution to the first volume of *Die Reihe*, edited by Herbert Eimert and Karlheinz Stockhausen (1928–). In 1952, Eimert published his *Lehrbuch der Zwölftontechnik*, now organizing his thinking around an ordered row (which had not played a role in his earlier *Atonale Musiklehre*). Eimert had begun working on establishing an electronic music studio in Cologne in 1951, and Stockhausen began composing electronic pieces there in 1953, after having spent a year working at the ORTF studio in Paris with Pierre Schaeffer. Eimert and Stockhausen founded *Die Reihe* in 1955, a journal that acted as the central voice of the European avant-garde and which over the next few years devoted attention to a number of topics. The first volume is devoted to electronic music, and Eimert's contribution offers a clear and well-argued statement of the ways in which electronic music extends the twelve-tone idea to all domains of musical creation, making it the perfect medium for integral serialism. A number of Stockhausen's early theoretical essays also appear in *Die Reihe*, including his important discussions of electronic music and serial procedures in "... wie die Zeit vergeht..." (See also **Chapter 20, pp. 717–18**.)

Despite the stated intention of many European serialist writers to move beyond Leibowitz's dodecaphonic approach, the general approach to the ordered series – in whatever domain – continued to be primarily motival. The emphasis tends to fall less on creating a single ordering that is projected in a number of domains and more on creating a number of orderings, each assigned – at least initially – to a single domain. The resulting serial counterpoint between domains is the result of elevating rhythm, timbre, and dynamics to the level of pitch in compositional importance, and marks a general distinction between the European approach advocated by Boulez, Stockhausen, and Eimert and the American one advanced by Babbitt and his students, which keeps pitch as the primary element. In this context it is interesting to note that

23 See Toop, "Messiaen/Goeyvaerts," for a valuable analytical account of the compositions arising from the the summer of 1951 at Darmstadt.

the approach to rhythmic independence put forward first by Boulez was anticipated by Berg's-student Fritz Heinrich Klein in 1925; Klein's theoretical article "Die Grenze der Halbtonwelt" (mentioned briefly above) describes his use of both a twelve- and an eleven-attack rhythmic motive in his 1921 composition, "Die Maschine."[24] In fact, at the conclusion of his 1964 reworking of his 1952 twelve-tone book, Eimert points out that not only Klein, but also both he and Golyscheff were working with rhythmic organization in a twelve-tone context.[25]

Milton Babbitt. In the United States the development of the twelve-tone idea followed the path toward extra-motival use of the row set down first by Hill. In one of Milton Babbitt's (1916–) first publications as a writer on music, the composer offers a review of Leibowitz's *Schoenberg et son école*. Babbitt's complaints regarding Leibowitz's work not only serve to highlight what was to become an important distinction between American and European approaches, but also touch on what would become the central tenets in Babbitt's later writing on dodecaphony. Babbitt makes two distinct but clearly related points. He argues that while it is fascinating to reflect on the historical aspects of Schoenberg's music and career, the fact is that this has nothing to do with what is most important about the twelve-tone idea; when Schoenberg hit upon his twelve-tone method, he discovered a rich musical context that offered a wealth of structural possibilities. In coming to terms with the consequences of Schoenberg's method, one discovers that the structure of any given row, combined with the standard four operations, produces a system of relationships that can be characterized theoretically and that create an extra-motival context that is newly established with each work. The problem with Leibowitz, as Babbitt sees it, is that his analyses never scratch the surface of this extra-motival structure, and that all the discussion of Schoenberg's place in history is beside the point.

In his "Some Aspects of Twelve-Tone Composition" – published in 1955, and thus in the wake of the first published theoretical articles from Boulez and Stockhausen – Babbitt continues to distinguish his approach from the European one, but now he sets his thinking in contrast not to Leibowitz's motival dodecaphonic orthodoxy, but rather to the new wave of continental serialists. Basing his theoretical remarks on his unpublished 1946 dissertation, "The Function of Set Structure in the Twelve-Tone System" (which was not accepted at Princeton University until 1992), Babbitt introduces two ideas that would come to be central to American twelve-tone theory in the decades that followed: combinatoriality and derivation. The first of these refers to any pair of the forty-eight possible rows in which the first six pcs of each together form an aggregate of all twelve possible pcs. The same property can arise using the first four pcs

24 See Headlam, "Fritz Heinrich Klein's 'Die Grenze der Halbtonwelt,'" for a comparison of Klein's essay with his composition "Die Maschine."

25 In his "Pioniere der Zwölftontechnik," Hans Oesch presents a detailed argument for Klein, Golyscheff, and Eimert as important precursors to post-World War II serialism.

of three rows (tetrachordal combinatoriality) or the first three pcs of four rows (trichordal combinatoriality). Babbitt lists the six "all-combinatorial" hexachords and discusses Schoenberg's use of "semi-combinatorial" hexachords in many of his twelve-tone works.[26] Derivation refers to a process whereby, for instance, the initial trichord of a row can be used to arrive at a new, "derived" row by employing the standard twelve-tone operations of transposition, inversion, retrograde, and retrograde-inversion.

In the articles that followed, Babbitt continued and extended his discussion of the structural properties of the twelve-tone system. In "Twelve-Tone Invariants as Compositional Determinants," for instance, he draws attention to the ways in which both segmental and non-segmental collections of pcs remain invariant under the standard operations. This is crucial, according to Babbitt, because the twelve-tone system is a "permutational" system, not a "combinational" one like tonality: while one key can be distinguished from another on the basis of content (some pcs are diatonic while others are not), twelve-tone rows differ only in terms of the ordering of identical contents (all twelve pcs). It is thus important to attend to the specific ways in which the pcs are reordered – when a collection of pcs from one row form map back into the same places in a second one, that constitutes a special property that can have compositional consequences. In order to keep track of both the pcs and the spots in the row they occupy, Babbitt represents each element in integer notation as an ordered pair: the first integer stands for order position, while the second represents the pitch class. The first element in a row beginning on G, for instance, might be 0,0, while the second is 1,9. Thus from the first element to the second, the G (represented by the second 0 in the first pair) moves to E (nine half steps up, represented by the 9 in the second pair). By using integer notation and assigning values to represent both pitch class and order position, Babbitt is able to reduce the number of operators in his system to two: transposition and inversion. A retrograde is simply an order-number inversion, while a rotation is an order-number transposition. A retrograde inversion is simply an instance of inversion applied to both pc and order-number domains.

By approaching the twelve-tone system in this way, Babbitt is able to argue that the row is not only extra-motival in Perle's pitch-oriented sense (though Babbitt does not use this term), but also extra-motival in any musical dimension the composer chooses. Serialization of non-pitch domains can be based on a single row, which having been formulated mathematically becomes an organizational structure that is no longer specifically pitch-oriented anyway. Babbitt's approach to rhythmic organization, which appears first in his "Twelve-Tone Rhythmic Structure and the Electronic Medium," relies on an order-number/pitch-class isomorphism and contrasts the polyphony of domains found in continental serialism with a more organic representation of the same

26 Space does not allow an extended or detailed consideration of Babbitt's twelve-tone thinking. For such an account, see Mead, *An Introduction to the Music of Milton Babbitt.* For a detailed account of Babbitt's influence on American serialism, see Peles, "Serialism and Complexity."

row structure, projected simultaneously in multiple domains. That Babbitt bases his thinking on Schoenberg's practice is also revealing in contrast to the theoretical positions of both Perle and Hill; rather than thinking of Schoenberg's practice as motival (and thus requiring a new dodecaphonic practice that would overcome this), Babbitt instead argues that Schoenberg's practice had always been extra-motival, or as he prefers to describe it, "contextual." With his "Remarks on the Recent Stravinsky" of 1964, Babbitt was also among the first to explore the theoretical dimensions of Stravinsky's twelve-tone practice, especially the rotational array – a dodecaphonic procedure Stravinsky likely developed from the approaches of Krenek and Perle discussed above.

American theory in the wake of Babbitt. Babbitt's theoretical writing, which continued to appear in the decades after the first important articles, was enormously influential for American composers and theorists. Along with Allen Forte, Babbitt was instrumental in establishing the conceptual bases for the discipline of music theory in the 1960s and 70s. While Forte's 1973 book, *The Structure of Atonal Music*, served as the basis for much work in atonal music generally, Babbitt's thinking was taken up and extended by a number of younger theorists. David Lewin's "A Theory of Segmental Association in Twelve-Tone Music," for instance, extends Babbitt's work on segmental invariants in Schoenberg's twelve-tone music, and his "A Study of Hexachord Levels in Schoenberg's Violin Fantasy" expands Babbitt's notions of combinatoriality and hexachordal invariants. Donald Martino's "The Source Set and Its Aggregate Formations" offers a detailed exploration of derivation, while Andrew Mead's study, "Some Implications of the Pitch Class/Order Number Isomorphism Inherent in the Twelve-Tone System," exhaustively explores the dialectic between order and pitch operations. Much of this work appeared in *Perspectives of New Music*, which was founded at Princeton in 1962, in part as a response to *Die Reihe*, and became the leading publication in American dodecaphonic theory for three decades. In fact, the 1960–90 period saw a tremendous explosion in writing and theorizing on twelve-tone music – a flood of dodecaphonic information and discussion like no other time in the history of twelve-tone theory.

While many articles or books could serve to represent this phase of theoretical activity, perhaps the most cumulative one is Robert Morris's *Composition with Pitch Classes* of 1987. In one volume, Morris pulls together much of the theory generated by American dodecaphonic theorists in the period since Babbitt's "Some Aspects," and while he casts his book as a composition treatise meant to appeal to a readership beyond that of twelve-tone composers and theorists, his study still serves as the best single introduction to American twelve-tone theory, and may, in time, be viewed as the culmination of Babbitt's project in dodecaphonic thinking. Morris's book, like John Rahn's *Basic Atonal Theory* of 1980, addresses both twelve-tone and atonal theory, betraying the influence that Babbitt's rigorous – and some would complain "mathematically oriented" – mode of inquiry has had beyond the bounds of serial theory since the early 1960s. Indeed, Babbitt's early support for Schenker's tonal theory helped fuel interest in an area that has been a central topic for American theorists since the beginnings of the discipline in the late 1950s, while his mathematical modeling has influenced recent neo-Riemannian theory.

The decline of twelve-tone theory?

We return at the end of this chapter to one of the points from which we started out: namely, the relationship between dodecaphonic music and theory. Most twelve-tone writing – no matter how descriptive it may be – at least carries with it a prescriptive aspect. Such a prescriptive dimension is useful so long as there are a significant number of composers who write music that somehow relates to dodecaphonic thinking. But as composers have turned to new ways of thinking about their music in recent years (and perhaps in reaction to modernism generally, with which dodecaphonic thinking is seen to be joined at the hip), the prescriptive component in twelve-tone theoretical writing has tended to recede. American music theory in the 1990s has tended to focus on new ways of understanding familiar dodecaphonic works (Schoenberg, Berg, Webern, Stravinsky) or on ways of understanding less familiar twelve-tone music (Hauer, Klein, Krenek). Thus the trend – at least in English-language twelve-tone writing – seems to be of theory following practice, treating the repertory it addresses no longer as a vital concern, but rather as a historical subject. This probably signals more a transformation of twelve-tone theory than its decline. Whatever the future of dodecaphonic theory may be, it would be difficult to deny that its past plays a central role in our understanding of concert music in the twentieth century.

Bibliography

Babbitt, M. "Remarks on the Recent Stravinsky," *Perspectives of New Music* 2/2 (1964), pp. 35–55; reprinted in *Perspectives on Schoenberg and Stravinsky*, ed. B. Boretz and E. Cone, New York, Norton, 1972, pp. 165–85

review of *Schoenberg et son école* and *Qu'est ce que la musique de douze sons?* by Réne Leibowitz, *JAMS* 3 (1950), pp. 57–60

"Set Structure as a Compositional Determinant," *JMT* 5 (1961), pp. 72–94; reprinted in *Perspectives on Contemporary Music Theory*, ed. B. Boretz and E. Cone, New York, Norton, 1972, pp. 129–47

"Some Aspects of Twelve-Tone Composition," *The Score and I.M.A. Magazine* 12 (1955), pp. 53–61

"Twelve-Tone Invariants as Compositional Determinants," *Musical Quarterly* 46 (1960), pp. 246–59; reprinted in *Problems of Modern Music*, ed. P. H. Lang, New York, Norton, 1962, pp. 108–21

"Twelve-Tone Rhythmic Structure and the Electronic Medium," *Perspectives of New Music* 1/1 (1962), pp. 49–79; reprinted in *Perspectives on Contemporary Music Theory*, ed. B. Boretz and E. Cone, New York, Norton, 1972, pp. 148–79

'Who Cares If You Listen?," *High Fidelity* 8 (1958), pp. 38–40; reprinted as "The Composer as Specialist," in *Esthetics Contemporary*, ed. R. Kostelanetz, Buffalo, NY, Prometheus Books, 1978, pp. 280–87

Words About Music, ed. S. Dembski and J. Straus, Madison, University of Wisconsin Press, 1987

Boulez, P. "An der Grenze des Fruchtlandes (Paul Klee)," *Die Reihe* 1 (1955); trans. S. Walsh in *Stocktakings from an Apprenticeship*, Oxford, Clarendon Press, 1991, pp. 158–87

"Eventuellement . . .," *La Revue musicale* 212 (1952), pp. 117–48; trans. S. Walsh in *Stocktakings from an Apprenticeship*, Oxford, Clarendon Press, 1991, pp. 111–40

"Propositions," *Polyphonie* 2 (1948), pp. 65–72; trans. S. Walsh in *Stocktakings from an Apprenticeship*, Oxford, Clarendon Press, 1991, pp. 47–54

"Schönberg is Dead," *The Score* 6 (1952), pp. 18–22; trans. S. Walsh in *Stocktakings from an Apprenticeship*, Oxford, Clarendon Press, 1991, pp. 209–14

"Stravinsky demeure," in *Musique russe*, ed. P. Souvtchinsky, Paris, 1953, pp. 151–224; trans. S. Walsh in *Stocktakings from an Apprenticeship*, Oxford, Clarendon Press, 1991, pp. 55–110

Eimert, H. *Atonale Musiklehre*, Leipzig, Breitkopf und Härtel, 1924

Grundlagen der musikalischen Reihentechnik, Vienna, Universal Edition, 1964

Lehrbuch der Zwölftontechnik, Wiesbaden, Breitkopf und Härtel, 1952

Eschman, K. *Changing Forms in Modern Music*, Boston, E. C. Schirmer, 1945

Forte, A. *The Structure of Atonal Music*, New Haven, Yale University Press, 1973

Hauer, J. M. "Atonale Musik," *Die Musik* 16/2 (1923), pp. 103–06

Deutung des Melos: Eine Frage an die Künstler und Denker unserer Zeit, Leipzig and Vienna, E. P. Tal, 1923

Lehrbuch der Zwölftontechnik: Vom Wesen des Musikalischen, Berlin-Lichterfeld, Schlesinger, 1923

"Offener Brief," *Die Musik* 17/2 (1924), p. 157

"Sphärenmusik," *Melos* 3 (1922), pp. 132–33

"Die Tropen," *Musikblätter des Anbruch* 6 (1924), pp. 18–21

Vom Melos zur Pauke: Eine Einführung in die Zwölftonmusik, Vienna, Universal Edition, 1925

Vom Wesen des Musikalischen, Vienna, Waldheim-Eberle A. G., 1920

Zwölftontechnik: Die Lehre von den Tropen, Vienna, Universal Edition, 1926

Headlam, D. "Fritz Heinrich Klein's 'Die Grenze der Halbtonwelt' and 'Die Maschine,'" *Theoria* 6 (1992), pp. 55–96

Hill, R. S. "Schoenberg's Tone-Rows and the Tonal System of the Future," *Musical Quarterly* 22 (1936), pp. 14–37

Klein, F. H. "Die Grenze der Halbtonwelt," *Die Musik* 17/4 (1925), pp. 281–86

Krenek, E. "Extents and Limits of Serial Techniques," in *Problems of Modern Music*, ed. P. Lang, New York, Norton, 1962, pp. 72–94

Music Here and Now, New York, Norton, 1939

"New Developments of the Twelve-Tone Technique," *Music Review* 4 (1943), pp. 81–97

Studies in Counterpoint, New York, G. Schirmer, 1940

"A Study of Cadential Formations in Atonal Music," paper presented to the Greater New York Chapter of the American Musicological Society, November 13, 1940

Schoenberg et son école, Paris, Janin, 1947; trans. D. Newlin as *Schoenberg and his School*, New York, Philosophical Library, 1949; reprint New York, Da Capo, 1975
Leibowitz, R. *Introduction a la musique de douze sons*, Paris, L'Arche, 1949
Lewin, D. "A Study of Hexachord Levels in Schoenberg's Violin Fantasy," *Perspectives of New Music* 6/1 (1967), pp. 18–32; reprinted in *Perspectives on Schoenberg and Stravinsky*, rev. edn., ed. B. Boretz and E. Cone, New York, Norton, 1972, pp. 78–92
"A Theory of Segmental Association in Twelve-Tone Music," *Perspectives of New Music* 1/1 (1962), pp. 89–116; reprinted in *Perspectives on Contemporary Music Theory*, ed. B. Boretz and E. Cone, New York, Norton, 1972, pp. 180–207
Martino, D. "The Source Set and Its Aggregate Formations," *JMT* 5 (1961), pp. 224–71
Mead, A. *An Introduction to the Music of Milton Babbitt*, Princeton University Press, 1994
"Some Implications of the Pitch Class/Order Number Isomorphism Inherent in the Twelve-Tone System, Part One," *Perspectives of New Music* 26/2 (1988), pp. 96–163
Messiaen, O. *Technique de mon langage musical*, Paris, Leduc, 1944
Morris, R. D. *Composition with Pitch Classes*, New Haven, Yale University Press, 1987
Oesch, H. "Pioniere der Zwölftontechnik," *Forum Musicologicum: Basler Studien zur Interpretation der alten Musik* 1 (1975), pp. 273–304
Peles, S. "Serialism and Complexity," in *The Cambridge History of American Music*, ed. D. Nicholls, Cambridge University Press, 1998, pp. 496–516
Perle, G. "Evolution of the Tone-Row: The Twelve-Tone Modal System," *Music Review* 2 (1941), pp. 273–87
The Listening Composer, Berkeley, University of California Press, 1990
Serial Composition and Atonality, Berkeley, University of California Press, 1962
Twelve-Tone Tonality, Berkeley, University of California Press, 1977
Rahn, J. *Basic Atonal Theory*, New York, G. Schirmer, 1980
Rufer, J. *Komposition mit zwölf Tönen*, Berlin, M. Hesses, 1952; trans. H. Searle as *Composition with Twelve Tones Related Only to One Another*, New York, Macmillan, 1954
Schoenberg, A. "Composition with Twelve Tones (1)," ed. and trans. D. Newlin in *Style and Idea*, New York, Philosophical Library, 1950; trans. L. Black in *Style and Idea: Selected Writings of Arnold Schoenberg*, ed. L. Stein, Berkeley, University of California Press, 1984, pp. 214–45
Spies, C. "Vortrag/12TK/Princeton," *Perspectives of New Music* 13/1 (1974), pp. 58–136
Stein, E. "Neue Formprinzipien," in *Arnold Schönberg zum fünfzigsten Geburtstag, Sonderheft der Musikblätter des Anbruch*, Vienna, Universal Edition, 1924, pp. 286–303; reprinted in *Von neuer Musik*, Cologne, Marcan-Verlag, 1924, pp. 59–77
Orpheus in New Guises, London, Rockliff, 1953
Stewart, J. L. *Ernst Krenek: The Man and his Music*, Berkeley, University of California Press, 1991
Stockhausen, K. ". . . wie die Zeit vergeht . . .," *Die Reihe* 3 (1957), pp. 15–40
Toop, R. "Messiaen/Goeyvaerts, Fano/Stockhausen, Boulez," *Perspectives of New Music* 13/1 (1974), pp. 141–69
Vogel, M. *Schönberg und die Folgen, Teil 1: Schönberg*, Bonn, Orpheus, 1984
Schönberg und die Folgen, Teil 2: Die Folgen, Bonn, Orpheus, 1997
Yasser, J. *A Theory of Evolving Tonality*, New York, American Library of Musicology, 1932; reprint New York, Da Capo Press, 1975

IIIC TIME

· 20 ·

The evolution of rhythmic notation

ANNA MARIA BUSSE BERGER

It is difficult to exaggerate the importance of rhythmic notation to the early history of Western art music. While the early chant repertories were by no means sung uniformly with even note values, our understanding of their rhythmic performance must remain speculative given the lack of any form of secure rhythmic notations.[1] It was only in the thirteenth century that musicians in Paris first established a rudimentary notation to indicate rhythmic patterns using a system of six rhythmic "modes." Over the next two centuries, as musical culture gradually evolved from one that was largely oral to one that was written, more precise rhythmic notations were developed to accommodate the increasingly complex polyphonic innovations of musicians. At the same time, though, it must not be overlooked that the development of increasingly precise rhythmic notations contributed to these innovations by allowing composers greater stylistic freedom. A good example can be seen in the emergence of the isorhythmic motet, which could not have come into existence without the development of new rhythmic notations. The principal innovation here was the "mensural" system by which ever more complex rhythmic relationships, allowing for duple or triple subdivisions of note values, could be expressed within the duration of a given unit of time. In the late fourteenth and early fifteenth centuries, rhythmic possibilities were further augmented through the use of a system of proportions. Eventually, however, a profusion of competing notational systems led to widespread confusion that the great theorist-reformer Tinctoris tried to eliminate in the late fifteenth century, although with only partial success. It is obviously not possible in this chapter to provide a comprehensive description and analysis of medieval rhythmic notation.[2] I will attempt here mainly to indicate the important conceptual changes of this notational evolution and its broader theoretical underpinnings and implications.

John of Garland

The first kind of rhythmic notation developed in the West originated in the thirteenth century and relied upon a system of modal notation. The most important treatise

1 For an excellent summary of the various theories of rhythmic interpretation for chant, see Hiley, *Western Plainchant: A Handbook*, pp. 373–85.

2 For a good introduction to this topic, see the recent entry "Notation; §3 History of Western Notation" in *NG2*, vol. xviii, pp. 84–140; see also Gallo, "Die Notationslehre"; Berger, *Mensuration and Proportion Signs*.

describing this system, and one upon which all others are based, is *De mensurabili musica* (c. 1250) by John of Garland (Johannes de Garlandia).[3] Garland was probably a *magister* at the University of Paris. (His name may refer to the *clos de Garlande*, a left-bank area in Paris.)[4] *De mensurabili musica* survives in three manuscripts.[5] Even though the earlier two manuscripts are transmitted anonymously, their wordings are quoted by later theorists. Only Jerome's version, a university exemplar, is attributed to Garland.[6] In the following discussion it should be kept in mind that there are sometimes considerable differences between the manuscripts.[7]

The term *musica mensurabilis* refers to rhythmically notated polyphonic music (as opposed to the "unmeasured" music of plainchant – *musica plana*). Garland subdivided measured music into three categories: discant, copula, and *organum purum*. Of these three, discant is most affected by rhythmic notation, which he defined as "the simultaneous sounding of different melodies according to mode and the equivalence of one to another."[8] Almost half of the treatise is devoted to a description of rhythm which is indicated through rhythmic modes, that is, the music of discant.

Garland defined the term *modus*, which he uses synonymously with *maneries*, as "that which runs together through the measurement of time, namely through longs and breves."[9] He distinguished six *species* of mode, that is, six ways in which longs (L) and breves (B) can alternate with one another (see Figure 20.1). Each mode establishes a rhythmic pattern in beats (or *tempora*) within a common unit of three *tempora* (a *perfectio*) that is repeated again and again. The first mode provides the model of the other modes, in that the "correct breve" (*brevis recta*) constitutes one beat (*tempus*), while the "correct long" (*longa recta*) constitutes two beats.

Garland calls Modes 1, 2, and 6 the "correct" or "proper" modes (*modi recti*) because they retain this duple proportion between breve and long. This idea is clearly derived from a long tradition of prose metrics taught in elementary Latin grammars of the period, which all agree that the normative relation between long and short syllables is duple – 2 : 1.[10] Modes 3, 4, and 5 are called "beyond measure" (*modi ultra mensuram*) because here the breve can be either one or two *tempora* long and the long now includes three tempora, which for Garland consists of an addition of a correct, that is, binary long with a correct breve. Garland gives further rules for the succession of two breves in Modes 3 and 4: if there are two breves, they must be made equivalent to a long,

3 See Reimer, *Johannes Garlandia: De mensurabili musica* for a modern edition. Additional medieval treatises based on Garland's text are St. Emmeram, *De musica mensurata* (1279), Anonymous IV, *De mensuris et discantu* (early thirteenth century), and the *Discantus positio vulgaris* (partly from 1225; the rest after 1280).

4 The theorist was not the same person as the poet and grammarian of the same name (see Reimer, *De mensurabili musica*, vol. 1, pp. 1–17).

5 MS Città del Vaticano, Biblioteca Apostolica Vaticana, vaticano latino 5325; MS Bruges, Stadsbibliotheek 528; and in a late thirteenth-century redaction by Jerome of Moravia in Paris, Bibliothèque Nationale, fonds latin 16663.

6 For a detailed description of the manuscripts see Haas, "Die Musiklehre," pp. 104–05.

7 Ibid., p. 148. 8 Reimer, *De mensurabili musica*, vol. 1, p. 35. 9 Ibid., p. 36.

10 Haas, "Die Musiklehre," p. 135.

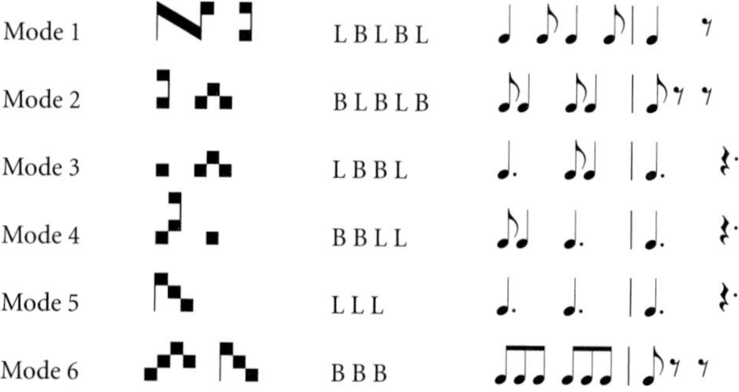

Figure 20.1 Garland's rhythmic modes

meaning the second of two breves is to be sung longer, that is, with the duration of two *tempora*. This process is called "alteration" (*alteratio*) by later theorists.[11]

In Garland's system, modes can also be perfect or imperfect depending upon the note values that end a given phrase (called an *ordo*).[12] The mode is considered perfect if an *ordo* begins with the same note value with which it began, while it is considered imperfect if it ends with a note value different from that with which it began. So as an example, a perfect Mode 1 *ordo* might be LBLBL as shown in Figure 20.1, while an imperfect Mode 1 *ordo* would be LBLB. An *ordo* is a modal phrase which counts the number of repetitions of the rhythmic pattern. So, if a pattern is repeated twice before a rest, it will be called second *ordo*.

Concerning the notation of the modes, Garland distinguishes between notation with text and notation without text. When the music is texted as in the motet or conductus, separate (unbounded) signs are used to designate each note. Figure 20.2 shows several of these signs, including the correct (*recta*) long (two *tempora*), the duplex long (four *tempora*), the plicated long (one *tempus*), the correct breve (one *tempus*), the semibreve (one-half *tempus*), and the plicated breve (one-quarter *tempus*).[13] Similarly, Garland introduced a notation for rests: a vertical line stretching one space on the staff indicates a correct breve rest, a vertical line through two spaces indicates a correct long rest.[14] Moreover, rests can be perfect (when the preceding mode is perfect) or imperfect (when the preceding mode is imperfect). A perfect rest preserves the mode, an imperfect rest changes it.[15] For example, a rest after an imperfect Mode 1 group will change the subsequent section into Mode 2.

Notation without text is based on chains of ligatures (the characteristic notations by which groups of notes are bound to one another). The rhythmic mode can generally be determined by the patterns of ligatures used. For example, Mode 1 is indicated

11 Reimer, *De mensurabili musica*, vol. I, pp. 38–39.

12 The *ordo* is only mentioned in MS Paris, B.N. 16663.

13 Reimer, *De mensurabili musica*, vol. II, p. 53. The *plica* is a short ascending or descending stroke added to the note shape that indicates a division of the *tempus*.

14 Ibid., vol. I, p. 66.

15 Ibid., p. 64.

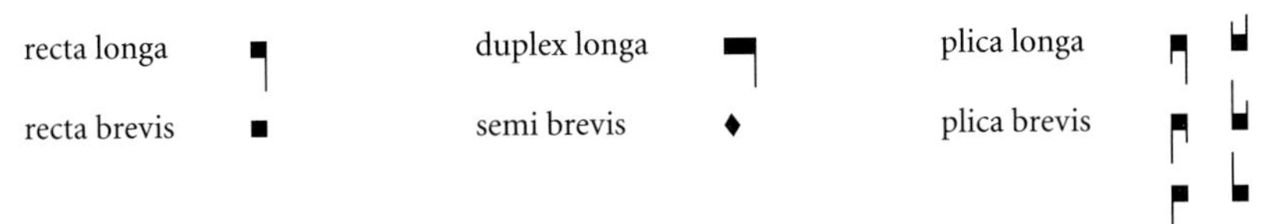

Figure 20.2 Garland's note shapes

by a three-note (*ternaria*) ligature followed by one or more two-note (*binariae*) ligatures (as shown in Figure 20.1).

It cannot be too strongly emphasized that the system of rhythmic modes was a highly contextual one, in which the interpretation of notation (and hence the determination of mode) was based upon the relation of parts to one another. This was particularly the case with the tenor voice in a motet. A ternary ligature might be transcribed as LBL, BLB, LLL, BBL, LLB, or BBB, depending on the context, and only the coordination with the other voices would allow one to determine the modal pattern.

Why did the Notre Dame musicians and theorists conceive rhythm primarily in terms of such repeated patterns? In looking for an answer, we must keep in mind the fact that musical culture until the middle of the thirteenth century was predominantly non-literate; music was conceived in the mind and sung by heart. As I have suggested elsewhere, the primary function of the rhythmic modes was mnemonic.[16] They fulfilled a purpose similar to the versification techniques popular in the thirteenth and fourteenth centuries. In the high Middle Ages, putting material into verse was the most common method of memorizing a subject. It would seem likely that musicians took the idea of repeated patterns from quantitative poetry and applied it to music.

If Garland can be seen as the principal codifier of the medieval rhythmic modes, he was ironically also the first to contribute to the eventual demise of this very system. By allowing individual note and rest shapes to specify certain rhythmic durations independent of the ligature, and by specifying the length of the note within a ligature, Garland helped to undermine the very system of strict metrical patterning he had created. It remained for the other great Notre Dame theorist, Franco of Cologne, to render the rhythmic modes wholly redundant.

Franco of Cologne

Franco's *Ars cantus mensurabilis* ("The Art of Mensurable Music") was probably written around 1280.[17] The author stresses in his prologue that now that plainsong has been explained theoretically by Boethius and practically by Guido, it is time to concentrate on mensural music. And indeed, in the following centuries, Franco is often celebrated, along with Boethius and Guido, as one of the most important music theorists – the

16 Berger, "Mnemotechnics and Notre Dame Polyphony."
17 Frobenius, "Zur Datierung von Franco's *Ars cantus mensurabilis*," pp. 122–27.

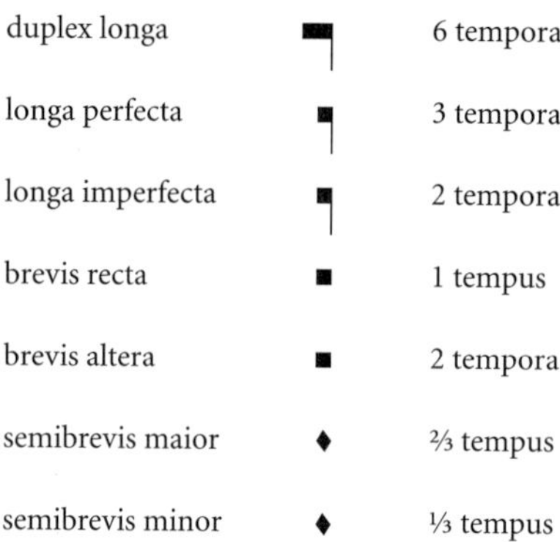

Figure 20.3 Franco's note shapes

"inventor" of mensural music. Little is known about his life. He was probably of German origin; a fourteenth-century manuscript from Saint-Dié describes Franco as a papal chaplain and preceptor of the Knights Hospitallers of St. John of Jerusalem at Cologne.[18] Two music theorists – the English author known as Anonymous IV and Jacques of Liège – also refer to him as a composer. (Jacques mentions a motet by Franco he heard in Paris, although no motets ascribed to Franco seem to have survived.[19])

It is not hard to understand why Franco's treatise was so popular throughout the Middle Ages and Renaissance: it is altogether one of the clearest and best-organized treatises. More importantly, though, it offers a radical improvement over the notational vagaries of Garland's rhythmic modes. Franco begins with the same material as Garland – the rhythmic modes, separate note values, rests, and ligatures – but he reinterprets these in fundamental ways. The most striking difference between Garland and Franco is that in Garland's system, the length of the individual note can only be gathered from the mode itself ("A figure is a representation of a sound according to its mode"). Franco inverts this relation by making the mode dependent upon – and determined by – the individual notes or *figurae* that have incontrovertible durational values: "A figure is a representation of a sound arranged in one of the modes. From this it follows that the figures ought to indicate the modes and not, as some have maintained, the contrary."[20]

Both theorists measured time with the perfect long, but Garland considered this unit to be composite, as the addition of an imperfect or correct long to a breve. Franco, however, considered the perfect long the "first and principal" unit, and all other rhythmic values derived from it. The ternary division of the perfect long, which he associated with the Holy Trinity, was to become the basic mensuration unit in French music theory. And when binary mensurations were described by fourteenth-century French theorists, they were considered secondary to ternary ones.

18 Saint-Dié, Bibl. Municipale, 42, fol. 43v.
19 Anonymous IV, ed. Fritz Reckow, vol. 1, p. 46; and Jacques of Liège, *Speculum musicae*, Book VII, p. 38. 20 *SR*, p. 229.

Mode 1	L L L (Garland's Mode 5) and	
	L B L B L (Garland's Mode 1)	
Mode 2	B L B L B	
Mode 3	L B B L B B L	
Mode 4	B B L B B L B B	
Mode 5	Breves and semibreves (Garland's Mode 6)	

Figure 20.4 Franco's modes

Figure 20.3 shows Franco's note shapes and their durational values.[21] Again, a comparison with Garland reveals that Franco has taken over all note signs from Garland but changed their names. In addition, the semibreve is no longer one-half of a breve, but one-third. Similarly, Franco enlarges the number of rests: a stroke covering three spaces is equivalent to a perfect long rest, a stroke covering two spaces to an imperfect long rest, a stroke covering one space to a breve rest, a stroke covering two-thirds of a space to a major semibreve rest, and one covering one-third space to a minor semibreve rest.[22] (Garland did not include semibreve rests.)

Since Franco considers the perfect long his primary measuring unit, he rearranges the rhythmic modes to reflect this priority. The mode which consists only of perfect longs (Garland's Mode 5) becomes the point of departure for all other modes, with the trochaic subdivision (Garland's Mode 1) considered a species of perfect longs. He also reduces the number of modes to five (see Figure 20.4).[23]

Franco expands Garland's rules for imperfection of the long and alteration of the breve with a number of his own rules. All of these rules are formulated in order to maintain the perfection. A summary of the rules is provided here:

1. First, as a basic rule, a long before a long is always perfect creating Mode 1 (see Figure 20.5a).
2. When a long is followed by a breve, the long becomes imperfect, unless it is separated by a little stroke, sign of perfection or division of mode, in which case the long remains perfect (see Figure 20.5b).[24]
3. When the long is separated from the breve by a little stroke or sign of perfection (*signum perfectionis* or *divisio modi*), the long remains perfect and the breve makes the following long imperfect (see Figure 20.5c).
4. If there are two breves between two longs, the second breve (*brevis altera*) is altered, becoming twice as long as the first breve (see Figure 20.5d).

21 Ibid. 22 Ibid., pp. 236–38. 23 Ibid., pp. 228–29. 24 Ibid., pp. 229–34.

(*a*) Perfect longs

(*b*) Imperfect longs

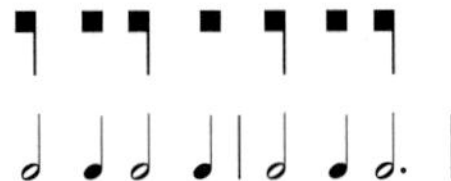

(*c*) Sign of perfection

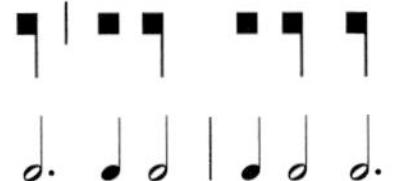

(*d*) Altered breves

(*e*) Semibreves between breves and longs

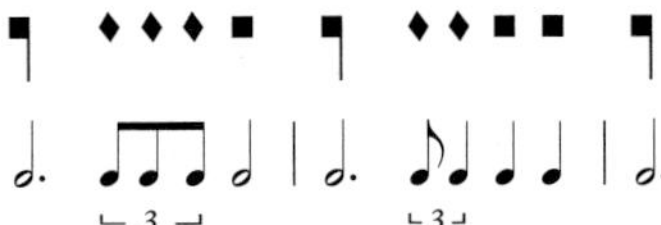

Figure 20.5 Franco's rules for imperfection and alteration

5. If there are three semibreves between breves or longs, they will all be minor semibreves, while if there are two, the first will be a minor semibreve, the second a major semibreve (see Figure 20.5e).

We have, then, in Franco a theorist who in his revisions of an already existing notational system places the separate note value rather than the modal pattern at the center. By notating rhythm using separate note shapes and ligatures, a singer could now read and perform a score without any knowledge of the rhythmic modes. In essence, then, the rhythmic modes have now been made obsolete. This conceptual revolution is inseparable from the fact that writing was becoming more important in the transmission of music. It is characteristic that Franco stresses the significance of notation in his prologue: the treatise was written "for the ready apprehension of our auditors and the thorough instruction of all copiers of mensural music."[25] But even though rhythm could now be understood without using the rhythmic modes, the rhythmic possibilities available to performers were still very much governed by the modal patterns, since Franco only allowed triple division of his basic note values. It remained for the next generation of French theorists to introduce binary mensurations.

Jehan des Murs

At the beginning of the fourteenth century a number of French composers and theorists gradually increased the number of possible note values. Most significantly, they introduced binary mensurations for all note values. These mensurations could be combined in various manners to produce metrical groupings that are the precursors of the modern system of simple and compound meters. Duple divisions, however, were not the unique discovery of fourteenth-century musicians. The duplex longa had always been divided into two equal parts. But now this division was transferred to the long,[26] the breve,[27] and the semibreve.[28] Several of the texts which describe these new mensurations refer to the composer Philippe de Vitry as the inventor of the new system. Whether this is true or not, de Vitry was certainly a well-known advocate of the "new art" of musical composition in the fourteenth century, of which mensural innovations play such a prominent role. Indeed, it is from the title of one of his treatises that the term *ars nova* was taken to describe this new style.[29] But it was Jehan des Murs, a contemporary – and personal acquaintance – of de Vitry, who offered the most comprehensive and systematic treatment of the new mensural innovations of the *ars nova*.

Jehan des Murs was born in the diocese of Lisieux, Normandy c. 1300. By the 1320s he was working in the Collège de Sorbonne in the rue Coupe-gueule. The next years find him at the monastery of Fontevrault in 1326 (Maine-et-Loire), Evreux (by 1332 or 1333), and back in the Sorbonne (1336). By 1342 he was a canon at the collegiate church of Mézières-en-Brenne (Indre). He accepted an invitation from Pope Clement VI to move to Avignon in 1344. A verse letter to Philippe de Vitry in which the latter

25 Ibid., p. 227. Note that I have kept Strunk's original translation of "auditor" for the Latin term *auditorum* rather than James McKinnon's translation as "readers." We must keep in mind that Franco was probably a teacher who would lecture to students.

26 In a short anonymous treatise possibly by Philippe de Vitry, entitled *Ars vetus*, p. 57.

27 In two motets from the appendix to the *Roman de Fauvel*, "Qui secuntur castra – Detractor est nequissima vulpis – Verbum iniquum et dolosum" and "O Philippe perlustris Francorum – Servant regem misericordia – Rex regum." The earliest theoretical explanation of imperfect time is given a few years later in the anonymous *Compendium musicae mensurabilis tam veteris quam novae artis*, p. 40.

28 In an appendix to two anonymous texts in Philippe de Vitry, *Ars vetus*, p. 57 and p. 63.

29 Gallo raises doubts about de Vitry's authorship and suggests the treatises might have been written down by his student (Gallo, "Die Notationslehre," p. 293). Also see Fuller, "A Phantom Treatise."

Figure 20.6 Jehan des Murs's note shapes

is called Bishop of Meaux, a position to which he was elevated in 1351, is the last document with which he can be associated.[30]

Des Murs was a prolific writer on music theory, and his many writings constitute a *summa* of medieval speculative and practical traditions. He was also the author of several astronomical and mathematical treatises.[31] In his first treatise on mensural notation, *Notitia artis musicae* (1321),[32] he introduces binary mensurations of the long, breve, and semibreve. (The *maxima* or *duplex longa*, it will be recalled, had always been divided into two parts.) But he is careful not to offend traditionalists. He stresses the superiority of perfect mensuration and does not yet detail his new notational system.

In his later treatise, *Libellus cantus mensurabilis* (c. 1340), he must have lost his fears of offending conservative theorists. It is the clearest and most influential presentation of the new mensural system. The *Libellus* was copied, translated, and quoted from extensively for the next hundred and fifty years, and used as a textbook in most schools and universities throughout the Middle Ages and Renaissance. The *Libellus* begins with a presentation of five basic note values: the *maxima*, the *longa*, the *brevis*, the *semibrevis*, and the *minima* (see Figure 20.6). With the exception of the minim, each value can be divided into either two or three parts.[33] Next, des Murs describes how the various divisions may be distinguished and combined with one another to form mensurations. Division of the long is termed the *modus*. If the division is triple (three breves), the mode is said to be perfect; if it is duple (two breves), the mode is imperfect. Division of the breve is termed the *tempus*. Again, if the division is triple (resulting in three semibreves) the *tempus* is said to be perfect, and imperfect if the division is in two. Finally, the division of the semibreve is termed *prolatio*, and it is distinguished by either *prolatio maior* (three minims) or *prolatio minor* (two minims). Des Murs offers four signs that can indicate these various mensurations of *tempus* and *prolatio* (see Figure 20.7). A complete circle indicates a perfect *tempus*, while an incomplete circle indicates an imperfect *tempus*; three *puncta* (points) in the center of the circle indicate major prolation, while two *puncta* indicate minor prolation. (Later in the fifteenth century, composers and

30 See also Michels, *Die Musiktraktate des Johannes de Muris*, pp. 1–14; and Gushee, "Jehan des Murs," *NG*, vol. IX, pp. 587–90. We chose to use here – as elsewhere – Jehan des Murs's vernacular name rather than the Latinized "Johannes de Muris."

31 For a detailed discussion of des Murs's work, see Michels, *Die Musiktraktate des Johannes de Muris*.

32 The treatise is known under *Notitia artis musicae*, although des Murs himself called it *Summa musice*. Michels provides a full edition of the treatise.

33 *Libellus cantus mensurabilis*, in *CS* 3, pp. 46–58.

(*a*) Tempus perfectum, prolatio maior ⨀

(*b*) Tempus perfectum, prolatio minor ⨀

(*c*) Tempus imperfectum, prolatio maior

(*d*) Tempus imperfectum, prolatio minor

Figure 20.7 Jehan des Murs's mensuration signs

theorists simplified the notation of the prolations by using a single *punctum* for major prolation and no *punctum* for minor.)

As for the rules guiding the interpretation of a given note value in context, des Murs largely follows Franco's guide. (For instance, a long followed by a breve in the perfect *modus* will still be understood as having the value of two breves, whereas if it is followed by two breves, it will remain perfect, and the two subsequent breves will be interpreted as *brevis recta* and *brevis altera*, respectively.) Rules governing the use of the *punctum divisionis* also remain the same.

The *Libellus* is also noteworthy for containing one of the first detailed discussions of diminution. In the late fourteenth century composers started to notate pieces in larger note values that were then diminished in performance. It is a topic which resulted in much confusion over the next two hundred years, to a large extent because des Murs's explanations were ambiguous. The question was by how much these note values were to be reduced: by one-half, by one-third, or by two-thirds? Consider the following passage by des Murs:

> Diminution of motets always takes place in the tenors, about which it should be noted first that in diminution the long often replaces the maxima, the breve replaces the long, the semibreve replaces the breve, and the minim replaces the semibreve. Secondly, it should be observed that when the tenor is in the imperfect mode, whether it is in perfect or imperfect time, the diminution of notes and rests only happens directly to a half. Thirdly, it should be observed that when the tenor is in perfect mode and imperfect time, diminution is also made directly to a half, as follows: for the long worth three breves are placed breves worth three semibreves. Fourthly, it should be observed that when the tenor is in perfect mode and perfect time, the diminution is made to a third (*per tertium*) and not to a half.[34]

In des Murs's time, diminution was used only in the tenors when these had slower note-values than the other parts. It was not yet associated with any particular mensuration sign. The theorist's rule thus seems straightforward: he recommends substitution of the next-smallest note value in the mensuration that is being replaced. This means that the original mensuration might not be preserved. Confusion arises,

34 *CS* 3, p. 58.

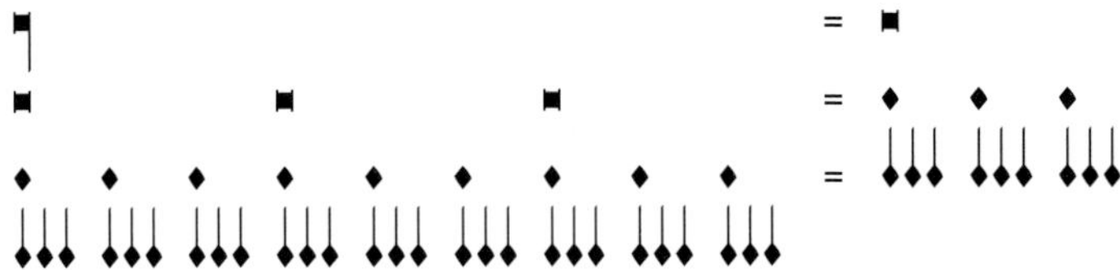

Figure 20.8 Diminution by two-thirds in Jehan des Murs

however, concerning mensurations which are perfect on every mensural level. Des Murs says they should be diminished "per tertium," which would normally be translated as "by one-third." But if one substitutes the longer value as a shorter one, the former is diminished by two-thirds (see Figure 20.8). The notated long, worth twenty-seven minims, is now equal to a perfect breve of nine minims. This, then, would suggest that "per tertium" should be translated as "to one-third." Indeed, two of the most important early fifteenth-century Italian theorists, Prosdocimo de' Beldomandi[35] and Ugolino of Orvieto,[36] both stress in their commentaries on the *Libellus* that "per tertiam partem" could easily be misunderstood as "diminution by one-third," when, in fact, diminution "to one-third" is intended.[37]

Confusion also arises over the interpretation of the so-called "cut signs," *tempus perfectum* and *imperfectum diminutum*, in particular the cut circle, a sign first employed by the composer Baude Cordier in the chanson "Amans, amés secretement" in the early fifteenth century. Theorists in the late fifteenth and early sixteenth centuries disagreed about the interpretation of this sign. Did it signify that the music should be diminished by one-half, by one-third, or simply sung a little faster? It should be noted, however, that no such confusion existed among Italian music theorists of the time as a result of Prosdocimo's and Ugolino's insistence that the cut circle is diminished exactly by one-half. Uncertainty only reigned in the north, where the explanations of Prosdocimo and Ugolino were unknown. Perhaps the blame may be placed upon Anonymous XII, whose treatise was written before 1471. In reference to this sign, the author of this treatise states, "such a song is sung fast, that is 'a breve for a semibreve, a semibreve for a minim, a long for a breve' . . ."[38] But if we apply this advice literally, that is, substitute a perfect breve with a perfect long, and a perfect semibreve with a perfect breve, we end up – just as in des Murs – with a diminution by two-thirds. Yet elsewhere in the same treatise, the author says that "a *cantus* of this kind does not have half removed, but only a third part (that is to say it is sung more quickly than if the stroke were not placed in the middle)."[39] Whether this misunderstanding originated with Anonymous XII or

35 *Expositiones tractatus practice cantus mensurabilis magistri Johannis de Muris*, ed. Gallo, p. 213.
36 *Declaratio musicae disciplinae*, ed. Seay, vol. II, p. 263.
37 See also the more detailed discussion of this issue in my *Mensuration and Proportion Signs*, pp. 125–47.
38 *Tractatus*, ed. Palmer, p. 86. 39 Ibid., p. 65.

not, subsequent generations of German theorists continued to report this erroneous interpretation of des Murs.[40]

It is significant that des Murs devotes considerable space to a discussion of color and talea.[41] For the isorhythmic motet was the first genre whose composition is dependent upon a written – that is, visual – notational system. A composer could not possibly prescribe diminution, inversion, and retrogrades without visualizing the notes or writing them down. Thus, we have within less than a hundred years of the invention of a system of rhythmic notation musical compositions that could not have been created without the very notation in which they were conceived and written. It is therefore not surprising that the early fourteenth-century theorist Jacques of Liège, who bitterly opposed the introduction of binary mensurations, complained that modern musicians are much too obsessed with notation. Such musicians, Jacques chided, should be called "writers of notes and text rather than singers."[42]

Des Murs's mensural system and the mensuration signs he described remained dominant through the end of the sixteenth century, with all their attendant advantages and disadvantages. On the one hand, his system offered composers great rhythmic freedom. Duple and triple divisions of notes could be juxtaposed quite easily. (Des Murs makes it clear that when different *tempora* or *prolationes* are set against one another, the minims remain equivalent.) On the other hand, the introduction of binary mensurations created a new ambiguity: the same note shape can indicate both binary and ternary values. Of course, des Murs was not oblivious to this problem.[43] Whereas in our contemporary mensural system, note values are always divided into two parts, and a division into three parts must be indicated as a triplet, fourteenth-century singers could only determine from the context or the mensuration sign if the note was perfect or imperfect.

Marchetto of Padua

There was another notational system also from the early fourteenth century that allowed for even greater interpretations of the same note-shape – and consequently even greater rhythmic variety. This was the so-called "Italian" school of mensural notation. While the Italian notational system never was able to rival in influence that of its French counterpart, it did provide interesting solutions to rhythmic questions that were not addressed by the French theorists. The most important theorist to detail this

40 Margaret Bent has claimed in "The Early Use of the Sign ⏀" that in the first half of the fifteenth century cut signs were not intended as signs of diminution, but functioned mainly to alert singers that something unusual was happening in the music. Her hypothesis has been challenged by Rob Wegman in "Different Strokes for Different Folks? On Tempo and Proportion in Fifteenth-Century Music."

41 *Libellus*, p. 58. 42 Jacques de Liège, *Speculum musicae*, vol. I. p. 11.

43 *Notitia artis musicae*, ed Michels, p. 75.

notation was Marchetto, a cantor at Padua Cathedral from 1305 to 1308.[44] Beginning in 1308, we find him in various cities in the Veneto. He died in Cesena in 1326.

Marchetto was active as both composer and theorist. He wrote two important treatises highly scholastic in tone and method. The *Lucidarium in artes musicae planae*, one of the most important treatises of Plainchant from the Trecento, was written in 1318 (see **Chapter 14, pp. 492–93**). His second treatise was *Pomerium in arte musicae mensuratae* ("The Garden of Mensural Music") and concerns mensural notation. He wrote the treatise probably between 1318 and 1326 at Cesena.[45]

As we have seen, Jehan des Murs had already placed the perfect *tempus* (represented by the perfect breve) at the center of his mensural system.[46] This is even more true of Marchetto. As seen in Figure 20.9, he divides the breve in four basic manners (*divisiones*). In the first division, *tempus perfectum secundum divisionem duodenariam* (shown by the letter "p" for perfect in Figure 20.9a) the breve is divided into three major semibreves, each of which is then divided on the second level into two minor semibreves, which, in turn, are divided on the third level into semibreves minimae. In *tempus imperfectum secundum ytalicos*, however (shown by the letters "i y" for "imperfectum" and "ytalici"), the breve is divided into up to eight parts (Figure 20.9b); in *tempus perfectum secundum divisionem novenarium* (shown by the letter n for *novenaria*) the breve is divided into nine parts (Figure 20.9c), while in *tempus imperfectum secundum gallicos* (shown by the letters "i g" for "imperfectum" and "gallici," that is, French) it is divided into six parts (Figure 20.9d).[47] Note that Marchetto's system will result in fractions with a denominator of twelve, that is, duodecimal fractions which are divisible into two or three parts. Just as in the French system, the breves of imperfect time are one-third shorter than those of perfect time.

Two other features of the Italian system may be noted. First, Italian theorists were already allowing for the binary division of note values in the late thirteenth century.[48] Second, in a group of semibreves which do not have the same length, the last will always be the longest, unless a stroke has been added. The values of the semibreves within a perfect or imperfect breve depend upon their quantity. If there are two semibreves in imperfect time, they will be equal (in modern notation, two quarter notes, as shown in Figure 20.10a). If there are four semibreves, they will likewise be equal (in modern notation, four eighth notes – Figure 20.10d). But if we have three semibreves in imperfect time, the last one will be twice as long as the first (in modern notation, two eighths and a quarter – Figure 20.10c).[49] If the composer wants the first to be longer, he has to add a descending stroke *via artis* to the first semibreve (see Figure 20.10b).

44 Other theorists are Prosdocimo de' Beldomandi (*Tractatus practice de musica mensurabili ad modum italicorum*, 1404) and Giorgio Anselmi (*De musica*, 1434).

45 There is a later short treatise entitled "Brevis compilatio."

46 *Notitia artis musicae*, trans. *SR*, pp. 264–65.

47 Marchettus de Padua, *Pomerium*, ed. Vecchi.

48 See Gallo, "Die Notationslehre," p. 305.

49 *Pomerium*, pp. 174–75.

(*a*) Tempus perfectum secundum divisionem duodenariam = 1/1

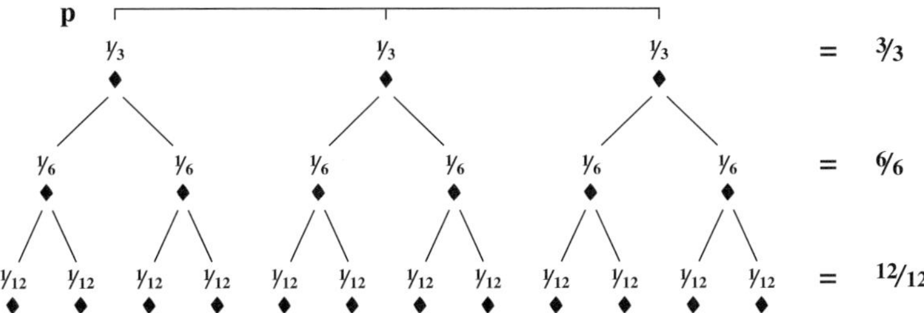

(*b*) Tempus imperfectum secundum ytalicos = 2/3

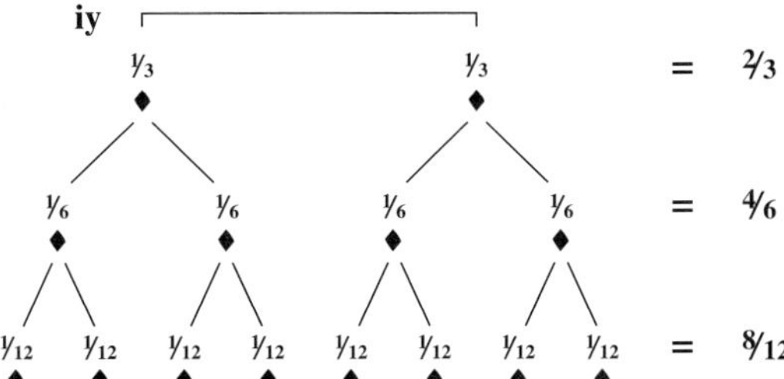

(*c*) Tempus perfectum secundum divisionem novenariam = 1/1

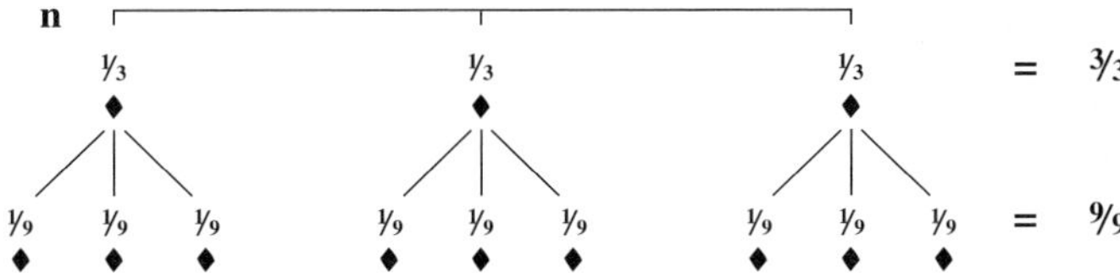

(*d*) Tempus imperfectum secundum gallicos = 2/3

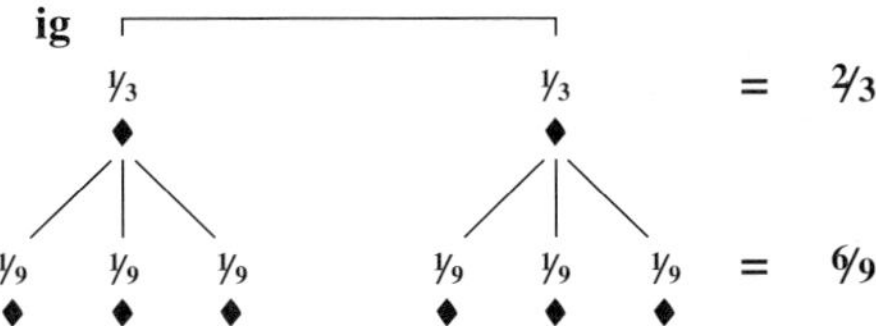

Figure 20.9 Marchetto's *divisiones* in his *Pomerium*

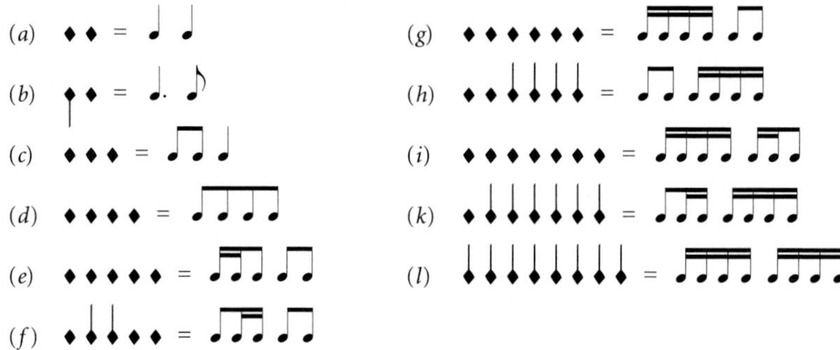

Figure 20.10 Marchetto's semibreves in *tempus imperfectum*

Similarly, if there are six semibreves in imperfect time, the last two will be eighth-notes and the other sixteenth (Figure 20.10g). A descending stroke added to a note makes the note longer (Figure 20.10b), an ascending stroke shorter (Figure 20.10f, h, k, and l). Italian theorists separate the semibreve groups by longer note values, a dot (*punctum divisionis*) or *pontelli*,[50] which are the Trecento's equivalent of the modern bar line.[51]

In short, the Italian notational system is built entirely around the central breve, which is multiplied in order to achieve longer note values (the long and maxima) and divided in order to achieve shorter ones (the semibreve and minim). But it is also a system with limitations: first, it has the same problem as des Murs's system: the same note shape can indicate many different values. Moreover, it does not allow syncopations which extend over the breve. This is probably the main reason why late fourteenth-century Italian theorists gradually replaced the *pontelli* marking breve measures and their divisions with the French system, which allowed syncopations reaching beyond the breve measures. Eventually, as we will see, the idea of the central breve was transformed into an equal breve to indicate proportions.

Excursus: Roman weights, measures and fractions

We have seen that the French and Italian mensural systems are based on a chain of decreasing note values each of which is either a multiple of the next smaller note or a divisor of the next larger one. Moreover, they are divisible into either two or three parts, while in the Italian system, the breve may be divided into as many as twelve smaller units. Why did medieval musicians choose these particular divisions and not

50 Ibid., pp. 62–67.

51 Bar lines start to be used consistently only in fifteenth- and sixteenth-century tablatures. See Apel, *The Notation of Polyphonic Music*, p. 9.

others? To answer this question, we can look at other measuring devices used in the Middle Ages, specifically, the Roman system of weights and measures.

It is important to remember that computation with Hindu-Arabic numerals was only very slowly introduced in Europe.[52] Although Leonardo Fibonacci sang its praises in his *Liber abaci* of 1202, with the exception of a few university-educated people, roman numerals continued to be used throughout medieval Europe. It was only 1494, for example, that the Medici account-books systematically adopted Hindu-Arabic numerals.

The Roman way to write integers is well known. Less known is the Roman system of fractions derived from their units of weights and currency, which was extraordinarily complicated.[53] Its most important feature is that it is based on duodecimal fractions. The largest Roman monetary unit, the *as* or *libra*, was divided into twelve *unciae*, which could themselves each be divided into twelve *scrupuli*. (The British pound sterling had utilized duodecimal divisions until 1971 – the shilling was divided into twelve pennies – and the sign for both the pound sterling and the Italian *lira* is an abbreviation of the word *libra*. Similarly, the word ounce is not only equivalent but also derives from the word *uncia*.) Length was measured through the same system: a *pes* (which corresponds to our foot) is also divided into twelve *unciae*, which is the source of our word inch. It is striking that all of the subdivisions involve the numbers two or three. When Romans wanted to use fractions involving the numbers 5, 7, and 11, they would either round them off to the closest duodecimal fraction or construct them artificially by adding or subtracting one of the fractions given above. So for example, 5/9 of a *libra* would be approximated as follows:

$$\frac{5}{9} = \frac{20}{36} = \frac{20}{3} \times \frac{1}{12} = \frac{20}{3} \textit{ unciae} = 6\tfrac{2}{3} \textit{ unciae} \sim 7 \textit{ unciae (septunx)}$$

Duodecimal divisions called *chronaca* were also used in the measuring of time. The year (called *libra*) is divided into twelve months, while each day is divided into twenty-four hours.[54] The hour (*hora*) was divided into four quarters (*momenta*) which were, in turn, divided into twelve *unciae*. In short, it is striking that the Romans, whether measuring length, currency, or time, employed similar hierarchies of fractions based on a duodecimal system, and even utilized the same names for these divisions.

As we have seen, Roman fractions seriously limited the arithmetic operations one could do. It is important to understand, then, that this system of fractions was in use throughout the Middle Ages. And it was a system that played a decisive influence upon music theorists, particularly in regard to their conceptualization and notation of

52 For a more detailed discussion see my *Mensuration and Proportion Signs*, pp. 33–50.

53 See also Menninger, *Number Words and Number Symbols*, pp. 158–62; and Friedlein, *Die Zahlzeichen und das elementare Rechnen der Griechen und Römer*.

54 See Ginzel, *Handbuch der mathematischen und technischen Chronologie: Das Zeitrechnungswesen der Völker*, vol. III, p. 97.

musical mensuration. For example, the Italian music theorist Nicolò Burzio still felt it necessary to include a section on Roman measurements in his *Musices opusculum* of 1487.[55]

We can see a possible influence in the very notations of the mensural system: the *uncia* in the Roman system is shown by a circle (an alternative sign is the stroke | or \). One half, the *semuncia*, is represented by a figure which resembles the semicircle, a C with a stroke below: Ç. One-quarter is indicated by the inverted C: Ɔ. The similarity of these signs to Jehan des Murs's mensuration signs is striking: the circle corresponds to perfect time, the semicircle to imperfect time. The inverted Ɔ corresponds to the *sesquitertia* proportion, which was not yet described by des Murs but appeared in manuscripts in the late fourteenth century. Rhythmically, this means that four notes are equal to three, that is, every note loses one-fourth of its value, just as in the system of Roman fractions Ɔ signals one-fourth of the *uncia*.

But even more important is the conceptual similarity between the mensural system and the Roman system of weights. First, the breve and the *uncia* are both at the center of their respective systems, and are each multiplied to produce larger values and divided to make smaller values. For example, the medieval scholar Gerbert of Aurillac (later Pope Sylvester II) describes multiplication and division of the identical *uncia* in exactly these terms.[56] In music, the theory of breve equality was popular throughout the late fourteenth to sixteenth centuries, the most famous proponent being Giovanni Spataro, who devoted an entire treatise to the subject.[57] To determine the minor and major mode, a breve is multiplied, while to determine the *tempus* and *prolatio*, it is divided. The length of the breve remains unchanged, while the other note-values vary, depending on the mensuration. Similarly, the value of the *uncia* remains unchanged, whether it is multiplied into *asses* or divided into *scrupuli*.

But there are other obvious correspondences between the Roman fractional system and the medieval mensural system. For example, in both systems each value is fractioned and becomes, in turn, a source of new fractions. As a result we have a chain of decreasing note-values, each of which can be divided: in music the maxima, long, breve, semibreve, and minim; in the Roman system the as, *uncia*, *scrupulus*, and *calcus*. Further, both systems are based on values divisible only by two and by three. The Italian system is most closely related to the Roman fractions in that it also uses duodecimal fractions. Finally, in the late fourteenth-century Italian system, semibreves with an ascending and descending tail are called *dragmae* just as one-eighth of the *uncia* is called a *dragma*. Medieval Italian musicians undoubtedly transferred the name from the system of fractions to the mensural system.

No particular signs were associated with the measurement of time. Yet a study of *chronaca* treatises provides an explanation for the origin of the signs for major and

55 Nicolaus Burtius, *Musices opusculum*, Book III, Chapter 19.
56 *Œuvres de Gerbert*, ed. Olleris, pp. 343–48, 393–96.
57 *Tractato di musica di Giovanni Spataro*.

minor prolation. The shortest time-unit which was thought to be indivisible was called *atomus*,[58] *momentum* or *punctum*.[59] Euclid defines the *punctum* in his *Elements* as the shortest geometric unit.[60] In mensural notation of the fourteenth century, the minim was considered the shortest note-value, the beginning of all time measurement. It is therefore not surprising that fourteenth-century musicians and theorists chose the *punctum* – the sign for the shortest geometric unit – to represent the minim, the shortest note-value: three dots represented three minims of major prolation, two dots two minims of minor prolation.

Proportions

We have seen with Jehan des Murs that when different mensuration signs had hitherto been combined, only the minims remained equal and unchanged. The larger rhythmic units such as the breve or semibreve varied in durational value depending upon the mensural context. By the late fourteenth and early fifteenth centuries, however, composers were using both the breve and semibreve as unchanging units of measurement. To this end, a system of rhythmic proportions was introduced to allow for the notation of such breve and semibreve equivalency. The first theorist to describe such a system was the Italian Prosdocimo de' Beldomandi in his *Tractatus practice cantus mensurabilis* of 1408.[61] Fifteenth-century theorists and composers commonly made use of the following temporal proportions: 2:1, 3:1, 4:1, 3:2, 4:3, 9:8, 9:4, and 8:3.[62] Johannes Tinctoris in his *Proportionale musices* of about 1473–74 dramatically expanded this list by describing twenty-five different rhythmic proportions along with their inversions.

Proportions are usually shown by a fraction in which a certain number of notes of the same kind in the numerator are made equal to a different number of the same kind of notes in the denominator. In Figure 20.11a, which is in imperfect *tempus*, minor prolation, the fraction 3/2 signals that three semibreves after the fraction are sung as fast as two before the fraction. The same proportion, usually called *sesquialtera*, can also be shown by the use of red notes, commonly called coloration and shown here by brackets below the notes (see Figure 20.11b). A number of theorists describe unusual Italian note shapes, but they were not used with much consistency (see Figure 20.11c, where two hollow semibreves each of which includes three hollow minims replace two black semibreves or four black minims, respectively).[63] Finally, mensuration signs may now receive a new interpretation. When ars nova theorists juxtaposed perfect and imperfect *tempora*, there was never any doubt that the minims remained equal. In other

58 Martianus Capella, *De nuptiis Philologiae et Mercurii*, 9971, p. 374; Isidore of Seville, *Etymologiae*, 13.2.3. 59 Berger, *Mensuration and Proportion Signs*, pp. 44–46.

60 Euclid, *Elements*, trans. Heath, p. 155. 61 *CS* 3, pp. 218–19.

62 For a detailed discussion of proportions, see my *Mensuration and Proportion Signs*, pp. 164–226.

63 See especially the *Tractatus figurarum* attributed to Philippus de Caserta.

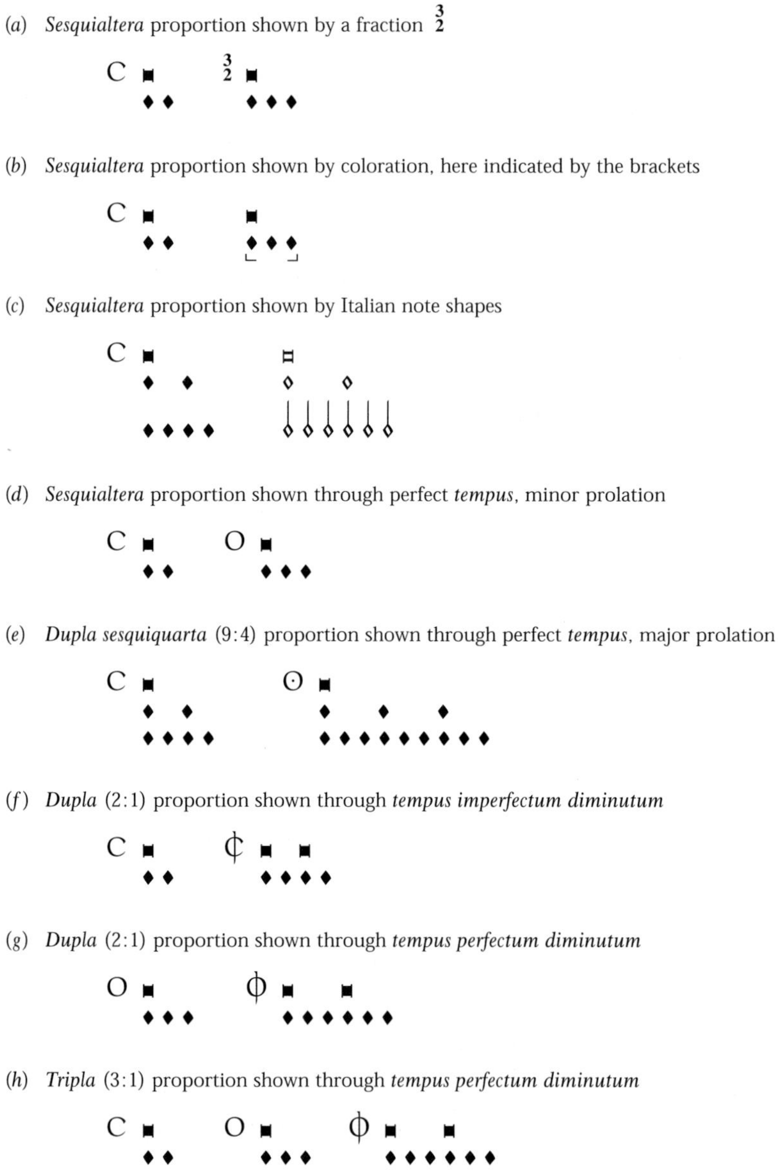

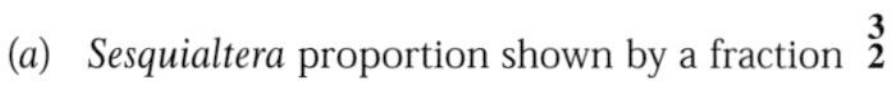

(*a*) *Sesquialtera* proportion shown by a fraction $\frac{3}{2}$

(*b*) *Sesquialtera* proportion shown by coloration, here indicated by the brackets

(*c*) *Sesquialtera* proportion shown by Italian note shapes

(*d*) *Sesquialtera* proportion shown through perfect *tempus*, minor prolation

(*e*) *Dupla sesquiquarta* (9:4) proportion shown through perfect *tempus*, major prolation

(*f*) *Dupla* (2:1) proportion shown through *tempus imperfectum diminutum*

(*g*) *Dupla* (2:1) proportion shown through *tempus perfectum diminutum*

(*h*) *Tripla* (3:1) proportion shown through *tempus perfectum diminutum*

Figure 20.11 Various ways to indicate proportions

words, perfect *tempus* was one semibreve or two minims longer than imperfect *tempus*. Now a *sesquialtera* proportion could be indicated by a mensuration sign (Figure 20.11d, where the circle signals that three semibreves are now equal to two under the semicircle).[64] A 9:4 proportion (*dupla sesquiquarta*) results when nine minims of perfect *tempus*, major prolation are set against four minims of imperfect *tempus*, minor prolation under equal breve (Figure 20.11e).[65] Similarly, a stroke through a mensuration sign may be used as a sign of diminution by one-half.[66] (Recall the confusion that had surrounded the interpretation of *tempus perfectum diminutum* discussed earlier.) Thus, two semibreves of imperfect *tempus*, minor prolation C are equal to four of *tempus imperfectum diminutum* ₵ and signal a 2:1 proportion (*dupla*) (Figure 20.11f). The same proportion pertains to the three semibreves of *tempus perfectum* O which are replaced by six semibreves in *tempus perfectum diminutum* ⏀ (See Figure 20.11g). Finally, in Figure 20.11h, a 3:1 or *tripla* proportion can occur: two semibreves under imperfect *tempus*, minor prolation C are set first against three semibreves of perfect *tempus* which results in a 3:2 proportion. Then the perfect *tempus* is diminished by one-half (when related to perfect *tempus*), which is signaled by the cut circle. Now six semibreves of *tempus perfectum diminutum* are equal to three perfect *tempus* and to two of imperfect *tempus*.[67]

Last, but not least, proportions may be shown by *modus-cum-tempore* signs. These signs consist of a circle or semicircle with or without a *punctum* for prolation followed by the number 2 or 3. Fifteenth- and sixteenth-century theorists offered two different interpretations for these signs: John Hothby, an English theorist who lived in Italy in the second half of the fifteenth century, took the geometric sign as indicating mode (mensuration of the long). A circle or semicircle indicated major mode (how many longs are in maxima), the first number referred to minor mode (how many breves are in a long) and the second number signaled *tempus*. The number 3 indicated a perfect mensuration, the number 2 an imperfect one.[68] For example, in Hothby's interpretation, O 23 would show perfect major, imperfect minor mode, perfect *tempus*, and minor prolation. In a different and less popular interpretation which was first described by the fifteenth-century Bruges theorist, Nicasius Weyts, the circle or semicircle always indicated *tempus*, while the numbers indicated major and minor mode.[69] Thus, Weyts would interpret O 23 as imperfect major mode, perfect minor mode, and perfect *tempus*.

64 The most famous proponent of using mensuration signs to indicate proportions was the early sixteenth-century Bolognese theorist Giovanni Spataro in his *Tractato di musica* (1531). For other theorists see my *Mensuration and Proportion Signs*, pp. 168–78.
65 See for example the anonymous Hebrew treatise *Exposition of the Proportions, according to the teaching of "mestre Joan Violant" [Vaillant], the Teacher of Paris*, pp. 58–76.
66 For a different interpretation see Rob Wegman, "What Is '*acceleratio mensurae?*,'" and my response to his argument in "Cut Signs in Fifteenth-Century Musical Practice."
67 See Florentius de Faxolis's *Liber musices*, written between 1484 and 1492; also see my *Mensuration and Proportion Signs*, pp. 68–69.
68 Hothby, *De cantu figurato*, p. 28.
69 Weyts, *Regule*, in *CS* 3, pp. 262–66.

It is clear, in any case, that these signs were used as signs of diminution by most theorists. First, almost all theorists treating these signs place the regularly recurring *tactus* or *battuta* on the breve rather than semibreve.[70] Second, most theorists consider the sign ○2 equal to the cut circle, which was certainly diminished. Third, many theorists called these signs proportion signs, which by their very nature are diminished. Finally, when ○2 or C2 appeared in a vertical relationship with ○ or C, the note values under ○2 and C2 were always diminished by half.

The use of proportions increased rhythmic possibilities considerably, and composers of the late fourteenth and early fifteenth centuries took full advantage of these new options.[71] But they also exacerbated interpretive ambiguities. When perfect and imperfect time were juxtaposed, which note value was to be the common unit of equal measurement – the breve or the minim? Did a stroke in the mensuration sign indicate diminution by one-half, one-third, or some other value? And how were the *modus-cum-tempore* signs to be interpreted? Finally, there was much confusion regarding the interpretation of proportion signs indicated by fractions. Were proportions cumulative or did they always relate back to the initial mensuration sign? Did the mensuration of the note-values that were being compared in the proportion have to match, or could you compare, for example, three perfect semibreves to two imperfect ones and still call the proportion *sesquialtera*? With the extraordinary growth of complex mensural relations used by composers throughout the late fourteenth and fifteenth centuries, and the equally bewildering profusion of signs to indicate these relations that varied widely depending upon geography, composer, and theoretical tradition, there was a desperate need for someone to step in and try to restore order by proposing a unified and coherent system. This was to be the great accomplishment of Johannes Tinctoris.

Johannes Tinctoris

Tinctoris was born near the Flemish town of Nivelles around 1435. As a youth, he evidently sang at Cambrai under the direction of Dufay. He soon moved to Orléans where he studied at the university and worked as an instructor for choirboys at the cathedral. We find him – probably in 1472 – in the service of King Ferdinand I of Naples as tutor to the King's daughter Beatrice. He met the other great Italian theorist of his day, Franchino Gaffurio, some time in the 1480s when both were in Naples. Tinctoris died in 1511 in Nivelles, having returned there after an active career travelling the continent for Ferdinand in search of singers for his chapel.

Tinctoris was the most prolific music theorist of the early Renaissance, authoring at least twelve treatises. Perhaps his most important and best-known treatise is his dic-

70 Berger, *Mensuration and Proportion Signs*, pp. 151–54.

71 Most of the pieces are transmitted in Modena, Biblioteca Estense, MS ÅM5.24 and Chantilly, Musée Condé 564.

Example 20.1 Cumulative proportions in Tinctoris, *Proportionale musices* (version of Perugia 1013, fol, 90v)

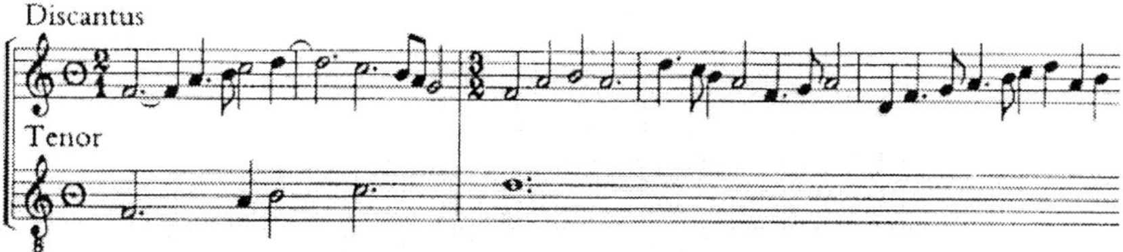

tionary of music, the *Diffinitorium musicae* published in Treviso in 1495. But it was in the domain of mensural theory that Tinctoris produced some of his most influential work. He wrote six treatises on the subject of mensural notation: *Proportionale musices* (c. 1473–74), *Liber imperfectionum notarum musicalium* (1474–75), *Tractatus de regulari valore notarum* (1474–75), *Tractatus de notis et pausis* (1474–75), *Tractatus alterationum* (after 1477), and *Scriptum super punctis musicalibus* (after 1471). His important treatise on counterpoint, the *Liber de arte contrapuncti* of 1477, might also be added to this list, as it contains some important discussions of mensural problems.

Tinctoris's reformist spirit touched virtually every aspect of mensural notation. Let us begin with his discussion of proportions. Before Tinctoris, two successive proportions, even when they were indicated by fractions, were not cumulative. Instead the second was related to the initial mensuration sign. For instance, suppose a piece in imperfect *tempus*, minor prolation uses first a 2:1 proportion and then a 3:2 proportion. Musicians before Tinctoris would relate the 3:2 proportion to the initial imperfect *tempus*, that is, as a simple *sesquialtera* proportion. Tinctoris, on the other hand, would multiply the 2:1 with the 3:2, resulting in a 6:2 or 3:1 fraction (*tripla* proportion). The reason was simple: before Tinctoris proportions were used interchangeably with mensuration signs and therefore were treated like mensuration signs, not fractions. Tinctoris, who was familiar with the new Hindu-Arabic arithmetic, recognized that any two numbers one on top of the other looked like a fraction, even though they represented a ratio, and could therefore be treated as such and multiplied just as in arithmetic.[72] In his *Proportionale musices*, Tinctoris gives an example in perfect *tempus*, major prolation which begins in the discant with a 2:1 proportion followed by a 3:2 proportion (see Example 20.1).[73] The 3:2 proportion is related not to the initial perfect *tempus*, major prolation, but to the 2:1 proportion, resulting in a 3:1 proportion achieved by multiplying the two initial proportions with each other: $2:1 \times 3:2 = 6:2$ or 3:1.

72 Johannes Tinctoris, *Proportionale musices*, p. 13; Seay trans., pp. 3–4.
73 Seay's transcription in *Proportionale musices* is incorrect. The following transcription is based on Perugia, Biblioteca Comunale, MS 1013, fol. 90v.

Example 20.2 Guillaume Dufay, "Qui cum patre," from *Missa Sancti Anthonii*; cited in Tinctoris, *Proportionale musices*, p. 58

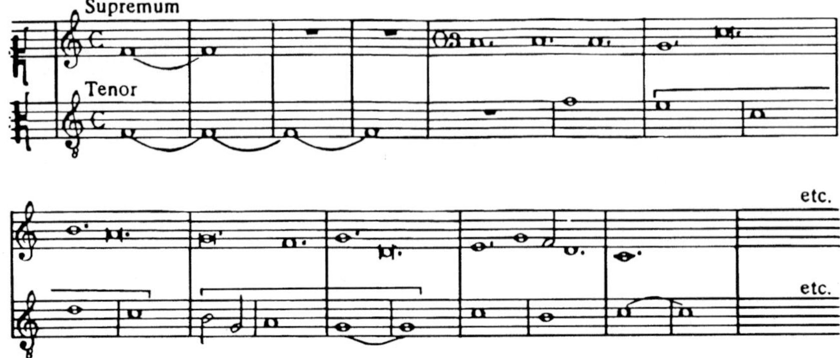

Before Tinctoris, theorists were not concerned that the mensurations of the compared note-values in a proportion had to match. For example, Ugolino of Orvieto and John Hothby both compared perfect to imperfect breves in their music.[74] Guillaume Dufay also juxtaposed three perfect breves with two imperfect breves (in his *Missa Sancti Antonii*), designating the proportion with the number 3, which stands for *sesquialtera*, or 3:2 (see Example 20.2). Indeed, Tinctoris was quite critical of Dufay's practice of comparing perfect with imperfect breves in proportions designed to compare notes of the same duple mensuration. He criticized him further for calling the relationship *sesquialtera* proportion, when in fact it is a *dupla sesquiquarta* or 9:4 proportion on the semibreve level. Finally, he disapproved of Dufay's use of signs: the derived proportion should have been indicated by ○ 9/4 to show the relationship of semibreves, rather than by the single number 3 (which, as Tinctoris explained, was meant to signal a 3/2 proportion showing the relationship of breves.

Why was Tinctoris so obsessed with comparing notes of the same mensuration? Again, a consideration of contemporaneous accounting systems outside of music may hold a clue: in the present case, a popular method employed in the commercial arithmetic books of the fifteenth and sixteenth centuries. One of the most important calculations taught in these treatises is the "Rule of Three," also known as the Golden Rule or the Merchant's Key, which is nothing but a simple means for calculating proportions between non-equivalent terms (see the window on p. 651).[75]

Just as a merchant should not confuse ounces with pounds, a composer should not confuse breves with semibreves. The Rule of Three thus may help the composer to determine the proper proportion between unequal durational values. To do this, we need first to answer two questions: (1) how many notes of a certain value (say, semi-

74 See my *Mensuration and Proportion Signs*, p. 197. 75 Ibid., pp. 198–210.

The Rule of Three

A medieval arithmetic treatise published anonymously in Treviso provides one of the first descriptions of calculating proportions using a technique known as the Rule of Three:

> The Rule of Three Things is this: that you should multiply the thing which you wish to know, by that which is not like it, and divide it by the other. And the quotient which arises will be of the nature of the thing which has no term like it. And the divisor will always be dissimilar (in weight, in measure, or in other difference) to the thing which we wish to know.
>
> In setting forth this rule, note that in every case which comes under it there are only two things of different nature, of which one is named twice, by two different numbers, and the other is named once, by one number alone.
>
> If 1 lira of saffron is worth 7 lire of pizoli, what will 25 lire of this same saffron be worth? Here are mentioned both the saffron and the money, but the saffron is mentioned twice by two different numbers, 1 and 25; and the money is mentioned once, by the number 7. So this is not called the Rule of Three Things because there are three things of different nature, for one thing is mentioned twice (trans. D. E. Smith, *A Source Book in Mathematics*, New York, 1959, p. 12).

If we apply the Rule of Three to the example given here, 7 is multiplied by 25, which makes 175. The latter number, in turn, is divided by 1, making again 175. There were two ways of arranging the figures. The first was used by medieval Arab mathematicians and taken over by Leonardo Fibonacci:

The most common way of notating these relationship in the Renaissance was linearly as follows:

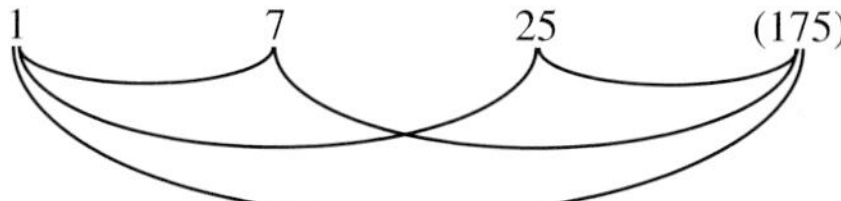

The curved lines indicate the relationship between the numbers. 1 stands to 7 in the same relationship as 25 to 175. Moreover, 1 to 25 stands in the same relationship as 7 to 175. The product of the first and the last number (1 × 175) is the same as that of the two middle numbers (7 × 25). The relationship indicated by the curves provides an important tool for checking whether the calculations are correct.

breves) after the proportion sign replace how many notes of the same value before it? and (2) What is the number of shortest notes within a perfection after the proportion sign? If the proportion sign takes the form of a fraction, the answer to the first question is obvious (it is indicated by the fraction). So in Figure 20.12, we have perfect *tempus*, minor prolation followed by a 4:3 (*sesquitertia*) proportion. We know therefore that we have to compare four to three semibreves. The answer to the second question, though, is not so obvious. Before Tinctoris, the mensuration of the compared note-

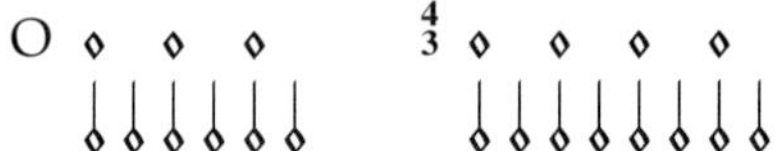

Figure 20.12 *Sesquitertia* (4:3) proportion after perfect *tempus*, minor prolation

value could change after the proportion sign, so that determining the number of short values within a perfection is not so easy. For example, a composer might well have compared imperfect semibreves before the proportion to perfect semibreves after the proportion.

On the other hand, once one decides with Tinctoris that the mensuration of the compared note-value remains the same, the Rule of Three serves to find this answer. In Figure 20.12 the shortest note value that both sections share is the minim. The section in ○ includes six minims within a perfection, the 4/3 (*sesquitertia*) section eight. The relationships are shown in Figure 20.13.

The number 3 relates to the number 6 as 4 to 8, and $3 \times 8 = 4 \times 6$. All the conditions for the Rule of Three are thus fulfilled.

Let us return to the Dufay example criticized by Tinctoris (Example 20.1). Dufay compares two imperfect breves with three perfect breves. None of the relationships discussed by Tinctoris would work in the *sesquialtera* example by Dufay. If we take minims as the shortest common value, we obtain the following numerical sequence that fulfills none of the conditions of the Rule of Three.[76]

2 3 8 18

Just as a merchant cannot conflate ounces with pounds, a composer has to change breves into semibreves before computing how many semibreves of the same mensuration are included respectively between C and ○ 3/2, namely 9 and 4. Only after labeling the proportion 9:4 can he obtain the correct computation for the Dufay example (see Figure 20.14). Four semibreves relate to nine as eight minims relate to eighteen. In short, Tinctoris was not a nit-picking theorist; rather, he applied the lessons he may have learned in commercial arithmetic to mensural proportions.

Tinctoris's discussion of the compared note-value in proportions from the Dufay example also leaves no doubt that he demands minim equality when perfect and imperfect time are juxtaposed. And it seems likely that the much-admired Dufay was not the only composer who faltered in this respect. Tinctoris is particularly critical of composers who use mensuration signs to indicate proportions, since such usage is almost always connected with breve equality.[77] Franchino Gaffurio echoed Tinctoris's criticism of those composers who favored breve equality directly in 1496: "Those who call a semibreve or *tempus imperfectum* greater in value because it equals half a breve, and

76 The 3:2 refers to Dufay's proportion (he writes only 3, but clearly means 3:2); the number 8 refers to the 8 minims (within two imperfect breves) before the proportion, the number 18 to the 18 minims (within three perfect breves) after the proportion. 77 *Proportionale*, pp. 46–47, 48.

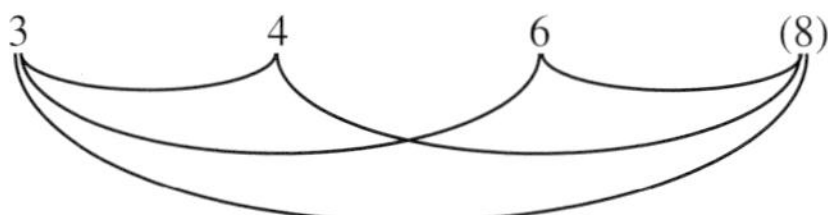

Figure 20.13 Calculations using the Rule of Three

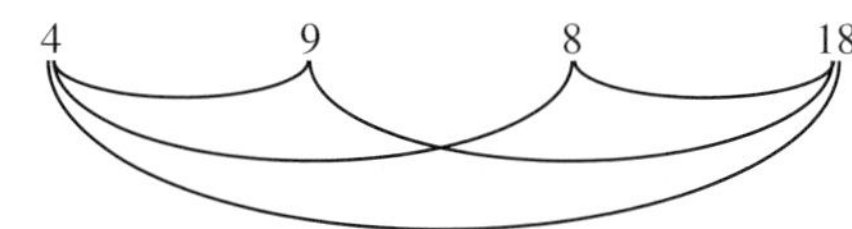

Figure 20.14 Calculations using the Rule of Three

lesser when it equals a third of a perfect breve, are in error, since one semibreve is always equal to another in the same prolation."[78] So successful were the mensural reforms of Tinctoris and Gaffurio that by the early sixteenth century breve equality was only a theoretical speculation, with the Italian theorist Giovanni Spataro as one of its few advocates.[79]

Another area that Tinctoris tried to reform was the use of the *modus-cum-tempore* signs (○ 3, ○ 2, C 3, and C 2). He was adamantly opposed to the use of these signs because they used the circle or semicircle to indicate *modus*, while he felt the geometric signs should be reserved exclusively for *tempus*. Moreover, according to Tinctoris, the numbers 2 and 3 could be signs of diminution only within a fraction.[80] The only *modus-cum-tempore* signs Tinctoris allowed consisted of rests to indicate mode, the circle or semicircle to indicate *tempus*, and a fraction or stroke to indicate the diminution by half.[81] Tinctoris's reforms in this area were less successful than with the equal breve. Musicians became confused about the meaning of the various signs and gradually abandoned the plethora of older mensuration signs. Indeed, the ever-reactionary Spataro lamented in a letter of 1529 to Giovanni del Lago: "in our times, the signs arranged by the ancients are held in little esteem . . . they only use this sign À; and of the proportions, they only use the *sesquialtera*."[82] By 1540, when Sebald Heyden published his treatise *De arte canendi*, it was no longer assumed that musicians were able to understand complex mensuration signs. He thus included transcriptions (*resolutiones*) of all pieces with complex time signatures translated into À. This suggests that musicians seemed to have lost the ability to interpret mensuration and proportion signs. For them every note-value was fundamentally binary in conception, just as it remains today in our modern notational system.

78 *Practica musice*, Book II, Chapter 8; Miller trans., p. 88.
79 *Tractato di musica*.
80 *Proportionale*, pp. 55, 45.
81 Ibid., p. 55; also see my *Mensuration and Proportion Signs*, pp. 157–63.
82 *A Correspondence of Renaissance Musicians*, ed. Blackburn et al., p. 336.

Bibliography

Primary sources

Amerus, *Practica artis musicae* (1271), ed. C. Ruini, *CSM* 25 (1977)

Anonymous IV, *De mensuris et discantu* (after 1280, poss. early 14th c.), ed. F. Reckow as *Der Musiktraktat des Anonymous IV*, 2 vols., *AfMw* 4–5 (1967); trans. J. Yudkin as *The Music Treatise of Anonymous IV: A New Translation*, *MSD* 41 (1985)

Anonymous VII, *De musica libellus* (postdates Franco), *CS* 1, pp. 378–83; see also S. Pinegar, "Exploring the Margins: A Second Source for Anonymous 7," *JAMS* 12 (1993), pp. 213–43

Anonymous XII, *Tractatus et compendium cantus figurati*, ed. J. Palmer, *CSM* 35 (1990)

Anonymous of St. Emmeram, see St. Emmeram, below

Anselmi, G. *De musica*, ed. G. Massera, Florence, L. Olschki, 1961

Burzio, N. *Musices opusculum*, ed. G. Massera as *Nicolai Burtii parmensis florum libellus*, Florence, L. Olschki, 1975; trans. C. Miller as N. Burtius, *Musices opusculum*, *MSD* 37 (1983)

Compendium mensurabilis tam veteris quam novae artis, ed. G. Reaney in *CSM* 30 (1982), pp. 33–41

Dietricus, *Regula super discantum* (c. 1275), ed. H. Muller as *Eine Abhandlung über Mensuralmusik in der Karlsruher Handschrift St. Peter pergamen. 29a*, Leipzig, B. Teubner, 1886

Discantus positio vulgaris (partly from c. 1225; the rest after 1280), ed. S. M. Cserba O.P. in *Hieronymus de Moravia O.P. Tractatus de Musica*, Regensburg, F. Pustet, 1935; trans. J. McKinnon in *SR*, pp. 218–22

Euclid, *The Thirteen Books of Euclid's Elements*, trans. T. Heath, New York, Dover, 1956

Exposition of the Proportions, according to the Teaching of "mestre Joan Violant" [Vaillant], the Teacher of Paris, Florence, Biblioteca Nazionale Centrale, MS Magl. III.70, ed. I. Adler in *Hebrew Writings Concerning Music*, Munich, G. Henle, 1975, pp. 55–77

Florentius de Faxolis, *Liber musices*, Milan, Biblioteca Trivulziana, MS 2146, fols. 42v–94v

Franco of Cologne, *Ars cantus mensurabilis* (c. 1280), ed. G. Reaney and A. Gilles, *CSM* 18 (1974); trans. O. Strunk in *SR*, pp. 226–45

Gaffurio, F. *Practica musice*, Milan, G. Le Signerre, 1496; facs. Farnborough, Gregg, 1967, Bologna, Forni, 1972 and New York, Broude, 1979; trans. C. Miller as *Practica musicae*, *MSD* 20 (1968); trans. I. Young as *The "Practica musicae" of Franchinus Gafurius*, Madison, University of Wisconsin Press, 1969

Gerbert of Aurillac, *Œuvres de Gerbert*, ed. A. Olleris, Clermont-Ferrand, F. Thibaud, 1867

Hothby, J. *De cantu figurato*, in *CS* 3 (1869), pp. 330–32

Jacques of Liège, *Speculum musicae*, ed. R. Bragard, *CSM* 3 (1955)

John of Garland, *De mensurabili musica*, ed. E. Reimer, *AfMw* 10–11 (1972); trans. S. Birnbaum as *Johannes de Garlandia Concerning Measured Music*, Colorado Springs, Colorado College Music Press, 1978; partial trans. in *SR*, pp. 223–26

Lambertus, *Tractatus de musica* (c. 1275), in *CS* 1 (1864), pp. 251–81

Marchetto of Padua, *Pomerium*, ed. G. Vecchi, *CSM* 6 (1961); partial trans. O. Strunk in *SR*, pp. 251–61

Brevis compilatio, ed. G. Vecchi in "Su la composizione del *Pomerium* di Marchetto da Padova e la *Brevis compilatio*," *Quadrivium* 1 (1956), pp. 153–205
Modena, Biblioteca Estense, MS Alpha M.5.24
Murs, J. de, *Libellus cantus mensurabilis*, in *CS* 3 (1869), pp. 46–58
Notitia artis musicae, ed. U. Michels, in *CSM* 17 (1972), p. 75; partial trans. O. Strunk in *SR*, pp. 261–69
Odington, Walter of, *Summa de speculatione musicae* (c. 1300), ed. F. F. Hammond, in *CSM* 14 (1970); Part IV trans. J. Huff, *MSD* 31, 1973
Prosdocimo de' Beldomandi, *Expositiones tractatus practice cantus mensurabilis magistri Johannis de Muris*, in *Prosdocimi de Beldemandis Opera*, ed. F. A. Gallo, Bologna, Antiquae musicae italicae studiosi, 1966
Tractatus practice de musica mensurabili ad modum italicorum, *CS* 3 (1869), pp. 228–48
St. Emmeram's Anonymous, *De Musica Mensurata* (1279); trans. and ed. J. Yudkin as *De Musica Mensurata: The Anonymous of St. Emmeram, Complete Critical Edition, Translation, and Commentary*, Bloomington, Indiana University Press, 1990
Spataro, G. *Tractato di musica di Giovanni Spataro musico bolognese nel quale si tracta de la perfectione de la sesqualtera producta in la musica mensurata exercitate*, Venice, B. de Vitali, 1531; facs. Bologna, Forni, 1970
Tinctoris, J., *Proportionale musices*, Brussels, Bibliothèque Royale, MS II 4147, fols. 101r–116v, and Ghent, Universiteitsbibliotheek, MS 70 (71), fols. 187r–206r; ed. A. Seay, *CSM* 22/2a (1978); trans. A. Seay as *Proportions in Music*, Colorado College Music Press, Colorado Springs, 1979
Tractatus figurarum (attr. Philippus de Caserta), ed. and trans. P. Schreur as *Treatise on Noteshapes*, Lincoln, University of Nebraska Press, 1989
Ugolino of Orvieto, *Declaratio musicae disciplinae*, ed. A. Seay, 3 vols., *CSM* 7 (1959–62)
Philippe de Vitry, *Ars nova*, ed. G. Reaney, A. Gilles, and J. Maillard as *Philippi de Vitriaco ars nova*, *CSM* 8 (1964); trans. L. Plantinga as "Philippe de Vitry's *Ars nova*: a Translation," *JMT* 5 (1961), pp. 204–23
Weyts, N., *Regule*, in *CS* 3 (1869), pp. 262–6

Secondary sources

Apel, W. *The Notation of Polyphonic Music, 900–1600*, 5th edn., Cambridge, MA, Harvard University Press, 1953
Bent, M. "The Early Use of the Sign ⦶," *Early Music* 24 (1996), pp. 199–225
"On the Interpretation of Cut Circle ⦶ in the Fifteenth Century." *JAMS* 53 (2000), 597–612
Berger, A. M. Busse, *Mensuration and Proportion Signs: Origins and Evolution*, Oxford University Press, 1993
"Cut Signs in Fifteenth-Century Musical Practice," in *Music in Renaissance Cities and Courts: Studies in Honor of Lewis Lockwood*, ed. J. Owens and A. Cummings, Warren, MI, Harmonic Park Press, 1997, pp. 101–12
"Mnemotechnics and Notre Dame Polyphony," *JM* 14 (1996), pp. 263–98
Blackburn, B. J., E. E. Lowinsky and C. A. Miller, eds., *A Correspondence of Renaissance Musicians*, Oxford, Clarendon Press, 1991

Friedlein, G. *Die Zahlzeichen und das elementare Rechnen der Griechen und Römer und des christlichen Abendlandes*, Erlangen, A. Deichert, 1869; reprint Wiesbaden, M. Sändig, 1968
Frobenius, W. "Zur Datierung von Fanco's *Ars cantus mensurabilis*," *AfMw* 27 (1970), pp. 122–27
Fuller, S. "A Phantom Treatise of the Fourteenth Century? The *Ars nova*," *JM* 6 (1985), pp. 23–50
Gallo, F. A. "Die Notationslehre im 14. und 15. Jahrhundert," in *Die mittelalterliche Lehre von der Mehrstimmigkeit*, *GMt* 5 (1984), pp. 257–356
Ginzel, F. K. *Handbuch der mathematischen und technischen Chronologie: Das Zeitrechnungswesen der Völker*, Leipzig, J. C. Heinrichs, 1906
Haas, M. "Die Musiklehre im 13. Jahrhundert von Johannes de Garlandia bis Franco," in *GMt* 5 (1984), pp. 91–158
Hiley, D. *Western Plainchant: A Handbook*, Oxford University Press, 1993
Menninger, K. *Number Words and Number Symbols: A Cultural History of Numbers*, trans. P. Broneer, Cambridge, MA, Harvard University Press, 1966
Michels, U. *Die Musiktraktate des Johannes de Muris*, *AfMw* 8 (1970)
Reaney, G. ed., *Early Fifteenth-Century Music*, 7 vols., American Institute of Musicology, 1955
Smith, D. E., *A Source Book in Mathematics*, 2 vols., New York, Dover, 1959
Wegman, Rob, "What is *acceleratio mensurae?*," *Music & Letters* 73 (1992), pp. 515–23
"Different Strokes for Different Folks? On Tempo and Diminution in Fifteenth-Century Music," *JAMS* 53 (2000), pp. 461–505

· 21 ·

Theories of musical rhythm in the eighteenth and nineteenth centuries

WILLIAM E. CAPLIN

Everyone agrees: it is difficult to talk about rhythm in music, or, for that matter, the temporal experience in general. Compared with spatial relations, which appear to us as fixed and graspable, temporal ones seem fleeting and intangible. As a result, the language of time and rhythm is complex, contentious, and highly metaphorical. Considering that theorists today continue to have difficulty dealing with the metrical and durational organization of music from the eighteenth and nineteenth centuries – our most familiar music – it should come as no surprise that theoretical writings from those centuries often present themselves as perplexing and in need of explication. Though their manner of formulation may at times seem odd or convoluted, these theorists nonetheless ask many of the same questions about musical rhythm that underlie current concerns: What is a metrical accent? How do the profusion of time signatures relate to each other? Do the groupings of measures create a sense of larger-scale rhythm? Can various durational patterns be organized according to some scheme or another? How does our understanding of musical rhythm affect performance, especially tempo, phrasing, and articulation?

Like many other domains of music theory, rhythmic theories are largely formulated in relation to a distinct compositional practice. Thus when compositional styles change, theorists respond by modifying their conceptions and formulating new ones in order better to reflect such transformations in practice. The high Baroque style, with its motoric pulses, regularized accentuations, and dance-derived rhythms, induced early eighteenth-century theorists to focus in detail on the classification of various metrical and durational patterns and to begin accounting for that most elusive concept – metrical accent. Later in the century, the emergence of the galant and Classical styles, with their emphasis on formal articulations, melodic prominence, and balanced phrasings, stimulated theorists to consider the rhythms projected by phrase groupings and cadential goals. And some nineteenth-century Romantic idioms, whose phrase rhythms are even more regularized and symmetrical, encouraged theorists to promote varying (and often competing) schemes of hypermetrical organization.

Though changes in musical style certainly prompted theoretical refinement and innovation, a strong conceptual inertia is evident in these writings. Thus early eighteenth-century rhythmic theory continued to be highly influenced by elements of the Renaissance mensural system, and it was not until much later in that century that an entirely modern conception of musical meter found systematic expression. This notion of meter then functioned as the basis for most nineteenth-century approaches. So, despite significant changes in compositional style, the sense of a "common practice" of rhythmic organization is reflected through strong conceptual continuities in the theoretical thought of both centuries.

Eighteenth-century theories: transition, innovation

Theories of rhythm in the eighteenth century (which more rightly includes the last two decades of the seventeenth century) concern themselves largely with describing and explaining the *modern system* of rhythm (as opposed to the earlier *mensural system* of the Middle Ages and Renaissance). In the first half of the century, rhythmic theories generally reflect Baroque practice but still incorporate considerable vestiges of the mensural system. Theorists of the time were highly preoccupied with classifying the numerous time signatures commonly employed and with trying to account for the phenomenon of metrical accent. Moreover, the Baroque use of conventionalized durational patterns (especially in dance-related genres) motivated some theorists to undertake complex taxonomies derived from the Greek poetic meters. The second half of the century saw the emergence of novel ideas that effected a decisive break with earlier conceptions. This new view posited a fundamental dichotomy between a strictly hierarchical organization of metrical accents (within which various forms of nonmetrical accentuation could occur) and the fully unconstrained use of varying durational values. The influence of the new galant style prompted later eighteenth-century theorists to regard the groupings of individual measures into phrases of varying lengths as distinctly "rhythmical," thus leading to the creation of sophisticated descriptions of phrase-structural procedures.

From the mensural system to the modern system

Prior to the seventeenth century, rhythm in Western music was organized according to the mensural system.[1] The (conceptual) starting point of the mensural system is a single *long* duration (which is sometimes doubled into a *duplex long*). A top-down process of division by three (*perfection*) or by two (*imperfection*) yields a faster level of motion consisting of *breves*. The same process divides the breve into two or three *semibreves*, and each semibreve into two or three *minims*. Various rules of perfection and imperfection permit a limited number of durational patterns to obtain among these values at a given level of motion. More complex durational relations arise through the use of *proportional signs*, which in the case of the *sesquialtera* (3:2), for example, stipu-

1 See **Chapter 20, passim** for details.

lates that three minims sound within the same time span as two prior minims. Thus unlike our modern system, in which the note values remain fixed and independent of the time signature, durations in the mensural system are contextually dependent to some extent upon the specific mensuration and proportion indicated by the signs.[2] The absolute duration of notes, and hence, their tempo, is determined by the *tactus*, which resides at the level of the semibreve (occasionally the breve). Each tactus embraces a single down-and-up motion of the hand (*thesis* and *arsis*) and moves at a moderate rate of speed, corresponding roughly to the pulse rate of a human at rest. In the case of a duple division of the semibreve, the tactus motions are equal in length; with a triple division, the tactus remains two-part, but the thesis lasts twice as long as the arsis.

During the seventeenth century, the mensural system gradually evolved into the modern system of note values and meters.[3] The breakdown of the older system occurred as part of a broader historical process (begun in the thirteenth century and continuing into the twentieth) of composers employing ever shorter note values. Eventually the long and the breve were rarely used, and the division of the minim (our half note) into values corresponding to quarter, eighth, and sixteenth notes created durational relations that could no longer be governed by the mensural principles of perfection and imperfection.[4] In order to indicate regular patternings of these shorter values, the traditional mensuration and proportional signs took on new meanings and were eventually transformed into our modern *time signatures*. Thus the mensuration signs C and ¢ (originally indicating *tempus imperfectum* and *tempus imperfectum diminutum* respectively) became general symbols for duple meter, while various triple-meter signatures evolved out of proportional signs, such as 3/2 and 3/4. The demands for an increasingly wider spectrum of tempos, especially within an individual movement, led to the mensuration and proportional signs specifying varying rates of tactus motion. In addition, tempo became more intimately linked to the length of the note values employed in a work, so that pieces using relatively long durational values (combinations of half notes and quarter notes) were meant to be performed more slowly than those using shorter note values.

Since the changes in compositional practice just sketched occurred gradually and over a long period of time, no one theorist of the seventeenth century stands out as articulating a consistent and comprehensive rhythmical system, though the contributions of Michael Praetorius (1614–19),[5] Marin Mersenne (1636–37),[6] Charles Butler (1639),[7] Giovanni Maria Bononcini (1673),[8] to name but a few, are frequently cited by historians. Instead, theoretical writings from this period present discrepant accounts on many issues and display a hotchpotch of conservative and progressive views. It is

2 Dahlhaus, "Entstehung des modernen Taktsystems," p. 223.

3 See Houle, *Meter*, Chapter 1. Houle's study, the principal English-language secondary source for rhythmic theories in the seventeenth and eighteenth centuries, has highly influenced my treatment of many issues in this chapter.

4 Ibid., p. 32.

5 Praetorius, *Syntagma musicum*.

6 Mersenne, *Harmonie universelle*.

7 Butler, *Principles*.

8 Bononcini, *Musico prattico*.

not until the eighteenth century that individual theorists, such as Johann Mattheson, Johann Philipp Kirnberger, and Heinrich Christoph Koch, put a more personal stamp on the theory of rhythm and began to formulate a more complete account of our modern system, though even with these theorists, remnants of earlier mensural practice continued to find expression.

Classification of meters

Musicians today are so familiar with the mechanics of note values, time signatures, and metrical organization in music of the high Baroque that it is perhaps surprising to discover how contentious these issues were for theorists of the period. Indeed, classifying the multitude of meters and their corresponding time signatures used by composers (plus many others that had largely become abandoned) became an obsession of these theorists.[9] Competing schemes based on varying underlying principles were vehemently attacked and defended. At least two basic issues regularly prompted debate: the number of primary divisions in a measure, and the nature of *compound* meters.

Primary divisions. The modern concept of meter evolved out of the mensural tactus (hence the German term for meter, *Takt*), with the duration of a whole measure (equivalent to a semibreve, the standard value of the tactus) functioning as the starting point of the metrical system. The measure then becomes divided into smaller parts at one or more levels of motion. Inasmuch as the complete measure represented the original tactus, the measure was often initially divided into two parts – thesis and arsis – and some theorists, especially in Germany, even held that all meters were fundamentally two-part in structure. Thus Mattheson, the most zealous upholder of this conservative position, presents a primary division of the measure into *equal* meters (our duple and quadruple meters) or *unequal* meters (triple). The latter are made up of two parts, the first (thesis) lasting twice as long as the second (arsis), just as in the original tactus theory.[10] Gradually, however, the notion that the primary divisions represent tactus motions gave way to a newer concept, namely, that the divisions "measure off," like a ruler, the time span of a measure.[11] The need for an exclusively binary division (tied to the original tactus hand motions) was eventually abandoned, and more forward-looking theorists, especially in France, placed three-part or four-part divisions on an equal footing with the original two-part division of the measure.[12]

9 See Houle, *Meter*, Chapter 2; Seidel, *Rhythmustheorien*, Chapter 2; Maier, *Theorie des Taktes*, Chapters 1–2; Schwindt-Gross, "Einfache Takte," pp. 206–12. Seidel's work is the most comprehensive investigation of rhythmic theories in the eighteenth and nineteenth centuries to date. I am highly indebted to many of his descriptions and interpretations. Maier's study is also a highly valuable source of information on late Baroque metrical theory.

10 Mattheson, *Neu-eröffnetes Orchester*, p. 78; *Der vollkommene Capellmeister* (Harriss trans., p. 365). See also Maier, *Theorie des Taktes*, pp. 17–21; Seidel, *Rhythmustheorien*, pp. 58–61; Houle, *Meter*, p. 45.

11 Maier, *Theorie des Taktes*, p. 16.

12 Houle, *Meter*, pp. 36–38.

Compound meters. In their efforts to make conceptual sense out of the wide variety of possible meters, many Baroque theorists distinguished between simple and compound meters. One major area of theoretical disagreement concerned the classification of the compound meters 6/4, 6/8, 9/8, 12/8, etc. Most theorists recognized that such meters have some kind of triple organization, and some, such as Tomás Baltazar Janovka, simply included them together with 3/2 and 3/4.[13] Other theorists, especially the highly vocal Mattheson, argued that 6/4, 6/8, and 12/8 are fundamentally two-part in nature and thus classified them with C, ¢, 2/4, etc.[14] Johann Gottfried Walther even proposed two completely different schemes so that some compound meters (6/4, 12/8, 24/16) could be viewed as either duple or triple.[15] These discrepancies in classification largely arise from theorists' taking different levels of musical motion as essential for defining the meter. Thus Mattheson's scheme focuses all attention on the first level of measure division (the duple organization of the dotted eighth notes), while Janovka attends primarily to the fastest meaningful level (in this case, the triple organization of the eighth notes).[16]

In general, theorists defined compound meters as the joining together of two or more simple meters. The results of such combination could yield, however, widely differing results. So, for example, Janowka and Johann David Heinichen considered 6/8, 9/8, and 12/8 meters to be compound because they combine together two, three, or four simple 3/8 meters.[17] For Friedrich Wilhelm Marpurg, however, 4/4 is the principal compound meter, consisting as it does of two 2/4 meters; 12/8 is also compound because it represents a triple subdivision of the compound 4/4. But Marpurg regards 6/8 and 9/8 as *simple* meters derived from 2/4 and 3/4 by triple subdivision.[18] Again, these discrepant accounts arise because the theorists focused their attention at differing levels of motion.[19]

Metrical accentuation

A central innovation of the modern system of rhythm is the explicit recognition that temporal events are differentiated through some notion of accentuation.[20] The concept of accent was initially linked to poetic theory and referred to the emphasis accorded a particular syllable either through its greater length or a more forceful pronunciation. A more specifically musical accentuation was articulated as early as 1636 (in some statements by Butler) but does not become an essential feature of rhythmic theory until

13 Janowka, *Clavis*, pp. 141–43; see Seidel, *Rhythmustheorien*, pp. 59–60; Maier, *Theorie des Taktes*, p. 33.
14 Mattheson, *Neu-eröffnetes Orchester*, p. 77; see Maier, *Theorie des Taktes*, p. 31.
15 Walther, *Praecepta*, pp. 29–33; see Maier, *Theorie des Taktes*, p. 29.
16 Maier, *Theorie des Taktes*, pp. 31–32; Seidel, *Rhythmustheorien*, p. 59.
17 Janowka, *Clavis*, pp. 141–43; Heinichen, *Generalbass*, p. 290; see Maier, *Theorie des Taktes*, pp. 33–36.
18 Marpurg, *Anleitung*, pp. 68–69; see Maier, *Theorie des Taktes*, pp. 36–38.
19 Maier, *Theorie des Taktes*, p. 35; see also Grave, "Metrical Displacement."
20 The mensural system would seem not to embody notions of accentuation, though that issue remains in dispute.

later in the seventeenth century.[21] As a general rule, accent was linked directly to meter; the idea of *nonmetrical* accentuation arose now and then but did not become an important component of rhythmic (and performance) theory until the nineteenth century. Theorists in the early part of the eighteenth century were particularly concerned with the terminology of indicating accentuation and with the actual patterns of accent associated with individual meters.

Terminology of accentuation. The wide variety of terms for accentuation used by Baroque theorists clearly reveal the conceptual difficulties attendant on metrical accent. From today's perspective, we might assume that the simplest way of talking about accentuation would be in reference to a greater intensity imparted to a beat. Yet early eighteenth-century theorists only sporadically mention dynamic differentiation as a cause for, or a result of, accentuation. Rather, their most typical way of expressing the idea derives from poetic theory, which, in reference to ancient Greek, differentiates longer and shorter syllables, generally in the proportion of 2 : 1 (long to short). Since the real length of the beats within a measure are equal, theorists speak of the *internal* length of notes (*Quantitas Intrinseca*) as distinct from their actual, *external* length. As Wolfgang Caspar Printz states,

> the position in the measure has a peculiar power and virtue which cause notes equal to one another, according to the time signature, to seem longer or shorter. This should be especially noted as much because of the text as because of consonance and dissonance.
>
> The apparent different length of notes that are equal according to their time or value, is called *Quantitas Temporalis Intrinseca*, or the inner duration.[22]

Printz's mention of an "apparent" difference in length between the notes implies that accent resides in our personal cognition of an event rather than in the event itself. Mattheson strikes a similarly psychological tone when he speaks of an accented note as having an "inner content and emphasis" (*innerliche Gehalt und Nachdruck*).[23] In other words, the mere position of the note within the measure is sufficient to impart accentuation in the absence of any real durational or dynamic differentiation.

Printz's linking of consonance and dissonance to metrical placement points to another aspect of accentuation reflected in terminology. Notes that function as metrically accented were frequently labeled *good*, those that are unaccented, *bad*. These strangely moral judgments about notes arose from the attempt to explain why consonances and dissonances have certain determinate metrical positions. As Walther put it, a good beat is "suitable for the placement of a caesura, a cadence, a long syllable, a syncopated dissonance, and above all a consonance (from which comes its name – *di*

21 Butler, *Principles*, p. 26; see Houle, *Meter*, p. 31.

22 Printz, *Phrynis Mitilenaeus*, vol. 1, p. 18; see Houle, *Meter*, pp. 80–81; Horn, "Johann David Heinichen," pp. 197–99.

23 Mattheson, *Critica musica*, vol. 1, p. 43; see Maier, *Theorie des Taktes*, p. 50; Seidel, *Rhythmustheorien*, p. 111.

buona)."[24] A related set of terms distinguishes accented notes as *struck* (*schlagend*) versus unaccented ones that are *passing* (*durchgehend*), again in obvious reference to consonance–dissonance placement.[25] Additional terms used by eighteenth-century theorists for metrical accentuation include *thesis* versus *arsis* (in extension of their original meaning as the first level of tactus division), *strong* versus *weak* (more typically used later in the century), and finally *accent* versus *unaccent* (with no necessary implication of dynamic stress).

Patterns of accentuation. The distribution of accents within the various meters was widely discussed by Baroque theorists. In the case of duple and quadruple meters, the accent analysis largely conformed to our modern understanding (i.e., first and third beats, accented; second and fourth, unaccented). For triple meter, however, no consensus was achieved, and a number of options proposed have no counterpart in today's practice. Every theorist, of course, attributed accent to the first beat, and many regarded the subsequent two beats as unaccented. But since metrical organization was conceived to relate intimately with consonance–dissonance practice, it became necessary to explain why, for example, the *syncope* (suspension) dissonance, which normally must occur on an accented beat, may be placed on the second beat of a triple meter. To accommodate this situation (as well as to explain, for example, the stress usually given to the second beat in a sarabande) some theorists posited the following pattern of accentuation in normative triple meter: – – ∪ (the dashes and cups refer to accents and unaccents respectively).[26] The attempt to correlate accent organization with the primary thesis–arsis division of the measure led theorists to propose another scheme, whereby the third beat receives accentuation through its association with the onset of the arsis: – ∪ – .[27] That this pattern along with the previous one results in two consecutive accents (either within the barline or from one bar to the next) seems not to have been of concern to these theorists. Today, however, such a situation is normally thought to violate fundamental principles of metrical organization, and thus we might want to recognize in these differing metrical interpretations an attempt by eighteenth-century theory to account for various types of *nonmetrical* accentuation.

Durational patterning, rhythmopoeia

A hallmark of Baroque style is the use of rhythmic motives (especially in instrumental, dance-derived genres) to provide surface uniformity and continuity and to help

24 Walther, *Musikalisches Lexicon*, p. 598; see Houle, *Meter*, p. 83.

25 Walther, *Praecepta*, p. 151; see Maier, *Theorie des Taktes*, p. 45. The idea of "striking" the note perhaps suggests a dynamic intensification, but this would be an erroneous interpretation, as the use of the term *schlagend* in seventeenth- and early eighteenth-century theory in fact derives from thorough-bass practice; see Maier, *Theorie des Taktes*, p. 146, n. 187.

26 Walther, *Praecepta*, p. 23; Scheibe, *Der critische Musikus*, p. 348.

27 Mattheson, *Critica Musica*, vol. I, p. 33; Walther, *Praecepta*, p. 23; Scheibe, *Der critische Musikus*, p. 348.

express the single *Affekt* responsible for achieving aesthetic unity in a movement. In response to this compositional practice, some theorists of the period attempted to classify the variety of durational patterns regularly appearing in compositions. They based their approaches on theories of Greek poetic meters, as transmitted through the humanistic revival of ancient thought and practice by late sixteenth- and early seventeenth-century writers.[28] This theory of *rhythmopoeia*, as it came to be known, defines various patterns of long and short durations using the traditional Greek metrical terms: for example, *iamb* for the pattern short–long; *trochee* for long–short; *anapest* for two shorts followed by a long; and so forth. The most important eighteenth-century exponents of *rhythmopoeia* are Printz and Mattheson, in that order chronologically. For practical reasons, however, it will prove easier to discuss Mattheson's approach first and then turn briefly to Printz's.[29]

Mattheson. Johann Mattheson's (1681–1764) extensive list of twenty-six durational patterns, which he calls *sound-feet* (*Klangfüße*) in analogy to the feet of poetic meters, represents the most complete extant theory of musical *rhythmopoeia* (see Example 21.1 for a sampling). As his brief musical examples reveal, Mattheson clearly found a way to accommodate many of the standard rhythmic (and melodic) motives that regularly appear in early eighteenth-century compositions, and at a level of general description, his labels are readily applicable to many passages. But from a stricter theoretical perspective, his account is problematic in a number of ways.

Any useful theory of durational patterning must, at minimum, specify criteria for durational differentiation and for pattern segmentation. As for the first issue, Mattheson appeals to the actual durational value of the notes to distinguish between those that are deemed long and short; thus his system, unlike that of Printz to be discussed shortly, makes no direct appeal to the internal length of the notes (i.e., their metrical accentuation). In some cases, however, assigning length or shortness to a note is ambiguous, and Mattheson brings metrical considerations to bear on the decision. For example, the pattern ♩.♪♩ yields the proportions 3 : 1 : 2. The dotted quarter is obviously a long; the eighth note, a short. If the final quarter note, which is manifestly longer than the preceding eighth, is considered long, then the pattern would be an *amphimacer* (– ∪ –; cups and dashes now referring to external length); if the final note is short, then a *dactyl* arises (– ∪ ∪). Mattheson opts for the second interpretation (as shown in Example 21.1, no. 5)[30] and justifies his choice by noting that the quarter note "seems to be twice as long according to its external aspect as the second or middle one; is nevertheless just as short in its intrinsic value, because of the upbeat of the

28 Houle, *Meter*, pp. 62–63. A similar neo-classical impulse led to the resurrection and adoption of ancient *rhetorica* teachings by theorists at the same time. See **Chapter 27, pp. 854–67**.

29 See Seidel, *Rhythmustheorien*, pp. 42–51, 63–66; Houle, *Meter*, Chapter 3.

30 Mattheson's metrical analyses contain a number of typographical errors: the *trochee* (pattern 4) should not be – – ∪, as he shows, but rather – ∪; the *iamb* (pattern 3) should be ∪ –, not ∪ – –; and the *bacchius* (pattern 9) should not be – – ∪, but rather ∪ – –.

Example 21.1 Examples of sound-feet from Mattheson, *Der vollkommene Capellmeister*, pp. 164–70

Feet of Two Syllables

2) Pyrrhic v v

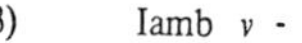

4) Choraeus or Trochee - - v

Feet of Three Syllables.

5) Dactyl. - v v

6) Anapaest. v v - - etc.

7) Molossus. - - - etc.

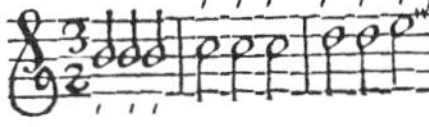

8) Tribrach. v v v

9) Bacchius. - - v

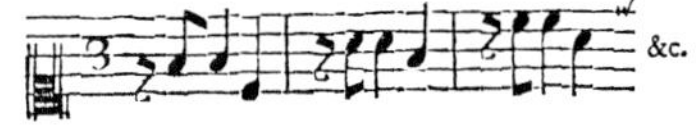

10) Amphimacer, - v -

allegro.

11) Amphibrachys, v - v

vivace.

12) Palymbacchius, - - v

andante.

measure."[31] Here, he appeals explicitly to meter, but his explanation is merely ad hoc. Indeed, Mattheson never arrived at a satisfactory and consistent relation of sound-feet to meter.

As for the second issue, that concerning the segmentation of sound-feet, Mattheson consistently delimits the durational patterning to the confines of the measure. Two problems result: the external lengths of notes frequently contradict their internal lengths (the *iamb* is but one example), and more importantly, it is not possible to account for rhythmic patterns that cross over the bar line, as manifestly arise throughout the Baroque (such as in the subject of Bach's C minor Fugue from the first book of the *Well-Tempered Clavier*).

Printz. Some of the issues that caused difficulties in Mattheson's theory of *rhythmopoeia* are handled more successfully by Wolfgang Caspar Printz (1641–1717). Unlike Mattheson's exhaustive listing, Printz's identifies six basic patterns (see Example 21.2) – *iambus*, *trochaeus*, *enantius* (or *contrarius*), *dactylus*, *nothrus* (or *spondaeus*), and *syncopaticus*. Within each category, Printz recognizes various versions (such as *iambus ecclesiasticus*, *hypochematicus*, *melismaticus*, and *proportionatus*) based largely on the lengths of the component durational values. His criteria for distinguishing long from short differ from Mattheson in that four of the patterns are based principally on the "internal" length of notes, not necessarily their actual "external" length. Thus the *iambus*, *trochaeus*, and *dactylus* have versions in which the notes making up the pattern are of equal duration. As regards segmentation, Printz is somewhat more flexible than Mattheson in that the *iambus* pattern is permitted to cross over the bar lines. Yet despite these theoretical advantages, Printz's theory also has some shortcomings. Not only are the number of his patterns quite limited (for example, he cannot account for the very common *anapest* figure: ∪ ∪ –), but internal contradictions within the theory appear as well. The *enantius* pattern is, like the *iambus*, made up of a short followed by a long, but in this case, it is the external length, not the internal one, that defines the pattern and its boundaries with respect to the measure. These problems, along with those identified in connection with Mattheson's approach, perhaps explain why *rhythmopoeia* reached a dead end with these theorists and why later theorists largely abandoned the attempt at providing a comprehensive theory of durational patterning.[32]

Origins of the Akzenttheorie

The medieval and Renaissance mensural system is rooted in an Aristotelian conception of temporality, whereby the passage of time is conceived as a succession of discrete,

31 Mattheson, *Der vollkommene Capellmeister*, p. 167 (Harriss trans., p. 355).

32 A later discussion of *rhythmopoeia* is found in Koch, *Introductory Essay*, pp. 66–69, but the topic plays little role in the subsequent development of his theories. Interest in durational patterning in music, inspired by ancient Greek metrical theory, was renewed late in the nineteenth century by Westphal, *Allgemeine Theorie*, and Wiehmayer, *Musikalische Rhythmik und Metrik*; see Smithers, "Theories of Rhythm," Chapter 4 and pp. 256–60. For a twentieth-century reincarnation of metrical poetics in music theory, see **Chapter 22, pp. 710–11**.

Example 21.2 Examples of *rhythmopoeia* from Printz, *Phrynis Mitilenaeus*, vol. III, pp. 100–07

individual *times* (in the plural) each marking a concrete type of cyclical motion (e.g., the rising and falling of the sun, the turning of a wheel). Whether it be the original mensural long, or later, the individual tactus, this basic unit delimits the essential time-spans of rhythmic motion. During the seventeenth century, a new conception of temporality emerged, one eventually codified by Newton, in which *time* (in the singular) is understood as an empty, homogeneous, and infinite span, waiting to be filled by any kind of motion.[33] It was not until the second half of the eighteenth century that a group of thinkers working closely together in Berlin – the music theorist Johann Philipp Kirnberger (1721–83), the aesthetician Johann Georg Sulzer (1720–89), and the composer Johann Abraham Peter Schulz (1747–1800) – articulated a theory of musical rhythm founded upon this newer concept of time.[34]

Unlike theorists in the first half of the eighteenth century, who regarded the entire measure as the starting point of a metrical theory, Kirnberger begins with an unlimited succession of undifferentiated and aesthetically insignificant stimuli, what we now typically call pulses or beats. These beats then become differentiated through accent:

> it is necessarily required that such a series of tones group themselves into units of equal length . . . These equally long and equally shaped units now constitute what one calls meter in music . . . It is also necessary to have accents, because without them the ear would have no cause to group the series of tones into equally formed units.[35]

Measures, in turn, can group together to build more complex, higher-level phrases or periods. This cumulative process of metrical units of one level grouping to form new units on a higher level gives rise to a hierarchical framework within which the actual music receives its metrical interpretation.[36]

In Kirnberger's theory, which Hugo Riemann later characterized as the *Akzenttheorie*, the individual measure no longer delimits fundamental rhythmic activity as did the earlier tactus-derived measure. The actual lengths of the notes need not correspond directly to metrical units at a given level, and the grouping of notes into motives need not be confined to the boundaries of the measure. And rather than being linked to the traditional Greek meters, durational values are free to assume a wide variety of patterns, always retaining, however, their metrical interpretation as defined by the hierarchy of accents and unaccents. By clearly separating metrical organization from durational and grouping organization, Kirnberger and his circle laid the aesthetic basis for a fundamental dichotomy, which has persisted until today, between rhythm, as unconstrained durational patterning, and meter, as rigid accentual hierarchy.

Meter: tempo and character

Though the foundations of Kirnberger's metrical theory effected a decisive break with earlier approaches, some residues of mensural theory still appear in his theories, especially the idea that the duration of notes is indicative of tempo. Indeed with

33 Dahlhaus, *Musiktheorie*, vol. II, p. 160.

34 Determining the actual "author" of the principal sources for this theory is difficult; for details, see Kirnberger, *Art*, p. xi. For the sake of convenience, Kirnberger will be identified here as the principal theorist, even for statements that may have actually been written by Sulzer or Schulz. Kirnberger's theories are discussed at length by Seidel, *Rhythmustheorien*, pp. 85–134.

35 Sulzer, "Tact," in *Allgemeine Theorie*, vol. IV, pp. 491–92.

36 In eighteenth-century thought, *metrical* interpretations were still largely confined to the boundaries of the measure; a more explicit notion of *hypermeter* is not formulated until the following century.

Kirnberger, this idea reaches its fullest expression; after him, it largely disappears from the theoretical literature, as the expressions Largo, Andante, Presto, and so forth entirely take over the role of tempo markings.

According to Kirnberger, an individual meter (with its unique time signature) specifies not only accent organization, but also tempo, articulation, and the general character of the musical passage set within that meter. Meters are also normally associated with certain genres and dance types. A given time signature defines a range of note values typically used with its meter. The external length of the notes suggests the *tempo giusto* (natural tempo) of the meter, a tempo that may be modified by Italianate expressions. An individual meter also implies its general style of articulation. For example,

> 2/2 meter, or rather *alla breve* . . . is most often used in church pieces, fugues, and elaborate choruses. It is to be noted about this meter that it is very serious and emphatic, yet is performed twice as fast as its note values indicate,[37] unless a slower tempo is specified by the adjectives grave, adagio, etc. The same is true of the 6/4 meter of two triple beats that is derived from 2/2 meter, but the *tempo giusto* of the meter is somewhat more moderate. Both meters tolerate no shorter note values than eighths.[38]

In the case of 3/4 meter, Kirnberger notes that

> [it] is not as common in the church style as 3/2; but it is used very often in the chamber and theatrical styles.
>
> Its natural tempo is that of a minuet, and in this tempo it does not tolerate many sixteenth notes, even less thirty-second notes, in succession. However, since it assumes all degrees of tempo from the adjectives adagio, allegro, etc., all note values that fit this tempo can be used, depending on the rate of speed.[39]

As these statements reveal, issues of duration, tempo, articulation, style, and genre are interwoven with those of meter. Later theorists, responding to contemporary compositional practice, largely separate these domains, especially the connection between meter and tempo.[40] The aesthetic basis of Kirnberger's concept of meter may mark the starting point of the new *Akzenttheorie*, but the fuller realization of his metrical theories represents the end of a line of thought reaching back several centuries.

Accent: metrical and nonmetrical

In describing the accent organization of the various meters, theorists in the second half of the eighteenth century continued to employ the wide variety of binary oppositions developed by Baroque theorists – long vs. short; good vs. bad; struck vs. passing; accented vs. unaccented. But another idea, one rarely expressed in earlier theory, gained in prominence throughout the century: that metrical accentuation is associated

37 Because of the older proportional tradition that the tactus of *alla breve* moves twice as fast as the normal semibreve tactus. 38 Kirnberger, *Art*, p. 386. 39 Ibid., p. 396.

40 Thus, from Beethoven on, composers could write very slow-moving works using mostly eighth, sixteenth, and thirty-second notes.

with an actual dynamic intensification supplied by the performer.[41] Thus Kirnberger regularly speaks of beats being *strong* or *weak*. That this distinction has performance implications is clear from statements like the following: "the pressure [of the bow] that marks the first note of the measure in each meter . . . determines . . . the downbeat of the measure, which always falls on the first beat of the measure."[42]

Theorists in the later part of the century also became more explicit about the possibility that accentuation could be applied to, or was even inherent in, events occupying metrically weak positions. This idea of a nonmetrical accent finds expression in Kirnberger's three-fold classification of musical accents (based on a similar model proposed by Sulzer for natural language) – *grammatical*, *oratorical*, and *expressive*. Grammatical accents directly pertain to meter: they are "the long and powerful tones that make up the main tones of each chord; they must be distinguished from other, passing tones . . . through [internal] length, through emphasis, and through greater perceptibility. These tones fall on the good beats of the measure."[43] On the contrary, the oratorical and expressive accents (the latter being a stronger, more emphatic version of the former) occur independently of meter: they are individual tones (or groups of tones) specially emphasized both compositionally (through musical figures, harmonies, or dissonances) and in performance (through dynamic intensification).[44] The *Akzenttheorie* thus lives up to its name by positing a wide variety of accents – some metrical, some not – that operate at multiple levels of motion. Left undiscussed by Kirnberger is the question of how these different accents actually exist together – both in performance and experientially – and even how to formulate a coherent theory of multiple accentuations. These questions emerge as central topics of discussion and debate in nineteenth-century theory.

Rhythm: phrase structure and melody

Although Kirnberger uses the term *rhythm* in its general sense,[45] he also employs it more narrowly along the lines of what we would today understand as the domains of phrase structure, melody, or even form. Just as individual beats can group into measures, so too can individual measures group into phrases (and phrases into periods), thereby projecting the *rhythm* of a melody. Unlike individual beats, whose grouping into measures arises by means of accent, the grouping of measures into phrases occurs when the flow of the melody is demarcated by *resting points* of varying degrees.[46] Some of these resting points are actual cadences, others are merely breaks in the melodic line

41 See Houle, *Meter*, Chapter 6. 42 Sulzer, "Tact," in *Allgemeine Theorie*, vol. IV, p. 495.

43 Sulzer, "Accent," in *Allgemeine Theorie*, vol. I, p. 18. Note that here Kirnberger employs almost every eighteenth-century term for metrical accent. 44 Ibid., pp. 18–19.

45 Especially in the article "Rhythmus," in Sulzer's *Allgemeine Theorie*.

46 Kirnberger, *Art*, p. 408. Thus Kirnberger's *rhythm* should not be understood as *hypermeter*, since the measures themselves are not construed as accented or unaccented; the idea of measures or phrases being metrically accented does not arise until the nineteenth century.

associated with "restful" chords (especially dominant harmony).[47] Kirnberger notes that "the best melodies are always those whose phrases have four measures,"[48] but he regularly discusses the possibility of phrases lasting three or five measures. Of particular theoretical importance are those cases where he demonstrates how an odd-numbered phrase derives from a more normative four-measure model.[49] In many respects, Kirnberger was influenced by the work of Joseph Riepel (1709–82), who effectively initiated the tradition of phrase-structural analysis. Kirnberger, in turn (along with Riepel), influenced Koch, who developed the most comprehensive account of phrase structure in eighteenth-century theory.

Riepel. Though little known until recent years, Joseph Riepel's (1709–82) reputation has grown significantly as historians have discovered that his writings, admittedly often convoluted and inconsistent, contain the core ideas of eighteenth-century phrase-structural theory.[50] Especially noteworthy is the wide variety of ways in which he characterizes the organization and content of phrases. He thus distinguishes them on the basis of their rhythmic activity (a concern rarely addressed by eighteenth-century theorists), their overall melodic contour, their underlying harmonic support, their degree of melodic closure, and their length in terms of measure numbers. Riepel establishes the four-measure phrase as a norm (at least for the minuet genre) and discusses ways in which such phrases can be expanded and altered. Although Riepel failed to shape his ideas into a systematic whole or to transmit much of his specialized terminology, his detailed analyses and critical commentary (on his own musical examples, admittedly) pointed the way for further developments by Kirnberger and Koch.

Koch. In the manner of much eighteenth-century theory, Heinrich Christoph Koch's (1749–1816) approach to "melodic" (i.e., phrase-structural, formal) organization is rooted in analogies with natural language (speech, poetry, rhetoric).[51] Just as language can be broken down into sentences, sentences into clauses, and clauses into parts of speech (subject, predicate), the melody of a composition can be divided into periods, phrases, and melodic segments.[52] At the basis of Koch's "mechanical rules of melody," as he calls them, are two notions: *melodic punctuation*, the demarcation of melodies through their resting points, and *rhythm*, the length and proportions of melodic sections with respect to their number of measures. Like Riepel and Kirnberger, Koch identifies the four-measure phrase as "most useful and most pleasing," but going

47 Kirnberger, *Art*, p. 404. 48 Ibid., p. 409. 49 Ibid., pp. 409–12.

50 Riepel, *Anfangsgründe*; see also Knouse, "Joseph Riepel"; London, "Riepel and Absatz"; Lester, *Compositional Theory*, pp. 258–72.

51 Koch's theories, especially as a stimulus for analyzing music of the Classical period, have received considerable scholarly attention in recent years; see Baker, "Heinrich Koch," pp. 1–48; Lester, *Compositional Theory*, pp. 285–99; Budday, *Grundlagen musikalischer Formen*; Sisman, "Small and Expanded Forms." Also see **Chapter 2, pp. 57–58** and **Chapter 27, pp. 881–82**.

52 Koch, *Introductory Essay*, p. 1.

Example 21.3 Basic phrases from Koch, *Introductory Essay*
(a) Example 1, p. 4

(b) Example 8, p. 7

(c) Example 10, p. 7

considerably further in theoretical scope and rigor, he provides a comprehensive framework for analyzing phrases of varying lengths. To that end, he proposes three main categories of phrase – *basic*, *extended*, and *compound*.

The basic phrase contains "only as much as is absolutely necessary for it to be understood and felt as an independent section of the whole."[53] The phrase normally consists of two two-measure segments, the first of which, continuing his linguistic analogy, Koch likens to a "subject," the second, to a "predicate" (see Example 21.3a). Each segment concludes with a "resting point of the spirit" (*Ruhepunct des Geistes*), sometimes an actual cadence at the very end of the phrase, sometimes a noncadential articulation internal to the phrase.[54] While every basic phrase expresses a sense of structural completeness, some are more complete than others. Thus Koch distinguishes between "internal" phrases and "closing" phrases on the basis of their "ending formulas"; his examples suggest that this difference is based on cadential strength, namely, between the weaker imperfect authentic cadence ending an internal phrase (as in Example 21.3b) and the stronger perfect authentic cadence ending a closing phrase (as in Example 21.3c).[55]

An extended phrase features "more than is absolutely necessary for its completeness."[56] Koch defines three techniques used to create the phrase extension: (1) repeat-

53 Ibid., p. 3.
54 When speaking of "resting points of the spirit," Koch acknowledges that the boundaries of grouping structures (to speak in today's terms) are impossible to define with explicit criteria, but rather ensue from "feeling" on the part of the listener; ibid., p. 4, note 7; see also p. 1, note 1.
55 Ibid., p. 7. 56 Ibid., p. 41.

Example 21.4 Extended phrases from Koch, *Introductory Essay*
(a) Example 133, p. 43

(b) Example 148, p. 46

(c) Example 180, p. 54

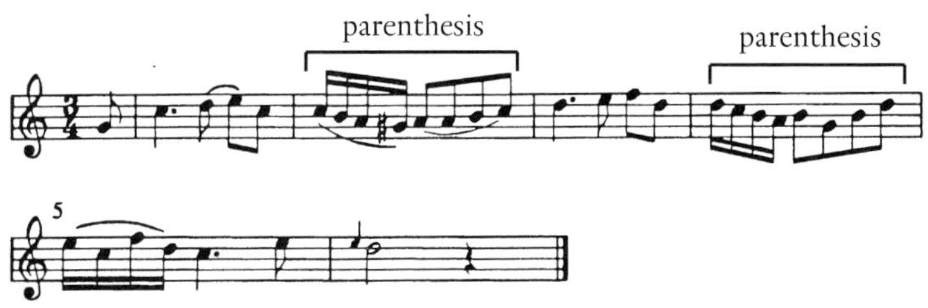

ing some part of the phrase, often the opening two measures (see Example 21.4a); (2) adding an appendix to the ending formula (see Example 21.4b); and (3) parenthetically inserting unessential melodic ideas between segments of a phrase (see Example 21.4c).[57] Though all of these extension techniques result in phrases that are literally longer than the basic phrases from which they (conceptually) derive, Koch stresses that for purposes of establishing the "rhythmic relations of phrases," the extended phrase is equal in length to its original basic phrase.[58]

A compound phrase consists of "two or more phrases, complete in themselves, [that] are combined so that externally they appear in the form of a single phrase."[59] This combination of phrases can occur in a variety of ways, the two most typical being cases (1) where the first phrase elides with the second, a procedure Koch rather colorfully calls

57 Ibid., pp. 41, 45, and 53. The identification of repetition, appendix, and parenthesis have been added to Examples 21.4a–c. 58 Ibid., p. 42. 59 Ibid., p. 3.

Example 21.5 Compound phrases from Koch, *Introductory Essay*
(a) Example 182, p. 55

(b) Example 188, p. 57

Example 21.6 Six-bar phrase from Koch, *Introductory Essay*, Example 53, p. 18

"strangling of the measure" (*Tacterstickung*) (see Example 21.5a), or (2) where the cadential punctuation of the first phrase is eliminated (see Example 21.5b, in which the "original" cadential ending of m. 4 is shown above the measure).[60]

From this discussion, one might have the impression that Koch's basic phrase would necessarily be four measures in length (or perhaps less), with phrases of five or more measures classified as extended or compounded. But Koch describes a number of basic phrases embracing five, six, and seven measures (such as in Example 21.6). He recognizes extended phrases only when they contain repetitions or interpolations of some kind. Thus the distinction between basic and extended is not essentially rooted in notions of phrase symmetry – an aesthetic criterion that finds primary expression in nineteenth-century thought – but rather on the degree to which the formal completion expressed by phrases is efficient or redundant. In this respect, Koch's emphasis on varying weights of cadential goals rather than on balanced phrasing is somewhat more

60 Ibid., pp. 54–57.

in tune with Classical practice than subsequent Romantic theories, which have tended to give a rather distorted view of Classical phrase structure as fundamentally symmetrical.

Nineteenth-century theories: consolidation, speculation

Nineteenth-century rhythmic theory is largely devoted to consolidating and expanding the late eighteenth-century *Akzenttheorie*. In the hands of some theorists, the notion that accent involves perceived dynamic changes led to practical applications of the theory with, in the case of Mathis Lussy, emphasis on matters of performance. But the earlier conception of accent as essentially cognitive, thus not necessarily tied to a performed intensification, stimulated Moritz Hauptmann to speculate on a more unified conceptual framework for the *Akzenttheorie*. Some nineteenth-century theorists continued to address issues of higher-level rhythm by developing the Kochian tradition of phrase-structural analysis in response to changes in musical style. Under the influence of the predominantly regularized phrase organization exhibited by Romantic styles, these theorists began to conceive of such higher-level processes as less properly "rhythmical" than "metrical" as they had been understood in the prior century. The principal concerns of nineteenth-century theorists culminate in Hugo Riemann's "system" of rhythm and meter, which combines a powerful critique of the *Akzenttheorie* with novel concepts of metrical organization within periodic structures.

The practical Akzenttheorie: *Mathis Lussy*

The conjunction of accent and dynamic intensification became so entrenched in nineteenth-century thought (and just why that occurred has yet to be fully answered) that a theory of rhythm implied at the same time a theory of performance. Numerous theorists stipulated that metrically strong positions within a bar be performed with greater intensity than metrically weak ones. A typical exemplification of this principle is offered by Adolph Bernhard Marx in his widely influential *Allgemeine Musiklehre*.[61] Using vertical strokes as symbols, he identifies varying gradations of accentuation within a measure and specifically instructs that the greater the accentuation, the louder the note should be performed. An extreme case is shown in Example 21.7, where up to four degrees of accent are identified. The manifestly unmusical results of performing such a passage in this way led even Marx to observe that the "law of accentuation" should not be taken too far.

More useful approaches to performance derived from refinements and expansions of

61 Marx, *Allgemeine Musiklehre*, p. 125. See Smithers, "Theories of Rhythm," pp. 17–21; this dissertation still remains the most extensive survey in English of nineteenth-century rhythmic theories.

Example 21.7 Performed accentuations from Marx, *Allgemeine Musiklehre*, p. 125

Kirnberger's three-fold classification of accents. The most comprehensive theory was presented by Mathis Lussy (1828–1910), who distinguishes among *metrical* accents, which are associated with our instinct, *rhythmic* accents, associated with our intelligence, and *expressive* (*pathétique*) accents, with our sentiments.[62] Lussy's "rules" for metrical accentuation entirely accord with traditional views, such as those of Marx. By rhythm, Lussy means any significant group of events, from simple motives to larger phrase-structural units, thus continuing the semantic tradition from the previous century. The rules for rhythmic accents derive from the desire to articulate the beginning and end of such groups. As one simple rule, admitting few exceptions, Lussy requires the first note of a group to be accented. The case of a group's final note is more complicated, and thus he details a variety of situations where that note is preferably accented or unaccented.[63] The expressive accent makes its effect primarily as a "surprise" or "exception" to the regularity of metrical and rhythmic accents. Consequently, Lussy can give no rules for their use and, instead, enumerates an extensive list of metrical, rhythmic, melodic, harmonic, and tonal situations that tend to call for expressive accentuation (such as syncopations, note repetitions, dissonances, and chromatic harmonies).[64] Typical of the nineteenth-century prizing of individual sentiments, and in accord with the title of his treatise, Lussy privileges the expressive accent over the other two types: "In spite of the importance of the bar, metrical accent must give way to rhythmical accent, and both must in turn give way to the expressive accent, which will always take the lead and rule the others."[65]

Though Lussy's treatise was highly influential, particularly upon teachers of performance, the actual theoretical content of his approach is problematic. (The most aggressive critique was launched by Riemann, whose views on the matter are examined below.) A central issue of concern is how the multitude of accents from various sources actually function in relation to each other. Although it might be the case that a performer would prioritize the accents in the manner prescribed by Lussy, the listener must somehow continue to perceive the metrical accents, or else the sense of meter would be lost. Since his concept of accent is tied so strongly to a literal dynamic

62 Lussy, *Musical Expression*, pp. 14–15. A later treatise by Lussy, *Le rythme musical*, develops some new topics but is largely based on *Musical Expression*. See Smithers, "Theories of Rhythm," pp. 79–142, for a detailed introduction to Lussy's theories. 63 Lussy, *Musical Expression*, pp. 116–22.
64 Ibid., Chapter 6. 65 Ibid., p. 15.

intensification, Lussy cannot explain how metrical accentuation can continue to be projected in the midst of powerful nonmetrical accents.

The speculative Akzenttheorie: *Moritz Hauptmann*

Despite the tendency to link accent to dynamics during the nineteenth century, a number of theorists nonetheless retained the eighteenth-century idea that accent is fundamentally a cognitive phenomenon independent of external intensification. Thus Gottfried Weber speaks of metrical accent as possessing an "internal weight" whether or not that metrically strong moment is actually performed with greater force.[66] Weber clearly derives his usage from earlier notions of *quantitas intrinseca*, except that now the issue involves not a conceptual differentiation of durations, but rather one of dynamics.

The disconnection of accent from dynamic intensification, as witnessed in Weber, permitted theorists to develop more speculative models of musical meter unencumbered by practical concerns of performance. The most theoretically sophisticated account of the *Akzenttheorie* is offered by Moritz Hauptmann (1792–1868), whose *Die Natur der Harmonik und Metrik* set a new standard for theoretical discourse. Rooted in the organicist ideology of Goethe, with external resemblances to Hegel's dialectic, Hauptmann's book attempted an entirely novel explanation for the fundamentals of musical rhythm and meter.[67]

For Hauptmann, the series of beats underlying the traditional *Akzenttheorie* is not a simple given. He thus subjects these beats to a rigorous analysis, one which might well be described as proto-phenomenological. He first notes the obvious fact that a single beat, by itself, cannot determine a portion of time; this requires a second beat, which demarcates the complete time-span. But the appearance of this second beat signals the beginning of a second time-span durationally equal to the first. "At the end of this second space we may expect a new [third] beat, which, however, cannot happen earlier than at that point of time without causing an interruption, a curtailment of the time determined for us by the [first] two beats."[68] Hauptmann represents this "projection of time" (to use Christopher Hasty's expression)[69] as shown in Example 21.8a. When the third beat occurs as expected, the resulting structure yields one complete unit of *two-timed* (duple) meter. From a dialectical perspective, this simple meter represents the notion of *unity* (akin to a Hegelian *thesis*).

A unit of *three-timed* (triple) meter arises when a fourth beat becomes incorporated

66 Weber, *Musical Composition*, vol. 1, p. 82; see Smithers, "Theories of Rhythm," p. 30.

67 See Seidel, *Rhythmustheorien*, pp. 135–56; Smithers, "Theories of Rhythm," pp. 39–78. Hauptmann's harmonic theories are discussed in **Chapter 14, pp. 459–62** and **Chapter 23, p. 736**.

68 Hauptmann, *Harmony and Metre*, p. 190.

69 Hasty, *Meter as Rhythm*, pp. 100–02, for a discussion of Hauptmann's ideas on the formation of meter.

Example 21.8 Metrical patterns from Hauptmann, *Harmony and Metre*

(a) p. 190

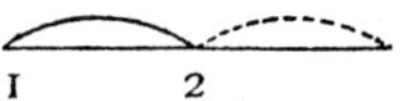

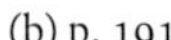
(b) p. 191

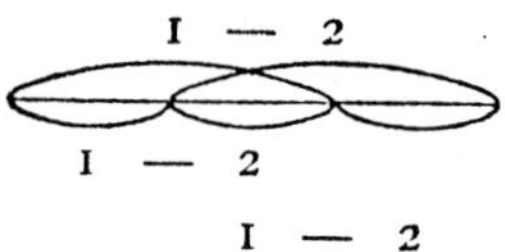

(c) p. 239

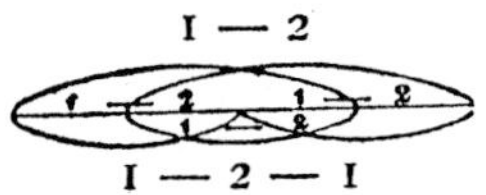

into the structure. As a result, the second time-span acquires conflicting interpretations: on the one hand, it continues to function as the "second" element in relation to the first, just as in a simple duple meter; on the other hand, this second time-span now functions as a "first" in relation to the third time-span, which "follows as echo of the second."[70] Moreover, two higher-level units now arise, but they overlap around the second time-span. (Example 21.8b shows the multiple interpretations of a single unit of triple meter.) The conflicting interpretation accorded the second time-span and the overlapping of the two higher-level units render triple meter representative of the dialectical notion of *opposition* (*antithesis*).

With quadruple meter, the addition of a fourth time-span allows the second time-span to become restored to a position of essential secondness, while the third span acquires a more primary meaning of "first" in relation to the fourth span, as "second." Moreover, the higher-level two-part units, which were interlocked (and thus internally conflicted) in triple meter, become fully whole in quadruple meter (see Example 21.8c). As a result of this complex interpretation of beats, quadruple meter represents the dialectical notion of *unified opposition* (*synthesis*).[71]

In so grounding quadruple meter, Hauptmann is responding to musical instincts, reflected in many classification schemes from the middle of the eighteenth century on, that this meter is genuinely distinct from duple meter and not merely a mechanical

70 Hauptmann, *Harmony and Metre*, p. 191. 71 Ibid., pp. 192–94.

combining together of two duple-meter units.[72] Indeed, Hauptmann not only discusses the difference between these metrical situations but also devotes considerable space to demonstrating why quintuple and septuple meters are entirely "artificial and inorganic."[73] For Hauptmann, the need to justify the organic unity of all truly artistic manifestations is paramount, and this concern leads him to formulations that might strike the modern reader as somewhat strange, if not downright bizarre. Nonetheless, his remarks on the phenomenology of time perception are highly insightful and mark a major theoretical advance in speculations on musical meter and rhythm.

Unlike the traditional *Akzenttheorie*, Hauptmann's concept of meter does not initially invoke the notion of accentuation. As he develops his theory, however, accent plays an increasingly important role. Indeed, his accent concept is highly original and of historical and theoretical significance. In characteristically dialectical language, Hauptmann writes: "A first element of time, which metrically can only be the first of a second equal to it, is, in regard to its second, *determining*; the second is *determined*. A first as against its second has the energy of beginning, and consequently the metrical accent."[74] Here, for the first time, the idea of metrical accent is entirely divorced from its traditional associations with poetic meter, durational differentiation, dynamic differentiation, internal length, and contrapuntal theory. Rather, a unit of time acquires accentuation essentially by being a *first* of some metrical unit and thereby possesses the "energy of beginning." As in the notion of *quantitas intrinseca*, Hauptmann conceives of accent as entirely internal to the musical event, not something that happens to it through some external force, such as dynamic intensification. The mere fact of metrical initiation is sufficient to produce our perception of accent.

Hauptmann easily applies his definition to the two parts of duple meter: the first part is accented; the second part unaccented. His analysis of triple and quadruple meters is more complicated, owing to the way in which he understands how these meters organize time. For triple meter, each metrical "1" is an accented member, each "2" an unaccented one (see again Example 21.8b). In combining these time-spans, Hauptmann rather mechanically adds together the accents and represents the resulting scheme as shown in Example 21.9a.[75] The first beat has double accentuation, the second beat has single accentuation, and the third beat is unaccented. The idea that two beats of a triple meter can be accented is not new, and thus when Hauptmann assigns accent to the first and second members of this meter he follows eighteenth-century traditions (as earlier discussed). His analysis of quadruple meter is more convoluted and

72 Not all theorists, however, recognize quadruple meter as a fundamental, distinct meter; see Weber, *Musical Composition*, vol. 1, pp. 71, 88, 90–91.

73 In this respect, Hauptmann follows the consensus of prior theorists regarding the undesirability of these asymmetrical meters. By mid-century, however, François-Joseph Fétis acknowledged the possibility of using quintuple meter "in the rhythmic system of future music" ("Du développement futur," p. 354); see Arlin, "Metric Mutation."

74 Haupmann, *Harmony and Metre*, p. 204.

75 Each dot represents a single degree of accentuation. Hauptmann also uses the caret and inverted caret to express varying grades of accentuation.

Example 21.9 Accent patterns from Hauptmann, *Harmony and Metre*
(a) p. 238

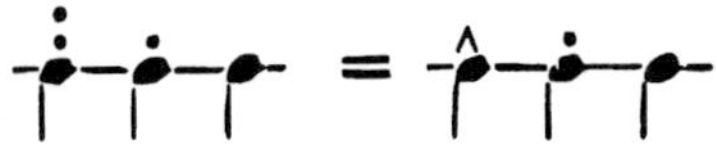

(b) p. 239

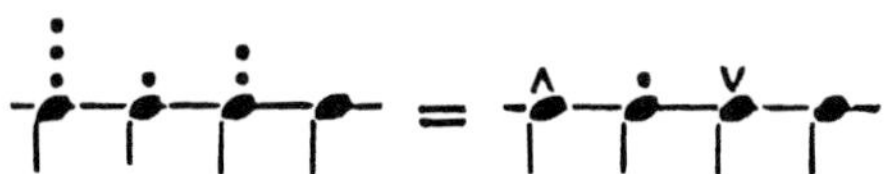

results in the pattern shown in Example 21.9b. Here, Hauptmann traditionally accords greater weight to the first beat than to the third, but he is unique among theorists in assigning accentuation to the second beat as well.

Having so vehemently argued that a metrical unit begins with an accent, Hauptmann reverses his position and claims that such a unit can start with a second, unaccented member. He justifies this turn around by invoking dualist notions that he used earlier in his treatise to account for the minor triad (and minor modality in general). In harmony, the major triad (and modality) achieves *positive unity*; on the contrary, the minor triad expresses *negative unity* because of its "backwards construction" (whereby the fifth of the chord is viewed as the logical starting point of harmonic organization).[76] In meter, a "major" or positive metrical unit begins with a first, accented time-span; a "minor" or negative meter begins with a second, unaccented span. This idea becomes clearer when Hauptmann represents the two forms in musical notation:

> In the metrical notion of major the first and second as positive unity is musically written: |♩♩|.
>
> In the metrical notion of minor the second and first as negative unity is musically written: ♩|♩.
>
> This beginning with the unaccented member is called the *upbeat*.[77]

Thus a metrical unit is not confined within the bar lines of a piece but rather can, through a negative accentuation, begin with an upbeat and cross over to the subsequent downbeat. It is clear, then, that Hauptmann's meter means more than the *Takt* of the traditional *Akzenttheorie*, for the analysis of a metrical unit involves not only an identification of accented and unaccented events but also the specific *grouping* of these differentiated events.

Like most nineteenth-century theorists of the *Akzenttheorie* tradition, Hauptmann observes that musical works contain many accents and unaccents in a wide variety of

76 Hauptmann, *Harmony and Metre*, pp. 14–17. For a discussion of Hauptmann's theory of harmonic dualism, see **Chapter 14, pp. 459–62.** 77 Ibid., p. 214.

Hauptmann's patterns of accentuation

Hauptmann holds that any basic (two-part) metrical formation may be "positive" by beginning with an accented element that progresses to an unaccented element (which he represents as "1—2") or may be "negative" by beginning with an unaccented element progressing to an accented one ("2—1"). Since he conceives of triple and quadruple meters as originating out of two-part metrical formations, he can generate a variety of accentual patterns by allowing each component formation to be positive or negative. In the case of triple meter, eight possible patterns may result; for quadruple meter, the total increases to thirty-two patterns. A selection of patterns for each meter are shown here. By "adding up" the various accented elements within a pattern, Hauptmann generates beats that have differing accentual weights. Thus in the triple pattern (b), the first beat has no accentuation, the second beat has double accentuation, and the third beat has single accentuation. Hauptmann further interprets this pattern to represent a metrical group that begins with an upbeat leading to the metrical downbeat and concluding with the second beat (which also has some accentual strength). In pattern (c), the first beat has single accentuation, the second beat, double accentuation, and the third beat remains unaccented. Here, Hauptmann sees the first beat as the metrical downbeat, with the second beat having stronger accentuation. Although Hauptmann presents these many metrical patterns in the abstract, he means them to represent actual musical situations. Thus pattern (c) just discussed would represent the special weight accorded the second beat in a sarabande, for example. Or a four-beat motive that features a crescendo anacrusis to a downbeat would take the form shown in pattern (k).

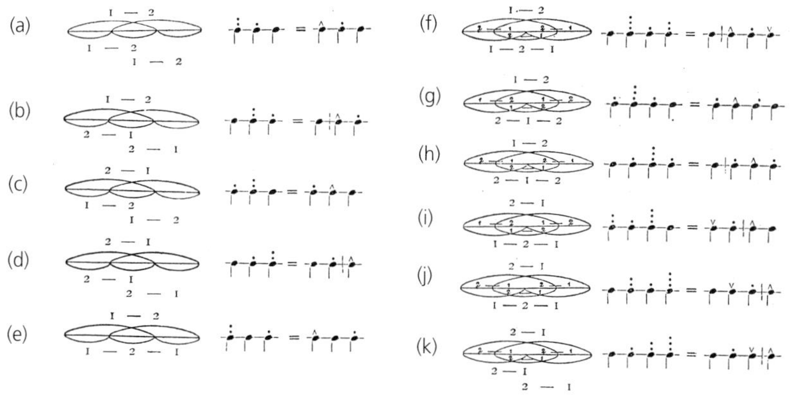

(a) I — 2 / I — 2 / I — 2

(b) I — 2 / 2 — I / 2 — I

(c) 2 — I / I — 2 / I — 2

(d) 2 — I / 2 — I / 2 — I

(e) I — 2 / I — 2 — I

(f) I — 2 / I — 2 — I

(g) I — 2 / 2 — I — 2

(h) I — 2 / 2 — I — 2

(i) 2 — I / I — 2 — I

(j) 2 — I / I — 2 — I

(k) 2 — I / 2 — I / 2 — I

patterns. By introducing the notion of negative meter, he can account for these numerous groupings and accents within the groups. His model generates all usable metrical forms, while excluding those that are not "natural" (or, as we would say today, not "stylistic"). The significance of his conceptions must not be undervalued: whereas many theorists distinguish among different types of accent (metrical, rhythmic, expressive), Hauptmann is the first to propose a truly unified theory of accent: "no accent can be an isolated determination, nor occur in a single portion of time as a solitary element not standing in an arrangement of accents and not in reciprocal relation with all the other parts of time in a metrical unity. Each single accent is always rooted

Example 21.10 Analysis of *rhythme* from Reicha, *Traité*, Example R[2]

in the metrical system."[78] Hauptmann recognizes that no matter how an accent may actually function, be it the first beat of a measure or a stressed second beat, the accent must ultimately be conceived in terms of one fundamental principle. Whereas Lussy presents a series of ad hoc rules and observations, Hauptmann attempts to establish a theoretically coherent system.

Higher-level rhythm

Symmetry. The eighteenth-century notion that phrase structure and melodic organization are essentially rhythmic phenomena (see the earlier discussion of Riepel, Kirnberger, and Koch) continued to find expression in early nineteenth-century theories, such as those of Jérôme-Joseph de Momigny, Antonín Reicha, Fétis, and Weber.[79] Indeed the word *rhythm* was specifically used by Reicha as a technical term for mid-level units of phrase organization (approximately four measures).[80] A distinguishing feature of these theories is the central role played by the aesthetic ideal of *symmetry*. To be sure, eighteenth-century theorists tended to privilege symmetrical phrase groupings; nonetheless, Koch's "basic" phrase, for example, could contain three or five measures, without necessarily being referred to a four-measure norm. Undoubtedly influenced by stylistic changes in early nineteenth-century music (Beethoven's phrase groupings are consistently more regular than those of Haydn and Mozart), contemporary theorists emphasized symmetry as a major component of rhythm.[81] As Weber notes, rhythm's "essential nature . . . consists in a perfect symmetry, as it respects the duration and the accent of the tones."[82] The analytical fallout of this emphasis can be witnessed in Reicha's *Traité de melodie*, where, in an effort to preserve the goal of a "square rhythm" (*rhythme carré*), a ten-measure melody is analyzed (rather unconvincingly) as three four-measure phrases (*rhythme*), whose third and sixth measures have overlapping functions (see Example 21.10).[83]

78 Ibid., p. 253.
79 It is not until somewhat later, with Marx, for example, that these concerns are associated more with form than with rhythm. See **Chapter 28, pp. 882–83**.
80 Baker, "*Ars poetica*," pp. 428–29; Fischer, "System and Impulse," pp. 36–39; London, "Phrase Structure," pp. 25–27. 81 London, "Phrase Structure," p. 21.
82 Weber, *Musical Composition*, vol. 1, p. 62.
83 See Baker, "*Ars poetica*," p. 432, who compares this analysis with another one based on the principles of Koch.

Hypermeter. As theorists came to consider higher-level rhythms to be essentially symmetrical, they increasingly characterized them as decidedly *metrical* in quality. Thus Reicha describes a rhythmic hierarchy in which entire measures and measure groupings mark off equivalent time-spans, just as do the individual beats of a measure.[84] Here, a rudimentary notion of hypermeter is clearly suggested, although, as George Fisher notes, "the conception . . . is durational rather than accentual; meter is defined by a succession of equal spans rather than by any accentual gestalt."[85] Momigny's version of the rhythmic hierarchy goes a step further by implicating more directly a sense of metrical accent. He starts with the motion from upbeat (*levé*) to downbeat (*frappé*), a fundamental pattern that he sees replicated at higher levels of musical structure.[86] A more explicit formulation of hypermeter is offered by Weber, in whose rhythmic hierarchy "the measures are distinguished from one another . . . in respect to their greater or lesser internal weight or accentuation, in the same way as the parts of measure are distinguished among themselves."[87] With Weber, the essential elements of a fully-functional hypermeter are set in place. The analytical application of hypermeter by early nineteenth-century theorists, however, remained scanty. It was not until Riemann, considerably later in the century, that a new model of hypermeter engendered a significant quantity of analytical work.

Critique of the Akzenttheorie: *Hugo Riemann*

The *Akzenttheorie*, initiated by Kirnberger, elaborated most practically by Lussy, and formulated most theoretically by Hauptmann, elicited its greatest critique in the writings of Hugo Riemann (1849–1919). Though following at first in the footsteps of Hauptmann, Riemann soon broke with his theoretical mentor and propounded what he believed to be a fundamentally new conception of rhythm and meter. According to Riemann, the *Akzenttheorie* is deficient in a number of respects. First, the theory is mistakenly premised on an analogy with the rhythm of natural language, whereby the idea of accented and unaccented syllables is transferred to musical tones. Second, the alternation of accents and unaccents implies that performers introduce abrupt changes in tone intensity, thus yielding a mode of musical phrasing that is "tasteless [and] contradictory to the practice of all good artists."[88] Third, the attempts by theorists, such as Lussy, to break away from the mechanical performance of metrical accents by proposing a variety of rhythmic and expressive accents results in a hotchpotch of ad hoc formulations and individual solutions lacking theoretical precision and (especially important for Riemann) any sense of *system*. As correctives, Riemann offers two new models of musical rhythm, the first

84 Reicha, *Traité*, p. 17, note 1. 85 Fisher, "System and Impulse," p. 38.

86 Momigny, *Cours complet*; see London, "Phrase Structure," p. 22; Seidel, *Rhythmustheorien*, pp. 199–204. 87 Weber, *Musical Composition*, vol. I, p. 87.

88 Riemann, "Die musikalische Phrasierung," in *Präludien und Studien*, vol. 1, p. 76.

Example 21.11 Dynamic shading from Riemann, *Musikalische Dynamik*, p. 11

of which appears most fully developed in his early treatise *Musikalische Dynamik und Agogik* (1884). A second model, reflecting Riemann's mature theory, is found scattered among a number of his other writings.

Musical dynamic and agogic. Riemann's initial model is based not on a series of undifferentiated pulses, as in the *Akzenttheorie*, but rather on the gradually changing intensity of two or three tones grouped into a *metrical motive*.[89] The most important feature of a metrical motive is its *dynamic shading* (*dynamische Schattierung*): a steady growth, a becoming, a "positive development" leads to a *dynamic climax* followed by a passing away, a dying off, a "negative development" (see Example 21.11). That the crescendo and decrescendo notations were meant as actual indications of tone intensity is obvious from much of Riemann's discussion; thus his, like Lussy's, is clearly a theory of musical performance, one rooted in a Romantic aesthetic of ultra-expressivity. That Riemann intended dynamic shading to be a theory of meter also becomes evident when he indicates in a number of statements, and in many examples throughout his treatise, that the dynamic climax of a metrical motive normally occurs at the tone immediately following the bar line.

Yet a closer examination reveals that his theory fails to function as a genuine metrical theory, for in a number of significant ways, the experiential phenomena embraced by the traditional concept of metrical accentuation finds no direct expression in Riemann's account.[90] For example, the primary metrical accent at the beginning of a 4/4 or 6/8 meter is realized by the dynamic climax, but in some cases, the *secondary* accents of traditional theory (e.g., the third quarter note in 4/4, the fourth eighth note in 6/8) may have the least intensity and thus function instead as the dynamic *nadir* (*Nullpunkt*) at the boundary between two motives (see Example 21.12).[91] In other instances, Riemann refers to the "displacement of the dynamics" without suggesting that the prevailing meter is at all disrupted, such as the syncopation shown in Example 21.13. Other examples of a displaced dynamic climax arise when Riemann brings melodic and harmonic issues into consideration, such as in Example 21.14, where the dynamic climax (as indicated by Riemann's addition of crescendo and decrescendo

89 Riemann's theory of musical dynamics is discussed by Seidel, *Rhythmustheorien*, pp. 161–67; Smithers, "Theories of Rhythm," pp. 187–229. 90 See Caplin, "Dynamic Shading."

91 Riemann unconventionally uses the time signatures 2/3 and 3/2 to represent 6/8 and 3/4 respectively (see *Musikalische Dynamik*, pp. 28–29).

Example 21.12 Dynamic shading from Riemann, *Musikalische Dynamik*, pp. 26, 29

Example 21.13 Displaced dynamic climax from Riemann, *Musikalische Dynamik*, p. 52

Example 21.14 Displaced dynamic climax from Riemann, *Musikalische Dynamik*, p. 188 (from Beethoven, Piano Sonata in D, Op. 10, No. 3, second movement, mm. 84–86)

signs) is shifted back to the last eighth note in the measures, presumably because of the intensity imparted by the diminished-seventh chords at these points. In these cases, the dynamic climax would seem to mark what traditional theories would recognize as nonmetrical accents (especially Lussy's expressive accents).

Riemann's theory is inadequate as an account of musical meter in another important respect: the dynamic shading of a metrical motive can reflect just a single structural level. In recognition of this limitation, Riemann introduces the concept of *agogic* accent – the minute durational extension of an individual note – to differentiate, for example, a 3/4 meter from a 6/8 meter (as shown by the carets in Example 21.15). But since an agogic accent is applicable to a single note only, it cannot be used to differentiate events at higher levels of metrical structure. Thus for a variety of reasons, the theory of musical dynamics failed to provide the basis for a comprehensive theory of meter. It is not surprising, therefore, that when Riemann turned his attention more to issues of higher-level rhythm in his mature theories, he proposed a revised model of

Example 21.15 Agogic accents from Riemann, *Musikalische Dynamik*, pp. 31–32

alternating accents and unaccents at multiple levels of structure, in other words, a kind of *Akzenttheorie*.

The mature theory. By the end of the nineteenth century, Riemann's theories of rhythm and meter had crystallized into a relatively unified view, one that found fairly consistent expression in a wide range of theoretical and pedagogical publications.[92] He continued to build upon many of his ideas of musical dynamics, but reformulated them in such a way that they could function as a framework for providing metrical (especially, hypermetrical) interpretations of musical content, from the simplest motive to the full eight-measure period. The new model finds various representations, but features essentially the same principles (see Example 21.16 for one such version).

For Riemann, the experience of music involves a mode of *active* listening (*Tonvorstellung*) whereby an initial musical idea is presented as a kind of *question*, which demands, and thus leads to, a concluding *answer*. This incessant progression toward a goal, which represents a moment of metrical strength (Riemann generally avoided

92 Such as *Rhythmik und Metrik*, *Große Kompositionslehre*, and *Vademecum der Phrasierung*. In addition to presenting his ideas in theoretical treatises, Riemann advanced his views in analytical studies on Bach's *Well-Tempered Clavier* and the piano sonatas of Mozart and Beethoven. Moreover, he produced the infamous "phrasing editions" (*Phrasierungsausgaben*) of these piano sonatas, in which the original phrase markings by Mozart and Beethoven are entirely replaced by those conforming to his own principles. Riemann's mature theory is discussed in Seidel, *Rhythmustheorien*, pp. 180–99; Smithers, "Theories of Rhythm," pp. 229–48; Apfel and Dahlhaus, *Studien*, vol. 1; and Waldbauer, "Riemann's Periodization."

Example 21.16 Metrical analysis of an eight-measure period from Riemann, "Neue Beiträge," p. 11

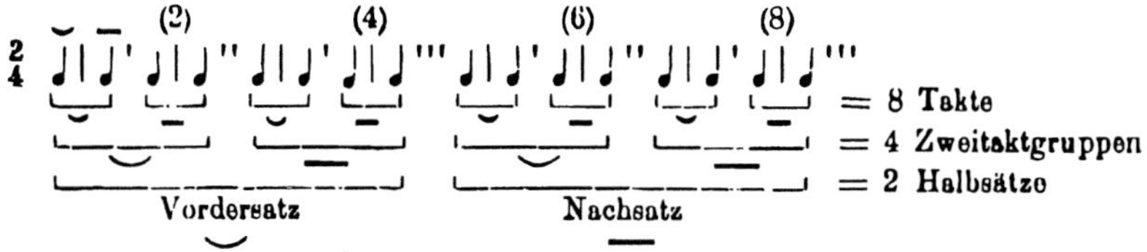

speaking of "accents"), characterizes rhythmical and metrical motion at all levels of formal structure. The elementary *metrical unit* is two-part, beginning with an upbeat (*Auftakt*) and leading to a downbeat.[93] (For Riemann, the traditional measure, beginning with an accented event, is a fiction.) The metrical unit replicates itself at successive levels in the hierarchy to the eight-measure period.[94] Like the *Akzenttheorie*, Riemann's model consists of alternating accented and unaccented events at multiple levels. But whereas the traditional scheme suggests beginning-accented groupings, Riemann's units are exclusively end-accented.[95] He never permits an event located on a metrically strong position to function as the first of a group. Even in cases where there is an obvious beginning on a strong beat, Riemann groups that beat back to some imaginary prior event. His dogmatism on this score has been, needless to say, the source of continual derision from later theorists.

In Riemann's mature theory, the general nineteenth-century tendency to interpret higher-level rhythms as hypermetrical achieved its most explicit formulation and extensive analytical application. His fundamental requirement that groupings be end-accented resulted in his analyzing the eight-measure normative period such that the even-numbered measures, the cadential ideas, and the consequent phrase are seen as the logical goals, and thus metrically stronger, in relation to preceding odd-numbered measures, initiating ideas, and antecedent phrase. Though Reimann seemed to have established an abstract, a priori model, he actually took pains to justify his analyses in terms of specific harmonic criteria, such as harmonic rhythm and *cadential action* (*Schlußwirkung*).[96] His hypermetrical interpretations, though roundly criticized in

93 Triple meters arise when the downbeat is doubled (*Musik-Lexikon*, pp. 936–37).
94 Example 21.16 shows a hierarchy consisting of eight one-measure units (*Takte*), four two-measure groups (*Zweitaktgruppen*), and two phrases (*Halbsätze*), consisting of antecedent (*Vordersatz*) and consequent (*Nachsatz*). The term *Vierhebigkeit*, originally referring to a "four-foot" metrical verse of German text, has been often been associated with Riemann's insistence on the four-square organization of musical meter (see Smithers, "Theories of Rhythm," p. 232). He uses the term rarely, however, in connection with his model of the eight-measure period and its analytical application for tonal music.
95 Riemann acknowledges that his views in this respect were anticipated by Momigny, who, as mentioned earlier, found an upbeat–downbeat progression at the basis of all rhythmic motion.
96 See Caplin, "Harmonic–Metric Relationships," pp. 348–72.

many quarters,[97] were nonetheless highly influential, not only on German theory, but on some twentieth-century North American thinkers as well.[98]

Riemann's "analytical sketch" of the slow movement ("Introduzione") of Beethoven's "Waldstein" Sonata, Op. 53, illustrates well his general approach to meter and phrasing (see Example 21.17). Riemann recognizes at the basis of the movement three eight-measure periods, whose beginnings he indicates with Roman numerals in mm. 1 (I), 10 (II), and 17 (III). Within each period, he identifies which measures relate to his abstract model using arabic numerals in parentheses (below the music, mixed in with the letter symbols for the harmonic functions).[99] He normally identifies only the even-numbered, metrically strong measures. But for the first and third periods, he also specifies m. 7, because in both periods, this "ideal" measure actually embraces two successive measures, labeled (‿7) and (7‿) (for mm. 7–8 and 27–28 respectively). This seventh measure initially brings a deceptive cadence and thus groups backwards (as indicated by the "‿" sign) as weak in relation to the preceding m. 6. But then the following measure, with its cadential preparation, also functions as a "seventh" measure, which groups forward (more in conformance with the model) with the following strong m. 8 containing the cadential arrival. As a result of this "doubling" of m. 7, the first normative 8-measure period is extended to nine measures.[100] The third period is likewise elongated because of a doubled m. 7, but in addition, this period is subjected to an even greater extension owing to the stretching out of the dominant of C major (mm. 21–26). Riemann understands this extension to create a repetition of mm. 5 and 6 of the normative period, as indicated in the analytical sketch with "6a" (at m. 24) and "6b" (m. 26).[101] This third period concludes at the very beginning of the following movement, thus creating an elided cadence when m. 8 of the period becomes m. 1 of the Rondo finale (8 = 1). A similar cadential elision occurs at the end of the second period (m. 27), which otherwise conforms to the eight-measure model.

As for the phrasing of the motivic material making up these periods, Riemann's "end-accented" approach is followed through obsessively: not a single collection of

97 His general approach is diametrically opposed to a more typically Viennese tradition (revealed in the metrical analyses of Bruckner and Schenker), in which the beginning-accented notated measure provides the model for the grouping of measures at higher levels. Theodore Wiehmayer's *Musikalische Rhythmik und Metrik* is the most significant German study to oppose Riemann's hypermetrical interpretations.

98 A distinctly "Princetonian" tradition, expressed in the writings of Roger Sessions, Edward T. Cone, and many of their students (Arthur J. Komar, William E. Benjamin, Robert P. Morgan, and Joel Lester), seems to have been significantly influenced by Riemann's notion that cadential articulation is a significant rhythmic goal, often with metrical qualities of strength or accent.

99 For a discussion and explanation of Riemann's harmonic analysis of this very movement, see **Chapter 25, pp. 799–800**. For a related analysis of another Beethoven sonata movement (in this case, the allegro from Op. 10, No. 1), see **Examples 28.1 and 28.2, pp. 894–97**.

100 Riemann acknowledges that this type of measure doubling is a "rare phenomenon" (*Beethovens Klavier-Solosonaten*, vol. III, p. 31).

101 In the accompaning text, Riemann explicitly refers to mm. 5a–6a and mm. 5b–6b (ibid.).

Example 21.17 Analytical sketch of Beethoven, "Waldstein" Sonata, second movement, from Riemann, *Beethovens Klavier-Solosonaten*, vol. III, pp. 32–33

Example 21.17 (*cont.*)

pitches is conceived to begin with an accented element. Thus both the opening bass F on the downbeat of m. 1 and the initial note in the melody C in the following eighth are grouped backwards to some imaginary event prior to the beginning of the piece. The subsequent motive begins with the upbeat thirty-second note and concludes with the first eighth-note E in the following measure (on the second eighth-note beat).[102] As a result, the motive "bridges over the rest" on the downbeat of m. 2. This mode of phrasing, which prohibits beginning-accented groups, is, of course, entirely discredited today. In fact, many performers, especially those influenced by the "historical performance practice" movement, tend to place high value on the composers' actual phrasing notations, which, in the case of the Baroque and Classical styles, tend to begin metrical units. Yet, just as the post-modern "new musicology" of recent years has revived the hermeneutic models of the nineteenth-century *fin-de-siècle*, so perhaps might a Riemann-like phrasing become fashionable again among performers.

The theoretical writings of Riemann stand at the end of an era in the history of rhythmic thought. The major issues that preoccupied theorists for two centuries received their most comprehensive and systematic exposition in his voluminous output. Those theorists at the beginning of the twentieth century who chose to continue pursuing issues of rhythm were inevitably drawn into continual debate with Riemann's ideas, even if the leading figures of that period (Schenker, Kurth, Tovey) generally eschewed the search for a systematic theory of rhythm (although each nonetheless had suggestive and rich ideas to contribute on the topic). Still other theorists found inspiration from new ideas on gestalt psychology, philosophy, and linguistics. But these are developments that constitute a separate chapter in the history of rhythmic theory.

102 Riemann notes that since the thirty-second-note figure becomes a clear motive in its own right in mm. 24–25, it should be indicated as originating at the beginning of the movement (ibid., p. 30).

Bibliography

Primary sources

Bononcini, G. M. *Musico prattico*, Bologna, G. Monti, 1673; facs. New York, Broude, 1969

Butler, C. *The Principles of Musik*, London, J. Haviland, 1639; facs. New York, Da Capo Press, 1970

Fétis, F.-J. "Du développement futur de la musique, Dans le domaine de rhythme," *Gazette musicale de Paris* 19 (1852), pp. 281–84, 289–92, 297–300, 325–27, 353–56, 361–63, 401–04, 457–60, 473–76

Hauptmann, M. *Die Natur der Harmonik und der Metrik*, Leipzig, Breitkopf und Härtel, 1853; trans. W. Heathcote as *The Nature of Harmony and Metre*, London, S. Sonnenschein, 1888

Heinichen, J. D. *Der General-Bass in der Composition*, Dresden, Heinichen, 1728; facs. Hildesheim, G. Olms, 1969 and 1994

Janowka, T. B. *Clavis ad thesaurum magnae artis musicae*, Prague, G.Labaun, 1701; facs. Amsterdam, F. Knuf, 1973

Kirnberger, J. P. *Die Kunst des reinen Satzes*, 2 vols., Berlin, Decker und Hartung, 1771–79; facs. Hildesheim, G. Olms, 1968 and 1988; trans. D. Beach and J. Thym as *The Art of Strict Musical Composition*, New Haven, Yale University Press, 1982

Koch, H. C. *Versuch einer Anleitung zur Composition*, 3 vols., Leipzig, A. F. Böhme, 1782–93; facs. Hildesheim, G. Olms, 1969 and 2000; partial trans. N. Baker as *Introductory Essay on Composition*, New Haven, Yale University Press, 1983

Lussy, M. *Le Rythme musical; son origine, sa fonction et son accentuation*, Paris, Heugel, 1883

Traité de l'expression musicale: accents, nuance et mouvements dans la musique vocale et instrumentale (1874), 4th edn., Paris, Fischbacher, 1882; trans. M. E. von Glehn as *Musical Expression; Accents, Nuances, and Tempo in Vocal and Instrumental Music*, London, Novello and Ewer, 1892

Marpurg, F. W. *Anleitung zur Musik überhaupt*, Berlin, A. Wever, 1763; facs. Leipzig, Zentralantiquariat der DDR, 1975

Marx, A. B. *Allgemeine Musiklehre* (1839), rev. edn., Leipzig, Breitkopf und Härtel, 1841

Mattheson, J. *Critica musica*, 2 vols., vol. I, Hamburg, Mattheson, 1722–23, vol. II, Hamburg, T. von Wierings Erben, 1725; facs. Amsterdam, F. Knuf, 1964

Das neu-eröffnete Orchestre, Hamburg, B. Schiller, 1713; facs. Hildesheim, G. Olms, 1993 and 1997

Der vollkommene Capellmeister, Hamburg, C. Herold, 1739; facs. Kassel, Bärenreiter, 1954; trans. and ed. E. C. Harriss as *Johann Mattheson's "Der vollkommene Capellmeister"*, Ann Arbor, UMI Research Press, 1981

Mersenne, M. *Harmonie Universelle*, Paris, S. Cramoisy, 1636–37; facs. Paris, Centre National de la Recherche Scientifique, 1963 and 1986

Momigny, J.-J. de, *Cours complet d'harmonie et de composition*, 3 vols., Paris, Momigny and Bailleul, 1803–06

Praetorius, M. *Syntagma musicum*, 3 vols., Wolfenbüttel, E. Holwein, 1614–20; facs. Kassel, Bärenreiter, 1958–59

Printz, W. C. *Phrynis Mitilenaeus, oder Satyrischer Componist*. 3 vols., Dresden, J. C. Mieth and J. C. Zimmerman, 1696

Reicha, A. *Traité de mélodie*, Paris, J. L. Sherff, 1814

Riemann, H. *L. van Beethovens sämtliche Klavier-Solosonaten*, 3 vols., 6th edn., Berlin, M. Hesse, 1925

Große Kompositionslehre, 2 vols., Berlin, W. Spemann, 1902–03

Musik-Lexikon, 5th edn., Leipzig, M. Hesse, 1900

Musikalische Dynamik und Agogik, Hamburg, D. Rahter, 1884

"Neue Beiträge zu einer Lehre von den Tonvorstellungen," *Jahrbuch der Musikbibliothek Peters* 23 (1916), pp. 1–21

Präludien und Studien, 3 vols., Leipzig, H. Seemann, 1895–1901; facs. Hildesheim, G. Olms, 1967

System der musikalischen Rhythmik und Metrik, Leipzig, Breitkopf und Härtel, 1903

Vademecum der Phrasierung, 2nd rev. edn., Berlin, M. Hesse, 1906

Riemann, H., ed., *Sonaten für Klavier, von Ludwig van Beethoven*, in Riemann, *Phrasierungsausgaben*, vol. II, Berlin, N. Simrock, 1885

Sonaten für Klavier, von W. A. Mozart, in Riemann, *Phrasierungsausgaben*, vol. 1, Berlin, N. Simrock, 1883

Riepel, J. *Anfangsgründe zur musicalischen Setzkunst*, 5 vols., Regensburg, Frankfurt, or Augsburg, variously E. F. Bader, J. L. Montag, J. J. Lotter, or J. C. Krippner, 1752–68

Scheibe, J. A. *Der critische Musikus*, Leipzig, J. C. Breitkopf, 1745

Sulzer, J. G. *Allgemeine Theorie der schönen Künste*, 2 vols., Leipzig, M. G. Weidmann, 1771–74; facs. Hildesheim, G. Olms, 1967

Walther, J. G. *Musikalisches Lexicon*, Leipzig, W. Deer, 1732; facs. Kassel, Bärenreiter, 1953

Praecepta der Musicalischen Composition, ed. P. Benary, Leipzig, Breitkopf und Härtel, 1955

Weber, G. *Versuch einer geordneten Theorie der Tonsetzkunst* (1817–21), 3rd edn., 4 vols., Mainz, B. Schott, 1830–32; trans. J. Warner as *The Theory of Musical Composition*, London, R. Cocks, 1851

Westphal, R. *Allgemeine Theorie der musikalischen Rhythmik seit J. S. Bach*, Leipzig, Breitkopf und Härtel, 1880

Wiehmayer, T. *Musikalische Rhythmik und Metrik*, Magdeburg, Heinrichshofen, 1917

Secondary sources

Apfel, E. and C. Dahlhaus, *Studien zur Theorie und Geschichte der musikalischen Rhythmik und Metrik*, 2 vols., Munich, E. Katzbichler, 1974

Arlin, M. "Metric Mutation and Modulation: The Nineteenth-Century Speculations of F.-J. Fétis," *JMT* 44 (2000), forthcoming

Baker, N. K. "An *Ars poetica* for Music: Reicha's System of Syntax and Structure," in *Musical Humanism and its Legacy: Essays in Honor of Claude V. Palisca*, ed. N. Baker and B. Hanning, Stuyvesant, NY, Pendragon Press, 1992, pp. 419–49

"Heinrich Koch and the Theory of Melody," *JMT* 22 (1976), pp. 1–48

Budday, W. *Grundlagen musikalischer Formen der Wiener Klassik. An Hand der zeitgenössischen Theorie von Joseph Riepel und Heinrich Christoph Koch dargestellt an Menuetten und Sonatensätzen (1750–1790)*, Kassel, Bärenreiter, 1983

Caplin, W. E. "Theories of Harmonic-Metric Relationships from Rameau to Riemann," Ph.D. diss., University of Chicago (1981)

"Riemann's Theory of Dynamic Shading: A Theory of Meter?," *Theoria* 1 (1985), pp. 1–24

Cooper, G. and L. B. Meyer, *The Rhythmic Structure of Music*, University of Chicago Press, 1960

Dahlhaus, C. "Zur Entstehung des modernen Taktsystems im 17. Jahrhundert," *AfMw* 18 (1961), pp. 223–40

Die Musiktheorie im 18. und 19. Jahrhundert, 2 vols., *GMt* 10–11 (1984–86)

Fisher, G. "System and Impulse: Three Theories of Periodic Structure from the Early Nineteenth Century," *Current Musicology* 49 (1992), pp. 29–47

Grave, F. K. "Metrical Displacement and the Compound Measure in Eighteenth-Century Theory and Practice," *Theoria* 1 (1985), pp. 25–60

Hasty, C. F. *Meter as Rhythm*, New York, Oxford University Press, 1997

Horn, W. "Johann David Heinichen und die musikalische Zeit: Die 'quantitas intrinseca' und der Begriff des Akzenttakts," *Musiktheorie* 7 (1992), pp. 195–218

Houle, G. *Meter in Music, 1600–1800*, Bloomington, Indiana University Press, 1987

Knouse, N. R. "Joseph Riepel and the Emerging Theory of Form in the Eighteenth Century," *Current Musicology* 41 (1986), pp. 46–62

Lester, J. *Compositional Theory in the Eighteenth Century*, Cambridge, MA, Harvard University Press, 1992

London, J. "Phrase Structure in 18th- and 19th-Century Theory: An Overview," *Music Research Forum* 5 (1990), pp. 13–50

"Riepel and Absatz: Poetic and Prosaic Aspects of Phrase Structure in 18th-Century Theory," *JM* 8 (1990), pp. 505–19

Maier, S. *Studien zur Theorie des Taktes in der ersten Hälfte des 18. Jahrhunderts*, Tutzing, H. Schneider, 1984

Schwindt-Gross, N. "Einfache, zusammengesetzte und doppelt notierte Takte: Ein Aspekt der Takttheorie im 18. Jahrhundert," *Musiktheorie* 4 (1989), pp. 203–22

Seidel, W. *Über Rhythmustheorien der Neuzeit*, Bern, A. Francke, 1975

Sisman, E. "Small and Expanded Forms: Koch's Model and Haydn's Music," *Musical Quarterly* 48 (1982), pp. 444–75

Smithers, H. "Theories of Rhythm in the Nineteenth and Twentieth Centuries with a Contribution to the Theory of Rhythm for the Study of Twentieth-Century Music," Ph.D. diss., Cornell University (1960)

Waldbauer, I. F. "Riemann's Periodization Revisited and Revised," *JMT* 33 (1989), pp. 333–92

· 22 ·

Rhythm in twentieth-century theory

JUSTIN LONDON

We have seen in the previous chapter how Riemann attempted to consolidate various trends in nineteenth-century rhythmic theory, synthesizing rhythm, meter, agogics, and phrase structure within his overarching theory of harmonic functionality. As was perhaps inevitable with such a comprehensive project, various tensions and problems remained in Riemann's mature theory. Many early twentieth-century theorists such as August Halm, Ernst Kurth, and Hans Mersmann were critical of Riemann's accentual theory, and so in part the history of rhythmic theory, at least at the beginning of the century, can be characterized as "a reaction to Riemann." In addition, there were other musical and intellectual developments which shaped twentieth-century rhythmic theory, among which can be mentioned:

1. There were new ideas of motion and time, from physics, philosophy, and psychology, that led a number of theorists to place musical energetics and motion at the center of their approach to rhythm.
2. Schenker's theory of tonality and tonal dynamics influenced a number of approaches to rhythm and the temporal unfolding of musical events, especially amongst North American theorists in the second half of the century.
3. Developments in linguistics and gestalt psychology influenced "architectonic" approaches to rhythm, engendering structuralist theories that emphasize the hierarchical aspects of rhythm and form.
4. Radical changes in musical style, especially the rise of atonality and serialism, demanded new conceptions of rhythm and meter. This led to various prescriptive theories of rhythm that were often developed (and commented upon) by the composers themselves.

This chapter will selectively review the work of theorists and musicians from each of these four areas. To be sure, these are loose categories, and many theorists have made significant contributions in more than one (e.g., Wallace Berry, who discussed motion and impulse as well as the hierarchic aspects of meter and phrase structure). Yet each is united by a common set of assumptions and concerns, and these are often revealed by the use of a shared terminology, a distinctive set of metaphors, and common descriptive strategies, including notational practices. These terms and metaphors will be noted at the head of each section, as they are markers for discursive engagement amongst theorists of the same and successive generations.

Rhythm, motion, and time

In the twentieth century a number of theorists have regarded motion and movement as the essential substrate of musical rhythm and form. These theorists sought to account for rhythm in terms of dynamic or "energetic" processes, rather than in the architectural arrangement of musical elements – in terms of temporal becoming, as opposed to being. Their emphasis on the kinetic qualities of music and musical experience was influenced by contemporaneous trends in philosophy and psychology, and in their work one finds references to phenomenology (Husserl, Heidegger, and Merleau-Ponty), gestalt psychology (Wertheimer and Koffka), and temporal philosophy (James, Bergson, Langer, and Whitehead). Common images and metaphors are of waves (in Kurth and Zuckerkandl), impulses (in Berry) and projection and expectation (in Neumann and Hasty), as well as a concern with the experience and understanding of musical duration and tone succession.

Kurth. In emphasizing rhythmic processes, rather than the forms created by those processes, these theorists stood in opposition to Riemann and his later emphasis on formal archetypes for rhythmic structure. Indeed, in some sense their approach harks back to Riemann's earlier conception of dynamic shading (see **Chapter 21, p. 684**). In Riemann's mature theory the fundamental rhythmic gesture is one of intensification and then relaxation, an upbeat-to-downbeat pairing that has its antecedents in Momigny's *levé–frappé* archetype. Moreover, each measure, pair of measures, and four-bar phrase is an element in an upbeat–downbeat relationship, and collectively they form a symmetrical, eight-bar rhythmic schema. Ernst Kurth (1886–1946) recognized many of these same elements, but rejected the rigidity of the eight-bar schema in favor of a more flexible and continuous approach to musical rhythm. Indeed, with Kurth we have what is probably the most thorough and far-reaching energeticist view of music ever articulated. (see **Chapter 30, pp. 939–44** for further discussion of Kurth's energeticist views).

Kurth accounts for rhythmic gestures from small to large in terms of a nested set of waves or wave-like motions. As Rothfarb has noted: "Short-range formal segments consist of localized surges called 'constituent waves,' which contribute to more broadly paced 'developmental waves.' These in turn mount toward huge 'symphonic waves.'"[1] All of these elements are understood through their relation to the larger symphonic wave. Kurth's views on motion and melody expressed here and in his earlier

1 Rothfarb, *Ernst Kurth as Theorist*, p. 191.

writings are very similar those of August Halm, who said simply "motion is the life of music."[2] Thus Kurth's waves are not temporal "containers" for various rhythmic forms, but rather consist of motion itself. From these waves one then gains a sense of musical space, a space that flows from the rhythmic shapes which themselves are the phenomenal traces of the symphonic waves: "The sense of space is always a reflection of the sense of form. For the sense of space, being evoked by formal processes in the first place, is also contingent upon the particular, stylistically variable type of formal processes for the nature of its aural experience."[3]

Zuckerkandl. Kurth's theory of rhythm and form influenced Lorenz's approach to Wagner and Kurt von Fischer's approach to Beethoven, as well as Toch's *The Shaping Forces of Music*. The theorist who most directly engaged Kurth's ideas of motion and the wave-metaphor to describe such motion, however, was Viktor Zuckerkandl (1896–1965). Zuckerkandl was born and educated in Vienna, and came to the United States prior to World War II. His work is equal parts philosophy, music cognition, and music theory. Zuckerkandl uses the image of a wave to build a theory of meter:

> A measure, then, is a whole made up, not of equal fractions of time, but of differently directed and mutually complementary cyclical phases. But since in time there can be no real going back, and hence, strictly speaking, no real cyclical motion either, since, therefore, every new beat does bring us to a new point in time, the process can be better understood and visualized as a wave . . . which also best corresponds to our sensation of meter. Our sympathetic oscillation with the meter is a sympathetic oscillation with this wave. With every measure we go through the succession of phases characteristic of wave motion: subsidence from the wave crest, reversal of motion in the wave trough, ascent toward a new crest, attainment of the summit, which immediately turns into a new subsidence.[4]

Note that these waves are both in the music and in the listening ear – the "sympathetic oscillations" noted above. Zuckerkandl gives an illustration of the metrical wave in the opening measures of Chopin's A major Polonaise (see Figure 22.1). He notes that "the tones fall upon the wave that they themselves have generated; the wave imparts its motion to the tones" (p. 171). In this way Zuckerkandl acknowledges the antinomy between rhythm and meter: "Such is the case in all metrical music. To put it metaphorically: the ground upon which the tones fall is itself in wave motion. The wave is the meter; rhythm arises from the different arrangements of the tones on the wave" (p. 172). Rhythm is the temporal gestalt that emerges from our interaction with tones and the metrical waves they generate. Like Kurth, Zuckerkandl acknowledged that larger, more complex waves could be composed of smaller component waves, though Zuckerkandl did not extend his waves to symphonic dimensions.

2 Halm, *Die Symphonien Anton Bruckners*; trans in Rothfarb, *Ernst Kurth as Theorist*, p. 8.

3 Kurth, *Bruckner*, p. 338; trans. in Rothfarb, *Ernst Kurth: Selected Writings*, p. 191.

4 Zuckerkandl, *Sound and Symbol*, p. 168. (All subsequent citations from Zuckerkandl will be from this work.)

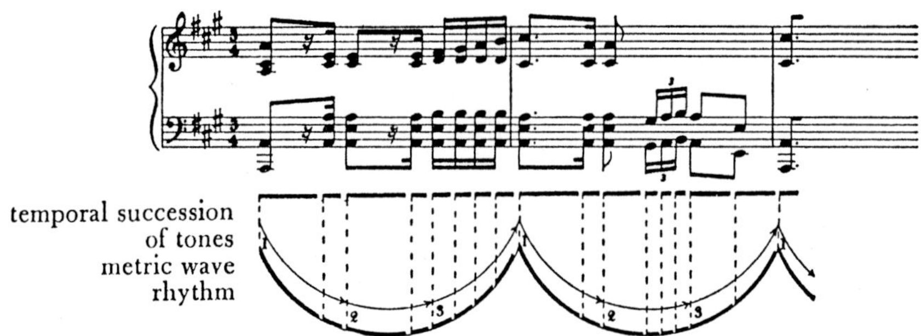

Figure 22.1 Metric wave analysis of Chopin, Polonaise in A major, from Zuckerkandl, *Sound and Symbol*, p. 171

Zuckerkandl's more radical claim is that metrical music makes time itself perceivable. First, he held that motion in its purest sense inhered in and was perceivable in music: "Tonal motion is the most real motion" (p. 139). But of course nothing really moves. So Zuckerkandl goes on to note: "We have come to know – music itself has taught us – that no objects and no object space are necessary to motion. For tonal motion begins precisely where all that – things and their space – comes to an end. But we can name one factor without which motion cannot be, that is, time" (p. 151). But where does this time exist? Zuckerkandl answers: "The time that is at work in music – whose work, indeed, music to an essential degree is – this time cannot be 'in me,' it is not 'my' time. It is where music is; I find it where I find music" (p. 245). Thus for Zuckerkandl, music "both is time and is a symbol of time."[5]

Berry. The Canadian composer and theorist Wallace Berry (1928–91) was also fundamentally concerned in his writings with rhythm and motion. His work in musical rhythm is in large part a response to that of Cooper and Meyer as well as Cone. For Berry, musical structure involves "the punctuated shaping of time and 'space' into lines of growth, decline, and stasis hierarchically ordered."[6] He then goes on to address the subject of motion:

> The concept of musical *motion* is critically allied to the concept of progressive, recessive, and static events and event-complexes. To the extent that motion is a useful concept in musical experience, it may be said to reside in factors of three kinds, of which the most important is that involving changing qualities in contiguous sonorous events. (p. 7)

The three kinds of factors Berry mentions are (1) periodic articulations, (2) intensity changes in successive sound events, and (3) changes in "height" relative to the ambitus of the pitch field. This last factor is akin to changes in intensity, but Berry notes that

5 Jacobs, in Macey, ed., *Encyclopedia of Time*, p. 454.

6 Berry, *Structural Functions in Music*, p. 5.

because it creates the illusion of a spatial field "it has [a] special significance and is usefully regarded as a distinct factor" (p. 8).

Berry's discussion of meter hinges upon his notion of *impulse*:

> *Meter, then, consists of units (large and small at various structural levels) formed by differentiations in the musical events* in what we shall describe as diverse "impulse functions." If there is differentiation it is expressed in some parameter or complex of parameters. *Meter is that aspect of structure articulated as accent-delineated groupings within the attack (event) sequence, and the proportional interrelations of such groups at all levels.* (p. 318, italics in original)

All musical parameters may thus contribute to the formation of metrical impulses, and a metrical impulse may inhere at the highest level of musical structure (cf. Cone's notion of a "structural downbeat"). Berry distinguishes four types of impulses: (1) *initiative impulses*, which "initiate a metric unit" and function as metrical accents, (2) *conclusive impulses*, which are the last in a reactive series and are metrically weak, (3) *reactive impulses*, which are relatively passive or absorptive and which carry the force of the initial initiative impulse, and (4) *anticipative impulses* which "direct energy toward an initiative [impulse]," and thus function as upbeats or anacruses (p. 327). The anticipative-initiative impulses are analogous to the arsis and thesis of Riemann's binary metrical taxonomy, and Berry's reactive and conclusive impulses would seem to capture the phases of subsidence and reversal in Zuckerkandl's description of the metrical wave. Unlike Zuckerkandl or Kurth, however, Berry seems more interested in isolating the various components of the metrical motion than in modeling their continuity.[7]

Neumann. While theorists like Kurth, Zuckerkandl, and Berry concerned themselves with categories and descriptions of motion, Friedrich Neumann (1915–) seems more concerned with the connection(s) between successive musical events. He begins his *Die Zeitgestalt* with an examination of the temporal relationship between a pair of durations. While this is similar to Riemann's basic categories of arsis and thesis, for Neumann their relationship is not given *a priori*, but arises from the emerging temporal relationship between them. He gives the following diagram and explanation (see Figure 22.2):

> Given the two events A and B, *two* discriminations are defined, one from A to B and one from B to a concomitant, unknown potential limit (S), such that the intervals A–B and B–(S) are, in fact, equal (ex. 2). The existence of this potential limit is immediately known to us when a third event C enters. We are then easily, and with great accuracy, able to say whether C coincides with (S) (ex. 3a), or if it enters earlier (ex. 3b) or later (ex. 3c) . . . An uninterrupted whole made up of two discriminations of equal duration and determined by two events and a potential limit we shall call a "*rhythmic pair.*"[8]

7 Note that in "Metric and Rhythmic Articulation in Music" Berry cites Riemann's *Musikalisches Dynamik und Agogik* (1884), but he does not cite Kurth or Zuckerkandl.

8 Neumann, *Die Zeitgestalt*, pp. 18–19; trans. in Hasty, *Meter as Rhythm*, pp. 96–97.

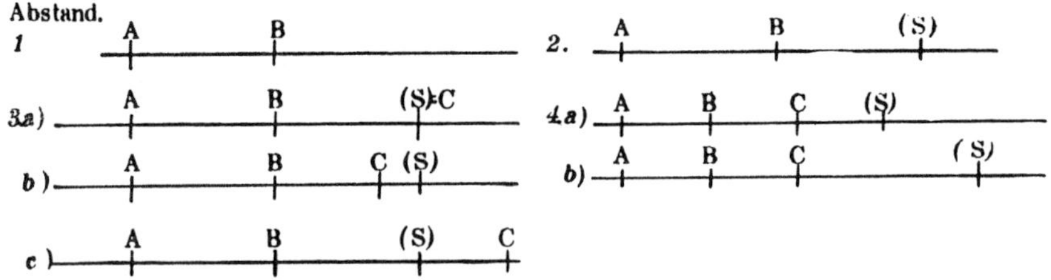

Figure 22. 2 Neumann's formation of a rhythmic pair (taken from Hasty, *Meter as Rhythm*, p. 97)

Neumann makes it clear that meter is wholly separate from rhythm, and that the rhythmic experience of equality is prior to any sense of meter-as-measurement. He goes on to describe the quality of motion and time within the rhythmic pair:

> Now further, in order to experience the temporal *content* of the rhythmic pair it is necessary that we set out and traverse the pair as a closed event that is surveyed in advance. Here two opposed qualities are revealed to us with some clarity. Namely, on the way from [point] A to [point] B temporal consciousness is directed predominantly toward the future, toward the arrival of B. This state we will label as *expectation* (*Erwartung*). From B to [a future point] S, however, the direction of our attention is reversed; consciousness glances back toward the past stretch A–B and avoids any thoughts of the coming potential limit (S) in order that the wholeness of the pair not be disturbed. This state we will label *recollection* (*Erinnerung*), and expectation and recollection form complementary qualities whose order may not be reversed without destroying wholeness. It lies in the nature of expectation that it *intensifies* with the growth of duration, and in the nature of recollection that it *dies away*.[9]

The distinction between expectation and recollection underlies the rhythmic distinction between "strong" and "weak" (or rhythmic accent vs. unaccent), but this maps onto rhythm and meter in different ways:

> In general . . . in the stronger parts recollection and immediate comprehension predominate, and in the weaker parts, expectation. An important consequence emerges in this connection. In the metrical the difference between stressed and unstressed parts is a *graduated* one, i.e., even the unstressed part has a certain stress, if, nevertheless, a weaker one. However, in the rhythmic, which looks toward content, stressed and unstressed parts *are set in logical opposition* – the unstressed point to the future, the stressed to the past.[10]

Thus it is because the motion from A to B engenders expectation, and B to (S) recollection, that the rhythmic pair naturally tends to be heard as weak to strong (as in Riemann). Furthermore, as Hasty has noted, "Neumann does not find it necessary to reduce other formations to an underlying *Paarigkeit*. Rather, by expanding the catalog

9 Ibid., pp. 19–20; p. 97. 10 Ibid., p. 39; p. 40.

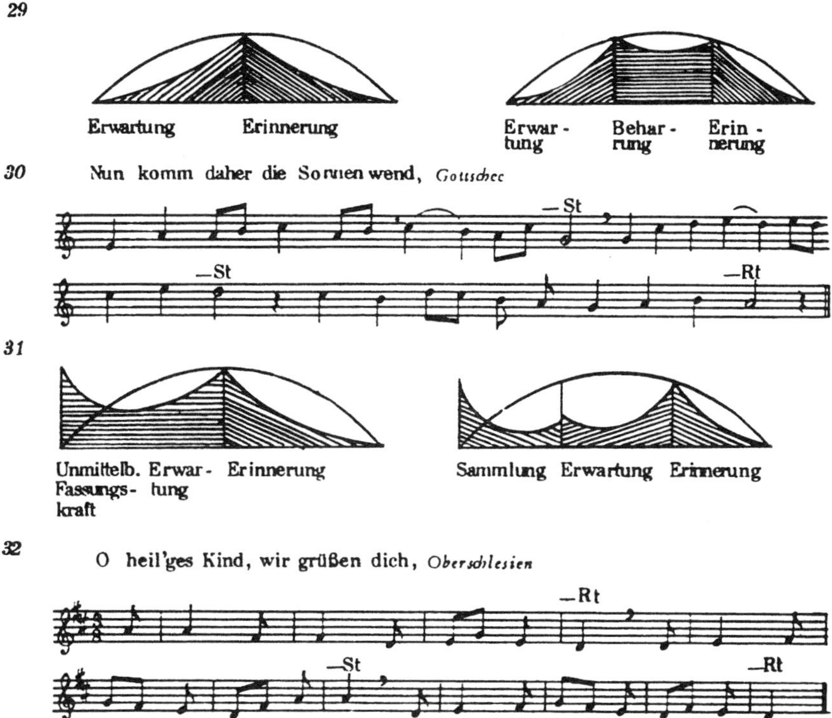

Figure 22.3 Neumann's dynamic shadings (taken from Hasty, *Meter as Rhythm*, p. 99)

of rhythmic qualities Neumann is able to describe three- or five-part schemes and variations within the two-part scheme as fully particular *Zeitgestalten* . . . These schemes include more complex tone sequences as well as 'time shapes' that encompass many bars."[11] Thus in addition to expectation (*Erwartung*) and recollection (*Erinnerung*), Neumann includes phases of persistence (*Beharrung*) and accumulation (*Sammlung*) (see Figure 22.3).

Neumann's approach and models for various *Zeitgestalten* informs Christopher Hasty's *Meter as Rhythm*, published in 1997. Hasty's approach to rhythm and musical time is also strongly influenced by Bergson's and Whitehead's discussions of time and temporal experience. When we listen to a tone, Hasty claims we have a sense of the musical present, a "feeling of growth, a feeling of continually new and expanding duration, and a feeling of [the] potential for becoming" (p. 72). A beginning such as a tone onset is for Hasty a "potential for duration." A second tone concretizes this

11 Hasty, *Meter as Rhythm*, p. 99.

potential into an actual duration, and if the duration is neither too long or too short (given the limits of our perceptual faculties), this "determinate duration" may be projected forward to anticipate the onset of a third event: "If durational determinacy is linked to the effect a duration has or can have on the formation of other events, we may speak of degrees or types of determinacy . . . A specific sort of determinacy characterizes the durations we call metrical" (p. 78). Contra Neumann, Hasty seeks to reunite rhythm and meter by viewing meter as a particular kind of rhythmic process. Like Neumann, Hasty has a variety of categories to describe different projective processes (e.g., *arsic* vs. *anacrustic* continuations of projective process, and a special category of *deferral*, akin to *Beharrung*, that is involved in the formation of triple meters). In addition, Hasty examines the ways in which projective potentials may be hierarchically embodied.

Clifton. Thomas Clifton (1935–78) also considered the problem of the musical present, though his concern was with the present of a broader scope. The phenomenological terms "protention," "retention," and "horizon" – which are taken from Husserl – are the keys to Clifton's account of the musical present. Clifton begins with retention, which is not to be confused with memory:

> Husserl characterizes retention as a kind of memory, called "primary remembrance" (*primäre Erinnerung*), distinguishable from the secondary sort of memory which is cut off from the felt present. Retention clings to events happening now, qualifying the real now with a wider, phenomenal now. Just as importantly, the retended object is modified by the actually present sensations of that object. Retention is a form of memory which is articulated with the present, the two interacting with and influencing the content of each. We say that retentions endure, while memories are invoked.[12]

If retention is the relationship between current and prior events in "the present," protention involves two analogous relationship(s) between current and subsequent events:

> Protention is the term for a future which we anticipate, and not merely await. Awaiting, like recollection, implies a disengagement from the present, whereas, experientially, the now which we perceive is colored by the way we intend a future. (p. 62)

Protention, then, is much like the projection of a definite duration (Hasty), the *Erwartung* phase of the *Zeitgestalt* (Neumann), the anticipative impulse (Berry), or the rising crest of a metrical wave (Zuckerkandl). Collectively protentions and retentions create a boundary around the "musical present" (see Figure 22.4). The "present" may mean this tone, or this motive, or this phrase, or this piece, or this concert:

> All three temporal modes are always there, but not there in the same way; they are always distinguishable, but also always relatable; and finally, all three temporal modes

12 Clifton, *Music as Heard*, p. 59.

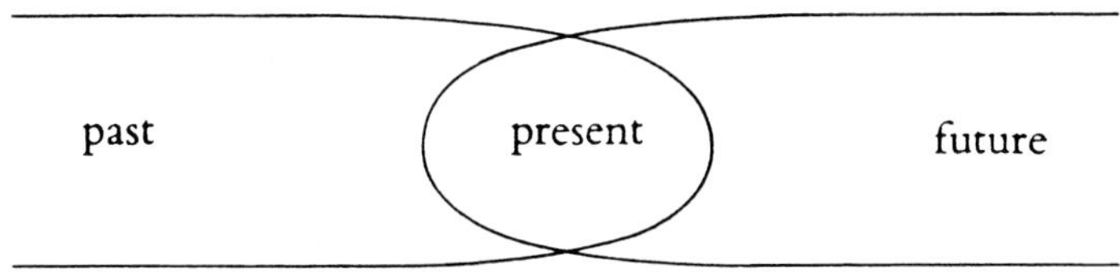

Figure 22.4 Musical horizons, from Clifton, *Music as Heard*, p. 65

are permeated with actualities and possibilities in varying degrees, so that the past is never completely irrevocable, and the future is never completely predetermined or undetermined. Merleau-Ponty said it much more simply: "The past . . . is not past, nor the future future." (p. 65)

Rhythm in Schenkerian theory

While Heinrich Schenker wrote voluminously on the nature of harmony, counterpoint, and form (see **Chapter 26, passim**), his comments on rhythm represent a very small portion of his work. While the first generation of Schenker's students (such as Ernst Oster and Felix Salzer) were concerned with editing and translating Schenker's texts as well as elaborating his theories of tonality and form, it was the following generation of students who extended Schenker's work in the rhythmic domain by fleshing out the brief remarks Schenker makes on rhythm and meter in *Free Composition* as well as by attending carefully to the rhythmic aspects of his analytical notation.

Following Schenker's dicta, many of the concepts and metaphors used by Schenkerian theorists to discuss rhythm are borrowed from the pitch domain. Thus one finds discussions of tonal rhythm, rhythmic and metrical "dissonance," and techniques of rhythmic (as opposed to pitch) reduction. Most of these theorists also share a common presumption that rhythmic structures are organized by or otherwise dependent on pitch organization. While Schenker and his followers are sensitive to differences amongst structural levels, their discussions of rhythm, like those of pitch, are strongly recursive.

Schenker's comments on rhythm and motion at the most abstract levels of structure are somewhat contradictory. On the one hand, he unequivocally states that:

The fundamental structure is arrhythmic.

Rhythm can no more exist in the fundamental structure than it can in a strict-counterpoint *cantus firmus* exercise.

Only when, through voice-leading transformations, linear progressions arise in the

> upper and lower voices of the middle ground, does a rhythmic ordering issue from the necessity of counterpointing the voices against each other. (p. 15)[13]

Yet elsewhere in *Free Composition* Schenker says that:

> Since it is a melodic succession of definite steps of a second, the fundamental line signifies motion, striving toward a goal, and ultimately the completion of this course. (p. 4)

Schenker's use of the term "signifies" is telling here – not that the line moves, or creates motion, but that the fundamental line is a sign of motion. Carl Schachter is able to accommodate this tension between arrhythmia and motion by making a distinction between *tonal* versus *durational* rhythm:

> What produces the patterned movement, the rise and fall of musical rhythm? I believe that there are two sources, one of them specifically musical, the other shared with other rhythmic phenomena. The purely musical one flows from the succession and combination of tones, *for the tonal system itself has rhythmic properties*.[14]

According to Schachter, tonal rhythm stems from the "recurrence of a tone after one or more different ones, the octave relationship, chordal and linear associations, consonance and dissonance," while durational rhythm stems from "a complex pattern of durations, emphases, and groupings which do not arise from the tones."[15] Thus Schachter is able to claim:

> Is the *Ursatz* arrhythmic, as Schenker maintained? My answer to this questions is a qualified no. I believe that progressions in the fundamental structure embody tonal, but not durational rhythm.[16]

Schachter goes on to note that tonal rhythm and durational rhythm may interact, as they "combine into a single continuum, sometimes supporting, sometimes diverging from, sometimes even contradicting one another."[17] In order to illustrate and explore their interaction, he develops a methodology of *durational reduction*, based on some principles first given in Schenker's *Der Tonwille* (see Example 22.1). Schachter says that durational reduction may be

> applied to and coordinated with significant structural levels of voice leading; in other words, durational reduction combined with a reduction, in Schenker's manner, of the tonal contents . . . By indicating tonal events in durational proportion and by specifying the larger metrical divisions, such an approach can sometimes clarify aspects of rhythmic organization not directly revealed by graphic analyses that deal mainly with voice leading and harmony.[18]

Schenker himself acknowledges the role durational rhythm plays in the creation of meter in his comments on repetition:

13 All quotations of Schenker are from *Free Composition* unless otherwise noted.
14 Schachter, "A Preliminary Study," p. 313. Here also Schachter acknowledges Zuckerkandl regarding the "rhythmic character of the scale" (p. 314). 15 Ibid., p. 313. 16 Ibid., p. 317.
17 Ibid., p. 313. 18 Schachter, "Durational Reduction," p. 198.

Example 22.1 Durational analysis of Beethoven, Op. 14, No. 1, from Schachter, "Durational Reduction," p. 216

Example 22.1 (*cont.*)

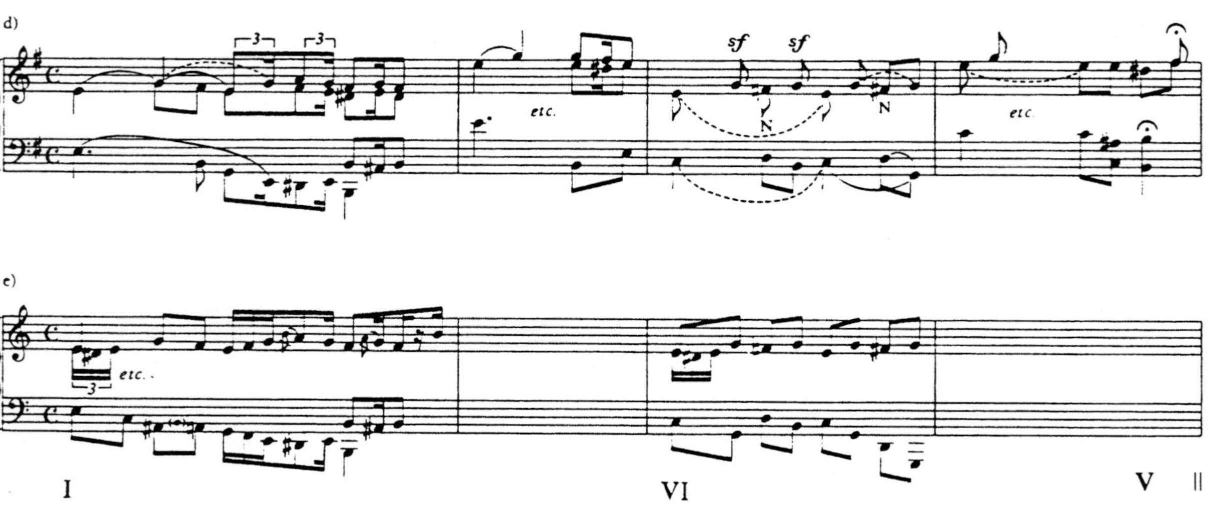

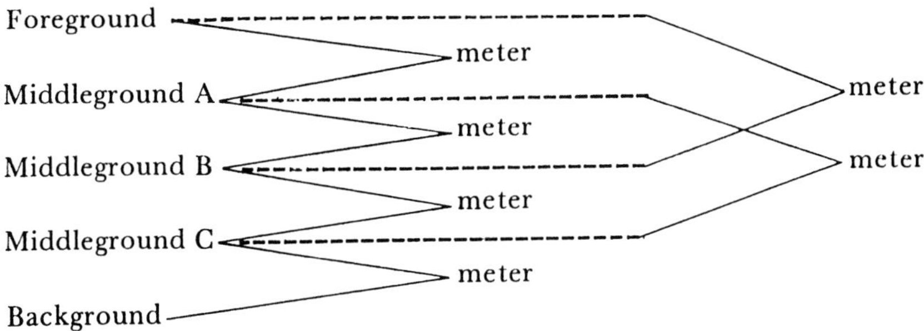

Figure 22.5 Interactions between rhythmic levels, from Yeston, *Stratification*, p. 67

> Repetition is also a prerequisite to meter and rhythm. Without repetition a metric scheme is inconceivable. But even repetitions that make up a metric scheme, like all foreground repetitions, are clarified and confirmed only by the background and middleground. (p. 118)

Schenker also states unequivocally that "all rhythm in music comes from counterpoint and only from counterpoint" (p. 15). Given that counterpoint involves the interaction between two or more melodic lines, in the case of rhythm one must speak of two or more tonal or durational "strata," to use the term coined by Maury Yeston. Yeston makes this contrapuntal condition clear in his statement: "A meter will never appear on any single stratum, but it will arise from the interaction of two strata, one of which must always be a middleground level" (p. 67).[19] Figure 22.5 gives Yeston's diagram for this interactive process, whereby a slower stratum, to use Yeston's term, "interprets" the organization of events on a faster level: "Hence the middleground is the interpretation of the foreground; it provides the accents by which foreground events may be grouped" (p. 68), and thus "all rhythmic patterns of middleground levels are determined exclusively by pitch criteria . . . chosen on the basis of principles of tonal structure" (p. 84).

Schachter moves away from Yeston's strict pitch-to-rhythm approach with respect to the formation of meter. Schachter notes that meter is "more closely bound to durational than to tonal rhythm," though of course "very frequently, however, aspects of tonal rhythm underscore the meter."[20] For Schachter, metrical accent is a phenomenal property of the music-as-heard:

> The listener's awareness of time spans automatically produces accents that punctuate his experience of the music; *these accents result from the heightened attention attracted by the boundary points of the spans* . . . The accents thus produced are true *metrical accents* –

19 All quotations of Yeston are from *The Stratification of Musical Rhythm*.
20 Schachter, "A Preliminary Study," p. 318.

> metrical because they arise directly out of the listener's awareness of the equal divisions of time that measure the music's flow.[21]

Schachter also notes that there are limits to meter and metrical accent, as there are limits on our perception of equivalent time spans: "Over very long spans of time, therefore, meter ceases to be directly available to the listener, who receives little or no help in determining whether the time intervals are really equivalent."[22]

Interactions between layers of durational and/or tonal rhythm may produce more complex aggregate rhythmic structures. Yeston lays out two broad categories of interaction between strata:

> The first is one in which the rate of any level of motion in a piece can be expressed as a simple multiplication or division (by an integer greater than 1) of the rate of any other level of motion in the piece. The resulting structure . . . may be characterized, metaphorically, as *rhythmic consonance* . . . The second broad category under discussion extends the convenient metaphor and may be characterized as *rhythmic dissonance* . . . [whenever] there are found to be two levels in a piece that cannot be expressed as a simple multiplication or division of each other. (pp. 77–8)

Yeston was not the first to apply the consonance/dissonance distinction to describe and categorize various rhythmic and metrical structures. Harald Krebs has noted that "both composers and theorists often have employed terms originally developed in connection with pitch theory" to describe rhythmic phenomena, and notes the use of rhythmic "dissonance" by Schillinger, Sachs, Hlawicka, and Cooper and Meyer (see Figure 22.6); similarly Schachter acknowledges the use of the term by Seeger.[23] Krebs then refines Yeston's definition of metrical dissonance:

> Metrical dissonance, unlike consonance, requires the presence of at least three levels – a pulse level and at least two interpretive levels that provide conflicting groupings of the pulses. The [metrical] conflict can arise in two ways. First, the cardinalities of the two interpretive levels may be different and not related by an integral common factor . . . [Second,] conflicting groupings of a pulse level can also arise from the non-aligned superimposition of at least two interpretive levels of the same cardinality.[24]

Schachter also considers "alternative and conflicting metrical patterns," including ambiguity of downbeat location, ambiguity of hypermetrical organization, and the interaction between simultaneous meters.[25] Krebs's expanded taxonomy of rhythmic and metrical dissonance has been given further discussion by Cohn, Kamien, and Samarotto.[26]

21 Schachter, "Aspects of Meter," p. 5. 22 Ibid., p. 16.
23 See Krebs, "Some Extensions," p. 99, and Schachter, "Aspects of Meter," p. 26.
24 Krebs, "Some Extensions," p. 103. 25 Schachter, "Aspects of Meter," pp. 29–36.
26 Cohn, "Dramatization of Hypermetric Conflict"; Kamien, "Conflicting Metrical Patterns"; Samarotto, "Strange Dimensions."

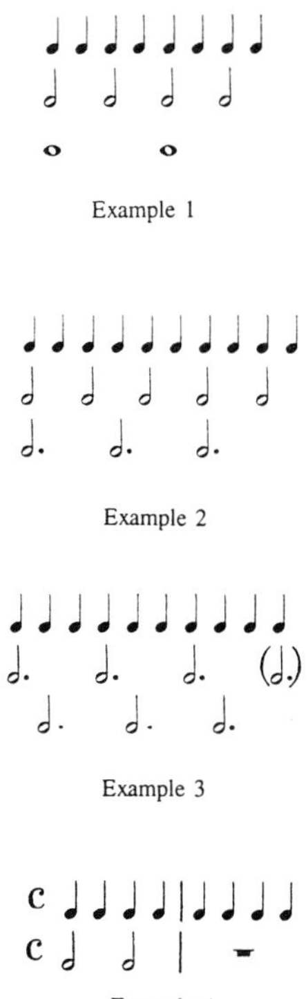

Figure 22.6 Varieties of metrical dissonance, from Krebs, "Some Extensions," p. 102

For Schenker, some rhythmic structures are normative:

> Since the principle of systole and diastole is inherent in our very being, metric ordering based on two and its multiples is the most natural to us. (p. 119)
>
> Measure orderings in odd numbers (such as 3 or 5) have their roots in a duple ordering in the background and middleground; this brings into clear relief the fact that metric schemes involving the numbers 3 and 5 are man-made and not as natural as duple orderings. (pp. 119–20)

Schenker then goes on to describe the process of rhythmic expansion (*Dehnung*):

> An expansion follows from one or more measures of a metric prototype. There must be an organic relationship. Despite the fact that prototype and derivation follow one another in direct succession, their relationship can be recognized only from the middleground and background. (p. 124)

William Rothstein has explored the relationships between rhythmic prototypes and their variants from a theoretical perspective that is equal parts Heinrich Schenker and

Heinrich Koch. Rothstein uses the term *phrase rhythm* to describe rhythmic structures that involve both phrase structure (which may contain both tonal and durational rhythms) as well as hypermeter.[27] He then discusses various techniques of phrase rhythm, including overlaps, elisions, prefixes, suffixes, and various types of internal expansions as they may be applied to prototypical phrases and hypermeasures.

Architectonic approaches to rhythm

Cooper and Meyer. A number of theorists, mainly North American and mainly from the last third of the century, have focused on the hierarchical aspects of meter and rhythm. Consider the following dictum by Grosvenor Cooper and Leonard Meyer, who collaborated on an influential study of rhythm and meter in 1960 while both taught at the University of Chicago:

> As a piece of music unfolds, its rhythmic structure is perceived not as a series of discrete independent units strung together in a mechanical, additive way like beads, but as an organic process in which smaller rhythmic motives, while possessing a shape and structure of their own, also function as integral parts of a larger rhythmic organization. (p. 2)[28]

In order to account for the relationship(s) between parts and wholes, the various parts must be identified, articulated, and related to each other. Such "architectonic" analyses indicate how units on one level nest to form higher-level structures, and they typically concern themselves with determinations of grouping, accent, and hierarchical super- and subordinate relationships. These analyses often represent the final state of a passage or piece, that is, rhythmic relationships as they are understood in retrospect. At the same time, many architectonic analyses of rhythm take a bottom-up (as opposed to a top-down) approach, starting with the smallest units of the foreground and then moving to larger and larger structural units, at times extending to the highest levels of form. From this view form becomes an aspect of rhythm; for example, Cone has claimed:

> Certain general rhythmic principles underlie common formal units . . . [and] the *same principles, working on higher levels* [italics mine] and more comprehensive formal sections, can ultimately be invoked to explain an entire composition as one all-embracing rhythmic impulse.[29]

Cooper and Meyer give a comprehensive account of rhythm and form that is based on a few accentual archetypes:

27 Rothstein, *Phrase Rhythm in Tonal Music*, p. 12.
28 All quotations of Cooper and Meyer are from *The Rhythmic Structure of Music*.
29 Cone, "Musical Form and Musical Performance," p. 39.

> Rhythm may be defined as the way in which one or more unaccented beats are grouped in relation to an accented one. The five basic rhythmic groupings may be differentiated by terms traditionally associated with prosody . . . Since, as noted above, rhythmic organization is architectonic, more extensive rhythmic structures – phrases, periods, etc. – as well as shorter, more obviously rhythmic motives exhibit these basic patterns. (p. 6)

They then list the basic patterns – iamb (Weak–Strong), anapest (W–W–S), trochee (S–W), dactyl (S–W–W), and amphibrach (W–S–W). These are not simply musical analogs to the poetic feet, as found in eighteenth-century theory (e.g., as shown in **Example 21.1, p. 665**) and even the earlier medieval rhythmic modes (as shown in **Figure 20.1, p. 630**). The patterns of Cooper and Meyer involve not durations, but beats, though duration plays a role in defining beats. In defining their archetypes as groups of beats, their analytical methodology commingles meter and rhythm. Beats are defined as pulses that are counted in a metrical context. Accent is more difficult to define – as they themselves acknowledge:

> One cannot at present state unequivocally what makes one tone seem accented and another not. For while such factors as duration, intensity, melodic contour, regularity, and so forth obviously play a part in creating an impression of accent, none of them appears to be an invariable and necessary concomitant of accent . . . Accent is a relational concept. There can be accents only if there are unaccents (weak beats) and vice versa. In this sense there is no such thing as a series of accents or a series of weak beats. If all stimuli are alike, there is only a series of pulses. An accent, then is a stimulus (in a series of stimuli) which is *marked for consciousness* in some way. (pp. 7–8)

Given this normative fluctuation between accent and unaccent, there will tend to be one or two weak beats between every strong beat, and this tendency constrains the number of possible grouping patterns.

Cooper and Meyer first examine rhythms on lower architectonic levels, that is, the ways in which each of the five basic groups can fit into various meters (e.g. S–W patterns in duple meter, then in triple meter, and so forth). They note how grouping and meter may or may not be congruent, how a passage may have more than one possible grouping (and how performance may effect grouping), how groups may overlap, and how even the simplest patterns often involve some hierarchic nesting amongst groups and subgroups. They then move on to composite groups on higher structural levels. Their treatment of a passage from the beginning of the first Bourrée of Bach's English Suite in A major is given in Figure 22.7. They continue to use their archetypes through the highest levels of structure, and conclude their book with an analysis of the first movement of Beethoven's Eighth Symphony as a giant anapest (pp. 183–203).

Lerdahl and Jackendoff. Of all of Cooper and Meyer's claims, it is their treatment of large spans of music as accented and unaccented that has received the most criticism,

Figure 22.7 Nested levels of rhythm in the Bourrée of Bach's English Suite in A major, from Cooper and Meyer, *The Rhythmic Structure of Music*, p. 69

and indeed, Meyer himself has backed away from this position.[30] Another aspect of Cooper and Meyer's theory that is both a strength and a weakness is how they have rhythm and meter inseparably intertwined. While they acknowledge that various grouping structures occur in and are dependent upon particular metrical contexts, Cooper and Meyer's analyses only indicate a single hierarchy – nested patterns of accentuation. In distinction to Cooper and Meyer, the music theorist and composer Fred Lerdahl and the linguist Ray Jackendoff collaborated on an important study of tonal music strongly influenced by theories of prosodic structure in language.[31] They treat rhythm and meter as independent though inter-related hierarchies: one of durational groups, and another of metrical time points.[32] Each is governed by its own set of well-formedness and preference rules. The grouping hierarchy, which extends recursively from the highest levels of structure down to the foreground, is an inclusive nesting of time spans. Groups must be contiguous, smaller groups must be wholly contained within larger groups, and larger groups are exhaustively partitioned into smaller groups. Under special conditions groups may overlap, but overlaps are understood as a surface transformation from an underlying non-overlapped structure.

Lerdahl and Jackendoff treat the metrical hierarchy as a pattern of beats.[33] Beats do

30 See Schachter, "A Preliminary Study," pp. 306–07; Kramer, "The Time of Music," pp. 88–89; and Meyer, "A Pride of Prejudices," p. 250.
31 All quotations from Lerdahl and Jackendoff are from *A Generative Theory of Tonal Music*. A broader discussion of the epistemological underpinnings of their theory is found in Chapter 3, pp. 99–102.
32 Moreover, in Lerdahl and Jackendoff's theory the rhythmic and metrical hierarchies are two components of a more comprehensive analytical system which also includes higher-level time-span and durational reductions (pp. 8–11).
33 Their treatment of the metrical hierarchy has its antecedents in Komar, *A Theory of Suspensions*.

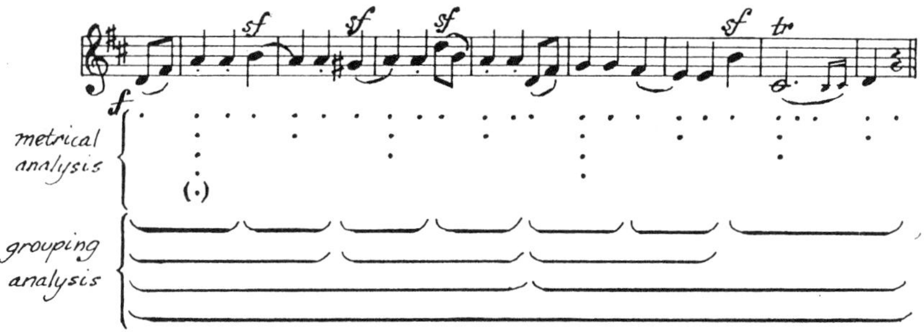

Figure 22.8 Meter–rhythm interaction in Haydn's Symphony No. 104, minuet, from Lerdahl and Jackendoff, *A Generative Theory of Tonal Music*, p. 26

not have duration; rather, they are "idealizations, utilized by the performer and inferred by the listener" that are read off the grouping structure. Metrical patterns thus arise in response to rhythmic regularities in the foreground (p. 37). As such, metrical levels must be isochronous (i.e., consist of equally spaced beats), and each metrical unit must consist of either two or three beats. Every articulation in the music must correspond to a metrical articulation at some level. As regularity is attenuated on higher levels of structure, so too is meter; as a result, Lerdahl and Jackendoff relegate the metrical hierarchy to the lower levels of structure (p. 21).

In Figure 22.8, the grouping hierarchy consists of a series of nested durations, while the metrical hierarchy is expressed by the pattern of dots immediately below the staff. Lerdahl and Jackendoff stress that "groups do not receive metrical accent, and beats do not possess any inherent grouping" (p. 26). Both the metrical and grouping patterns emerge through the operation of a set of preference rules assigned to each hierarchical domain. While Lerdahl and Jackendoff's well-formedness rules delimit what grouping and metrical structures are possible, the preference rules choose among possible structures to a maximally preferable analysis of the meter and grouping in a given context. These preference rules take into account symmetry, parallelism, gestalt principles of pattern formation, and style-specific syntactic cues. While the well-formedness rules are held to be universal, the preference rules may be tailored to a particular musical culture or style.

Lerdahl and Jackendoff's separation of rhythm and meter also helps clarify the definition of accent. Cooper and Meyer make a distinction between accent and stress: "Stress . . . means the dynamic intensification of a beat, whether accented or unaccented. Thus a stress, no matter how forceful, placed on a weak beat will not make that beat accented" (p. 8). Stress is analogous to Lerdahl and Jackendoff's *phenomenal accent*, and they include not only dynamic emphasis but also relative length, sudden changes in timbre or texture, and so on. They further distinguish between *structural accent*, "caused by the melodic/harmonic points of gravity in a phrase or section," and *metrical accent*, created by the hierarchical persistence of a beat (p. 17). Each category of accent tends to accrue to a particular hierarchical level: phenomenal accents are most salient on the foreground, metrical accents on the levels immediately above the foreground, and structural accents on middleground and higher levels. Lerdahl and Jackendoff's three types of accent are similar to David Epstein's categories of stress, rhythmic accent, and metrical accent.[34] While Lerdahl and Jackendoff distinguish structural and metrical accents on the basis of the difference between time-span and time-point relationships, Epstein's accentual categories stem from his distinction between a "chronometric time" consisting of beats, measures, and metrical accents versus an "integral time" which contains pulses, rhythmic groups, and hence both rhythmic accent and stress.

Extending the metrical hierarchy above the notated barline gives rise to hypermeter, a term generally ascribed to Edward Cone, wherein individual measures "behave as a single beat."[35] Beethoven's "Ritmo di tre battute" in the Scherzo of the Ninth Symphony is an obvious example, but hypermeter is more than a notational conceit.[36] In a true hypermeter, meter is operative beyond the musical foreground, though theorists differ as to just how far meter may extend to higher levels of structure. Lerdahl and Jackendoff have argued for a hypermeter of limited scope, usually no more than two to four *hyperbeats* (pp. 21–25). Their use of the term "hyperbeat" refines Cone's definition, as it is not measures (that is, spans of time) which function as the elements of a hypermeasure, but the metrically accented beats at one level which form hyperbeats on the next-highest level. Like Lerdahl and Jackendoff, Joel Lester has argued that extensive hypermeters are relatively rare, and cautions against confusing regularity of phrase structure with hypermeter proper.[37] In contrast, Arthur Komar, Wallace Berry, and Jonathan Kramer have given analyses of the metrical hierarchy for entire movements.[38] Figure 22.9 gives Kramer's analysis of the first movement of Beethoven's Sonata in C minor, Op. 13, which is quite detailed.

Kramer. Kramer explicitly relaxes Lerdahl and Jackendoff's metrical well-formedness rules, which require isochronously spaced beats and downbeats – note the irregular spacing of "beats" on levels b and c in Figure 22.9.[39] Instead, he focuses on the creation of higher-level metrical accents which serve to articulate each hyper-measure. These hyper-accents are high-level points of initiation; indeed, Kramer's conception of metrical accent draws on Berry's concept of impulse noted above. By defining higher-level metrical accent in terms of an initiation which accrues to a time point, Kramer is able to avoid the problem of accented spans that arose in Cooper and Meyer's rhythmic analysis of entire movements.

34 Epstein, *Beyond Orpheus*, pp. 60–62. 35 Cone, *Musical Form and Musical Performance*, p. 79.
36 Even in the Beethoven Scherzo hypermeter is more than a notational conceit. See Cohn, "The Dramatization of Hypermetric Conflicts." 37 Lester, *The Rhythms of Tonal Music*, pp. 163–67.
38 Komar, *Theory of Suspensions*; Berry, *Structural Functions*; Kramer, *The Time of Music.*
39 All Kramer quotations are from *The Time of Music* Kramer's analysis of Op. 13 is indebted to Komar's analysis of the same piece – see *Theory of Suspensions*, pp. 151–61.

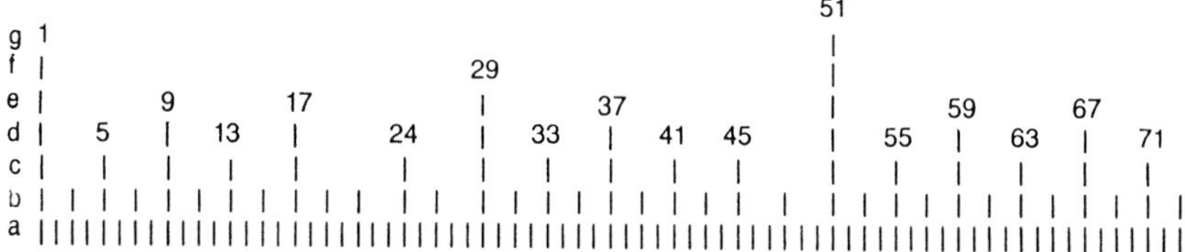

Figure 22.9 Hypermetric analysis of the entire second movement of Beethoven's Op. 13, from Kramer, *The Time of Music*, p. 119

Kramer's discussion of musical rhythm, meter, and form is notable not only for its treatment of architectonic structure, but also for its treatment of what might be termed "anti-architectonic" music – the rhythmic analysis of pieces which resist listening and analysis in terms of the relationships between their parts and wholes. He outlines a continuum of temporal coherence and order, from the most continuous, contiguous, and teleological arrangement of musical elements to the most fragmentary and dissociated musical structures. He begins with a definition of *linearity*: "Let us identify linearity as *the determination of some characteristic(s) of music in accordance with implications that arise from earlier events of the piece*" (p. 20). Kramer is careful to distinguish between linearity versus continuity: "nonlinearity should not be equated with discontinuity, since discontinuities can acquire their force by violating linear as well as nonlinear implications" (p. 22). Likewise, linearity, though typical of tonal compositions, may also be present in atonal compositions (e.g., in pieces or sections that are characterized by a constant thickening of texture, increase of dynamics, or acceleration). Linear time may involve more than a simple chain of syntactic entailments. Kramer describes the possibility of *multiply directed linear time*, one that "depends on underlying linearity being perceptible even when not presented in linear order" (p. 46).

A composition may abandon linearity all or in part. According to Kramer, *nonlinearity* is the "principle of composition and listening in which events are understood as outgrowths of general principles that govern entire pieces" (p. 453) and is exhibited by "pieces in which the texture, motivic material, and rhythmic figuration are virtually constant," as in the case of many minimalist compositions (p. 40). A piece that is almost or entirely nonlinear creates a radically different kind of temporality: "A nonlinear composition in moment time does not really begin. Rather, it simply starts, as if it had already been going on and we happened to tune in on it . . . [similarly, it] ceases rather than ends" (p. 50). Thus pieces like Stockhausen's *Gesang der Jünglinge* or Ives's *The Unanswered Question* involve high degrees of nonlinearity, as do pieces that are composed and/or performed with various degrees of indeterminacy.[40]

40 On varying types of indeterminacy, see Cage, "Indeterminacy," in *Silence*, pp. 35–40.

When there is no fundamental linearity and when the music is markedly discontinuous, the result is *moment time*, a term Kramer uses following Stockhausen's notion of *moment form*:

> These forms do not aim toward a climax, do not prepare the listener to expect a climax, and their structures do not contain the usual stages found in the development[al] curve of the whole duration of a normal composition . . . They are forms in a state of always having already commenced, which could go on as they are for an eternity . . . an eternity that is present in every moment.[41]

While moment time may seem extreme, beyond it lies *vertical time*. A piece which attempts to create vertical time contains a single, static moment as its entire essence. Such pieces have no hierarchical structure whatsoever – there are no parts, nor relationships among them, only a singular whole. The result, according to Kramer, "is a single present stretched out into an enormous duration, a potentially infinite "now" that nonetheless feels like an instant. In music without phrases, without temporal articulation, with total consistency, whatever structure is in the music exists between simultaneous layers of sound, not between successive gestures" (p. 55). Thus, the apprehension of vertical time involves the absence – indeed, the very impossibility – of temporal arrangement. It is the absence of time itself, and as Zuckerkandl has noted:

> Should time vanish, all motion must instantly vanish too, tonal motion not excepted. A God enthroned beyond time in timeless eternity would have to renounce music . . . [as] temporal omnipresence would make the revelation of audible beauty impossible. It argues against God's timelessness. Are we to suppose that we mortals, in possessing such a wonder as music, are more privileged than God? Rather, to save music for Him, we shall hold, with the Greeks, that God cannot go behind time. Otherwise what would He be doing with all the choiring angels?[42]

Rhythm in post-tonal music

The discontinuity and nonlinearity that is characteristic of post-tonal compositions creates many challenges for rhythmic theory and analysis. One way of meeting these challenges is to focus on the compositional process, rather than analytically tracing the complex surfaces and forms which result. Indeed, it is not surprising that rhythm in post-tonal music receives extended attention in the writings of composers of multiserial or totally serialized music (e.g., Stockhausen, Babbitt, Krenek, Boulez), since for these composers rhythm was an important element in their systematic treatment of all musical parameters. More surprisingly, perhaps, is the extent to which many of these

41 Stockhausen, *Texte zur elektronischen und instrumentalen Musik*, p. 199, cited in Kramer, *The Time of Music*, p. 201. 42 Zuckerkandl, *Sound and Symbol*, p. 151.

composers were versed in temporal philosophy. Thus we find composers such as Koechlin, Stravinsky, Boulez, Sessions, and Carter citing the likes of Bergson, Langer, Suvchitsky, or de Selincourt in their own remarks on the rhythmic aspects of composition and musical structure. Other theorists and composers have confronted the challenge of post-tonal rhythmic theory and analysis more directly, and have addressed such topics as the description and segmentation of a rhythmic surface in post-tonal music and the metrical implications of the twelve-tone system. Many of these writers (e.g., Babbitt, Lewin, Morris, and Roeder) have developed sophisticated theories of rhythm and tools for rhythmic analysis using the language and methods of mathematical group theory.

A basic doctrine of post-tonal theory and analysis is that there are essential isomorphisms between pitch and time, and so there are substantive parallels between pitch and temporal phenomena. As we have already noted, Schachter has remarked that the "tonal system itself has rhythmic properties."[43] Composers of post-tonal music extend this notion to assignations of rhythmic and quasi-rhythmic properties rooted in the chromatic pitch universe. For example, Stockhausen does not even separate rhythm and pitch into ontologically separate domains. Rather, he notes that pitches and rhythms both involve periodic phases between successive impulses, with a threshold of about one-sixteenth of a second as the boundary between the two:

> Our sense-perception divides acoustically-perceptible phases into two groups; we speak of *durations* and *pitches* . . . Until a phase-duration of approx. $^1/_{16}$″, we can still just hear the impulses separately; until then, we speak of "duration," [even] if of one that becomes extremely short. Shorten the phase-duration gradually to $^1/_{32}$″, and the impulses are no longer separately perceptible . . . one [now] perceives the phase-duration as the "pitch" of the sound. (p. 10)[44]

Stockhausen draws parallels between the overtone series for pitch and categorical values for duration (see Figure 22.10). He claims: "What is such a series of proportions, $^1/_1$, $^1/_2$, $^1/_3$, . . . $^1/_{12}$ . . . , when applied to time-phases? . . . That is nothing more nor less than a *harmonic or overtone series*" (p. 16).

Just as one may have a complex tone which contains several composite partials, so too one may speak of composite rhythm or meter, what Stockhausen terms a *formant spectrum* (pp. 17–18). This leads him to claim that:

> The difference between *metre* and *rhythm* is exactly that which we discern between the "fundamental tone" and the "tone-colour" of sound-spectra; the fundamental phase (metric fundamental) is defined by the periodic main intensity-maxima (the heaviest accents), and these result from the formant-structure . . . Shifting the basic metric period is thus akin to modulation, while changes of patterning within the basic period are not. (pp. 19–20)

43 Schachter, "A Preliminary Study," p. 314.
44 All quotations of Stockhausen are from " . . how time passes . . ."

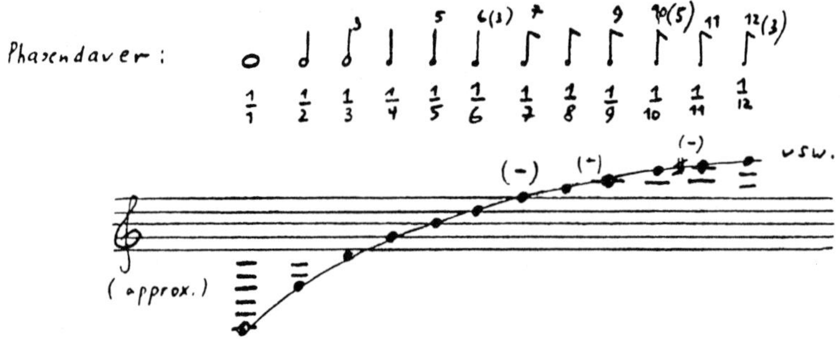

Figure 22.10 Rhythmic durations as a harmonic series, from Stockhausen, "How Time Passes," p. 16

Elliott Carter has explicitly termed such shifts of the basic metric period "metric modulations," though Carter often uses a series of shifts, along with coordinated changes in the notated durations, to create an effect whereby one part of the texture seems to maintain a steady beat while another continuously speeds up or slows down.[45] Stockhausen also suggests that one may partition the range of perceptible durations into various octaves, just as one may partition the range of audible pitch space:

> The composition of durations has at its disposal a *chromatic scale of durations over approx. seven octaves*, between 8″ and 1/16″, and in every 2 : 1 relationship, the chromatic scale of twelve durations, fixed by metronome markings, repeats itself. Together with the seven or eight pitch-octaves, *musical time* would thus be circumscribed in fourteen or fifteen *time-octaves*, in which the composer proportions phase-relationships both in the sphere of duration and in that of pitch. (p. 21)

Going beyond Stockhausen's time-octaves, Boulez draws the distinction between "smooth" versus "striated" varieties of space for pitches and time for durations: "pulsation is for striated time what temperament is for striated space; it has been shown that, depending on whether partition is fixed or variable, defined space will be regular or irregular; similarly, that the pulsation of striated time will be regular or irregular, but systematic."[46] Thus just as the semitone partitions the octave into sub-modules, so too do pulses divide a larger module into smaller units of time. The difference between a constant versus a shifting tempo is the difference between two different modularities of musical time:

> *Straight time*, corresponding to straight space, will, whatever the partition, observe a constant module; in other words, the original values being comprised between two limits, the derived values will be comprised between the multiples of the relationship defined by these two limits. *Curved time*, on the contrary, will cause the derived values

45 Carter, "Music and the Time Screen," in *The Writings of Elliott Carter*, pp. 349–50.
46 Boulez, *Boulez on Music Today*, p. 91.

> to depend upon a function of the relationship defined by these two limits . . . Whatever the module, *regular time* will be that in which partition remains fixed; *irregular*, where partition varies (according to a defined numerical proportion or to the tempo).[47]

Messiaen claimed there are isomorphisms between symmetrical scale forms (his modes of limited transposition) and his symmetrical durational patterns, what he termed "non-retrogradable rhythms":

> Modes which cannot be transposed beyond a certain number of transpositions, because one always falls again into the same notes; rhythms which cannot be used in retrograde, because in such a case one finds the same order of values again – these are two striking impossibilities . . . Immediately one notices the analogy of these two impossibilities and how they complement one another, the rhythms realizing in the horizontal direction (retrogradation) what the modes realize in the vertical direction (transposition). After this first relation, there is another between values added to rhythms and notes added to chords . . . Finally, we superpose our rhythms . . . [and] we also superpose our modes.[48]

> These modes are divisible into symmetrical groups; these rhythms, also, with this difference: the symmetry of the rhythmic groups is a retrograde symmetry. Finally, the last note of each group of these modes is always *common* with the first of the following group; and the groups of these rhythms frame a central value *common* to each group.[49]

While composers struggled individually to find ways to extend the principles of serialism beyond the pitch domain, there were marked differences between European and North American approaches to the serialization of rhythm. Milton Babbitt has given an extended discussion of the issues of rhythm within the context of serial technique. Given that a twelve-tone series is essentially a series of intervals, and thus a function of the relative difference between successive pitches, he notes that one cannot simply translate pitch-differences to durational differences:

> There is no apparent basis for constructing duration classes by designating as elements of the same durational equivalence class those durations which differ by a multiple of 12 or any other number. The temporal analog of pitch interval is translatable only as "the difference between durations." Even without arguing the dubious perceptual status of this notion, the ordered succession of such differences remains invariant under transposition if and only if one assumes difference classes as a result of applying transposition modularly, and therefore embracing the assumption of duration classes in its most unrealistic form.[50]

Babbitt thus recognizes some limits to the pitch–time isomorphism. As a result, he focuses on orderings of and relationships between time-points within a measure which has twelve distinct positions – and so one may speak of time-point equivalence classes:

> The notion of meter is made an essential part of the systematic structure. The equivalence relation is statable as "occurring at the same time point with relation to the

47 Ibid., p. 93. 48 Messiaen, *The Technique of My Musical Language*, p. 13. 49 Ibid., p. 21.
50 Babbitt, "Twelve Tone Rhythmic Structure and the Electronic Medium," p. 161.

measure." The "ascending" ordered "chromatic scale" of twelve time points, then, is a measure divided into twelve equally spaced time points.[51]

While Babbitt discussed the various ways pitch-class operations such as transposition, inversion, and the like can be applied within this particular context (i.e., a multi-serial composition), Robert Morris describes how these operations can be applied to any ordered series of time points.[52] Given some reference point 0, and a minimum duration which defines the interval between time-points, one may then consider a set of time-points derived from this series (see Figure 22.11).

The series in Figure 22.11a may be transposed *n* units to the right or left by adding or subtracting n to the value of each time point in the set. The set as a whole may be subject to augmentation or diminution (multiplied by some value of n), retrograded (multiplying each value by -1, which Morris labels as inversion since -1 is the inversion operator in pitch and pitch-class space), or both, as in Figure 22.11b. Note how in both Figures 22.11a and 22.11b the various operations preserve the durational shape of the original time-point set. In Example 22.11c we see how these time-point series, sets, and operations may also be mapped into a modular time-point space. Here the series {3578} is transformed by a variety of multiplicative operations. In a modular space these operations do not preserve the durational shape of the series; indeed, in the last instance, the operation maps two values onto the same location, reducing the number of elements by one.

In contrast to the accounts given above, other theorists, particularly in North America, have sought analytical methodologies independent of the compositional process. To be sure, as in the analysis of pitch relationships, a tenet of post-tonal rhythmic analysis is that "beneath the complex surface exists a considerable degree of regularity."[53] For example, Allen Forte developed a method for systematically searching for patterns of duration by cataloguing and ordering all possible correlations between note onsets and offsets through his "proportional graphs," a linear representation of all of the durations in the musical texture expressed in terms of the smallest common duration present, and "attack–release partitions," an ordered presentation of the aggregate pattern of durations and silences, again expressed in terms of the smallest common durational unit.[54] These graphs and partitions may then be used in the search for durational patterns, including rhythmic motives (which may be manifest on different structural levels) as well as symmetrical orderings of durations and durational complexes. In many instances, by backtracking from durational regularities one can find important pitch configurations and relationships (i.e., viewing rhythmic configurations as the durational residue of a pitch-to-rhythm compositional process). Forte also notes that pitch and rhythm may relate to each other on a more equal and more complicated footing: "the pitch-class set structure of [some of Webern's] works . . . is

51 Ibid., p. 162. 52 Morris, *Composition with Pitch Classes*, pp. 299–307.
53 Forte, "Aspects of Rhythm in Webern's Atonal Music," p. 90. 54 Ibid., p. 90.

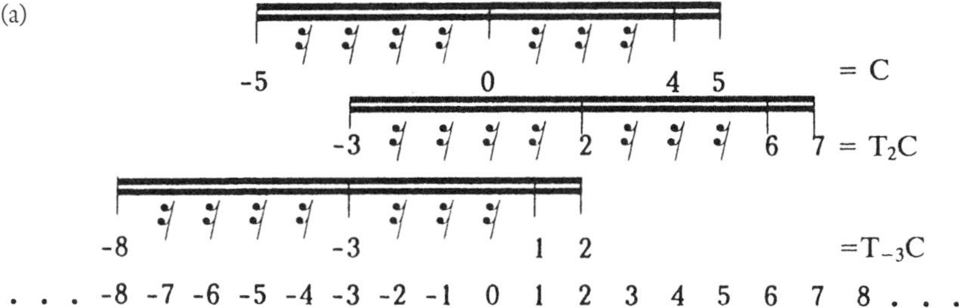

(b)

-4 -1 0 2 = D

-8 -2 0 4 = M2D

-4 0 2 8 = M-2D

-2 0 1 4 = ID

. . .-8 -7 -6 -5 -4 -3 -2 -1 0 1 2 3 4 5 6 7 8 9 . . .

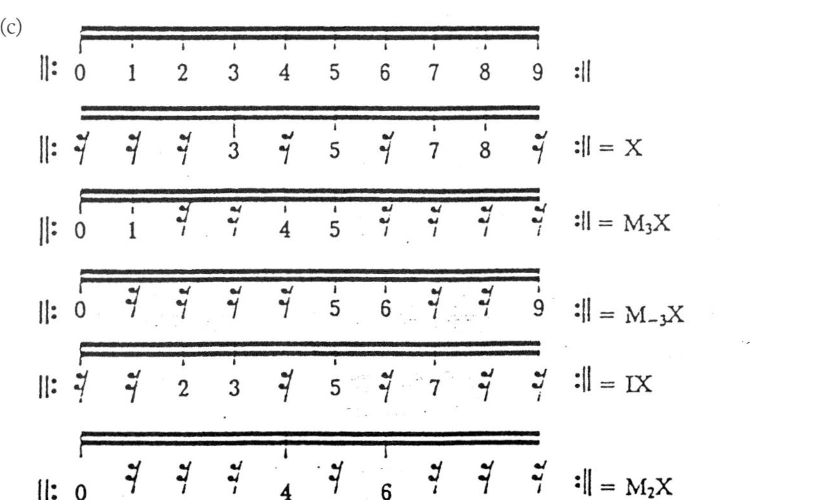

Figure 22.11 Manipulations of time-point series, from Morris, *Composition with Pitch Classes*, pp. 300–03

intimately allied to the fundamental rhythmic structures of the work. Perhaps even more important, it can be tentatively concluded that the relations among pitch-class sets in terms of intersections, unions, and complements have structural analogues in the relations among rhythmic formations in terms of combinations and partitions of durations."[55]

While Forte specifically eschews any appeal to meter in his account of durational patterns, Martha Hyde argues for the cogency of meter in serial music. Her principal thesis is that

> In tonal music, well-defined principles determine the equivalence or commensurability of pitch events and so regulate the articulation of rhythmic strata derived from them. These tonal principles – such as the rules of voice-leading and harmonic progression, or the role of triadic structure – can produce middleground pitch events that recur regularly, providing an important source of rhythmic accent. An analogous process operates in Schoenberg's twelve-tone music: structural principles determine analogous functions for various pitch events, recurrence of these analogous pitch events produces middleground rhythmic strata, and, as in tonal music, middleground strata make up a key source of rhythmic organization.[56]

Thus Hyde's methodology is overtly and strongly pitch-to-rhythm, and her main task is to show how specific recurrences of various pitch-class sets form a middleground stratum (following Yeston) which serves to organize lower-level articulations and produce metrical accents through their interaction.

David Lewin has developed a general approach to rhythm, including post-tonal rhythm, using the tools of mathematical group theory.[57] Different types of rhythmic relationships may be considered in the context of various conceptual spaces: ordered time-points, modularly ordered time-points, durational quotients, durational quotients in a modular durational space, durational differences, and durational differences in modular duration space. In each type of musical space one may explore various categories of equivalence classes and transformations. For example, precedence relationships can be considered in the first time-point space, while tempo differences (i.e., the same pattern of durations performed at different tempi) may be construed relative to the first durational space. Lewin also notes how different compositional approaches to rhythm, such as Babbitt's system of twelve beat-classes, or Carter's proportionally modulating tempi, correspond to particular rhythmic spaces – a modular time-point space and a proportional duration space, respectively (p. 23). In so doing, Lewin neatly sorts out how different approaches to musical time will give rise to different classes of similarity relationships.

Lewin is also sensitive to the ontological and epistemic difficulties various rhythmic spaces entail. As he points out, there is a fundamental "bootstrapping problem" for

55 Ibid., p. 109. 56 Hyde, "A Theory of Twelve-Tone Meter," p. 25.
57 All quotations of Lewin are from *Generalized Musical Intervals and Transformations*.

rhythmic and metrical analysis, since there are no absolute values for durations or beats, as there are for pitches: "The notion of '*an*' abstract conceptual time-unit, a unit by which we measure [duration] . . . is a notion fraught with methodological problems" (p. 62). Similarly, in pursuing various isomorphisms between pitch and rhythmic operations, one may give rise to analytical concepts that are strongly counter-intuitive, such as when a transformation gives rise to a negative duration, since "it is not clear what intuition we could possibly be modeling, when we stipulate a duration *t* that lasts not only less than no time at all, but also *measurably* less than no time at all" (p. 29). Thus the ability to conceive of certain temporal spaces and compositional operations within them does not always translate into musically intelligible relationships, and analytical claims that are rooted in those kinds of rhythmic spaces should be treated cautiously.

In *Meter as Rhythm*, Christopher Hasty also takes a generalized approach to rhythm and meter that is independent of tonal structure. Hasty, drawing upon the process-oriented temporal philosophies of Alfred North Whitehead and Henri Bergson, among others, argues for a projective approach to musical time. In particular, he conceives of meter as a product of the projective fields engendered by a series of durations (or hierarchical complexes of duration). Rather than searching for an underlying order or simplicity, as do Forte and Hyde, Hasty seeks to explain precisely how the musical surfaces of some post-tonal music are rhythmically complex, as well as why such complexity is often difficult to perceive and understand. A complex rhythmic surface is one which thwarts our innate ability to make temporal projections, as we routinely do when confronted with a regular series of relatively short temporal articulations. In some cases durational complexity may attenuate our sense of projection, while in others it may defeat it entirely.[58]

As can thus be seen, theories of musical rhythm have varied widely over the course of the twentieth century. Different kinds of theories and analytical methodologies have arisen depending upon a theorist's commitment to a particular repertoire and its musical syntax, in other cases commitment to a psychologically informed view of musical structure, and yet in other cases commitment to a particular temporal philosophy. As the work of music theorists in the domain of rhythm, motion, and time has become even less insulated, the boundaries separating the four areas of rhythmic theory laid out at the beginning of this chapter have become quite blurred at the century's end. And while millennial predictions are almost always precarious, at the beginning of the twenty-first century we seem to be witnessing the re-emergence of purely speculative approaches to musical rhythm, the likes of which have not been seen since the days of Hauptmann and Riemann.

58 For an instance of the former (attenuation) see Hasty's discussion of Webern's Op 22, pp. 257–75; for an instance of the latter (obliteration) see Hasty's discussion of Lutoslawski's *Jeux Vénitiens*, pp. 293–95.

Bibliography

Babbitt, M. "Twelve Tone Rhythmic Structure and the Electronic Medium," in *Perspectives on Contemporary Music Theory*, ed. B. Boretz and E. Cone, New York, Norton, 1972, pp. 148–79

Benjamin, W. E. "A Theory of Musical Meter," *Music Perception* 1 (1984), pp. 355–413

Bergson, H. *Matière et mémoire*, trans. N. Paul and W. Palmer, New York, Macmillan, 1911

Berry, W. *Structural Functions in Music*, Englewood Cliffs, Prentice Hall, 1976

Boulez, P. *Thoughts on Music Today*, trans. S. Bradshaw and R. Bennett, Cambridge, MA, Harvard University Press, 1971

Bregman, A. S. *Auditory Scene Analysis: The Perceptual Organization of Sound*, Cambridge, MA, MIT Press, 1990

Cage, J. *Silence*, Middletown, CT, Wesleyan University Press, 1961

Carter, E. "Music and the Time Screen," in *The Writings of Elliot Carter*, ed. E. and K. Stone, Indiana University Press, 1977, pp. 343–65

Clifton, T. *Music as Heard*, New Haven, Yale University Press, 1983

Cohn, R. L. "The Dramatization of Hypermetric Conflicts in the Scherzo of Beethoven's Ninth Symphony," *19th-Century Music* 15 (1992), pp. 188–206

Cone, E. T. *Musical Form and Musical Performance*, New York, Norton, 1968

Cooper, G. and L. B. Meyer, *The Rhythmic Structure of Music*, University of Chicago Press, 1960

Epstein, D. *Beyond Orpheus*, Cambridge, MA, MIT Press, 1979

Shaping Time: Music, the Brain, and Performance, New York, Schirmer, 1995

Forte, A. "Aspects of Rhythm in Webern's Atonal Music," *MTS* 2 (1980), pp. 90–109

"Foreground Rhythm in Early Twentieth Century Music," *MA* 2 (1983), pp. 239–68

Hasty, C. F. "Rhythm in Post-Tonal Music: Preliminary Questions of Duration and Motion," *JMT* 25 (1981), pp. 183–216

Meter as Rhythm, New York, Oxford University Press,1997

Husserl, E. *Lectures on Internal Time-Consciousness* (1928), trans. J. S. Churchill, Indiana University Press, 1964

Hyde, M. M. "A Theory of Twelve-Tone Meter," *MTS* 6 (1984), pp. 14–51

Kamien, R. "Conflicting Metrical Patterns in Accompaniment and Melody in Works by Mozart and Beethoven: A Preliminary Study," *JMT* 37 (1993), pp. 311–48

Komar, A. J. *Theory of Suspensions*, Princeton University Press, 1971

Kramer, J. D. "Postmodern Concepts of Musical Time," *Indiana Theory Review* 17 (1996), pp. 21–61

The Time of Music, New York, Schirmer, 1988

Krebs, H. "Some Extensions of the Concepts of Metrical Consonance and Dissonance," *JMT* 31 (1987), pp. 99–120

Kurth, E. *Bruckner*, 2 vols., Berlin, M. Hesse, 1925; facs. Hildesheim, G. Olms, 1971

Lerdahl, F. and R. Jackendoff, *A Generative Theory of Tonal Music*, Cambridge, MA, MIT Press, 1983

Lester, J. *The Rhythms of Tonal Music*, Carbondale, Southern Illinois University Press, 1986

Lewin, D. *Generalized Musical Intervals and Transformations*, New Haven, Yale University Press, 1987

Lochhead, J. M. "Temporal Structure in Recent Music," *Journal of Musicological Research* 6 (1986), pp. 49–93
Macey, S. L., ed., *Encyclopedia of Time*, New York, Garland, 1994
Merleau-Ponty, M. *Phenomenology of Perception*, London, Routledge and K. Paul, 1962
Messiaen, O. *The Technique of my Musical Language*, 2 vols., trans. J. Satterfield, Paris, A. Leduc, 1956
Meyer, L. B. *Emotion and Meaning in Music*, University of Chicago Press, 1956
"A Pride of Prejudices, or Delight in Diversity," *MTS* 13 (1991), pp. 241–51
Morgan, R. P. "The Theory and Analysis of Tonal Rhythm," *Musical Quarterly* 64 (1978), pp. 435–73
Morris, R. D. *Composition with Pitch Classes*, New Haven, Yale University Press, 1987
Neumann, F. *Die Zeitgestalt: Eine Lehre vom musikalischen Rhythmus*, 2 vols., Vienna, P. Kaltschmid, 1959
Riemann, H. *System der musikalischen Rhythmik und Metrik*, Leipzig, Breitkopf und Härtel, 1903
Roeder, J. "A Calculus of Accent," *JMT* 39 (1995), pp. 1–46
Rothfarb, L. *Ernst Kurth as Theorist and Analyst*, Philadelphia, University of Pennsylvania Press, 1988
Rothfarb, L. (trans.), *Ernst Kurth: Selected Writings*, Cambridge University Press, 1991
Rothstein, W. N. *Phrase Rhythm in Tonal Music*, New York, Schirmer,1989
Samarotto, F. "Strange Dimensions: Regularity and Irregularity in Deep Levels of Rhythmic Reductions," in *Schenker Studies II*, ed. C. Schachter and H. Siegel, Cambridge University Press, 1997
Schachter, C. "Rhythm and Linear Analysis: A Preliminary Study," in *The Music Forum* 4, ed. F. Salzer and C. Schachter, Columbia University Press, 1976, pp. 281–334
"Rhythm and Linear Analysis: Durational Reduction," in *The Music Forum* 5, ed. F. Salzer and C. Schachter, Columbia University Press, 1980, pp. 197–232
"Rhythm and Linear Analysis: Aspects of Meter," in *The Music Forum* 6, ed. F. Salzer and C. Schachter, Columbia University Press, 1987, pp. 1–59
Schenker, H. *Free Composition* (1935), trans. and ed. E. Oster, New York, Longman, 1979
The Masterwork in Music (1925–30), 3 vols., ed. W. Drabkin, trans. I. Bent et al., Cambridge University Press, 1994–97
Sessions, R. *Harmonic Practice*, New York, Norton, 1951
Stockhausen, K. *Texte zur elektronischen und instrumentalen Musik*, Cologne, DuMont, 1963
". . . wie die Zeit vergeht . . .," in *Die Reihe* 3, Vienna, Universal, 1957; trans. C. Cardew as ". . . how time passes . . .," in American edition of *Die Reihe* 3, Bryn Mawr, T. Presser, 1959, pp. 10–14
Toch, E. *The Shaping Forces in Music*, New York, Criterion Music, 1958
Westergaard, P. *An Introduction to Tonal Theory*, New York, Norton, 1975
Yeston, M. *The Stratification of Musical Rhythm*, New Haven, Yale University Press, 1976
Zuckerlandl, V. *Sound and Symbol: Music and the External World*, New York, Pantheon Books, 1956

·23·

Tonality

BRIAN HYER

As a music-theoretical term, "tonality" was first used by Alexander Choron in 1810 to describe the arrangement of the dominant and subdominant above and below the tonic and thus to differentiate the harmonic organization of modern music (*tonalité moderne*) from that of earlier music (*tonalité antique*).[1] One of the main conceptual categories in Western musical thought, tonality most often refers to the orientation of melodies and harmonies toward a referential (or tonic) pitch class. In the broadest possible sense, however, it refers to systematic arrangements of pitch phenomena and relations between them.

Usage

A number of musical and discursive factors have contributed to a veritable profusion of definitions for the term.[2] To begin with, there has been considerable indecision about what musical domain the term covers: whether it applies to both Western and non-Western music, or whether, within Western musical traditions, the term can be restricted to the harmonic organization of music from the so-called common practice (1600–1910) or includes all music that evinces a basic difference between consonance and dissonance. There have also been some basic theoretical disagreements about whether its constituent musical elements are melodies or harmonies: however narrow the definition given to the term, the domain of tonal music is so enormous, diverse, and complex that one can choose almost any combination of musical phenomena and theoretical principles as the basis for discussion. In addition to these musical problems, enormous discursive difficulties have arisen from the conceptual languages used to

The present chapter is a revised version of the article written for *NG2*.

1 Choron, "Sommaire de l'Histoire de la Musique," pp. xxxvii–xl; "Summary of the History of Music," pp. xxvii–xxix. In the "Sommaire de l'Histoire de la Musique," Choron contrasts *tonalité moderne* with *tonalité ecclésiastique*. He first drew the more oppositional distinction between *tonalité moderne* and *tonalité antique* in a footnote to his translation of Johann Georg Albrechtsberger's *Gründliche Anweisung zur Composition* (1790). See Albrechtsberger, *Méthode élémentaire de composition* (trans. Choron), p. 18.

2 An invaluable guide to the evolving uses of the term *tonalité* is Michael Beiche's "Tonalität" (1992) in *HmT*.

describe tonal phenomena, theoretical vocabularies that vary dramatically according to the aesthetic and epistemological commitments of the writer. A further complication (and recurrent tension) has to do with whether the term refers to the objective properties of the music – its fixed, internal structure – or the cognitive experience of listeners, whether tonality is inherent in the music or constitutes what one recent author describes as "a form of consciousness."[3]

It is nevertheless possible to sort the various uses of the term into two basic categories, corresponding to its noun and adjective forms, and while its noun forms suggest a greater degree of abstraction and are therefore more controversial, in practice the two forms often converge:

(1) As an adjective, the term is often used to describe the systematic organization of pitch phenomena in both Western and non-Western music. Tonal music in this sense includes music based on, among other theoretical structures, the eight ecclesiastical modes of medieval and Renaissance liturgical music, the *slendro* and *pelog* collections of Indonesian gamelan music, the modal nuclei of Arabic *maqām*, the scalar peregrinations of Indian *raga*, the constellation of tonic, dominant, and subdominant harmonies in the theories of Rameau, the paired major and minor scales in the theories of Weber, or the 144 basic transformations of the twelve-tone row. Perle thus refers to his complexes of interrelated row forms as "twelve-tone tonalities."[4]

(2) As a noun, then, the term is sometimes used as an equivalent for what Rousseau called a "sistême musical," a rational and self-contained arrangement of musical phenomena: Sainsbury, who translated Choron into English in 1825, thus rendered the first occurrence of *tonalité* as "system of modes" before matching it with the neologism "tonality." While tonality *qua* system constitutes a theoretical (and thus imaginative) abstraction from actual music, it is often hypostatized in musicological discourse, converted from a theoretical structure into a musical reality. In this sense, it is understood as a Platonic form or prediscursive musical essence that suffuses music with intelligible sense, that exists prior to its concrete embodiment in music, and can thus be theorized and discussed apart from actual musical contexts.

(3) Within Western musical traditions, "tonal" is often used in contrast with "modal" and "atonal," the implication being that tonal music is *dis*continuous as a form of cultural expression from modal music (before 1600) on the one hand and atonal music (after 1910) on the other.

(4) At the same time, music historians sometimes describe premodern music as being "tonal" on the grounds of (1) above. Here it has been assumed that important historical *con*tinuities underlie music before and after the emergence of musical modernism around 1600 and that the crucial difference between *tonalité ancienne* and *tonalité moderne* is one of emphasis rather than kind. In this sense, tonality is a generic term that

3 Norton, *Tonality in Western Culture: A Critical and Historical Perspective*.
4 Perle, "The Three Tonalities," in *Twelve-Tone Tonality*, pp. 143–51.

refers to music based on the eight modes of the Western church as well as the major-minor complexes of common-practice music, repertoires that share common melodic gestures and cadential formulas, coordinate successions of intervals or harmonies with conditions of dissonance and consonance, and evince a basic textural stratification into a treble melodic voice over a supporting bass line with inner voices that fill out harmonic sonorities.

(5) Tonal phenomena are musical phenomena (harmonies such as the tonic, dominant, and subdominant, cadential formulas, harmonic progressions, melodic gestures, formal categories) arranged or understood in relation to a referential tonic, which imbues the music – in the case of C major – with C-ness.

(6) In a psychophysical sense, tonal phenomena are musical phenomena perceived or preinterpreted in terms of the categories of tonal theories. Here the point is that listeners tend to hear a given pitch as, for instance, an A above middle C, an augmented fourth above E♭, the minor third in an F♯ minor triad, a dominant in relation to D, or $\hat{2}$ (where the caret designates a scale degree) in G major rather than a mere acoustical frequency, in this case 440 Hz.

(7) As a noun, the term is sometimes used, trivially, as a synonym for "key." E minor and A♭ major are thus said to be two different "tonalities." While Choron derived *tonalité* from *ton*, the French word for key, the concept reaches further than the pitch-class content of a particular major or minor scale to describe the relations governing them, relations responsible for the orientation of the music toward the referential tonic. Tonality in this sense means "keyness."

(8) Perhaps the most common use of the term, then, in either its noun or adjective forms, is to designate the arrangement of musical phenomena around a referential tonic in European music from about 1600 to around 1910. However this arrangement is conceptualized, musicians agree that there are two basic genera, major and minor, each with different but analogous musical and expressive properties. It gives rise, moreover, to abstract relations that control melodic motion and harmonic succession over long expanses of musical time. In its power to form musical goals and regulate the progress of the music toward these moments of arrival, tonality has become the principal musical means in Western culture by which to manage expectation and structure desire. In this sense, tonality is understood to define the essential condition of modern Western music: it determines the coordination of harmony with melody, meter with phrasing, texture with register, and thus encompasses – within its historical domain – the whole of music. This use of the term will form the main concern of this chapter.

Rhetoric

Fétis, who popularized the notion of tonality in the 1830s and 40s, defined tonality as the sum total "collection of necessary relations, both successive and simultaneous, between the notes of the scale."[5] He imagined these relations as forces of musical "attraction." In particular, the "minor fifth" between $\hat{4}$ and $\hat{7}$ formed an "appellative consonance" in which both notes summon (*appeler*) their notes of resolution. $\hat{4}$, that is, strives toward $\hat{3}$, while $\hat{7}$ strives toward $\hat{1}$: if $\hat{4}$ and $\hat{7}$ were both notes of "attraction" within the scale, $\hat{3}$ and $\hat{1}$ were notes of "repose." Fétis, who characterized each degree of the scale in terms of relative attraction and repose, was uncertain about whether these melodic tendencies were prior to the scale or arose from it, but it is clear that *tonalité* and the scale were inseparable, the scale being its material form. These inherent melodic tendencies – which he regarded as "les lois de tonalité" – were charged with harmonic implications: while $\hat{4}$ and $\hat{7}$ belong to the "natural" harmony of the dominant seventh, $\hat{3}$ and $\hat{1}$ belong to the tonic, the chord of resolution. $\hat{4}$ and $\hat{7}$ thus operate like needles on a musical compass to orient the listener toward the tonic within a given scalar environment.

For Fétis, the dominant seventh was the crucial musical element in *tonalité moderne*, the "birth" of which he registered in a Monteverdi madrigal, *Stracciami pur il core* of 1592.[6] While the historical and musical validity of the claim is arguable, the time and place he gives for the origin of modern tonality – around 1600 in the music of Monteverdi – has become firm musicological lore. Fétis, however, mishandled his discussion of the madrigal: the dominant seventh in question does not in fact resolve to the tonic over a change in bass. He later made the same claim, however, about another madrigal, *Cruda Amarilli* of 1605, this time more persuasively.[7] His comments on *Cruda Amarilli* renew the terms of an earlier polemic over dissonance treatment in this madrigal between Artusi and Giulio Cesare Monteverdi, of which Fétis was well aware. He notes that an unprepared dominant seventh occurs above G in m. 13 of Example 23.1 and cadences to a tonic above C on the downbeat of m. 14: because it is unprepared, the dominant seventh in m. 13 is heard as vertical (and therefore autonomous) harmony rather than a collection of simultaneous intervals. Here the dominant seventh derives its intense attraction for the tonic from the presence of $\hat{4}$ (F in the *canto*) and $\hat{7}$ (B in the *tenore*), which move to $\hat{3}$ and $\hat{1}$ on the downbeat of the next bar. Yet for Fétis, the dominant seventh has no real tonal significance *per se*, but rather forms a mere pretext for bringing $\hat{4}$ and $\hat{7}$ together. He regards the dominant as the most common harmonic support for the appellative minor fifth, not as an essential scale degree.

Though Fétis claimed that the idea of *tonalité* came to him as a revelation under a tree in the Bois de Boulogne on a warm spring afternoon in 1831, he borrowed most of its basic tenets – not to mention the term itself – from earlier writers. In fact, both the word and concept had been in circulation for over two decades before Fétis embraced it in the 1830s: Castil-Blaze included a definition for *tonalité* in his *Dictionnaire de*

5 Fétis, *Traité complet de la théorie et de la pratique de l'harmonie*, p. 22.
6 Fétis, *Esquisse de l'histoire de l'harmonie* (Arlin trans., pp. 30–32).
7 Fétis, *Traité complet de la théorie et de la pratique de l'harmonie*, pp. 165–67.

Example 23.1 Monteverdi, "Cruda Amarilli" (1605), mm. 9–14

musique moderne (1821), but the term also occurs in Geslin's *Cours d'harmonie* (1826) and Jelensperger's *L'harmonie au commencement du 19ᵉ siècle* (1830). It now appears certain that the first author to use the term was Choron, who coined it in the *Sommaire de l'histoire de la musique* (1810) to describe the constellation of tonic, dominant, and subdominant harmonies familiar to musicians since Rameau. Monteverdi, Choron tells us moreover, invented the dominant seventh around 1590, was the first composer to introduce it without preparation, and was the first composer to use the "minor fifth" as a consonance: "and so tonal harmony came to be." Fétis's debt to Choron thus extends to include the notion of appellative consonance, the distinction between *tonalité ancienne* and *moderne*, and the claim that Monteverdi invented the dominant seventh.

Fétis was at a loss to account for the "mysterious" forces of attraction that operate within the scale other than to insist that these appellative tendencies were "purement métaphysique" – an expression he borrowed from Momigny.[8] If nowadays appeals to metaphysics tend to fall on deaf ears, Fétis was nevertheless broaching a crucial issue: most if not all tonal theories recognize that tonal phenomena are not static and motionless, but rather possess (or seem to possess) dynamic qualities that, however crucial to musical experience, resist causal explanation and are better understood in cultural terms. These qualities occasion intricate aggregates of metaphors and verbal images, some of which compare these relations of musical attraction to forces of nature: for Rameau, the attraction of the dominant to the tonic was gravitational in nature, a metaphor he elaborated to discuss relations between harmonies – and the motions of these harmonies toward the cadential goal – in general. At the same time, these forces

8 See Momigny, "Musique," vol. II, p. 178a.

of attraction have often been translated into animistic language, which attributes intelligence and intention to tonal phenomena: to regard the scale degree below the tonic as the *note sensible*, for instance, is to ascribe sentience to it. Henry Cowell thus defines tonality as "a musical homing instinct,"[9] while Schoenberg imagines relations of melodic attraction in tonal music in terms of "the instinctual lives of tones."[10] Rameau seemed to suggest that this instinct was sometimes sexual: on occasion, he personifies the tonic as the object of musical desire, the musical being "to whom all our wishes tend."[11] For d'Alembert, in contrast, this musical desire was more olfactory in nature: the "sourness of the dominant," he wrote, "desires the sweetness of the tonic."[12]

If the dominant desires resolution to the tonic, the tonic then assumes a passive role in relation to the dominant, which in this sense governs – *dominates* – the tonic. Schoenberg (in *Harmonielehre*, 1911) contended that this view of the tonic was erroneous, insisting that the tonic controls the dominant, not *vice versa*. Schoenberg, that is, inverted the relation between them and opposed an active tonic with a passive dominant, a notion implicit in a number of earlier writers. In *Die Lehre von den Tonempfindungen* (1863), Helmholtz thus describes the tonic as the main note (*Hauptton*), a note that has dominion or maintains control (*Herrschaft*) over all the others.[13] Political images of this sort are pervasive in theories of tonal music: to describe relations between harmonies in terms of dominance and subordinance, as Rameau did, is to conceive them in terms of relations between persons, in terms, that is, of social power. Sometimes these metaphors are extended to become entire musical societies: Schoenberg, for instance, imagined the tonic as a sovereign who rules over the other harmonies and the dominant as his vassal, going before his liege to announce and prepare for his arrival, an idea he embroiders at considerable length.[14] Momigny, in contrast, had earlier imagined the tonic as a queen: the tonic is "the purpose of all purposes, the end of all ends," for "it is to her that the scepter of the musical empire is entrusted."[15] Perhaps the most elaborate of these social simulacra, however, is one of the earliest. In the *Grundregeln zur Tonordnung insgemein* (1755), Riepel compares the six diatonic harmonies in C major to the social and economic organization of a rural farm, where C major was the bailiff or master (*Meyer*), G major the overseer (*Oberknecht*), A minor the head maid (*Obermagd*), F major the day laborer (*Taglöhner*), E minor the chamber maid (*Untermagd*), and D minor the errand girl (*Unterläufferin*).[16] Riepel, that is, separates the six diatonic harmonies in C major into two hierarchical orders, one masculine and agricultural (major harmonies), the other feminine and domestic (minor harmonies), both operating under the watchful supervision of the master. Momigny

9 Cowell, "New Terms for New Music," pp. 22–23.
10 Schoenberg, *Harmonielehre*.
11 Rameau, *Génération harmonique*, pp. 108–09.
12 D'Alembert, *Elémens de Musique théorique et pratique*.
13 Helmholtz, *Die Lehre von den Tonempfindungen*, p. 395; *On the Sensations of Tone*, p. 240.
14 Schoenberg, *Harmonielehre*, pp. 36–37; *Theory of Harmony*, pp. 32–33.
15 Momigny, *Cours complet d'harmonie et de composition*, vol. 1, p. 47.
16 Riepel, *Grundregeln zur Tonordnung insgemein*, pp. 65–67.

described the seven notes of the major and minor scales in this sense as a "hiérarchie naturelle" under the "authorité" of the tonic, whereas Schenker would later write, in contrast, of a more egalitarian "stable community of tones."[17] Hence the peculiar insistence in tonal theories of the eighteenth and nineteenth centuries on laws and principles: for Fétis, *tonalité* was "le principe régulateur des rapports." These musical laws were meant both to regulate musical phenomena and to constrain compositional practice. Despite the intended comparisons with natural laws, then, these *Gesetze der Tonalität* were social in basis: there is a strong correlation between tonal theories and conservative political ideologies.

In the discursive rhetoric of tonal theories, the tonic tends to be framed in images of presence and plenitude. Marpurg (in his translation of d'Alembert) was the first writer to describe the tonic as a musical "home," an image that has remained in circulation ever since.[18] Perhaps the most resilient metaphor for the tonic, however, has been that of a musical "center." Helmholtz, building on Rameau's gravitational rhetoric, would later describe the tonic as the center (*Schwerpunkt*) of a tonal mass (*Tonmasse*). As a center, the tonic forms a geometrical *punctum* in a spatial arrangement of harmonies: in one of the more ingenious metaphors for the harmonic organization of tonal music, Tovey compared tonality in music to linear perspective in painting, where the tonic forms a musical "vanishing point," the focal center of an abstract configuration of musical relations.[19] Spatial intuitions like these are crucial to the tonal imagination: when Momigny likens the arrangement of scale degrees around the tonic to the orbits of planets around the sun, he equates the tonic with the gravitational center of the solar system but also conceptualizes the entire arrangement as a series of concentric circles.[20] Here the premise is that one can abstract relations between harmonies from music and plot them as distances between points in two or more dimensions. This urge to spatialize musical phenomena has its immediate origins in registral intuitions of above and below: for Rameau, the dominant lies a perfect fifth above the tonic, the subdominant a perfect fifth below, which allows him to imagine the tonic as a center, at a point equidistant between the two dominants. In actual musical contexts, however, the tonic forms a conclusion, not a center – it arrives at the *ends* of phrases, formal sections, and entire pieces. Even the idea that the dominant lies a perfect fifth above the tonic is true only in a theoretical sense, since in numerous musical contexts the dominant fundamental often lies a perfect fourth *below* – rather than a perfect fifth *above* – the tonic.

In most tonal theories, relations between harmonies are woven together to form a mental grid, an abstract representation Fétis describes as the "basis for all music," that which underlies tonal music and renders it intelligible. The notion that the tonic

17 Schenker, *Harmonielehre*, pp. 54–55; *Harmony*, p. 40.
18 D'Alembert, *Systematische Einleitung in die musikalische Setzkunst nach den Lehrsätzen des Herrn Rameau*, p. 27. 19 Tovey, "Musical Form and Matter," p. 167.
20 Momigny, *Cours complet d'harmonie et de composition*, vol. 1, p. 26.

occupies a referential or locus position on an abstract mental grid of harmonic relations, for instance, is crucial to the intuition that some harmonies are more distant from the tonic than others. Schoenberg thus speaks of "remote regions" within larger musical geographies: for Schoenberg, the musical universe divides into spatial enclosures – territories – of harmonies.[21] Implicit here is the idea that tonality constitutes a material substance that has a certain extension in space and time. The discursive reliance of tonal theories on images of containers in particular is remarkable: musicians often speak of music being "in" C major as if C major were a receptacle with an interior volume that somehow contains and gives shape to the music within it. In this sense, tonal music comes to have a diatonic inside and chromatic outside, often understood in terms of an opposition between the rational and irrational, or between the domestic and foreign. Histories of nineteenth-century music are often narrated in terms of a progressive initiative to absorb and incorporate more and more chromaticism into the diatonic confines of the key. Schoenberg's term for the enlarged harmonic resources of late Romantic music was "expanded tonality," a description that attributes an almost Cartesian *res extensa* to music.

Theory

While both Choron and Fétis drew on the same basic theoretical resources, there are subtle but crucial differences between their accounts of *tonalité*. In contrast to Choron, who emphasizes relations between harmonies, Fétis places more stress on the order and position of pitches within a scale. This difference in emphasis corresponds to the two main historical traditions of theoretical conceptualization about tonal music: the function theories of Rameau and Riemann on the one hand and the scale-degree theories of Weber and Schenker on the other. All tonal theories can be understood in terms of one tradition or the other, or as a hybrid (as with Fétis) of both. Two basic traits common to both discursive traditions are (1) the notion that tonal music has an ideational content, where harmonies refer either to a tonic (in *Funktiontheorien*) or to a scale (in *Stufentheorien*), both of which are understood to underlie the music and render it intelligible; and (2) the use of a metalanguage – whether discursive labels such as "dominant" or "subdominant," or cyphers such as roman numerals – to express the referential orientation of these harmonies.

In *Génération harmonique* (1737), Rameau conceived relations between harmonies in terms of cadences. In the imperfect cadence, Example 23.2a, the fundamental bass (or *B.F.*, for *basse fondamentale*) ascends a perfect fifth from the subdominant to the tonic. In the perfect cadence, Example 23.2b, the fundamental bass descends a perfect fifth

21 Schoenberg, *Structural Functions of Harmony*, p. 19. For a reproduction of Schoenberg's "Chart of the regions," see **Chapter 25, p. 804**.

Example 23.2 After Rameau, *Génération harmonique* (1737)

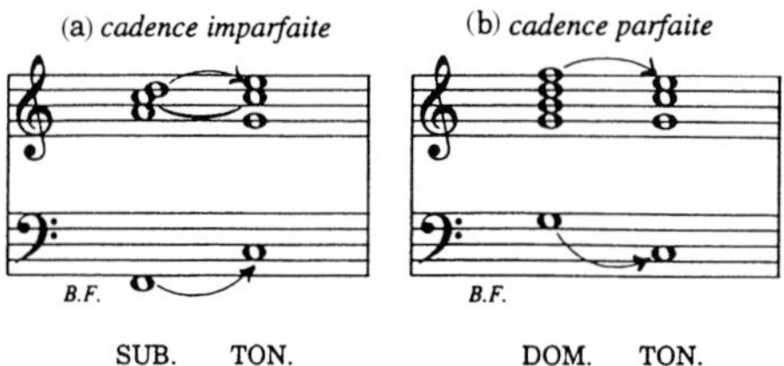

from the dominant to the tonic (cf. **Plates 24.1** and **24.2, pp. 762, 763**). As a constellation, these three harmonies (the tonic, dominant, and subdominant) comprise what Rameau called the "mode." His theories differ from older traditions of *modalité* in their emphasis on the harmonic dimension of music: *tonalité* for Rameau – if one can use the expression – was more harmonic than melodic in nature. A crucial factor in this musical system was the addition of dissonances to the dominant and subdominant: Rameau added a major sixth (D in Example 23.2a) to the subdominant, a minor seventh (F in Example 23.2b) to the dominant, both of which resolve to the same note (in this case E) above the tonic – the note of resolution determines whether the mode is major (as in Example 23.2) or minor. These dissonances accord the tonic, dominant, and subdominant distinctive harmonic identities and characteristic musical behaviors: the added dissonances increase the pressure on the dominant and subdominant to move to the tonic. Rameau often describes these harmonic relations in quasi-Newtonian language: the tonic, that is, exerts a gravitational pull on the dominant and subdominant, an invisible force that binds these three harmonies together.

Rameau was concerned, then, both with the identities of harmonies (as tonics, dominants, or subdominants) and their succession: he coordinates harmonic succession with consonance and dissonance, tension and resolution. For some writers, the notion that harmonies are not mere adjacencies, but that one moves to the next, constitutes the defining trait of tonality. In his influential *Untersuchung über die Entstehung der harmonischen Tonalität* (1966), Dahlhaus extends this concern for succession from harmonies to intervals and thus locates the historical origins of tonality in the music of Josquin and his contemporaries.

If function theories begin with the prior assertion of a referential tonic, scale-degree theories use the major (or minor) scale as their referential point of departure. Though adumbrated in the theories of Kirnberger, Vogler, and Koch, it was Weber who (in the *Versuch einer geordneten Theorie der Tonsetzkunst zum Selbstunterricht*, 1830–32; see also **Chapter 25, pp. 782–88**) gave them their definitive form and who was responsible for their tremendous pedagogical success: scale-degree theories remain the dominant conceptual language for tonal music in Europe and North America. Weber uses the pitch classes of the major and minor scale to construct diatonic triads and seventh chords on

Example 23.3 After Weber, *Versuch einer geordneten Theorie der Tonsetzkunst zum Selbstunterricht* (1830–32), §149

(a) Diatonic harmonies in major

(b) Diatonic harmonies in minor

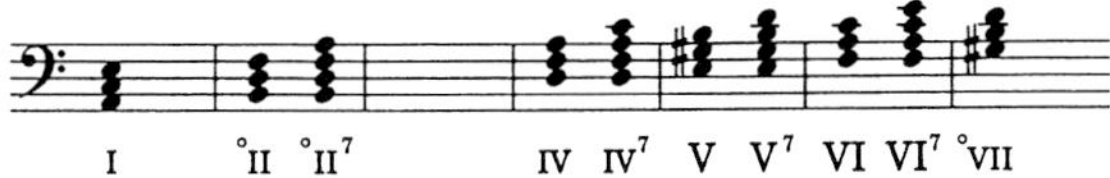

the melodic degrees of each scale: Example 23.3a tabulates the results for major, Example 23.3b for minor. He then uses roman numerals to number these *Stufen* from one through seven: large roman numerals designate major triads, small roman numerals designate minor triads, and degree signs designate diminished harmonies. Weber assigns these roman numerals to actual harmonies on the basis of pitch-class content: a succession of harmonies coheres (makes musical sense) when each chord can be traced back via the mechanism of chord inversion to the same major or minor scale. A recurrent source of vexation in scale-degree theories is *Mehrdeutigkeit*, or multiple meaning: because harmonies assume roman numerals on the basis of pitch-class content rather than musical behavior (as in function theories), there are no hard and fast criteria to determine which major or minor scale a particular harmonic configuration refers to: a C major triad, for instance, can be heard as I in C major, IV in G major, V in F major, or VI in E minor; one must take contextual factors into account in order to narrow down the possibilities to a single roman numeral.

In both discursive traditions, tonal theories have tended to concentrate on harmonies to the virtual exclusion of all other musical considerations: register, texture, instrumentation, dynamics, etc., are taken into account only to the extent that these parameters articulate or bring out relations between harmonies. Yet this separation of harmonic from other musical considerations is artificial. Meter in particular is crucial to the subordination of dissonant harmonies to consonant ones: Rameau understood that the clear and unambiguous assertion of a tonic depended on the *mesure*. While most theorists concentrate on harmonic and sometimes melodic considerations, tonality is perhaps best conceptualized as a *tertium quid* in which melody, harmony, and meter all combine into a single musical nexus.

An important historical development in function theories occurred around 1850 with the formal integration of mediants into the aggregate of tonic, dominant, and subdominant harmonies. Though common in earlier theories, mediants did not become the locus of intense theoretical concern until a number of writers began to use them as functional alternatives to roman numerals. In *Die Natur der Harmonik und Metrik* (1853), Hauptmann represented the musical infrastructure of C major as *F–a–C–e–G–b–D*, where large letters designate dominant-related perfect fifths and small letters their mediant major (or minor) thirds. In this arrangement of intervals and pitch classes, each string of three consecutive letters forms a diatonic triad: the tonic *C–e–G*, dominant *G–b–D*, and subdominant *F–a–C*, of course, but also the mediant *e–G–b* and submediant *a–C–e*. In this case, E minor mediates between the tonic and dominant above, while A minor mediates between the tonic and subdominant below – the submediant is a mediant below the tonic. This further differentiation of dominant-related harmonies into mediants enabled functional theories to account for secondary triads (for which scale-degree theories were able to assign roman numerals), but also to account for the harmonic practice of Romantic music, which began to privilege third relations over the opposed tonics and dominants of Classical harmonic practice. These third relations received their most complete representation in Plate 23.1, which Ottokar Hostinský (whose harmonic theories are unremembered) included in his *Die Lehre von den musikalischen Klängen: Ein Beitrag zur aesthetischen Begründung der Harmonie-Lehre* (1879). In this sonorous grid of interwoven harmonic consonances, horizontal strands of perfect fifths criss-cross with diagonal strands of major thirds (upper left to lower right) and minor thirds (lower left to upper right). While similar grids were common before Hostinský, he was the first to integrate major thirds and minor thirds in the same diagram and thus to give them equal prominence.

It was Riemann who coined the term *function* in *Vereinfachte Harmonielehre* (1893) to describe relations between dominant and subdominant harmonies and the referential tonic: he borrowed the word from mathematics, where it was used to designate the correlation of two variables, an *argument* and a *value*. In contrast to scale-degree theories, function theories are concerned more with harmonic identities than with chord progressions. For Riemann, more than one chord could represent a given tonal function: a D minor triad, for instance, can be heard as the subdominant parallel (or **Sp**) in C major by virtue of the interval (the major third F–A) it maintains in common with the subdominant F major (or S). D minor and F major are in this sense two possible values for the same subdominant function. Riemann recognized three basic harmonic transformations (or *Verwandtschaften*) of a given tonic, dominant, or subdominant function: the *Variant*, which correlates major and minor triads having the same ground note (C major/C minor), the *Parallel*, which correlates major and minor triads a minor third apart (C major/A minor), and the *Leittonwechsel*, which correlates major and minor triads a major third apart (C major/E minor). When applied to the tonic, dominant, and subdominant in C major, the result is Example 23.4, in which the three main tonal functions overlap: A minor, for instance, can be heard either as the tonic parallel (**Tp**) or the subdominant *Leittonwechsel* (**S̸**) depending on which function – **T** or **S** – controls the musical context.

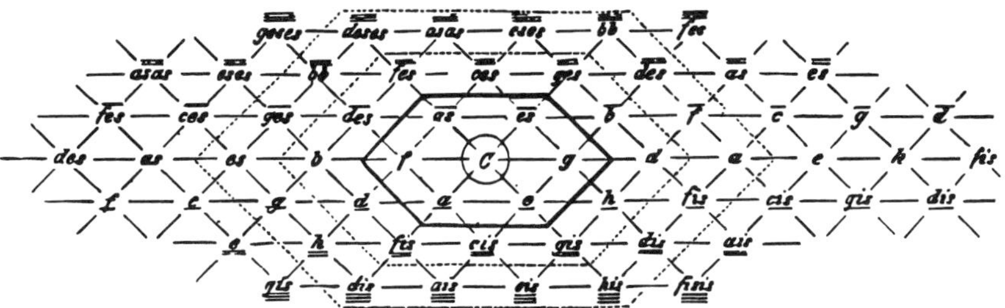

Plate 23.1 Grid of tonal relations (*Tonnetz*), from Hostinský, *Die Lehre von den musikalischen Klängen* (1879), p. 67. In Riemannian terms, letter names designate fundamentals of *Variant*-related major and minor triads. Dominant-related perfect fifths run horizontally from left to right; *Leittonwechsel*-related major thirds run diagonally from lower right to upper left; *Parallel*-related minor thirds run diagonally from lower left to upper right. Because Hostinský assumes just intonation, no two pitches with the same letter name are equivalent. Hence the lines above and below the letter names designate pitch differences in syntonic-comma increments.

Riemann, who identified the *Dominante* with the perfect fifth, the *Leittonwechsel* with the major third, and the *Parallel* with the minor third, thus recognized Plate 23.1 as a powerful realization of his harmonic theories and reproduced the diagram (without attribution) in the "Ideen zu einer 'Lehre von den Tonvorstellungen.'"[22] There he uses uses his three prime functional transformations to reconstruct the diagram as a multidimensional musical terrain in which each letter represents the groundtone of a *Variant*-related major or minor triad: in this torus of harmonic consonances, the horizontals represent dominant-related perfect fifths, which intersect at diagonals with *Parallel*-related minor thirds and *Leittonwechsel*-related major thirds. Like Hostinský, Hauptmann, and most other theorists in the functional tradition, Riemann advocated the use of just intonation, which accounts for the lines above and below the pitch letters in the diagram. If viewed through the filter of equal temperament (to which there was no real alternative in the musical practice of the time) and enharmonic equivalence, the diagram expresses a musical universe saturated with with major and minor triads on all chromatic twelve semitones. Even though Riemann restricted their application to the music of Bach and Beethoven, his harmonic theories constitute a remarkable expression of the chromatic tonal relations in late Romantic music.

Scale-degree theories accounted for chromaticism by means of what Schenker called mixture (*Mischung*), which refers to contexts in which the music gains access to or borrows harmonies from the parallel major or minor. In order to increase the harmonic resources of C major, for instance, one can replace A minor (or VI) with A♭ major (or

22 Riemann, "Ideen zu einer 'Lehre von den Tonvorstellungen,'" p. 20. For the dualist underpinnings of Riemann's harmonic theory, see **Chapter 14, pp. 458–65**; for more on his theory of functions, see **Chapter 25, pp. 796–800**.

Example 23.4 Functional harmonies in C major, after Riemann, "Dissonanz," *Musik-Lexikon*, 8th edn. (1916)

♭VI), borrowed from the parallel minor. In *Harmonielehre* (1906), Schenker goes on to describe how, in the music of late Romanticism, major and minor fuse together: he combines the notes of both the major and minor scale into a single chromatic scale and then places – as in Figure 23.1 – major and minor triads (via mixture) on each degree. Schoenberg likewise heard late Romantic music in terms of "a transition from twelve major and twelve minor tonalities (*Tonarten*) to twelve chromatic ones," a historical transition "fully completed in the music of Wagner."[23]

Practice

Historians do not agree on how and when the transition from Renaissance modal polyphony to the harmonic tonality of the Baroque occurred. Harold S. Powers has even argued that modality and tonality coexist as musical properties on separate epistemological planes, in which case it is meaningless to imagine a transition from one to the other; modality and tonality in this sense are no longer competing or mutually exclusive means of musical organization.[24] Even within the terms of this argument, however, we can register a reduction in musical practice from eight or more modes in *Cinquecento* music to a mere two in music of the *Seicento*. In historical retrospect, this reduction occurs as a gradual emergence of a paired *cantus durus* and *cantus mollis* from the labyrinthine complications of Renaissance modal theories, a transition completed in *Das neu-eröffnete Orchestre* (1713), where Mattheson lists alternative major (*dur*) and minor (*moll*) modes for all twelve semitones within the chromatic octave (see also **Chapter 13, p. 427**) In the music of Mattheson's contemporaries, however, mutations of earlier modal procedures continue to exist alongside newer means of tonal organization, but also in conjunction with numerous hybrid practices: there are a large number of Bach chorales, for instance, that accord modal melodies *dur* or *moll* harmonizations.

There *is* a consensus, however, that the emergence of a newer major-minor modal ethos coincides with a radical simplification of musical texture that involves the strat-

23 Schoenberg, *Harmonielehre*, p. 466; *Theory of Harmony*, p. 389.
24 Powers, "Is Mode Real?," pp. 9–14.

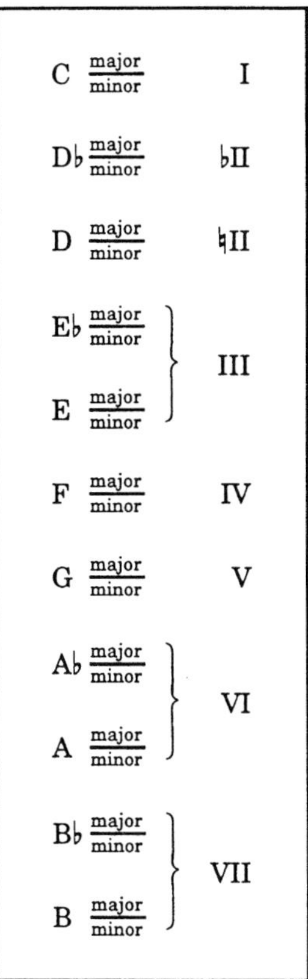

Figure 23.1 C $\frac{\text{major}}{\text{minor}}$, after Schenker, *Harmonielehre* (1906), p. 395

ification and sedimentation of the dense, interwoven imitation of late Renaissance music into harmonic sonorities above a *basso continuo*. A crucial effect of this transformation was to isolate and draw attention to chords as discrete musical entities: from now on, Western music would be heard as successions of harmonies rather than collections of simultaneous intervals. In both theory and practice, the harmonic triad – a musical structure in which the fundamental unifies the intervals above and lends its pitch class to the entire configuration – becomes the basic perceptual element of tonal music. The final, mediant third, and dominant fifth – the three constituents of the *trias harmonica* – were used not only as normative sonorities but also to determine medial cadences: the harmonic triad thus took precedence over the distribution of semitones within the modal octave as a means of structuring the pitch domain. It is in this context that the *clausula formalis* of earlier music was reinterpreted as the dominant-to-tonic

Example 23.5 *Clausula formalis* (with bass accompaniment)

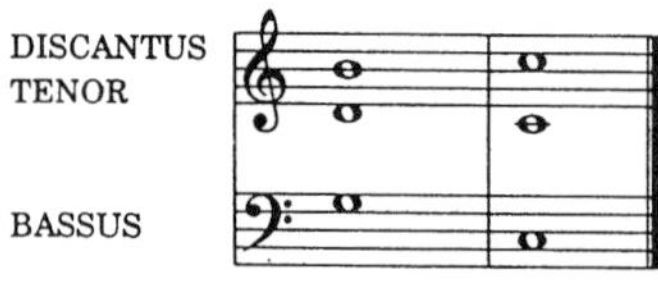

cadence. In Example 23.5, the bass G – the dominant fundamental – is the one note capable of forming consonances with both D and the *subsemitonum* B in the penultimate bar: the dominant-to-tonic cadence, in other words, arises from the melodic exigencies of the voice leading. In the newer harmonic orientation of German Baroque music it becomes a rhetorical device, a conventional gesture used to punctuate mosaic-like successions of phrases and *ritornelli*.

The preoccupation with the moment-to-moment resolution of dissonance in Rameau's theories mirrors the sensuous harmonic sonorities and episodic nature of French Baroque music. These dissonances urge the fundamental bass forward, but gravitational momentum in this music nevertheless tends to be local in significance, directed toward an immediate cadential goal. It is an improvisational, accompanimental harmonic practice, one that responds to the expressive needs of the moment: rapid transitions from one tonic to the next (Rameau was inclined to hear any triad without a dissonance as a tonic) organize the music into additive series of modulations connected together via chains of dominants in which tonal coherence has more to do with the dramatic action on stage (or the *sentiment* of a poetic image) than an abstract musical design.

Harmonies in Classical music (Haydn, Boccherini, Mozart, Beethoven), like those in Baroque music, tend to be clear and unambiguous in their references to the tonic, whether a chord or a scale degree. Whole passages and even entire pieces can be heard as large-scale harmonic progressions in which the music assumes a sense of almost inevitable momentum and progress toward a distant but forehearable harmonic goal. Pieces are thus sometimes said to develop from within, out of certain tensions inherent in the musical material. These tonal tensions constitute a musical logic analogous to that of premise (antecedent) and conclusion (consequent) that allows listeners to predict both the immediate course of events and the modulations that articulate the larger musical argument. In this sense the harmonic organization of Classical music can even be understood (after Fichte and Hegel) as a dialectic in which the dominant opposes (or even negates) the tonic: the dominant and tonic, that is, enter into a rational, contrastive musical logic homologous with other oppositions between dissonance and consonance, tension and resolution, etc. In the sonata, the reprise in particular constitutes a moment of synthesis in which music heard earlier in the dominant recurs in the tonic and thus assumes an altogether different musical significance. In this sense, the tensions that underlie tonal music form what Rose Rosengaard Subotnik has described as the musical equivalent of reason.[25] Because of this quasi-objective musical logic, Classical music gives the appearance of being universally intelligible to all listeners within its cultural reach.

However evident this musical logic appears to us now, certain aspects of Classical harmonic practice were not theorized until well after the fact. Schoenberg, for instance, conceptualized the firm sense of closure in this music in terms of "monotonality," the idea that, no matter how extended in duration, pieces of music retain their allegiance to the original tonic from beginning to end (*Structural Functions of Harmony*, 1954). Schenker, who elaborated the same basic idea, heard modulations as temporary "tonicizations" of non-tonic scale degrees rather than permanent departures from the original tonic. This allowed him to regard entire pieces as recursive hierarchies of harmonies, progressions within progressions. In Plate 23.2, his musical picture of the Moderato from the Haydn Piano Sonata in G minor, Hob. XVI:44 (c. 1771–3), tonicized scale degrees control isolated contexts as local tonics while retaining their original identities as non-tonic harmonies in the large-scale progression that governs the piece as a whole: the large-scale III at m. 13 in Plate 23.2a is thus heard as I in B♭ major in Plate 23.2b, where it controls its own I–II–V–I progression between m. 13 and m. 20.[26] Schenker viewed pieces as melodic projections (or prolongations) of the tonic in the form of an a priori *Ursatz*, in which both the bass and the melodic *Urlinie* (outlined with whole notes and carets in the upper voice of Plate 23.6a) move within the intervals of the tonic triad. Within this contrapuntal framework, tonicizations of non-tonic scale degrees, however near or remote, have their rationale not as autonomous harmonies, but in the coincidental confluences of melodic lines. The bass, in particular, moves from I through III to V before returning to I at the beginning of the reprise, a large-scale arpeggiation of the tonic that Schenker equates with *Tonalität*. The crucial moments in this long-range elaboration of the tonic coincide with the main formal divisions of the sonata: I with the so-called first theme (*erster Gedanke*), III with the second theme (*zweiter Gedanke*), the motion from III to V with the development (*Durchführung*), and the return to I with the reprise (*Wiederholung*). In this sense, the tonic controls and coordinates not just the large-scale harmonic and melodic organization of the piece, but also the succession of textural contrasts that characterize sonata form in its various generic guises: the tonic seems to saturate the music and reach down to its very core, determining its points of internal articulation.

In its use of distinctive harmonic sonorities and remote tonal relations, the harmonic focus in Romantic music is on the particular, concrete, sensuous, and contingent. In drawing attention to these unusual harmonies, the music tarries over the

25 Subotnik, "Tonality, Autonomy, and Competence in Post-Classical Music," pp. 154ff.
26 Schenker, "On Organicism in Sonata Form," p. 34. For further information on the theory and notation of Schenker's analytical graphs, see Chapter 26, pp. 816–31.

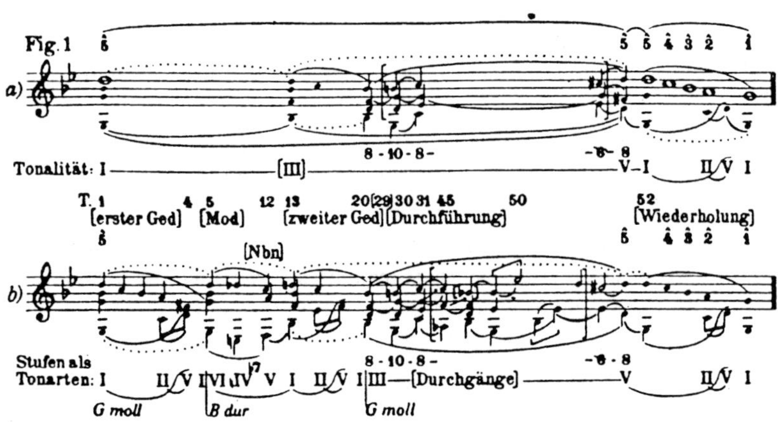

Plate 23.2 Schenker's analysis of Haydn's Sonata in G minor, Hob. XVI:44; from *The Masterwork in Music*, vol. II, p. 24

present moment and distracts the listener from large-scale tonal relations. At the same time, motivic chromaticism destabilizes the careful coordination between the melodic and harmonic dimensions that characterized Classical music, freeing music from the requirement to close on the original tonic: numerous pieces from Schubert on begin and end on different tonics. At first the two termini were a major or minor third apart, as in *Ganymed*, D. 544 (1817), which moves from A♭ major through C♭ major to F major. With Wagner, however, relations between the two tonics become less diatonic and increasingly remote: Act 3 of *Tristan und Isolde* (1859), for instance, begins in F minor but concludes in B major; the dictum that pieces close on the original tonic was an aesthetic rather than a cognitive requirement. As Romantic music turned away from the autonomous, self-contained, and absolute, it began to depend more and more on the extrinsic and extramusical for its coherence: poems, dramatic narratives, programmatic conceits, visual imagery. Tonal relations become increasingly "associative" in nature, unique to a given piece. Hence the overall motion from E♭ minor in the Prologue to *Götterdämmerung* (1874) to B minor at the end of Act 1 can be heard in the context of the entire *Der Ring des Nibelungen* to effect a transition from the natural world of the Norns to the evil (because cultural) realm of the Gibichungs.[27] It is this thematic relation between the two tonics rather than any intrinsically musical logic that accounts for the tonal coherence of the music.

The aesthetic predilection for sensuous sonorities and striking progressions in late

27 Bailey, "The Structure of the *Ring* and Its Evolution," pp. 59–60.

Romantic music led to what Kurth (in the *Romantische Harmonik und ihre Krise in Wagners "Tristan"* of 1923) called "absolute effect," where chromatic harmonies stand out as figures against a more normative diatonic ground (see also **Chapter 30, pp. 941–42**). These chromatic harmonies were characteristic of the "alteration style," which he diagnosed in terms of three factors: (1) chord alteration, where a chord tone is raised or lowered a semitone, (2) melodic displacement, where a dissonant neighbor replaces a regular chord tone, and (3) chromatic progression, where chromaticism inflects the interval of bass progression between harmonies. In combination with one another, these three factors tend to occlude references to the tonic and obliterate the distinction between the chromatic figure and the diatonic ground. In general, references to the tonic become increasingly ambiguous and occasional: in the music of *Tristan* (which for Kurth represented a "crisis" in Western music), cadential dominants and tonics are few and far between and the connections between them are for the most part melodic rather than harmonic. Kurth heard these interspersed functional harmonies as pillars (*Grundpfeiler*) supporting a texture of melodic chromaticism more non-tonal (if not *a*tonal) than tonal. On occasion, this chromaticism resulted in the "repression of the tonic," the indirect assertion of the tonic in music where the tonic itself remains in abeyance. In the first three bars of the opening phrase of *Tristan*, the music moves to a dominant seventh above E, which refers to an absent A minor tonic (see **Example 25.8, p. 792**). Kurth hears the entire *Vorspiel* to Act 1 as a series of increasingly violent "oscillations" between the dominant and subdominant in A minor that never once in over fourteen minutes of music touches on the tonic.[28]

In late Romantic music, moments of orientation toward the tonic become allusive and fragmentary, a condition that Schoenberg – an ever-reliable source of neologisms – termed "floating tonality."[29] In the sequential continuation of the *Tristan* Prelude, the music moves out of A minor to the dominant in C minor, and so on. In the historical wake of *Tristan*, music underwent an atomization in which non-tonal harmonies cluster around isolated dominants and tonics. This tonal disintegration has often been understood as a dissolution from within, an organic process in which the forces of melodic attraction that gave rise to tonality led to its inevitable destruction. For Kurth, major and minor triads were suffused with leading-tone energies in which the major third (above the ground tone in the major triad) presses upward, while the minor third (above the ground tone in the minor triad) presses downward. In the historical development of the musical material, these leading tones came to overwhelm the triads that gave rise to and at first contained them, resulting in an amorphous, centrifugal chromaticism that neutralizes and obscures more centripetal references to the tonic. Coherence in this music is no longer tonal but melodic and (above all) motivic in

28 Kurth, *Romantische Harmonik und ihre Krise in Wagners "Tristan"*, pp. 235–36.
29 Schoenberg, "Über schwebende und aufgehobene Tonalität," *Harmonielehre*, pp. 459–60; "Concerning Fluctuating and Suspended Tonality," *Theory of Harmony*, pp. 383–84.

Example 23.6 Wagner, *Parsifal* (1881), Act 2, mm. 993–1001

nature: it makes far more sense to hear the *Tristan* chord as a verticalization of the melodic minor third from G♯ to B (the Yearning motive) and the diminished third from F to D♯ (the Suffering motive) than to hear it as an altered dominant (Kurth) or subdominant (an augmented sixth chord above F) in A minor.

In extreme cases, the motivic chromaticism of late Romantic music negates all reference to the tonic and veers over the precipice into atonality. In Example 23.6, the climactic bars in Act 2 of *Parsifal* (1881), Wagner loads harmonies with dissonances that render them ambiguous and referentially inoperative: while the music is littered with tonal debris – seventh and ninth chords familiar from more conventional tonal contexts – those harmonies fail to coalesce around a tonic. Sustained bass notes immobilize the harmonies above them and arrest forward momentum: the music wanders between functionless harmonies that neutralize rather than progress to one another, sonorities that seem to float in the music, without a goal, without direction. Dissonant harmonies are either severed from their resolutions or resolve back into themselves: with his agonized "Amfortas!," Parsifal resolves the minor ninth F in m. 994 to a no less dissonant, no less wrenching E in m. 996. As Adorno noted in his discussion of these measures in the *Versuch über Wagner* (1938), dissonances in Romantic music "stand for negation and suffering."[30] Amfortas's open wound thus becomes symbolic of what some listeners (Adorno among them) have heard as the death throes of tonality.

30 Adorno, *Versuch über Wagner*, pp. 61–62; *In Search of Wagner*, p. 67.

Historiography

The diachronic account of tonal music given in the preceding section is most often related in terms of musical evolution or continuous progress, a master narrative in which the historical course of tonal music is directed toward its own end, depicted either as a completion or (as is more common) a tragic demise. In either case, the *telos* of these stories reflects (perhaps ironically) the strong forward momentum toward a cadential goal so often thought to be an essential attribute of tonal music. While these histories are sometimes recounted as technological allegories in which tonality collapses, breaks down, or wears out from overuse, it is more common to imagine them as genetic narratives, organic processes of growth and decay, birth and death.

Ideas of evolution and progress make powerful claims on the historical imagination, claims consistent with a musical aesthetic that privileges (as Romanticism did) the new and original. This aesthetic led both composers and listeners to fetishize striking harmonies and to associate chromaticism with the irrational, foreign, and erotic. This fascination with harmonic color can be understood in quantitative terms as an increase in chromaticism and dissonance, either a progression toward some utopian *Zukunftsmusik* (Schoenberg regarded the progressive increase in dissonance as an "emancipation" of musical resources) or toward a musical apocalypse; both Choron and Fétis forewarned their readers of an impending atonal catastrophe.

Popular accounts of this musical evolution follow the familiar lines of biological evolution, with its concern for selection and adaptation. These stories assert, more or less explicitly, that there were forces at work within tonal music analogous to those that determine the form and development of an organism. Perhaps the most important of these were the energetic tendencies of the semitone, which accounted for the earlier mutation of modality into tonality (for Fétis, the occurrence of the appellative minor fifth between $\hat{4}$ and $\hat{7}$ in both the C and A mode explained the reduction of the six ecclesiastical modes to two) but also the later mutation of tonality into atonality. This historical process is further understood to be unidirectional and irreversible, in which relations between successive stages are both genetic and causal. In biological terms, the evolution of tonal music is both specific (in which newer phenomenal forms – harmonies – differentiate themselves from older ones) and general (in which more complex phenomenal forms replace simpler ones).

There are, however, good reasons to question this historical narrative, as there are to dispute the application of evolution to cultural phenomena in general. First, the notion of a musical evolution ignores the crucial factor of mediation: composers write music with an awareness of their roles as agents of historical change and make compositional decisions in an effort either to transform the music of their own time or to maintain the *status quo*. Their active interference in the historical course of events undermines attempts to explain musical change on the basis of some genetic, self-regulating musical process. Second, the notion of an evolution in tonal music tends to compress the messy diversity of contemporaneous compositional practices into a single historical mainstream. Hence all the metaphors of trunks and branches, rivers and tributaries: Tovey, whose commitment to evolution was self-conscious and emphatic, described this unilineal compression as "the mainstream of music." As a result, accounts of musical evolution smooth over historical discontinuities, either failing to register divergent practices or dismissing them as inconsequential departures from the main music-historical current. Third, such accounts tend to privilege later forms of harmonic phenomena over earlier ones: later harmonic practices, that is, are thought to be more complicated, more advanced, and therefore better with respect to the common tonal language of the historical mainstream. Chopin is thus heard to be progressive in relation to his contemporaries, while Rakhmaninov, in his own historical milieu, is regressive. This attitude lies at the root of the prejudice, common in academic music circles, that atonal music is somehow more complicated and more difficult (and therefore worthier of sustained critical attention) than tonal music, which is believed to be simpler and easier in comparison.

However compelling within the narrow confines of a certain historical tradition, from a broader perspective the notion that tonality somehow dissolved is implausible, for tonal music has never faded from cultural attention. It continued to thrive in what are sometimes considered to be conservative idioms within Western art music, but also in popular music, commercial music, and – despite ongoing experiments with atonal procedures – jazz, where it has never loosened its grip on the musical imagination. To insist on the dissolution of tonality as a historical fact is to confuse a historical phenomenon for a cognitive one. In the West and elsewhere, tonal music remains the music most people listen to most if not of all the time. It makes little sense to argue that tonality broke down around 1910 when we still listen to the music of Beethoven and Cole Porter. In this sense, tonality is still very much a part of the historical present, perhaps even more so – given the wide dissemination of Western music through electronic media and the globalization of mass culture – than ever before. News of its demise, like Mark Twain's, seems premature.

At the same time, however, composers, music historians, and music theorists have tended to exaggerate the importance of tonality as a theoretical construct. The entire historical account in the previous sub-section could be rewritten without reference to the idea: the history of tonality is better understood in terms of specific harmonic practices rather than immutable laws. Before 1910, moreover, tonality – as a construct that informs the production and consumption of music – had a modest historical provenance. Liszt, who corresponded with Fétis, was perhaps the first composer (besides Fétis himself) to create music with a conscious awareness of the notion, and it would not be until Schoenberg that it assumes crucial historical significance. Almost all of the tonal music written during the three previous centuries emerged without reference (tacit or otherwise) to the concept now thought to define its essential condition.

Tonality, then, is an ideological as well as a theoretical construct: from the very beginning, the term has been used primarily for historiographical purposes. Both Choron and Fétis, for instance, cite the birth of the dominant seventh in the music of Monteverdi as the decisive event in the historical separation of *tonalité moderne* from *tonalité antique* (Choron) or *ancienne* (Fétis). In this sense, one can equate modality with musical premodernism, tonality with modernism, high modernism with its putative dissolution, and its re-emergence in the avant garde of the late twentieth century (however changed in musical and cultural significance) with post modernism. According to this scenario, tonality virtually coincides with the age of Western modernism, the great era of representation that stretches from the philosophical meditations of Descartes to the general crisis of representation in the arts around 1910. It thus forms a precise analog to linear perspective in painting as one of the main cognitive structures in Western culture: in their respective media, tonality and linear perspective are responsible for the effect of subjectivity – the notion that an individual embodies a historical consciousness – so crucial to modernity. Heinrich Besseler in fact traced the origins of tonality back to the use of *fauxbourdon* in the 1430s,[31] the same decade in which Brunelleschi demonstrated the basic geometrical principles of linear perspective from within the central portal of the Santa Maria del Fiore in Florence.

Tonality, for Choron, was in fact "entirely modern." It was the culmination, "the goal and the result," of a teleological process. He regarded each historical era as a succession of progressive stages: "formation, development, progress toward perfection, permanence, and decline."[32] This process was cyclical: it was the coincidence of decline and formation that separated one historical age from another. Choron believed that the guiding spirit of each age (and here Hegelian language is appropriate) manifests itself in the objective tendencies of the musical material, hence the epochal division between *tonalité antique* and *moderne*. He heard the music of his time as the apex in the historical curve of modernism: he believed that his contemporaries could look back on "the progressive rise" of *tonalité moderne* and "the attainment of its present state of perfection." The current age was one of "permanence," a plateau from which one could cast a sad glance at the future of music and its inevitable historical descent.

Fétis (who read Hegel) understood this historical process as the progressive actualization of immutable laws. He believed that tonality was a metaphysical principle, a fact not of the inner structure or formal properties of music, but of human consciousness, which imposes a certain cognitive organization – a certain set of dynamic tendencies – on the musical material. As a metaphysical principle, then, tonality does not itself evolve, but rather remains invariant and universal, true for all people and for all time. He thus regarded what he felt to be the undeniable historical progress of Western music as a series of discrete advances toward completion, the ever more perfect realization of a musical absolute.

31 Besseler, "Tonalharmonik und Vollklang," p. 135.
32 Choron, "Summary of the History of Music," p. vi.

Fétis arranged these historical transformations (as he called them) into a teleological series that culminated in the music of his contemporaries.[33] The first of these was the *ordre unitonique*, the music of plainchant: the *tonalité ancienne* of liturgical music was, for Fétis, placid and dispassionate, free of appellative tendencies and thus incapable of modulation. He heard the onset of the *ordre transitonique* around 1600 in the music of Monteverdi, whose invention of the dominant seventh allowed for a wide range of modulations and marked the birth of *tonalité moderne*. Intense and subjective, transitonic music was well suited to the dramatic requirements of opera. The historical transition to the *ordre pluritonique* in the music of Mozart and Rossini was more subtle. Remarkable for its chromaticism, pluritonic music represented the culmination and perfection of *tonalité moderne*. In their orientation around diminished seventh and augmented sixth harmonies (both of which Fétis considered to be deformations of the dominant seventh), the volatile appellative tendencies of this tonal language allowed for remote modulations appropriate to the violent emotions of the age. The historical logic behind this progression of tonal orders gave Fétis the confidence to predict the future course of music: he believed that the chromaticism of the *ordre pluritonique* would dissolve into the ambiguous enharmonism of an *ordre omnitonique*, premonitions of which could be detected in music as far back as Mozart. Fétis, however, listened in on "the insatiable desire for modulation" in the omnitonic music of Berlioz and Wagner with revulsion: in their music, the intense appellative energies of pluritonic music neutralize and even negate themselves, weakening the gravitational forces on which *tonalité moderne* – with its clear references to the tonic – relies. For Fétis, *musique omnitonique* was sensual, decadent, and dangerous. It was music in historical decline.

Tonalité was in fact the site of a remarkable number of cultural anxieties, worries about the future of music, but also (and perhaps surprisingly) about race. For Fétis, there was a strong anthropological dimension to *tonalité*: he believed that different human societies were attracted to different pitch repertoires because of their different mental capacities, which were, moreover, a function of "cerebral conformation."[34] Fétis asserted that primitive (non-Western) societies were limited to simpler scales because of their simpler brain structures, while the more complex psychological organizations of Indo-Europeans permitted them to realize, over historical time, the full musical potential of *tonalité*; his theories were similar in their biological determinism to the racial theories of Gobineau. His inquiries into non-Western music advanced the academic agenda of Orientalism, an ambitious international attempt to research the languages, social organizations, sciences, and arts of non-Western societies, those under European rule in particular. In its most common forms, this research

33 Fétis devotes a separate chapter to each historical transformation in Book III of the *Traité complet de la théorie et de la pratique de l'harmonie*, pp. 151–200. He includes a précis of the argument on pp. xlii–l of the preface.

34 Shellhous, "Fétis's *Tonality* as a Metaphysical Principle," pp. 234–36.

was used to bolster vast and often irrational generalizations about race, intelligence, emotional temperament, social organization, and various forms of cultural expression. A strong motive behind these generalizations was the tacit fear that various African and Eastern cultural practices constituted a threat to European notions of social self-identification: in contrast to the modern West, the Orient appeared to European writers as a primitive or even animalistic realm of sexual desire, religious violence, and racial terror. In general, these writers organized knowledge about the East into cross-cultural comparisons that served to denigrate non-Western others and thus associated the Oriental with marginalized elements in their own societies – the ignorant, backward, degenerate, insane, and the feminine.[35] Fétis's contribution to Orientalism was to associate pitch repertoires with racial characteristics. His accounts of non-Western music, however – which he collected in the *Histoire générale de la musique depuis les temps les plus anciens jusqu'à nos jours* (1869–76) – conceal emotive assertions within the neutral language of factual description. Because of its dearth in appellative semitones, Fétis contended (in the *Traité complet*) that the pentatonic music of "la race jaune ou mongolique" – the music of the Chinese, Japanese, Koreans, Manchus, and Mongols – was "grave and monotonous." Arab, Persian, and Indian music, in contrast, was "langoureuse et sensuelle," befitting "the manners and mores (*mœurs*) of the nations that conceived it." Fétis believed that the dangerous excess of microtonal inflections in the pitch repertoires of the Levant was consistent with the expressive content of their music, which consisted of nothing but "amorous songs and lascivious dances."[36]

While the essentialization of race in terms of pitch repertoires has since been discredited, the practice remains part of the genealogical heritage of tonality. But the main point here is that the concept of tonality, as an ideological construct, serves to articulate and promote a far from disinterested view of the historical past. The notion of a tonal evolution or progress, in particular, has been appropriated for both conservative and radical aesthetic agendas: decisions about what constitute historical continuities or discontinuities are never empirical. Conservative ideologies, drawn to the hierarchical organization of harmonies in tonal music, have often advanced the concept of tonality (as Fétis did) as a means of regulating compositional practice or to naturalize Western music as a form of cultural expression. Some writers have also used the notion of its demise to warn of a cultural decline, or to argue for a return to traditional musical values. An almost random selection of more or less recent books on twentieth-century music, for instance, yields chapters titled "Tonality as Order" and "The Twilight of Tonality." Use of the term in accounts of modern music often expresses a sense of profound loss and infinite nostalgia, even among proponents of the new. Within this discursive tradition, the onset of atonal music in the avant garde around 1910 constitutes a decisive (and for some listeners irreparable) rupture in the history of Western music.

35 The standard account is of course Edward W. Said's *Orientalism*, on which the present discussion relies. 36 Fétis, *Traité complet de la théorie et de la pratique de l'harmonie*, p. xxi.

The concept of tonality has also been an important one for radical ideologies. Here the seminal figure is Schoenberg, who relies on the idea of a progressive development in musical resources to compress divergent *fin-de-siècle* compositional practices into a single historical lineage in which his own music brings one historical era to a close and begins the next: he appealed to notions of musical evolution and progress to position himself as the sole legitimate musical heir to Brahms. Twelve-tone music could thus be heard either as the natural and inevitable culmination of an organic motivic process (Webern) or a historical *Aufhebung* (Adorno), the dialectical synthesis of late Romantic motivic practice on the one hand with a musical sublimation of tonality as pure system on the other. It could be heard and understood in this sense as a simultaneous completion and negation of tonal practice. Schoenberg thus depicted himself as Siegfried to (paradoxically?) Brahms's Wotan, the hero who shattered the sacred musical spear (with its contractual obligations to the tonic) and blazed a path to the new world order, rebuilt from the ruins of musical tradition. "The Atonal Revolution" proclaims a chapter in another recent volume on modern music.

From this point of view, the rise and fall of tonality is far from a neutral account of music history, but serves, rather, to situate atonal and twelve-tone music as the focus of musicological (if not cultural) attention. The fierce commitment of music historians and music theorists to ultramodernist narratives of evolution and progress buttresses the hegemonic position of a serialism long since on the wane. It allows its advocates to characterize composers who continue to pursue tonal idioms as regressive, but also to exclude popular music – which continues to embrace tonal materials – from music curricula: narratives of evolution and continuous development are conspicuous for their silences and elisions. The failure of these narratives to account for the continuous use and renewal of tonal resources in Bartók, Porter, Coltrane, and Britten (among numerous other composers) alongside the music of Schoenberg, Berg, and Webern (not to mention the arcane experimentalism of Babbitt, Boulez, and Stockhausen) is remarkable.

Yet as Adorno pointed out, the dissolution of the distinction between consonance and dissonance – a distinction crucial to all theories of tonal music – into the closed, algebraic structures of serialism constituted a doubtful "emancipation." Now that popular and commercial music has overwhelmed and displaced "serious" music in cultural significance, and in view of an ongoing re-emergence of tonal idioms within the postmodern avant garde, the narrative of continuous tonal evolution no longer seems as credible as it once did and has begun to loosen its grip on the music-historical imagination. In the absence of the musical and cultural polemics that were responsible for the tremendous prestige of the concept, musicologists – whether historians or theorists – will turn to the description of tonal music in terms of contingent harmonic practices rather than immutable laws that inhere in or arise from the musical material and determine its ultimate historical fate.

Bibliography

Adorno, T. *Versuch über Wagner* (1938), Frankfurt, Suhrkamp, 1952; trans. R. Livingstone as *In Search of Wagner*, London, Verso, 1981

Albrechtsberger, J. G. *Gründliche Anweisung zur Composition*, Leipzig, Breitkopf, 1790; trans. A. Choron as *Méthode élémentaire de composition*, 2 vols., Paris, Courcier, 1814

D'Alembert, J. *Elemens de musique, théorique et pratique, suivant les principes de M. Rameau*, Paris, David l'aîné, Le Breton, and Durand, 1752; facs. New York, Broude, 1966; Ger. trans. F. Marpurg as *Systematische Einleitung in die musikalische Setzkunst nach den Lehrsätzen des Herrn Rameau*, Leipzig, Breitkopf, 1757; facs. Leipzig, Zentralantiquariat der DDR, 1980

Bailey, R. "The Structure of the *Ring* and Its Evolution," *19th-Century Music* 1 (1977), pp. 48–61

Besseler, H. "Tonalharmonik und Vollklang," *Acta* 24 (1952), pp. 131–46; trans. as "Tonal Harmony and Full Sonority," in *Counterpoint and Compositional Process in the Time of Dufay*, ed. K. Moll, New York, Garland, 1997, pp. 129–48

Choron, A. E. "Sommaire de l'Histoire de la Musique," in *Dictionnaire historique des Musiciens*, ed. Choron and F. J. Fayolle, Paris, Valade and Lenormant, 1810; facs. Hildesheim, G. Olms, 1971; trans. J. Sainsbury as "Summary of the History of Music," in *Dictionary of Musicians from the Earliest Ages to the Present Time*, London, Sainsbury, 1825; facs. New York, Da Capo Press, 1966

Cowell, H. "New Terms for New Music," *Modern Music* 5/2 (1928), pp. 21–7

Dahlhaus, C. *Untersuchungen über die Entstehung der harmonischen Tonalität*, Kassel, Bärenreiter, 1968; trans. R. Gjerdingen as *Studies on the Origin of Harmonic Tonality*, Princeton University Press, 1990

Fétis, F. J. *Traité complet de la théorie et de la pratique de l'harmonie*, Paris, Schlesinger, 1844; 11th edn., Paris, Brandus, 1875

Esquisse de l'histoire de l'harmonie, Paris, Bourgogne and Martinet, 1840; trans. M. Arlin as *Esquisse de l'histoire de l'harmonie: An English-Language Translation of the François-Joseph Fétis History of Harmony*, Stuyvesant, NY, Pendragon Press, 1994

Histoire générale de la musique depuis les temps les plus anciens jusqu'à nos jours, 4 vols., Paris, Didot Frères, 1869–76

Geslin, P. *Cours d'harmonie*, Paris, Geslin, 1826

Hauptmann, M. *Die Natur der Harmonik und der Metrik*, Leipzig, Breitkopf und Härtel, 1853; trans. W. Heathcote as *The Nature of Harmony and Metre*, London, S. Sonnenschein, 1888

Helmholtz, H. *Die Lehre von den Tonempfindungen als physiologischer Grundlage für die Theorie der Musik* (1863), 4th edn., Braunschweig, F. Vieweg, 1877; trans. A. J. Ellis as *On the Sensations of Tone as a Physiological Basis for the Theory of Music*, 2nd edn., London, Longman and Green, 1885; reprint New York, Dover, 1954

Hostinský, O. *Die Lehre von den musikalischen Klängen: Ein Beitrag zur aesthetischen Begründung der Harmonie-Lehre*, Prague, H. Dominicus, 1879

Jelensperger, D. *L'harmonie au commencement du 19me siècle*, Paris, Zetter, 1830

Kurth, E. *Romantische Harmonik und ihre Krise in Wagners "Tristan"* (1919), 3rd edn., Berlin, M. Hesse, 1923; facs. Hildesheim, G. Olms, 1968 and 1998

Momigny, J.-J. "Musique," in *Encyclopédie méthodique de Musique*, ed. N. E. Framery, P. L. Ginguené, and Momigny, Paris, Agasse, 1818; reprint New York, Da Capo Press, 1971

Cours complet d'harmonie et de composition après une théorie neuve et générale, 3 vols., Paris, Bailleul, 1806

Norton, R. *Tonality in Western Culture: A Critical and Historical Perspective*, University Park, Pennsylvania State University Press, 1984

Perle, G. *Twelve-Tone Tonality*, Berkeley, University of California Press, 1977

Powers, H. S. "Is Mode Real? Pietro Aron, the Octenary System, and Polyphony," *Basler Jahrbuch* 16 (1992), pp. 9–53

Rameau, J. P. *Génération harmonique*, Paris, Prault fils, 1737

Riemann, H. "Ideen zu einer 'Lehre von den Tonvorstellungen,'" *Jahrbuch der Musikbibliothek Peters* 21 (1914), pp. 1–26; trans. R. Wason and E. West Marvin as "Riemann's 'Ideen zu einer Lehre von den Tonvorstellungen': An Annotated Translation," *JMT* 36 (1992), pp. 69–117

Riepel, J. *Grundregeln zur Tonordnung insgemein*, vol. II of *Anfangsgründe zur musikalischen Setzkunst*, Frankfurt, Wagner, 1755; facs. Vienna, Böhlau, 1996

Said, E. W. *Orientalism*, New York, Pantheon, 1978

Schellhous, R. "Fétis's *Tonality* as a Metaphysical Principle: Hypothesis for a New Science," *MTS* 13 (1991), pp. 219–40

Schenker, H. *Harmonielehre*, Stuttgart, Cotta, 1906; reprint Vienna, Universal, 1978; abridged trans. E. M. Mann Borgese, ed. O. Jonas as *Harmony*, University of Chicago Press, 1954

"Vom Organischen der Sonatenform," in *Das Meisterwerk in der Musik*, vol. II, Munich, Drei Masken, 1926; trans. W. Drabkin as "On Organicism in Sonata Form," in *The Masterwork in Music*, vol. II, Cambridge University Press, 1996

Schoenberg, A. *Harmonielehre* (1911), 3rd edn., Vienna, Universal, 1922; trans. R. Carter as *Theory of Harmony*, Berkeley, University of California Press, 1978

Structural Functions of Harmony (1954), rev. edn. L. Stein, New York, Norton, 1968

Subotnik, R. R. "Tonality, Autonomy, and Competence in Post-Classical Music," *Critical Inquiry* 6 (1979), pp. 153–63

Tovey, D. F. "Musical Form and Matter" (1934), in *The Mainstream of Music*, London, Oxford University Press, 1949

Weber, G. *Versuch einer geordneten Theorie der Tonsetzkunst* (1817–21), 3rd edn., 4 vols., Mainz, B. Schott, 1830–32; trans. J. Warner as *The Theory of Musical Composition*, London, R. Cocks, 1851

24

Rameau and eighteenth-century harmonic theory

JOEL LESTER

The more complex a natural entity is, and the more interrelated its components are, the harder it often is for us to comprehend how it could have evolved from completely independent constituent elements. Human vision, for instance, is so immensely complex, with numerous specialized parts both in the eye itself and in the way that the brain processes visual signals, that it is difficult to imagine how each component evolved both separately and in interaction with its affiliates before the final, highly integrated developmental stage existed. The same is true of complex cultural systems that have evolved over long periods of time, among which is harmonic tonality. Virtually every aspect of harmonic tonality (tertian harmonies as primary compositional structures, contrapuntal voice leading connecting those harmonies, the bass as a harmonic foundation, notions of root generation, harmonic motion directed toward cadential goals, the interaction of diatonic scales and chromaticism, and the interaction of harmony and counterpoint with rhythm and meter) arose before tonal harmonic syntax existed. Even though those components interact quite intricately in tonal music, each arose within different musical contexts, and each was explained autonomously by teachings having long, independent theoretical traditions.

The individual who first recognized that all those components interacted to create a sense of tonality was the French theorist and composer Jean-Philippe Rameau (1683–1764). Although Rameau proposed some original ideas, a major part of his theorizing in the treatises he published between 1722 and 1761 consisted of reformulating and combining long-standing concepts into a single harmonic, directional perspective. Rameau is an instance of that relatively rare theorist who was a major composer as well. Because of this, as much as he pursued theoretical ideas for their own consistency, he generally remembered that the function of a theory of harmony was to explain music as he understood it compositionally. This chapter traces many of these concepts and their attendant pedagogical traditions as inherited by the early eighteenth century, and then considers Rameau's brilliant accomplishment of consolidating them into a unified (if not completely stabilized) harmonic theory. Lastly, this chapter surveys the evolving legacy of this now-dominant heritage in the late eighteenth century and beyond.

Seventeenth-century antecedents of tonal harmonic theory

Chordal theory

Crucial to any theory of harmonic tonality is the notion that the basic harmonic unit is the chord, not the interval – that harmonic intervals are best understood as the components of chords, not that chords merely arise from combinations of intervals. As with many of the components that were eventually combined to form a tonal harmonic perspective, this notion arose in several independent theoretical traditions. In 1558, the great Venetian theorist Gioseffo Zarlino (1517–90), whose encyclopedic treatises are primary sources for understanding musical thinking of the sixteenth century, explained that

> the variety of harmony . . . does not consist solely in the variety of the consonances which are formed between two voices, but also in the variety of the harmonies – which [variety] is determined by the position of the note which makes a third or tenth above the lowest voice of the composition. Either these [intervals] are minor, and the harmony which arises is determined by or corresponds to the arithmetic proportion or division; or they are major, and such a harmony is determined by or corresponds to the harmonic mean. On this variety depends all the diversity and perfection of harmonies.[1]

To be sure, Zarlino's statement is far from the modern conception of the "triad" (a term not coined until after his death), let alone any notion of the equivalence of triadic inversions. First, his assertion that a crucial aspect of harmony is determined by the quality of intervals over the bass must be considered in the context of the priority he ascribed to the tenor voice as a compositional determinant. Because Zarlino proclaimed the importance of the tenor in most aspects of musical structure, he could hardly have accorded triadic inversions a central role in his theorizing. What later theorists call a first-inversion triad was for him the result of having a sixth instead of fifth over the bass: C–E–A arose as a modification of C–E–G, not as an inversion of A–C–E; C–E–A was, after all, a "major" chord with two major imperfect consonances over the bass, not a "minor" chord rearranged. For these reasons, Zarlino could hardly have placed the triadic structure of harmonies at the center of his conception of musical simultaneities. In fact, his cited description of "perfect harmony" (*harmonia perfetta*) appears amidst a discussion on how to avoid improper harmonies in textures with multiple voices: cross relations and improper diminished and augmented intervals. "Perfect harmony" was a rule of thumb for him – a way of checking a texture to make sure the harmonies were not improper. Nonetheless, Zarlino's authoritative enunciation that the essential nature of a harmony was defined by the quality of the third over the bass probably called this trait to the attention of many musicians.

Other late sixteenth-century theorists came to recognize through other avenues the primacy of chords over intervals. For example, the German organist Johannes Avianius

1 Zarlino, *Le istitutioni harmoniche*, Part III, Chapter 31; Rivera, "Harmonic theories" discusses tentative antecedents of Zarlino's recognition of these harmonies.

(d. 1617) recognized in 1581 that even single intervals were best understood as part of a chord. Two of his compatriots, Joachim Burmeister (1564–1629) and Johannes Magirus (c. 1550–1631), recognized in 1599 and 1611, respectively, that 5/3 and 6/3 chords were the sole consonant harmonies. Contemporaneous Iberian guitarists found the same chords to be the basis of the new *rasgueado* (strummed) style of guitar playing, and gave these sonorities formal status by including them in the abbreviated *alfabeto* notation.[2]

Around 1610, two German theorists consolidated this thinking into a harmonic theory by pairing this chordal recognition with the already extant notion of intervallic inversion. In 1608, Otto Siegfried Harnisch (c. 1568–1623) recognized that 6/3 and 6/4 chords were essentially rearrangements of the basic 5/3 sonority. Just a couple of years later, Johannes Lippius (1585–1612) formalized this insight by dubbing these three verticalities (and all their spacings and voicings) with the single name *trias harmonica* (reflecting for Lippius – a theologian as well as a music theorist – that the musical triad, like the Holy Trinity, represents a triune unity in that three notes and three intervals form a single sonority). By the end of the seventeenth century, it had become commonplace for musicians to recognize at least 5/3 and 6/3 triads as permutations of the same harmony. Even Johann Joseph Fux in 1725 explained the inversional relationship between these two forms of the triad when he begins the study of three-part modal species counterpoint in *Gradus ad parnassum*.

Thorough-bass practice

The recognition of 5/3 and/or 6/3 chords by sixteenth- and early seventeenth-century writers as the primary harmonic building blocks of musical structure precedes and derives from a different set of traditions than the growth of one of the most important and characteristic features of early Baroque musical practice: the thorough bass.[3] Thorough-bass practice and pedagogy contributed greatly to the widespread recognition in the seventeenth century that a 5/3 chord (the one simultaneity that usually required no figuring at all) was the primary stable harmonic unit. And although the concept of thorough bass was fundamentally at odds with theoretical notions of chordal inversions (since in thorough bass, chords are conceptualized from the bass note, not from a root), in practice it promoted such notions, since keyboardists inevitably became aware that the same right-hand chord could be played over differing signatures. For instance, C–E–G could be played in the right hand over an unfigured bass C, as well as over an E figured with 6/3 and a G figured with 6/4. By the end of the seventeenth century, thoroughbass manuals frequently suggested such mnemonics to simplify the realization of chord signatures. Likewise, performers of strummed instruments such as the guitar, lute, and theorbo (all popular instruments in seventeenth-century continuo bands) learned to realize chordal signatures without regard to the actual acoustical bass note sounded.

2 Described in Christensen, "The Spanish Baroque Guitar and Seventeenth-Century Triadic Theory."
3 See also the discussions in Chapter 3, pp. 62–63, and Chapter 17, pp. 441–47.

But as much as these practical suggestions might seem to be based on a theory of chordal inversion, such was not necessarily the case. A thorough-bass manual that suggested that C–E–G was the proper right hand for a bass C with no figuring, an E with 6/3, and a G with 6/4, might continue (as did Keller, *Rules for playing a thorough bass*, 1705) by noting that C–E–G was also the proper right hand for a bass A with 7 – a chord that is obviously not inversionally related to a C major triad. Nonetheless, certain pitch similarities between different chords became widely recognized as rules of thumb. In effect, everyday practice made musicians familiar with chordal relationships that theorists rarely addressed formally.

The thorough bass was also important in bringing to light another fundamental feature of tonal music: that specific sonorities regularly occurred over given bass notes. As early as 1619, for instance, the German musician Michael Praetorius (d. 1621), who borrowed thorough-bass and composition rules from an Italian manuscript treatise of a generation earlier, explained that a bass-note B (*b durus*) could not suffer the diminished fifth of a 5/3 chord, demanding instead a 6/3. Early in the seventeenth century, this was generalized into a norm for imputing a 6/3 chord to any bass note that was solmizated as *mi*, thus including not only the *subsemitonum* (leading tone) of a key, but also the mediant of any major key or a chromatically raised (secondary) leading tone. During the seventeenth century, thorough-bass manuals for keyboardists, guitarists, lutenists, and theorbists developed a host of rules and mnemonics (especially scale fragments) to illustrate such normative bass harmonizations. Indeed, so commonplace were many of these harmonizations in Baroque musical practice, that it was possible – and relatively easy – to offer guidelines for the realization of completely unfigured bass lines (as found, for examples, in the thorough-bass treatises of Lorenzo Penna [1672] and Johann David Heinichen [1711 and 1728]). Admittedly, those guidelines generally yielded rather formulaic harmonizations. But at the same time, they also helped codify norms of harmonic coherence (especially for composers, who, after all, always faced an "unfigured bass" when they began to compose).

Seventeenth-century versions of these rules offer harmonic patterns apart from placement within a key. By the early eighteenth century, Heinichen, reflecting the growing systematization of tonal harmonic norms, reduced the number of rules and differentiated between recommendations based on patterns and recommendations based on scale-step placement within a key.[4]

A separate pedagogical tradition bypassed such rules by simply presenting model bass scales and other bass patterns with the common harmonies they support. In 1716, the French guitarist François Campion (d. 1748) canonized a normative harmonization of both ascending and descending major and (melodic) minor scales under the rubric of the Rule of the Octave ("Règle de l'octave"), shown in Example 24.1.[5] Through the

4 Lester, *Compositional Theory in the Eighteenth Century*, Chapter 3, explores rules for unfigured basses.
5 A full history of the Rule of the Octave appears in Christensen, "The Rule of the Octave in Thorough-Bass Theory and Practice." Also see Chapter 13, pp. 442–44.

Example 24.1 Campion's "Rule of the Octave," *Addition au Traité de l'accompagnement et de composition*, p. 44

"Rule" (or many of its variants), countless eighteenth-century musicians learned the common scale-step placements of harmonies within a key, and how they interacted with one another. Campion, implicitly recognizing that harmonic norms were different when the bass moved by skip rather than by step (as in the "Rule"), also included other progressions illustrating additional common and less common harmonies, and explained their normative scale-step location. These guidelines, found in both theoretical and practical literature in the seventeenth and eighteenth centuries, helped to codify and promote musical intuitions of the harmonic norms that became part of a coalescing tonal syntax. Still, they could by themselves hardly be considered to constitute a theory of harmony.

Cadential progressions

A separate component of tonal harmonic thinking – the recognition of the directionality of certain harmonic norms – first arose in the mid-sixteenth century in connection with cadential voice leadings. Two leading Italian theorists, Nicola Vicentino (1511 – c. 1576) in 1555 and Zarlino in 1558, recognized that certain combinations of two or more voices created such a strong expectation of imminent arrival on a specific cadential goal that a clear sense of directionality was perceived even when the goal itself was absent – an effect they called "evading the cadence." This thinking posited that forces underlying musical continuity might be greater than the local resolution of dissonances. Consider, for instance, the seventh in a typical 7–6 suspension preceding a cadential octave (say, a C–B over a D before an octave C). A contrapuntal perspective explains that the seventh (C) resolves locally to the sixth (B); the resolution is a single note in a two-voiced context. But from Vicentino's and Zarlino's perspective of cadential drive, that consonant sixth is not so much a single note relatively at rest because it resolves a preceding dissonance, but rather an interval that drives toward an anticipated resolution upon an octave (on C, in this case). Their argument premises that musical motion arises from the entire harmonic context, and that the mere presence of a consonance does not necessarily indicate a point of repose.[6]

Major and minor key systems

A further ingredient of changing theoretical perspectives in the sixteenth and seventeenth centuries that laid the foundation for later theories of harmonic tonality was the emergence of major and minor key systems. While the history of this emergence is detailed elsewhere in this volume (see **Chapter 13, pp. 430–46**), it is worth emphasizing here that the evolving recognition of a transposable major-minor key system during the seventeenth and early eighteenth centuries involved a profound reorientation for musicians involving a fundamentally new harmonic perspective, one in which keys were now defined not only by the pitch-class upon which the *finalis* fell and by the octave species of the modal scale, but by the quality of triad built upon that final. Significantly, Lippius, the theorist who coined the term *triadis*, is also the first to argue that the essential difference between the modes is that quality of triad built upon the final. But major and minor keys were not universally recognized as the basis of contemporary music. Several traditions in German-speaking areas continued to insist well into the eighteenth century that the traditional modes were the basis of all music.[7]

The generative fundamental

Complementing these changing aspects of practical music theory during the seventeenth century were important developments in the understanding of musical intervals and acoustics. For instance, the traditional hierarchy of interval rations canonized by Zarlino within his *senario* was inadequate to theorists (beginning with Lippius in 1610) who posited major and minor triads as the source of consonance. Most problematic was the perfect fourth, which ranked ahead of the major or minor third in consonance value when measured by interval ratio, yet was a dissonance when it appeared over the bass. Not long after Lippius published his treatise, the great French philosopher René Descartes (1596–1650) penned his *Musicae compendium* (c. 1618), in which he differentiated consonances from one another based on their relationship to a generating interval. The octave (2 : 1), Descartes argued, was divided into a perfect fifth (3 : 2) and a perfect fourth (4 : 3). The fifth was a direct interval, because it was acoustically built on the lower tone of the octave; the fourth, by contrast, was merely the "shadow" of the fifth, filling in the space between the fifth and the octave. This reasoning likewise placed the

6 Their thinking also reflects a dynamism recognized by theorists since the Middle Ages for intervals to resolve to intervals of increasing perfection: the seventh (dissonance) resolving to the sixth (imperfect consonance) resolving to the octave (perfect consonance). This theory lies at the root of the older notion of "interval perfection" that is so characteristic of the dynamic of medieval contrapuntal theory, as well as the law of "closest approach" cited by Renaissance theorists. The dynamism is intensified when the two voices of this *clausula formalis* are supplemented by additional voices (as shown in **Example 23.5, p. 740**).
7 The interactions between evolving recognition of major-minor keys and maintenance of the modes is chronicled in Lester, *Between Modes and Keys*.

major third (5 : 4) as a primary interval, since it too was directly "generated" by the fundamental string. But it failed to explain how a minor third could form the lowest interval of a triad, since by this reasoning a minor third should be the "shadow" of the major third, filling in the distance between a major third and a perfect fifth. (This was to become a Gordian knot of speculative music theory addressed by innumerable theorists thereafter, and never satisfactorily resolved.)

In any event, the notion of the undivided string serving as a fundamental generator and progenitor of all subsequent string divisions was an appealing and potent one for music theorists of the seventeenth century imbued with neo-Platonic notions of hierarchy and unity.[8] The French scientist and avid music theorist Marin Mersenne wrote extensively on the ontological paradox entailed by positing unity (the undivided string) as the source and generator of diversity (all subsequent intervals and harmonies).[9] The notion of a generative fundamental also received surprising confirmation when scientists corroborated what many musicians had long noticed: a resonating string when carefully listened to seemed to generate a series of faint tones that corresponded to the natural "harmonic" series. The "discovery" of the harmonic overtone series by Joseph Sauveur in the early eighteenth century thus seemed to lend credence to notions of a musical "fundamental generator." (See also **Chapter 9, pp. 251–54.**)

All these diverse notions – chords as fundamental compositional units, the inversional identity of harmonies, the system of transposable major and minor keys, the directionality of cadential progressions, the rise of standardized scale harmonizations, theories of the generative fundamental – emerged in the course of the seventeenth century within differing (and often contradictory) traditions of practice, pedagogy, and speculative theory. What was needed was someone to unify these notions within a single system of harmonic theory. This was to be the accomplishment of Rameau.

Rameau

Jean-Philippe Rameau epitomizes the intellectual aspirations of the eighteenth-century Enlightenment. Likened by his contemporaries to both Descartes and Newton, Rameau sought to reduce a complex body of empirical data (harmonic practice), hitherto discussed in a bewildering welter of partial and often contradictory approaches, to a rational system governed by a single principle.[10] His resulting system – first appearing in the *Traité de l'harmonie* of 1722, but evolving in many essentials in another half dozen treatises over the next forty years – builds on these premises: (1) the consonant, root-position triad and the dissonant seventh chord built by adding a note

8 See Christensen, *Rameau and Musical Thought*, pp. 71–203, for more on the history of the "generative fundamental" in music theory. 9 Ibid., pp. 84–87.

10 The most comprehensive discussion of Rameau's music theory appears in Christensen, *Rameau and Musical Thought* (esp. Chapters 5–7). Lester (in *Compositional Theory in the Eighteenth Century*) also offers a useful summary.

to that triad are the source of all harmonies (through inversion and other processes); (2) the chordal root (the *son fondamental*) is the generator of triads and seventh chords; (3) motion from one chord to another is best understood as a progression of these chord roots (called the *basse fondamentale* or "fundamental bass") with the resulting voice leading being the proper connection of the notes of chords; and (4) the fundamental bass constitutes directed motion that leads to a sense of key and, ultimately, tonal coherence because of the identity or similarity between fundamental-bass motions and the directionality of cadences. By forging a single system that included many individual strands of seventeenth-century music theory, Rameau instilled so much greater explanatory power into each that the power of his entire approach overcame the previously perceived inadequacies of various of the strands, and was able to solve problems that older theory could not.

For instance, by including seventh chords as well as triads in the category of invertible chords generated by a fundamental, he easily explained the resolution of many dissonances hitherto deemed anomalous. Thus, Rameau's approach explains why the fifth in a 6/5 chord is a dissonance: its essence is not as a consonant fifth over the bass, but rather as the seventh over the fundamental bass of the chord. And Rameau was easily able to explain other common dissonances that seemed to defy the norms of resolution, such as the fourth over the bass in a V^4_3 chord resolving to I (a fourth that remained as a common tone between the two harmonies instead of resolving downward like most dissonances). Rameau showed that this so-called "irregular fourth" was actually the dominant's fundamental sound. The invertibility of chords – seventh chords as well as triads – thus became not just a curious trait of chords to be used as a mnemonic, but a path to understanding the behavior of harmony and voice leading.

We will now consider the substance of Rameau's theory in more detail.

The generation of chords

In Book I of the *Traité*, Rameau offers an elaborate procedure for deriving all chords from divisions of a single monochord string. Essentially, Rameau argued that Zarlino's *senario* provides all the basic components one needs to construct any chord – perfect fifths and major or minor thirds. By combining these constituent intervals in appropriate ways, Rameau generated the two basic building blocks of harmony: the triad and seventh chord. And from these, he derived all other harmonies. Each chord can thus be seen as directly "generated" from the monochord string, which thus serves as the fundamental "principle" of harmony. To be sure, Rameau's logic at times becomes tortuous. For instance, he was not able to overcome the problem Descartes had already brought to light of generating the minor third directly from the octave. (If Rameau was to posit the minor triad as equal in validity to the major triad, he needed some consistent method of generating the minor third.) Nor could he convincingly justify indispensable notions such as the identity of octaves (to justify the inversional "equivalence" of chords) or the generation of irregular seventh chords such as the diminished seventh.

Nonetheless, his essential argument was clear: the monochord string serves as a kind of generative fundamental sound (*son fondamental*) for the two fundamental chord types of tonal music, the consonant triad and the dissonant seventh chord.

The fundamental bass

In Book II of the *Traité*, Rameau shows how these chords are used in practice, how they may be animated, so to speak, in temporal succession. He writes out the succession of chord roots as the "fundamental bass" (*basse fondamentale*). The result may look like a continuo bass line. But it is not meant to be played; rather, it depicts the succession of the chords' generators.

Rameau reached back to an ancient explanation of motion in contrapuntal theory – the need for a dissonance to resolve to a consonance, combined with a mechanistic model of motion that owed much to Enlightenment theories of material causation – to explain how chords connected to one another. Essentially, Rameau elevated the role of dissonance – and particularly the fundamental dissonance of a seventh chord – as the prime motivator of harmonic motion, the force that mechanically propelled one harmony to the next. His paradigm for this progression was the "perfect" cadence (as he labeled the "authentic" cadence). Indeed, the very first example that Rameau presented in music notation in his *Traité de l'harmonie* illustrates the *Cadence parfaite*: the motion from a dominant seventh chord to its tonic, shown here in Plate 24.1.

The content, annotations, and graphics of this example illuminate numerous aspects of Rameau's theories. One striking point is Rameau's use of multiple staffs, one for each voice part. Despite his belief that the chord is the essential unit of musical structure, Rameau was always aware of the voice leading that arises as the notes of one harmony move to the notes of the next. He argued repeatedly that only by understanding the underlying chord progression could one fully grasp the essence of the part writing.

Second, the progression is a dominant seventh progressing to the tonic by the fundamental motion of a perfect fifth – not, for instance, a dominant seventh framed by two tonic chords. Rameau believed that the factor motivating a chord to progress in a directed fashion to another chord is the presence of dissonance. The tonic triad, which contains no dissonances, is a point of repose with no particular urge to move anywhere. The dominant seventh, by contrast, contains – according to Rameau – two dissonances whose resolutions propel the chord toward its tonic. The very term he coined to refer to what we call the dominant seventh chord – the *dominant-tonique* – underscores its dynamic role in defining the following chord as a tonic goal. One of the dissonances is the seventh, which Rameau calls the "minor dissonance," in homage to a voice-leading tradition dating back at least to Zarlino in which notes that form minor intervals (here, a minor seventh over the bass) supposedly tend to descend; the other dissonance for Rameau is the leading tone, dubbed the "major dissonance" because of the corresponding tendency for major intervals (here, the major third over the root of the chord) to ascend. The order of argument here (as well as the presence of only two chords in his

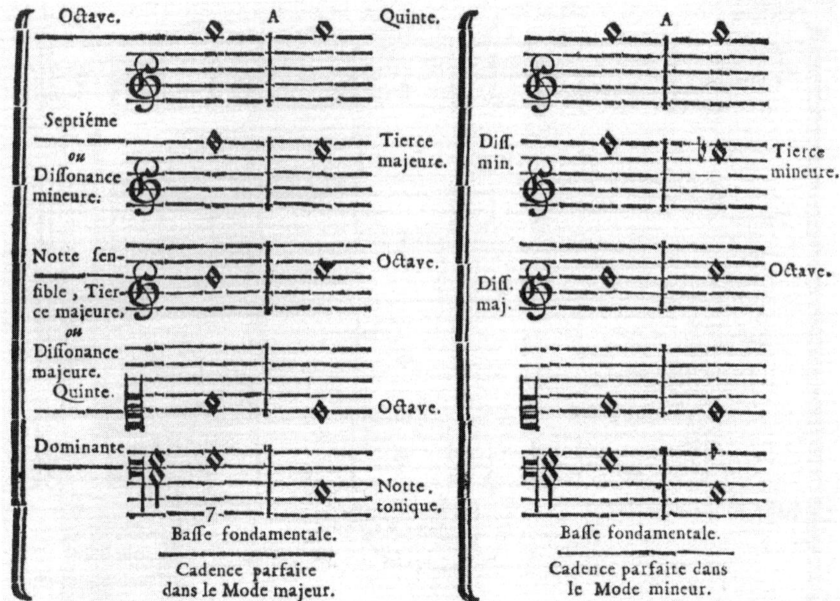

Plate 24.1 The perfect cadence, from Jean-Philippe Rameau, *Traité de l'harmonie*, Book II, Chapter 5, p. 57

example of the cadence) reveals Rameau's notion of how a sense of key is formed: the dissonances in the dominant seventh chord propel the chord toward its consonant resolution in the triad a fifth lower; that progression defines the tonic as the point of repose. And it is the sense of motion from one chord to the next connected by a fundamental motion of the perfect fifth – and not merely the content of the individual harmonies – that is the essence of the cadence. This imparts a dynamism to Rameau's theory of tonality; a key is not merely a given pitch field within which harmonies and melodies move, but a harmonic focus that emerges from the dynamic of the progression.

The Perfect Cadence is one of the two basic cadential types that Rameau proposes. The other is the Irregular Cadence (*cadence irregulière*): a chord built on the fourth degree of the scale moving to a tonic, in which an added sixth makes the first chord dissonant, propelling it toward a resolution, as shown in Plate 24.2.

Like the Perfect Cadence, the Irregular Cadence follows the normative motion of a perfect fifth in the fundamental bass, albeit ascending rather than descending. And like the Perfect Cadence, the Irregular Cadence reflects the mechanistic model of a dissonance impelling a chord toward consonant resolution. (Rameau's arguments for justifying the added sixth as a dissonance comparable to the seventh in the *dominante-tonique* required some subtle reasoning to be discussed below.)

Rameau considers these cadences not only as the progressions that end phrases (which is the way we generally use the term "cadence" nowadays), but as the models

Plate 24.2 The imperfect cadence, from Jean-Philippe Rameau, *Traité de l'harmonie*, Book II, Chapter 7, p. 65

for directed harmonic motion in general. He saw all music as basically a series of interconnected cadences, in which most cadential conclusions are *evaded* (adopting and adapting from Zarlino) because one (or both) of the chords has been altered to avoid a complete resolution: one or both chords might be inverted, the chord of conclusion might itself contain a seventh or an added sixth, or the third in a dominant seventh might be minor to remove the drive of the leading tone (in which case it is no longer a "dominant-tonic," but merely a simple "dominant" chord since it no longer has the power to define the following chord as the tonic of a key). In all cases, though, the music is driven onward by the motivating force of the dissonant seventh (or occasionally, the added sixth) involving largely fifth motion in the fundamental bass until a final point of consonant repose is attained at the tonic.

With Perfect, Irregular, and evaded cadences, Rameau tried to show how the fundamental bass proceeded primarily by fifths and thirds – the very intervals generated from the fundamental string. He thereby explored the recently developed sense of tonal directionality that differentiated the music of his time from that of earlier generations. He was so enthralled by his ability to explain directed harmonic motion involving triads and seventh chords moving by fourths and fifths as a series of real or evaded cadences that he attempted to extend these insights to all the chordal types and all types of harmonic connections.

"All chordal types" for Rameau meant those indicated in thorough-bass signatures. Thorough bass generally indicated chords to be played along with bass notes: consonant chords on the beat, and also suspensions. Simultaneities that arose from various sorts of motion in any of the voices after the beat (metrically weak passing tones, neighbors, escape tones, and the like) were rarely indicated in the thorough-bass figuring, and are generally absent from Rameau's theory. But simultaneities with suspensions were central to Rameau's theorizing. The modern consensus that chordal dissonances (sevenths and ninths, for instance) should be differentiated from nonharmonic tones that appear at the beginning of a chord (suspensions, appoggiaturas, and accented passing tones) was an issue that could not be conceptualized before Rameau focused on functional chords. Rameau felt it was his obligation to explain the behavior not only of triads and seventh chords and their inversions, but also of the various suspension sonorities that were commonly labeled in thorough bass.

Chords by supposition

Rameau did this through a controversial and problematic aspect of his theory: what he called "chords by supposition." The basic principle is that the seventh chord should be the model for resolutions of all dissonant chords: a dissonance should behave like a seventh. This category includes what we nowadays call ninth chords, various types of suspensions, appoggiaturas, and motions over a pedal. Essentially, Rameau posited the bass of such chords to be "supposed" (or perhaps "sub-posed") below the true fundamental lying above it and upon which a seventh chord – one of the fundamental chord types – could be formulated. So, for example, he argued that a ninth chord built upon G (G–B–D–F–A) is actually a seventh chord on B (B–D–F–A), with the G "supposed" below the true fundamental. Likewise, he posited that a chord with a suspended fourth (e.g., A–D–E) was a seventh chord built upon E (E–G–B–D) with A "supposed" a fifth below the fundamental E (and the third and fifth of the seventh chord on E imputed).[11] Example 24.2 shows how the suspended fourth (D in m. 2) can be read as a dissonant "seventh" above the authentic root E that is disguised by the "supposed" fundamental of A in the bass. Thus, the resolution of this fourth down a step to a consonant third is in fact nothing less than a concealed version of the paradigmatic seventh chord resolving via the descending fundamental-bass motion of the fifth.

Although Rameau occasionally commented that he developed the category of chords by supposition merely to explain suspensions, his extensive discussions of supposition gave the impression that he had invented a new category of verticalities. Supposed chords became a highly contentious point in controversies involving Rameauian theory later in the eighteenth century.

Irregular motion in the fundamental bass

The fundamental bass quite effectively explained the directionality of many harmonic progressions as real or imitated cadences: especially root progressions by fifth. But

11 Further information on Rameau's theory of "supposition" appears in Christensen, *Rameau and Musical Thought*, pp. 123–29, and Lester, *Compositional Theory*, pp. 108–15.

Example 24.2 A 4–3 suspension explained as a chord by supposition, from Jean-Philippe Rameau, *Traité de l'harmonie*, Book II, Chapter 10, p. 76

Rameau allowed that the fundamental bass may move by the other intervals contained in the triad – by major and minor thirds. Since such tertian motion involved only consonant triads, Rameau felt challenged to reconcile such progressions with his stricture that all non-tonic chords must necessarily contain a dissonant seventh, and such sevenths ought to resolve by fifth motion in the fundamental bass. A succession of consonant triads entailed a succession of individual "tonic" harmonies, since the defining seventh of any non-tonic harmony was lacking. Only in his later writings did Rameau begin to distinguish levels of tonic hierarchy, referring to an overall "reigning tonic" (*ton regnant*) of a piece distinct from more localized tonicizations. Tertian motion in the fundamental bass also led to a number of secondary cadential progressions (such as the "interrupted" cadence) and various "chromatic" and "enharmonic" progressions that Rameau carefully itemized.

Even more vexing were fundamental-bass progressions that seemed to move by step – in clear violation of his dictum that fundamental-bass motion ought to be composed of those consonant intervals that comprised the vertical triad. He attempted to solve these problems by proposing "interpolated" (concealed) fundamental basses and implied dissonances. So, for example, in Example 24.3 the fundamental bass from the third beat of m. 2 to the downbeat of m. 3 would seem to suggest an ascending second – from C to D. Rameau interpolates an A (the last quarter note in the fundamental bass in m. 2) between C and D, thereby explaining the progression into the C chord as a descending fifth motion (G-dominant seventh to C triad) and the progression into the following D chord (in m. 3) as another descending fifth motion.

Rameau frequently invoked this interpretation to explain the progression from a subdominant chord to the dominant. In that case, the subdominant would carry its characteristic dissonance, the added sixth; that chord would then be reinterpreted as a supertonic seventh-chord as it moved to the dominant. In his publications after the *Traité*, Rameau used the term "double employment" (*double emploi*) of the dissonance for this interpretation. On the one hand, "double employment" allowed him to interpret common progressions like I ii^{6}_{5} V^{7} without any step progressions in the fundamental bass – seemingly by a sleight of hand. On the other hand, "double employment" confirms that Rameau's primary interest was in the directionality of chordal *progressions*.

Rameau's analyses

Although most examples in Rameau's treatises are abstract progressions, he does occasionally use real pieces of music to illustrate and test his ideas. Among his more extensive analyses are one of his own vocal fugues in Chapter 44 of Book III of his *Traité* of 1722, and two analyses of a monologue from *Armide* by Jean-Baptiste Lully: once in his *Nouveau système de musique théorique* of 1726, and again (with a different explanation of many progressions) in his *Observations* of 1754.[12]

To illustrate "How to compose a basso continuo below a treble" in his *Traité* (Book III, Chapter 41), he composed the sarabande-like excerpt in Example 24.3, with this commentary:

> Once you have composed the fundamental bass, pay attention to the design of your treble, its affect, its movement, and all other particulars, and then try to include the same expressions in the new bass you are composing. Avoid final cadences where the melody does not require them, and draw from the fundamental chords those notes you judge appropriate, notes that will harmonize completely with the treble . . . In the first and second measures of the fundamental bass, there are two equivalent progressions [i.e., C to G]. I reserve for the second measure the progression most closely related to the cadence, because here [i.e., on the downbeat] is where the cadence occurs normally; notice that the cadence is irregular here [i.e., with the rising fundamental-bass fifth C–G] and perfect in the fourth measure [i.e., with the falling fundamental-bass fifth G–C]. In the basso continuo in the first measure, I use a stepwise progression, which harmonizes completely with the treble. To continue conjunctly in the second measure, I use a note on the second beat which forms a seventh with the fundamental bass and is resolved by a third over the fundamental bass, all of this of course harmonizing with the treble. I continue the stepwise progression in the bass until a perfect cadence occurs [into m. 4], where I follow [in the basso continuo] the progression of the fundamental bass . . . I figure a ninth on the first

12 Verba discusses these Lully analyses and the reasons for their differences in "The Development of Rameau's Thoughts."

Example 24.3 Setting a bass to a treble, from Rameau, *Traité de l'harmonie*, Book III, Chapter 41, p. 325

note of the sixth measure, for this note is found a third below or a sixth above the note in the fundamental bass, and is therefore allowed in the harmony only by supposition. Thus, by observing the seventh chord carried by the note in the fundamental bass, I can see that this latter may carry only the ninth chord, even though the ninth does not actually appear in the treble. Note, however, that the fifth which does appear in the treble is part of the ninth chord, and that the supposed ninth is prepared and resolved in accordance with all the rules.

This method of melodic harmonization and explanation was unprecedented in 1722. Rameau does not talk of counterpoint or thorough-bass progressions. Instead, he demonstrates how all but three of the fundamental-bass motions are the sorts of directed harmonic motions that he calls "cadential" – that is, by rising or descending fourths and fifths. (The exceptions are the *double emploi* progressions in mm. 2 and 5 and the stepwise motion into m. 7. The *double emploi* progressions show, in Rameau's analysis, how the given chord is approached and left as a cadential-type progression.) By analyzing the chord-to-chord directionality of much of this excerpt as cadential-type progressions, Rameau can focus on when these progressions should articulate a relatively conclusive cadence (as at mm. 4 and 8), and when they should be voiced so as to facilitate the flow of the music.

In addition, Rameau is able to explain details of the outer-voice counterpoint. Rameau must have been particularly proud of his explanation of the appoggiatura dominant in m. 6. Even though the melodic F♯ forms a seemingly consonant fifth with the bass, it does not belong to the same harmony as the bass B. The dissonant note that he is most concerned about is the inner-voice C (the seventh of the D^7 in the fundamental bass) – a suspension from the preceding harmony that resolves to an inner-voice B at the end of the measure. That motivates the progression at this point, creating the flow the phrase that extends to the final cadence in m. 8.

While Books I and II of the *Traité de l'harmonie* contain important and consequential work (the third and fourth books applying fundamental bass to composition and accompaniment, respectively), Rameau continued to refine his ideas and explore further aspects of harmonic and tonal theory in another half-dozen treatises and many shorter works and polemical writings published over the next four decades. Some of these later books were largely speculative in nature (such as the *Nouveau système de musique théorique* of 1726, the *Démonstration du principe de l'harmonie* of 1750, or the *Observations sur notre instinct pour la musique* of 1754); others are almost entirely practical in orientation (the *Dissertation sur les différentes métodes d'accompagnement* of 1732 and the *Code de musique pratique* of 1761); and still others are like the *Traité* in combining both (the *Génération harmonique* of 1737).

Rameau's theories after the Traité

In practical matters, there were several important additions to Rameau's theory after the *Traité*. Among the most important are the introduction of the *subdominant* (*sous-dominante*) and the term for *double emploi* in the *Nouveau système* (1726), both of which became central to his theory of tonality in the *Génération harmonique* (1737), even though both notions are already implicitly present in his *Traité*. Beginning with the *Génération harmonique*, he posits the tonal organization of a key as the tonic surrounded by an upper and lower fifth – a dominant and subdominant. He referred to this organization as the *triple proportion* because each tone is the third harmonic of the previous one and thus each note arises as a triple ratio of the previous one. In C major, for instance, if F equals 1, then F, C, and G are 1:3:9. This provided him with three harmonic functions (although Rameau never used the term "function"): the tonic, represented by a triad; the dominant, whose function it was to descend by fifth and which carried a seventh; and the subdominant, whose function it was to ascend by fifth and which carried an added-sixth chord.

In line with the newly discovered symmetry of this harmonic arrangement, Rameau posited the sixth above his subdominant as derived from the same dissonant third added above the dominant to create the dissonant seventh, but now placed *below* the subdominant (shown in Fig. 24.1; see also **Example 23.2, p. 734**). Both dissonances tended to the third of the tonic for resolution. But unlike the mechanistic model of dissonant dominant sevenths that motivate harmonic directionality in the *Traité*, the model of the triple proportion in the *Génération harmonique* emphasizes the gravitational power of the central tonic to draw its dominant subordinates toward itself.[13]

13 Concerning Rameau's quite explicit reliance upon Newtonian theories of gravitation to model his notion of tonal attraction, see Christensen, *Rameau and Musical Thought*, pp. 185–93.

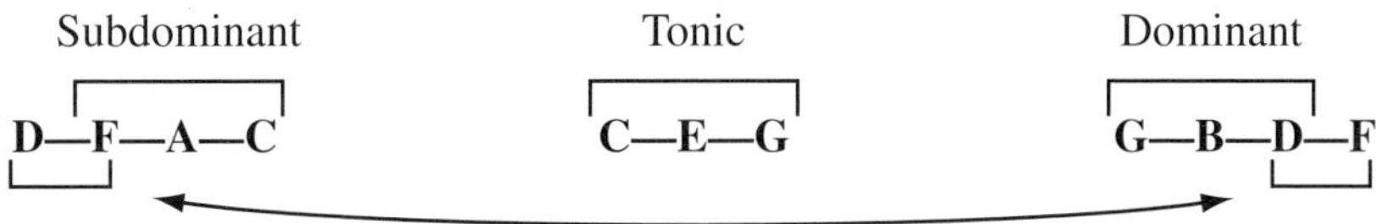

Figure 24.1 Rameau's demonstration of the symmetrical relation between subdominant and dominant with added minor third

With these primary functions in place, Rameau now offered insights into the relationship between the diatonic scale and a key. Plate 24.3, from the *Démonstration du principe de l'harmonie* of 1750, illustrates how Rameau utilized his new ideas to show the origins of the major scale in harmony. In effect, this was his reformulation of the "Rule of the Octave" from a thorough-bass scale to the harmonic basis of a melodic scale. Rameau thereby argued that the scale (melody) originates in harmony, not the other way around. This would be a critical argument in his debate with Rousseau concerning the respective priorities of melody and harmony.

The graphic shows Rameau's interpretation of the harmonic foundation of the C-major scale. The notes of C major (*ut*, *re*, *mi*, etc.) appear in the second line from the top. G (*sol*) is repeated, because Rameau in this interpretation finds the scale to arise from two tetrachords (shown above the example by the arches over C–F and G–C), with a 'disjunction' between them ('ici la disjonction') to cover the three consecutive whole tones ('Trois tons de suite'). The interval between each tone appears above each pair of notes: two types of whole tones (the 'major tone' [9:8] and 'minor tone' [10:9]) and one 'major semitone' (16:15). Each tetrachord is harmonized as a triple proportion ('Basse fondamentale en proportion triple'): 3:9:27 for F, C, and G in the lower tetrachord, and 9:27:81 for C, G, and D in the upper tetrachord.

Acoustical revisions and resonance

Rameau applied much of his energy over his final four decades (that is, when he was not composing the operas and ballets that made him the most important French composer of the eighteenth century) to finding a systematic or natural basis for his practical theories, and to debating with the leading philosophers and scientists of the day over these aspects of his theories. In the *Traité*, he based his harmonic theories on the ratios that derive from harmonic and arithmetic division of a vibrating string. Shortly after the *Traité* was published, he became aware of the acoustical research of Joseph Sauveur demonstrating that the ratios that arose from the harmonic division of a vibrating string were in fact audible in the resonance of that string (the *corps sonore* or "resonant body," as Rameau called it). As Father Bernard Castel, an influential friend of Rameau's, put it in a 1722 review of the *Traité*, "Nature gives us the same system that M. Rameau discovered in numbers."[14]

14 Ibid., p. 133. On Sauveur's discovery, see Chapter 9, pp. 252–53.

ECHELLE DE L'OCTAVE DIATONIQUE
du Mode précédent

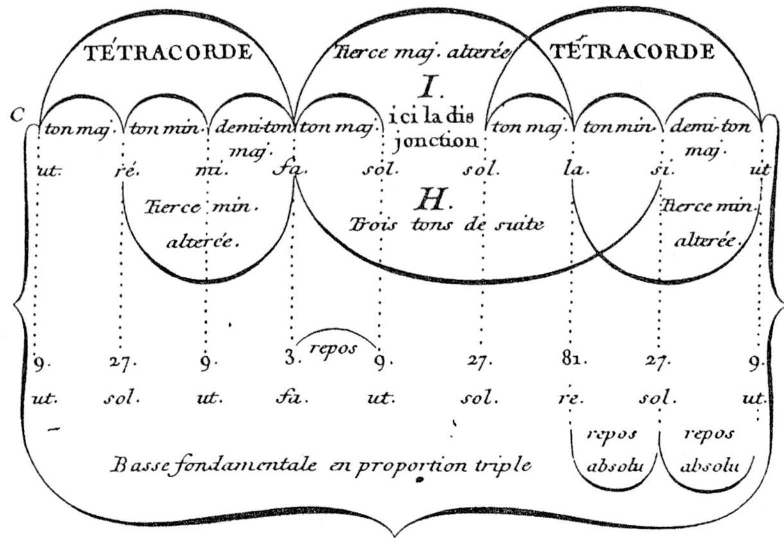

Comme les rapports des sons diatoniques avec la Basse fondamentale sont les mêmes qu'auparavant; exepté où le Mode change, comme je l'expliquerai: J'ai seulement écrit le nom des intervales qu'il y a de l'un de ces sons à l'autre.

Plate 24.3 The octave scale, from Rameau, *Démonstration du principe de l'harmonie*, Plate C

The importance of this realization for Rameau cannot be underestimated. "Nature" was a potent talisman of Enlightenment thought in all areas. Rameau's realization that much of what he had deduced painstakingly from the ratios of a vibrating string actually occurred in Nature caused him to redefine the very basis of harmonic theory, in essence changing it from a Cartesian deductive system to a Newtonian empirical system. The preface of the *Traité* states in Cartesian fashion that "Music is a science which should have definite rules; these rules should be drawn from an evident principle; and this principle cannot really be known to us without the aid of mathematics." He had totally recast these axiomatic statements by the time he wrote his *Génération harmonique* in 1737: "Music is a physico-mathematical science; sound is its physical object, and the ratios found between different sounds constitute its mathematical object." Invoking numerous empirical demonstrations and experiments as a proof for the *corps sonore* (patterned self-consciously upon the model of Newtonian optics), Rameau believed his musical theories were now on a par with the most advanced scientific discoveries of the age.[15] Indeed, during this period, he assiduously cultivated the support of leading scientists and scientific academies.

He also interacted with many of the leading figures of the French Enlightenment: Voltaire (1694–1778, one of whose librettos Rameau set in 1745), Jean-Jacques Rousseau (1712–78, who wrote some of the musical articles for the *Encyclopédie* that Rameau had been asked to write), Denis Diderot (1713–84, who helped Rameau author his *Démonstration*), and Jean Le Rond d'Alembert (1717–83, who, although he knew little about music, published a widely distributed précis of Rameau's theories in 1752). As influential as these *philosophes* were to Rameau in the development of his theories, Rameau's ideas also inspired the *philosophes* in the development of their own thoughts on a range of metaphysical and aesthetic issues.

If Rameau delighted in finding a "natural" basis for music in the *corps sonore*, his accomplishment proved precarious. The *corps sonore* was no more able to offer a direct generation of the minor triad than were the string divisions with which Rameau originally struggled. (At one point in the *Génération harmonique* Rameau suggested the existence of a putative "undertone" series of partials replicating an arithmetic division of the octave as a "natural" origin for the minor triad; but he quickly abandoned this idea when d'Alembert showed the acoustical evidence of such a series to be illusory.) Nor could the *corps sonore* offer a convincing explanation for the subdominant harmony. In the triple proportion, the subdominant (as the lowest number in the proportion) and not the tonic seemed to be generator of the key. The source of the problem is that the subdominant note does not exist in the harmonic series over the tonic. If the subdominant had had its origin explained by an arithmetic series, Rameau could not have claimed that the *corps sonore* bore a causal relationship with tonal structures.

In his final fifteen years, Rameau struggled with these and many other speculative issues, often engaging in bitter polemical wars with the *philosophes*. Despite Rameau's impeccable tonal intuitions, he was no match in such intellectual arguments, and by the end of his life he was widely perceived as defensive and misguided – the very opposite of the "enlightened" *musicien-philosophe* he was initially celebrated to be. (It certainly did not help matters that in his last years, Rameau's writings took a markedly mystical turn, with quasi-Rosicrucian speculations over the omnipotence of the *corps sonore*.)

Rameau was hardly alone among musicians in the eighteenth century in seeking a "scientific" basis for common musical structures. The violinist and composer Giuseppe Tartini (1692–1770), for instance, like Rameau, wrote practical works (on violin playing and ornamentation) as well as theory treatises of a highly speculative nature. Drawing upon his experience as a violinist, Tartini thought that the acoustic phenomenon of the "third sound" (*terzo tuono*; what is now called a first-order difference tone) might offer an alternative source of harmony to Rameau's *corps sonore*.

15 For more on the epistemological vacillations of Rameau, see **Chapter 3, pp. 85–88, 91**.

He developed this theory in his 1754 treatise, whose title claimed to treat music "according to the true science of harmony" (see also Chapter 9, pp. 254–56). But like Rameau and all others who have attempted such "scientific derivations," Tartini failed at the basic task of deriving the major and minor triads in a consistent manner. Nor did his theories offer the comprehensive explanation of musical practice that Rameau's fundamental bass did, despite the latter's shortcomings as a strictly "scientific" theory.

Accomplished musicians such as Rameau and Tartini always understood that their primary theoretical mission was to explain the musical practice of their time. For instance, when Rameau found his speculative side arguing against his practical music knowledge, he frequently invoked "license" to explain a usage. Nonmusicians (such as d'Alembert and the eminent mathematician Leonhard Euler [1707–83], whose music-theory treatise appeared in 1739), by contrast, often began from the premise that, as stated in 1753 by the Swiss painter and scientist Jean-Adam Serre (1704–88), "artists who are most accomplished in their art are ill-suited . . . to give the public a true theory." One of Rameau's pupils, Pierre-Joseph Roussier (c. 1716–92), went so far as to criticize Rameau in 1765 for having included in his theorizing "concepts of practice and routine from which he was unable to completely free himself, as they had been unfortunately inculcated into him since early childhood." As intriguing it may be to trace Rameau's speculative thinking as it interacted with the trends of the age, his practical theorizing was what transformed forever the manner in which musicians thought about musical structure.

Rameau's legacy

Rameau's theory of the fundamental bass – if not the *corps sonore* – spread rapidly throughout Europe, even though few non-French musicians cited Rameau by name or seem to have read his works first-hand. For instance, Heinichen's 1728 discussion of seventh chords is based on Rameau's *Traité*. John Frederick Lampe (c. 1703–51), a German opera composer who moved to London in 1725, clearly differentiated in 1737 between a "natural bass" (equivalent to Rameau's fundamental bass) and the thorough bass, and he graphically illustrated how a key was organized by the tonic flanked symmetrically by its dominant and subdominant. By the middle of the eighteenth century, Rameau's theories had clearly influenced the fundamental perspective on musical structure of most musicians – even those who claimed to reject his theories. For instance, C. P. E. Bach (1714–88) loudly decried Rameauian theory in a letter from the 1770s; but in his 1762 thorough-bass manual, he begins by discussing 5/3, 6/3, and 6/4 chords – an ordering of harmonies that does not appear in pre-Rameau thorough-bass manuals.[16] Attributions of chord roots, the primacy of triads and seventh chords as

16 Christensen argues that Bach's vocal animosity toward Rameau is based as much on political tensions (associated with Bach's rivalry with another Rameau acolyte in Berlin, Christoph Nichelmann) as

basic harmonies, the importance of the subdominant as a functional complement to the dominant, harmonic progression being determined by root progressions – these and other features became part of common musical parlance. In dozens of treatises published in the second half of the eighteenth century, theorists throughout Europe worked within the Rameauian paradigm of the fundamental bass.

Many of these theorists attempted to refine aspects of Rameau's arguments that they perceived as faulty or under-developed. For instance, Johann Philipp Kirnberger (1721–83), a Berlin theorist who had studied briefly with J. S. Bach, attempted to clarify Rameau's theory of *supposition* by distinguishing between "essential" dissonant sevenths that belonged to some "dominant" harmony and could be introduced without preparation, and "accidental" dissonances arising from suspensions, and hence needing to be introduced through voice-leading preparation. This was an early stage in the historical process of differentiating chords from simultaneities formed by nonharmonic tones.

During this period, terminological problems precluded a clear statement of the general topic of nonharmonic tones. Traditional German terminology derived from *stile antico* counterpoint or thorough-bass traditions differentiated *Hauptnoten* or principal notes that occurred on the beat from *Nebennoten* or subsidiary notes that occurred after the beat, ignoring whether *Nebennoten* were consonant or dissonant, or chord tones or nonharmonic tones. Friedrich Wilhelm Marpurg (1718–95), a prolific writer based in Berlin, differentiated a note's harmonic and metrical status by referring in 1755 to notes on weak metrical points as harmonic subsidiary notes (*harmonische Nebennoten*, as in repetitions or arpeggiations) versus passing (*durchgehende*) or changing notes (*Wechselnoten*). But not until the nineteenth century did generic terms for nonharmonic or foreign tones allow the clear distinction that is universally understood today.

Despite the many theoretical disputes engendered by Rameau's speculative writings, the practical value of the fundamental bass for teaching composition and analysis proved attractive to musicians across Europe. Kirnberger and Christoph Nichelmann (1717–62, another pupil of J. S. Bach's), who claimed their ideas were based on J. S. Bach's teaching, analyzed Bach compositions using the fundamental bass.[17] Mozart employed the fundamental bass in the mid-1780s when he taught harmony and composition to two pupils. Even discussions of thorough bass or counterpoint were couched in harmonic terms. Heinrich Christoph Koch (1749–1816) used the term "species counterpoint" to refer to a graded series of increasingly complex chordal vocabularies to be used in harmonization exercises. Johann Georg Albrechtsberger (1736–1809), one of Beethoven's composition teachers in the early 1790s, recast Fuxian species counterpoint in 1790, explaining that before writing a counterpoint to a *cantus*

on fundamental theoretical differences. See Christensen, "Nichelmann contra C. Ph. E. Bach." Also see Christensen, "C. P. E. Bach's *Versuch* and its Context in Eighteenth-Century Thorough-Bass Pedagogy."

17 Kirnberger, "Die wahren Grundsätze"; Nichelmann, "Die Melodie"; excerpts of analyses by both theorists of music by J. S. Bach appear in Lester, *Compositional Theory*, pp. 221, 248.

firmus, the student should first examine the harmonies underlying that *cantus firmus*. (See also **Chapter 18, pp. 583–84.**)

Various writers invented analytical symbols to refer to the harmonies of a key. The Irish theorist John Trydell (c. 1715–76) proposed labeling chord roots by "harmonical figures" in 1766 (an invention disseminated via the 1771 edition of the *Encyclopaedia Britannica*); the German theorist and composer Abbé Vogler (1749–1814) used a few roman numerals later that decade; and Gottfried Weber (1779–1839) made roman numerals standard musical symbols in 1817. By the early nineteenth century, this led to the *Stufentheorie* (scale-step theory) that defined the role of a harmony by its placement in the key. Another strand of Rameauian thinking – his discussions of the roles of tonic, dominant, and subdominant chords in defining a key – influenced a number of eighteenth-century thinkers, such as Christoph Gottlieb Schröter (1699–1782), Georg Andreas Sorge (1703–78), and Johann Friedrich Daube (c. 1730–97). But a full-blown theory of harmonic functions did not flower until the work of Hugo Riemann (1849–1917) late in the nineteenth century. Still other theorists in the nineteenth century – notably in Austria – retained the fundamental bass as a pedagogical tool, albeit infused with elaborated interpolations and elisions in order to accommodate the increasingly chromatic harmonic language explored by nineteenth-century composers. Thus, *Stufentheorie*, the fundamental bass, and functional theory – three primary strands of nineteenth-century harmonic theory – all trace their roots to Rameau.

At the same time, even though Rameau had focused on the nature of harmonic motion, and various eighteenth-century perspectives articulated the interactions between underlying structures and musical surfaces, later eighteenth-century harmonic theory bequeathed to the nineteenth century an unfortunate preoccupation with verticalities at the expense of the role of linear factors in musical structure, and provided no conceptual framework within which to discuss the interaction of local structures (chord-to-chord and larger progressions) with phrasing and form. These topics were left for later generations and perspectives – and, in some fundamental ways, remain open today.

In summary, eighteenth-century harmonic theory – largely Rameauian theory and its legacy – transformed earlier thinking about how pitches interacted, and laid the groundwork for conceptualizations about harmony, voice-leading, and the forces that give directionality to tonal music, leaving a profound legacy of solutions and challenges that still reverberate today. Even more resonant, however, was the intellectual legitimacy with which Rameau stamped his ambitious project. Largely because of the personal influence of Rameau, harmonic theory came to be understood as a science – indeed, a cutting-edge science attracting the attention of the leading scientists, mathematicians, and philosophers of the day. Only rarely in the history of the West has music theory (or even music) been so close to the vortex of cultural discourse in its profound synthesis of practical and speculative concerns. Not until the mature works of Schenker nearly two centuries after Rameau's *Traité* was a theorist to offer a substantially different yet compelling vision of musical structure of comparable power and influence.

Bibliography

Primary sources

D'Alembert, J. *Elemens de musique, théorique et pratique, suivant les principes de M. Rameau*, Paris, David l'aîné, Le Breton, and Durand, 1752; facs. New York, Broude, 1966; 6th edn., Lyon, J.-M. Bruyset, 1779; facs. Les introuvables, Editions d'aujourd'hui, 1984; Ger. trans. F. Marpurg as *Systematische Einleitung in die musikalische Setzkunst nach den Lehrsätzen des Herrn Rameau*, Leipzig, Breitkopf, 1757; facs. Leipzig, Zentralantiquariat der DDR, 1980; partial trans. T. Blacklock under "Music" in *Encyclopaedia Britannica*, 2nd edn., 1784

Avianius, J. *Isagoge in libros musicae poeticae*, Erfurt, G. Baumannus, 1581; partial reprint and trans. B. Rivera, "The *Isagoge* (1581) of Johannes Avianius: An Early Formulation of Triadic Theory," *JMT* 22 (1978), pp. 43–64

Brossard, S. *Dictionnaire de musique*, Paris, Ballard, 1703; facs. Geneva, Minkoff, 1992

Burmeister, J. *Hypomnematum musicae poeticae*, Rostock, S. Myliander, 1599

Campion, F. *Traité d'accompagnement et de composition, selon la règle des octaves*, Paris, Aux depens d'Estienne Roger, 1716; facs. Geneva, Minkoff, 1976; trans. L. Dragone as "François Campion's Treatise on Accompaniment: A Translation and Commentary," *Theoria* 6 (1992), pp. 135–62

Addition au traité de l'accompagnement, Paris, Boivin and Le Clair, 1730

Daube, J. R. *General-Bass in drey Accorden*, Leipzig, J. B. Andrä, 1756; trans. B. Wallace as "J. F. Daube's *General-Bass in drey Accorden* (1756): A Translation and Commentary," Ph.D. diss., University of North Texas (1983)

Descartes, R. *Compendium musicae*, Utrecht, G. Zijll and T. ab Ackersdijck, 1650; in *Œuvres de Descartes*, vol. x, ed. C. Adam and P. Tannery, Paris, L. Cerf, 1908; facs. Strasbourg, Heitz, 1965 and New York, Broude, 1968; trans. W. Robert as *Compendium of Music*, American Institute of Musicology, 1961

Frère, A. *Transpositions de musique*, Amsterdam, E. Roger, 1710

Fux, J. J. *Gradus ad Parnassum*, Vienna, Van Ghelen, 1725; reprint, ed. A. Mann, Kassel, Bärenreiter, 1967; facs. New York, Broude, 1974; partial trans. A. Mann as *Steps to Parnassus*, New York, Norton, 1943; rev. edn. *The Study of Counterpoint*, New York, Norton, 1965

Harnisch, O. S. *Artis musicae delineatio*, Frankfurt, Stein, 1608

Heinichen, J. D. *Neu erfundene und gründliche Anweisung*, Hamburg, B. Schiller, 1711

Der General-Bass in der Composition, Dresden, Heinichen, 1728; facs. Hildesheim, G. Olms, 1969 and 1994

Janowka, T. B. *Clavis ad thesaurum magnae artis musicae*, Prague, G. Labaun, 1701; facs. Amsterdam, F. Knuf, 1973

Keller, G. *A compleat method for attaining to play a thorough bass*, London, J. Cullen, 1705

Kirnberger, J. P. *Die Kunst des reinen Satzes*, 2 vols., Berlin, Decker und Hartung, 1771–79; facs. Hildesheim, G. Olms, 1968 and 1988; trans. D. Beach and J. Thym as *The Art of Strict Musical Composition*, New Haven, Yale University Press, 1982

Die wahren Grundsätze zum Gebrauch der Harmonie, Berlin, Decker und Hartung, 1773; facs. Hildesheim, G. Olms, 1970; trans. D. Beach and J. Thym as "'The True Principles for the Practice of Harmony' by Johann Philipp Kirnberger," *JMT* 23 (1979), pp. 163–225

Lampe, J. F. *A plain and compendious method of teaching thorough bass*, London, J. Wilcox, 1737; facs. New York, Broude, 1969

Lippius, J. *Disputatio musica (prima–tertia)*, 3 vols., Wittenberg, J. Gormanus, 1609–10

Synopsis musicae novae, Strassburg, K. Kieffer, 1612; trans. B. Rivera as *Synopsis of New Music*, Colorado Springs, Colorado College Music Press, 1977

Magirus, J. *Artis musicae*, 2nd edn., Braunschweig, Magirus, 1611

Malcolm, A. *A Treatise of Musick*, Edinburgh, s.n., 1721; facs. New York, Da Capo Press, 1970

Marpurg, F. W. *Anleitung zum Clavierspielen*, Berlin, A. Haude and J. C. Spener, 1755; facs. New York, Broude, 1969, and Hildesheim, G. Olms, 1970; trans. E. Hayes as "F. W. Marpurg's 'Anleitung zum Clavierspielen,'" Ph.D. diss., Stanford University (1977)

Anleitung zur Musik überhaupt, Berlin, A. Wever, 1763; facs. Leipzig, Zentralantiquariat der DDR, 1975

Mozart, W. A. *Barbara Ployers Theorie- und Kompositionsstudien bei Mozart*, facs. in *W. A. Mozart als Theoretiker*, ed. R. Lach, Vienna, A. Hölder, 1918; facs. in *Barbara Ployers und Franz Jakob Freystädtlers Theorie- und Kompositionsstudien bei Mozart*, Kassel, Bärenreiter, 1989

Thomas Attwoods Theorie- und Kompositionsstudien bei Mozart, ed. D. Heartz and A. Mann, Kassel, Bärenreiter, 1969

Nichelmann, C. *Die Melodie nach ihrem Wesen sowohl, als nach ihren Eigenschaften*, Danzig, J. C. Schuster, 1755

Penna, L. *Li primi albori musicali* (1672), 3 vols., Bologna, G. Monti, 1684; facs. Bologna, Forni, 1969

Praetorius, M. *Syntagma musicum*, 3 vols., Wolfenbüttel, E. Holwein, 1614–20; facs. Kassel, Bärenreiter, 1958–59

Rameau, J.-P. *Traité de l'harmonie*, Paris, Ballard, 1722; facs. New York, Broude, 1967, and in vol. I of *The Complete Theoretical Writings of Jean-Philippe Rameau* (hereafter *CTW*), ed. E. Jacobi, American Institute of Musicology, 1967–72; trans. P. Gossett, as *Treatise on Harmony*, New York, Dover, 1971

Nouveau système de musique théorique, Paris, Ballard, 1726; facs. *CTW* 1; trans. G. Chandler as "Rameau's 'Nouveau système de musique théorique': An Annotated Translation with Commentary," Ph.D. dissertation, Indiana University (1975)

Dissertation sur les différentes métodes d'accompagnement, Paris, Boivin and Le Clair, 1732; facs. *CTW* 5; trans. D. Hayes as *Dissertation on the Different Methods of Accompaniment*, Ann Arbor, UMI Research Press, 1974

Génération harmonique, Paris, Prault fils, 1737; facs. *CTW* 3; trans. D. Hayes as *Harmonic Generation*, Ann Arbor, UMI Research Press, 1974

Démonstration du principe de l'harmonie, Paris, Durand and Pissot, 1750; facs. *CTW* 3; trans. R. Briscoe in "Rameau's 'Démonstration du principe de l'harmonie' and 'Nouvelles réflexions': An Annotated Translation," Ph.D. diss., Indiana University (1974)

Observations sur notre instinct pour la musique, Paris, Prault fils, Lambert, and Duchesne, 1754; facs. *CTW* 3

Code de musique pratique, Paris, Imprimerie royale, 1761; facs. *CTW* 4

Riemann, H. *Vereinfachte Harmonielehre: oder, Die Lehre von den tonalen Funktionen der Akkorde*, London, Augener, 1893; trans. H. Bewerung as *Harmony Simplified; or, the Theory of the Tonal Functions of Chords*, London, Augener, 1896

Roussier, P.-J. *Observations sur différens points d'harmonie*, Geneva, d'Houry, 1765

Schröter, C. G. *Deutliche Anweisung zum General-Bass*. Halberstadt, J. H. Gross, 1772

Serre, J.-A. *Essais sur les principes de l'harmonie*, Paris, Prault fils, 1753; facs. New York, Broude, 1967

Sorge, G. A. *Anleitung zur Fantasie*, Lobenstein, Sorge, 1767

Tartini, G. *Trattato di musica secondo la vera scienza dell'armonia*, Padua, Stamperia del seminario, 1754; facs. New York, Broude, 1966, and in *Le Opere di Giuseppe Tartini* 2/1, Padua, Casa editrice dott. A. Milani, 1973; trans. F. Johnson as "Tartini's *Trattato*," Ph.D. diss., Indiana University (1985)

Trydell, J. *Two essays on the theory and practice of music*, Dublin, B. Grierson, 1766

Vicentino, N. *L'antica musica ridotta alla moderna prattica*, Rome, A. Barre, 1555; facs. Kassel, Bärenreiter, 1959

Vogler, G. J. *Tonwissenschaft und Tonsezkunst*, Mannheim, Kurfürstliche Hofbuchdruckerei, 1776; facs. Hildesheim, G. Olms, 1970

Weber, G. *Versuch einer geordneten Theorie der Tonseztkunst*, 3 vols., Mainz, B. Schott, 1817–21

Werckmeister, A. *Die nothwendigsten Anmerkungen und Regeln wie der Bassus continuus oder General-Bass wol könne tractiret werden*, Aschersleben, G. E. Struntz, 1698; facs. Michaelstein, Kultur- und Forschungsstätte Michaelstein, 1985

Zarlino, G. *Le istitutioni harmoniche*, Venice, Franceschi, 1558; facs. New York, Broude, 1965; trans. of Part III by G. Marco, ed. C. V. Palisca as *The Art of Counterpoint*, New Haven, Yale University Press, 1968

Secondary Sources

Buelow, G. *Thoroughbass accompaniment according to Johann David Heinichen*, 2nd edn., Ann Arbor, UMI Research Press, 1986

Christensen, T. "Nichelmann contra C. Ph. E. Bach: Harmonic Theory and Musical Politics at the Court of Frederick the Great," in *Carl Philipp Emanuel Bach und die europäische Musikkultur des mittleren 18. Jahrhunderts*, ed. H. Marx, Göttingen, Vandenhoeck and Ruprecht, 1990, pp. 189–220

"The Spanish Baroque Guitar and Seventeenth-Century Triadic Theory," *JMT* 36 (1992), pp. 1–42

"The Rule of the Octave in Thorough-Bass Theory and Practice," *Acta* 64 (1992), pp. 91–117

Rameau and Musical Thought in the Enlightenment, Cambridge University Press, 1993

"C. P. E. Bach's Versuch and its Context in Eighteenth-Century Thorough-Bass Pedagogy," in *Carl Philipp Emanuel Bach: Musik Für Europa. Bericht über das Internationale Symposium vom 8 März bis 12. März 1994 in Frankfurt (Oder)*, ed. H.-G. Ottenberg, Frankfurt (Oder), 1998, pp. 352–77

Lester, J. *Between Modes and Keys: German Theory 1592–1802*, Stuyvesant, NY, Pendragon Press, 1989

Compositional Theory in the Eighteenth Century, Cambridge, MA, Harvard University Press, 1992

Rivera, B. "Harmonic Theories in Musical Treatises of the Late Fifteenth and Early Sixteenth Centuries," *MTS* 22 (1979), pp. 43–64

Shirlaw, M. *The Theory of Harmony*, London, Novello, 1917

Verba, C. "The Development of Rameau's Thoughts on Modulation and Chromatics," *JAMS* 26 (1973), pp. 69–91

Music and the French Enlightenment: Reconstruction of a Dialogue, New York, Oxford University Press, 1992

· 25 ·

Nineteenth-century harmonic theory: the Austro-German legacy

DAVID W. BERNSTEIN

Today most scholars agree that Rameau was the founder of modern harmonic theory. As we have seen in the previous chapter, Rameau attempted to synthesize in his many writings a multiplicity of ideas – both old and new, speculative and practical – into a unified theory of tonal harmony grounded upon a single underlying principle, the *corps sonore* (see **Chapter 24, pp. 759–71**). If he did not succeed in creating a truly systematic and stable theory of harmony owing to his many differing and often contradictory theoretical arguments and intellectual borrowings, he nonetheless bequeathed to the nineteenth century a number of compelling and richly suggestive ideas that would inspire theorists in their own efforts.

In this chapter, we will look at the evolution of harmonic theory in the nineteenth century. This is of course a vast and complex topic. Given the profound changes in harmonic language between 1800 and 1900 – a period covering the end of Viennese Classicism and closing with Schoenberg's first tentative steps beyond the tonal system – it is not surprising that theorists expended extraordinary energy and efforts in their attempts to rationalize this shifting practice. As it is impossible here to describe all of these efforts in detail, we will limit our scope to the development of Austro-German harmonic theory, a tradition which arguably encompasses some of the most innovative and influential writings on this topic for the entire century. Within this tradition, three individual trajectories can be traced back by differing routes to Rameau's own theory: scale-degree (*Stufen*) theory, fundamental-bass theory, and function theory. While all of these trajectories intersect in various ways (as they surely do in Rameau's own writings), each will be treated individually by focusing on a few representative advocates of each view: Vogler and Weber for scale-degree theory, Sechter and Mayrberger for fundamental-bass theory, and Riemann for function theory. We will then consider several polemics generated by these colliding trajectories in the early twentieth century and conclude with an examination of Schoenberg's attempt to find a mediation in his own theory of harmony.

Scale-degree theory

One of the central tenets of Rameau's harmonic theory was that every chord was generated from some fundamental sound belonging to a scale degree of a given key. But as scholars have long reminded us, clear notions of chordal scale degrees can be found in the seventeenth century (see **Chapter 13, pp. 441–47**; and **Chapter 24, pp. 756–57**). Thorough-bass pedagogues, for instance, supplied rules for a performer to select harmonies above an unfigured bass. These rules, often based on deciding which harmonies were appropriate for the individual scale degrees in a key, show a growing awareness of tonal relations. Eighteenth-century thorough-bass manuals often included paradigmatic harmonizations of ascending and descending diatonic bass lines, called the *règle de l'octave*, which assigned specific harmonies to the diatonic scale degrees in major and minor.[1] Rameau, as we have seen, was a significant contributor to the development of scale-degree theory. In his *Traité de l'harmonie*, for example, he differentiated between seventh chords above the fifth scale degree of a key (called *dominante-tonique*) and those that would appear above other non-tonic scale degrees (called simply *dominante*). The added-sixth chord, however, was restricted to the fourth scale degree of a key – a chord he would in later writings christen the *sous-dominante* (see **Chapter 24, p. 768**). The designation of a given chord was determined by its structure, i.e., whether it was a simple triad or contained one of Rameau's two characteristic dissonances. But according to Carl Dahlhaus, such generalized designations do not properly constitute a full theory of chordal scale degrees (*Stufentheorie*) ince they fail to make functional distinctions between all the harmonies built on the tones of the diatonic scale.[2] Other theorists after Rameau attempted to offer an expanded correlation between chord types and scale degrees, including Georg Andreas Sorge (1703–78) in his *Compendium harmonicum* (1760), and a lesser known Irish theorist named John Trydell (1715–76) in a treatise entitled *Two Essays on the Theory and Practice of Music* (1766).[3] But the first systematic *Stufentheorie* came in a series of treatises by an eccentric German musician and teacher named Georg Joseph Vogler.

Vogler. Abbé Georg Joseph Vogler (1749–1814) studied speculative music theory in Padua with Francesco Antonio Vallotti (1697–1780), through whom he undoubtedly became acquainted with the writings of Rameau and Giuseppe Tartini. Following his studies in Italy, Vogler established a public conservatory in Mannheim in 1776 for which he published several treatises, including his *Tonwissenschaft und Tonsezkunst* (1776).[4] His activities as a composer, theorist, and organ builder took him to such cities as Stockholm, Copenhagen, Munich, Prague, and Vienna.[5]

Influenced by the same Cartesian rationalism promulgated by Rameau, Vogler maintained that the science of music was drawn from a single principle. All necessary musical proportions, Vogler argued, could be derived from the resonance of the vibrating string. But unlike Rameau, Vogler exceeded Zarlino's *senario* of six partials and reached up to the sixteenth partial. In order to make these higher partials audible and

1 See **Example 24.1, p. 757** and **Chapter 13, p. 443**. 2 Dahlhaus, *Studies*, p. 26.
3 Lester, *Compositional Theory*, pp. 207–08.
4 Graves, *In Praise of Harmony*, pp. 3–4. Graves's book offers the most comprehensive discussion of Vogler's music theories, especially Chapters 1 and 2, pp. 13–84. 5 Ibid., pp. 5ff.

comprehensible, Vogler devised an instrument called the *Tonmaass*, consisting of eight strings with up to sixteen fixed bridges. By plotting out the various ratios engendered by these higher partials, Vogler was able to derive the "natural" major scale from the eighth through sixteenth partials, containing both a raised fourth and a natural seventh: f, g, a, b(♮), c, d, e(♭), e♮, and f. The natural scale served as a model for the "artificial" major and minor scales, which Vogler derived from triads one and two fifths above "fundamental" triads on F and D (F–A–C, C–E–G, G–B–D and D–F–A, A–C–E and E–G–B).

Vogler's next step was to form triads on the remaining degrees of these "artificial" scales. Every major, minor, and diminished triad that could be placed over a scale degree in a major or minor scale was considered by Vogler to be fundamental. (Unlike Rameau, he did not concern himself with an acoustical generative explanation for minor or diminished triads.) To designate the scale-degree placement of these chords, Vogler introduced roman numeral designations. Although earlier theorists had proposed analogous notations and terminologies for identifying chordal scale degrees, Vogler was the first theorist to use roman numerals consistently.[6]

The primacy of the triad is reinforced by Vogler's system of "reduction" through which even the most complex simultaneity may be explained as a simple triad (*Wohlklang*) by virtue of several categories of displacement: suspension, anticipation, appoggiatura, etc.[7] Vogler's system of reduction, which he applied in analyses of his own works,[8] is noteworthy for its strong demarcation between harmony and voice-leading. In fact, several scholars have suggested that his theory of reduction anticipates Heinrich Schenker's notion of structural levels.[9]

Vogler analyzed his chords according to their behaviour in a series of archetypal cadential formulations called *Schlussfälle*. Critical for Vogler was the chromatic leading tone in helping to define a cadence. In his *Handbuch zur Harmonielehre* (1802), Vogler lists ten such cadences possessing various degrees of closure: I–V, V–I, IV–I, VII–I, and ♯IV–V in major; V–I, I–V, ♯VII–I, ♯IV–V, and II–V in minor.[10] The diminished chord on ♯IV in major (F♯–A–C in C major) and the irregular triad on ♯IV in minor (D♯–F–A in A minor) are both derived from Vogler's "natural" scale, and are analogously cadential (*Schlussfallmässig*) to the dominant as the leading-tone chord is to the tonic.

In his *Tonwissenschaft und Tonsezkunst*, Vogler claimed that modulations are best limited to keys with only one additional sharp or flat if a work is to maintain its tonal unity. Thus, from C major, one may modulate to five keys: A minor, G major, E minor,

6 Properly speaking, Vogler designated only the leading-tone chord (VII) in his *Tonwissenschaft und Tonsezkunst* (p. 82). It was only in his later *Handbuch* (1802) that he applied roman numerals to all scale degrees. For earlier uses of roman numerals, see **Chapter 24, p. 774**.

7 Vogler, *Handbuch*, p. 6. For a discussion of Vogler's "reduction" theory, see Graves, "Abbé Vogler's Theory of Reduction."

8 See, for example, Vogler's *Zwei und dreisig Präludien* (translated in Bent, *MANC*, vol. II, pp. 132–45).

9 Morgan, "Schenker and the Theoretical Tradition," p. 88; Graves, "Abbé Vogler's Theory of Reduction," p. 64.

10 Vogler, *Handbuch*, Table II ("zehn Schlussfälle").

11 Vogler, *Tonwissenschaft und Tonsezkunst*, pp. 70–72.

Example 25.1 Progressions from Vogler's *Handbuch zur Harmonielehre* (Table VII) illustrating "multiple meaning"

a.

b.

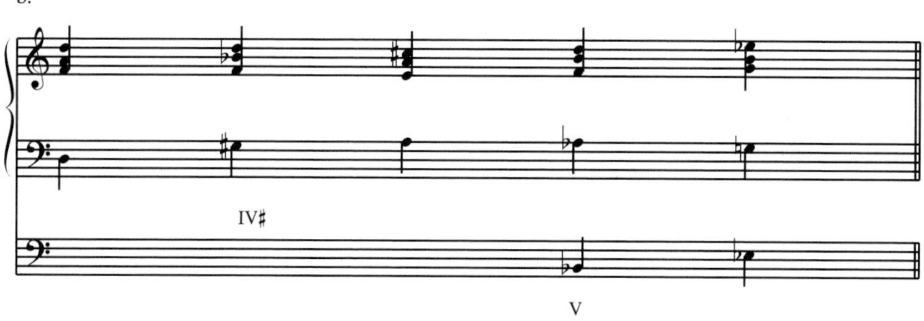

D minor, and F major.[11] However, as a church organist well versed in the art of improvisation, he understood the need to consider modulation to keys beyond this restriction. Thus, Vogler admitted the possibility of modulation to the major and minor keys on every degree in the chromatic scale.[12] And in an essay entitled "Summe der Harmonik" (1778–81) as well as in his *Handbuch zur Harmonielehre*, we find exhaustive lists of modulations to chromatically related keys.[13] These discussions of chromatic relations were forward-looking; they established an avenue of research that was continued at mid-century by such "progressive" theorists as Carl Friedrich Weitzman (1808–80) and H. J. Vincent (1819–1901).[14]

Modulation, in Vogler's system, may exploit the "multiple meaning" (*Mehrdeutigkeit*) of chords. He described two types of multiple meaning. The first occurs when a chord on a given scale degree is reinterpreted as belonging to a different degree of a new key. The second takes place by means of enharmonic reinterpretation; a diminished seventh chord, for example, may be enharmonically respelled, thus resolving in four different

12 Ibid., p. 84. 13 See, for example, Vogler, *Handbuch*, Tables IX–XI.

14 For further discussion of Weitzmann and Vincent, see Wason, "Progressive Harmonic Theory." Also see **Chapter 10, p. 286**.

keys (see Example 25.1a). Similarly, a chord built on the raised fourth degree of his "natural" scale with an added seventh (e.g., G♯–B♭–D–F in D minor) may be respelled as a dominant seventh chord (A♭–B♭–D–F in E♭ major)[15] (see Example 25.1b).

Vogler's awkward system of harmonic theory suffered from numerous logical and empirical problems, and it cannot be said to have enjoyed any subsequent support by theorists. However, a few practical elements of his theory did have a more lasting influence: roman numeral notation was adopted by subsequent generations of theorists; and his ideas concerning modulation and multiple meaning supplied them with a strategy to explain increasingly intractable chromatic progressions.

Weber. Most music theorists in the early nineteenth century tended to eschew the speculative side of harmonic theory in favor of more practical considerations. Typical was the German theorist and composer Gottfried Weber (1779–1839). In his three-volume *Versuch einer geordneten Theorie der Tonsetzkunst* (1817–21), Weber criticized music theorists for lagging miserably behind musical practice. He believed that theory depends on practice for its very substance. Weber's model was the music of the Viennese Classical tradition, his theory was guided by standards that he derived from careful examination of this repertory as well as from his own taste and aesthetic judgment. The predominant method he employed was thus descriptive and empirical rather than deductive as was the case for theorists in the more speculative tradition of harmonic theory exemplified by Rameau.[16]

The use of the word "systematic" (*geordneten*) in the title of Weber's *Versuch* is somewhat misleading, for, as stated in his preface, a scientifically grounded systematic theory of music is not possible, since musical theory cannot be reduced to a single first principle. The "systematic" aspect of the *Versuch* lies more in its organization, the natural order and unencumbered presentation of its contents. Weber was among the most adamant critics of those theorists who rely upon acoustics for their systems. He rejected both mathematical and physical explanations for musical relations as useless pedantry. Composers such as Mozart, Haydn, Bach, or Palestrina, Weber declared, had little use for the knowledge that a perfect fifth is in the ratio of 2:3.[17] The scale is obviously not derived from the overtone series, *pace* Vogler, since it cannot produce all the notes of the diatonic scale in tune. He also chided theorists such as Rameau, Marpurg, and d'Alembert for attempting to derive the minor triad from nature.

Weber was particularly critical of Vogler's student Justin Heinrich Knecht (1752–1817)[18] for his large and unwieldy number of chords and complicated notational system.[19] Instead, Weber posited only seven fundamental chord types: three

15 Vogler, *Handbuch*, Tables VII and VIII. Vogler supplied the chordal roots in the lowest staff when they do not appear in the bass. Note that Vogler's natural seventh chord built on IV♯ in Example 25.1b would be described by later theorists as an inversion of a ("German") augmented sixth chord built on $\hat{6}$.

16 Rummenhöller, "Der deskriptive Theoriebegriff."

17 Weber, *Versuch* (2nd edn.), vol. 1, p. 21.

18 Knecht, *Elementarwerk der Harmonie*.

19 Weber, *Versuch*, vol. 1, p. 194.

triads (minor, major, and diminished) and four seventh chords (dominant, minor, major, and half-diminished). As did several eighteenth-century theorists, Weber considered the diminished seventh to be a minor ninth chord with a missing root and not a true fundamental chord. Most other chords, according to Weber, are derived from those seven fundamental harmonies through chromatic alteration, linear embellishment, or the addition of tones. But not all harmony is reducible to these seven chords. Weber acknowledged more complex, yet independent harmonies, such as major and minor ninth chords. Their existence was based upon examples from the literature in which the dissonant ninth, in his view, is not treated as a suspension.

Weber presented his theory of chordal scale degrees following his discussion of the fundamental harmonies and their transformations. In Weber's judgment, the tonic, dominant, dominant seventh, and subdominant chords express a key in its simplest form. These harmonies, as well as the remaining diatonic chords, are built upon the degrees of the major and minor scales. Weber utilized Vogler's roman numeral notation, but he refined it by using upper and lower cases so as to be able to distinguish the qualities of triads. The result is fourteen fundamental harmonies (triads and seventh chords) in the major mode and ten in minor. (A listing of Weber's fundamental harmonies along with their roman numeral symbols may be found in **Example 23.3, p. 735.**)

Weber's next concern was – like Rameau's – how these harmonies may progress from one to another. He calculated that there exist more than six thousand possible progressions.[20] Many of these progressions are unusual or harsh-sounding. However, Weber was reluctant to provide the reader with rules for determining acceptable and unacceptable progressions, since some of the less agreeable-sounding progressions might be usable within a specific musical context. He criticized fundamental-bass theory for its focus on generalized prescriptions for harmonic succession as doomed to failure. Theory should never set arbitrary limitations for art, he argued; it is through the analysis of works of art that theory should deduce its rules.[21] For example, Weber cited the rule, dictated by fundamental-bass theory, prohibiting the descent of the fundamental bass by step. He offered a counterexample with a passage from Mozart's Requiem where the fundamental bass descends from IV to iii to ii to I (albeit as parallel 6/3 chords).[22]

Weber invoked the empirical judgment of the ear to define a key in terms of relationships around the tonic:

> When our ear perceives a succession of tones and harmonies, it naturally endeavours to find, amidst this multiplicity and variety, an internal connection – a relationship to a common central point. For, as, in every art, the mind spontaneously desires to find a certain unity in the multiplicity – a centrality of the manifold parts – so it does here. The

20 Ibid., vol. II, p. 173. 21 Ibid., p. 204.
22 Ibid., p. 204. The example in question is the "Domine Jesu" movement. A similar progression of step-wise fundamental-bass motion (in this case ascending) can be seen in m. 3 of Example 25.2 below.

> ear everywhere longs to perceive some tone as a principal and central tone, some harmony as a principal harmony, around which the others revolve as accessories around their principal, that is, around the predominant harmony.[23]

The tonic, conceived in this manner, is the central point, an axis in relation to which the remaining harmonies are disposed. A key exerts its identity through the presence of chords built upon its scale degrees, and it continues to exert this identity by a kind of inertia (*Trägheit*) until a new chord not belonging to the original key is heard and establishes a new tonal center. Thus, unlike Rameau, Weber never held a unifying conception of tonality in which various modulations could be subsumed within a single governing key. For Weber, each modulation constituted a real change of key. Example 25.2 illustrates this approach in an analysis of a march from Mozart's *Die Zauberflöte*. The letters identify the chord tones: R = root, T = third, and F = fifth; the solid slashes indicate non-harmonic tones. There are modulations from F major to C major (mm. 5–8), and back to F major (m. 9), which is then interrupted by "slight digressions" (not shown) into G minor (m. 11) and D minor (m. 13). The excerpt concludes with a "digression" to C major (which proceeds immediately back to F major).

During the eighteenth century, German theorists sometimes referred to relationships between keys using the term *Verwandtschaft*. Keys were typically classified according to similarities in pitch content between diatonic collections.[24] Such discussions found their way into nineteenth-century treatises, including Weber's *Versuch*. His graphic illustration of key relations (*Tonartenverwandtschaften*) is shown in Plate 25.1.[25]

Weber classified keys according to their *Verwandtschaftgrade* or degrees of relationship with the tonic: first-degree relationships occur between adjacent keys on the horizontal and vertical axes of Weber's chart. For example, G major, F major, A minor, and C minor are related to C major in the first degree. Keys immediately adjacent to those related to the tonic in the first degree stand in a second-degree relationship to the tonic. Thus, D major, G minor, E♭ major, A major, F minor, D minor, E minor, and B♭ major are all related to C major in the second degree. Third-degree relationships occur between the tonic and keys adjacent to those keys related to the tonic in the second degree. B minor, E major, F♯ minor, B♭ minor, A♭ major, and E♭ minor all stand in a third-degree relationship to C major.

Weber's tonal grid exhaustively measures all key relationships according to their proximity to any tonic key, and thus supplants the more limited conceptual mapping of key relations afforded by the eighteenth-century musical circle (see **Plate 13.1, p. 445**). It is one of the first of many such tonal charts (or *Tonnetze*) conceived by theorists, including Arthur von Oettingen (**Figure 14.3, p. 463**), Ottokar Hostinský (**Plate 23.1, p. 737**) and Arnold Schoenberg (see below, Plate 25.2). Like Schoenberg, Weber takes

23 Weber, *Theory of Composition*, vol. I, pp. 253–54.

24 For example, see Kirnberger, *The Art of Strict Musical Composition*, pp. 123–27. For a survey of eighteenth- and nineteenth-century discussion of *Verwandtschaft* and particularly several interesting circular models depicting degrees of relationships in all twenty-four major and minor keys, see Werts, "The Musical Circle of Johannes Mattheson."

25 Weber, *Versuch*, vol. II, p. 81.

Example 25.2 Weber's analysis of a passage from Mozart's *Die Zauberflöte* from *The Theory of Musical Composition*, vol. I, Fig. 232, p. 399

into account both similarities in pitch content and parallelisms in scalar structure. The keys on the vertical axes relate by the cycle of fifths, and thus according to their scalar pitch content. The keys on horizontal axes are organized by parallel and relative major/minor relationships; they are grouped by their structural similarities (such as a common dominant and root of the tonic triad, as in the case with C major and C minor). The scale, however, retains its organizing role in Weber's theory. His discussion of key relationships remains consistent with the orientation of his approach to harmony as a theory of chordal scale degrees.

Vogler's concept of "multiple meaning" (*Mehrdeutigkeit*) becomes a critical component in Weber's analytical theory; he applied the notion far beyond the more limited domain envisioned by Vogler to model the cognitive choices an ideal listener faces when closely attending to any given musical progression.[26] Weber's approach to multiple

26 For a detailed discussion of these applications, see Saslaw, "Gottfried Weber and Multiple Meaning."

TABELLE

der Tonartenverwandtschaften.

C	a	A	fis	Fis	dis	Dis	his	His	gisis
F	d	D	h	H	gis	Gis	eis	Eis	cisis
B	g	G	e	E	cis	Cis	ais	Ais	fisis
Es	c	C	a	A	fis	Fis	dis	Dis	his
As	f	F	d	D	h	H	gis	Gis	eis
Des	b	B	g	G	e	E	cis	Cis	ais
Ges	es	Es	c	C	a	A	fis	Fis	dis
Ces	as	As	f	F	d	D	h	H	gis
Fes	des	Des	b	B	g	G	e	E	cis
Bes	ges	Ges	es	Es	c	C	a	A	fis
Eses	ces	Ces	as	As	f	F	d	D	h
Ases	fes	Fes	des	Des	b	B	g	G	e
Deses	bes	Bes	ges	Ges	es	Es	c	C	a

Plate 25.1 Weber's chart of key relationships from the *Versuch*, (2nd edn.) vol. II, p. 81

meaning is clearly to be seen in his celebrated analysis of the introduction of Mozart's "Dissonance" Quartet (K. 465), a passage whose clashing dissonances and meandering modulations confounded contemporary critics.[27] The first four measures of the quartet are shown in a reduction in Example 25.3.

The opening C in the cello is ambiguous, according to Weber, and shows the multiple meaning a single pitch may project. The listener, upon hearing the solitary C, does not

27 Weber's analysis appears in the 1830–32 edition of his *Versuch*, vol. III, pp. 196–226.

Example 25.3 Mozart, "Dissonance" Quartet (K. 465), first movement, mm. 1–4, reduction

know whether the key is C major or C minor. The A♭ played by the viola on the last beat creates yet another ambiguity; Weber claimed that it is unclear whether the interval formed with the C is an augmented fifth (C–G♯) or a minor sixth (C–A♭). In the former interpretation, G♯ is an incomplete neighbor of A. The latter may be construed as part of an A♭ major triad (I in A♭ major or VI in C minor) or an F minor triad (iv in C minor or i in F minor). The entrance of the E♭ by the second violin in m. 2 narrows down the possibilities to the first set of interpretations. But Weber notes that it remains to be seen whether the A♭ is in fact a chord tone or an embellishment of the following G. When the A♭ does in fact proceed to G, the first violin sounds at the same time an A♮, thus creating a "startling" cross relation with the A♭. The resultant harmony itself possesses multiple meanings; as a half-diminished seventh chord (A–C–E♭–G) it may be registered either as vii^{ø7} in B♭ major or ii^{ø7} in G minor. When the G in the viola part moves to F♯ and the E♭ moves to D in the second violin, this ambiguity is temporarily resolved; the ear realizes that G was in fact not a chord tone. The harmony in m. 2 is actually a D^{7} chord, the dominant of the dominant in C minor to which it resolves in m. 3. Weber's harmonic analysis, which extends through m. 8, continues to track an idealized listener's perception of the passage chord by chord. The result is an analysis that is historically noteworthy for its elegant descriptive language and its quasi-phenomenological awareness of musical harmony as it unfolds in time.[28]

Weber's roman numeral notation system achieved widespread popularity in the second half of the nineteenth century, appearing in treatises, for example, by Ernst Friedrich Richter, Salomon Jadassohn, and Simon Sechter.[29] His ideas also migrated to France, where they were incorporated first by Daniel Jelensperger (1830), and then later in Gustave Lefèvre's *Traité d'harmonie* (1889). An English translation by James Warner in 1842 introduced Weber's practical approach to harmony to British readers. (His influence is particularly evident in the writings of the most important Victorian theorist, Ebenezer Prout.) And a subsequent reissue of Warner's translation in Boston helped to establish a roman numeral style of harmonic analysis in America during the

28 Ian Bent provides a most illuminating discussion of this famous analysis by Weber as an introduction to his translation of this excerpt in *MANC*, vol. I, pp. 157–60.

29 Richter, *Lehrbuch*; Sechter, *Grundsätze*; Jadassohn, *Melodik und Harmonik*. See also **Chapter 2, p. 64**.

nineteenth century (especially in the writings of Percy Goetschius and George W. Chadwick).[30]

Viennese fundamental-bass theory

Rameau's primary legacy to the nineteenth century, as already suggested, lay not so much in the specifics of his theory of the fundamental bass as in the more expansive notions of harmonic tonality he bequeathed, well exemplified in the *Stufentheorie* of Weber. Nonetheless, aspects of Rameau's fundamental bass survived well into the nineteenth century. This was especially so in Vienna, where arguably the most full-blown theory of the fundamental bass ever conceived was taught by Simon Sechter.

Sechter. A respected church organist and renowned contrapuntist, Simon Sechter (1788–1867) became perhaps the most influential teacher of music theory in Vienna during the nineteenth century, eventually earning a prestigious appointment at the Vienna Conservatory, where he taught, among others, the young composer Anton Bruckner. (See also **Chapter 2, p. 62.**) His theoretical works, most notably his *Grundsätze der musikalischen Komposition* (1853–54), helped to revitalize Viennese harmonic theory, which had hitherto been dominated by a rather regressive reliance upon classical figured-bass pedagogy. Disseminated by his many students, Sechter's teachings eventually found their way into twentieth-century treatises on harmony by Schoenberg and Schenker.[31]

Sechter brought to the thorough-bass teachings of his contemporaries an infusion of both fundamental-bass theory and chordal scale-degree theory.[32] Not unlike Weber, Sechter begins his *Grundsätze* with the scale, and he proceeds to an examination of the chords formed on each of its degrees. Sechter lists both triads and seventh chords as fundamental harmonies. (And as with most other *Stufentheorie* pedagogues, Sechter does not try to justify the generation of these chords in any scientific way.) Since he conflates the three traditional forms of the minor scale into one, he arrives at thirteen diatonic triads in a minor key and seven in a major. To label these harmonies, Sechter utilizes both letter notation and the roman numerals popularized by Vogler and Weber. A key, according to Sechter, is articulated by the presence of a scale's diatonic degrees. This is most clearly seen in the "Sechterian Chain" (*Sechtersche Kette*) of descending fifths shown in Example 25.4a, which represents for Sechter the paradigmatic and ideal harmonic motion of tonal music. In Example 25.4b, the paradigmatic

30 For a survey of late nineteenth-century American harmonic theory see Thompson, *History of Harmonic Theory in the United States*; Baron, "At the Cutting Edge: Three American Theorists" examines another, more "radical" tradition during the same period.

31 A story comprehensively narrated by Robert Wason in *Viennese Harmonic Theory*.

32 Dahlhaus, *Studies*, p. 33; Wason, *Viennese Harmonic Theory*, p. 33.

Example 25.4
(a) "Sechterian chain" of falling fifths

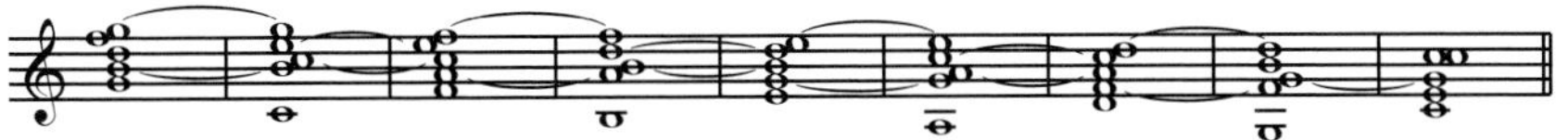

(b) Sechter's "reciprocal effect"

falling fifth fundamental-bass motion appears with its reversal, i.e., an ascending fifth progression, yielding what Sechter termed a *Wechselwirkung* – a "reciprocal effect."

As mentioned above, Sechter does not try to justify the generation of harmonies through recourse to the harmonic overtone series, as would Rameau, although ironically, he authored a treatise on acoustics.[33] Sechter's debt to Rameau, however, is clear. As did Rameau, Sechter attributes a fundamental tone to every chord. The progression of these tones by the fundamental bass was limited to the intervallic structure of Rameau's *l'accord parfait*, that is, by ascending or descending fifths and thirds. Fundamental-bass movement by a diminished fifth or the "impure" fifth between the second and sixth degrees are prohibited. (Sechter was a staunch advocate of just tuning, and the fifth between $\hat{2}$ and $\hat{6}$ in a justly tuned major scale is unusably narrow.) In cases where the fundamental bass ascends or descends by a step, Sechter adopts a technique that Rameau had occasionally used by interpolating a concealed fundamental (*Zwischenfundament*) between the two bass tones (see **Chapter 24, pp. 765–66**). As illustrated in Example 25.5a, an interpolated fundamental D mediates between F and G. In Example 25.5b, a descending fundamental-bass progression from G to F is explained as an elided sequence of fifths, with an interpolated fundamental of C implied. In both cases, the "impermissible" fundamental-bass progression of a major second is shown in fact to proceed by the permissible intervals of a perfect fifth or imperfect third.[34]

Example 25.6 shows the elaboration of a simple descending fifth fundamental bass; first with a passing seventh, then with a voice exchange between the bass and tenor, and finally with passing harmonies.[35] Example 25.7 is a more complicated chromatic

33 Sechter, *Abhandlungen über die musikalischen akustischen Tonverhältnisse*.
34 We should note here, as Wason points out (*Viennese Harmonic Theory*, p. 39), that Sechter probably was exposed to Rameau's theories through the writings of Johann Philipp Kirnberger and J. A. P. Schulz. Both Kirnberger and Schulz employed varieties of "passing harmonies" and interpolated basses far more extravagantly than did Rameau.
35 Sechter, *Grundsätze*, p. 38.

Example 25.5
(a) Ascending fundamental bass progression by step with "concealed" fundamental

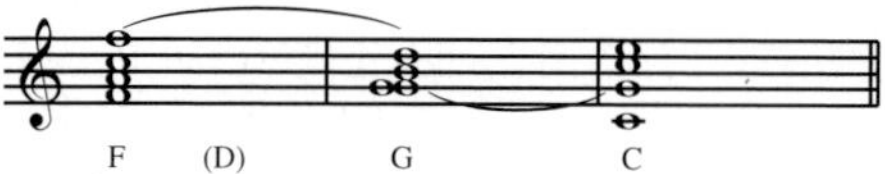

(b) Descending fundamental bass progression by step with "concealed" fundamental

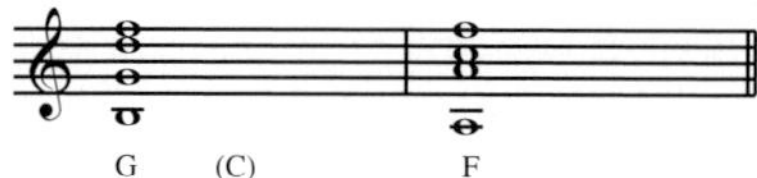

Example 25.6 Diatonic elaboration of a fundamental bass progression from Sechter's *Grundsätze*, p. 38

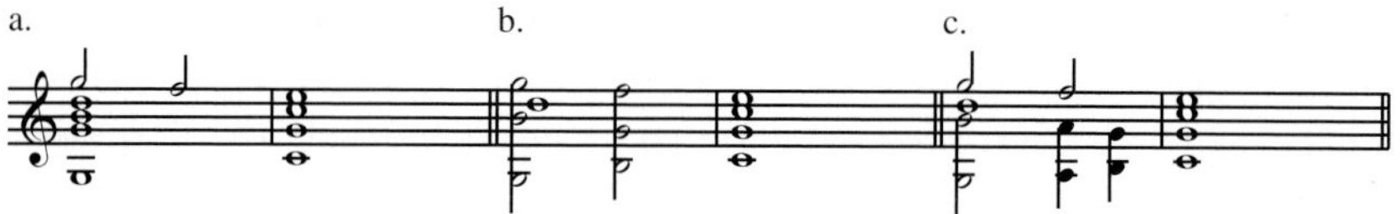

Example 25.7 Chromatic elaboration of a fundamental-bass progression progression from Sechter's *Grundsätze*, p. 200

elaboration of a descending fifth fundamental-bass progression.[36] The D and E major triads in m. 1 (as well as the G and A major triads in m. 2, and the C and D major triads in m. 3) are "subsidiary" harmonies (*Nebenharmonien*), not part of the authentic fundamental bass.

Scale-degree thinking likewise permeates Sechter's approach to chromaticism. Sechter considered chromatic chords to be essentially diatonic in nature, viewing

36 Ibid., p. 200.

them not – like Weber – as some kind of altered diatonic prototype, but rather as containing notes belonging to some neighboring key. Chromatic chords were consequently "hybrid chords" (*Zwitterakkorde*) made up of notes derived from multiple keys, an example being the augmented sixth chord. (We will see below an application of Sechter's notion of hybrid chords when considering the theories of Karl Mayrberger.)

Despite his extensive discussion of chromaticism, Sechter does not cite any contemporaneous music involving advanced chromaticism in his *Grundsätze*; his treatise is essentially anachronistic, a fusion of thorough-bass theory with Rameau's fundamental bass. As a result of his insistence upon just intonation, his views concerning modulation are also conservative. Published during a decade which would include the composition of Wagner's *Tristan*, the blinkered explanations of chromatic harmony in Sechter's *Grundsätze* proved to be of little help in deciphering the complexities increasingly to be heard in nineteenth-century harmony. This treatise espoused an essentially eighteenth-century view at a time when musical language was expanding in new directions. But, as recent scholarship has shown, by developing the implications of the concealed fundamental and possible extensions of fundamental-bass progressions (such as those given in Examples 25.6 and 25.7), Sechter opened up the possibility of conceiving scale degree in terms of broader spans.[37] In so doing, he can be said to have paved the way for the discussion of *Stufen* in Heinrich Schenker's *Harmonielehre* (1906) and his later theories of prolongation and structural levels.[38]

Sechter's influence continued after his death through the teachings of his student Anton Bruckner (1824–96). Bruckner, who also would hold a teaching position at the Vienna Conservatory and lectured at the University of Vienna,[39] promoted the conservative theories of his mentor despite his own compositional innovations. He did, however, introduce several new ideas into Sechterian theory, most notably his treatment of the ninth chord, which he considered a fundamental harmony rather than the result of a suspension.[40] The task of reconciling the growing rift between Viennese musical theory and contemporary musical practice, however, was left to several other theorists, among whom was Karl Mayrberger.

Mayrberger. Karl Mayrberger (1828–81) can be credited as the first music theorist to attempt a comprehensive analysis of the harmonic techniques employed by Wagner, and one approved, no less, by the composer himself. His analysis of selected leitmotives from *Tristan und Isolde* first appeared in the *Bayreuther Blätter* and was later expanded and published in monograph form.[41] Keenly aware of the radical developments in harmonic language taking place in the nineteenth century, Mayrberger

37 Wason, *Viennese Harmonic Theory*, pp. 45ff.
38 See Wason, "Schenker's Notion of Scale-Step in Historical Perspective."
39 Bruckner, *Vorlesungen über Harmonie und Kontrapunkt an der Universität Wien.*
40 Wason, *Viennese Harmonic Theory*, pp. 71ff.
41 Mayrberger, *Die Harmonik Richard Wagners.*

Example 25.8 Mayrberger's analysis of the *Tristan Prelude*, mm. 1–3

mm. 1 2 3

Fundamentals: A D B E
Scale Degrees:
A–Minor: 1. 4. 2. 5.
E–Minor/Major: 5. 1.

attempted to adapt Sechterian fundamental-bass theory to contemporary practice. In the foreword of his monograph on *Tristan*, he presents a view of harmonic evolution that might have come from Fétis:

> The harmonic language of the present day is on a footing essentially different from that of the past. Richard Wagner has pointed the musical world along the path that it must henceforth travel. The sixteenth century knew only the realm of the diatonic. In the eighteenth century, the diatonic and the chromatic existed side by side, equal in status. The nineteenth century, in the work of Beethoven, Schubert, Weber, and Spohr, gravitated more and more towards chromaticism. But with Richard Wagner an altogether new era begins: major and minor intermingle, and the realm of the diatonic gives way to that of the chromatic and the enharmonic.[42]

Like Sechter, Mayrberger considered all three forms of the minor scale when laying out the available diatonic triads and seventh chords in the minor mode. So, for example, all of the following chords could be attributed to "D minor" by using its raised and lowered sixth and seventh scale degrees: B♭–D–F–A, B–D–F–A, C–E–G–B♭, C♯–E–G–B♭, and F–A–C♯–E. Following the tenets of Sechterian theory, Meyrberger considered chromatic chords as composite diatonic chords or "hybrid chords" (*Zwitterakkorde*) whose chromatically inflected pitches stem from keys other than the tonic. B–D♯–F–A, in A minor, for example, is an altered seventh chord on the second degree whose D♯ is borrowed from E minor.

The same harmony occurs most notably in Mayrberger's analysis of the opening of the *Tristan Prelude* (see Example 25.8). His interpretation reveals that the entire opening section conforms to fundamental bass progressions sanctioned by Sechterian theory. In the first phrase (mm. 1–3), the opening leap from A to F occurs over a fundamental bass which ascends a fourth from A to D. The E in the first measure is a passing tone and the G♯ in m. 2 is a lower neighbor, derived diatonically from A

42 Mayrberger, "The Harmonic Style of Richard Wagner," p. 226. For Fétis's views on the evolution of harmony, see Chapter 23, pp. 748–49.

Example 25.9 Mayrberger's analysis of the *Tristan Prelude*, mm. 5–7

mm. 5 6 7

Fundamentals:	B	E	A	D	G
Scale Degrees:					
A–Minor:	2.	5.	1.	4.	
D–Minor:			5.		
C–Minor/Major:				2.	5.
G–Minor/Major:				5.	1.

minor. The harmony in m. 2 is thus, as noted above, a "hybrid" chord (B–D♯–F–A) and is registered in two keys: the second scale-degree in A minor and the fifth scale-degree in E minor/major.[43] The fundamental bass thus moves down a third to B and up a fourth to E. The A♯ in measure three is a chromatic embellishment, which he terms "melodic chromatic" as opposed to the "harmonic chromatic" of D♯ in m. 2 (chromatic pitches which are members of a given harmony).[44]

In the second phrase (Example 25.9), Mayrberger interprets the G♮ in m. 5 as a chord tone, the seventh of a tonic harmony in A minor or of a dominant in D. He cannot treat the note as a passing tone as he did with the E♮ in m. 1, since this would result in the "illegitimate" fundamental-bass progression of a descending second from E to D in mm. 5 and 6. He thus likens the entire progression in the second phrase to a succession of dominant seventh chords with a fundamental bass proceeding from B to E, A, D, and ending on G. As in the initial phrase, the first note in the upper voice in m. 6 is a chromatic embellishment; here the *Tristan* chord is a doubly hybrid chord, borrowing its chromatic pitches from three keys: A minor, C major/minor, and G major/minor.

Mayrberger did not label the opening of the third phrase (Example 25.10), no doubt because he viewed it as a continuation of the G fundamental at the end of the second phrase. (This interpretation would thence require a "concealed" fundamental bass E in order to avoid the fundamental-bass progression of an ascending second from G to the A in m. 10.) His rendering of the third appearance of the *Tristan* chord reduces this

43 Many analysts today would argue that the G♯ rather than the A is the true chord tone. (This view is supported by the voice exchange between the soprano and tenor in mm. 2 through 3.) In fact, several of Mayrberger's contemporaries favored the latter interpretation. Cyrill Kistler (1848–1907), known for his adaptation of Moritz Hauptmann's theories to Wagner's music, analyzed the *Tristan* chord as a minor triad with a diminished seventh (G♯–B–D♯–F). See Kistler, *Harmonielehre*, p. 82. See also Jadassohn, *Melodik und Harmonik bei Richard Wagner*, p. 27; Arend, "Harmonische Analyse des Tristanvorspiels," pp. 160–69; Schreyer, *Harmonielehre*, pp. 223ff.

44 Mayrberger, "The Harmonic Style of Richard Wagner," p. 228.

Example 25.10 Mayrberger's analysis of the *Tristan Prelude*, mm. 8–11

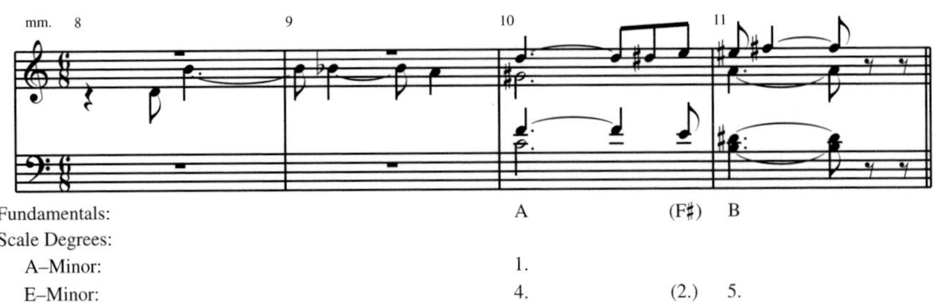

harmony to an A minor triad despite the similarities with the first and second phrases; the D is a freely suspended eleventh which resolves upwards through a chromatic passing tone D♯ to E; the G♯ and F are also suspensions.[45] The phrase concludes with a progression from A to B through a "hidden" fundamental F♯.

Mayrberger's *Tristan* analysis demonstrates that the rigid limitations of fundamental-bass theory were not easily adaptable to the complexities of Wagnerian harmony. This is especially apparent in his interpretations of passages with ascending chromatic bass progressions. For example, on the progression from an F major to an F♯ minor triad (as occurs in for example in the "Motive of the ailing Tristan"), Mayrberger applied the notion of a "harmonic ellipsis," a theoretical concept which he added to the panoply of Sechterian analytical tools. Just as in rhetoric where a word or phrase can be omitted without altering the meaning of a passage, this phenomenon can occur in music, according to Mayrberger, when the resolution of a dissonance is elided, yet at the same time its resolution is fully understood by the listener. This principle also applies to chords which, as Mayrberger explains, "function in a purely mediating capacity between two harmonies."[46] Mayrberger claimed that the progression from F major to F♯ minor could then be understood by virtue of an interpolated diminished seventh chord (B–D–F–A♭). The "insertion" of this harmony allows for an acceptable diatonic fundamental-bass progression from F to B. The interpolated chord then can be enharmonically reinterpreted as an E♯ diminished seventh chord (E♯–G♯–B–D) allowing a fundamental-bass interpretation of E♯–C♯ that finally resolves to the F♯ minor chord. Such theoretical hypotheses seem to stretch aural credulity and exemplify the growing crisis faced by music theorists in the second half of the nineteenth century as they sought to reconcile theoretical traditions rooted in the eighteenth century with the increasingly complex harmonic practices of composers like Wagner.

45 Ibid., p. 229. 46 Ibid., p. 242.

German function theory

Rameau first employed the term subdominant (*sous-dominante*) for the chord built on the fourth scale degree in his *Nouveau système* (1726) (see **Chapter 24, p. 768**). But it was only in his *Génération harmonique* of 1737 that Rameau fully explored the functional importance of the subdominant, treating it as an equal and symmetrical counterpart to the *dominante* (having dropped the earlier and more cumbersome appellation *dominante-tonique* as a descriptive for the fifth scale degree). Each of these chords has its own characteristic dissonance: a seventh for the dominant, and an added sixth for the subdominant. Each may also form a cadence with the tonic: the subdominant ascends a perfect fifth (or descends a perfect fourth) in an imperfect cadence (*cadence imparfaite*); the dominant descends a perfect fifth (or ascends a perfect fourth) in a perfect cadence (*cadence parfaite*). In his *Nouveau système*, Rameau represented this symmetrical relationship by the geometric proportion 1:3:9. The tonic (3) is flanked on opposite sides by its subdominant (1) and dominant (9) (see **Example 23.2, p. 734** and **Figure 24.1, p. 769**).

Perhaps the most significant implication of Rameau's new theory of three primary harmonies is seen in his reconceptualization of tonality; he now began to conceive of a key in terms of harmonic relationships around a tonal center. With his *Génération harmonique*, he moved away from a Cartesian mechanistic explanation of tonality based on the linking of dissonant and consonant chords to an entelechial model inspired by Newtonian gravitational theory.[47] In this latter sense, tonality results from the forces of attraction between the tonic and its dominant and subdominant harmonies.

Rameau's hypostatization of the tonic, dominant, and subdominant as fundamental harmonic functions had a significant impact upon a number of subsequent German music theorists, including Johann Friedrich Daube (*General-Bass in drey Accorden*, 1756), Christoph Gottlieb Schröter (*Deutliche Anweisung zum General-Bass*, 1772), and Heinrich Christoph Koch (*Versuch einer Anleitung zur Composition*, 1782–93).[48] For Daube and Schröter, as the titles of their treatises would suggest, Rameau's reduction of all chordal harmonies to three fundamental prototypes was primarily of utilitarian value for the learning of the thorough bass. (Essentially, any signature could be "realized" by playing one of these three fundamental chord types, albeit with occasional necessary modifications.) For Koch, the value of Rameau's theory lay more in its compositional implications. The writing of harmony was immensely simplified by thinking of the three primary functions as "essential" (*wesentlich*), while chords on the second, third, and sixth degrees were "incidental" (*zufällig*).

47 Christensen, *Rameau and Musical Thought*, pp. 132ff.

48 Georg Andreas Sorge (1703–78) also adumbrated a version of harmonic functionalism influenced by Rameau in his *Vorgemach* (1745), although it was not one he ever developed systematically.

But despite its widespread adoption by German theorists in the later eighteenth century, Rameau's theory of three primary harmonies did not seem to inspire any theorist to consider more deeply the tonal, functional problems with which Rameau wrestled in his *Génération harmonique*. Rameau's ideas here would remain largely dormant until resurrected almost a century later by a remarkable group of German speculative theorists, led by Hugo Riemann (1849–1919).

Riemann. Properly speaking, "functionality" in tonal music concerns the behavior of chords in relation to the tonic. A function theory differs from a theory of chordal scale degrees (*Stufentheorie*) in that the former goes beyond the description of chords according to their position within the scale and constitutes a systematic ratiocination of chordal relationships around a tonal center. The theoretical underpinning for Riemann's theory of function, what he referred to as its "musical logic," lies in the dualistic interpretation of the *Klang*: the harmonic entities that may be derived – either acoustically or psychologically – from the resonance of a fundamental sound. Riemann postulated a "dual" basis for harmony by claiming that the *Klang* generates – as Rameau claimed in the *Génération harmonique* – both a major and a minor harmony. The minor harmony is a symmetrical inversion of the major harmony in that the major triad consists of a fifth and a major third above the principal tone, while the minor triad is formed by the same intervals below. (Riemann's dualism is discussed in more detail in Chapter 14, pp. 465ff.) Dualism becomes entangled with functional theory in that dominant and subdominant harmonies become reciprocally generated from the tonic *Klang*: the dominant as based upon the "over" fifth, and the subdominant based upon the "under" fifth.

In an intellectual evolution that is comparable again only to Rameau's, Riemann's theory of tonal functions emerged laboriously over a career that lasted more than forty years.[49] In his earliest writings, beginning with his dissertation, "Über das musikalische Hören" (1873), later published as a monograph entitled *Musikalische Logik* (1874), the influence of Moritz Hauptmann looms conspicuously. Like Hauptmann, Riemann was concerned with the logic of chordal relationships, and he developed the dialectical model of harmonic functions that Hauptmann had earlier outlined in which a "thetic" tonic is contrasted with an "antithetic" subdominant leading to a "synthetic" dominant.[50] Riemann described the remaining, "secondary" harmonies in terms of their

49 A detailed discussion of Riemann's harmonic theory and its evolution may be found in Harrison, *Harmonic Function*, pp. 252–92. Also see Mooney, "'Table of Relations' and Music Psychology in Hugo Riemann's Chromatic Theory"; Seidel, "Die Harmonielehre Hugo Riemanns." A less systematic, although nonetheless revealing comparison between Riemann's functional theory and earlier traditions of fundamental-bass theory and *Stufentheorie* is given in Dahlhaus, *Studies on the Origin of Harmonic Tonality*, Chapter 1, esp. pp. 47–59.

50 Riemann, *Musikalische Logik*, pp. 52–53. Further discussion of Hauptmann's theories may be found in Chapter 14, pp. 759–62.

association with one (and in some cases two) of these three primary chords, an approach which foreshadows his later classification of tonal harmonies according to three functional categories. In another early treatise, entitled *Musikalische Syntaxis* (1877), Riemann abandoned much of Hauptmann's dialectical terminology; instead, he centered the unity of a harmonic progression around the tonic or "thesis" which may combine with chords from two "sides." A one-sided thesis consists of either all major or all minor harmonies; a two-sided thesis combines both major and minor chords.

Riemann's mature theory of tonal functions appeared first in his *Vereinfachte Harmonielehre* (1893; translated as "Harmony Simplified") and then in the third edition of his *Handbuch der Harmonielehre* (1898). As in his early writings, he continued to utilize a notational system that described the acoustical derivation of chords based upon dualist premises. For example, "$^+$" denotes a major or *Oberklang*; "$^\circ$" stands for a minor or *Unterklang*. C^+ represents a major triad generated above a C fundamental; $^\circ C$ is a minor triad generated downward from its "prime," C (C–A♭–F). But now he grouped all harmonic possibilities within a key into three functional prototypes based on the dualistic model of the *Klang*: tonic (T), dominant (D), and subdominant (S). He then developed an analytical nomenclature to show the relationships of any chord to one of the three functional categories that, if at times pushing aural credulity in its audacious reductionist sweep, is also impressive in its appealing symmetries and undeniable logical unity. (Riemann's function symbols are summarized in the window on p. 798).

The tonic, dominant, and subdominant harmonies are shown to constitute the three pillars of the tonal system; all the remaining harmonies are derivatives of these three primary chords. (Even a single note should suggest affiliation to one of these three functions through the principle of *Klangvertretung* or "chord representation.") The association of the primary and secondary chords within a key depends upon Riemann's concept of "apparent consonance" (*Scheinkonsonanz*). For example, the *Subdominantparallel* ("Sp" or A–F–D in C major) results from an added sixth (D) and omitted fifth of the subdominant harmony (F–A–C). The D is a dissonance, according to Riemann, since it is contingent on the fifth, C. Although the D sounds as if it were a consonance, it is actually an "apparent consonance" because it is not a member of the *Klang* (F–A–C). In the same manner, the mediant (B–G–E) or Dp (*Dominantparallel*) is derived from the dominant (the D is displaced by the E) and the submediant or Tp (*Tonikparallel*) (E–C–A) is derived from the tonic (the G is displaced by the A). Similarly, "leading-tone-change" chords (*Leittonwechselklänge*) are alterations of the three primary harmonies. The tonic "leading-tone-change" chord (B–G–E) or T̸ is an altered tonic in which the "leading tone" B substitutes for the C as the generative root of the chord; the subdominant "leading-tone-change" chord (E–C–A) or S̸ is likewise an altered subdominant in which the E replaces the F as root, while the dominant "leading-tone-change" chord (F♯–D–B) or D̸ is an altered dominant in which an F♯

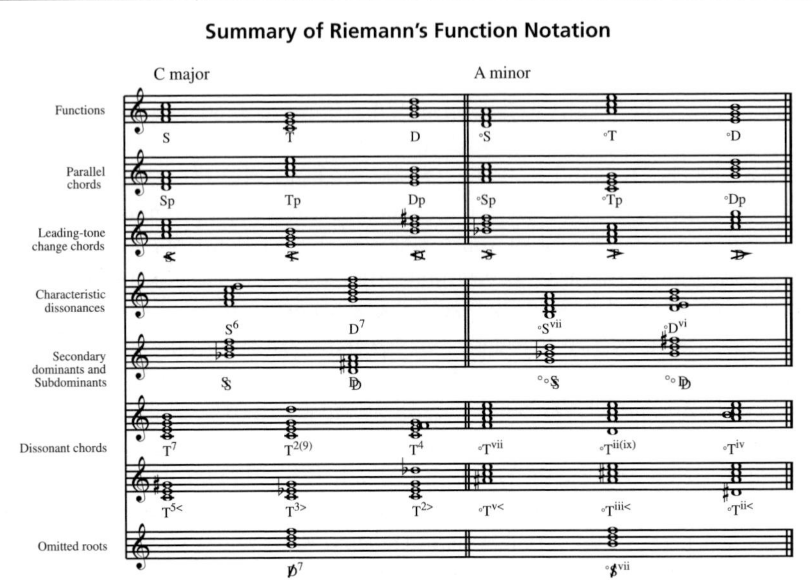

S, T, D = major subdominant, tonic, and subdominant functions.
°S, °T, °D = minor subdominant, tonic, and dominant functions.
Sp, Tp, Dp = "major" parallel chords (*Parallelklänge*). The fifth above the root of a major chord is replaced by a sixth.
°Sp, °Tp, °Dp = "minor" parallel chords (*Parallelklänge*). The fifth below the prime of a minor chord is replaced by a sixth.
S̸, T̸, D̸ = "major" leading-tone change chords (*Leittonwechselklänge*). The root of a major chord is replaced by its leading-tone.
S̸, T̸, D̸ = "minor" leading-tone change chords (*Leittonwechselklänge*). The prime of a minor chord is replaced by its leading-tone.

Arabic numbers refer to intervals (both consonant and dissonant) above the root of a major chord. Roman numerals refer to intervals (both consonant and dissonant) below the prime (the highest note) of a minor chord.
"<" raises a note.
">" lowers a note.
"/" through a number or letter indicates that note is omitted.
Đ or (D) = secondary dominant
S̶ or (S) = secondary subdominant

substitutes for the G. (The resulting chain of interlocking triads is illustrated in **Example 23.4, p. 738**, transposed to G major.) In addition, Riemann outlines a systematic network of chordal transformations by which all the various functions could be connected, constituting a kind of functional harmonic syntax. (See **Table 14.1, p. 471** for an itemization of these transformations.)

$\not{S}$ — $D^{7}_{5>}$ — T (E major)
. . $^{3>}$ = $^{\circ}$S — D^{7} — T (B major)
. . $^{5>}_{3>}$ = $\not{D}\!D$ — D — T (F major)
Sp — D — T (F major)

Figure 25.1 "Cadences" in the first period of the slow movement from Beethoven, "Waldstein" Sonata, Op. 53

Riemann's analysis of the introduction from the slow movement of Beethoven's "Waldstein" sonata illustrates an application of his functional theory and its attendant notational system (see **Example 21.17, pp. 689–90**).[51] The introduction is divided into three periods (as indicated by roman numerals above the staff).[52] The first period, constituting mm. 1 through 9, contains four cadences. The first ends on the dominant (D) of A minor (m. 2). The opening tonic is repeated (the notated ellipse indicates a repeated function) and re-interpreted as the "minor" subdominant parallel of A minor ("= °Sp" in m. 1 indicates this change in function) which moves to an augmented-sixth chord functioning as a secondary dominant in that key (DD). The next cadence proceeds to the dominant of E minor (m. 4). In m. 3, the third of the dominant in m. 2 is lowered ($^{3>}$), and this harmony is reinterpreted as the minor subdominant of B minor which moves to a secondary dominant in E minor. The third cadence ends on the dominant of F major (m. 6). This progression begins in m. 5 by repeating the dominant from the previous measure with a lowered fifth and third ($^{5>}_{3>}$ – the root, G, is implied), which then becomes a secondary dominant in F major. The secondary dominant is chromatically altered to become an augmented-sixth chord by lowering its fifth and omitting its root ($\not{D}\!D^{7}_{5>}$) and moves to a dominant and then a dominant seventh in m. 6. The fourth cadence ends on the tonic of F major (m. 9), approached from its subdominant parallel and dominant harmonies.

In the commentary accompanying his analysis, Riemann notes that the four progressions in the first period look back to the opening movement which begins with a phrase (mm. 1–4) also employing a secondary dominant.[53] In this case, the secondary dominant in m. 2 resolves on the dominant of C major in m. 3 (T–DD–D). The second phrase (mm. 5–8) transposes the progression so that it concludes on the subdominant. Riemann claims that the two phrases may also be interpreted in the keys of G and F major. Similarly in the second movement the four cadences in the first period imply the keys of E major, B major, and F major (Figure 25.1).[54]

51 Riemann, *Ludwig van Beethoven sämtliche Klavier-Solosonaten*, vol. III, pp. 32–3. Another example of Riemann's Beethoven analyses is shown in **Examples 28.1–2, pp. 894–97**.

52 The arabic numbers in parentheses below the staff refer to the phrase structure. For more on this notation, see **Chapter 21, p. 688**.

53 Riemann, *Ludwig van Beethoven sämtliche Klavier-Solosonaten*, vol. III, p. 30.

54 Ibid. See Smith, "The Functional Extravagance of Chromatic Chords," for a modern approach to the functional ambiguities in this passage.

The second period, m. 9 through 17, largely consists of a repeated tonic in F major according to Riemann's analysis. Reference to the actual score shows that his interpretation takes into account the chromatic and diatonic embellishment of tonic harmony in this passage (see, for example, m. 10 in the score). Despite the obvious harmonic orientation of his theory, Riemann was not willing to label every simultaneity as a chord.[55] He also observed the similarities between the first and third periods (mm. 17–28). Noteworthy departures from the opening period include the dominant chord with a lowered ninth and omitted root ($\not{D}^{9>}$) in m. 21, the extended minor subdominant (°S) in mm. 22 through 24 (with an added raised "under" ninth [$°S^{ix<}$] in m. 22), and the dominant seventh in mm. 24 and 25 (which is chromatically altered in m. 26 and becomes a dominant seventh with a raised root [$D^{7}_{1>}$], reinterpreted as a dominant with a lowered ninth and omitted root [$\not{D}^{9>}$] of the A minor triad or tonic parallel (Tp) in m. 27).

Riemann's harmonic theory gained unprecedented influence during his lifetime. To be sure, there was considerable resistance to the more dogmatic aspects of his dualistic premises. (As discussed in Chapter 14, Riemann was eventually compelled to move away from a purely acoustical argument on behalf of his theory of dualism to a more psychological, almost idealist justification.) Yet his theory of functionality became widely adopted throughout Europe and, indeed, is still clearly to be seen in harmony textbooks in Germany, Scandinavia, and Russia today.[56] No theorist since Rameau had offered a more compelling, comprehensive, and ultimately influential body of theoretical writings. Still, Riemann's theory was not without its critics.

Fin-de-siècle polemics and synthesis

The crucial stylistic changes taking place in music at the turn of the century presented a formidable challenge to harmonic theorists, as the received models of functionalism, scale-degree theory, and fundamental-bass theory seemed ill suited for the new music. The writings of two theorists – Georg Capellen and Arnold Schoenberg – well illustrate some of these challenges.

Capellen. As we have seen in **Chapter 14**, harmonic dualism was a dominating idea in German music theory during the last half of the nineteenth century. Beginning with mid-century treatises by Hauptmann and Oettingen, dualism later became the focus of Riemann's exhaustive theoretical work. At the turn of the century, the dualist school was sustained by theorists such as Herman Schröder, the author of an ambitious trea-

55 For Riemann's discussion of "figurative" dissonance, see *Harmony Simplified*, pp. 107–20.

56 For a comprehensive history of the reception of Riemann's theory, see Imig, *Funktionsbezeichnung in den Harmonielehren seit Hugo Riemann*. Also see **Chapter 2, pp. 64–65**.

tise on symmetrical inversion.[57] But dualism was not without its critics. Georg Capellen (1869–1934), a theorist as well as a composer, authored several treatises and articles criticizing the dualist element of early twentieth-century music theory.[58] One of Capellen's targets was naturally the leading proponent of harmonic dualism, Hugo Riemann.[59] Capellen proposed a "monistic" theory of harmony, thereby using a terminology that directly challenged the harmonic dualism of his opponent. His theory began with the overtone series, a single underlying principle which accounted for major and minor as well as all other harmonic phenomena. He maintained that the symmetrical relationship between major and minor triads is imperceptible and therefore invalid, explaining that the ear

> rejects the inversion that is noticeable by the eye, since it hears all the tones in a simultaneity from the bottom up (in terms of the fundamental) according to the law of gravity, which is also valid in music. *The external difference in direction entails a more profound difference in type.*[60]

Riemann replied with an article in his own defense,[61] but Capellen's criticism of harmonic dualism was reflected in the next generation's dissatisfaction with both the over-complexity of Riemann's theory and his failure to provide a sound explanation for the dualistic representation of the *Klang*.[62] In Europe, aside from the dualistic systems of Hermann Erpf (1891–1969) and Sigfried Karg-Elert (1877–1933),[63] harmonic dualism ended with Riemann.[64]

In another series of polemical exchanges, Capellen questioned the basic assumptions of Sechter's fundamental-bass theory and its suitability to Wagnerian analysis.[65] He considered the Sechterian approach to chromaticism too conservative; its emphasis on the diatonic scale resulted in theoretical contrivances such as "hybrid chords" with notes derivable from three and more scales[66] (see above, p. 791). In contrast, Capellen represents the more "German" stem of nineteenth-century harmonic theory with its ontological roots in the generative *Klang* to account for all harmonies. In a treatise entitled *Fortschrittliche Harmonie- und Melodielehre* (1908), Capellen outlined a theory of

57 Schröder, *Die symmetrische Umkehrung in der Musik*. For a discussion of Schröder's treatise as well as writings on symmetrical inversion by Georg Capellen and Bernhard Ziehn, see Bernstein, "Symmetry and Symmetrical Inversion."

58 Capellen, *Die Zukunft der Musiktheorie*; "Die Unmöglichkeit und Überflussigkeit der dualistischen Molltheorie Riemanns."

59 Capellen, *Die Zukunft der Musiktheorie*, p. 72.

60 Ibid., p. 74.

61 Riemann, "Das Problem des harmonischen Dualismus."

62 Imig, *Funktionsbezeichnung in den Harmonielehren seit Hugo Riemann*, pp. 135ff.

63 Erpf, *Studien zur Harmonie und Klangtechnik der neueren Musik*; Karg-Elert, *Polaristische Klang- und Tonalitätslehre*.

64 As we have seen in **Chapter 14, pp. 473–74**, however, revised theories of harmonic dualism have received some advocacy recently by a few American music theorists.

65 Capellen, "Harmonik und Melodik bei Richard Wagner"; *Ist das System S. Sechters*. For an essay examining Capellen's critique, see Bernstein, "Georg Capellen on *Tristan und Isolde*."

66 Bernstein, "Georg Capellen on *Tristan und Isolde*," p. 47.

harmony based upon the first nine partials of the overtone series. As with Catel some one hundred years earlier, an acoustically verifiable major ninth chord provided the raw material for a multiplicity of chordal types and relations.[67] Capellen even went as far as to claim that harmonies larger than a ninth chord (which he called *Doppelklänge*) may be generated by two concurrent fundamentals.

Schoenberg. As we have just seen, Capellen represented a tradition of monistic *Klang* theory that can be traced at least back to Vogler (and ultimately, as we have seen earlier, to Rameau). Although he did not rely upon acoustics, the monistic approach to harmonic generation was also taken up by Arnold Schoenberg (1874–1951). In a chapter on non-harmonic tones in his *Harmonielehre* (1911), Schoenberg rejected the distinction between harmony and figurative dissonance, claiming that there are

> no non-harmonic tones, no tones foreign to harmony, but merely tones foreign to the harmonic system. Passing tones, changing tones, suspensions, etc. are, like sevenths and ninths, nothing else but attempts to include in the possibilities of tones sounding together – these are of course, by definition, harmonies – something that sounds similar to the more remote overtones.[68]

Thus, according to Schoenberg, we can hear virtually any simultaneity as a chord. This theoretical assumption was consistent with his notion concerning the "emancipation of dissonance."[69] By challenging traditional distinctions between consonance and dissonance, a myriad of new harmonic configurations was thereby sanctioned, both tonal and nontonal, including chromatically altered chords, chords based on the whole-tone scale, fourth chords, and chords with six or more tones. Schoenberg examines these materials in his *Harmonielehre*, a treatise which demonstrates links between late nineteenth-century chromaticism and nontonal music. He saw the evolution of harmonic language as a process by which dissonant harmonies were gradually discovered, the figurative dissonances of one era becoming the harmonic dissonances of the future.[70] He supported this claim with examples from the music of Bach and Mozart in which several of his own nontonal harmonies appear as embellishing dissonances.[71]

Schoenberg's progressive approach to harmonic theory, as may be expected, aroused considerable opposition. This was particularly to be seen in the writings of a fellow Viennese theorist, his contemporary Heinrich Schenker. Unlike Schoenberg, Schenker was not concerned with the harmonic practice of his own time; he rejected Wagnerian harmony and blamed contemporary composers for the downfall of musical culture, describing its present catastrophic state as a veritable "Herculaneum and Pompeii of

67 For an overview of Capellen's theory of harmony, see Bernstein, "Georg Capellen's Theory of Reduction," pp. 86–92. For more on Catel, see **Chapter 2, pp. 60–61**.

68 Schoenberg, *Theory of Harmony*, p. 321. This statement and the commentary associated with it provoked one of Schenker's strongest critiques of Schoenberg.

69 Ibid., p. 21.

70 Ibid., p. 320.

71 Ibid., p. 324. See also Bernstein, "Georg Capellen's Theory of Reduction," pp. 108–09.

music."[72] Schenker was equally displeased with the development of harmonic theory. In a scathing attack on Rameau and his successors (among whom he would have included Schoenberg), he criticized theorists for overemphasizing vertical structure rather than voice leading.[73] The resultant de-emphasis of what Schenker called "the temporal-horizontal axis of musical motion" contributed to a "creeping paralysis in music" and to the demise of musical art.

If Schoenberg's *Harmonielehre* has a clear affiliation with the tradition of "monistic" harmonic theory traceable to Vogler, there are also other aspects of his theory that suggest a more synthetic approach in which the composer appears to be reconciling various strands of Viennese fundamental-bass theory and scale-degree theory.[74] It appears, for instance, that Schoenberg may have studied Sechterian fundamental-bass theory at the University of Vienna with Bruckner in the mid-1890s,[75] and his approach to harmonic progression points to Bruckner's influence.[76] In his *Harmonielehre*, Schoenberg's discussion of modulation includes a reference to Sechter's concept of "turning points" (*Wendepunkte*) in the minor mode.[77] Both Sechter and Schoenberg considered the minor mode in terms of its three forms: harmonic, melodic, and natural minor. As a result, the minor mode includes cross-related pitches on its sixth and seventh degrees (for example, F♯ and F♮ and G♯ and G♮ in A minor). According to Sechter's voice-leading rules, the lower member of each cross-related pair must descend, the higher member must ascend. Schoenberg applied Sechter's notion of *Wendepunkte* to the entire scale, thus allowing for the possibility of cross-related pairs on every diatonic degree. In modulating smoothly, a nondiatonic pitch, or "substitute," may occur only if its cross-related diatonic counterpart is "neutralized" by resolving stepwise in its proper melodic direction.[78] For example, in a modulation from D major to A major, the G♮ must proceed to F♯ before the introduction of a G♯.

Schoenberg considered modulation as a movement from one diatonic collection to another. This emphasis on the scale is evident in his discussion of tonality in his *Structural Functions of Harmony* (1948), a pedagogical text written after Schoenberg had emigrated to California in 1934. There he explains that "a tonality is expressed by the exclusive use of all of its tones. A scale (or part of one) and a certain ordering of its harmonies affirm it most definitely."[79] In a manner reminiscent of Sechter's "hybrid"

72 Schenker, *Counterpoint*, vol. 1, p. xvii. Schenker's criticisms of Schoenberg's theories are examined in Dunsby, "Schoenberg and the Writings of Heinrich Schenker"; Simms, "New Documents in the Schoenberg–Schenker Polemic." For a more extensive discussion of Schenker's theory of harmony, see Chapter 26, p. 812. 73 Schenker, "Rameau or Beethoven," p. 2.

74 See, for example, Wason, *Viennese Harmonic Theory*, pp. 136ff.; Tittel, "Wiener Musiktheorie," pp. 196ff. 75 Orel, *Ein Harmonielehrekolleg*, pp. 4ff.

76 Wason, *Viennese Harmonic Theory*, pp. 136–37.

77 Schoenberg, *Theory of Harmony*, pp. 98–99. For Sechter's discussion of *Wendepunkte*, see his *Grundsätze*, vol. 1, pp. 55–57.

78 Dineen, "Schoenberg's Concept of Neutralization," discusses this topic in detail.

79 Schoenberg, *Structural Functions of Harmony*, p. 11.

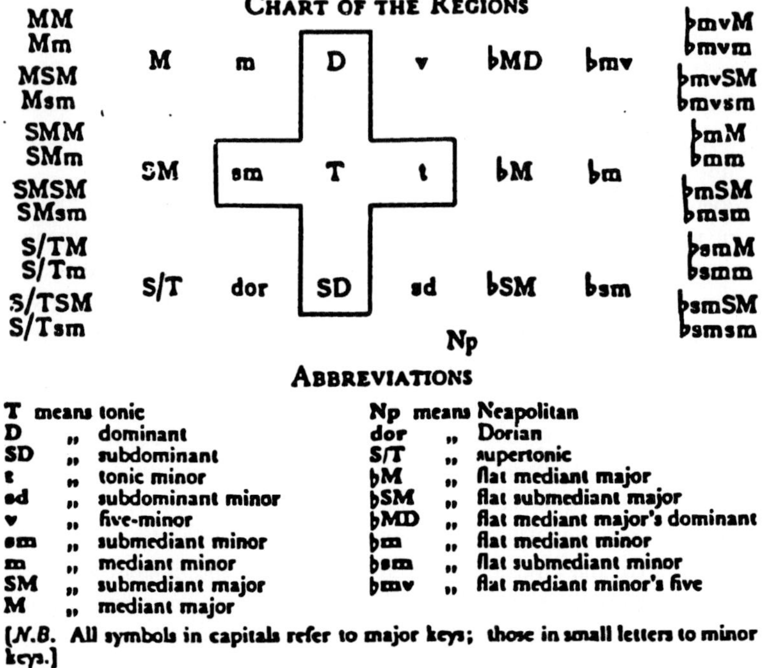

Plate 25.2 Schoenberg's "Chart of the Regions" from *Structural Functions of Harmony*, p. 20.

chords, Schoenberg's derivation of chromatic harmonies also depends upon the scale. Chromatic harmonies, which Schoenberg terms "transformations," result from replacing diatonic pitches with tones borrowed from another key. Thus a chord such as D–F♯–A♭–C in C major obtains its chromatic pitches, F♯ and A♭, from respectively, G major and C minor (or F minor).

Schoenberg did not conceive of modulation as motion from one key to another. Rather, he considered every digression away from the tonic to still be within the original tonality. In a given tonal work there exists only a single tonality; movement away from the tonic constitutes motion to one of its "regions" rather than a modulation to different key.[80] Schoenberg called this approach to tonality "monotonality," which he represented by a chart of the regions (Plate 25.2).

In an earlier sketch of this chart, Schoenberg organized the regions according to the diatonic scale degrees, which he designated with roman numerals.[81] Although the later version of his chart omits the roman numerals and replaces it with nomenclature that

80 Ibid., p. 18.
81 Schoenberg, *The Musical Idea*, pp. 338–39. For a discussion of this earlier sketch, see Bernstein, "Schoenberg Contra Riemann," pp. 27ff.

suggests a functional orientation, the scale remains its organizing principle. Regions on the vertical axes are arranged according to fifth relations; their proximity results from minimal changes in pitch content from one region to another. The horizontal axes are organized according to relative major–minor and parallel major–minor relationships and thus are grouped according to similarities in pitch content and parallelisms in scalar structure. Schoenberg's chart is thus in agreement with Gottfried Weber's table of key relationships (see **Plate 25.1, p. 786**).

Although Schoenberg criticized Riemann's theory of tonal functions,[82] it would be a mistake to overlook his ties to this theoretical tradition. Schoenberg described the I–IV–V–I cadence dialectically, in a manner reminiscent of Hauptmann. The tonic, according to Schoenberg, "asserts" the tonality, which is "challenged" by the subdominant, which in turn is "refuted" by the dominant and "confirmed" by the final tonic.[83] Such tonal dialectics are consistent with other binary oppositions found elsewhere in Schoenberg's writings, such as balance and imbalance, or centripetal and centrifugal tendencies. Even the disputed theory of harmonic dualism seems to be given some voice in Schoenberg's writings, as in the following description of dominant and subdominant functions in C major:

> Here the dependence of C on G, with which, strictly speaking, the force of the C is exerted in the same direction as that of the F, may be considered like the force of a man hanging by his hands from a beam and exerting his own force against the force of gravity. He pulls on the beam just as gravity pulls him, and in the same direction. But the effect is that his force *works against* the force of gravity, and so in this way one is justified in speaking of two opposing forces.[84]

Both Schoenberg and Riemann defined tonality in terms of a network of functional relationships around a tonal center; Riemann's *Tonnetz* and Schoenberg's chart of the regions are schematic representations of axially organized tonal space.[85] Schoenberg described his notion of tonal space in a lecture presented at Princeton University in 1934:

> In formulating the notion concerning the *unity of musical space* I relied on the assertion that had already been made by previous theoreticians, namely: chords are the vertical product of the overtones, but the scale is the horizontal product. I carried this thought to its conclusion and consequently arrived at the concept whereby the vertical and the horizontal, harmonic and melodic, the simultaneous and the successive were in reality comprised within one unified space.

Thus, for Schoenberg, tonal space is multi-dimensional. Not unlike Riemann, who in a principle of *Klangvertretung*, suggested the unity of pitch, harmony and tonality, Schoenberg's concept of musical space extends from scale degree and chordal roots to tonal regions.

82 See Bernstein, "Schoenberg Contra Riemann."
83 Schoenberg, *The Musical Idea*, p. 311.
84 Schoenberg, *Theory of Harmony*, pp. 23–24.
85 For a discussion of the *Tonnetz*, see **Chapter 10, pp. 283–84**.

As a result of Schoenberg's unified view of musical space, harmonic motion constitutes not so much a calculus of quantifiable steps away from some defined tonic center as a more dynamic notion of tension and release. On reading the following passage, full of energeticist rhetoric, one might imagine it to be by Ernst Kurth:

> The paths of harmony are tortuous; leading in all directions, approaching a starting point and leaving it again and again, leading astray, as they lend to a different point a momentary meaning that they soon take back again and again, producing climaxes that they know how to exceed, calling forth gigantic waves which ebb without coming to a standstill.[86]

For Schoenberg, a pitch, chord, or region represents a tonal function which can create a state of rest or unrest, by either establishing or undermining the tonic, a property which he defined in terms of centripetal and centrifugal tendencies.

While not properly a consequence of harmonic theory, Schoenberg's original ideas concerning motivic and thematic development must be seen in the context of his broader notions of musical space and unity. Like a harmonic progression, motives and themes for Schoenberg can create states of rest and unrest. The juxtaposition of dissimilar motivic or thematic materials creates imbalance and a potential for change in the same manner as the introduction of foreign elements within a tonal region creates unrest. Using a terminology similar to his centrifugal and centripetal tendencies, Schoenberg explained that thematic materials which are stable have "concentric" tendencies; unstable themes or "loose formations" have "eccentric" tendencies. The latter contain phrases which lack obvious motivic associations and, as a result, exhibit a strong propensity for subsequent motivic development. Motive and harmony are thus both elements of Schoenberg's unified tonal space; they work in tandem to present what he termed a composition's "musical idea."[87] His synthesis of Austrian and German harmonic theory with this sophisticated approach to thematic development and motivic unity was a culminating point in the history of the Austro-German theoretical tradition.

86 Schoenberg, *The Musical Idea*, p. 309. For more on "energeticist" theories of tonality in the twentieth century, see **Chapter 30, p. 927.**

87 For a useful introduction to this concept, see Schoenberg, *The Musical Idea*, pp. 15–21 (the translator's introduction). Also see **Chapter 29, pp. 912–13** for more on Schoenberg's concept of motive.

Bibliography

Primary sources

D'Alembert, J. "Réflexions sur la théorie de la musique" (1777), in *Œuvres et Correspondances inédites de d'Alembert*, Geneva, Slatkine, 1967

Arend, M. "Harmonische Analyse des Tristanvorspiels," *Bayreuther Blätter* 24 (1901), pp. 160–69

Bruckner, A. *Vorlesungen über Harmonie und Kontrapunkt an der Universität Wien*, ed. E. Schwanzara, Vienna, Österreichischer Bundesverlag für Unterricht, Wissenschaft, und Kunst, 1950

Capellen, G. "Die Unmöglichkeit und Überflussigkeit der dualistischen Molltheorie Riemanns," *Neue Zeitschrift für Musik* 97 (1901), pp. 529–31, 541–43, 553–55, 569–72, 585–87, 601–03, 618–19

"Harmonik und Melodik bei Richard Wagner," *Bayreuther Blätter* 25 (1902), pp. 3–23

Die Zukunft der Musiktheorie (Dualismus oder "Monismus"?) und ihre Einwirkung auf die Praxis, Leipzig, C. F. Kahnt, 1905

Ist das System S. Sechters ein geeigneter Ausgangspunkt für die theoretische Wagnerforschung?, Leipzig, C. F. Kahnt, 1902

Ein neuer exotischer Musikstil an Notenbeispielen nachgewiesen, Stuttgart, C. Grüninger, 1906

Erpf, H. *Studien zur Harmonie und Klangtechnik der neueren Musik*, Leipzig, Breitkopf und Härtel, 1927

Halm, A. *Harmonielehre*, Leipzig, G. J. Göschen, 1902

Hauptmann, M. *Die Natur der Harmonik und der Metrik*, Leipzig, Breitkopf und Härtel, 1853; trans. W. Heathcote as *The Nature of Harmony and Metre*, London, S. Sonnenschein, 1888

Helmholtz, H. *Die Lehre von den Tonempfindungen als physiologischer Grundlage für die Theorie der Musik* (1863), 4th edn., Braunschweig, F. Vieweg, 1877; trans. A. J. Ellis as *On the Sensations of Tone as a Physiological Basis for the Theory of Music*, 2nd edn., London, Longmans and Green, 1885; reprint New York, Dover, 1954

Hostinský, O. *Die Lehre von den musikalischen Klängen: Ein Beitrag zur aesthetischen Begründung der Harmonie-Lehre*, Prague, H. Dominicus, 1879

Hynais, C. "Die Harmonik Richard Wagners in Bezug auf die Fundamentaltheorie Sechters," *Neue musikalische Presse* 10 (1901), pp. 50–53, 67–69, 81–82, 97–100

Jadassohn, S. *Melodik und Harmonik bei Richard Wagner*, Berlin, Verlagsgesellschaft für Literatur und Kunst, 1899

Jelensperger, D. *L'Harmonie au commencement du 19me siècle*, Paris, Zetter, 1830

Karg-Elert, S. *Polaristische Klang- und Tonalitätslehre*, Leipzig, Leuckhart, 1931

Kistler, C. *Harmonielehre*, 3rd edn., Heizbronn, C. F. Schmidt, 1899

Knecht, J. H. *Elementarwerk der Harmonie*, Munich, Falter, 1814

Kurth, E. *Die Voraussetzungen der theoretischen Harmonik und der tonalen Darstellungssysteme*, Bern, M. Drechsel, 1913

Romantische Harmonik und ihre Krise in Wagners "Tristan", 3rd edn. Berlin, M. Hesse, 1923; facs. Hildesheim, G. Olms, 1968 and 1988

Lefèvre, G. *Traité d'harmonie*, Paris, E. Niedermeyer, 1889

Louis, R. and L. Thuille, *Harmonielehre*, 7th edn., Stuttgart, C. Grüninger, 1907

Mayrberger, K. *Lehrbuch der musikalischen Harmonik*, Pressburg [Bratislava], G. Heckenast, 1878

Die Harmonik Richard Wagners an den Leitmotiv aus "Tristan und Isolde" erläutert, Bayreuth, Bayreuther Patronaterverein, 1881; trans. I. Bent as "The Harmonic Style of Richard Wagner, Elucidated with Respect to the Leitmotifs of 'Tristan and Isolde,'" in *MANC* vol. I (1994), pp. 226–52

Oettingen, A. von, *Harmoniesystem in dualer Entwickelung*, Dorpat, W. Gläser, 1866

Polak, A. J. *Die Harmonisierung der indischer, türkischer und japanischer Melodien; neue Beiträge zur Lehre von den Tonempfindungen*, Leipzig, Breitkopf und Härtel, 1905

Rameau, J.-P. *Traité de l'harmonie reduite à ses principes naturels*, Paris, Ballard, 1722; trans. P. Gossett as *Treatise on Harmony*, New York, Dover, 1971
Richter, E. F. *Lehrbuch der Harmonielehre*, Leipzig, Breitkopf und Härtel, 1853
Riemann, H. *Musikalische Logik*, Leipzig, C. F. Kahnt, 1874
Musikalische Syntaxis, Leipzig, Breitkopf und Härtel, 1877
"Die Natur der Harmonik," *Sammlung musikalischer Vorträge* 4/40 (1882), pp. 157–90; trans. J. C. Filmore as "The Nature of Harmony," in *New Lessons in Harmony*, ed. J. C. Filmore, Philadelphia, T. Presser, 1887
Vereinfachte Harmonielehre, oder die Lehre von den tonalen Funktionen der Akkorde, London, Augener, 1893; trans. H. Bewerung as *Harmony Simplified*, London, Augener, 1896
Grosse Kompositionslehre, 2 vols., Berlin, Spemann, 1902–03
"Das Problem des harmonischen Dualismus," *Neue Zeitschrift für Musik* 17 (1905), pp. 3–5, 23–26, 43–46, 67–70
"Ideen zu einer 'Lehre von den Tonvorstellungen,'" *Jahrbuch der Musikbibliothek Peters* 21 (1914), pp. 1–26; trans. R. Wason and E. West Marvin as "Riemann's 'Ideen zu einer Lehre von den Tonvorstellungen': An Annotated Translation," *JMT* 36 (1992), pp. 69–117
"Neue Beiträge zu einer Lehre von den Tonvorstellungen," *Jahrbuch der Musikbibliothek Peters* 23 (1916), pp. 1–21
L. van Beethovens sämtliche Klavier-Solosonaten: Ästhetische und formal-technische Analyse mit historischen Notizen, 3 vols., Berlin, M. Hesse, 1917–19
Schenker, H. "Rameau or Beethoven? Creeping Paralysis or Spiritual Potency in Music?," in *The Masterwork in Music*, vol. III (1930), W. Drabkin, trans. I. Bent et al., Cambridge University Press, 1997, pp. 1–9
Counterpoint, 2 vols. (1910–22), trans. and ed. J. Rothgeb, trans. J. Thym, New York, Schirmer, 1987
Schoenberg, A. *Harmonielehre* (1911), 3rd edn., Vienna, Universal, 1922; trans. R. Carter as *Theory of Harmony*, Berkeley, University of California Press, 1978
Coherence, Counterpoint, Instrumentation, Instruction in Form (Zusammenhang, Kontrapunkt, Instrumentation, Formenlehre), trans. and ed. S. Neff, trans. C. Cross, Lincoln, University of Nebraska Press, 1994
The Musical Idea and the Logic, Technique, and Art of Its Presentation (Der musikalische Gedanke, und die Logik, Technik, und Kunst seiner Darstellung), bilingual ed. and trans. P. Carpenter and S. Neff, New York, Columbia University Press, 1995
Structural Functions of Harmony, ed. H. Searle, New York, Norton, 1954; rev. ed. L. Stein, New York, Norton, 1969
Schreyer, J. *Harmonielehre*, Dresden, Holz and Pahl, 1905
Schröder, H. *Die symmetrische Umkehrung in der Musik*, Leipzig, Publikationen der International Musikgesellschaft, 1902
Sechter, S. *Die Grundsätze der musikalischen Komposition*, 3 vols., Leipzig, Breitkopf und Härtel, 1853–54; vol. I trans. and ed. C. Müller as *The Correct Order of the Fundamental Harmonies: A Treatise on Fundamental Basses, and their Inversions and Substitutes*, New York, W. A. Pond, 1871
"Abhandlungen über die musikalischen akustischen Tonverhältnisse," MS, Library of the Gesellschaft der Musikfreunde, Vienna
Vogler, G. J. *Tonwissenschaft und Tonsezkunst*, Mannheim, Kurfürstliche Hofbuchdruckerei, 1776; facs. Hildesheim, G. Olms, 1970

"Summe der Harmonik," *Betrachtungen der Mannheimer Tonschule* 3 (1780–81), pp. 1–117; 4 (1781), pp. 318–32
Handbuch zur Harmonielehre und für den Generalbass, Prague, K. Barth, 1802
Zwei und dreisig Präludien für die Orgel und für das Fortepiano, Munich, Falter, 1806; partial trans. I. Bent as "Prelude No. 8 (in D minor)" from *Thirty-two Preludes for Organ or Piano, together with an Aesthetic, Rhetorical and Harmonic Analysis*, in *MANC*, vol. I, pp. 132–45
Weber, G. "Ueber eine besonders merkwürdige Stelle in einem Mozart'schen Violinquartett aus C," in *Versuch einer geordneten Theorie der Tonsetzkunst*, vol. III, Mainz, B. Schott, 1830–32, vol. III, pp. 196–226; trans. I. Bent as "A Particularly Remarkable Passage in a String Quartet in C by Mozart, K. 465 ('Dissonance')," in *MANC*, vol. I, pp. 157–83
Versuch einer geordneten Theorie der Tonsetzkunst, 3 vols., Mainz, B. Schott, 1817–21; 2nd edn., 4 vols., 1824; 3rd revised edn., 4 vols., 1830–32; trans. J. Warner as *The Theory of Musical Composition*, 2 vols., Boston, J. Wilkens and R. Carter, 1842–46; revised trans. by J. Bishop, London, R. Cocks, 1851
Weitzmann, C. F. *Die neue harmonielehren im Streit mit der alten*, Leipzig, C. F. Kahnt, 1861
Ziehn, B. *Harmonie- und Modulationslehre*, Berlin, C. Friedrich, 1887

Secondary sources

Baron, C. K. "At the Cutting Edge: Three American Theorists at the End of the Nineteenth Century," *International Journal of Musicology*, 2 (1993), pp. 193–247
Bernstein, D. W. "Georg Capellen on *Tristan und Isolde*: Analytical Systems in Conflict at the Turn of the Twentieth Century," *Theoria* 4 (1989), pp. 34–62
"Georg Capellen's Theory of Reduction," *JMT* 37 (1993), pp. 85–116
"Symmetry and Symmetrical Inversion in Turn-of-the-Century Theory and Practice," in *Music Theory and the Exploration of the Past*, ed. C. Hatch and D. W. Bernstein, University of Chicago Press, 1993, pp. 377–404
"Schoenberg Contra Riemann: *Stufen*, Regions, *Verwandschaft*, and the Theory of Tonal Function," *Theoria* 6 (1992), pp. 23–53
Burnham, S. "Method and Motivation in Hugo Riemann's History of Harmonic Theory," *MTS* 14 (1992), pp. 1–14
Christensen, T. *Rameau and Musical Thought in the Enlightenment*, Cambridge University Press, 1993
"The Rule of the Octave in Thorough-Bass Theory and Practice," *Acta* 64 (1992), pp. 91–117
"The Schichtenlehre of Hugo Riemann," *In Theory Only* 6 (1982), pp. 37–44
Dahlhaus, C. *Untersuchungen über die Entstehung der harmonischen Tonalität*, Kassel, Bärenreiter, 1968; trans. R. Gjerdingen as *Studies on the Origin of Harmonic Tonality*, Princeton University Press, 1990
"Schoenberg and Schenker," in *Schoenberg and the New Music: Essays by Carl Dahlhaus*, trans. D. Puffett and A. Clayton, Cambridge University Press, 1987, pp. 134–40
Dineen, P. "Schoenberg's Concept of Neutralization," *Theoria* 2 (1987), pp. 13–28
Dunsby, J. "Schoenberg and the Writings of Heinrich Schenker," *Journal of the Arnold Schoenberg Institute*, 2/1 (1977), pp. 26–33

Goehr, A. "The Theoretical Writings of Arnold Schoenberg," *Perspectives of New Music*, 14 (1975), pp. 3–16

Federhofer, H. *Akkord und Stimmführung in den musiktheoretischen Systemen von Hugo Riemann, Ernst Kurth und Heinrich Schenker*, Vienna, Österreichische Akadamie der Wissenschaften, 1981

Grave, F. K. "Abbé Vogler's Theory of Reduction," *Current Musicology* 29 (1980), pp. 41–69

Grave, F. K. and M. G. Grave, *In Praise of Harmony: The Teachings of Abbé Georg Joseph Vogler*, Lincoln, University of Nebraska Press, 1987

Harrison, D. *Harmonic Function in Chromatic Music: A Renewed Dualist Theory and an Account of Its Precedents*, University of Chicago Press, 1994

Hyer, Brian, "Reimag(in)ing Riemann," *JMT* 39 (1995), pp. 101–03

Imig, R. *Systeme der Funktions-Bezeichnung in den Harmonielehren seit Hugo Riemann*, Düsseldorf, Gesellschaft zur Förderung der systematischen Musikwissenschaft, 1970

Kirnberger, J. P. *Die Kunst des reinen Satzes*, 2 vols., Berlin, Decker and Hartung, 1771–79; facs. Hildesheim, G. Olms, 1968 and 1988; trans. D. Beach and J. Thym as *The Art of Strict Musical Composition*, New Haven, Yale University Press, 1982

Lester, J. *Compositional Theory in the Eighteenth Century*, Cambridge, MA, Harvard University Press, 1992

Lewin, D. "A Formal Theory of Generalized Tonal Functions," *JMT* 26 (1982), pp. 23–60

Mickelsen, W. C., trans. and ed., *Hugo Riemann's Theory of Harmony: a Study* (trans. of *Geschichte der Musiktheorie im IX.–XIX. Jahrhundert*, vol. III), Lincoln, University of Nebraska Press, 1977

Mooney, M. K. "'Table of Relations' and Music Psychology in Hugo Riemann's Chromatic Theory," Ph.D. diss., Columbia University (1996)

Morgan, R. P. "Schenker and the Theoretical Tradition," *College Music Symposium* 18 (1978), pp. 72–96

Orel, A. *Ein Harmonielehrekolleg bei Anton Bruckner*, Berlin, Verlag für Wirtschaft und Kultur, 1940

Rummenhöller, P. "Der deskriptive Theoriebegriff Gottfried Webers," in *Musiktheoretisches Denken im 19. Jahrhundert*, ed. P. Rummenhöller, Regensburg, G. Bosse, 1967, pp. 11–17

Saslaw, J. "Gottfried Weber and Multiple Meaning," *Theoria* 5 (1990–91), pp. 74–103

Saslaw, J. and J. P. Walsh, "Musical Invariance as a Cognitive Structure: 'Multiple Meaning' in the Early Nineteenth Century," in *Music Theory in the Age of Romanticism*, ed. I. Bent, Cambridge University Press, 1996, pp. 211–32

Seidel, E. "Die Harmonielehre Hugo Riemanns," in *Beiträge der Musiktheorie des 19. Jahrhunderts*, ed. M. Vogel, Regensburg, G. Bosse, 1966, pp. 39–92

Simms, B. "New Documents in the Schoenberg–Schenker Polemic," *Perspectives of New Music* 16 (1977–78), pp. 110–24

Smith, C. J. "The Functional Extravagance of Chromatic Chords," *MTS* 8 (1986), pp. 94–139

Spies, C. "Vortrag/12TK/Princeton," *Perspectives of New Music* 13 (1974), pp. 58–136

Thompson, D. M. *A History of Harmonic Theory in the United States*, Kent, OH, Kent State University Press, 1980

Tittel, E. "Wiener Musiktheorie von Fux bis Schoenberg," in *Beiträge zur Musiktheorie des 19. Jahrhunderts*, ed. M. Vogel, Regensburg, G. Bosse, 1966, pp. 163–201

Vogel, M. *Der Tristan-Akkord und die Krise der modernen Harmonielehre*, Düsseldorf, Gesellschaft der systematischen Musikwissenschaft, 1963

"Arthur v. Oettingen und der harmonische Dualismus," *Beiträge zur Musiktheorie des 19. Jahrhunderts*, ed. M. Vogel, Regensburg, G. Bosse, 1966, pp. 103–32

Wason, R. W. "Progressive Harmonic Theory in the Mid-Nineteenth-Century," *Journal of Musicological Research* 8 (1988), pp. 55–90

Viennese Harmonic Theory from Albrechtsberger to Schenker and Schoenberg, Ann Arbor, UMI Research Press, 1985

"Schenker's Notion of Scale-Step in Historical Perspective: Non-Essential Harmonies in Viennese Fundamental Bass Theories," *JMT* 27 (1983), pp. 49–73

Werts, D. "The Musical Circle of Johannes Mattheson," *Theoria* 1 (1985), pp. 97–131

Zeleny, W. *Die historischen Grundlagen des Theoriesystems von Simon Sechter*, Tutzing, H. Schneider, 1979

· 26 ·

Heinrich Schenker

WILLIAM DRABKIN

Long after his major writings on harmony, counterpoint and analysis began to appear, Heinrich Schenker (1868–1935) remains one of the most important and influential theorists in the history of Western music. His achievements have often been compared to those of eminent thinkers of his age working in other fields, e.g., his Viennese compatriots Sigmund Freud in psychology and Albert Einstein in physics. His influence, modest (though not negligible) in his own lifetime, has grown steadily since the middle of the last century and shows no signs of abating. Already a paradigmatic figure in North American universities by the 1970s, he has since exerted a powerful influence in British and, more recently, European academic circles. Indeed, the interest shown in his life's work is, in some respects, comparable to that of some of the twentieth century's leading composers, and in this respect his reputation as a theorist is unequaled.

That which is called "Schenkerian theory" is a complex set of regulatory principles that were initially intended to explain the tonal music of the eighteenth and nineteenth centuries; it is at the same time a synthesis of many traditions, embracing Fuxian counterpoint, the thorough-bass teaching of Carl Philipp Emanuel Bach and late nineteenth-century harmonic theory. It is at once a sophisticated explanation of tonality, but also an analytical system of immense empirical power. Schenker's ideas and work touch on, or have implications for, virtually every topic addressed in this volume.

This chapter includes a synopsis of Schenker's life and works, an explanation of the rudiments of his theory, remarks on its historical background, and a survey of its reception both as a pedagogical tool and as a basis for further investigation of a wide range of music.[1]

Life and writings

The few sources for Heinrich Schenker's childhood and adolescence suggest that he came from a poor but intellectually supportive Jewish family in Galicia (Poland),

1 Related aspects of Schenker's theory are discussed in numerous other chapters in the volume. In particular, see **Chapter 3, pp. 89–90** (on Schenker's epistemology), **Chapter 22, pp. 703–10** (on implications of Schenkerian theory for the analysis of rhythm and meter), and **Chapter 23, pp. 741–42** (on Schenker's broader views of tonality).

attended the Gymnasium in the capital city of Lemberg (L'viv in present-day Ukraine) and completed his schooling in Brezežany, where he also had music lessons from the celebrated Chopin pupil Karl Mikuli. After taking the *Matura* examinations, he enrolled as a law student at the University of Vienna in 1884, gaining a doctorate in law there six years later. In his last three years at university, he also attended classes at the Vienna Conservatory, where his teachers included Anton Bruckner.

After graduation, Schenker embarked on a musical career which included composition, journalism and accompanying. He gave up composing while in his early thirties, after realizing that he would never be able to equal the achievements of the masters whom he admired above all else, and for most of his life he earned a living as a piano teacher in Vienna, devoting himself in his free time to music theory and analysis. His publications were financially supported by friends, and by people whom he taught or with whom he shared thoughts on music, and this enabled him to abandon his work in music journalism and to write in a more serious way from the early years of the twentieth century until the end of his life.[2]

His published work includes critical editions, a treatise on ornamentation, and commentaries for facsimile editions of composer autographs. But it is by his detailed analyses of music and the working out of a comprehensive theory of tonality – the two types of writing commingle in textbooks, monographs, pamphlets, yearbooks, and critical commentaries – that he has become widely known. Schenker's analyses exemplify, over a broad range of the literature and in considerable detail, a view of music that has gained sufficient esteem in North America (and more recently in parts of Europe) to establish itself as one of the foremost approaches to musical structure.

Although Schenker is best known for a highly specific view of music, and a method for describing how music behaves, his writings cover a broad range of approaches and embrace editorial technique, performance practice, and criticism. A theoretical project, built around the four-volume *Neue musikalische Theorien und Phantasien*, spans a thirty-year period yet shows a remarkable degree of consistency. The first three volumes in the series are based on the traditional disciplines of harmony and counterpoint: *Harmonielehre* (1906) and a two-volume *Kontrapunkt* (1910, 1922). The fourth volume, *Der freie Satz* (1935), was initially conceived as the third volume of *Kontrapunkt* but marks a more radical break with the traditional study of the contrapuntal species with reference to a cantus firmus; it is more a book about analytical method than composition technique.

The texts devoted primarily to the analysis of whole pieces include a monograph on Beethoven's Ninth Symphony (1912) and the periodical publications *Der Tonwille* (1921–24) and *Das Meisterwerk in der Musik* (1925–30). Though *Tonwille* and *Meisterwerk* are largely devoted to small- to medium-length studies, sometimes of short keyboard

2 To date, the fullest account of Schenker's life is contained in the opening chapter of Federhofer, *Heinrich Schenker, nach Tagebüchern und Briefen*, pp. 1–47.

pieces or sonata movements, they also contain longer analyses of three major works from the Classical symphonic repertory: Beethoven's Fifth Symphony (1921–23), Mozart's Symphony in G minor, K.550 (1926), and Beethoven's *Eroica* Symphony (1930). Two of these are, in effect, Beethoven symphony monographs which, together with the book on the Ninth, constitute a trilogy on the symphonic output of the composer he esteemed above all others.

As it was primarily as a piano teacher that Schenker earned a living, one should not be surprised to find his work addressed as much to practical musicians as to the world of scholarship. The majority of his longer essays include detailed suggestions on performance; these invariably follow, and are derived from, the analysis of the score, sometimes supported by the evidence of the sources. Schenker frequently stated that an inspired performance of a work could only be obtained by way of following its compositional growth from the background to the foreground. It is clear, from his extant remarks on performance, that this did not amount to an "analytical" style of playing, whereby elements of a structural "background" are brought out crudely. (The opposite is closer to the truth: foreground dissonances require greater weight than the consonances from which they are derived.[3]) Schenker's long-projected *Kunst des Vortrags*, never completed but recently brought out in English translation as *The Art of Performance*, expresses concerns as much in tune with his earlier writings as with the later theoretical formulations.[4]

If Schenkerian analysis entails a profound and detailed understanding of the relationship of the notes of a piece to one another, then an essential condition of an analysis is an accurate text of the piece. This was a problem of life-long concern: in the days in which the texts of musical works were overlaid by editors with additional dynamic and articulation marks, and when the notes themselves were often changed arbitrarily, the understanding of a work could begin in earnest only after it had been established what the composer had actually written.[5] (In this activity Schenker was assisted by his pupils Otto Erich Deutsch and Anthony van Hoboken, both of whom followed distinguished careers as musicologists.) The search for the best musical text, a salient feature of the *Erläuterungsausgaben* of Bach's Chromatic Fantasy and Fugue and four of Beethoven's late sonatas, extends to Schenker's other editorial work, his commentary on a facsimile reproduction of the "Moonlight" Sonata, and the essays on Mozart's G minor Symphony and Beethoven's *Eroica*. With Beethoven and, to a lesser extent, Haydn, an additional measure of the composer's purported intentions was sometimes provided by the transcription and interpretation of sketches. The practical texts

3 Referring to the Bach C major Prelude, he wrote to a pupil that "the dissonances . . . should always be played *louder* than the consonances"; see Drabkin, "A Lesson in Composition," p. 247. See also Rothstein, "Schenker as an Interpreter of Beethoven's Piano Sonatas."

4 Recent studies in this field include Burkhart, "Schenker's Theory of Levels"; Schachter, "Twentieth-Century Analysis."

5 This matter is treated briefly in *Tonwille*, vol. III, pp. 24–25 and vol. VI, pp. 38–40, and at greater length in the essay "Weg mit dem Phrasierungsbogen" in *Meisterwerk*, vol. I.

include a commentary on ornamentation in eighteenth-century music, an edition of the complete Beethoven piano sonatas, and a two-volume selection of keyboard works by Carl Philipp Emanuel Bach.

The parsing of this prodigious *oeuvre* should not, however, obscure the fact that, for Schenker, many aspects of music – theory, analysis, performance, manuscript study, and the preparation of editions – were interrelated and hence discussible in an integrated format. For contemporary musicians outside the academy, e.g., concert pianists and piano teachers, the *Erläuterungsausgaben* were his most important contributions to the literature of music, providing in an integrated format an authoritative text of the music, an analysis, commentary on the autograph score and other primary textual sources, remarks on performance, and discussion of the secondary literature. Their musical insights were recognized by performers with no particular theoretical ideology.[6]

Where not accompanied by the musical text, a typical analytical essay nevertheless includes some or all of the following: observations on the text of the piece (including, where relevant, alternative readings in the autograph score and early sketches), suggestions for performance that arise from the analysis, remarks on modern editions and arrangements, and a survey of the secondary literature. As Schenker's stature as a theorist grew, and he became more convinced of the rightness of his views on music, he became less concerned with attacking the writings of other scholars. The Ninth Symphony monograph (1912) was expressly concerned with the opinions of earlier commentators, as its subtitle makes clear;[7] but the *Eroica* essay (1930) mentions only two studies peripherally concerned with the work's structure, and does so only briefly.

In both his published writings and private communications, Schenker decried the mixing of politics with music; the immortality of great music was itself proof that political beliefs had little to do with musical values. Yet the notion of hierarchy, of a strict ordering of the tones of a composition, is so thoroughly consistent with his deeply conservative outlook on life and culture that it is difficult to uncouple his theory entirely from two of his most consistently expressed ideological stances: (1) the centrality of the German people in European culture, underscored by their preeminence in music, and (2) the steady decline of culture and political order in Europe since the late eighteenth century, ultimately resulting in the complete demise of musical art by the beginning of the twentieth century. Schenker admitted only two foreign composers into the pantheon of German music, Chopin and Domenico Scarlatti. Although he encouraged his private pupils in composition, he found nothing favourable in either mainstream modern music or the tonally accessible jazz and popular music of his time.

6 See, for example, Paul Badura-Skoda, "A Tie," in which Schenker's analysis of the Piano Sonata in A♭, Op 110, is championed, three-quarters of a century after its publication, as "a monument of precision and insight, by far the best analysis ever made of one of the last Beethoven sonatas" (p. 87).
7 *Eine Darstellung des musikalischen Inhaltes unter fortlaufender Berücksichtigung auch des Vortrages und der Literatur* ("a representation of its musical contents, together with a running commentary on performance and the critical literature").

He reserved his harshest polemics for the atonal composers, yet made no qualitative distinction between the work of contemporary composers as stylistically diverse as Debussy, Strauss, Schoenberg, and Hindemith.[8]

That *Der freie Satz* is not only his *opus ultimum* but also a posthumous work – it was published some months after his death in January 1935 – has had important consequences for our understanding of Schenker's work. Although it is the text on which his reputation is based, and remains the basis of explanations of his theory and of the analytical and graphing techniques that arise from it, it would be a mistake to regard it as the definitive formulation of Schenkerian theory. For one thing, it is generally reckoned as incomplete, especially with regard to the discussion of form, metrics and rhythm, and style and genre. Second, the earlier writings, though they are formatted differently and use terminology in a different way (especially the words *Urlinie* and *Zug*), shed a great deal of light on Schenker's analytical technique; they are sometimes preferred to the later writings, whose insights can sometimes seem tangled inside an elaborate theoretical web. This means that a single account of Schenker's contribution to music theory is an illusory goal, even if *Der freie Satz* remains the largest repository of his analytical work and is probably the best vantage-point from which to view it.

Outline of the theory

If one were to attempt to reduce Schenker's understanding of music to a single concept, "hierarchy" would perhaps be the best choice. For Schenker, music – great music – is tonal, and hence a composition is governed ultimately by its principal chord, the tonic triad; all other harmonic functions are subordinate to the tonic, and analysis must always make a distinction between essential and passing harmonies. Similarly, the notes of a melody can be described as either essential or transitional. Moreover, the notion of essential versus passing, of harmonic versus non-harmonic, applies not only to the surface of the music but informs the deeper levels, too: a harmony might be essential at one level but transitional at another, a passing note at one level might be the start of an important "linear progression" at another.

8 Only two modern works were subjected to analysis by counter-example: a passage from Stravinsky's Piano Concerto and the whole of Reger's Variations and Fugue on a theme of Bach, Op 81. Both appear in *Meisterwerk*, vol. II.

Schenker's polemics proved an embarrassment to his disciples, many of whom were forced to flee Nazi Germany in the late 1930s. After 1945, Schenker's ideological position was untenable to a German nation trying to come to terms with the horrors it had recently perpetrated, and for a long time afterwards the offending passages from his texts were excised from later editions and translations of his writings, or relegated to an appendix. The more virulent parts of his published work, above all the sections of *Tonwille* and *Meisterwerk* devoted to miscellaneous "thoughts on art and its relationships to the general scheme of things," have until recently been ignored altogether, though some writers have argued that Schenker's polemics are inseparable from his theory; see Cook, "Schenker's Theory of Music as Ethics"; "Heinrich Schenker, Polemicist"; Bent, "Schenker e la missione del genio germanico."

Example 26.1 *Harmonielehre*, Example 153: Analysis of aria "Buß und Reu" from Bach's *St Matthew Passion*

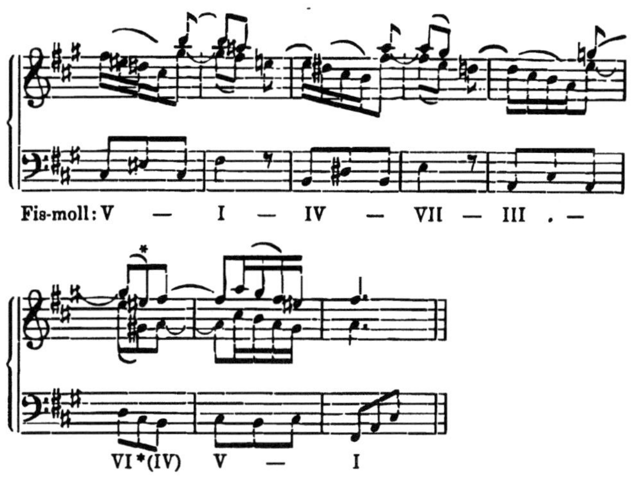

I shall outline the essentials of Schenker's theory using four further concepts: *Stufe*, *Schicht*, *Prolongation* (*Auskomponierung*), and linearity. Additional terms will be introduced in relation to these.

Stufe

This term is often translated as "scale degree" or "scale step," expressions that have a melodic connotation. But *Stufe* is a harmonic concept, one which provides a means of distinguishing important harmonies from transitional ones (*Durchgänge*); thus it provides a means of assigning different values to what might otherwise appear to be instances of the same chord. It makes an early appearance in Schenker's writings – in the *Harmonielehre* of 1906 – and represents an important milestone in his development of a hierarchical view of musical structure. In discussing the ritornello of an aria from Bach's *St. Matthew Passion* (see Example 26.1), Schenker showed how only one of two C♯ major chords could be understood as a true dominant of F♯ minor, a "V. Stufe":[9]

> At * we see the appearance of a complete triad on C♯, which could represent the dominant harmony ("*die V. Stufe*"), but the listener would have been directed most specifically by the rhythm of the falling fifths I–IV–VII–III etc. to viewing this triad as merely a passing configuration of three voices; even if we were to ignore the fact that the inversion of the fifths supports this view, and that there is no need to invoke a V here since one appears *ex officio* in the very next measure, there is no question of it having the weight of

9 *Harmonielehre*, p. 187; see also Federhofer, *Akkord und Stimmführung*, pp. 66–67.

a *Stufe*. Each of the three voices in fact has its own reason for passing this point. The D in the bass passes through C♯ to B as a possible [root of] IV; the suspended fourth G in the soprano passes through E♯ en route to its resolution, F♯; and finally the suspended E in the inner voice moves through G♯ to A in parallel sixths with the soprano. Thus their coming together must be taken for what it truly is: a contrapuntal accident.

The example shows a clearly hierarchical view of musical design: what is transitional must, by definition, be dependent on the points enclosing it. The starred C♯ major chord cannot be mistaken for a true dominant, since it acts as a passing chord between two chords along the cycle of falling fifths, VI on the first beat and IV^7 (substituting for II) on the third.

In Schenker's later writings, the status of a chord is dependent on the perspective from which it is viewed. A passing harmony at a higher structural level (*Schicht*) could gain the weight of a *Stufe* at a lower level. In the analyses the roman numbers are often laid out simultaneously in differing degrees of detail, sometimes with parentheses enclosing a lower-level progression (see Examples 26.5 and 26.6, below).

Schicht

Musical content is created by an unfurling of the tonic triad, referred to in some of Schenker's writings as the *Klang in der Natur*: the "chord of Nature," i.e., harmony in its natural state. This is achieved in the first instance by "horizontalizing" the contents of this chord as a simple two-voice setting. The upper voice, called the *Urlinie*, makes a diatonic stepwise descent from a note in the tonic triad to its root, and hence traverses the interval of a third, a fifth or an octave (see Example 26.2). The lower voice, called the *Bassbrechung* ("bass arpeggiation"), starts with the root and moves to the fifth degree and back to the root. It is no accident, for Schenker, that the roots of both the mediant (the "relative major" in minor keys) and the dominant belong to the tonic triad: this enables Schenker to argue even more forcefully that the tonic triad not only represents harmony in its natural state but also contains the essentials of harmonic motion, i.e., what other theorists would have called the "principal modulations."

The configuration of *Urlinie* supported by bass arpeggiation is called the *Ursatz*. It not only represents the melody in its most rudimentary form, the scale, but also the basic harmonic progression underlying most eighteenth- and nineteenth-century music: I–V–I in roman numeral terms. [10] (In this respect, the *Ursatz* is a stronger abstraction of tonal music than Fuxian note-against-note counterpoint, which prefers stepwise motion in both parts, especially at the cadence.)

10 The use of careted arabic numbers for melodic steps is analogous to that of roman numerals for the harmonic *Stufen*, and is explained in a footnote to an analytical graph in *Tonwille*, vol. III. The *Tonwille* analyses show a liberal use of these symbols, with hierarchy shown by different sizes of number; by the time of *Der freie Satz*, there was only one fundamental descent of the *Urlinie*, i.e., one descending line indicated by careted numbers.

Example 26.2 The three forms of the Schenkerian *Ursatz* (cf. *Der freie Satz*, figs. 1, 9–11)

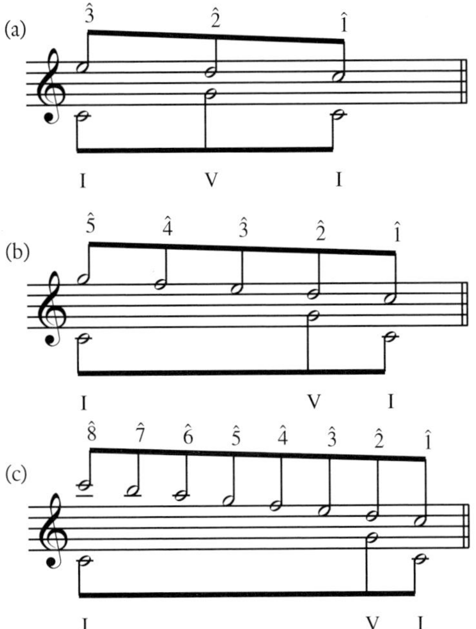

The *Ursatz*, which represents the contents of a tonal work at the most basic level, called the *background* (*Hintergrund*), gives rise to more elaborate harmonic-contrapuntal designs. These in turn generate further development, in stages, until the final elaboration is reached, which is the piece itself with all its details of rhythm and tempo, dynamics and articulation, and scoring. This level is called the *foreground* of a composition (*Vordergrund*). Between the extremities of background and foreground lies the *middleground* (*Mittelgrund*), an area whose scope and complexity is dependent on the size and nature of the composition.

The top staves of Examples 26.2a–c show that the linear descent in the upper voice of the *Ursatz* traverses the space of a third, a fifth, or an entire octave. Because of the perfect alignment of the upper and lower voices in Example 26.2a, this form of the *Ursatz* is given pride of place in most explanations of Schenkerian theory. Indeed, the *Ursatz* from $\hat{3}$ most clearly illustrates the notion of hierarchy (see Example 26.3). The tonic triad, Schenker's chord of Nature, is given in Example 26.3a; it is stretched out (or "horizontalized") by the successive presentation of its root and third (26.3b) and by the filling of the space between these with a passing note (26.3c). The passing note, which is initially dissonant against the prevailing harmony, is converted to a

Example 26.3 Derivation of the *Ursatz* from $\hat{3}$ from the tonic C major chord

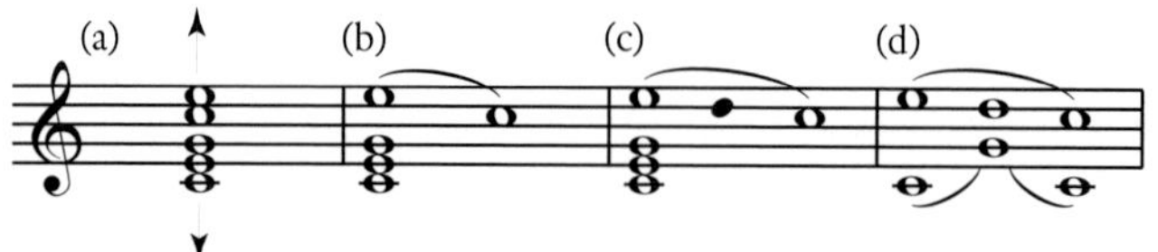

consonance by the arpeggiation of the bass from the first to the fifth step of the scale (26.3d). The resultant harmony – the dominant – thus acquires the status of a fundamental harmony – a *Stufe* – and is then able to generate further elaborations. At subsequent levels these processes are repeated: passing notes are given consonant support and become harmonies in their own right.

As Schenker himself explained:

> The dissonant passing tone . . . so long as it retains its dissonant quality . . . cannot at the same time give rise to a further elaboration; only the transformation of a dissonance into a consonance can make elaboration possible . . . The *Ursatz* exhibits the first transformation of a dissonant *Urlinie* tone into a consonance: above all, $\hat{2}$ is changed into a consonance $\hat{2}$/V by the counterpointing bass arpeggiation of the tonic triad.[11]

Although Schenker's terminology implies a tripartite division, each term – background, middleground, foreground – in fact embraces more than one distinct structural level. His statement early in *Der freie Satz* that "the *background* in music is represented by a contrapuntal structure which I call the *Ursatz*"[12] is already a simplification; as we have seen (Example 26.3), there is a musical construction – the tonic chord – that is conceptually prior to the *Ursatz*. At the other end, the "foreground" of a piece is the totality of its notes and associated markings, i.e., the score; but the term is conventionally used to describe a simplification of the piece in which the melodic contour, harmony, and phrase rhythm are clearly discernible. Example 26.4b, which reproduces part of Schenker's most detailed analytical "graph" of the first movement of Mozart's G minor Symphony, can easily be read as a simplification of the start of the symphony in a way that line (*d*) from Example 26.4a, which it elaborates, cannot.[13] The motion of the upper voice is, with few exceptions, reduced to quarter-notes and half-notes; the piece is presented in a two-stave piano format, with some indications of scoring. To distinguish between the two notions of musical foreground, Schenker generally used the term *Urlinie-Tafel* for the graph of the foreground in this simplified notation, and *Ausführung* or *letzte Ausführung* ("final elaboration," "realization") when referring to the actual score.

That the middleground also comprises several hierarchically conceived layers is clear

11 *Der freie Satz*, §§169–70. 12 Ibid., Part I, Chapter 1, section 3. 13 *Meisterwerk*, vol. II.

both from Schenker's analyses and from his terminology. In Example 26.4a, lines (*a*), (*b*), (*c*), and (*d*) each represent a middleground layer; had he published this analysis a few years later, he would have labeled them "1. Schicht" (="first [middleground] layer"), "2. Schicht," "3. Schicht," and "4. Schicht," respectively. In the well-known graphic analysis of Bach's Prelude in C from the *Well-Tempered Clavier*, Book 1,[14] the initial elaboration of the *Ursatz* is still marked "1. Schicht," even though no further middleground layers intervene between it and the *Urlinie-Tafel*.[15]

Prolongation and *Auskomponierung*

Though these terms are central to his theory, Schenker never provided clear definitions of either, nor did he attempt to distinguish between them. *Prolongation* suggests the creation of content by stretching out the constituent elements (representing specific musical events) in a given layer. In the analysis of the Bach prelude, for instance, the fall of an octave from e^2 to e^1 is a prolongation of the first note, or "primary tone," of the *Urlinie*, $e^2 = \hat{3}$. *Auskomponierung* (literally, "composing out") is the process by which prolongation is achieved: the word, constructed by analogy with the German *ausarbeiten* ("to work out, develop"), implies that temporal events have the potential to generate further content; that is, material contained in (or implied by) an event in a higher level can be "unlocked" by the process of elaboration. In the Bach prelude, the $\hat{3}$ that is initially prolonged by the drop of an octave is further elaborated by being filled with stepwise motion: the linear descent "composes out" the octave.

Linked to the concepts of *Prolongation* and *Auskomponierung* is a favorite metaphor of Schenker's, *Saat-Ernte*, by which musical structure is made analogous to organic growth: "from seed to harvest." The commentary on the first movement of Mozart's G minor Symphony makes reference to two instances: the interval of a sixth, "planted" in the viola part in m. 1, "germinates" in the first violin in mm. 3 and 7 (this relationship is shown in the *Urlinie-Tafel*: see the square brackets in Example 26.4b); in mm. 10–11 the descending third from a^2 to f♯^{2}, itself the inversion of the original sixth, resolves to the fourth in the next measure. With the key-note, g^2, in the upper voice, this fourth is the "harvest" of the original planting.[16]

Another term used in this connection is *Diminution*. By this Schenker sought to emphasize the historical validity of his theoretical work, through the connection

14 See, for example, Cook, *Guide to Musical Analysis*; Drabkin et al., *Analisi schenkeriana*. Derivative examples are found in Jonas, *Einführung*; Forte and Gilbert, *Introduction to Schenkerian Analysis*; Neumeyer and Tepping, *Guide To Schenkerian Analysis*; Cadwallader and Gagné, *Analysis of Tonal Music*. See also Drabkin, "A Lesson in Analysis," which includes Schenker's preliminary sketches for this graph.

15 Another Schenkerian graph illustrating levels of musical structure (in this case of a Haydn piano sonata) may by seen in Plate 23.2, p. 742. There, the subsumption of middleground modulations within a background voice-leading structure is clearly to be seen.

16 *Meisterwerk*, vol. II, p. 118.

Example 26.4 Extracts of graphic analyses from "Mozart: Sinfonie G-moll," *Das Meisterwerk in der Musik*, vol. II

(a) from fig. 1, layer analysis of first movement

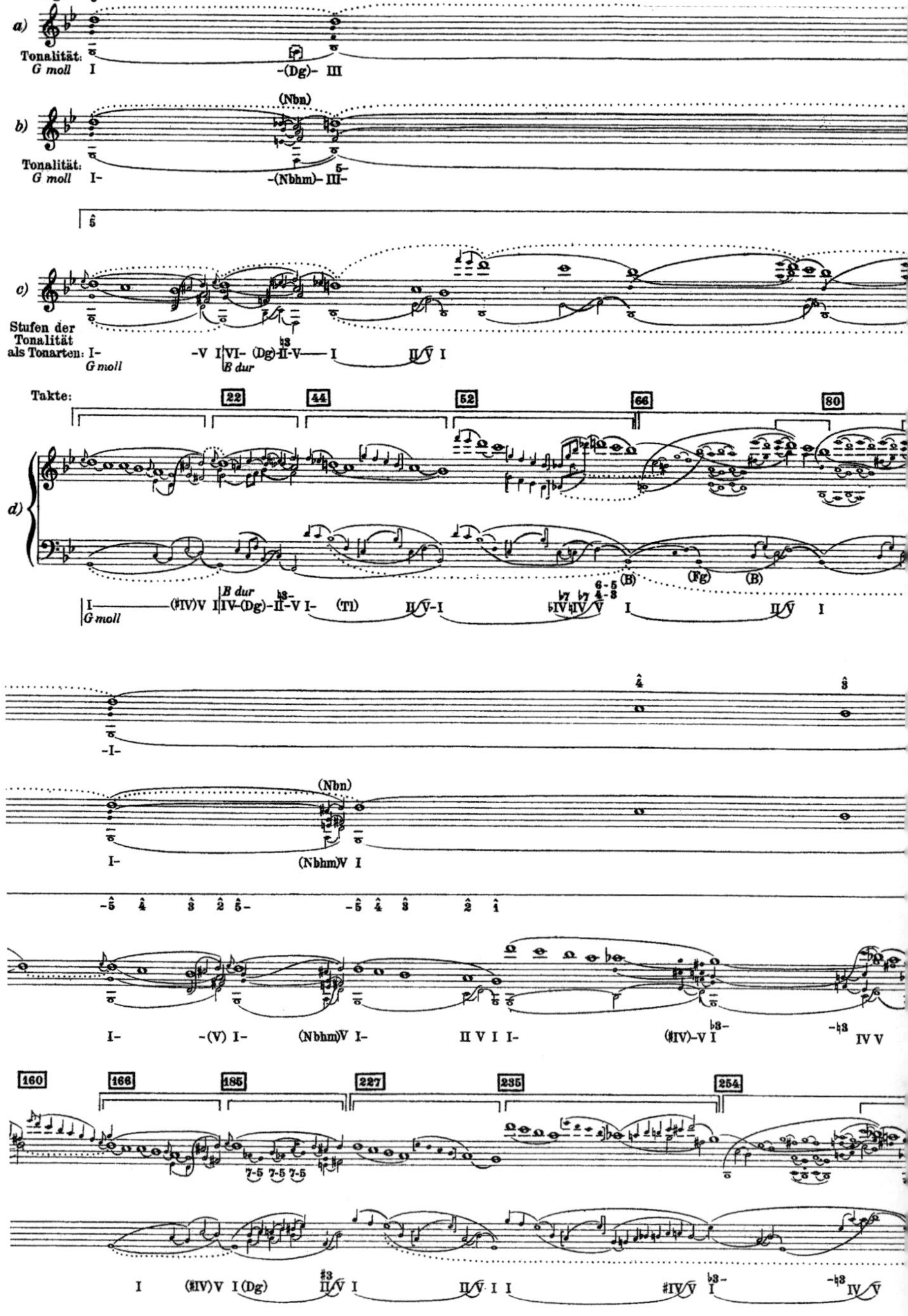

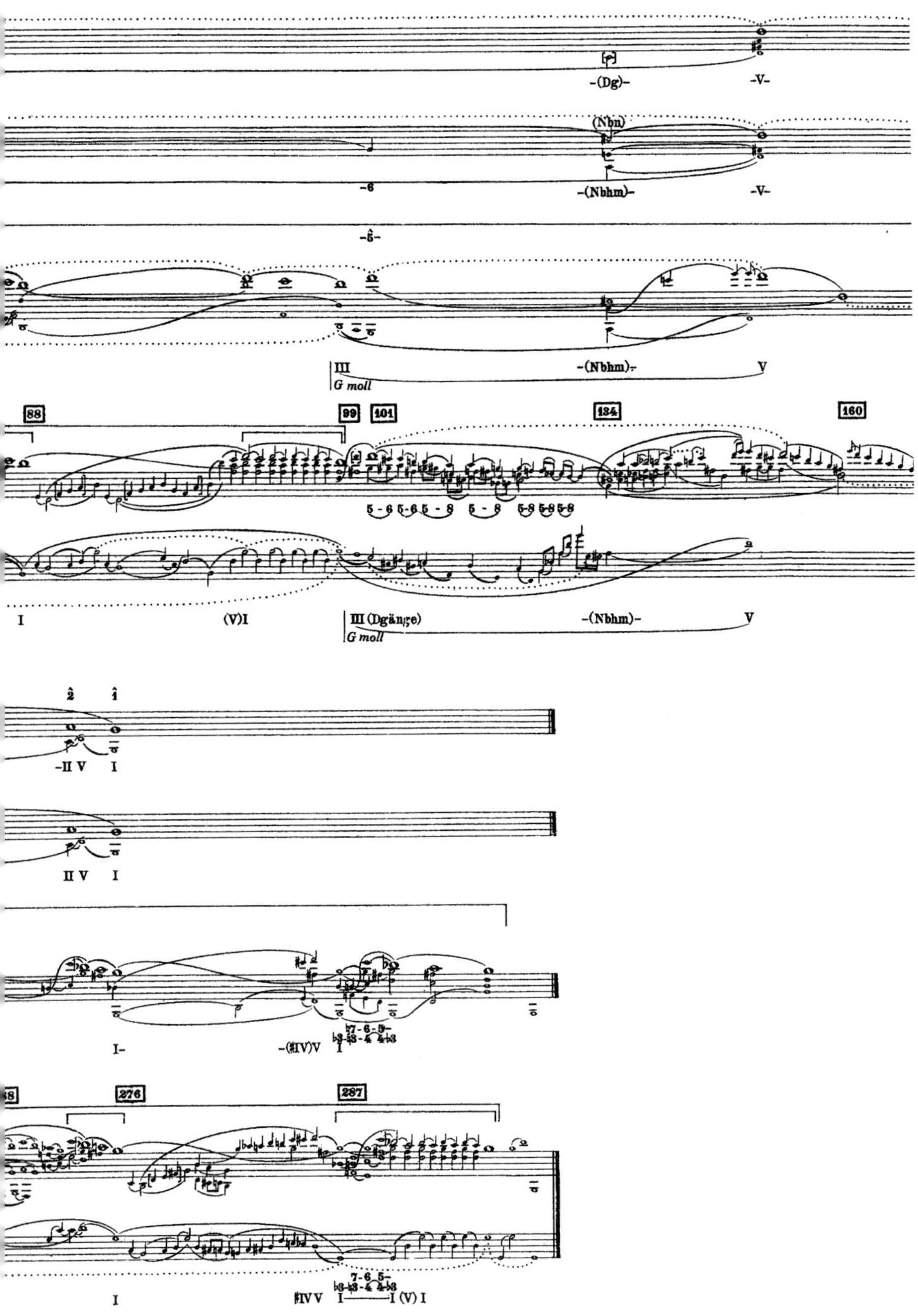
-(Dg)-
-V-
(Nbn)
-6
-(Nbhm)-
-V-
-5̂-
III
G moll
-(Nbhm)-
V
88
99
101
134
160
5 - 6 5-6 5 - 8 5 - 8 5-8 5-8 5-8
I
(V)I
III (Dgänge)
G moll
-(Nbhm)-
V
2̂
1̂
-II V
I
II V
I
I-
-(♯IV)V
I
276
287
I
♯IV V
I
I (V) I

Example 26.4 (*cont.*)
(b) from the *Urlinie-Tafel* of the first movement

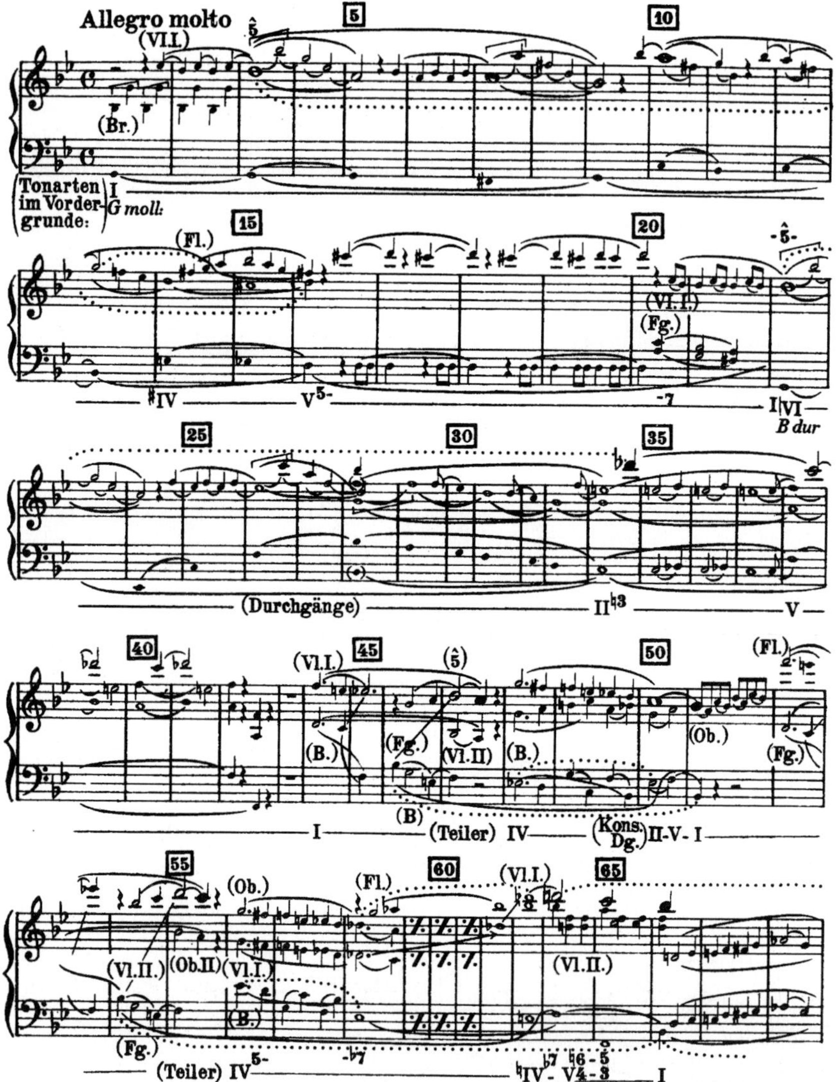

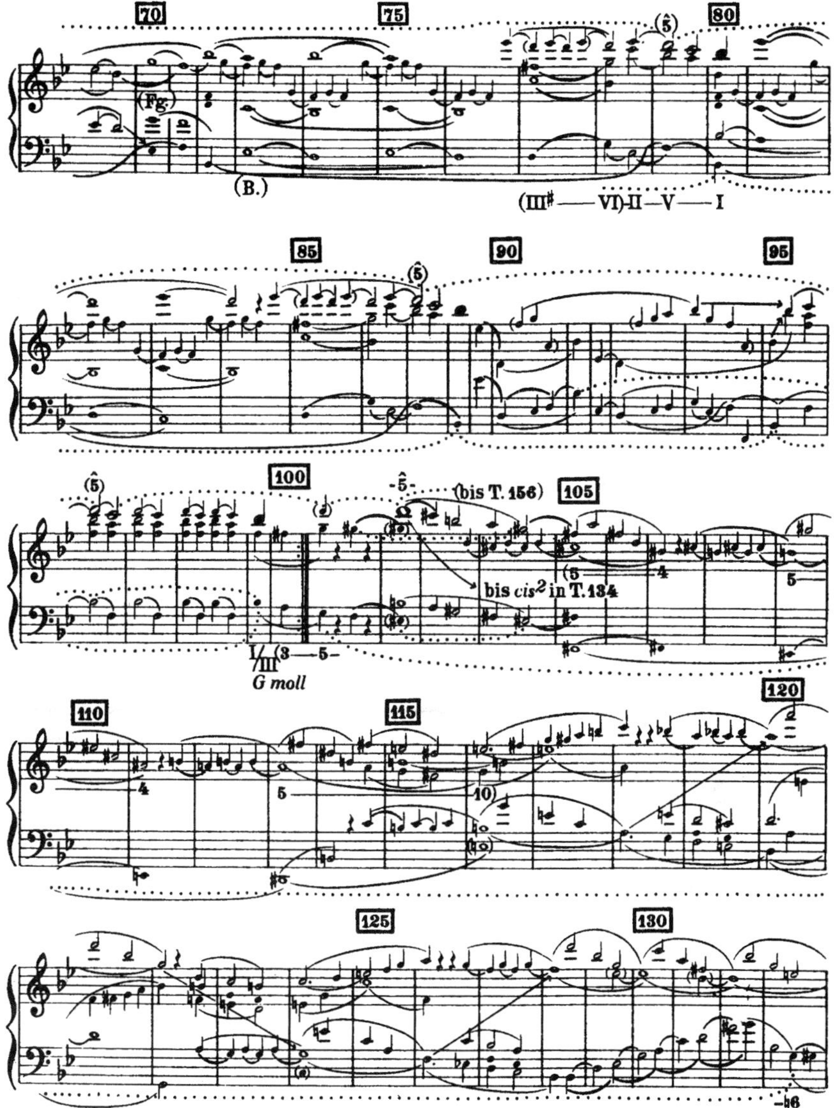
70
75
80
(Fg.)
(B.)
(5̂)
(III♯ — VI)-II — V — I
85
90
95
(5̂)
(5̂)
100
-5̂-
(bis T. 156)
105
bis cis2 in T. 134
I/III (3 — 5 —
G moll
110
115
120
125
130

Example 26.5 *Der freie Satz*, fig. 87/5: Mozart, Sonata in A, K. 331, first movement, mm. 1–8

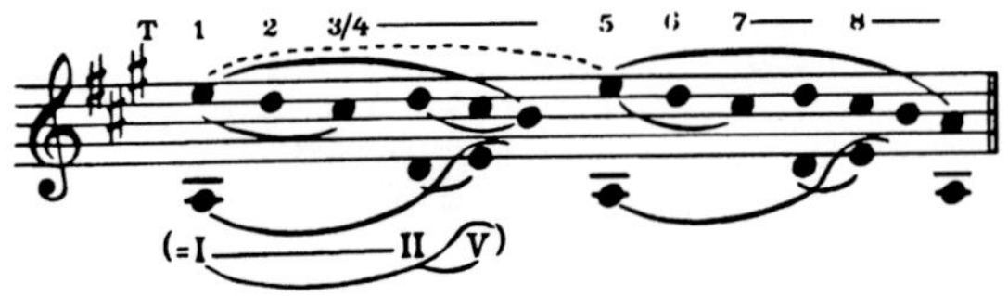

between structure and detail. If "diminution" means, for historians of seventeenth- and eighteenth-century music, the practice of ornamentation or the elaboration of a framework (e.g., an Adagio written skeletally in long note values) or a chord progression (e.g., the realization of a cadenza or the improvising of a prelude), then *Auskomponierung* could be understood as diminution, with the additional requirement that the elaborations must not be applied arbitrarily but are needed to promote the overall unity of a composition (or, in Schenker's preferred term, its "synthesis").[17] In the Bach prelude, for instance, the rising fourths e^2–a^2 and d^2–g^2 (in mm. 4–7) are diminutions of the upper-voice movement from e^2 to d^2. The fourth in the bass in mm. 8–9, though it gives the illusion of V–I in G major, is also a diminution of a conceptual stepwise descent, from a to g; synthesis is promoted by the repetition of the same interval, D rising to a G, in different voices.

In *Der freie Satz* much is also made of "concealed repetition," achieved by making a short figure or an interval in the foreground the basis of an extensive elaboration later in the piece. Schenker's essays sometimes refer specifically to "diminution motives," i.e., figures that are consistently applied at various structural levels. In his essay on the G minor Symphony, the upward leap of a sixth and its inversion, the descending third, are identified as motives characteristic of the foreground of the first movement (represented in Example 26.4b). At higher levels the stepwise descent of a second, in pairs, is a characteristic diminution technique (compare the start of levels (*c*) and (*d*) in Example 26.4a); the original neighbor figure in the melody, E♭ slurred to D in the violin parts, is also an expression of this two-note linearity.[18]

Prolongation can also be achieved by repeating material, and musical form is often created by the repetition of portions of the *Ursatz* itself. A technique of fundamental importance in this respect is *Unterbrechung*, the "interruption" of the progress of the *Ursatz* at $\hat{2}$/V, which necessitates a new beginning. All constructions based on antecedent and consequent phrases can be understood as elaborations of interrupted struc-

17 For discussion – and illustrations – of diminution techniques in earlier music theory, see Chapter 17, pp. 544–48.

18 The term *Diminutionsmotiv* appears as such only in the analysis of Bach's Largo for solo violin (*Meisterwerk*, vol. I), but its spirit informs other analyses. In the Mozart symphony essay, for instance, Schenker describes the *Diminution* of the various structural levels as having their "own special motivic characteristic[s]" (*Meisterwerk*, vol. II, p. 117).

Example 26.6 Sonata-form movements as elaborations of interrupted *Urlinien*
(a) *Der freie Satz*, fig. 154/5a: Beethoven, *Pastoral* Symphony, first movement

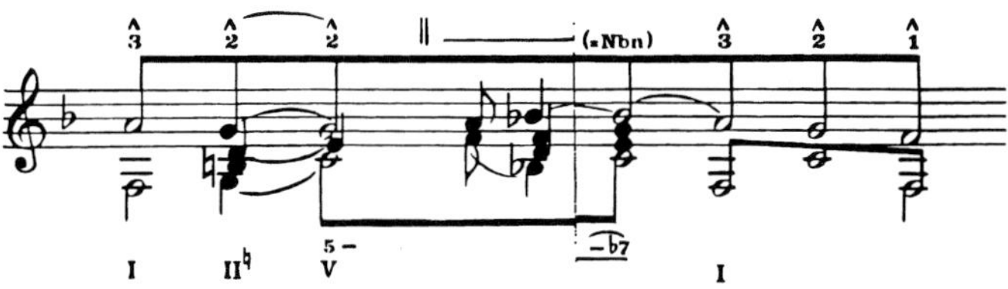

(b) *Der freie Satz*, fig. 47/1: Mozart, Sonata in C, K. 545, first movement

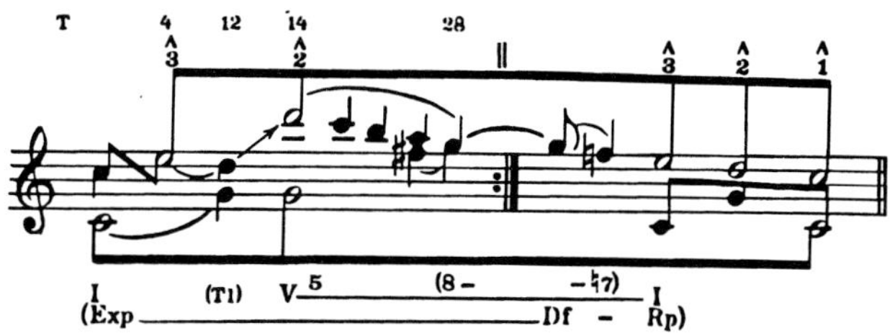

tures. In the first-movement theme from Mozart's Sonata in A, K. 331, mm. 1–5 show a linear progression from e² that is expected to end at a¹; it is interrupted after four measures, and must begin again in order to reach its goal (see Example 26.5).

Since the first arrival of $\hat{2}$/V marks the halfway point in the structure, Schenker refers to it as the *teilende Dominante* ("dividing dominant") or simply *Teiler* ("divider").[19] In doing so, he invites comparison with themes that, though they do not have an interrupted structure in the upper voice, are similarly constructed in two halves with the first ending on a dominant. One such example is the second-group theme of the first movement of Mozart's G minor Symphony, at mm. 44–51: the dominant in m. 47 is marked "Teiler" or "Tl" in the analytical graphs (Example 26.4), since it lacks the harmonic weight of a *Stufe*.[20]

19 *Der freie Satz*, §89.

20 The use of the term *Teiler* in both contexts suggests that, for Schenker, the second half of a symmetrically designed theme has greater structural weight The dotted line linking the two e²s in Example 26.5 further implies that the first four measures of the Mozart theme elaborate the primary tone of the linear descent, i.e., the e² in m. 1; this would mean that the first arrival on V has less structural weight than the V of the V–I cadence in m. 8. This end-oriented view of interruption is consistent with Schenker's theory in general, and with his explanation and use of the term *Teiler*. It is contradicted, however, by other graphs in *Der freie Satz* and by the text (§90), which stipulates that, in an interrupted structure, the first arrival on the dominant is the more important of the two. The editors of the English edition of *Der freie Satz* attempt an explanation of this difficulty (see *Free Composition*, p. 37, note 6); for a fuller discussion of the problem of hierarchy in interrupted structure, see Smith, "Musical Form and Fundamental Structure," esp. pp. 267–69.

At a higher level, e.g., in a complete two-part song form, the entire first part may be represented as a descent to $\hat{2}$ supported by I–V, with the second part traversing the same ground but ending on the $\hat{1}$/I. In sonata form, the first arrival on $\hat{2}$/V marks the start of the conventionally termed "second group"; the development section will then convert this dominant to a V^7, for instance by elaborating the space of a third lying immediately above the fifth of the dominant (V^{5-7}), as in Example 26.6a (a middleground graph of the opening movement of Beethoven's *Pastoral* Symphony), or as a passing seventh of an 8–7 progression superimposed above $\hat{2}$, as in Example 26.6b (a middleground graph of Mozart's Sonata in C, K. 545, first movement). In both cases the resulting seventh can also be understood as an upper neighbor note to the $\hat{3}$.[21]

Form can also be created with the large-scale application of prolongation techniques normally associated with the foreground. For instance, a minuet or scherzo movement, with a trio section in the parallel key, could be understood in terms of *Mischung* ("modal mixture"): elaboration of the tonic by alternation with its tonic minor, i.e., as a $I^{\natural 3-\flat 3-\natural 3}$ progression.[22] Similarly, a trio section cast in the subdominant key could be explained as a prolongation of the tonic by a neighbor note and its supporting *Nebennotenharmonie* ("neighbor-note harmony"), e.g., $\hat{4}$ (supported by IV) elaborating $\hat{3}$-($\hat{2}$–$\hat{1}$) on either side.[23]

Musical elaboration is also assisted by changes of register. In the Bach Prelude in C major, the descent of the upper voice of the *Ursatz* is the shortest line between two notes of the tonic triad, a third. But at the next structural level, an octave descent to e^1 and an ascent from d^1 are shown to unfold from the original upper voice. These processes, which involve a change of the register governing prolongations, are called *Tieferlegung* and *Höherlegung*, commonly rendered as "descending register transfer" and "ascending register transfer," respectively. When the two are employed in pairs, a registral linkage is created, called *Koppelung* ("coupling"). In a short, summarizing graph of the Prelude in *Der freie Satz*, Fig. 49/1, shown here as Example 26.7, the register transfers are indicated by the "crossed" beaming of e^2–e^1 and d^1–d^2 but are not so labeled. Nor are the registers specifically marked as having been "coupled," though this is self-evident from the symmetry of the graph.[24]

21 *Der freie Satz* – fig. 154/5a. and fig. 47/1. In Example 26.6a, the representation of sonata form as $\hat{3}$ $\hat{2}$ || – (Nbn) $\hat{3}$-$\hat{2}$–$\hat{1}$ is a hybrid form of prolongation, a conflation of interruption and neighbor-note elaboration; $b\flat^1$ (= Nbn) is, strictly speaking, an incomplete neighbor to the a^1 that follows it but, taking a larger view of the analysis, it refers also to the a^1 at the start of the graph.

In Example 26.6b, the outlines of sonata form are indicated in parenthesis beneath the harmonic analysis; Schenker dates the recapitulation ("Rp," for *Reprise*) not from the reprise of the opening theme – unconventionally – in F major (m. 42), but from the definitive return of the tonic which follows.

22 *Der freie Satz*, fig. 28a. 23 Ibid., figs. 35/1 and 40/1.

24 In the more formal analysis of the Prelude, published in the *Fünf Urlinie-Tafeln*, Schenker confusingly labeled the descending and ascending register transfers "Kopp[elung] abw.[ärts]" and "Kopp.[elung] aufw.[ärts]," respectively, i.e., descending and ascending "coupling." At that time, he had still not worked out a clear relationship between the concepts *Höherlegung*, *Tieferlegung*, and *Koppelung*.

Example 26.7 *Der freie Satz*, fig. 49/1: new middleground graph of Bach's Prelude in C

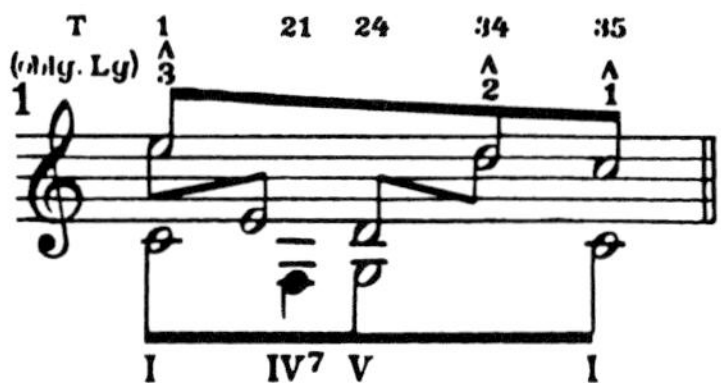

The principle of hierarchy is, however, still in force, with one register taking precedence over the other. In the Bach prelude, the upper voice starts on e^2 and ends on c^2, so its higher octave predominates in the background, despite the long progression into the lower register and the extensive elaboration of the interval d^1–f^1; Schenker called this the *obligate Lage* ("obligatory register").

The Mozart piano sonata movement (Example 26.6b, above) also shows how register can promote musical synthesis by creating a long-range connection. In the exposition the second group is set in a higher register, its upper voice governed by the linear progression d^3–g^2. The dominant of the second group is elaborated as a dominant seventh in the development, g^2 passing through f^2. When this seventh resolves, the original starting point, e^2, is regained, and in this way Mozart returns to the initial register without actually making an exact recapitulation of the opening theme.

Linearity

The notion that "coherence" and "connection" are closely related (in German, the word *Zusammenhang* can be used for both) finds a special resonance in Schenker's view of musical structure: even those writers who have kept a respectful distance from Schenkerian analysis or have categorically rejected its principles have nevertheless been attracted by the search for connections between musical events resulting from pitch identity or proximity.

A succession of diatonic steps joining two voices in a chord, or in adjacent chords, is called a *Zug* (plural *Züge*; the term is most commonly translated as "linear progression," or simply "progression"). In the first elaboration of the chord of Nature, the upper voice – the *Urlinie* – is a *Zug*, since it joins two notes of the tonic triad. And when the passing d^2 of an e^2–d^2–c^2 *Urlinie* (see Example 26.3c) is turned into a consonance by the support of g in the bass, i.e. $\hat{2}$ supported by V, it is capable of generating further content by the application of a new linear progression. This is shown in Schenker's analysis of the Mozart sonata movement (Example 26.6b, above): the $\hat{2}$, after being transferred to a higher octave, itself becomes the starting point of a linear progression encompassing a fifth. The new progression, an elaboration of the dominant harmony (*Auskomponierung der V. Stufe*), is Schenker's way of saying that the second group (mm. 14–28) of the exposition is in the dominant key of G major.

Schenker qualified his linear progressions by the size of interval they embraced. The *Urlinie* of the Mozart sonata movement is a *Terzzug* ("third-progression"); the line from $\hat{2}$ is called a *Quintzug* ("fifth-progression"). As is the case for many techniques of prolongation, linear progressions may exist at any structural level, and they are sometimes transformed from one level to the next. In the first movement of the G minor Symphony (see Example 26.4, above), the *Urlinie* embraces a fifth, d^2–g^1. The first subject (antecedent phrase, mm. 1–21) is graphed as a fourth-progression at level (c), which is extended to a sixth in (d).

Since linear progressions join registral spaces, they give the effect of a play among the polyphonic voices. An elementary way in which this works is at the beginning of a composition, where an ascending line may lead up to the primary tone of the *Urlinie*, e.g. $\hat{1}$–$\hat{2}$–$\hat{3}$ or $\hat{3}$–$\hat{4}$–$\hat{5}$, and thus fill the space between the "alto" and "soprano" of the opening harmony; Schenker called this progression an *Anstieg* (usually translated as "initial ascent"). Another common technique is *Übergreifen*, a kind of registral leapfrogging by the superposition of one or more descending linear progressions to form a series of steps. *Übergreifen* (now translated by most English-speaking theorists as "reaching over") enables a composer to reach a higher register, or to regain the primary tone of an earlier linear progression, or to create an ascending line from a series of short descending progressions. In the Mozart symphony movement, the modulation to B♭ in mm. 22–42 is assisted by a series of short *Übergreifzüge* finishing with a neighbor-note figure. The overall effect is an elaboration of the third, d^2–e^2–f^2 (see also Example 26.4a, level *d*) and Example 26.4b).[25]

measure:	22	24	26	28	34	38
				f^2 ⌒	e♮^{2}	f^2
			e♭^{2} ⌒	d^2		
	d^2 ⌒	c^2				

Because their points of origin and their goals are clear, linear progressions show unity in musical movement. But linearity in a Schenkerian sense can also mean the connection between widely spaced occurrences of the same note, e.g. the d^2 at the start of the Mozart symphony movement and the d^2 in m. 16, at the first *forte*, or even the d^2 at m. 44 in the second group. Whereas earlier theorists demonstrated musical relatedness more by thematic similarity or the derivation of one theme from another, Schenker demonstrated that a single note, correctly positioned and supported, might be enough to confer synthesis over a large musical time-span. It is this aspect of Schenker's work

25 Although the term *Übergreifzug* contains the word *Zug*, such a "progression" often consists of just two notes, rather than the minimum of three needed for linear progressions that act on their own.

in particular that has attracted the attention of many twentieth-century theorists who are not wholly sympathetic to a layered view of musical structure, or are mistrustful of what they perceive to be an excessive reliance on graphic representation.[26]

Historical and intellectual background

Schenker's published writings tell us little about the source of his insights into music. On the contrary, they give every indication that he regarded them very much as his sole property, developed over years of private engagement with the canonic repertory of Western music, without recourse to the academy or the contemporary music scene. This is well encapsulated in a postscript to some analyses of short keyboard works by Bach, which includes the following statement:

> Blessed by the grace of our greatest, I have held up a mirror to music, as no ancient, medieval or modern philosopher, no musician, music historian or aesthetician – or any of these considered together – has been able to do. I am the first to explain its internal laws, to comprehend the vivacious ear of the German masters and their capacity for invention and synthesis. I have explained their daring invention in the realm of hearing, as had previously been experienced only in the realm of the other senses. And I have, so to speak, revealed for the first time by verbal communication the realm of hearing, as our masters understood it, and so have enriched human existence by a new dimension.[27]

These sentiments are expressed more succinctly in the inscription on his gravestone in the Central Cemetery in Vienna: "Here lies the man who perceived the soul of music, and who proclaimed its laws as the masters understood them, as no one had done before."

On the assumption that every intellectual idea has its genealogy, scholars have attempted to trace Schenker's conception of music theory back to its cultural, philosophical and musical roots. According to a lifelong friend, Moriz Violin, the music of Mozart and Beethoven and the literature of Schiller and Goethe were an important part of his childhood upbringing.[28] Schenker's extensive quotations of eighteenth- and nineteenth-century German writers bear witness to an intellectual background that may have been as much literary as it was musical.

Extracts from the works of Goethe figure in almost every publication; Schenker quoted him more often than any other writer, and he may have found inspiration for the concept of a structural background in Goethe's scientific writings; indeed, the very word *Ursatz* has strong resonance with the *Urpflanze* of Goethe's botanical studies. William Pastille has suggested that the relationship of species counterpoint to the

26 Rosen, *The Classical Style*; Meyer, *Explaining Music*; Narmour, *Beyond Schenkerism*.
27 *Tonwille*, vol. 5, p. 55. 28 Federhofer, *Heinrich Schenker, nach Tagebüchern und Briefen*, p. 4.

behavior of parts in "real" music, crucial to Schenker's view of musical structure, recalls Goethe's concept of the *Urphänomen*; and, further, that Schenker's long-range, or "structural" hearing is closely related to Goethe's more visionary type of perception – *Anschauung* – that comes from beholding things within a theoretical framework rather than noting their surface features.[29]

Concerning philosophical influences, one notes above all Schenker's indebtedness to Immanuel Kant. As Kevin Korsyn has shown, there is a strong kinship between the Kantian notion of causality and Schenker's *Synthese*, a "synthesis" by which the musical mind conceives tones as bound to one another in much the same way as the philosophical mind comprehends events as following one another in a particular order.[30] The familiar criticism of Schenker, that his theoretical program and particularly his analytical graphing technique ignore the function of time in music, falls away if one accepts that Schenkerian synthesis implies time-consciousness; thus true musical perception is a form of Kantian "transcendental apperception," in which temporal ordering is an indispensable ingredient.[31] Both Kant and Schenker also shared a view of genius as the means "through which Nature gives rules to art";[32] for Schenker the gift of genius was innate, God-given.

The influence of Arthur Schopenhauer is more elusive, and has not been researched systematically. Quotations from his writings are scarce; one was used as a prop on which to hang the anti-imperialist sentiments vented by Schenker in the aftermath of the First World War.[33] The idea of musical tones having a "will," and that they are intrinsically bound to behave in a certain way, is expressed in the first volume of *Kontrapunkt* (1910)[34] and enshrined in the series title *Der Tonwille*, which marks the start of Schenker's most ambitious project in analysis. That he saw in Schopenhauer (and, by extension, in Kierkegaard and Nietzsche) a kindred spirit is suggested by two quotations from *The World as Will and Representation*, which are drawn together to provide an analogy between the true creative artist, who is able to achieve insight with direct expression, and the scholar who strives for truth and wisdom for its own sake, unmediated by the authority conferred by academic stature or other such approval ratings.[35]

Schenker's unshakable faith in his own theories of music led him to denigrate the writings of most of his contemporaries. This led to a general view of Schenker as an iconoclast, a theorist working entirely outside of tradition, a point that is reinforced by his isolation from Viennese academic musical life. His contemptuous references to "die Theorie" in a pair of essays on sonata form and fugue from 1926 underscore his

29 Pastille, "Music and Morphology"; see esp. pp. 34–38.

30 Korsyn, "Schenker and Kantian Epistemology." 31 Ibid., pp. 34–35. 32 Ibid., p. 7.

33 *Tonwille*, vol. 1, p. 13.

34 "Thus tones cannot produce any desired effect just because of the wish of the individual who sets them, for nobody has the power over tones in the sense that he is able to demand from them something contrary to their nature Even tones must do what they must do!" *Counterpoint*, vol. I, p. 14. The energeticist context of Schenker's views is explored further in Chapter 30, pp. 936–39.

35 *Tonwille*, vols. 8–9, p. 48; see also Federhofer, *Heinrich Schenker, nach Tagebüchern und Briefen*, p. 89.

isolation from mainstream theory teaching as exemplified, for instance, in the work of Hugo Riemann and the series of handbooks published by Max Hesse in Berlin, which featured Riemann's writings.[36] His surveys of the secondary literature, a regular feature of his analytical essays of the 1910s and 1920s, are taken up by extensive quotation from and ridicule of contemporary scholarship and journalism. The few authors who are singled out for praise – and then only briefly – were either personal friends, such as Otto Vrieslander and August Halm, or writers with only loose links to theoretical traditions: thus E. T. A. Hoffmann is lauded for his declaration of interest in Beethoven for the sake of the music alone, the Beethoven scholar Gustav Nottebohm for making the contents of the sketchbooks accessible to a wider public. Otherwise, one must go back to eighteenth-century music theory for palpable connections.

Jean-Philippe Rameau's notion that all modulations arise in relation to a single tonic is an important forerunner to the concept of *Tonalität*, the "home key" to which all the fundamental harmonies, or *Stufen*, are ultimately related;[37] on the other hand, the extraction of a *basse fondamentale* as a synthesis of vertical organization and chord progression must have seemed inimical to someone concerned above all with linear connections, in both melodic and bass lines. Rameau accepted the seventh above the fundamental as a component of a chord, whereas Schenker followed the precept of Johann Joseph Fux that all dissonance in music must be introduced and resolved properly.[38] And as Schenker came to view his concept of musical structure in nationalist terms, Rameau's Frenchness became an unalterable blot on his character.[39]

Fux's *Gradus ad Parnassum* was widespread in Europe, and was known to have figured prominently in the musical training – and teaching – of Schenker's heroes, including Haydn, Mozart, Beethoven, and Brahms (see the extensive discussion in **Chapter 18, pp. 579–84**). It is thus hardly surprising to find him coming to terms with it in the two volumes of *Kontrapunkt*. But while Schenker praised the *Gradus* for its insights into vocal music, he was critical of what he perceived as Fux's distrust of instrumental music, with its creative uses of voice-leading principles, coupled with a failure to distinguish clearly between counterpoint as a pedagogical discipline and composition as a creative act. Indeed, it is Schenker's profound insights into the relationship between the contrapuntal species and what happens in "real" music, from Bach to the end of the nineteenth century, that represent his greatest triumph as an analyst. His defense of consecutive major thirds in a Wagner *Leitmotiv* as the "lovely fruit of the composing-out of scale degrees!" is not merely emblematic of his view of instrumental part-writing as counterpoint, but simply and perfectly encapsulates the need to reconcile the rules governing harmony in short stretches with the opportunities for synthesis offered by musical linearity. (It is also a useful counter-example to the widespread

36 The essays, on the subjects of sonata form and fugue, appear in *Meisterwerk*, vol. II. Hesse also published analyses by Hugo Leichtentritt of the music of Chopin; these were ridiculed in the two Chopin essays in *Meisterwerk*, vol. I.

37 Christensen, *Rameau*, p. 177, note 29.

38 *Meisterwerk*, vol. III, p. 17.

39 Ibid., pp. 13–15.

Example 26.8 *Counterpoint*, vol. 1, Example 203: extract from Wagner's *Rheingold*, scene 4

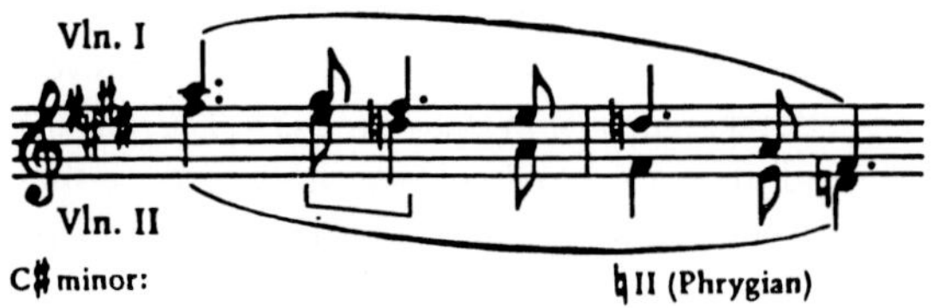

belief that Schenker had little sympathy for Wagner's music.[40]) As Example 26.8 shows, the persistence of g♯² above the Neapolitan sixth chord shows that the home key prevails in spite of the lower-order demands for a flattening of this note to avoid an augmented fourth (false relation) between the moving parts.[41]

Perhaps the most important of all of Schenker's predecessors was Carl Philipp Emanuel Bach, above all for his *Versuch über die wahre Art das Klavier zu spielen* of 1753–62, with its emphasis upon linearity in continuo playing and the need "to hold the register together" in the realization of a chord progression.[42] But when it came to offering a tribute to Bach's role in musical art, it was not his advice to the accompanist but his skills as an improviser and composer that Schenker dwelt on at length, by showing how Bach's suggestions for improvisation technique are firmly underpinned by such concepts as arpeggiation, voice-exchange, and what he called "parallelism," the consistent application of motivic patterns to the middleground. By subjecting the free fantasia in D printed at the end of the *Versuch*, and other short pieces, to the same type of voice-leading analysis he used elsewhere, Schenker granted Bach the same canonical status he conferred on only a handful of other masters.[43]

Nearer to his own time, Schenker may have been influenced by the lively debate sparked by the republication of Eduard Hanslick's *The Beautiful in Music* in 1885. Alan Keiler has suggested that Schenker's early views on the origin of music were influenced by critiques of Hanslick by two younger scholars attached to the University of Vienna, Friedrich von Hausegger and Robert Hirschfeld. Hausegger's *Die Musik als Ausdruck* in particular has strong resonances in Schenker's views on the origins of music and its significance for the study of history, as expounded in an important early essay, "Der Geist der musikalischen Technik" (1895).[44]

40 On the possible indebtedness of Schenkerian theory to the writings of Wagner, see Cook, "Heinrich Schenker, Polemicist."

41 For further illustrations, and a fuller explanation of Schenker's contrapuntal agenda, see Dubiel, "When You Are a Beethoven," pp. 291–340. Also see the discussion in **Chapter 18, pp. 592–94**.

42 *Meisterwerk*, vol. II, p. 118.

43 *Tonwille*, vol. 4, pp. 10–13; *Meisterwerk*, vol. I, pp. 13–30. Schenker also honored Bach in a two-volume edition of selected keyboard works.

44 Keiler, "Origins of Schenker's Thought," esp. pp. 292–94.

Reception and influence

Schenker seems to have enjoyed a considerable following in his own lifetime (for a long time posterity underestimated it), but it was nothing like the renown his theories were to bring him after his death in 1935: textbooks, courses, seminars, and conferences on Schenkerian theory; the establishment of major research archives based round his private papers; and a seemingly endless supply of voice-leading graphs in journals and books, supporting a range of theoretical, analytical, and historical viewpoints.

Schenker's final years saw the rise of National Socialism; three years after his death, Hitler's troops marched into Vienna and supervised the annexation of Austria to the Third Reich. Amidst the most difficult circumstances, two of Schenker's pupils, Oswald Jonas and Felix Salzer, kept the Schenkerian flame alive through their own writings;[45] the leading article of a short-lived periodical they co-edited perpetuates the notion of "mission" Schenker had expressed years earlier in the inaugural issue of *Der Tonwille*.[46] The efforts of Professor Reinhard Oppel to disseminate Schenkerian theory at the Leipzig Conservatory, and of Felix-Eberhard von Cube to establish a thriving Schenker Institute in Hamburg, quickly ran aground as the Nazis closed in on Jewish-based teaching. Faced with the imminent annihilation of European Jewry, and with it European Jewish thought, Jonas and Salzer emigrated to America where another pupil of Schenker's, Hans Weisse, had established an outpost of Schenkerian teaching at the David Mannes School of Music in New York. Transplanted to the New World, Schenkerian analysis began to thrive in the teaching programs of conservatories and university music departments, and in the research of a new generation of theorists and their pupils.[47]

Much of the early activity was concentrated around pedagogy. There had been concern among Schenker's circle that his writings were too difficult: Jonas's first book, published while Schenker was still alive, bears the subtitle "Introduction to the teaching of Heinrich Schenker," and was intended for readers without prior knowledge of his methods.[48] The publication of Salzer's *Structural Hearing* in 1952 represented a greater milestone, in that it made available to English readers literally hundreds of voice-leading graphs together with brief analyses covering a wide repertory; it became

45 Jonas, *Das Wesen des musikalischen Kunstwerkes* (1934); Salzer, *Sinn und Wesen* (1935). Around this time Adele Katz, a pupil of Hans Weisse, wrote the first exposition of Schenkerian analysis in English ("Schenker's Method"), and later expanded his theories in book form, *Challenge to Musical Tradition* (1945).

46 That is, Schenker's "Die Sendung des deutschen Genies" of 1921 became "Die historische Sendung Heinrich Schenkers" in 1937.

47 For a brief history of Schenkerism in North America, see Rothstein, "Americanization"; for a comprehensive survey of the literature on Schenkerian analysis until 1985, see David Beach's bibliographical articles.

48 *Das Wesen des musikalischen Kunstwerkes: eine Einführung in die Lehre Heinrich Schenkers*. The title and subtitle were reversed when the book was reissued in German in 1972, and trans. into English ten years later.

the principal Schenker textbook for the postwar generation. The long-awaited translation of Schenker's last work in 1979, under the bilingual title *Free Composition (Der freie Satz)*, helped standardize Schenkerian terminology in English; but because this book was heralded as marking a breakthrough in North American Schenker pedagogy, its polemic passages were relegated to an appendix, and a number of established Schenkerians were enlisted to help clarify the more difficult parts of the theory and to suggest routes into the text.[49] The utility of *Free Composition* was, however, overestimated, and the past two quarter-centuries have witnessed a rapid, unabated growth in the number of explanatory textbooks on Schenkerian analysis.[50]

Not surprisingly, the attempt to render Schenker's work accessible has also led to new developments in his theories. Although Schenker himself stressed that his work was artistic, not scientific, succeeding generations of theorists felt the need for it to be more internally consistent. One sees not only a more scientific approach, as early as Forte's seminal essay of 1959, but also numerous attempts to come to terms with ambiguities and inconsistencies in the theory. Both the sanctity of the two-voice *Ursatz* and the primacy of the descending $\hat{3}$–$\hat{2}$–$\hat{1}$ *Urlinie* have been challenged,[51] and theorists now generally accept the possibility that a piece may admit more than one valid Schenkerian reading.[52]

Forte's essay identified the study of rhythm in relation to voice-leading analysis as a major area in need of investigation. Some fruitful work in this area was undertaken by Arthur Komar and Maury Yeston,[53] but it was with Carl Schachter's three-part study of rhythm and linear analysis that Schenkerian voice-leading graphs were first harnessed systematically with rhythmic analyses. Subsequent developments in this field have been made by Fred Lerdahl and Ray Jackendoff in their investigations into grouping and meter, and in William Rothstein's study of phrase rhythm.[54]

The number of voice-leading analyses of instrumental works is legion, but that of the operatic, choral, and solo song repertory has been much more restricted. Schenker

49 In addition to the translator's preface, there is a translation of Jonas's preface to the second German edition, an "introduction" to the English edition by Allen Forte, a range of clarificatory footnotes by John Rothgeb supplementing those by Jonas and Oster, and a glossary of technical terms. See also Schachter, "Commentary on *Free Composition*."

50 These include Westergaard, *Introduction to Tonal Theory*; Neumeyer and Tepping, *Guide to Schenkerian Analysis*; Cadwallader and Gagné, *Analysis of Tonal Music*. The most widely used textbook has been Forte and Gilbert, *Introduction to Schenkerian Analysis*, thanks largely to its scope, organization, and systematic set of student exercises, together with a companion *Instructor's Manual* which provides solutions to many of the exercises.

The 1980s also saw the proliferation of textbooks on analytical method in which the explication of Schenker's theories figures prominently: Cook, *Guide to Musical Analysis*; Bent, *Analysis*; Dunsby and Whittall, *Music Analysis*. For more on Schenker's influence on the pedagogy of music theory in North America, see **Chapter 2, p. 72**.

51 Neumeyer, "The Ascending *Urlinie*"; "The Three-Part *Ursatz*"; "The *Urlinie* from $\hat{8}$"; Beach, "The Fundamental Line from Scale Degree 8"; Chew, "The Spice of Music."

52 Federhofer, *Akkord und Stimmführung*, Chapter 4; Drabkin et al., *L'analisi schenkeriana*, pp. 91–93; Schachter, "Either/Or"; Drabkin, "Consonant Passing Note."

53 Komar, *Theory of Suspensions*; Yeston, *The Stratification of Musical Rhythm*.

54 Lerdahl and Jackendoff, *A Generative Theory of Tonal Music*; Rothstein, *Phrase Rhythm in Tonal Music*. See also **Chapter 3, pp. 99–102**; and **Chapter 22, pp. 703–10**.

himself published few analyses of works in these genres, though a brief comment on Schubert's *Am Meer* offers one of the clearest examples of the relationship of words to music from a Schenkerian viewpoint.[55] Some of Schenker's closest followers have made major contributions to the bearing of a sung text on the analysis of music,[56] though in much of the best work in the field, the Schenkerian approach is one of a number of coordinated methods.[57]

Just as an adequate theory of the relationship between voice-leading and rhythm had to await the reception of Schenkerian theory by a younger generation of scholars, so the matters concerning musical form have been integrated into voice-leading theory only recently. If Schenker's ideas on form were, characteristically, full of insight, his graphic representations were inconsistent even – as Charles Smith persuasively showed – within an ostensibly unified presentation such as the music examples for *Der freie Satz*.[58] In particular, Schenker had failed to clarify the relative status of the two parts of an interrupted structure, and was inconsistent in his mapping of the conventionally termed parts of a form ("second group," "recapitulation" etc.) onto graphic representations of the middleground.

Another project that Schenker barely touched on in his writings was the overall coherence of a multi-movement work, or a set of variations, i.e., pieces in which a separate *Ursatz* could be said to govern individual components. Recent writers have attempted to make sense of variation sets as "single pieces" in a Schenkerian sense,[59] and some have gone so far as to show how an entire sonata might be embraced by a single *Ursatz*, or how a set of bagatelles or character pieces form a coherent sequence in terms of their voice-leading.[60]

The field of contrapuntal music has proved more resistant to voice-leading analysis (Schenker's own studies of fugues by Bach and Brahms notwithstanding), and has only recently begun to receive the attention that it deserves.[61] Schenker provided substantial analyses neither of string quartets nor of solo concertos; given the preeminence of these genres in the oeuvre of Schenker's composers of "genius," it is surprising that little Schenkerian research has been undertaken in these repertories.

Schenker's deeply held belief that music was in decline was mainly expressed in general attacks on contemporary society. The shorter of his analytical counter-examples, a voice-leading analysis of an extract from Stravinsky's Piano Concerto, proved something of a model for later writers, including Adele Katz and Felix Salzer, whose influential *Structural Hearing* includes voice-leading analyses of works by Bartók, Hindemith, Prokofiev, Ravel and Stravinsky. The linearity of much late nineteenth- and twentieth-century composition may have been a significant factor. On the other

55 *Meisterwerk*, vol. I, pp. 199–200.

56 Jonas, *Das Wesen des musikalischen Kunstwerks* contains an important analysis of Schubert's *Der Lindenbaum*. See also Schachter, "Motive and Text."

57 See in particular Webster, "Mozart's Arias."

58 Smith, "Musical Form and Fundamental Structure."

59 Salzer, "Mozart's Divertimento, K 563"; Marston, "Analysing Variations."

60 Dunsby, "Multipiece"; Marston, "Trifles or Multi-Trifle?"; *Beethoven's Sonata in E, Op 109*, p. 253.

61 Renwick, *Analyzing Fugue*, "Hidden Fugal Paths."

hand, changes to the concepts of consonance and dissonance around 1900 make the principle of tonal hierarchy far more difficult to apply systematically to this repertory. Thus linear connections are made more on the basis of temporal proximity, with duration a key factor in determining the starting points and goals of progressions. And background structures take on new "dissonant" figurations, e.g., a $\sharp\hat{4}$–$\hat{3}$–$\hat{2}$–$\hat{1}$ *Urlinie* for the first movement of Bartók's Fourth Quartet.[62]

The linear analysis of "pre-Baroque" music has a longer and fuller history, beginning during Schenker's life with the study of medieval and Renaissance polyphony by his pupil Felix Salzer.[63] The changes to Schenkerian doctrine necessitated by the surface designs of early repertories are no less extensive than those for contemporary music. For early medieval polyphony the concepts of consonance, dissonance and part-writing result in much graphic analysis underpinned by chains of consecutive fifths or octaves, something which Schenker would have found inimical. Yet it has been claimed for the late secular songs of Guillaume de Machaut that "cadences [act] as the focus of directed progressions extended over considerable stretches of music."[64]

With consonance and dissonance treatment broadly codified in the Renaissance, the analysis of much sixteenth-century music is on surer ground, and examples of sensitive Schenkerian readings have appeared with some frequency.[65] There remains, however, the problem of large-scale unity in works that are conceived in accordance with the syntax of a sacred text. As Donald Tovey put it in a trenchant discussion of High Renaissance polyphonic texture, "Sixteenth-century music is aesthetically equivalent to the decorating of a space, but not to structure on an architectural scale," and it is consequently a mistake to "expect a high note in one place to produce a corresponding one long after Palestrina has effected all that he meant by it and directed his mind elsewhere."[66]

Schenker's admiration of the music of Johann Strauss and his efforts to promote it by providing voice-leading graphs of his more famous waltzes in *Der freie Satz* suggests that, his outright dismissal of jazz and other forms of popular music notwithstanding,[67] he saw the difference between good and bad as greater than that between serious and popular. The application of Schenkerian theory to jazz, American popular song, and non-Western music has flourished in recent years; it remains to be seen how post-modernist arguments against the contemplation of music outside its cultural context affect Schenkerian and other theoretically based approaches to all repertories of music in the twenty-first century.[68]

62 Travis, "Bartók's Fourth Quartet." 63 Salzer, *Sinn und Wesen.*

64 Leech-Wilkinson, "Machaut's *Rose, lis*," p. 23.

65 See, for example Bergquist, "Mode and Polyphony"; Novack, "Fusion of Design and Tonal Order"; Mitchell, "Lasso's Prophetiae Sibyllarum." 66 Tovey *Musical Textures*, pp. 30–31.

67 *Meisterwerk*, vol. II, p. 107; vol. III, p. 119.

68 The first Schenkerian study of a non-Western repertory was Loeb, "Japanese Koto Music." For approaches to popular music, see for example Gilbert, *The Music of Gershwin*; Forte, *American Popular Ballad*; Everett, "The Beatles as Composers." The issues concerning Schenkerian analysis of jazz solos are aired in Larson, "Schenkerian Analysis of Modern Jazz."

Bibliography

Primary sources: Schenker's principal writings

Ein Beitrag zur Ornamentik, Vienna, Universal, 1904; rev. 2nd edn., 1908; trans. H. Siegel as "A Contribution to the Study of Ornamentation," *Music Forum* 4 (1976), pp. 1–139

Harmonielehre (Neue musikalische Theorien und Phantasien I), Stuttgart, Cotta, 1906; reprint Vienna, Universal, 1978; abridged trans. E. M. Borgese, ed. O. Jonas as *Harmony*, University of Chicago Press, 1954

J. S. Bach, Chromatische Phantasie und Fuge: kritische Ausgabe, Vienna, Universal, 1910; trans. H. Siegel as *J. S. Bach's Chromatic Fantasy and Fugue: Critical Edition with Commentary*. New York, Longman, 1984

Kontrapunkt (Neue musikalische Theorien und Phantasien II), 2 vols., Vienna, Universal, 1910–22; trans. and ed. J. Rothgeb, trans. J. Thym as *Counterpoint*, 2 vols., New York, Schirmer, 1987

Beethovens neunte Sinfonie, Vienna, Universal, 1912; trans. J. Rothgeb as *Beethoven's Ninth Symphony*, New Haven, Yale University Press, 1992

Beethoven: Die letzten fünf Sonaten: kritische Ausgabe mit Einführung und Erläuterung, Vienna, Universal, 1913 (Op. 109), 1914 (Op. 110), 1915 (Op. 111), 1920 (Op. 101); rev. 2nd edn., ed. O. Jonas, Vienna, Universal, 1971–72 (Op. 106 not completed or published)

Ludwig van Beethoven: Sonate Op. 27, Nr. 2, MS; facs. with sketches and commentary, Vienna, Universal, 1921

Der Tonwille, 10 issues, Vienna, A. J. Gutmann, 1921–24

Das Meisterwerk in der Musik: ein Jahrbuch, 3 vols., Munich, Drei Masken, 1925, 1926, 1930; ed. W. Drabkin, trans. I. Bent et al. as *The Masterwork in Music*, 3 vols., Cambridge University Press, 1994–97

Fünf Urlinie-Tafeln (Five Analyses in Sketch Form), Vienna, Universal, 1932; facs. ed. F. Salzer as *Five Graphic Music Analyses*, New York, Dover, 1969

Johannes Brahms: Oktaven und Quinten u. a., MS; facs. with commentary, Vienna, Universal. 1933; trans. P. Mast as "Brahms's Study, Octaven u. Quinten u. A., with Schenker's Commentary Translated," *Music Forum* 5 (1980), pp. 1–196

Der freie Satz (Neue musikalische Theorien und Phantasien III), Vienna, Universal, 1935; rev. 2nd edn., ed. O. Jonas, Vienna, Universal, 1955; trans. and ed. E. Oster as *Free Composition*, New York, Longman, 1979; reprint edn. Stuyvesant, NY, Pendragon Press, 2001

The Art of Performance, trans. and ed. H. Esser, trans. I. Scott, New York, Oxford University Press, 2000

Heinrich Schenker als Essayist und Kritiker: Gesammelte Aufsätze, Rezensionen und kleinere Berichte aus den Jahren 1891–1901, ed. H. Federhofer, Hildesheim, G. Olms, 1990

Secondary sources

Babbitt, M. review of *Structural Hearing* by Felix Salzer, *JAMS* 5 (1952), pp. 260–65

Badura-Skoda, P. "A Tie is a Tie is a Tie: Reflections on Beethoven's Pairs of Tied Notes," *Early Music* 16 (1988), pp. 84–88

Beach, D. "A Schenker Bibliography," *JMT* 13 (1969), pp. 2–37

"A Schenker Bibliography: 1969–1979," *JMT* 23 (1979), pp. 275–86

"The Current State of Schenkerian Research," *Acta* 57 (1985), pp. 275–307
"The Fundamental Line from Scale Degree 8: Criteria for Evaluation," *JMT* 32 (1988), pp. 271–94
"The Cadential Six-Four as Support for Scale-Degree Three of the Fundamental Line," *JMT* 34 (1990), pp. 81–99
Beach, D., ed., *Aspects of Schenkerian Theory*, New Haven, Yale University Press, 1983
Bent, I. *Analysis*, with glossary by W. Drabkin, Basingstoke, Macmillan, 1987
"Heinrich Schenker e la missione del genio germanico," *Rivista italiana di musicologia* 26 (1991), pp. 3–34
Bergquist, P. "Mode and Polyphony around 1500: Theory and Practice," *Music Forum* 1 (1967), pp. 99–161
Blasius, L. *Schenker's Argument and the Claims of Music Theory*, Cambridge University Press, 1996
Burkhart, C. "Schenker's Theory of Levels and Musical Performance," in *Aspects of Schenkerian Theory*, ed. D. Beach, New Haven, Yale University Press, 1983, pp. 95–112
Cadwallader, A., ed., *Trends in Schenkerian Research*, New York, Schirmer, 1990
Cadwallader, A. and D. Gagné, *Analysis of Tonal Music: A Schenkerian Approach*, New York, Oxford University Press, 1998
Chew, G. "The Spice of Music: Towards a Theory of the Leading Note," *MA* 2 (1983), pp. 35–53
Christensen, T. *Rameau and Musical Thought in the Enlightenment*, Cambridge University Press, 1993
Cook, N. *A Guide to Musical Analysis*, London, Dent, 1987
"Schenker's Theory of Music as Ethics," *JM* 7 (1989), pp. 415–39
"Heinrich Schenker, Polemicist: A Reading of the Ninth Symphony Monograph," *MA* 14 (1995), pp. 89–105
Cube, F.-E. von, *The Book of The Musical Artwork*, ed. and trans. D. Neumeyer, G. Boyd and S. Harris, Lewiston, E. Mellen, 1988
Drabkin, W. "A Lesson in Analysis with Heinrich Schenker," *MA* 4 (1985), pp. 241–58
"Felix-Eberhard von Cube and the North-German Tradition of Schenkerism," *Proceedings of the Royal Musical Association* 111 (1986), pp. 180–207
"Schenker, the Consonant Passing Note and the First Movement of Beethoven's Sonata Opus 26," *MA* 15 (1996), pp. 149–89
Drabkin, W., S. Pasticci, and E. Pozzi, *Analisi schenkeriana*, Lucca, Libreria Musicale Italiana, 1995
Dubiel, J. "'When You are a Beethoven': Kinds of Rules in Schenker's *Counterpoint*," *JMT* 34 (1990), pp. 291–340
Dunsby, J. "The Multipiece in Brahms: *Fantasien*, Op. 116," in *Brahms: Biographical, Documentary and Analytical Studies*, ed. R. Pascall, Cambridge University Press, 1983, pp. 167–89
Dunsby, J. and A. Whittall, *Music Analysis in Theory and Practice*, London, Faber, 1988
Everett, W. "The Beatles as Composers: The Genesis of *Abbey Road*, Side Two," in *Concert Music, Rock, and Jazz since 1945*, ed. E. West Marvin and R. Hermann, Rochester, NY, Rochester University Press, pp. 172–228
Federhofer, H. *Akkord und Stimmführung in den musiktheoretischen Systemen von Hugo Riemann, Ernst Kurth und Heinrich Schenker*, Vienna, Österreichische Akademie der Wissenschaften, 1981

Heinrich Schenker, nach Tagebüchern und Briefen in der Oswald Jonas Memorial Collection, Hildesheim, G. Olms, 1985

Forte, A. "Schenker's Conception of Musical Structure," *JMT* 3 (1959), pp. 1–30

The American Popular Ballad of the Golden Era, 1924–1950, Princeton University Press, 1996

Forte, A. and S. Gilbert, *Introduction to Schenkerian Analysis*, New York, Norton, 1982

Gilbert, S. *The Music of Gershwin*, New Haven, Yale University Press, 1995

Jonas, O. *Das Wesen des musikalischen Kunstwerkes: eine Einführung in die Lehre Heinrich Schenkers*, Vienna, Saturn, 1934; 2nd edn., Vienna, Universal, 1972; trans. J. Rothgeb as *Introduction to the Theory of Heinrich Schenker*, New York, Schirmer, 1982

Jonas, O. and F. Salzer, eds., *Der Dreiklang: Monatsschrift für Musik*, 9 issues, Vienna, Krystall, 1937–38; facs. Hildesheim, G. Olms, 1989

Katz, A. "Heinrich Schenker's Method of Analysis," *Musical Quarterly* 21 (1935), pp. 311–29

Challenge to Musical Tradition: A New Concept of Tonality, New York, A. Knopf, 1945

Keiler, A. "The Origins of Schenker's Thought: How Man is Musical," *JMT* 33 (1989), pp. 273–95

Komar, A. *Theory of Suspensions*, Princeton University Press, 1971

Korsyn, K. "Schenker and Kantian Epistemology," *Theoria* 3 (1988), pp. 1–58

Kosovsky, R. *The Oster Collection: Papers of Heinrich Schenker: A Finding List*, New York Public Library, 1990

Lang, R. and J. Kunselman, *Heinrich Schenker, Oswald Jonas, Moriz Violin: a Checklist of Papers in the Oswald Jonas Memorial Collection*, Berkeley, University of California Press, 1999

Larson, S. "Schenkerian Analysis of Modern Jazz: Questions about Method," *MTS* 20 (1998), pp. 209–41

Leech-Wilkinson, D. "Machaut's *Rose, lis* and the Problem of Early Music Analysis," *MA* 3 (1984), pp. 9–28

Lerdahl, F. and R. Jackendoff, *A Generative Theory of Tonal Music*, Cambridge, MA, MIT Press, 1983

Loeb, D. "An Analytic Study of Japanese Koto Music," *Music Forum* 4 (1976), pp. 335–93

Lubben, J. "Schenker the Progressive: Analytic Practice in *Der Tonwille*," *MTS* 15 (1993), pp. 59–75

Marston, N. "Trifles or a Multi-Trifle? Beethoven's Bagatelles, Op. 119, Nos. 7–11," *MA* 5 (1986), pp. 193–206

"Analysing Variations: The Finale of Beethoven's String Quartet Op. 74," *MA* 8 (1989), pp. 303–24

Meyer, L. B. *Explaining Music: Essays and Explorations*, Berkeley, Univeristy of California Press, 1971

Mitchell, W. J. "The Prologue to Orlando di Lasso's Prophetiae Sibyllarum," *Music Forum* 2 (1970), pp. 264–73

Morgan, R. P. "Schenker and the Theoretical Tradition: The Concept of Musical Reduction," *College Music Symposium* 18 (1978), pp. 72–96

Narmour, E. *Beyond Schenkerism: the Need for Alternatives in Music Analysis*, University of Chicago Press, 1977

Neumeyer, D. "The Ascending *Urlinie*," *JMT* 31 (1987), pp. 275–303

"The Three-Part *Ursatz*," *In Theory Only* 10 (1987), pp. 3–29

"The *Urlinie* from $\hat{8}$ as a Middleground Phenomenon," *In Theory Only* 9 (1987), pp. 3–25

"Fragile Octaves, Broken Lines: On Some Limitations in Schenkerian Theory and Practice," *In Theory Only* 11 (1989), pp. 13–30

Neumeyer, D. and S. Tepping, *A Guide to Schenkerian Analysis*, Englewood Cliffs, NJ, Prentice Hall, 1992

Novack, S. "Fusion of Design and Tonal Order in Mass and Motet: Josquin Desprez and Heinrich Isaac," *Music Forum* 2 (1970), pp. 188–263

"The Analysis of Pre-Baroque Music," in *Aspects of Schenkerian Theory*, ed. D. Beach, New Haven, Yale University Press, 1983, pp. 113–33

Pastille, W. "Heinrich Schenker, Anti-Organicist," *19th-Century Music* 8 (1984), pp. 29–36

"Music and Morphology: Goethe's Influence on Schenker's Thought," in *Schenker Studies*, ed. H. Siegel, Cambridge University Press, 1990, pp. 29–44

Renwick, W. *Analyzing Fugue: A Schenkerian Approach*, New York, Pendragon Press, 1995

"Hidden Fugal Paths: A Schenkerian View of Handel's F major Fugue (Suite II)," *MA* 14 (1995), pp. 49–67

Rosen, C. *The Classical Style: Haydn, Mozart, Beethoven*, London, Faber and Faber, 1971

Rothstein, W. "Heinrich Schenker as an Interpreter of Beethoven's Piano Sonatas," *19th-Century Music* 8 (1984), pp. 3–28

Phrase Rhythm in Tonal Music, New York, Schirmer, 1989

"The Americanization of Heinrich Schenker," in *Schenker Studies*, ed. H. Siegel, Cambridge University Press, 1990, pp. 193–203

Salzer, F. *Sinn und Wesen der abendländischen Mehrstimmigkeit*, Vienna, Saturn, 1935

"Die historische Sendung Heinrich Schenkers," *Der Dreiklang* 1 (1937), pp. 2–12

Structural Hearing, New York, C. Boni, 1952

"The Variation Movement of Mozart's Divertimento K. 563," *Music Forum* 5 (1980), pp. 257–315

Schachter, C. "Rhythm and Linear Analysis," 3 parts, *Music Forum* 4 (1976), pp. 281–334; 5 (1980), pp. 197–232; 6 (1987), pp. 1–59

"A Commentary on Schenker's *Free Composition*," *JMT* 25 (1981), pp. 115–42

"Motive and Text in Four Schubert Songs," in *Aspects of Schenkerian Theory*, ed. D. Beach, New Haven, Yale University Press, 1983, pp. 61–76

"Either/Or," in *Schenker Studies*, ed. H. Siegel, Cambridge University Press, 1990, pp. 165–79

"Twentieth-Century Analysis and Mozart Performance," *Early Music* 19 (1991), pp. 620–26

Unfoldings: Essays in Schenkerian Analysis, New York, Oxford University Press, 1999

Schachter, C. and H. Siegel, eds., *Schenker Studies 2*, Cambridge University Press, 1999

Siegel, H., ed., *Schenker Studies*, Cambridge University Press, 1990

Smith, C. J. "Musical Form and Fundamental Structure: An Investigation of Schenker's *Formenlehre*," *MA* 15 (1996), pp. 191–297

Snarrenberg, R. *Schenker's Interpretive Practice*, Cambridge University Press, 1997

Tovey, D. F. *Musical Textures*, London, Oxford University Press, 1941

Travis, R. "Tonal Coherence in the First Movement of Bartók's Fourth String Quartet," *Music Forum* 2 (1970), pp. 198–371

Wason, R. "Schenker's Notion of Scale-Step in Historical Perspective: Non-Essential Harmonies in Viennese Fundamental Bass Theory," *JMT* 27 (1983), pp. 49–73

Viennese Harmonic Theory from Albrechtsberger to Schenker and Schoenberg, Ann Arbor, UMI Research Press, 1985

Webster, J. "The Analysis of Mozart's Arias," in *Mozart Studies*, ed. C. Eisen, Oxford, Clarendon Press, 1991, pp. 101–99

Westergaard, P. *Introduction to Tonal Theory*, New York, Norton, 1975

Yeston, M. *The Stratification of Musical Rhythm*, New Haven, Yale University Press, 1976

Yeston, M., ed., *Readings in Schenker Analysis and Other Approaches*, New Haven, Yale University Press, 1977

PART IV

DESCRIPTIVE TRADITIONS

IVA MODELS OF MUSIC ANALYSIS

· 27 ·

Music and rhetoric

PATRICK McCRELESS

Rhetoric is the original metalanguage of discourse in the West.[1] From the fifth century BCE until around 1800 it served the educated classes as the most prestigious and influential means of conceptualizing and organizing language, and articulating how it can best be effective, persuasive, and elegant. Given that rhetoric shares with music the structured unfolding of sound in time, aspects of performance and delivery, and even a rudimentary notion of the "work" (the *oration* in rhetoric, the *composition* in music), it was natural and even inevitable that analogies would be drawn between the two. Analogies between rhetoric and music were common even in antiquity: Quintilian, for example, pointed to the expressivity of music as a model for the orator.[2] In later times it was rhetoric that more frequently served as a model for musicians. Although musico-rhetorical analogies occurred sporadically in the music theory of the medieval period, they began to play a more extensive role only in the sixteenth century, when musicians appropriated rhetoric, by then a central element in the humanistic education of the time, as a model for the teaching of musical composition. It was the theorists of a uniquely German musico-rhetorical tradition who imported the apparatus of rhetoric directly into music theory, in effect making it a metalanguage for music as well as for language by interpreting it as a model for musical composition. What distinguished this German effort in the long history of the interaction between rhetoric and music was precisely that it went beyond the mere drawing of analogies to a thoroughgoing attribution of specific musical substance to rhetorical terms and concepts. The ultimate success of this musico-rhetorical enterprise is open to question: music theory eventually outgrew rhetoric and developed its own vocabulary, systems, and metalanguages. Yet this peculiarly German moment, roughly the years 1550–1800, when rhetoric and music came closest together, has left a permanent stamp on Western music theory, and it is this moment upon which the present chapter will focus.

1 For the notion of rhetoric as a global metalanguage of language in the West, I am indebted to Barthes, "The Old Rhetoric."

2 For Quintilian on music, see *Institutio oratoria*, vol. 1, pp. 165–77. See the bibliography at the end of this chapter for a modern edition and translation of Quintilian and other central primary sources of rhetoric.

The classical tradition

The term *rhetoric*, in modern English usage, may refer simply to the art of persuasion, or to the art of effective speaking and writing. Less innocently, it may refer to *artificial eloquence*, the calculated use of language to impress, sway, or even deceive. The term may also refer to the classical discipline in which both of these meanings have their root: the art of rhetoric, as developed in antiquity, and as taught in the West for 2,500 years as a coherent and stable system of organizing language. As Barthes has pointed out, the modern notion of rhetoric is thus two-sided: it is both a "grandiose system which a whole civilization, in its extreme breadth, perfected . . . in order to think its language," and "an ideological object," from which modern objectivity dictates that we "take an indispensable critical distance."[3]

The substance of rhetoric has remained remarkably consistent throughout its history. Aristotle, the first theorist of rhetoric, defines it as "the art of extracting from every subject the proper degree of persuasion it allows," or as "the faculty of speculatively discovering what in each case are the available means of persuasion."[4] The five traditional parts of rhetoric – *inventio*, *dispositio*, *elocutio*, *memoria*, and *pronunciatio* – were firmly established by the early Roman period (c. 100 BCE), and have retained their organizing force ever since. In classical rhetoric, these parts provided a comprehensive discipline for the orator. Of the five, the first three – *inventio*, *dispositio*, and *elocutio* – constitute the conceptual core of rhetoric. *Inventio* addresses the problem of developing ideas for a speech. In the classical tradition, this means less "inventing" a subject out of nothing, in the manner of the nineteenth-century artistic genius, than "discovering" in a subject or case what is already there: what ideas to extract, seize upon, and develop. Once these ideas or topics are discovered, it is *dispositio* that determines their linear ordering and arrangement into a persuasive whole. *Dispositio* also has its own taxonomy for the organization of a speech, including the *exordium* (introduction), *narratio* (statement of facts), *partitio* or *propositio* (division, or the statement of what is agreed upon and what contested, and of the orator's plan of action), *confirmatio* (proof of the arguments), to *refutatio* (refutation of the opponent's arguments), and *peroratio* or *conclusio* (peroration or conclusion).[5] *Elocutio*, the third primary component of classical rhetoric, is the source of style and expression, of figure and trope, and of the eloquence,

3 Barthes, "The Old Rhetoric," p. 47. Richard A. Lanham makes a similar point when he draws a distinction in Western thought between the "rhetorical" view of life and what he calls the "serious" view of life – between language as an instrument of persuasion and language as an instrument of truth. This opposition, he claims, "goes far to explain two persistently puzzling facts about the history of rhetoric: why it has been so deplored and why it has so endured." See Lanham's *The Motives for Eloquence: Literary Theory in the Renaissance*, pp. 4–5. The opposition in fact goes back to Plato, who in his two dialogues that deal most explicitly with rhetoric – *Gorgias* and *Phaedrus* – rejects rhetoric, which deals only with opinion, in favor of philosophy, which deals with truth.

4 Aristotle, *The Art of Rhetoric*, cited in Barthes, "The Old Rhetoric," p. 21.

5 See Vickers, *In Defence of Rhetoric*, pp. 62–67, for a more detailed exposition of the five parts of rhetoric.

even grandiloquence, that we naturally associate with rhetoric. For the classical writers, *elocutio* embodied an *excess;* assuming a stable base of the normal mode of linguistic communication, they saw in the heightened usage of language a means of persuasion – hence their referring to the figures and tropes as *ornamenta*, *flores*, and *colores*. The remaining two parts of rhetoric – *memoria* and *pronuntiatio* – deal with aspects of "performance," memory and delivery, and thus address the technique of making the fully conceptualized oration persuasive to an audience.

Western rhetoric claims its origins in property disputes that arose in the Greek community at Syracuse, in Sicily, around 485 BCE. The means of persuasion developed to argue such cases quickly distilled into a concrete and teachable discipline. Of the five parts of rhetoric, the first to achieve canonical stature was *dispositio* (Gk. *taxis*), which had already begun to be codified before rhetoric migrated to Athens later in the fifth century BCE. In the rhetoric of Gorgias and other Sophists we find the roots of *elocutio* – a heightened sense of style, and the use of tropes and figures. By 393 BCE, Isocrates (436–338 BCE), who established a school of rhetoric in Athens, was writing down and polishing his speeches – an act of crucial importance, inasmuch as a perennial dispute in rhetoric turns on the question of whether it is an oral art of persuasion, negotiated in real time in front of a live audience as an act with a civic function (what George Kennedy, the distinguished historian of rhetoric, calls "primary rhetoric"), or whether it is a written, academic discipline, a discipline of poetics or pedagogy, carried out entirely in writing (Kennedy's "secondary rhetoric").[6]

Plato, to whom we owe the first extensive critique of rhetoric, distrusted it in both its oral and its written forms. In the dialogues *Gorgias* and *Phaedrus* he mounted against rhetoric the most scathing attack it has ever known, seeing in it only flattery, deception, and illusion – "artificial eloquence," as it were – as opposed to philosophy, which was for him a dialectical pursuit of eternal truths. Plato's student Aristotle, unlike his teacher, saw value in rhetoric: elevating *doxa* (opinion) to a status equal to that of *episteme* (knowledge), he placed it on the same level as Plato's dialectic. In his *The Art of Rhetoric* (c. 335 BCE), the first surviving text on rhetoric, Aristotle continued the Greek tradition and contributed most significantly in the area of *inventio*, for which he developed the notion of *topics*, or "places," which serve to generate and sustain the ideas of a speech.

The Roman rhetoric of the anonymous *Rhetorica ad Herennium* (c. 85 BCE), and of Cicero (seven treatises on rhetoric, 87–44 BCE) and Quintilian (*Institutio oratoria*, 92–94 CE), inherited and developed Aristotle's theories, and gave increased emphasis to aspects of delivery – *memoria* and *pronuntiatio*. Quintilian's justly famous work, which was written about a century after rhetoric had already begun to decline in

6 Kennedy, *Classical Rhetoric and Its Christian and Secular Tradition from Ancient to Modern Times*, pp. 4–5. The secondary literature on rhetoric and its history is enormous. The books by Kennedy and Vickers noted here and in footnote 5 are the best modern introductions in English. The bibliography provides a small selection of other valuable sources.

public discourse in Rome, is the *summa* of classical oratory: it approaches rhetoric from the point of view of pedagogy, education, and ethics, and it summarizes and systematizes the entire Greco-Roman tradition in practical language and in admirable detail. The Roman oratory of Cicero and Quintilian turned on two vital and interrelated distinctions, one philosophical and one aesthetic, each of which would play a crucial role in later rhetorical thought, and in the Renaissance and Baroque appropriation of rhetorical theory for the arts. On the philosophical side is the binary opposition between *res* and *verba*, between the substance of an argument and the verbal means used to make that argument. The distinction differentiates between an idea itself and the figures and tropes – the linguistic excesses, as it were – used to enliven, dramatize, or "mark" the idea and make it serve the larger persuasive goal. The conceptual task here is to achieve a balance between figure and idea, so that the former accentuates the latter without overwhelming it, to produce eloquence rather than grandiloquence. The not unrelated aesthetic distinction made by Roman oratory is Cicero's triadic view of what rhetoric attempts to accomplish: *docere*, *movere*, and *delectare* – to teach, to move, and to delight. Here, content and essence are enriched by an aesthetic dimension; however, such a dimension must not be allowed to function on its own, but must operate in service of an argument.

The history of rhetoric for the next two thousand years traces a path of successive declines and renewals. The early Christian church appropriated classical rhetoric for its own ends. But the task now was preaching a revealed truth as persuasively as possible, not convincing an audience of the value of one among many opinions. The Middle Ages also brought a turn from rhetoric as public discourse to rhetoric as writing and as disputation – from "primary" to "secondary" rhetoric, in the historical model of Kennedy. However, with the Renaissance, rhetoric experienced a spectacular revival. The Renaissance humanists juxtaposed the classical ideals of rhetorical eloquence and civic participation with the baleful scholasticism and inwardness of their more immediate predecessors, and rediscovered many of the classical texts that had been lost or only partially preserved. A manuscript of Quintilian's *Institutio* was discovered in 1416 and was quickly copied and distributed around Europe, and Aristotle's *The Art of Rhetoric* and a number of lost treatises of Cicero were recovered as well. With the ancient rhetorical sources as their model (especially Quintilian), the Renaissance humanists returned to the Roman practice of making rhetoric the foundation of education, and it became the centerpiece of the advanced teaching of language. In this latter function the connection between rhetoric and poetics, already begun in the Middle Ages, was continued and expanded, especially in the early Renaissance, in which the "totalizing function of poetics… [was] able to give unity to and synthesize within itself the whole spectrum of disciplines."[7] Among those disciplines are painting, for which Leon Battista Alberti initiated a long tradition of rhetorically based crit-

7 Barilli, *Rhetoric*, p. 60.

icism in his *De pictura* of 1435, and music, which in the late Renaissance saw the flowering of a musico-rhetorical tradition.

Over the course of the Renaissance and into the seventeenth century a growing interest in the passions and their representation and expression in rhetoric and poetics led to an elevation of *movere* over *docere* and *delectare*, and a corresponding elevation of *elocutio* at the expense of *inventio* and *dispositio*.[8] This concern with *elocutio* entailed an increasingly frenzied obsession with the centerpiece of *elocutio* – the figures. As Vickers notes, tongue-in-cheek, "the Renaissance pursued *elocutio* with enormous zest."[9] Schoolboys all over Europe memorized scores of rhetorical figures, carefully noting them in texts that they studied, as a final stage in learning to use them themselves. It was in fact an overemphasis on the figures that eventually led to the death of rhetoric. The once vital tradition of civic rhetoric had given way to the dry recitation and identification of figures with strange-sounding names in Greek and Latin. By the early eighteenth century, even though rhetoric remained at the center of most European educational systems, it had hardened into an oppressive orthodoxy and had lost its vitality. Rhetoric continued to decline as a central cultural force in the later eighteenth century, and its demise is traditionally pinpointed to the beginning of the nineteenth century. It remained for the twentieth century to resurrect it: as intellectual history, as a pedagogy of writing, as a model for speech communication, as an instrument of mass culture in politics and advertising, and as a refined tool for literary and other textual criticism. Rhetoric is again respectable, although, as throughout its history, it continues to embody the tensions between philosophy and persuasion, *res* and *verba*, intellectual integrity and ideology.

Rhetoric and music in the Renaissance

When and why did rhetoric enter music history – or, more specifically, when and why did it enter music theory? As we already know, the separate streams of rhetorical history and musical history coalesced most fruitfully in the period from the High Renaissance to the end of the eighteenth century. A broad look at the historical flow of the two arts makes it clear why this confluence happened when it did. On the rhetorical side, the Renaissance witnessed a dramatic resurgence of interest in rhetoric; it quickly colonized the entire educational system in the teaching of language. Brian Vickers estimates that around 2,000 books on rhetoric were published between 1400 and 1700, usually in editions of between 250 and 1,000 copies. This flood of publication fed the teaching of rhetoric in schools throughout Europe, to the point that it achieved its widest distribution and greatest influence ever.[10] And since rhetoric was the omnipresent metalanguage of language – indeed, it was arguably the only metalanguage of anything at

8 Vickers, *In Defence of Rhetoric*, p. 282. 9 Ibid., p. 283. 10 Ibid., p. 256.

the time – it is hardly surprising that its concepts, systems, and terms were co-opted by the arts. The critical language of painting developed by Alberti and others in the fifteenth century, of music developed by Joachim Burmeister and the German theorists of the seventeenth century, and of poetry developed by writers like Sir Philip Sidney (*An Apology for Poetry*, 1595) all naturally derive from the rhetorical thinking that dominated Renaissance discourse.

On the musical side, a central feature of the new styles of the sixteenth century (*musica reservata*) and the seventeenth century (*le nuove musiche*) was a concern for a close relation between text and music. The trend toward using rhetoric as a model for the arts, already well underway in the visual arts and poetry, led many musicians to adopt the classical oration as a model for composition. Zarlino, for example, takes the title of his theoretical *summa* of High Renaissance vocal polyphony, *Le istitutioni harmoniche* (1558), directly from Quintilian. And in his discussion of setting a counterpoint to a *soggetto*, he cites classical works on oratory (Plato, Aristotle, Cicero, and Quintilian) and poetry (Hermogenes and Horace), and he suggests that the composer follow Horace's dictum that the poet (or composer) should write things both pleasing and useful – also a central concept to rhetoric.[11] Yet Zarlino stands as a characteristic example of the anomaly that, whereas rhetoric permeated critical thinking in the visual arts and poetics throughout Europe, it gained a strong foothold in music only in the German tradition. Even a cursory look at the work of Italian, French, and British theorists reveals their devotion to rhetoric to be superficial at best. Unlike the German theorists, they do not attempt to correlate rhetorical principles with music-theoretical ones. Most importantly, they develop no *Figurenlehre*, or doctrine of musical figures. Nor does their work offer much in the way of substantive discussion of *inventio* or *dispositio*. Italian music theory, beginning in the sixteenth century, and French and British theory, which did not develop a strong indigenous tradition until the seventeenth century, do their music-theoretical business in musical, not rhetorical terms. A few theorists, notably Charles Butler in England and Marin Mersenne in France, do draw strong analogies between rhetoric and music, but they do so without giving these analogies detailed theoretical substance.

We have seen how, in the early sixteenth century, the theory of music was broadly divided into two parts: *musica theorica* (speculative theory, as a numerical, quadrivial discipline dealing with tuning ratios and the like) and *musica practica* (practical theory, focusing on composition, counterpoint, and mensural notation), although frequently individual treatises, such as Zarlino's *Le istitutioni harmoniche*, dealt with both (see in particular **Introduction, pp. 7–8**; also **Chapters 2** and **5, passim**). In German theory, however, which was at the time just beginning to establish itself, there was virtually no active tradition of *musica theorica* throughout the sixteenth century, despite Luther's

11 Zarlino, *The Art of Counterpoint*, pp. 51, 87.

adherence to the speculative, mathematical cosmogony of that tradition. In Reformation Germany, it was the practical skills of singing and performance that were taught in the Lutheran *Lateinschule*, the centerpiece of the humanistic educational system developed and implemented by Luther and his education minister, Philipp Melanchthon. What was lacking in this practical curriculum was the advanced teaching of counterpoint and composition – skills essential to a fledgling cantor or composer – that had developed so strongly in the Italian tradition of *musica practica* culminating with Zarlino. Such skills could only be acquired by students in private lessons. What stepped in to fill this void was, on the one hand, the dissemination of Zarlino's compositional pedagogy, and on the other, *musica poetica*, a creative new branch of music theory developed by German pedagogues.

The origin of the *musica poetica* theoretical tradition may be dated to 1537, when the German schoolmaster Nikolaus Listenius (born c. 1510), in his treatise *Musica*, introduced the term as a complement to *musica theorica* and *musica practica*, thus completing the Aristotelian triad of categories concerning the activities of the human mind (the theoretical, the practical, and the poetic or creative). For purposes of the present chapter, the tradition may be said to include those German treatises that are addressed to the composer as *musicus poeticus*, or that in any way appropriate rhetoric as a compositional pedagogy or descriptive taxonomy, or both. *Musica poetica* flourished side by side with other theoretical approaches, most notably an early seventeenth-century manuscript tradition, once thought to have begun with Sweelinck, through which Zarlino's counterpoint was spread through German-speaking areas, and a similar later tradition, centering on Reinken, that dealt with double counterpoint and other complex contrapuntal practices. Furthermore, the *musica poetica* tradition was hardly a monolithic system: Dressler's unpublished *Praecepta musicae poeticae* of 1563 allies conventional contrapuntal and modal theory, and it is the first to suggest a parallel between the beginning, middle, and end of a musical piece and the *exordium*, *medium*, and *finis* of an oration; Calvisius's *Melopoiia* of 1592 teaches Zarlinian counterpoint and modal theory but not rhetorical figures; Burmeister's *Musica poetica* of 1606 offers a pedagogy only of a chorale-like homophony, but introduces his rhetorical figures to analyze works of imitative polyphony; Lippius's *Synopsis musicae novae* of 1612 offers a triad-based compositional pedagogy and uses rhetoric to describe musical form, but it makes no use of musico-rhetorical figures; Nucius's *Musices poeticae sive de compositione cantus* of 1613 and Kircher's *Musurgia universalis* of 1650 follow the tradition of musical figures established by Burmeister, but they write as Catholics, not Protestants, and Kircher writes for scholars, not practical composers; Herbst's *Musica poetica* of 1643 cobbles together a variety of compositional approaches, including rhetoric; Bernhard provides a useful marriage of counterpoint in the new Italian style and figures in the manner of Burmeister; and so forth. Later, in the eighteenth century, as the notion of *musica poetica*, with the composer as *musicus poeticus*, became outdated, the tradition lived on in those theoretical works that continued to use musical figures. Rhetoric was central to this tradition, and it functioned as an important strand in German theory for over two hundred years.

Rhetoric and Baroque musical poetics

Sporadic isolated references to rhetoric as a model for musical composition appeared in various treatises over the course of the sixteenth century (e.g., the treatises of Listensius and Dressler noted above), but these did not yet constitute a full-fledged musico-rhetorical tradition. The more thoroughgoing rhetoricization of *musica poetica* awaited two central figures who emerged around the beginning of the seventeenth century: Joachim Burmeister (1564–1629) and Johannes Lippius (1585–1612). Characteristically for the period, both were educators: Burmeister a schoolteacher and church cantor in the North German port of Rostock, Lippius a doctor of theology and traveling scholar who had accepted a position in theology at the University of Strassburg the year before his death. Their principal works – Burmeister's *Musica poetica* (1606) and Lippius's *Synopsis musicae novae* (1612) – stand as the fountainheads of the *musica poetica* tradition for several reasons. First, each offers a comprehensive approach to music and musical composition in a way that sixteenth-century *Lateinschule* texts could not. Second, each contains elements of startling originality and subsequent importance to the development of music theory: Burmeister's pioneering examples of musical analysis, and Lippius's revolutionary theory of the *trias harmonica*. Most significant in the present context, though, both treatises bring rhetoric and rhetorical terminology into music theory in a detailed and systematic manner.[12] Each represents the work of an intellectual musician who was widely read in music theory and in the humanistic disciplines such as rhetoric, and who was positioned to bring the two productively together.

Lippius. Lippius, the younger of the two theorists, is a perhaps a less important figure than Burmeister in the *musica poetica* tradition with respect to the development of a rhetorical theory, but more important in other areas – reinstituting for German theory the medieval cosmogony of music, whereby music as sounding number links the macrocosm of God's created universe and the microcosm of human existence; establishing music as an encyclopedic science; and articulating a clear theory of the *trias harmonica* (see **Chapter 24, p. 755**). In the area of musical rhetoric, Lippius, who modeled *Synopsis musicae novae* on his own treatise on rhetoric, offered for the first time a thorough exposition of how the five parts of classical rhetoric – *inventio, dispositio, elocutio, memoria*, and *pronunciatio* – could serve as a model for conceiving a musical piece

12 Burmeister's *Musica poetica* has long been available in facsimile. Both Burmeister's *Musica poetica* and Lippius's *Synopsis musicae novae* are available in modern English translations by Benito Rivera. See also Ruhnke, *Joachim Burmeister*; Dammann, *Der Musikbegriff im deutschen Barock*; Rivera, *German Music Theory in the Early Seventeenth Century*; Bartel, *Musica poetica*.

and working it out. Yet he did not elaborate any single part of musical rhetoric in detail; and since he named no musical figures (even though he recognized some of the same configurations upon which his contemporary Burmeister conferred rhetorical terms), at least one scholar has left him out of the *musica poetica* tradition.[13]

Burmeister. Burmeister has now become one of the most written about figures in the history of music theory – in the early years of the twentieth century because he was recognized as the founder of the *Figurenlehre* tradition, more recently because he is seen as the founder of musical analysis. It has now become fashionable, even among the most sympathetic scholars, to question whether Burmeister was a brilliant innovator or an obsessive pedant: was the invention of the musical figures a great conceptual leap forward? or did it represent the imposition of a once vital but now petrified and repressive discipline on a newly developing art that deserved better, and that has ever since had difficulty relieving itself of the ballast thereby imposed upon it? Whatever our judgment of the intellectual and musical merits of his case, we can hardly deny the surge of energy that he infused into the nascent discipline of *musica poetica* – a process that required a full two centuries to play out. The same could perhaps be said of Lippius, of course, with respect to his revival of *musica theorica*. But it is striking for us today to step back and view the full import of Burmeister's work for the subsequent history of music theory. From the helter-skelter fashion in which rhetoric was invoked by German music pedagogues in the sixteenth century, we find at the turn of the seventeenth century, with the advent of Burmeister's work, a whole taxonomy of musical figures suddenly emerging full-blown out of virtually nothing, and then, over the next two centuries, spawning more and more competing sets of rhetorical topoi and figures pressed into the service of music theory.

Burmeister's musico-rhetorical theory appears in his *Hypomnematum musicae poeticae* (1599), *Musica autoschediastike* (1601), and finally, in its best-known form, in the *Musica poetica* of 1606. His classic presentation of the figures occurs in the twelfth and fifteenth chapters of the sixteen-chapter *Musica poetica*. Chapter 12 presents twenty-seven musical figures, with definitions and examples from the music of composers such as Clemens non Papa and Orlando di Lasso, while Chapter 15 presents an analysis of Lasso's motet *In me transierunt*. From these two chapters, it is perfectly clear how his work relates to the classical rhetorical tradition. He essentially ignores *inventio*, *memoria*, and *pronunciatio*. *Dispositio* is discussed briefly in Chapter 15, "The Analysis or Arrangement of a Musical Piece." Here Burmeister posits the threefold model, *exordium–medium–finis*, already introduced by Gallus Dressler – except that Burmeister calls the *medium* or middle section *ipsum corpus carminis*, "the body of the song itself."[14] The analysis of the Lasso motet then is given as an example of this arrangement.

13 Dietrich Bartel omits Lippius entirely from his account of rhetoric in the *musica poetica* tradition.
14 Burmeister, *Musical Poetics* (Rivera trans., pp. 202–03). Also see Dressler, *Praecepta musica poeticae*; Ruhnke, *Joachim Burmeister*, p. 137; Bartel, *Musica poetica*, p. 80.

But Burmeister's real commitment is not to *dispositio*; it is to *elocutio* and his newly invented figures, or *ornamenta*. What motivated Burmeister to develop a whole system of figures, more or less *ex nihilo*? First, as George Buelow has noted, stylistic changes in the music of the late fifteenth and sixteenth centuries toward a more declamatory, rhetorical, text-sensitive model challenged music theory to grow beyond its conventional concerns with the elements of *musica theorica* and *practica* and to develop a vocabulary to deal with music conceived more closely according to a text.[15] Second, in the German *Lateinschule* tradition, music theory had become virtually synonymous with a constricted notion of *musica plana* – one limited virtually to the teaching of musical notation and solmization. Thus, Burmeister surely wanted not only to provide young composers and cantors with a systematic pedagogy not available in the schools, but also to restore music theory to intellectual respectability; what better way to do so than to map the academically prestigious discipline of rhetoric onto music? Third, inasmuch as rhetoric, as taught in his time, was used not only as a prescriptive method for speaking and writing, but also for text exegesis, Burmeister clearly reasoned that his figures could function as a kind of analytical tool. A motto of rhetorical pedagogy was *praeceptum – exemplum – imitatio*: learn a principle, find and memorize an example of it, then imitate it. For the young composer, the figures would anchor this precept in actual musical techniques, in musical reality.

The conceptual apparatus that Burmeister imported from rhetorical *elocutio* operates on a number of fronts. He lays at the very foundation of his *Figurenlehre* the rhetorical notion of figure as excess: a figure constituted heightened language, now heightened music. An essential feature of an *ornamentum* or figure is that "it departs from the simple manner of composition, and with elegance assumes and adopts a more ornate character."[16] A cursory look over his figures (see Table 27.1), makes clear what is implicit here: that the underlying norm of the music is presumed to be diatonic, rhythmically, regular, and homophonic – more or less in the style of the chorale; the figures serve, then, to enliven and elaborate this fundamental level of expression.[17] Also taken from rhetoric, of course, are the Greek terms that he adapts for most of his musical figures. Insofar as possible, he finds rhetorical terms that create a plausible analogy with a given musical technique. Thus, *hypallage*, a reversal of words in rhetoric ("Fair is foul, and foul is fair," from Shakespeare's *Macbeth*) becomes the inversion of a fugue subject. *Hyperbole*, an overstatement of the truth, becomes an overstepping of the highest note of the modal ambitus of a melodic voice. But it soon becomes obvious that music and musical concepts, not rhetoric, are driving the system. For occasionally Burmeister will invoke a quasi-rhetorical term

15 Buelow, "Rhetoric and Music," p. 250.
16 Burmeister, *Musical Poetics* (Rivera trans., pp. 154–57).
17 Bartel makes this point in *Musica poetica*, p. 84. For Burmeister's figures, see Burmeister, *Musical Poetics* (Rivera trans., pp. 154–97).

figurae harmoniae	
fuga realis	imitation in all voices
metalepsis	*fuga* with two subject (double fugue)
hypallage	*fuga* with inversion in several voices
apocope	*fuga* not completed in all voices
noema	homophonic section for text declamation
analepsis	repeated *noema* on the same scale degree
mimesis	*noema* in some parts while others are silent, then *noema* in other parts
anadiplosis	repeated *mimesis*
symblema	passing tone on a weak beat
syncopa/syneresis	dissonant syncopation on strong beat
pleonasmus	combination of *symblema* and *syneresis*, or increase of syncopations before a cadence
auxesis	increase of number of voices and heightening of pitch in association with repetition of a section of text
pathopoeia	use of semitones foreign to a key
hypotyposis	enlivening of a particular word or section of text
aposiopesis	*Generalpause*
anaploce	repetition of a short section by a second choir
figurae harmoniae	
parembole	passage in which two or more voices have a point of imitation, while another voice is free
palilogia	repetition of a melodic fragment on the same scale degree
climax	repetition of a melodic fragment on another scale degree (sequence)
parrhesia	passing 7th or 4th
hyperbole	overstepping of modal ambitus in upper register
hypobole	overstepping of modal ambitus in lower register

Table 27.1 Burmeister's figures from the *Musica poetica*, 1606

figurae tam harmoniae quam melodiae	
congeries	succession 5-6-5-6 3-3-3-3
fauxbourdon	fauxbourdon
anaphora	imitation in some, but not all voices of a polyphonic piece
fuga imaginaria	canon
supplementum	decoration of a final melodic note through chordal progression under or over a pedal

Table 27.1 (*cont.*)

for which there is little rhetorical precedent: thus he appropriates *symblema*, which does not appear in rhetorical treatises, and he uses the rare term *hypobole* for the exceeding of the lowest note of the melodic ambitus of a given voice. And in four cases (*fuga realis*, *fuga imaginaria*, *supplementum*, and *fauxbourdon*) he designates as figures terms that are neither Greek nor rhetorical. Yet rhetoric remains central in that it provides the names for most of the figures, and it also provides the basis for Burmeister's division of them into three classes. Rhetoric traditionally distinguished between figures of words (*figurae dictionis* or *verbi*) and figures that involved whole phrases, clauses, or sentences (*figurae sententiae*). Burmeister's harmonic–melodic division of musical figures attempts, not entirely successfully, to replicate these categories, and he adds a third, combined category to deal with figures that he considers both harmonic and melodic.

From the analytical – not compositional – perspective of late twentieth- and twenty-first century music theory, it is easy to dismiss Burmeister's conceptualization of the figures. Brian Vickers has rejected the validity of musical *Figurenlehre* altogether because the semantic dimensions of the rhetorical figures cannot map literally onto the musical ones. And it takes little effort to find other faults as well.[18] Modern musicians would probably divide the figures, not into classes based on harmony and melody, but into classes based on function: contrapuntal figurations (e.g., *symblema*, *syncopa*, *fauxbourdon*), fugal techniques (*fuga realis*, *hypallage*, *anaphora*), repetition or sequential

18 For Vickers's critiques, see "Figures of Rhetoric/Figures of Music?" and *In Defence of Rhetoric*, pp. 360–74. For a persuasive argument that the central tradition of the pedagogy of music composition in seventeenth-century Germany does not revolve solely around the rhetorically based *Figurenlehre*, see Forchert, "Heinrich Schütz und die *musica poetica*"; "Bach und die Tradition der Rhetorik." Forchert traces the central tradition of Protestant compositional pedagogy from Calvisius to Johann Crüger to Herbst – none of whom mentions figures – in the first half of the century, and then to Bernhard, who adopted the Italian pedagogy as well as *Figurenlehre*, in the second half of the century. For skeptical views of the value of *Figurenlehre* for analysis, see Harrison, "Rhetoric and Fugue"; Williams, "Encounters with the Chromatic Fourth"; The Snares and Delusions of Musical Rhetoric."

figures (*palilogia*, *auxesis*, *climax*), figures regarding modal ambitus (*hyperbole*, *hypobole*), textural figures (*noema*), expressive figures (*hypotyposis*), and so forth. Even with the division of the figures into more logical categories, what we are left with is still a purely descriptive taxonomy. Certainly by modern standards, an analysis by Burmeister's method could do little but name the figures according to his definitions. Yet this process of *naming*, whatever we may think of it, surely extended his power as a music theorist over the music in his purview: naming phenomena that previously had no names reifies and classifies compositional techniques, and enables the theorist to partition musical pieces into discrete classes of events.

Example 27.1, an analysis in the manner of Burmeister of a verse from Lasso's setting of Psalm 143 (one of his *Seven Penitential Psalms*), shows how such a process of naming might look. The setting of the Psalm verse, like virtually any late Renaissance imitative polyphony, is full of figures of all sorts; they are not difficult to identify. From our present analytical point of view, Burmeister's musical rhetoric may appear as limited in value; it offers us a set of strange Greek and Latin names for a hodge-podge of unrelated techniques for which music theory since the early seventeenth century has developed a better conceptual grasp and a less arcane terminology. Still, as a critical tool to show how a work communicates a text and how it is rhetorically persuasive, Burmeister's figures arguably give us an original and insightful method of connecting musical gesture and meaning in the vocal music of the sixteenth century. On the other hand, such a taxonomic system risks flattening such music out into an endless series of descriptive terms. Unlike modern analytical systems, Burmeister's theory does not make it possible to reveal a deep structure, a teleology, or a master narrative for a vocal work. It proceeds along the textual and musical surface, identifying figures as they occur, as well as features such as cadences, periods, and modal identity, but it has no real means of tying all the descriptive details together.

For all these weaknesses, Burmeister's – and Lippius's – rhetorical models help us to focus upon some of the central stylistic and compositional issues of *musica poetica* in the seventeenth and eighteenth centuries – issues that were at least in part recognized at the time, and that can shape our response to this tradition: the relation of an implicit plain style to a rhetorically heightened style, the relation of *dispositio* to the form of a musical piece, the degree of correspondence between rhetorical figures and their musical analogues, the conceptual basis for the classification of figures, the relation of figures to the textual expression of passion and affect, and the broader, fundamental question of whether rhetorical thinking drove the music-theoretical enterprise, or whether music theory proceeded on its own terms, taking up rhetorical theory because it was there, but adapting it according to the conceptual needs of music.[19]

19 A number of scholars – notably Heinz Brandes in the 1930s, and more recently, Dietrich Bartel – have emphasized that German theorists designated as rhetorical figures musical techniques that were already acknowledged as significant in purely musical terms. See Brandes, *Studien zur musikalischen Figurenlehre*, p. 27; Bartel, *Musica poetica*, p. 58.

Example 27.1 Analysis of verse 13 of Lasso's setting of Psalm 143, *Seven Penitential Psalms*, using Burmeister's figures

Example 27.1 (*cont.*)

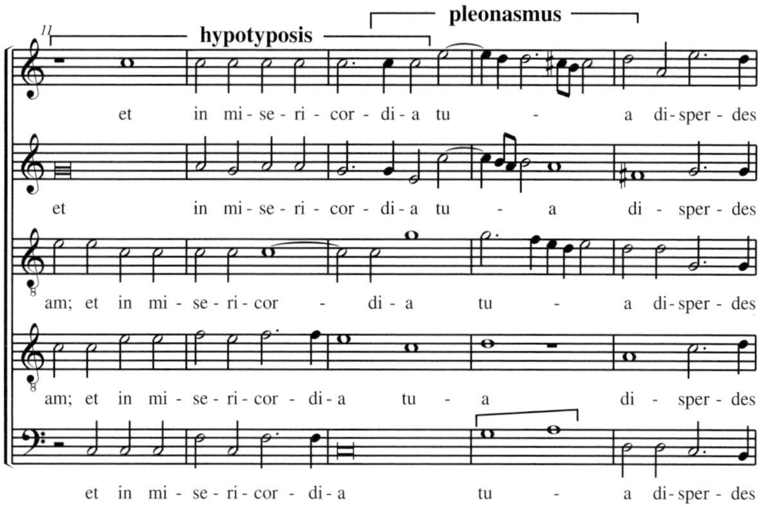

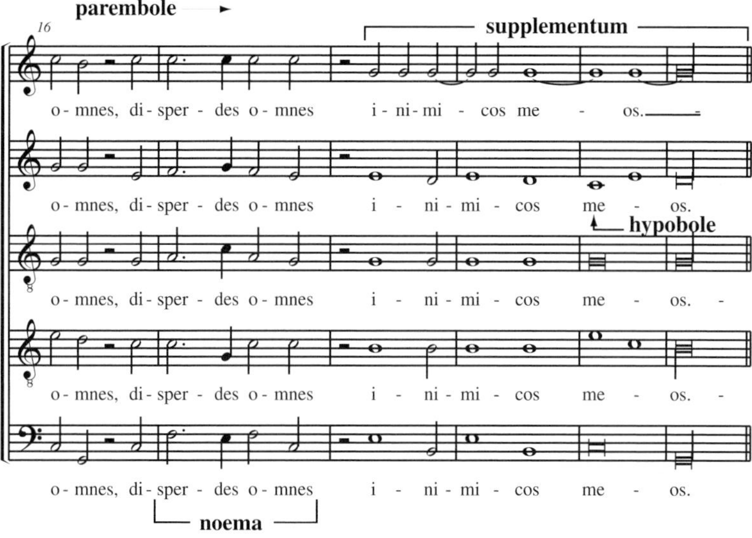

Christoph Bernhard

A new stage of musico-rhetorical theory was initiated in the mid-seventeenth century by Christoph Bernhard (1628–92), a North German who was a student of Heinrich Schütz but also studied in Italy in the 1650s, and who definitively adapted the *Figurenlehre* to the newer Italian styles.[20] Bernhard was not the first German theorist after Burmeister to use musical figures in the teaching of composition. A number of theorists in the first half of the century took up and elaborated Burmeister's idea, including Johannes Nucius (1613), Joachim Thuringus (1624), and Athanasius Kircher (1650).[21] But it was Bernhard who ultimately was most successful and influential in adapting the notion of musical figures to a radically changing musical style in the seventeenth century.

Bernhard, working in North Germany in the decades just after the publication of Kircher's *Musurgia universalis* in 1650, made style the very foundation of his classificatory system. He retained, perhaps unconsciously, an underlying link to the Burmeister tradition, in that he saw musical figures as ornamenting a plain, diatonic musical style. But now, that plain style is explicitly identified as an actual style in the real musical world: the *stylus gravis*, the *prima prattica.* Bernhard's *stylus gravis* is not completely unornamented, as was Burmeister's presumed underlying diatonic homophony, for it allows four simple figures, which are for him contrapuntal elaborations: the unaccented and accented passing tones, and the suspension and rearticulated suspension (*transitus*, *quasi-transitus*, *syncopatio*, *quasi-syncopatio*; see Table 27.2 for Bernhard's figures in the *Tractatus*). Style in fact becomes the criterion for the classification of figures. In the *Tractatus*, Bernhard recognizes, in addition to the *stylus gravis*, two more modern styles – the *stylus luxurians communis* (*seconda prattica*, church style) and the *stylus luxurians theatralis* (*seconda prattica*, theatrical style). For each of these styles he gives a list of acceptable expressive figures, virtually all of which are dissonant figurations of the *seconda prattica*, with the more radical treatments of dissonance being reserved for the theatrical, as opposed to the church, style.[22]

Bernhard's *Figurenlehre* has the advantage over Burmeister's – and over those of his other predecessors as well – of being more logically consistent. His set of figures is no longer a grab-bag of unrelated devices (of melody, harmony, counterpoint, texture,

20 Bernhard's works involving rhetorical figures are the *Tractatus compositionis augmentatus*, a manuscript treatise dating from around 1660, and the *Ausführlicher Bericht vom Gebrauche der Con- und Dissonantien*, from the late 1660s. Of the two, the *Tractatus* is the principal text, and was widely distributed and copied throughout Europe in the latter part of the seventeenth century. For modern editions of Bernhard's treatises, see *Die Kompositionslehre Heinrich Schützens*, ed. Müller-Blattau (German), and the English translations by Walter Hilse in *Music Forum* 3.

21 On the *Figurenlehre* of Nucius, Thuringus, and Kircher, see Bartel, *Musica poetica*, pp. 99–111.

22 In his later treatise, *Ausführlicher Bericht vom Gebrauche der Con- und Dissonantien*, Bernhard retreated from his earlier stylistic classifications in the *Tractatus*, since the categories drawn there were more applicable to Italian than to German music. See Bartel, *Musica poetica*, pp. 116–17. For Bernhard's figures, see Bernhard, *Tractatus*, pp. 56–121.

Stylus gravis	
transitus	passing tone on weak beat
quasi-transitus	passing tone on strong beat
syncopatio (ligatura)	suspension
quasi-syncopatio	note repeated on strong beat
Stylus luxurians communis	
superjectio	upper neighbor
anticipatio notae	anticipation
subsumptio	lower escape tone
variatio	long note decorated with several shorter notes (*passaggio*)
multiplicatio	repetition of a dissonant note
prolongatio	figure in which a dissonance has a longer duration than the preceding note
syncopatio catachrestica	ornamented resolution of suspension
passus duriusculus	rise of fall of a (chromatic) semitone
saltus duriusculus	use of large or dissonant leaps not used in *stylus gravis*
mutatio toni	mixing of modes, either with authentic and plagal in the same voice, or going from one mode to another in composition
inchoatio imperfecta	beginning a composition with a dissonant interval
longinqua distantia	wide separation of one voice from another
quaestitio notae	cutting of the end of a note in order to seek the next note from a lower neighbor
cadentiae duriusculae	"strange dissonances" before final two notes of a cadence

Table 27.2 Bernhard's figures from the *Tractatus compositionis augmentatus*, c. 1660

Stylus luxurians theatralis	
extensio	extreme lengthening of a dissonance
mora	inverted resolution of a suspension
ellipsis	suppression of a normally required consonance
abruptio	breaking off of a vocal line instead of achieving expected consonant resolution
transitus inversus	situation in recitative in which (passing) dissonance is on the strong beat or part of the measure, consonance on the weak; expanded version of *quasi-transitus*
heterolepsis	leap into another voice

Table 27.2 (*cont.*)

imitation, form, silence, and so forth) that articulates expressive meaning by representing the heightening of some unstated norm. Rather, it is an organized collection of contrapuntal treatments that acquire meaning precisely because they represent the expressive ornamentation of a specific figure in the simpler *stylus gravis*. Bernhard sees the newer style literally in rhetorical terms: he writes of "the newly established and lately further embellished *stylus recitativus*, that . . . may indeed be compared to a rhetoric, in view of the multitude of figures."[23] He makes this rhetorical – and *his*torical – connection explicit in his presentation of the figures, in that for each figuration in the new *stylus luxurians*, he gives a hypothetical origin in the *stylus gravis* (see Example 27.2). Bernhard, as Bartel aptly notes, "updates the *Figurenlehre*, placing it squarely in the context of mid-seventeenth-century stylistic trends without breaking ties to the past."[24] His figures, like Burmeister's, had the prescriptive intent of reifying for young composers – though also composers of a later generation – techniques that they might not otherwise have thought of. Used descriptively, as an analytical tool, they are best tailored for the recitative style. Again, like Burmeister's figures, they may seem to the modern analyst to focus too exclusively on the musical surface, as will be evident from the analysis of an excerpt from Buxtehude's cantata *O dulcis Jesu* in Example 27.3. But they do help to clarify real compositional techniques resulting from the German adaptation of the *seconda prattica*, and they stand as testament to the contribution of an original and musical mind to the *Figurenlehre* tradition.

Yet Bernhard's connection to the classical traditions of German rhetoric is less

23 Bernhard, *Bericht* (Hilse trans., p. 90). 24 Bartel, *Musica poetica*, p. 118.

Example 27.2 Bernhard, *Tractatus compositionis augmentatus* (Hilse translation, p. 117). Examples 1a, 2a, and 3a give excerpts from the *stylus luxurians theatralis*. Examples 1b, 2b, and 3b give the more fundamental *stylus gravis* or *prima prattica* figurations that underlie the more ornate *seconda prattica* ones.

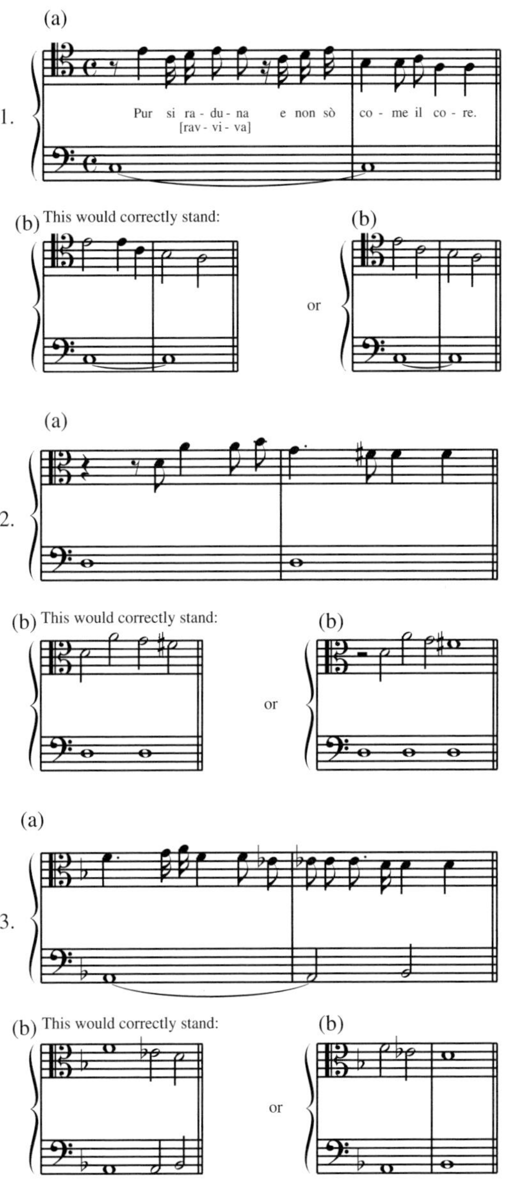

Example 27.3 Analysis of Buxtehude's Cantata *O dulcis Jesu*, mm. 249–61, using Bernhard's figures (no *prima prattica* or *stylus gravis* figures are marked here, only *seconda prattica* figures of the *stylus luxurians communis* and the *stylus luxurians theatralis*)

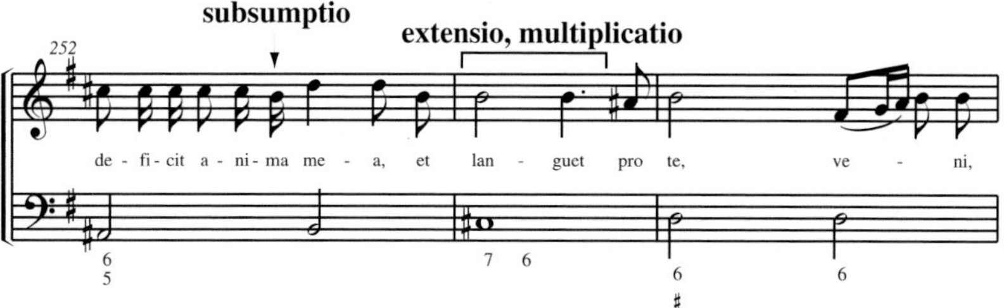

robust than his description of the recitative style as a "rhetoric" may suggest. He completely lacks the intellectual pretensions of Lippius and Burmeister, and he translates everything into musical terms. He retains, of course, the commitment to text-setting and loyalty to rhetoric that we would expect from a *musica poetica* theorist. But he often sounds far more like a musician speaking to musicians in a musical language than a musician co-opting rhetoric for use in a different art. Consider, for example, the matter of language. Bernhard, along with Herbst, was one of the first *musica poetica* theorists to write his treatises in German rather than in Latin. The change to the vernacular for music-theoretical treatises began to take place in the German tradition fifty to a hundred years after it did in other European countries. Seemingly unimportant in itself, the shift bespeaks a weakening of the ties to classical humanism, with its foundations in Greek and Latin, that were so dominant in Luther's day, and in the time of Lippius and Burmeister. Furthermore, although Bernhard does use Latin rather than German terms for his figures, it is significant that he does not use the more esoteric Greek names. None of Burmeister's original designations survive in Bernhard at all; and indeed, of all the musical devices to which the earlier theorist's rhetorical names referred, only the passing tone and the suspension remain in Bernhard's work. That such a radical change could take place in what is ostensibly the same tradition in a mere fifty years suggests, of course, that the tradition was by no means the hardened doctrine that it is sometimes thought to be. But it also suggests that in German theory, rhetoric, as a metalanguage for music, was beginning to give way to a more purely *musical*, or music-theoretical, metalanguage: that rhetoric, in European musical culture in general, and German musical culture in particular, provided a way for music theory to reorient itself in the wake of radically new musical styles, but that the descriptions that it offered for musical phenomena were not so precise as those later developed in musical terms. Supporting this view is the fact that Bernhard's names for figures are not really rhetorical terms at all: they are either standard musical terms of the time (e.g., *transitus* for passing tone, *syncopatio* for suspension) or Latin names that aptly describe a particular technique. Although they project the flavor of rhetoric, they seem far removed from the academic and humanistic patina of Burmeister's figures. Indeed, one is tempted to wonder if Bernhard's musical roots, like those of Schütz, really lie in Italy – in Zarlinian counterpoint and in the *seconda prattica* – rather than in Germany, and that his adaptation of musical figures was simply a way of packaging Italian ideas in a manner compatible with German tradition.[25]

25 On the claim that Schütz's musical roots lie in Italy rather than Germany, see Forchert, "Heinrich Schütz und die Musica poetica," p. 11.

It is hardly surprising that Bernhard, with his clear exposition of the relation between simple and more elaborate contrapuntal figurations, is the one theorist of the German musico-rhetorical tradition – and also the only theorist of the seventeenth century – singled out by Schenkerian theory as having something to say to us today: hence the translation of the entirety of the *Tractatus* in *The Music Forum*, a publication devoted for the most part to Schenkerian studies.

The waning of the rhetorical tradition

The final third of the seventeenth century and the first third of the eighteenth offer evidence of the apparent continued vitality of the *Figurenlehre.* Although no strikingly original thinkers emerged, each writer on the figures had a distinctive angle and list of figures. In general, the tendency, initiated by Bernhard, to write treatises in the vernacular rather than Latin gained strength, although works still appeared in Latin well into the eighteenth century. The principal *Figurenlehre* theorists of the period were Wolfgang Caspar Printz (1696), Johann Georg Ahle (1695–1701), Tomás Janowka (1701), Mauritius Vogt (1719), and Johann Gottfried Walther (1708 and 1732). Of these five, the most original and influential was Printz. Unlike previous writers, Printz was only interested in melodic, not harmonic or contrapuntal, figures. Indeed, none of his figures is a musico-rhetorical figure from the older *musica poetica* tradition; rather, they are melodic divisions or diminutions (*Zertheilungen* or *Manieren*), often simple embellishments or ornaments, given names from the new Italian style (e.g., *tremolo, groppo, trillo, passaggio*). Printz's work marks the beginning of a historical process in which melodic embellishments and ornaments were added to the lists of musico-rhetorical figures. This harbingers the melody-dominated style that would come to the fore in the eighteenth century, when the older musico-rhetorical figures become conflated with the *Manieren,* the simple melodic diminutions (various types of turns, scalar passages, and so forth) that would be so central to both vocal and instrumental music in the *galant* period.

By the time of Johann Mattheson, whose active career encompassed fully the first six decades of the eighteenth century, the musico-rhetorical tradition had begun an irreversible decline. Not that rhetoric itself was dead: it continued to be taught, albeit in a rather pedantic manner, in the German schools, and to play a fundamental role in education. But the powerful forces that had welded Reformation theology, classical humanism, and a few remnants of a medieval worldview together into a stable cultural system for almost two centuries were waning, just as the rational philosophy and aesthetic of the Enlightenment were emerging. The Swiss critic and pedagogue Johann Gottsched did his part to preserve what he could of the older system by bringing rhetoric fully into the vernacular: his popular *Ausführliche Redekunst* (1736; four more editions by 1759) was a complete rhetoric that brought classical sources, especially Cicero, into line with the seventeenth-century French poetics that was so admired in contemporary German literary circles, all in a dual-language edition with modern German and Latin on facing pages. Gottsched purveyed a rather Cartesian view of the affects and the passions, but his thorough vernacularization of rhetoric did much to bring it out of the humanistic world of the Reformation and into the world of the Enlightenment. It would in fact be Gottsched's Germanized rhetoric that Johann Georg Sulzer would put to musical use in the 1770s in his enormously influential *Allgemeine Theorie der schönen Künste.*

Mattheson. The work of Johann Mattheson (1681–1764), an exact contemporary of Gottsched, marks a critical turn in the musical appropriation of rhetoric. From the outset Mattheson brings a new point of view to music. As an occasional composer of church music working within the Lutheran tradition, Mattheson retained his loyalty to that tradition while at the same time questioning, indeed waging war against those elements within it that he considered old-fashioned. Chief among these were the medieval cosmogony of music as mathematical art, and any overemphasis on harmony and counterpoint at the expense of melody. For Mattheson the purpose of music was to express the passions, a goal toward which the language arts, such as rhetoric, were a better guide than the exact sciences, and toward which melody was a more effective musical means than harmony. He thus assigned to rhetoric and rhetorically conceived melody central roles in his compositional teaching. He claimed to be the first theorist to give melody its due, and he offered a thorough grounding in "melodic science" in his *Kern melodischer Wissenschaft* of 1737 – a rhetorically based approach to melodic composition that he incorporated two years later, virtually without alteration, in Part II of his magnum opus, *Der vollkommene Capellmeister.*[26]

Mattheson's original approach to musical rhetoric is first evident in that he turns his attention away from *elocutio* and the figures – the core of the *musica poetica* tradition in the seventeenth century – toward *inventio* and *dispositio.* (Paradoxically, he makes this turn in music precisely at the time that rhetoric proper was well on the way to complete ossification in its obsession with the figures.) Near the end of his exposition of melodic rhetoric, he briefly discusses the figures as a viable means of melodic expression.[27] Yet he seems just to note them in passing: he refers to a few figures, but provides only one example. He gives the strong impression that the figures, useful as they are, have been too much written about, that most musicians know them anyway, that many of them are out of date, and that musical fashion concerning the *ornamenta* changes so quickly that it is hardly worth mentioning them. In contrast, he devotes a long and detailed discussion to a central topic of *inventio:* the use of the *loci topici* as a means of inspiring melodic ideas. Mattheson's discussion here is not entirely original; Johann David Heinichen had already devoted over fifty pages to a detailed musical application of the *loci* in his *Neu-erfundene und gründliche Anweisung* of 1711. Yet the point here is less that of which theorist developed the idea first, than that of the shifting of rhetorical focus in music from *elocutio* to *inventio*. Mattheson, whose theories of melody laid the foundation for later eighteenth-century theories of form, also attempted to employ *dispositio* as a model for musical form: his famous analysis of a Marcello aria using the classic parts of *dispositio* harks back to the simpler *exordium–medium–finis* model of Dressler. To be sure, as a number of scholars have shown, the mapping does not really work; but it serves notice that the eighteenth century's interest in rhetoric would be

26 Mattheson's *Der vollkommene Capellmeister* is available in facsimile, and in an English translation by Ernest C. Harriss. 27 Mattheson, *Der vollkommene Capellmeister* (Harriss trans., pp. 469–84).

principally as a metaphor to guide the shaping of musical form.[28] Furthermore, Mattheson's well-known application of grammatical (more than rhetorical) terminology to musical phrase structure would provide the starting point for Riepel and Koch in the second half of the century.

By the middle of the eighteenth century it no longer makes sense to continue linking the musico-rhetorical element in German theory to its *musica poetica* or *Figurenlehre* roots. The aim of these two traditions, we recall, had been the musical heightening of a text, either in general, or by means of the figures in particular. This text-expressive goal became increasingly incompatible with the newer *galant* and *empfindsam* style as the eighteenth century progressed, not only because of the associated change in musical aesthetics, but also because of the growing emancipation of instrumental music from vocal music. To be sure, theorists throughout the century, from Mattheson to Heinrich Christoph Koch, maintained the priority of vocal over instrumental music: Mattheson, in a famous quip, dubs vocal melody the mother, instrumental melody the daughter.[29] Yet even though Mattheson's expositions of *inventio* and of *dispositio* were based on examples of vocal composition or analysis, his melodic theories are equally applicable to instrumental music.

Scheibe. With Johann Adolf Scheibe's (1708–76) *Der critische Musicus* (a musical journal published in individual issues 1736–45; collected publication 1745) the process of bringing the musico-rhetorical figures into the Enlightenment becomes complete. Ironically, Scheibe's progressive work was published in the same year as the *Tractatus musicus* of the Catholic priest and composer Meinrad Spiess, the last German theorist who could be said to believe wholeheartedly in the now outdated *musica poetica* synthesis. Scheibe projects an entirely different worldview. The composer whom Scheibe addresses is not the devout *musicus poeticus* but the instrumental composer of the mid-century Enlightenment. And the rhetoric that he brings to bear on the task is not that of the classical authors, or of those authors as interpreted by Lutheran humanism, but the modernized and Germanized rhetoric of Gottsched; Scheibe even takes his title from Gottsched's early work on poetics, *Versuch einer critischen Dichtkunst* (1730). Like Gottsched, Scheibe gives the names of the figures in both German and Latin. Like Gottsched, Scheibe projects a somewhat Cartesian, quasi-mechanistic view of the emotions and their expression. And it is Scheibe who most concisely articulates a central historical phenomenon embodied in the evolution of the musical figures: that the expressive meaning originally linked with a text in vocal music can eventually be liberated to function independently in instrumental music.

Scheibe, who has long been maligned for his criticism of J. S. Bach, is in fact arguably the most musically sensitive of the musico-rhetorical theorists of the eighteenth century. No other theorist of the century gives figures (listed in Table 27.3) that so

28 See, for example, Hoyt, review of Bonds, *Wordless Rhetoric*. Also see **Chapter 28, pp. 881–83**.
29 Mattheson, *Der vollkommene Capellmeister*, pp. 133 ff. (Harriss trans., p. 418).

(NB: German terms taken from Gottsched)

exclamatio (Ausruf): musical exclamation

dubitatio (Zweifel): an intentionally ambiguous rhythmic or harmonic progression

ellipsis (Verbeißung): breaking off of a passage which one begins but does not completely finish

hyperbaton (Versetzung): transfer of a note or phrase from its natural position to a different position

repetitio (Wiederholung): repetition of a passage; repetitions should not all be in the same key

paranomasia (Verstärkung): "occurs when an already expressed sentence, word, or saying is repeated with a new, singular, and emphatic addition"

distributio (Zergliederung): "occurs when the principal theme of a composition is presented in such a manner that each of its parts is successively and thoroughly elaborated"

antithesis (Gegensatz): "occurs when a few passages are contrasted with each other in order to bring out the main subject more clearly"

suspensio (Aufhalten): "occurs when a passage begins from a remote point and progresses for a considerable time through numerous digressions in such a manner that the listener cannot ever discern the intention of the composer"

interrogatio (Frage): musical question

epistrophe (Wiederkehr): "occurs when the ending of one passage is repeated at the end of another passage"

gradatio (Aufsteigen; earlier writers called it *climax*): "occurs when one progresses by step from a weak passage to stronger ones, thereby gradually increasing the importance and emphasis of the expression or music"

Harmonishce Figuren

transitus (regularis, irregularis)

syncopatio/ligature

Fuge

Table 27.3 Scheibe's figures from *Der critische Musicus*, 1745; translations from Bartel.

aptly capture the rhetorical, declamatory character of the German music of the *empfindsam* style, and indeed of Haydn, Mozart, and Beethoven at the end of the century.[30] Example 27.4 offers a Scheibe-based figural analysis of the beginning of the Rondo finale of Beethoven's Piano Sonata in D major, Op. 10, No. 3. Scheibe's figures elegantly map onto many of the features of the music that are most engaging to us as listeners: the questioning character of the opening motive; the centrality of repetition, and the ways in which altered repetition conveys meaning; the elements of hesitation and surprise; the tendency of the music to start and stop, or to rush along in one direction, then suddenly veer off in another. Though still essentially descriptive, and tied to the musical surface rather than its underlying structure, Scheibe's figures offer a path into the expressive and affective qualities of the music that modern structuralist analyses often miss.

The later eighteenth century

The second half of the eighteenth century witnessed the final stages of the musico-rhetorical tradition. Many theorists and critics continued to ply the metaphor of rhetoric as a model for music. Mark Evan Bonds has meticulously documented such references to rhetoric in musical writings, in both the German and the other European traditions, throughout the eighteenth century and early nineteenth century.[31] But radical changes are evident in the ways that rhetoric is conceived of and used for musical purposes. As Bartel has noted, most essential is the now full transformation from a rationalist, objective aesthetic to an expressive, subjective one – or, in the well-known formulation of Morris Abrams, the shift from a mimetic to an expressive aesthetic.[32] With this shift the *Figurenlehre* tradition becomes defunct. In this regard, Friedrich Blume has rightly claimed that "the art of musical rhetoric is . . . gradually lost in the generation of Bach's sons, which replaced outlived oratorical formulas by the natural outpouring of the human heart."[33]

Even so, the death of the *Figurenlehre* is not necessarily coextensive with the death of musical rhetoric in general. A central thinker here is the conservative Swiss aesthetician Johann Georg Sulzer (1771–79) who, further developed the work of Mattheson within the confines of the aesthetics of Gottsched. Sulzer loosely appropriated the basic rhetorical concepts of *inventio*, *dispositio*, and *elocutio* – now expressed in the vernacular as *Erfindung*, *Anlage*, and *Ausarbeitung* – as descriptive categories for the process of creating artworks, musical or otherwise. Heinrich Christoph Koch (1782–93, 1802), who took on the mantle of Mattheson at the end of the century as the principal

30 For Scheibe's figures, see *Der critische Musikus*, pp. 683–99.

31 Bonds, *Wordless Rhetoric*, esp. Chapter 2, "Rhetoric and the Concept of Musical Form in the Eighteenth Century."

32 Bartel, *Musica poetica*, p. 157; Abrams, *The Mirror and the Lamp*.

33 Blume, *Renaissance and Baroque Music*, p. 105; cited in Bartel, *Musica poetica*, p. 157.

theorist of melody, and thus of musical form, enshrined these terms in music theory as stages of the compositional process.[34]

A number of features characterize this swan-song of musical rhetoric. First, as was already perfectly evident by mid-century, the rhetorical tradition was eventually going to have to adapt to the cultural fact that instrumental music was gradually gaining a solid footing that would put it on a level of prestige equal to – and, by the early nineteenth century, higher than – that of vocal music. The last *Figurenlehre* theorist, the music historian Johann Forkel (1788), tried to respond to this challenge by making a final effort to save the figures: going beyond Scheibe, he detached the figures completely from texted vocal music and claimed that they were not derived from the rhetorical figures of language, but were fundamental and analogous forms of human expression. A second response was common among theorists, Forkel included: to adapt to music the notion of a subject, or idea, of an oration – embodied in rhetoric in the *status* theory of the ancient Romans, with its *loci topici.* Late eighteenth-century compositional theory is full of discussions of the *Idee*, *Gedanke*, *Thema*, or *motivo*. Again, as in Mattheson's analysis of Marcello, the analogy seems to fit, but it only works at a high level of generality – when rhetoric serves more as a metaphor than as an arbiter of specific musical techniques. Indeed, were it conceived loosely enough, one could adapt the notion of subject in rhetoric to underlie thematic usage in standard instrumental forms such as sonata form, as Forkel did in the late eighteenth century, and as Bonds has done, from a historical and critical perspective, two hundred years later. Ultimately such usages of rhetoric led to the final divorce of rhetoric and music.

The last musico-rhetorical act of the late eighteenth-century theorists was to distinguish musical rhetoric from musical grammar, to split off compositional process and melodic form from the details of counterpoint and harmony. Forkel, for example, separates the two as follows:

> In concatenating musical expressions into a coherent whole, one must attend to two points in particular: first, the connection of individual notes and chords into individual phrases, and second, the successive connection of multiple phrases . . . The precepts for joining individual notes and chords into individual phrases are part of musical grammar, just as the precepts for joining multiple individual phrases are a part of musical rhetoric.[35]

By the early nineteenth century, the split was complete. But at this point, despite the rhetorical terminology, music theory was on its own: thanks to the tradition that extended from medieval *discantus* treatises through Zarlino to Fux and Kirnberger, it had a theory of counterpoint; thanks to Lippius, the thorough-bass tradition, Rameau, and German theorists such as Marpurg, Sorge, Daube, and Kirnberger, it had a theory

34 For translations of passages involving rhetoric and compositional process in Sulzer and Koch, see Christensen and Baker, *Aesthetics and the Art of Musical Composition*; see also Christensen's and Baker's introductory essays. See also Bent, "The Compositional Process in Music Theory."

35 Forkel, *Allgemeine Geschichte der Musik*, vol. 1, p. 21; cited in Bonds, *Wordless Rhetoric*, p. 72.

Example 27.4 Analysis of Rondo of Beethoven's Sonata in D major, Op. 10, No. 3, mm. 1–34, using Scheibe's figures

Example 27.4 (*cont.*)

of harmony; and thanks to Mattheson, Riepel, and Koch, it had a theory of melody – or for us, a theory of form. Thus, just as instrumental music eventually separated itself from vocal music, so did music theory wean itself of musical rhetoric. Whatever references we find to musical rhetoric after 1800 describe but the shell of what it once was. The nineteenth century combined Koch's musical rhetoric and grammar into a single entity, musical *structure* – a term that, according to Carl Dahlhaus, is datable back to E. T. A. Hoffmann's review of Beethoven's Fifth Symphony in 1810.[36] What the late eighteenth century tended to call rhetoric gradually began to be subsumed under what the nineteenth century called structure, to the point that musical rhetoric disappeared altogether. It was left to twentieth-century musicology to recover, underneath the nineteenth-century concepts of expression, organicism, and structure, the rhetorical roots of the music and music theory of the preceding centuries.

36 Dahlhaus, *The Idea of Absolute Music*, p. 7.

Bibliography

Primary sources: rhetoric

Ad C. Herennium. De ratione dicendi (Rhetorica ad Herennium), with Eng. trans. H. Caplan, Loeb Classical Library, Cambridge, MA, Harvard University Press, 1954

Aristotle, *The Art of Rhetoric*, trans. and ed. H. C. Lawson-Tancred, London and New York, Penguin Books, 1991

Cicero, *De inventione; De optimo genere oratorum; Topica*, with Eng. trans. H. M. Hubbell, Loeb Classical Library, Cambridge, MA, Harvard University Press, 1949

De oratore, 2 vols., Books I and II trans. E. Sutton and H. Rackham, Book III trans. H. Rackham, Loeb Classical Library, Cambridge, MA, Harvard University Press, 1942–48

Gottsched, J. C. *Ausführliche Redekunst nach Anleitung der Griechen und Römer wie auch der neuern Ausländer*, Leipzig, Breitkopf, 1736; facs. Hildesheim, G. Olms, 1973

Plato, *Gorgias; Phaedrus*, trans. and ed. J. Nichols, Jr., Ithaca, Cornell University Press, 1998

Quintilian, *Institutio oratoria*, 4 vols., with Eng. trans. H. Butler, Loeb Classical Library, Cambridge, MA, Harvard University Press, 1920

Secondary sources: rhetoric

Barilli, R. *La retorica*, Milan, A. Mondadori, 1983; trans. G. Menozzi as *Rhetoric*, Minneapolis, University of Minnesota Press, 1989

Barner, W. *Barockrhetorik: Untersuchungen zu ihren geschichtlichen Grundlagen*, Tübingen, Niemeyer, 1970

Barthes, R. "The Old Rhetoric: An *Aide-mémoire*," in *The Semiotic Challenge*, trans. R. Howard, New York, Hill and Wang, 1988

Conley, T. *Rhetoric in the European Tradition*, New York, Longman, 1990
Fumaroli, M. *L'Age de l'éloquence: Rhétorique et "res literaria" de la Renaissance au seuil de l'époque classique*, Geneva, Droz, 1980; reprint Paris, A. Michel, 1994
Kennedy, G. A. *Classical Rhetoric and Its Christian and Secular Tradition from Ancient to Modern Times*, Chapel Hill, University of North Carolina Press, 1980
A New History of Classical Rhetoric, Princeton University Press, 1994
Lanham, R. A. *The Motives of Eloquence: Literary Theory in the Renaissance*, New Haven, Yale University Press, 1976
Lausberg, H. *Handbook of Literary Rhetoric: A Foundation for Literary Study*, trans. M. Bliss, A. Jansen, and D. Orton, ed. D. Orton and R. Anderson, Boston, Brill, 1998
Vickers, B. *In Defence of Rhetoric*, Oxford University Press, 1988

Primary sources: music

Ahle, J. *Musikalisches Frühlings-, Sommer-, Herbst-, und Winter-Gespräche*, Mühlhausen, Pauli und Brückner, 1695–1701
Bernhard, C. *Ausführlicher Bericht vom Gebrauche der Con- und Dissonantien, Tractatus compositionis augmentatus in Die Kompositionslehre Heinrich Schützens in der Fassung seines Schülers Chr. Bernhard*, ed. J. Müller-Blattau, 2nd edn., Kassel, Bärenreiter, 1963; trans. W. Hilse as "The Treatises of Christoph Bernhard," *Music Forum* 3 (1973), pp. 1–196
Burmeister, J. *Hypomnematum musicae poeticae*, Rostock, S. Myliander, 1599
Musica autoschediastike, Rostock, C. Reusner, 1601
Musica poetica, Rostock, S. Myliander, 1606; facs. Kassel, Bärenreiter, 1955; trans. B. Rivera as *Musical Poetics*, New Haven, Yale University Press, 1993
Butler, C. *The Principles of Musick*, London, Haviland, 1636; facs. New York, Da Capo Press, 1970
Dressler, G. *Praecepta musicae poeticae*, MS, 1563; ed. B. Engelke in *Geschichts-Blätter für Stadt und Land Magdeburg* 49–50 (1914–15), pp. 213–50
Forkel, J. *Allgemeine Geschichte der Musik*, Göttingen, Schwickert, 1788; facs. Graz, Akademische Druck- und Verlagsanstalt, 1967
Heinichen, J. *Neuerfundene und gründliche Anweisung*, Hamburg, B. Schiller, 1711
Herbst, J. *Musica poetica*, Nuremberg, Dümler, 1643
Janowka, T. B. *Clavis ad thesauram magnae artis musicae*, Prague, G. Labaun, 1701
Kircher, A. *Musurgia universalis*, Rome, Corbelletti, 1650; facs. Hildesheim, G. Olms, 1970
Lippius, J. *Synopsis musicae novae*, Strassburg, Kieffer, 1612; trans. B. Rivera as *Synopsis of New Music*, Colorado Springs, Colorado College Music Press, 1977
Listenius, N. *Musica*, Wittenberg, G. Rhau, 1537
Mattheson, J. *Kern melodischer Wissenschaft*, Hamburg, Herold, 1737
Der vollkommene Capellmeister, Hamburg, C. Herold, 1739; facs. Kassel, Bärenreiter, 1954, 1999; trans. and ed. E. C. Harriss as *Johann Mattheson's "Der vollkommene Capellmeister"*, Ann Arbor, UMI Research Press, 1981
Mersenne, M. *Harmonie universelle*, Paris, S. Cramoisy, 1636–37; facs. Paris, Centre National de la Recherche Scientifique, 1963 and 1986
Nucius, J. *Musices poeticae*, Nysa, C. Scharffenberg, 1613; facs. Kassel, Bärenreiter, 1978

Printz, W. *Phrynis Mitilenaeus, oder Satyrischer Componist*, 3 vols., Dresden, J. C. Mieth and J. C. Zimmerman, 1696

Scheibe, J. *Der critische Musicus*, Leipzig, B. C. Breitkopf, 1745; facs. Hildesheim, G. Olms, 1970

Spiess, M. *Tractatus musicus compositorio-practicus*, Augsburg, J. J. Lotters Erben, 1745

Thuringus, J. *Opusculum bipartitum*, Berlin, Runge, 1624

Vogt, M. *Conclave thesauri magnae artis musicae*, Prague, G. Labaun, 1719

Walther, J. *Musikalisches Lexikon*, Leipzig, Deer, 1732; facs. Kassel, Bärenreiter, 1953

Praecepta der musicalischen Composition, MS 1708; new edn., ed. P. Benary, Leipzig, Breitkopf und Härtel, 1955

Zarlino, G. *Le istitutioni harmoniche*, Venice, Franceschi, 1558; facs. New York, Broude, 1965

Secondary sources: music

Bartel, D. *Musica Poetica*, Lincoln, University of Nebraska Press, 1997; rev. from *Handbuch der musikalischen Figurenlehre*, Regensburg, Laaber, 1985

Bent, I. "The Compositional Process in Music Theory, 1713–1850," *MA* 3 (1984), pp. 29–55

Blume, F. *Renaissance and Baroque Music*, New York, Norton, 1967

Bonds, M. E. *Wordless Rhetoric: Musical Form and the Metaphor of the Oration*, Cambridge, MA, Harvard University Press, 1991

Brandes, H. *Studien zur musikalischen Figurenlehre im 16. Jahrhundert*, Berlin, Triltsch und Huther, 1935

Buelow, G. "Johann Mattheson and the Invention of the *Affektenlehre*," in *New Mattheson Studies*, ed. G. Buelow and H. J. Marx, Cambridge University Press, 1983

"The *Loci Topici* and Affect in Late Baroque Music: Heinichen's Practical Demonstration," *Music Review* 27 (1966), pp. 161–76

"Music, Rhetoric, and the Concept of the Affections: A Selective Bibliography," *Notes* 30 (1973), pp. 250–59

Butler, G. "Fugue and Rhetoric," *JMT* 21 (1977), pp. 49–109

"Music and Rhetoric in Early Seventeenth-Century English Sources," *Musical Quarterly* 66 (1980), pp. 53–64

Christensen, T. and N. Baker, eds. and trans., *Aesthetics and the Art of Musical Composition in the German Enlightenment: Selected Writings of Johann Georg Sulzer and Heinrich Christoph Koch*, Cambridge University Press, 1995

Dahlhaus, C. *The Idea of Absolute Music*, trans. R. Lustig, University of Chicago Press, 1989

"Der rhetorische Formbegriff H. Chr. Kochs und die Theorie der Sonatenform," *AfMw* 35 (1978), pp. 155–77

Dammann, R. *Der Musikbegriff im deutschen Barock*, 2nd edn., Regensburg, Laaber, 1984

Eggebrecht, H. H. "Zum Figur-Begriff der Musica poetica," *AfMw* 16 (1959), pp. 57–69

Federhofer, H. "Christoph Bernhards Figurenlehre und die Dissonanz," *Musikforschung* 42 (1989), pp. 110–27

Forchert, A. "Bach und die Tradition der Rhetorik," in *Alte Musik als ästhetische Gegenwart: Bach, Händel, Schütz. Bericht über den internationalen musik-wissenschaftlichen Kongreß Stuttgart 1985*, vol. I, ed. D. Berke and D. Hanemann, Kassel, Bärenreiter 1987, pp. 169–78

"Heinrich Schütz und die Musica poetica," *Schütz-Jahrbuch* 15 (1993), pp. 7–24
Gurlitt, W. "Musik und Rhetorik," *Helicon* 5 (1944), pp. 67–86
Harrison, D. "Rhetoric and Fugue: An Analytical Application," *MTS* 12 (1990), pp. 1–42
Hoyt, P. review of *Wordless Rhetoric: Musical Form and the Metaphor of the Oration* by M. E. Bonds, *JMT* 38 (1994), pp. 123–43
Kirkendale, U. "The Source for Bach's *Musical Offering*: The *Institutio oratoria* of Quintilian," *JAMS* 33 (1980), pp. 88–111
Kirkendale, W. "Ciceronians versus Aristotelians on the Ricercar as Exordium, from Bembo to Bach," *JAMS* 32 (1979), pp. 1–44
"Circulatio-Tradition, *Maria lactans*, and Josquin as Musical Orator," *Acta* 56 (1984), pp. 69–92
Krones, H. "Rhetorik und rhetorische Symbolik in der Musik um 1800: Vom Weiterleben eines Prinzips," *Musiktheorie* 3 (1988), pp. 117–40
Neubauer, J. *The Emancipation of Music from Language: Departures from Mimesis in Eighteenth-Century Aesthetics*, New Haven, Yale University Press, 1986
Palisca, C. "*Ut oratoria musica:* The Rhetorical Basis of Musical Mannerism" (1972), in *Studies in the History of Italian Music*, New Haven, Yale University Press, 1994
Reidemeister, P. and V. Gutmann, eds., *Alte Musik: Praxis und Reflexion*, Winterthur, Amadeus, 1983
Rivera, B. *German Music Theory in the Early Seventeenth Century*, Ann Arbor, UMI Research Press, 1980
Ruhnke, M. *Joachim Burmeister: Ein Beitrag zur Musiklehre um 1600*, Kassel, Bärenreiter, 1955
Schering, A. "Die Lehre von den musikalischen Figuren," *Kirchenmusikalisches Jahrbuch* 21 (1908), pp. 106–14
Sisman, E. *Haydn and the Classical Variation*, Cambridge, MA, Harvard University Press, 1993
"Pathos and the *Pathétique*: Rhetorical stance in Beethoven's C-minor Sonata, Op. 13," *Beethoven Forum* 3 (1994), pp. 81–106
Street, A. "The Rhetorico-Musical Structure of the 'Goldberg' Variations: Bach's *Clavierübung IV* and the *Institutio oratoria* of Quintilian," *MA* 6 (1987), pp. 89–131
Unger, H. H. *Die Beziehungen zwischen Musik und Rhetorik im 16.–18. Jahrhundert*, Würzburg, Triltsch, 1941; facs. Hildesheim, G. Olms, 1969
Vickers, B. "Figures of Rhetoric/Figures of Music?," *Rhetorica* 2 (1984), pp. 1–44
Williams, P. "Encounters with the Chromatic Fourth, or More on Figurenlehre," *Musical Times* 126 (1985), pp. 276–77 and 339–44
"The Snares and Delusions of Musical Rhetoric: Some Examples from Recent Writings on J. S. Bach," in *Alte Musik: Praxis und Reflexion*, ed. P. Reidemeister and V. Gutmann, Winterthur, Amadeus, 1983

· 28 ·

Form

SCOTT BURNHAM

This chapter will trace some of the major strands of a tradition of musical thought that reaches from the late eighteenth century to our own time: the analysis of large-scale tonal form. Whereas a fascination with formal analysis undertaken purely for its own sake is mostly a twentieth-century phenomenon, the emphasis on form has been a central preoccupation of music-theoretical writings ever since the "work concept" (consolidated around 1800) decisively shifted theoretical focus to whole works of music and thus to overall form.[1] As notions of organic musical process became more prevalent, musical form became less self-evident, more in need of elucidation. Mainstream music criticism in the early nineteenth century was increasingly characterized by intuitive professions of aesthetic unity (the urge to demonstrate such unity analytically was only faintly in evidence at first); this trend was of a piece with a romanticized view of the creative artist as a second Creator, whose unifying spirit was thought to hover over the great variety that could now be brought together within the selfsame work. In short, form became more than a matter of conventional arrangement: it was the extensive manifestation and discernible logic of the creative imagination.

At the same time, the pedagogical context of music-theoretical writing broadened: the *Satzlehre* tradition became that of the *Kompositionslehre*, as theoretical treatises were now concerned with promoting the composition of entire pieces in the available forms. The analysis of musical forms began in this context as a pedagogical exercise in emulation, and the works of Haydn, Mozart, and Beethoven were increasingly held up as exemplary. But by the end of the nineteenth century, the business of formal analysis began to be undertaken as a kind of research program – what was primarily at stake was no longer the education of a young composer but rather the viability of theories of music that attempted to determine what were felt to be the natural laws of music. Pedagogy gave way to taxonomy, emulation to contemplation.

The sprawling tradition of the so-called *Formenlehre* (doctrine of forms) obviously involves a welter of forms and even of methods, but the analysis of what we call sonata form has surely been the central strand. To tell a story of the codification of sonata form is by and large to tell a story of the theory of musical form in the last two centuries. Thus the analysis of sonata form will serve in this chapter as a connecting thread. That

1 Goehr, *The Imaginary Museum of Musical Works.*

thread will connect Heinrich Christoph Koch's 1790s late-Enlightenment theory of harmonic articulation with the distinctly Idealist and thematic approach of A. B. Marx, and it will continue on through the Naturalist functional taxonomies of Hugo Riemann, the differently motivated functional analyses of Arnold Schoenberg and Erwin Ratz, and the empirical, style-conscious analyses of Donald Francis Tovey. The chapter will conclude with a brief consideration of some late twentieth-century recuperations and extensions of these earlier orientations.

Phrase, form, and rhetoric at the close of the eighteenth century

Heinrich Christoph Koch. The influential treatise of Heinrich Christoph Koch (1749–1816), the *Versuch einer Anleitung zur Composition* (1782–93), makes an appropriate point of departure for this survey.[2] For Koch sought to transcend one of the defining theoretical debates of the eighteenth century, the debate over the primacy of melody or harmony, by positing that the primal material (*Urstoff*) of music was the interdependence of melody and harmony.[3] With this fundamental precept in hand, Koch proceeded to describe various kinds of musical phrases in consuming detail, attending closely to the relations of cadential (harmonic) articulation and melodic behavior. This in turn provided him with a way to process many individual realizations of binary form, particularly that of the Classical-style minuet.

In the still strong wake of a long tradition of rhetorical approaches to music, Koch worked hard to demonstrate that musical phrases were analogous to grammatically sound sentences. Like sentences, musical phrases are both self-sufficient and flexibly configured; they possess subjects and predicates and are articulated by different strengths of punctuation; they can accommodate a variety of interpolations, extensions, and compressions without sacrificing their fundamental coherence and comprehensibility. In addition, Koch was concerned about the ways such phrases may or may not follow each other. He extracts some generalized rules for continuations after various types of phrase-ending. For example: two phrases that end with the same harmony (two I-phrases or two V-phrases) may not follow back to back with different melodic sections.[4] If the same melody is used, the effect will be that of a reinforcing repetition, but if a different melody is used the effect will inevitably be static. This type of observation demonstrates the interdependence of melody and harmony in Koch's approach to form.

Another example of his sensitivity to the role of melodic content within a musical form is his injunction to precede the return of the "main phrase" toward the end of a composition with a V-phrase rather than a I-phrase, so as not to weaken the entrance

2 For English translations, see Koch, *Introductory Essay on Composition* (contains material from vols. III and IV of the original) and Baker and Christensen, eds., *Aesthetics and the Art of Musical Composition* (contains material from vol. II of Koch's treatise). 3 See Baker, "Der Urstoff der Musik."

4 Koch, *Introductory Essay*, p. 110.

of the main phrase but rather to allow it to arouse "the greatest attention at once as a main phrase."[5] This clearly underlines the aesthetic importance for Koch of the simultaneous return of main key and main melody.

Koch deals exhaustively and nearly exclusively with small-boned binary forms such as the minuet; what he has to say about sonata form comes only toward the end of the last volume of his treatise and is characterized by a tangible shift in his method from a generative approach to a conformational approach, from a step-by-step tracking of individual phrases to a more cursory description of the conventions of large-scale form and genre.[6] In fact, Koch's description of sonata form is more accurately a description of the genre of the symphony and its "first allegro."

In contrast to slow movements with their more highly defined melodic sections, symphonic first movements entail frequent compounding of phrases, a more continuous melody, and a sense of inner power and emphasis: "a noble, or more often, forceful feeling" must be presented with momentum and unhindered by extreme detail.[7] In other words, there are fewer checks to the harmonic and melodic flow than tend to occur in slow movements or minuets.[8] (It might be argued that Koch, with his elaborate apparatus of cadential articulation, was supremely equipped to recognize this enhanced type of motion – as a marked contrast to the highly punctuated minuet forms – yet less well equipped to track it step by step.)

When discussing the form of the symphonic first allegro, Koch invokes his central aesthetic premise about the compositional process, which he had essayed at length in the first volume of his treatise. For Koch (following Johann Georg Sulzer's *Allgemeine Theorie der schönen Künste*, 1771–74), the composition of a piece of music takes place as a three-part process: the invention of the plan (*Anlage*), containing the core material of the movement; its sketched-out realization (*Ausführung*), including all the sections of the form; and the final details of its elaboration (*Ausarbeitung*). What we would call the sonata-form exposition is conceived by Koch as a single main period (*Hauptperiod*), which also functions as the *Anlage* for the entire movement; the second section of Koch's binary conception of the form consists of two large periods (our development and recapitulation). Koch thus makes the important claim that a sonata-form exposition is not simply an arrangement of themes and transitions but rather can be heard as an integrated, self-sufficient utterance (the *Hauptperiod*), and – perhaps more conse-

5 Ibid., p. 98. 6 Bonds, *Wordless Rhetoric*, p. 27.

7 Koch, *Introductory Essay*, pp. 197–99 and 229–30. The pertinent sections of Koch's essay on various Classical genres is excerpted in *SR*, pp. 807–19.

8 Sulzer compared the genre of the symphony to a Pindaric ode. See Bonds, "The Symphony as Pindaric Ode."

9 Conceptualizing the exposition as a single *Hauptperiod* allows Koch to embrace an entire exposition without leaving the logical framework of a single period. See Ritzel, *Die Entwicklung der "Sonatenform"*, p. 175. For Sulzer's earlier description of the symphonic allegro, see Baker and Christensen (eds.), *Aesthetics and the Art of Musical Composition*, pp. 105–08. On Sulzer's tripartite compositional process see ibid., pp. 66–80. Also see **Chapter 27, pp. 872–73**.

quentially – as the product of invention (the *Anlage*).[9] In other words, the sonata form is marked as a form that does not consist of the syntactically logical ordering of thematic sections but rather is heard – qua form – to be the product of inspiration. What was once the province of melody becomes the province of form.

Theme and development: the early nineteenth century

In Koch's treatise, analysis per se is not the point – there it is more a matter of describing and illustrating possibilities for the student of composition. Of interest for the history of music analysis is the way Koch chooses to focus on the level of the phrase and the influential analytical terminology he developed to describe the melodic content and harmonic closure of phrases. In the first few decades of the nineteenth century, on the other hand, formal analysis began to be undertaken as a kind of demonstrative exercise that could stand apart from the programmatic flow of a composition treatise. Whereas Koch did not feel compelled to map out an entire large-scale movement, or to engage in any analysis apart from what he needed to illustrate at any given instance, here we begin to observe a more strictly analytical impulse, made explicit in the urge to account comprehensively for every bar of a movement.

Such analyses often parse the movement into phrases or periods, at times including some form of Rameau's fundamental bass as an analytical gloss of the harmonic content. At the end of *System der Musik-Wissenschaft und der praktischen Komposition* (1827) by Johann Bernhard Logier (1777–1846), for example, stand analyses of movements from a Corelli concerto and a Haydn string quartet. Underneath a condensed score of each movement, Logier provides a figured-bass analysis and a fundamental bass on a separate staff. He accompanies each analysis with a prose account of the layout of melodic ideas and the various modulations, and, in the case of the Haydn movement, adds a supplementary hermeneutic narrative that compares the musical action to the animadversions of a spirited family discussion.[10]

Several theorists working in France carried on Koch's rhetorically influenced analytical reduction of phrases into smaller units, while incorporating other features of a distinctly progressive stamp. Jérôme-Joseph de Momigny (1762–1842), in his *Cours complet d'harmonie et de composition* (1803–06), offers detailed and lengthy analyses of the opening movements of Mozart's Quartet in D minor, K. 421 and Haydn's Symphony No. 103.[11] These analyses lay out a series of flexibly extended, often non-symmetrical periods (in the Mozart example, each period is analyzed rhythmically on an almost beat-to-beat level, as Momigny marks a succession of what he calls *cadences*

10 Logier, *Logier's Comprehensive Course*, pp. 233–49.
11 Momigny's analysis of the Haydn symphony can be found in *MANC*, vol. II, pp. 127–40.

mélodiques, a kind of musical respiration of upbeats leading to downbeats). Of great interest for the history of formal analysis is the way in which Momigny labels the different periods by their contextual function and character. Thus there are debut periods, intermediary periods, and complementary periods. And he also uses labels that denote character and texture, as in the *période de verve* and the *période mélodieuse*. The result is an analysis that conveys a lively sense of a piece of music as an expressive series of dramatic events, from the smaller melodic level of local upbeats and downbeats to the large-scale succession of periods of quite varied characters. Momigny's approach is also indicative of the growing preoccupation with the nature of musical themes; no longer is the material construction of the period the prevailing point of focus. Related to this concern for thematic character is the hermeneutic impulse that runs so strongly in Momigny's analyses: he actually provides an interpretive text underlay for the Mozart quartet movement (thus indicating his sense of the music as operatic and tragic, for he adapts Dido's lament from the *Aeneid*); for the Haydn, he constructs a fairly elaborate narrative about the effects of a thunderstorm on a country village.[12]

Anton Reicha. Anton Reicha (1770–1836), composer, theorist, and unusually influential teacher (he taught at the Paris Conservatoire from 1818 into the 1830s, and his students included Berlioz and Liszt), wrote several composition treatises that featured formal analyses, including the *Traité de mélodie* (1814) and the *Traité de haute composition musicale* (1824–26). It has been argued by Birgitte Moyer that Reicha emphasizes the period in the 1814 treatise and the theme in the later treatise, thus mirroring the general change in emphasis between the late eighteenth and early nineteenth centuries.[13] In the earlier treatise, for example, Reicha submits Mozart's "Non so più," from *The Marriage of Figaro*, to a melodic analysis in which he labels the different phrases, periods, and parts, and vindicates different types of cadences.[14] In addition to noting these things on a single staff, Reicha provides a numerical reduction of the aria:

Part I: 4;–4;–3;–3.–6;–4;–6:–6. Part II: 4;–4;–3;–3.–4;–4;–6;–8.–4;–4;–4;–8:–4;–6.

The numbers represent the number of bars within each phrase; the semicolons denote half cadences; the colons denote what Reicha calls interrupted cadences; and the periods denote the full cadences at the end of each musical period (thus there are two periods in Part I and three periods in Part II). Reicha's reduction reveals the proportions of the aria at a glance. Moreover, by arranging all the bars of a piece of music into the musical analogy of coherently articulated clauses, sentences, and paragraphs, Reicha posits a model of musical form that bears some relation to the unfolding and completion of an extended spoken and/or written utterance, such as an oration. The coherence of musical form is held to reside in its similarity to the large-scale rhythm of prose composition.

12 Translated in *SR*, pp. 826–48. 13 Moyer, "Concepts of Musical Form," p. 46.
14 This analysis can be found in *MANC*, vol. 1, pp. 146–51.

Reicha returns to Mozart in his 1824 treatise, in which he analyzes the overture to *The Marriage of Figaro*. This happens within the section on the so-called *grande coupe binaire*, Reicha's name for what we call sonata form. His theoretical treatment of sonata form emphasizes above all the development of themes: he prefaces his discussion of the form with an excursus on the nature of musical ideas (*idées musicales*) and the creative process, and he engages in a kind of interactive analysis of the Mozart overture by composing several different development sections for it (the overture stands as a sonata form without development section). Before doing this, he analyzes Mozart's exposition by identifying nine *idées musicales* within it. Some are simply motives, or even cadential motives. Reicha defines the *idée musicale* as a theme or motive that speaks to our sentiment, flatters our ear, can be retained easily, and inspires the wish to be heard again. He also claims that it takes as much *génie* to develop ideas as it does to invent them.

It is important to keep in mind, as Peter Hoyt has suggested, that Reicha conceived of the "développement" of musical ideas not exclusively as a process of transformation but as a process of unfolding that can include almost anything that happens to the musical ideas after they are first sounded – thus such "développement" actually takes place in every section of the form.[15] Nevertheless, Reicha's emphasis on the unfolding development of thematic ideas (as well as his exercise of composing actual development sections) would begin to have the effect of shifting the center of gravity of the sonata form to the development section.

Reicha's diagram of the *grande coupe binaire* represents his largely thematic sense of the form (see Plate 28.1). The prevailing shapes in the diagram house thematic sections; the arcs above denote coherent parts and sections, in a manner suggestive of musical phrase markings. Of particular interest is Reicha's identification in the exposition of a "second principal idea" that is found in the new tonic.[16] The overall design of the diagram reflects both binary and ternary elements. Note that the "development" section is separated off and placed above the second section of the second part. This allows the diagram to show the parallelism of the first part with the second section of the second part. The middle section is thus isolated as a special section, standing apart from the more strictly thematic sections. The fact that Reicha calls the first division of this middle section "développement principal" indicates that he thinks of the whole movement as manifestly developmental and of this section as principally so.[17] Finally, the homologous shape of the middle section suggests that it appears as a condensed

15 Hoyt, "The Concept of *Développement*," p. 149.

16 Although Reicha was by no means the first theorist to reify a second thematic area: already in 1796 Francesco Galeazzi had discussed in detail the "characteristic" or "intermediate passage" of sonata allegros that correspond roughly to Reicha's second principal idea. Galeazzi's discussion is translated in SR, pp. 819–26.

17 See also Hoyt, "The Concept of *Développement*," on why Reicha finds it necessary at one point to state that an exposition should precede the development. Doing so indicates the possibility that development and exposition could be equated with one another, both being involved in the *développement* of musical ideas.

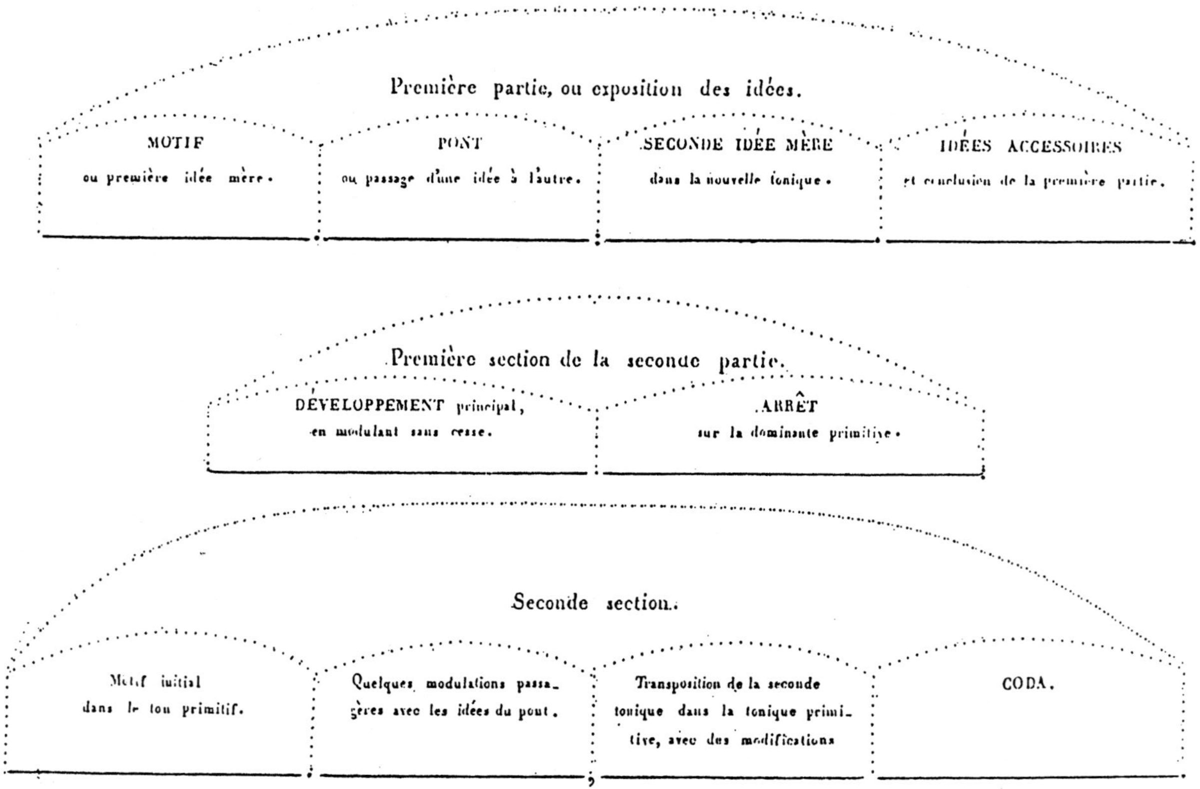

Première partie, ou exposition des idées.

MOTIF
ou première idée mère.

PONT
ou passage d'une idée à l'autre.

SECONDE IDÉE MÈRE
dans la nouvelle tonique.

IDÉES ACCESSOIRES
et conclusion de la première partie.

Première section de la seconde partie.

DÉVELOPPEMENT principal,
en modulant sans cesse.

ARRÊT
sur la dominante primitive.

Seconde section.

Motif initial
dans le ton primitif.

Quelques modulations passagères avec les idées du pont.

Transposition de la seconde tonique dans la tonique primitive, avec des modifications

CODA.

Plate 28.1 Diagram of *grande coupe binaire* from Reicha, *Traité de haute composition musicale*, vol. II (1826), p. 300

afterthought to the first part and/or a condensed pre-thought to the second section of the second part – its relation to the other two sections is complex and interpenetrating. Thus Reicha's diagram makes the "principal development" central while preserving a binary view of the form.

Adolph Bernhard Marx. The development section is much more consequentially at the center of Adolph Bernhard Marx's (1795–1866) hugely influential conception of sonata form, from the third volume (1845) of his four-volume treatise *Die Lehre von der musikalischen Komposition, praktisch-theoretisch* (1837–47). We owe to Marx not only the very name of sonata form but also the long prevailing sense of the form as a ternary design, with the development section as its crucial middle term.

The development section acts for Marx as the primary locus of mobility within the very form that he distinguishes above all others for its mobility. (Thus Marx takes up and amplifies Koch's emphasis on the enhanced flow of sonata form.) But Marx goes further yet in his aggrandizement of sonata form and motion: he positions sonata form at the culmination of his derivation of musical forms. The originary basis of Marx's derivation is the fundamental formula rest–motion–rest (*Ruhe–Bewegung–Ruhe*), a ternary impulse embodied in every formed musical utterance, from the simple four-bar *Satz* all the way to sonata form. Thus sonata form may be said to realize – as fully as possible – the underlying formal impulse in music.

Marx's synchronically conceived derivation of musical forms – probably the most fully developed and influential *Formenlehre* of the nineteenth century – was to a considerable degree motivated by the needs of his pedagogical system. He wanted to present the available forms in a progressive fashion, from simple to complex. But the way each formal stage moves to the next is dialectical and teleological: each stage is said to solve a problem inherent in the previous stage, and each in turn creates a new problem. The only form said to lack any problems is sonata form; thus it ends the derivation. (Strictly speaking, the fantasia comes after the sonata form in Marx's treatise, but it is detached from the derivation of earlier forms and floats in a realm of compositional freedom.)

In Marx's conceptualization, sonata form behaves like an organism: its subsections are not, like those of the minuet forms, individual organisms but rather begin to function as interdependent and indispensable organs of a larger organism (the whole form). Marx describes the main *Satz* (our first-theme group) as inherently incomplete and in need of a complementary subsidiary *Satz* (our second-theme group). In a famous formulation of this relationship, Marx characterizes the first theme as masculine and the second as feminine.[18] While Marx's gendering of the two principal theme groups of sonata form has invited much interpretive comment, it is perhaps more germane to realize that with this complementary relationship of first and second theme Marx

18 Marx, *Die Lehre*, vol. III, pp. 272–73.

A. B. Marx's derivation of musical forms

Marx first posits two fundamental categories of musical utterance: the closed *Satz* and the open-ended *Gang*. He then derives the period from the *Satz*, as a balanced and firmly closed-off pair of *Sätze*. From here he goes on to construct binary and ternary forms, up to and including the Classical-style Minuet and Trio, which completes this family of forms. He then posits another – and higher – family of forms, the motion-oriented rondo forms. The characteristic feature of this family of forms is the *Gang*.

Marx's rondo forms can be represented schematically as follows (MS-main *Satz* [*Hauptsatz*]; SS-subsidiary *Satz* [*Seitensatz*]; CS-closing *Satz* [*Schlusssatz*]; G-*Gang*):

First rondo form		MS G MS	
Second rondo form		MS SS (G) MS	
Third rondo form		MS SS1 G MS SS2 G MS	
Fourth rondo form	MS SS1 G	MS SS2 G	MS SS1
Fifth rondo form	MS SS1 G CS	SS2 G	MS SS1 G CS
Sonata form	MS SS1 G CS	(2nd Part)	MS SS1 G CS

Marx refers to the three large sections of sonata form not as exposition, development, and recapitulation but simply as First Part, Second Part, and Third Part. These designations help Marx show the relation of sonata form to the foregoing fourth and fifth rondo forms, in which he also distinguishes three large parts. The above schematic is clearly thematically oriented; it gives no sense of the dynamic underpinning of Marx's theory of form.[a]

[a] For some recent interpretations of Marx's derivation of forms, see Burnham, "The Role of Sonata Form"; Schmalfeldt, "Form as the Process of Becoming," esp. pp. 42-47; and Spitzer, "Marx's 'Lehre' and the Science of Education."

understands sonata form as bringing forth its own continuation in a way that additive forms do not. Themes are heard to lead to each other, to require each other.

For Marx, the thematic sections of sonata form are destabilized, mobilized for the sake of the whole. Here is what he says about the course of the main *Satz*: "[sonata form] displaces the main *Satz*, transforms it, blends it with the remaining sections of the piece into an inwardly unified whole; it will not let the main *Satz* stand still, as happens in the rondo, but rather moves it, to other keys, to other *Sätze* and *Gänge*."[19]

Marx includes close to one hundred pages of sonata-form examples in his composition treatise, treating one subsection of the form at a time (main *Satz*, progression to the subsidiary *Satz*, subsidiary *Satz*, etc.). He emphasizes the First Part (our exposition) overwhelmingly, in particular the linking and interrelationship of its principal themes, leaving only six pages for the Second Part (development) and three pages for the Third Part (recapitulation)! Beethoven is now the primary analysand; Marx cites examples from over twenty of his piano sonatas (but in accordance with his section-by-section approach, Marx analyzes no single movement of Beethoven's in its entirety).

19 Marx, *Musical Form in the Age of Beethoven*, p. 102. A more condensed translation of Marx's discussion of sonata form is found in *SR*, pp. 1223–31.

Like Reicha, Marx offers a primarily thematic view of the form, although with a different emphasis. Whereas Reicha dwells on the creative process and the development of musical ideas, Marx concentrates on the thematic behavior of the exposition. His analytical path is something like Koch's, for he works from left to right, addressing each compositional choice as it arises, with close and abiding attention to matters of thematic character, closure, and continuation. Utterances that are firmly closed are generally followed by new material; more open-ended utterances are subject to a process of expansion and continuation. This is why the main themes in a sonata form more often assume the looser, "unmarked" form of the *Satz* than the more symmetrical and conclusive, "marked" form of the period (whose closure demands to be followed by a new idea rather than some process of expansion and continuation – which is why periodic themes work so well as rondo themes).

Marx insists repeatedly that the nature and type of the opening theme determine the way it is continued, and ultimately the type of overall form. For example, Marx describes the first eight bars of Beethoven's Op. 31, No. 3 piano sonata as an already developed *Satz* (the first bar is repeated and the next motive is repeated and led forth), which "must now be imprinted in accordance with the increased importance of its purpose and the richness of its content." Thus Beethoven takes off from the final tone of his opening *Satz* with a *Gang* that leads to several repetitions of the *Satz* in different registers. "In this way, the [entire main *Satz*], hovering above and below its original position, immediately assumes the mobility that characterizes sonata form."[20]

Marx clearly eschews a parsing sort of analysis, offering instead a prose commentary striking for its phenomenological immediacy. Such commentary works well with Marx's concern for the mechanics of continuation, of moving forward. The attention of both Marx and Reicha to the compositional invention involved in the overall unfolding of a sonata-form movement distinguishes them from Koch's more explicitly dichotomous understanding of the compositional process as inspired invention followed by a more or less mechanical working out of the rest of the form. Reicha emphasizes thematic development; Marx emphasizes the logical flow of theme groups in the exposition.

Thematic character and behavior was of fundamental importance to Momigny, Reicha, and Marx, characterizing their progressive view of musical form. And yet these theorists clearly build on the earlier work of Koch. Momigny and Reicha were committed to the kind of parsing that Koch's terminology and theoretical understanding made possible, while Marx shares with Koch a concern for the articulated flow of an unfolding form and for the nature and effects of harmonic closure. But in the main, the central preoccupation of formal theory and analysis has definitely migrated from a harmonic emphasis to a more strictly thematic emphasis.

20 Marx, *Musical Form in the Age of Beethoven*, p. 104.

The masters as models

Cristle Collins Judd has amply demonstrated that the use of music examples within theory treatises is not a transparent practice but rather carries important aesthetic, cultural, and intellectual meanings.[a] The theorists surveyed in this chapter increasingly rely on examples culled from the same group of acknowledged "masters": Haydn, Mozart, and Beethoven. The predominant use of examples from these composers testifies not only to their contemporaneous stature but also to a sense that the Viennese sonata style itself had become the prevailing model for musical composition.

Emulation has often been a watchword for compositional pedagogy. Carl Czerny and Johann Christian Lobe even felt that a bar-by-bar modeling of an existing composition was the surest route to the mastery of form. The result is an exercise in syntactical paraphrase, in which new thematic ideas are composed to fit the model's phrase lengths and cadences. In defense of this prescription, Czerny draws an analogy to the practice of copying as a pedagogical exercise in the visual arts, or translation as a means for a budding author to master his language.[b] The point was both to internalize the conventions of the prescribed form and to develop versatility in thematic invention. Czerny himself demonstrates by composing a sonatina movement that preserves the exact dimensions of a movement by Mozart, from his four-hand piano sonata in D major, K. 381.[c]

Recent scholarship has shown that there was much more compositional modeling in the actual practice of composers like Mozart, Beethoven, and Schubert than we had previously taken account of (and a growing amount of theoretical attention is being lavished here as well, often under the aegis of a theory of intertextuality, such as Harold Bloom's "anxiety of influence"[d]). Clearly, the modeling of masters was important, and it laid the foundation for the use of the same class of masterworks as objects for analysis. As the Viennese Classical style receded historically, the analysis of masterworks became more and more important as a practice in its own right.

[a] Judd, *Reading Renaissance Music Theory: Hearing with the Eyes.*

[b] Czerny, *School of Practical Composition*, vol. I, p. 46. [c] Ibid., pp. 43-46.

[d] See for example, Bonds, *After Beethoven*, or Korsyn, "Towards a New Poetics of Musical Influence." The emphasis on intertextuality offers a way to continue to employ our most effective analytical methods while attempting to get beyond the ideology such methods were arguably designed for, namely, the ideology of the autonomous work.

The functional logic of organic form: from the mid-nineteenth century to the mid-twentieth century

However one wishes precisely to construe Eduard Hanslick's 1854 formulation of music as "tönend bewegte Formen,"[21] the words carry the force of a slogan, one that encouraged a renewed emphasis on musical form as a bulwark of the growing ideology of absolute music: to study form is to confirm the autonomy of music as an end unto itself rather than as a means of expressing extramusical content. As the nineteenth century grew older, form became increasingly reified in music-theoretical thought as a

21 Hanslick, from section 3, "Das Musikalisch-Schöne," in *Vom Musikalisch-Schönen.*

general category worthy of study even apart from the study of composition (the word *Formenlehre* itself, for example, came into broad use only late in the century).

A large part of the reason for this shifting emphasis has to do with the establishment of the Viennese Classical style as the essential basis of modern Western music. With the work of Marx, one senses the excitement of accounting for a nearly contemporaneous phenomenon, one that still seemed new, viable, and engagingly opaque: the music of Beethoven. Around mid-century and later, a classicizing urge may be detected in the theory and analysis of musical form, for theorists continued to focus primarily on the now historical Classical style. As a result, sonata form begins to be treated somewhat more abstractly and schematically; less stress is placed on the great variety of ways the form could be realized. The view is no longer from ground level but from a generalizing distance.

For the several generations of theorists discussed in the first section of this chapter, the theory of sonata form is perforce a theory of genre: for Koch, the genre of the symphony and "first movement allegro" form; for Marx, the genre of the (Beethovenian) piano sonata. But despite its nearly exclusive reliance on Beethoven's piano sonatas, Marx's influential treatment of sonata form had the effect of creating a reified formal construct. The creation of such a construct is in itself a neo-Classical gesture; only well after the heyday of the Viennese Classical style would sonata form become more an object to be defined than a practice to be described.[22]

Johann Christian Lobe. Johann Christian Lobe's (1797–1881) analysis in 1850 of the first movement of Beethoven's Op. 18, No. 2 string quartet can be seen as linking the earlier theorists with the classicizing urge of the succeeding generations.[23] In the manner of Reicha, Lobe's analysis consists of a single staff of music mapped out to show the formal divisions. On the staff itself Lobe represents what he calls the "principal melodic strand." The number of bars in each phrase as well as the key centers are indicated under the staff, the larger formal groups above the staff. A classicizing tendency is revealed in the way that Lobe conceives of the compositional process involved in creating a movement in sonata form. He understands the exposition as a series of theme groups: first theme group; transition group; song group; and closing group. With this frame in place, Lobe encourages the student to invent "self-sufficient ideas" for each group "with as yet no regard for their continuation or combination" – this is the first stage of composition. Next, the composer takes each idea and tries to find as many ways of presenting it as he can, creating a host of variants, which can be used or discarded in the next stage. In the third and final stage, the student selects the best variants and links them together. Within this scheme, Lobe lays the most stress by far on the invention of thematic variants (the art of harmonic figuration forms the longest

22 As Charles Rosen puts it: "Sonata form could not be defined until it was dead." Rosen, *The Classical Style*, p. 30. 23 This analysis appears in *MANC*, vol. I, pp. 197–220.

chapter in his treatise). Gone almost entirely is Marx's detailed concern with moving from one section of the form into the next. What remains, however, is Marx's schematic: Lobe's sonata form is a succession of "period-groups"; motion is no longer the distinctive characteristic. Thus the form is understood more as an object containing thematic stations than as a dynamically unfolding process.

Lobe's emphasis on creating musical cells that can be endlessly elaborated also reveals another agenda increasingly featured in theories of form: the urge to make the organic metaphor more and more palpable in analysis. Apart from the idea of motives as seeds, one of the principal methodological manifestations of the organicist perspective is the analysis of formal functions. Musical form is here figured as an organism in which every part has a specific function. As Arnold Schoenberg put it, "form means that a piece is *organized*; i.e. that it consists of elements functioning like those of a living *organism*."[24]

Hugo Riemann. The most comprehensive theory of functions in music was developed by Hugo Riemann (1849–1919) in a series of writings that spanned the last quarter of the nineteenth century and the first twenty years of the twentieth century. Theorist, historian, aesthetician, analyst, Riemann was a broad and imposing presence in German musicology, the epitome of the multi-faceted musical thinker and *Vielschreiber*. One of the enabling characteristics of this kind of writer is a secure and abiding modus intellegendi, if not modus operandi. Like many figures in intellectual history who have found an Answer, Riemann never tired of rounding up all the questions that could now be settled.

Riemann's Answer was his putative discovery of a natural logic for music, in which every bar and every harmony possess a classifiable function. In his *Grundriss der Kompositionslehre (Musikalische Formenlehre)* of 1905, Riemann includes fully developed functional analyses of the entire first movement of Beethoven's Ninth Symphony and the development section of the first movement of his Fifth Symphony. These are undoubtedly meant to serve as showpiece demonstrations of Riemann's analytical method. But an even more impressive, indeed summational, achievement is Riemann's three-volume set of analyses of all of Beethoven's piano sonatas, written during the last years of the First World War.[25] In justifying the need to analyze Beethoven's piano sonatas, Riemann lays stress on the importance of a proper understanding of form: "It will be of great use to realize that the work of the ever ripening Master is characterized not by the destruction of Form but, on the contrary, by an always firmer designation of the actual underpinning (*Gerüst*), upon which the subsidiary material (*Beiwerk*) is placed."[26]

The essential formal underpinning in Riemann's analyses is the eight-bar period. Riemann conceives of the period as a prototypical construction in which each bar has

24 Schoenberg, *Fundamentals*, p. 1. 25 Riemann, *Beethovens Klavier-Solosonaten*.
26 Riemann, from unpaginated Foreword to 1st edn. of *Beethovens Klavier-Solosonaten*.

a specific function: m. 8 is the final cadence, which answers the medial cadence of m. 4 (making the entire period into a large-scale upbeat and downbeat pattern); mm. 7 and 3 are upbeat penultimates to 8 and 4; mm. 1–2 and 5–6 are the initial upbeat pairs to which the cadential pairs form answers (for a discussion of Riemann's eight-bar period, see **Chapter 21, p. 687**). Riemann understands his prototype to be both "natural" and "historical." As he puts it,

> The continuing operation of the artistic fantasy – in its productive as well as receptive modes – with categories that are given naturally and come into being historically, categories which divest artistic creation of any and all arbitrary caprice and make it into a matter of logical necessity – this is a fact of our inner life whose significance cannot be overestimated.[27]

By making the eight-bar period into such an a priori category, Riemann takes part in a growing effort to promote the Viennese Classical style as the natural and essential state of Western music.[28]

At first glance, Riemann's analytical application of these ideas to Beethoven's piano sonatas seems a zealous taxonomic exercise, involving the classification of every bar and every harmony. Examples 28.1 and 28.2 present Riemann's analysis of the exposition from the first movement of Beethoven's Piano Sonata in C minor, Op. 10, No. 1. Periods are marked with roman numerals; bars are assigned various numbers (representing the stations of the eight-bar period) and are connected with several types of slurs denoting elisions, interruptions, etc.; harmonies are labeled in accordance with Riemann's theory of harmonic function. [29]

But despite the initial impression given by such an analysis, Riemann is not just marking out eight-bar plots, or tucking Beethoven's music into so many eight-bar Procrustean beds. Note, for instance, the rebarring of mm. 32ff., where 3/4 bars are grouped by twos into a series of 6/4 bars (at Riemann's Period IV). On the face of it, this may seem an ad hoc device to which Riemann must resort in order to generate eight-bar periods that better fulfill his sense of function. But Riemann's analytical augmentation marks a fundamental change in phrase rhythm, and it is sensitive to the way the piece now seems to unclench and breathe (he sees the one-bar rest as helping shift gears to this new sense of time).

Moreover, although Riemann posits an array of functions that happen in a certain order, these functions can be freely deployed within that order. For example, consider the repeated 6s in the excerpt from the second-theme group shown in Example 28.2. Again, this is not simply an ad hoc device. It amounts instead to hearing these bars as iterations that delay an imminent arrival – the arrival, or 8-function, is always perceived to be just a bar away (note particularly the effect of the three consecutive downbeat 6/4 chords – cadential antepenults – that Riemann marks as 6d, 6e, and 6f).

27 Ibid. 28 See Burnham, "Method and Motivation," pp. 12–14.

29 Riemann, *Beethovens Klavier-Solosonaten*, vol. I, pp. 279–83. See Ian Bent's valuable précis of Riemann's phrase-structure analysis in Bent, *Analysis*, pp. 90–93. On Riemann's harmonic theory and notation, see **Chapter 25, pp. 796–800**.

Example 28.1 Riemann's analysis of mm. 1–55 of Beethoven's Piano Sonata in C minor, Op. 10, No. 1, from Riemann, *L. van Beethovens sämtliche Klavier-Solosonaten*, vol. 1, pp. 279–83

Example 28.1 (*cont.*)

The repeated 6s are eventually brought to a cadence, at the beginning of the section marked "Epiloge," and are then followed by two 7–8 pairs and finally by two 8s, as if commensurately answering the collected tension of all those cadential delays.

The result of all this is that Riemann hears the entire second-theme group as realizing the function of a single period. From this one perceives that the eight-bar period, as deployed by Riemann, is an extremely flexible analytical tool, very much alive to the rhythmic impulse of the Classical style. This is no attempt to regularize Beethoven's phrasing by taxonomical fiat but rather a bid to hear his phrasing as enacting a coherent set of underlying functions, to hear Beethoven's much-vaunted dramatic momentum as ultimately grounded in natural law.

Arnold Schoenberg. A more strictly organicist approach to the functional analysis of musical form was practiced in a later generation by Arnold Schoenberg (1874–1951) and his students. Some twenty years after Riemann's death in 1919, Schoenberg was teaching composition in Los Angeles; his intended textbook on musical composition was completed well after his own death by several of his students and published in 1967 as *Fundamentals of Musical Composition*. Here Schoenberg stresses the contrastive functions of the subsidiary parts of larger forms ("Large forms develop through the generating power of contrasts"[30]), parts which behave like organs in a larger organism. They include the main theme (which could take the form of a period, a sentence [*Satz*], or a small ternary form), transitions, the "lyric theme," the coda, and the group of subordinate

30 Schoenberg, *Fundamentals*, p. 178.

Example 28.2 Riemann's analysis of mm. 56–105 of Beethoven's Piano Sonata in C minor, Op. 10, No. 1, from Riemann, *L. van Beethovens sämtliche Klavier-Solosonaten*, vol. 1, pp. 279–283

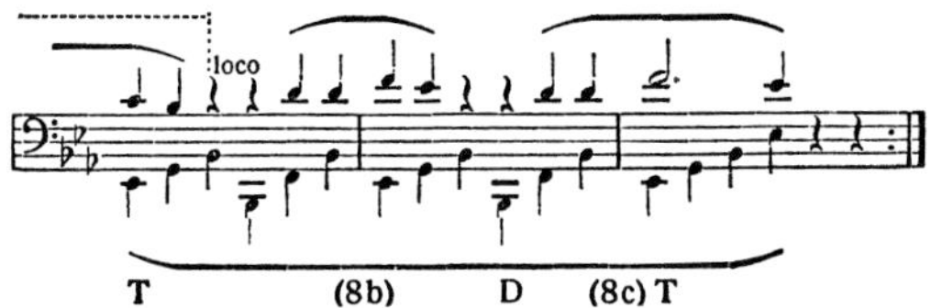

Example 28.2 (*cont.*)

themes (a "looser construction" consisting of the repetition or juxtaposition of relatively short segments and manifesting a "lesser degree of internal development"[31]). In an approach reminiscent of that of A. B. Marx, Schoenberg illustrates different types of each of these formal parts with examples from Beethoven's piano sonatas.

Erwin Ratz. In the 1960s, Erwin Ratz (1898–1973) elaborated and consolidated Schoenberg's functions into his more comprehensively developed *Einführung in die musikalische Formenlehre*, crowned with a thoroughgoing analysis of Beethoven's "Hammerklavier" Sonata, Op. 106. Following Schoenberg's lead, Ratz posits two general formative principles: tight construction (main theme, closing theme) and loose construction (subsidiary group, transition, development). But the most striking aspect of Ratz's book is his extension of these largely Beethovenian categories backward in time to the music of Bach. Through close analysis of Bach's inventions and fugues, Ratz finds historical precedents for the functionally differentiated formal categories in Beethoven's music, noting thematic formations that are *Satz*-like, sections that are developmental, and the contrastive principles of loose and tight construction at work throughout. (Ratz's urge to construct a larger Germanic musical practice flowing from Bach to Beethoven is reminiscent of August Halm's 1913 attempt to reduce modern Western music to two "cultures": fugue and sonata, represented by Bach and Beethoven respectively. Halm went on to add a third, and synthesizing, term to this pair: the music of Bruckner.[32])

Challenges to *Formenlehre*: Tovey and Schenker

Donald Francis Tovey. Another important and contending strand of early twentieth-century formal analysis was not functionally but empirically conceived, not German but English. Pianist, critic, and analyst Donald Francis Tovey (1875–1940), though enormously influential throughout the twentieth century as a writer about music, is not generally thought of as a theorist of musical form. And indeed, he has no explicit theory

31 Ibid., p. 184. 32 Halm, *Von Zwei Kulturen.*

of form, no *Formenlehre* per se: his fundamental preoccupation is not form but style (he much prefers to generalize about the latter, and never does so without a specific composer's practice in mind – this is why, at the heart of his *Encyclopaedia Britannica* article "Sonata Forms," he provides an account of the individual sonata-style practices of Haydn, Mozart, and Beethoven). And yet he holds definite views about the overall effect and sense of Classical-style sonata form, which he characterizes not by invoking some quasi-Idealist conception of form and thematic content but with the more empirically grounded scenario of temporal drama.

Tovey's fundamental emphasis on the dramatic fitness of sonata form thus brings with it an implicit attitude about musical form, most pronounced when Tovey attacks what he felt were popular misconceptions brought about by (largely Germanic) theories of form. In particular, Tovey reacted vigorously against what he called the jelly-mould view of sonata form, in which thematic content would be poured into pre-set frames. For Tovey, neither the grouping of themes nor their motivic content can of themselves provide the key to logical coherence or to balance in sonata forms.[33] "The art of movement is the crux of the sonata problem," he claims, not the content or arrangement of themes.[34] In contrast to the more Germanic notion of organic growth from an "ideal" thematic seed, Hanslick's view of structure as a consequence of a theme, or the functional view of organ-like parts serving a collective whole, Tovey's sense of musico-formal logic has to do with the differentiated movement of phrases – his analyses move with the music, phrase by phrase, raising issues of proportion, freedom, and expansion. "We know nothing of form until we begin to study proportions and details," he avows.[35] He shifts the emphasis from thematic content and its destiny to the way that individual forms move through time.

To see how this attitude translates into analytical practice we may turn to Tovey's *A Companion to Beethoven's Piano Sonatas* (1931), a collection of closely detailed formal analyses of all the sonatas. Tovey presents his analyses in outline-style prose, enumerating what he regards as the "facts" in a flat, paratactic, and largely reportorial style. He refers to this process as précis-writing. In order to create the interesting possibility of a comparison with the Riemann analysis already discussed, we shall consider Tovey's analysis of the same music, the first-movement exposition of Beethoven's piano sonata, Op. 10, No. 1. (See the text excerpted in the window, p. 899.)

Tovey's analysis takes note of the following items:

1. key and form
2. each phrase
   (a) length of phrase
   (b) subdivisions of phrase
3. labeling of themes, motives, and some harmonies

33 Tovey, "Some Aspects," p. 275.
34 Tovey, "Sonata Forms," p. 232.
35 Tovey, *A Companion*, p. 8.

D. F. Tovey's analysis of Beethoven's Op. 10, No. 1

SONATA IN C MINOR, Op. 10, No. 1

Allegro molto e con brio: C minor

First group

Bars 1-8. – Eight-bar theme in two 4-bar steps, containing figures (a) and (b)

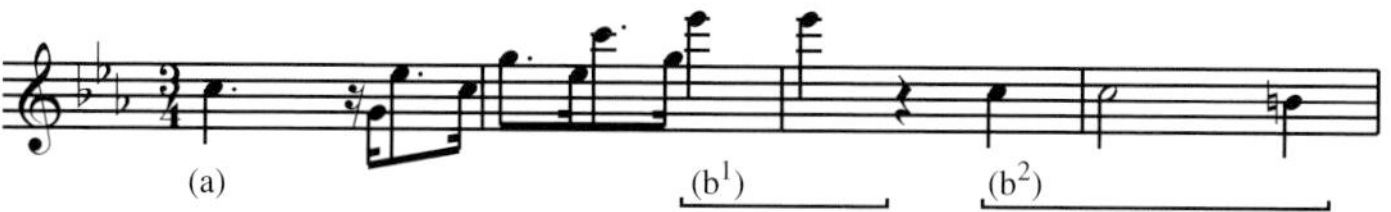

9-21. – Arising out of (b2) a new cantabile develops by threefold repetition of a 2-bar figure, expanded the third time to 4 bars of downward scale. At bar 17 a new 2-bar group leads in three steps, broken with rests, into the next period. The whole passage from bar 9 proves that bar 9 is unaccented, a fact not forced on the listener until the broken phrases mark the rhythmic grouping from bar 17 onwards…[here Tovey engages in a lengthy polemic against abstruse rhythmic theories that speak against "the impressions of human listeners"]

22-31. – First theme resumed, as if to make a counterstatement, but compressed, with omission of (b2), into three 2-bar steps, followed by a new 4-bar close (the last bar silent).

Transition

32-47. – New theme in 4-bar sequential steps, starting in A♭ (VI.) and passing through F minor (iv.) and D♭ (♭II.) and then (continuing regular descent of bass) in 4 more bars, closing on to dominant of E♭ (III.).

48-55. – Eight bars dominant preparation (4+4 with variation) leading to

Second group: E♭ (III.)

56-93. – Large paragraph articulated as follows:

56-63. – Eight-bar tonic-and-dominant theme (4+4).

64-69. – Variation of above diverging after 6th bar into

70-77. – New continuation in broader single 8-bar phrase.

78-85. – Variation of this 8-bar phrase diverging after 4th bar into 2+2

bars carrying its rising steps twice a bar around the dominant (as $^6_4$) and followed by

86-93. – Further hovering around the $^6_4$ with figure (a) for 4 bars,

followed by 4 bars of final $^6_4$ and resolution closing into

94-105.—Cadence theme, tonic-and-dominant in two self-repeating 4-bar phrases (2+2) with insistence twice on last 2 bars.

Exposition repeated.

(Tovey, *A Companion to Beethoven's Piano Sonatas*, pp. 44-45)

Because Tovey refuses to generalize about musical form and process, his analyses are sometimes regarded as mere descriptions, a kind of bar counting. But Tovey maps out the progress of the movement with succinct precision; he possesses the critic's gift for salient detail, and a careful reading of any one of his analyses will begin to reveal something like an underlying theory of the Classical style. (The reader should also consult

Tovey's striking précis-style analysis of the first movement of Beethoven's *Eroica* Symphony in his *Britannica* article, done on a single musical staff by notating the "principal melodic thread," and creating a special notation for Beethoven's frequently prolonged harmonies: "by means of it the reader will be enabled to apprehend, almost at a glance, the inexhaustible expansive and contractile power of Beethoven's phrase-rhythm."[36])

For Tovey, such a précis (whether in prose or in music notation) is better than an abstract ground plan; music is not amenable to such ground plans.[37] These and other "a priori fancies," he argues, hinder the ear from recognizing subtleties.[38] Although Tovey specifically distances himself from the work of Riemann, their approaches to analysis bear some similarities in terms of the guiding principle of musical logic. Like Riemann, Tovey is obviously preoccupied with phrase lengths and accents – but whereas Riemann classifies every bar in accordance with what Tovey would deem an a priori fancy (namely, the eight-bar period), Tovey charts the behavior of phrases against what he knows about existing musical styles. Tovey is much more literal than Riemann – there is no eight-bar ideal construction underlying any number of bars on the surface; there is only one phrase followed by the next. But Tovey often groups phrases in ways similar to Riemann – for example, he characterizes the second-theme group of Op. 10, No. 1 as a "large paragraph." (A quick way to gain a vivid sense of the different intellectual and musical grain of these two writers is to think about the difference between hearing this second-theme group as a paragraph and hearing it, in Riemann's sense, as an expanded period.)

Whereas Riemann stresses natural laws, Tovey stresses aesthetic values, as determined empirically. Theoretical abstraction has no explicit place in his enterprise; aesthetic presence is the point. His précis-style analyses are meant to appear anti-abstract; they assume an air of "sticking to the facts." And though they may seem to sit oddly with the type of writing he indulged in for his more famous *Essays in Musical Analysis*, they form an important part of his overall analytical program of technical analysis and description. In his article "Some Aspects of Beethoven's Art Forms," Tovey lists three things that are fundamental to what he calls sonata style: key system, phrase system, and dramatic fitness. The first two of these can be "reduced to technical analysis" (as we have seen); the last can only be discussed through description and analogy but in fact "constitutes the all-pervading distinction between the sonata style and the earlier non-dramatic, architectural, and decorative styles which culminated in Bach and Handel."[39] In Tovey's empirically grounded aesthetic approbation of individual works, musical form is a function of style, and style is a function of historically situated aesthetic needs.

Ultimately, Tovey assumes a place in the proud tradition of English practical criticism. His attempt to debunk the traditional *Formenlehre* is motivated by a studied

36 Tovey, "Sonata Forms," p. 220. 37 Tovey, *A Companion*, pp. 280–81. 38 Ibid., p. 3.
39 Tovey, "Some Aspects", p. 275.

aversion to theory. Another and exceedingly different attempt to discredit the *Formenlehre* tradition can be seen in the work of Austrian music theorist Heinrich Schenker.

Heinrich Schenker. For members of the Anglo-American theory community, it is in fact Heinrich Schenker (1868–1935) and not Tovey who looms as the great antihero of the *Formenlehre* tradition, for Schenker did more than anyone else to discredit the enterprise of taxonomic formal analysis as schematic and empty. Whereas Tovey seeks to chase away all a priori phantoms by clinging to the temporal surface of music and its empirical daylight, Schenker plunges into theory, positing and exploring great depths below that surface. Consequently, few serious admirers of Schenker's work could return to the traditional business of formal analysis without feeling as though they were wading in the shallows. Specifically, Schenker tried to debunk the entire *Formenlehre* tradition by claiming that true form was a deeply organic function of the *Ursatz*, that it emerged out of the primal background of an individual piece much as human features soon emerge from a primitive embryo. But Charles Smith has recently argued that for all his and his disciples' claims to the contrary, Schenker's analyses actually support – are even predicated upon – traditional formal classifications. For Smith, traditional "formal classification provides the most accessible and dependable route to the structural background."[40] In what follows, we shall see that the last years of the twentieth century did in fact witness a resurgence of the taxonomic classification of the elements of sonata form.

Recuperations of *Formenlehre*: the late twentieth century

Leonard Ratner. In a now classic article of 1949, Leonard Ratner (1916–) called for a change of emphasis in our view of Classical-style sonata form, dismissing the thematic model as a dubious legacy of the nineteenth century and urging a return to Koch's (and others') largely harmonic conception of the form.[41] Some thirty years later, in 1980, with the harmonic view now so accepted as to be unquestioned, Ratner published *Classic Music*, his own comprehensive answer to his earlier summons. The culminating description of sonata form in *Classic Music* encapsulates many still current assumptions and is worth quoting at length:

> Viewed as a harmonic plan, organized by periods and colored by rich thematic content, classic sonata form has something of the character of a forensic exercise, a rhetorical discourse that reflects in its own way the spirit of 18th-century philosophy. The opposing keys are the premises to be argued; their respective positions are set in the exposition,

40 Smith, "Musical Form and Fundamental Structure," p. 280.
41 Ratner, "Harmonic Aspects of Classic Form."

> and their forces are represented by their respective thematic material. The victory of the tonic, a foregone conclusion, is signaled by the incorporation of the melodic content of the second key into the tonic at the end of the movement. The analogy with the enlightened absolutism of the 18th century is very attractive; in each case, authority enforces its hierarchical supremacy, incorporating opposing elements into their proper place in the scheme as a resolution of conflict.[42]

In attending to harmony as the fundamental parameter of sonata form, Ratner posits a tonal plot that has proved irresistible: the form becomes an argument whose premises are not themes but opposing key centers (themes merely "color" the action), and the inevitable result is the home key's victorious resolution of this conflict. Most late twentieth-century accounts of sonata form ratify the broad claim of this view, though they may differ in their particulars. Charles Rosen states that "the principle of *recapitulation as resolution* may be considered the most fundamental and radical innovation of sonata style"; James Webster emphasizes the double return of home key and main theme as the "central aesthetic event" of the form; Leonard Meyer refers to the return of the home key as the "syntactic climax"; and Edward T. Cone considers the obligatory appearance in the tonic of any important thematic material originally presented in another key to constitute the "sonata principle."[43] In addition, Ratner's harmonic plot works well with the tonal theory of Schenker – the opposing key area can be conceptualized as a "structural dissonance," allowing the overall form to assume the logical coherence and unequivocal closure of a harmonic cadence.

Ratner's call to return to a harmonic view of sonata form after some hundred or more years of a primarily thematic orientation lends the conceptual history of sonata form the overall shape of sonata form itself. And yet our present-day standpoint cannot be understood as an exact recapitulation of Koch's "exposition." Instead, we have chosen to amplify the conflict–resolution aspect of harmonic return, creating a plot-like scenario that may in fact be closer to the model of oppositional contrast underlying the nineteenth-century thematic view.[44]

Historical style and convention. Perhaps most striking about Ratner's position is his resolute attempt to understand sonata form as a product of its original cultural and intellectual milieu; this in itself stands as a distinct challenge to the *Formenlehre* tradition, which increasingly tended to treat the form ahistorically, as a timelessly valid aesthetic product.[45] The move away from a theoretical and ahistorical conception of musical form toward a more historically informed and concrete approach has had a lasting effect on the practice of criticism and analysis in Anglo-American musical

42 Ratner, *Classic Music*, p. 246.

43 Rosen, *Sonata Forms*, p. 284; Webster, "Sonata Form"; Meyer, "Exploiting Limits," p. 189; Cone, *Musical Form*, pp. 76–77.

44 Hoyt, "The False Recapitulation and the Conventions of Sonata Form," pp. 338–40.

45 Ratner's informed invocation of Koch also had the supplementary effect of encouraging a significant rise of scholarly interest in theorists of the late eighteenth and early nineteenth centuries.

thought (conceptual discussions of form have maintained a strong presence in Germany, however, particularly in the writings of Carl Dahlhaus).[46] Because of this (and also because of the still powerful legacy of Tovey) the analysis of sonata forms now tends to be undertaken less with reference to some abstract concept of form and more with reference to historical style and convention.

As Charles Rosen wrote in 1971, arguing against an abstract notion of form: "An understanding of the sense of continuity and the proportions of classical style would enable us largely to dispense with a further discussion of 'sonata form.'"[47] And more recent writings show clearly to what extent we have become attracted to treatments of form that highlight a play of conventions. These include the psychological and statistical approaches to musical style of Leonard Meyer and Robert Gjerdingen; semiotic approaches, as in Ratner's topical method and its various extensions in the work of Wye Jamison Allanbrook, Kofi Agawu, Robert Hatten, and Melanie Lowe; William Rothstein's detailed analytical survey of the evolution of phrase rhythm (which returns to Koch via Schenker); and William Caplin's ambitious revival of taxonomic *Formenlehre*, building on Schoenberg's and Ratz's functional approach to form. Finally, a new theory of sonata form, put forth by James Hepokoski and Warren Darcy, assumes an explicitly late twentieth-century orientation by conceptualizing stylistic conventions as a series of available options and defaults, selected from a menu not unlike that of a computer program.[48]

All these enterprises entail ever more closely detailed classifications of the stylistic conventions of sonata-form practice: if we have left the Idealist philosophical roots of the *Formenlehre* tradition well behind us, we are clearly more preoccupied with the mechanics of sonata forms than ever before. It is this preoccupation that continues to connect us to the rest of the tradition, for one could argue that the entire sweep of the *Formenlehre* tradition coheres around the need to understand sonata form as the chief (and natural) accomplishment of Western tonal music.

Sonata form has proved to be a cultural product with an astonishing shelf life; each new age understands it as vitally implicated in its own concerns. Sonata form has served as the Enlightenment form that maintains balance, symmetry, and hierarchy; the Idealist form that best merges form and content, best solves the problem of unity and diversity; the Romantic form that reconciles opposites and can accommodate irony; the Naturalist form that best embodies the natural laws of music; the organicist form that behaves most like an organism with functional organs; and finally, the modernist and postmodernist metaform that can comment on itself and its conventions.

46 See Schmalfeldt, "Form as the process of becoming."

47 Rosen, *The Classical Style*, p. 53.

48 Meyer, *Explaining Music*; Gjerdingen, *A Classic Turn of Phrase*; Ratner, *Classic Music*; Allanbrook, *Rhythmic Gesture in Mozart*; Agawu, *Playing with Signs*; Hatten, *Musical Meaning in Beethoven*; Lowe, "Expressive Paradigms"; Rothstein, *Phrase Rhythm in Tonal Music*; Caplin, *Classical Form*; Hepokoski and Darcy, "The Medial Caesura."

To study the history of musical *Formenlehren*, then, is to revisit these various cultural stations. Linking them all is an abiding fascination with the large-scale rhythm of return and recollection played out in sonata form. Sonata form can thus be heard to sound an overarching theme of modern Western culture, of the *Abendland*: the problem of time and its passing, conceived as a process both linear and cyclical. The perennial appeal of sonata form speaks to the cultural coherence of the modern period, and it is safe to say that the eclipse of sonata form as a theoretical preoccupation will come about only as the result of a much greater kind of eclipse, in which the cultural lights of the last few centuries fall under the shadow of some brave new sense of human temporality.

Bibliography

Primary sources

Agawu, V. K. *Playing with Signs: A Semiotic Interpretation of Classic Music*, Princeton University Press, 1991

Allanbrook, W. J. *Rhythmic Gesture in Mozart: Le Nozze Di Figaro and Don Giovanni*, University of Chicago Press, 1983

Baker, N. K. and T. Christensen, eds., *Aesthetics and the Art of Musical Composition in the German Enlightenment: Selected Writings of Johann Georg Sulzer and Heinrich Christoph Koch*, Cambridge University Press, 1995

Caplin, W. E. *Classical Form: A Theory of Formal Functions for the Instrumental Music of Haydn, Mozart, and Beethoven*, New York, Oxford University Press, 1998

Cone, E. T. *Musical Form and Musical Performance*, New York, Norton, 1968

Czerny, C. *Die Schule der praktischen Tonsetzkunst*, 3 vols., Bonn, Simrock, c. 1849; trans. J. Bishop as *School of Practical Composition*, 3 vols., London, R. Cocks, c. 1849; facs. New York, Da Capo Press, 1979

Darcy, W. and J. Hepokoski, "The Medial Caesura and its Role in the 18th-Century Sonata Exposition," *MTS* 19 (1997), pp. 115–54

Gjerdingen, R. *A Classic Turn of Phrase: Music and the Psychology of Convention*, Philadelphia, University of Pennsylvania Press, 1988

Halm, A. *Von Zwei Kulturen der Musik*, Munich, G. Müller, 1913

Hanslick, E. *Vom Musikalisch-Schönen: Ein Beitrag zur Revision der Ästhetik der Tonkunst*, Leipzig, R. Weigel, 1854

Hatten, R. *Musical Meaning in Beethoven: Markedness, Correlation, and Interpretation*, Bloomington, Indiana University Press, 1994

Koch, H. C. *Versuch einer Anleitung zur Composition*, 3 vols., Leipzig, A. F. Böhme, 1782–93; facs. Hildesheim, G. Olms, 1969 and 2000; partial trans. N. Baker as *Introductory Essay on Composition*, New Haven, Yale University Press, 1983; vol. I trans. N. Baker in Baker and Christensen, eds., above

Lobe, J. C. *Lehrbuch der musikalischen Komposition*, 4 vols., Leipzig, Breitkopf und Härtel, 1850–67

Logier, J. B. *A System of the Science of Music and Practical Composition*, London, J. Green, 1827; rev. edn., ed. C. Stein as *Logier's Comprehensive Course in Music, Harmony, and Practical*

Composition, Boston, C. Fischer, 1888; A. B. Marx as *System der Musik-Wissenschaft und der praktischen Komposition*, Berlin, H. A. W. Logier, 1827
Lowe, M. "Expressive Paradigms in the Symphonies of Joseph Haydn," Ph.D. diss., Princeton University (1998)
Marx, A. B. *Die Lehre von der musikalischen Komposition*, 4 vols., Leipzig, Breitkopf und Härtel, 1837–47
Musical Form in the Age of Beethoven: Selected Writings on Theory and Method, ed. and trans. S. Burnham, Cambridge University Press, 1997
Meyer, L. *Explaining Music: Essays and Explorations*, Berkeley, University of California Press, 1973
"Exploiting Limits: Creation, Archetypes, and Style Change," *Daedalus* 109 (1980), pp. 177–205
Momigny, J.-J. de *Cours complet d'harmonie et de composition*, 3 vols., Paris, Momigny and Bailleul, 1803–06
Ratner, L. G. *Classic Music: Expression, Form, and Style*, New York, Schirmer, 1980
"Harmonic Aspects of Classic Form," *JAMS* 2 (1949), pp. 159–68
Ratz, E. *Einführung in die Musikalische Formenlehre*, 2nd edn., Vienna, Universal, 1968
Reicha, A. *Traité de mélodie*, 2 vols., Paris, Reicha, 1814
Traité de haute composition musicale, 2 vols., Paris, Zetter, 1824–26
Riemann, H. *Grundriss der Kompositionslehre (Musikalische Formenlehre)*, Leipzig, M. Hesse, 1905
L. van Beethovens sämtliche Klavier-Solosonaten: Ästhetische und formal-technische Analyse mit historischen Notizen, 3 vols., Berlin, M. Hesse, 1917–19
Rosen, C. *The Classical Style*, rev. edn., New York, Norton, 1997
Sonata Forms, rev. edn., New York, Norton, 1988
Rothstein, W. *Phrase Rhythm in Tonal Music*, New York, Schirmer, 1989
Schenker, H. *Der freie Satz*, Vienna, Universal, 1935; rev. 2nd edn., ed. O. Jonas, Vienna, Universal, 1955; trans. and ed. E. Oster as *Free Composition*, New York, Longman, 1979
Schoenberg, A. *Fundamentals of Musical Composition*, ed. G. Strang, New York, St. Martin's, 1967
Tovey, D. F. *A Companion to Beethoven's Piano Sonatas*, London, Associated Board of the Royal Schools of Music, 1931
"Some Aspects of Beethoven's Art Forms," in *The Main Stream of Music and Other Essays*, Oxford University Press, 1949, pp. 271–97
"Sonata Forms," *Musical Articles from the Encyclopaedia Britannica*, Oxford University Press, 1949
Webster, J. "Sonata Form," *NG*, vol. xvii, pp. 497–508

Secondary sources

Baker, N. K. "Der Urstoff der Musik: Implications for Harmony and Melody in the Theory of Heinrich Koch," *MA* 7 (1988), pp. 3–30
Bent, I. *Analysis*, London, Macmillan, 1987
Bonds, M. E. *After Beethoven: Imperatives of Originality in the Symphony*, Cambridge, MA, Harvard University Press, 1996

"The Symphony as Pindaric Ode," in *Haydn and His World*, ed. E. Sisman, Princeton University Press, 1997, pp. 131–53

Wordless Rhetoric: Musical Form and the Metaphor of the Oration, Cambridge, MA, Harvard University Press, 1991

Burnham, S. "Method and Motivation in Hugo Riemann's History of Harmonic Theory," *MTS* 14 (1992), pp. 1–14

"The Role of Sonata Form in A. B. Marx's Theory of Form," *JMT* 33 (1989), pp. 247–71

Goehr, L. *The Imaginary Museum of Musical Works: An Essay in the Philosophy of Music*, Oxford University Press, 1992

Hoyt, P. A. "The Concept of *Développement* in the Early Nineteenth Century," in *Music Theory in the Age of Romanticism*, ed. Ian Bent, Cambridge University Press, 1996, pp. 141–62

"The 'False Recapitulation' and the Conventions of Sonata Form," Ph.D. diss., University of Pennsylvania (1999)

Judd, C. C. *Reading Renaissance Music Theory: Hearing with the Eyes*, Cambridge University Press, 2000

Korsyn, K. "Towards a New Poetics of Musical Influence," *MA* 10 (1991), pp. 3–72

Moyer, B. "Concepts of Musical Form in the Nineteenth Century with Special Reference to A. B. Marx," Ph.D. diss., Stanford University (1969)

Ritzel, F. *Die Entwicklung der "Sonatenform" im musiktheoretischen Schrifttum des 18. und 19. Jahrhunderts*, Wiesbaden, Breitkopf und Härtel, 1968

Schmalfeldt, J. "Form as the Process of Becoming: The Beethoven-Hegelian Tradition and the 'Tempest' Sonata," *Beethoven Forum* 4, Lincoln, University of Nebraska Press, 1995

Smith, C. J. "Musical Form and Fundamental Structure: An Investigation of Schenker's *Formenlehre*," *MA* 15 (1996), pp. 191–297

Spitzer, M. "Marx's 'Lehre' and the Science of Education: Towards the Recuperation of Music Pedagogy," *Music and Letters* 79 (1998), pp. 489–526

Thaler, L. *Organische Form in der Musiktheorie des 19. und beginnenden 20. Jahrhunderts*, Munich, E. Katzbichler, 1984

Thematic and motivic analysis

JONATHAN DUNSBY

Western music, with its origins in liturgical chant, can be said to be inherently melodic: the word "theme" was in use in the seventeenth century, and "motif" (later, "motive') became a common term in art, literature, and music criticism two centuries ago.[1] In the nineteenth century the common English translation of the German word *Motiv* was "figure," and the definition of this in 1906 (Parry, at a time when recognizable music theory might be said to have become clearly underway) was comprehensive and prescient:

> It is in fact the shortest complete idea in music; and in subdividing works into their constituent portions, as separate movements, sections, periods, phrases, the units are the figures, and any subdivision below them will leave only expressionless single notes, as unmeaning as the separate letters of a word.[2]

This definition is almost as all-embracing as was to be Bent's definition some seventy years later of "analysis" itself (see p. 913 below), and this indicates that "motive" has been a critical element of the whole modern music-analytical enterprise. The definition also captures, and anticipates, a central impetus in music theorizing as a language analogy.[3] The subject of this chapter has been, then, overtly or implicitly universal in Western music-theoretical writings. Its treatment here will be constrained by the dual aims of concision and plenitude. The conceptual and compositional background will be restricted sharply to recent centuries, and the invocation of "theme" and "motive" will be examined in just three readily identifiable areas: developing variation, set theory, and the one which needs least detailed exposure but perhaps greater critique, semiotics. However, these areas – rooted respectively in the ideology of Romantic organicism, the would-be scientific method of logical positivism and the structural anthropology of twentieth-century linguistics – offer a broad conspectus which may represent something not only of the pith but

1 For an extensive inventory of the term in music-theoretical literature, see the entry "Motiv" in *HmT*.
2 Parry, "Figure," p. 36.
3 Etymologically, "theme" passed from Greek, through Latin to early English with the consistent conceptual sense of a proposition or a topic, and in music theory has always represented the view of music as a kind of discourse. In rhetoric, "figure" was some special kind of expression of a "theme," as in "metaphor," "hyperbole," and the like. If the term "figure" was anchored in the idea of discourse, it nevertheless became a special term in nineteenth-century art criticism and referred more to design than to discourse, a parallel of obvious interest to musicians.

also of the extent of musicians' pre-occupation with the phenomenon of the musical "line."

Conceptual and compositional background

The human being comes to life equipped with a natural ability to vocalize, and vocalization, but for such a special effect as "harmonic" singing, is monodic. Traditionally it has been held that song must have been the earliest form of human music, hence for example Reaney's throwaway first line: "the history of song is obviously as old as the history of mankind."[4] In fact it is now thought that this genealogy of human song is unfounded:

> From current paleobiological points of view, the idea is far from being merely a random speculation that instrumental production of intentional sounds or pre-forms of music had its origin in the same or earlier periods when mankind is believed to have begun singing and speaking. Consequently, the fabrication of acoustical artifacts in the form of instrumentally produced signals and gestures does not necessarily represent a later or more advanced level of human evolution and culture than vocal calls and melodies.[5]

Even if we were to speculate that from its earliest manifestation human music was communal and even multiphonic, this does not alter the underlying physiological fact that human sound production is of a single line, equated uniquely with language, and specifically with phonology by Roman Jakobson,[6] or uniquely with the string of conceptual "meaning" in general, notably by Claude Lévi-Strauss.[7] Thus we must bear in mind constantly the distinction between communication theory that considers a single "string" of information (and a piece of music in all its multivalent parameters may be considered to be such a single string of information) and, within music theory, the concepts "theme" and "motive" which apply to individual lines of music. Although the term "communication theory" carries specifically twentieth-century resonances, the image of music as being a string of information goes back deep into the history of musical aesthetics and rhetoric, and in a technical analytical sense was contemporaneous with the early manifestations of post-Baroque theories of form. Bent for instance mentions Bernard Lacépède's 1785 publication *Le Poétique de la musique*, in which sonata form is likened "to the three overarching phrases of a drama: presentation–complication–resolution."[8] Later here we shall encounter in Schoenberg's concept of "developing variation" highly evolved thinking of this kind, and indeed Bent elsewhere notes the commonly perceived links throughout eighteenth-,

4 Reaney, *A History of Song*, p. 15. 5 Wallin, *Biomusicology*, p. 349.

6 For a specialist but gratefully written account of key aspects of Jakobson's thinking and its impact see Culler, *Structuralist Poetics*, especially pp. 55–74.

7 Lévi-Strauss's most widely known work in this respect is perhaps *The Raw and the Cooked*, which specifically equates the narratives of music with the narratives of mythology. 8 *MANC*, vol. 1, p. 128.

nineteenth-, and twentieth-century theorizing about the general qualities of musical continuity, or line.[9]

From the earliest stage of modern music theory there has been a consistent interaction between these two conceptions of line. Early analysts of motive did not have the intention merely of breaking music into its smallest components, but of examining how those components were used (poietically) to form musical structure and perceived (esthesically) as structuring. This interplay of part and whole, and of composition and appreciation, is illustrated delightfully by Czerny's glowing account some five years after Beethoven's death of the first movement of the "Waldstein" sonata. Czerny offers five aspects of the "remarkable unity and symmetry of the whole of this movement" of which two are relevant here: "it is not overlaid with too many different melodies; for it consists only of four ideas"; and "the ideas, which are judiciously chosen, are always beautifully connected with each other."[10] It is reasonable to see Beethoven's music as the creative source of a new nineteenth-century consciousness of how musical ideas can be connected. Hoffmann's 1810 review of the Fifth Symphony is often cited as the first torch in this phalanx of critical illumination deriving from Goethean organicism and marching on to this day.[11] The concentration on the "ideas" of a piece and how they are "connected" was shortly to be radically theorized in Hanslick's *Vom Musikalisch-Schönen* of 1854.[12] Hanslick's main intention was to show that musical "meaning" resides purely in the life of "tones." This prototypically structuralist, post-Kantian venture offered a pan-thematic view of music that can be regarded as the aesthetic bedrock of the next century and a half of theorizing.[13] Though often characterized as the ultimate formalist in music theory, Hanslick was also – and, it might be thought, not as a strictly necessary consequence of his philosophical formalism – the ultimate "thematicist," of which the following quotation gives some impression:

> The independent, aesthetically not further reducible unit of musical thought in every composition is the theme. The ultimate determinations which one ascribes to music as such must always be manifest in the theme, the musical microcosm . . . Since the composition follows formal laws of beauty, it does not improvise itself in haphazard ramblings but develops itself in organically distinct gradations, like sumptuous blossoming from a bud. This bud is the principal theme, the actual material and content (in the sense

9 Bent, *Music Theory in the Age of Romanticism*, p. xii. 10 *MANC*, vol. I, p. 196.

11 On Hoffmann's review, see Bent, *Music Theory in the Age of Romanticism*, pp. 115–19; and see Burnham's *Beethoven Hero* for some account, speculative rather than forensic, of the impact of Beethoven's music – in this case, the *Eroica* Symphony – on subsequent music theory. DeNora argues in *Beethoven and the Construction of Genius* that Beethoven's special identity was evident in musico-sociological discourse during the decade before the *Eroica* and the Fifth (see esp. pp. 179–85); thus for example it is likely that the opinions of such as the precocious Czerny (1791–1857) were forming ahead of Hoffmann's influence.

12 There are two English versions of this title. *The Beautiful in Music* is the more familiar, if only because Cohen's translation appeared as long ago as 1891. In this writer's opinion, Cohen's translation is linguistically vastly superior to Payzant's of 1986 entitled *On the Musically Beautiful*; yet the Payzant publication is valuable for its footnotes and perhaps above all for its detailed index, and thus it is used here.

13 See Grey's "Metaphorical Modes" for an example of recent discussion of the place of Hanslick.

> of subject matter) of the whole tonal structure. Everything in the structure is a spontaneous continuation and consequence of the theme, conditioned and shaped by it, controlled and fulfilled by it . . . The composer puts the theme, like the principal character in a novel, into different situations and surroundings, in varying occurrences and moods – these and all the rest, no matter how sharply contrasted, are thought and shaped with reference to it.[14]

If we can thus trace back some of the concerns of thematic and motivic analysis in modern theory to the organicism and formalism of the nineteenth century, another important cultural force, the dissolution of tonality, also feeds back into this kind of analytical practice. That Second Viennese composers solved the crisis of atonality by resorting to serial composition is too obvious to state, except that we need to be aware of a particular inflection of this development, an inflection perceived acutely by Webern, whose music has appeared as the object of theorizing so often since the middle of the twentieth century, but whose critical insight too was of the finest. In Webern's *The Path to the New Music* it is argued that the "form" of the twelve-note row along with its levels of transposition "occupy a position akin to that of the 'main key' in earlier music . . . This analogy with earlier formal construction is quite consciously fostered; here we find the path that will lead us again to extended forms."[15] In other words, tonality had been replaced as a method of extended composition, in Webern's view, by the dodecaphonic approach of which it would be perverse to deny that it is in some sense "thematic," that is, characterized by an ordered series of intervals. Indeed in Webern's own typical use of the row in either three- or four-note self-referential partitions, the "motive" is the substrate of the "theme" – and if one were to add "just as in Beethoven," no-one might have assented more vigorously than Webern himself.[16]

If a purview such as the above can justifiably be stretched across recent music-theoretical history – "recent" meaning roughly in the period from Beethoven onwards – the justification must rely to some extent on the support of a contextual understanding of music:[17] there must always be a place for hermeneutical "interpretation" of musical continuity, or so became the credo of the nineteenth century in the writings of such as Berlioz, Kretzschmar, and Schumann; still a force in nineteenth-century analysis was the tradition of rhetoric, too, where we find in thinkers such as Koch and Marx a retrieval in hermeneutical garb of basic human psychology and especially human language; and no theory of musical "line" could ever be expected to float free of concepts of "form," which had a totalizing grip on musical thought from Romanticism

14 Hanslick, *On the Musically Beautiful*, pp. 80–82.

15 Webern, p. 54. This quotation will be well known to those familiar with the secondary literature on Second Viennese issues. Among recent citations it is to be found in Wason's "Signposts," the first three pages of which offer an admirable overview of the point at issue here.

16 Bailey's *The Twelve-note Music of Anton Webern* was the first – and as a definitive publication may be the last – thorough technical study of the composer's row usage.

17 In a decidedly programmatic statement, Lerdahl and Jackendoff, writing of "themes, motives, and other musical ideas," assert in *A Generative Theory* that "it would be pointless to discuss them without a theory of the structures in which they are embedded" (p. 286).

onwards. Scheibe and Reicha often take a particularly prominent role in accounts of the relatively modern history of form, yet only a few decades ago nineteenth-century formal theory was seen to be anchored in eighteenth-century, Enlightenment theorizing whose explanatory power in truth may not have been subsequently equalled: Allen wrote tellingly in *Philosophies of Music History* of how "the Nature-philosophy of Rousseau" meets "the Nature-philosophy of his contemporary Rameau" who "managed to fix eighteenth-century concepts of natural harmony and natural form in theory teaching for a century and a half."[18] All such factors – interpretation, rhetoric, form or, as Allen repeatedly calls it, "persistence" – were part of the tool-kit needed to assimilate Western music in a way that Adorno perhaps uniquely laid bare:

> Analysis retaliates against musical works of art by pointing out that they are truly "composed," assembled from components; the illusion they generate – that of an absolutely integrated being, of the necessary sequence of the whole and its flow – offsets their own constituent parts. Analysis, being the destruction of that illusion, is critical. Enemies of analysis are well aware of that. They want nothing to do with it, fearing that in forfeiting the illusion of the absolute meaningfulness of the whole they will be robbed of some secret within the artwork which they think they hold and must protect, but which is largely synonymous with that illusion.[19]

Developing variation

Had Adorno left his comments at that, they would amount to no more than the familiar shadow cast on the heady structuralist optimism of 1960s cultural theory by the then-enduring, inherited counter-culture of idealism, positivism, rationalism, and similar critical positions whose adherents were unwilling to subscribe to the notion of the "death of the author"[20] and could not see any alternative in dialectics. Nevertheless, Adorno clearly is espousing a dialectical approach since to the forlorn thesis above he immediately opposes the antithesis that promises a music-theoretical synthesis:

> This does not mean, as prejudice would have it, that *less* analysis is needed, but rather *more*, a second reflection. It is not enough to establish analytically the constituent elements, nor even the most concrete primary cells, the so-called "inspired ideas." Above all it is necessary to reconstruct what happens to those ideas, or to use Schoenberg's phrase, to write the "history of a theme."[21]

The metaphor, if that is what we choose to call it, of modern Western music telling a kind of thematic story was crystallized above all in Schoenberg's concept of "developing variation," which drew together the strands of Goethean organicism and

18 Allen, *Philosophies of Music*, p. 307. 19 Adorno, *Alban Berg*, p. 37.

20 Barthes's famous essay "The Death of the Author" was first published in French in 1968 (in the journal *Mantéia*); it is available in English in, for example, Barthes's *Image–Music–Text*, pp. 142–48.

21 Adorno, *Alban Berg*, p. 37.

Hanslick's insistence on the "self-subsistent" status of musical ideas;[22] music is seen by Schoenberg as having a "life," but a life that requires a "second reflection" (see Adorno, above) in which the purely musical relationships are somehow understood in and of themselves.[23] "Variation" grounds musical meaning in a kind of living identity, since obviously something varied is by definition something also recognized; "development," on the other hand, implies the avoidance of literal repetition – such avoidance being an aspect of musical composition that Schoenberg equated clearly and continually in a lifetime of music-theoretical writing with "higher" musical value, all the more ripe for deeper musical meaning and, of course, ripe for the need of deeper understanding including "reflection." Composers, Schoenberg insisted, should be "connecting ideas through developing variation, thus showing consequences derived from the basic idea and remaining within the boundaries of human thinking and its demands of logic."[24]

Schoenberg aimed at developing variation in his own composition, and found it everywhere in the compositions of the past that he considered worthy of study and influence. Despite his reverence of J. S. Bach, and his awareness of the profundity found in "early music" by those of his contemporaries whose opinions he valued, found for example in Isaac by his pupil Webern, Schoenberg's main canon of compositional masterpieces began with Haydn and Mozart, and there is no doubt that he saw the music of Brahms as the crowning achievement of the First Viennese School in which he found all the validation he needed for the aesthetics of his own kind of modernism. It is no accident that to date the most extensive study of developing variation is largely devoted to Brahms's compositional manner (Frisch, *Brahms and the Principle of Developing Variation*), and in fact Schoenberg's analysis of Brahms's song "O Tod," the third of the Four Serious Songs, Op. 121 (*Style and Idea*, pp. 431–35), is not only discussed by Frisch (pp. 151–56) but is emblematic of the entire Schoenbergian project to demonstrate at the level of theme and motive a maximal balance of unity and diversity (a project taken up by the Schoenberg-influenced critic Hans Keller throughout the latter's extensive writings; see below, pp. 913–14).[25] The aetiology of this kind of

22 Hanslick, *On the Musically Beautiful*, p. 28.

23 Thus Schoenberg is partaking of the tradition of structural interpretation which can be traced back above all to Momigny (see Bent, *Analysis*, pp. 20–25) but from which the linguistic and indeed poetic tropes are expressly excluded, which without doubt paves the way for unheralded degrees of theoretical abstraction in Forte and Nattiez as discussed below.

24 Schoenberg, "Criteria," p. 130.

25 There is no need to repeat here the arguments conducted in the musicological literature since the 1950s bemoaning the lack of focus in Second Viennese theorizing: it is true for example that there is no single source to which one can point as a repository of Schoenberg's explanation of musical structure, in the way that one can invite students of Schenkerian methods to study the latter's *Free Composition* (cf. the remarks in Chapter 19, pp. 609–10); nevertheless, Schoenberg's *Fundamentals* is recommended as a most concentrated yet elaborate – and musically satisfying – compendium of illustrated argument, of which Part I, "Construction of Themes" (pp. 1–118), provides a great deal of flesh for the bones picked here. The Brahms Op. 121 songs are discussed in analytical detail, including comments on Schoenberg's approach, in Whittall's "The *Vier ernste Gesänge*." Schoenberg's large, but inchoate, would-be treatise was eventually published as *The Musical Idea*, despite doubts expressed for many years by Schoenberg

thinking in Wagner's *Leitmotiv* technique, and its twentieth-century flowering in a dodecaphonic context,[26] provide us with some sense of the historical sweep of the line of thought. In this context, what is perhaps most striking is that we see in the twentieth-century assimilation of First Viennese practice, and Second Viennese self-awareness, a fixation on the thematic, on melody as the true voice of modern Western music under theoretical scrutiny. This is well, if perhaps incidentally, expressed in Boss's summary ("Schoenberg's Op. 22 Radio Talk") of what developing variation meant in a tonal context:

> Developing variation affects various kinds of motives, as well as phrases. Specific variations change intervallic and rhythmic features of a motive or phrase such as pitch succession, harmonic succession, tonal context, duration succession, or metrical context. Along with the feature, each variation changes aspects of the feature, and the number of aspects changed serves as an index of remoteness from the original motive. Two considerations govern the successions of motive-forms produced by variation: later forms should fulfill the implications of earlier forms, and the succession should delimit a segment of the musical form and enable that segment to perform its function within the form. (p. 130)

Evidently, "a contextual understanding of music" as mentioned above is at a premium in Boss's encapsulation, which introduces the "harmonic" early on and ends with "form"; but from the viewpoint of developing variation it is the motive that is characterized as the life-blood of music, and this is an authentically Schoenbergian position.

What has been said so far about the role of theme and motive in the context of developing variation may give the impression that such patterns of musical invention are audible or visible for all in a musical surface, and that analysis is merely a freely available process of dissection. This impression is fostered by Bent's now-famous definition of music analysis in general: "The resolution of a musical structure into relatively simpler constituent elements, and the investigation of the functions of those elements within that structure."[27] Yet we have already encountered Adorno's assertion that analysis requires a "second reflection," and Cook dramatizes the issue starkly and without apology: "Music as it appears to the listener and music as it appears to the analyst may not necessarily be quite the same thing. The relationship between the two is one of the most problematic issues in the whole business of musical analysis."[28] Much more subtly, but also decisively, Keller provided a psychological grounding for

scholars, for example in Goehr's "Schoenberg's 'Gedanke' Manuscript" (1977), about the validity of finalizing material on Schoenberg's behalf. An apparently modest but most significant document about the early development of Schoenberg's concepts was published and discussed in Cross's "Schoenberg's Earliest Thoughts" – here we first see his desire to forge a new, modern account of "the purpose of the motive" (p. 127). For relatively recent applied research in this area, see Collisson, "Grundgestalt, Developing Variation."

26 See the discussions of developing variation in Haimo, *Schoenberg's Serial Odyssey*, especially pp. 73–105. 27 Bent, *Analysis*, p. 1. 28 Cook, *A Guide*. p. 16.

Schoenbergian "thematicism" (see above, p. 912) and many believe that the definitive Kellerian statements and exemplifications are to be found in his essay on Mozart's chamber music, which begins with a series of confident premises indicating not only the object of thematic analysis – above all, that of developing variation – but the actual work that this will always require:

> What usually goes by the name of analysis is nothing of the sort. Most critics have never grasped the essential difference between analysis and description. Description gives a verbal account of what you hear and is essentially unnecessary. Can anyone seriously suggest that a music-lover has to be told that a contrasting theme is a contrasting theme?
>
> Verbal or symbolic analysis shows, on the other hand, the elements of what you hear. In a great piece, these are always the elements of unity, not of diversity, because a great piece grows from an all-embracing idea. Great music diversifies a unity; mere good music unites diverse elements. As soon as you have analysed the unity of a great work, its variety explains itself, whereas when you describe its, or indeed any work's, diversity, nothing is explained at all . . . It will be the *latent* basic motifs, and generally the unitive forces behind the *manifest* music, on which my analytic observations will concentrate. The most uncomfortable questions, hardly ever as much as touched upon, will clamour for an answer: why or how does the contrasting second subject necessarily belong to the first? why is a particular movement an integral part of a particular work and of no other? and so forth.[29]

Inevitably the work of analysis of the general kind being discussed here has been seen as heuristic, and it is in the nature of discovery procedures to be capable of being taken to extremes. This is just how the work of Rudolph Réti has been characterized (see Figure 29.1), critics having often preferred to see him as obsessed with "latent" thematic unity rather than as the discoverer of real, if hidden compositional secrets. That those secrets appear to be "real" and are of abiding fascination justifies Réti's place in the history of theory – thus for example Cook devotes more than thirty pages to the exposition of Réti's ideas about the underlying thematic patterns in Beethoven.[30] It is perhaps Réti in particular, however, who can stimulate us to take a step back from exposition at this point and ask whether there is any serious flaw in what may be broadly termed Schoenbergian thematicism (see n. 23). If there is a flaw, the consensus seems to find it in the very resistance of diversity, of variation itself, to codification, posing a question which must end by asking what are the *limits* of music theory.[31] In respect of

29 'The Chamber Music," pp. 90–91. In this essay Keller offers dozens of actual musical examples of thematic relationships which selective quotation here would misrepresent, not least because part of the conviction of Keller's argument lies in his accumulation and marshalling of evidence. In this respect Keller's essay is a forerunner of Frisch's more extensive, though hardly more insightful exposition in *Brahms and the Principle of Developing Variation*.

30 Cook, *A Guide*, pp. 89–115. There is also some review of Réti's analytical work in Bent's *Analysis*: see in particular pp. 85–88. A fascinating but today little-known precursor to Réti's style of motivic analysis is found in Cassirer, *Beethoven und die Gestalt*.

31 Street's "Superior Myths" is an iconoclastic meditation on the limits of modern music-analytical practice; see also Dunsby, "Criteria of Correctness."

Figure 29.1 Rudolph Réti and hidden theme. In this analysis of the opening of Beethoven's String Quartet in E♭ major, Op. 135, Réti aims to demonstrate that music may entail a covert thematic continuity, rather like the plot of a play. From *The Thematic Process in Music*, Example 331, p. 211

thematicism, there is no nicer relevant position than that taken by Leonard Meyer in a paper that originated as a keynote address to the Society for Music Theory in 1988:

> It is indisputable that a succession of motivic variants often occurs in, say, the exposition sections of nineteenth-century sonata-form movements. The nature and order of such changes can as a rule be readily explained in relation to typical sonata-form procedures. But the theorists and critics who use the term "developing variation" seem to be making a much stronger claim – though it is seldom explicitly formulated. The implicit claim is that the process of change makes musical sense in and of itself – that developing variation is not merely a set of techniques for motivic manipulation, but a specific and independent structural/processive principle. But I have not, thus far, been able to find any discussion of the constraints that govern the nature of the succession of variants, although such a theory would appear to be a *sine qua non* of an adequate account of diachronic motivic change – of development and variation.[32]

To this it might be objected that, at least as far as tonal masterpieces are concerned, there is certainly some claim among adherents of Schenkerian analysis to be relying on

32 Meyer, "A Pride of Prejudices," pp. 244–45.

a theory of "diachronic motivic change," in the sense that musical elaboration which cannot be shown to be organically coherent is not worth the salt.[33] If that is a polemic to be considered elsewhere, it seems to remain the case that "it was through his ever-deepening awareness of how 'motive' functions in tonal structure that Schenker was encouraged to formulate his theory of organic coherence . . . [An] awareness of the nature and function of motivic connection may be not only the starting-point for a voice-leading analysis, but also one of its most valuable results. Recent literature suggests that the combination of Schenkerian 'organicism' and 'thematicism' in its various forms is a trend for the future."[34]

Pitch-class sets

"The spontaneous expression of the imagination, the melodic idea," writes the composer Alexander Goehr, "does not seem to alter its form significantly through the ages. There is not such a great difference between a fourteenth-century melodic idea and one by Webern."[35] It was in this spirit that we noted earlier how in serial music (Webern's in particular) motive is the substrate of the theme. "Composers," that is, "have increased the influence of their ideas from foreground relationships to the most trivial aspects of the background."[36] Most evidently this was the case in the serial organization of musical themes using the same pitch material as in the accompaniment, as in the surrounding counterpoint, or as in a heterophonic texture. Serial composition of this kind, albeit radically misunderstood in many theory and critical sources in the 1920s and 30s, was promulgated from the beginning as a poietic, creative impulse; this caused critical resentment, inevitably,[37] but what is of more interest theoretically is that music theory became confronted with a first-order challenge. In theorizing about Beethoven the writers of the nineteenth century and beyond were continually exposed to the question of what the purpose might be of a chain of re-scrutiny of canonical music: Wagner writing to explain his own compositional evolution in the white heat of the mid-Romantic discovery of new musical languages, for instance; Tovey explaining music to the ordinary early twentieth-century listener as a legacy of the great democratizing and educating ideals of Victorian Britain; or Schenker, finishing nearly a century after Wagner began, passing on a kind of secret knowledge concerning an essentially lost art – all of them carrying out tasks of, as it were, aeonic separation. Now, however, at the time when Schoenberg was consider-

33 Among the wide discussion in recent decades of the coherence of Schenkerian theory, which it is not appropriate to discuss here, there have been a number of striking shifts away from Schenkerian orthodoxy, and these do tend to revert to the "old" questions of thematicism; Cohn's "The Autonomy of Motives" is an outstanding case where it is admitted that "to acknowledge the autonomy of motives is to abandon the proposition . . that the *Ursatz* is the sole source of unity" (p. 168).

34 Dunsby and Whittall, *Music Analysis*, p. 101.

35 Goehr, *Finding the Key*, p. 64.

36 Ibid.

37 See for example Blom, "How it Started," p. 22.

ing thematic and motivic structure in the music of the past, there was a common currency of theoretical purpose since the questions to be asked of post-tonal and atonal music were by and large similar ones. They still are: "It is when we shift our analytical focus to post-tonal music that the freedom of manoeuvre gained by detaching surface and depth becomes increasingly attractive . . . it is not clear whether this new music even has a single deep structure, let alone one capable of fusing surface gestures into an organic totality."[38]

The early history of the attempt to understand post-tonal pitch structure, with all the concomitant significance this has for ideas of theme and motive in the new repertoire, was characterized by years of false starts – years dated by Bernard in "Chord, Collection and Set" specifically as 1911 to 1964, and demonstrating "duplicated effort, reinventings of the wheel, and seemingly inexplicable conceptual leaps";[39] the early days of pitch-class consciousness amounted to a history of failure, driven by artistic fashion rather than intellectual progression, and we must be clear that Allen Forte's version of pitch-class set theory, first fully codified in 1973, was a matter of specific vision and invention, not the dutiful development of inherited concepts.[40] What emerged in the Forte-inspired literature from the 1970s onwards was a picture of organized sound in which there is an inherent link between theme (and its motives) and harmony, to a degree of coherence that may lead one to understand Goehr's use of the word "trivial" of fundamental aspects to a compositional background, if trivial refers to a compositional background so deep in the musical fabric that it is no longer of specific artistic interest – although its theoretical interest cannot be doubted.[41] This delving into the ingredients of some canonical twentieth-century music[42] showed that exactly the picture of integration and organicism claimed of the best of earlier music was to be found again even after the massive cultural fracture caused by early twentieth-century musical modernism. Whereas cultural historians and to some extent music theorists have naturally tended to concentrate on explaining this "fracture" largely in terms of the evolution of post-tonal, atonal, and dodecaphonic pitch content and structure, those pursuing analytical work recognized from early on that thematic and motivic matters would perforce be at a premium in this new context. Even if the following diagnosis by Lester amounts to a slight overstatement (doubtless in the interests of pedagogical clarity), it is nevertheless emblematic of a momentous trend in twentieth-century theory: "in nontonal works of the twentieth century . . . tonal voice leading and harmonies no longer provide a basis for the pitch structure of

38 Fink, "Going Flat," p. 114. 39 Bernard, "Chord, Collection, and Set," p. 12.

40 *The Structure of Atonal Music* is but one of Forte's many publications in this area, but it remains the definitive statement of his version of pc set theory. "Pitch-Class Set Genera" was Forte's next decisive step in this field of research, which is reviewed, amplified and revised in Ayrey's "Symposium."

41 The Schenkerian *Ursatz* similarly states the obvious – that all tonal masterpieces are tonal – but has the potential to reveal inexhaustible insights into the way in which individual pieces of music "work" or "go," bearing in mind Adorno's call for *more* analysis (see above, p. 911).

42 And a wider canon, as mentioned in Dunsby's "Fortenotes," p. 177.

a piece. In their place, motivic relationship among groups of pitches generate melody and harmony. Analysis of this music entails locating these motives, and understanding the way they are used."[43]

The Structure of Atonal Music took on the huge question of "whether this new music even has a single deep structure" (see above, p. 917). It did so at two levels. First, Forte addressed the question of whether all music which can be understood as using the full range of the twelve-note universe – music, that is, which continually recycles the pitches available in the complete twelve-note total chromatic aggregate – was susceptible to comparison in terms of its pitch content: the crucial issue was whether like could be compared with like, theme with theme, motive with motive, and of course chord with chord (a question which is as inherently semiotic as it is Fortean – see pp. 920–22 below). In order to tame the massive combinatorial potential of the twelve-note universe Forte defined a pitch-class set according to two constraints, one of which is unproblematic, another of which lies at the heart of the theoretical polemics that have been such a fascinating aspect of this kind of theorizing over some four decades. The unproblematic constraint is "transpositional equivalence," which asserts that the notes, say, C–D–E are the "same" as the notes F–G–A in that the one is a literal transposition of the other (both collections carry the designation "set 3–6"[44]), and anyone familiar with the concept of "scale" in modern Western music is perfectly used to moving around pitch universes in this way, so that for example the melodic minor scale on F – which uses nine of the possible twelve chromatic pitches, with those on the sixth and seventh degrees of the scale being variable depending on the order in which the scale is presented – is understood as being specifically equivalent to the melodic minor scale on, say, B. The other constraint is "inversional equivalence," which asserts not only that the notes, say, C–D–E are the "same" as the notes F–G–A but that the notes, say, D–E–F are the "same" as the notes E–F–G, in that D–E–F places a semitone (interval class 1 or ic1) in order after a tone (ic2), as does E–F–G (understood as the succession G–F–E, ic2 followed by ic1). One only has to consider set 3–11 (0, 3, 7), which may represent, say, the notes C–E–G (otherwise known as a major triad) or D–F–A (where, if A is "7," F follows, downwards as it were, at four semitones' distance as "3," and D at a further three semitones' distance as "0" – and otherwise known as a minor triad), to understand the glaringly simple point that many crucial kinds of musical identity familiar in common-practice harmony, where inversional equivalence is not a general property of pitch relations, are necessarily missing in pc set theory where inversional equivalence is assumed by definition. Non-inversional relations – for instance, distinctions between major and minor triads – need to be "missing" in pc set theory so that within reason like can be compared with

43 Lester, *Analytical Approaches*, pp. 9–10. Although dating from the early 1980s, Hasty's "Segmentation and Process" remains one of the most relevant, carefully argued, and musically sensitive accounts of "the division of a musical work into structural components" (p. 54).

44 The set names, which have become a music-theoretical *lingua franca*, were first laid out in *The Structure of Atonal Music*, "Appendix 1: Prime Forms and Vectors of Pitch-Class Sets," pp. 179–81.

like, as stated above: all possible sets as just defined, from three up to nine elements, amount to a mere 208 items.[45]

The second level at which *The Structure of Atonal Music* addressed the question of "deep structure" concerned the systematic relations between pc sets. The analysis of Webern's Op. 7, No. 3 (see **Figure 10.7, p. 293**) shows how the set content of an entire piece, albeit in this case a short composition for violin and piano, may be displayed in an inventory of pc sets disposed in such a way as to enable precise specification of the relations between each set and every other set. In summary, where it can be shown that in any particular analysis a piece of music displays an array of pc sets in which all or most sets can be shown to be, in an abstract sense, derived from one or two sets in particular, these particular sets may be considered to be special, "nexus" sets and the pitch structure as a whole may be said to be "connected."[46] In order to begin a pc set analysis at all, the music must be "segmented" (reminding us of Bent's very definition of analysis as the "resolution of musical structure into relatively simpler constituent elements"; see above, p. 913), and much of the controversy surrounding pc set theory in the late twentieth century has centered on what may rightly be thought of as a somewhat uneasy concatenation of analysis and theory: the theory, as will be evident even from the compact account above, is systematic, relatively abstract, "programmatic", or "totalizing" as it might be called, and perhaps fairly characterized as quasi-scientific. The analytical practice on which it depends if it is to have worthwhile outcomes has understandably tended to make applications of the theory seem not so much quasi-scientific as pseudo-scientific, not least perhaps because this practice seems to exclude composers' intentions.[47] Yet in the end, it is argued, music theory of this kind may be

45 Two fairly simple examples of how this theory translates into analytical practice as a system of motivic designation, in Schoenberg's Piano Piece, Op 19, No. 6 and Webern's Piece for Violin and Piano, Op. 7, No. 3, are explained in Dunsby and Whittall, *Music Analysis*, pp. 140–42. A lucid, step-by-step account of the rudiments of pc set analysis is to be found in Cook, *A Guide*, pp. 124–51; for more detail in a pedagogical context, see Lester, *Analytical Approaches*, pp. 66–172; for thorough exposition and exemplification see Simms, "A Theory of Pitch-Class Sets." In 1985 Forte provided a comprehensive review, in "Pitch-Class Set Analysis Today," of his theory and practice and their critical reception up to that time. Finally, see the brief discussion in **Chapter 10, pp. 291–94**.

46 See Forte, *The Structure of Atonal Music*, p. 114. In "Pitch-Class Set Genera" Forte was to put forward a revised theory of connectedness, in which set relations are quantified in relation not to hexachords but to trichords, providing, according to Dunsby in "Fortenotes," pp. 178–79, "an explanation of the semitonal, or half-step universe that really is a theory, in that it not only frees us from the philosophically distracting world of compositional practice . . . but also frees itself from the statistical spin of the hexachord in theory."

47 Haimo hopes to persuade us in "Atonality, Analysis, and the Intentional Fallacy" that this particular issue is somehow the main cause of a "bitter debate" (p. 168) surrounding Forte's ideas on pc-set matters. However, one may surely ask where in the history of music theory any worthwhile debate has been resolved by the discovery and agreement over a composer's "intention" – intention being such a fundamentally contingent entity that it can hardly be expected to form the bedrock of the musicological interpretation of past works of art. And one may point to the danger of edifying a rather simple if perpetually intractable philosophico-analytical question – whether and how it matters what people such as composers mean by what they do – at the expense of downgrading an inherently complex and, some would say, more urgently necessary inquiry into how intelligent processing actually takes place at all; see Rahn's "Some Remarks on Network Models of Music" for a recent, intense discussion of such "processing" in a music-theoretical context.

not so much "substituting its own scientific jargon for the personal, living experience of music that had presumably drawn the theorists to it in the first place,"[48] as demonstrating that the theory of music is always likely to be stamped with the fact that it is the theory of an art. In this respect pc set theory may be regarded as one of the most instructive developments in music theory in recent centuries, since it has addressed fundamental issues seriously and thoroughly, beyond the ephemeral world of contemporaneous critical commentary, and demonstrated that the shock of the new may not be so shocking or so new:

> The separating out of pitch collections for analysis involves extraction of melodic as much as chordal formations, and indeed mixtures of these two as well as what might better be called "aggregates" or "clusters" of notes. This process is itself one of extreme *delicacy*, for the entire analysis rests on its being carried out with *musical sensibility*. While phrase marks, rests and the like may offer clues, the task demands much more.[49]

The semiotic perspective

In considering Forte's heuristics we asked above "whether like could be compared with like, theme with theme, motive with motive," and this question lies at the heart of the study of signs, be it called semiotics or semiology. Music semiotics – if not derived from, then certainly inspired by, twentieth-century linguistic science[50] – can be called the study of the thematic process par excellence, a sustained meditation by a goodly number of music theorists on what we called initially "the general qualities of musical continuity, or line."[51] This thinking rests on criteria that have formed a consistent protocol for semiotic analysis, where "signs" are taken to be the elements of any object (of, say, a written sentence, or a piece of music heard) and semioticians study their interrelations accordingly:

(1) The sign, until scientific research may convince us to the contrary, is regarded as "arbitrary" or "unmotivated," and what this means in music-theoretical practice is

48 Cook, *Music*, p. 96. 49 Bent, *Analysis*, p. 108.

50 One of the most influential books in the intellectual history of the early twentieth century, Saussure's *Course in General Linguistics*, has been the epistemological starting point for the study of sign systems throughout the arts and human sciences, as Saussure himself – in all modesty – accurately predicted (pp. 16–17).

51 In *Linguistics and Semiotics* Monelle offers an informative recent picture of the general semiotic project in music theory; another milestone was Tarasti's *A Theory of Musical Semiotics*. Agawu's article "The Challenge of Semiotics" offers closer and more recent argument, and his earlier book *Playing with Signs* spread a semiotic perspective over a much larger canvas, without, however, fully convincing such as Treitler (see "Language and the Interpretation of Music," especially pp. 28–32). It must be noted that semiotics has not found its way into all corners of music theory, or indeed into some of its codifications: thus whereas it figures significantly in, say, Bent's *Analysis* and Cook and Everist's *Rethinking Music*, the highly influential Hatch and Bernstein *Music Theory* pursues other agendas entirely, which might be thought a regrettable lack but must also be taken at face value as part of the reality of an ongoing discipline.

that music cannot be examined for any inherent "meaning" in its elements, hence the inclination to look for structures – perhaps motivic structures or pc-set relations as outlined above.

(2) Sign relations are always in one aspect "synchronic," that is, they exist free of the constraints of time and indeed "place" or any other empirical determinant. Thus for example it becomes an analytical requirement to explain, not the derivation of a musical idea (which may be borrowed from earlier art, such as are many of J. S. Bach's themes, or which may elicit an established cultural response, hence, say, our tendency not to walk out after hearing the first theme of a Classical symphony), but its function within the work of art being examined.

(3) Sign relations are always in another aspect "diachronic," since every sign has a history, whether within a work of art, or viewed more widely as part of a culture in time (cf. the parenthetical remark immediately above).

(4) Taking these three criteria together it follows that signification is either "paradigmatic," to do with one sign appearing rather than another at a particular point in a structure, "merely synchronically," it might be informally said; or "syntagmatic," to do with how a sign relates to what came before and what comes after, diachronically, be it within a few seconds of connected perception, or within a hundred years of human culture. The paradigmatic tells us about the *identity* of a sign, and the syntagmatic tells us about its structural *function*.

It is a hallmark of such studies that comparisons, that is, music-analytical statements about similarity and difference, are *explicit*, so that for example the approximations and excesses of informal critical language as well as the positivism of "pure" (one might even say, non-Schenkerian) formal theory are equally shunned, the one because of the semiotic ideal of *precision*, the other because of the ideal of *consistency*.[52] The "explicit" entails not only the metaphors and metalanguages themselves of technical musical description and explanation, but also their epistemological status: it entails the attempt at a continuous awareness of what kind of knowledge they are and from what kind of knowledge they are derived; in the semiotic "tripartitional" analysis of any signifying process knowledge is regarded as being inevitably some combination of the poietic, the esthesic, and the "neutral."[53] It is an incidental result of this interrogatory character of music semiotics that any particular inquiry can necessitate the processing of relatively large amounts of information.[54]

How distinct such processing may be from traditional methods has been a topic of

52 When we consider semiotics in such a concise perspective, the question naturally arises whether it amounts to anything more than what has often been called common sense; the main intention of this brief section is to indicate that it can and should amount to more.

53 Perhaps the most important tripartitional semiotic manifesto was Molino's "Musical Fact," originally published in *Musique en Jeu* in 1975. Molino's work in general sociological theory has been a sustaining influence on the work of Nattiez from *Fondements* to *Music and Discourse*.

54 One classic example of many pages of music-semiotic research devoted to a short piece for solo flute is Nattiez's "Varèse's 'Density 21.5.'" A more compact, and extremely instructive, example of semiotic music-analytical research is to be found in Morris's "A Semiotic Investigation," p. 926.

long debate since the 1960s. On the one hand, it is certainly true that "the pursuit of melodic similarities by Ruwet and Nattiez as a form of paradigmatic analysis is nothing if not a brand of thematic or motivic analysis"; but there must be some degree of overstatement in Agawu's basic "challenge" here that "only political or institutional interests, rather than epistemological concerns, would lead one to continue to uphold the autonomy of a field of musical semiotics."[55] This last claim is unduly insensitive to the heuristic edge in much of the research in applied music semiotics. Right from the foundational work, especially in Ruwet's "Methods of Analysis," the sincere attempt was to arrive at results that could not otherwise be achieved, to find otherwise hidden form.[56] In the *Geisslerlied* analysis presented there for example (see Figure 29.2), and much discussed in the secondary literature,[57] it is vital to bear in mind that the object of analysis, a medieval flagellant song, comes down to us with essentially no poietic or indeed esthesic information, no historical attachments telling us about the compositional intention, the proposed manner of performance, the probable attitude of any listener, and so on. Ruwet was using the instincts of a major linguistic scholar – his main métier – faced with an unknown language, asking how best to make sense of it, to find some key to the beginnings of translation into a known language. In this sense the segmentation he provides, and the methodology that can apply to any similar need for segmentation in other contexts, is designed to be immune from the vagaries of "musical sensibility" (Bent; see above, p. 920) in the interests of a result more akin to, if not scientific truth, then at least linguistic fact – which we may define in specialist terminology as an intersubjective recognition of semantic pertinence, but which may just as well be characterized as the laying bare of meaning, as opposed to its bald assertion. It is especially in ethnomusicology, where typically and often by definition the raw material is effectively "unknown," that one might expect semiotic analysis of the musical line to be at a premium. Writing about Arom's *African Polyphony*, Nattiez claimed that "as one of the most ambitious and successful analytical ventures ever pursued in ethnomusicological research, it could be said to mark 'the return to analysis in ethnomusicology.' "[58]

Conspectus

The "poietic" (creation) and "esthesic" (reception) poles of signification have often been illustrated as boxes surrounding the operational – call it analytical – "neutral" level of observation. To the question, what lies outside these boxes in human experience?, it

55 Agawu, "The Challenge of Semiotics," pp. 159 and 153 respectively. 56 See n. 52.

57 It must be admitted that Dunsby and Whittall, in *Music Analysis*, commented on the "infuriating banality of studies of early chant" by Ruwet (p. 216); thus the claim here is not that that Agawu's position is incomprehensible, but rather that the cool light of history may cast matters more positively.

58 Nattiez, "Simha Arom," p. 241.

Figure 29.2 Nicolas Ruwet and hidden form. Ruwet's widely discussed analysis of a medieval flagellant song, originally published in *Langage, musique, poésie* (1972), demonstrates the sharp focus that a semiotically disciplined approach to "signification" may yield. Although the ordered pitches of this music are known, there is no other historical evidence about the articulation of the song, and it is only through rigorous comparison with clear transformation rules that a picture of its inherent internal "form" is possible. Cited in Ruwet, "Methods of Analysis in Musicology" (1987), Example 1a, p. 21

may be that the best answer is to appeal to philosophy and anthropology, with the origin of the poietic amounting to an ontological issue, and the result of the esthesic amounting to a sociological one. Where music comes from, in other words, is probably a less important and interesting question than the question of where human awareness itself comes from; and the role of music in our lives is again one important corner of the underlying challenge to understand the nature and consequences of human activity in general. In attempting to understand something of the place of thematic analysis in this grand human scenario, it has been abundantly clear throughout this investigation that the true measure of one approach compared with another is its epistemological grounding. For example there is no doubt that the way developing variation was discussed by musicians throughout the twentieth century assumed a shared knowledge of a shared body of music, a "canon" as it came to be called in the 1980s. Set theory posited a different form of shared knowledge, since it asserted that there is a chromatic universe that developed from tonal music and that formed the "vocabulary" of important ways of composing in the twentieth century. This composing, especially of "atonal" music, could nevertheless be "athematic," and the very notion of "harmonic" is challenged by the fact that many, some would say all, aspects of pc set structure are inaccessible to direct musical experience (which characteristic no more undermines the "reality" of pc set structure than does the fact that when we speak we are unaware of the grammatical structures essential in our making any kind of linguistic sense to others). Even less, as it were, "anchored" epistemologically is the position of semiotics, a critique that proposes no prior knowledge of the structure and "meaning" of particular pieces of music, but on the contrary prefers to suspend any intuitions of such knowledge in order to make a forensic investigation that is, like a scientific theorem, replicable and falsifiable. While different theorists, including of course different readers of this text, will have their own epistemological point of view and suspicion of one or another approach to music analysis, the very fact that this suspicion, in the context of informed debate and artistic openness, is unlikely to be uniform tells us that thematic theory has not been a whimsical trend in music theory, but touches directly on our artistic values. By definition, then, one can hardly say which way thematic theory is heading, the only realistic prediction being that however the musical canon is to develop, musicians are likely to seek to unearth the patterns, correspondences, compositional mechanisms, and perceptual strategies of the future.

Bibliography

Adorno, T. *Alban Berg: Master of the Smallest Link* (1968), trans. J. Brand and C. Hailey, Cambridge University Press, 1991

Agawu, V. K. *Playing with Signs: A Semiotic Interpretation of Classic Music*, Princeton University Press, 1991

"The Challenge of Semiotics," in *Rethinking Music*, ed. N. Cook and M. Everist, Oxford University Press, 1999, pp. 138–60

Allen, W. D. *Philosophies of Music History: A Study of General Histories of Music 1600–1900*, New York, Dover, 1962

Arom, S. *African Polyphony and Polyrhythm: Musical Structure and Methodology*, trans. M. Thom et al., Cambridge University Press, 1991

Ayrey, C., ed., "Pitch-Class Set Genera: A Symposium," *MA* 17 (1998), pp. 161–244

Bailey, K. *The Twelve-note Music of Anton Webern*, Cambridge University Press, 1990

Barthes, R. *Image–Music–Text*, trans. S. Heath, London, Fontana, 1977

Bent, I. *Analysis*, London, Macmillan, 1987

Music Theory in the Age of Romanticism, Cambridge University Press, 1996

Bernard, J. "Chord, Collection, and Set in Twentieth-Century Theory," in *Music Theory in Concept and Practice*, ed. J. Baker, D. Beach, and J. Bernard, University of Rochester Press, 1997, pp. 11–51

Blom, E. "How it Started: The Nineteenth Century Pioneers," in *Twentieth Century Music*, ed. R. Myers, London, Calder, 1968, pp. 13–22

Boss, J. "Schoenberg's Op. 22 Radio Talk and Developing Variation in Atonal Music," *MTS* 14 (1992), pp. 125–49

Burnham, S. *Beethoven Hero*, Princeton University Press, 1995

Cassirer, F. *Beethoven und die Gestalt*, Stuttgart, Deutsche Verlags-Anstalt, 1925
Cohn, R. "The Autonomy of Motives in Schenkerian Accounts of Tonal Music," *MTS* 14 (1992), pp. 150–70
Collisson, S. "Grundgestalt, Developing Variation, and Motivic Processes in the Music of Arnold Schoenberg: An Analytical Study of the String Quartets," Ph.D. diss., University of London (1994)
Cook, N. *A Guide to Musical Analysis*, London, Dent, 1987
Music: A Very Short Introduction, Oxford University Press, 1998
Cook, N. and M. Everist, eds., *Rethinking Music*, Oxford University Press, 1999
Cross, C. "Schoenberg's Earliest Thoughts on the Theory of Composition: a Fragment from c. 1900," *Theoria* 8 (1994), pp. 113–33
Culler, J. *Structuralist Poetics: Structuralism, Linguistics, and the Study of Literature*, Ithaca, Cornell University Press, 1975
DeNora, T. *Beethoven and the Construction of Genius: Musical Politics in Vienna, 1792–1803*, Berkeley, University of California Press, 1995
Dunsby, J. "Criteria of Correctness of Music Theory and Analysis," in *Theory, Analysis and Meaning in Music*, ed. A. Pople, Cambridge University Press, 1994, pp. 77–85
"Fortenotes," *MA* 17 (1998), pp. 177–81
Dunsby, J. and A. Whittall, *Music Analysis in Theory and Practice*, London, Faber, 1988
Fink, R. "Going Flat: Post-Hierarchical Music Theory and the Musical Surface," in *Rethinking Music*, ed. N. Cook and M. Everist, Oxford University Press, 1999, pp. 102–37
Forte, A. *The Structure of Atonal Music*, New Haven, Yale University Press, 1973
"Pitch-Class Set Analysis Today," *MA* 4 (1985), pp. 29–58
"Pitch-Class Set Genera and the Origin of Modern Harmonic Species," *JMT* 32 (1988), pp. 187–271
Frisch, W. *Brahms and the Principle of Developing Variation*, Berkeley, University of California Press, 1984
Goehr, A. "Schoenberg's 'Gedanke' Manuscript," *Journal of the Arnold Schoenberg Institute* 2 (1977), pp. 4–25
Finding the Key: Selected Writings of Alexander Goehr, ed. D. Puffett, London, Faber, 1998
Grey, T. "Metaphorical Modes in Nineteenth-Century Music Criticism: Image, Narrative, and Idea," in *Music and Text: Critical Enquiries*, ed. S. Scher, Cambridge University Press, 1992, pp. 93–117
Haimo, E. *Schoenberg's Serial Odyssey: The Evolution of His Twelve-tone Method, 1914–1928*, Oxford, Clarendon Press, 1990
"Atonality, Analysis, and the Intentional Fallacy," *MTS* 18 (1996), pp. 165–99
Hanslick, E. *The Beautiful in Music*, trans. G. Cohen (1891), introduced by M. Weitz, Indianapolis, Bobbs-Merrill, 1957; reprint New York, Da Capo, 1974
On the Musically Beautiful, trans. G. Payzant, Indianapolis, Hackett, 1986
Hasty, C. "Segmentation and Process in Post-Tonal Music," *MTS* 3 (1981), pp. 54–73
Hatch, C. and D. Bernstein, eds., *Music Theory and the Exploration of the Past*, University of Chicago Press, 1993
Keller, H. "The Chamber Music," in *The Mozart Companion*, ed. H. C. Robbins Landon and D. Mitchell, New York, Norton, 1969
Lerdahl, F. and R. Jackendoff, *A Generative Theory of Tonal Music*, Cambridge, MA, MIT Press, 1983

Lester, J. *Analytical Approaches to Twentieth-Century Music*, New York, Norton, 1989
Lévi-Strauss, C. *The Raw and the Cooked: Introduction to a Science of Mythology*, vol. 1, trans. J. and D. Weightman, London, J. Cape, 1969
Meyer, L. B. "A Pride of Prejudices; Or, Delight in Diversity," *MTS* 13 (1991), pp. 241–51
Molino, J. "Musical Fact and the Semiology of Music," trans. J. Underwood, *MA* 9 (1990), pp. 105–55
Monelle, R. *Linguistics and Semiotics in Music*, Chur, Harwood, 1992
Morris, D. "A Semiotic Investigation of Messiaen's 'Abîme des oiseaux,'" *MA* 8 (1989), pp. 125–58
Nattiez, J.-J. *Fondements d'une sémiologie de la musique*, Paris, Union générale d'éditions, 1975
"Varèse's 'Density 21.5': A Study in Semiological Analysis," trans. A. Barry, *MA* 1 (1982), pp. 243–340
Music and Discourse: Toward a Semiology of Music, trans. C. Abbate, Princeton University Press, 1990
"Simha Arom and the Return of Analysis to Ethnomusicology," *MA* 12 (1993), pp. 241–62
Rahn, J. "Some Remarks on Network Models on Music," in *Musical Transformation and Musical Intuition: Eleven Essays in Honor of David Lewin*, ed. R. Atlas and M. Cherlin, Roxbury, MA, Ovenbird Press, 1994, pp. 225–35
Reaney, G. "The Middle Ages," in *A History of Song*, ed. D. Stevens, London, Hutchinson, 1960, pp. 15–64
Réti, R. *The Thematic Process in Music*, London, Faber, 1961
Ruwet, N. "Methods of Analysis in Musicology," trans. M. Everist, *MA* 6 (1987), pp. 3–36
Saussure, F. de, *Course in General Linguistics* (1915), trans. W. Baskin, ed. C. Bally and A. Sechehaye, New York, Philosophical Library, 1959
Schenker, H. *Free Composition* (1935), trans. and ed. E. Oster, New York, Longman, 1979
Schoenberg, A. "Criteria for the Evaluation of Music," in *Style and Idea*, London, Faber, 1975, pp. 124–36
Fundamentals of Musical Composition, ed. G. Strang, London, Faber, 1970
The Musical Idea and the Logic, Technique, and Art of its Presentation, trans. and ed. P. Carpenter and S. Neff, New York, Columbia University Press, 1995
Simms, B. "A Theory of Pitch-Class Sets," in *Models of Analysis: Early Twentieth-Century Music*, ed. J. Dunsby, Oxford, B. Blackwell, 1993, pp. 114–31
Street, A. "Superior Myths, Dogmatic Allegories: The Resistance to Musical Unity," *MA* 8 (1989), pp. 77–123
Tarasti, E. *A Theory of Musical Semiotics*, Bloomington, Indiana University Press, 1994
Treitler, L. "Language and the Interpretation of Music," in *Music and Meaning*, ed. J. Robinson, Ithaca, Cornell University Press, 1997, pp. 23–56
Wallin, N. *Biomusicology: Neurophysiological, Neuropsychological and Evolutionary Perspectives on the Origins and Purposes of Music*, Stuyvesant, NY, Pendragon Press, 1991
Wason, R. "Signposts on Webern's Path to Atonality: *The Dehmel Lieder* (1906–08)," in *Music Theory in Concept and Practice*, ed. J. Baker, D. Beach, and J. Bernard, University of Rochester Press, 1997, pp. 409–32
Webern, A. *The Path to the New Music*, Bryn Mawr, T. Presser, 1963
Whittall, A. "The *Vier ernste Gesänge* Op. 121: Enrichment and Uniformity," in *Brahms: Biographical, Documentary and Analytical Studies*, ed. R. Pascall, Cambridge University Press, 1983, pp. 191–207

IVB MUSIC PSYCHOLOGY

· 30 ·

Energetics

LEE ROTHFARB

As a rubric for music-theoretical literature focused on music's dynamic qualities, "energetics" is unrestrictively broad in scope on the one hand, and restrictively narrow on the other. It is broad because ever since ancient times authors have identified motion as a fundamental aspect of music, and narrow because specific references to "energy" in music, or analogies with force, power, or similar concepts from the domain of physics, are historically limited, appearing first with regularity in the decades straddling 1900. In fact, the term energetics was first coined in 1934 by an historian of aesthetics, Rudolf Schäfke, who proposed it as a way of characterizing the work of several theorists active in the early twentieth century, primarily Heinrich Schenker, August Halm, and Ernst Kurth, although the nature and language of certain contemporaries, likewise German-speaking (Arnold Schering, Hans Mersmann, Kurt Westphal), associate them with energetics.[1] As Schäfke points out (p. 395), if authors had long recognized the primacy of motion and tonal flux in music, they did not thematize motion to the same degree as did the energeticists, or isolate it from music's affects. If we set aside for a moment the long line of pre-twentieth-century writings that contain traces of energetics and focus instead on those that represent its maturity, the following five characteristics will be useful for orienting ourselves to the subject, bearing in mind that some may be more pronounced in a given author's work than others:

1. Thematization of "force." This metaphor leads to various characterizations of music: as a biology of tones (Schenker); an organism (Fritz Jöde); a drama of forces (Halm); an interplay of potential and kinetic energies (Ernst Kurth); invocations of musical spatiality and contours of force (Ernst Kurth, Hans Mersmann, Kurt Westphal, Victor Zuckerkandl); alternating phases of tension and release (Arnold Schering).
2. Musical logic. References to musical logic (*Gesetzmäßigkeit*) mean understanding the succession of events in a piece as unfolding according to properties residing exclusively within the tones, and forces arising from their combinations, apart from

1 Rudolf Schäfke, *Geschichte der Musikästhetik*, pp. 393–450. Schäfke had earlier proposed the term energetics in a lecture entitled "Musikästhetik und musikalischer Einführungsunterricht."

extramusical factors (text or program). The emphasis on internal logic aims at separating the logical from the psychological, thus aligning energeticists with Edmund Husserl's anti-psychologistic viewpoint. Indeed, in 1920 Mersmann posited a new analytical methodology which he explicitly called phenomenological. Halm described his own aesthetic writings in much the same way. Around 1920, the aesthetician Arthur W. Cohn discerned the new mode of musical understanding in Halm's and others' work, and identified its philosophical and methodological roots in phenomenology (Husserl, Hans Scheler).[2]

3. Centrality of form. Energeticist analysis focuses heavily upon musical form. It does so by specifying the functional significance of interdependent formal units, and by showing how those units are integrated into a dynamic whole. In viewing form as the result of a holistic, dynamic synthesis, energeticists distinguish themselves from nineteenth-century "formalists" as well as from "atomistic" (thematic) analysts who fall short of, or make little or no attempt at, synthesis.
4. Antihistoricism. Because energeticists hold to premises asserted as natural "law," and ignore all extramusical, social, and biographical factors in their consideration of music, they tend to take an absolutist (non-relativistic) stance on the evolution of music. Like Husserl, they claim apodictic certainty for their analyses independent of any historical consideration and thus view their work as a foundation for authoritative criticism.
5. Cultural-ethical mission. In a time of political turmoil, cultural decline, and attendant utopian ambitions, energeticists saw themselves as missionaries with the sacred duty of rescuing and reviving a moribund musical culture. They saw their task as saving the canon of masterworks and its creators from vulgarization at the hands of popularizing critics and misguided readers, as well as educating a new generation of musical amateurs and professionals to understand, appreciate, and become committed advocates for high musical art.

Prerequisite to discussing energetics is an understanding of the idea of musical motion, a phenomenon which is at once intuitively plain to listeners, yet on close study conceptually problematic. A basic question is: what moves in music? In attempting to answer that question, another, even more fundamental, one arises: what constitutes movement in music? As Victor Zuckerkandl and others have stressed, tones do not move. In a melody, the archetypal example of musical motion, a tone of some frequency is replaced by a new one of a different frequency. The first one does not move to become the second; rather, the second instantaneously supplants the first. The succession involves two distinct tones (pitch plateaus) and an abrupt shift from one to the other.

2 Mersmann, "Versuch einer Phänomenologie der Musik," pp. 226–69 (Halm mentioned on p. 227); Mersmann, "Zur Phänomenologie der Musik," pp. 372–97; Halm, "Von meinem Schaffen," p. 301; "Über mein musikalisches Schaffen," *Von Form und Sinn der Musik*, p. 289; Cohn, "Das Erwachen der Ästhetik," pp. 669–79 (mentions Halm pp. 669, 673); "Das musikalische Verständnis," pp. 129–35 (mentions Halm p. 135).

There is no continuous transition between plateaus as is characteristic of motion – or at least not motion in the usual sense of *loco*motion (change of place). Musical motion does not qualify as locomotion because a tone, as an aural object, does not change locale.[3]

Even more puzzling than the idea of musical motion, perhaps, is the idea of an impelling force – the energy of energetics – that induces the changes perceived as musical motion. Motion, even of the qualitative, non-spatial sort ("change") implies a motive force (Aristotle's efficient cause). Kurth posits such a motive force to be psychological – a kind of psychic energy. A composer's psychic flow, embodied in the music, manifests itself primarily in melody, notably in "linear" counterpoint (Bach), but also in harmonic contrasts (dominant–subdominant, major–minor) and, most powerfully, in highly chromatic harmony (Wagner and Bruckner), which magnifies the melodic energy of the leading tone. Schering likewise proposes a mental source – the unceasing tension-release cycles of the mind – symbolized in music by rhythmic, intervallic, melodic, and harmonic configurations aimed at effecting a "psychic resonance" in aural experience. Zuckerkandl considers but then dismisses both Theodor Lipps's "pulse theory" and associationist explanations for musical dynamism, and propounds instead a theory which casts tones as "dynamic symbols." The energy that inhabits the symbols springs from directional forces inherent in the scale (of traditional tonality), which he conceives as a "dynamic field," a referential frame within which tones move.

The ideas of Kurth, Schering, and Zuckerkandl all rely on symbolism, an oft-visited subject in late nineteenth-century aesthetics. The attraction of symbolist ideas to the energeticists should be clear. If the idea of concrete mimetic content in music proved precarious (whether of specific images or generalized affections), a symbolic interpretation might offer a way of rescuing music from sheer formalism. But if such symbolic content was to be communicable and generally comprehensible, a theory of intersubjectivity was required. In the late nineteenth and early twentieth centuries, such a theory was found in "empathy" (*Einfühlung*), first alluded to in the writings of Johann Gottfried von Herder, and later developed in aesthetics by Hermann Lotze, Friedrich T. Vischer, Robert Vischer, Johannes Volkelt, and Theodor Lipps, and in the historical hermeneutics of Wilhelm Dilthey and Johann Gustav Droysen. In the Hanslickian formalist world, where content tended to dissolve into form, symbolism and empathic aural experience were the keys to salvaging the notion of musical content.[4] Tones, as dynamic symbols, as organisms, as sonic embodiments of psychic energy, attract and repel, strive toward and away from each other. A motive may ascend to power, vanquishing others, may "live its fate like a personage in a drama" (Schenker), in a symbolic "drama of forces" (Halm), as a "symbol of interior life" (Schering).[5]

3 See Scruton, *The Aesthetics of Music*, pp. 19–20.

4 Hanslick, *On the Musically Beautiful*, p. 80 ("in music we see content and form . . . fused in an obscure, inseparable unity").

5 Schenker, *Harmony*, p. 13; Halm, *Von zwei Kulturen*, p. 50; Schering, *Musikalische Bildung*, p. 83. Unless otherwise noted, all translations are my own.

Precursors of energetics in music

As noted above, there were many precursors to energeticist thought in the history of music theory. In the following section, we will consider a few of them, with an understanding that our selection and discussion will be more illustrative than systematic.

Musical dynamics in Greek thought

We began this chapter with the observation that motion was considered by ancient writers to be a quintessential attribute of music. Motion was of course required to create sound and for air to propagate it. But motion was also associated with time, which was conceived of as measured, ordered motion.[6] The characteristic quality of tones in music is change of various sorts: of location, frequency, amplitude, speed, duration, timbre, density, complexity, and so forth. As understood by ancient Greek writers, change is the source of motion, where motion means change that is quantitative (in size or number), qualitative (in nature or constitution), spatial (of location), and temporal. Conversely, everything that is in motion is necessarily changing.

The extraordinary ethical power of music was thought to derive from its inherent motion – motion being the recognized foundation of existence. Aristoxenus, the first author to attempt a sustained technical discussion of music, is also the first to go beyond metaphysical speculation and theorize concretely about musical motion. In explaining how the voice moves when singing melody, he touches several times on a unique functional quality of notes – which he calls *dynameis* – determined by their position within the tetrachord: "in respect of the magnitudes of intervals and the pitches of notes, the facts about melody seem to be in some ways indeterminate, but in respect of functions (*dynameis*), forms and positions they appear to be determinate and ordered."[7] The very word itself makes plain that Aristoxenus's notion of melody is related to a modern energeticist conception, where each note, as a scale degree, has an identity and directional tendency.

Although Aristoxenus refers only cursorily to *dynameis*, he has clearly identified a distinctive attribute of tones that imbues them with dynamic individuality ("The functions [*dynameis*] of the notes can change while the magnitude remains the same"). Melodies, too have dynamic qualities that we may apprehend through reason ("Understanding melodies is a matter of following with both hearing and reason things as they come to be . . . for it is in a process of coming to be that melody consists").[8] Aristoxenus's theory of dynamic functionality in tones is remarkably modern when compared with Zuckerkandl's conclusions: "The experience of tonal motion has

6 The Pythagoreans and, later, Plato and Aristotle equated time with motion (*Timaeus*, 37d–38a; Aristotle, *Physics*, Book IV, Chapter 11, 219a; also Plotinus, *Ennead* III, sections 7–8).

7 Aristoxenus, *Elementa Harmonica*, Book II, in Barker, *Greek Musical Writings*, vol. II, p. 180.

8 Barker, *Greek Musical Writings*, vol. II, pp. 150, 151, 152, 155.

its origin not in differences of pitch but in differences of dynamic quality. The whole argument about the spatial character of pitch differences [Aristoxenus's 'magnitudes'] does not even touch the problem."[9]

Dynamism in medieval counterpoint

The preoccupation during the Middle Ages with regulating part-movement in multi-voiced textures highlighted the dynamic qualities of tones. Treatises in the fourteenth and fifteenth centuries speak of imperfect consonances and dissonances "requiring" or "demanding" a subsequent perfect consonance, as in the cadential interval progressions of the major sixth resolving outward to an octave (the *clausula formalis*), the minor third resolving inward to the unison and the major third resolving outward to the perfect fifth. Each species of consonance requires a specific, subsequent consonance according to its nature.[10] Jacques of Liège is explicit on the matter (*Speculum musicae*, 1321–25): "an imperfect concord strives (*nititur*) to attain a more perfect concord;" and Ugolino of Orvieto (*Declaratio musicae disciplinae*) speaks of how an imperfect consonance "ardently burns" to achieve perfection, "to which it is driven (*coacta movetur*)."[11] Subsequent writers on counterpoint follow in their predecessors' conceptual and verbal footsteps (Tinctoris, 1477; Gaffurio, 1496). It is not hard to imagine that in so describing those cadential progressions, counterpoint teachers had in mind and ear the characteristic semitone connection, which puts the imperfect in close proximity to the allied perfect consonance to which each tends.

Of course fourteenth- and fifteenth-century references to an interval that desires, requires, or seeks (*appetit*) a subsequent one do not mean that writers thought of the intervals as energetic in a modern sense. For medieval thinkers, imperfect intervals lack something, which they metaphorically seek in their successors in order to achieve completeness (perfection). We might, however, interpret a little further from an Aristotelian view. First, treatises of this time set as an objective for good counterpoint changing interval quality, from perfect to imperfect and vice versa.[12] The transition from one interval to the next involves change, the root of musical motion. Qualitative changes in a succession of intervals thus exemplify a type of motion and not just of imperfect elements seeking perfection. Further, in instructing that a discrete passage of counterpoint must begin and end with a perfect consonance, treatises imply that successions of intervening imperfect consonances, collectively seeking perfection, are transient links between perfect consonances. From an Aristotelian view, the transient, imperfect consonances might be thought of individually and cumulatively as the

9 Zuckerkandl, *Sound and Symbol*, p. 93.

10 See Sachs, *Der Contrapunctus im 14. und 15. Jahrhundert*, pp. 66, 67, 82, 109.

11 Jacques of Liège, *Speculum musicae*, vol. IV, pp. 122–23; Ugolino of Orvieto, *Declaratio musicae disciplinae*, vol. II, p. 12. David Cohen cites these passages in "Arisotelian Physics and the Early Concept of Harmonic Progression." Translations are his.

12 Sachs, *Der Contrapunctus*, pp. 59, 113, 114; Dahlhaus, *Origin of Harmonic Tonality*, pp. 71–80.

efficient cause of, i.e., the initiators of the motion toward, perfections. The transience amounts to mobility (the arrivals at perfections, stability), where each imperfect interval manifests a dynamic impulse.

Musical rhetoric as energetic metaphor

Throughout the Baroque era, one of the most commonly invoked metaphors in discussions of music was the oration. Just as an effective oration should sway opinions and move minds, an effective musical work should arouse affections. To this end, techniques of rhetoric were often called upon by theorists as a model for the composer to emulate. To a musical rhetorician, a piece of music is an oration in sound, for Christoph Bernhard a *Rede in der Music*, for Mattheson a *Klang-Rede*.[13] Music unfolds in a sequence of logically arranged periods that lead the listener through a series of "arguments" so that, ultimately, "the proposition [may] be more clearly grasped." The movement arising from the purposive development inherent in the rhetorical *dispositio* suggests a dynamic image of a musical work.[14]

The rhetorical approach to understanding music was so well established by the time Mattheson published his *Der vollkommene Capellmeister* that it was possible for him to rely on rhetorical design for explaining untexted, instrumental music, and to maintain that "even if words were not used," still the music may have its effect.[15] A composer of instrumental music "must know how without the words to express sincerely all the emotions of the heart through selected sounds and their skillful combination in such a way that the auditor might fully grasp and clearly understand therefrom, as if it were actual speech, the impetus (*Trieb*), the sense, the meaning, and the expression . . ." Mattheson's use of *Trieb* (from *treiben*, to drive forward) is striking because it suggests that he imagines a force that underlies the hierarchically organized phrase syntax and propels the music through an unfolding rhetorical trajectory.[16]

Heinrich Christoph Koch (1749–1817) carried the music-rhetorical tradition to its height. Like Mattheson, Koch's language also implies a dynamism powering the musico-rhetorical process, particularly in connection with the symphony. The initial section of the symphony, for example, exhibits phrases that "are linked so that their phrase-endings are less perceptible." (See also **Chapter 28, pp. 881–82**) Koch further notes: "For the most part, a melodic section is directly connected with the caesura tone of the preceding phrase." Owing to continuous elisions, the melodic sections "flow more forcefully (*stärker fortströmen*)," and momentum is thereby built up and sustained. In contrast to the sonata, which "must present the finest nuances of feelings," the symphony distinguishes itself "through force and energy (*Kraft und Nachdruck*)."[17] Koch

13 Bernhard, *Tractatus compositionis augmentatus*, p. 82; Mattheson, *Der vollkommene Capellmeister*, p. 380 (Part II, Chapter 9).

14 The history of rhetoric in music is discussed in **Chapter 27, passim**.

15 Mattheson, *Der vollkommene Capellmeister*, pp. 424, 426 (Part II, Chapter 12, §§30, 36).

16 Ibid., p. 425 (Part II, Chapter 12, §31).

17 Koch, *Introductory Essay on Composition*, pp. 199 (§101), 203 (§108).

isolates such force and energy not for their analytical or compositional interest, but for their importance to the rhetorical unfolding of a work. In counseling students to arrange sections in sequence "as though they could not possibly follow otherwise," he seems to be aware as well that the force is guided by logic, imbuing a work with a sense of inevitability.[18]

A. B. Marx and the dynamics of form

Fifty years after Koch, Adolf Bernhard Marx (1795–1866) continued the rhetorical tradition but modified it, crucially, into an organicist view of musical form, which rose to prominence and eventually superseded the rhetorical one during the first half of the nineteenth century. The emphasis shifts away from listener response toward the music's internal growth processes, which reflect a composer's spiritual motion. The distinction between the two approaches is subtle but important.[19] Both are based on the premise of a logically founded sequence of events. But in the organicist view there is added attention to the processes of germination and growth across the piece, and it is the focus on those dynamic processes that associates Marx's analyses, and those of the organicist tradition generally, with energetics.

Marx characterizes a primary period (*Hauptsatz*) as "the first-determined entity, in initial freshness and energy, further the more energetic, marked and more ideally structured element." A main thematic section (A) should convey a sense of growth toward the ensuing section (B). "A period (*Satz*) is not internally satisfying if it evokes a *spiritual motion* that it cannot fulfill, if it alludes to a content that it is unable to exhaust within its own context" (emphasis mine).[20] It is the composer's interior spiritual motion, a residual energy embodied in the music, that makes a period incomplete and require continuation. At the modified return of A and an appended section, the music traces Marx's normative dynamic schema, *Ruhe–Bewegung–Ruhe* (rest–motion–rest), where the initial *Ruhe* contains not only the motivic germ but also, and crucially, the dynamic spark ("spiritual motion") that initiates the formal process by driving toward the *Bewegung*, and where the final *Ruhe* arises from, and appears as the outcome of, the preceding music.[21]

Tonal harmonic theory

Because musical form deals with the overall flow of a musical work, it lends itself naturally to dynamic interpretations. But energeticist views of music are not limited to ideas about musical form. Harmony treatises of the eighteenth and early nineteenth

18 Koch, *Versuch einer Anleitung zur Composition*, vol. II, p. 56: "all parts are connected such that they follow one another as though they could not possibly follow otherwise" (my translation).

19 Bonds, *Wordless Rhetoric*, pp. 132–49.

20 Marx, *Lehre von der musikalischen Komposition*, vol. III, pp. 273, 92–93. Translations mine.

21 Ibid., p. 99. For more on Marx's ideas on form, see **Chapter 28, pp. 887–89**.

centuries rely implicitly, in some cases quite explicitly, on the notion of impelling forces to explain tone movements and chord progressions. Jean-Philippe Rameau, for instance, speaks of the "perfect cadence" – a falling-fifth fundamental bass applied to the model *clausula formalis* (major sixth resolving outward to the octave) – in much the same way that medieval theorists spoke of interval dynamics: the movement from a less to a more perfect sonority.[22] However, as Thomas Christensen observes, Rameau introduces a new mechanistic element to his theory as presented in his *Traité de l'harmonie* (1722) by positing the dissonant seventh as the primary motivating force of the fundamental bass, the "tonal equivalent of Galileo's *vis motrix*." Dissonance becomes a harmonic force that disrupts the equilibrium of consonance and furnishes an impetus that drives any harmonic progression. Rameau analogizes the resolution of dissonance with the motion of colliding solids, which absorb and transfer motion from/to one another.[23] In his *Génération harmonique* (1737) he replaces this mechanistic model with a gravitational one; in what may be described as a Newtonian conception of tonality, the symmetry of a dominant and subdominant around the tonic creates a force that draws chord progressions toward a center of gravity. (See **Chapter 23, p. 734.**)

If Rameau can be credited with formulating a view of tonality based on forces arising from the polar opposition of dominant and subdominant, it was François-Joseph Fétis (1784–1871) who more than a century later proposed a theory of energy-laden tones operating in a dynamic force field (*Traité complet*, 1844). Fétis's pitch "affinities" (*affinités*) "give to the successions of one type or another a character of necessity that is designated in general by the name of *tonality*."[24] Accordingly, the theory of harmony is concerned with "discovering and revealing the laws of affinities which determine the characteristics of tonality," and with "establishing the laws of succession, by reason of the affinities."[25]

The melodic and harmonic affinities of tones are not merely abstract notions but rather technically defined properties of scale degrees. Fétis specifies the relative reposefulness of each degree and how accompanying tones may enhance or diminish its properties. Combining scale degree $\hat{4}$ with $\hat{7}$, for instance, which forms an augmented fourth or diminished fifth, produces an "appellative consonance" (*consonance appellative*), in that it "summons" certain resolutions. Sounding like Kurth, he says "It is remarkable that these intervals characterize modern tonality by the energetic tendencies (*tendances énergiques*) of their constituent notes."[26] Finally, Fétis coins the term "attractional" (*attractif*) for intervals formed by altered (nonscalar) notes. When such intervals are used, our enjoyment of the music is outside of the otherwise "perfect rapport with tonality among the sounds." The result is "agitations, impassioned movements, and

22 Rameau, *Treatise*, Book I, pp. 62–66. For more on Rameau's theory of the fundamental bass, see **Chapter 24**.

23 Christensen, *Rameau and Musical Thought in the Enlightenment*, pp. 106, 107–08 Also see **Chapter 24, pp. 762–4.**

24 Fétis, *Traité complet*, p. 2 (§§5–6).

25 Ibid., pp. 3 (§9), 4 (§13). For more on Fétis's dynamic concept of *tonalité* see **Chapter 23, pp. 129–30.**

26 Fétis, *Traité complet*, pp. 8–9 (§25).

nervous crises, expressed by the contact of diverse tonalities and by the alternations of consonances and dissonances."[27] Kurth could easily have written that sentence to describe *Tristan* in *Romantische Harmonik*, published nearly eighty years later and at a vast cultural distance.

One of Fétis's little-known composition students, Albert-Joseph Vivier (1816–1903), similarly espoused a dynamic view of tones, intervals, chords, and tonality. However, he modified Fétis's basic assumption from a system that was scale-generated to one that was chord-generated, and carried the idea of tone affinities and attractional harmonies to their logical, tonality-threatening conclusions.[28] For Vivier, the tonic is the only truly reposeful chord; all others are in motion toward the tonic. This is because he interprets all chords composed of scale degrees other than 1, 3, and 5 as either appoggiatura or suspension formations leaning toward the tonic. Indeed, the last edition of Vivier's *Traité* (1903) dispenses altogether with the notion of nonharmonic tones and replaces it with "attractions," and even recognizes nontertian sonorities as fundamental.[29] Consequently, all chords, altered *and* diatonic, become neighbor-note displacements of the tonic.

> Basing ourselves on the consideration that consonant and dissonant chords have a marked tendency constantly to return to the perfect chord of the first degree – that is to say, that they are subject to a real influence of attraction toward the chord of repose – we demonstrate that almost all chords are derived, directly or indirectly, from the perfect chord of the first degree.[30]

As Renata Groth has observed, Vivier's conception of harmony is one grand dynamic process (*Bewegungsvorgang*).[31]

Riemann's theory of musical dynamics and agogics

Hugo Riemann's (1849–1919) extensive writings on harmonic theory are generally well known.[32] Less familiar perhaps is Riemann's study of phrasing, based on "musical dynamics and agogics," in which dynamics means tone volume, not tone motion. To interpret phrasing, Riemann links dynamics to changes affecting a variety of musical parameters, primarily rhythm but also melodic contour and harmony.[33] Such changes reflect a pervasive musical life-force (*Lebenskraft*). "The smallest components into which musical structures may be analyzed – tone groups of two or three units – . . . represent . . . a small organism of a peculiar life-force. It is thus justified that they receive

27 Ibid., p. 10 (§28). 28 Vivier, *Traité complet* (1862).

29 Groth, *Die französische Kompositionslehre*, p. 57; see also her "Harmonik und Tonalität in der Interpretation des belgischen Theoretikers Albert-Joseph Vivier (1816–1903)."

30 Vivier, *Traité complet*, p. ii (cited in Groth, *Die französische Kompositionslehre*, p. 64.) Translation mine.

31 Groth, *Die französische Kompositionslehre*, pp. 64, 65.

32 See **Chapter 25, pp. 796–800**; and **Chapter 14, pp. 465–71** for further discussion of Riemann's tonal theories.

33 See **Chapter 21, pp. 683–91** for an introduction to Riemann's theory of dynamics and agogics.

the name motive (element of motion)." The performer who has "*recognized and felt the rich content in animated force and motion in* [compound] *metrical-rhythmic formations . . . will fill the individual shapes with musical life so that they come to full and clear effect*" (emphasis Riemann's). In addition to metrical-rhythmic disposition, melodic contour affects the interpretive use of dynamics. Ascending melodies with *crescendo* imply "increased life-force with diminishing mass (expanding upward)," while ascending melodies with *diminuendo* imply "decreasing life-force (dissipation)"; analogous qualities were assigned to descending melodies that *crescendo* or *diminuendo*.[34] Even rests have dynamic value (Chapter 6); they indicate a growth or decline in the life-force established contextually by the melodic contour and phrasing. Interior rests (those within a phrase as opposed to at its beginning or end) sustain the energy of the ongoing musical activity (§32).

The energeticist school

The work of theorists reviewed in the preceding paragraphs all share an underlying assumption of musical dynamism that emerges with varying emphasis and specificity in their writings. As we have seen, dynamism is a nearly universal *topos* in music-theoretical writings since the ancient Greeks. But as Schäfke also correctly noted, it was only at the turn of the twentieth century that a fully explicit school of "energetic" thought can be identified. In the following sections, we will consider in more detail the ideas of several of these theorists, beginning with the work of August Halm and Heinrich Schenker, and then moving on to Ernst Kurth, who arguably articulated the most comprehensive and thorough-going theory of energetics. We will then look at the writings of Arnold Schering, Hans Mersmann, and Kurt Westphal, concluding with a brief consideration of some more recent music-theoretical writings in which distinct resonances of energeticist thought may be detected.

August Halm and Heinrich Schenker. The ideas of August Halm (1869–1929) and Heinrich Schenker (1868–1935) are the framework and reference points for Schäfke's energetics. A significant motivation for both men in viewing music and writing about it as they did was a perceived collapse of traditional German music culture. This collapse, in their view, entailed not only the decline of compositional technique but also the degeneration of professional music criticism, music-educational conviction, aesthetic values and, with those convictions and values, the corruption of public understanding and appreciation of the revered German musical canon.[35] They sought to stem what they believed to be this alarming cultural and critical erosion of their generation.

34 Riemann, *Musikalische Dynamik und Agogik*, pp. 11, 69, 173. See also Bent, *Analysis*, p. 80.
35 See Rothfarb, "Music Analysis, Cultural Morality, and Sociology in the Writings of August Halm"; "The 'New Education' and Music Theory, 1900–1925."

Halm's vitalist conception of music displaces from the center of analytical interest an emerging preoccupation with the moods, emotions, personality, and life of the composer and listener, and focuses attention on intrinsic musical processes as manifest in the tonal ebb and flow, tension and release, interior dynamic escalations and attenuations of small and large scope. This thematization of musical forces is clear in his earliest publication, a harmony manual published in 1900. There, we learn that the essence of music is "life and motion"; the major third is the "impelling force (*Trieb*) and germ of movement"; and that dominant–tonic progressions, music's primal "dynamic impulse (*Bewegungsanstoß*)," possess their own "energy." Chords are not "inanimate stones placed arbitrarily one after another but rather animate relationships, motion and tendency, organic growth."[36] The key to understanding music is a "knowledge of musical processes, of the function of musical forces as they operate in chords and chord progressions, in forms." For Halm, those forces were not something imaginary or obscure but rather "the actually concrete element" in music.[37] Similarly, Schenker's *Harmonielehre* (1906) acknowledges the "biological urges" of tones, and the "force of the scale-step" that subsumes several chords into one unit. The theory of the *Urlinie* is founded on the idea that it "conceals within itself the seeds of all forces that shape tone-life," and "imparts life to the motive, the melody." It "signifies motion, striving toward a goal, and ultimately the completion of this course."[38] Like that of their predecessors reaching back to antiquity, the language of Schenker and Halm is rooted in a dynamic conception of music. But their development of this idea is more thoroughgoing, deliberate, and technically specific than that of authors of past centuries.

Musical forces are for Halm and Schenker not mere metaphors invoked for poetic or heuristic purposes. Both theorists explain in detail harmonic and melodic techniques by which forces manifest themselves, and the logic that governs them. For Halm, art is a "piece of world order," music an illustration of "*Logos* manifest in tones," the "rationality" of musical construction "the most important discovery of human musicality." This inner logic springs from harmony as it operates in traditional tonality.[39] Music's autonomous logic frees it from externally imposed programs and imagery, as well as from common emotionalizing. Halm demonstrates this logic through analyses, among them discussions of the C major prelude from Book 1 of Bach's *Well-tempered Clavier*, Beethoven's "Waldstein" and "Tempest" sonatas, and the development section from the *Pastoral* Symphony.[40] For Schenker, too, "music is emancipated from every external obligation" (words, stage, narrative); "tones mean nothing but themselves . . . as

36 Halm, *Harmonielehre*, pp. 14, 26, 27, 52.

37 Halm, "Reden bei Gelegenheit musikalischer Vorträge," p. 62; *Einführung in die Musik*, p. 139.

38 Schenker, *Harmony*, pp. 6, 155, 158; *Tonwille* pp. 1, 23; *Free Composition*, p. 4.

39 Halm, *Von zwei Kulturen*, p. 251; unpaginated diary entry of 1923 (Deutsches Literaturarchiv, Marbach, protocol 69458); "Rationale Musik!," pp. 153, 155; *Beethoven*, p. 321.

40 Halm, "Musikalische Logik," pp. 486–87, 545–47; "Musikalische Bildung," *Von Form und Sinn der Musik*, pp. 212–14; *Von zwei Kulturen*, pp. 38–81, 84–107, 107–11. See my "Hermeneutics and Energetics"; "The 'New Education' and Music Theory"; "Beethoven's Formal Dynamics: August Halm's Phenomenological Perspective."

living beings with their own social laws." Counterpoint in three, four, and more voices exhibits "causalities" whose necessity increases in free counterpoint owing to scale-steps, which have their own "immanent logic of development." What matters when "dealing with a work of art is to perceive with all senses the necessity unique to it."[41] Musical logic as a reflection of rationality was for Halm a sign that music, with its internal forces, has cosmic significance as a "spiritual power" (*geistige Macht*) that is vital for nourishing and promoting the human intellect and, hence, for enriching and sustaining culture.[42]

Halm and Schenker believed the intrinsic logic of tonality and the raw musical forces governed by it were universally valid and timeless. They often express their ideas, therefore, in the form of ahistorical pronouncements. "We do not hear historically," Halm proclaims, "and we should not do so, either . . . Further, we do not need any historical knowledge in order to feel the value of music, or even to judge it." Art that was good from the start "is still so today and remains so for always." In evaluating pictorial art we do not consult calendars or historical tables. Why, then, asks Halm, do we insist on doing it with music? "The next thing that is urgently necessary is an antihistorical sense."[43] Schenker was likewise contemptuous of the historicist perspective: "What is the use, in musical histories, monographs, and biographies, of focusing chiefly on only the extraneous events, when they can never help us understand the art-work itself?" He dismisses the notion of *Zeitgeist* as "a real nuisance and plague in our literature . . . when that other, more important, care that should be devoted to the works themselves is lacking." While "empires can doubtless come and go . . . languages can die and give way to new ones . . . tonal art . . . remains, after a centuries-long evolution, an art based in its ultimate products on laws immutable from nation to nation, from race to race, from century to century . . . tonal art will never rest on laws different from those discovered in it by the great Masters!"[44] Halm's and Schenker's absolutist outlook may be as much a reaction against the compositional experiments of the early twentieth century that threatened the tonal system as a reaction to nineteenth-century historicism.[45]

Following Kant, Halm recognizes form as the abiding guarantor of aesthetic value. It is the "will" and "drive of music," the ebb and flow of musical forces in a "drama of forces" that is played out in the logical arrangement of a work's components and their constituents, all of which have dynamically defined formal functions.[46] As the "purpose of the [composer's] spiritual effort," form is "that which is communicable," in contrast to psychological or poetic content, which is not reliably communicable.

41 Schenker, *Counterpoint*, vol. I, pp. 15, 16; *Counterpoint*, vol. II, pp. 6–7; *Harmony*, p. 158; *Beethoven's Ninth Symphony*, p. 7. 42 Halm, "Musik und Leben," *Von Form und Sinn der Musik*, p. 241.

43 Halm, *Beethoven*, p. 93; *Von zwei Kulturen*, p. 233; "Musikgeschichtliches: Ein Vergleich," *Von Grenzen und Ländern der Musik*, pp. 221–22.

44 Schenker, *Counterpoint*, vol. I, p. xxiv; *Beethoven's Ninth Symphony*, p. 19.

45 Halm, "Rationale Musik!," *Von Form und Sinn der Musik*, p. 80; Schenker, *Harmony*, pp. 59, 69, 136, 137. 46 Halm, *Beethoven*, p. 119 (*Wille* and *Trieb*); *Von zwei Kulturen*, p. 50 (*Drama von Kräften*).

The "cultivation of musical form – the consistent if often also self-denying willingness to recognize the will of music and to adhere to it alone" – is for Halm the only remedy for the intoxication of egocentric engagement with music, which focuses on inner experiences and emotions.[47] For Schenker, form is likewise a dynamic process, conceived within the framework of structural levels. Musical form, he explains, is "in an almost physical-mechanical sense . . . an energy transformation – a transformation of the forces which flow from the background to the foreground through the structural levels." While Schenker says this near the end of *Free Composition*, in the section on "Form in General" (§301), the idea of energy coursing through the structural levels derives from statements made early in the treatise (§§29–30), where we learn that the transformation levels represent "motion from foreground to background or the reverse," and that "all growth . . . finds its fulfillment only through the control of the fundamental structure (*Ursatz*) and its transformations." These "constitute a delaying, a retardation (*Aufhaltung*)," which creates tension in the transformations from background to foreground, the "final goal" of the motion.[48] That Schenker conceives form dynamically is a natural outgrowth of his theory of the *Urlinie*, which – as pointed out above – he had envisioned already in 1921 as embodying "the seeds of all forces that shape tone-life."

Ernst Kurth. The Viennese-born Ernst Kurth (1886–1946) trained as a musicologist at the University of Vienna under Guido Adler, and taught at the University of Bern from 1913 up to his death at age sixty. From the start of his academic career, Kurth boldly explores new paths in a habilitation study, *The Requirements for a Theory of Harmony* (1913). Invoking Carl Stumpf's idea of "concordance," for instance, he challenges inherited notions of dissonance as categorically distinct from consonance. Kurth proposes instead a psychological interpretation of chords where the "fusion" (*Verschmelzung*) of stacked thirds and the resultant "feeling of gravity" (*Schwerkraftempfindung*) weighing upon a fundamental may transform an acoustically dissonant sonority into a psychologically satisfying resolution, as with the dominant seventh in m. 3 of the *Tristan* Prelude. "Not mere sound sensation (*Klangempfindung*) decides whether a cadence is possible," Kurth declares, "but also the sensation of force (*Kraftempfindung*)."[49] A harmonic force of gravity produced by fusion stabilizes sonorities, even discordant ones. In addition, Kurth introduces in this work ideas developed later in monographs on Bach's "linear" counterpoint, Wagner's chromatic harmony, and Bruckner's symphonic form. *The Requirements* portrays music as suffused with

47 Halm, "Musikalische Erziehung I," *Von Form und Sinn der Musik*, p. 203; "Unsere Zeit und Beethoven," *Von Form und Sinn der Musik*, p. 160.

48 Schenker, *Free Composition*, pp. 162, 18, 19.

49 Kurth, *Die Voraussetzungen der theoretischen Harmonik*, pp. 28 (*Schwerkraftempfindung*), pp. 35, 36, 54–55 (*Tristan* opening), 61, 70 (*Klangempfindung* and *Kraftempfindung*), p. 73. See also my commentary in "Ernst Kurth's *The Requirements for a Theory of Harmony*" and "Ernst Kurth's *Die Voraussetzungen der theoretischen Harmonik* and the Beginnings of Music Psychology." For background on Stumpf, see Chapter 9, pp. 262–65.

energy, both kinetic (melodic) and potential (harmonic). The onset of a melody, and particularly melodic ornaments, illustrate an "initial melodic energy," the dominant–tonic cadence an "initial tonal energy" as a basic element in a "harmonic-tonal play of forces" (*Kräftespiel*). In fact, all musical activity may be viewed as such a play of forces, and Kurth frequently speaks of music as such in connection with kinesthesia (*Bewegungsempfindung*), a primal element of melody: "The beginning of all melody is the activity of kinesthesia."[50]

Kurth's *Foundations of Linear Counterpoint* (1917) is the first of three analytical monographs. Its first sentence encapsulates the book's aesthetic premise and analytical agenda: "Melody is motion," and later, "Melody is streaming force." "It is misguided," Kurth holds, "to highlight only the acoustic-sonic phenomena – tone production and the tones themselves with all their latent harmonic relationships – as the essential and actually significant factors of melody without paying attention to connections with sensations of a dynamic procedure between the tones."[51] For Kurth, as for certain philosophers (Theodor Lipps, Henri Bergson), melody occurs between the tones, in the sweep of kinetic energy that flows through them and becomes dammed up, as potential energy, in chords. "The fundamental content of melody is, in the psychological sense, not a succession of tones . . . but rather the element of *transition* between the tones. . . Transition is motion" (p. 2). Melody first arises, explains Kurth, in the "sensation of force" that flows through the chain of tones. Kinetic energy is a "more general phenomenon" than rhythm, he insists, which depends on melodic energy. The simplest manifestation of melodic energy is the developmental motive (*Entwicklungsmotiv*), a "distillation of melody down to pure symbols of motion," found typically in developmental passages (e.g., in fugal "episodes"), but not exclusively.[52] These melodic kernels are shaped to express various dynamic tendencies, e.g., ascending or descending drives, upward or downward spirals, swaying or oscillating, and are integrated into local contexts based on the overarching dynamic profile.

Contrary to the interpretation of Bach's polyphony as a contrapuntally elaborated harmonic succession, Kurth's linear-dynamic approach to the music often reveals polyphonic subtleties that tend to be neglected in harmonic normalizations and reductive analyses. Good examples of Kurth's keen analytical acumen may be found in his discussions on "real" and "apparent" voices (pp. 328–48), on the staggering and highlighting of linear high and low points (pp. 361–82), and on the "Influence of Dynamics on Harmonic Relationships" (pp. 374–94). In a pair of excerpts from J. S. Bach's *Inventio* in D major (mm. 1–4, 12–17), Kurth points out how the composer first presents the melodic apexes of the motive as consonances, and enhances them later, in an

50 Kurth, *Die Voraussetzungen*, pp. 71, 122 (kinetic and potential energy), 65, 123 (initial melodic energy), 20, 106, 126, 128 (play of forces), 125, 129 (initial tonal energy), 60, 67 (melody and kinesthesia).

51 Kurth, *Grundlagen*, pp. 1, 10. All translations from Kurth mine. See my *Ernst Kurth As Theorist and Analyst*; *Ernst Kurth: Selected Writings*.

52 Kurth, *Grundlagen*, p. 436, also pp. 417–38; "Zur Motivbildung Bachs."

Example 30.1 Bach, Inventio in D major, mm. 1–4

episodic passage, by transforming them into dissonances (*Foundations*, p. 382) (see Examples 30.1 and 30.2).

Harmony in this linear-dynamic view is pervaded with potential energy ("von Energien durchsetzt," pp. 68, 70), the counterpart of kinetic energy (p. 11). Melody is the streaming force, chordal tension the "restrained force" (p. 69). Like Fétis and Vivier, Kurth speaks of an attraction between tones, which he characterizes as a "gravitational force." The result is a "cohesion" among energy-laden tones momentarily "caught" in chords, which represent an "equilibrium of forces" (pp. 61, 62). The stepwise continuation of a chordal dissonance is thus, according to Kurth, not so much a resolution (*Auflösung*) as a release (*Auslösung*) of constrained forces (p. 63; cf. *The Requirements*, p. 69). In sum, then, Bach's polyphony is to be understood not merely as a melodic animation of a preexisting harmonic framework but rather as a "conflict of reciprocally interacting undercurrents" (pp. 141–42). Just as the surface of a fluid body, e.g., a drop of water, can be understood only by studying its interior constitution and the gravitational forces that shape its surface, so too a theory of tonal polyphony such as Bach's must begin with the undercurrents, with the forces that give rise to the surface properties and configurations.[53]

Kurth's *Romantic Harmony and its Crisis in Wagner's Tristan* (1920) broadens and escalates the energeticist program based on both the style and the aesthetics of musical Romanticism.[54] In Schopenhauerian language, Kurth locates the origin of Romantic harmony in the tumultuous, unceasing ebb and flow of psychic forces. Kurth's first utterance in *Romantic Harmony* captures the essence of the entire volume: "Harmonies are reflexes from the unconscious." The remainder of his book serves essentially as a clarification and elaboration of this thesis. The familiar sonic experience we call music "is in reality merely its fading away." "Music is a natural force within us, a dynamic of volitional impulses . . . Sound is dead. That which lives in it is the will toward sound" (pp. 1, 3). "Every sonority is merely an aurally grasped image of certain energetic tendencies"; the very nature of harmony is "the influx of unconscious energies into sound" (pp. 11, 13).[55] Contrary to conventional theory, and similar to the catchy verbal distinction drawn earlier between the sensation of sound (*Klangempfindung*) and the

53 Kurth, *Grundlagen*, p. 9. 54 Kurth, *Romantische Harmonik*, pp. 14–43.
55 Compare *Grundlagen*, p. 30: "The resting tone is will toward motion."

Example 30.2 Bach, Inventio in D major, mm. 12–17

sensation of force (*Kraftempfindung*), for Kurth chords are not simply sound (*Klang*) but rather primarily urge (*Drang*) (p. 11). The agenda for music theory, then, is clear: "to observe the *transformation* of certain *tension* processes into *sounds*. Only in this way is it possible to awaken . . . an empathy (*Einfühlen*) and sympathetic reverberation with the animated *creative* forces, and so to restore once again the connection . . . between theory and art" (p. 2). Nowhere in all of Kurth's work is his vitalism more pervasive or pronounced than here.

In Kurth's world of Romantic harmony, tones coalesce through cohesion and gravitational force into "sensuous" (tertian) harmonies, or associate in "energetic" (altered and nontertian) harmonies, which in disintegrating release potential energy as they lead either to yet other energetic or sensuous harmonies. Abundant musical examples illustrate the foundations and nuances of chromatic harmony as effects of melodic, harmonic, and tonal energy. Single chromatic inflections in tonicizations signify the incursion of leading-tone energy, in modal mixture the technique of "shading." Multiple inflections in highly chromatic chords and in sonorities composed of multiple "neighbor-note insertions" indicate heightened energy levels characteristic of the "intensive" alteration style. "Tension chords," straightforward and obscure progressions, coloristic "absolute" chords and progressions used for their jolting effect, small- and large-scale sequences, narrow and broad modulatory plans – these and other techniques arise from the turbulence of sonified psychic energies. The discussion of the Preludes to Acts 1 and 3 of *Tristan* exemplify well Kurth's analytical thinking and style (pp. 315–25). Those analyses illustrate characteristic ideas on, among other things, tension chords, chromatic sequences, and tonal organization.[56]

If *Foundations* is Kurth's treatise on counterpoint and *Romantic Harmony* one on chromatic harmony, then the landmark 1,300-page, two-volume *Bruckner* (1925) is one on form, developed primarily with that composer's symphonies in mind, but applicable in principle far more broadly.[57] Despite its problems – analyses are based on heavily

56 See Bailey, *Prelude and Transfiguration from Tristan and Isolde*, pp. 186–204; Kurth, *Romantic Harmony*, pp. 45–53, 62–67, 318–27, 315–18.

57 Analyses of each movement of the nine symphonies, as well as of Bruckner's other instrumental and choral works appear in *Bruckner*, vol. II.

edited, obsolete first editions – *Bruckner* remains valuable for showing how energeticist ideas make intelligible what many contemporaries considered unintelligible and formless. Kurth teaches that form is "the reciprocal effect, held in constant suspension, of force and its control in outlines," a "control of force through space and time" (vol. I, pp. 234, 239). It is "neither the pure streaming of the formation process nor the pure fulfillment of borders, but rather the transition, the active transformation of the former into the latter . . . neither flux nor outline, but rather the lively struggle aimed at grasping something flowing by holding on to something firm." "The conflict between becoming and being is the never-ceasing primordial tension of the concept of musical form" (vol. 1, pp. 239–240). Kurth's ideas hark back to those of organicists, with their emphasis on internal growth, and even to those of the rhetoricians except that the focus is now on energy, forces, and tension, rather than on affect. As hackneyed as some of Kurth's rhetoric may seem to a reader today, for a musician in 1925 trained in the traditional schools of static harmonic analysis and formal taxonomy, his writings must have been fresh and inspiring.

The central image in Kurth's concept of form is the force-wave (*Kraftwelle*), escalatory and deescalatory undulations that shape the musical flow. In Bruckner's wave dynamics (*Wellendynamik*), local phases of growth and decline (component and mediatory waves, (*Teilwellen*, *Zwischenwellen*) build toward – and discharge – accumulated energy in, apex waves (*Gipfelwellen*), which subside in a series of reverberatory waves (*Nachwellen*). Melodic, harmonic, rhythmic, tonal, and orchestrational activity signify forces that wax and wane in undulatory phases. Kurth's analysis (vol. 1, pp. 280–90) of the opening (mm. 1–31) from the Finale of Bruckner's Sixth Symphony illustrates a gradual intensification that discharges in the first full statement of the theme (at m. 29). Motivic contours and patterning, melodic direction, phrasing, articulation, registration, and orchestration promote an overall heightening of tension.

An isolated tremolo frames Example 30.3, Kurth explains, and gives the passage a dynamic symmetry (vol. 1, pp. 281–82). It remains throughout as an undercurrent of anticipatory tension while the violins, starting in a high register, drift passively downward in as yet indistinct melodic gestures. Before the music ebbs toward the suspenseful quivering of the tremolo, Kurth detects hints of restrained energy in the rise and fall outlined by F–A–E at the close of the bass line (mm. 6–7) and, roughly at the midpoint of the passage, in the momentary upsurging clarinet line (m. 4) before it is subsequently absorbed by the violins' descending fourth (a^1–e^1). In sum, Example 30.3 illustrates a microcosmic symphonic wave whose content is best explained not in technical language, but rather, dynamically, as a design of energetic impulses, "a first casting of symphonic mist" (vol. 1, p. 283).

We have devoted several paragraphs to Kurth's work because it is so thoroughly energeticist in concept, analytical practice, and expression, more than that of Schenker, and even more than that of Halm, whose writings strongly influenced

Example 30.3 Bruckner, Sixth Symphony, Finale, mm. 1–7 (reduction)

Kurth, but who nevertheless remains an embryonic energeticist by comparison.[58] Other writers contemporaneous with Kurth, however, articulated ideas in which music was also considered as a network of interacting forces, in particular Arnold Schering and Hans Mersmann, both students of Kretzschmar (and Mersmann a student of Schering as well).

Arnold Schering. For Arnold Schering (1877–1941), all musical activity boils down to the "operation of the basic psychological law of tension and release," whether in tempo and rhythm (fast/slow), melody (ascending/descending), register (high/low), harmony (dissonant/consonant), key (remote/near), and so forth. As with Kurth, musical motion springs from a "play of forces," which constitutes the "bridge to our mental experience." Music is a "symbol" (*Sinn-Bild*) of life, or human will, and our experience of it is a "psychic resonance" with its origins. Even the alternation of sound and silence is a "small drama of human will."[59] Through hermeneutics, "we arrive at an image of an animated organism by thinking of it as possessing inner motive forces. We believe ourselves to be confronted with a system of active forces of dynamic, rhythmic, melodic, [and] harmonic nature." In essence, music is based on "nothing other than a continuous balancing of feuding sonic and dynamic principles."[60] To demonstrate the musical forces in action Schering offers several analyses, two of which are particularly interesting: Bach's G minor fugue from *The Well-tempered Clavier*, Book 1 (*Musikalische Bildung*, pp. 103–09), and first movement of Beethoven's String Quartet, Op. 74 (pp. 118–38). At the opening of the latter (see Example 30.4), Schering infers an

58 Allen Forte views Kurth as the main figure in "tension" theory (*Dictionary of Twentieth-Century Music*, p. 75). See also Bent, *Analysis*, pp. 46–47.
59 Schering, *Musikalische Bildung*, pp. 5, 78; 16–17 (*Kräftespiel*, *Menschenwille*), pp. 83, 18; "Music is thus simply the audible expression of will" (p. 17). Translations mine.
60 Schering, "Zur Grundlegung," p. 169.

Example 30.4 Beethoven, String Quartert, Op. 74, first movement, mm. 1–13

affect of melancholy and brooding based on the *sotto voce*, unstable inversions of the $E\flat^7$ chord, an applied dominant to an energetically slack subdominant, abrupt stop and pause in m. 2. Other musical events attempt to undermine and counter the affect, including the ascent from a♭ to d♭ in the first-violin in mm. 1–2, second, a steep ascent to $a\flat^1$ in mm. 9–10, and an ascending sequence in mm. 11–13 indicating a "pleading" for relief.

Although Schering maintains that "specific constructive laws . . . lie latent in the tones" of the dynamic organism, the language of his analyses emphasizes music's origins in psychic life, its musical manifestation as symbols, and its psychological reverberations as affects in attuned and comprehending listeners ("We listen to a communication of feeling from a remote source"). The unspecifable feelings of tension conveyed symbolically in music "have the same reality" as real emotions, which are likewise often nonspecific. The logic with which symbolic feelings or moods unfold in music resembles the course of our emotional life: "We recognize in [tone connections] the reflection of our own volitional and life and moods."[61]

61 Ibid., pp. 169, 170; *Musikalische Bildung*, pp. 17, 80.

From all of this it is clear that, for Schering, our enjoyment and understanding of music depend on empathy (*Einfühlung*), a dominant theme in aesthetics in the late nineteenth and early twentieth centuries. Kurth, too, relies on empathy as a vehicle for analysis. The various technical categories for examining Bach's polyphony are intended "as a *guide for gaining empathic entry* (*Einfühlung*) into Bach's instrumental counterpoint . . . The most essential goal in identifying and observing artistic logic is the awakening and stimulating of that art of instinctive feeling (*Erfühlens*)." As mentioned earlier, *Romantic Harmony* also speaks of "empathy (*Einfühlen*) and sympathetic reverberation with the animated *creative* forces" as the basis for a theory of harmony.[62]

Schering no doubt learned about empathy from two leading empathy theorists of the time, first Theodor Lipps (1851–1914) at Munich, where Schering enrolled in 1900 for a semester, and later Johannes Volkelt (1848–1930), one of Schering's teachers – and later a colleague – at Leipzig University. At the heart of Volkelt's empathy theory is the notion of symbolism and the belief that in aesthetic experience feelings dominate over semantic and conceptual meanings. Empathy results from a fusion of perception and feeling. In aesthetic perception, we encounter both actual and symbolic meanings. Aesthetic behavior chiefly involves responses to symbolic meanings. These can take the form of images or concepts, as they do in plastic, graphic, and literary arts. But in music, most abstract of the arts, the predominant symbolisms are that of feeling and mood (*Gefühlssymbolik*, *Stimmungssymbolik*). Unlike other arts, music dispenses with mediatory concepts, which are otherwise necessary for symbolic meaning. "Disregarding all mediation," Volkelt explains, "certain melodies and harmonies have in and of themselves similarity with cheerful, melancholy, impish, yearning, and other moods."[63] Here we have instances of "pure acoustical empathy," which begins with kinesthetic sensations, and ends in symbolic moods. Conflating Volkelt's ideas on empathy with Kretzschmar's ideas on affective hermeneutics, Schering developed a mode of analysis that begins with musical statics and dynamics and ends in a symbolic drama of affects.

Hans Mersmann. One of the first music theorists to attempt a phenomenology of music, Hans Mersmann (1891–1971) acknowledges Halm as his initial inspiration, as well as the musical hermeneutics of Kretzschmar and Schering. The theoretical research of Edmund Husserl, originator of phenomenology, and two of his chief exponents, Max Scheler and Moritz Geiger, left Mersmann dissatisfied because a "pure" phenomenology, though praiseworthy and powerful, is not possible in Mersmann's program of *applied* aesthetics (=analysis).[64] His point of departure is "the question concerning forces." Having identified them, "laws are sought according to which the

62 Kurth, *Grundlagen*, pp. 349–50; *Romantic Harmony*, p. 2.

63 Volkelt, *System der Ästhetik*, vol. 1, pp. 177–78, 250, 117, 208, 280.

64 Mersmann, "Versuch einer Phänomenologie," pp. 227n, 228n; "Zur Phänomenologie," p. 375. All translations mine.

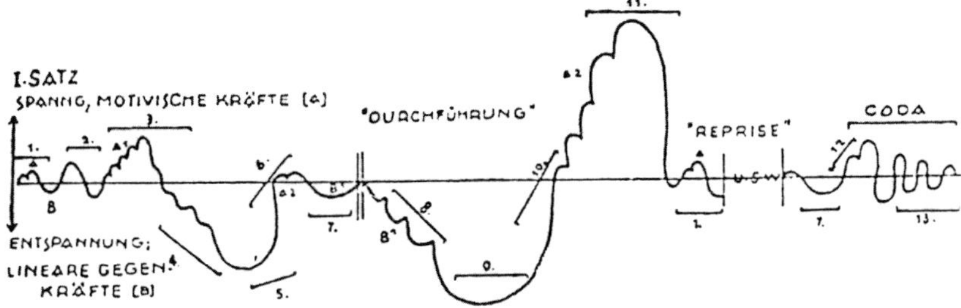

Figure 30.1 Mersmann's graph of Haydn, Sonata in E♭ major, Hob. XVI:49, first movement

forces arise and develop. This development, the evolution of the forces, is the main issue." Like Schering, Mersmann recognizes and interprets the activity of musical forces based on contrasts of tension and release. "The fundamental phenomena of an art work," he writes, "are based on a continual succession of tension and release phases, which penetrate each other in the most varied dimensions." The objective is "to comprehend all phenomena of the art work as an evolution of fundamental forces."[65]

Mersmann demonstrates his applied music phenomenology in an analysis of Haydn's E♭ major Piano Sonata, Hob. XVI:49, whose dynamic evolution is spawned by the contrasting forces featured in the two initial gestures of the piece: an essentially arpeggiated, ascending motive (mm. 1–2, with pick-up), and a scalar, descending motive that rebounds upward at its end (mm. 2–3 with pick-up). "Everything in the sonata, at least in its first movement, is based on the contrast of these two forces" ("Versuch," p. 259). Mersmann graphs the interaction between the two sets of motivic characteristics in a contour diagram of the piece (p. 261) that depicts mounting and dissipating tension across the movement (see Figure 30.1).

In a note on the diagram, he explains that such graphic force-profiles were developed in workshops given at a continuing education school in Berlin, which is interesting because Schering, Halm, and Kurth were also involved in teaching musical amateurs. Their energeticist concepts, language, and analytical strategies appealed to a broad, cultured but nonprofessional audience. However, behind the general accessibility of energeticist literature lies the sophistication of its philosophical and aesthetic assumptions.[66]

Kurt Westphal Form is also the subject of Kurt Westphal's (1904–) study of the Viennese Classical music. He undertakes to clarify the notion of musical form and the underlying concept of "unity."[67] He dismisses attempts to derive formal unity additively

65 Ibid., pp. 230, 376.
66 Ibid., 261n. Cf. Schering, preface to *Musikalische Bildung*; also Rothfarb, *Ernst Kurth as Theorist and Analyst*, pp. 5–6, 10, 17, 19.
67 Westphal, *Der Begriff der musikalischen Form*, pp. 9–16.

by piecing together motives, phrases, etc. As with the gestaltists, he stresses the need to approach form holistically, by postulating a dynamic whole from which parts may be resolved analytically, but only as functional components that promote a synthetic whole. For Westphal that whole is a dynamic phenomenon, characterized as a "processive curve" (*Verlaufskurve*), which "holds the parts together, determines the function that they fulfill for the whole, creates relationships among the parts, and imparts meaning to them with respect to the greater whole to which they belong" (pp. 47–49).

Westphal's processive curve, like Kurth's force-wave, is made up of constituents whose function depends on the overall, multilevel tectonic structure to which a component belongs; the dynamic disposition of local curves can be only be evaluated relative to larger ones. Westphal illustrates the idea with an excerpt from the first movement of Mozart's Piano Sonata, K. 284 (mm. 17–21). The dynamic function of the passage – a "vamping" on an A major chord as dominant of D – might be construed as hovering, the drive of the preceding passage (mm. 13–16) being momentarily held in suspension. However, the overarching processive curve of the music to m. 21 indicates an ongoing dynamic escalation, a continuous rise in tension from m. 1 on. The accumulated tension streams into mm. 17–21, which are swept along in an ascending dynamic spiral and thus do not hover. The sense of suspension that the passage might have conveyed in another context is superseded by the encompassing curve.[68]

Westphal's theory of form, like Schering's, Kurth's, and Halm's, relies on listeners' resonance with, and mental processing of, musically intrinsic, shaping forces. We are drawn into and empathically participate in the musical flow. Music theory and cognitive psychology intersect frequently, explicitly or implicitly, in energeticist writings. Establishing a theory of music, Kurth affirms, involves not merely hearing and investigating sonic events as technical or acoustical phenomena, but rather delving deeper, "to the primordial processes in ourselves . . . The forces activated in us are projected from within onto the surface, where they take shape . . . Musical activity merely expresses itself in tones, but it does not reside in them."[69] Similarly, for Westphal "form as evolutionary curve cannot be read from the anatomical structure of the work of art (insofar as that structure is visible in the organization, arrangement, succession of components). Rather, it acquires its reality in the aural process, a reality which is therefore a purely psychic one."[70]

Late twentieth-century reverberations

Although the orientation of the twentieth-century energeticists discussed here is toward technical analysis, they do not attempt to concretize their psychological

68 Ibid., p. 60. 69 Kurth, *Grundlagen*, p. 7. See also *Musikpsychologie*, pp. x, 10.
70 Westphal, *Begriff*, p. 52.

speculations, or to quantify their analytical findings about the details of music's dynamic properties or about the contours of a work as a whole (Westphal's curves, Kurth's waves, Halm's drama of forces). Instead, based on intuitively sensed intensities they interpret musical events energetically, and narrate a work as a series of functionally defined, interrelated dynamic events that we follow empathically. The emphasis is on revealing and explicating qualitative characteristics and their psychic resonance rather than on quantifying or systematizing them. Those latter tasks have fallen to more modern-day authors, music theorists and psychologists. Among others, Steven Larson, Fred Lerdahl, and Carol Krumhansl have published studies aimed at quantifying and experimentally testing for awareness of music's dynamic properties. Steven Larson has defined three specific musical forces ("musical gravity," "musical magnetism," and "musical inertia") and built computer models based on an algorithm that quantifies their interaction. Fred Lerdahl proposes a similar algorithm as a part of his method for calculating tonal tension, and Carol Krumhansl reports the results of aural experiments that show how listeners segment musical experience and respond to musical tension over time. Both of the last two studies center on the first movement of Mozart's Piano Sonata in E♭ major, K. 282. Interestingly, Krumhansl's data corroborate the results of Lerdahl's analytical methodology, which is based on the hierarchical branching model developed in *A Generative Theory of Tonal Music*.[71]

The legacy of Schering, Halm, Kurth, Mersmann, and Westphal is still strongly evident in the work of Victor Zuckerkandl and Wallace Berry, the former in the aesthetic, the latter in the analytic domain. With Halm, Zuckerkandl calls the dynamic qualities of tones "the proper musical quality," having nothing to do with the exterior, "physical event" of tones, but rather with interior qualities perceived in consciousness.[72] For Zuckerkandl as for Schering, tones are dynamic symbols (chap. 6): "The meaning of a tone . . . lies not in what it points to but in the pointing itself . . . When meaning sounds in a musical tone, a non-physical force intangibly radiates from its physical conveyor." In the same special sense in which we speak of religious symbols, "we can speak of the tones of music as dynamic symbols. We hear forces in them as the believer sees the divine being in the symbol" (*Sound and Symbol*, pp. 68, 69). Like Kurth, Zuckerkandl calls "Musical contexts . . . *motion* contexts, kinetic contexts." Tones are musical only insofar as they are "conveyors of a motion that goes through them and beyond them. When we hear music, what we hear is above all motions" (p. 76).

The forces we hear in tones are, according to Zuckerkandl, directional tendencies (the symbolic "pointing" attribute), which result in a continuous sense of expectancy, an idea that anticipates the work of Leonard Meyer and Eugene Narmour (implication–realization model of perception). "No musical tone is sufficient unto itself. . . .

71 Larson, "Musical Forces"; Lerdahl, "Calculating Tonal Tension"; Lerdahl and Jackendoff, *A Generative Theory of Tonal Music*; Krumhansl, "A Perceptual Analysis of Mozart's Piano Sonata K. 282."
72 Zuckerkandl, *Sound and Symbol*, pp. 21–23.

[A]s each musical tone points beyond itself... we too... listen tensely and expectantly for each next tone" (p. 94). The directional tendencies are produced against the background of the (traditional tonal) scale as "dynamic field," conceived along the lines of Fétis and Vivier, where scale degrees are either reposeful (stable) or possess attractional forces (pp. 95–104).

While Zuckerkandl's book, with its few, simple examples, is accessible to music lovers and amateurs, Berry's detailed inquiry into *Structural Functions in Music* is clearly for professionals and advanced students of music theory. The study aims at acquiring "a better understanding of [musical] structure and experience," and to deal comprehensively with "syntactic process in which music can be said to have meaning."[73] "Meaning" here refers to "contextually shaped processes of mounting and receding intensity," which are "of fundamental importance in the musical experience" where "*thought and feeling* are cofunctionally engaged" (p. 26, emphasis Berry's). Such processes involve change in one or more musical parameters (pitch, harmony, key, rhythm, texture, etc.). Like Mersmann and Westphal, Berry sets out to explore music's "actions" as evident structural and expressive properties within an "intensity" curve, where "*intensities develop and decline*, and... analogous feeling is induced" (p. 4, emphasis Berry's).

In three large chapters, on tonality, texture, and rhythm and meter, Berry presents numerous analyses that illustrate by various graphical means the progressive, recessive, static, and erratic (irregular) phases that create intensity curves. In comparison to his energeticist forerunners, whose repertorial scope is comparatively limited (mainly Bach, Beethoven, Bruckner), Berry deals with music from Gregorian chant up to our own day (Berio, Boulez, Carter, Nono). In the chapter on tonality, analyses reveal the dynamics of tonal action: expanding a key's resources toward remote regions ("progression"), and narrowing toward tonic ("recession," pp. 84–85, 86–87). Mozart's Piano Sonata, K. 332, first movement, is a good example (p. 45), as is Liszt's third *Transcendental Etude* (pp. 57–59, with Fig. 1-2). Tension (instability) and release (stability) again play a key role. In a process similar to Lerdahl's tension calculation, though not as precisely defined, Berry offers a profile of tonal relations among near and distant keys in two songs of Hugo Wolf (Fig. 1-4, p. 83).[74]

The work of many other twentieth-century music theorists can also be aligned with energeticist thought. Paul Hindemith, for instance, classified chords based on their interval content yielding sonorities of varying harmonic tension. According to their degree of intensity, a succession of sonorities (tonal or nontonal) may exhibit "harmonic fluctuation." Franz Brenn's concept of form as wave-dynamics recalls that of Ernst Kurth whose notion of form as wave-dynamics is foreshadowed by Leo Funtek.[75] The psychological dimension of energetics and its emphatic foundation evident in the work of Schering, Halm, and Kurth has been developed by a number of American

73 Berry, *Structural Functions*, p. 1. 74 Ibid., pp. 85–86, 138–42.

75 Hindemith, *Unterweisung im Tonsatz*, vol. 1, p. 120; Brenn, *Form in der Musik*, p. 28.

music theorists. As already pointed out, the implication–realization model of cognition developed by Leonard Meyer and Eugene Narmour is in its teleological ramifications clearly energetic. Using Mark Johnson's and George Lakoff's image schemas of body movement, Janna Saslaw is able to analyze language such as that used by Riemann and show its reliance on metaphors of internally experienced forces. Work by Lawrence Zbikowsky has also attempted to incorporate energeticist notions within his broad conceptual models of musical cognition.[76] In a similar vein, writers such as Fred Maus, Marion Guck, and Gregory Karl have developed narrative approaches to the analysis of music that rely upon energeticist notions of dramatic agency and dynamic empathy.[77]

If the subjective element of energetic analysis is vulnerable to criticism (Halm, we recall, tried to purge all qualities of affect, mood, feeling, program, and personality from his analyses), it nonetheless seems to be difficult to avoid in practice. Unless analysis is to be no more than a lifeless, formalistic taxonomy of musical events, it seems desirable and perhaps inevitable that description will engage not only reason but also feeling. "Taking the step from the musical to the psychological is unavoidable," Schäfke reminds us; "The images of force through which the present sees music cannot lay claim to objective and generally valid truth."

Today, we may recognize in Schäfke's comments some of the same criticisms that have recently been leveled at formal theoretical analysis by critics both within and without the field of music theory. More and more, the heavily positivistic, formalist approaches to musical description that so characterized the enterprise of music analysis in the late twentieth century seems to be receding. If such formal structural analysis has by no means been fully displaced – and we should hope that it never will be if music theory hopes to claim any form of continuity as coherent intellectual tradition – then energeticist theory still can have a salutary influence as a fruitful historical point of reference. And with epistemological adjustments, it may also serve as a model for the evolving critical methods of contemporary music analysis.

76 Meyer, *Explaining Music*; Narmour, *The Analysis and Cognition of Melodic Complexity*; Saslaw, "Forces, Containers, and Paths"; Zbikowski, "Metaphor and Music Theory."
77 Karl, "Musical Plot"; Guck, "Analytic Fictions"; Maus, "Music as Drama."

Bibliography

Primary sources

Babb, W., trans., and C. Palisca, ed., *Hucbald, Guido, and John on Music: Three Medieval Treatises*, New Haven, Yale University Press, 1978
Barker, A. *Greek Musical Writings*, 2 vols., Cambridge University Press, 1984–89

Bernhard, C. *Tractatus compositionis augmentatus*, ed. J. Müller-Blattau, Kassel, Bärenreiter, 1963

Berry, W. *Structural Functions in Music*, New York, Dover, 1987

Brenn, F. *Form in der Musik*, Freiburg, Switzerland, Universitätsverlag, 1953

Cohn, A. W. "Das Erwachen der Ästhetik," *Zeitschrift für Musikwissenschaft* 1 (1918–19), pp. 669–79

"Das musikalische Verständnis: Neue Ziele," *Zeitschrift für Musikwissenschaft* 4/3 (1921), pp. 129–35

Fétis, F.-J. *Traité complet de la théorie et de la pratique de l'harmonie*, 6th edn., Paris, G. Brandus, 1858

Funtek, L. *Bruckneriana*, Leipzig, Verlag für Literatur, Kunst und Musik, 1910

Guck, M. A. "Beethoven as Dramatist," *College Music Symposium* 29 (1989), pp. 8–18

"Analytical Fictions," *MTS* 16 (1994), pp. 217–30

Halm, A. *Beethoven*, Berlin, Hesse, 1927

Einführung in die Musik, Berlin, Deutsche Buch-Gemeinschaft, 1926

Harmonielehre (1900), Leipzig, Göschen, 1905

"Musik und Leben," in *Von Form und Sinn der Musik*, ed. S. Schmalzriedt, Wiesbaden, Breitkopf und Härtel, 1978, pp. 240–44

"Musikalische Bildung," in *Von Form und Sinn der Musik*, ed. S. Schmalzriedt, Wiesbaden, Breitkopf und Härtel, 1978, pp. 211–27

"Musikalische Erziehung I," in *Von Form und Sinn der Musik*, ed. S. Schmalzriedt, Wiesbaden, Breitkopf und Härtel, 1978, pp. 200–03

"Musikalische Logik," *Der Kunstwart* 18 (1905), pp. 486–87, 545–47

"Musikgeschichtliches, Ein Vergleich," in *Von Grenzen und Ländern der Musik*, Munich, G. Müller, 1916, pp. 217–22

"Rationale Musik!," in *Von Form und Sinn der Musik*, ed. S. Schmalzriedt, Wiesbaden, Breitkopf und Härtel, 1978, pp. 78–82

"Reden bei Gelegenheit musikalischer Vorträge," in *Wickersdofer Jahrbuch 1908*, ed. G. Wyneken and A. Halm, Jena, Diederichs, 1909, pp. 62–67

"Über mein musikalisches Schaffen," in *Von Form und Sinn der Musik*, ed. S. Schmalzriedt, Wiesbaden, Breitkopf und Härtel, 1978, pp. 284–91

"Unsere Zeit und Beethoven," in *Von Form und Sinn der Musik*, ed. S. Schmalzriedt, Wiesbaden, Breitkopf und Härtel, 1978, pp. 152–64

"Von meinem Schaffen," *Das hohe Ufer* 1/12 (1919), pp. 289–304

Von zwei Kulturen der Musik (1913), 3rd edn., Stuttgart, E. Klett, 1947

Hanslick, E. *On the Musically Beautiful*, trans. G. Payzant, Indianapolis, Hackett, 1986

Hindemith, P. *Unterweisung im Tonsatz*, vol. I, Mainz, B. Schott, 1937

Jacques of Liège, *Speculum musicae*, ed. R. Bragard, *CSM* 3 (1955)

Karl, G. "Structuralism and Musical Plot," *MTS* 19 (1997), pp. 13–34

Koch, H. C. *Versuch einer Anleitung zur Composition*, 3 vols., Leipzig, A. F. Böhme, 1782–93; facs. Hildesheim, G. Olms, 1969 and 2000; partial trans. N. K. Baker as *Introductory Essay on Composition*, New Haven, Yale University Press, 1983

Krumhansl, C. L. "A Perceptual Analysis of Mozart's Piano Sonata K. 282: Segmentation, Tension, and Musical Ideas," *MP* 13 (1996), pp. 401–32

Kurth, E. "Zur Motivbildung Bachs: Ein Beitrag zur Stilpsychologie," *Bach-Jahrbuch* (1917), pp. 80–136

Bruckner, 2 vols., Berlin, M. Hesse, 1925

Die Voraussetzungen der theoretischen Harmonik und der tonalen Darstellungssysteme, Bern, Drechsel, 1913; reprint Munich, Katzbichler, 1973; trans. L. Rothfarb as "Ernst Kurth's *The Requirements for a Theory of Harmony:* An Annotated Translation with an Introductory Essay," Master's Thesis, University of Hartford, 1979

Grundlagen des linearen Kontrapunkts: Bachs melodische Polyphonie (1917), 5th edn., Bern, Krompholz, 1956

Musikpsychologie, Berlin, M. Hesse, 1931

Romantische Harmonik und ihre Krise in Wagners Tristan, 3rd edn., Berlin, M. Hesse, 1923; facs, Hildesheim, G. Olms, 1968 and 1998

Larson, S. "Musical Forces, Step Collections, Tonal Pitch Space, and Melodic Expectation," in *Proceedings of the Third International Conference for Music Perception and Cognition* (Université de Liège, 1994), ed. Irène Deliège, Liège, European Society for the Cognitive Sciences of Music, 1994, pp. 227–29

Lerdahl, F. "Calculating Tonal Tension," *MP* 13 (1996), pp. 319–63

Lerdahl, F. and R. Jackendoff, *A Generative Theory of Tonal Music*, Cambridge, MA, MIT Press, 1983

Marx, A. B. *Die Lehre von der musikalischen Komposition*, 4 vols., Leipzig, Breitkopf und Härtel, 1837–47

Mattheson, J. *Der vollkommene Capellmeister*, Hamburg, C. Herold, 1739; facs. Kassel, Bärenreiter, 1954; trans. and ed. E. C. Harriss as *Johann Mattheson's "Der vollkommene Capellmeister"*, Ann Arbor, UMI Research Press, 1981

Maus, F. "Music as Drama," *MTS* 10 (1988), pp. 56–73

Mersmann, H. "Versuch einer Phänomenologie der Musik," *Zeitschrift für Musikwissenschaft* 5 (1922–23), pp. 226–69

"Zur Phänomenologie der Musik," *Zeitschrift für Aesthetik und allgemeine Kunstwissenschaft* 12 (1925), pp. 372–97

Meyer, L. B. *Explaining Music: Essays and Explorations*, Berkeley, University of California Press, 1973

Narmour, E. *The Analysis and Cognition of Melodic Complexity: The Implication–Realization Model*, University of Chicago Press, 1992

Rameau, J.-P. *Treatise on Harmony* (1722), trans. P. Gossett, New York, Dover, 1971

Reymann, R. M. "François-Joseph Fétis, *Traité complet de la théorie et de la pratique de l'harmonie*, An Annotated Translation of Book I and Book III," Master's Thesis, Indiana University (1966)

Riemann, H. *Musikalische Dynamik und Agogik*, Hamburg, D. Rahter, 1884

Saslaw, J. "Forces, Containers, and Paths: The Role of Body-Derived Image Schemas in the Conceptualization of Music," *JMT* 40 (1996), pp. 217–43

Schenker, H. *Beethoven's Ninth Symphony* (1912), trans. J. Rothgeb, New Haven, Yale University Press, 1992

Counterpoint (2 vols., 1910–22), trans. J. Rothgeb and J. Thym, New York, Schirmer, 1987

Free Composition (1935), trans. and ed. E. Oster, New York, Longman, 1979

Harmony (1906), trans. E. M. Borgese, ed. O. Jonas, University of Chicago Press, 1954

Der Tonwille 1 (1921)

Schering, A. "Musikalische Symbolkunde," *Jahrbuch der Musikbibliothek Peters* 42 (1935), pp. 15–30

"Zur Grundlegung der musikalischen Hermeneutik," *Zeitschrift für Ästhetik und allgemeine Kunstwissenschaft* 9 (1915), pp. 168–75
Musikalische Bildung und Erziehung zum musikalischen Hören, Leipzig, Quelle und Meyer, 1911
Ugolino of Orvieto, *Declaratio musicae disciplinae*, 3 vols., ed. A. Seay, *CSM* 7 (1959–62)
Vivier, A.-J. *Traité complet d'harmonie théorique et pratique*, Paris and Brussels, J. B. Kotto, 1862
Volkelt, J. *System der Ästhetik*, 3 vols., Munich, C. H. Beck, 1905–14
Westphal, K. *Der Begriff der musikalischen Form in der Wiener Klassik*, Leipzig, Kister und Siegel, 1935; reprint ed. W. Kolneder, Giebing, Katzbichler, 1971
Zbikowski, L. "Metaphor and Music Theory: Reflections from Cognitive Science," *Music Theory Online* 4/1 (1998)
Zuckerkandl, V. *Sound and Symbol*, 2 vols., trans. W. R. Trask, New York, Pantheon Books, 1956

Secondary sources

Agawu, V. K. "Does Music Theory Need Musicology?," *Current Musicology* 53 (1993), pp. 89–98
Bailey, R., (ed.), *Prelude and Transfiguration from Tristan and Isolde*, New York, Norton, 1985
Bent, I. *Analysis*, New York, Norton, 1987
Bonds, M. E. *Wordless Rhetoric: Musical Form and the Metaphor of the Oration*, Cambridge, MA, Harvard University Press, 1991
Christensen, T. *Rameau and Musical Thought in the Enlightenment*, Cambridge University Press, 1993
Cohen, D. "'The Imperfect Seeks its Perfection': Harmonic Progression, Directed Motion, and Aristotelean Physics," *MTS* 23 (2001), pp. 139–69
Dahlhaus, C. *Studies on the Origin of Harmonic Tonality*, trans. R. Gjerdingen, Princeton University Press, 1990
Groth, R. "Harmonik und Tonalität in der Interpretation des belgischen Theoretikers Albert-Joseph Vivier (1816–1903)," in *Bericht über den internationalen musikwissenschaftlichen Kongress Bayreuth 1981*, Kassel, Bärenreiter, 1984, pp. 543–47
Die französische Kompositionslehre des 19. Jahrhunderts, *AfMw* 22 (1983)
Liebert, A. *Die Bedeutung des Wertesystems der Rhetorik für das deutsche Musikdenken im 18. und 19. Jahrhundert*, Frankfurt am Main, P. Lang, 1993
Rivera, B. *German Music Theory in the Early 17th Century*, Ann Arbor, UMI Research Press, 1980
Rothfarb, L. "Ernst Kurth's *Die Voraussetzungen der theoretischen Harmonik* and the Beginnings of Music Psychology," *Theoria* 4 (1989), pp. 10–33
"Hermeneutics and Energetics, Music-Theoretical Alternatives in the Early 1900s," *JMT* 36 (1992), pp. 43–68
"Music Analysis, Cultural Morality, and Sociology in the Writings of August Halm," *Indiana Theory Review* 16 (1995), pp. 171–96
Ernst Kurth as Theorist and Analyst, Philadelphia, University of Pennsylvania Press, 1988

"The 'New Education' and Music Theory, 1900–1925," in *Music Theory and the Exploration of the Past*, University of Chicago Press, 1993, pp. 449–72

"Beethoven's Formal Dynamics, August Halm's Phenomenological Perspective," *Beethoven Forum* 5 (1996), pp. 65–84

Rothfarb, L., trans. *Ernst Kurth, Selected Writings*, New York, Cambridge University Press, 1991

Sachs, K.-J. *Der Contrapunctus im 14. und 15. Jahrhundert: Untersuchung zum Terminus, zur Lehre und zu den Quellen*, *AfMw* 13 (1974)

Schäfke, R. *Geschichte der Musikästhetik in Umrissen*, Berlin, M. Hesse, 1934

Scruton, R. *The Aesthetics of Music*, Oxford, Clarendon Press, 1997

· 31 ·

The psychology of music

ROBERT GJERDINGEN

The psychology of music is a subfield of psychology that addresses questions of how the mind responds to, imagines, controls the performance of, and evaluates music. The history of this subfield has been greatly influenced by the major trends and developments in the parent discipline, and the organization of this chapter follows the traditional rubrics of that history. Earlier in the twentieth century there was a frequent distinction made between *Tonpsychologie* (the study of vibration, the ear, and the sensation of sound) and *Musikpsychologie* (the study of music as a form of cognition). Though the distinction seems less clear-cut today, this chapter recognizes its historical force and focuses on the latter category, with the former receiving extended treatment in **Chapter 9, passim.**

Since at least the seventeenth century, proponents of one or another theory of music have frequently used the psychology of music as a touchstone. They assert propositions in the general form of "musical relationship has a valuation because there exists a relevant phenomenon or principle in the psychology of music." For example, one might view Rameau as having asserted that "the fifth and third, as progressions of the fundamental bass have the qualities of being good, natural, and fitting because Sauveur and other acousticians have shown these intervals to be present in every musical tone, as a macrocosm within a microcosm." Or Riemann could be viewed as having asserted that "harmonic relationships based on progressions of a major third or perfect fifth between the chordal 'roots' have the qualities of being directly intelligible and foundational because Helmholtz and other physiologists have shown that the frequency analysis of the inner ear privileges these intervals." Developments in the psychology of music thus shift and reestablish the ground on which are based propositions in the theory of music.

As a less well-known example of how the discourse of a music theory can have its roots in psychological principles and premises, one might consider a treatise on harmony (1862) by Abramo Basevi.[1] Basevi, widely recognized as one the nineteenth century's most astute critics of Italian opera, and of Verdi in particular, felt a growing divide between theoretical precepts handed down from the eighteenth century and the

1 Basevi, *Introduzione ad un nuovo sistema d'armonia* [Introduction to a New System of Harmony].

actual musical practice of his time (p. 4).[2] To reconcile the expressive techniques of his day with the stricter traditions of the past, he proposed two principles borrowed from the psychological literature: "sensation" and "perception" (p. 5). Laws of sensation are applicable to tones *per se* and outside of a particular musical context. Laws of perception depend on learning and expectation. Thus, while sensation is constant over the centuries, perception changes (p. 10). Basevi goes so far as to assert that a sound "perceived" has sufficient psychological force to trump a sound "sensed" (p. 11). In this book ostensibly about harmony, Basevi restates and encapsulates the nineteenth-century debate over the importance, but also the limits, of sensation as an explanation for human cognition. His wise and, for music studies, innovative contrasting of sensation and perception (what today might be termed "bottom-up" and "top-down" factors), though rarely cited, comes close to the actual practice of musical explanation evidenced in most classrooms.

The foundations of modern psychology

The study of the mind has long been the province of philosophy. Many passages in ancient Greek texts can be read as addressing psychological questions, and the work of Aristoxenus (fourth century BCE) on musical problems displays an empirical bent easily mistaken for current formulations. But it is with philosophical texts of the seventeenth century that historians see the new orientation toward sensing and thinking that would develop into the foundations of modern psychology.

We have inherited so much of the world-view of these authors that their originality can be difficult to convey. One is reminded of the schoolboy who objected to reading Shakespeare because it was full of clichés. A contemporary of Shakespeare and Monteverdi was the philosopher Sir Francis Bacon (1561–1626). In his *Advancement of Learning* (1605), he departs from the long canonist tradition of music as a science of numerical relationship and focuses instead on music as both sensation and a mode of conveying ideas or feelings. Though the schoolchild of today will likely say that music is "about feelings," the idea was not a cliché in 1605:

> Is not the precept of a musician, to fall from a discord or harsh accord upon a concord or sweet accord, alike true in affection? Is not the trope of music, to avoid or slide from the close or cadence, common with the trope of rhetoric of deceiving expectation? Is not the delight of the quavering upon a stop in music the same with the playing of light upon the water? (Second Book, v, 3)

Bacon expounds on emotions, expectations, and the quality of sensations as if they were the very stuff of music, whereas only a few generations earlier any reference to

2 See, for example, Della Corte, *La critica musicale e i critici*.

such topics could have occurred only in a poetic context. The change was evident to Bacon's generation. Music historians may well hear echoes of Monteverdi's *prima* and *seconda prattica* when, in Bacon's *Novum Organum* (1620, "A New Instrument"), they read:

> Let there exist, then . . . two sources, and two distributions of learning, and in like manner two tribes . . . of philosophers . . . Let us wish that [the cultivators of received dogma] prosper as they desire in their undertaking, and attain what they pursue. But if any individual desire . . . to penetrate still further . . . to know to a certainty and demonstration, let him, as a true son of science . . . join with us. (Preface)

Bacon's program has come to be known as British empiricism, and his "true sons of science" seized upon music as an integral part of mental life. One of them, John Locke (1632–1704), a contemporary of Corelli, clearly articulated subjects that remain central to the psychology of music. His *Essay Concerning Human Understanding* (1690) takes up auditory imagery, the holistic nature of a melody, attention, performance, and memory by association:

> Sounds also, besides the distinct cries of birds and beasts, are modified by diversity of notes of different length put together, which may make that complex idea called a tune, which a musician may have in his mind when he hears or makes no sound at all, by reflecting on the ideas of those sounds, so put together silently in his own fancy. (Book II, Chapter 18, Sec. 3)
>
> Thus a triangle, though the parts thereof compared one to another be relative, yet the idea of the whole is a positive absolute idea. The same may be said of a family, a tune, etc. (Book II, Chapter 25, Sec. 6)
>
> Custom settles habits of thinking . . . which, by often treading, are worn into a smooth path, and the motion in it becomes easy, and as it were natural . . . A musician used to any tune will find that, let it but once begin in his head, the ideas of the several notes of it will follow one another orderly in his understanding, without any care or attention, as regularly as his fingers move orderly over the keys of the organ to play out the tune he has begun, though his unattentive thoughts be elsewhere a wandering. (Book II, Chapter 33, Sec. 6)

Though Locke and others posed many of the core questions of the psychology of music in the seventeenth century, so little was then known about the nature of vibration, the ear, the nervous system, and the brain that even the most ardent "sons of science" did not venture to answer them empirically. Seventeenth-century achievements in mechanics did lay the foundations for eighteenth-century discoveries about the physics of vibrating strings. And the eighteenth-century fixation on matters of taste, sense, and sensibility (*Empfindsamkeit*) did lay the foundation for nineteenth-century studies of sensations (*Empfindungen*). But the beginnings of successful attempts to use evidence gleaned from carefully controlled experiments to connect the musical mind with its sensate body date only from the second half of the nineteenth century.

Structural psychology and act psychology

Auguste Comte (1798–1857, father of "positivism"), displaying the hubris, teleology, and obsession with progress characteristic of many nineteenth-century authors, held that explanations (and civilization generally) pass through distinct stages.[3] The first is theological, in which explanations are grounded in the supernatural. The second is metaphysical, in which explanations depend on positing universals and other grand abstractions. Finally, the third and ultimate stage is positivism, in which one "seeks to coordinate observable facts and find descriptive laws of natural events."[4] Comte's prescriptions are caricatures, and yet they capture the general program that animated the pursuit of science in European universities, especially in the second half of the nineteenth century, and especially in German-speaking lands. Carefully controlled observation would lead to accurate description which in turn would lead to the proper understanding of the laws of nature.

Strictly speaking, the nineteenth-century German university did not recognize psychology, much less the psychology of music, as a discipline. Instead, psychology constituted a problem attacked from "above" by philosophy and "below" by physiology. Wilhelm Wundt (1832–1920), son of a Lutheran pastor, was trained as a physiologist and held an important chair in philosophy at Leipzig, where he established in 1879 what is widely regarded as the first modern psychological research laboratory. His laboratory became the center of "structural psychology," which charted the physiological constituents of consciousness. As a onetime assistant to the brilliant physicist and physiologist Hermann von Helmholtz (whose work is discussed in **Chapter 9, pp. 257–62**), Wundt had adopted the widely prevalent idea that individual nerves carry "specific nervous energies" to the brain (1874). Each signal represents a unique sensation, and an inventory of all such sensations would catalogue the elements of consciousness, just as the periodic table today catalogues the elements of matter.[5]

Franz Brentano (1838–1917), a Dominican priest and professor of philosophy in Würzburg and later Vienna, founded the more loosely defined "act psychology," which focused on the acts and processes that he felt were the overt products of consciousness (1874). His philosophical influence became more widely disseminated through famous students such as Edmund Husserl (1859–1938), Sigmund Freud (1856–1939), Christian von Ehrenfels (1859–1932), and the philosopher Carl Stumpf (1848–1936). Stumpf rose quickly to prominence. After completing the first volume of his *Tonpsychologie* in Prague (1883), he was given professorships at increasingly prestigious universities, eventually establishing an institute of psychology in Berlin that came to

3 Comte, *Cours de philosophie positive*. 4 Brennan, *History and Systems of Psychology*, p. 87.

5 Edwin G. Boring, professor of psychology at Harvard during the first half of the twentieth century, wrote what are widely acknowledged as the great histories of the early days of psychological experiment. His work forms the basis of most general histories of psychology, and the clarity that he brought to this most difficult topic is remarkable. Three of his many works are listed in the Bibliography, p. 979.

rival Wundt's. (For a synthesis of Stumpf's ideas, see **Chapter 9, pp. 262–65.**) Wundt and Stumpf embodied different sides of several sociological, intellectual, and professional faultlines of the late nineteenth century. In 1890, these two giants, like Wagner's Fafner and Fasolt, began a great battle over what seemed like a small problem in the psychology of music.

A student of Wundt's, Carl Lorenz, had published a paper in which he reported that subjects in an experiment made comparisons of the sizes of musical intervals which suggested that the perception of tone height was more linear than logarithmic (1890). Thus the estimated middle of an arbitrary musical interval would lie closer to the arithmetic than to the geometric mean, a result that would contradict not only the newly minted and highly prized psychosensory laws of Ernst Weber (1795–1878) and Gustav Fechner (1801–87), but also the whole history of music theory with its elaborate calculations of "harmonic" means (see Figure 31.1).

Stumpf started the fight.[6] His considerable background in music (he had composed by age ten, established the Berlin *Phonogramm Archiv*, and was mentor to the ethnomusicologist Erich von Hornbostel) and his standing as the author of *Tonpsychologie* (vol. I, 1883; vol. II, 1890) were not the only underpinnings of his discontent. Stumpf, like Wundt, believed in the careful observation of one's own mind – introspection – as a linchpin of psychological inquiry. But against Lorenz's 110,000 observations of non-experts he set the intuitions of his own and other highly trained musical minds as being equally valid. Stumpf the philosopher and musician knew the truth of what the physiologist could only approximate, and he viewed empirical psychology as merely propaedeutic to "higher philosophical concerns."[7]

Stung by Stumpf's sixty-seven-page refutation of Lorenz, Wundt counterattacked (1892). His assertion that "whoever would further the psychology of tone must have something more than musical experience" was aimed directly at Stumpf, though Wundt himself was famous for advocating introspection as a starting point. Wundt's laboratory, in a variety of studies, had been attempting to define what his student Edward Titchener (1867–1927, later professor at Cornell) described as the "full resources of the normal mind" (1896). "The structural psychology of Wundt and Titchener had a threefold aim: to describe the components of consciousness in terms of basic elements, to describe the combinations of basic elements, and to explain the connections of the elements of consciousness to the nervous system."[8] Titchener reported 11,600 "conscious elements" of audition (i.e., discriminable pitches), each "distinct from all the rest, and altogether simple and unanalyzable. Each one may be blended or connected with others in various ways, to form *perceptions* and *ideas*." For Wundt, the manner in which a musical expert "blended or connected" the basic elements was a problem separate from establishing the identity of those elements through

6 Stumpf, "Vergleichung der Tondistanzen." 7 Ash, *Gestalt Psychology*, p. 31.

8 From Titchener, *An Outline of Psychology* (1896), quoted in Brennan, *History and Systems of Psychology*, p. 149.

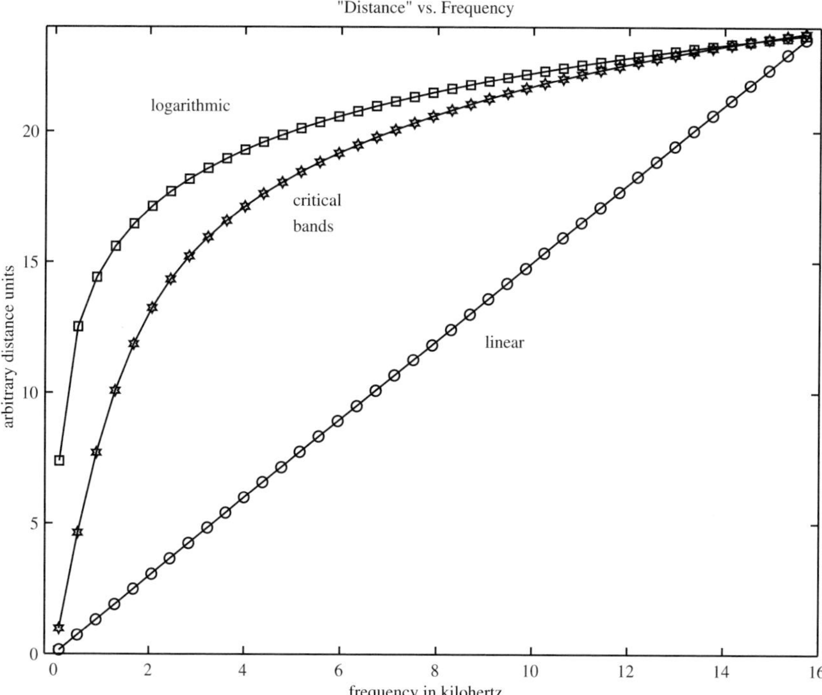

Figure 31.1 The controversy between Wundt and Stumpf centered on finding the proper function for relating two frequencies to their perceived musical distance. As traditionally defined, musical intervals have a logarithmic relationship to frequency (e.g., two frequencies in the ratio of 2:1 will be perceived as being an octave apart, regardless of the specific frequencies involved). Lorenz's experiments suggested that in some cases a linear relationship existed between two frequencies and their perceived distance (e.g., the frequencies 1,200 and 1,100 Hz, which are 100 Hz apart, might seem to be the same distance apart as the frequencies 200 and 100 Hz). The modern measure of musical distance is based on "critical bands" and falls between the functions advocated by Stumpf and Wundt.

experimentation. If Stumpf did not like those results, then perhaps he was, to use Bacon's metaphor, in the wrong tribe.

Four more rejoinders were published, each more shrill and exasperated in tone.[9] At a century's distance, all the fuss about measuring intervals may seem overblown, more a function of male territoriality than of science. Yet the positions sharpened in that engagement continued to assert themselves. The field itself eventually split, with the Wundtians pursuing the "bottom-up" investigation of the auditory system

9 See Boring, "The Psychology of Controversy."

(*Tonpsychologie*) and the Stumpfians developing "top-down," Gestalt psychology (see below) and what Ernst Kurth (1886–1946) termed *Musikpsychologie* (1931). Musicians still deride psychologists for not being adequately "musical," and psychologists still labor at establishing the psychological foundations of musicians' poorly defined intuitions.[10] Syntheses that reconcile opposing positions often come decades after the dispute. Today, for example, we may surmise that Lorenz's subjects were revealing the importance of "critical bands,"[11] "an intermediate measure between frequency and log frequency"[12] that is determined by the fine-scale neurophysiology of the inner ear (see Figure 31.1). Wundt's obsession with controlled observation was indeed pointing toward a better understanding of the "basic elements," yet Stumpf was right in distinguishing them from the "perception and ideas" of the expert. In the same regard, Stumpf's statistical analysis of differences in the way Lorenz's subjects responded to situations where a "middle" pitch could or could not fall on a scale tone (e.g., the major third c^1–e^1 has a middle pitch of d^1, whereas the minor third e^1–g^1 has a middle pitch that falls outside of the standard twelve chromatic pitches) became typical of modern techniques of using computational measures to distinguish "nature" from "nurture" ("Vergleichung der Tondistanzen," 1890). In Comte's terms, perhaps both sides in the Stumpf–Wundt controversy had too quickly posited universals that obscured the coordination of "observable facts" and delayed the discovery of more encompassing "descriptive laws of natural events."

American functionalism

In contrast to Wundt's structuralism, "the American psychologists who had been trained in Germany imposed a functional interpretation on structural psychology when they returned to America . . . Functionalism was an orientation in psychology that emphasized mental processes rather than mental content and that valued the usefulness of psychology."[13] As an early example of this different orientation, we may look to the 1910 dissertation at the University of Chicago by W. Van Dyke Bingham (1880–1952). Bingham was a student both of James Angell (1869–1949, who had studied with William James [1842–1910] at Harvard and in Germany at Halle with Erdmann) and of Hugo Münsterberg (1863–1916, who was a student of Wundt and whom James then brought to Harvard). Angell's influential *Psychology* (1904) proclaimed that "our purpose is . . . to adopt a biological point of view . . . and to attempt . . . to see just how the mind aids in the adjustment of the psychophysical human organism to its environment."

For his topic, Bingham chose the "melody problem." He set out a series of hypotheses concerning melodic "unity," "relationship," and "tonality," and then tested his

10 Gjerdingen, "An Experimental Music Theory?"
11 Plomp and Levelt, "Tonal Consonance and Critical Bandwidth."
12 Huron and Sellmer, "Critical Bands."
13 Brennan, *History and Systems of Psychology*, p. 164.

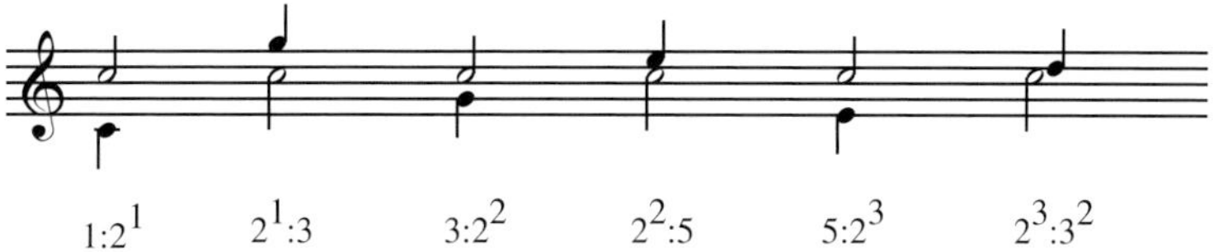

Figure 31.2 The "Lipps–Meyer" Law predicts an "effect of finality" for a melodic interval that ends on a tone which, in terms of an idealized frequency ratio, can be represented as a power of two. There are an infinite number of such ratios, but Lipps, Meyer, and others of that time usually restricted their discussions to the "normal" intervals of the diatonic scale. As shown on the staff, the open noteheads represent the notes with an "effect of finality" as predicted by the law.

hypotheses with a series of experiments. In melody studies from this period, a much-discussed issue was the "law of the number 2" (see Figure 31.2). This law – the assertion that in pairs of tones, if one of the tones has, as its number when the interval is expressed as a ratio, a power of 2, then that tone functions as a psychological "center of gravity" – was first proposed by Theodor Lipps (1851–1914, also a logician) and taken up by Max Meyer (1873–1967), who in 1896 completed the first dissertation in Berlin supervised by Stumpf. The status of these scholars notwithstanding, Bingham's experiments suggested that "the law of finality of two-tone melodies did not tell the whole story."[14]

> Two melodically "related" tones tend to establish a tonality. (p. 34)

> The tonality consists in the *attitude* of which the image is merely the superficial manifestation or sensory core. One can image the tone of 320 d.v. [= Hz] as a tonic in the key of *e* or as a median in the key of *c*, and the auditory image will be identical in the two cases, but not the total psychosis. There will be an entirely different organization of expectations, an entirely different attitude, an entirely different set of anticipations and demands, a preparedness for one set of experiences, but not for another. (p. 37)

What Bingham describes as his "motor theory of melody" is couched strongly in Angell's terms of an "organism" and its "environment":

> Every melody, like every other experience which is a "whole," must have . . . "a beginning, a middle and an end." A motor theory of melody finds the "beginning" in the upsetting of established muscular tensions which the onset of the tonal sequence involves . . . The "middle" includes the taking of the proper "attitude," the organization of a set of incipient responses, and then, as the tonal sequence proceeds, the making of these responses explicit and overt in the acts of responding to the successive tones. Each tone demands a specific act of adjustment for which a general and also a more or less specific preparation has already been made, and each contributes in turn to the furthermore definite organization of the total attitude. If a tone appears which is of such a

14 Bingham, *Studies in Melody*, p. 34.

> pitch that an entirely new adjustment is necessary, that tone is unrelated: unity is destroyed; the succession of tones is not a melody. But if the new tone is so related to its predecessors that it institutes a response which is in part a continuation of the act already in progress, the unity is preserved . . . The "end" comes only with the arrival of a phase of the complex ongoing activities in which the balanced tensions can merge into each other and harmoniously resolve their opposing strains. This becomes possible when a sufficiently definite set of expectations has been aroused and then satisfied. (pp. 81ff.)

Bingham's discourse has clear affinities with that of Angell's most famous student, James B. Watson (1878–1958), whose earlier dissertation was entitled *Animal Education: The Psychical Development of the White Rat* (1903) and who was the great early exponent of behaviorism. But it also foreshadows the much later doctoral work at Chicago by Leonard Meyer (see below).

The most American of American functionalists was, ironically, born in Sweden. Carl Seashore (1866–1949, né Sjöstrand) came as a boy to a Swedish-American settlement in Boone County, Iowa. He worked summers on the family farm, learned English, and qualified to attend the Swedish Lutheran college of Gustavus Adophus in Minnesota (Seashore's father was a lay minister). After graduating as valedictorian (1891), he went off to Yale to study with George Ladd (1842–1921, a Protestant minister) and Edward Scripture (1864–1945, student of Wundt). Yale granted him its first Ph.D. in psychology, and he was later recognized as "easily the most distinguished" of the graduates of that laboratory.[15] Seashore returned to Iowa and developed in Iowa City the most extensive program in the psychology of music that the world had yet seen. He published extensively, became Dean of the Graduate School (1908; Stumpf had become Rector in Berlin), and led the way in adapting or building new technology for the study of musical performance. A $200,000 research grant by the Bell Laboratories in the 1930s gives some indication of the magnitude of his enterprise.[16]

American psychologists in the age of Teddy Roosevelt lived in a different society than their German counterparts in the age of Kaiser Wilhelm. Applied psychology, directed at raising the masses, was not a priority in a German educational system where "powerful and well-established social mechanisms . . . governed the selection . . . both of individuals and of programs."[17] German scholars were an elite and tended to report studies based on relatively few subjects (in Stumpf's case, often on Stumpf alone). But in the New World, "instead of functioning as a repository of preindustrial patterns, as it did in Germany, . . . education [in America] quickly adapted itself to provide an almost perfect reflection of the requirements of the new industrial order. The chief

15 Boring, *A History of Experimental Psychology*, p. 528.

16 A short but valuable biography of Seashore was prepared by John Kendall, then head of the psychology department at Gustavus Adolphus College, and published October 21, 1977 in *Faculty Notes*, an in-house publication at Gustavus. I would like to thank the Gustavus archivist, Chester Johnson, for his kind assistance in providing me with this material.

17 Danziger, "Social Context and Investigative Practice," p. 27.

agents of this process were the new educational administrators who provided applied psychology with its most important and most reliable market."[18]

Seashore's *Psychology of Musical Talent* (1919), a monograph "addressed to students of applied psychology" (p. vii), established his public reputation and offered valuable tools to the educational administrator. Francis Galton (1822–1911), a close relative and advocate of Charles Darwin (1809–82), had pioneered the study of inherited traits and abilities through statistical methods. As Seashore says, "The stress of [World War I] forced our army to adopt psychological methods for the selection and rating of the human energies of men for assignment to service and for promotion. When the best results are demanded in any occupation, haphazard procedure must give way to procedure on the basis of ascertained facts. When Music shall come to her own she will come to the musically gifted: to that end musical talent must be revealed and encouraged" (p. vii). And who better to administer these tests than an educational administrator: "For the large cities, the most natural solution is the employment of a consulting supervisor of music, who shall be given general charge of the organization of surveys, the adjustment of the curriculum for the introduction of the tests and exercises, the planning of follow-up work, the giving of individual counsel and more intensive examinations, and the adjustment of groupings for instruction in the public schools on the basis of ascertained talent" (pp. 280ff.).

The Seashore tests were designed to measure specific "capacities or abilities for the hearing of music tones,"[19] and thus constitute a legacy of Wundt's inventory of "specific nervous energies." For instance, pitch discrimination was measured by two pure tones "sounded in quick succession . . . The listener is to tell whether the second tone was higher or lower than the first. Thus, the problem is reduced to its simplest form."[20] Pure tones had been produced by large sets of precision tuning forks, the preserve of elite research institutions. The most prized of these, by the Parisian Rudolph Koenig (1832–1901), were wonders of the scientific world. At the Philadelphia Centennial Exposition (1876) he exhibited a set of 670 forks ranging from one five feet high, with a pitch of 16 Hz, to a tiny one that vibrated at nearly 20,000 Hz.[21] Against this expensive European craftsmanship Seashore offered "a phonograph record which is economical, standard, durable, and relatively foolproof in use."[22]

Seashore summed up the work of his laboratory in *The Psychology of Music* (1938). Its frontispiece presents a photograph of "The Henrici Harmonic Analyzer, a symbol of the science of music." Its gleaming wheels, carefully machined armatures, and six mysteriously glowing orbs portend not just an efficient mechanical means of approximating the Fourier integral, but the pride and power of modern science brought to bear on long-standing problems of the musical mind. In their day, Seashore's energy and enthusiasm were highly infectious. He promised a Brave New World where there

18 Ibid., p. 26. 19 Seashore, *Psychology of Music*. 20 Seashore, *Psychology of Musical Talent*.
21 Boring, *Sensation and Perception*, pp. 328ff. 22 Seashore, *Psychology of Music*, p. 56.

would be few limits on what "scientific procedure in the interpretation, evaluation, and education of the musical mind" could achieve. "Scientific procedure" would:

1. give us "a psychology of music"
2. furnish us with "a technique for the development of musical esthetics"
3. form "a basis for the analysis and evaluation of musical talent"
4. develop a basis for "an intimate relationship between music and speech"
5. lay "the foundation of musical criticism, musical biography and autobiography, and music theory in general"
6. furnish "the foundation for the essential facts for the construction of the curriculum"
7. give "music its true place and influence" (p. 12)

This minister's son felt deeply that science improved the lot of mankind. "It is a wonderful thing," he marveled, "that science makes it possible to discover, measure, and explain the operations of the musical mind in the same attitude that the astronomer explains the operation of the stars" (p. xi). Yet a reader with experience of what the science and the institutionalization of psychology brought about in the years after 1938 may find it difficult to share fully in Seashore's enthusiasms. Standardized tests intended to uncover the talent hidden in farmboys like Seashore can begin to look like means of discrimination in the urban ghetto. Moreover, Seashore's own tests did not reliably predict an individual's subsequent success or failure.

"Pure" research into hearing could be integrated into the technical means of the modern state. For example, the Gestalt psychologist Wertheimer and the ethnomusicologist Hornbostel (see below), both from Stumpf's institute, adapted theories of sound localization into battlefield devices for locating enemy artillery positions and served during the First World War as reserve officers of the Prussian Artillery Testing Commission.[23] Paul Farnsworth (1899–), an early critic of Seashore's tests, declared him "one of the most ardent hereditarians psychology has produced, and his books quite clearly reflect this nativistic bias."[24]

While the boosterism of the jazz-age American Heartland, skewered by the novels of Sinclair Lewis, may ring hollow today, Seashore's numerous achievements nevertheless remain truly impressive. His studies of the nuances of musical performance (vibrato, phrasing, dynamics, etc.), aided by the same technology that had made possible talking motion pictures, are models of their kind. He also tried to encourage research into areas that still present great obstacles:

> Success or failure in music depends upon the capacity for living in a tonal world through productive and reproductive imagination. The musician lives in a world of images. (p. 5)

23 Ash, *Gestalt Psychology*, pp. 187ff. 24 Farnsworth, *Social Psychology of Music*, p. vi.

> This subject [auditory imagery] has received too little attention in recent years, largely owing to the extreme behavioristic attitude which ignores the existence of the mental image and partly owing to the fact that it is a phenomenon which does not lend itself accurately to psychophysical measurements. (p. 161)

And he was a pioneer in the field of experimental aesthetics. His credo, "The artistic expression of feeling in music consists in esthetic deviation from the regular – from pure tone, true pitch, even dynamics, metronomic time, rigid rhythms, etc. All of these deviations can be measured" (p. 9), would likely be shared by many of today's leading scholars in the study of musical performance.

Gestalt psychology

As mentioned earlier, John Locke was among the first to note that "the idea of the whole" as "a positive absolute idea" could be applied to a melody. Ernst Mach (1838–1916, for whom the Mach numbers of supersonic flight are named) revisited the topic. Thinking about how two melodies might be perceived as "the same," and using the newer vocabulary of psychophysics, he remarked that "we can choose the melodies in such a way that not even two partial tones in them are the same. And yet we recognize the melodies as the same."[25] Mach, however, could not, in the spirit of physiology, find a "sensation" that accounted for the "affinity of form." Christian von Ehrenfels (1859–1932, student of Brentano) "restructured the discussion by taking melody as his paradigmatic case for deciding what such forms 'are in themselves' (*an sich seien*). Noting, as had Mach, that we can recognize two melodies as identical even when no two notes in them are the same, he argued that "these forms must therefore be something *different* from the sum of the elements. They must have . . . 'Gestalt quality.'"[26]

Ehrenfels's holistic notion of "Gestalt quality" struck a chord with musicians. It reinstituted *Vorstellungen* (conceptions or ideations) above *Empfindungen* (sensations), a shift that Hugo Riemann (1849–1919) eventually followed in replacing his early reliance on Helmholtz's term *Tonempfindungen* with a new emphasis on *Tonvorstellungen*.[27] Ehrenfels himself was a musician and devotee of Wagner, to the extent that he undertook a pilgrimage on foot to Bayreuth for the 1882 premiere of *Parsifal*. In his view, the tone painting in Wagner's music dramas "provides an inestimable wealth of material for the comparison of Gestalt qualities of all kinds."[28] And for the young musician-psychologists under the tutelage of Stumpf (the arch musician-psychologist), Ehrenfels's new concept seems to have been irresistible.

25 Mach, "Vom räumlihen Sehen."
26 Ehrenfels, "Über Gestaltqualitäten." See also Ash, *Gestalt Psychology*, pp. 87–88.
27 Riemann, "Ideen zu einer 'Lehre von den Tonvorstellungen.'"
28 Ash, *Gestalt Psychology*, p. 91.

The three young scholars who developed Gestalt psychology were all closely connected with Stumpf. Max Wertheimer (1880–1943) grew up playing piano and violin in a German-speaking Jewish family in Prague. He studied with Brentano at Prague and then with Stumpf in Berlin, becoming friends with Hornbostel and attending musicological lectures by Max Friedlaender (1852–1934). In 1910 he wrote to a friend that he intended to study melody as a Gestalt.[29] Kurt Koffka (1886–1941) came from the well-to-do family of a Protestant Berlin lawyer and a Jewish mother. He completed a 1908 dissertation under Stumpf on the theory of rhythm (expressed in visual patterns). Koffka's studies showed that "'grouping,' determined or structured by an 'accent,' was fundamental for the experience of rhythm." He argued that "the then current theory of rhythm, which stressed kinesthetic sensations, did not explain the role of grouping, but only shifted the problem to another level of explanation."[30] Wolfgang Köhler (1887–1967), youngest of the three, was highly musical and like Wertheimer played both piano and violin. With his solid training in the physical sciences (he had worked with the quantum physicist Max Planck) Köhler made a breakthrough in the study of *Klangfarben* (tone colors) by placing a tiny mirror on the surface of his eardrum and studying the patterns of light reflected when a beam was directed onto it while he listened to loud tones. His 1909 dissertation on the subject appeared the same year as Arnold Schoenberg's *Five Pieces for Orchestra*, Op. 16, with its *Klangfarbenmelodie*.

The Gestalt psychologists did not invent the study of parts and wholes. Nor were they the first to notice that certain arrangements of stimuli seem to enhance the perception of the whole. Georg Müller (1850–1934), for example, reported in 1904 that stimuli characterized by factors of nearness, symmetrical position, or "inclusion in common contours," seemed to possess a higher "degree of coherence." But the Gestalt school elevated these observations to general laws supported by experimental data. In a 1923 formalization of precepts first announced in 1914, Wertheimer transformed Müller's "inclusion in common contours" into the Law of Good Continuation. Likewise he postulated a Law of Proximity, a Law of Similarity, a Law of Closure, and a Law of *Prägnanz* (i.e., we perceive the best and simplest organization afforded by circumstances). The experimental data, as one might expect of Stumpf's students, did not emphasize voluminous statistics on groups of inexpert subjects. *Psychologische Forschung*, the Gestalt organ edited first by Koffka and then by Wertheimer, had "the lowest proportion of studies with data referring to group rather than to individual performance of the major German psychology journals for the years 1920 to 1930."[31] And the Gestalt research program favored what today would be termed "robust" phenomena. As a student of the period jokingly put it, "A Gestalt theoretical experiment was geared up so that it would work in 100 percent of the cases, and if it did not work, well throw it out the window."[32]

29 Ibid., p. 108. 30 Ibid., p. 109.
31 Danziger, "Social Context and Investigative Practice," p. 28. 32 Ash, *Gestalt Psychology*, p. 222.

Though Stumpf himself was not an eager adherent, he had already made "Gestalt qualities" the subject of his seminar in the winter of 1906–07, and he went to great lengths to ensure his Gestaltist students a prominent place in the post-war Weimar Republic. First, in a spectacular feat of academic-political maneuver during the chaos following the Kaiser's abdication, he managed to move his institute into a wing of the imperial palace. Many key experiments of the Gestalt school were performed in grand spaces only recently vacated by the ladies-in-waiting. Then, Stumpf artfully arranged for Köhler, still a young man, to succeed him in Germany's most prestigious chair. The years between Köhler's 1922 ascension in Berlin and his forced resignation in the 1930s represent the high-water mark of the Gestalt school. Koffka, fluent in English, left Germany in 1927. Wertheimer, who recognized the danger for Jews under the Nazi regime, departed in 1933. Köhler, the unimpeachably Teutonic German, stood for a while against the toadyism of pro-Nazi academics and published the last anti-Nazi article permitted in a German newspaper. All three eventually came to America: Wertheimer to the New School for Social Research, Koffka to Smith College, and Köhler to Swarthmore and then Dartmouth.

In what seems like a puzzling missed opportunity, the first generation of Gestalt psychologists did not make music a focus of their experiments. To be sure, musical subjects were mentioned frequently as exemplifications of Gestalt ideas – the holistic nature of melody, the grouping of rhythms, the triad as a unity. Hornbostel attempted a synthesis ("Psychologie der Gehörerscheinungen") in 1923 but did not venture much beyond the domain of psychoacoustics. These most musical of psychologists focused their actual work much more on visual than on auditory phenomena. Though Wertheimer composed music at an early age, his name is associated with the study of apparent motion in visual perception, not with the psychology of music. Of their few students to study aesthetic questions, the best known – Rudolf Arnheim (1904–) – chose the visual arts (films and painting) over music. Only for their intellectual grandchildren would the art of music become a major focus.

Behaviorism

Tones were there at the birth of behaviorism – the dogs that salivated in the Russian laboratory of Ivan Pavlov (1849–1936) were conditioned to expect food after hearing a tone. And the American evangelist who redirected psychology away from the subjective study of mind and toward the objective study of overt behavior – John Watson (1878–1958) – studied at the University of Chicago in the same environment as the melody specialist W. Van Dyke Bingham (see above). Yet music, as opposed to an isolated tone, did not fit easily into the stimulus–response paradigm of behaviorism. The emphasis of behaviorists on "comparative psychology," meaning the study of animal behavior, left little or no place for music. And definitions of rewards (the food for

Pavlov's dogs) in terms of motivations, urges, and so forth were not easily adapted to questions of why a particular phrase in a string quartet sounded better in the key of G major than in A♭ major. As an internal aesthetic activity, music could have few overt behaviors beyond tapping one's foot or occasionally humming along with a tune.

Music does function within social events, however, and those social events or circumstances do produce overt behaviors. That shift in focus – from music as "art for art's sake" to music as a component of "important public acts" – formed the starting point for Charles Diserens's *Influence of Music on Behavior* (originally a dissertation in psychology at the University of Cincinnati). Diserens declared:

> Our purpose then is to study the influence of music on the organism. We approach music from the practical rather than the aesthetic standpoint, regarding it as a necessity, a possible means of re-education and human reconstruction for all, rather than a mere subject of unproductive pleasure, or an object for criticism from the learned few . . . Music was always associated with social life, or rather the functioning of the organs of society. It was never "an end is itself," but subordinate to important public acts, magic, ritual, ceremony, or labor. (p. 16)

If the social human is the analogue of Pavlov's dog, and social functions the motivations, then music is part of a complex of stimuli that should produce a measurable organic response analogous to the dog's salivation. Diserens had begun a series of experiments in 1921–22 "to determine the influence of music upon certain typical forms and aspects of behavior which are of importance in the ordinary activities of daily life." Using apparatus related to the modern polygraph, he measured fatigue, endurance, accuracy of movement, speed of movement, effects on handwriting, perception of optical illusions, "suggestibility," color selection, respiration, and reflexes. He concluded that in spite of many questions and problems raised by the experiments, one could nevertheless conclude that "all activities tested are considerably accelerated by music" (p. 209), a finding not easily interpreted but still suggestive of how music could aid in industrial efficiency and production. The ubiquitous background music of today's commercial environments has its roots in behaviorism.

Diserens went farther than most in his behaviorist approach to music. Yet his interest in music's social functions was less a leap into a twentieth-century dehumanized science than a reinterpretation of nineteenth-century inclinations to view music as part of society's moral and ethical fabric. These musico-social functions retained their status as "higher" subjects and typically came toward the end of textbooks in the psychology of music. Like the formulaic presentation of topics in a medieval music treatise, where one often began with *Sonus est* . . ., the psychology-of-music textbook from the 1920s onward had a typical order of presentation that also began with the nature of sound. After presenting the elements of vibration; the rudiments of psychoacoustics; the qualities of a tone, of tones in pairs, and of larger combinations of tones; and the nature of rhythm; the author would then proceed to the higher subjects. These were musical aesthetics, musical talent, issues of performance, and music in society.

Good examples of this presentational scheme, which in many respects still functions today, are the texts of Max Schoen (1888–1957, a Seashore student) and James Mursell (1893–1963). Schoen's "survey for teacher and musician" (1940) provides an excellent summary of the studies done on musical prodigies, in particular Stumpf's work with Pepito Areola and Geza Révész's (1878–1955) with Ervin Nyiregyházy.[33] Mursell was not unique for his time in addressing the subject of race. Both he and Seashore[34] note that studies of the musical ability of schoolchildren did not show any consistent racial differences. Mursell's adoption of a Gestalt approach to describing musical patterns and his postulation of a small set of rhythmic feet as the core constituents of rhythm reappears in the writings of Leonard Meyer (see below), who took his bachelor's degree (in philosophy) in 1940 at Mursell's Columbia University.

Cognitive psychology

Behaviorism might be called the "era of the white rat" in honor of that animal's role in countless studies. But even during behaviorism's heyday, careful observers had begun to notice that the humble rat seemed to do more than just respond to isolated stimuli. A 1948 article by Edward Tolman (1886–1959, University of California at Berkeley), "Cognitive Maps in Rats and Men," suggested that rats could learn the general organization of their environment, a knowledge apparently gleaned from a process akin to thinking. If rats could think, then perhaps so could men. Other studies began to highlight innate limitations or biases in human cognition. In an experiment that presented listeners with a rapid alternation of two tones,[35] George Miller (1920–, Princeton University) demonstrated that, as the interval between these tones widened, one heard a shift from the trilling of one main tone to a tremolo effect of two separate tones. The change in the response seemed more a Gestalt-like rethinking of the stimulus than a simple response. Miller's most famous article, "The Magical Number Seven, Plus or Minus Two," further demonstrated innate properties of how the brain "processes" information in memorable "chunks" of from five to nine items. The influential *Cognitive Psychology* (1966) of Ulric Neisser (1928–) helped give a name to what eventually replaced behaviorism as the dominant orientation in psychology. Cognitive psychologists attempt to specify, through the interpretation of statistical data obtained from experiments, how the mind works. And they often express that working in terms of "mental structures" and "mental processes." In his book on memory,[36] Sir Frederic Bartlett (1886–1969) had introduced this distinction to explain how the memory of a story is first encoded (a process) into a *schema* (a structure) and then subsequently decoded (another process) as a recollection that may depart in significant

33 Stumpf, "Akustische Versuche"; Révész, *Nyiregyházy*.
34 Mursell, *Psychology of Music*; Seashore, *Psychology of Music*.
35 Miller and Heise, "Trill Threshold."
36 Bartlett, *Remembering*.

ways from the original experience. A similar conceptual model, though in mathematical form, appeared in Claude Shannon's (1916–) influential general theory of communication,[37] in which the notion of "information" explains how abstract senders and receivers of messages negotiate "signals," "noise," "coding," and "decoding." The work of the French scholar Jean Piaget (1896–1980) on children's learning, the American Noam Chomsky (1928–) on language, the discovery of neurons that respond to higher-level percepts,[38] and the "artificial intelligence" of digital computers further helped to foster a view of the mind as a complex modular system that couples a formidable array of inherited capabilities ("hardware") with learned adaptations specific to its environment ("software").

In the psychology of music, two great figures emerged in the early postwar years. Both had fought the Nazis, one from the West in the major battles of the American army, and the other from within the French Resistance (which led to later imprisonment in Auschwitz). Both took the precepts of the Gestaltists for granted, though with reservations. Both were musically sophisticated and sufficiently knowledgeable of avant garde and ethnic musical styles to recognize that the facts of psychoacoustics are not fully determinative of musical culture. And both wrote their respective treatises with such grace, breadth of vision, and insight as to prompt a recent text to list them, along with the treatise of Helmholtz, as the "three books that form a nucleus of what we consider most important in the psychology of music."[39]

The first, Leonard Meyer (1918–), provided what Seashore had dreamed of – "a technique for the development of musical esthetics."[40] Meyer's 1954 dissertation and 1956 book, *Emotion and Meaning in Music*, focuses on "those aspects of meaning which result from the understanding of and response to relationships inherent in the musical progress."[41] His work combines Gestalt precepts, a theory of emotion, and an emphasis on learned expectations. Meyer quotes Koffka and Wertheimer, claiming that "the work of the Gestalt psychologists has shown beyond a doubt that understanding is not a matter of perceiving single stimuli, or simple sound combinations in isolation, but is rather a matter of grouping stimuli into patterns and relating these patterns to one another" (p. 6). Yet after presenting the Gestalt laws in relation to musical patterns, he cautions that "even within the confined limits of a particular style," it does not seem likely that "a precise and systematic account of musical perception solely in Gestalt terms is possible. Even given additional empirical data about aural perception, certain basic difficulties in the application of Gestalt principles to any specific music process would still remain. These difficulties do not derive from any basic weakness in Gestalt laws per se but from the fact that the number, interdependence, and subtlety of the variables involved in musical perception make the establishment of a system of analytical

37 Shannon, "Mathematical Theory of Communication."

38 Hubel and Wiesel, "Receptive Fields."

39 Dowling and Harwood, *Music Cognition*, p. xii.

40 Seashore, *Psychology of Music*, p. 12.

41 Meyer, *Emotion and Meaning*, p. 3.

Figure 31.3 Meyer (1956) provided musical examples of the "Law of Good Continuation," a basic precept of Gestalt psychology. "The perception of a line or motion initiates a mental process, and it is this mental process which, following the mental line of least resistance, tends to be perpetuated and continued" (p. 92). "Continuity always operates within a particular cultural stylistic context . . . Harmony often plays an important part in determining our expectations of melodic continuation. A common example of this is the melodic progression upward through the triad" (pp. 101–02) as in the tune "Three Blind Mice."

rules of thumb impossible." In particular, "musical perception" depends critically on "the sensitive responses of experienced listeners" (p. 86) (see Figure 31.3).

Meyer's theory of emotion draws on a tradition begun by John Dewey (1859–1952, University of Chicago and Columbia University) and is then given a more neurological formulation in 1949 by Donald Hebb (1904–85, McGill University). As Meyer states it, "Emotion or affect is aroused when a tendency to respond is arrested or inhibited" (p. 14). This "conflict" theory of emotion has parallels with Seashore's concept of expressive deviation in performance, though Meyer takes pains to distinguish the two (pp. 201ff.). For Meyer, Seashore lacked a theory connecting deviations to affective experience. Meyer provides that theory, as well as a related theory of musical meaning: "If on the basis of past experience, a present stimulus leads us to expect a more or less definite consequent musical event, then that stimulus has meaning." The similarity to his theory of emotion is obvious. Meyer remarks, "Once it is recognized that affective experience is just as dependent upon intelligent cognition as conscious intellection, that both involve perception, taking account of, envisaging, and so forth, thinking and feeling need not be viewed as polar opposites but as different manifestations of a single psychological process" (p. 39).

The second great postwar psychologist of music was Robert Francès (1919–). Like Meyer, he completed his bachelor's degree in philosophy and turned his dissertation into his most famous publication, *La Perception de la musique* (1958).[42] And like Meyer, Francès concerns himself with questions of musical aesthetics:

> There is a type of musical perception that has little in common with simple audition; it is to that we devote our efforts here. In all of its complexity, it is identified with a part of the aesthetic experience, insofar as that embraces equally both experience and creation. We can conceptualize it only as a process of development, and never as simply falling under a "stimulus-response" schema. We must distinguish between the effects

42 Trans. Dowling as *The Perception of Music*.

of acculturation – unreflective, involuntary, and resulting from almost passive familiarity with works – and the effects of education, where perceptual development is supported by the acquisition of concepts and symbols that provide for the definition of forms, their elements and articulations. (Dowling trans., pp. 2–3)

To empirically validate this differentiation between "simple audition," acculturation, and education, Francès devised sixteen experiments containing many of the techniques that would become standard in the field. His second experiment revisited a topic that was important in Seashore's laboratory – deviations from "correct" intonation during musical performance.[43] Measurements of phonograph recordings by such famous violinists as Kreisler, Elman, and Menuhin had clearly shown intonational deviations, many of which seemed to confirm the notion of inflected "tendency tones." Francès wanted to investigate the psychology of these deviations:

Until now, those phenomena have in effect been presented either as facts, based on the analysis of instrumental playing and vocal interpretation, or as consequences deduced from the precepts of harmonic writing . . . For a theory of the development of musical perception such as ours . . . [it is important to see] in what measure the precepts of writing have been transformed into perceptual tendencies, resulting in the tonal integration of tones into a whole . . . If we take as a base the tempered tuning of a piano, and lower the pitch of two of its notes, we would expect this alteration to be less noticeable to the listener when those notes contribute to a structure where they are subject to descending influences (in keeping with the tendencies defined earlier), than where they are subject to ascending influences . . . [From the empirical results of tests on 22 musically trained subjects] we can conclude that the global impression of correct intonation was greater in the first piece (where the flatting of the critical notes conformed to the descending influences they had each time they occurred) than in the second piece (which exerted ascending influences on the same notes). (pp. 55ff.)

In this and other experiments, Francès shows that listeners develop mental structures similar to, though not identical with, patterns described in music theory. These structures derive from the "second nature" of experience and not from the facts of acoustics. Francès emphasizes learned expectations: "The functions of each scale degree . . . are normatively defined by the theory of classical harmony, but through frequent use they come to determine expectancy reactions – momentary perceptions entirely saturated with knowledge or containing a small degree of uncertainty" (p. 78). When expectancies cannot be learned, "acculturation" may prove difficult. He is among the first to raise a cautionary flag about the perception of twelve-tone music. From his sixth experiment, which had among its subjects impressive specialists in serial music, he concludes that "Serial unity lies more on the conceptual than on the perceptual level; . . . when thwarted by melodic motion, rhythm, and the harmonic grouping of tones, it remains very difficult to hear."

Students of the psychology of music in the 1960s and 1970s were influenced by the

43 See Small, "An Objective Analysis."

work of Meyer and Francès, by the studies of Paul Fraisse (1911–), whose 1956 *Les Structures rythmiques* integrates concepts of musical rhythm into the larger framework of human time perception, and by the exciting work being done in language, vision, psychoacoustics, neurophysiology, and the study of mental representations. Not since the time of Stumpf had so many fine dissertations been written on important themes of music perception.

The promise to understand the nature of pattern perception in melody, left unfulfilled by the original Gestaltists, was taken up by three major scholars who began publishing in the late 1960s and early 1970s. Diana Deutsch (1938–), a native Londoner transplanted to the University of California at San Diego, studied melody and memory, developing in the process a number of fascinating musical "illusions" that provide auditory analogues of the optical illusions important to the study of vision. Her vigorous advocacy of the psychology of music resulted in a landmark volume, *The Psychology of Music* (1982; 2nd edn., 1999), and the founding of an interdisciplinary journal devoted to the subject, *Music Perception* (1983–). W. Jay Dowling (1941–), an American working at the University of Texas at Dallas, demonstrated the intimate connections between memories of scale step, interval, contour, and rhythm in a series of studies summarized in the first such textbook designed for students in cognitive psychology, his *Music Cognition* (1986). And Albert Bregman (1936–), a Canadian working at McGill University, approached the broader problem of how the brain makes sense of any sonic landscape. He interpreted the perception of melody and counterpoint as special cases of "auditory scene analysis," which became the title of a 1990 survey of his work.

In the later 1970s and early 1980s, psychologists placed harmony and tonality back onto center stage, a position these subjects had enjoyed in the days of Helmholtz and Stumpf. In the process, many psychologists became de facto music theorists, and some music theorists became de facto psychologists. First, the psychologists.

Roger Shepard (1929–), a cognitive psychologist widely known for his work on mental representations, had revisited in the 1960s the so-called pitch spiral advocated by Geza Révész and first imagined by Drobisch.[44] Shepard viewed this spiral, whose two components are chroma (pitch class) and height (octave), as a mathematically precise specification of a mental representation.[45] His student Carol Krumhansl (1947–) greatly extended this line of inquiry though a series of "probe tone" experiments summarized in her *Cognitive Foundations of Musical Pitch* (1990). In the typical experiment, a subject hears a musical context followed by a single pitch – the "probe" – and is asked to rate, on a scale from 1 to 7, how well that tone fits into the musical context. As one might expect, probe tones in the key of the musical context receive better subjective ratings than tones outside of the key. But the data showed that subjects responded with specific and consistent ratings for all twelve pitches in any major

44 Révész, *Zur Grundlegung der Tonpsychologie*; Drobisch, "Nachträge."
45 Shepard, "Circularity in Judgments of Relative Pitch."

or minor key. A further mathematical correlation of the major and minor key "profiles" resulted in a proposed mental representation of the subjective distances between keys, one that captures many of the rules of thumb reported in harmony texts.

In developing a theory to predict the subjective pitch of arbitrary groups of inharmonic overtones (e.g., the overtones of a bell), the German psychoacoustician Ernst Terhardt (1934–, Technical University, Munich) found himself positing subjective or "virtual" fundamental pitches that bear comparison to the chordal roots posited in the eighteenth century by Rameau or Tartini. But whereas Rameau proposed one or at most two roots for chords, Terhardt's algorithm proposes a probability of root salience for each of twelve possible root pitches;[46] it assumes recorded sound as its input and takes into account the relative intensities of individual partials. An adaptation of the algorithm designed for score-based inputs has been proposed by his student Richard Parncutt (1957–).[47]

Among music theorists with interests in psychology, the composer and music theorist Fred Lerdahl (1943–, Columbia University), in concert with the linguist Ray Jackendoff (1945–, student of Chomsky), is noted for the publication of *A Generative Theory of Tonal Music* (1983). It provides a formalization of musical intuitions about harmony and rhythm, and serves as an analogue of the "generative" grammars in language studies. The book has spawned a large number of studies as cognitive psychologists have attempted to find empirical validation of its many provocative "preference rules" – rules similar to Gestalt laws in the sense that they codify preferred modes of perceptually organizing complex musical patterns (see also **Chapter 3, pp. 99–102**; and **Chapter 22, pp. 712–14**). And like Francès, Lerdahl has stressed the limitations in human musico-cognitive abilities as crucial factors in the difficulties that many serial and post-serial musics have had in gaining an audience.[48] Leonard Meyer has remained active, and after relocating to the University of Pennsylvania in the 1970s, founded the so-called "Penn" school of music theory, with its strong focus on listeners. Among his students, Eugene Narmour (1939–) has developed Meyer's analysis of melodic expectations into the formalized "implication–realization" model of melody (see Figure 31.4).[49]

Robert Gjerdingen (1952–) has developed Meyer's notion of "archetypes" into the study of historical schemata. And Justin London (1959–) has extended Meyer's work on rhythm and meter in a number of studies.[50]

Cognitive science

Since the 1980s, the phrase "music cognition" has begun to replace "psychology of music" in reference to the processing of musical information by the normal adult

46 Terhandt et al., "Algorithm." 47 Parncutt, *Harmony*. 48 Lerdahl, "Cognitive Constraints."
49 Meyer, *Explaining Music*; Narmour, *Analysis and Cognition of Basic Melodic Structure*; and *Analysis and Cognition of Melodic Complexity*.
50 Gjerdingen, "An Experimental Music Theory?"; London, "Some Examples"; "Rhythm," *NG2*, vol. XXI, pp. 277–308.

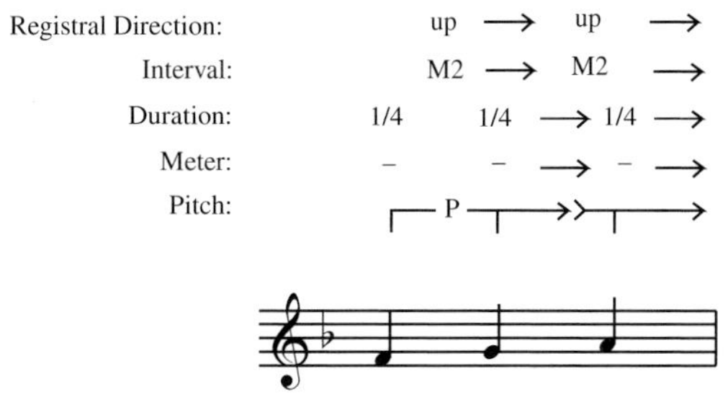

Figure 31.4 Narmour's implication–realization model (1990, 1992), building on many precepts of Leonard Meyer, attempts a rigorous "bottom-up" analysis of how each musical feature contributes to the setting up or realizing of expectations for closure or forward progress. The figure shows a process (P), which is the result of expectations for forward progress set up by the several musical features. Whether – or the extent to which – the third pitch is perceived as ongoing or closed depends on contextual factors such as harmony and the particular weighting of all the other features.

mind. In part the change recognizes the diversity of psychology itself, there now being such recognizable specializations as music therapy, the developmental psychology of music, the psychology of learning, the social psychology of music, and the psychology of emotions. But this change to "music cognition" also reflects the new status of "cognitive science." Cognitive science has as its object the study of the human mind, as does psychology. But what distinguishes cognitive science is its interdisciplinary approach and its focus on a confluence of new technologies. In relation to studies of music, these technologies are: (1) computational models of dynamical systems, neural networks, cellular automata, and other nonlinear systems not amenable to succinct verbal description; (2) *in vivo* recordings of neuronal firing patterns in the auditory systems of animals; and (3) computer-assisted imaging of the working human brain.

Gestalt theorist Wolfgang Köhler had speculated in the 1930s that the stable percept of a Gestalt was facilitated by the establishment in the brain of a stable "field" of neuronal activity analogous to the field equations in the theory of electromagnetism. Similarly the Canadian psychologist Donald Hebb had shown in the 1940s how assemblages of neurons could learn, and respond to, specific patterns of stimulation. These ideas found renewed interest in the 1980s in a branch of cognitive science known as "connectionism" or "neural networks." Diana Deutsch (1969) was the first to suggest how assemblages of neurons could process the basic constituents of scales, chords, and keys. Jamshed Bharucha (1956–, student of Krumhansl) and Gjerdingen (student of Narmour and Meyer) applied neural-network algorithms of the 1980s to music-psychological problems in a series of exploratory papers,[51] using simple inputs derived from a score-like representation of music pitch. Later studies have used recorded

51 Bharucha, "Music Cognition"; Bharucha and Olney, "Tonal Cognition"; Gjerdingen, "Using Connectionist Models"; "Categorization of Musical Patterns."

sound as input and shown how a concept like key could self-organize in response to regularities in the acoustic signals of real music.[52]

Hebb's legacy in Montreal is reflected in the prominence of McGill University and the Neurological Institute of Montreal in brain imaging. Robert Zatorre (1955–) and Isabelle Peretz (1956–) are two cognitive scientists who study and report on the response of the brain to musical stimuli. Good summaries of this research can be found in the second edition of Deutsch's *The Psychology of Music* (1999).

Limitations of space have required the omission of several important subjects and a large number of important scholars. The rich tradition of time, rhythm, and meter studies would require its own narrative, since it forms part of the study of motor behavior and control. (See, however, **Chapter 22, pp. 696–703.**). The important work of British researchers on the roles of music in everyday life, and the fascinating study of musical performance, which has continued to grow since Seashore's time, could not be covered in this short exposition. The texts cited above, however, should provide ample references to these and other areas of research. The impressive work of an active and talented cohort of younger scholars has not been included because the import of their work belongs to the field's future, not its past.

The first scholar to study systematically human memory, Hermann Ebbinghaus (1850–1909), once quipped, "Psychology has a long past, but only a short history." He was distinguishing between venerable traditions of thinking about the mind and the short period in which hypotheses about the mind's behavior had been empirically tested. Music, as "an internal, subjective entity springing from mental operations,"[53] has figured prominently in psychology's long past through the disciplines of philosophy and music theory, in psychology's short history through its subfield of the psychology of music, and shows every sign of forming an ongoing constituent of cognitive science.

52 Leman, "Ontogenesis of Tonal Semantics."

53 Serafine, *Music as Cognition*, p. 233.

Bibliography

Angell, J. R. *Psychology*, New York, Holt, Rinehart & Winston, 1904

Aristoxenus, *Elementa rhythmica*, trans. and ed. L. Pearson as *Elementa rhythmica: The Fragment of Book II and the Additional Evidence for Aristoxenean Rhythmic Theory*, Oxford, Clarendon Press, 1990

Ash, M. G. *Gestalt Psychology in German Culture, 1890–1967*, Cambridge University Press, 1995

Bacon, F. *The twoo bookes of Francis Bacon: of the proficience and advancement of learning, divine and humane (Advancement of Learning)*, London, H. Tomes, 1605

Novum Organum, London, 1620

Bartlett, F. *Remembering: A Study in Experimental and Social Psychology*, Cambridge University Press, 1932

Basevi, A. *Introduzione ad un nuovo sistema d'armonia*, Florence, Tofani, 1862

Bharucha, J. J. "Music Cognition and Perceptual Facilitation: A Connectionist Framework," *MP* 5 (1987), pp. 1–30

Bharucha, J. J. and K. L. Olney, "Tonal Cognition, Artificial Intelligence and Neural Nets," *Contemporary Music Review* 4 (1989), pp. 341–56

Bingham, W. V. D. *Studies in Melody*, Baltimore, Review Publishing Company, 1910

Boring, E. G. "The Psychology of Controversy," *Psychological Review* 36 (1929), pp. 107–13

Sensation and Perception in the History of Experimental Psychology, New York, Appleton-Century, 1942

A History of Experimental Psychology, 2nd edn., New York, Appleton-Century-Crofts, 1950

Brennan, J. F. *History and Systems of Psychology*, 3rd edn., Englewood Cliffs, NJ, Prentice Hall, 1991

Brentano, F. *Psychologie vom empirischen Standpunkt*, Leipzig, 1874

Comte, A. *Cours de philosophie positive*, 2nd edn., Paris, 1864

Cooper, G. W. and L. B. Meyer, *The Rhythmic Structure of Music*, University of Chicago Press, 1960

Danziger, K. "Social Context and Investigative Practice in Early Twentieth-Century Psychology," in *Psychology in Twentieth-Century Thought and Society*, ed. M. Ash and W. Woodward, Cambridge University Press, 1987

Della Corte, A., *La critica musicale e i critici*, Turin, Unione Tipografico, 1961

Deutsch, D., ed., *The Psychology of Music*, New York, Academic Press, 1982; 2nd edn. 1999

Diserens, C. M. *The Influence of Music on Behavior*, Princeton University Press, 1926

Dowling, W. J. and D. L. Harwood, *Music Cognition*, New York, Academic Press, 1986

Drobisch, M. W. *Nachträge zur Theorie der musikalischen Verhältnisse*, Leipzig, Hirzel, 1855

Ehrenfels, C. von, "Über Gestaltqualitäten," *Vierteljahrschrift für wissenschaftliche Philosophie* 14 (1890), pp. 249–92

Farnsworth, P. R. *The Social Psychology of Music*, New York, Dryden Press, 1958

Francès R. *La Perception de la musique*, Paris, J. Vrin, 1958; trans. W. J. Dowling as *The Perception of Music*, Hillsdale, NJ, L. Erlbaum, 1988

Gjerdingen, R. O. "An Experimental Music Theory?" in *Rethinking Music*, ed. N. Cook and M. Everist, Oxford University Press, 1999, pp. 161–70

"Using Connectionist Models to Explore Complex Musical Patterns," *Computer Music Journal* 13 (1989), pp. 67–75; reprinted in *Music and Connectionism*, ed. P. M. Todd and D. G. Loy, Cambridge, MA, MIT Press, 1991, pp. 138–49

"Categorization of Musical Patterns by Self-Organizing Neuronlike Networks," *MP* 8 (1990), pp. 339–70

Hebb, D. O. *The Organization of Behavior: A Neuropsychological Theory*, New York, Wiley, 1949

Helmholtz, H. *Die Lehre von den Tonempfindungen als physiologischer Grundlage für die Theorie der Musik* (1863), 4th edn., Braunschweig, F. Vieweg, 1877; trans. A. J. Ellis as *On the Sensations of Tone as a Physiological Basis for the Theory of Music*, 2nd edn., London, Longman and Green, 1885; reprint, New York, Dover, 1954

Hubel, D. H. and T. N. Wiesel, "Receptive Fields, Binocular Interaction and Functional Architecture in the Cat's Visual Cortex," *Journal of Physiology* 160 (1962), pp. 106–54

Huron, D. and P. Sellmer, "Critical Bands and the Spelling of Vertical Sonorities," *MP* 10 (1992), pp. 129–50

Krumhansl, C. L. *Cognitive Foundations of Musical Pitch*, New York, Oxford University Press, 1990

Kurth, E. *Musikpsychologie*, Bern, Krompholz, 1931

Leman, M. "The Ontogenesis of Tonal Semantics: Results of a Computer Study," in *Music and Connectionism*, ed. P. Todd and G. Loy, Cambridge, MA, MIT Press, 1991, pp. 100–27

Lerdahl, F. "Cognitive Constraints on Compositional Systems," in *Generative Processes in Music*, ed. J. Sloboda, Oxford University Press, 1988, pp. 231–59

Lerdahl, F. and R. Jackendoff, *A Generative Theory of Tonal Music*, Cambridge, MA, MIT Press, 1983

Locke, J. *An Essay Concerning Human Understanding*, London, T. Basset, 1690

London, J. "Some Examples of Complex Meters and Their Implications for Models of Metric Perception," *MP* 13 (1995), pp. 59–77

Lorenz, C. "Untersuchungen über die Auffassung von Tondistanzen," *Philosophische Studien* 6 (1890), pp. 26–103

Mach, E. "Vom räumlichen Sehen" (1865), in *Populärwissenschaftliche Vorlesungen*, Leipzig, 1911

Meyer, L. B. *Emotion and Meaning in Music*, University of Chicago Press, 1956

Explaining Music: Essays and Explorations, Berkeley, University of California Press, 1973

"Exploiting Limits: Creation, Archetypes and Change," *Daedalus* 109 (1980), pp. 177–205

Meyer, M. F. *The Musician's Arithmetic; Drill Problems for an Introduction to the Scientific Study of Musical Composition*, Columbia, University of Missouri Press, 1929

Miller, G. A. "The Magical Number Seven, Plus or Minus Two," *Psychological Review* 63 (1956), pp. 81–97, and 101 (1994), pp. 343–451

Miller, G. A. and G. A. Heise, "The Trill Threshold," *Journal of the Acoustical Society of America* 22 (1950), pp. 637–38

Mursell, J. L. *The Psychology of Music*, New York, Norton, 1937

Narmour, E. *The Analysis and Cognition of Basic Melodic Structures: The Implication–Realization Model*, University of Chicago Press, 1990

The Analysis and Cognition of Melodic Complexity: The Implication–Realization Model, University of Chicago Press, 1992

Parncutt, R. *Harmony: A Psychoacoustical Approach*, New York, Springer, 1989

Plomp, R. and W. J. M. Levelt, "Tonal Consonance and Critical Bandwidth," *Journal of the Acoustical Society of America* 38 (1965), pp. 548–60

Révész, G. *Zur Grundlegung der Tonpsychologie*, Leipzig, Veit, 1913

Ervin Nyiregyházy: psychologische Analyse eines musikalisch hervorragenden Kindes, Leipzig, 1916; trans. Révész as *The Psychology of a Musical Prodigy*, London, Kegan Paul, Trench, Trubner and Co., 1925

Riemann, H. "Ideen zu einer 'Lehre von den Tonvorstellungen,'" (1914); reprint in *Frankfurter Zeitschrift für Musikwissenschaft* 2 (1999), pp. 1–31; trans. R. Wason and E. West Marvin in *JMT* 36 (1992), pp. 69–117

Schoen, M. *The Psychology of Music: A Survey for Teacher and Musician*, New York, Ronald Press, 1940

Seashore, C. E. *The Psychology of Musical Talent*, Boston, Silver, Burdett, 1919
Psychology of Music, New York, McGraw-Hill, 1938
Serafine, M. L. *Music as Cognition: The Development of Thought in Sound*, New York, Columbia University Press, 1988
Shannon, C. E. "A Mathematical Theory of Communication," *Bell Systems Technical Journal* 27 (1948), pp. 379–423, 623–56
Shepard, R. N. "Circularity in Judgements of Relative Pitch," *Journal of the Acoustical Society of America* 36 (1964), pp. 2345–53
Small, A. "An Objective Analysis of Artistic Violin Performance," *University of Iowa Studies in the Psychology of Music* 4 (1936), pp. 172–231
Stumpf, C. *Tonpsychologie*, 2 vols., Leipzig, S. Hirzel, 1883–1890
"Vergleichung der Tondistanzen," *Zeitschrift für Psychologie* (1890), pp. 419–85
Terhardt, E., G. Stoll and M. Seewann, "Algorithm for Extraction of Pitch and Pitch Salience from Complex Tonal Signals," *Journal of the Acoustical Society of America* (1982), pp. 679–88
Titchener, E. B. *An Outline of Psychology*, New York, Macmillan, 1896
Tolman, E. C. "Cognitive Maps in Rats and Men," *Psychological Review* 55 (1948), pp. 189–208
Watson, J. B. "Animal Education: The Psychical Development of the White Rat," Ph.D. diss., University of Chicago (1903)
Wundt, W. *Grundzüge der physiologischen Psychologie*, Leipzig, W. Engelmann, 1874

Index of authors

Index of subjects